The New VEGETABLES, HERBS & FRUIT

Matthew Biggs, Jekka McVicar and Bob Flowerdew

The New VEGETABLES, HERBS & FRUIT

An Illustrated Encyclopedia

FIREFLY BOOKS

To Henry John William and Chloe Elizabeth
Matthew Biggs

To Mac, Hannah and Alistair
Jekka McVicar

To all those who helped make our glorious
fruits from such humble beginnings
Bob Flowerdew

A FIREFLY BOOK

Published by Firefly Books Ltd. 2016

Design copyright © 2008 Kyle Cathie Ltd
Text pages 12–209, 440–441, 557, 549, 616–619,
636–639, 653, 662–667 ©1997, 2002, 2008, 2016
Matthew Biggs; Text pages 212–439, 442–439, 620–
627, 672–675 ©1994, 1997, 1999, 2002, 2007, 2009,
2016 Jekka McVicar; Text pages 444–548, 550–556,
558–613, 628–631 ©1995, 1997, 2000, 2002, 2009,
2016 Bob Flowerdew

First printing

Publisher Cataloging-in-Publication Data (U.S.)

A CIP record for this title is available from the Library of
Congress

**Library and Archives Canada Cataloguing in
Publication**

A CIP record for this title is available from Library and
Archives Canada

Published in the United States by
Firefly Books (U.S.) Inc.
P.O. Box 1338, Ellicott Station
Buffalo, New York 14205

Published in Canada by
Firefly Books Ltd.
50 Staples Avenue, Unit 1
Richmond Hill, Ontario L4B 0A7

Interior Design Geoff Hayes
Editorial team Caroline Taggart, Hannah Coughlin,
Claire Rogers and Tara O'Sullivan

Color reproduction by ALTA London
Printed and bound in China by C&C Offset Printing
Co., Ltd

This edition was first published in Great Britain in 2016 by Kyle Books,
an imprint of Kyle Cathie Ltd, 192–198 Vauxhall Bridge Road, London,
SW1V 1DX

Matthew Biggs, Jekka McVicar, and Bob Flowerdew are hereby identified
as the authors of this work in accordance with Section 77 of the
Copyright, Designs and Patents Act 1988.

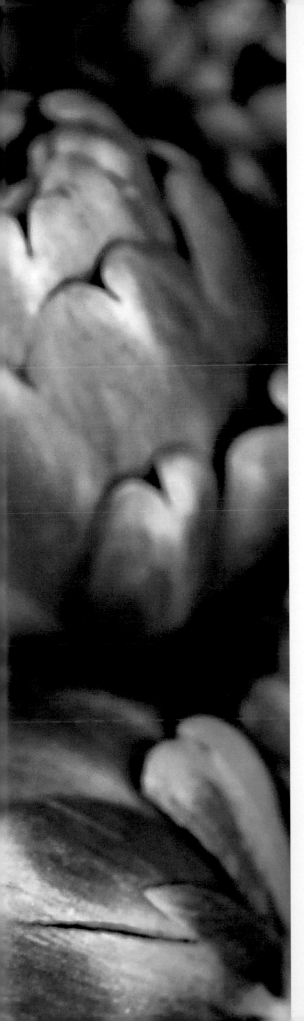

CONTENTS

Introduction	6
Vegetables A to Z	10
Herbs A to Z	210
Fruits	442
Orchard Fruits	444
Soft, Bush-, and Cane Fruits	484
Tender Fruits	524
Tropical and Subtropical Fruits	550
Shrub and Flower Garden Fruits	572
Nuts	594
Practical Gardening	614
Glossary	682
Seed Sources	684
Selected bibliography & other resources	686
Index	688
Acknowledgments	702

INTRODUCTION

A flourishing, productive garden, containing vegetables, herbs, and fruit plants, is a testament to diligent, imaginative gardening and a promise of a delicious harvest to come. The range of color, texture, scent and flavor offered by these plants is unrivaled, and there is space in any garden — even in a window box — for a selection of edible and useful plants.

Vegetables, herbs, and fruit have always been essential to humanity. They are the basis of the food chain — even for meat-eaters — and are a vital component in creating tempting, palatable meals, as well as providing unique flavoring and aromas. All provide essential vitamins and minerals for a balanced diet, and many herbs have the added dimension of being used medicinally.

Vegetables and herbs can be widely defined. Vegetables are those plants where a part, such as the leaf, stem, or root, can be used for food. Herbs, similarly, are those plants that are used for food, medicine, scent, or flavor. Fruits tend to be the sweet, juicy parts of the plants, containing the seed. There is considerable overlap between the three types of plant — one further distinction is that fruits are generally sweet, or used in sweet dishes, while vegetables are savory, although this is by no means clear-cut.

For centuries throughout the world, productive gardens have been the focal point of family and community survival. Our earliest diet as hunter-gatherers must have included a wide range of seeds, fruits, nuts, roots, leaves, and any moving thing we could catch. Gradually, over millennia, we learned which plants could be eaten and how to prepare them — as with the discovery that eddoes were edible only after being washed several times and cooked to remove the injurious calcium oxalate crystals. Fruit trees and bushes sprang up at the camp sites of nomadic people and were waiting for them when they returned, growing prolifically on their fertile waste heaps. Vegetables and herbs were collected from the surrounding countryside, and gradually were domesticated. Cultivated wheat and barley have been found dating from 8000 to 7000 BCE, and peas from 6500 BCE, while rice was recorded as a staple in China by 2800 BCE.

With domestication came early selection of plants for beneficial characteristics such as yield, disease resistance, and ease of germination. These were the first cultivated varieties, or "cultivars." This selection has continued extensively and by the 18th century in Europe, seed selection had become a fine art in the hands of skilled gardeners. Gregor Mendel's work with peas in 1855–64 in his monastery garden at Brno in Moravia yielded one of the most significant discoveries, leading to the development of hybrids and scientific selection. Most development has centered on the major food crops. Minor crops, such as sea kale, have changed very little, apart from the selection of a few cultivars. Others, like many fruits, are similar to their wild relatives, but have fleshier, sweeter edible parts. Herbs have in general had less intensive work done on selection; many of the most popular and useful herbs are the same as or closely related to plants found in the wild.

The Vegetable Garden, Coombe by Paul Riley, 1988

Food plants have spread around the world in waves, from the Roman Empire, which brought fruits such as peaches, plums, grapes and figs from the Mediterranean and North Africa to northern Europe, to the influx of plants such as potatoes and corn from the New World in the 15th century. In between, monasteries guarded fruits, vegetables, and herbs for their own use and for their medicinal value. During the famine and winter dearth of the Middle Ages and beyond, the commonplace scurvy and vitamin deficiencies would have seemed to many people almost miraculously cured by monks' potions containing little more than preserved fruits, vegetables, or herbs full of nutrients and vitamin C. In 1597 John Gerard wrote his *Herball*, detailing numerous plants and their properties, and giving practical advice on how to use them.

Productive gardening developed on several levels. The rich became plant collectors and used the latest technology to overwinter exotic plants in hothouses and greenhouses. Doctors followed on in the traditions of the monasteries and had physic gardens of medicinal herbs. Villagers had cottage gardens filled with fruit trees and bushes, underplanted with vegetables and herbs.

In the 20th century, the expense of labor and decrease in the amount of land available meant that productive gardening declined. Home food production revived during World War II, but the availability of ready-made foods afterwards again hit edible gardening at home. The later years of the 20th century saw a reaction against the

St Paul de Vence by Margaret Loxton

blandness and cost of mass-produced food. There was also an increasing awareness of the infinite variety of herbs, and their use in herbalism, cosmetics, and cooking all over the world.

The wider realization that we had polluted our environment and destroyed much of the ecology of our farms, countryside, and gardens was to bring about a real revolution. A mass revulsion against chemical-based methods was mirrored in the rise of organic production and the slowly improving availability of better foods. Vegetarianism also increased as many people turned away from meat, in part because of factory farming. These trends have meant that there is now an increased demand for fruits and vegetables, often organically produced or with a fuller flavor, and supermarkets now offer a huge range all year round.

But there has also been a move towards people growing their own. The health benefits, ecology, and economy of gardening appeal to a greener generation. An increased awareness of alternative medicine, including herbalism and aromatherapy, has revived interest in a range of herbs. With food processors, juicers, and freezers, it is easier than ever to store and preserve what we harvest. In addition, the genetic richness represented by the huge range of food plants has been recognized and organizations such as the Henry Doubleday Research Association in the UK, Seed Savers Exchange in the U.S., and Seed Savers International are working to safeguard and make available the old and rare varieties.

The availability of different gardening techniques also offers great opportunities at home. Dwarfing fruit rootstocks, varieties that store well or resist disease, glass or plastic cover, and controlled heating in greenhouses give us scope to grow a huge variety of crops, even in a small garden. The earlier and later seasons, combined with gardening under cover, also mean that we can be planting and harvesting for a larger proportion of the year.

This book is intended to guide the reader in choosing which vegetables, herbs, and fruits to grow, and then in producing a crop successfully. The vegetable and herb sections are arranged alphabetically by the botanical Latin name. The fruit section is grouped into five chapters covering different types of fruit plants — Orchard Fruits; Soft, Bush, and Cane Fruits; Tender Fruits; Shrub and Flower Garden Fruits; and Nuts — according to how they are usually grown in temperate gardens.

Under each plant, after a brief introduction covering origins and history, the most useful and recommended varieties are given, followed by details of cultivation, including propagation, growing under glass and in containers, a maintenance calendar, pruning and training (if needed), dealing with pests and diseases, companion planting, and harvesting and storing. Information and ideas are given for using the plant, including recipes and medicinal and cosmetic uses. If any part of the plant is toxic or harmful in any way, a detailed warning is given. If the plant is of particular ornamental or wildlife value in the garden, this is indicated. The fruit and vegetable sections cover some of the more exotic tropical and subtropical crops that can, with variable success, be grown under cover.

The end of the book covers the practical aspects of making a productive garden, including planning your plot and preparing the soil, creating an ornamental edible garden, crop rotation, pollination, propagation and growing in containers, maintenance, companion planting, and dealing with pests, diseases and weeds. A yearly calendar details the tasks in the productive garden month by month, although precise dates will vary according to frost times in different regions.

There is nothing more satisfying to the soul, eye, and stomach than a garden well stocked with produce. This book will help you to grow what you want with confidence, and perhaps to experiment and try out new plants and flavors.

A Note on Botanical Names

While most gardeners refer to plants by their common names, one plant may have several common names, or a common name in different parts of the world refers to different plants. Botanical names are vital for clearly identifying plants. The system of botanical names used today is known as the Binomial System and was devised by the 18th-century Swedish botanist Carl Linnaeus (1707–78). In this system, each plant is classified by using two words in Latin form. The first word is the name of the genus (e.g., *Thymus*) and the second the specific epithet (e.g., *vulgaris*): together they provide a universally known name (e.g., *Thymus vulgaris*).

The Binomial System has been developed so that the entire plant kingdom is divided into a multibranched family tree according to each plant's botanical characteristics. Plants are gathered into particular families according to the structure of their flowers, fruits, or seeds. A family may contain one genus or many. The Cannabaceae family, for example, to which cannabis and hops belong, consists of only 11 genera, while the Asteraceae contains over 800 genera, including *Achillea* (mace and yarrow), *Arnica* and *Artemisia* (southernwood, wormwood, etc.) to name a few, and over 13,000 species.

Plants are cultivated for the garden from the wild to improve their leaf or their flower or their root. This can be done either by selection from seedlings or by spotting a mutation. Such plants are known as cultivars (a combination of "cultivated varieties"). Propagation from these varieties is normally done by cuttings or division. Cultivars are given vernacular names, which are printed within double quotes, e.g., *Thymus* "Doone Valley," to distinguish them from wild varieties whose name are written in Latin form in italics, e.g., *Thymus citriodorus aurea*. Sexual crosses between species, usually of the same genus, are known as hybrids and are indicated by a multiplication sign, e.g., *Rheum × hybridum*.

Finally, a problem that seems to be getting worse: Many plants are undergoing reclassification and long-established names are being changed. This is the result of scientific studies and research whereby it is found either that a plant has been incorrectly identified or that its classification has changed. This book uses the latest information available, and where there has been a recent change in the botanical name, the previous one is shown in brackets.

Large kitchen gardens were formerly attached to great houses: *Vegetable Garden at Charlton Park* by Thomas Robins, c. 1745

VEGETABLES
A-Z

MUSHROOMS, EDIBLE FUNGI

Simple organisms growing on decaying substrate or symbiotically with living plants, some with edible fruiting bodies. Half hardy/tender. Value: low in calories, moderate potassium, linoleic and folic acid, carbohydrates, iron, niacin, and B vitamins.

Fungi are extraordinary organisms: lacking both chlorophyll and root systems, they are more akin to molds and yeasts than to traditional vegetable plants. The fleshy mushroom, or bracket, that you eat is a fruiting body, dispersing spores in order to reproduce in the same way that plant fruits disperse seeds. Instead of drawing nutrients through roots, however, a fungus is sustained by a network of fine — often microscopic — threads (known collectively as the *mycelium*). This can extend over vast distances into rotting wood, soil, or some other preferred medium. To help identify a fungus it is important to know the particular substrate on which it depends, or the higher plant species with which it lives in symbiosis (certain fungi, for example, grow only in the vicinity of specific trees such as birch or oak); when attempting to cultivate any kind of mushroom, you must provide similarly congenial conditions.

However, few of the many thousand fungus genera are amenable to cultivation. Even in nature, fruiting is wildly unpredictable: the organism depends on precise moisture and temperature variables to produce fruiting bodies, and more generally is sensitive to environmental changes such as recent air pollution and high nitrate levels.

Their erratic behavior and mysterious origins — allied with the deadly toxins some contain — have given rise to a "love-hate" attitude towards fungi. Some have been collected as "wild food" since ancient times. The Romans esteemed them as a delicacy and the rich employed collectors to find the most desirable species.

However, Gerard, writing in his *Herball*, remained unimpressed: "few … are good to be eaten and most of them do suffocate and strangle the eater." John Evelyn advised that all types of mushrooms should be kept well out of the kitchen.

By the late 17th century, varieties of *Agaricus* began to be grown in underground caves in the Paris region, in which giant heaps of manure were impregnated with soil taken from areas where field and horse mushrooms grew naturally. For many centuries cultivated mushrooms were a delicacy enjoyed only by the wealthy, and from the 18th century most stableyards had a shady corner where there was a mushroom bed. Some garden owners had outhouses converted to provide ideal growing conditions: George IV had a large mushroom house at Kensington Palace in London. In seasons when wild or cultivated crops were plentiful, surplus mushrooms were conserved in the form of sauces and ketchups, and only recently has the role of mushroom sauce in the kitchen been usurped by tomato sauce.

Cultivated *Agaricus* species have remained popular in northern Europe and the English-speaking world, yet elsewhere they are eclipsed by other mushrooms. In Japan, velvet shank, nameko, oyster, and shiitake mushrooms are established as the cultivated varieties, and some of them are slowly becoming popular in other countries.

A number of species are commercially available, some of them to amateur growers, and usually work by inoculating the growing medium with *mycelium* or "spawn." Home growing of many fungus species is still in its infancy, but it is gaining ground each year. As adventurous gardeners and mushroom eaters increasingly experiment, advances in mushroom cultivation will also help to conserve wild species.

Ensure fungi are correctly identified before eating

 species

The following lists include several of the more common and better known edible fungi.

Commonly available for home cultivation
These fungi are grown commercially and can occasionally be bought from specialized suppliers as kits, "spawn" or impregnated dowels for inoculating logs. A notable advantage of buying mushrooms in this form is that you are assured of their identity. You should follow suppliers' detailed cultivation instructions carefully to increase the chances of success. Some producers have their own selected strains of these fungi.

Agaricus bisporus (cultivated mushroom, champignon de Paris) has a smooth white to brownish cap and white stem and flesh. Excellent flavor raw and cooked. This accounts for 60 percent of the world's mushroom production. Available as kits or spawn (see "Cultivation" p. 16). Commercial growers are developing new races with color variation in the cap: watch out for them in the future as kits.

Flammulina velutipes (enokitake, velvet shank, velvet foot, winter mushroom) occurs naturally on dead wood and is grown commercially on sawdust, particularly in Japan. Small tan-yellow caps on dark brown stems. Do not eat stems and wipe or peel off any stickiness from the caps before cooking.

Hericium erinaceus (lion's mane, bearded tooth, hedgehog, pom pom, monkey head) produces large, rounded clusters of icicle-like growths that taste like lobster — delicious fried with butter and onions. Grows in the wild from wounds on living hardwoods such as beech, and can be cultivated on stumps or logs.

Cultivated mushrooms are easy to grow

Lentinula edodes (shiitake) is a small to medium sized mushroom with light brown stem and pale to dark reddish-brown cap. Documents record this strongly flavored gourmet mushroom being eaten in AD199 and it is the second most important cultivated fungus. In the U.S. and Japan it is grown commercially on logs of chestnut, oak, or hornbeam. Different forms tolerate warmer or colder conditions, and include "Snowcap," a thick-fleshed form with a long fruiting season, grown on large logs, and "West Wind," which is ideal for inexperienced growers, yielding well over a long period.

Pholiota nameko (nameko, viscid mushroom) is among the four most important fungi cultivated in Japan. Grows in clusters on tree trunks or wood chips. Orange-brown caps atop paler stems are 2–2½ in. in diameter. It is pleasantly aromatic.

Pleurotus (or oyster mushroom) is a genus with a number of distinct species and strains. Popular in Japan and Central Europe, they are increasingly available in kit form, or can be grown from plugs of spawn. Eat when small, discarding the tough stem. Sauté in butter until tender, season, then add cream or yogurt. The first two are fairly common in the wild and are also offered in seed catalogs.

Pleurotus ostreatus (oyster mushroom) has large fan-shaped caps, slate-blue to white in color and with white or pale straw-colored gills; used coffee grounds (sterilized as the coffee is brewed) are becoming a popular medium for inoculating with the spawn.

P. cornucopiae (golden oyster) has a white stem with a cream cap turning to ocher-brown. Grows on the cut stumps of deciduous trees, usually elm or oak. Other species may be harder to find, and some need warmth to fruit.

P. ergyngii (king pleurotus) has a concave cap, whitish becoming gray-brown. It tastes sweet and meaty and grows in clusters on the decaying roots of plants in the carrot family. It can be grown on chopped straw.

P. flabellatus is an oyster mushroom with pink caps. *P. pulmonarius* has brown or gray caps. *P. samoneus-tramineus* from Asia is pink-capped. *P. sajor-caju* has brown caps.

Stropharia rugosoannulata (king stropharia, wine cap, burgundy) is a brown-capped, violet-gilled fungus

Chanterelles

commonly cultivated in eastern Europe; it is claimed to be capable of growing in vegetable gardens. It requires a substrate of humus containing rotting hardwood or sawdust. Grow spawn from reputable sources: look-alikes include the deadly *Cortinarius* species.

Volvariella volvaceae (Chinese or straw mushroom, paddy straw, padi-straw) has a gray-brown cap, often marked with black, and a dull-brown stem. Grown on composted rice straw, it is regarded as an expensive delicacy in China and other Asian countries. Needs high temperatures and humidity to grow well. Harvest when it is immature.

Naturally occurring edible fungi
Many edible species of fungi may be found growing in your garden if it happens to provide the host trees or other conditions that form their natural habitat. In the U.S. and Continental Europe, fungi collected in the wild are often sold in markets; but local pharmacists or health inspectors are on hand to verify that those on sale are edible species and some states provide training in identification.

NEVER EAT WILD FUNGI UNLESS YOU HAVE FIRST HAD THEIR IDENTITY CONFIRMED BY AN EXPERT

Agaricus arvensis (horse mushroom) and ***A. campestris*** (field mushroom) are cousins of the cultivated mushroom, found in clusters or rings in grazed or mown grassland. Dome-shaped white "buttons" open to wide caps. Horse mushrooms can grow to soup-plate size with thick, firm flesh smelling of aniseed; the gills are pale grayish-pink darkening to chocolate-brown. Field mushrooms are smaller and rather more delicate in stature, with a "mushroomy" smell; their deep-pink gills become dark brown to black at maturity.

Boletus edulis (porcini, cep, penny bun) grows on the ground near trees, favoring pine, beech, oak, and birch forests. The rounded, bun-like brown cap (often covered with a white bloom when young) sits on a bulbous whitish stem — also edible. Tube-like pores (rather than gills) beneath the cap are white, turning dull yellow at maturity. This delicious, fleshy fungus is highly prized in European markets and can be eaten fresh, pickled, or dried. Related species of *Boletus* are also edible.

Cantharellus cibarius (chanterelle) is funnel-shaped; egg yolk-yellow caps, fading with age, are thick and fleshy with gill-like wrinkles running down from the cap underside into the stem. Has a mild peppery aftertaste when eaten raw; and an excellent flavor when cooked. True chanterelles grow on soil in broad-leaved forest: similar-looking species are highly toxic.

Hirneola auricula judae, syn. ***Auricularia auricula-judae*** (wood ear) looks like a human ear and is date-brown, drying to become small and hard. Found on living and dead elder, beech, and sycamore. Can be dried and reconstituted with water. Popular in Taiwan and China.

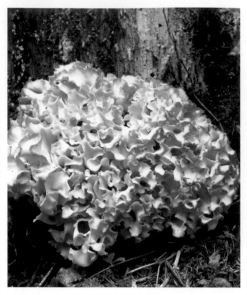

Wild — and free!

Hypholoma capnoides, syn. ***Nematoloma capnoides***, is a gilled fungus found growing in clusters on conifer stumps. Caps ¾–2½ in. in diameter are pale ocher with a buff-colored margin. Check identity carefully: other *Hypholoma* species are suspect.

If you can't grow your own, try the market for a wide range of varieties

MUSHROOMS, EDIBLE FUNGI

Oyster mushrooms

dirt and insects — rinsing in water is advised.) Found on well-drained soils under deciduous trees, particularly in ash and elm woods, in gardens and near old hedges. Other edible species include **M. rotunda**, found on heavier soil, and **M. vulgaris**, on richer soil. Some similar-looking mushroom species are highly toxic.

Sparassis crispa (cauliflower mushroom, brain fungus) has a folded, rounded fruiting body, creamy-white when young, which looks more like a cauliflower than a mushroom. It tastes nutty, with a spicy fragrance. Found at the base of pines and other conifers. As with morels, rinse to remove any debris.

Tuber melanosporum (the Perigord or black truffle), often found in oak woods, is highly desirable and the most valuable truffle. Pigs and trained dogs are used to sniff them out. Truffle-inoculated trees and hazel are now available to amateur gardeners but need specific growing conditions to flourish.

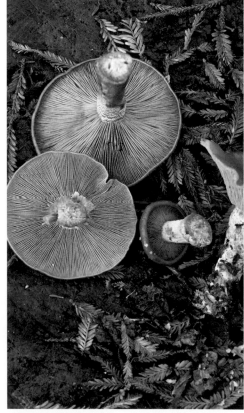

Pick fungi at their prime

Laetiporus sulfureus, syn. **Polyporus sulfureus** (chicken of the woods) is a bracket fungus found on many hardwoods and softwoods, often on sweet chestnut, oak, and beech. Has the flavor of chicken breast and is an orange to sulfur-yellow color. Eat young, but only try a little the first time: it can cause nausea and dizziness in some people. The largest ever found weighed 100 pounds.

Langermannia gigantea (giant puffball) can be enormous: large and round with white skin, it sits on the ground like a giant soccer ball. The biggest ever recorded, according to the *Guinness Book of Records*, was 8¾ ft. in circumference and weighed 49 pounds! It is found on soil in fields, hedgerows, forests, and gardens, often near nettles. Eat when young, while the flesh is pure white; it tastes good sliced, dipped in breadcrumbs, and fried. Other related (and smaller) species of puffball are also edible while they remain white all through.

Lepista nuda (blewit, wood blewit, blue-stalk) is medium to large with a light cinnamon-brown to tan cap; the gills and stems are violet to lavender. It is found in forests, parks and hedges. It can be grown in leaf debris around compost piles. Better eaten young, it is well flavored and particularly good in stews or fried. Never eat raw: cook thoroughly to remove traces of cyanic acid.

Marasmius oreades (fairy ring mushroom) is found on lawns in a "ring" of dark green grass with dying grass in the center. Small with a bell-shaped light tan-colored cap, matching gills and similar stem. Good in omelets. Beware: Similar-looking species are toxic.

Morchella esculenta (common morel) is a delicious fungus that emerges annually in spring, earlier than most fall-fruiters. The hollow cap has a surface covered in honeycomblike pits and varies from round to conical in shape. (The many crevices of the cap often harbor

Boletus edulis — delicious

 cultivation

Propagation

Nameko mushrooms favor moist toilet rolls or arrive with packs of clean straw which the fungi grow on. It is also possible to cultivate mushrooms in the garden; the spawn of field mushrooms grow in rich soil and are an ideal candidate for cultivating around the compost pile, while blewit mushrooms thrive in a mixture of well-rotted leaf mold and pine needles. They are also grown using kits or on heaps of rotted horse manure.

It is also possible to buy mushroom growing kits or "logs" supplied with dowels inoculated with spores of fungi like shiitake, which are hammered into holes drilled in the logs, or to buy the dowels and use logs of beech, birch, oak, or similar wood that have been harvested at home. Put them in the shed, cellar, or a shady corner of the garden, in conditions similar to those enjoyed by shade-loving plants and cover them with damp burlap.

Mushroom logs take 6 months to a year to become productive; flushes of growth appear when temperatures drop in fall, though shiitake logs can be shocked into production in summer by plunging them into cold water.

Each log crops for about 3 years.

Growing

Humidity is essential for success, along with a plentiful supply of organic matter. Choose a shady position and, on a damp day in spring or fall, "plant" blocks of spawn, about the size of a golfball, 2 in. below the soil and 12 in. apart. A good crop of mushrooms often appears when spent mushroom compost is used as a mulch around other crops.

Maintenance

Indoor crops can be planted any time of the year. Plant spawn outdoors in spring or fall.

Protected Cropping

Indoor crops grow well in an airy shed, cellar, greenhouse, or cold frame. They do not need to be grown in the dark.

Container Growing

See "Propagation."

Harvesting and Storing

The first "button" mushrooms are ready for harvesting 4 to 6 weeks after "casing"; there may be another 2 weeks before the next "flush."

Harvesting lasts for about 6 weeks. To harvest, twist and pull mushrooms upwards, disturbing the compost as little as possible, removing broken stalks and filling holes with "casing."

Mushrooms last in a ventilated plastic bag in the salad drawer of a refrigerator for up to 3 days. Most species can be dried. Thread them on to a string and hang them over a radiator or in an airing cupboard, then store in a cool dry place. Reconstitute with water or wine.

After the final harvest, you can use the spent mixture as a mulch; you should never try to respawn for a second crop.

Pests and Diseases

Mushroom fly can be a problem; pick mushrooms when young.

 medicinal

Reportedly, edible fungi lower blood cholesterol, stimulate the immune system, and deactivate viruses. Shiitake mushrooms are particularly effective. Wood-ear has been used in herbal medicine for treating sore throats.

 warning

If you gather wild mushrooms, be certain of their identity before eating. Best of all, collect with an expert. Those that are highly toxic are often similar to edible species. Mistakes can be fatal.

Feeling hungry yet?

culinary

Fungi should always be eaten fresh as the flavor is soon lost and the quality deteriorates. Avoid washing most kinds: the fruit bodies absorb water, spoiling the texture and flavor. Simply clean the surface by wiping with a damp cloth or brushing off any dirt. Peel only when necessary.

Both caps and stems of *Agaricus* species can be eaten. With some other fungi, stems may be discarded as inedibly tough. Check for any special instructions on preparation: some fungi, for instance, are toxic unless cooked.

Harvested cultivated mushrooms at the "button" stage can be eaten raw, added to salads; more mature caps can be baked, broiled, or fried whole, or sliced and stir-fried, made into soups, pies or stuffings, added to stews or the stockpot, or used as a garnish. Other fungi can be prepared in many similar ways. Large fruit bodies can be stuffed.

Try frying in butter and a little lemon juice for 3 to 5 minutes. Brush with oil and seasoning and broil each side for 2 to 3 minutes. Add yogurt or cream before serving, or dip in breadcrumbs and fry. Garlic mushrooms are especially delicious.

Mushroom Soup
Serves 4

Open-capped cultivated mushrooms make a good alternative to the wild variety.

5 tablespoons butter
4 shallots, finely minced
1 clove garlic, crushed
1 pound field mushrooms, cleaned and sliced
4 cups chicken stock
1 tablespoon all-purpose flour
Dash soy sauce
A little heavy cream
Salt and freshly ground black pepper

Heat 3 tablespoons of the butter in a heavy-bottomed pan and sauté the shallots until softened; add the garlic and cook for 1 minute more. Add the mushrooms and stir to coat well. Pour in the stock

Mushroom Mélange

and bring to a boil. Season and cover, simmering for 10 to 15 minutes, until the mushrooms are cooked. Remove from the heat.

In a separate pan, heat the remaining butter and stir in the flour to make a roux. Cook for 2 minutes and remove from the stove. Use a blender to mix the roux with the soup (this may need to be done in batches). Add soy sauce, check seasoning, and serve with cream.

Broiled Shiitake Mushrooms
Serves 4

Allow 2 mushrooms per person for a first course to be served with Italian bread.

8–12 shiitake mushrooms
6 tablespoons olive oil
1 sprig fresh rosemary
1 tablespoon fresh thyme leaves
2 tablespoons balsamic vinegar
2 tablespoons Barolo wine
1 small onion, finely minced
4 slices Italian bread, toasted
1 tablespoon butter
1 clove garlic, crushed
Salt and freshly ground black pepper

Wash the shiitakes, ensuring the gills are free from dirt. Discard the stems and add to a stockpot. Dry the caps. Leave the mushrooms in a marinade of oil, rosemary, thyme, vinegar, wine, onion, and seasoning for 30 to 45 minutes, turning them occasionally.

Broil the marinated caps under a preheated broiler for 5 minutes each side, brushing with the marinade juices. Serve on slices of toasted Italian bread, buttered and rubbed with garlic. Pour over a little of the juices on each helping.

Mushroom Mélange
Serves 4

1 pound oyster mushrooms
1 pound shiitake mushrooms
4 tablespoons butter
2 cloves garlic, crushed
2 shallots, finely minced
4 tablespoons white wine
½ cup heavy cream
4 tablespoons grated Parmesan
Salt and freshly ground black pepper

Wash the mushrooms well and chop them, including the stalks. Melt the butter in a heavy pot, add the garlic and shallots and allow them to soften over a gentle heat. Add the mushrooms and stir well. Pour in the wine and the heavy cream and bring the mixture to simmering point. Then cover and leave to stew for 15 minutes.

Pour into a greased sauté pan, season with salt and pepper and sprinkle over the Parmesan. Put under a preheated broiler on the highest setting for 3 to 5 minutes until the cheese is melted.

Serve immediately.

Allium cepa. Alliaceae

ONION

Biennial; grown as annual for swollen bulbs. Half hardy. Value: small amounts of most vitamins and minerals.

A vegetable of antiquity, the onion was cultivated by the Egyptians not only as food, but also to place in the thorax, pelvis or near the eyes during mummification. Pliny recorded six varieties in Ancient Rome. The onion was highly regarded for its antiseptic properties, but many other legends became attached to it. In parts of Ireland it was said to cure baldness: "Rub the sap mixed with honey into a bald patch, keep on rubbing until the spot gets red. This concoction if properly applied would grow hair on a duck's egg." Many varieties have been bred over the centuries; some, like the "Kelsae," are famous for their size, while newer varieties have incorporated hardiness, disease resistance and color.

 varieties

Varieties of *Allium cepa* fall into several different groups according to their color, shape, and use. The bulb or common onion has brown, yellow, or red skin and is round, elongated, or flattened. (Grouped with these are Japanese onions, a type of the perennial *Allium fistulosum*, which are grown as an annual for overwintering.) Bunching onions or scallions are harvested small, and pickling varieties (also known as "silverskin," "mini," or "button" onions) are allowed to grow larger.

Bulb or Common Onions
"Ailsa Craig," an old favorite, is a large variety; round and straw-colored with a mild flavor. "Buffalo" is high-yielding and good for sowing in summer and harvesting the following year. The round, firm bulbs are well flavored. "Chippolini" are small, round, and flattened old-fashioned Italian onions that are used for boiling and for creamed onions. "Red Baron" is a gorgeous dark-red-skinned onion with a strong flavor and red outer flesh to each ring. Good for storing. "Senshyu Semiglobe Yellow" is a Japanese onion with a deep yellow skin and good taste. "Sturon," an old, high-yielding variety, has straw-colored skin and an excellent resistance to running to seed. "Stuttgarter Giant" is a reliable variety with flattened bulbs and a mild flavor. A good keeper and slow to bolt. "Super Star," a hybrid All-America Selections Winner, is a day-neutral variety, so it grows well throughout North America. Uniform, large, white onions are mild, but do not store well. The "Kelsae," a large, round onion with mild flesh, does not store well. "Torpedo" is a spindle-shaped onion that is mild-flavored, but does not store well.

"Walla Walla Sweet" is a long-day West Coast classic that may be sown in spring, or in fall where winter temperatures do not drop below −10°F. Fall-sown seeds grow to form huge and exceptionally sweet bulbs. "Yellow Granex Hybrid 33" is the variety grown in Georgia and sold as the famous Vidalia sweet onion. Very sweet, with light-yellow flesh, this short-day southern onion requires up to 125 days to mature.

Bunching, Spring or Salad Onions, or Scallions

"Ishikura," a cross between a leek and coarse chives, is prolific, tender, and a rapid grower with upright, white stems and dark green leaves. It can be left in the ground to thicken and still retains its taste. "Red Baron" offers consistent red color from its base to its lower leaves regardless of weather. It may be sown continuously for spring and summer harvest. "Redmate" is a colorful variety with a red base, and ideal for livening up salads. It can be thinned to 3 in. apart for mild bulb onions. "Southport White Bunching," produces a mild white scallion that matures quickly and can be sown spring through summer. Stems are bright white with strong tips. "White Lisbon" is a tasty, popular, and reliable variety. It is fast-growing and very hardy

Pickling Onions

"Brown Pickling SY300" is a pale brown-skinned early variety. It stores well and remains firm when pickled. "White Paris" is a popular, excellent cocktail onion, which grows rapidly and thrives in poor soil. Sow from midspring and lift when the size of your thumbnail. "Purplette" produces a very attractive small burgundy bulb with a pastel pink color even when cooked or pickled.

 cultivation

Onions require an open, sunny site, fertile soil, and free drainage. Sets (immature bulbs that have been specifically grown for planting) are more tolerant than seedlings and do not need a fine soil or such high levels of fertility. Pickling onions tolerate poorer soil than other types. Rotate crops annually.

Two distinct types of onion are grown in North America: Long-day types require extended periods of summer sunlight to form bulbs and so are grown in the northern U.S. and Canada. Short-day onions mature only in the shorter summer days of the south. Because they require a longer growing period, the latter are usually grown in fall and overwintered. **Zones 3 to 11.**

Propagation

Onion sets have several advantages over seed. They are quick to mature, are better in cooler areas with shorter growing seasons, they grow well in poorer soils, and are not attacked by onion fly or mildew, though onion maggot (the larvae of onion fly) can attack the roots. They are easy to grow and mature earlier, but are more expensive and prone to go to seed. (Buying modern varieties and heat-treated sets about ¾ in. in diameter reduces that risk.) There is a greater choice of varieties when growing from seed. If planting is delayed, spread out sets in a cool, well-lit place to prevent premature sprouting. It is possible to save your own sets from bulbs grown the previous year. Plant onion sets when the soil warms from late winter to midspring. Sets that have been heat treated should not be planted until late spring. Plant in shallow rows or push them gently into the soil until only the tips are above the surface. For medium-sized onions, plant 2 in. apart in rows 10 in. apart; for larger onions space sets 4 in. apart in rows.

Sow seed indoors in late winter at 50–60°F in seed trays, pots or packs (six seeds in each pack). Harden off the seedlings carefully by gradually increasing ventilation, then plant out in early spring when the seedlings have two true leaves. When transplanting those raised in packs and pots, ensure that the roots fall into the planting hole and that the base of the bulb is about ½ in. below the surface.

Onions can be sown outdoors in a seedbed in early to midspring in cool temperate zones. Use cloches or row covers to ensure the soil is warm, as cold, wet soil leads

Scallions add bite to salads

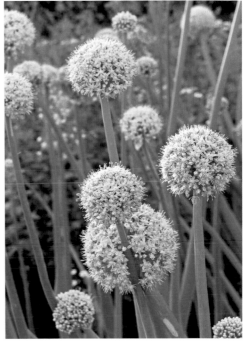

Onion flowers are beautifully ornamental

to poor germination and disease. Use treated seed to protect against fungal disease.

When the soil is moist and crumbly, rake in a general fertilizer about 2 weeks before sowing and firm up the seedbed, then sow onions ½–¾ in. deep in rows 12 in. apart. Once they germinate, thin to 1–1½ in. apart for medium-sized onions and 3–4 in. for large onions. Thin when the soil is moist to deter onion fly. Plant multi-sown blocks 10–12 in. apart. Plant firmly.

Sowing times for Japanese onions are critical; sown too early, they go to seed; sown too late, they are too weak to survive the winter. To cover for losses over winter, sow seeds about 1 in. apart in rows 12 in. apart. Top-dress with nitrogen in midwinter. Sow pickling onions in spring, either broadcast or in rows the width of a hoe and about 4 in. apart. Thin according to the size of onions required and harvest them when the leaves have died back.

Sow salad or bunching onions thinly, watering the rows before sowing in dry weather. Rows should be 4 in. apart; thin to ½–1 in., when the seedlings are large enough to handle, for good-sized onions. For a regular supply sow at 2- to 3-week intervals through late spring and early summer, watering thoroughly during dry weather.

Growing

Dig thoroughly during early winter, incorporating liberal quantities of well-rotted manure or potting mix if needed. Do not grow on freshly manured ground. Lime acid soils. Before planting, rake the surface level, removing any debris and adding a general granular fertilizer to it at 2 oz. per square yard.

Maintenance

Spring Plant sets or seeds. Keep weed-free, particularly in the early stages of growth.
Summer Mulch to reduce water loss and weeds. Watering is only vital during drought.
Fall Dig early fall.
Winter Push back any sets that have been lifted by frost or birds.

Protected Cropping

Onions do not need protection, although early sowings in cold weather and overwintering onions benefit from cloching or from floating row cover in exceptionally cold or wet weather.

For mild-winter areas of the U.S., early sowings of bunching onions or scallions can be made in late summer or early fall and protected with cloches during severe weather for harvesting the following spring.

Onions drying on a metal rack

Rows of onion plants growing in the U.S.

Harvesting and Storing

Harvesting commences when the tops bend over naturally and the leaves begin to dry out. Do not bend the leaves over. Allow the bulbs and leaves to dry out while still in the ground during fine weather; wait until the dried foliage rustles before lifting. In adverse weather, spread out the bulbs on burlap or in trays in cold frames, cloches or a shed, turning them regularly. Handle bulbs carefully to avoid damage and disease. Before storing, be sure to remove any damaged, soft, spotted or thick-necked onions and use them immediately. Onions can be stored in trays, net bags, or pantyhose, or tied to a length of cord as onion ropes in a cool place.

Harvest salad or bunching onions before the bases swell. During dry weather, water before harvesting to make pulling easier.

Making an Onion Rope

Storing onions on a rope enables the air to circulate, reducing the possibility of diseases. It is attractive and a convenient method of storage. You can braid the stems to form a rope, as with garlic, but they are usually too short and are better tied to raffia or strong string. Firmly tie in two onions at the base, then wind the leaves of each onion firmly round the string, with each bulb just resting on the onions below. When you reach the top of the string, tie a firm knot around the bulbs at the top, then hang them up to dry. Cut onions from the rope as they are needed.

Pests and Diseases

If birds are a nuisance, protect plants with bird netting or netting. The larvae of onion fly tunnel into bulbs, causing the stems to wilt and become yellow. Seedlings and small plants may die. Cultivate the ground thoroughly over winter. Remove and destroy affected plants, rotate crops, sow under mesh. White rot can be a problem, particularly on salad onions. White mold like cotton balls, dotted with tiny, black spots, appears around the base. Leaves turn yellow and die. It is almost impossible to eradicate. Remove affected onions with as much of the soil around them as possible, dispose of plants and any debris — do not put them on the compost pile. Avoid spreading contaminated soil on tools or boots. Grow on a new site and from seed.

When attacked by stem wireworm, bulbs become distorted, crack, soften, then die. Grow plants from seed; rotate crops; in severe cases do not grow in the same place again. Dispose of plant debris thoroughly and remove any affected plants.

 ## companion planting

Parsley sown with onions is said to keep onion fly away.

 ## container growing

Bulb onions can be grown in containers, but yields will be small and not really worth the trouble.

 ## medicinal

Used as an antiseptic and diuretic, the juice is good for coughs and colds. The bulbs and stems were formerly applied as poultices to carbuncles.

culinary

So indispensable are onions for flavoring sauces, stocks, stews, and casseroles that there is hardly a recipe that does not start with some variant of "fry (or sauté or sweat) the onion in the oil or fat until soft …" They also make a delicious vegetable or garnish in their own right: roasted or boiled whole, cut into rings, battered, and deep-fried, or sliced and slowly softened into a meltingly sweet "marmalade." Finely minced raw onion adds zing to dishes like rice salad; you can also use the thinnings to flavor salads.

Bunching onions are perfect for salads, pastas, soups and quiches. In France they are chopped, sautéed in butter and added to chicken consommé with vermicelli. Pickled onions are an excellent accompaniment to bread, strong cheese and pickled beet — the traditional "Ploughman's Lunch." Besides being pickled, pickling varieties can be used fresh in salads and stir-fries, added to stews, or else threaded on to kabob skewers for barbecuing.

Onion Pie
Serves 4

This Alsatian dish is full of flavor and very filling. Enjoy it with a simple fresh green salad.

½ cup olive oil
4 cups onions, sliced into rings
¼ pound bacon, diced
1 cup heavy cream
3 eggs, lightly beaten
Salt and freshly ground black pepper
Shortcrust dough to line an 8–9 in. pie tin

In a heavy pan, heat the oil and sauté the onions until soft but not browned. Drain well on paper towels. Add the bacon to the pan and cook briskly for a couple of minutes, then drain off the fat. Next, mix the cream and the eggs and season well. Then stir in the onions and the bacon and fill the dough case.

Preheat the oven to 425°F and bake for 10 to 15 minutes, turning the heat down to 375°F for an additional 15 minutes, or until the filling is set. Serve warm.

Onion and Walnut Muffins
Makes 20

This wonderful recipe comes from chef Wally Malouf's *Hudson Valley Cookbook*.

1 large onion, peeled and quartered
2 sticks unsalted butter, melted
2 large eggs
6 tablespoons sugar
1 teaspoon kosher salt
1 teaspoon baking powder
2½ cups shelled walnuts, coarsely crushed
3 cups all-purpose flour

Preheat the oven to 425°F. Purée the onion finely in a food processor and measure it to achieve 8 oz. Beat together the butter, eggs, and sugar and add the onion purée. Stir in the remaining ingredients one by one and mix thoroughly. Fill the muffin tins almost full. Bake them for 20 minutes, or until they are puffed and well browned. Serve warm.

Allium cepa (Aggregatum Group). Alliaceae

SHALLOT

Small onion, grown as an annual, forming several new bulbs. Hardy. Value: small amounts of most vitamins and minerals.

Shallots are hardy, mature rapidly, are good for colder zones, tolerate heat, and will grow on poorer soils than common onions. Sets are more expensive than seed and are inclined to bolt unless they are heat-treated; buy virus-free stock which is higher-yielding and vigorous, or save healthy bulbs of your own for the following year.

Shallots are mild enough to be added whole to dishes

 ## varieties

"Atlantic" can be sown early and produces heavy yields of moderate to large bulbs which are crisp, tasty and store well. "Creation F1," a seed-grown variety, is delicious, highly resistant to bolting, and stores well. "Longor" is a French variety with elongated bulbs and mild flesh. "Giant Yellow Improved" is well worth considering. The bulbs have yellow-brown skins and are consistently large and high-yielding. "Golden Gourmet" is a mild-tasting shallot for casseroles and salads. It is reliable and high-yielding, stores well, and produces good edible shoots. "Hative de Niort" is an extremely attractive variety with elongated, pear-shaped bulbs, dark brown skins, and white flesh. "Pikant" is prolific and resistant to bolting. Its skin is dark reddish-brown, the flesh strongly flavored and firm. "Mikor" has large elliptical bulbs, crisp white flesh, and a superb taste. "Sante" is large and round with brown skin and pinkish-white flesh, packed with flavor. Yields are high and it stores well. However, it is inclined to bolt and should only be planted from mid- to late spring when conditions improve. "Red Sun" is red with firm skin and a crisp and mild flavor that is ideal for salads.

 ## cultivation

Propagation

The ideal size for sets is about ¾ in. diameter, which will result in a high yield of good-sized shallots; larger sets will produce a greater number of smaller shallots. Plant from late winter or early spring, as soon as soil conditions are suitable. Shallots can also be planted from late fall to midwinter for early crops. Cover the soil with cloches, floating row cover, or crop covers 2 weeks before planting to warm the soil.

If the weather is unfavorable, bulbs can be planted in 4-in. pots of potting mix and transplanted when conditions improve.

Space sets 9 in. apart with 12–15 in. between the rows. Make small holes with a trowel rather than pushing bulbs into the ground (the compaction this causes, particularly in heavier soils, can act as a barrier to young roots). Leave the tips of the bulbs just above the soil. Alternatively, plant in rows, ½ in. deep, 7 in. apart, then cover with soil.

F1 hybrids that are grown from seed produce one bulb, rather than several. From early to midspring, as soon as soil conditions allow, sow seed thinly ½ in. deep in wide rows, the width of a hoe, thinning until there is 1–2 in. around each plant. If spaced farther apart, clusters of bulbs are more likely to form.

Unlike onions, shallots develop in small clusters

Undersized shallots can be grown for their leaves, or you can pick a few leaves from those being grown for bulbs. Plant from fall to spring under cloches for earlier crops, in seed trays or pots of potting mix under cover and outdoors when the soil becomes workable. Each bulb should be about 1 in. apart. **Zones 3 to 11.**

Growing

Shallots flourish in a sheltered, sunny position on moist, free-draining soil, preferably one that has been manured for the previous crop.

Before planting, level the soil and rake in a general fertilizer at 4 oz. per square yard. If you are sowing sets, a rough tilth will suffice, but seeds need a seedbed of a finer texture.

Water during dry periods and keep crops weed-free, particularly while becoming established. Use an onion hoe with care, as damaged bulbs cannot be stored.

Maintenance

Spring Plant sets when soil conditions allow. Sow seed when the soil warms up.
Summer Keep crops weed-free. Water during dry periods.
Fall Dig in well-rotted organic matter if needed. Plant sets for early crops.
Winter Plant sets from late winter onwards.

Protected Cropping

Shallots are extremely hardy, but benefit from temporary protection under cloches or floating row cover in periods of severe winter weather, particularly if the soil is poorly drained.

Harvesting and Storing

From midsummer onwards, as the leaves die back, carefully dig the bulbs and in dry weather leave them on the surface for about a week to dry out; otherwise dry them as onions. Do not cut off the green foliage as this may cause fungal infection, spoiling the bulbs for storage. Break up the bulbs in each clump, remove any soil and loose leaves, then store them in a dry, cool, well-ventilated place. Store on slatted trays, in net bags or in old pantyhose. Harvest shallots grown for their foliage when the leaves are about 4 in. high.

Pests and Diseases

Shallots are usually free of pests and diseases. Bolting may be a problem in early plantings or if temperatures fluctuate. Use resistant varieties for early plantings. Bulbs infected with virus are stunted and yields are poor. Use disease-free stock. If mildew is a problem, treat as for onions.

Birds can be a nuisance, pulling sets from the ground. Sprinkling a layer of fine soil over the tips can help; otherwise protect the crop with bird netting or similar bird scarers.

Bulbs lifted by frost should be carefully replanted immediately.

Wireworms and onion fly should be treated in the same way as for onions.

 ## companion planting

Shallots make good companions for apples and strawberry plants; storing sulfur, they are believed to have a fungicidal effect.

 ## container growing

Shallots will grow in large pots or containers of soil-based potting mix. Add slow-release fertilizer to the mix and put a good layer of broken crocks or polystyrene in the bottom of the pot, for drainage. Keep plants well watered in dry periods.

 ## culinary

Shallots have a milder taste than onions; generally, the yellow-skinned varieties are larger and keep better, while red types are smaller and have the best flavor. The bulbs can be eaten raw or pickled and the leaves used like scallions.

Shallots can be finely minced and added to fried steak just before serving. Do not brown them, as it makes them bitter. Béarnaise sauce is made by reducing shallots and herbs in wine vinegar before thickening with egg and butter.

LEEK

Biennial grown as annual for blanched leaf bases. Hardy. Value: good source of potassium and iron, smaller amounts of beta carotene and vitamin C, particularly in green leaves.

The Bible mentions "the cucumbers, and the melons, and the leeks, and the onions and the garlic" which grew in Egypt, where the leek was held as a sacred plant, and to swear by the leek was the equivalent to swearing by one of the gods.

Giant leek contests have been held in pubs and clubs throughout the north-east of England since the mid-1880s. At one show in 1895, W. Robson was awarded a second prize of £1 and a sheep's heart; now the world championship has a first prize of over £1,300 ($2,000). At its peak, the European Community produced over 7 million tons per year.

 varieties

Older varieties are divided into two main groups, long thin and short stout types. In many modern cultivars, such differences are less obvious. There are also early, midseason and late varieties.

"King Richard" is a high-yielding, mild-tasting, early variety with a long shank. Good for growing at close spacing for "mini leeks". "Autumn Mammoth 2 — Argenta" matures in late fall and can be harvested until midspring. A high-yielding leek with a medium shank length and thick stems. "Leekool" will produce heavy crops of dark blue-green leaves atop white shanks, even from direct sowing. "Rikor" is a new early and vigorous variety for baby leeks from direct sowing. "Laura" is an extra hardy leek for overwintering. Its upright leaves are deep blue.

 cultivation

Leeks flourish in a sunny, sheltered site on well-drained, neutral to slightly acid soil. **Zones 5 to 10.**

Propagation

Leeks need a minimum soil or potting mix temperature of at least 45°F to germinate, so you will achieve more consistent results, particularly with early crops, when they are sown under cover. For rapid germination, sow early varieties indoors during late winter at 55–60°F in trays, pots or packs of potting mix. Repot those grown in trays or pots, spacing them about 2 in. apart, when two true leaves are produced, or when they begin to bend over. Harden off gradually before planting out in late spring.

Leeks can also be sown in unheated greenhouses, in cold frames, or under cloches. Sow seeds from late winter to early spring, repot, harden off, and transplant in late spring.

Although all varieties are suitable, later sowings of midseason and later types are particularly successful in seedbeds. Warm the soil using cloches, black plastic, or floating row cover and rake the seedbed to a fine tilth. Sow thinly in rows 6 in. apart and 1 in. deep, providing protection during cold spells. They can also be sown directly in the vegetable plot, 1 in. deep in rows 12 in. apart, thinning when seedlings have two or three leaves. Sowing seeds in packs — either in pairs or singly — keeping the most vigorous of the two, and multi-sowing 3 to 5 per cell, avoids the necessity of "pricking out" or thinning.

Growing

Fertile, moisture-retentive soil is essential, so dig in plenty of organic matter the fall or winter before planting, particularly on light soils. On heavy soils, add organic matter to improve drainage as crops are poor on heavy or waterlogged soil. Rake, level, and firm the soil before planting in spring. As they are a long-term, high-nitrogen crop, apply a general fertilizer, fish, blood, and bone or ammonium sulfate at 2–3 oz. per square yard, 1 or 2 weeks before planting.

Transplant leeks when they are 6–8 in. tall. Trim the leaf tips back if they drag on the ground, but not the roots, as is often recommended. If the soil is dry, water the area thoroughly before planting. Planting 6 in. apart in rows 12 in. apart provides a high yield of moderately sized leeks. Planting them 3–4 in. apart in rows gives a high yield of slim leeks. A spacing of 6–7 in. each way provides a reasonable crop of medium-sized leeks. Leeks grown in packs should be planted 9 in. apart each way.

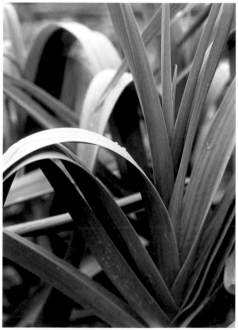

Leeks growing in a vegetable bed

LEEK

There are two methods of planting to ensure well-blanched stems. I find the first method better, as deeply planted leeks are more drought-resistant and soil is less likely to fall down between the leaves. Make a hole 6–8 in. deep with a dibble, drop the plant into it, and fill the hole with water (this washes some soil into the bottom of the hole), but do not fill any further.

Alternatively, plant leeks 3 in. deep and several times through the season pull the hill up around the stems, 2–3 in. at a time, with a draw hoe. Stop hilling when the plants reach maturity and make sure that the soil does not fall down between the leaves. Hilling is easier on light soil.

Whichever method you use, after planting, water gently with a seaweed-based fertilizer. If there is a dry period after planting, water leeks daily until the plants are well established and thereafter only during drought conditions. Hand weed or hoe carefully to keep down weeds, using an onion hoe around younger plants to avoid any damage. In poorer soils, feed weekly in summer with a liquid fertilizer.

Maintenance
Spring Repot leeks grown indoors; sow seed outdoors.
Summer Transplant seedlings, water, and feed. Keep crops weed-free by hoeing or mulching.
Fall Harvest crops as required.
Winter Harvest mid- and late-season crops. Sow seed indoors in late winter.

Protected Cropping
Apart from early sowings in the greenhouse or cold frame or under cloches and floating row cover, leeks are an extremely hardy outdoor crop.

Harvesting and Storing
Early varieties are ready for lifting from early to midfall, midseason types from early to midwinter and lates from early to midspring. Dig leeks carefully with a garden fork and dispose of any leaf debris to reduce the risk of disease in the future. Late varieties taking up space in the vegetable garden that is needed for spring planting can be stored for several weeks in a shallow, angled trench 6–8 in. deep; cover them lightly with soil and leave the tops exposed. If inclement weather is likely to hinder harvest, they can be lifted and packed closely together in a cold frame. The top should be raised to provide ventilation on warmer days.

Pests and Diseases
Leeks share many diseases with onions. Leek rust appears as orange pustules on the leaves during summer and is worse in wet seasons. Foliage developing later in the season is healthy. Feed with high-potash fertilizer, remove infected plants and debris. Improve drainage; do not plant leeks on the site for 4 to 5 years; grow partially resistant varieties like "Autumn Mammoth," "Titan" or "Gennevilliers-Splendid." Slugs can damage; collect them at night, use biological control, set traps, or use aluminum sulfate pellets. Mature leeks usually survive slug damage. Stem wireworm causes swelling at the base and distorted leaves. Destroy affected plants and rotate crops. Leaf rot is common during periods of high humidity, particularly on high-nitrogen soils.

White spots appear on leaf tips, followed by shrivelling. Spray with fungicide, increase spacing between plants to improve air circulation, and apply high-potash fertilizer.

 companion planting

Leeks grow well with celery. When planted with onions and carrots they discourage onion and carrot fly. Grow leeks in your rotation program alongside garlic, onions and shallots, unless you are in the northern U.S. where leeks require the full growing season. If they are grown at a 12 in. spacing; their upright growth makes them ideal for intercropping with lettuces like "Tom Thumb," with land cress or winter purslane.

 culinary

Leeks can be boiled, baked or steamed, made into terrines, cooked in casseroles, or added to pasta dishes. They are a useful addition to soups and an important ingredient in "cock-a-leekie" soup and in French Vichyssoise. Braise in stock with a little wine added and bake in a medium oven. Partially cook trimmed leeks in boiling water, drain well and roll in slices of good country ham and lay them in a dish; cover with a well-flavored cheese sauce and bake in a hot oven until well browned. Slice or chop young leeks and use raw as a scallion substitute in salads.

Leek and Ricotta Pie
Serves 4

4 largish leeks, trimmed and roughly chopped
2 tablespoons olive oil
2 cloves garlic, finely minced

1 cup ricotta
2 tablespoons pine nuts
3 tablespoons raisins, softened in warm water
1 egg
Salt and freshly ground black pepper

For the Dough:
1 stick butter
2 cups all-purpose flour
3 tablespoons water
Pinch salt

Make the dough by crumbling the butter into the flour and then adding water to make a dough. Add the salt and sprinkle with flour. Wrap in plastic wrap and chill in the refrigerator for 30 minutes.

Steam the leeks gently for about 10 minutes and drain.

Preheat the oven to 375°F. In a heavy skillet, heat the oil and gently fry the garlic. Then add the leeks and stir to coat well with oil; allow them to cook for about 5 minutes, stirring occasionally.

Remove from the heat. In a bowl mix the ricotta with the pine nuts and raisins, and bind with an egg. Add the leeks, mix well, and season.

Gently roll out the dough to fit a 8 inch pie tin. Prick the base and bake blind for 10 to 15 minutes. Fill the pie with the leek and ricotta mixture and continue cooking for 30 minutes. Serve with a green salad.

Allium sativum. Alliaceae

GARLIC

A garlic field in Aomori, Japan

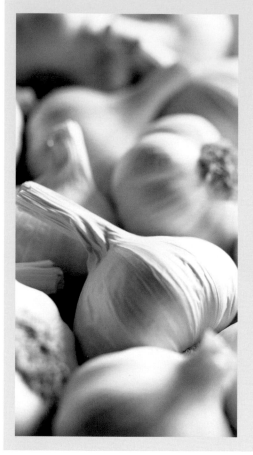

Perennial grown as annual for strongly aromatic bulbs. Half hardy. Value: contains small quantities of vitamins and minerals.

Prized throughout the world for its culinary and medicinal properties, garlic, now known only as a cultivated plant, is thought to have originated in western Asia. It has been grown since Egyptian times and for centuries in China and India. Its reputation as a "cure-all" has been endorsed by modern science. The Egyptians placed it in their tombs and gave it to the slaves who built the pyramids to ward off infection, while Hippocrates prescribed it for uterine tumors. In medieval Europe it was hung outside doors to deter witches. Today almost 3 million tons per annum are produced globally.

In areas with heavy soil, cloves can be planted any time over winter in pots or packs containing soilless potting mix, and can be planted out as soon as soil conditions are favorable. Plant cloves vertically with the flattened base plate at the bottom, twice the depth of the clove with at least 1 in. of soil above the tip. On good soils, planting up to 4 in. deep increases the yield. When planting, you should handle the cloves lightly: do not press them into the soil as this reduces root development. The amount of leaf growth dictates the size of the mature bulb which develops during long summer days. **Zones 3 to 10.**

Growing
Garlic favors an open, sunny position on light, well-drained soil. On heavier soil, grow in ridges or improve the drainage by working organic matter in to the topsoil.

Garlic is less successful in areas of heavy rainfall. On poor soils, it is beneficial to rake in a general fertilizer about 10 days before planting. Garlic can be grown on soil manured for the previous crop as well as limed acid soils.

Rotate the crop and do not grow in sites where onions have been planted the previous year. Keep the bulbs weed-free throughout the growing season.

Maintenance
Spring Mulch to suppress weeds. Water if necessary.
Summer Keep weed-free.
Fall Plant cloves.
Winter Plant cloves in containers for planting out in the spring.

Protected Cropping
Garlic can be grown in an unheated greenhouse for an early crop.

 varieties

There are two main categories of garlic; soft necks, which don't produce a flower stalk, and hard necks, which do. Hardnecks, also known as "gourmet" garlics, have a greater color range and taste but don't store well.

Softneck
"Germidor" crops early, producing large cloves and purple bulbs. "Inchelium Red" is a regular winner in taste tests. "Long Keeper" is well adapted to a cool, temperate climate. The bulbs are white-skinned and firm. "Solent Wight," producing large cloves with a mild flavor, is heavy-cropping with an appealing bouquet.

Hardneck
"Chesnok Red" is robustly flavored, "Brown Tempest" and "Purple Moldovan" are renowned for their taste and "Spanish Roja" is sought after by enthusiasts.

 cultivation

Propagation
Garlic is usually grown from healthy, plump bulb segments (cloves) saved from a previous crop. Where possible, buy nematode- and virus-resistant stock.

Plant cloves, a minimum of ½ in. diameter, in late fall or early spring, at a depth of 1 in. and 4 in. apart, with the rows 6–8 in. apart.

Garlic is surprisingly hardy and needs a cold, dormant period of 1 or 2 months when temperatures are 0 to 32–50°F to yield decent-sized bulbs; for this reason it is generally better planted in late fall. A long growing period is also beneficial for the ripening process.

Harvesting and Storing

From mid- to late summer, as soon as the leaves and stems begin to yellow, lift the bulbs carefully with a fork and leave them to dry off in the sun. Delaying harvest causes the bulbs to shrivel and increases the possibility of disease during storage. Handle them delicately as they are easily bruised.

In inclement weather, dry them under cover on trays. Store them in cool, dry conditions indoors or in a shed or garage. Hang them in bunches tied by the leaves, in string bags or braid the stems together. Plants that have gone to seed are still able to produce usable bulbs for the kitchen.

Pests and Diseases

Onion flies lay their eggs around the base of garlic: the larvae tunnel into the bulb and the plant turns yellow and dies. Rotate crops, dig the plot over winter, grow under covers, and apply chemicals to the soil before growing.

Downy mildew is a common problem in wet seasons. Gray patches appear on the leaves. White rot, a gray fungus on the roots, turns the leaves yellow. Lift and destroy infected plants, and do not grow garlic, onions or shallots on the site for 8 years.

Stem and bulb wireworm seedlings become blunted, bloated and distorted, and stems rot. Dig and destroy affected plants. Rotate crops.

 ## companion planting

Planted beside rose bushes, garlic controls greenfly. Good companions are lettuce, beets, summer savory, Swiss chard, and strawberries. It should not be planted with peas and beans.

 ## container growing

Garlic can be grown in pots, windowboxes, or containers, in a moisture-retentive, free-draining potting mix. Water the plants regularly to produce decent-sized bulbs and place the container in a sunny position to allow the bulbs to develop.

 ## medicinal

Garlic has powerful antiviral, antibacterial, and antifungal properties, and is effective for digestive complaints, bowel disorders, and insect stings. It contains two chemicals that combine to form the bactericide allicin, which gives it the characteristic odor. Modern herbalists believe a cold will be cured by rubbing garlic on the soles of feet. What a combination of odors! Current research indicates its ability to reduce blood cholesterol levels and the chance of heart attack. There is also a lower incidence of colonic and other types of cancer where it is part of the daily diet.

 ## culinary

Garlic is used as a seasoning in dishes from curries to pasta — whole plants can be added to salads! Harvest very young leaves of wild garlic, a few per plant as a milder substitute.

Jean-Christophe Novelli's Honey-glazed Lamb
Serves 4

4 lamb knuckles or shanks
Olive oil
Salt and freshly ground black pepper
2 carrots, cut into chunks
2 onions, cut into chunks
2 leeks, cut into chunks
2¼ cups celeriac, cut into chunks
1 head of garlic, broken into cloves
Handful of mixed fresh herbs, like rosemary, bay and thyme

For the Red Wine Sauce:
2–3 tablespoons shallots, sliced
1 tablespoon celery, sliced
½ cup button mushrooms, sliced
2 tablespoons unsalted butter
1 tablespoon finely minced mixed fresh herbs, like tarragon, parsley and basil
1 cup plus 1 tablespoon red wine
Juice of ½ a lemon
2 teaspoons honey

Remove the excess fat from the knuckles and trim the meat away to expose the bone, reserving the meat trimmings. Heat a little oil in a roasting pan on the stovetop. Season the knuckles and place into the pan. Add the chunks of carrot, onion, leek, and celeriac and brown the meat quickly all over. Meanwhile, bring a large pan of salted water to a boil. Lift the knuckles from the roasting pan, and plunge into the water. Blanch for 1 to 2 minutes to help it retract around the bone and keep it in one piece during cooking.

Drain and put in a clean pan with the vegetables, garlic, and herbs, together with enough water to cover the meat. Bring to a boil, lower the heat, and simmer gently for about 1½ hours to the point where the meat is almost falling off the bone. Remove the knuckles from the stock and reserve the stock.

Preheat the oven to 325°F. Sweat the sliced vegetables in a little of the butter to soften them without browning. Add the reserved meat trimmings and the chopped herbs and cook for an additional 2 to 3 minutes. Pour in the red wine and bubble until reduced by half. Add 2 cups of the reserved lamb stock and reduce again by half. Cut the remaining butter into small pieces and whisk these in, a few at a time. Season to taste and pass through a fine strainer. Pour half of the sauce into the roasting pan. Stir in the lemon juice and honey. Add the knuckles and coat with this glaze. Cook in the oven for about 20 minutes, removing every 5 minutes or so to baste the knuckles.

Just before the knuckles come out of the oven, heat through the remaining sauce. Place each knuckle or lamb shank on a warmed plate, pour on a little sauce, and serve with mashed potatoes and seasonal vegetables of choice.

Pestou

This is a version of the classic garlic and basil butter, which is extremely good over pasta and which the Italians eat with fish. For ¼ cup butter, have 2 plump garlic cloves, 5 to 6 sprigs of fresh basil, 2 tablespoons Parmesan, and a pinch of salt. Pound the garlic in a mortar, tear the basil leaves roughly, then add to the garlic with the butter and cheese. Pound to mix.

AMARANTH

Amaranthus spp. Amaranthaceae

Also known as Pigweed, Kiwicha, Chinese Spinach, Calaloo, Bayam. Half hardy annual.

Value: extremely rich in protein; contains carotene, zinc, phosphorus and calcium, some of the vitamin B complex, and vitamin E.

Amaranth was a staple grain of the Incas and Aztecs as long ago as 6000 BCE until it was banned by the Spanish, who forced them to grow European crops in a form of "botanical colonialism," and it retreated to the high Andes. The seeds remain viable for centuries — when archeologists sowed seeds found in an Aztec ruin, they germinated and grew successfully.

It is also an excellent ornamental plant, which was prized by Victorians in their bedding schemes and is known as "Love Lies Bleeding." With high levels of protein and minerals, the Amaranth has been compared favorably with milk and has become an important nutrient source in tropical highlands.

Amaranths share an extremely efficient type of photosynthesis, similar to some cacti and succulents, which allow them to grow efficiently in high temperatures, intense sunlight and under dry conditions.

 varieties

"A 452" has leaves and flowers in shades of gold, green, red and purple. "Bolivia" reaches up to 7 ft., the upright, red flower-heads followed by deep purple seeds. "Golden" is early maturing, with rich golden seeds. "Plainsman" is a short growing variety with maroon seed-heads followed by high volumes of dark purple seeds. "Popping" is a selection for use as a "popping" grain.

Amaranthus caudatus is successful in cool conditions and the most important species for grain, reaching up to 7 ft. or more at maturity, depending on the variety. Broad, lance-shaped leaves appear from side branches and main stem. Extravagant upright or hanging flower- and seed-heads, often called "cat's tails," produce up to 500,000 seeds per plant.

Amaranthus gangeticus — the greatest variety of those grown for their leaves — is found in India. "Asia Red" is colored bright red with tender and delicious leaves and shoot tips — ideal for hotter climates. There are several selections of fast-growing "Bayam" with dark green leaves and tender stems. The top-quality dwarf variety "Tender Leaf" reaches 8 in. tall, was developed in Taiwan, and is ideal as a "cut and come again" crop for harvesting at any stage.

Amaranth growing in Bhutan

cultivation

Propagation

To extend the growing season, sow amaranth indoors, several per pack, from midspring at 68°F, lightly but thoroughly, covering the seeds with potting mix or an opaque cover as they need darkness to germinate.

Germination is rapid, usually within 4 days and is aided by fluctuating day and night temperatures. When they are about ½ in. tall, thin to leave the strongest seedling before planting outdoors once the danger of frost has passed, and protecting with cloches for 2 to 3 weeks to acclimatize.

Alternatively, in warmer climates, broadcast or sow seed in rows outdoors once the danger of frost has passed, into a seedbed raked to a fine tilth, mixing the fine poppy-like seeds with sharp sand to aid sowing, then thin to the final spacing.

Planting distance varies according to the climate. In cool temperate conditions, varieties grown for grain should be 20 in. apart, and up to 3 ft. apart in warmer climates or under the protection of a greenhouse or plastic tunnel where plants grow larger.

Cuttings from nonflowering side shoots of established or bought plants root easily. For a continuous supply of "cut and come again" seedlings of leafy varieties, sow at 2-week intervals throughout the season.

Growing

Amaranths prefer a sunny position in light, moist, rich, free-draining soil similar to that enjoyed by pumpkins and squashes, but are tolerant of most soils, providing they are not waterlogged. Incorporate well-rotted organic matter, grit, or sharp sand into the soil if necessary before planting. The plants are drought-tolerant once established and perform well in poor soils, though crops are reduced. Critical periods for watering are at germination and pollination, though regular watering during drought increases the size of the plant and consequently the crop. Amaranths are not frost-hardy — the most tolerant cultivars withstand temperatures down to 39°F, growing best at 70–82°F. Plant them with brassicas (cabbage-family crops) in your crop-rotation scheme. Hoe around young plants to break up the soil and keep them weed-free; they are easily overwhelmed by weed seedlings, though the leaves rapidly grow large enough to suppress weed growth.

Maintenance

Spring Sow seeds.
Summer Keep crops weed-free, water if necessary, harvest leaves. Harvest seeds from late summer.
Fall Harvest seeds.
Winter Order seeds for next year.

Protected Cropping

Sow seeds under cover to extend the growing season for "leaf" or "grain" varieties. Growing plants to maturity in greenhouses or plastic tunnels in cooler climates results in larger plants and increased production of leaves and seeds, particularly in poor summers.

Harvesting and Storing

Plants take 16 to 24 weeks from sowing to harvest and yield well, even in poor summers. Harvest when the first seeds start to ripen and fall when rubbed between the fingers — usually from September; leave it too late and they will be lost during harvesting. Pull up the plants or cut off the seed-heads then strip the grains with your fingers and riddle into a bucket before drying the seeds. Store the seeds in dry conditions in jars or paper bags.

Harvest leaves from those being grown primarily for their seeds when plants are well established and the loss of a few leaves does not check their growth. Frequent harvesting delays flowering and encourages leaf and stem growth. Thinned seedlings can be used as transplants or pot herbs. Varieties grown for their leaves should be harvested before flowering, and are harvested at various stages as micro-greens, "cut and come again" seedlings or young plants.

Pests and Diseases

Seedlings can suffer from "damping off" if they are sown too densely.

 container growing

Varieties grown as "cut and come again" crops for their leaves can be grown in growing bags or containers of moisture retentive, free-draining potting mix, with drainage holes in the base.

 medicinal

Betalaina, a yellow or green dye is obtained from red flowering varieties and used as a food coloring and for clothing. Medicinally, it has several uses; it is a diuretic, astringent, and is applied to skin sores.

 culinary

The leaves, stems, and young shoots can be eaten raw, in soups, stir-fries, or salads, steamed or lightly cooked like spinach and young leaves as micro-greens. The seeds have a nutty flavor when "popped" like corn and can be added to rice, or ground as a wheat substitute in unleavened chapattis or tortillas; when used in baking bread it should be mixed with wheat as amaranth is gluten-free. Because of its high nutritional value, it is considered good for children, the ill, and the elderly.

CELERY

Apium graveolens var. *dulce.* Umbelliferae

Biennial grown as annual for fleshy leaf stems and leaves. Hardy. Value: low in carbohydrate and calories, high in potassium.

The species is a biennial plant, native to Europe and Asia. It is usually found on marshy ground by rivers, particularly where the water is slightly saline. Its Latin generic name *Apium* is derived from the Celtic *apon*, water, referring to its favored habitat, while *graveolens* means heavily scented, alluding to its aroma. The stems of the wild plant are very bitter, distinguishing it from var. *dulce* — meaning sweet or pleasant — from which the culinary varieties have been bred. Celery became popular in Italy in the 17th century and during the following 200 years spread throughout Europe to North America. "Trench celery" (so called from the method used for blanching the stems) is very hardy and is harvested from late fall to early spring, while the more recently developed self-blanching and American green types have a shorter growing season and are less hardy, cropping from midsummer until midfall. Less succulent, but full of flavor, is the smaller-stemmed "cutting celery."

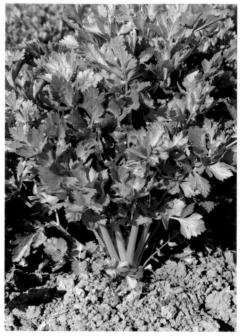

The dense foliage of celery suppresses weed growth

 varieties

English Trench or Pascal Celery

This is grouped into white, pink, and the hardier red varieties: "Giant Pink" is a hardy variety harvested from mid- to late winter. The crisp, pale pink stalks blanch easily. "Giant Red" is hardy and vigorous and the outer stalks turn shell-pink when blanched. "Giant White" is an old, tall, white celery variety with crisp stems and a solid, well-flavored heart. It needs good growing conditions to flourish. "Hopkins Fenlander" is a late-maturing green celery with good flavor. Its sticks are of medium length and free from string. "Standard Bearer" red celery has the reputation of being the latest of all to reach maturity.

Self-blanching and American Green Celery

These include: "Celebrity", an early-maturing variety with long, crisp stems and a nutty-flavored heart. It has good bolting resistance and is one of the least stringy self-blanching varieties. "Golden Self Blanching" is compact with firm golden-yellow hearts which are crisp and tasty. Does not become stringy. "Greensleeves," a green variety, produces tasty green sticks. "Ivory Tower" is "stringless" and well flavored. "Lathom Self Blanching" is a vigorous, well-flavored early variety with crisp stems.

"Tall Utah Triumph" has long, succulent, tender green stems. It crops from late summer to early fall but the season can be extended by growing under cloches.

Leaf, Cutting or Soup Celery

This produces leaves and stems over a long period and is very hardy. It is usually sold as seed mixes, but cultivars are available: "French Dinant" is excellent for drying and full of flavor. "Soup Celery d'Amsterdam" is aromatic and prolific, producing thin stems and lots of leaves. "Thai Bai Khuen Chai" is spicy and leafy with thin stems. Its strong flavor is good in Thai soup, salads, curries, and stir-fries.

 ## cultivation

Celery is a crop for cool temperate conditions, flourishing at 59–70°F on an open site. It requires rich, fertile soil which is constantly moist yet well drained and a pH of 6.5 to 7.5. Lime acid soils before planting if needed. **Zones 5 to 10.**

Propagation

Sow celery from mid- to late spring, in trays of moist seed potting mix, sprinkling the seed thinly over the surface; do not cover it with potting mix, as light is needed for germination. Keep the tray in a propagator or in a greenhouse at 55–60°F; germination can take several weeks, so be as patient as possible.

When two true leaves appear, transplant the seedlings into trays of moist seed potting mix about 2½ in. apart or individually into 3-in. pots and allow them to establish. Harden off before planting outdoors from late spring to early summer when they have five to seven true leaves.

Low temperatures after germination sometimes cause bolting later in life; temperatures should not fall below 50°F for longer than 12 hours until the seedlings have become established. They are particularly sensitive at transplanting size, so cover them with cloches and do not try to slow down the growth of advanced seedlings by putting them outdoors. It is much better to trim plants back to about 3 in. with sharp scissors and keep them in the warm until outdoor temperatures are satisfactory. Cutting back also seems to lead to more successful transplanting. Planting in packs of seed potting mix lessens transplanting shock, which can also result in bolting. If you are unable to

provide the necessary conditions, you may be able to find transplants at a nursery.

Celery can also be sown *in situ* but germination is usually erratic and it is not worth the trouble. Celery's low germination rate can be improved by "fluid sowing" (pre-soaking seeds before sowing). If possible, use treated seed to control celery leaf spot. Several sowings at 3-week intervals lengthens the harvesting season.

Sow cutting celery in trays of seed potting mix from late spring to late summer before hardening off and planting out 12 in. apart each way. Alternatively, multi-sow in packs, about 6 to 8 seeds in each, and plant each pack group 8 in. apart. Leave a few plants to go to seed the following year, then transplant self-sown seedlings at the recommended spacing.

Growing

The planting method is different for trench celery and self-blanching types. "Trenching" celery can only be done in temperate regions where the climate allows overwintering. Dig a trench 15–20 in. wide and 12 in. deep in late fall or early spring and incorporate as much well-rotted manure or compost as you can find. If more than one trench is needed, their centers should be 4 ft. apart. Trench celery can also be grown by filling

in the trench to a depth of about 3–4 in. and leaving the remaining soil alongside for hilling. A week or 10 days before planting, rake a balanced general fertilizer at a rate of 2–3 oz. per square yard into the bottom of the trench. Celery is easier to manage when planted in single rows with plants 12–18 in. apart. If you plant in double rows, set the plants 9 in. apart in pairs, rather than staggered. This makes blanching easier. Water thoroughly after planting.

Blanch with "collars." Use 9–10 in. strips of thick paper like newspaper, corrugated cardboard, brown wrapping paper, or thick black plastic. (Ideally this should be lined with paper to prevent sweating.) I have also seen tile drainpipes and plastic guttering being used to good effect.

Plants can also be blanched by hilling plants when they are about 12 in. high. Before you start, tie the stems loosely, just below the leaves, using raffia or soft string and make sure the soil is moist, watering if necessary (or hill up after rain). Draw soil up the stems about 3 in. at a time, repeating this two or three times at 3-week intervals until only the tops of plants are exposed. Do not hill up higher than the leaves, neither should you let soil fall into the heart of the plant. If heavy frosts are forecast in winter, place hay, straw, or other protective material over plants to keep in good condition for as long as possible.

Celery being grown on a commercial scale

Celery blanched by wrapping cardboard around the stem

Begin blanching when plants are about 12 in. high, tying the collar quite loosely around the plant to give it room to expand and leaving about one third of the plant exposed. Further collars can be added every 2 to 3 weeks as the plants grow.

Remember to unwrap them periodically to remove any slugs hiding beneath. If collars are used in exposed sites, support them by staking. Cover the top of the stake with a flower pot, film canister, or table tennis ball to avoid inflicting any damage to your eyes.

Labor-saving self-blanching types do not need hilling. They also tolerate a wider range of soils, and are particularly good where the ground is heavy and trenching or waterlogging would be a problem. They are, however, shallow-rooted and should be fed and watered regularly throughout the growing season. Self-blanching celery is planted at ground level. Dig in generous amounts of well-rotted organic matter in spring before planting. The spacing varies according to your requirements and plants should be arranged in a square pattern, not staggered rows. Spacing about 6 in. apart gives a high yield of very tender, small-stemmed shoots; 11 in. apart each way, the optimum spacing, gives high yields of longer, well-blanched shoots and 9 in. apart each way gives moderate stem growth. Plant with the crown at soil level and put straw around the outer plants when they mature to help blanching.

For good-quality crops celery must be watered copiously throughout the growing season and the soil should not be allowed to dry out. Apply up to 5 gallons per square yard per week during dry periods. Mulching with straw or compost once plants have established conserves moisture and suppresses weeds. Feed with a granular or liquid general fertilizer about 4 to 6 weeks after transplanting. Rotate crops, but do not plant next to parsnips, as both are attacked by celery fly. Avoid anything that checks plant growth throughout the season as this can cause bolting, so transplant the seedlings when the soil is warm, water and feed them regularly, and always mulch or hoe round the plants very carefully.

Maintenance

Spring Prepare the ground for planting. Sow seed and plant earlier crops out under cloches.
Summer Plant out in early summer, keep soil moist and weed regularly. Check for pests and diseases.
Fall Harvest with care using a sharp knife or garden fork.
Winter Cover with straw, bracken or similar materials to allow harvest to continue during heavy frosts.

Protected Cropping

Protect newly transplanted plantlets with cloches or floating row cover for several weeks after planting, until they become established. This is particularly necessary in cooler conditions.

Harvesting and Storing

Cut or dig celery carefully with a garden fork, easing the roots from the ground. Hay, straw or other protective material placed over trenches assists digging in frosty weather. Self-blanching celery can be harvested from midsummer to early fall. Before the first frosts, lift and store any remaining plants and put them in a cool, frost-free shed. They will keep for several weeks. Harvest cutting celery regularly from about 5 weeks after planting.

Pests and Diseases

Celery leaf miner or celery fly larvae tunnel through the leaves leaving brown blisters. Severe attacks check growth. Grow under crop covers, pinch out affected leaves, do not plant seedlings which have affected leaves. Check plants in late spring and late summer. Do not plant near to parsnips as they can be affected.

Slugs are a major problem, particularly on heavy soil. Use biological control, traps, hand pick, or use aluminum sulfate–based slug pellets. Carrot flies attack the roots and stem bases, stunting growth. Grow under floating row cover until harvest or put fine mesh netting barriers 45–72 in. high around the crop before or straight after transplanting.

Celery leaf spot shows as brown spots on older leaves, spreading to younger ones. Severe attacks can stunt growth; use treated seed, rotate crops or use copper-based fungicide.

Celery pale leaf spot (early blight) appears as tiny yellow spots on the leaf surfaces with accompanying gray mold in damp conditions. This disease spreads rapidly. Spray with Bordeaux mixture, be vigilant and destroy all plant debris at the end of the season.

 companion planting

Celery helps brassicas by deterring damaging butterflies. It grows well with beans, tomatoes, and particularly leeks. If left to flower, celery attracts beneficial insects.

 medicinal

Cultivated varieties are said to be beneficial in the treatment of rheumatism and as a diuretic.

culinary

Usually eaten raw rather than cooked, celery adds welcome crunchiness to salads, particularly in winter months. It is a key ingredient of the famous Waldorf Salad, made with equal quantities of chopped red-skinned apples and celery, combined with walnuts and bound with mayonnaise.

Celery with cheese-sticks filled with cream cheese or pâté are an appetizing "nibble." The "heart" is particularly tasty. Cook celery in soups and stews, or stir-fry. Braise hearts by simmering in boiling water for 10 minutes, then cook in a covered dish for 45 minutes in a low oven to accompany roasts.

Add leaves, like parsley, to meat dishes. Fresh or dried leaves flavor soups and stuffings. Cutting celery is a flavoring for salads, soups and stews; the seeds can also be used.

Celery will stay fresh in a plastic bag in the refrigerator for up to 3 days. Do not stand in water for long periods, or the freshness is lost.

Freeze celery by washing and cutting the sticks into 1 in. lengths, blanch for 3 minutes, cool, drain and pack into plastic bags. Use frozen celery only in cooked dishes.

Celery and Zucchini with Blue Cheese Dip
Serves 4

2 tablespoons olive oil
1 teaspoon chile powder
½ teaspoon paprika
1 clove garlic, crushed
4 fresh basil leaves, roughly chopped
4 zucchini, sliced lengthwise into quarters
Fresh chives, to garnish
4 stalks celery, cut into 3-in. lengths

For the Dip:
4 tablespoons cottage cheese
2 tablespoons crumbled blue cheese
4 tablespoons yogurt
Salt and freshly ground pepper

In a heavy skillet over a gentle heat, mix the oil with the chile powder, paprika, garlic and basil. Turn up the heat and fry the zucchini slices, cut side down, until browned and turn them to brown the second side. In a small bowl mix together all the dip ingredients. On 4 small plates, arrange a fan of alternating zucchini and celery sticks and fill the center with the dip. Garnish with finely snipped chives and serve.

Apium graveolens var. *rapaceum*. Umbelliferae
CELERIAC

Also known as Celery Root. Biennial usually grown as annual for edible root. Hardy. Value: rich in potassium; moderate amounts of vitamin C.

This swollen-stemmed relative of celery has long been popular in Europe. It was introduced to Britain in the early 18th century by the writer and seedsman Stephen Switzer, who brought seed from Alexandria and wrote about the vegetable in his book, *Growing Foreign Kitchen Vegetables*. It is an excellent, versatile winter vegetable, hardier and more disease-resistant than celery, but with similar flavor and aroma.

encourage them to go to seed later in the season. Maintain the temperature and cut off the tops of the plants with sharp scissors to 3 in. — the ideal size for transplanting. **Zones 4 to 10.**

Growing
Celeriac needs rich, fertile, moisture-retentive soil and is ideal for damper parts of the garden. In fall, incorporate as much well-rotted manure or potting mix as possible. Space plants 12–15 in. apart each way. Do not bury the crowns; they should be planted at ground level. Plant firmly and water thoroughly and continually. In midsummer remove the outer leaves to expose the crown and encourage the bulb to develop, and remove side shoots if they appear.

Maintenance
Spring Plant out seedlings — harden off. Keep weed-free.
Summer Water in dry weather. Mulch to conserve moisture; feed weekly with a liquid manure, particularly in poorer soils.
Fall Begin harvesting. Cover with straw.
Winter Prepare ground. Sow seeds indoors.

Protected Cropping
Celeriac only benefits from protection when it is at the seedling stage.

Harvesting and Storing
Celeriac can be harvested through the winter in mild climates. Harvest when the plants are 3–5 in. diameter, though they can be lifted when larger with no loss of flavor. Ideally they should remain in the ground until required. Before the onset of severe winter weather, protect plants with a layer of straw or with floating row cover to prevent the ground from freezing. If the soil is heavy, the site exposed or needed for another crop, lift and remove the outer leaves, keeping the central tuft attached; cut off the roots and store in a cool shed in boxes of damp peat substitute or sand.

Alternatively, lift and "heel in" or transplant the crop in another part of the garden, laying them close together in a trench and covering the bulbs with soil. They last for several weeks when stored in this manner.

Bulbs can be frozen; cut into cubes, blanch for 3 minutes, dry, store in plastic bags and put in the freezer. They will keep for a week in the salad drawer of a refrigerator.

 varieties

The lowest part of the stem, known as the "bulb," is eaten; the roots that grow below are removed. "Alabaster" is high-yielding with upright foliage, round bulbs and has good resistance to running to seed. "Balder" has round, medium-sized roots, which have excellent flavor when eaten cooked and raw. The "bulb" of "Brilliant" is smooth with white flesh and does not discolor. "Iram" is a medium-sized "bulb" with few side shoots. It stores well and the flesh remains white when cooked. "Marble Ball," a well-known variety, is medium-sized, globular and strongly flavored. It also stores well. "Monarch" is a popular variety with smooth skin and succulent flesh. "Prinz" has white-fleshed roots with an aromatic flavor and is also resistant to leaf disease and bolting. "Tellus" grows quickly and remains white after boiling. It has firm flesh and a smoother skin than many varieties.

 cultivation

Propagation
Celeriac needs a long growing season. Sow in late winter to early spring in a propagator at 65°F or in mid- to late spring in a cold greenhouse, under cloches, or in a cold frame. Plant seeds in peat substitute-based potting mix either several to a pot or in seed boxes or packs.

Germination is notoriously erratic. Repot strong seedlings when they are about ½ in. tall and large enough to handle. Plant them into single 3-in. pots, packs, or in seed trays at 2½-in. intervals, keeping the temperature at 55–60°F. Harden off when the weather becomes warm in late spring and plant outdoors once there is no danger of frost.

Celeriac is sensitive to cold at the transplanting stage; do not try to slow the growth of fast-growing seedlings by lowering the temperature, as this will

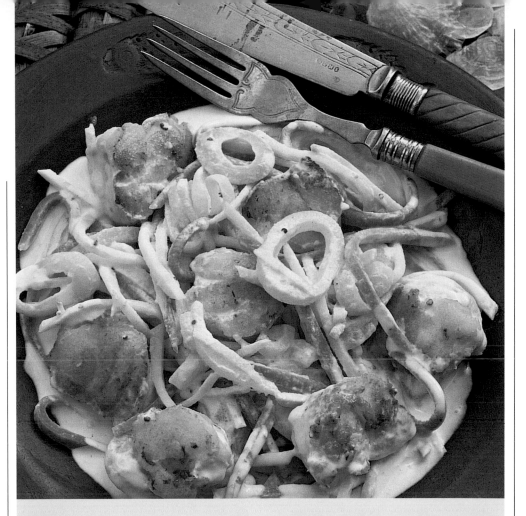

Pests and Diseases

Celeriac has the same problems as celery. Protect against slugs; use aluminum sulfate–based slug pellets, pick off slugs at night and encourage natural predators. Slugs congregate under lettuce leaves or wet paper; pick off and destroy. Carrot fly is often a pest when established on carrots. Grow under floating row cover or place a barrier 30 in. high of fine netting or plastic, erected before or just after sowing. Keep it in place until harvesting time. Celery fly is less of a problem than on celery. Pick off any brown, blistered leaflets or grow under floating row cover.

 ## companion planting

Celeriac grows well where legumes have been planted the previous year and benefits from being placed alongside beans, brassicas, leeks, tomatoes, and onions.

 ## medicinal

Celeriac oil has a calming effect and is a traditional remedy for skin complaints and rheumatism. It is also said to restore sexual potency after illness! Celeriac is rich in calcium, phosphorus, and vitamin C.

 ## warning

Celeriac is a diuretic. Pregnant women and those with a kidney disorder should avoid eating it in large quantities.

"Prinz"

 ## culinary

Containing only 14 calories per 4 oz., celeriac is excellent for anyone on a diet.

Scrub the bulb well to remove dirt before peeling. It discolors rapidly when cut; put immediately into acidified water. Grated celeriac can be added raw to winter salads. Alternatively, blanch the slices or cubes in boiling water for a few seconds beforehand. In France it is cut into cubes and mixed with mayonnaise and Dijon mustard to make *céleri-rave rémoulade*.

The bulb adds flavor to soups or stews and is good with lamb or beef, puréed or seasoned with pepper, salt, and butter, it is an ideal accompaniment for stronger-flavored game.

The leaves are strongly flavored and can be used sparingly to garnish salads or dried for use in cooking. The stems can be cooked and eaten like sea kale. Celeriac can be made into delicious fries: boil a whole, peeled root in salted water until just tender and then cut into fries and fry in a mixture of butter and oil until lightly browned. These fries make an excellent accompaniment to game or plain broiled steaks.

Boiled and sliced, celeriac can be covered with a cheese sauce well flavored with French mustard. It also makes an excellent soup.

Monkfish with Celeriac
Serves 4

1½ pounds monkfish, cut into chunks
½ cup celeriac, cut into julienne strips
1 large onion, finely sliced
1 carrot, peeled and cut into julienne strips
1 stick butter
1 tablespoon flour
2 teaspoons French mustard
2 tablespoons Greek yogurt
1 tablespoon heavy cream
Salt and freshly ground black pepper

Season the monkfish and prepare the vegetables. Heat half the butter in a heavy skillet and cook the monkfish gently for about 7 to 8 minutes, turning it until just tender. Remove from the pan and keep warm. Using the rest of the butter, add the vegetables to the pan, and sauté until soft. Stir in the flour and cook for a couple of minutes; then add the mustard, yogurt, and cream. Stir well and heat through gently. Put the fish pieces in, stir to coat well and serve piping hot.

BURDOCK

Also known as Edible Burdock, Gobo. Hardy biennial, grown as an annual. Value: moderate levels of dietary fiber plus vitamin B, potassium, calcium, and inulin.

After walking his dog one day in the early 1940s, inventor George de Mestral noticed that burdock seeds had attached themselves to his woollen clothes and the fur of his dog; when analyzing them under a microscope, he discovered that the sharply hooked "burrs" were firmly linked to the loops of fur and material. After much research, he devised the famous fastening system Velcro®, which is widely used today. Burdock is naturalized throughout the world; the Chinese introduced it to Japan and neatly packed boxes are a feature of Japanese food markets. The famous French seedsmen Vilmorin-Andrieux, in their book, *The Vegetable Garden*, noted that, "although it cannot be termed delicious, it is certainly not a bad vegetable and is, therefore, deserving of serious consideration." It has an unusual but rather pleasing flavor — perhaps you should give it a try!

Burdock roots close up

 ## varieties

Arctium lappa is a large biennial up to 4 ft. tall, notable for its large, rough, heart-shaped leaves. Roots can be up to 8 ft. long and 1 in. thick. The small, thistle-like flower heads are followed by prickly burrs. However, avoid cultivating wild burdock as a crop as the roots are comparatively small. "Mitoya Shirohada" has roots that are white and smooth with a tender texture and just over 3¼ ft. long. "Takinogawa Long" has small leaves and large roots. "Watanabe Early" is ideal for spring sowing, matures rapidly and has roots around 3 ft. long.

 ## cultivation

Propagation

Soak seeds overnight or scratch the seed coat before sowing and place them on the surface as they need light to germinate. Sow in fall but not too early in the season; smaller plants are more resistant to winter weather and larger over-wintering plants usually bolt in spring. Alternatively, sow in spring when temperatures are at a minimum of 68°F, placing three seeds 16 in. apart, with 20 in. between rows, then thin in late winter, leaving the strongest seedling. Another option is to germinate seeds indoors and transplant before a "taproot" starts to form; packs are ideal for this.

Growing

Burdock grows well in temperate and warm, humid climates at temperatures from 68–77°F and is most successful on moisture-retentive, free-draining, light or sandy soils for increased rooting depth and easy lifting of the roots. It is less successful on heavier soils, though it can be grown successfully in raised beds or ridges. Clear the site before planting, incorporating copious amounts of well-rotted organic matter as deeply as possible and adding bone-meal to encourage root growth. Keep young plants weed-free until the foliage is large enough to prevent them from germinating. Water plants well during drought.

Burdock is vigorous and spreading, demanding high levels of nutrients and water and should be sited well away from other plants.

Maintenance

Spring Sow seeds indoors or outdoors if soil is warm.
Summer Water well and keep weed-free.
Fall Lift roots.
Winter Protect over-wintering seedlings under cloches.

Protected Cropping

Plants can be started off indoors before transplanting them outdoors.

Harvesting and Storing

Plants sown in fall or spring are ready for harvest the following fall. Dig the first roots when the foliage dies back after the first frosts; it may not be possible to dig out whole roots because of their length, but those that remain in the ground will not become a problem. Lifting roots when they are immature, up to 18 in. long, ensures they are tender. Cover plants with straw or similar materials in winter; the roots can then still be lifted when the surrounding soil is frozen. Alternatively, lift all roots after the first frosts and store in boxes of damp sand or wrapped in paper in the salad drawer of a refrigerator.

Pests and Diseases

Burdock is pest- and disease-free.

container growing

Burdock is not suitable for most containers because of the size of the plant above and below ground, but raised beds should provide adequate space.

medicinal

Burdock contains a chemical that encourages lactation and is also used as a hair and scalp conditioner, blood purifier, diuretic, and for the treatment of skin conditions.

Burdock growing in a field

culinary

Burdock is a major ingredient in Root Beer. Young roots, which are of a better quality, can be eaten raw or stir-fried, whereas older roots are boiled until soft or added to casseroles. One seed catalog even suggests it can be fried with red bell peppers and makes a good accompaniment to baked beans! The young leaves and stem can be lightly cooked; immature flower stems can also be harvested and eaten before flowering.

In Japan, the roots are pickled and served with sweet sauce, or shredded and braised with several ingredients, including carrot, sake, and sesame oil, in a dish called *kinpira gobo*. Burdock *makizushi* is sushi filled with pickled burdock root instead of fish. Soak older roots in water for an hour before use, to purge any bitterness, adding a dash of vinegar to prevent discoloration. Older roots taste earthy and become woody and less palatable with age. Buy burdock in Asian or health food stores — or get it for free when out in the countryside. This dish comes from southern Italy.

Bucatini with Burdock, Artichokes, and Peas
Serves 4

1 burdock root, about 10 in. long
Balsamic vinegar
1 pound bucatini pasta
1 tablespoon olive oil
1 shallot, finely minced
1 small onion, finely minced
3 to 4 cloves garlic, crushed
Zest of 1 lemon
4 to 6 marinated artichoke hearts
½ pound peas
1 large handful basil leaves
½ cup chicken or vegetable stock
2 tablespoons butter
Salt and freshly ground black pepper
Freshly grated pecorino cheese, to serve

Peel the burdock root if you prefer, but remember the vitamins are right under the skin and it has more flavor with the skin left on. Cut into matchstick-sized pieces, cover with water, stir in a couple of teaspoons of balsamic vinegar, and leave to soak for 30 minutes.

Cook the pasta in boiling, salted water until *al dente*, then drain. Meanwhile, strain the burdock. Heat a large, heavy-bottomed frying pan over a medium heat and pour in the olive oil. Sauté the shallot and onion for 2–3 minutes, then add the garlic, lemon zest and burdock root and cook until the vegetables are softened and lightly colored. Add the artichoke hearts, peas, basil and the butter, and sauté for a further 5 minutes. Combine the vegetables with the drained pasta, season with salt and pepper and serve sprinkled with cheese.

Armoracia rusticana. Cruciferae

HORSERADISH

Perennial herb sometimes grown as annual for its strong-flavored fleshy roots. Hardy. Value: rich in vitamin C and calcium, moderate in carbohydrates.

Thought to be native of southern Russia and the eastern Ukraine, horseradish is now found throughout the temperate zones of the world. Cultivated since classical times, horseradish was probably carried around Europe by the Romans, who used it as a medicine and flavoring. Parkinson noted in 1640, "it is too strong for tender and gentle stomaches," yet it was extensively eaten by country folk in Germany; it is known in France as *moutarde des Allemands*. Its hardiness and ability to regenerate from the smallest particle of root have ensured its success — and sometimes makes it a pernicious weed both in and outside the garden. The common name "horseradish" distinguishes it from the salad radish, "horse" signifying coarse.

sand in a cool, frost-free shed. In midspring, make holes with a dibble 2 ft. apart, deep enough for the top of the root cutting to be covered with soil to a depth of 2–3 in.; insert a piece of root into each hole with the thickest end up and fill with soil.

Growing

Horseradish dislikes heavy shade but grows on any soil with reasonable drainage; roots flourish in deep, rich, well-drained soils. Dig in well-rotted organic matter the winter before planting; where crops are rotated, horseradish should follow a heavily manured crop like beans. After planting, apply a general fertilizer, water as needed, particularly during drought. Keep weed-free.

Roots are at their hottest when eaten fresh

 varieties

The species *Armoracia rusticana* grows up to 3 ft. tall; the broad, oblong, dark green leaves have serrated margins. The thick tapering roots penetrate 24 in. or more into the soil. *Armoracia rusticana* "Variegata" has leaves splashed with cream and is of ornamental merit, though its flavor is not as good as the species.

 cultivation

As horseradish is difficult to eradicate once established, lift all plants from late fall to early winter, keeping some side roots for propagation the following spring. Alternatively, let it grow as a perennial for some years and divide in spring.

Propagation

Grow from root cuttings or young plants. In late fall or winter lift crowns, remove side shoots of pencil thickness about 6–8 in. long and store them in damp

Maintenance

Spring Plant root cuttings.
Summer Feed, water, and keep the crop weed-free.
Fall Lift whole crowns, keep large roots for use in the kitchen, use others for propagation.
Winter Prepare the ground for replanting.

Harvesting and Storing

Lift and harvest the crowns in fall when the flavor is strongest and use stored roots over winter and spring. As exposure to light causes greening, store roots in the cool and dark. In summer, lift roots as required.

Pests and Diseases

Do not plant in soil affected by clubroot. Horseradish pale leaf spot — near-white spots with dark margins on the leaves — does not affect the roots and no treatment is needed.

companion planting

It is said to improve the disease resistance of potatoes.

container growing

Restrict the growth of horseradish as a perennial by planting in a bucket or garbage can (with drainage holes in the base) sunk into the ground. Use soil with plenty of rotted organic matter or a soilless potting mix with a moderate fertilizer content. Water well. Divide in fall and winter as necessary.

medicinal

Horseradish is a diaphoretic, digestive, diuretic, and stimulant. Modern research has indicated antimicrobial activity against some micro-organisms. It is also said to staunch bleeding, prevent scarring, and cure stomach cramp. In folk medicine the vapor from grated roots was inhaled to treat colds. It is rich in vitamin C, sulfur, potassium, and calcium.

warning

Grate horseradish using the shredder attachment of a food processor to prevent your eyes watering.

culinary

The root stays fresh for about 2 weeks in the salad drawer of a refrigerator, but it is better to freeze grated root in plastic bags and use as required. Trim off the rootlets, scrub or scrape under the cold tap to remove soil. Finely grate or use a food processor, discarding the central core. Or store by grating into white vinegar (red wine or cider vinegar discolors the root).

Horseradish sauce, made with milk or oil and vinegar, is the traditional accompaniment for roast beef, asparagus, and smoked fish like mackerel. Fold into whipping cream, yogurt, or sour cream and season with salt, sugar, and a little vinegar to make horseradish cream. Don't grate until just before serving or it will lose its flavor. My father made his horseradish sauce just before the roast beef was carved: a teaspoonful was absolutely lethal and sent us running for a glass of cold water! Serve with ham, on baked potatoes, or cold meats. Grated horseradish can be used in steak tartare, or added to coleslaw, dips, and sauces. Blended with butter and chilled it is an alternative to garlic butter to accompany broiled steak.

Apricot and Horseradish Sauce

Serve this more delicate sauce to accompany roast chicken. To serve it with fish, use fennel rather than tarragon.

1 pound apricots, pitted
Juice of ½ a lemon
Superfine sugar
1 to 2 tablespoons freshly grated horseradish
1 tablespoon fresh tarragon, chopped
Salt and freshly ground white pepper

Soften the apricots in a little water and purée. To the purée, add the lemon juice, sugar to taste, horseradish, and tarragon. Season to taste.

ASPARAGUS

Long-lived perennial grown for slender young shoots and ornamental foliage. Fully hardy. Value: high in potassium and folic acid, moderate source of beta carotene, and vitamin E.

The genus *Asparagus* provides us with a range of robust foliage houseplants and one of the world's most desirable vegetables. The delicious taste, succulent texture, and suggestive shape of the emergent shoots combine to create an eating experience verging on the decadent which has been celebrated for over 2,000 years. Pliny the Elder describes cultivation methods used by the Romans for producing plants with blanched stems, and mentions a cultivar of which three "spears" weighed a pound. These spears were once believed to arise from rams' horns buried in the soil. Wild asparagus grows in North America, Europe, Asia, and northwest Africa, in dry meadows, sand dunes, limestone cliffs, and volcanic hillsides.

in late winter at 55–60°F directly into packs, pots, or trays. Repot, harden off, and plant outdoors in early summer. Male plants are the more productive, so the following year, remove any females (identifiable by their red berries) before they shed their fruits. Transplant the remaining male crowns into their permanent position in midspring the following year.

Growing

The fall or winter before planting, dig in plenty of well-rotted organic matter; lime acid soil to create a pH of 6.5 to 7.5. It is vital to remove perennial weeds. Fork over the soil 1 or 2 weeks before planting and rake in a general fertilizer at approximately 6 oz. per square yard.

One-year-old crowns establish quickly; 2- and 3-year-old crowns tend to suffer from a growth check after transplanting. Plant in midspring, once the soil is warm. The roots desiccate quickly and are easily damaged, so cover with burlap until ready to plant, then handle with care.

Either plant in single rows with the crowns 12–18 in. apart or in beds with 2 or 3 rows 12 in. apart. For several beds, set them 3 ft. apart. Before planting dig a trench 8 × 12 in. and make a 1½ in. mound of soil in the base; plant crowns along the top, spreading out the roots, and cover them with 2 in. of sifted soil. As the stems grow, gradually cover with soil; by fall, the trench should be filled with soil. Keep beds weed-free by hand weeding or hoeing carefully to avoid damaging the shallow roots. On more exposed sites, support the "ferns" when windy to avoid damage to the crown, and water during dry weather.

After harvesting, apply a general fertilizer to nurture stem growth and build up the plants for the following year. In fall, when stems have turned yellow, cut back

 varieties

"Connover's Colossal," an early, heavy-cropping, old variety producing large, tasty spears, is suitable for light soils and freezes well. "Franklin" crops heavily, and has thick spears. A few can be harvested from 2-year-old crowns. "Jersey Giant" is a hybrid resistant to most diseases, producing top-quality spears. "Jersey Knight" is similar to "Jersey Giant," but 99 percent of the plants are male for heavier cropping. "Martha Washington," an established favorite in the U.S., crops heavily, has long spears and is rust-resistant.

 cultivation

Asparagus thrives in an open, sheltered position on well-drained soil. As a bed it can be productive for up to 20 years, thorough preparation is essential. **Zones 3 to 8.**

Propagation

Asparagus can be grown from seed, though it is easier and less time-consuming to plant crowns. Soak seed for 2 days before sowing in midspring, 1 in. deep in rows 18 in. apart. Thin seedlings when they are 3 in. tall until they are 6 in. apart. Alternatively, sow indoors

The fall fruits of Connover's Colossal

to within 1–2 in. of the surface and tidy up the bed. Ferns can be shredded and composted. Each spring apply a general fertilizer as growth begins. Mulching with manure has little value beyond suppressing weeds and conserving moisture.

Maintenance

Spring Sow seed and plant crowns. Harvest late spring.
Summer Keep weed-free and water as necessary. Stop harvesting by midsummer.
Fall Cut back yellowing ferns and tidy beds.
Winter Prepare new beds. mix in organic matter and remove perennial weeds.

Protected Cropping

Protect the crowns from late frosts with floating row cover or cloches.

Harvesting and Storing

Recent research shows that a small harvest the first year can remove apical dominance and increase subsequent yield. Harvesting lasts for 6 weeks in the first year and 8 weeks in subsequent years. Do not harvest after midsummer: it can result in thin spears the following year. When spears are 4–7 in. long, cut them obliquely about 1–2 in. below the surface with a sharp knife or a serrated asparagus knife.

Pests and Diseases

The black and yellow adults and small grayish larvae of asparagus beetles appear from late summer, stripping stems and foliage. Control by removing dying foliage.

 companion planting

Where growing conditions allow, asparagus is compatible with tomatoes, parsley, and basil.

 medicinal

Asparagus is used to treat rheumatism, gout, and cystitis. Anyone who lacks the enzyme to break down asparagine produces urine with a strong odor — a disconcerting but harmless phenomenon.

 warning

The berries are poisonous.

 culinary

Asparagus spears should be used as fresh as possible, preferably within an hour of harvesting. They can be refrigerated in a plastic bag for up to 3 days. To freeze, tie into bundles and blanch thick spears for 4 minutes, thin for 2. Freeze in a plastic container.

Asparagus is best eaten steamed or boiled and served hot with butter. Also good cold with vinaigrette, Parmesan or mayonnaise. Asparagus tips can be added to salads and pizza toppings.

To boil, wash spears, peel away the skin below the tips, and soak in cold water until all have been prepared. Sort into stalks of even length (perhaps 20 stalks if thin varieties and 6 to 8 if thicker-stemmed), and tie with soft string or raffia, one close to the base and another just below the tip. Stand bundles upright in boiling salted water, with the tips above water level. Cover and boil gently for 10 to 15 minutes until *al dente*, then drain and serve. Don't overcook: the tips should be firm, and the spears should not bend when held at the base. The water can be used in soup.

Jean-Christophe Novelli's Steamed Asparagus
Serves 4

1 pound butter
4 egg yolks
1 tablespoon white wine vinegar
1 vanilla bean, split and seeds scraped out
20 asparagus spears
Salt and freshly ground black pepper
Toasted almonds

To make a hollandaise sauce, melt the butter and keep warm. Place a bowl over a pan of boiling water. Put the egg yolks, vinegar, and vanilla seeds in the bowl and whisk until the mix is light and fluffy. Take off the heat and slowly whisk in the butter, a little at a time, until all is incorporated. Season to taste.

Steam the asparagus until still slightly crunchy, spoon a generous spoonful of hollandaise on top and garnish with some toasted almonds.

Barbarea verna. Brassicaceae
LAND CRESS

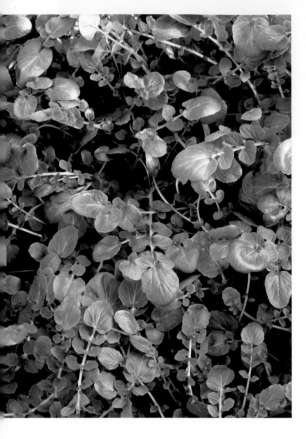

Also known as American cress, Early Yellowrocket. Biennial or short-lived perennial grown as annual for young leaves. Hardy. Value: low in calories, good source of iron, calcium, beta carotene and vitamin C.

The genus *Barbarea* was known as *herba Sanctae Barbarae*, the "herb of St Barbara," patron saint of miners and artillerymen and protectress from thunderstorms! Land cress is a fast-growing, hardy biennial with a rosette of deeply lobed, shiny leaves and yellow flowers. Native to southwestern Europe, it has been grown as a salad crop since the 17th century; by the 18th century, extensive cultivation had died out in England. In America, it is still a popular annual crop.

Pests and Diseases
Flea beetle may affect plants; grow under fabric.

 companion planting

Makes a good edging plant for borders. Can be grown between taller crops, like grains and brassicas.

 container growing

Grow in moisture-retentive, peat-substitute potting mix, water well, and feed with a dilute general liquid fertilizer every 3 weeks.

 culinary

Use its peppery-tasting leaves as a watercress substitute — as a garnish, in salads, and sandwiches. Or cook them like spinach and make into soup. Good in rice, pasta salads, and stir-fries.

cultivation

Land cress grows in wet, shady conditions, but is best in moist fertile soil; in summer plant in light shade, under deciduous trees. **Zones 3 to 9.**

Propagation
Sow as soon as the soil becomes workable, in early spring to early summer for a summer crop, and in mid- to late summer for fall to spring crops. Sow in seed trays or packs for transplanting when large enough to handle, or in rows ½ in. deep, thinning the seedlings to 6–8 in. Germination takes about 3 weeks in spring but in midsummer half that time. If a few plants are left to go to seed in late spring, the following year they will seed freely; transplant seedlings into rows and water well.

Growing
Before sowing, dig in well-rotted manure or compost. Transplant seedlings sown in late summer indoors. In heat and drought they go to seed, so water often. Pick flower stalks as they appear.

Maintenance
Spring Sow seed, water well.
Summer Water as necessary so plants do not run to seed.
Fall Sow winter crops and transplant plantlets indoors.
Winter Prepare beds for spring sowing; harvest protected crops.

Protected Cropping
Improve the quality of fall and winter crops by growing in an unheated greenhouse or cold frame, or under cloches.

Harvesting
Harvest after 7 weeks when plants are 3–4 in. long. Pick or cut the tender young leaves about 1 in. above ground. Do not harvest heavily until the plant is established. Soak in water to loosen dirt, then wash it off.

Cress, Anchovy, and Barley Salad
Serves 4

1 ½ cups pearl barley
4 tablespoons virgin olive oil
2 tablespoons white wine vinegar
2 tablespoons finely minced fresh dill
4 anchovy fillets, roughly chopped
12 oz. cress, washed and dried
1 cucumber, diced
Salt and freshly ground pepper

Cook the barley in boiling water until tender and drain. Let sit. Make the dressing: mix the oil and vinegar with the dill and seasoning. In a separate bowl, mix the barley with the anchovy, add the cress and cucumber, and pour over the dressing. Toss well.

Beta vulgaris subsp. *cicla.* Chenopodiaceae

SWISS CHARD

Also known as Silver Chard, Silver Beet, Sea Kale Beet. Biennial grown as annual for leaves and midribs. Hardy. Value: high in sodium, potassium, iron, and exceptional source of beta carotene, the precursor of vitamin A.

The umbrella name "leaf beet" includes Swiss chard and also encompasses perpetual spinach or spinach beet. (The "true" spinach and New Zealand spinach both belong to other genera.) A close relative of the beet, leaf beet is an ancient vegetable cultivated for its attractive, tasty leaves. Native to the Mediterranean, it was well known to the Greeks, who also ate its roots with mustard, lentils, and beans. Aristotle wrote of red chard in the fourth century BCE, and Theophrastus recorded both light and dark green varieties. The Romans introduced it to central and northern Europe and from there it slowly spread, reaching the Far East in the Middle Ages and China in the 17th century. The name "chard" comes from the French *carde* and derives from the resemblance of the leaf stalks to those of globe artichokes and cardoons. In 1597 John Gerard wrote in his *Herball*, "… it grew with me to the height of eight cubits and did bring forth his rough seeds very plentifully." If the measurement is correct, his Swiss chard would be approximately 13 ft. tall. I wonder where that variety is today, was his yardstick wrongly calibrated, or had it simply bolted?

"Fordhook Giant"

 varieties

Swiss chard has broad red or white leaf stems and midribs. "Bright Lights" has a bright colored stems and green or bronze leaves. Delicious! "Erbette," an Italian variety, is well flavored and has an excellent texture. It is good as a "cut and come again" crop. "Fordhook Giant" has huge, glossy green leaves with white veins and stems. It is tasty and high-yielding, producing bumper crops even at high temperatures. "Lucullus" is vigorous and crops heavily, producing pale yellow-green leaves with succulent midribs. Tolerant of high temperatures, it does not bolt.

"Perpetual Spinach," or spinach beet, is smaller, with narrower stems and dark, fleshy leaves, and is very resistant to bolting. Good for fall and winter cropping. "Rhubarb Chard" ("Ruby Chard") is noted for its magnificent bright crimson leaf stalks and dark green puckered leaves. Ideal for the ornamental border or "potager," it needs growing with care, as it is prone to bolting.

 cultivation

Though they tolerate a wide range of soils, the best growing conditions are sunny or lightly shaded positions in rich, moisture-retentive, free-draining soil. In poor soil, bolting can be a problem, so dig in plenty of well-rotted organic matter the winter before planting. The ideal pH is 6.5 to 7.5 and acid soils should be limed.

The ideal growing temperature is 60–65°F, though the range of tolerance is remarkably broad. They survive in winter temperatures down to about 7°F and are more tolerant of higher summer temperatures than true spinach, which is inclined to bolt. **Zones 3 to 10.**

Propagation

For a constant supply throughout the year, make two sowings, one in midspring for a summer harvest and another in mid- to late summer. The later crop is usually lower-yielding.

Sow three to four seeds in hills 9 in. apart, about ½ in. deep. Swiss chard needs 18 in. between the rows, and perpetual spinach 17 in. Thin seedlings when large enough to handle to leave the strongest seedling.

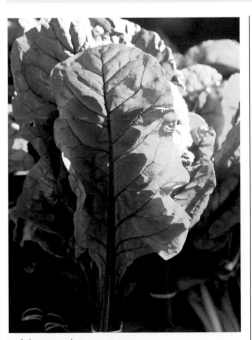

Both leaves and stems are tasty

SWISS CHARD

Alternatively, sow in packs or trays and transplant to their final spacing when they are large enough to handle. Swiss chard is particularly successful as a "cut and come again" crop. Prepare the seedbed thoroughly and broadcast or sow seed in rows the width of a hoe.

Growing
Keep crops weed-free by hoeing or, preferably, mulching with well-rotted organic matter and keep the soil continually moist. In dry conditions, plants will need 2½ to 3½ gallons per week, but are surprisingly drought-tolerant. A dressing of general granular or liquid fertilizer can be given to plants needing a boost.

Maintenance
Spring Sow the first crop in midspring; thin, leaving a strong seedling.
Summer Weed, water, and feed as necessary. Sow a second crop in mid- to late summer. Harvest as needed.
Fall Protect with cloches or row covers in late fall for good-quality growth.
Winter Dig over the area where the following year's crop is to be planted. Harvest overwintering crops.

Protected Cropping
Though they are hardy enough to withstand mild-climate winters outdoors, plants protected in cloches, cold frames, plastic tunnels, or floating row cover produce better crops of higher-quality leaves.

Harvesting and Storing
Seeds sown in midspring are ready to harvest from early to midsummer. Harvest the outer leaves first, working towards the center of the plant and cutting at the base of each stem: snapping them off is likely to disturb the roots. Choose firm leaves and discard any that are damaged or wilted. Pick regularly to ensure a constant supply of tender regrowth, so harvest even if you are unable to use them — they are certain to be welcomed by friends.

They can also be grown as "cut and come again" crops from seedling stage through to maturity. Cut seedlings when about 2 in. tall. After two to three crops have been harvested, allow them to regrow to about 3 in.

Semi-mature plants are harvested leaf by leaf and mature plants can be cut about 1 in. above the ground; from this, new growth appears.

Swiss chard and perpetual spinach are best eaten straight from the plant. Leaves (minus the stalks) keep in a refrigerator in the salad compartment or in plastic bags for 2 to 3 days.

Pests and Diseases
They are relatively trouble-free, though beware of downy mildew when dense patches of seedlings are sown for "cut and come again" crops. It appears as brown patches on leaves. Birds sometimes attack seedlings, so protect crops; growing plants under brassicas or beans also gives them some protection.

 ## companion planting

They grow well with all beans except runners, and flourish alongside brassicas, onions, and lettuce. Herbs like sage, thyme, mint, dill, hyssop, rosemary, and garlic are also compatible.

 ## container growing

Swiss chard can be grown in containers and makes a fine ornamental feature. Either transplant seedlings or sow directly into soilless potting mix, or garden soil, with added organic matter.

 ## medicinal

Leaves are vitamin- and mineral-rich with high levels of iron and magnesium. In folk medicine the juice is used as a decongestant; the leaves are said to neutralize acid and have a purgative effect. Beware of eating it in large quantities!

 ## culinary

Perpetual spinach can be lightly boiled, steamed, or eaten raw. Swiss chard takes longer to cook: try it steamed and served with butter. Soup can be made from the leaves and its midribs cooked and served like asparagus, or added to pork pies. "Rhubarb Chard" tastes milder than white-stemmed varieties.

Spinach Beet Fritters
Serves 4

These robust fritters go well with salmon or cod.

1 ½ lbs perpetual spinach, well washed
Pat of butter
2 large eggs, separated
1 tablespoon grated Parmesan
1 teaspoon grated lemon zest
Salt and freshly ground black pepper
Pinch of nutmeg
Olive oil, for frying

Prepare the leaves, removing the midribs, and chop roughly. Cook in the water that clings to the leaves until wilted — 2 to 3 minutes — and drain well. Chop finely and return to the pan with the butter, cooking until all the liquid evaporates. Let cool for 5 minutes and stir in the egg yolks, Parmesan, and lemon zest. When almost cold, fold in the stiffly beaten egg whites and season with salt, pepper, and nutmeg to taste.

Drop spoonfuls into hot fat, heated in a heavy skillet, and cook for a minute or two, turning halfway.

Drain well and serve hot.

BEET

Beta vulgaris subsp. *vulgaris.* Chenopodiaceae

Beets come in beautiful colors

Also known as Red Beet, Beetroot. Biennial grown as annual for swollen root and young leaves. Hardy. Value: slightly higher in carbohydrates than most vegetables, good source of folic acid and potassium.

Beets are a form of the maritime sea beet which has been selected over many centuries for its edible roots. From the same origin come mangels (a cattle fodder), the beet used for commercial sugar production and Swiss chard. Grown since Assyrian times, the vegetable was highly esteemed by the ancient Greeks and was used in offerings to Apollo. There were many Roman recipes for beets, which they regarded more highly than the greatly revered cabbage. It appeared in 14th-century English recipes and was first described as the beets we know today in Germany in 1558, though it was a rarity at that tlme in northern Europe. The typical red coloration comes from its cell sap, but there are also varieties in other colors.

 varieties

Beets are grouped according to shape — round or globe-shaped, tapered or long, and flat or oval. To reduce the amount of thinning needed, breeders have introduced "monogerm" varieties (see "Propagation").

Globe
"Boltardy" is a delicious, well-textured, smooth-skinned variety and an excellent early cropper as it is very resistant to bolting. Good in containers. "Bonel" has deep red, succulent, tasty roots and is high-yielding. It crops over a long period and is resistant to bolting. "Detroit 2 Little Ball" produces deep red, smooth-skinned "baby beet," which are ideal for pickling, canning, or freezing. A good crop for late sowing and for storing. "Monogram" is dark red, well-flavored and vigorous, with smooth skin and rich red flesh. It is a "monogerm" variety. "Monopoly" is also a "monogerm" and is resistant to bolting, with a good color and rough skin. "Pablo" is a tasty early with uniform roots and smooth skin. Also bolting resistant. "Regala" has very dark roots and is quite small, even at maturity. An excellent variety for containers, and resistant to bolting.

Tapered
"Cheltenham Green Top" is a tasty, old variety with rough skin and long roots. It stores well. "Cheltenham Mono" is a tasty, medium-sized "monogerm" which is resistant to bolting, good for slicing and stores well.

Others
"Albina Vereduna" ("Snowhite") is a wonderful globe-shaped white variety, with smooth skin and sweet flesh.

BEET

It also has the advantage that it does not stain. The curly leaves can be used as "greens" and are full of vitamins. It does not store well and is prone to bolting. "Barbabietola di Chioggia" is a mild, traditional Italian variety. Sliced, it reveals unusual white internal "rings" and gives an exotic look to salads. When cooked, it becomes pale pink. Sow from midspring. "Burpee's Golden" has beautiful orange skin and tasty yellow flesh. It looks great in salads, keeps its color when cooked, does not bleed when cut, and the leaves can be used as "greens." It stores well, has good bolting resistance and is better harvested when small. "Cylindrica" has sweet-tasting, dark, oval roots that have excellent keeping qualities and good flavor. Because of its shape, it is perfect for slicing and cooks well. Harvest when young. "Egyptian Turnip Rooted" ("D'Egypte," "Egyptian Flat") has smooth roots with deep red, delicious flesh. An American introduction, it was first grown around Boston about 1869. "Forono" is very tasty with large, cylindrical roots, smooth skin, and good color. Slow to go woody, it is ideal for summer salads and stores well. Susceptible to bolting, it should be sown from midspring.

Varieties of "mini vegetables" include "Pronto," "Action," and "Monaco."

 cultivation

Propagation

In most varieties, each "seed" is a corky fruit containing two or three seeds, so a considerable amount of thinning is required. "Monogerm" varieties, each containing a single seed, reduce such a work load. They also contain a natural inhibitor that slows or even prevents germination. Remove this by soaking seeds or washing them in running water for 30 to 60 minutes before sowing. At soil temperatures below 45°F germination is slow and erratic. To overcome this, sow early crops in packs, "fluid sow," or sow in rows or stations after warming the soil with cloches. These can be left in place after sowing until the weather warms up. Use bolting-resistant varieties until midspring; after that, any variety can be used.

Sow the first crops under cloches from late winter to early spring ½–1 in. deep and 1 in. apart with 9 in. between rows. Thin to a final spacing of 4 in. between plants. Alternatively, sow two to three seeds in hills 4 in.

apart, thinning to leave the strongest seedling when the first true leaf appears. Round varieties can be "multi-sown" in a cool greenhouse planting three seeds per pack, thinning to four to five seedlings, then planting the packs 4 in. apart when about 2 in. high. Early crops can also be sown thinly in broad flat seedings ½–1 in. deep, in a similar way to peas.

Thin as soon as seedlings are touching and keep thinning as plants grow: those large enough can be used whole. If you grow beets under floating row cover or a similar cover (put in place once the seedlings have established), yields can be increased by up to 50 percent. Remove protection 4 to 6 weeks after sowing. From midspring, if the weather is warm seeds can be sown without the protection of cloches, thinning to 3–4 in. apart.

Beets grown for pickling need to be about 2 in. in diameter. Sowing in rows 3 in. apart and thinning plants to 2½ in. apart will give you the correct size.

From late spring to early summer sow the main crop, using any round or long variety. Harvest throughout the summer and for winter storing. Sow in rows or in hills thinning to leave a final spacing of 3 in. apart in rows 8 in. apart or 5–6 in. in and between the rows.

For a constant supply of beets, sow round cultivars indoors from late winter at 4-week intervals for midspring crops; and for a late fall crop sow from early to midsummer in mild areas (for lifting during winter thin to 4 in.). For winter storage sow in late May, early June. **Zones 3 to 9.**

Growing

Beets need an open site with fertile, well-drained light soil which has been manured for the previous crop. The pH should be 6.5 to 7.5, so acidic soils will need liming. Fall-maturing varieties tolerate heavier conditions and long-rooted varieties require a deeper soil. The best quality roots grow in moderate temperatures around 61°F.

Sprinkle a slow-release general fertilizer at 2–3 oz. per square yard, 2 to 3 weeks before sowing, raking the seedbed to a fine tilth. For good-quality beets, it is important to avoid any check in growth; at the onset of drought, water at a rate of 3 gallons per square yard every 2 weeks. Do not overwater as this results in excessive leaf growth and small roots. If watering

is neglected, yields are low, roots become woody and when it rains or you water suddenly, the roots will split. Keep weed-free and hoe with care as damage causes the roots to bleed: use an onion hoe or mulch round the plants. Mulching with a 2 in. layer of well-rotted potting mix or spent mushroom compost will conserve moisture.

Maintenance

Spring Sow early crops indoors or cloches. Midspring crops can be sown without protection.
Summer Sow successively every month, harvest earlier crops, keep the plot weed-free, and water as required. Sow main crops.
Fall Lift later crops and those for storage.
Winter In mild areas leave overwintering crops outdoors and protect with straw or similar materials. Alternatively, lift and store indoors.

Protected Cropping

Grow early crops indoors in packs and transplant under cloches. Alternatively, grow under cloches or crop covers and remove these about 6 weeks after sowing.

Harvesting and Storing

Beets take 60 to 90 days to mature. They must always be harvested before they become woody and inedible. Harvest salad beets from late spring to midfall and maincrop varieties from midsummer

"Boltardy"

onwards. Early varieties are best harvested when the size of a golf ball; when later crops reach that size, lift every other plant and use for cooking, leaving the rest for lifting when they reach baseball-size.

Lift roots carefully with a fork, shake off soil, and twist off the leaves. Do not cut off the leaves: it causes bleeding and makes a terrible mess! Use any damaged roots immediately. Lift beets for storage by midfall and put in stout boxes of moist peat substitute, sand, or sawdust, leaving a gap between each root. Store in a cool, frost-free shed or garage. Roots should keep until midspring the following year but check regularly and remove any that deteriorate. The long-rooted types are traditionally grown for storage, although most varieties store successfully.

In mild areas and on well-drained soil, they can be left over winter, but need a dense protective covering of straw or similar material before the frosts. This also makes lifting easier.

Pests and Diseases

Beets are generally trouble-free but may suffer from the following problems:

Black bean aphid forms dense colonies on the leaves. Yellow blotches between the veins, the symptom of manganese deficiency, appear on older leaves first and can be a problem on extremely alkaline soil.

Rough patches on the surface of the root and waterlogged brown patches and rings at its center are a sign of boron deficiency. There may also be corky "growths" on the shoots and leaf stalks.

Make sure that beet seedlings are protected against birds. Slugs make holes in leaves. The problem is worse in damp conditions.

 ## companion planting

Beets flourish in the company of kohlrabi, carrots, cucumber, lettuce, onions, brassicas, and most beans (not runners). Dill or Florence fennel planted nearby attracts predators. Because they combine well with so many other crops and small roots mature within 9 to 13 weeks, beets are good for intercropping and useful catch-crops.

 ## culinary

The roots are eaten raw — try them grated as a crudité — or cooked and served fresh or pickled. Young "tops" can be cooked like spinach and used as "greens." They add color and flavor to salads, particularly the red, yellow, white, and bi-colored varieties. Bean and beet salad is particularly tasty. Wash in cold water, keeping root and stems intact: do not "top and tail" or damage the skin, as bleeding causes loss of flavor and color. Boil for up to 2 hours in saltwater, depending on the size, then carefully rub off the skin. It is delicious served hot as a vegetable, otherwise cool for pickling or for a fresh salad.

Beets can also be baked, and are the basis for borscht soup when cooked with white stock. They also make excellent chutney and wine.

Freeze small beets which are no more than 2 in. across. Wash and boil, skin and cool, then cut roots into slices or cubes and freeze in a rigid container. You should use within 6 months.

In a plastic bag or salad compartment of the refrigerator, they stay fresh for up to 2 weeks.

Spicy Beet Salad
Serves 4

1 ½ pounds beets, washed and trimmed
Juice of ½ a lemon
½ teaspoon ground cumin
½ teaspoon ground cinnamon
½ teaspoon paprika
1 tablespoon orange flower water
2 tablespoons olive oil
Salt and freshly ground black pepper
2 tablespoons chopped fresh parsley
Lettuce (colored varieties mixed with green leaves such as corn salad)

Cook the beets in a steamer for 20 or 30 minutes until tender. Peel and slice them when cool, reserving the liquid that accumulates on the plate.

Toss them in lemon juice and coat with the spices, orange flower water and olive oil, together with the liquid. Season, cover and chill. To serve, toss with the parsley and arrange on individual plates on a bed of lettuce leaves.

 ## container growing

Unless growing for exhibition, grow only globe varieties in containers — about 8 in. deep — or troughs or growing bags. Sow seed thinly ½–1 in. deep from midspring to midsummer, thinning to 4–5 in. apart. Water regularly, harvest when the size of a tennis ball and keep weed-free.

 ## other uses

The foliage is attractive and ideal for inclusion in an ornamental border or "potager," particularly varieties like

"Bull's Blood." The leaf mineral content is 25 percent magnesium, making it useful on the compost pile.

 ## medicinal

Used in folk medicine as a blood tonic for gastritis, piles, and constipation; mildly cardio-tonic. Recent research has shown that taking at least one glass of raw beet juice a day helps control cancer. It is regarded as a "superfood."

 ## warning

The sap stains clothes. To remove, rub the stain with a slice of pear and wash as usual.

Brassica juncea. Brassicaceae

MUSTARD GREENS

Also known as Oriental Mustard. Hardy annual or biennial. Value: rich in vitamin A and C, moderate calcium, iron potash, and phosphorous.

Commonly grown in Europe for mustard seed, mustard greens have their greatest diversity of shape and form in central Asia and the Himalayas which, along with the warm, central-Chinese province of Sichuan, India, and the Caucasus, are thought to be one of the ancient areas of domestication. Sanskrit records show that mustard greens have been cultivated since 3000 BCE and there have been an astonishing range of selections for their desirable characteristics. Among them are forms with tumescent swellings on the leaf stems, fleshy tap roots, large stems, multi-shoots, green stems, and curled leaves plus heading varieties both large and small. This selection process is set to continue long into the future, as oriental mustard strengthens its position as an indispensable crop for oriental cuisine.

 varieties

Commonly grown groups include:

Giant-leaved Mustard
This is very hardy. "Green Chirimen" has green, blistered leaves, while "Miike Giant" is broad-leaved and vigorous with mildly-flavored, crinkled leaves and purple veins. "Osaka Purple" is fast growing, the large green leaves becoming purple in cold weather. It is easy to grow and cold-hardy.

Wrapped Heart
These varieties grow better when there are high temperatures immediately after sowing. "Amsoi" produces tender greens with a mustard tang which are often used for pickling. "Chicken Heart" is a semi-heading variety and well flavored. "Kekkyu Takana" forms a small head and the mild flavor becomes stronger as it matures.

Leaf Mustard
Sow in summer and fall. "South Wind" has purple-tinted, undulating leaves and is heat tolerant and good for stir-fries.

Green in the Snow
This is fast growing and cold tolerant with frilly leaves. Young leaves are moderately spicy, older leaves should be cooked. Sow in fall, can be grown as a "cut and come again" crop.

Curled Mustard
These are hardy but also tolerant of high temperatures. "Green Wave" is an All-American Selection; it grows to 2 ft. tall with dark green, frilly-margined leaves. It is highly productive, slow to bolt and the flavor is hot.

Swollen Stem Mustard
These have unusually shaped or formed stems or leaf stems. "Horned Mustard" has bright green, frilly leaves with a distinct "horn" in the center of the stem. The leaf buds are also delicious. "Tsa Tsai Round" is unusual in that it forms thick, rounded, tumescent-like stems that are up to 6 in. diameter and ½ pound in weight below the leaves. It is a cool-season crop.

MUSTARD GREENS

"Osaka Purple"

 cultivation

Propagation

Sow seeds thinly *in situ* and thin to the required spacing; summer and fall sowings can also be made in packs for planting out. Sow according to the ultimate size of the variety or the stage of growth at harvest. Young plants should be 4–6 in. apart; mature at 12 in. apart in and between rows. Large varieties with spreading heads being grown to maturity should be 18 in. apart.

Growing

Grow in an open, sheltered site in fertile soil of any kind, add well-rotted organic matter if necessary; they need plenty of moisture when in growth as they "bolt" in dry conditions. All of the mustard varieties are cool season crops, though the resistance to cold and heat varies according to the variety. Sow from mid- to late summer for growing to maturity outdoors, or under cover, or in spring, for harvesting as "cut and come again" crops. Sow successionally to extend the harvesting season.

Maintenance

Spring Sow outdoors when the soil is warm and friable.
Summer Sow crops for harvesting at maturity from midsummer where frosts occur and late summer where frost free. Harvest "curly leaved" and "headed" types or "cut and come again."
Fall Harvest.
Winter Harvest crops outdoors or indoors.

Protected Cropping

Oriental mustards make good fall-sown crops for unheated greenhouses or plastic tunnels.

Harvesting and Storing

Cut and use fresh as required.

Pests and Diseases

They suffer from most of the usual brassica problems including flea beetle, cabbage root fly, and slugs.

 container growing

Some varieties can be grown as "cut and come again" seedling crops in growing bags or large containers. They tend to be slow growing and are not as productive as other types of Asian vegetables using this method.

 culinary

Mustard greens are renowned for their spicy and peppery flavor which varies according to the plant's age and variety. They can be used raw or cooked in stir-fries and soups, combine well with crab, can be made into pickles, and the leaves and shoots can be dried for winter eating. The inner leaves are milder and used in salads; the outer leaves are stronger flavored and usually cooked.

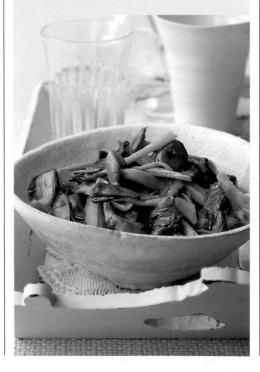

Brassica napus (Napobrassica Group). Brassicaceae

RUTABAGA

Also known as Swede, Swedish turnip. Biennial grown as annual for swollen root and young leaves. Hardy. Value: small amounts of niacin (vitamin B) and vitamin C, low in calories and carbohydrates.

Rutabaga is one of the hardiest of all root crops and is the perfect winter vegetable for cool temperate climates. An abbreviation of "Swedish turnip," its name indicates its origins. Eaten in France and southern Europe in the 16th century, it went to Britain from Holland in 1755 and rapidly became popular as the "turnip-rooted cabbage." Along with the turnip, it was first used as winter fodder for sheep and cattle, improving milk production during a traditionally lean period. During times of famine, rutabagas were eaten by country folk and still have the reputation among many as peasant food.

To despise them is your loss; they are robust, undemanding and one of the easiest vegetables to grow. New varieties are disease-resistant, tasty and a wonderful accompaniment to sprouts as a winter vegetable — particularly when mashed with butter, cream, and spices.

 varieties

"Acme" has round roots with pale purple skin but its tops are prone to powdery mildew. "Angela" produces purple roots and is resistant to powdery mildew. "Lizzy" is a round variety with purple tops and yellow flesh, a soft texture, and sweet, nutty flavor. "Marian" is purple with yellow flesh and is very tasty and quick-growing. "Magres" has deliciously flavored yellow flesh and is mildew resistant. "Virtue" has red skin and sweet flesh.

 cultivation

Propagation
Rutabagas need a long growing season and should be sown from early spring in cooler climates to early summer where temperatures are warmer and germination and growth are rapid. Sow in rows 1 in. deep and 16–18 in. apart, thinning seedlings to 9–12 in. apart. Thin when they are no more than 1 in. high, when the first true leaves appear, to ensure that the roots develop properly. Firm the soil after thinning.

Growing
Rutabagas prefer a sheltered and open site in fertile, well-drained but moisture-retentive soil. Good drainage is essential. Summer sowings can be made in moderate shade, provided they receive sufficient moisture. Rutabagas prefer a pH of 5.5 to 7.0, so very acid soil will need liming. If the ground has not been manured for the previous crop, till in fall, incorporate plenty of well-rotted organic matter and allow the soil to "weather" over winter.

About a week prior to sowing, remove any weeds or debris and rake general fertilizer into the soil at 3 oz. per square yard. In common with other brassicas, rutabagas grow poorly on loose soil, so rake the soil to a fine tilth and firm it with the head of a rake or by carefully treading. If the soil is dry, water thoroughly before sowing and stand on a planting board to avoid compacting the soil. Mark each row with stakes or twigs, and label and date the crop.

Keep crops weed-free by hand weeding and careful hoeing. Rutabagas need a constant supply of water throughout the growing season, otherwise they tend to go to seed or produce small, woody roots. Sudden watering or rain after a period of drought causes the roots to split, so they will need up to 2 gallons per square yard a week in dry periods. This improves the size and quality but usually reduces the flavor. Rotate rutabagas with other brassicas.

Rutabaga tops can be blanched for eating raw as a winter salad vegetable. Lift a few roots in early to midwinter, cut back the leaves, and plant the roots under the greenhouse benches, or stand them upright in boxes or wooden trays filled with peat substitute, humus-rich garden soil, or with a thick layer of straw. Cover with upturned boxes or black plastic to exclude the light and put them in a cellar, garage, or shed. After 3 to 4 weeks shoots will appear and can be cut when they are 4–5 in. long.

Maintenance
Spring Warm soil under cloches for early sowings.
Summer Water crops and keep weed-free.
Fall Harvest early varieties.
Winter Lift and store crops before severe weather starts.

Protected Cropping
Cover ground with cloches, floating row cover, or black plastic for 2 to 3 weeks in late winter to early spring to warm the ground before sowing early crops. Seedlings should be protected until they are well-established.

Harvesting and Storing
Harvest begins any time from early to midfall. Rutabagas are extremely hardy and can be left in the ground until needed, though it is advisable not to leave them for too long or they will become woody. Lift when they are about the size of a grapefruit. They can be stored in boxes in a garage or cool shed. Twist off the leaves and place roots between layers of peat substitute, sawdust, or sand in a stout box.

Smaller rutabagas are more tasty and succulent, so begin lifting as soon as the roots are large enough to use, before they reach their maximum size.

Pests and Diseases
Rutabagas are affected by the same problems as turnips.

Powdery mildew is common. It appears as a white powdery deposit over shoots, stems, and leaves, causing stunted growth. In severe cases leaves become yellow and die. It is more of a problem when plants are dry at the roots and if it is cold at night and warm and dry in the day.

Rutabagas are susceptible to clubroot — to be avoided at all costs. Roots swell and distort, young plants wilt on hot days but recover overnight, growth is stunted, and crops ruined. It is more of a problem on poorly drained, acid soils. Spores remain in the soil for up to 20 years.

Flea beetles are tiny and black and some have yellow stripes. They nibble leaves of seedlings, checking growth.

 ## companion planting

Rutabagas grow well with peas.

 ## medicinal

Rutabagas have been used in folk medicine for the treatment of coughs, kidney stones, and whooping cough, though their efficacy has not been recorded.

A mature crop ready to be harvested

 ## culinary

Rutabagas can be sliced or cubed and roasted like parsnips, or added to casseroles and stews. Otherwise, they are delicious mashed with potatoes and served with meat or fish.

To boil, peel off the outer "skin," cut into slices or cubes and boil for 30 minutes. Drain thoroughly before serving.

Neeps
Serves 4

This is the traditional accompaniment for haggis and tatties (mashed potatoes), washed down with plenty of whisky, on Burns Night in Scotland.

1 ½ pounds rutabagas
Salt and black pepper
Pinch nutmeg
Butter or olive oil

Clean the rutabagas, cut them up, and boil in enough water to prevent them from burning until tender. Process in a blender or put through a strainer, discarding the juices. Season, and reheat with either butter or olive oil.

Brassica oleracea (Acephala Group). Brassicaceae

KALE

Also known as Borecole, Collards, Colewort, Sprouts. Biennial grown as annual for young leaves and shoots. Hardy. Value: good source of calcium, iron, beta carotene, vitamins E, and C.

Kales are exceptionally robust, and an ideal winter crop. Also, they are untroubled by common brassica problems. A primitive cabbage, kales are among the earliest cultivated brassicas (the Romans grew several types), with many similarities to the wild *Brassica oleracea* on the western coasts of Europe.

The Celtic "kale" derives from *coles* or *caulis* used by the Greeks and Romans to describe brassicas; the German Kohl has the same origin. First recorded in North America by 1669, kales are thought to have been introduced much earlier.

curly leaves and is ready to harvest 6 to 8 weeks after sowing. It crops for a long period so grow as "cut and come again." "Tall Green Curled" ("Tall Scotch Curled") is excellent for freezing, and shows good resistance to clubroot and cabbage root fly. "Thousand Head" is a plain-leaved, tall, old variety for harvesting through winter and spring. Exceptionally hardy.

Collards (or Greens)
These have smooth, thinner leaves than true kale that taste milder and are more heat-tolerant. "Blue Max" is tender and mild-flavored. "Green Glaze" is attractive, delicious, and quite frost hardy. "Hevi-crop" has deep, blue/green leaves and is very high-yielding. "Top Bunch" is upright and bolting resistant with blue-green savoyed leaves, good yields and good flavor.

 cultivation

Propagation
Sow in early spring in trays of moist seed potting mix or packs, or outdoors in seedbeds in milder areas, for summer crops. Sow from late spring for fall and winter

 varieties

Varieties are classified into groups, including the true kale, Siberian kale, and Collards. These are popular in the southern states of America and other warm climates. Kales vary in height from dwarf types, about 12–16 in. high, to tall varieties growing to 3 ft. and spreading to 2 ft. "Nero de Toscana" is famous for its ornamental value but the "peppery" leaves are good steamed, stir-fried, or in salads.

Siberian Kale, Rape Kale, or Curled Kitchen Kale
(*Brassica napus* Pabularia Group)
This is a relative of the rutabaga or swede, grown for the leaves, not the roots. It is variable in form and color, with broader leaves than kale, which are sometimes curled or frilled. It must be sown *in situ*, not transplanted, and crops when true kales have finished. "Hungry Gap" is a late cropper, robust and very reliable. "Laciniato," an

Italian variety, has deeply cut, flat leaves. "Ragged Jack" has pink-tinged leaves and midribs. "Red Russian" has tender and frilly leaves which have excellent flavor. "True Siberian" is fast-growing, with blue-green frilly leaves and harvests continually throughout winter.

Kale (Scotch Kale, Curly-leaved Kale or Borecole)
True kale usually has dark green or glaucous leaves with heavily frilled margins. "Darkibor" is exceptionally hardy with dark green, curled leaves. "Dwarf Blue Curled Vates" ("Dwarf Blue Curled Scotch") is low-growing with glaucous leaves and is also hardy and slow to bolt. "Dwarf Green Curled" is compact, hardy, and easy to grow; ideal for the small garden or windswept sites. "Fribor" with dark green leaves and "Redbor" winter well. "Pentland Brig," a cross between curly and plain-leaved kale, is grown for the texture and flavor of its young leaves, side shoots, and immature flower heads (which are cooked like broccoli). "Showbor" is a "mini vegetable." "Spurt" produces tender, deep green,

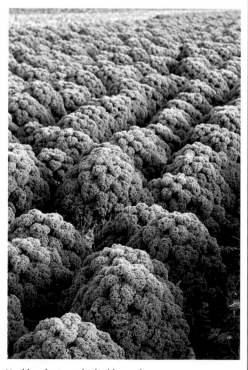

Healthy plants packed with goodness

Kale can be highly ornamental

crops. Alternatively, sow thinly in rows ½ in. deep *in situ*, gradually thinning to final spacing, or sow three seeds in hills at the final spacing, thinning to leave the strongest seedling. When 4–6 in. high, water the rows the day before, then transplant in the early evening, keeping the lowest leaves just above the soil surface. Water well with diluted liquid fertilizer after planting and until they become established. The final spacing for dwarf varieties should be 18 in. apart, with taller types 24–30 in. apart.

Collards are sown in late spring in areas with cool summers and in late summer in hotter climates. Sow Siberian kale thinly in early summer, *in situ*, in rows 18 in. apart, thinning when large enough to handle to a final spacing of 18 in. apart. **Zones 3 to 9.**

Growing

Kales are very hardy: some survive temperatures down to 5°F; others tolerate high summer temperatures. They grow in poorer soils than most brassicas, but flourish in a sunny position on well-drained soil with moderate nitrogen levels. Excessive nitrogen encourages soft growth, making plants prone to damage. Lime acid soils.

Prepare the seedbed when the soil is moist. Lightly fork the surface, remove any weeds, then firm (but do not compact) the soil.

Overwintering crops need top-dressing with high-nitrogen liquid or granular fertilizer at 3 oz. per square yard in spring to encourage side shoots.

Keep crops weed-free, water thoroughly before the onset of dry weather, mulch with a 2 in. layer of organic matter, and in fall, firm or hill up round the base of taller plants to prevent wind rock. On more exposed sites, they may need staking.

Kales are good where peas, early potatoes, or very early crops have been grown. Rotate with other brassicas.

Maintenance

Spring Sow early crops under cover; in midspring sow in trays or packs, or outdoors in a seedbed.
Summer Transplant seedlings, feed, and water well during dry spells. Keep weed-free. Harvest regularly.
Fall Firm round plant bases; stake if necessary.
Winter Harvest regularly.

Protected Cropping

Make early sowings as a "cut and come again" crop in the greenhouse bed or in mild areas outdoors under cloches, from mid- to late winter. Sow in rows the width of a hoe, broadcast thinly, or sow sparingly in rows, thinning to 3 in. apart.

Sow kale under cover in mid- to late winter for transplanting from midspring onwards when soil conditions are suitable.

Harvesting and Storing

Harvest by removing young leaves with a knife when they are 4–5 in. long. Cut from several plants for an adequate picking.

Harvest regularly for constant young growth and a long cropping season; older shoots become bitter and tough. Harvest early sowings of "cut and come again" crops when about 2–3 in. high, or thin to 4 in. and harvest when 5–6 in. high.

Pests and Diseases

Kale is resistant to cabbage root fly and clubroot, and is usually ignored by pigeons. Take precautions against whitefly, cabbage caterpillar, and flea beetle. Caterpillars eat irregular holes in the leaves: check regularly for eggs, squashing them. Beware of infestations of cabbage aphids, which check growth and may kill young plants.

 companion planting

Kale can be planted with corn and peas.

 culinary

Young leaves of later varieties taste better after exposure to frost.

Wash well and boil in 1 in. of water for 8 minutes at most. Serve with butter or white sauce — an excellent accompaniment for poached eggs, fried fish, bacon, and other fatty meats. Kale is also good with plain fish dishes such as salmon or cod. In parts of North America kale is served with hog jowls, and the juice is eaten with hot corn bread.

Kale can also be used in salads, soups, and stews; it can be creamed, or braised with onions, parsley, spices, and bacon or ham.

Before freezing, blanch young shoots for 1 minute, then cool, drain, and chop. Kale stays fresh for about 3 days in the refrigerator or in a plastic bag.

Stir-fried Kale
Serves 4

1½ pounds young kale
3 tablespoons peanut or olive oil
Salt and freshly ground black pepper
Juice of ½ a lemon

Thoroughly wash and dry the kale in a salad spinner. Chop it roughly. Pour the oil in a wok or heavy skillet over high heat and, when the oil is steaming, toss in the kale and cook for 3 minutes, stirring constantly. Season and add the lemon juice, adding shavings of lemon peel for decoration if you wish. Serve piping hot with stews or roasted meats.

CAULIFLOWER

Brassica oleracea (Botrytis Group). Brassicaceae

**Annual grown for immature flowerheads. Hardy or half hardy.
Value: good source of vitamin C, traces of most other vitamins.**

Cauliflowers are believed to have originated in Cyprus and the oldest record dates from the sixth century BCE. One thousand years later they were still widely grown there, being known in England as "Cyprus coleworts." A Jewish-Italian traveler wrote from Cyprus in 1593 that cabbages and cauliflowers were to be found growing in profusion, and, "For a quattrino one can get more almost than one can carry." Gerard in his *Herball* of 1597 calls them "Cole flowery." Moorish scholars in 12th-century Spain described three varieties as introductions from Syria, where cauliflowers had been grown for over a thousand years and were much developed by the Arabs. Even in 1699, John Evelyn suggested that the best seed came from Aleppo (now Halab, in northern Syria). Cultivation methods improved after 1700, and by the end of the 18th century the cauliflower was highly regarded throughout Europe. Dr Johnson is said to have remarked, "Of all the flowers in the garden, I like the cauliflower." But Mark Twain wrote disdainfully, "Cauliflower is nothing but cabbage with a college education." This, of course, is a matter of opinion.

Purple cauliflower — great for dips!

 ## varieties

There are four main groups for spring, summer, fall and winter, but many overlap the seasons.

"All the Year Round" is sown in late fall or spring for spring or summer harvest. It produces good-quality white heads and is excellent for successional sowing. "Alverda" has yellow-green heads. Sow late spring to midsummer for fall cropping. "Autumn Giant 3" has beautiful white, firm heads. Excellent for late fall and winter cropping. "Cheddar" (summer — fall) has orange-yellow flowerheads. "Clapton" is clubroot resistant and takes 85 days to harvest. "Dok Elgon" has firm, snow-white heads and is a reliable variety for early and late fall cropping. "Emeraude" (late summer — fall) has bright green curds. "Graffiti" (summer — fall) has deep purple curds. "Mystique" (spring) grows large white heads that are firm, crisp, and have outstanding flavor. "Purple Cape" is a hardy, overwintering purple type for cropping from late winter to midspring. Good raw or cooked; the head turns green when boiled. "Romanesco Veronica", also in catalogs under "Broccoli," has a tender stem like asparagus — delicious! "Snowball Self Blanching" is high-yielding and the leaves naturally blanch the curds. "Veitch's Autumn Giant" is a huge plant with large leaves and massive heads that grow to 12 in. in diameter; very tasty and also stores well. "White Rock" produces plenty of leaves to protect the curd and is a very versatile variety.

Foliage protects from sun or frost

 cultivation

Propagation

Start off crops as described in "Protected Cropping" unless stated. Plants are ready for transplanting when they have five to six leaves; water before moving and retain as much soil as possible around the roots.

Sow successionally to ensure regular cropping all year round. Sow early summer crops in midfall and leave them to overwinter under cover. Harden off in late winter, transplant from midspring as soon as the soil is workable and warm.

Space plants 20 in. apart with 24 in. between the rows or with 20 in. between the rows and plants. Protect with crop covers until established.

Sow summer cauliflowers in early spring under cover or in a seedbed outdoors if the soil is warm and workable, for transplanting in midspring and harvesting from midsummer to fall. Spacing as above.

Sow early fall cauliflowers in midspring for transplanting in early summer and harvesting from late summer to early fall. Space 21 in. apart in and between rows, or 20 in. between plants and 24 in. between rows.

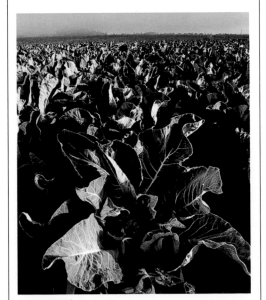

A promising harvest

Sow fall cauliflowers in late spring for transplanting in midsummer and harvesting from mid- to late fall. Space plants 24 in. apart in and between rows.

If you have available space and live in a mild climate, sow overwintering cauliflowers, but remember that they can be in the ground for almost a year. Sow in seedbeds outdoors and transplant in midsummer. Winter cauliflowers for harvesting from midwinter to early spring should be 26 in. apart each way; those for cutting from midspring to early summer should be spaced 24 in. apart in and between the rows. Most varieties need frost protection to avoid damage to the heads. **Zones 3 to 9.**

Growing

Cauliflowers need a sheltered sunny site on deep, moisture-retentive, free-draining soil with a pH of 6.5 to 7.5. Dig in plenty of well-rotted organic matter in fall before planting and lime acid soils where necessary. Avoid planting overwintering types in frost pockets. Rake over the area before planting; the ground should be firm, but not compacted. Keep plants well watered from germination to harvest, as checks in growth spoil the quality of the heads. They need at least 4 gallons of water per square yard every 2 weeks.

Cauliflowers also need moderate nitrogen levels, though excessive amounts encourage soft leafy growth. Overwintering cauliflowers require low nitrogen levels, or they will be too soft to survive colder weather.

Keep crops weed-free with regular hoeing or mulching. Bend a few leaves over the heads of summer varieties to protect them from sunshine; do the same with winter crops to protect plants from frost and snow. Leaves can be easily tied in place with garden twine.

If the weather is hot and dry, water plants every now and then to maintain humidity and cool temperatures. Unwrap heads occasionally to check for hiding pests. Rotate crops.

Maintenance

Spring Sow early crops indoors and outdoors in seedbeds. Keep well watered and weed-free. Transplant.
Summer Sow indoors or outdoors in seedbeds. Transplant, harvest.
Fall Sow overwintering crops. Harvest.
Winter Prepare ground for the following year. Harvest.

Protected Cropping

Sow under a cold frame or under cloches and thin after germination to about 2 in., or sow two to three seeds in hills at the required spacing and thin to leave the strongest seedling. Grow on in the seedbed or transplant into small pots or packs. Alternatively, sow directly in small pots or packs, and germinate in a propagator or an unheated greenhouse according to the time of year. Repot when they are large enough to handle. Ventilate on warm days, then harden off and transplant as required.

Harvesting and Storing

Harvest cauliflowers successionally while they are small, rather than waiting until they all mature. If the heads become brown or if florets start to separate, it is almost too late: cut them immediately. Harvest in the morning, except in frosty conditions when you should wait until the frost has melted. Cauliflowers can be stored for up to 3 weeks by lifting whole plants, shaking the soil off the roots, and hanging upside down in a cool shed; mist the heads occasionally to maintain freshness.

Freeze tight heads only. To prepare, divide into sprigs, blanch for 3 minutes in water with a squeeze of lemon juice. Cool, drain, pack, and freeze in plastic bags.

Cauliflowers will store, wrapped, in the salad drawer of a refrigerator for up to 1 week.

Pests and Diseases

Beware of clubroot, cabbage root fly, caterpillars, and birds.

 companion planting

Plant with rosemary, thyme, sage, onions, garlic, beet, and chards.

 medicinal

This is another vegetable reputedly good for reducing the risk of cancer, especially of the colon and stomach.

CAULIFLOWER

 culinary

Separate into florets, boil or steam and serve with cheese or white sauce and grated nutmeg, or flaked almonds. Alternatively, dip in batter, fry, and eat as fritters.

Sprigs can be served raw with mayonnaise and other dips, or added to soups, soufflés, and pickles.

Cauliflower with Chiles and Black Mustard Seeds
Serves 4

In Indian cuisine, cauliflower can be cooked into curries but it is more often served dry, as in this recipe from southern India, given to me by the chef at Madras' Chola Hotel. For this dish, buy washed or white dal.

5 tablespoons vegetable oil
½ teaspoon asafetida
1 teaspoon black mustard seeds
1 teaspoon urad dal
2 dried hot red chiles, left whole
6 fresh hot green chiles, left whole
1½ pounds cauliflower, broken into bite-size florets
Salt
2 tablespoons fresh coconut, grated

Cauliflower with Chiles and Black Mustard Seeds

Either use a karhari or a heavy skillet. Heat the oil over high heat and add the asafetida, then the mustard seeds. When the seeds pop, add the dal; this will turn red, at which point add the chiles and cook until the red ones start to darken. Then stir in the cauliflower and cook for a minute or so. Add a tablespoon of water, season with salt, and keep stirring, adding more water as necessary; you will probably need to cook for 4 to 5 minutes, using 4 to 5 tablespoons of water. At this point, turn the heat right down and cook, covered, for an additional 5 minutes, until all the liquid has evaporated. Take care not to let the cauliflower burn.

Stir in the coconut and serve, discarding the chiles unless you like really hot food. You have been warned!

Cauliflower Soufflé
Serves 4

1 pound cauliflower florets
1 tablespoon butter
1 tablespoon all-purpose flour
½ cup milk
3 large eggs, separated
4 tablespoons grated cheddar
Pinch of nutmeg
Salt and freshly ground pepper

Steam or boil the cauliflower in salted water until just tender. Drain and dice finely. Keep warm. In a heavy pot, make a roux from the butter and flour and cook for 1 minute. Stir in the milk and bring to a boil, stirring constantly, to thicken the sauce. Then remove from the heat and stir in the egg yolks. Beat well and add the cheddar and cauliflower, seasoning well. Whisk the egg whites until stiff, then, using a metal spoon, fold into the cauliflower mixture.

Pour into a buttered soufflé dish and cook on the middle shelf of a preheated oven at 375°F, until the top is gloriously browned.

This should take about 30 to 35 minutes. Serve the soufflé immediately.

CABBAGE

Brassica oleracea (Capitata Group). Brassicaceae

Biennial grown as annual for leaves and hearts. Half hardy/hardy. Value: rich in beta carotene and vitamin C — especially green varieties and outer leaves; outer leaves contain vitamin E.

The Latin *Brassica* comes from *bresic*, the Celtic word for cabbage, a plant cultivated for centuries in the eastern Mediterranean and Asia Minor. The Romans believed that cabbages rose from Jupiter's sweat as he labored to explain two contradicting oracles — esteeming wild and cultivated cabbages as a cure-all as well as recommending them to prevent unseemly drunkenness.

Many varieties have been developed over the centuries. Heat-tolerant types were bred in southern Europe, while many hard-headed varieties were introduced by the Celts and Scandinavians. White cabbages appeared after 814 CE and German literature records the cultivation of red cabbages in 1150; in the 16th century Estienne and Liébault believed these were made by watering cabbages with red wine or by growing them in hot places. By the 13th century "headed cabbage" was well known, and three kinds of "Savoy" were mentioned in a German herbal of 1543.

"January King"

 varieties

Cabbages are usually grouped according to the season when they are harvested. They range from fairly loose-leaved heads of pointed or conical shape to rounded "ball" shapes with varying degrees of densely packed leaves.

Spring
Spring cabbages traditionally have pointed heads, but there are now round-headed types. For "spring greens," use their immature leaves or choose a leafy variety bred for this purpose.

"Duncan" is high yielding so grow for leaves or small solid heads in June. "Offenham 1 Myatts Offenham Compacta" is a tasty, very early spring cabbage and has dark green leaves. "Pixie" is another very early spring variety that has tight, compact hearts; ideal for small gardens.

Early Summer/Summer
"Derby Day" is an excellent "ball-head" cabbage for harvesting from early summer. "Hispi" is reliable, with pointed heads of good quality and taste. It matures rapidly and is ideal for close spacing. "First of June" is a dark-leaved variety with a compact head, good for successional sowing in summer. "Ruby Ball" is an ornamental and colorful red cabbage, very reliable and particularly excellent for use in salads. "Kalibos," also red, is slug-resistant and good for small gardens.

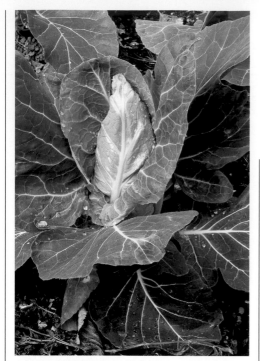
A heart is forming

Late Summer/Fall
"Golden Acre," a ball-headed variety, is compact and sweet-tasting and ready in 12 weeks. It tolerates close spacing, is high-yielding, and grows well on poorer soils. "Kilaton" is delicious, good quality, and club root-resistant. "Kilaxy" produces compact, tasty heads, stands well, and is also club root-resistant. "Stonehead" has a tightly packed head and is early-maturing. It is resistant to yellow and black rot.

Winter/Winter Storage
Winter cabbages are usually ball- or drum-headed. The white-leaved Dutch cabbage (used primarily for coleslaw) matures from mid- to late fall and can be cut for storage or left to stand in mild conditions. The extremely hardy, tasty, and attractive Savoy types with puckered green leaves mature from midfall to late winter.

"January King 3" is an excellent drum-head Savoy type, which is extremely hardy and frost-resistant, maturing in midfall to early winter. "Multiton" is a winter-storage cabbage and "Savoy Express" is small, sweet, and ideal where space is limited.

 cultivation

Propagation
Seeds sown in trays, packs, or seedbeds will be ready for transplanting about 5 weeks after sowing. Spacings can be modified according to the size of "head" required. Closer spacing means a smaller head while wider spacing produces slightly larger heads.
Sow spring cabbage from mid- to late summer; transplant from early to midfall. Space 10–12 in. apart in and between the rows. Protect with cloches or crop covers over winter to encourage earlier cropping. For "spring greens," grow suitable varieties with 10 in. in and between the plants, or space spring cabbage plants 4–6 in. apart and harvest when immature.

Sow cabbages for summer and fall harvest successionally, with "earlies" and "lates" for an extended cropping season (see "Varieties"). You should make the first sowings in a propagator or heated greenhouse at 55–60°F from late winter to early spring, repot, and transplant in mid- to late spring. Follow these with sowings in cold frames or a seedbed under cloches or crop covers. Make further sowings without protection until late spring.

Transplant from early to midsummer, spacing plants 14–20 in. apart depending on the size of head you are after.

Sow winter-maturing varieties successionally from mid- to late spring under cover or outdoors for transplanting from early to midsummer. Space about 18 in. apart. **Zones 3 to 9.**

Growing
Cabbages flourish at around 59–68°F and should not be transplanted at temperatures above 77°F, while some overwintering varieties survive temperatures

Cabbage plants in a vegetable patch

down to 14°F. They flourish in a rich, fertile, moisture-retentive soil with a pH of 5.5 to 7.0. Dig in plenty of well-rotted organic matter several weeks before planting and lime the soil if necessary. Rake the soil level before planting and ensure that it is firm but not compacted.

Do not fertilize spring cabbages after planting, as this encourages soft growth and the nutrients are washed away by winter rains. Wait until early to midspring and sprinkle a general granular fertilizer round the plants, or liquid feed.

Summer, fall, and winter cabbages need a dressing of fertilizer after transplanting and will benefit from an additional granular or liquid feed in the growing season. To increase stability, hill up spring and winter cabbages as they grow.

Provided growing conditions are good and plants healthy, you can produce a second harvest from spring or early summer varieties. After cutting the head, cut a cross shape ½ inch in the stump, which will sprout a cluster of smaller cabbages.

Keep cabbages moist and weed-free with regular hoeing, hand weeding, or mulching. Rotate cabbages with other brassicas.

Maintenance
Spring Sow and transplant summer, fall, and winter cabbage. Harvest.
Summer Sow spring cabbage. Harvest.
Fall Transplant spring cabbage. Harvest.
Winter Sow summer cabbages. Harvest.

Harvesting and Storing
Spring cabbages are ready to harvest from mid- to late spring. Summer and fall varieties are ready to harvest from midsummer to midfall. Winter types can be harvested from late fall to midspring in milder climates. Spring and summer varieties are eaten immediately after harvest.

Dutch winter white cabbages and some red cabbages can be lifted for storing indoors. Choose those that are healthy and undamaged and dig them up before the first frosts for storage in a cool, slightly humid, frost-free place.

Remove the loose outer leaves and stand the heads on a slatted shelf or a layer of straw on the shed floor. Alternatively, suspend them in nets. They can also be stored in a spare cold frame if it is well ventilated to discourage rotting. They should store for up to 5 months.

Freeze only the best quality fresh crisp heads. Wash, shred coarsely, blanch for about 1 minute, and pack into plastic bags or rigid plastic containers.

Wrapped in plastic wrap in a refrigerator, cabbages stay fresh for about a week.

Pests and Diseases

Cabbages suffer from the common brassica problems, including cabbage root fly, clubroot, aphids, and birds.

 ## companion planting

Cabbages thrive in the company of herbs like dill, mint, rosemary, sage, thyme, and chamomile. They also grow well with many other vegetables including onions, garlic, peas, celery, potatoes, fava beans, and beets.

Like all brassicas, they benefit from the nitrogen left in the soil after legumes have been grown. The belief that they do not grow well with vines, oregano, and cyclamen stems from Classical times. In the 16th century, it was well known that "Vineyards where Coleworts grow, doe yeeld the worser Wines."

 ## medicinal

Eating cabbage is said to reduce the risk of colonic cancer, stimulate the immune system, and kill bacteria. Drinking the juice is alleged to prevent and heal ulcers. Some active principles are partly destroyed on cooking, so cabbage is much more nutritious eaten raw.

According to folklore, placing heated cabbage leaves on the soles of the feet reduces fever; placed on a septic wound, they draw out pus or a splinter.

 ## culinary

Traditionally cabbage is cooked by boiling — preferably as briefly as possible — in a small amount of water, to preserve the nutrients. Add the cabbage to boiling water, which should not stop boiling while you place the younger leaves from the heart on top of the older leaves below. Cover, cook briefly for 3 minutes, then drain. Or steam for about 6 to 8 minutes.

Stir-frying, the oriental way, is almost as fast; alternatively, bake, braise, or stuff. Use as a substitute for vine leaves in dolmades.

Eat shredded white or red cabbage raw in salads. Coleslaw is a mixture of shredded cabbage, carrot, apple, and celery with French dressing or a mayonnaise/sour cream blend; its name derives from "cole," the old name for cabbage, and the Dutch *slaw*, meaning salad.

Pickle red cabbage in vinegar and white cabbage in brine (as *sauerkraut*).

Czerwona Kapusta
Serves 6

The Polish and Czechs are extremely keen on red cabbage. This dish combines subtle flavors to make a refreshing change from our usual ways of cooking the vegetable.

2 pounds red cabbage, finely sliced
salt and freshly ground black pepper
1 tablespoon butter
1 tablespoon all-purpose flour
½ cup red wine
2 teaspoons sugar
Pinch ground cloves
Pinch ground cinnamon

Put the cabbage in a colander and sprinkle with 1 teaspoon salt; leave for 15 minutes then rinse well under cold water. Transfer to a pan of boiling water and simmer gently until the cabbage is just cooked. Drain and keep warm. Reserve a little of the liquid.

Heat the butter in a pot over medium heat and mix in the flour to make a roux. Cook for 2 minutes without burning. Dilute with the cooking liquid to make a thick sauce and stir in the cabbage. Season and add the red wine, sugar, cloves, and cinnamon. Mix well and simmer for an additional 5 minutes. Serve.

Czerwona Kapusta

Colcannon
Serves 4

Probably the most famous Irish dish, some believe this was traditionally made with kale but today it is commonly made with cabbage. Use a Savoy.

1 pound potatoes, peeled and cooked
1 leek, cleaned, sliced and cooked in a little cream or milk
1 pound cabbage, sliced and cooked
4 tablespoons butter
Salt and freshly ground black pepper

Mash the potatoes and season them before stirring in the slices of leek and juices in which they were cooked. Then add the cabbage and mix thoroughly over low heat. Arrange on a warmed serving dish and make a hole in the center. Keep warm. Partly melt the butter, season, and pour it into the cavity. Serve immediately, piping hot.

BRUSSELS SPROUTS

Biennial grown as annual for leafy buds and "tops." Hardy. Value: excellent source of vitamin C, rich in beta carotene, folic acid, vitamin E, and potassium.

First recorded as a spontaneous sport from a cabbage plant found in the Brussels region of Belgium around 1750, this vegetable had reached England and France by 1800. The Brussels version may not have been the first occurrence: a plant described as *Brassica capitata polycephalos* (a many-headed brassica with knob-like heads) was illustrated in D'Alechaps's *Historia Generalis Plantarum* in 1587. A stalwart among winter vegetables in cool temperate climates, sprouts are extremely hardy and crop heavily, but are rather fiddly to prepare. As with all vegetables, home-grown ones taste far better than those bought from a store. If you have never eaten sprouts harvested fresh from the garden, try them: they are absolutely delicious.

 ## varieties

Sprouts are divided into early, midseason and late varieties, harvested from early to midfall, midfall to midwinter and midwinter to early spring respectively. "Earlies" are shorter and faster-growing than the hardier "lates," which are taller with higher yields. To extend the season, grow one variety from each group if you have space; alternatively, grow midseason and late types for midwinter to early spring crops, when other vegetables are scarce.

Although older open-pollinated varieties are very tasty, it is generally accepted that the modern, compact F1 hybrids are a better buy. They produce a heavy crop of uniform "buttons" all the way up the stem, which remain in good condition for a long period without "blowing"; plants are also less likely to fall over.

"Braveheart" is vigorous, high yielding and easy to pick, with a nutty flavor. "Falstaff" is a vigorous, high-yielding red cultivar with tasty "buttons." The red coloration disappears when boiled so steaming is a good method of cooking. "Noisette" is a "gourmet" sprout with a nutty flavor. "Oliver" (very early) is a high-yielding variety with large, tasty sprouts and good resistance to powdery mildew. "Rampart" (late) has tasty sprouts that last for a long time before "blowing" but tend to become bitter late in the season. It has good resistance to powdery mildew and some resistance to ringspot. "Romulus" grows tall and vigorous, crops well, and is very reliable and tasty. "Rubine," a red form, is worth a place in an ornamental border and produces small crops of good-tasting sprouts.

BRUSSELS SPROUTS

 cultivation

Sprouts need a sheltered, sunny spot; wind rock can be a problem in exposed sites. Soil should be moisture-retentive yet free-draining, with a pH of 6.5.

Propagation

Sow early varieties from late winter to early spring, midseason varieties from mid- to late spring and late varieties from midspring. Sow seeds thinly, 1 in. deep in a half tray of moist seed or multi-purpose potting mix, and put them in an unheated greenhouse, cold frame, or sheltered spot outdoors to germinate. Transplant seedlings when they are large enough to handle into a larger seed tray, in potting or multi-purpose potting mix, about 1½ to 2 in. apart.

Sowing in packs reduces root disturbance when transplanting. Put two seeds in each pack and retain the strongest after germination. Sow early varieties from late winter in a propagator at 50–55°F and transplant them into their permanent position after hardening

Brussels sprouts can be harvested in fall and winter

off. Some taller varieties are prone to falling over when grown in packs, but when planted deeply, a long tap root develops.

The previous two methods are preferable to sowing in a seedbed, which takes up space that could be used for other crops, and leaves seedlings vulnerable to pests and diseases; I do not recommend it. If necessary, warm the soil with cloches or black plastic. Protect earlier sowings from cold weather; later sowings can be made without shelter. Water before sowing if the soil is dry. Level, firm, and rake the seedbed to a fine tilth before sowing seed thinly, 1 in. deep in rows 8 in. apart, thinning seedlings to 3–4 in. apart when they are large enough to handle. Transplant into their final position when they are about 4–6 in. tall. Gradually harden off those grown under cover before planting them in their final positions.

Growing

Dig in plenty of well-rotted manure or potting mix several months before planting, particularly on light, poor or heavy soils. The ground should not be freshly manured, as excessive nitrogen causes sprouts to fail to form heads.

Plant earlier, smaller varieties about 24 in. apart each way, those of moderate size 30 in. apart and taller varieties 3 ft. apart. Wider spacing encourages larger sprouts, improves air circulation, and reduces fungal problems, while closer spacing means smaller, compact

"buttons" which will mature at the same time. Plant with the lowest leaves just above the soil surface. Tug a leaf — if the whole plant moves it has not been planted firmly enough. On light soils, make a drill 3–4 in. deep, plant sprouts in the bottom, and refill it with soil. The extra support makes the plants more stable. Water immediately after transplanting for 3 to 4 weeks until plants have become established and, if available, mulch with straw to a depth of 2–3 in.

Keep the beds weed-free. Watering is not normally needed once plants are established except during drought, when each plant can be given up to ½ cup per day to maintain the growth necessary for good cropping. Remove any diseased or yellowing leaves as they appear. Hilling round the stem base to a depth of 3–5 in. provides support against winter winds, although tall varieties will usually need staking. In exposed gardens, even dwarf varieties need staking.

"Topping" by removing the growing point is only beneficial for fall-maturing F1 cultivars being grown for freezing. Plants can be topped when lowest sprouts reach ½ in. diameter, to encourage even development of sprouts on the stem. When left untopped, sprouts can be picked over a longer period.

Grow sprouts on a 3- or 4-year rotation, preferably following peas and beans (where they benefit from the nitrogen left in the soil). In late summer, feeding with a liquid high-potash fertilizer gives plants a useful boost.

The tops can be eaten, too

BRUSSELS SPROUT

Plant small lettuces like "Little Gem" between sprouts for summer and fall cropping, and winter purslane or land cress for early winter crops.

Dig plants immediately after harvesting, put leaves on the compost pile, and shred the stems.

Maintenance
Spring Sow outdoors in seedbeds, thin, and keep weed-free.
Summer Transplant outdoors and water during drought.
Fall Harvest early varieties; stake tall varieties if needed.
Winter Sow early varieties indoors. Harvest later crops.

Protected Cropping
Earlier sowings made outdoors in a seedbed should be protected with cloches or floating row cover. Continued protection with floating row cover provides a physical barrier against pests such as cabbage root fly, flea beetle, aphids, and birds.

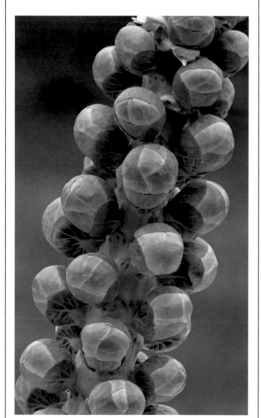
Harvest sprouts that are tightly closed

Harvesting and Storing
Pick sprouts when those at the base are walnut-sized and tightly closed. Snap them off with a sharp downward tug or cut with a knife, removing split sprouts and any yellow, diseased leaves. When harvest is over, the tops can be cooked as cabbage. During severe winter weather, lift a few plants to hang in a shed where they can be easily harvested. They will last for several weeks.

Pests and Diseases
Sprouts are very robust yet subject to the usual brassica problems. Downy mildew shows as yellow patches on the leaves, with patches of fluffy mold on the underside in humid conditions. Remove all affected leaves or dust with sulfur. If downy mildew appears on seedlings, improve ventilation and increase spacing.

Powdery mildew is a white powdery deposit over shoots, stems, and leaves. In severe cases, plants become yellow and die. It is more of a problem when plants are dry at the roots. Water and mulch, remove diseased leaves and spray with fungicide.

Clubroot, affecting members of the Brassicaceae family, is a disease to be avoided at all costs. Roots swell and distort, young plants wilt on hot days but recover overnight, growth is stunted and crops ruined. It is more of a problem on poorly drained, acid soils. Spores remain in the soil for up to 20 years. Never buy brassicas from unknown sources: grow them yourself. Potting plants on into 4–6 in. pots allows the roots to become established before they are planted out, which lessens the effects of clubroot. Improve drainage; lime acid soils to create a neutral pH. Hilling often encourages new roots to form and reduces the effects. Remove all diseased plants, with the whole root system if possible, and destroy them.

Ringspot is worse in cool wet seasons and on well-manured land. It is most evident on older leaves as round brown spots with dark centers. Remove and burn any affected plants and rotate crops.

 companion planting

When planted among maturing onions, sprouts benefit from their root residues and the firm soil.

 culinary

Steam or boil sprouts briskly for the minimum time required to cook through — they should not turn mushy. Small sprouts can be shredded in salads — "Rubine" and "Falstaff" are particularly attractive.

They can be stored for up to 3 weeks in a plastic bag in the refrigerator. Freeze sprouts only if they are small. Blanch for 3 minutes, cool, and drain before drying and packing them into plastic bags.

Stir-fried Sprouts
Serves 4

This can look quite spectacular made with a red variety such as "Falstaff" or "Rubine."

2 tablespoons vegetable oil
2 tablespoons soy sauce
1 pound Brussels sprouts, trimmed and finely sliced
2 tablespoons hazelnuts, roughly ground
Salt and freshly ground black pepper

Heat the oil in a wok, stir in the soy sauce and, over high heat, cook the sprouts for 2 to 3 minutes. Sprinkle over the hazelnuts. Season and serve.

Brassica oleracea (Gongylodes Group). Brassicaceae

KOHLRABI

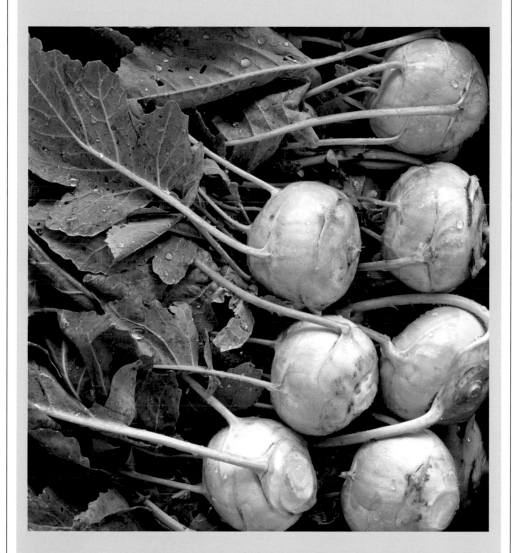

Biennial grown as annual for rounded, swollen stems. Hardy. Value: rich in vitamin C, traces of minerals.

This odd-looking vegetable with a distinctive name has a rounded, swollen stem which, with the leaves removed, looks like a sputnik! Its common name, derived from the German *Kohl*, meaning cabbage, and *Rabi*, turnip, accurately describes its taste when boiled. Raw, it has a fresh, nutty flavor. Found in northern Europe in the 15th century, it may already have existed for centuries, as a similar-sounding vegetable was described by Pliny around 70 CE. This highly nutritious, tasty vegetable is more drought-resistant than most brassicas, succeeding where rutabagas and turnips fail. It deserves to be more widely grown and eaten.

 varieties

"Blusta" is fast-maturing, has a sweet, nutty flavor, and is resistant to bolting. "Domino", an early variety, is good for growing under cover. "Kongo" is top quality; fast-growing, very sweet and juicy, and has high yields. "Korist" produces a good-sized crop of mildly flavored, tender, juicy bulbs. "Lanro" is a white-fleshed, green-skinned variety. Juicy and mild-flavored, it is a good mini vegetable. "Olivia" produces good-sized bulbs and is crisp and mild-flavored. "Trero" is sweet, uniform, vigorous, and slow to become "woody." "White Vienna" has a pale green skin and is delicately flavored.

 cultivation

Propagation

Sow successionally for a regular harvest. Early sowings in seed or multi-purpose potting mix in a propagator at 55–65°F can be made during midwinter to early spring. Transplant after hardening off in midspring when they are no more than 2 in. high; if you let them grow taller or sow seed when soil temperatures are below 50°F, they are liable to go to seed. Protect with cloches or floating row cover until the plants are established.

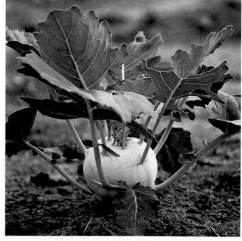

Pick when small for the finest flavor

"Purple Vienna"

Water the rows before sowing and sow later crops thinly in rows ½ in. deep in rows 12 in. apart. Thin seedlings when they are about 1 in. high and the first true leaves appear, to a final spacing 6–8 in. apart. Prompt thinning is vital, as growth is easily checked. Alternatively, plant three seeds together in hills 6 in. apart and thin to leave the strongest seedling. Kohlrabi can also be grown successfully in packs and then transplanted at their final spacing.

Kohlrabi grown as a mini vegetable is ideal for the small garden. Sow cultivars like "Rolano," "Logo," "Korist," and "Kolibri" and thin to about 1 in. apart between the plants and rows. Harvest after 9 to 10 weeks when about the size of golf balls.

Growing
The ideal situation is a sunny position on light, fertile, humus-rich, well-drained soil. Incorporate organic matter the winter before planting if necessary and lime acid soils to create a pH of 6 to 7. The ground must be firm before planting, as (in common with other brassicas), kohlrabi does not grow well on loose soil. Lightly fork the area, removing any debris, then gently tread down the surface or firm it with the head of a rake. Finally, rake in a general fertilizer at 3 oz. per square yard and level. Kohlrabi must receive a constant supply of water throughout the season. This is because if growth is checked they can become "woody." During drought periods, they need up to 2 gallons per square yard of water per week. If growth slows down, liquid feed with a high-nitrogen fertilizer. Keep crops weed-free and mulch with potting mix to suppress weeds and retain moisture. Rotate kohlrabi with brassicas.

Maintenance
Spring Prepare the seedbed and sow seed *in situ* under cloches.
Summer Sow regularly for successional cropping. Sow hardier purple varieties later in the season. Weed and water as necessary.
Fall Sow in midfall and protect with cloches for early winter harvest.
Winter From late winter, sow early crops in packs or trays. Prepare the ground for outdoor sowings.

Protected Cropping
Early and late outdoor crops should be protected with cloches or crop covers.

Harvesting and Storing
Kohlrabi matures rapidly and is ready for harvest 2 months after sowing. Lift when plants are somewhere in size between a golf and a tennis ball. Larger "bulbs" tend to become woody and unpalatable, but this is less of a problem with newer cultivars.

Harvest as required. In severe weather they can be stored in boxes of sand or sawdust. Remove the outer leaves, keeping the central tuft of leaves to keep them fresh. Some flavor tends to be lost during storage.

Pests and Diseases
As it matures quickly, kohlrabi is untroubled by many of the usual brassica problems, including clubroot.

Birds can cause severe damage, particularly to young plants. You should protect crops with netting, cages, humming wire, or with bird scarers.

Flea beetles — tiny and black — nibble holes in leaves of seedlings, checking growth. Dust plants and the surrounding soil thoroughly with rotenone or another insecticide when symptoms appear. They can also be controlled by brushing a yellow sticky trap or piece of wood covered in glue along the tops of the plants: the insects jump out, stick to the glue, and can be disposed of.

Cabbage root fly larvae cause stunted growth, wilting and death. Protect the seedlings when transplanting with 5-in. squares of plastic, cardboard or rubberized carpet underlay, slit from edge to center, and fitted around the stems. This stops adults from laying eggs.

 ## companion planting

Kohlrabi grows well with beet and onions.

 ## container growing

Kohlrabi are ideal for containers, particularly when grown as "mini vegetables." Plant in a soilless potting mix with a moderate fertilizer content and maintain a regular supply of water. Feed every 2 to 3 weeks with a general liquid fertilizer.

 ## culinary

There is no need to peel tiny kohlrabi, but peel off the tough outer skin of older globes before cooking. Young ones can be trimmed, scrubbed, and boiled whole or sliced for 20 to 30 minutes, then drained, peeled, and served with melted butter, white sauce, or mashed.

Boiled kohlrabi can be made into fritters by frying with egg and breadcrumbs. Add kohlrabi to soups and stews, serve stuffed, cook like celeriac, or eat in a cheese sauce. It complements basil and is excellent steamed.

Kohlrabi globes can also be eaten raw, grated, or sliced into salads, and the leaves are good boiled.

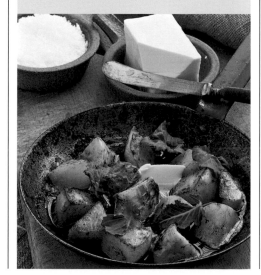

Brassica oleracea (Italica Group). Brassicaceae
BROCCOLI

Also known as Sprouting Broccoli, Calabrese. Annual or biennial grown for immature flowerheads. Hardy or half hardy. High in beta carotene, vitamin C, folic acid, and iron. Moderate levels of calcium.

Said to have originated in the eastern Mediterranean, early forms of broccoli were highly esteemed by the Romans and described by Pliny in the first century CE. It spread from Italy to northern Europe, arriving in England in the 18th century. Philip Miller in his *Gardener's Dictionary* of 1724 called it "sprout cauliflower" or "Italian asparagus."
Broccoli is an Italian word, derived from the Latin *brachium*, meaning "arm" or "branch." Calabrese, a similar plant with the same botanical origin, grown for its larger immature flowerheads, also takes its name from the Italian — meaning "from Calabria." This delicious vegetable was introduced to France by Catherine de Medici in 1560, spreading from there to the rest of Europe. "Green broccoli" was first mentioned in North American literature in 1806, but was certainly in cultivation long before that. It is said to have been introduced by Italian settlers and is extensively grown around New York and Boston.

"Purple Sprouting Early"

 varieties

Old varieties of perennial broccoli are still available; outstanding among them all is "Nine Star Perennial," a multi-headed variety with small white heads. Cropping improves if unused heads are removed before they go to seed.

Sprouting Broccoli
This excellent winter vegetable produces a succession of small flowerheads for cropping over a long season from early winter to late spring and is suitable for poor soils and cold areas. "Purple" varieties are hardier than the "white," which have a better taste and crop later, but tend to be less productive. Sow "Summer Purple" in early spring, "Rudolph" from early to late spring and "Cardinal" in late spring for a harvest lasting almost 12 months.

"Bordeaux," if sown early, can produce an early flowering harvest from July. "Purple Sprouting Early" is easy, prolific, and extremely hardy and can be eady for harvesting from late winter. "Purple Sprouting Late" is similar, but ready for picking from midspring. "White Sprouting" is delicious, with shoots like tiny cauliflowers and "White Sprouting Early" is the white equivalent of "Purple Sprouting." "White Sprouting Late" is ready to harvest from midspring.

Calabrese
Also known as American, Italian, or green sprouting broccoli, this produces a large central flowerhead surrounded by smaller sideshoots, which develop after the main head has been harvested. Maturing about

3 months after sowing, it crops from summer until the onset of the first frosts.

"Broccoletto" is quick-maturing and sweet, with a single head. "Fiesta" is excellent for summer and fall cropping with large, domed heads of small buds. "Flash" produces small to medium buds over a long season. "Green Sprouting," an old Italian variety, matures early. "Paragon Enhanced" has hybrid, umbrella like spears, and tender, slim, sweet-tasting stems. "Ramoso" ("DeCicco"), an old Italian variety for spring or fall cropping, produces heads over a long period. Tasty, tender, and freezes well. "Trixie" is high yielding with domed heads of small buds.

cultivation

Propagation

Prepare the seedbed for sprouting broccoli by raking the soil to a fine texture. Sow over several weeks from mid- to late spring, planting the earlier varieties first. Sow thinly in rows in a seedbed, 12 in. apart and ½ in. deep, thinning to 6 in. apart before transplanting at their final spacing. Alternatively, sow two to three seeds in hills 6 in. apart, thinning to leave the strongest seedling.

For early spring crops, sow early maturing cultivars indoors in trays from late summer to early fall. Transplant seedlings when they are about 5 in. tall into an unheated greenhouse or cold frame. Harden off and transplant outdoors from late winter to midspring. Alternatively, sow two seeds per pack and thin to leave

Ready for harvesting

the stronger seedling. The final spacing for plants should be about 26–30 in. apart in and between the rows. It is worth noting that they take up a lot of space and have a long growing season!

Calabrese can be sown successively from midspring to midsummer for cropping from early summer to fall. It does not transplant well and is better sown *in situ*. Sow two to three seeds at "stations," thinning to leave the strongest seedling. Close spacing suppresses side shoots and encourages small terminal spears to form, which are useful for freezing. Wider spacing means higher yields. While they can be as close as 3 in. apart with 24 in. between rows, the optimum spacing is 6 in. apart with 12 in. between the rows. **Zones 3 to 10.**

Growing

Sprouting broccoli thrives in a warm, sunny position. Soil should be deep, moisture-retentive, and free-draining. Nitrogen levels should be moderate; excessive amounts encourage soft, leafy growth. You should avoid shallow or sandy soils and windy sites. Sprouting broccoli tends to be top-heavy, so hill up round the stem to a depth of 3–5 in. to prevent wind rock, or stake larger varieties. Firm stems loosened by wind or frost.

Keep crops weed-free with regular hoeing or mulch with a 2 in. layer of organic matter. Water crops regularly before the onset of dry weather: do not let them dry out. Calabrese needs at least 4 gallons per square yard every 2 weeks, though a single thorough watering 2 to 3 weeks before harvesting is a useful option for those under watering restrictions!

Feed with a general liquid fertilizer, or sprinkle and water in ½ oz. per square yard of granular fertilizer after the main head has been removed to encourage side shoots to grow.

Maintenance

Spring Sow early broccoli indoors and later crops in seedbeds. Sow calabrese.
Summer Water crops and keep weed-free. Feed calabrese after harvesting the terminal bud.
Fall Harvest calabrese, remove, and dispose of crop debris.
Winter Harvest broccoli in mild climate areas.

Steam florets to keep the color and goodness

Harvesting and Storing

Cut sprouting broccoli when the heads have formed, well before the flowers open, when the stems are 6–8 in. long. Regular harvesting is essential, as this encourages side-shoot formation and should ensure a 6- to 8-week harvest. Never strip the plant completely, or let it flower, as this stops the side shoots forming and makes existing "spears" woody and stronger tasting.

Sprouting broccoli can be stored in a plastic bag in the refrigerator. It will keep for about 3 days. To freeze, soak in salted water for 15 minutes, rinse and dry. Blanch for 3 to 4 minutes, cool and drain. Pack it in containers and freeze.

Cut the mature central heads of calabrese with a sharp knife, while still firm and the buds tight. This encourages growth of side shoots within about 2 to 3 weeks. Pick regularly as for sprouting broccoli.

Calabrese can be stored in the refrigerator for up to 5 days, and freezes well.

companion planting

Plant with rosemary, thyme, sage, onions, garlic, beet, and chards.

culinary

Remove any tough leaves attached to the stalks and wash florets carefully in cold water before cooking. For the best flavor cook immediately after picking in boiling salted water for 10 minutes, or steam by standing spears upright in 2 in. of gently boiling water for 15 minutes with the pan covered. Drain carefully and serve hot with white, hollandaise, or béarnaise sauce, melted butter, or vinaigrette. An Italian recipe book recommends braising calabrese in white wine or sautéing it in oil and sprinkling with grated Parmesan cheese. In Sicily, it is braised with anchovies, olives, and red wine. Broccoli fritters are dipped in batter, then deep-fried.

Stir-fried florets can be blanched for 1 minute and fried with squid and shellfish. On a more mundane (but practical) level, broccoli and calabrese can be used as a fine substitute in cauliflower cheese.

Penne with Broccoli, Mascarpone and Dolcelatte
Serves 4

1 pound broccoli florets
½ cup mascarpone cheese
1 cup dolcelatte cheese
2 tablespoons crème fraîche
1 tablespoon balsamic vinegar
1 tablespoon dry white wine
3½ cups penne
2 tablespoons capers
4 tablespoons black olives
1 tablespoon hazelnuts, crushed
Salt and freshly ground black pepper

Steam the broccoli florets over a pan of boiling water for 2 to 3 minutes. Run under cold water and let sit. In a heavy pan, gently heat the mascarpone, dolcelatte, crème fraîche, vinegar, and wine.

Add the broccoli florets. Cook the pasta until it is just tender and drain well. Pour over the hot sauce, sprinkle with the capers, olives, and hazelnuts and toss well. Adjust the seasoning and serve.

TURNIP

Biennial grown as an annual for globular, swollen root, and young leaves. Hardy. Value: low in calories and carbohydrate; small amounts of vitamins and minerals.

This ancient root crop was known to Theophrastus in 400 BCE and many early varieties were given Greek place names. Pliny listed 12 distinct types under *rapa* and *napus* — which became *naep* in Anglo-Saxon, and together with the word "turn" (meaning "made round"), gave us the common name. Introduced to Canada in 1541, the turnip was brought to Virginia by the colonists in 1609 and was rapidly adopted by the native Americans. In Britain they have found a role in folklore. In Northern Ireland, turnips were made into lamps for Halloween (October 31), and in the Shetland Islands of Scotland slices were shaped into letters and put into a tub of water for young revellers to retrieve with their mouths; they usually tried to pick the initial of someone they loved.

 ## varieties

Earlies

"Oasis" has virus-resistant white roots and is delicious when raw. "Purple Top Milan" produces flattish roots with purple markings and white flesh. Tender when young, early maturing, and good for overwintering, it has an excellent flavor. "Primera" is succulent and full of flavor. "Snowball" is a delicately flavored, fast-maturing white variety with cut leaves. "Tokyo Cross" is an excellent F1 hybrid that matures rapidly, in about 35 to 40 days, and produces small, tasty white globes. A "mini vegetable" that is also tasty when larger, it is suitable as a late summer to early fall crop.

Maincrops

"Golden Ball" ("Golden Perfection" or "Orange Jelly") is a small, round yellow variety that should be grown quickly to keep the flesh succulent. Tasty, hardy, excellent for storing. "Green Globe" is white-fleshed with round roots; excellent for turnip tops. "Shogoin" (Japanese for "greens" or "root") is crispy and great for cooking and pickling.

 ## cultivation

Turnips flourish at about 68°F and prefer a sheltered, open site in light, fertile, well-drained but moisture-retentive soil. Summer sowings can be made in moderate shade provided they receive sufficient moisture. Turnips prefer a pH of 5.5 to 7.0; very acid soil will need liming.

Propagation

Sow early turnips in midspring, as soon as the ground is workable, or in late winter or early spring under cloches or floating row cover.

Prepare the seedbed carefully and sow early turnips thinly about 1 in. deep, in rows 9 in. apart. Then thin to a final spacing of 4–5 in. They can also be grown in a grid pattern: mark 5 in. squares in the ground with a stick and sow three seeds where the grid lines cross, thinning after germination to leave the strongest seedling.

Sow maincrop varieties from mid- to late summer in rows 1 in. deep and 12 in. apart, thinning to 4–5 in. apart. It is important to thin seedlings when no more than 1 in. high, when the first true leaves appear, to ensure the roots develop properly. Firm the soil after thinning; do not thin turnips grown for tops.

When growing for their tops, prepare the seedbed and broadcast seed over a small area or sow thinly in rows 4–6 in. apart as soon as soil conditions allow. Sow early cultivars in spring for summer cropping and hardy varieties in late summer or early fall. Small seedlings of "maincrops" overwinter and grow rapidly in spring, making them a useful early crop, particularly when

"Purple Top Milan"

covered with cloches or floating row cover. To ensure a prolonged harvest, make successional sowings of "earlies" from early spring until early summer.

Growing

If the ground has not been manured for the previous crop, till in fall, working plenty of well-rotted organic matter into the soil, and allowing it to weather over winter. About a week to 10 days before sowing, remove any weeds or debris and rake general fertilizer into the soil at 2 oz. per square yard. In common with other brassicas, turnips grow poorly on loose soil, so rake the soil to a fine tilth and firm it with the head of a rake or by carefully treading. If the soil is dry, water thoroughly before sowing and stand on a planting board to avoid compacting the soil. Mark each row with stakes or twigs, and label and date the crop.

Keep crops weed-free by hand weeding or careful hoeing. Turnips must have a constant supply of water throughout the growing season, otherwise they tend to go to seed or produce small woody roots, while sudden watering or rain after a period of drought causes them to split. They will need up to 2 gallons per square yard per week during dry periods. This improves the size and quality of the crop, but usually reduces the flavor. Turnips should be rotated with crops other than brassicas.

Maintenance

Spring Prepare seedbed, sow early varieties under cloches.
Summer Sow earlies every 2 to 3 weeks for successional cropping. Keep crops weed-free and water as necessary. From mid- to late summer, sow maincrop varieties.
Fall Sow "earlies" under cloches mid- to late fall. Thin maincrop varieties.
Winter Harvest and store maincrop turnips.

Protected Cropping

Cover ground with cloches, floating row cover, or black plastic for 2 to 3 weeks in late winter to early spring to warm the ground before sowing early crops. In late summer, protect sowings of early cultivars. Maincrop turnips grown for their tops can be grown under cloches after sowing in fall and picked during winter.

"Shogoin"

Harvesting and Storing

Harvest early varieties when young and tender. Gather those to be eaten raw when they are the size of a golf ball; any time up to tennis ball-size if they are to be cooked. Hand pull them in the same way as radishes. Maincrop turnips that are lifted in midfall for winter use are much larger, hardier, and slower to mature. To keep the flavor, harvest at maturity as they soon become woody and unpalatable. Turnips can be left in the soil and lifted as required using a garden fork. Keep them in a cool place and use within a few days. In cold wet climates, roots are better lifted to prevent deterioration. Twist off the leaves, remove any soil, put the roots between layers of dry peat substitute, sawdust or sand in a box, then store in a cool shed or refrigerator.

Turnips grown for their tops can be harvested when about 4–6 in. high, cutting about 1 in. above ground level. Keep soil moist and they will resprout several times before finally going to seed.

Pests and Diseases

Flea beetles, tiny and black, with or without yellow stripes, nibble holes in leaves of seedlings, checking growth. Large infestations of mealy aphid may kill young plants or cause black "sooty mold" on leaves. Cabbage root fly larvae feed on roots; transplanted brassicas are particularly vulnerable. Powdery mildew, a white deposit over shoots, stems and leaves, causes stunted growth. In severe cases, leaves yellow and die.

 ## companion planting

Growing with peas deters aphids. Turnips are useful for intercropping between taller crops and for catch-cropping.

 ## container growing

Fast-maturing early varieties grow well in large containers of well-drained, soil-based potting mix with added organic matter. Water crops well.

 ## medicinal

The liquor from turnips sprinkled with turbinado sugar was used in folk medicine to cure colds.

 ## culinary

Both turnips and their leaves (turnip tops) are tasty. Eat early turnips raw in salads or boiled, tossed in butter and chopped parsley. Peel maincrop turnips before cooking. They are good mashed, roasted, and in casseroles and soups.

Glazed Turnips

Use small, young turnips. Scrub them and cut into ½ in. dice (or use whole). Drop into boiling water for 3 minutes. Drain. Melt a little butter and olive oil in a skillet, add the turnips, sprinkled with a little sugar, and fry over high heat, stirring constantly, until browned and caramelized. This is particularly delicious with the "Snowball" variety.

Turnip Tops

Wash well, removing stringy stalks. Chop roughly into manageable pieces. Steam over boiling water until just tender. Serve warm, tossed in olive oil and lemon juice vinaigrette, sprinkled with a finely minced garlic clove. Or cook like spinach: put the washed leaves in a pan, add salt, pepper, and a small pat of butter, and steam for 10 minutes in only the water remaining on the leaves. Drain thoroughly and serve immediately.

Brassica rapa var. *chinensis*. Brassicaceae
BOK CHOY

Also known as Pak choi. Hardy biennial, grown as an annual. Value: rich in carotenes, calcium, fiber, potassium, and folic acid.

Bok choy, translated as "white vegetable" from Cantonese, has been grown in China since the 5th century CE, cultivated in Europe since the 18th century and is one of the most familiar oriental vegetables. Relatively few varieties are grown in the west; there are 20 varieties in Hong Kong alone and many more on mainland China and Taiwan. In 1751 a friend of the Swedish Taxonomist Carl Linneaus brought seeds to Europe, at the same time as Jesuit missionaries handed similar races to German scientists working in Russia, where it also spread rapidly.

Bok choy

 varieties

Joy Larkcom, in her definitive work, *Oriental Vegetables*, a "must-have" book for anyone interested in the ingredients and cultivation of vegetables for eastern cuisine, identifies four types based on their appearance.

Chinese White Types
These have thick, light to deep green leaves, usually curving outwards, with wide, white, short, and straight leaf blades, often overlapping at the base. They vary in their cold tolerance and tendency to bolt. "Joi Choi" is slow to bolt and has good frost resistance.

Soup Spoon Types
These are vigorous and versatile, tolerating warm or cool conditions and have narrow "waists" with thin leaves and leaf stalks; the leaves are shallowly concave, like soup spoons. Most are tall, reaching around 18 in. when mature, and have the best flavor. "Japanese White Celery Mustard" is particularly delicious.

Green Leaf Stalk Types
These varieties produce broad, light green leaf stalks on compact, robust, fast-growing plants.

Canton Types
The smallest bok choy come from this group, with dense, white leaf stalks and compact, deep green leaves; they can be harvested as young greens and have a fine flavor. They are more warm-weather tolerant than most and inclined to go to seed in cold weather. "Canton Dwarf" is compact with dark green leaves.

 cultivation

Propagation
Sow seeds about ½ in. deep and spaced according to the recommendations on the seed packet, which is dictated by the size of the plant required at harvest. Sow small varieties up to 2 in. apart with 7 in. between rows; large plants should be up to 18 in. apart.

Growing
Most are cool season crops for late summer and fall, growing best between 59–68°F. Spring-sown seedlings are best grown as "cut and come again" or for harvesting as young plants. Alternatively, choose cold-tolerant varieties like "Tai Sai." Protect early sowings with crop covers.

Most varieties only tolerate light frost though green-stalk varieties are much tougher. They thrive in rich, fertile, well-drained soil and bolt if the soil dries out though "Canton" and green-stemmed varieties are the most resistant to drought; keep the soil constantly moist and grow in shade during summer.

Maintenance
Spring Sow seedling crops under cover; harvest early sowings.
Summer Sow seeds in shade and harvest earlier crops.
Fall Sow seedling crops under cover.
Winter Sow indoors.

Protected Cropping
Grow early- and late-season crops indoors. In winter, seed can be sown in packs at 68°F and temperatures lowered by 50 percent after germination.

Harvesting and Storing
Pick when the leaves are fresh and crisp, either by removing a few leaves from plants as required or cutting them off at the base, so they can resprout.

Pests and Diseases
They are susceptible to all the standard brassica problems. Flea beetle is a major problem; grow crops under floating row cover or mesh to avoid cabbage root fly, slugs, cutworm, and powdery and downy mildew.

 medicinal

Dried leaves have been used to alleviate the effects of dysentery.

 culinary

Bok choy has a mild flavor in the way that Swiss chard does. Wash well with several changes of water before use. Bok choy leaves, from "cut and come again" to mature leaves, stems, and flower shoots are used in stir-fries, soups, and salads, and are an ingredient in many forms of oriental cooking including pickles. Young flower heads from "bolting" plants can be used as a "choy sum" substitute.

Tempting, tender, and tasty

Brassica rapa var. *japonica.* Brassicaceae

MIZUNA & MIBUNA GREENS

Hardy annual. Value: rich in vitamin A and C, folic acid, and antioxidants.

Mizuna greens are a Chinese vegetable but have long been cultivated in Japan. They are fast growing, productive over a long period of time, and can tolerate several degrees of frost without damage; making them an excellent all-round crop for cool conditions. Both mizuna and mibuna greens have the characteristics of the parent plant, thought to be a natural hybrid which occurred in times past. There is chromosome evidence from *brassica rapa,* the "turnip" which has several leafy forms, particularly in Italian cooking where they are known as *cima de rapa,* and *Brassica juncea* or Chinese mustard that is grown as an oil seed in China and Japan.

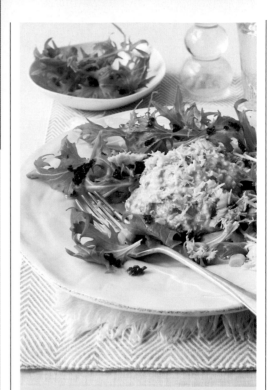
Crab salad served on mizuna leaves

Mizuna greens add texture and taste to salads

 ## varieties

Mizuna greens form a vigorous clump of finely-cut, dark green leaves with white, juicy stems. "Mibuna" greens have long been cultivated in Japan; they have slender stems and long strap-like leaves of varying length, which are dark or light green. They are normally referred to as "early" or "late" according to the timing of their sowing and harvest.

 ## cultivation

Propagation
Sow outdoors from late spring and late summer to early fall or under cover, either direct sown or sown in seed trays or a seedbed; transplant 2 to 3 weeks later. For small plants sow 1½ in. apart, for medium-sized 7 in. and large up to 18 in. apart.

Growing
Both are tolerant of cool, wet conditions and dislike extreme heat; drought may stunt plants and make the leaves tough. Mibuna and mizuna greens are cool weather plants and ideal for early- and late-season sowings; both need an open, sunny site in moisture-retentive soil with shade if sown in summer. Improve the soil by adding well-rotted organic matter if necessary. Keep plants weed free and watered when necessary to ensure a constant supply of young leaves.

Maintenance
Spring Sow seedlings under cover when the soil warms; sow in trays for transplanting into cloche- or floating-row-cover-warmed soil.
Summer Sow in shade, harvest regularly, and keep crops well watered.
Fall Sow under cover for "cut and come again" seedling crops.
Winter Harvest. Ventilate the greenhouse on hot days.

Protected Cropping
Mizuna and mibuna greens flourish in unheated greenhouses, cloches or cold frames over winter and tolerate low, winter light levels.

 ## culinary

Use mizuna and mibuna greens in stir-fries and salads. Mizuna can be used in soups, steamed, with fish or poultry, seeds can be dry roasted for use in curries and pickles, sprouted seeds can be used in salads. Use fresh to retain the highest level of nutrients. Wash in several changes of water and dry thoroughly before use. Leaves can be stored for up to 5 days in the salad compartment of a refrigerator.

Harvesting and Storing
Mibuna and mizuna greens can be grown as "cut and come again" crops, juvenile, or mature plants. Harvest regularly for a constant supply of tender leaves, up to five cuts can be made per plant, according to the level of maturity and time of year. Older leaves gradually become more fibrous.

Pests and Diseases
Flea beetles and slugs can be a problem, grow under floating row cover or mesh.

 ## container growing

They are ideal for growing in containers and growing bags, provided there is adequate space to form a good root system.

Brassica rapa var. *komatsuna*. Brassicaceae
KOMATSUNA

Also known as Japanese Mustard Spinach, Turnip Tops. Hardy annual or biennial. Value: rich in calcium, vitamin A, C, folic acid, and antioxidants.

This oriental vegetable of Japanese origin is another leafy form of the wild turnip; with large, wide, dark green, often glossy leaves it is believed to have been developed from bok choy. Valued for its versatility, it is grown as a food crop in Taiwan and Korea, and as a fodder crop in several Asian countries. It is tough, vigorous, fast growing, impervious to the effects of all but the worst weather, and is an ideal winter crop in cool climates.

 varieties

"Green Boy" is often listed as a form of bok choy. It is heat tolerant with dark green leaves and thick leaf stems. "Hybrid Kojisan" is top quality with bright green leaves. "Komatsuna" is an all-season variety, with fleshy, rounded, green stems, and dark green leaves; disease and heat resistant, best in early spring or late summer. Originally found growing near Tokyo. "Nozawana" is highly cold- and heat-tolerant with long green leaves. It is popular in Japan for pickling. The variety "Summer Fest" is similar. "Natsu Rakuten—Summer Fest" hybrid, has thick, dark green leaves and an upright habit. Sow spring to fall. "Red Komatsuna" is ideal as micro- or baby greens; the flat, round leaves are tinted red above and green with red veins below. It is heat-tolerant. Sow spring to fall. "Tokyo Early" has glossy leaves and thin, light green stalks and is slow to bolt. Sow from spring to fall. "Toriksan" is heat-tolerant.

 cultivation

Propagation
Sow seeds in wide rows or broadcast, thinning seedlings to leave 1 in. between "cut and come again" plants. The spacing of crops growing to maturity depends on the variety; large plants should be up to 18 in. apart in and between the rows, those being harvested at other stages of growth can be spaced accordingly and "thinnings" can be eaten at any stage.

Growing
Komatsuna greens are easy to grow, very prolific and almost the perfect winter-hardy crop, recovering from temperatures down to 7°F. This characteristic ensures that they are less likely to "bolt" in cold spring weather than other "oriental" vegetables. They need an open, sunny site and rich, fertile, moisture-retentive soil;

incorporate well-rotted organic matter if necessary before planting. Sow 1/8–1/2 in. deep and keep plants well watered at all times.

"Cut and come again" seedlings can be sown in spring and fall under cover and in late spring and summer outdoors. Crops being grown to maturity can be sown in late summer and transplanted under cover in fall or midsummer, if being grown outdoors, so they are well established before the onset of winter.

Maintenance
Spring Make early sowings under unheated protection; harvest mature crops.
Summer Sow in packs or trays in late summer for transplanting under protection.
Fall Make late sowings under unheated protection.
Winter Harvest crops.

Protected Cropping
Although very hardy, the quality of the leaves is improved when crops are grown under protection. Protect early and late sowings under cloches, in cold frames, or in a cold greenhouse.

Harvesting and Storing
Harvest seedlings from 4 in.; cut juvenile plants back to 1 in. above ground level and they will regrow. Water plants well to boost regrowth and feed with dilute liquid fertilizer. Cut leaves from mature plants as needed.

Pests and Diseases
Plants are susceptible to the usual cabbage-family problems like slugs, flea beetle, and pigeons. Grow under floating row cover and protect mature plants with netting.

 container growing

Growing bags or containers of organic-based potting mix can be used for growing "cut and come again" or semi-mature crops.

 culinary

Komatsuna greens have a mellow flavor between spinach and Asian mustard. They can be eaten from "cut and come again" to maturity; flowering shoots can be eaten too and are sweet and juicy. Steam or lightly boil younger leaves as spinach; older leaves taste stronger and are more like cabbage — they become stronger and hotter as they mature, so are better cooked. Eat young leaves raw in salad, stir-fry, boil, pickle, add to soups, or braise.

Broth with Komatsuna and Tofu
Serves 2

2 sheets deep-fried tofu
1/4 pound komatsuna, cleaned and trimmed
Pinch of salt

For the Broth:
2 cups dashi stock
1 tablespoon sake
1 tablespoon mirin
2 tablespoons light soy sauce
Pinch of salt

Put the tofu in a colander and pour boiling water over it to remove the excess oil. Cut lengthwise in half and slice thinly.

Discard any roots of the komatsuna and wash it well. Bring a large pan of water to a boil and add a pinch of salt. Blanch the komatsuna and transfer immediately to a bowl of cold water. Squeeze the komatsuna dry and chop it into 1 in. lengths.

Put all the ingredients for the simmering broth into a large pan and bring to a boil. Add the tofu and simmer over medium heat for 2 minutes before adding the chopped komatsuna. Simmer for another 2 to 3 minutes and serve.

CHINESE CABBAGE

Also known as Chinese Leaves, Celery Cabbage, Pe Tsai, Peking Cabbage. Annual or biennial grown as annual for edible leaves, stems and flowering shoots. Half hardy. Value: moderate levels of folic acid and vitamin C.

Chinese cabbage was first recorded in China around the fifth century CE, and has never been found in the wild. It is thought to have been a spontaneous cross in cultivation between the bok choy and the turnip. Taken to the East Indies and Malaya by Chinese traders and settlers who established communities and maintained their own culture, in the 1400s Chinese cabbage could be found in the Chinese colony in Malacca. By 1751 European missionaries had sent seeds back home, but the vegetable was regarded as little more than a curiosity. Another attempt at introduction was made by a French seedsman in 1845, but the supply became exhausted and the seed was lost. In 1970 the first large-scale commercial crop was produced by the Israelis and distributed in Europe; about the same time it was marketed in the United States as the Napa cabbage, after the valley in California where it was grown. It has become a moderately popular vegetable in the West.

 varieties

There are many groups, but three have become popular: the "tall cylindrical," the "hearted" or "barrel-shaped," and the "loose-headed."

The cylindrical type has long, upright leaves and forms a compact head, which can be loosely tied to blanch the inner leaves. It is slow-growing, takes about 70 days from sowing to harvest, and is most susceptible to bolting. This type is sweet and stores well.

Hearted types have compact, barrel-shaped heads with tightly wrapped leaves and a dense heart. They mature after about 55 days and are generally slow to bolt.

Loose-headed types are lax and open-headed, often with textured leaves. The "self-blanching" ones have creamy centers and textured leaves. They are also less liable to bolt than headed types. "Jade Pagoda" is cylindrical with a firm, crisp head. It takes about 65 days to mature and is cold-tolerant. "Kasumi", a barrel type, has a compact head and is resistant to bolting. "Monument" is strong, vigorous, uniform, and very tasty. "Nerva" is similar, matures quickly, and has dark green leaves with dense heads. "Ruffles" is delicious and early-maturing, with lax, pale green heads and a creamy white heart. However, early sowings are liable to bolt. "Shantung" has a spreading habit, with tender, light green leaves, and a dense heart. "Tip Top" is an early variety for spring planting and can be harvested around 70 days after sowing. It is vigorous and produces good-sized heads. "Wa Wa Sai" is sweet and very tender. Sow closely for baby leaves.

cultivation

Propagation

A cool-weather crop, Chinese cabbage is more likely to bolt in late spring and summer. Use resistant varieties or sow after midsummer. The chance of bolting increases if young plants are subjected to low temperatures or dry conditions, or suffer from transplanting check.

Sow the main crop *in situ* from mid- to late summer, two to three seeds per "station," spaced 12–14 in. apart in and between the rows. Thin to leave the strongest seedling. Alternatively, sow sparingly in rows and thin.

Otherwise it can be sown in packs or pots, transplanting carefully to avoid root disturbance when there are four to six leaves. If the soil is dry, water thoroughly. Broadcast or sow loose-headed types as "cut and come again" seedlings.

Make first sowings in a cold greenhouse or cold frame in early spring, sow outdoors under cloches or row covers as the weather improves and the soil becomes workable. Summer sowings tend to grow too rapidly and become "tough," unless it is a cool summer. Make the last sowing under cover in early fall.

Cut seedlings when they have reached a few inches tall, leaving them to resprout. Seeds can also be sprouted, as for alfalfa. **Zones 3 to 10.**

Growing

Chinese cabbage needs a deep, moisture-retentive, free-draining soil with plenty of organic matter. Excessively light, heavy, or poor soils should be avoided unless they are improved by incorporating organic matter or grit. Alternatively, grow in raised beds or on ridges. Dig the soil thoroughly before planting; acid soils should be limed, as the ideal pH is 6.5 to 7.0. Slightly more alkaline soils are advisable where there is a risk of clubroot.

Chinese cabbage prefers an open site, but tolerates some shade in midsummer. Rotate Chinese cabbage with other brassicas.

Water crops thoroughly throughout the growing season; do not let them dry out. They are shallow-rooted and so need water little and often. Mulching is also

Chinese cabbage harvest in Thailand

advisable. Erratic watering can result in damage to the developing head, encouraging rots. Sprinkle general fertilizer around the base of transplants or feed with a general liquid fertilizer as necessary to boost growth — this is particularly important on poorer soils. Keep crops weed-free.

In late summer, tie up the leaves of hearting varieties with soft twine or raffia. (With self-hearting varieties, this is unnecessary.)

Maintenance

Spring Sow early "cut and come again" seedling crops under cover. Sow later crops outdoors.
Summer Sow in rows from mid- to late summer. Water a little and often, mulch, and keep weed-free. Harvest.
Fall Sow quick-maturing varieties or "cut and come again" crops outdoors; sow later crops under cover.
Winter Harvest "cut and come again" crops grown under cover.

Protected Cropping

Earlier crops can be achieved by sowing bolting-resistant cultivars from late spring to early summer. They need temperatures of 68–77°F for the first 3 weeks after germination to prevent bolting. Harden off, transplant, then protect the plants with cloches or with row covers.

Late summer-sown crops should be transplanted under cover. Space plants about 5 in. apart and grow them as a semi-mature "cut and come again" crop.

Harvesting and Storing

In fall, cold-tolerant varieties can stay outside for several weeks provided it is dry. Protect from wet and cold using cloches. Lift developing crops and replant in cold frames, or uproot and lay plants on straw, bracken or similar, covering them with the same material if temperatures fall below freezing point. Ventilate on warm days.

CHINESE CABBAGE

Harvest as "cut and come again" seedlings, semi-mature or mature plants and for the flowering shoots. Cut seedlings when they are 1–2 in. tall. Semi-mature or mature plants can be cut with a sharp knife about 1 in. above the ground and will then resprout; after several harvests they will send up a flower head. Harvest the flowering shoots when they are young, before the flowers open. Harvest mature heads when they are firm.

Chinese cabbage keeps in the refrigerator for several weeks. Wash thoroughly before storing. Heads can be stored in a cool, frost-free shed or cellar for up to 3 months. When storing, check plants every 3 to 4 weeks and remove any diseased or damaged leaves immediately.

Pests and Diseases
Chinese cabbage can be affected by any of the usual brassica pests and diseases. You should take precautions in particular against flea beetle, slugs, snails, caterpillars, clubroot, and powdery mildew. Crops grow well under floating row cover or fine netting.

 ## companion planting

Plant with garlic and dill to discourage caterpillars. Main crops are ideal after peas, early potatoes, and fava beans; late crops are good companions for Brussels sprouts. It is good for cropping between slower-growing vegetables.

Chinese cabbages are sometimes grown as sacrificial crops so that slugs, flea beetles, and aphids are attracted to them rather than other crops.

 ## container growing

The fast-growing varieties give the best results. Use a 10 in. pot or container and soilless potting mix with added organic matter and a thick basal layer of drainage material. Sow seeds ½ in. deep and 1 in. apart in shallow pots or packs in midspring. Transplant seedlings singly into pots when they have three to four leaves.

 ## warning

To minimize the risk of listeria, you should never store Chinese cabbage in plastic bags.

 ## culinary

Cook Chinese cabbage only lightly to retain the flavor and nutrients. Steam, quickly boil, stir-fry — or eat raw. (Seedlings are better cooked.) Leaves blend well in raw salads of lettuce, green bell pepper, celery, mooli, and tomato. They also make a delicious warm salad, stir-fried and mixed with orange. Otherwise use in soups, cook with fish, meat, poultry, and use in stuffing.

Outer stalks can be shredded, cooked like celery and tossed in butter. In Korea, China, and Japan heads are used to make fermented and salted pickles.

Sweet and Sour Chinese Cabbage
Serves 4

2 tablespoons olive oil
1 onion or several shallots, sliced
2 tablespoons white wine vinegar
2 teaspoons sugar
6 tablespoons chopped tomatoes in their juices
1½ pounds Chinese cabbage, finely shredded
Salt and freshly ground black pepper

Heat the oil in a heavy-bottomed pan and cook the onions until soft. Stir in the vinegar, sugar, and tomatoes and blend well. Add the Chinese cabbage and seasoning. Cook for 10 minutes with the lid on, stirring occasionally, until the cabbage is tender.

Serve hot.

Capsicum annuum. Solanaceae
BELL PEPPER & CHILI

Also known as Sweet Pepper, Pepper, Capsicum, Pimento, Chilli Peppers, and Chile Peppers. Annuals and short-lived perennials grown for edible fruits. Tender. Value: very rich in vitamin C and beta carotene.

Both hot and mild peppers come from one wild species, which is native to Central and South America. The name capsicum comes from the Latin *capsa*, meaning "a box." It is thought that the hot types were the first to be cultivated; seeds have been found in Mexican settlements dating from 7000 BCE, and the Aztecs are known to have grown them extensively. They are one of the discoveries made in the New World by Columbus. He thought he had discovered black pepper, which at the time was extremely expensive, and used the name "pepper" for this new fiery spice. Spanish and Portuguese explorers then distributed the new kinds of peppers around the world.

Sweet peppers were introduced to Spain in 1493 and were known in England by 1548 and Central Europe by 1585. The Spanish use red sweet peppers to make the spice pimentón and for stuffing green olives. Chili peppers are notorious for their fieriness. Their heat is caused by the alkaloid capsaicin, which is measured in Scoville Units. Mild chilies are around 600 units. Beware the "Dorset Naga" and "Bhut Jolokia," both measured at over one million units!

 ## varieties

The larger, bell-shaped, mild-tasting sweet bell peppers eaten as vegetables are members of the *Capsicum annuum* Grossum Group. Green when immature, different cultivars ripen to yellow, orange, red, or "black."

"Hungarian Hot Wax"

The smaller, hotter chilies used for flavoring are classed in the *C. a.* Longum Group.

Sweet bell peppers
"Big Bertha" is one of the largest bell peppers, growing to 7 in. long by 4 in. wide. Excellent for growing in cooler climates and for stuffing. "California Wonder" has a mild flavor, is good for stuffing, and crops well over a long period. "Calwonder Wonder Early" grows well in short seasons and is prolific. "Gypsy" is an early cropper with slightly tapered fruits and is also resistant to tobacco mosaic virus. "Redskin" is compact and ideal for pots and growing bags. "Sweet Chocolate" is an unusual chocolate-brown color and good when frozen whole.

Chili peppers
"Anaheim" produces tapered, moderately hot fruits over a long period. The moderately hot yellow fruits of "Hungarian Hot Wax" ripen to become crimson and are good for salad and stuffing. "Italian White Wax" has pointed fruits which pickle well and are mild-tasting when young. "Large Red Cherry" is extremely hot, with flattened fruits ripening to cherry red. Good for drying and ideal in curries, pickles, and sauces. "Serrano" is extremely hot with orange-red fruits. It is prolific and can be dried. "Tabasco Habañero" is extremely hot — beware! "Tam Jalapeño" has a good, mild flavor and is high yielding. "Thai Burapa" is small and pointed; ideal for Asian dishes. "Thai Denchai" tapering to 5 in., is great for all Thai dishes. "Tunisian Baklouti" has large, tapering pods and is hot.

BELL PEPPER & CHILI

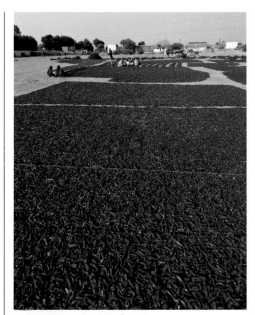

Chili peppers drying in India

 cultivation

Propagation

Sow seed indoors from late winter to midspring in trays, packs or pots of moist seed potting mix at 70°F. Lower temperature gradually after germination. Transplant into 3-in. pots when three true leaves appear, repotting again into 4–5 in. pots when sufficient roots have formed. Move plants into their final position when about 4 in. high and the first flowers appear.

Harden off outdoor crops in cool temperate zones and transplant in late spring to early summer when the soil is warm and there is no danger of frost.

Space standard varieties 15–18 in. apart; dwarf varieties should be spaced 12 in. apart. **Zones 4 to 11.**

Growing

Sweet bell peppers and chilies flourish outdoors in warmer climates. More successful under cover in cooler zones, they can be grown outside in mild areas or warm microclimates but benefit from protection with cloches or floating row cover. Chilies tend to be more tolerant of fluctuating temperatures and high or low rainfall and grow in marginally less fertile soil. Blossom drops when night temperatures fall below 60°F. Soil should be moisture-retentive and free-draining on

ground manured for the previous crop. Alternatively, dig in plenty of well-rotted organic matter in fall or winter prior to planting. Rake in a granular general fertilizer at 4 oz. per square yard before planting.

Keep the soil moist and weed-free; mulching is recommended. Feed with a general liquid fertilizer if plants need a boost. Excessive nitrogen can result in flower drop.

If branches are weak and thin, when the plant is about 12 in. tall remove the growth tips from the stems to encourage branching. Normally, they branch naturally. Support with a stake if necessary.

Maintenance

Spring Sow seeds under cover. Transplant when the danger of frost is passed or grow in an unheated greenhouse.
Summer Keep crops weed-free; dampen the greenhouse in warm weather. Harvest.
Fall Cover outdoor crops where necessary. Harvest.
Winter Prepare the ground for outdoor crops.

Protected Cropping

Crops are better grown indoors, plastic, cold frames, or cloches in cool temperate climates. In greenhouse beds, prepare the soil as for "Growing." Keep it moist but not waterlogged and mist with tepid water to maintain humidity and help fruit set.

Sow in midspring for growing in a greenhouse and in late spring for under cloches. Ventilate well during hot weather. If you are growing dwarf varieties on a sunny windowsill, turn pots daily to ensure even growth.

Plants grown under cloches may outgrow their space: rigid cloches can be turned vertically and supported with stakes. Alternatively, use plastic sheeting.

Harvesting and Storing

Harvest with scissors or hand pruners when sweet bell peppers or chilies are green, or leave on the plant for 2 to 3 weeks to ripen and change color. Picking them when they are green increases the yield.

Peppers may be stored in a cool, humid place for up to 14 days at temperatures of 55–58°F. Towards the end of the season, uproot plants and hang them by the roots in a frost-free shed or greenhouse; fruits will continue to ripen for several months.

The heat of chilies increases with the maturity of the fruit. Fresh chilies keep for up to 3 weeks in the refrigerator in a paper bag. Or store them in an airtight jar in a dark cupboard. Chilies can either be dried and used whole or ground into powder. Both sweet bell peppers and chilies freeze successfully.

Pests and Diseases

Red spider mite can be a nuisance under cover. Slugs can damage seedlings, stems, leaves, and fruits. Remove any decaying flowers or foliage immediately.

 companion planting

Capsicums grow well with basil, okra, and tomatoes.

 container growing

Grow under cover or outdoors. Plant in 8–10 in. pots of soilless potting mix with moderate fertilizer levels or in growing bags. Dwarf varieties can be grown successfully in pots on windowsills. Keep the potting mix moist but not waterlogged and mist with tepid water, particularly during flowering to assist fruit set. Water frequently in warm weather, less at other times.

 medicinal

Capsaicin increases the blood flow and is used in muscle liniments. It is said to help the body metabolize alcohol, acts as expectorant, and prevents and alleviates bronchitis and emphysema. 10 to 20 drops of red-hot chili sauce in a glass of water daily (or hot spicy meals three times a week) can keep airways free of congestion, preventing or treating chronic bronchitis, and colds. It stimulates endorphins, killing pain and inducing a sense of wellbeing.

 warning

Ventilate the kitchen when using chilies. If you have sensitive skin, wear rubber gloves to handle them and always avoid touching your eyes or other sensitive areas after handling.

culinary

Bell peppers add both color and taste to the table. They can be eaten raw in salads, roasted or barbecued, fried or stir-fried, stuffed with rice, fish or meat mixtures, and used in countless casseroles and rice dishes.

Chilies are used in chile con carne, curries, and hotpots. Removing the internal ribs and seeds reduces the heat intensity. Paprika is the dried and powdered fruits of sweet bell peppers. Cayenne pepper is dried and ground powder made from chilies.

If chili is too strong, it can cause intestinal burning — cucumber, rice, bread, and beans are good antidotes. By coating the tongue, the fat content of yogurt and butter soothes a chili-burned mouth. Water only makes things worse.

If you're uninitiated at eating chili peppers, start with small doses and build up tolerance of heat. Excessively hot peppers can cause jaloproctitis or perianal discomfiture.

Mrs Krause's Pepper Hash
Serves 6

William Woys Weaver, in *Pennsylvania Dutch Country Cooking*, quotes this recipe from Mrs Eugene F. Krause of Bethlehem, who lived in the early part of the 20th century and was renowned for her peppery hashes.

6 green bell peppers, seeded and finely minced
6 red bell peppers, seeded and finely minced
4 onions, finely minced
2 small pods hot chili peppers, seeded and finely chopped
1 ½ tablespoons celery seeds
1 ½ cups cider vinegar
1 ¼ cups brown sugar
1 ½ teaspoons kosher salt

Combine the bell peppers, onions, hot chili peppers, and celery seeds in a non-reactive preserving pan. Heat the vinegar in a non-reactive pan and dissolve the sugar and salt in it. Bring to a fast boil, then pour over the pepper mixture. Then cook over medium heat for 15 minutes, or until the bell peppers begin to discolor. Pack into hot sterilized preserving jars, seal, and place in a 15-minute water bath. Let the pepper hash mature in the jars for 2 weeks before using.

Jean-Christophe Novelli's Andalouse of Sole
Serves 6

For the piperade:
Carton of sun-dried tomato juice
½ pound sun-dried tomatoes
3 star anise

Fresh thyme
1 ½ cups olive oil
1 large zucchini, sliced at an angle
2 medium eggplants, sliced at an angle, then halved
8 large shallots, peeled
8 baby fennel, trimmed
2 red bell peppers, seeded and cut in half
2 yellow bell peppers, seeded and cut in half
2 green bell peppers, seeded and cut in half
10 red cherry tomatoes
1 head of garlic, cloves separated and peeled
Sugar
Freshly ground salt and pepper
Good handful of black olives
20 basil leaves

For the Sole Fillets:
6 large sole fillets
olive oil
1 vanilla bean, split and seeds scraped out

To Serve:
Handful of mixed fresh herbs
Freshly grated Parmesan
2 tablespoons truffle oil

To make the piperade, start by heating the tomato juice in a pan with the sun-dried tomatoes, star anise, and thyme and cook steadily until it's reduced by one third.

Heat the olive oil in a pan. Add the vegetables, garlic, a little sugar, and the sun-dried tomato juice and season. Cover with a tight-fitting lid and leave over low heat until the vegetables are just soft to the touch. Remove the vegetables from the heat and add the olives and basil to warm through.

Preheat the broiler. Brush the sole fillets with a little olive oil and the vanilla seeds. Season and broil for about 2 to 3 minutes on each side, skin-side up first. If the fillets are quite thick, they may require 4 minutes on each side.

Carefully arrange the vegetables on the plates. Place a sole fillet on each dish and garnish with fresh herbs, grated Parmesan, and a splash of truffle oil.

Mrs Krause's Pepper Hash

CHRYSANTHEMUM GREENS

Chrysanthemum coronarium. Compositae

Also known as Shungiku, Chop Suey Greens. Hardy annual. Value: rich in vitamin B, moderate vitamin C, and minerals.

There are few Chrysanthemums or their close relatives with culinary value. *Tanacetum balsamita*, a stalwart of the cottage garden, was once classified in the same group and, in times past, its leaves were used to flavor ale while Dioscorides notes that the stalks and leaves of marguerites were "eaten as other pot herbes are." It is a mystery how an attractive plant of Mediterranean hillsides, valued as an ornamental for its pretty flowers, spread east to China, Vietnam, and Japan, where its foliage became widely eaten as "greens." It is not only the leaves that are used; the Japanese dip the flowers in sake and eat them at the beginning of a meal to confer health and long life.

Wash thoroughly before eating

 culinary

Eat young aromatic shoots and stems raw, in salads, sushi, or with pickles; leaves can be cooked or steamed, dipped into tempura batter, and deep-fried. Try not to overcook the leaves as they can become bitter. Kikumi, a Japanese pickle, is made from the edible flower petals. Garnish stews with young leaves. Harvest just before use as the leaves wilt quickly.

Chrysanthemum in bloom

 varieties

There are no cultivars; just three forms are in cultivation. One has pale green, finely-cut, almost feathery leaves, with good low- and high-temperature tolerance and a strong flavor. Another, bushier, high-yielding plant with broader, thicker, shallowly-lobed leaves is tender and mildly flavored; the third, which is intermediate in appearance between the two, is fast growing, bushy, and high-yielding, thriving in both warm and cool climates.

 cultivation

Propagation

Sow, in rows or broadcast thinly, lightly covering the seed, every 2 to 3 weeks during spring and fall for a constant harvest. Allow 6 in. in and between the rows for larger plants. Thinning is not usually required, for young plants, unless sowing is particularly dense, when they should thinned to 2 in. apart. Plants can also be grown from soft tip cuttings taken from over-wintering plants in spring.

Growing

Chrysanthemum greens are primarily a cool-season crop, tolerating low light levels and withstanding light frosts. They are at their best in spring and fall as temperatures over 77°F impart bitterness to the leaves. They tolerate most soils but prefer a well-prepared seedbed on rich, fertile, moisture-retentive soil in full sun and a cool, shady position in summer. Plants can be grown as small "cut and come again" seedlings or leaves harvested from larger individual plants. Keep plants well watered and weed-free by hoeing or hand weeding to prevent competition from annual weeds which suppresses growth.

Maintenance

Spring Sow outdoors once the danger of frost has passed. Harvest winter crops.
Summer Make the final sowings of the season outdoors around 10 weeks before the last frost.
Fall Sow winter crops indoors; harvest earlier crops.
Winter Harvest earlier sowings.

Protected Cropping

Sow seeds indoors in fall for cropping over winter in an unheated greenhouse and in early spring for early crops.

Harvesting and Storing

As "cut and come again" crops, the first harvest can be made from 4 weeks after sowing during midsummer; plants recover rapidly and several cuts can be made from each sowing. Alternatively, cut back the top 8 in. of more mature plants leaving them to re-sprout from the base or pick side shoots from individual plants. Shoots can be harvested from flowering plants without any loss of quality and the flowers eaten in salads.

Pests and Diseases

It is pest- and disease-free.

 container growing

Can be grown in containers or growing bags throughout the season and respond well to cutting back.

 medicinal

Leaves have a calming effect on the stomach and are used as an expectorant.

Cicer arietinum. Papilionaceae

CHICKPEA

Also known as Dal, Egyptian Pea, Garbanzo, Gram. Annual grown for seed sprouts, seeds, young shoots, and leaves. Tender. Value: high in protein, phosphorus, potassium, most B vitamins, iron, and dietary fiber.

Chickpeas originated in the northern regions of the fertile crescent. Evidence of their ancient use as a domesticated crop was found at a site in Jericho and dated to around 6500 BCE. Seeds excavated in Greece indicate that the chickpea must have been introduced to Europe with the first food crops arriving from the Near East. Today it is cultivated worldwide in subtropical or Mediterranean climates as a cool-season crop, needing about 4 to 6 months of moderately warm, dry conditions to flourish. It is the world's third most important pulse after peas and beans, and 80 percent of the crop is produced in India. It is eaten fresh or dried, made into flour, used as a coffee substitute and grown as a fodder crop. The plant grows about 12 in. tall, with compound leaves of up to eight toothed leaflets. Its tiny white- or blue-tinged flowers are followed by a small flat pod containing one or two round seeds, each with a small "beak" — hence the common name "chickpea."

 varieties

The following are Indian cultivars: "Annegeri" is a semi-spreading, high-yielding variety with yellowish-brown seeds. It is deep-rooting and likes good soil but a coarse tilth is adequate. "Avrodhi" has medium-sized brown seeds and is wilt-resistant. "Bheema," a semi-spreading variety, has large, light brown, smooth seeds and is suitable for drought-prone or low-rainfall areas. "Brown Seeded" is good for the home gardener, particularly in short, dry seasons. "Kabuli Black," with two black seeds per pod, is very hardy, vigorous and fast maturing. It has some tolerance of cold soils and is drought-resistant.

 cultivation

Chickpeas need a fertile, well-drained soil in full sun.

Propagation
Seeds can be broadcast or sown in rows during winter in Mediterranean regions or after the rains in subtropical climates. Broadcasting is very simple. Prepare the soil using the "stale seedbed" method, raking and levelling, allowing the weeds to germinate and hoeing them off before sowing. Then sprinkle the seed evenly, raking the soil twice — first in one direction, then again at 90 degrees to ensure even coverage.

Chickpeas can also be sown 2½ to 4 in. deep with the rows 20 in. apart, thinning to 10 in. between plants after germination. Alternatively, sow three to four seeds in hills 10 in. apart, and thin to leave the strongest seedling standing.

Growing
Dig over the area thoroughly before planting, adding organic matter to poor soil. Rake over the area to create a fine tilth and water well before sowing if the seedbed is dry. Alternatively, soak the seeds for an hour. Keep crops weed-free during the early stages; as plants mature, their spreading habit naturally stifles weed growth.

Chickpeas are drought-tolerant, but watering just before flowering and as the peas begin to swell improves productivity. Rotate with other legumes and leave the roots in the ground after harvest to provide nitrogen for the following crop.

The flowers are delicate and pretty

Maintenance

Spring Dig over the planting area, adding organic matter where needed.
Summer Keep crops weed-free. Water in prolonged drought, just before flowering and as the peas swell.
Fall Harvest crops.
Winter Dig over the planting area, adding organic matter where needed.

Protected Cropping

In cooler climates, sow seeds in early spring into small pots of moist seed potting mix in a greenhouse or on a windowsill. Harden off in late spring and plant outdoors once there is no danger of frost. Growing crops in cloches or plastic tunnels increases the yield.

Harvesting and Storing

Crops are ready after about 4 to 6 months. Harvest when leaves and pods turn brown; don't leave it too late, or the seeds will be lost when the pods split. Cut the stems at the base and tie them together before drying upside down in a dry, warm place. Collect the dry seeds and store in airtight jars. Peas can also be harvested fresh for cooking, but fresh ones deteriorate rapidly and should be used as soon as possible.

Sprouting Seeds

Always buy untreated chickpeas for sprouting, as seed sold for sowing is often treated with chemical dressings. Soak seeds overnight or for several hours in boiling water, tip into a strainer, and rinse. Put several layers of moist paper towel or blotting paper in the base of a jar and cover with a layer of seed. Cut a square from a pair of tights or piece of muslin and cover the top, securing with a rubber band. Place in a bright position, away from direct sunshine, maintaining constant temperatures around 68°F. Rinse the seed three to four times a day by filling the jar with water and pouring off

again. Harvest after 3 to 4 days when the "sprouts" are about ½ in. long.

Pests and Diseases

Plants can suffer from root rot. They turn black and finally dry up, leaves fall, and the stems desiccate. Ensure the soil is well drained and destroy affected crops immediately. The acidic secretions from the glandular hairs are a good defense against most pests. Gram pod borer caterpillars feed on the crop from seedlings to maturity, damaging seedpods and the immature seeds. Spray with pyrethrum.

 container growing

They can be grown in containers, but seed production levels do not make them a worthwhile proposition as a crop plant.

 culinary

With a protein content of 20 percent, chickpeas are an important meat substitute and good for children and expectant and nursing mothers. Chickpeas are used fresh or dried. They are ground into "gram flour" (used in vegan cooking), and the ground meal is mixed with wheat and used for chapatis. Whole chickpeas are fried, roasted (to eat as a snack), and boiled. To make hummus, grind boiled chickpeas into a paste, mix with olive or sesame oil, flavor with lemon and garlic, and eat on pita bread or crackers. Chickpeas are also used to make dal and are found in spicy side dishes, vegetable curries, and soups. The young shoots and leaves are used as a vegetable and cooked like spinach — boiled in soups, added to curries, or fried with spices.

Puréed Chickpeas
Serves 4

1 cup dried chickpeas, soaked overnight
2 tablespoons olive oil
1 onion, sliced finely
3 garlic cloves, crushed
¾ cup tomatoes, peeled, seeded, and chopped
Salt and freshly ground black pepper

 medicinal

The leaves are astringent and used to treat bronchitis. They are also boiled and applied to sprains and dislocated bones; the exudate is used for indigestion, diarrhea, and dysentery. The seeds are a stimulant, tonic, and aphrodisiac. In Egypt they are used to gain weight, and to treat headaches, sore throat, and coughs. Powdered seed is used as a facepack and also in dandruff treatment.

 warning

The whole plant and seed pods are covered with hairs containing skin irritants. You must always wear gloves when harvesting.

Drain the chickpeas, put in a heavy-bottomed pot, cover with fresh water, and cook until tender. This will take up to 1½ hours, depending on the age of the chickpeas. Drain. Purée in a food processor.

Heat the oil in a skillet, sauté the onion until softened, add the garlic, and cook for 30 seconds longer. Add the tomatoes and simmer for 5 minutes before adding the chickpea purée. Season well and serve immediately.

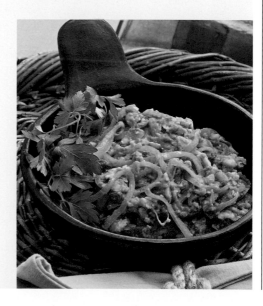

Cichorium endivia. Asteraceae

ENDIVE

Also known as Escarole, Chicory, Batavian Endive, Grumolo. Annual or biennial grown as annual for blanched hearts and leaves. Value: rich in iron, potassium, and beta carotene; moderate vitamin A and B complex.

The origins of this plant are obscure, but it was certainly eaten by the Egyptians long before the birth of Christ and is one of the bitter herbs used at Passover. Mentioned by Ovid, Horace, Pliny, and Dioscorides, it was valued by the Greeks and Romans as a cultivated plant. It was introduced to England, Germany, Holland and France around 1548 and was described by several writers.

 varieties

There are two types. The upright Batavian, scarole, or escarole has large, broad leaves. Curly or fringed frisée is a pretty plant, with a low rosette of delicately serrated leaves. Curled varieties are generally used for summer cropping; the more robust broad-leaved types tolerate cold, are disease-resistant and grow well in winter.

"Broad Leaved Batavian" has tightly packed heads of broad, deep green leaves that become creamy-white when blanched. "En Cornet de Bordeaux," an old variety, is very tasty, extremely hardy, and blanches well. "Green Curled Ruffec," a curly type, is tasty blanched and makes a good garnish. Very hardy and cold resistant. "Green Curled" ("Moss Curled") produces compact heads of dark green, fringed leaves. "Lassie" yields a large amount of deeply cut, well-flavored leaves. "Pancalieri" has very curly, dark green leaves with creamy white hearts. "Salad King" is prolific and extremely hardy, with large, dark green, finely cut leaves.

"Sanda" is vigorous and resistant to tip burn, cold, and bolting. "Scarola Verde" has a large head of broad, green and white leaves. However it may bolt in hot weather. The pale, green leaves of "Toujours Blanche" are deeply cut and finely curled. "Très Fine Maraichère" ("Coquette") has finely cut, curled leaves that are mild and delicious, and it grows well in most soils. "Wallone Frisée Weschelkopf" ("Wallone") has a large, tightly packed head with finely cut leaves. It is vigorous, hardy, and good as a "cut and come again."

 cultivation

Propagation

Sow thinly, ½ in. deep *in situ* or in a seedbed, pots or packs to transplant. Allow 12–15 in. between plants and rows.

Endive germinates best at 68–72°F. Sow early crops under cover and shade summer crops. Sow from early to midsummer for fall crops, in late summer for winter crops, using curled or hardy Batavian types. Sow all year round for "cut and come again" seedlings or semi-mature leaves, making early and late sowings indoors.

Growing

Endive needs an open site, though slimmer crops tolerate a little shade. Soils should be light, moderately rich and free-draining; this is particularly important for winter crops. If necessary, dig in plenty of well-rotted organic matter before planting. Excess nitrogen encourages lush growth and makes plants prone to fungal diseases.

Endive is a cool-season crop, flourishing between 50–68°F, yet it withstands light frosts; hardier cultivars withstand temperatures down to 15°F. Higher temperatures tend to encourage bitterness, though "curled" types are heat-tolerant. Young plants tend to bolt if temperatures fall below 41°F for long.

Keep crops weed-free; mulch and water thoroughly during dry weather, as dryness at the roots can cause bolting. Use a general liquid fertilizer to boost growth if necessary.

Blanch to reduce bitterness and make leaves more tender. Many newer cultivars have tight heads and some blanching occurs naturally. Damp leaves are likely to rot, so choose a dry period or dry plants under cloches for 2 to 3 days. Draw the outer leaves together and tie with raffia 2 to 3 weeks before harvest, placing a tile, piece of cardboard, or dinner plate over the center

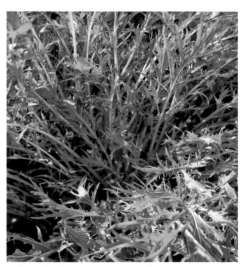

Endive is invaluable in winter salads

of the plant, and covering with a cloche to keep off the rain. Alternatively cover the whole plant with a bucket or a flower pot with its drainage holes covered. Blanching takes about 10 days. Blanch a few at a time; they rapidly deteriorate afterwards.

Maintenance

Spring Sow early crops indoors or cloches. Harvest late crops under cover.

Summer Sow curly varieties outdoors in seedbeds for transplanting, or *in situ*. Keep early-sown crops weed-free and moist. Harvest.

Fall Sow outdoors and under cover. Harvest.

Winter Sow under cover and harvest.

Protected Cropping

Sow hardy cultivars under cover in trays or packs at 68°F in midspring for early summer crops. After germination, maintain a minimum temperature of 41°F for 3 weeks after transplanting — this is to prevent bolting.

For winter and early spring crops, transplant in early fall from seed trays or packs under cover. Sow "cut and come again" crops under cover in early spring, and in early fall.

Endive grows better than lettuce in low light and is also a useful crop for the greenhouse in winter.

Harvesting and Storing

Harvest endive from 7 weeks after sowing, depending on cultivar and season.

"Cut and come again" seedlings may be ready from 5 weeks. With some cultivars, only one or two cuts may be possible before they go to seed. Pick individual leaves as needed or harvest them using a sharp knife about 1 in. above the ground, leaving the root to resprout. The whole plant can be lifted in fall and put in a cool, dark place to blanch.

Leaves do not store well and are better eaten fresh. They last about 3 days in a plastic bag in the salad drawer of a refrigerator.

Pests and Diseases

Protect plants from slugs and control aphids.

Keep winter crops well watered and mulched to prevent tip burn.

Eat endive immediately after harvest

 culinary

Endive is used mainly in salads with — or instead of — lettuce and other greens; the slightly bitter taste and crisp texture gives it more of a "bite" than the usual lettuce combinations. It suits strongly flavored dressings. Crisp bacon bits or croutons are often included. With mature endive, use the inner leaves for salads; the outer ones can be cooked as greens. Endive can also be braised. Try serving it shredded and dressed with hot crushed garlic, anchovy fillets, and a little olive oil and butter.

Warm Red and Yellow Bell Pepper Salad
Serves 6

The slightly bitter taste of curly endive (escarole or frisée) is ideal combined with other salad greens, such as corn salad or watercress in winter months. The sweetness of the bell peppers in this dish happily complements the endive.

1 large endive, washed and roughly chopped
Big bunch corn salad, washed
2 large red bell peppers
3 tablespoons olive oil
3 cloves garlic, crushed
1 tablespoon chopped fresh herbs
Salt and freshly ground black pepper

For the dressing:
3 tablespoons extra virgin olive oil
1 tablespoon white wine vinegar
Salt and freshly ground black pepper

Arrange the greens in a large bowl. Core and deseed the bell peppers and cut them into thin strips. Heat the oil in a heavy pan and sauté the bell peppers, stirring constantly. Add the garlic after 5 minutes and cook for an additional minute.

Add the bell peppers to the salad. Make the dressing and toss in the herbs and seasoning. Serve the salad alongside plain broiled fish or chicken.

 companion planting

Endive is good for intersowing and intercropping.

container growing

Sow directly or transplant into large containers of soilless potting mix with added well-rotted organic matter. Keep potting mix moist and weed-free. Use a general liquid fertilizer to boost growth if necessary.

Cichorium intybus. Asteraceae
CHICORY

Chicory is a traditional ingredient in Belgium

Also known as Witloof, Belgian Endive, Succory, Sugar Loaf Chicory, Radicchio. Hardy perennial grown as annual for blanched leaves or root. Very hardy. Value: moderate levels of potassium.

A native of Europe through to central Russia and western Asia, chicory has been cultivated for centuries. Pliny tells us that cichorium is a Greek adaptation of the Egyptian name; he also noted its medicinal use as a purgative and the blanching of leaves for salads.

Large-rooted varieties have long been used dried, ground and roasted as a substitute for coffee — particularly popular in England during the Napoleonic wars when a blockade of the French coast cut supplies. It has a distinctive fragrance and is often drunk by those who like the taste of coffee without the caffeine. John Lindley, in the 19th century, recorded that roasted endive was adulterated with a multitude of substances as diverse as marigolds, oak bark, mahogany sawdust, and even baked horse liver!

 varieties

Chicory has a distinctive, slightly bitter flavor. Most varieties are hardy and make a good winter crop with colorful, attractive leaves. There are three types. "Forcing" chicories like "Witloof" (that is, whiteleaf) produce plump, leafy heads (known as "chicons") when blanched. Red endive or radicchio includes older cultivars which respond to the reduced daylength and lower temperatures of fall by turning from green to red; newer cultivars are naturally red and heart earlier. "Non-forcing" or "sugarloaf" types produce large-hearted lettuce-like heads for fall harvest.

"Brussels Witloof" ("Witloof de Brussels") is one of the most famous forcing types which is also grown for its root. "Catalogna Frastagliata" is upright with thin, white ribs. "Large Rooted Magdeburg" ("Magdeburg"), like "Brussels Witloof," is grown for its root, which is used to make coffee, but young leaves can also be harvested. "Orchidea Rossa" is crunchy with good flavor and texture; delicious eaten steamed, roasted or raw. "Palla Rossa Zorzi Precoce" is a radicchio with a tangy, delicate flavor. It colors better in cool weather. "Radicchio di Treviso Black Svelta" has dark red, upright leaves with white midribs.

"Rossa di Treviso," another radicchio, has crisp, green leaves that become deep red and veined with white in cooler conditions. It dates back to the 16th century and tolerates light frost. "Rossa di Verona" is a radicchio with a spreading habit and withstands considerable frost.

 cultivation

Propagation

Sow seed of forcing varieties thinly in late spring to early summer in rows ½ in. deep and 9–12 in. apart. Thin when the first true leaves appear to 8 in. apart.

Sow early radicchio under cover in seed trays and packs before hardening off and transplanting from midspring for summer harvest, using early maturing types first. Sow for fall harvest from early to midsummer, and in mid- to late summer for transplanting under cover in fall and cropping over winter. Thin to 9–15 in. in and between the rows.

Non-forcing or sugarloaf types can be broadcast or sown in wide rows under cover in late winter. When the soil warms and the weather improves, sow successionally outdoors until late summer. Sow the final crop during early fall under cover.

Thin to a final spacing of 9–12 in. in and between the rows. For a semi-mature "cut and come again" winter crop, sow seed from mid- to late summer and transplant indoors in fall.

Growing

Chicories prefer an open, sunny site, but tolerate a little shade. Soil should be fertile and free-draining, with organic matter added for the previous crop; avoid recently manured ground, this causes the roots to fork.

Radicchio tolerates most soils except gravel or very heavy clay. The ideal pH is 5.5 to 7. Rake soil to a fine texture before sowing. Apply a general balanced fertilizer at 2 oz. per square yard.

Keep weed-free with regular hoeing or mulching. Water thoroughly during dry weather to prevent bolting. Force appropriate varieties *in situ* if soil is light and winters are mild.

In late fall to early winter, cut back the leaves to 1 in. above ground level. Form a ridge of friable soil 6–8 in. high over the stumps and cover with straw or leaf mold. After about 8 to 12 weeks, when the tips are appearing, remove the soil and cut the heads off at about 1 in. above the neck. Keep the potting mix moist while the "chicons" are growing.

Maintenance

Spring Sow early radicchio under cover, transplant from midspring. Sow sugarloaf types as "cut and come again" crops.

Summer Harvest early radicchio and sow maincrop. Sow sugarloaf outdoors for "cut and come again" and fall maincrop.

Fall Harvest radicchio crops sown early to midsummer; sow late crops for winter. Lift forcing types or force outdoors. Sow sugarloaf indoors.

Winter Force roots indoors successionally until spring. Sow sugarloaf indoors.

Protected Cropping

Non-forcing varieties can be grown indoors, for early or late crops.

In fall, cover outdoor crops of radicchio with cloches, row covers, or similar to extend the growing season.

Forcing

Force "chicons" indoors if soil is heavy, if winters are severe, or for earlier crops. In mid- to late fall when the foliage dies down, lift roots carefully, discard any forked or damaged ones and keep those that are at least 1–2 in. in diameter at the top. Cut off the remaining leaves to within ½ in. of the crown, trim back the side and main roots to about 8–9 in. Pack horizontally in boxes of dry sand, peat substitute, or sawdust and store in a cool, frost-free place. For forcing, remove a few roots from storage at a time. Plant about five to six roots in a 9-in. pot of sand or light soil, ensuring that ½ in. of the crown is above the surface. Surround the roots with moist peat or potting mix, leaving the crown exposed above ground.

Radicchio

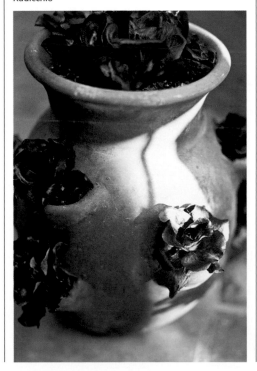

Water sparingly and cover with a black plastic bag, an empty flower pot with the holes blocked up, or an empty box. Maintain temperatures of 50–60°F. They can also be blanched in a dark cellar or shed or under greenhouse benches (see "Growing"). The blanched "chicons" should be ready for cutting within 4 weeks, depending on the temperature. Roots may resprout, producing several smaller shoots which can then be blanched.

Harvesting and Storing

Harvest chicories grown for roots after the first frost. Cut heads of mature sugarloaf varieties with a sharp knife 1 in. above the soil in late fall; use immediately or store in a frost-free place.

Allow the plants to resprout as a "cut and come again" crop under cloches.

Pick radicchio leaves as required, taking care not to over-harvest, as this weakens plants. Alternatively, cut the whole head and leave the roots to resprout.

"Chicons" can be stored in the refrigerator, wrapped in foil or paper to prevent them from becoming bitter. Non-forcing endive will stay fresh for up to 1 month.

Pests and Diseases

Though seldom troubled by pests and diseases, crops can rot outdoors in cold weather.

 companion planting

The blue flowers of endive are attractive in the ornamental border.

 container growing

Chicories can be grown in large containers or growing bags as "cut and come again."

 medicinal

Endive is said to be a digestive, diuretic, and laxative, reducing inflammation. A liver and gall bladder tonic, it is used for rheumatism, gout, and hemorrhoids. Culpeper suggests its use "for swooning and passions of the heart."

CHICORY

 culinary

All types of chicory make a wonderful winter salad, particularly if you mix the colors of red, green, and white. Add tomatoes or a sweet dressing to take away some of the bitter taste. Home-grown chicons stored in the dark tend to be less bitter.

For a delicious light supper dish, pour a robust dressing (made with lemon juice rather than vinegar) over the leaves, add some anchovy fillets, crumbled hard-boiled eggs, and top with a handful of kalamata olives.

As an accompaniment to cold meat and game, eat with sliced oranges, onion, and chopped walnuts.

With roast meats, braise chicory with butter, lemon juice, and cream. Radicchio can also be braised, but loses its color.

To make a chicory coffee substitute, dry roots immediately after harvest and grind thoroughly.

Chicory with Ham and Cheese Sauce
Serves 4

4 heads chicory
8 slices smoked Bayonne ham
2 tablespoons butter
2 tablespoons all-purpose flour
2 teaspoons Dijon mustard
½ cup milk
4 tablespoons grated Gruyère cheese
Light cream
Salt and freshly ground black pepper

Blanch the chicory heads in a pan of salted water for 5 minutes, drain, and gently squeeze out as much water as you can. Cut each chicory in half and wrap in a slice of the ham. Then arrange in one layer in an ovenproof dish.

Preheat the oven to 400°F. Make the cheese sauce: Melt the butter in a heavy pan and stir in the flour. Cook for 2 minutes, then stir in the mustard. Pour in the milk gradually, stirring vigorously as the sauce thickens, then add the cheese and enough cream to accomplish a smooth consistency. Stir over a gentle heat for 5 minutes to let the cheese melt. Season to taste.

Pour the cheese sauce over the chicory wrapped in ham and cook in the oven for 20 minutes until nicely browned. Serve immediately.

Braised chicory

Braised Chicory
Serves 4

The French, especially in the southwest and in Provence, braise chicory or Belgian endives and serve them with roasted meats such as lamb and beef.

2 tablespoons butter
1 red onion, finely minced
2 slices bacon, diced
4 heads chicory, trimmed
½ cup chicken stock and white wine combined
Juice of ½ a lemon
Salt and freshly ground black pepper

Liberally coat the sides and bottom of a heavy, lidded casserole with half the butter and heat the remaining butter in a small pan over a medium flame. Gently fry the onion and bacon, and let sit.

Arrange the chicory in the casserole. Add some of the stock and white wine, season with salt and pepper, and cover. Allow to sweat over low heat until just turning color. Roll them over and cook on the other side.

Add a little more liquid as required. The liquid should evaporate from the chicory by the end, so that they are browned and tender (you may have to remove the lid for a short while). Add the onion and bacon and quickly heat up. Drizzle over the lemon juice, season and serve immediately.

Endive with Ham and Cheese Sauce

Colocasia esculenta var. antiquorum. Araceae

EDDOE

Perennial grown as annual for edible tubers. Tender. Value: rich in starch, magnesium, potassium, and vitamin C.

This variety of taro, native of India and Southeast Asia, was first recorded by the Chinese 2,000 years ago. It is now grown throughout the humid tropics. Eddoes flourish in moist soil alongside rivers and streams. The central tuber is surrounded by clusters of smaller tubers which are harvested, making it different from the single-tubered dasheen. The brown, hairy tubers can weigh up to 5 pounds, and when they are sliced reveal flesh which is usually white but can also be yellow, pink, or orange. Their taste is similar to a garden potato but with an attractive nutty flavor. Tubers should never be eaten raw as all varieties contain calcium oxalate crystals, a skin irritant.

 culinary

Tubers can be boiled, baked, roasted, puréed, and made into soup. They can also be fried.

Protected Cropping

If you have space in a greenhouse or plastic tunnel, it is worth trying to grow eddoes. Plant presprouted or chitted tubers in spring into growing bags or 8–12 in. pots containing peat-substitute potting mix. Maintain heat and high humidity: dampen the greenhouse floor or mist plants with soft tepid water. Throughout the southern part of the U.S., no special structure is needed to grow these.

Harvesting and Storing

Eddoes take 5 to 6 months to mature. Harvest when the stems begin to turn yellow and die back. Lift tubers carefully with a garden fork; select some for eating and save others for replanting. If they are undamaged and dried carefully, tubers can be stored for several months.

Pests and Diseases

Eddoes grown outdoors are generally problem-free but when grown indoors they are susceptible to aphids and fungal leaf spots; red spider mite can also be a problem, particularly when humidity is low.

Downy mildew can attack tubers after they have been lifted so it is important to ensure that they are dried well before being stored. Dispose of infected tubers and do not use them for propagation.

 varieties

"Euchlora" has dark green leaves with violet margins and leaf stems. "Fontanesii" produces leaf stems which are dark red-purple or violet. Its leaf blades are dark green with violet veins and margin.

 cultivation

Propagation

In the humid tropics, eddoes can be planted any time. In temperate climates, grow in a greenhouse or plastic at a minimum temperature of 70°F, and plant in spring. Plant small tubers or a tuber section containing some dormant buds in individual holes 24–30 in. apart. Cuttings consisting of the top of a tuber with several leaves and a growth point can be planted directly into the soil and will establish rapidly. Add general fertilizer to the planting hole. **Zones 9 to 11.**

Growing

Eddoes need humus-rich, slightly acid, moisture-retentive soil, in sunshine or partial shade. Cultivate the soil before planting and remove any weeds.

Maintenance

Spring Plant tubers if protected cropping.
Summer Feed every 3 to 4 weeks with a high-potassium fertilizer; additional nitrogen may be needed. During drier periods, irrigate as needed to ensure swelling of the tubers and hill up. Keep weed-free.
Fall Harvest as required.
Winter Prepare beds for the following year's crop if growing in a greenhouse.

 warning

When handling and peeling eddoes, be sure to wear gloves or cover the hands with a layer of cooking oil to prevent a nasty rash.

Colocasia esculenta var. *esculenta.* Araceae

DASHEEN

Also known as Elephant's Ear, Arvi Leaves, West Indian Kale, Taro, Coco Yam. Herbaceous perennial grown for its edible leaves, shoots and tubers. Tender. Value: tuber rich in starch; leaves high in vitamin A, good source of B2.

In cultivation for around 7,000 years, dasheen is said to have been first grown in India on terraces where rice now flourishes. The common name derives from *de Chine* (from China): the root was imported from Southeast Asia following a competition organized by the Royal Geographical Society to find a cheap food source for the slaves on West Indian sugar plantations.

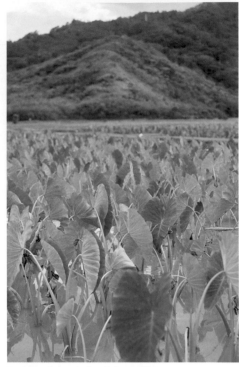

Dasheen thrives in flooded conditions

 varieties

Dasheen has a cylindrical main tuber with fibrous roots and a few side tubers. The upright stems up to 6 ft. tall are topped with large, heart-shaped leaves with prominent ribs on the underside. Cultivated types rarely flower and are grouped by the color of their flesh, ranging from pink to yellow, and leaf stems of green, pinkish purple to almost black.

 cultivation

Propagation
Dasheen is propagated from "tops" with a small section of tuber, small side tubers, or "suckers." Plant 24 in. apart with 40 in. between rows, or 2–3 ft. apart; add general fertilizer to the hole before planting. **Zones 9 to 11.**

Growing
Dasheen tolerates quite heavy, fertile, moisture-retentive soil rich in organic matter with a pH of 5.5 to 6.5. Dig in potting mix or well-rotted manure if necessary. As dasheens need plenty of water and tolerate waterlogging, they are ideal for areas by streams and rivers. Where the water table is high, mound or ridge planting is advized. Irrigate heavily during dry weather.

In well-manured soil, a second crop can be planted between the rows 12 weeks before the main crop is harvested.

Maintenance

Spring Plant presprouted tubers with protection.
Summer Keep crops well fed and watered and weed-free.
Fall Harvest crops.
Winter Prepare for the following year.

Protected Cropping

Plant pre-sprouted tubers in spring into greenhouse beds. Keep temperatures around 70°F, and maintain high humidity by misting plants with soft tepid water or wetting down the greenhouse floor. Do not worry about over-watering.

Feed every 3 to 4 weeks with a high potassium fertilizer; extra nitrogen may be needed if growth slows.

 ## container growing

Dasheens can be grown as a "novelty" crop in 8–12 in. pots of peat-substitute potting mix. Soak thoroughly after planting and stand the pot in a shallow tray of tepid water throughout the growing season. Treat as for "Protected Cropping."

Dasheen roots

 ## culinary

Tubers can be roasted, baked, or boiled, served with spicy sauces, and in stews. Larger tubers, which tend to be dry and coarse, should be braised and cooked slowly.

Leaves (with midrib removed) can be stuffed, boiled, or steamed and eaten with a pat of butter. Avoid particularly large leaves; they are often tough. In the West Indies, Callaloo Soup is made from dasheen leaves, okra, crab meat, and coconut milk. Young blanched shoots can be eaten like asparagus.

Pests and Diseases

Taro leaf blight causes circular water-soaked spots on leaves followed by collapse of the plant. Those grown in greenhouses are susceptible to aphids. Red spider mite and downy mildew can also be a problem. Take the necessary precautions.

Harvesting and Storing

Dasheens take 7 to 11 months to mature. Harvest by lifting the main tuber, saving some of the small side tubers for eating and others for replanting. Undamaged tubers can be dried and stored for up to 4 weeks, while washed leaves keep for several days in a refrigerator.

Palusima

This is a Western Samoan or Polynesian dish. Allow about ½ pound per person. Peel and chop roughly, then parboil in plain salted water for 5 to 10 minutes. Drain, then boil until reduced in coconut milk (enough to come to half the height of the dasheen in the pan) until thickish. Mash. Stuff the mashed dasheen into parboiled leaves and secure with a toothpick. (Alternatively, wrap it in banana leaves, and even spinach or cabbage.) Bake for 15 minutes in a lightly greased dish in a preheated oven at 350°F. Serve with any good white fish such as cod.

 ## warning

Although selection has, over the years, reduced calcium oxalate levels in the skin of dasheen, it is extremely important to wear gloves or to cover the hands with a layer of cooking oil. This prevents skin irritation when peeling the vegetables.

Always make sure dasheens are cooked thoroughly before eating.

Crambe maritima. Brassicaceae

SEA KALE

Perennial grown for its blanched young shoots. Hardy. Value: an excellent source of vitamin C.

Found on the seashores of northern Europe, the Baltic, and the Black Seas, sea kale was harvested from the wild and sold in markets long before it came into cultivation. In Victorian times it was seen as an aristocrat of the vegetable garden and widely cultivated by armies of gardeners in the enormous kitchen gardens attached to great houses. Today it is rarely grown, perhaps because the scale on which it was forced for Victorian tables gave it a reputation for being labor-intensive. However, it is easy to grow at home, and quite delicious; so it is high time it experienced a revival!

Two essentials: healthy plants and a blancher

 varieties

"Lily White" crops heavily with pale stems and has a good flavor. Unnamed selections of the wild species are also available from nurseries.

 cultivation

Propagation
Sea kale can be grown from seed, but it is usually propagated from crowns or root cuttings from the side roots, taken in fall after the leaves have died back. These are called "thongs." Buy them from a nursery or select roots that are pencil-thick and 3–6 in. long.

Make a straight cut across the top of the root and an angled cut at the base (so top and bottom are distinguishable). Store in sand until planting.

Growing
Sea kale needs a sunny position on deep, rich, well-drained light soil with a pH of around neutral. The winter before planting, dig in some well-rotted potting mix; on heavier soils, add organic matter, or plant on a raised bed.

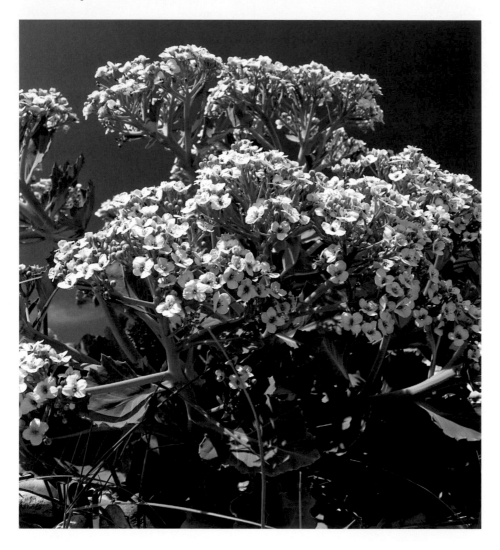

SEA KALE

Sea kale should crop for about 5 to 7 years before it needs replacing, so it is vital to prepare the ground thoroughly. 2 weeks prior to planting, rake in a general fertilizer. Before planting, in early spring, rub off all the buds to leave the strongest bud and plant thongs or crowns 18 in. apart, covered with 1–2 in. of soil.

Water regularly, feed occasionally, remove flower stems as they appear and keep weed-free. In fall, cut down the yellowing foliage. From late fall until midwinter, cover the crowns with a bucket, flower pot (cover the drainage holes), or sea kale forcer and surround with manure, straw, or leafmold. Stop harvesting in late spring, rake in a general fertilizer and mulch with well-rotted manure or potting mix. Water well in dry periods. Delaying harvest until the second year lets plants become established.

Maintenance
Spring Force crops outdoors.
Summer Water in dry weather, feed occasionally, keep weed-free.
Fall Remove the yellowing foliage.
Winter Lift crowns for forcing.

Sea kale being forced

Protected Cropping
For an early crop, lift crowns after leaves die back, trim the main root to 12 in. and remove the side shoots; plant 4 in. apart in boxes or three per 9 in. pot filled with rich soil from the sea kale bed or soilless potting mix with a high fertilizer content. Cover with upturned pots, plastic, or anything opaque. Keep the potting mix moist. They should be ready in 5 to 6 weeks at temperatures of 48–55°F; from 60–70°F they will be ready earlier. Keep them in a cellar, boiler house or under greenhouse benches and maintain a constant supply by lifting crowns regularly. In frosty weather lift and store crowns in moist sand until required. Dispose of exhausted crowns after use.

Harvesting and Storing
When blanched sprouts are 3–8 in. long, remove the soil from around the shoots and cut through the stems with a sharp knife, removing a tiny sliver of root. Crops forced outdoors can be harvested in late fall to early spring. After harvesting, discard the exhausted roots of those forced indoors.

Pests and Diseases
Do not plant in beds infected with clubroot. Flea beetles make round holes in the leaves; cover with mesh or floating row cover.

 other uses

Sea kale is attractive in the flower border. It forms a compact rosette of large, wavy-edged, glaucous leaves, with large bunches of white, honey-scented flowers towering above the foliage in summer.

 culinary

Better eaten fresh, sea kale lasts for 2 to 3 days in the salad compartment of the refrigerator.

Wash stems and tie them into bundles using raffia and steam or lightly boil them until tender overcooking toughens the stems and makes them less palatable.

Victorians served sea kale on folded napkins or on toast, drenched in white sauce or melted butter.

Sea kale is also delicious served as a starter with béchamel or hollandaise sauce, or covered in lemon-flavored melted butter.

Young flowering shoots can be eaten once they are lightly boiled.

Sea Kale Gratinée
Serves 4

1 ½ pounds sea kale, washed well

For the béchamel sauce:
3 tablespoons butter
2 tablespoons all-purpose flour
1 teaspoon French mustard
½ cup milk or crème fraîche
4 tablespoons grated strong cheddar cheese
Salt and freshly ground black pepper

Rinse the sea kale well, tie into bundles, and cook until *al dente* in boiling salted water. Drain well. Arrange in an ovenproof dish.

Make the béchamel sauce, flavoring with the cheddar cheese. Pour the sauce over the sea kale and bake in a preheated oven, 400°F for 15 minutes. Serve hot.

Crithmum maritimum. Apiaceae
SAMPHIRE

Also known as Rock Samphire, Sea Fennel, Sea Samphire. Low-growing maritime perennial. Half hardy. Value: good source of iron and vitamin C; moderate iodine.

Rock samphire is found on the shores and cliffs of Europe. Its name comes from "sampiere," a contraction of the French *herbe de St Pierre* — the fisherman Saint's herb. Collected from the wild for centuries, by the English Tudor period it was widely cultivated in gardens. William Turner wrote: "Creta marina groweth much in rockes and cliffes beside Dover." This precarious habitat is mentioned in *King Lear*, where harvesters dangle over the cliffs from a rope. Robert Turner in 1664 described similar dangerous activities on the 650-ft. cliffs of the Isle of Wight, "yet many adventure it though they buy their sauce with the price of their lives." Samphire was sent in casks of seawater to London, where wholesalers paid four shillings a bushel, but for the privilege of collecting it and gulls' eggs the Lord of the Manor exacted an annual rent.

 varieties

Crithmum maritimum has a woody base, with stems to 24 in. and lobed, gray-green leaflets. The white/cream flowers grow in flat clusters and are followed by small oval fruits. The leaves have an aromatic odor which has been likened to the smell of furniture polish!

 cultivation

Propagation
Plants are propagated from fresh seed sown in fall or spring in a sheltered position. Transplant when large enough to handle, or divide plants in spring. **Zones 6 to 9.**

Growing
Its natural habitat is in sand; if you create a satisfactory habitat in a coastal garden, natural colonies may form. Plants often inhabit dry stone walls. They flourish in well-drained, sandy or gritty soil, which is constantly moist and protected from full heat. An open east- or south-facing position is ideal. Mulch with seaweed, or burn seaweed and sprinkle with the sodium-rich debris. If possible, water with seawater or sea salt solution.

Maintenance
Spring Sow seed in gritty potting mix or in shallow rows.
Summer Keep soil moist with a saline solution. Harvest.
Fall Harvest. Protect crops during colder weather.
Winter Mulch with straw or leaves.

Protected Cropping
As a succulent plant, rock samphire needs frost protection. Cover with leaves, straw or cloches.

Harvesting and Storing
Harvest young shoots and leaves by cutting or pulling. Young spring growth is the most tender. Do not harvest excessively from each plant. It is best eaten immediately after harvesting, but will last for up to 2 days in a refrigerator.

Pests and Diseases
Usually trouble-free.

 container growing

Grow in containers of gritty potting mix. Water regularly in summer; in cooler climates, bring plants indoors during the winter.

 medicinal

John Evelyn noted "its excellent vertues and effects against the Spleen. Cleansing the Passages and sharpning appetite." It was also recommended as a kidney, bladder, and general tonic and as a treatment for "stones." It is said to be a diuretic, to improve digestion, and has been used to encourage weight loss.

 culinary

This plant is difficult to find in the U.S., but if you can, wash thoroughly in running water before use. Tender young shoots and leaves can be eaten fresh or cooked as a vegetable. They are added raw to salads or dressed with oil and lemon juice as an hors-d'oeuvre.

Pickle young shoots, leaves, and stems by filling a jar with samphire cut into 1 in. lengths, add peppercorns and a little grated horseradish, pour over a boiling mixture of equal parts dry hard cider and vinegar, and infuse for an hour before sealing. Pickled, it is used as a garnish and as a caper substitute. In Italy it is known as *roscano.*

Cucumis sativus. Cucurbitaceae

CUCUMBER

Climbing or scrambling annual, grown for elongated or round succulent fruits. Tender. Value: moderate potassium and small amounts of beta carotene.

The wild species from central Asia is now rare in nature, yet the world-renowned salad crop has been cultivated for centuries. The first record was in Mesopotamia around 2000 BCE in the earliest known vegetable garden, and cucumbers were grown in India a thousand years later. The Romans in the 1st century CE cultivated them in baskets or raised beds mounted on wheels so they could be moved around "as the sun moved through the heavens." When the day cooled, they were moved under frames or into cucumber houses glazed with oiled cloth known as *specularia*. Tiberius found them tasty and was said to have eaten them every day of the year.

Early varieties were quite bitter and were boiled and served with oil, vinegar, and honey. They were a common ingredient in soups, stews, and as a cooked vegetable until the 19th century. Eighteenth century English recipes include cucumbers stuffed with partly cooked pigeons (with head and feathers left on: the idea was to make the head appear attached to the cucumber); the whole was then cooked in broth, and the heads garnished with barberries. Cooks in Georgian England obviously had a rather bizarre sense of humor!

Columbus introduced cucumbers to the New World. They are recorded as being planted in Haiti in 1494 and grown by English settlers in Virginia in 1609. About the same time, French writers Estienne and Liébault warned: "Beware that your seed be not olde, for if it be 3 years olde, will bring forth radishes." Obviously their soil was as fertile as their imagination.

 varieties

Your seed catalog will give an idea of the huge number of cultivars to choose from. There are "greenhouse cucumbers" (though many indoor varieties can grow outdoors in a sheltered position in cooler zones and grow outdoors in warm zones); "row" or outdoor types, which need protection as seedlings but can be grown outdoors in cool temperate zones; pickling cucumbers or gherkins; round varieties; Japanese climbing and bushy types.

Greenhouse or Indoor Cucumbers
"Crystal Apple" is a small, round, yellow cucumber that is prolific and easy to grow in the unheated greenhouse or outdoors. "Danimas" is a vigorous, "all-female" mini-cucumber, ideal for a slightly heated or cold greenhouse. "King George" produces good-quality, long, dark fruit. "Flamingo" yields masses of fruit so only requires a few plants. "Telegraph" is popular and reliable with smooth skin and good-sized fruits.

Outdoor or Ridge Cucumbers
"Bianco Lungo di Parigi" produces moderately-sized fruits with creamy-white skin. "Boothby Blonde" has been grown for generations by the Boothby family of Maine — tasty, crisp, and mild. Harvest at 3 in. long. Many older varieties have been grown from the seed saved from the previous year's crop. "Burpless Tasty Green" is tender, delicious, crisp, and the best. "Bush Champion" produces bushy, dark green fruit; ideal for patios. "Long Green Improved" is robust and highly productive with large, tasty fruits that can also be used for pickling. "Long White Paris" is sweet and easy to digest with low acidity. "Marketmore" is smooth, tasty and excellent for cooler conditions.

Pickling Cucumbers or Gherkins
"Athene" is for outdoors or an unheated greenhouse or frame. The sweetness of "Beit Alpha" is ideal for salads or pickling. "Gherkin" is fast-growing, with masses of small prickly fruits. "Midget" is a prolific and compact variety. "National Pickling" is short, blunt-ended with small, smooth fruits. It is vigorous and heavy-yielding

Crystal Apple with male and female flowers

and was introduced in 1929 by the National Pickle Packers Association in Britain. "Vert Petit de Paris" is a French heritage variety with good flavor and yield. "West Indian Gherkin" is a reliable cropper whatever the weather. Use peeled in a salad, or cook unpeeled in a relish or pickle.

 cultivation

Propagation
When growing outdoor cucumbers, sow two seeds edgeways ½ to 1 in. deep in a 2–3 in. pot from midspring. Place in a propagator or heated greenhouse at 68°F.

Retain the stronger seedling after germination, keep moist with tepid water and tie up small stakes. Feed with a general liquid fertilizer to boost growth.

Give plants plenty of light and harden off before transplanting with care to avoid checks, when the danger of frost has passed. Allow 36 in. between plants. Protect with cloches or floating row cover until established.

Sow successively to extend the cropping season. Alternatively, pregerminate or sow two to three seeds, ½ to 1 in. deep *in situ* under jelly jars or cloches from late spring to early summer when the

soil temperature is around 68°F. Thin to leave the strongest seedling.

The second method is preferable, as cucumbers do not transplant well. **Zones 3 to 11.**

Growing
Most areas in the U.S. have plenty of heat units to grow cucumber simply by planting them directly in garden soil with no special pretreatment. If you would prefer special treatment for "row" cucumbers, a few weeks before planting, dig out holes or longer ridges at least 18 in. wide and 12 in. deep. Half fill with well-rotted manure or good garden potting mix, then return the excavated soil, mounding it to about 6 in. above ground level.

Better fruits are obtained when plants are grown against supports, though traditionally they are left to trail over the ground.

Once plants have produced five to six leaves, pinch out growing points of the stems, allow 2 laterals to form and pinch out the growing tips again. Row cucumbers are insect-pollinated, so do not remove male flowers as you would with greenhouse cultivars.

Grow gherkins like row cucumbers, or train them up some netting.

Train Japanese cultivars up trellis, stake tripods, wire, or nylon netting. Nip out the growing point when stems reach the top of the support. Water regularly; feed with a high-potassium fertilizer every 2 weeks when fruits are forming.

Keep crops weed-free and the soil moist.

Maintenance
Spring Sow under cover from midspring.
Summer Plant row cucumbers outdoors once frost is past. Maintain high temperatures and humidity indoors. Train and harvest.
Fall Harvest.
Winter Store in a cool place.

Protected Cropping
Sow under cover or in a propagator from midspring at 70–75°F. To avoid erratic germination, seeds can be pre-germinated on moist paper towels in a covered plastic container, then placed in an airing cupboard or propagator. After about 3 days, when the seeds have

germinated, sow in 3 in. pots of seed potting mix. Sow from late spring if no heat can be provided. Fill 3 in. pots with seed potting mix and press the seed down edgewise into each pot about ½ in. deep.

Greenhouse cucumbers need a humid atmosphere and temperatures around 70°F. Soils should be rich, moisture-retentive and free-draining, so incorporate well-rotted organic matter if you are planting in the greenhouse bed. Even better, grow in 10 in. pots of soil-based potting mix with added organic matter, in growing bags, or in untreated straw bales with a bed of compost in the center.

Insert a stake at the base of the plant and tie it into the roof structure of the greenhouse. Tie in the main stem and remove the growth tip when it reaches the roof, pinching out the laterals two leaves beyond each fruit.

Greenhouse cucumbers should not be pollinated or they become bitter: remove male flowers. Female flowers are identified by the swelling behind each one. Or choose "all-female" cultivars.

Feed every 2 weeks with high-potassium fertilizer once fruits begin to swell. Outdoor cucumbers can be grown in cold frames or a cold greenhouse in cooler climates. They are better trained above the ground. Ventilate well on warm days and mist regularly.

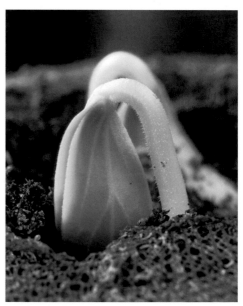

A cucumber seedling

CUCUMBER

Plenty to enjoy and give away

Harvesting and Storing

Fruits should never be harvested until they are fully ripe, and the 16th-century practice of leaving fruit on until they were mottled brown and yellow with a rich flavor may be to your taste!

Outdoor cucumbers crop midsummer to early fall: cut with a sharp knife when they are large enough to use. For maximum yields, you should pick fruit regularly. Cucumbers last for several days in the crisper in the refrigerator. Cover the cut end with plastic wrap and use as rapidly as possible. Like squash, they can be stored in nets in a cool place.

Pests and Diseases

Spotted and striped cucumber beetles can cause bacterial wilt and sudden death of the plants. Red spider mite, aphids, slugs, and powdery mildew can also be troublesome. Cucumber mosaic virus shows as mottled, distorted leaves. Burn young infected plants and leaves from older plants. Older plants may recover, though yields will be lower.

 culinary

Eat while the stalk end is still firm. Some people remain adamant that peeled cucumbers are best: others think the flavor and appearance of the skin enhance the vegetable.

They are frequently sliced and eaten in salads, and are good in sandwiches with salmon. Mix with yogurt and mint as a side dish to Middle Eastern dishes or curries. Make into a delicious cold soup.

To eat them as a vegetable, peel, seed, dice, and stew them in a little water and butter for 20 minutes, until soft. Thicken with cream and serve with mild- or rich-flavored fish.

Cucumber and Cream Cheese Mousse
Serves 4

½ a cucumber, in chunks
8 oz. cream cheese
1 to 2 tablespoons mint leaves
2 teaspoons white wine vinegar
2½ teaspoons gelatin
½ cup vegetable stock
Salt and freshly ground black pepper
Radicchio leaves and sprigs of fresh mint, to serve

Put the cucumber into a blender with the cream cheese, mint, and vinegar and purée until smooth. Dissolve the gelatin in a little stock over low heat. Let cool, then stir in the balance of the stock. Add this to the cream cheese, season and blend.

Chill for at least 2 hours before serving, arranged individually with radicchio leaves, garnished with a few fine slices of cucumber and sprigs of mint.

 companion planting

Row cucumbers thrive in the shade of corn or sunflowers, and grow well with peas and beans, beets, or carrots.

Climbing cucumbers flourish, scrambling over corn and beans.

 container growing

Sow indoor types in pots or growing bags (see "Protected Cropping"). Smooth-skinned varieties can be grown in a growing bag or container 12 in. wide by 8 in. deep in a sunny position outdoors. Sow three seeds 1 in. deep in late spring or early summer.

Thin out to leave the strongest seedling; pinch out growing tips when the plant develops six to seven leaves. Train the side shoots on netting or stakes. Keep soil moist. Feed with high-potash fertilizer when fruits form. "Bush Champion" is ideal.

 medicinal

Cucumbers were used by the Romans against scorpion bites, bad eyesight, and to scare away mice.

Wives wishing for children wore cucumbers tied around their waists, and they were carried by midwives and thrown away once the child was born.

Cucurbita maxima, Cucurbita moschata and *Cucurbita pepo.* Cucurbitaceae

PUMPKIN & SQUASH
COURGETTE, ZUCCHINI, POTIRON

"On the coast of Coromandel
Where the early pumpkins blow
In the middle of the woods
Lived the Yonghy-Bonghy-Bo …"
Edward Lear (1812–88)

Annuals grown for edible fruits, often colorful, which can be extremely large. Tender. Value: high in beta carotene, moderate amounts of vitamin C and folic acid.

The name "pumpkin" appeared in the 17th century, shortly before Perrault wrote Cinderella, the tale about a poor girl whose fairy godmother turned a pumpkin into a golden coach which took her to the ball. "Pumpkin" comes from the Greek word for melon — *pepon* or "cooked by the sun" — while one French name, *potiron*, means "large mushroom," from the Arabic for morel mushrooms. "Squash" is an abbreviation of the native North American Indian word *askutasquash*, meaning "eaten raw or uncooked."

The squashes originated in the Americas and are believed to have been cultivated for between five and 10 thousand years. Wild forms were originally gathered for their seeds and were only later found to have sweet flesh. Many varieties arrived in Europe soon after the discovery of the New World in the 16th century. Not only were they eaten, but the seeds were pounded in oatmeal and applied to the

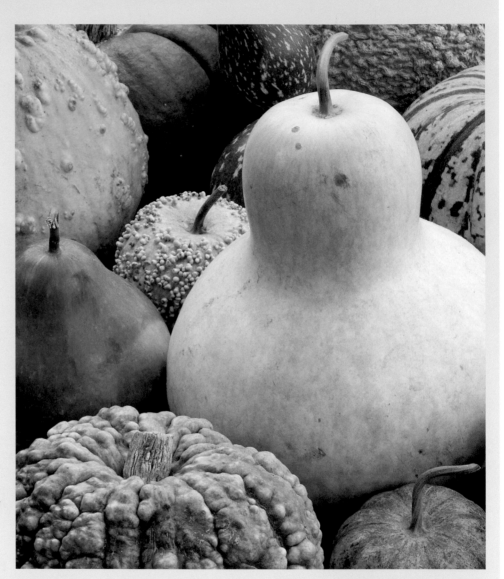

face, to bleach freckles and other blemishes.

Estienne and Liébault wrote in 1570: "To make pompions keep long and not spoiled or rotted, you must sprinkle them with the juice of a houseleek." In the 17th century they were mashed to bulk up bread, or boiled and buttered.

This group contains a wealth of edible and outstandingly ornamental fruits. One of the most beautiful sights in the kitchen garden is that of pumpkins ripening in golden sunshine during the fall.

PUMPKIN & SQUASH

Provide enough space to spread

 varieties

Members of the genus *Cucurbita* are bushy or trailing annuals — sometimes extremely vigorous plants — bearing a wide range of edible and/or ornamental fruit. The fruits from all of these species are often grouped together according to their shape or time of harvest — crookneck, summer squash, winter squash, and so on; in practice, categories overlap and some are multipurpose, being served differently when young and when mature. Additional confusion arises because of local variation in what is grown and what it is called. Here they are classed according to species.

The *Cucurbita maxima* group has large, variable fruits and includes most traditional pumpkins and winter squashes, containing several ornamentals like the banana, buttercup, hubbard, and turban types. They tend to have hard skins when mature, and keep well; the yellow flesh needs cooking. They flourish in low humidity from 68–80°F, though some tolerate cooler conditions.

"Dill's Atlantic Giant" is not for the faint-hearted as it can grow to 2,000 pounds. "Pink Banana" is long, broad and curved, with pale pink skin. "Big Max" is a massive pumpkin with rough, red-orange skin and bright flesh. It is excellent for pies, exhibitions, and as a "giant" vegetable. "Buttercup" is delicious with firm, dense, sweet flesh. The skin is dark green with pale narrow stripes and the flavor is perfect for soups, roasting and pumpkin pie. "Crown Prince" is small with tender orange flesh. It's tasty and keeps well. "Queensland Blue" is an attractive small variety with blue-gray skin — very tasty. "Turk's Turban" ("Turk's

Cap") is a wonderful ornamental squash; orange with cream and green markings. The name aptly describes the shape. "Warted Hubbard" is a round/oval fruit with extraordinary dark green, warty skin and orange-yellow flesh. It keeps well. "Whangaparoa Crown" pumpkin is a hard, gray-skinned variety with a pronounced crown and orange flesh. It also stores well.

Cucurbita pepo embraces summer squashes (including zucchini and their larger version, the marrow), non-keeping winter pumpkins and ornamental gourds such as custard squash, plus straight and crook-necked types. The fruits are usually soft-skinned, especially when young, and may be served raw when small. One variety, "Little Gem," is slow to mature, taking about 4 months. It doesn't perform well in cooler conditions but is good for storage.

Summer Squash

"Early Golden Summer" Crookneck is an early cropper with bright yellow fruits and excellent flavor. Harvest when 4 in. long. "Early Prolific Straight Neck" is yellow with finely textured flesh. Pick at 6 in. "Vegetable Spaghetti" ("Spaghetti Squash") is pale yellow when mature. Boil or bake fruits whole and then scoop out the flesh inside; it looks like spaghetti. "White Patty Pan" ("White Bush" Scallop) has an unusual flattened

Marrow or *Cucurbita pepo*

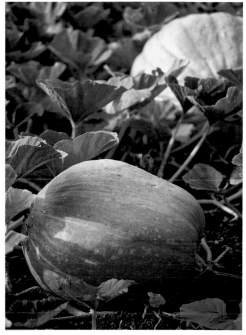

Even the "Atlantic Giant" starts small

shape with a scalloped edge. It is better harvested and cooked whole when about 3 in. in diameter. It is bushy and ideal for small gardens. "Yellow Bush" Scallop is an old variety with bright yellow skin and coarse, pale yellow flesh that has a distinctive flavor.

Marrow

This elongated type of summer squash has long been popular in Britain.

"Long Green Trailing" is a prolific, long-fruited, dark green variety — fine quality and flavor. "Tiger Cross" is an early, green bush-type that crops well and yields good-quality fruits. Resistant to cucumber mosaic virus. "Badger Cross" is compact, high yielding, and crops early. Ideal for containers or small gardens.

Zucchini

Varieties of marrow bred for picking small, the following are all bush types and ideal for the smaller garden. "Ambassador" is high-yielding with dark green fruit and reliable cropping. "Defender" produces high yields of midgreen fruits. Harvest regularly. Resistant to cucumber mosaic virus. "De Nice à Fruit Rond," a round variety, should be picked when the size of a golf ball — delicious flavor. "Partenon" fruits without pollination and is good for early crops or in

PUMPKIN & SQUASH

cool weather. "Spacemiser" is a compact and prolific gourmet variety. "Supremo" produces very tasty, dark green fruit.

Winter Squash

These usually have white or pale yellow flesh, whereas pumpkins have coarse, orange flesh. "Ebony Acorn" ("Table Queen") is early-cropping with thin, dark green skin and sweet, pale yellow flesh; delicious baked with honey. It is a semi-bush but can be temperamental. "Jack-Be-Little" is a miniature pumpkin with deep ribbed, orange-skinned fruits with a diameter of 2–3 in. You can eat them but they are often more attractive as an fall decoration. "Small Sugar" has rounded orange fruits growing to 7 in. diameter. The flesh is tender, yellow, and excellent in sweet or savory dishes. It matures from late fall.

Cucurbita moschata includes the early butternut, butternut, Kentucky Field, and crookneck squashes, harvested in fall and winter. They are large, rounded and usually have smooth, tough skin. Possibly one of the earliest species in cultivation, they are widely grown and found throughout the tropics. Particularly heat-tolerant.

"Butternut" has pale tan, club-shaped fruits with bright orange flesh. It succeeds in cooler areas and the flavor improves with keeping. "Early Butternut" is a curved, narrow fruit with a swollen tip. This bush variety matures rapidly and keeps well. "Neck" squash, with straight or curled necks, is tasty, high-yielding, and the best for pies. "Triple Treat" is a bright orange, round fruit. Its seeds are particularly good eaten raw, fried, or roasted. It is easy to carve and is therefore a variety that is often grown for Halloween. "Waltham Butternut" has a smooth, pale tan skin, yellow-orange flesh, and a nutty taste. It is very good for storing and yields extremely well.

 cultivation

Propagation

Sow *in situ* or in pots in cooler climates as seeds do not germinate if the soil is below 56°F.

From mid- to late spring, sow one seed edgeways, about 1 in. deep in a 3 in. pot or pack of moist multi-purpose or seed potting mix and place in a propagator or on a warm windowsill, preferably at 68–77°F. After germination transplant the seedlings when they are large enough to handle into 5 in. pots, taking care not to damage the roots. Keep potting mix moist but not waterlogged. Harden off gradually and transplant from late spring to early summer when the danger of frost has passed. Protect with cloches until the plants are established.

Alternatively, sow *in situ* when the soil is warm and workable and there is no danger of frost, from late spring to early summer. Dig out a hole at least 12–18 in. square and half fill with well-rotted manure 7–10 days before planting. Sow two to three seeds 1 in. deep in the center of the mound with a jam jar or cut the base from a plastic bottle and use as a crop cover. After germination, thin to leave the strongest seedling, remove the cover and mark the position with a stake so you know where to water the plant among the mass of stems. Alternatively, prepare the ground as described and transplant seedlings.

Space cultivars according to their vigor. Sow bush varieties on mounds or ridges, 2–3 ft. apart with 3–14 ft. between rows. Trailing varieties should be 4–6 ft. apart with 6–12 ft. between rows.
Zones 3 to 11.

Even the flowers are edible

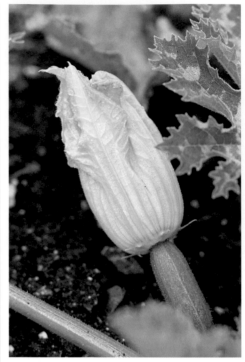
Only female flowers produce fruit

Growing

Pumpkins and squashes need a sunny position in rich, moisture-retentive soil with plenty of well-rotted organic matter and a pH of 5.5 to 6.8.

It is a good idea to plant through a black plastic mulch laid over the soil with the edges buried to hold it in place. This warms the soil, suppresses weeds, conserves moisture, and protects ripening fruit. A thick layer of straw or floating row cover are useful alternatives, or you can lay the ripening fruit on a roof tile, a piece of board, or similar to protect it from the soil and prevent rotting.

Hand-pollination is recommended, particularly in cold weather when insect activity is reduced. Female flowers have a small swelling, the embryonic squash, immediately behind the petals, while male flowers have only a thin stalk.

When the weather is dry, remove a mature male flower, fold back or remove the petals, and dust pollen on to the stigma of the female flowers. Alternatively, transfer the pollen with a fine paintbrush. Periods of hot weather can reduce the ratio of female to male flowers.

Plants need copious amounts of food and water, particularly when flowers and fruits are forming, up to 2 gallons of water per week, but they should never be allowed to become waterlogged.

Feed with a liquid general fertilizer every 2 weeks. Plants grown with a black plastic mulch also need an occasional foliar feed to boost growth.

Pinch out tips of main shoots of trailing varieties when they reach 24 in. to encourage branching and trim back those that outgrow their position.

Small trailing types can also be trained over trellis or supports. Where space is limited, push a circle of pegs into the soil and trail the stems around the pegs.

To guarantee large fruits, allow only two to three to develop on each plant.

Keep crops weed-free.

Maintenance
Spring Sow seeds indoors or outdoors.
Summer Feed and water copiously; keep crops weed free. Harvest zucchini and marrows.
Fall Harvest pumpkins and winter squashes, allow to ripen, and protect from frost.
Winter Store winter squashes until midwinter or later.

Protected Cropping
In cooler climates or to advance growth, sow seed indoors and transplant. Protect with cloches or crop covers until they are well established. Use bush varieties for earlier crops.

Harvesting and Storing
Pick zucchini and summer squashes when they are about 4 in. long and still young and tender. Marrows are harvested when they have reached full size. Push your thumbnail gently into the skin near the stalk; if it goes in easily then the marrow is ready for harvest.

Cut them from the stem, leaving a short stalk on the fruit, and handle with care to avoid bruising. Harvest regularly for continual cropping.

They can be stored in a cool place for about 8 weeks. Zucchini can be kept in a plastic bag in the refrigerator and will stay fresh for about a week. Zucchini are suitable for freezing. Cut into ½ in. slices, blanch for

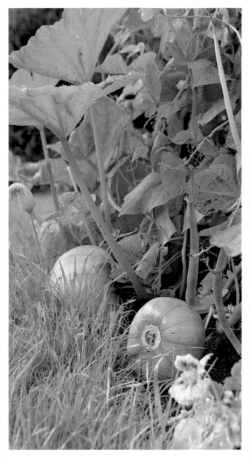

Plenty of sunshine ensures early ripening

2 minutes, cool, drain, and dry. Freeze in plastic bags. Flesh of winter squashes and pumpkins can be cooked, then frozen, without any loss of flavor.

Towards the end of the growing season, remove any foliage that shades the fruits. Harvest pumpkins and winter squashes from late summer to fall, though they must be brought into storage before the first heavy frosts. On maturity, the foliage rapidly dies, the skin hardens, and stem starts to crack.

After harvest, leave them outdoors for about 14 days, as cold weather improves the taste and sugar content, hardening the skin, and sealing the stem. Protect from heavy frost with a covering of hay, straw, or similar.

In cooler areas, they can be ripened in a greenhouse or on a sunny windowsill. Pumpkins will last until midwinter when stored in a frost-free shed.

Store winter squashes at a minimum temperature of 50°F; they can last for up to 6 months. Some Japanese varieties will last even longer.

Pests and Diseases
If fruits show signs of withering, water and feed more often. Aphids, powdery and downy mildew, and slugs can be a problem.

Cucumber mosaic virus causes yellow mottling and puckering of the leaves and rotting of the fruit. Destroy infected plants immediately and control aphids, which transmit this virus.

 ## companion planting

Grow zucchini and marrow alongside corn for support and shade, and with legumes, which provide essential nitrogen.

 ## container growing

Zucchini, marrows, bush varieties of other squashes and those that are moderately vigorous can be grown in growing bags or containers that are at least 14 in. by 12 in. deep. Use a soilless potting mix with additional well-rotted organic matter. Sow indoors to transplant later or sow directly outdoors. Keep plants well watered and do not allow the potting mix to dry out. Plants can be grown up strong stakes 7 ft. tall. Pinch out growing points when stems reach the top; tie the main stem and side shoots firmly to the supporting stakes.

Hand-pollinate for successful cropping.

 ## other uses

Pumpkins are hollowed out and made into Halloween "Jack o' Lanterns." Mature marrows can be used for wine making.

 ## medicinal

In Ethiopia, seeds from squashes are used as laxatives and purgatives; they are used worldwide to expel intestinal worms. Eating winter squash and pumpkin is said to reduce the risk of prostate cancer.

 ## warning

Be careful when lifting large squashes: bend from the knees, not the back!

PUMPKIN & SQUASH

culinary

Flowers of all varieties can be used in salads or stuffed with rice or ground meat and fried in batter. Prepare the meat, rice, and batter before picking the flowers, as they wilt quickly. They can also be puréed and made into soup. Young shoots are steamed or boiled. Pumpkin flesh is used for pies; their seeds are deep-fried in oil, salted, and are known as "pepitos." The fruits can be stuffed, steamed, stir-fried, added to curries, made into jam or pickles, and the seeds are edible too.

Pumpkin Kibbeh
Serves 4

A centerpiece of many Middle Eastern meals, these "balls" should be served warm, rather than hot. This recipe was given to me by Arto der Haroutunian.

1 cup freshly boiled pumpkin flesh
2 cups bulgar wheat
1½ cups all-purpose flour
1 onion, finely minced
Salt and freshly ground black pepper

For the filling:
2 shallots, finely minced
½ pound spinach, washed
¾ cup cooked chickpeas, drained
½ cup walnuts, chopped
½ cup dried apricots
¼ teaspoon sumac
1 tablespoon lemon juice
Salt and freshly ground black pepper
Oil for frying

In a large bowl, purée the pumpkin, using a fork. Sift the bulgar and flour into the bowl and mix in the onion and seasoning. Leave in a cool place for 10 to 15 minutes. If the dough is too hard to handle, you may need to add a tablespoon of water and knead well.

To make the filling, sauté the shallots in the oil until they just turn brown. Mix in the spinach and allow to wilt, stirring constantly, for a couple of minutes. Then add the rest of the ingredients, mixing well.

Make the kibbehs with wet hands to prevent the mixture from sticking. Form the bulgar and pumpkin

mixture into oval patties — they should be about 3 in. long and just big enough to stuff. Create an opening at one end and fill each kibbeh with the spinach and apricot stuffing. Using your fingers, seal up the ends.

Fry the kibbehs in hot oil for a couple of minutes on each side and drain on paper towel. There should be enough to make between 20 and 24 kibbehs.

Zucchini Omelette
Serves 2

5 eggs
²/₃ pound zucchini
4 tablespoons olive oil
1 tablespoon fresh (purple) basil leaves
1 tablespoon fresh thyme leaves
Salt and freshly ground black pepper

Whisk the eggs with salt and pepper and let sit. Slice the zucchini into coarse dice. Heat half the oil and sauté the zucchini for a couple of minutes. Then remove from the heat.

In an omelette pan, heat the balance of the oil and pour in the eggs, zucchini, and herbs. Stir gently over low heat while the omelette sets. Turn it on to a plate and slide back into the pan to cook the second side for a minute or so until nicely browned. Serve as a refreshing Sunday supper dish.

Zucchini Omelette

Acorn Squash with Balsamic Vinegar

Acorn Squash with Balsamic Vinegar
Allow ¼ pound of acorn squash per person. Cut in half and remove the seeds and fibers. Place in a buttered ovenproof dish and pour over 1 tablespoon balsamic vinegar, 2 tablespoons honey and 1 tablespoon lemon juice for each serving. Cook in a preheated oven, 350°F for 40 minutes, turning over halfway.

Custard Marrow with Bacon and Cheese
Serves 2 to 4

4 cups custard marrow, roughly diced
2 tablespoons butter
1 small onion, finely sliced
3 oz. Canadian bacon, diced
¼ cup crème fraîche
4 tablespoons grated mature cheddar cheese
Salt and freshly ground black pepper

Steam the custard marrow until just tender. Keep warm. Make a sauce by heating the butter and cooking the onion until softened. Add the bacon and continue cooking for 5 minutes, stirring from time to time. Mix in the crème fraîche, the custard marrow, and seasoning and pour into a greased ovenproof dish. Top with the cheese and cook in a preheated oven, 425°F, for 15 minutes.

Cynara cardunculus. **Asteraceae**

CARDOON

Also known as Cardon. Perennial grown as annual for "heart" and blanched leaf midribs. Half hardy. Value: rich in potassium.

This close relative of the globe artichoke is found in the wild through much of the Mediterranean and North Africa. Cultivated versions are valued as a vegetable and in the ornamental garden. When grown as a food crop, the stems are blanched during fall in a similar manner to celery. Its delights have been enjoyed for centuries; it was grown before the birth of Christ and was esteemed by the Romans, who paid high prices for it in their markets as an ingredient for stews and salads. Cardoons reached England by 1658 and North America by the following century, but never established themselves as a major crop, despite their popularity in Europe. Today they are more likely to be found in the herbaceous border, where the bold angular foliage and tall candelabras of thistle-like purple flowers are outstanding.

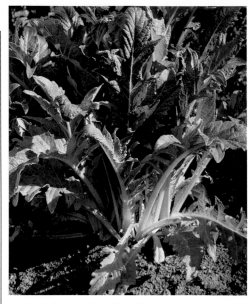

The leaves are ready for blanching

 varieties

"Gigante di Romagna" is a reliable variety with long stalks. "Gobbo di Nizza Monferrato" is a large plant with a strong celery flavor. Use in soups or eat fried, sautéed or raw, dipped in olive oil. "Plein Blanc Inerma Ameliora" grows to 4 ft. tall, with white ribs that are well textured and tasty.

 cultivation

Cardoons need a sunny, sheltered site on light, fertile, well-drained soil. **Zones 3 to 10.**

Propagation

Sow *in situ* in midspring, planting three to four seeds 1 in. deep in hills 20 in. apart with 5 ft. between rows. Thin after germination to retain the strongest seedling. In cooler areas or if spring is late and the soil is yet to warm up, sow indoors. Place three seeds in 3 in. pots or packs of moist seed potting mix in a propagator or greenhouse at 55°F. Thin, leaving the strongest seedling, then harden off before planting outdoors in mid- to late spring, when there is no danger of frost. Water well after planting and protect from scorching sunshine until they have established.

Growing

The fall or early spring before seed sowing or planting out seedlings, double dig the site, adding well-rotted organic matter. Alternatively, plant in trenches 15 to 20 in. wide and 12 in. deep; dig these in late fall or early spring, incorporating plenty of rotted manure or potting mix into the base and refilling to 3–4 in. below the surface. Leave the remaining soil alongside for hilling. Before planting, rake in general fertilizer at 4 oz per square yard.

In late summer or early fall, on a day when the leaves and hearts are dry, begin blanching: pull stems into a large bunch (wear long sleeves and gloves for protection), and tie with raffia or soft string just below the leaves. Wrap cardoons with "collars" of newspaper, corrugated cardboard, brown wrapping paper or black plastic tied firmly around the stems. Tile drainpipes and plastic guttering are just as effective at excluding the light. Support collars with a stake, particularly on exposed sites. Alternatively, cardoons can be hilled up. Cover stems with dry hay or straw held firmly at several points with twine and cover with soil, banked at an angle of 45°. The first method is easier, cleaner and quicker.

Cardoons need a regular water supply from early summer through to early fall, and feeding with liquid general fertilizer every 2 weeks. Keep them weed-free by hand weeding, hoeing or, preferably, mulching with a 2 in. layer of organic matter once plants are established.

Maintenance

Spring Sow seeds *in situ* or indoors.
Summer Feed and water regularly. Keep weed-free.
Fall Harvest crops using a sharp knife. Prepare the planting bed.
Winter Store in a cool, dry place until required.

Protected Cropping
Protect transplants or seedlings under cloches or floating row cover if late spring frosts are forecast.

Harvesting and Storing
Blanching takes about 3 to 4 weeks. When ready to harvest, lift plants with a garden fork, trim off roots, and remove outer leaves. Cardoons can remain in the ground until needed, but protect with straw or other insulating material in moderate frosts. If hard frosts are forecast, lift and store in a cool shed or cellar.

Pests and Diseases
Cardoons are robust and have few problems. They can be affected by powdery mildew, worst when plants are dry at the roots and if nights are cold and days warm and dry. Mice will eat the seeds. An old remedy is to dip the seeds in paraffin; concentrated liquid fertilizer is better. Otherwise buy humane traps or a cat!

 ## container growing

Grow in large containers of soilless potting mix with added organic matter or in free-draining, moisture-retentive soil. Allow plenty of room for leaves to grow. Water and feed regularly: do not let the potting mix dry out. Blanch using "collars."

Cardoons make attractive ornamentals

 ## culinary

The leaf midribs and thinly sliced hearts are eaten raw in salads, in soups and stews or as an alternative to fennel or celery. They can be boiled in salted water with a squeeze of lemon juice for about 30 minutes until tender. Once cardoons are cut, drop them into water with a squeeze of lemon juice, as the cut surfaces do tend to blacken.

The dried flowers are used as a substitute for rennet in Spain and some parts of South America.

Lamb Tagine with Cardoons
Serves 4

Tagines (or stews) are popular in northern Africa. Cardoons give this traditional Moroccan dish a rich flavor.

1 ½ pounds lamb, in chunks
3 cloves garlic, crushed
1 teaspoon ground ginger
Pinch saffron
¼ teaspoon turmeric
2 to 3 tablespoons vegetable oil
2 tablespoons chopped fresh cilantro
1 onion, peeled and sliced
1½–2 pounds cardoons
2 preserved lemons, quartered
4 tablespoons black olives
Juice of 2 lemons
Salt and freshly ground black pepper

Put the lamb, garlic, ginger, saffron, turmeric, oil, chopped cilantro, and onion in a heavy pan and mix well. Pour over a cup or two of water and bring to a boil.

Skim, if need be, then simmer, covered, for 1 hour, adding more water if necessary, to just cook the lamb.

Then add the cleaned cardoons and enough water to cover them (this is important), and continue cooking for an additional 30 to 40 minutes.

Stir in the preserved lemon quarters and the olives and enough lemon juice, to taste, and ensure the tagine is well mixed. Taste and adjust the seasoning before serving piping hot.

Cynara scolymus. Asteraceae
GLOBE ARTICHOKE

Also known as French artichoke, green artichoke. Tall, upright perennial grown for edible flower buds. Half hardy. Value: 85 percent water; half carbohydrate indigestible inulin, turning to fructose in storage; moderate iodine and iron content.

Originating in the Mediterranean, globe artichokes were grown by the Greeks and Romans, who regarded them as a delicacy. The common name comes from the Italian *urticoclos*, deriving from *cocali*, or pine cone — an apt description of the appearance of the flower bud. Artichokes waned in popularity in the Dark Ages, but were restored to favor when Catherine de Medici introduced them to France in the 16th century. From there they spread around the world. Globe artichokes reached the United States in 1806, traveling with French and Spanish settlers.

In Italy, its bitter principal flavors the aperitif Cynar, which is popular as a vermouth and definitely an acquired taste!

Growing to about 4–5 ft. tall, with a 3 ft. spread, attractive leaves and large thistle-like flowers, globe artichokes always look wonderful in the flower border and make excellent dual-purpose plants.

 varieties

"Green Globe" has large green heads with thick, fleshy scales and needs winter protection in cooler climates. "Gros Camus de Bretagne" is only suitable for warmer climates, but is worth growing for its large, well-flavored heads. "Purple Globe" is hardier than the green form but not as tasty. "Purple Sicilian" has small, deep purple-colored artichokes that are excellent for eating raw when they are very young. However it is not frost-hardy. "Gros Vert de Laon" is hardy with an excellent flavor and "Violetta di Chioggia," a purple-headed variety, is excellent in the flower border.

 cultivation

Artichokes need an open, sheltered site on light, fertile, well-drained soil.

Propagation
Artichokes can be grown from seed or divided, but are usually propagated from rooted "suckers" — shoots arising from the plant's root system. Suckers are bought or removed from established plants in midspring. They should be healthy, about 8–9 in. long and well rooted,

"Purple Globe"

GLOBE ARTICHOKE

with at least two shoots. Clear soil from around the roots of the parent plant and remove them with a sharp knife, cutting close to the main stem between the sucker and parent plant. Alternatively, divide established plants in spring by lifting the roots and easing them apart with two garden forks, a spade or an old knife and replanting the sections; these, too, should have at least two shoots and a good root system. To keep your stocks vigorous and productive, renew the oldest one third of your plants every year. This extends the cropping season, too, as mature plants are ready for harvest in late spring to early summer and young plants in late summer.

Sow seed in trays of moist seed potting mix in an unheated greenhouse during late winter or outdoors in early spring. Thin to leave the strongest seedlings and harden off before planting out at their final spacing in late spring. Once flower buds have been produced, retain the best plants for harvest and for future propagation, discarding the rest.

Growing
If necessary, improve the soil by digging in plenty of well-rotted organic matter in spring or fall before planting. This prevents summer drought and winter waterlogging, conditions that globe artichokes dislike. Before planting, rake in general fertilizer at 4 oz. per square yard.

Plant suckers or divisions 24 in. apart with 60–72 in. between each row, trimming the leaves back to 12 in., which helps to reduce water loss, and shading them from full sun until they are established. Water thoroughly after planting and during periods of dry weather, applying a high-potash liquid fertilizer every 2 weeks when the plants are actively growing.

Keep the beds weed-free and mulch with organic matter in spring. During fall and winter, if heavy frosts are forecast, protect plants by hilling with soil, then covering them with a thick layer of straw, bracken or other organic insulation. Remove the covering in spring.

Maintenance
Spring Divide or remove suckers from existing plants and replant.
Summer Keep weed-free and water thoroughly during drought.
Fall In areas with moderate temperatures, retain

leaves and stems as frost protection.
Winter If severe frost is forecast, remove the decayed leaves, hill up, and protect plants with insulating material. Remove the materials in spring before growth begins.

Harvesting and Storing
Each flowering stem normally produces one large artichoke at the tip and several smaller ones below. Artichokes can be quite productive from seed-started plants the first year, so a few flower heads will be produced in the first year. You can remove these so that the energy goes into establishing the plant, but if you cannot resist the temptation, harvest in late summer. In the second and third years more stems will be produced and are ready for cutting in midsummer. Harvest when the scales are tightly closed, removing the terminal bud first with 2 or 3 in. of stem, then the remaining side buds as they grow large enough. Alternatively, remove the lower artichokes for eating when they are about 1½ in. long.

Once the scales begin to open, globe artichokes become inedible.

Buds ready to enjoy

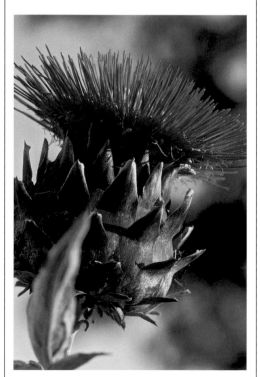
Bees are attracted to the flowers

Pests and Diseases
Slugs attack young shoots and — the problem is worse in damp conditions. Keep the area free of plant debris, use biological controls, sprinkle aluminum sulfate–based slug pellets around plants or make traps from plastic cartons half-buried in the ground and filled with milk or beer. Lay roof tiles, newspaper, old lettuce leaves, or other tempting vegetation on the ground and hand pick regularly from beneath. Or put a barrier of grit around plants, or attract predators such as birds to the garden. Lettuce root aphid can be a problem. Creamy yellow aphids appear on the roots during summer, sucking sap and weakening plants. Water well in dry weather; spray with soft soap.

 ## medicinal

Artichokes are highly nutritious and are especially good for the liver, aiding detoxification, and regeneration. They reduce blood sugar and cholesterol levels, stimulating the gall bladder and helping the metabolism of fat. Artichoke is also a diuretic and used to treat hepatitis and jaundice. It was formerly used as a contraceptive and aphrodisiac, but its potency is not recorded!

culinary

Artichokes can be stored for up to a week in a plastic bag in a refrigerator.

The edible parts are the fleshy base of the outer scales, the central "heart" and the bottom of the artichoke itself. Wash the artichoke thoroughly before use and sprinkle any cut parts with lemon juice to prevent them from turning black. Boil artichokes in a non-metallic pan of salted water with lemon juice for 30 to 45 minutes, until soft. Check if they are ready by pushing a knife through the heart, or try a basal leaf to check it for tenderness.

Eat artichokes by hand, pulling off the leaves one by one and dipping the base in mayonnaise, hollandaise, lemon sauce, melted butter, or plain yogurt before scraping off the fleshy leaf base between your teeth. Pull off the hairy central "choke," or remove it with a spoon, and then eat the fleshy heart.

Bottoms can be a garnish for roasts, filled with vegetables or sauces. Cook "Cypriot-style" with oil, red wine, and coriander seeds, or toss in oil and lemon dressing as an hors-d'oeuvre. Make a salad of cubed artichoke bottoms and new potatoes (leftovers are suitable), and season well. Toss in mayonnaise and crumble over finely chopped hard-boiled egg and good-quality black olives. Sprinkle with chives and flat-leaved parsley. Whole baby artichokes can be battered and deep-fried or cooked in oil. Eat them cold with vinaigrette.

A 17th-century herbalist and apothecary wrote that even the youngest housewife knew how to cook artichokes and serve them with melted butter, seasoned with vinegar and pepper. Florence White, a founder of the English Folk Cookery Association and member of the American Home Economics Association, gives a recipe for artichokes in *Good Things in England* (1929) from the time of Queen Anne:

A Pie of Artichoke Bottoms

"Line a dish with fine dough. Put in the artichoke bottoms, with a little finely minced onion and some finely minced sweet herbs. Season with salt, pepper and nutmeg. Add some butter in tiny pieces. Cover with dough and bake in a quick oven. When cooked, put into the pie a little white sauce thickened with yolk of egg and sharpened with tarragon vinegar."

Artichokes Cypriot-style

Risotto with Artichokes

Risotto with Artichokes
Serves 6

Rose Gray and Ruth Rogers give this recipe in their wonderful *River Café Cookbook*:

8 small globe artichokes, prepared and trimmed
(chokes removed if at all prickly)
2 garlic cloves, peeled and finely minced
3 tablespoons olive oil
4 cups chicken stock
1 stick butter
1 medium red onion, very finely minced
1 ½ cups risotto rice
¼ cup extra dry white vermouth
1 cup freshly grated Parmesan
Kosher salt and freshly ground black pepper

Cut the artichokes in half and slice as thinly as possible. Fry gently with the garlic in 1 tablespoon of the olive oil for 5 minutes, stirring continuously, then add ½ cup water, salt, and pepper and simmer until the water has evaporated. Let sit.

Heat the chicken stock and check for seasoning. Melt 1 tablespoon of the butter in the remaining oil in a large heavy-bottomed pot and gently fry the onion until soft, about 15 to 20 minutes. Add the rice and, off the heat, stir for a minute until the rice becomes totally coated. Return to the heat, add 2 or so ladlefuls of hot stock or just enough to cover the rice, and simmer, stirring, until the rice has absorbed nearly all the liquid. Add more stock as the previous addition is absorbed. After about 15 to 20 minutes, nearly all the stock will have been absorbed by the rice; each grain will have a creamy coating, but will remain *al dente*.

Add the remaining butter in small pieces, then gently mix in the vermouth, Parmesan, and artichokes, being careful not to overstir.

Daucus carota complex *sativus*. Apiaceae

CARROT

Swollen-rooted biennial grown as annual for edible orange-red roots. Hardy/half hardy. Value: extremely rich in beta carotene (vitamin A); small amounts of vitamin E.

Though there are white, yellow, purple and violet carrots, most of us are more familiar with orange carrots, which have been known only since the 18th century. Domestication is thought to have occurred around the Mediterranean, Iran and the Balkans. The Greeks cultivated them for medicinal uses, valuing them as a stomach tonic. In Roman and early medieval times, carrots were branched, like the roots of wild types; the conical-rooted varieties seem to have originated in Asia Minor around 1000 CE. Moorish invaders took them to Spain in the 12th century; they reached North-West Europe by the 14th and England in the 15th century. Gerard mentions only one yellow variety, purple ones being most popular — even though, when cooked, they turned into a nasty brown color.

The Elizabethans and early Stuarts used flowers, fruit and leaves as fashion accessories for hats and dresses and carrot tops were highly valued as a substitute for feathers, particularly when they colored up in fall. European explorers took the carrots across the Atlantic soon after the discovery of the New World and they were growing on Margarita Island, off the coast of Venezuela, in 1565, arriving in Brazil before the middle of the 17th century. They were grown by early colonists in Jamestown, Virginia in 1609.

Said to make you see well in the dark and make your hair curly, they are now highly valued as a rich source of vitamin A.

CARROT

varieties

There is a huge choice of carrot varieties; many new varieties have been bred for increased sweetness and higher beta carotene content. Carrots are grouped into categories according to their root shape and harvesting time. This is indicated on the packet or in the catalog.

"Adelaide" is one of the earliest to mature, with cylindrical, stump-shaped roots that are deep orange in color. "Amsterdam Forcing 3" is fast-maturing and produces small, good-quality roots with little core. Ideal for early sowings under unheated cover and good for "finger" carrots. "Fall King 2" is an excellent "maincrop" with top-quality roots up to 12 in. long. Ideal for eating fresh or winter storage. "Bangor" produces large, top-quality cylindrical roots with excellent color and flavor. It resists greening and cracking and stores well and is one of the best maincrops for the gardener. "Belgian White" is a tasty white variety for summer harvesting. "Carson" has a rich, crunchy orange core and is one of the best "Chantenay" hybrids for flavor — a good "maincrop" for fall use and winter storage. "Eskimo" has excellent cold tolerance, so is good for late cropping or storing in the ground. Rich in vitamin A, it also has good resistance to cavity and leaf spot and is suitable for deep freezing. "Giant Flakee" is a reliable old "maincrop" with huge, juicy roots and exceptional flavor. "Healthmaster" grows up to 10 in. long and is said to contain up to 35 percent more beta carotene than any other carrot. The roots are deep

"Parmex" — ideal for children

Eat carrots immediately for the finest flavor

orange-red and are resistant to cracking and greening. "Honeysnack" is juicy and delicious. The creamy-yellow roots reach 12 in. and are perfect for slicing or cutting into cubes for snacks or salads. The early-maturing Nantes variety "Jeanette" has a high level of pest and disease resistance and so is ideal for organic growers. It is well flavored, vigorous and ideal for salads. "Kazan" "Fall King" hybrid is one of the best late varieties for color and flavor and stores well. "Kingston" is one of the best for taste, color and uniformity. Another Nantes type, "Maestro," is vigorous, resists pests (including carrot fly) and is good for organic production. "Mokum" is high-yielding, very juicy, crisp and sweet, so ideal for juicing or eating fresh. Grow early indoors or in containers. "Nantes Frubund" is the first fall sowing carrot. It is very cold-resistant and ideal for early spring crops. "Parmex," a round- rooted type, is ideal for shallow or stony soils. "Paris Market Baron" is a similar shape. "Parano" is a very early bunching type with a smooth skin and delicious cylindrical roots that are ideal for salads. Good carrot fly resistance. "Samurai" ("Red Samurai") has sweet, slender, red-skinned roots with pink-tinted flesh that retains its color after steaming and lends color to a salad. "Purple Dragon" is similar but with an orange core. "Sugarsnax 54" and earlier-maturing "Tendersnax" both have long, juicy, tender roots that are tantalisingly sweet. Ideal juiced, in salads or lightly cooked. "Flyaway," "Sytan" and "Resistafly" are reliably carrot fly-resistant and "Edible leaf carrot" is grown for the leaves which are good in salads.

cultivation

Propagation

Germination is poor at soil temperatures below 45°F: warm the soil before sowing early crops. Another option is available for the small Paris Market varieties — sow three to four seeds per pack and plant out after hardening off in midspring.

Carrot seed is very small and is easier to sow when mixed with sand or "fluid sown." Sow sparingly to reduce thinning and associated problems with carrot fly.

Seeds should be sown 1 in. deep in rows 6 in. apart; allow 4 in. between plants in the rows for early crops and 1½ to 2½ in. apart for maincrops, depending on the size of roots you require.

Sow all but the "Berlicum" and "Fall King" types from mid- to late spring for cropping from late summer to early fall.

Sow "Chantenay," "Fall King" and "Berlicum" types from mid- to late spring for mid- to late fall crops. Sow "Fall King" and "Berlicum" types in late spring for mid- to late winter harvesting. **Zones 3 to 10.**

Growing

Early carrots need an open, sheltered position; maincrops are less fussy. Soils should be deep, light and free-draining, warming early in spring, and with a pH of 6.5 to 7.5. Carrots are the ideal crop for light sandy soils — you should be able to push your index finger right down into the seedbed.

Let's hope they all germinate

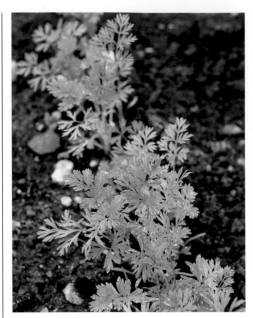

Thin when the soil is damp

Avoid walking on prepared ground to ensure maximum root growth.

Dig in plenty of well-rotted organic matter in the fall before planting. On heavy or stony soils, grow round or short-rooted varieties, or plant in raised beds or containers.

Rake the seedbed to a fine texture about 3 weeks before sowing and use the "stale seedbed" method, allowing the weeds to germinate and hoeing off before sowing.

Keep crops weed-free at first by mulching, hand weeding or careful hoeing, to avoid damaging the roots. In later stages of growth, the foliage canopy will suppress weed growth.

Keep the soil moist to avoid root splitting and bolting. Water at a rate of 3–5 gallons/ sq. yd. every 2 to 3 weeks, taking particular care with beds surrounded by barriers as a protection against carrot fly, as these create an artificial rain-shadow.

Maintenance
Spring Sow crops successively from midspring when the soil is workable.
Summer Harvest early crops, sow maincrops. Keep well watered.

Fall Sow under cover for a midspring crop. Harvest.
Winter Harvest and store.

Protected Cropping
Sow "Nantes" types in an unheated greenhouse, under cloches or floating row cover in midfall for a midspring crop. Sow "Paris Market," "Nantes" and "Amsterdam Forcing" in midspring for early to midsummer crops.

Harvesting and Storing
Early cultivars are ready to harvest after around 8 weeks, maincrops from 10 weeks. In light soils, roots can be pulled straight from the ground, but on heavier soils they should be eased out with a garden fork. Water the soil beforehand if it is dry.

On good soils, maincrop carrots can be left in the ground until required. Cover with a thick layer of straw, bracken or similar material before the onset of inclement weather to make lifting easier.

Alternatively, lift roots, cut or twist off foliage and store healthy roots in boxes of sand in a cool, dry, frost-free place for up to 5 months. Check regularly and remove any that are damaged.

Freeze finger-sized carrots in polyethene bags. Top and tail, wash and blanch for 5 minutes. Cool and rub off the skins.

Carrots will stay fresh for about 2 weeks in a cool room or for 2 months in a plastic bag in the refrigerator.

Pests and Diseases
Carrot fly is the most serious problem. Attracted by the smell of the juice from the root, their larvae tunnel into the roots, making them inedible. Leaves turn bronze. Sow resistant cultivars, sow sparingly to avoid thinning, thin on a damp overcast day (or water before and after), pinch off the tops of thinnings just above the soil level and dispose of them in the compost pile. Lift and dispose of affected roots immediately. Lift "earlies" by early fall and maincrops by midfall. Since these pests do not fly very high, grow carrots under floating row cover or mesh, or surround with a barrier of fine netting or fleece 24 in. high, or grow in raised beds or boxes.

Root and leaf aphids can also be a problem.

Carrot juice is tasty and packed with goodness

 ## companion planting

Intercropping carrots with onions reduces carrot fly attacks; leeks and salsify have also been used with some success.

Mixing with seeds of annual flowers also seems to discourage carrot fly.

Carrots grow well with lettuce, radishes and tomatoes and encourage peas to grow. They dislike anise and dill. If left to flower, carrots attract hoverflies and other beneficial predatory insects to the garden.

 ## container growing

Choose short-rooted or round varieties for containers, window boxes or growing bags. Sow in soilless potting mix; keep moist throughout the growing season.

 ## medicinal

Reputed to be therapeutic against asthma, general nervousness, dropsy and skin disorders.

Recent research suggests that high intake of beta carotene may slow cancerous growths. Beet and carrot juice is reported to prevent diarrhea.

culinary

Young carrots are sweet and can be eaten raw. Older carrots need to be peeled and the hard core discarded. Grated, they can be made into salads They're especially good mixed with raisins and chopped onion and tossed in a French dressing or mayonnaise, thinned with some extra virgin olive oil.

Try freshly plucked baby carrots, rinsed under the tap, topped and tailed, very lightly boiled in as little water as possible, then sprinkled with chopped parsley, a little sugar and freshly ground black pepper, or just a pat of butter. Add a sprinkling of sugar, a tablespoon of butter and a pinch of salt, cover and gently steam until tender. Cook in a cream sauce seasoned with tarragon, nutmeg and dill, or steam with mint leaves.

Cut into sticks as raw snacks, slice for stews and casseroles, pickle, stir-fry, use for jams, wine and carrot cake. Carrots are an essential ingredient in stocks, soups and many sauces.

Balkali Havuçi

Balkali Havuçi
Serves 4

Serve this Armenian-Turkish dish with pilaf and salad; it can be topped with a dollop of yogurt.

1 pound fava beans, shelled
1 onion, chopped
2 carrots, cut into 1 in. discs
2 cloves garlic, finely minced
2 tablespoons chopped fresh dill or mint
1 teaspoon salt
Freshly ground black pepper
Pinch sugar
3 tablespoons extra virgin olive oil

Rinse the beans. Put 1¼ cups water into a large pot and bring to a boil; add the onion and beans, bring to a boil, cover and simmer until tender.

Stir in the remaining ingredients and cook until the vegetables are just tender, about 20 minutes more. Serve hot with chunks of good bread as a starter.

Carrot and Raisin Cake
Serves 10 to 12

This spicy dough mixture can also be used to make cookies; drop heaping tablespoonfuls of dough on to a lightly greased baking sheet 2 in. apart and bake for 12 to 15 minutes until golden. Cool on a rack.

1½ cups all-purpose flour
2 teaspoons baking powder
1 teaspoon ground cinnamon
Pinch mace
Pinch salt
2 heaping tablespoons seedless raisins
½ cup carrots, grated
Zest of ½ an orange
2 tablespoons orange juice
½ butter
⅔ brown sugar
2 large eggs

Sift the flour, baking powder, spices and salt into a large bowl and let sit. Mix the raisins, carrots, orange zest and juice and let sit. Cream the butter and sugar thoroughly in a mixer and beat until light. Add the eggs, one at a time, with the blender on slow. Combine the batter with the flour and carrot mixtures and blend well.

Pour into a greased and lined 8 in. pan and bake in a preheated oven (350°F) for 40 to 60 minutes. Test with a skewer to ensure the cake is cooked and allow to cool in the pan for 15 minutes before turning out onto a wire rack.

Dioscorea alata. Dioscoreaceae
YAM

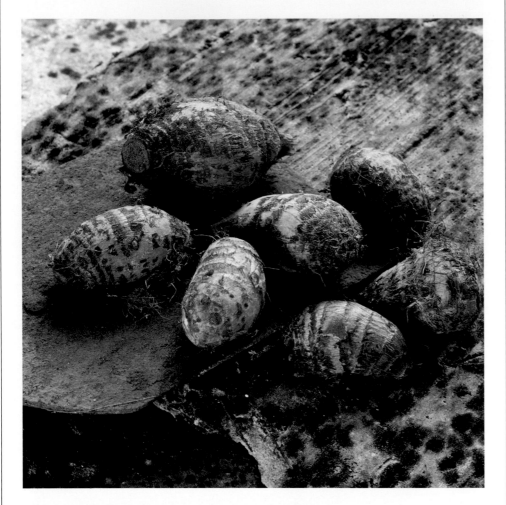

Also known as Greater Yam, Asiatic Yam, White Yam, Winged Yam, Water Yam. Twining climber grown for large edible tubers. Tender. Value: rich in carbohydrate and potassium; small amounts of B vitamins.

The "greater yam" is believed to have originated in east Asia and is widely cultivated as a staple crop throughout the humid tropics. It was said to have reached Madagascar by 1000 CE and by the 16th century Portuguese and Spanish traders had taken it to West Africa and the New World. Christopher Columbus knew of the plant as *nyame* and the tubers were used for ships' supplies, because they stored for several months and were easy to handle. There are hundreds of different forms producing tubers with an average weight of 10–20 pounds, although specimens with massive tubers up to 136 pounds have been recorded. In the U.S., sweet potatoes are often referred to as yams, but they are actually different plants.

 varieties

Dioscorea alata has square, four-winged or angled twining stems with pointed, heart-shaped, leaves. Small bulbils are often produced on the stems. The tubers are brown on the outside with white flesh, vary in size and are usually produced singly. There is a great number of cultivars which vary in the color and shape of the stems, leaves and tubers.

"White Lisbon," one of the most widely grown, is high-yielding, shallow-rooted and tasty and it will store for up to 6 months. "Belep," "Lupias," "Kinbayo" and "Pyramid" are also high-yielding.

 cultivation

Propagation

Yams are usually planted on banks, mounds or ridges at the end of the dry season while they are still dormant, as they need the long rainy season to develop. Small tubers, bulbils or sections with two to three buds or "eyes" taken from the tops of larger tubers are used for propagation. The latter are preferable, as they sprout quickly and produce higher-yielding plants.

They can be "sprouted" in a shady position before planting 6 in. deep and 12–36 in. apart on mounds 48 in. across or ridges 48 in. apart. Spacing depends on the site, soil and the variety. **Zones 8 to 11.**

Growing

Yams need a humid, tropical climate, 60–70 in. of rain in a 6- to 12-month growing season and a site in sun or partial shade. Soils must be rich, moisture-retentive and free-draining, as yams can survive drought but not waterlogging. Dig in plenty of well-rotted organic matter before planting and grow plants up trellising, arbors, poles or netting at least 6 feet high, or allow them to grow into surrounding trees.

Keep crops weed-free.

Tropical crops do not grow well below 68°F. Growth increases with temperature and the crucial time for rain is 14 to 20 weeks after planting, when food reserves are nearly depleted and the shoots are growing rapidly.

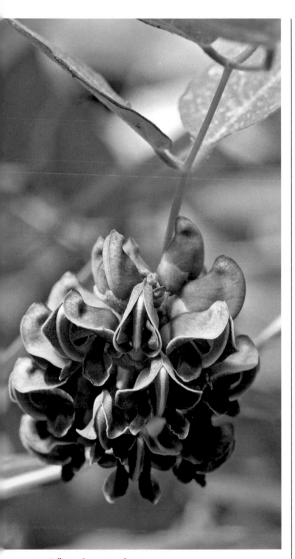

A flowering yam plant

watering during the resting season as the stems die back, gradually increasing the amount in spring when plants resume active growth.

Harvesting and Storing

Depending on the variety and weather conditions, tubers are ready to harvest from 7 to 12 months after planting as the leaves and stems die back. Lift them carefully, as damaged tubers cannot be stored.

Tubers are normally dried on a shaded vertical frame or in an open-sided shed before being stored in a dark, cool, airy place where they can last for several months. Do not store yams at temperatures below 50°F.

Pests and Diseases

Leaf spot appears as brown or black spots on stems and leaves. Storage rot can be a serious problem and yam beetles feed on tubers and damage the shoots of newly planted sets. Scale insect also causes problems.

companion planting

Grows well with taro, ginger, corn, okra and cucurbits.

medicinal

Yams have been used as a diuretic and expectorant.

warning

All yams except *Dioscorea esculenta* contain a toxin, dioscorine, which is destroyed by thorough cooking.

culinary

Yam can be peeled and then boiled, mashed, roasted and fried in oil. In West Africa, they are pounded into *fufu* in a similar way to manioc, and are added to a thick soup made of spices, meat, oil, fish and vegetables. Yams are tasty cooked with palm oil, candied, casseroled with orange juice or curried. They can be peeled and boiled in water with a pinch of salt, then brushed with melted butter and broiled or barbecued until brown; serve with more butter.

In China, they are mashed with lotus root, wrapped in lotus leaves and steamed.

They can also be peeled, rubbed with oil and baked at 350°F for 1 1/2 hours, then slit like a baked potato and eaten with seasoned butter or a similar filling.

Yellow Yam Salad

Serves 6

3 pounds yellow yams
1 large onion, sliced
3 tablespoons chopped chives
1 green bell pepper, seeded and diced
½ cup mayonnaise
½ teaspoon cayenne pepper
Salt and freshly ground black pepper

4 hard-boiled eggs, chopped
1 tablespoon black olives, pitted and sliced

Clean the yams and cook in boiling salted water until tender but firm. Drain and allow to cool slightly, then cut into cubes. Add the onion, chives and bell pepper and mix well.

Season the mayonnaise with the cayenne, salt and pepper and stir into the yam mixture, folding in the eggs and olives carefully.

Check the seasoning. Chill for an hour before serving.

Maintenance

Spring Increase watering as new shoots appear when growing under cover.
Summer Maintain high temperatures and humidity.
Fall Reduce watering as stems turn yellow.
Winter Keep potting mix slightly moist.

Protected Cropping

If you are able to provide an environment and cultural conditions similar to those described under "Growing," yams can be grown indoors. The minimum temperature for active growth is 68°F; dampen greenhouse paths and mist with tepid water during summer, and reduce

Eleocharis dulcis. Cyperaceae

WATER CHESTNUT

Half-hardy aquatic perennial. Value: good source of potassium, B6 and fiber; high in carbohydrates.

Eleocharis dulcis has been cultivated for centuries. It has become naturalized on the edge of paddy fields in China and Southeast Asia, is popular in oriental cuisine and is used for making salt in Zimbabwe. Like the tiger nut and lotus root, the water chestnut is notable for remaining crisp even after cooking or canning — this is because its cell walls are cross-linked and strengthened by the presence of aromatic phenolic compounds that also give plants such as cloves their fragrance.

 varieties

Eleocharis dulcis is a tropical or subtropical marginal plant, with dense tufts of thin, hollow, sedge-like leaves that grow to 3¼ ft. tall.

 cultivation

Propagation
Use water chestnuts bought from specialized suppliers or the market; choose ones free of wrinkles and soft spots. Plant in 6 in. pots of soilless potting mix with the base submerged in warm water in a heated propagator or on a sunny windowsill, at a minimum of 79°F, from midspring. Transfer them into their final position as temperatures rise. Alternatively, plant them by hand directly into their final position, 12–16 in. apart, once the danger of frost has passed.

Growing
Water chestnut needs an open, sunny site and to be grown in water. Use a wading pool, an old bathtub or similar, or create a temporary pond by digging a hole or trench in the ground and lining it with polyethylene. The "pond" should be deep enough to allow an 8 in. layer of loam or garden soil (with a low organic matter content) to be spread over the base with 4 in. of water above. If a wading pool is being used, sweep the standing area before inflating and put a layer of old carpet, corrugated cardboard or similar under the base to prevent it from being punctured by stones.

Plant water chestnut when the soil and water has warmed; a small pond or swimming pool heater boosts water temperatures and is useful in cooler summers. It needs plenty of warmth to grow, at least 6 months in temperatures from 86–95°F is ideal, though it can crop in cooler conditions.

Maintenance
Spring Plant corms in a pot and put in a warm place.
Summer Keep water levels topped up in the container.
Fall Harvest corms.
Winter Store propagation material in damp conditions.

Protected Cropping
In cooler climates, growing in a greenhouse or in polyethene tunnels encourages heavier cropping. Starting crops off under protection, even if they are then grown outdoors, extends the growing season.

Harvesting and Storing
Tubers form from late summer and are ready to harvest when the stems turn yellow and die down in fall. Allow the water to evaporate, then drain any remaining water; it is easier to harvest tubers when soil is moist, rather than waterlogged. Store tubers for propagation the following year in a damp, frost-free place.

Pests and Diseases
There are no problems with pests and diseases.

 medicinal

Chinese herbalists use water chestnuts for sweetening breath. The juice of the tuber is said to be bactericidal.

 culinary

The onion-shaped tubers of the water chestnut are sweet, nutty and crisp. Remove the papery tunic before cooking them, or eating them raw or lightly cooked. A familiar ingredient in Chinese cooking, they can be seasoned or combined with other vegetables and are eaten in chop suey. Soaked lightly in salted water and threaded on to thin bamboo stalks, they are sold by street vendors in China. Dried tubers are ground into flour that is used for thickening, coating vegetables or giving a crispy coating to deep-fried food. They store for up to 2 weeks in a plastic bag in the refrigerator, but are better eaten fresh.

Stir-fried Shrimp with Vegetables
Serves 4

½ pound raw tiger shrimp, peeled
1 teaspoon salt
1 tablespoon egg white
2 tablespoons cornstarch paste
2½ cups vegetable oil
⅓ lb. snow peas
1 carrot, peeled and finely sliced
3 ounces water chestnuts from a can, drained and sliced
3 ounces straw mushrooms from a can, drained and halved lengthwise
2 scallions, cut into ½ in. pieces
2 tablespoons peeled and finely sliced fresh ginger
½ teaspoon sugar
1 tablespoon light soy sauce
2 teaspoons rice wine
A few drops sesame oil

Cut the shrimp in half lengthwise and remove the black vein. Mix the shrimp with the salt, egg white and cornstarch paste.

Heat the oil in a wok, then deep-fry the shrimp for 1 minute until they turn pink. Remove them with a slotted spoon on to some paper towel to drain.

Pour off the oil, leaving roughly 1 tablespoon in the wok. Add the snow peas and carrot and stir-fry for about 1 minute. Then add the rest of the vegetables, the ginger, sugar, soy sauce and rice wine and stir well. Stir-fry for 1 more minute.

Drizzle over the sesame oil and serve piping hot with noodles or boiled rice.

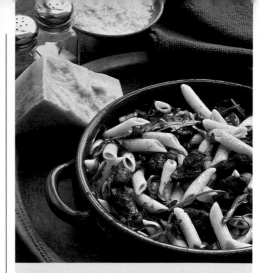

Eruca vesicaria subsp. *sativa.* Brassicaceae

ARUGULA

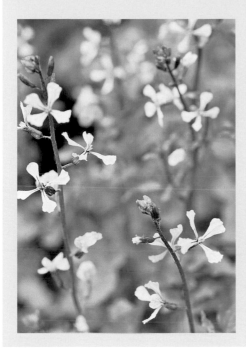

Also known as Rocket Salad, Roquette, Italian Cress, Rucola, Rocket. Annual grown for tender edible leaves. Hardy. Value: high in potassium and vitamin C.

Arugula has been cultivated since Roman times and is native to the Mediterranean and Eastern Asia, though it grows in many areas. *Eruca* **means "downy-stemmed";** *vesicaria,* **"bladder-like," describes the slender seed pods. Introduced to North America by Italian settlers, the spicy leaves were particularly popular in Elizabethan England.**

 ## varieties

Eruca vesicaria subsp. *sativa,* an erect plant growing to 3¼ ft., has hairy stems, broadly toothed leaves and cross-shaped, creamy flowers. "Apollo" and "Runway" are fast growing forms and "Sky Rocket" combines the flavor of wild arugula with the fast growth of salad arugula.

 ## cultivation

Propagation
Sow seed successionally every 2 to 3 weeks, from midspring to early summer, in rows ½ in. deep and 12 in. apart. Thin when large enough to handle, until 6 in. apart. Arugula germinates at fairly low temperatures. In warmer climates sow in winter or early spring. **Zones 3 to 9.**

Growing
Arugula needs rich, moisture-retentive soil in partial shade. It may need extra shading in hot weather, otherwise it produces less palatable leaves. Keep weed-free and water regularly.

Maintenance
Spring Sow seeds from midspring; thin when large enough to handle.
Summer Continue sowing until midsummer. Water and feed as necessary. Harvest regularly to encourage tender growth and keep from bolting.
Fall Harvest, prepare the ground for the following year's sowing and sow seeds for protected crops.
Winter Harvest winter crops.

Protected Cropping
Although arugula is a hardy plant, protect against severe frosts with cloches. Sow fall/winter crops from late summer in a cool greenhouse, cold frame, or under cloches.

Harvesting
Plants are ready to harvest after 6 to 8 weeks. Pick frequently to encourage a regular supply of good-quality leaves and to prevent plants from running to seed in hot weather. Discard any damaged leaves. Either pull leaves as required or treat as a "cut and come again" crop, cutting the plant 1 in. above the ground.

Pests and Diseases
Arugula is usually trouble-free, but flea beetle can damage seedlings. Protect with floating row cover or mesh.

 ## culinary

The increasingly popular leaves are delicious in salads — younger leaves are milder. They can be lightly boiled or steamed, added to sauces, stir-fried, sautéed in olive oil and tossed with pasta. The flowers are edible and can decorate salads.

Penne with Merguez and Arugula
Serves 4

1 pound penne
2 tablespoons olive oil
⅔ lb. merguez sausages, cut into bite-size pieces
1 red onion, thinly sliced
2 tablespoons dry white wine
12 cherry tomatoes, halved
3 ounces arugula leaves, washed and shredded
Salt and freshly ground black pepper
¼ cup freshly grated Parmesan

Bring a pan of salted water to a boil and cook the penne. Meanwhile, heat the oil in a large skillet, add the merguez and onion and fry for 2 to 3 minutes. Add the wine and simmer for 10 minutes. Then add the tomatoes. When the pasta is cooked, drain well and toss in the sauce with the arugula. Mix well, season and serve at once with Parmesan.

 ## container growing

Arugula is not the perfect plant for pots, but it can be grown in a soil-based potting mix with low fertilizer levels with added peat-substitute compost. Sow seed *in situ.* Water thoroughly.

 ## medicinal

Young leaves are said to be a good tonic and are used in cough medicine. Dioscorides described arugula as "a digestive and good for ye belly."

Foeniculum vulgare var. *azoricum.* Apiaceae

FENNEL

Also known as Florence Fennel, Sweet Fennel, Finocchio. Biennial or perennial grown as annual for pungent swollen leaf bases, leaves and seeds. Half hardy. Value: good source of potassium; small amounts of beta carotene.

This outstanding vegetable with a strong aniseed flavor, swollen leafbases (known as "bulbs") the texture of tender celery, and delicate feathery leaves has been cultivated for centuries as an ornamental vegetable. Its close relative, wild fennel, which lacks the swollen base, is used as an herb. When Portuguese explorers first landed on Madeira in 1418, they found the air fragrant with the aroma of wild fennel, so the city of Funchal was named after *funcho*, the Portuguese name for the plant. Florence fennel was popular with the Greeks and Romans, whose soldiers ate it to maintain good health — while the ladies used it to ward off obesity. In medieval times, seeds were eaten during Lent to alleviate hunger, and dieters still chew raw stalks to suppress their appetite. The first records of its cultivation in England date from the early 18th century, when the third Earl of Peterborough cultivated and ate it as a dessert.

In 1824 Thomas Jefferson received seeds from the American consul in Livorno and sowed them in his garden in Virginia. He enthused: "Fennel is beyond every other vegetable, delicious … perfectly white. No vegetable equals it in flavor." However, it has become a weed in those countries where conditions are particularly favorable.

 varieties

"Amigo" is early cropping and vigorous with medium, white bulbs. "Heracles" is fast-maturing and produces top-quality bulbs. "Perfection," a French variety, has medium-sized bulbs and a delicate aniseed flavor. Resistant to bolting, it is ideal for early sowing. "Pronto" is an early variety with round, white bulbs. "Sirio," from Italy, is compact with large, sweet white bulbs and matures rapidly. "Sweet Florence" is moderately sized and should be sown from midspring to late summer. "Victoria" produces dense, top-quality, greenish-white bulbs. "Zefa Fino" is particularly vigorous and ornamental with uniform bulbs of excellent quality.

 cultivation

Propagation
Fennel thrives in a warm climate and is inclined to bolt prematurely if growth is checked by cold, drought or transplanting. For early sowings, choose cultivars that are bolt-resistant.

Grow successionally from late spring to late summer for summer and fall crops. Sow thinly in rows ½ in. deep and 18–20 in. apart, thinning when seedlings are large enough to handle to a final spacing of 9–12 in. apart.

Where possible, fennel is better sown *in situ* to reduce problems with bolting. Flats are preferred for plants started under cover. Growing in trays is fine if transplants are treated carefully enough. **Zones 4 to 10.**

Growing
Fennel flourishes in temperate to subtropical climates, though mature plants can withstand light frosts. The largest bulbs are formed during warm, sunny summers. Plants should be grown as rapidly as possible, so incorporate a slow-release general fertilizer into the soil before planting at 1–2 oz/sq. yd.

Plants need a sunny, warm, sheltered position and well-drained, moisture-retentive, slightly alkaline soil. A light, sandy soil with well-rotted organic matter dug in the winter before planting is ideal. Stony soils and heavy clays should be avoided. Never allow the soil to

A fine filigree of fennel foliage

dry out; mulch in spring and hand weed around bulbs to avoid damage.

When the stem bases start to swell, hill soil to half their height to blanch and sweeten the bulbs. Or tie cardboard "collars" round the base.

Maintenance

Spring Sow early crops under cover. Warm the soil with cloches before sowing early crops outdoors.
Summer Keep the soil constantly moist and weed-free. Harvest mature bulbs.
Fall Cover later crops in order to prolong the growing season.
Winter Transplant later sowings for an early winter crop.

Protected Cropping

Cover early outdoor crops with cloches. Sow from midspring, in cell-packs or trays of seed compost at 60°F. Pot seedlings grown in trays when very small, with a maximum of four leaves, into 3 in. peat pots. Transplant in the pots a month after hardening off.

Harden off and plant out those grown in cell-packs at a similar size. Late sowings can be made for transplanting under cover in early winter. Plants do not always produce "bulbs," but the leaves and stems can still be used in cooking.

Harvesting and Storing

Harvest about 15 weeks after sowing or 2 to 4 weeks after hilling, when the bulbs are about 2–3 in. across and slightly larger than a tennis ball. Cut the bulb with a sharp knife, just above the ground, and the stump should resprout, producing small sprigs of ferny foliage. Bulbs do not store and should be eaten when fresh.

Leaves can be harvested throughout summer and used fresh in salads, or deep-frozen.

Pests and Diseases

Slugs can damage young plants. Lack of water, fluctuating temperatures and transplanting can cause bolting.

 companion planting

Allow a few plants to flower; they are extremely attractive to a large number of beneficial insects which prey on garden pests.

Fennel has a detrimental effect on beans, kohlrabi and tomatoes.

 container growing

Grow single plants in a container at least 10 in. wide by 12 in. deep containing soilless potting mix with added sharp sand. Apply a general liquid fertilizer monthly from late spring to late summer.

 medicinal

An infusion aids wind, colic, urinary disorders and constipation. Recent research indicates that fennel may reduce the effects of alcohol.

Use in an eye bath or as a compress to reduce inflammation. Chew to sweeten breath or infuse as a mouthwash or gargle for gum disease and sore throats, to alleviate hunger and ease indigestion.

 warning

Do not take excessive doses of the oil; nor should it be given to pregnant women.

 culinary

Use bulbs in the same way as celery, removing green stalks and outer leaves. For salads, slice inner leaf stalks and chill before serving. (To ensure that bulbs are crisp, slice and place in a bowl of water and ice cubes in the refrigerator for an hour.)

Fennel can be parboiled with leeks and is suitable for egg and fish dishes. Steam, broil or boil and serve with cheese sauce or butter. Infuse fresh leaves in oil or vinegar, add to a bouquet garni or snip as a garnish over soups or salads. Gives characteristic flavor to *finocchiona*, an Italian salami, and the French liqueur, *fenouillette*.

Fennel Sautéed with Peas and Red Bell Peppers
Serves 4

2 tablespoons olive oil
2 sweet red bell peppers, seeded and cut in strips
1 pound fennel, trimmed and finely sliced
2 cloves garlic, crushed
½ pound peas, shelled
Salt and freshly ground black pepper

In a wok or heavy-bottomed skillet heat the oil, add the bell peppers and fennel and cook for 10 to 15 minutes over a moderate heat until crunchy, stirring occasionally. Add the garlic and peas and continue cooking for 2 minutes. Season and serve.

Glycine max (syn. *Glycine soja*). Leguminosae

SOY BEAN

Also known as Edamame, Soya Bean. Annual grown for seed sprouts and seeds. Half hardy. Value: rich in potassium, protein, fiber, vitamins E, B and iron. Seed sprouts are rich in vitamin C.

One of the most nutritious of all vegetables, this Asian native is thought to have been the plant that Chinese emperor Shen Nung used to introduce people to the art of cultivation. It is mentioned in his *Materia Medica* from around 2900 BCE. Soy beans were first known in Europe through Engelbert Kaempfer, physician to the governor of the Dutch East India company on an island off Japan in 1690–92. The Japanese guarded their culture, but, by bribing the guards and picking plants along the route, Kaempfer was able to get his botanical specimens. Benjamin Franklin sent seeds back from France to North America in the late 18th century. One of the first Americans to be interested in soy beans was Henry Ford, who saw their potential for manufactured goods and is said to have eaten soy beans at every meal, had a suit made from "soy fabric" and sponsored a 16-course soy bean dinner at the 1934 "Century of Progress" show in Chicago.

 varieties

Glycine max is an herb, usually with trilobed leaves and white to pale violet flowers. The pods, containing two to four seeds, are mainly on the lower parts of the stem. "Black Jet" is early-maturing and one of the best. The seeds have a good flavor and it is ideal for a short growing season. "Friskeby V," a Swedish variety, is ideal for cool climates and "Hakucho Early," an early dwarf Japanese variety, produces three small seeds per pod but is high yielding. "Lammer's Black" is the best bean for short seasons, producing heavy crops of thin-skinned, tasty seeds. Perhaps the earliest green soybean is the 2-foot-tall "Envy," good for fresh shelling or drying. "Butterbean" is said to be the finest tasting of all.

 cultivation

Propagation
Sow when danger of frost has passed and the soil has warmed. Sow two to three seeds 1 in. deep in heavy soil and 1¼ in. deep in lighter soils in hills 3–4 in. apart with 18–24 in. between rows. After germination, thin, leaving the strongest seedling. Alternatively, sow thinly and thin to the final spacing when large enough. **Zones 4 to 10.**

Sprouting Seed
Seeds can also be sprouted. Use untreated seed and remove any that are damaged or moldy. Soak overnight in cold water. The following morning rinse them thoroughly. Put a layer of moist paper towel over the base of a flat-bottomed bowl or "seed sprouter." Spread over a layer of soya beans ½ in. deep and cover with plastic wrap. Exclude light by putting the bowl in a dark cupboard or wrapping it in newspaper or tinfoil. Temperatures should be 68–75°F. Check that the absorbent layer stays damp, rinsing morning and night. They should be ready to harvest in 4 to 10 days, when shoots are 1–2 in. long. Remove sprouts from the shell, and rinse well before eating.

Growing
Soya beans flourish in an open site with rich, free-draining soil and a pH of 5.7 to 6.2, although there are now cultivars to suit most soils. Where necessary, lime soils and dig in well-rotted organic matter before planting. They are not frost hardy;

Just a little taster

they prefer 68–75°F; exceeding 100°F may retard growth. Keep plants well watered during drought and early stages of growth. Remove weeds regularly, or suppress by mulching in spring.

Maintenance

Spring Sow seeds under cover or outdoors when there is no danger of frost.

Summer Keep crops weed-free. Water during drought.

Fall Harvest before the pods are completely ripe.

Winter Hang in bunches in a cool shed and collect seed when the pods open.

Protected Cropping

In cooler climates, sow seeds in pots, packs or trays of seed potting mix, planting out when the soil is warm. Harden off before transplanting and protect under cloches until established. In cooler climates, sow crops in a heated greenhouse.

Harvesting and Storing

Soy needs a hot summer and fine fall for the seeds to ripen. Harvesting should be carefully timed so that the seeds are ripe but the pods have not yet split. If conditions are unfavorable, pull up plants when the pods turn yellow and hang up to ripen in a dry place. Do not harvest when plants are wet, as the seeds are easily bruised. Harvest for green beans as soon as pods are plump and the seeds are almost full size.

Pests and Diseases

Fungal diseases can be a problem if plants are harvested when wet and pods are bruised or broken.

 container growing

This is only worth growing in containers as a "novelty" crop. Use 8–10 in. pots and soilless potting mix with moderate fertilizer levels, adding well-rotted organic matter. Keep well watered and weed-free.

 other uses

Soy oil is used in a range of products, including ice cream, margarine, soaps, and paint; milk substitute is made from the crushed beans, and fermented they make soy sauce and tofu, and also Worcestershire sauce. Also firefighting foam and meat substitute. A valuable plant indeed!

 medicinal

Said to control blood sugar levels, lower cholesterol, regulate the bowels, and relieve constipation.

 warning

Soy beans should be cooked before drying; they can cause stomach upset.

 culinary

Used mainly when green or sprouted for salads or stir-fries. Remove shell by plunging into boiling salted water for 5 minutes, then allow to cool and squeeze out the seeds. Cook for 15 minutes, then sauté with butter. Juvenile pods can be cooked and eaten whole.

Soak dried beans before eating. A shortcut is to cover with water in a kettle, boil for 2 minutes, allow to stand for 1 hour, then cook until tender.

Soy Bean and Walnut Croquettes

Serves 4

4 ounces soy beans, soaked and well rinsed
1 onion, finely minced
1 clove garlic, crushed
5 teaspoons butter
1¼ cup walnuts, whizzed in the liquidizer
½ teaspoon dried thyme
½ cup wholewheat breadcrumbs
1 tablespoon tomato paste
2 tablespoons chopped fresh parsley
½ teaspoon mace
1 egg
Salt and freshly ground black pepper

Wholewheat flour
1 egg, beaten
Dried breadcrumbs
Vegetable oil, for frying

Cook the beans until very tender, drain, then mash with a fork, enough to break them up. Fry the onion and garlic in the butter for 10 minutes, then remove from the heat and stir in the beans. Add the walnuts and thyme, together with the breadcrumbs, tomato paste, parsley, mace, and egg. (You may need to add more liquid; otherwise use fewer breadcrumbs.) Mix well and season to taste.

Using your hands, shape into small croquettes, then roll in the flour, dip into the egg and roll in the crumbs. Fry in hot oil until crisp and drain on paper towel. Serve hot. Particularly good with a spicy tomato sauce.

Helianthus tuberosus. Asteraceae
JERUSALEM ARTICHOKE

Also known as Girasole, Sunchoke. Tall perennial for edible tubers. Hardy. Value: high in carbohydrate but mostly inulin, turning to fructose in storage; moderate vitamin B1, B5, low in calories.

This vegetable is not from Jerusalem, nor is it any relative of the globe artichoke. "Jerusalem" is said to be a corruption of the Italian *girasole* or "sunflower" — a close relative; the nutty-flavored tubers were thought to taste similar to globe artichokes, hence the adoption of that name. Frost-hardy, these tall, upright perennials are native to North America, where they grow in damp places. The tubers contain a carbohydrate which causes flatulence; in 1621 John Goodyear wrote that "they stirre and cause a filthie loathsome wind within the bodie." In the 1920s they were a commercial source of fructose and were expected to replace beet and cane as a source of sugar.

 ## varieties

"Boston Red" has large, knobbly tubers with rose-red skin. "Dwarf Sunray" is a short-stemmed, crisp, tender variety that does not need peeling. It flowers freely and is good for the ornamental border. "French Mammoth White" is round, white-skinned and frost-hardy. "Fuseau," a traditional French variety, has long, smooth, white tubers. The plants are compact, reaching 4½ to 6 ft. "Gerrard," purple-skinned and round, is smooth and easy to peel. "Golden Nugget" has tubers that are good for slicing. "Originals" produces traditional rounded tubers and also makes an excellent windbreak or temporary screen in the garden. "Stampede" is a quick-maturing variety with large tubers and is also very cold hardy. The tubers of "Sun Choke" have a fresh nutty flavor and are excellent raw in salads, cooked or creamed.

 ## cultivation

Jerusalem artichokes prefer a sunny position, but will grow in shade. They tolerate most soils, though tubers are small on poor ground; the best are grown on sandy, moisture-retentive soil.

They will grow in heavy clay provided it is not extremely acid or subject to winter waterlogging. The fibrous root system makes them useful for breaking up uncultivated ground. The tall stems make excellent temporary screens or windbreaks in sheltered areas, but need staking in more exposed sites. **Zones 4 to 11.**

Propagation
Tubers bought from the grocery store can be used for planting. Choose tubers the size of hen's eggs, and plant from early to late spring, when the soil becomes workable, 4–6 in. deep, 12 in. apart and 36 in. between rows; cover the tubers carefully. During harvest, save a few tubers to replant or leave some in the soil to sprout the following year.

Growing
Incorporate organic matter in fall or early winter before planting. Hill up the base of stems to improve stability when plants are 12 in. high. Water during dry weather. Remove flower buds as they appear. Shorten stems to 5–6 ft. in late summer to stop them from being blown over; on windy sites they may also need staking. On

JERUSALEM ARTICHOKE

Jerusalem artichoke makes a wonderful windbreak

poor soil, feed with liquid general fertilizer every 2 to 3 weeks.

Maintenance

Spring Plant tubers.
Summer Keep weed-free, water and stake if necessary. Remove flower buds.
Fall Cut back stems and begin harvesting.
Winter Save tubers for next year's crop.

Harvesting and Storing

In fall, as the foliage turns yellow, cut back stems to within 3–6 in. of the ground. Use the cut stems as a mulch to protect the soil from frost, making lifting easier; alternatively, cover with straw.

Lift tubers from late fall to midwinter. They keep better in the ground, but in cold climates or on heavy ground, lift in early winter and store for up to 5 months in a cool cellar in moist peat substitute or sand.

Pests and Diseases

Slugs tend to hollow out tubers. Set traps, aluminum sulfate pellets, or pick off manually.

Sclerotinia rot causes stem bases to become covered with fluffy white mold. Lift and burn diseased plants; water healthy plants with fungicide. Cutworms eat stems at ground level; damaged plants wilt. Keep crops weed-free, cultivate well or sprinkle an appropriate insecticide in the soil before planting.

 medicinal

The carbohydrate inulin is difficult to digest; tubers are low calorie and suitable for diabetics.

 warning

Jerusalem artichokes can become invasive. After harvesting, lift even the smallest tuber from the ground.

 culinary

Jerusalem artichokes are versatile vegetables when the weather is cold: they can be kept in the ground until you want to cook them and then dug up root by root. Fresh tubers have a better flavor, but they become more digestible if stored; they will keep in a plastic bag in the salad drawer of the fridge for anywhere up to 6 months.

There is no need to peel them painstakingly unless you want a very smooth, creamy-white purée — the vitamins are, after all, just below the skin. (If you do want them peeled, steaming or boiling knobby varieties makes the job easier.) To serve as a vegetable, scrub tubers immediately after picking, boil for 20 to 25 minutes in their skins in water with a teaspoon of vinegar; peel before serving if desired. The addition of a little grated nutmeg always does wonders in bringing out the unusual flavor.

To make rissoles, form boiled, mashed artichokes into flat cakes and deep-fry. Jerusalem artichokes can also be fried, baked, roasted or stewed — or eaten raw. Artichokes gratinéed in a sauce made with good,

strong cheddar make an excellent accompaniment to plain meat dishes such as baked ham or roast lamb. Parboil the artichokes and drain when they are just tender. Roughly slice and layer into a dish. Pour over a béchamel sauce flavored with French mustard and well-matured cheese and bake in a hot oven (400°F) until browned.

Artichoke Soup

Serves 4

1 pound Jerusalem artichokes
2 tablespoons olive oil
2 large onions, sliced
1 large clove garlic, crushed
2½ cups chicken stock
Strip of orange peel
Salt and freshly ground black pepper
4 tablespoons thick cream

Scrub the artichokes, discard any hard knobs and roughly chop. Heat the oil in a heavy-bottomed pan and add the onions. Cook until translucent, add the garlic, continue cooking for a couple of minutes and add the artichokes. Toss well to coat with oil and pour in the chicken stock. Bring to a boil, add the orange peel and

season. Cover and simmer for 15 to 20 minutes, until cooked. Remove from the heat, discard the peel and blend in a food processor. Return to the pan, adjust the seasoning, stir in the cream and serve.

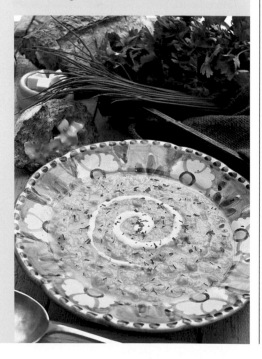

OKRA

Hibiscus esculentus (syn. *Abelmoschus esculentus*). Malvaceae

Also known as Lady's Fingers, Bhindi, Gumbo. Annual grown for its edible pods. Tender. Value: rich in calcium, iron, potassium, vitamin C, and fiber.

The okra, a close relative of the ornamental hibiscus, with slender edible pods, has been cultivated for centuries. It is thought to have originated in northern Africa around the upper Nile and Ethiopia, spreading eastwards to Saudi Arabia and to India. One of the earliest records of it — growing in Egypt — describes the plant, its cultivation and uses. It was introduced to the Caribbean and southern North America by slaves who brought the crop from Africa; the name "gumbo" comes from a Portuguese corruption of the plant's Angolan common name.

 ## varieties

"Cow Horn" has a good flavor and texture and is slow to go fibrous. "Clemson Spineless" is a popular, reliable variety with high yields of dark, fleshy pods over a long period. It grows well under cover. "Dwarf Green Long Pod" is only about 3 ft. tall but crops well, producing dark green, spineless pods. "Emerald" grows prolifically, with deep green pods on tall plants. It sets pods early and is slow to go "seedy." "Little Lucy" a dwarf variety growing to 2 ft. is ideal for containers. Its attractive flowers and 4 in. pods are held erect above the plant. "Mammoth Spineless Long Pod" is vigorous and high yielding, with pods that stay tender for a long time. It is excellent fresh or canned. "Red Velvet," another spectacular red variety, is vigorous, reaching 4–5 ft. "Star of David," an Israeli variety growing to 6–8 ft. tall, is very tasty and high-yielding. The pods grow to 9 in. long, but are better eaten when small; great in soups and stews.

 ## cultivation

A garden plant for the tropics and warm temperate climates, okra can be tried outdoors in cooler climates during hot summers, though success is better guaranteed if it is sown under cover. **Zones 4 to 11.**

Propagation

Soak the seeds in warm water for 24 hours before planting. My friend Robert Fleming, who gardens in Memphis, Tennessee, has been successful with several other methods that reduce germination time from 15 to 5 days: soak the seed in bleach for 45 to 60 minutes, rinse, then plant; pour boiling water over seed, soak overnight, then plant; or place three seeds in each section of an ice-cube tray, allow to freeze for a few hours, then plant.

When soil temperatures are about 60°F, sow seeds in rows about 24 in. apart, leaving the same distance between plants. Alternatively, sow in hills 8–12 in. apart, thinning to leave the strongest seedling. Plant seedlings grown in trays or cell-packs into 3 in. pots when they are large enough to handle and later harden them off ready for transplanting when they are about 4–6 in. tall.

Growing

Okra needs a rich, fertile, well-drained soil, so incorporate organic matter several weeks before sowing. Put a stake in place before transplanting and tie in the plant as it grows, pinching out the growing tip on the main stems when plants are around 9–12 in. tall to encourage bushy growth. Apply a general liquid fertilizer until plants become established, then change to a liquid high-potash feed every 2 weeks or sprinkle sulfate of potash around the plant base. In cool temperate conditions, warm the soil for several days before planting outdoors, spacing plants 24 in. apart once the danger of frost has passed.

Maintenance

Spring Sow seeds under cover or outdoors in warmer climates when the soil is warm enough. Pinch out the

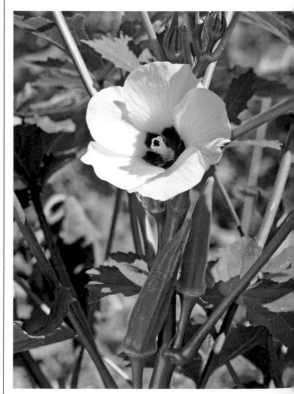

Okra growing in Southern India

growth tips as they appear.

Summer Water, feed, and tie in plants to their supporting stakes. Keep crops weed-free. Harvest young pods.

Fall Protect outdoor crops in cooler zones to extend the cropping season.

Winter Prepare the ground for the following season.

Protected Cropping

In cooler climates, plant okra in heated greenhouses or polyethene tunnels from early spring, waiting until midspring if heat is not provided. Plant them about 24 in. apart in beds or borders. Insert a supporting stake before planting.

Temperatures should be a minimum of 70°F with moderate humidity. Feed plants every 2 weeks with a liquid general fertilizer, changing to a high-potash fertilizer once they are established.

Harvesting and Storing

Harvest with a sharp knife or scissors while seed pods are young, picking regularly for a constant supply of new pods. Handle gently: the soft skin marks easily. Pods keep for up to 10 days wrapped in a plastic bag in the salad drawer of the fridge.

Pests and Diseases

Precautions should be taken against heavy infestations of aphids, which weaken and distort growth, and powdery mildew, which stunts growth and, in severe cases, causes death. This is more of a problem when plants are underwatered. Whitefly can cause yellowing, stickiness and mold formation on the leaves. They form clusters on the leaf undersides and fly into the air when the foliage is disturbed.

companion planting

Okra flourishes when it is grown with melons and cucumbers, as it enjoys the same conditions.

container growing

Okra can be grown in 10 in. pots or growing bags, in peat-substitute potting mix, under cover or outdoors. Water regularly and feed every 2 weeks with a high potassium liquid fertilizer during the growing season.

medicinal

The mucilage from okra is effectively used as a demulcent, soothing inflammation. In India, infusions of the pods are used to treat urinogenital problems as well as chest infections.

Okra is also added as an ingredient of artificial blood plasma products.

culinary

Okra is used in soups, stews, and curries, can be sautéed or fried and eaten to accompany meat or poultry. To deep-fry, remove the stalks, trim round the "cone" near the base, simmer for about 10 minutes, drain and dry each pod, then deep-fry until crisp. In the Middle East, pods are soaked in lemon juice and salt, then fried and eaten as a vegetable. In Indian cooking, bhindi is used as a vegetable or as a bhaji to accompany curries.

Okra should not be cooked in iron, brass or copper pans, otherwise it will discolor.

Overcooked, the pods become very slimy. Any "gluey" texture can be overcome by adding a little lemon juice to the pan and the fine, velvety covering over the pod can easily be removed by scrubbing the pod gently under running water.

Okra can also be eaten raw in salads or used as a "dip." Wash pods, carefully trimming off the ends. To reduce stickiness, soak them for about 30 minutes in water with a dash of lemon juice, then drain, rinse and dry.

Okra seed oil is also used in cooking.

Gumbo
Serves 4

This spicy Creole dish is known for its good use of okra.

1 pound okra
1 tablespoon olive oil
½ pound cooked ham, cubed
1½ cup onion, finely sliced
1 cup celery, chopped
1 red bell pepper, seeded and chopped
2 teaspoons tomato paste
1 pound tomatoes, skinned and chopped
1 dried chile, finely minced
Salt and freshly ground black pepper

Trim the stalk ends of the okra to expose the seeds, then soak for 30 minutes in acidified water.

In the meantime, heat the oil and gently cook the ham, onion, celery, and bell pepper until the onion begins to color. Add the tomato paste, tomatoes, and dried chile, mix in well, and cook over high heat for a minute or so.

Stir in the drained okra and seasonings. Cover and cook gently until stewed. Add a little water if the mixture gets dry. Serve with plain broiled chicken.

Ipomoea aquatica. Convolvulaceae
WATER SPINACH

Also known as Swamp Cabbage, Aquatic Morning Glory, Bindweed, Water Convolvulus, Kangkong, Ung Choi, Rau Muong, Entsai Water Spinach. Tropical aquatic/semi-aquatic perennial. Value: high in vitamin A, calcium, phosphorus and potassium.

This close relative of the sweet potato has a long history of cultivation in southeastern China, probably originated in southern India, grows throughout the tropics and has become a pestilent weed, now banned, in America. Once a staple crop of the poor in Vietnam, it gradually became an important ingredient of Vietnamese cuisine and has potential as a food crop for rabbits grown for meat production in Cambodia. It was first mentioned in *Nanfang Zaomu Zhuang*, a Vietnamese botanical work of the 5th century CE, and is a worthwhile "novelty" crop for those who like to grow horticultural and culinary oddities.

"Pak Quat" flowers

 varieties

There are two types: "Ching Quat" is narrow leaved with green stems and white flowers, "Pak Quat" has broad, arrow-shaped leaves, white stems and pink flowers. The former is more cold-tolerant and robust; the latter is of better culinary quality.

 cultivation

Propagation

In temperate climates they are best grown from seed sown just below the surface of soilless potting mix at 72°F; plant several seeds in a 9 in. pot, standing in a tray of tepid water from midspring. Alternatively, sow directly into their final position from midspring or start off in packs, transplanting to the final position when they are at least 4 in. high. They can also be propagated from 12 in. long stem cuttings with five or more joints on the stem and the basal cut just below a node, in water or damp sand.

Growing

Water spinach can be grown as an aquatic or in waterlogged potting mix or rich soil, in a sheltered, sunny site. It stops growing and starts flowering as day length shortens, so is grown as an annual. Transplant seedlings into soilless potting mix in an old sink or wading pool, topped up with water, depending on the volume required. Temperatures should be around 77°F from midspring. Growth stops below 50°F and lower temperatures can be damaging to water spinach. Plants grown in soil should be spaced in blocks, with

WATER SPINACH

A farmer in Vietnam collecting water spinach plants

Harvesting and Storing

Harvest regularly, removing the tips to encourage tender regrowth or cut back plants to within a few inches of the base to encourage regrowth of young, tender shoots. Towards the end of the season, the whole plant can be lifted for harvesting.

Pests and Diseases

None in cooler climates; they suffer from the same diseases as sweet potato in warmer climates.

 container growing

Grow plants in old sinks or wading pools of water to ensure plenty of soft, tender growth.

 medicinal

In Burma, the plant is used as an emetic for opium poisoning; also used as a diuretic and to treat constipation.

around 6 in. between rows. Keep the soil moist, or growth becomes coarse. Add well-rotted potting mix to aid water retention.

Maintenance

Spring Sow seeds and take cuttings.
Summer Keep potting mix moist and water levels topped up. Harvest regularly.

Fall Harvest regularly.
Winter Buy seed for next year.

Protected Cropping

Water spinach is best grown in a plastic tunnel or greenhouse in cooler climates.

 culinary

Use immediately after harvesting, as the water-filled stems wilt rapidly. Water spinach is used extensively in Chinese and Malayan cuisine. It is mucilaginous, slightly sweet and takes up the surrounding flavors during cooking. The crispy stems are made into a pickle in the Philippines. The edible young shoots and leaves are eaten raw or cooked and eaten like spinach. Eat water spinach as the Chinese do, with fermented bean curd or shrimp sauce; it can also be fried with garlic, chiles and dried shrimp or with squid and sweet, spicy sauce.

Chicken and Water Spinach with Spicy Peanut Sauce
Serves 4

1⅓ lbs. water spinach, stems discarded, washed
  and dried
2 cooked chicken breasts, shredded
1 tablespoon oil

3 cloves garlic, finely minced
1 tablespoon Thai red curry paste
½ cup thick coconut milk
1 tablespoon fish sauce (nam pla)
1 teaspoon palm sugar, finely shaved,
  or brown sugar
4 tablespoons dry-roasted peanuts, coarsely ground
Salt

In a large pot of boiling water quickly blanch the water spinach for about 2 minutes. Drain and cool it under running water to stop the cooking process, then drain again. Arrange on a large platter and sprinkle with the shredded chicken.

Heat the oil in a small pan and stir-fry the garlic for a minute or so until fragrant, then add the red curry paste and continue cooking for another 30 seconds. Pour in the coconut milk and bring up to simmering point. Stir in the fish sauce and the sugar, then add the peanuts, seasoning with salt to taste.

Pour over the water spinach and chicken and serve.

Ipomoea batatas. Convolvulaceae
SWEET POTATO

Also known as Kumara, Louisiana Yam, Yellow Yam, Yam. Trailing perennials grown as annuals for starchy roots and leaves. Tender. Value: excellent source of beta carotene, rich in carbohydrates, moderate potassium and vitamins B and C. Yellow and orange types rich in vitamin A.

The "sweet potato" is unrelated to the "Irish" potato and the "yam" but is a relative of the bindweed, in the Morning Glory family. The names became interchangeable when the USDA (United States Department of Agriculture) ruled that canned sweet potatoes must also be labeled as yams. Sweet potato was cultivated in prehistoric Peru and is now found throughout the tropics; it is also a staple crop in Polynesia. Its arrival there is something of a mystery; some suggest it was taken there by Polynesians who visited South America, others think it arrived on vines clinging to logs swept out to sea. It was cultivated in Polynesia before 1250 and reached New Zealand by the 14th century. Columbus observed sweet potato growing in the West Indies and introduced it to Spain, where it was widely cultivated, predating the "Irish" potato by nearly half a century, and De Soto later found sweet potato in what is now Louisiana. Native Americans were reportedly growing sweet potato in present-day Georgia when English settlers arrived. It was grown in Virginia in 1648.

Closely related to Morning Glory

 varieties

There are hundreds of sweet potato varieties worldwide. They are classified under three groups: dry and mealy-fleshed, soft and moist-fleshed, and coarse-fleshed types used as animal feed. White or pale types are floury with a chestnut-caramel flavor, while yellow and orange varieties are sweet and watery.

"Centennial" grows vigorously (to 16 ft.) and prolifically in short seasons. Its high-quality tubers have bright copper-orange skin and deep orange flesh. The deep orange flesh of "Georgia Jet" has a superb flavor. It matures early and is very reliable. "T65" has creamy-white flesh and is the most reliable in cool climates. "Beauregard Improved" is a virus-free clone, smaller than T65, but with orange flesh and a more pronounced flavor. "Tokatoka Gold" is large, rounded and smooth-textured, and popular in New Zealand.

 cultivation

Propagation
Take cuttings from healthy shoots 8–10 in. long. Cut just below a leaf joint, remove basal leaves. Alternatively, pack several healthy tubers in a tray of moist and sharp sand, vermiculite or perlite in a warm greenhouse, or plant into hotbeds. When shoots reach 9–12 in. , cut them off 2 in. above the soil and take the cuttings as described above. Three potatoes should produce about 24 cuttings, enough for a 30 ft. row.
Zones 5 to 11.

SWEET POTATO

 culinary

A sweet potato contains roughly one and a half times the calories and vitamin C of the "Irish" potato. Before cooking, wash carefully and peel or cook whole. Parboil and cut into "fries," grate raw and make into fritters or roast with a joint of meat.

Glazed with butter, brown sugar and orange juice, sweet potatoes accompany Thanksgiving dinner. In Latin America and the Caribbean they are used in spiced puddings, casseroles, soufflés and sweetmeats. The leaves can be steamed.

Tzimmes
Serves 4

This one-pot meal is based on Olga Phklebin's recipe from *Russian Cooking* but adapted to our ingredients.

1 to 2 sweet potatoes, depending on size
2 large potatoes
Olive oil

2 pounds stewing steak, cubed
1 large onion, chopped
2 carrots, chopped
3 cups vegetable stock
3 tablespoons honey
½ teaspoon ground cinnamon
1 tablespoon all-purpose flour
Chopped fresh parsley, to garnish
Salt and freshly ground black pepper

Peel both sorts of potato and cut roughly. Heat the oil in a heavy pan and sauté the meat well to brown it on all sides. Remove from the pan and keep warm. Brown the onion, adding the carrots and the meat and sufficient stock to cover. Season with salt and pepper and bring to a boil, then simmer for 45 minutes.

Stir in the potatoes, the honey, cinnamon and more seasoning if required. Bring back to a boil and simmer for an additional 45 minutes, covered. If the stew is too liquid, allow it to boil fast at this stage. Remove ⅓ cup of the stock and mix with the flour. Pour this back into the pot, bring to a boil and cook for an additional

30 minutes or until the meat is tender and the potatoes are cooked. Sprinkle with parsley and serve with a green salad.

In the humid tropics and subtropics, cuttings are rooted *in situ* at the start of the rainy season. Plant on ridges 6–12 in. high and 3–5 ft. apart. Just below the ridge top, insert cuttings 9–12 in. apart, leaving half of the stem exposed. Or plant small tubers 3–4 in. deep along the top of the ridge. On sandy, free-draining soil plant cuttings and tubers on level ground.

Growing
Sweet potatoes thrive in a tropical or subtropical climate with an annual temperature of 70–77°F. Light frost kills leaves and damages tubers. Ideal annual rainfall is 30–48 in., with wet weather in the growing period and dry conditions for the tubers to ripen. Tuber production is fastest and sugar production highest when day lengths exceed 14 hours.

Soils should be moisture-retentive and free-draining with a pH of 5.5 to 6.5. If necessary, dig in well-rotted organic matter before planting. In cool climates, plant cuttings outdoors when there is no danger of frost. Plant through black polyethene after hardening off. Once established, sprinkle a high-potash granular fertilizer around plants. Occasionally lift vines from the ground to prevent rooting at the leaf joints. Rotate crops.

Maintenance
Spring Take cuttings under cover, keep warm and moist.
Summer Keep cuttings weed-free, water well and feed. Prune as necessary.
Fall Harvest. Save some tubers for the next crop.
Winter Keep potting mix slightly moist.

Protected Cropping
Grow under cover in cool-temperate climates at a minimum temperature of 77°F.

Take cuttings as normal from healthy shoots of mature plants, and insert about four cuttings around the outside of a 6 in. pot filled with cuttings potting mix. Keep moist with tepid water. Transplant into a greenhouse bed once a good root system has formed. Water regularly. Prune stems longer than 24 in. to encourage sideshoots and also from late winter to thin out congested growth.

Harvesting and Storing
In good conditions, tubers ripen in 4 to 5 months. Lift when slightly immature; otherwise wait until vines begin to yellow. Lift carefully to avoid bruising. Use fresh or store, once dried, in a cool dark place. Properly cured, sweet potatoes will store for several months.

Pests and Diseases
Sweet potato scurf is the most severe disease problem. Leaves can also suffer from leaf spot and sooty mold. Black rot appears at the base of the stem and brown rot on the tuber. Check stored tubers regularly. Also susceptible to whitefly or red spider mite under cover.

 container growing

Grow in soilless potting mix with moderate fertilizer levels in containers 12 in. deep and 15 in. wide. Provide supports.

 medicinal

Sweet potatoes and their leaves contain antibacterial and fungicidal substances and are used in folk medicine. In Shakespeare's day they were sold in crystallized slices with sea holly ("eringo") as an aphrodisiac. In *The Merry Wives of Windsor*, Falstaff cries: "Let the sky rain potatoes … hail kissing-comforts and snow eringoes." The Empress Josephine introduced sweet potatoes to her companions, who were soon serving them to stimulate the passion of their lovers. The results are not recorded!

Lactuca sativa. Asteraceae
LETTUCE

Annual grown for edible leaves. Half hardy to hardy. Value: rich in beta carotene, particularly outer leaves.

The garden lettuce is believed to be a selected form of the bitter-leaved wild species *Lactuca serriola*, which is found throughout Europe, Asia and North Africa. The ancient Egyptians were said to have been the first to cultivate lettuces and there are examples of tomb wall paintings depicting a form of Romaine lettuce, which is said to have originated on the Greek island of the same name. They believed it was an aphrodisiac and also used its white sap and leaves in a concoction alongside fresh beef, frankincense and juniper berries as a remedy for stomach ache. The Romans, too, attributed medicinal properties to the lettuce and the Emperor Augustus erected an altar and statue in its honor; they believed that it upheld morals, temperance and chastity. The Romans were said to have introduced it to Britain with their conquering armies and even after many centuries the lettuce is still regarded as the foundation of a good salad.

varieties

The many cultivars are divided into three main categories — head, leaf, and Romaine types. They can be grown all year round, and many modern cultivars are disease-resistant (see pp. 663–664).

Head Lettuce
More tolerant of drought and drier soils than the other kinds, this group includes "Butterhead" types, with soft buttery-textured leaves which are usually grown in summer, and "Crisphead" types, which have crisp leaves forming compact hearts.

Butterhead
"Action" has thick, pale green leaves and is resistant to mosaic virus and downy mildew. "All Year Round" is tasty and compact, with pale green leaves. It is slow to bolt and hardy. "Arctic King" is highly resistant to cold and ideal for fall or early spring sowing. "Avon Defiance" is an excellent, high-yielding, dark green lettuce which withstands drought and high temperatures. It is ideal for summer crops, particularly those sown from mid- to late summer, and is resistant to root aphid and downy mildew. "Buttercrunch" has compact, crisp, dark green heads and a beautiful "buttery" heart. It is slow to bolt and heat-resistant. "Cassandra" is top quality with pale green leaves and large "hearts." Resistant to downy mildew and lettuce mosaic virus, it is good for growing all year round. "Dolly" is a large lettuce for midsummer to midfall cropping. It has good resistance to downy mildew and

Pandero

"Sangria"

lettuce mosaic virus. "Kwiek," a large-headed variety for winter cropping, is resistant to downy mildew. Sow in late summer for harvesting in midwinter or force as an early spring crop. "Musette" has dark green, succulent leaves and is resistant to root aphid, lettuce mosaic virus and downy mildew. "Sabine" is resistant to root aphid and downy mildew. The outer leaves of "Sangria" are tinged red, the inner a pale green and it has some resistance to mildew and mosaic virus. "Soraya" also has some resistance to downy mildew and lettuce mosaic virus. "Valdor," which has firm, dark green hearts, is a very hardy lettuce for overwintering outdoors. "Yugoslavian Red" has red tips to the leaves and a bright greeny-yellow heart. It is mild-flavored and ideal for the ornamental vegetable garden.

Crisphead

"Avoncrisp" has some resistance to mildew and root aphid, but can suffer from "tip burn." "Iceberg" is ideal for spring or summer sowing and has very crisp tender leaves with large ice-white hearts (the heart has the best-quality leaves). "Malika" grows very rapidly and should be harvested soon after it matures. It has some resistance to mildew and bolting. "Premier Great Lakes" is large, crisp and matures rapidly. It is heat- and "tip-burn"-resistant. "Saladin" is excellent for summer cropping and is resistant to mildew and bolting. "Vienna" has crisp, medium-sized heads of fresh, green leaves and is resistant to leaf aphids and mildew. "Webb's Wonderful" is extremely popular, and rightly so. It is a good-quality lettuce which lasts well at maturity.

Leaf Lettuce

These are loose leaf varieties which sometimes form an insignificant head. Cut to resprout, or remove single leaves as needed. They stand longer before bolting than other types and can be grown at any time of year; however, growth is slower in winter.

"Cocarde" is a large, bronze, "oak leaf" type with an excellent flavor. "Grand Rapids" has crinkled, pale green leaves and is resistant to tip burn. "Lollo Blonda" is similar to "Lollo Rossa," but with fresh pale green leaves and some resistance to lettuce root aphid. "Lollo Rossa" adds color to salads. The leaves are tinged red with serrated, wavy margins and it is good mixed with romaine or iceberg lettuces. It is also attractive as an edging plant in the flower border or vegetable plot. "Oak Leaf" has several different color forms, from pale green to brown. It is tasty and ornamental. "Red Salad Bowl" has bronze-green to crimson leaves. "Ruby" is crinkled and pale green with deep red tints and has good heat resistance. "Salad Bowl" was one of the first leaf lettuces with masses of green, deeply lobed leaves which are crisp but tender. Good resistance to bolting.

Romaine

These flourish in humus-rich, moist soil, take longer to mature than other varieties and are better in cooler weather. Some can overwinter outdoors or be grown as leaf lettuce if closely spaced. They are generally very tasty.

"Bubbles" has heavily textured leaves and is mildew resistant. "Chartwell" is one of the tastiest and sweetest with firm hearts. It is downy mildew resistant and slow to bolt. Grows well in hot weather. "Counter" is very sweet and crisp and is resistant to tip burn, downy mildew and bolting. "Freckles" is very tasty, with attractive, red mottling over the leaves. It is warm weather-tolerant and slow to bolt. "Lobjoits Green," is a large, good-quality, old variety which is deep green, crisp and tasaty. It can be grown as closely as leaf lettuce but is subject to tip burn. "Little Gem" is a compact, quick-maturing, semi-Romaine with a firm, sweet heart. It is ideal as a catch crop, for early crops under cover and for small gardens and has remained a popular variety since the late 19th century. "Nymans" has burgundy leaves that blend towards a bright green heart. It is slow to bolt and has good mildew resistance. "Pandero" is a well flavored, red-leaved baby romaine. It is mildew-resistant and

ideal as a colorful "cut and come again." "Parris Island" has upright conical heads with light green outer leaves and a white heart. They have a wonderful flavor. "Valmaine" is good for growing as a "cut and come again" or for close planting and use as leaf lettuce. "Winter Density" has dark green heads and crisp, refreshing leaves, and also outstanding cold hardiness.

 ## cultivation

Propagation

Germination is poor, particularly with Butterhead types, if soil temperatures exceed 77°F, with the critical period being a few hours after planting. During hot weather sow in late afternoon or evening, when soil temperatures are lower, water after sowing to reduce soil temperature, shade before and after sowing, germinate in trays or cell-packs in a cool place and transplant, or fluid sow. Lettuces do not transplant well in dry soil and hot weather; where possible, summer sowings are better made *in situ* or in packs. Sow thinly in rows ½ in. deep; seeds sown too deeply are slow or fail to germinate. Thin to the final spacing when plants are large enough to handle (overcrowding checks growth and can cause bolting). In cool

Sow lettuce early, then transplant

Beauty in a bell jar

weather, thinnings can be transplanted if lifted with care to avoid root damage.

Sow those grown in trays or cell-packs in soilless potting compost to maintain strong growth and harden off before transplanting when they have four to five true leaves. Do not transplant when the weather is hot and dry, unless shading can be provided, and do not plant them too deeply.

Sow summer crops from midspring to midsummer. Sow winter-hardy varieties from late summer to early fall, thinning to the final spacing in spring. As they do not last long after maturity, maintain a continuous supply of lettuce by sowing successively, about every 2 weeks, just as the seedlings from the previous sowing appear. Thin when the seedlings are large enough to handle, where possible staggering them in a triangular pattern to make optimum use of the area.

Space small lettuces 8 in. apart in and between the rows, butterheads with about 11 in. in and between the rows, or 10 in. apart in rows 12 in. apart. Crispheads should be planted 15 in. apart or 12 in. apart with the rows 15 in. apart. Plant "Salad Bowl" or Romaine about 14 in. apart in and between the rows.

Leaf lettuce can also be grown as "cut and come again" seedlings, providing two or three harvests before bolting, while summer crops tend to go to seed more rapidly. Make sure you sow thinly.

Romaine varieties like "Lobjoits Green" can be grown as leaf lettuce. Sow in rows 5 in. apart, thinning to 1 in.

Sow weekly from late spring to early summer and again in three consecutive weeks from late summer. This technique was developed at the Horticulture Research International in the United Kingdom. **Zones 3 to 11.**

Growing

Lettuces prefer cool growing conditions, from 50–68°F, and need an open, sunny site on light, rich, moisture-retentive soil, with a pH of around neutral. They struggle on dry or impoverished soil, so dig in plenty of well-rotted organic matter the fall before sowing or grow on ground manured for the previous crop. Lightly fork in a base dressing of general fertilizer at 2 oz./sq. yd. about 10 days before sowing and create a seedbed by raking to a fine tilth.

Hoe and hand weed regularly to remove any weeds. A constant supply of moisture is vital for success. Lettuce needs 4 gallons/sq yd per week in dry weather. Water in the mornings on sunny days so that the water evaporates quickly, reducing the risk of disease. If water is scarce, apply only on the last 7 to 10 days before harvest.

Boost growth of winter-hardy outdoor crops with a liquid general fertilizer in midspring and use the same treatment for slow-growing crops at any time of year. Rotate crops every 2 years to avoid the build-up of pests and diseases.

Maintenance

Spring Sow crops indoors or outdoors under cloches in early spring. Sow later crops outdoors. Harvest early crops.
Summer Sow successionally and harvest overwintered crops. Keep crops weed-free; water as needed. Harvest.
Fall Sow and protect crops under cloches. Harvest.
Winter Sow crops under cover. Harvest.

Protected Cropping

Sow from late winter to early spring in cell-packs or trays for transplanting under cloches or cold frames from mid- to late spring. Alternatively, they can be sown *in situ* in cold frames or under cloches for growing on or transplanting outdoors in a protected part of the garden and covered with floating row cover.

Protect late-spring and summer transplants under floating row cover until they become established and protect late summer sowings under floating row cover to maintain the quality of fall crops. Grow hardier varieties under floating row cover or in a greenhouse or a cold frame over winter, ideally with a gentle heat around 45°F.

Germination is better in cool conditions

Lettuce seedlings in a vegetable garden

LETTUCE

Sow from late summer to midfall for transplanting. Earlier sowings can be made outdoors in a seedbed for transplanting; others can be sown in cell-packs or seed trays. Ventilate well to avoid disease problems.

Harvest from late fall to midspring. Cover outdoor winter-hardy crops with glass or floating row cover to ensure a good-quality crop and provide protection during severe weather.

Sow early crops of "cut and come again" seedlings under cover in late winter or spring, and also from midfall.

Harvesting and Storing
Summer maincrop lettuces are ready to harvest from early summer to midfall, around 12 weeks after sowing. Romaines stand for quite a time in cool weather but Butterheads deteriorate within a few days of maturity. Crispheads last for about 10 days before deteriorating. Leaf lettuces can be picked over a long period. Harvest hardy overwintered outdoor crops from late spring to early summer.

Harvest "cut and come again" seedlings about 4 weeks after sowing and Romaine types grown as leaf lettuce about 1 in. above the ground when they are 3–5 in. high. A second crop can be harvested from 3 to 8 weeks later, depending on the growing conditions.

Cut mature lettuces at the base, just below the lower leaves. Do not squeeze hearting lettuces to check if they are ready for harvesting, as this can damage the leaves: press them gently but firmly with the back of your hand. Pull single leaves from leaf lettuce as required or cut 1 in. above the base and allow the plant to resprout.

Store lettuce in the refrigerator in the salad drawer or in a plastic bag for up to 6 days. Romaine lettuce stores the longest.

Pests and Diseases
Root aphids appear in clusters on the roots and are usually covered in a white powdery wax. The symptoms are stunted growth and yellowing leaves; plants may collapse in hot weather. They are less of a problem in cool, damp conditions. Pick and destroy affected plants or grow resistant varieties.

Aphids can also be a problem.

Leaf tips become brown and dry when affected by tip burn, caused by sudden water loss in warm weather. Water well and shade, if necessary; do not allow lettuces to grow excessively large; grow resistant varieties where possible.

Botrytis or gray mold can be a problem in cool, damp conditions. Do not plant seedlings too deeply, handle transplants carefully to avoid damage, thin early, remove diseased material, improve ventilation and spray with a systemic or copper-based fungicide. Grow resistant varieties.

Bolting or going to seed is caused by check during transplanting, drought, temperatures over 70°F, or long days; otherwise lettuces will only bolt after hearting. Grow resistant varieties or leaf lettuce.

Pigeons and sparrows can damage seedlings. Grow under floating row covers, tie thread between bamboo stakes, use humming line or other deterrents.

Lettuce mosaic virus is a disease that causes the leaves to become puckered and mottled; veins become transparent and growth is stunted — more of a problem on overwintering crops. Destroy those that are affected, control aphids and grow resistant varieties.

 ## companion planting

Lettuces grow well with cucumbers, onions, radishes and carrots. Dill and chervil protect them from aphids.

 ## container growing

Compact varieties are suitable for growing in pots, containers and window boxes. Use a soil-based potting mix, mix in a slow-release granular fertilizer and water regularly. Sow either *in situ* or in moduls for transplanting.

 ## medicinal

Lettuce is used as a mild sedative and narcotic, and lettuce soup is reported to be effective in treating nervous tension and insomnia. Lettuce sap dissolved in wine is said to make a good painkiller.

Lettuce soothes inflammation — lotions for the treatment of sunburn and rough skin are made from its extracts.

Lettuce can also be used as a poultice on bruises or taken internally for stomach ulcers and for irritable bowel syndrome.

It is also antispasmodic and can be used to soothe coughs and bronchial problems; it is reputed to cool the ardor.

culinary

Wash leaves thoroughly before use. Use fresh or wilted in salads, braise with butter and flavor with nutmeg or braise with peas and shallots and serve with butter. Stir-fry with onions and mushrooms, steam and add to chicken soup or make cream of lettuce soup and garnish with hardboiled eggs and a sprinkling of curry powder. Stalks can be sliced and steamed.

Cypriot Salad
Serves 2

1¾ ounces haloumi cheese, cut into thin slices
3 to 4 large lettuce leaves, torn into pieces
4 medium tomatoes
¼ cucumber, sliced
¼ yellow bell pepper, cored, seeded and diced
Handful of fresh Italian parsley, roughly chopped
10 black olives, pitted
½ red onion, thinly sliced

For the Dressing:
2 tablespoons extra virgin olive oil
1 tablespoon white wine vinegar
1 to 2 teaspoons lemon juice
Kosher salt and freshly ground black pepper

Toast the cheese under a medium broiler on a nonstick baking sheet until golden brown. Turn once and brown the other side. Mix with the other ingredients in a large salad bowl. Shake all the dressing ingredients together in a glass jar until well combined. Pour over the salad, gently toss to mix and serve immediately.

Lettuce-wrapped GroundShrimp
Serves 6 to 8 as a side dish

30 raw shrimp, shelled and deveined
¼ teaspoon salt
2 teaspoons cornstarch
2 tablespoons egg white
1 crisp lettuce (Webb's or iceberg)
4 tablespoons peanut or vegetable oil
50g Sichuan zhacai, trimmed and finely minced
1 teaspoon crushed garlic

Cypriot Salad

Mince the shrimp coarsely and put in a large mixing bowl. Season with salt. Add the cornstarch and egg white and stir in the same direction until the egg white is absorbed and the mixture is elastic. Refrigerate, covered, for 1 hour.

Arrange the separated lettuce leaves, preferably cup-shaped, on a plate on the dining table.

Heat a wok until hot. Add 1 tablespoon of oil and the Sichuan *zhacai* (pickled mustard stem, from specialized stores) and cook for a few seconds, stirring. Scoop on to a dish and keep nearby. Wipe the wok clean.

Reheat the wok until the smoke rises. Add the rest of the oil and coat the wok with it. Add the garlic and the shrimp, stirring vigorously. Add the *zhacai* and continue cooking until the shrimp turn pink and are cooked. Then place on a plate next to the lettuce.

To serve, each person takes a lettuce leaf, spoons some shrimp mixture into the center and wraps the lettuce around it: perfect finger-food.

Papaya Salad
Serves 4

2 cloves garlic, peeled
3 to 4 small fresh red or green chiles
2 yard-long beans or 20 green beans, chopped into
  2 in. lengths
1 cup fresh papaya, peeled, seeded
1 tomato, cut into wedges
2 tablespoons nam pla (Thai fish sauce)
1 tablespoon granulated sugar
2 tablespoons lime juice
A selection of firm seasonal green vegetables, e.g.,
  iceberg lettuce, cucumber and cabbage, to serve

Pound the garlic in a large mortar, then add the chiles and pound again. Add the long beans, breaking them up slightly. Cut the papaya into fine slivers. Now take a spoon and stir in the papaya. Lightly pound together, then stir in the tomato and lightly pound again.

Add the fish sauce, sugar and lime juice, stirring well, then turn into a serving dish. Serve with fresh raw vegetables — any leaves, such as white cabbage, can be used as a scoop for the spicy mixture.

Braised Lettuce
Serves 4

4 to 5 lettuces, trimmed
A little oil or butter
¼ cup bacon, roughly diced
1 carrot, roughly diced
1 red onion, sliced
1 ¼ cups vegetable stock
2 tablespoons chopped fresh thyme and parsley
Salt and freshly ground black pepper

In a pot of salted water, cook the lettuces for 5 minutes. Drain and refresh in cold water. Drain again and remove as much liquid as possible: you can blot the leaves lightly with paper towel.

Grease an ovenproof dish and sprinkle the base with the bacon, carrot, onion and seasoning. Arrange the lettuces neatly in the dish and pour in the stock. Cover the dish with buttered paper and braise in a preheated oven, 350°F, for 30 to 40 minutes.

Remove the lettuces and other ingredients and keep hot. Then reduce the cooking liquid and pour it over the vegetables. Sprinkle with the fresh herbs and serve very hot.

Papaya Salad

Lactuca sativa var. *augustana.* Asteraceae

CELTUCE

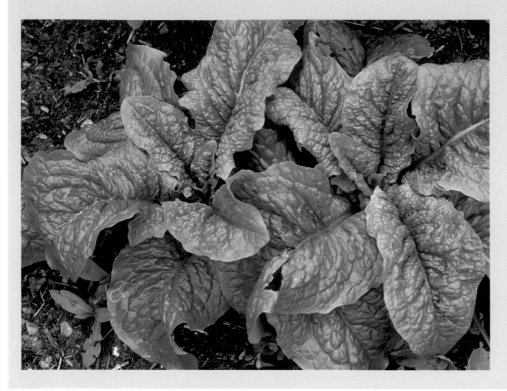

Also known as Stem Lettuce, Asparagus Lettuce, Chinese Lettuce. Annual grown for edible leaves. Value: little nutritive value; low in carbohydrate and calories; a source of potassium.

Introduced from China, where it has been grown for centuries, this "oriental vegetable" consists of a short-stemmed mutation lettuce. It has been listed in European catalogs since 1885, but the name "celtuce" was adopted by an American seed company that first offered seeds in 1942. It aptly describes its characteristics: the stems are used like celery; the leaves make a lettuce substitute.

 ## varieties

"Zulu" is a variety for cooler climates, with narrow, dull-textured leaves. Others are sold in seed mixes of broad, dull, glossy or red-leaved varieties.

 ## cultivation

Celtuce needs well-drained, rich, fertile soil, with a pH of 6.5–7.5, around neutral. Celtuce tolerates a range of temperatures from light frosts to over 80°F.

It tends to bolt prematurely in extremely hot conditions, but is still more heat-resistant than lettuce. Grow celtuce as a winter crop in mild areas. **Zones 4 to 10.**

Propagation
For successional cropping, sow every 2 weeks from midspring until midsummer in rows ½ in. deep and 12 in. apart. When large enough to handle, thin to 3½ in.

Germination is poor in temperatures above 80°F. In hot summers, sow in seed trays or cell-packs in a cool, partially shaded position. Cell-packs tend to produce better plants than seed trays; weak seedlings rarely produce good stems. Transplant when three to four leaves have been produced, generally after 3 to 4 weeks.

Mulch after planting to conserve moisture and suppress weeds; the shallow roots are easily damaged by hoeing.

Growing
In poor soils, add copious amounts of organic matter the winter before planting. Celtuce grows well on light soil, but develops a stronger root system and more robust plants on heavier soils.

Water well as leaves develop, to keep them tender. As the stems develop, reduce watering, but take care to keep the supply steady: if the soil becomes too wet or too dry, the stems may crack. Feed with a liquid general fertilizer every 3 weeks.

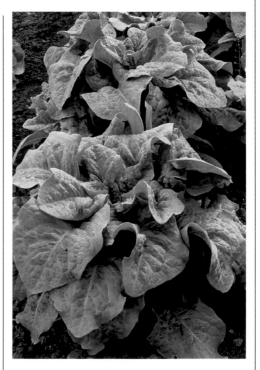

Why not give it a try?

Maintenance
Spring Sow seed.
Summer Water and remove weeds.
Fall Transplant seedlings for winter crops.
Winter Grow under cover; harvest mature crops.

Protected Cropping
Grow in cloches, unheated greenhouses, tunnels or under floating row covers to extend the season. Raise early crops by sowing and planting under cover in early spring and late crops by transplanting summer-sown seedlings under cover in fall.

Harvesting and Storing
Harvest 3 to 4 months after sowing, when 12 in. high and 1 in. diameter. Cut the stalks, pull up the plant or cut it off at ground level. Trim the leaves from the stem but do not touch the top rosette of leaves, in order to keep the stem fresh.

Celtuce stems can be kept for a few weeks if stored in cool conditions.

Pests and Diseases
Celtuce is susceptible to the same problems as lettuce. Pick off slugs, set traps or use aluminum sulfate pellets. Downy mildew is worse in cool, damp conditions: treat with fungicide, and remove infected plants and debris at the end of the season.

 ## companion planting

Plant with chervil and dill to protect from aphids. Interplant between slower-growing crops such as cauliflower, self-blanching celery or Chinese chives.

 ## container growing

Sow in containers or pots in a soilless potting mix with moderate levels of added fertilizer.

 ## culinary

Celtuce is excellent raw and cooked. Prepare the stems by peeling off the outer layer. Cut into thin slices for salads, or into larger pieces for cooking. In salads, it can either be eaten raw or cooked and cooled, served with a spicy dressing.

Cook lightly, for 4 minutes at most. Stir-fry with white meat, poultry, fish, other vegetables, or on its own seasoned with garlic, chile, pepper, soy or oyster sauce. It is also delicious served with a creamed sauce or baked *au gratin*. In China it is used in soups and pickles. Young leaves can be cooked like "greens."

Crispy Spring Rolls
Serves 4 to 6

½ pound fresh beansprouts, washed and husked
½ cup bamboo shoots
½ pound celtuce stems
½ cup white mushrooms
½ cup carrots
Vegetable oil, for frying
1 teaspoon sugar
1 tablespoon light soy sauce
1 tablespoon rice wine
20 frozen spring roll skins, defrosted
1 tablespoon all-purpose flour mixed with
   1 tablespoon water
Salt and freshly ground black pepper

Prepare the beansprouts and roughly chop all the other vegetables to the same size. Heat a little oil in a wok until smoking and stir-fry the vegetables for a minute, then add the sugar, soy sauce, rice wine and seasoning, and cook for an additional minute or two. Let sit to cool.

Cut the spring roll skins in half diagonally. Place a teaspoon of the vegetable mixture in the center of each and roll up neatly, folding in all the corners. Place on a lightly floured plate and brush the upper edge with a little flour paste to seal.

Heat enough oil to deep-fry until steaming and drop in the spring rolls for 3 to 4 minutes, until crispy, cooking in batches. Drain and serve with chile sauce.

Lagenaria siceraria. Cucurbitaceae

CALABASH

Also known as Bottle Gourd, Calabash Gourd, Doodhi, White-flowered Gourd, Trumpet Gourd. Vigorous annual climber grown for edible young fruits, shoots and seeds. Tender. Value: little nutritive value; a moderate source of vitamin C; small quantities of B vitamins and protein.

Early evidence for the cultivation of this versatile tropical gourd comes from South America around 7000 BCE, though it is thought to have originated in Africa, south of the Sahara, or India. Some sources suggest that it may have dispersed naturally by floating on oceanic currents from one continent to another: experiments have found that seed will germinate after surviving over 7 months in seawater. One of the earliest crops cultivated in the tropics, these gourds with their narrow necks have developed in many shapes and sizes, some reaching up to 7 feet long. The young fruits are edible, but mature shells become extremely hard when dried and have been used to make bottles, kitchen utensils, musical instruments, floats for fishing nets and even gunpowder flasks. In the past *Lagenaria* leaves were used as a protective charm when elephant hunting.

 ## varieties

Lagenaria siceraria is a vigorous annual, climbing or scrambling by means of tendrils to more than 30 ft. The leaves are broad and oval with wavy margins. Its solitary, fragrant, white flowers open in the evenings. Its fruits are pale green to cream or yellow, with a narrow "neck," and contain white, spongy flesh and flat, creamy-colored seeds. The names of selected forms (like "bottle," "trumpet," "club" or "powderhorn" gourd) relate to their use and appearance.

 ## cultivation

They flourish in warm conditions, around 68–86°F and plenty of sunshine, but will grow outdoors in warm temperate climates where humidity levels are moderate to high. Plants need to be trained over supporting structures. **Zones 4 to 11.**

Propagation
Soak seeds overnight in tepid water before sowing on mounds of soil about 12 in. apart, containing copious amounts of well-rotted manure. Plant three seeds, edgeways, and thin to leave the strongest seedling.

Seeds can be sown in a nursery bed and transplanted when they have two to three leaves. Seeds are usually sown at the start of the rainy season.

Growing
Calabash needs fertile, well-drained soil, preferably with a pH of 7. Add a granular general fertilizer to the planting hole or sprinkle it around the germinated seedling.

Train the stems into trees, or over fences, arbors or frames covered with 6 in. mesh netting. Erect stakes or trellis on the beds or among the groups of mounds. Alternatively, grow plants in beds 4–6 ft. square, planting a seedling at each corner and training towards the center. Pinch out the terminal shoots when they are 1–1½ in. long, to encourage branching. The best yields are obtained in warm-climate areas with rainfall around 28–48 in. per annum, but they grow well in drier regions if they are kept watered well. Feed with a high-nitrogen fertilizer every 3 weeks during the growing season, keep crops weed-free and mulch with a layer of organic matter.

Plants can grow extremely rapidly in hot weather: 2 ft. in 24 hours has been recorded. Where conditions are suitable they can be grown all year round. To grow outdoors in cooler climates, harden off under cloches or cold frames and plant in a sheltered, sunny position when the danger of frost has passed.

In colder zones, the chance of success is greater in hot summers; they should reach edible size, though they rarely have a long enough season to mature fully.

Maintenance
Spring Sow seeds indoors in warm conditions.
Summer Train vines over trellis or netting. Water regularly; feed as necessary. Wet down the greenhouse to maintain humid conditions and harvest young fruits.
Fall In cooler climates, harvest mature gourds for preserving before the onset of the first frosts.

Protected Cropping
In cool, temperate climates, sow seeds 6 to 8 weeks before the anticipated planting out time. Sow two to three seeds in a 6 in. pot of peat-substitute potting mix in late winter or early spring at 70–75°F.

Germination takes 3 to 5 days. If the ideal temperatures cannot be achieved and maintained, delay sowing until mid- to late spring. Transplant when seedlings are 4–6 in. high. They will grow at temperatures down to 50°F, but flourish at high temperatures and in humid conditions in bright, filtered light.

CALABASH

Dampen the greenhouse floor at least twice a day, depending on outside weather conditions. Dig in plenty of well-rotted manure and horticultural grit or sharp sand into the greenhouse bed, or grow in containers.

Keep the compost constantly moist, using lukewarm water, and feed with a liquid general fertilizer every 2 weeks. Train up a trellis, wires or netting. Flowers will appear from early summer and only one or two should be allowed to grow to maturity.

Harvesting and Storing

Vines begin to fruit 3 to 4 months after planting. Harvest immature fruits when a couple of inches long, 70 to 90 days after sowing. Mature fruits can be harvested and dried slowly as ornaments.

Pests and Diseases

This very robust plant is rarely troubled by disease. Whiteflies can occasionally be a problem when plants are grown under cover. In warm, humid climates, anthracnose appears as pinhead-sized, water-soaked lesions on the fruits, combining to form a small black mass. Fruit rot can also be a problem. Spray with a

copper-based compound and remove badly affected leaves. Harvest fruits carefully to avoid damage.

 container growing

Repot as plants grow, until they are in 12 in. pots, or grow in large containers of soilless potting mix with added organic matter and horticultural grit or sharp sand to improve drainage. Keep the compost moist, with lukewarm water. Growth is better restricted when they are grown in pots and is preferable in the greenhouse bed, increasing the chance of successful fruiting.

Stop the shoot tips when the stems are 5 ft. long and train the side stems along a wire. (It is worth noting that even with this method, plants still need a considerable amount of space.) Hand-pollination ensures a good crop. (Male and female flowers are on the same plant: females are recognizable by the ovary at the back of the flower, covered in glandular hairs.) Once a flower has formed, allow two more leaves to appear, then pinch out the growing tip. If it is a male flower or a fruit is not going to form, cut the stem back to the first leaf. A replacement will be formed.

The ornamental gourd tunnel in Rosemoor Gardens, UK

 culinary

Young fruits, which are rich in pectin, are popular in tropical Africa and Asia. They have a mild, somewhat bland taste, are peeled before eating and any large seeds removed. They can be cubed or sliced, sautéed with spices to accompany curries and other Indian dishes and added to stews or curries. Young shoots and leaves can be steamed or lightly boiled. Seeds are used in soups in Africa and are boiled in salt water and eaten as an appetizer in India. The seed oil is used for cooking.

medicinal

The fruit pulp around seeds is emetic and purgative and is sometimes given to horses! Juice from the fruit is used to treat baldness; mixed with lime juice, it is used for pimples; boiled with oil, it is used for rheumatism. Seeds and roots are used to treat dropsy and the seed oil used externally for headaches.

GREATER GALANGAL

Languas galanga (syn. *Alpinia galanga*). Zingiberaceae

Also known as Greater Galingale, Siamese Ginger. Herbaceous perennial; rhizomatous rootstock used as flavoring. Tender. Value: negligible nutritive value.

Two species, greater and lesser galangal, have been grown for centuries for their pungent, aromatic roots, which are used as spices and medicinally. The earliest records date from around 550ce, while Marco Polo noted its cultivation in southern China and Java in the 13th century. In the Middle Ages it was known as "galangale," a name also used for the roots of sweet sedge, whose violet-scented rhizomes are used in perfumery.

The word galangal came from the Chinese, meaning "a mild ginger from Ko," a region of the Canton province. It is an essential ingredient of many Malaysian and Thai dishes. The spicy rhizomes have a somewhat different use in the Middle East, where they have been used to "spike" horses!

 ## cultivation

The plant is an herbaceous perennial with pale orange-flushed cream bulbous rhizomes. Stems grow to 7 ft. tall, with dark green lance-shaped leaves to 20 in. long. Flowers are pale green and white with pink markings; the fruit is a round red capsule. There are many different races in cultivation, including types with red and white rhizomes. Lesser galangal is regarded as superior, as it is more pungent and aromatic, but is uncommon in cultivation.

Propagation

Sow fresh seed in pots of peat-substitute compost at 68°F. Keep the compost moist, using lukewarm water, and transplant seedlings when they are large enough to handle. In tropical and subtropical regions they can be sown outdoors in a seedbed (for ground preparation, see "Growing").

Divide rhizomes in spring, when the young shoots are about 1 in. long. Remove young, vigorous sections from the perimeter of the clump, using a sharp knife, dust the cuts with fungicide and transplant just below the soil or compost surface. Soak thoroughly with lukwarm water and maintain high humidity and temperatures.

Growing

Galangal grows outdoors in tropical or subtropical climates, thriving in sunshine or partial shade. It needs a rich, free-draining soil, so dig in plenty of well-rotted potting mix and allow the ground to settle for a few weeks before planting. Allow 3 ft. between plants. Keep crops weed-free and water during dry periods. Mulch with well-rotted compost when plants are well established.

Protected Cropping

In temperate zones, plants can be grown in a heated polyethylene tunnel or greenhouse in bright filtered light, with a minimum temperature of 58°F. Maintain high humidity by misting plants with lukewarm water and "damping down" paths. Prepare borders as for "Growing" and allow 3 ft. between plants.

Keep the compost constantly moist with lukewarm water and reduce watering in lower temperatures.

Remove flower stems before they flower and reduce watering. The foliage gradually becomes yellow and

culinary

Before use, scrape or peel off the skin. The raw chopped or minced root is used in Malaysian and Indonesian dishes with bean curd, meat, poultry, fish, curries, and sauces. It is also used as a marinade to flavor barbecued chicken. The fruits are a substitute for cardamom, the buds can be pickled, and the flowers are eaten raw with vegetables or pickles in parts of Java. In Thai cooking, it is preferred to ginger. In medieval England, a sauce was made from bread crusts, galangal, cinnamon, and ginger pulverized and moistened with stock. It was heated with a dash of vinegar and strained over fish or meat.

Galangal Soup
Serves 4

This Vietnamese recipe has many variations. First, make a stock from the following, by simmering for about 3 hours, topping up as necessary:

4 cups water
1 chicken carcass

4 bulbs lemongrass, bruised
5 in. piece galangal, peeled and sliced
1 onion, roughly sliced
2 red dried chiles
6 kaffir lime leaves
Salt and freshly ground black pepper

Then strain the stock through some fine cheesecloth. Reheat in a heavy pot, adding the meat from the

chicken carcass, chopped finely, together with 1 tablespoon of fish sauce and 4 tablespoons of lime juice.

Simmer for 5 minutes, then add 1 cup shiitake mushrooms, left whole. Simmer for an additional 3 minutes, then stir in ½ cup thick coconut milk. Do not allow to reboil, and check the seasoning. Serve hot.

---

dies back in winter. The compost should remain slightly moist throughout the dormant period. Increase watering when new shoots emerge the following spring. Feed regularly with a liquid general fertilizer every 2 weeks while the plant is actively growing. Mulch plants grown in borders annually in spring with well-rotted manure.

Harvesting and Storing
Rhizomes are ready to harvest after 3 to 4 years. Dig plants towards the end of the growing season and remove mature rhizomes, retaining younger ones for transplanting. It is a good idea to divide and replant a few each year to ensure a constant supply.

Galangal is better used immediately after harvest but will keep for at least a week in a cool place. Alternatively, it can be frozen whole in a plastic bag and segments removed as required. Keep dried roots in airtight containers in a cool dark place.

Pests and Diseases
Red spider mites can be a problem indoors. Check plants regularly, as small infestations are easily controlled. Speckling, mottling, and bronzing of the leaf

surface are the usual symptoms; in later stages, fine webbing appears on leaves and stems. They prefer hot, dry conditions. Control by maintaining high humidity or spray with rotenone or a similar insecticide.

 container growing

Plants can be grown in containers under cover in a compost mix of 2 parts each of loam and leaf mold, 1 part horticultural grit or sharp sand, and 3 parts medium-grade bark. Repot and divide in spring when the rhizomes outgrow their allotted space.

 medicinal

Plants contain cineol, an aromatic, antiseptic substance. The essential oil acts as a decongestant and respiratory germicide and digestive aid. In India it is used as a breath purifier and deodorant, and a paste is made from the rhizomes to treat skin infections. It is also said to be an aphrodisiac. Infusions are taken after childbirth.

 other uses

Roots of lesser galangal are used in Russia for flavoring tea and a liqueur called Nastoika. The rhizomes produce a yellow or yellow-green dye.

KAEMPFERIA GALANGA
(Chinese keys)

The rhizomes, common in the markets of Southeast Asia, produce a distinctive cluster of finger-like roots that are pale brown with bright yellow flesh and a pungent aroma. They have a very strong taste and should be used sparingly in green curry paste, sauces, soups, and curries.

The rhizomes may be eaten raw when young, or steamed and eaten as a vegetable. Young shoots are cooked as a vegetable, pickled, or eaten raw. Chinese keys are used as a carminative, stomachic, expectorant, analgesic, and to treat dandruff and sore throats.

LENTIL

Lens culinaris. Leguminosae

Also known as Split Pea, Dhal, Masur, Dal. Annual herb grown for edible, flattened seeds. Tender. Value: rich in protein, fiber, iron, carbohydrate, zinc and B vitamins.

Presumed to be native to southwest Europe and temperate Asia, lentils are one of the oldest cultivated crop plants. Carbonized seeds found in Neolithic villages in the Middle East have been dated at 7000 to 6000 BCE, and it is believed that they were domesticated long before that. By 2200 BCE plants appeared in Egyptian tombs; they are referred to in the Bible as the "mess of pottage" for which Esau traded his birthright (Genesis 25: 30, 34). The English "lens," describing the glass in optical instruments, comes from their Latin name — its cross-section resembles a lentil seed. Christian Lent has the same origin, as it was traditionally eaten during the fast.

Grown throughout the world, lentils have become naturalized in drier areas of the tropics. Because of their relatively high drought tolerance, they are suitable for semi-arid regions. The quick-maturing plant is rarely more than 18 in. tall and has branched stems, forming a small bush. The white to rose and violet flowers lead to two to three seeded pods.

 ## varieties

Lentils have been selected over many centuries for their size and color. Today many different races and cultivars exist. Two main races predominate: the larger, round-seeded types usually grown in Europe and North America, and the smaller, flatter-seeded types common in the East.

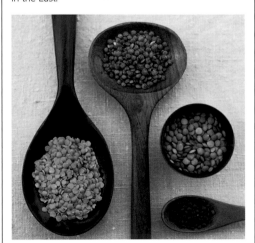
The choice is yours

Frequently encountered is the split red or Persian lentil, which is extremely tender and quick to cook.

Among round-seeded types grown in Europe, the "Lentille du Puy," a tiny green form, is the tastiest and tenderest. Similar but coarser is the "Lentille Blonde" or "Yellow Lentil" commonly grown in northern France, while German or Brown Lentils are coarser still and need lengthy cooking to make them tender. Of varieties grown in North America, "O'Odham" has flat gray-brown to tan-colored seeds and "Tarahumara Pinks" from Mexico has mottled seeds and thrives well in semi-arid conditions.

 ## cultivation

Propagation
Prepare the seedbed by removing any debris from the soil surface and raking to a moderate texture. Sow in spring, when the soil is warm, in rows 1 in. deep, thinning seedlings to 8–12 in. apart with 18 in. between rows. They can also be broadcast and then thinned after germination to 8–12 in. apart.
Zones 5 to 11.

Growing
Lentils are not frost-hardy but flourish in a range of climatic conditions. They prefer a warm, sunny, sheltered position on light, free-draining, moisture-retentive soil. Sandy soils with added well-rotted organic matter are ideal, though equally good crops are grown on silty soil.

Keep crops weed-free and irrigate if necessary during periods of prolonged drought. Excessive watering can lead to over-production of leaves and poor cropping.

Lentils can be grown as a "novelty" crop in cool temperate climates, but yields are not high enough to make it worthwhile on a large scale.

Maintenance
Spring Prepare the seedbed and sow when soil is warm.
Summer Keep crops weed-free and irrigate if needed.
Fall Harvest before the seeds split.
Winter Store seeds or pods in a cool dry place, for use as required.

culinary

As their protein content is about 25 percent, lentils are an important meat substitute. They also have the lowest fat content of any protein-rich food.

Soak lentils overnight, drain and replace the water. Boil rapidly for 10 minutes, then simmer for 25 minutes until tender. Use in soups, thick broth or grind into flour.

Lentils are commonly used for "dhal." Seeds are moistened with water and oil and dried before milling two to three times, each time separating the "chaff" from the meal.

Puy Lentils with Roasted Red Bell Peppers and Goat Cheese
Serves 4

3 red bell peppers
3/4 cup Puy lentils
1 red onion
1 carrot
Sprig each of fresh parsley, marjoram and thyme

2 tablespoons sun-dried tomatoes, chopped
6 ounces crumbled goat cheese
1 tablespoon freshly chopped herbs

For the Dressing:
4 tablespoons extra virgin olive oil
1½ tablespoons lemon juice
Salt and freshly ground black pepper

Roast the bell peppers on a baking sheet in a preheated oven at 475°F, for 30 minutes. Put them into a plastic bag in the fridge. When cooled, deseed and peel the bell peppers, then cut into strips. Let sit.

Wash the Puy lentils thoroughly and cook them, covered in 1½ cups water, with the whole onion, carrot and herbs. These lentils cook faster than other types, in about 15 minutes. Drain. Roughly chop the onion and add back into the lentils. Discard the carrot and herbs. While still warm, add the tomatoes and goat cheese and stir gently. Season.

Make the dressing and toss the lentil mixture in it. Arrange the lentils with the slices of red bell pepper on individual plates.

Sprinkle with the herbs and serve.

Protected Cropping
In cool temperate climates, sow seeds in spring in trays, pots or cell-packs of seed compost. Keep compost moist and repot when seedlings are large enough to handle. Harden off before planting outdoors when the soil is warm and workable and there is no danger of frosts. Protect plants under cloches until they are properly established. Seeds can be sprouted.

Harvesting and Storing
Lentils take about 90 days to reach maturity. Harvest as foliage begins to yellow, before the pods split and the seeds are shed. Lift the whole plant and lay on trays or mats in the sunshine to air-dry or put them in an airy shed. When the pods dry and split, remove the seed and store in a cool, dry place.

Pests and Diseases
Lentils suffer from few pests and diseases. Leaf rust can occur; burn plants after harvest and use treated seed.

Companion Planting
Lentils can be grown as a "green manure."

 container growing

Grow in containers of soilless potting mix with moderate fertilizer levels. Water well and keep the plants weed-free. To avoid the need for transplanting, seeds can be sown in a container which can then be moved outdoors into a suitable sunny spot after germination.

 other uses

Dried leaves and stems are used as forage crops. Lentils have also been used as a source of commercial starch in the textile and printing industries, the by-products being used as cattle feed. Plants are used fresh, or dried as hay and fodder.

 warning

Never eat lentils raw.

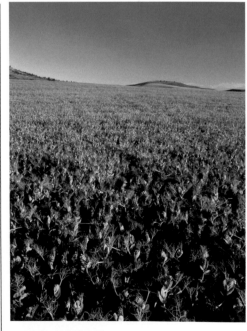

A protein-packed field

TOMATO

Lycopersicon esculentum. Solanaceae

Also known as Love Apple. Short-lived perennial grown as annual for fleshy, succulent berry. Half hardy. Value: rich in beta carotene and vitamin C; some vitamin B.

The wild species is believed to have originated in the Andean regions of north and central South America, spreading to Central and North America along with corn during human migrations over 2,000 years ago. The fruits had been cultivated in Mexico for centuries when European explorers found them growing under local names including *tomati*, *tomatl*, *tumatle* and *tomatas*. When they were first brought to Europe around 1523, tomatoes were considered to be poisonous, due to their strong odor and bright white, red and yellow berries, and were grown only as ornamentals. Dodoens in his *Historie of Plants* of 1578 records, "This is a strange plant and not found in this country, except in the gardens of some herborists … and is dangerous to be used."

In Europe, it was first used for food in Italy. Like many vegetable introductions from the New World, it was considered to be an aphrodisiac. The Italian name *pommi dei mori* was corrupted during translation to the French *pomme d'amour* or "apple of love," as it was thought to excite the passions. Not all believed it to have this effect. Estienne and Liébault wrote that tomatoes were boiled or fried, but gave rise to wind, choler and "infinite obstructions" — hardly an inducement to romance!

The use of tomatoes by North American settlers was not recorded until after Independence, but they were regularly used as food by Italian immigrants to New England and French settlers living in New Orleans, who were making ketchup by 1779. Thomas Jefferson was certainly growing them in his garden in 1781 and they were introduced to Philadelphia 8 years later.

TOMATO

varieties

Most greenhouse varieties are "indeterminate," with a main stem that can become several yards long — these are usually grown as "cordons." Many of those grown outdoors are bush types which do not need supporting and can be grown under crop covers or cloches. Low-yielding, dwarf varieties are good for pots or window boxes.

As you will see from any seed catalog, there are many hundreds of tomato varieties. Those for cultivation under cover in a cold greenhouse and outdoor varieties are generally interchangeable. They range in size from the large ribbed, "beefsteak" types to small "cherry," "pear-shaped" and "currant" tomatoes in a fantastic range of colors including mottled, dark skinned, pink and yellow.

"Ailsa Craig" grows well indoors/outdoors. It is a reliable, tasty, heavy-cropping variety. "Alicante," another indoor/outdoor variety, crops heavily and matures early. It produces smooth, tasty fruit and does well in growbags. The large, black-tinted fruit of "Black Krim" have a delicious, smoky flavor. It sets well in

"Yellow Pear"

heat but is also prone to cracking. However, don't let that deter you. "Brandywine" is a delicious old variety and the fruit can become quite sizeable. The skin is rosy pink or tinged slightly purplish-red. It performs best in cooler climates. "Dombito" is an excellent variety that produces large, round, sweet "beefsteak" fruits; perfect for salads or slicing. "Gardener's Delight" is extremely popular, producing long trusses of delicious, sweet, "cherry" tomatoes over a long period. It grows indoors but has better flavor outdoors, is ideal for containers and generally trouble-free. "Ildi" is very prolific indeed, producing masses of tiny fruits. "Jaune Flammée" is deep orange and shaped like an apricot; prolific, tasty and good for drying. "Marmande" is a delicious outdoor variety with deep, red ribbed fruits. It crops early and is resistant to fusarium and verticillium wilt. "Oaxacan Pink" has small, flattened, pink fruits. "Orange Banana" has orange fruit up to 4 in. long, which are excellent for drying. "Red Alert" is an early bush variety for the greenhouse or outdoors with small, sweet, oval fruits. "Roma VF" is an outdoor bush "plum" tomato, ideal for paste, ketchup, canning, soups or juice. It crops heavily and sometimes needs supporting, and has high resistance to fusarium and verticillium wilt. "San Marzano," another Italian tomato, also crops heavily and is good for soups, sauces or garnishing salads. "Shirley" is grown commercially and has good-quality, tender, tasty, disease-resistant fruit.

Withstanding lower temperatures than most types, it does not suffer from "greenback," is highly resistant to tobacco mosaic virus, leaf mold and fusarium and is therefore an ideal tomato for organic growers. "Siberia" is a bush variety that crops extremely early, around seven weeks after transplanting and sets fruit at temperatures as low as 38°F. "Stupice" crops heavily and extremely early, producing fruit with an excellent balance between sweetness and tartness; delicious! "Sungold" is one of the sweetest tomatoes ever produced.

"Tasty Evergreen" has light yellow to green skin and the flesh remains green when ripe; succulent, tender and sweet. "Tigerella" produces tasty, small orange-red fruits with pale stripes and crops well over a long period. "Tiny Tim" is compact, bushy and ideal for pots, window boxes and hanging baskets. The fruits are cherry-sized and tasty. "Tumbler" was originally bred for hanging baskets. It has flexible, hanging stems, and the bright red fruits ripen quickly and are sweet to the taste. "Wapsipinicon Peach" has fuzzy skin like a peach and was a taste test winner in the U.S.; delicious and sweet — recommended. "Yellow Pear" is well described by its name. The dense clusters of fruit are sweet-tasting and have few seeds and the plants are vigorous and high-yielding. "Yellow Perfection" crops early and is prolific, producing tasty, bright yellow fruits — an excellent tomato.

Modern greenhouse varieties such as "Aromata," "Moravi" and "Merlot" are significantly disease-resistant compared with older sorts.

Roma

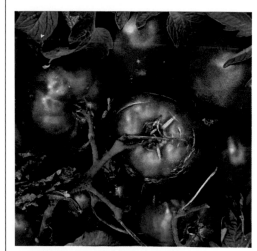
The "Black Krim" has a fabulous flavor

There's plenty of light by the window

 cultivation

Propagation
A minimum temperature of 60°F is needed for germination, but seedlings can tolerate lower night temperatures if those during the day are above this level.

In cool climates, for growing in heated greenhouses, sow from midwinter. For growing outdoors or in an unheated greenhouse, sow seed indoors ¼ in. deep in trays of seed potting mix, 6 to 8 weeks before the last frost is due or sow two to three seeds in 3 in. pots or packs, thinning to leave the strongest seedling. **Zones 3 to 11.**

Transplant tray- or pack-grown seedlings into 3 in. pots when two to three leaves have formed, keeping the plants in a light, well-ventilated position. Harden off carefully and plant out when there is no danger of frost and air temperatures are at least 45°F with soil temperatures at a minimum of 50°F.

Transplant, with the first true leaves just above the soil level, when the flowers on the first truss appear. Do not worry if your plants have become spindly; planting them deeply stimulates the formation of roots on the buried stems, making the plants more stable.

Tomatoes can also be fluid-sown from midspring *in situ* or in a cold frame for transplanting after warming the soil. Germinate on moist paper towel at 70°F, sowing when the rootlets are a maximum of ⅕ inch long (see advice on fluid sowing, p. 645). Sow outdoors in rows and thin to leave the strongest seedling or in hills at their final spacing. Cover the rows with potting mix and protect them with cloches until the first flowers appear.

When sowing in cold frames, sow seed in rows 5–6 in. apart, thinning to 4–5 in. apart in the rows. Transplant carefully when the plants are 6–8 in. tall.

Alternatively, buy plants grown individually in pots rather than packed in boxes or trays, using a reliable supplier. Plant indeterminate types 15–18 in. apart, or in double rows with 36 in. between each pair of rows. Bush types should be planted 18–24 in. apart and dwarf cultivars 8–12 in. apart, depending on the variety.

Closer spacing produces earlier crops; wider spacing generally produces slightly higher yields.

Growing
Outdoor tomatoes need a warm position, ideally away from buildings for better air circulation, in a moisture-retentive, well-drained soil. Add well-rotted organic matter where necessary and lime acid soils to create a pH of 5.5 to 7. If tomatoes are grown in very rich soil or are fed with too much nitrogen they produce excessive leaf growth at the expense of flowers and fruit. Fruit will not set at night temperatures below 55°F and day temperatures above 90°F. Night temperatures around 76°F may well cause blossom to drop. Tomatoes should be fed with a liquid general fertilizer until established, then with a high-potash fertilizer to encourage flowering and fruiting.

Keep crops weed-free by hoeing and hand weeding, taking care not to damage the stems, or mulch with a layer of organic matter.

Keep them constantly moist but not waterlogged; erratic watering causes the fruits to split and also encourages blossom end rot, particularly when plants are grown in containers or growing bags. Use tepid water. In dry conditions or when the first flowers appear they need about 3 gallons water each week. Careful watering and feeding is essential (be restrained!), particularly near harvest time to ensure that the fruits are not excessively watery and have a good flavor. Feed with tomato fertilizer according to the manufacturer's instructions.

Be prepared to recycle and improvise

Long shoots need supporting with stakes, strings or a frame. Using a sharp knife or by pinching between the finger and thumb, remove sideshoots when they appear and "stop" plants by removing the growing tip two to three leaves above the top truss when three to five trusses have been formed or when the plant has reached the top of the support. The number of trusses on each plant depends on the growing season: in shorter growing seasons, leave fewer trusses. Remove leaves below the lowest truss to encourage air circulation, but not too many.

In seasons when ripening is slow, remove some of the leaves near to the trusses with a sharp knife, exposing fruits to the sunshine.

To keep the fruit clean and stop fruit from rotting, grow bush tomatoes on a mulch of straw, felt or crop covers laid over the soil. Black polyethylene or even a split garbage bag (with the edges anchored by burying them in the soil) absorbs heat, warms the soil, conserves moisture and helps fruit to ripen. Rotate crops annually.

Maintenance

Spring Sow crops under cover and, later, outdoors.
Summer Keep crops watered, fed and weed-free. Shade and ventilate as necessary. Remove any sideshoots. Harvest.
Fall Ripen later outdoor crops under cloches or indoors.

Protected Cropping

In cooler climates, more reliable harvests can be achieved by growing tomatoes in an unheated greenhouse or polyethylene tunnels. Rotate crops to avoid the build-up of pests and diseases and sterilize or replace the soil every 2 to 3 years, or use containers. To assist pollination and fruit set, particularly of plants grown indoors, mist occasionally and tap the trusses once the flowers have formed; do this around midday if possible. (It is not so important for outdoor crops, as wind movement assists pollination.) Shade greenhouses before the heat of summer and ventilate well in warm conditions.

A fascinating innovation is the "Wall-o-Water," a series of connected plastic tubes filled with water which absorbs heat during the day and warms by radiated heat at night. This is reusable and offers protection down to 16°F, extending the growing season and warming the soil. Adding roughly 1 part bleach to

A tomato plant supported by a trellis

500 parts water will prevent the formation of algae on the inside of the tubes.

For tomatoes at Christmas, take cuttings in midsummer from sideshoots 5 in. long and root them in a container of sharp sand or perlite and water. When roots appear they can be potted into 4 in. pots and grown on under cover. Or simply start a new crop from seed to avoid propagating diseases along with the tomatoes.

Protect newly planted outdoor tomatoes with cloches or floating crop covers until they become established. Once the first flowers are pushing against the cover, make slits along the center; about 7 to 10 days later slit the remainder of the cover and leave as a shelter alongside the plants. "Indeterminate" varieties can then be tied to stakes.

Harvesting and Storing

Harvest fruits as they ripen, about 7 to 8 weeks after planting for bush types and 10 to 12 weeks for indeterminate varieties. Lift and break the stem at the "joint" just above the fruit. Outdoor crops should be harvested before the first frosts. Towards the end of the season, indeterminate varieties with unripe fruit can be lifted by the roots and hung upside down in a frost-free shed to ripen.

Alternatively, they can be detached from their support, laid on straw and covered with cloches or put in a drawer or a paper bag with a ripe banana or apple (the ethylene these produce ripens the fruit). Bush and dwarf types can be ripened under cloches.

Tomatoes can be cooked and bottled in airtight jars. To freeze, skin and core when ripe, simmer for 5 minutes, then sift, cool and pack in a rigid container.

Tomatoes stay fresh for about a week at cool room temperature.

Dry large "meaty" tomatoes in the sun or the oven. Cut into halves or thirds and put skin side down on a tray and cover with a gauze frame as a protection from insects. Ideal drying conditions are in warm, dry windy weather, but they should be brought indoors at night if dew is likely to form. Humid conditions are not suitable for outdoor drying. Oven-dry just below 145°F until tomatoes are dried but flexible. Stored in airtight containers in a cool place, they can last for up to 9 months. Before use, put the tomatoes in boiling water or a 50:50 mix of boiling water and vinegar and allow them to stand until soft. Drain and marinate for several hours in olive oil with added garlic to suit your taste. They last in the marinade for about a month and are excellent with pasta and tomato sauce.

Growing bags can be productive

Pests and Diseases

Blossom end rot appears as a hard, dark, flattened patch at the end of the fruit away from the stalk. This indicates a deficiency in calcium, usually caused by erratic watering. It is often a problem with plants grown in growing bags or containers. Water and feed regularly, particularly during hot weather. Erratic watering causes fruit to split, which may also happen with sudden growth after overcast weather. Pick and use split fruits immediately.

Greenback — hard, green patches appearing near the stalk, caused by sun scorch and overheating — is more of a problem with plants growing in the greenhouse. Sometimes this becomes an internal condition known as whitewall. Shade and ventilate well, water regularly and feed with a high-potash liquid fertilizer.

Curled leaves are caused by extreme temperature fluctuations between day and night. It is often a problem in greenhouses: shade, ventilate and dampen. Close ventilation before temperatures drop.

"Alicante"

Whitefly, aphids and red spider mite can be a problem. Early blight and septoria leaf spot are serious problems: dark blotches with lighter margins appear on the leaves. Spray with a copper fungicide or grow resistant varieties.

Plants with verticillium wilt droop during the day and usually recover overnight. Lower leaves turn yellow and cut stems have brown markings on the inside. The best control is to grow resistant cultivars, but you can also avoid planting when the soil is cold, rotate crops regularly, replace the soil, mist regularly and shade. Mounding moist potting mix round the stem encourages the formation of a secondary root system. The symptoms and control of fusarium wilt are similar.

Tobacco mosaic and other viruses show as mottling on the leaves, some of which may be misshapen; inside the fruit is browned and pitted and growth is stunted. Dispose of affected plants, wash your hands and sterilize tools by passing them through a flame. Grow the following year's plants in sterilized compost or in growbags. Resistant varieties are also available.

The tomato hornworm is a large (3½ to 4 in. when mature) pale green or brown caterpillar with white and black markings that feeds on the leaves of tomatoes and related plants. It has eight V-shaped markings down each side. Hand picking or sniping the hornworms in half with scissors gives good control.

The symptoms of magnesium deficiency are yellowing between the leaf veins, older leaves being affected first. Spray, drench or sprinkle magnesium sulfate around the base. Wherever possible, grow disease-resistant varieties.

 ## container growing

Tomatoes are excellent for containers, pots or growing bags, indoors or outside where they can be included in "edible" displays in window boxes, pots and hanging baskets.

Grow in 9 inch pots of soilless potting mix with high fertilizer levels. For requirements see "Growing" and "Protected Cropping." Bushy varieties are ideal. Plants in containers dry out rapidly, so careful feeding and watering is essential. Water regularly and remember to label your plants.

Marigolds can help keep whitefly away

 ## companion planting

Grow with French marigolds to deter whitefly. Tomatoes grow well with basil, parsley, alliums, nasturtiums and asparagus.

medicinal

Tomatoes contain lycopene and are believed to reduce the risk of cancer and appendicitis.

In American herbal medicine, tomatoes have been used to treat dyspepsia, liver and kidney complaints and are also said to cure constipation.

 ## warning

Some doctors believe that tomatoes aggravate arthritis and may be responsible for food allergies. The leaves and stems are poisonous.

culinary

In salads, tomatoes are particularly good with mozzarella, basil, and olive oil. They are also good with chives. Some people prefer to peel them first, by immersing in boiled water for 1 minute to loosen the skins. Use in soups, stews, sauces, and omelets.

Tomatoes are wonderful broiled: cut them in half and cover the cut surface with olive oil, pepper, and sugar. Broil for 5 minutes. Alternatively, glaze them with wine and brown sugar and broil.

Try a BLT — a bacon, lettuce, and tomato sandwich. Eat "currant" and "cherry" varieties as a snack. Use "beefsteak" varieties as a garnish with steak or hollow out and stuff with shrimp, potato salad, cold salmon, cottage cheese, or egg salad filling. Serve hot or cold.

Green tomatoes can be sliced, dipped in batter and then breadcrumbs, and fried in hot oil, made into chutney or jam, or be added to orange marmalade.

Jean-Christophe Novelli's Gazpacho Soup
Serves 6

1 pound very ripe cherry tomatoes
2 large over-ripe tomatoes
2 tablespoons truffle oil
1/3 cup olive oil
4 teaspoons white wine vinegar
Unrefined superfine sugar
Salt and freshly ground black pepper
1 pound bright red bell peppers, chopped
6 sprigs fresh cilantro

Place the tomatoes, truffle oil, and olive oil in a blender and add half the vinegar, 2 teaspoons sugar, and a little seasoning. Blitz together, thin with water if necessary, and season to taste. Put through a fine strainer and chill for at least 2 hours.

Rinse out the blender, then whizz the peppers with 3 tablespoons water to a purée. Pass through a fine strainer and stir in 1½ tablespoons sugar and the remaining vinegar. Put the sifted purée in a pan and simmer until reduced to a syrup. Allow to cool to room temperature.

Stuffed Tomatoes

To finish, carefully pour the chilled gazpacho soup into a bowl, drizzle some red bell pepper syrup over the surface, and serve garnished with cilantro.

Stuffed Tomatoes
Serves 4

In times gone by Catholics all over Europe ate these on fast days, when meat was not allowed.

4 large ripe tomatoes
3 cups white breadcrumbs (day-old bread)
2/3 cup milk
2 eggs, lightly beaten
2 cloves garlic, finely crushed
2 tablespoons chopped fresh basil
2 tablespoons finely minced fresh parsley
1 onion, finely minced

2 tablespoons toasted breadcrumbs
5 to 6 tablespoons grated Gruyère cheese
Olive oil
Salt and freshly ground black pepper

Remove a slice from the top of each tomato and scoop out the pulp. Season the insides of the tomatoes with salt and pepper, and arrange in a greased baking dish.

Preheat the oven to 350°F. To make the stuffing, combine the white breadcrumbs with the milk and eggs in a bowl and add the garlic, herbs, and onion. Season with salt and pepper and fill the tomatoes. Sprinkle over the toasted breadcrumbs and Gruyère and drizzle over a little olive oil to prevent burning. Bake until the tomatoes are tender, about 30 minutes.

Manihot esculenta (syn. *M. utilissima*). Euphorbiaceae
CASSAVA

Also known as Tapioca, Yucca, Manioc. Tall herbaceous perennial grown for edible tubers and leaves. Tender. Value: mainly starch; small amounts of vitamin B, C and protein.

One of the most important food crops in the humid tropics, cassava is believed to have been cultivated since at least 2500 BCE. Unknown as a wild plant, it may have originated in equatorial South America in the Andean foothills, the Amazon basin or regions of savannah vegetation. The earliest archaeological records, from coastal Peru, date from 1000 BCE. Tubers contain highly toxic cyanide, which is removed by cooking; accounts tell of starving European explorers eating raw manioc and dying at the moment they thought sustenance had been found. The indigenous Indians tipped their arrows and blowpipe darts with its toxic sap; Arawak Indians committed suicide by biting into uncooked tubers rather than be tortured by the Conquistadors.

The Portuguese brought the crop to West Africa, whence it quickly spread, reaching Sri Lanka in 1786, India in 1794 and Java by 1835. An estimated 62 million tons of cassava is produced annually, much of it in West Africa, where it is eaten as "fufu."

 varieties

Manihot esculenta is tall and branched and its stems become woody with age. The leaves are long-stalked, with 5 to 9 lobes; toxic latex is present in all parts of the plant. The swollen tubers are cylindrical or tapering, forming a cluster just below the soil surface, and weigh 10–20 pounds.

There are two types. "White Cassava" is sweet, soft and used as a source of starch; yellow varieties are bitter and usually grown as a vegetable. The more primitive bitter varieties contain larger quantities of cyanide, which is washed out by boiling in several changes of water before cooking. In recent selections of "sweet" varieties, most of the toxin is in the skin, and tubers are edible after simple cooking.

There are well over 100 different forms with local names. "Nandeeba," quick to mature, and "Macapera," used for boiling, are both from Brazil.

 cultivation

Propagation
Take cuttings from mature stems 6–12 in. long; plant 4 ft. apart in rows 3 ft. apart or "pits" 3–3½ ft. square in a grid pattern. Planting cuttings upright, leaving the top 2 in. exposed, gives best results. Plant cuttings at the start of the rainy season. **Zones 9 to 11.**

Growing
Cassava flourishes where the warm rainy season is followed by a dry period. It has good resistance to drought; in a constantly wet climate there is excessive stem growth and tuber formation is poor. Soils should be deep, rich and free-draining. It is often grown on ridges or mounds as it dislikes waterlogging. Dig deeply before planting, adding well-rotted organic matter. Hill up as necessary. Cassava is a heavy feeder and cannot usually be grown for more than 3 years on the same ground.

Maintenance
Spring Dig in organic matter before planting.
Summer Plant cuttings at the start of the rainy season.
Fall Keep weed-free.
Winter Harvest at maturity.

CASSAVA

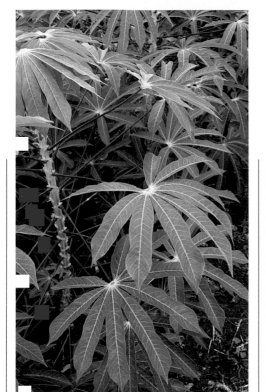

Typically tropical

Protected Cropping

In cool temperate zones, plants can be grown as a "novelty crop" in a hothouse. Prepare the borders and cultivate as for "Growing." Water well during the growing season and reduce watering during winter.

Harvesting and Storing

Varieties are harvested from 8 months to 2 years after planting, depending on the locality and variety. Harvest when plants have flowered and the leaves are yellow. Lift the whole plant and carefully remove the tubers. They store for up to 2 years in the ground, but should be used within 4 to 5 days of lifting.

Pests and Diseases

Whiteflies and fungal diseases can be a problem.

Bacterial diseases, scale and cassava mosaic are a real problem in Africa. Plants are highly resistant to locusts.

 other uses

Cassava is also a source of starch for the manufacture of plywood, textiles, adhesives, and paper.

 warning

All parts of the plant contain toxic latex. Prepare tubers thoroughly before eating. Inhabitants of Guyana take chiles steeped in rum as an antidote to cassava poisoning, but do not rely on it!

 culinary

The fresh root is equivalent in starch to 33 percent of its weight in rice and 50 percent in bread, but its nutritional value is unbalanced and high consumption often leads to protein deficiency.

Wash thoroughly and remove the skin and rind with a sharp knife or potato peeler. Boil in several changes of water and allow to dry before cooking.

It can be eaten mashed or boiled as a vegetable or made into dumplings and cakes. Mix with coconut and sugar to make cookies. The juice from grated cassava is boiled down and flavored with cinnamon, cloves and brown sugar to make "cassareep," a powerful antiseptic and essential to the West Indian dish, Pepperpot. Tapioca flour is made from ground chips.

In Africa, the fresh root is washed, peeled, boiled and pounded with a wooden pestle to make "fufu." Cook cassava chunks in boiling water for 45 to 50 minutes, drain, cool, pound into dough and shape into egg-sized balls to add to soups and stews as a traditional African accompaniment.

Roots of "sweet" forms can be roasted like sweet potato, baked or fried in slices.

Young leaves can be boiled or steamed and eaten with a pat of butter.

Cassava Fries (Singkong)

These thin, crispy wafers are perfect served as a snack or as a garnish. Allow ½ pound per person to accompany a plain meat course.

Slice the cassava very thinly and leave to dry. Heat some peanut or vegetable oil (do not allow it to smoke)

in a wok or a deep pan. Deep-fry one to three slices at a time by immediately submerging each below the surface of the oil. Remove quickly from the heat and drain well on layers of paper towels.

Cooked Singkong can be stored in an airtight container for several weeks, but is best served at once.

Medicago sativa. Papilionacae
ALFALFA

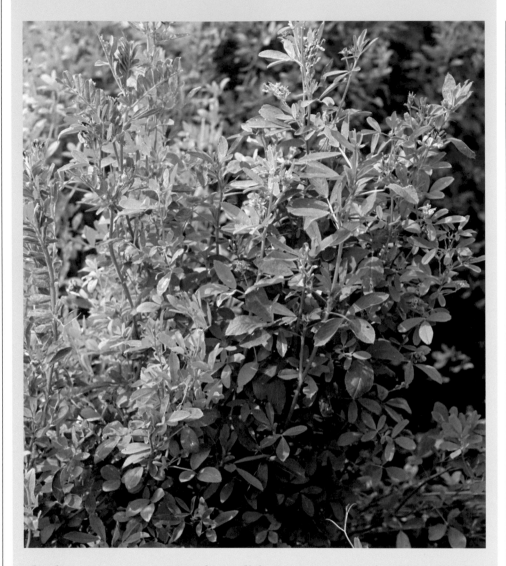

Also known as Lucerne, Purple Medick. Grown as annual or short-lived perennial for seed sprouts and young leaf shoots. Hardy. Value: good source of iron and protein.

"Medick" comes from the Latin *Herba medica*, the Median or Persian herb, imported to Greece after Darius found it in the kingdom of the Medes. It was a vital fodder crop of ancient civilizations in the Near East and Mediterranean, and known in Britain by 1757. Today, alfalfa is valued by gardeners as a green manure as well as a nutritious vegetable. Its blooms in the wildflower meadow are rich in nectar, while the leaves are a commercial source of chlorophyll.

 varieties

The species *Medicago sativa* is a fast-growing evergreen legume with clover-like leaves; growing ultimately to 3–4 ft., it has spikes of violet and blue flowers. It produces quality crops on poor soils, as it is highly effective at fixing nitrogen in the root nodules.

Penetrating up to 20 ft. into the ground, the roots draw up nutrients and aerate the soil. Agricultural varieties are available. If you want to sprout alfalfa seeds, buy untreated seed; that sold for sowing as a crop is usually chemically treated.

 cultivation

Alfalfa can be grown as a short-lived perennial, a "cut and come again" crop or as seedsprouts. It tolerates low rainfall and can be grown in any soil, in temperate to subtropical conditions or at altitude in the tropics.

Propagation
Sow in spring or from late summer to fall. Thin those grown as perennials to 10 in. apart when large enough

Alfalfa flowering in California

culinary

Young shoot tips and sprouted seeds can be used raw in salads or cooked lightly.

For a tasty salad, try it with hard-boiled eggs (1 per person), anchovies and capers served on a bed of endive and radicchio leaves. To stir-fry, pour a little oil in a pan, add the alfalfa, stir briskly for 2 minutes; serve immediately.

 companion planting

Alfalfa accumulates phosphorus, potassium, iron and magnesium; it keeps grass green longer in drought.

 container growing

Sow "cut and come again" crops in a bright open position in a soilless potting mix with low fertilizer levels; water pots regularly.

 medicinal

An infusion of young leaves in water is used to increase vitality, appetite and weight. The young shoots, rich in minerals and vitamin B, are highly nutritious and the seeds appear to reduce cholesterol levels.

to handle. Sow "cut and come again" crops, spaced evenly, by broadcasting or in shallow rows 4–5 in. wide. **Zones 3 to 9.**

Growing
Prepare seedbeds in winter, fork the area, remove debris and stones, rake level. Keep weed-free until established. Cut perennials to within a few inches of the base after flowering and renew every 3 to 4 years, as old plants become straggly.

Maintenance
Spring Sow seed outdoors.
Summer Harvest young shoots from perennials.
Fall Sow protected crops.
Winter Prepare seedbed.

Protected Cropping
Sow alfalfa seeds under cloches, floating row cover in late summer to fall to harvest a winter crop.

Harvesting
Harvest "cut and come again" crops when about 2 in. long a few weeks after sowing. Cut back plants regularly to encourage new growth; they provide young growths for many harvests.

Sprouting Seeds
To sprout alfalfa, soak seeds overnight or for several hours, tip seeds into a strainer and rinse. Put several layers of moist paper towel in the base of a jar and cover with a ¼ in. layer of seed. Cut a square from a pair of tights or piece of muslin to cover the top, securing with a band. Place in a bright position, away from direct sun, maintaining constant temperatures around 68°F. Rinse seed daily by filling the jar with water and pouring off again. Harvest shoots after 3 to 7 days, when they have nearly filled the jar. Wash and dry sprouts and use as required; do not store more than 2 days, as salmonella develops quickly.

Pests and Diseases
Rabbits can be a problem.

Healthy eating for all

Momordica charantia. Cucurbitaceae
BITTER MELON

Also known as Karela, Bitter Gourd, Balsam Pear, Fu Gua, Momordica, Peria. Annual climber grown for edible fruits and leaves. Tender. Value: fruit a good source of iron, ascorbic acid and vitamin C; leaves and young shoots contain traces of minerals.

This strange-looking fruit with skin the texture of a crocodile has been grown throughout the humid tropics for centuries. Rudyard Kipling's description in Mowgli's "Song Against People" conveys the plant's vigor, as it climbs to 13 ft. with the aid of tendrils:

I will let loose against you the fleet-footed vines,
I will call in the Jungle to stamp out your lines.
The roofs shall fade before it, the house-beams shall fall;
And the Karela shall cover it all.

The strongly vanilla-scented flowers are followed by the elongated fruit. When ripe, it splits at the tip into three sections, exposing brown or white seeds surrounded by blood-red pulp. Fruits are best eaten young.

Go on, try it!

 varieties

Male and female flowers are borne on the same plant. Male flowers are 2–4 in. long; females are similar, but with a slender basal bract. The fruit can grow up to 10 in.— which ripens to become orange-yellow, though a white variety is grown in India and eastern Asia. **Zones 8 to 11.**

"Baby Doll" has top-quality, small fruit and is easy to grow. "Bankok Large" produces dark green fruit of excellent quality and "Japan Green Spindle" produces spindle-shaped fruit. "Taiwan Large" is high-yielding. "Taiwan White" is highly ornamental with white fruit and "Winter Beauty" is creamy white in color.

 cultivation

Propagation
In humid tropical climates, sow at the start of the rainy season, placing two to three seeds outdoors in hills 3 ft. apart, in and between the rows. Thin after germination, leaving the strongest seedling. Water plants as needed.

The first flowers appear 30 to 35 days after sowing. In temperate zones, sow seed in early spring indoors at 68°F in peat-substitute compost. Keep the compost moist with lukewarm water and repot as necessary when roots become visible through the drainage holes.

Growing

Bitter melons flourish in moderate to high temperatures with sunshine and high humidity. Plant in beds or mounds of rich, moisture-retentive, free-draining soil. Dig in plenty of well-rotted manure or similar organic matter before sowing.

Pinch out the terminal shoots when they are 1–1½ in. long to encourage branching, then train the stems into trees or over fences, trellis or frames covered with 6 in. mesh netting. Keep plants moist and weed-free.

Maintenance

Spring Sow seed indoors in peat-substitute compost.
Summer Keep plants well fed and watered.
Fall When cropping finishes, add leaves and stems to your compost pile.
Winter Prepare the greenhouse bed for the following year's crop.

Protected Cropping

Grow under cover in temperate zones. Plants need hot, humid conditions in bright light. When growing plants in the greenhouse bed, prepare the soil as for "Growing."

Growth is better restricted in borders and containers. Stop the shoot tips when the main stems are 5 ft. long, training the lateral stems along wires or trellis.

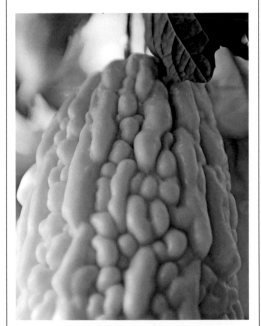

Appearances are deceiving

Once a flower has formed, allow two more leaves to appear, then pinch out the growing tip. If it is a male flower or a flower does not form, cut the stem back to the first leaf to allow a replacement to form. Flowers should be hand-pollinated.

You should dampen the greenhouse floor regularly during hot weather.

Harvesting and Storing

The first fruits appear about 2 months after sowing, are yellow-green in color and should be harvested when they are about 1½ in. long. They can be eaten when longer.

Fruits can be kept in a cool dark place for several days or stored in the salad drawer of a refrigerator for 4 weeks. Karela can also be sliced and dried for use out of season.

Pests and Diseases

Fruit fly is common; spray with contact insecticide or protect the fruits with a piece of paper wrapped around the fruit and tied with string around the stalk. Red spider mite is a common pest under cover. Leaves become mottled and bronzed. Check plants regularly; small infestations are easily controlled — isolate young plants. The mite prefer hot, dry conditions, so keep humidity high or use biological control.

 container growing

Plants can be grown indoors in containers containing a rich, well-drained potting mixture of equal parts soilless potting mix and well-rotted organic matter with added peat and grit.

Keep the compost moist with lukewarm water and feed every 2 weeks with a liquid general fertilizer.

 medicinal

The fruits are said to be tonic, stomachic and carminative and are an herbal remedy for rheumatism, gout, and diseases of the liver and spleen. In Brazil, the seeds are used as an anthelmintic. Its fruits, leaves and roots are used in India and Puerto Rico for diabetes. In India, leaves are applied to burns and used as a poultice for headaches and the roots used to treat hemorrhoids. In Malaya they are used as a poultice for elephants with sore eyes.

 culinary

Remove the seeds from mature fruit, and remove any bitterness by salting. Young fruits do not need to be salted.

Bitter melons are ideal diced in curries, chop suey or pickles, stuffed with meat, shrimps, spices and onions and fried or added to meat and fish dishes. Mature fruits can be parboiled before being added to a dish or cooked like zucchini and eaten as a vegetable.

Young shoots and leaves are cooked like spinach.

Pelecing Peria
Serves 4

Sri Owen gives this recipe in her marvellous book, *Indonesian Food and Cookery*. Some of the ingredients need determination to track down, but it is worth the trouble.

3 to 4 karela (peria)
Salt
6 cabé rawit (or hot red chiles)
3 candlenuts
2 cloves garlic
1 piece terasi (shrimp paste, available at Thai stores)
1 tablespoon vegetable oil
Juice of 1 lime

Cut the karela lengthwise in half, take out the seeds, then slice like cucumbers. Put the slices into a colander, sprinkle liberally with salt and leave for at least 30 minutes. Wash under cold running water before boiling for 3 minutes with a little salt.

Pound the cabé rawit, candlenuts, garlic and terasi in a mortar until smooth. Heat the oil in a wok or skillet and fry for about 1 minute. Add the karela and stir-fry for 2 minutes; season with salt and lime juice. Serve hot or cold.

Oxalis tuberosa. Oxalidaceae
OCA

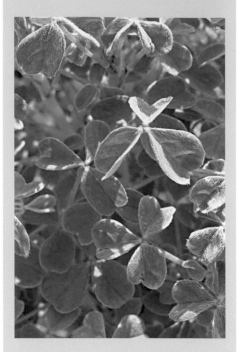

Also known as Iribia, Cuiba, New Zealand Yam. Perennial grown for tubers. Half hardy. Value: 85 percent water; some carbohydrates; small amounts of protein.

This is common in the high-altitude Andes from Venezuela to northern Argentina, where it is second only to the potato in popularity. At the northern end of Lake Titicaca, more than 150 steep terraces dating from the Incas are still cultivated. Oca is grown in New Zealand, where it was introduced from Chile in 1869. Today it is rarely found in European or American gardens, though it was once grown as a potato substitute. Tubers form in fall when day lengths are less than 9 hours.

 varieties

Oxalis tuberosa is bushy to 10 in. tall, with tri-lobed leaves and orange-yellow flowers. It produces small tubers 3–4 in. long which are yellow, white, pink, black or piebald.

 cultivation

Propagation
Plant single tubers or slice into several sections, each with an "eye" or dormant bud, and dust the cut surfaces with fungicide. Plant 5 in. deep and 12 in. apart with 12 in. between rows.

In frost-free climates plant in midspring; in cooler areas propagate under cover in 5–8 in. pots of compost before planting out once frosts have passed. **Zones 7 to 9.**

Growing
Oca flourishes in deep fertile soils, so incorporate organic matter before planting. Hilling before planting increases the yield.

Maintenance
Spring Plant tubers.
Summer Water as necessary.
Fall Tubers can be lifted when needed.
Winter Store tubers in sand.

Protected Cropping
Where early or late frosts are likely, grow under cover to extend the harvest season. Plant in midspring in greenhouse beds. Harvest from midfall to early winter.

Extend outdoor cropping by protecting with floating row cover or cloches.

Harvesting and Storing
Tubers are formed in fall and can be stored in sand in a dry frost-free place. Lift just before the first frosts or protect with fleece and harvest later.

Pests and Diseases
Slugs are often a problem.

 culinary

Tubers have been selected over the centuries for flavor and reduced levels of calcium oxalate crystals, which otherwise render them inedible. Leave them for a few days to become soft before eating. In South America they are dried in the sun until floury and less acid. If dried for several weeks, they become sweet, tasting similar to dried figs.

The acidity can be removed by boiling in several changes of water. The flavor of tubers even improves once frozen. Oca can be eaten raw, roasted, boiled, candied like sweet potato and added to soups and stews. Use leaves and young shoots in salads or cook them like sorrel.

Oca and Bacon
Clean 1 pound oca and cut into cubes. Boil in salted water until just tender; drain and combine with ½ pound bacon that has been diced and fried. Coat with mayonnaise, sprinkle over fresh chives and season. Serve warm.

 container growing

Oca grows well in containers, although yields are lower. Tubers should be planted in spring in 12 in. pots in soilless potting mix with moderate fertilizer levels, with added organic matter. Regular watering is vital, particularly as tubers begin to form. Allow the compost surface to dry out before rewatering. An occasional feed with liquid fertilizer helps to boost growth.

 companion planting

Oca grow well with potatoes and can be grown under runner beans, corn or crops of a similar height.

 warning

Prepare correctly before eating to remove calcium oxalate crystals.

Pachyrrhizus erosus. Leguminosae
JICAMA

Also known as Yam Bean, Potato Bean, Mexican Water Chestnut, Dou Shou, Sha Kot. Tender, vining perennial. Value: low in starch and calories, high in fiber, a good source of vitamin C and potassium.

Originating in tropical America and naturalized in Florida, the Jicama is very popular in the local cuisine of southern China and the Philippines. In Mexico, it is one of four foods included in rituals for the "Festival of the Dead" celebrated on November 1st, alongside sugar, tangerines and peanuts.

Grown as a novelty crop in cooler climates, its attractive flowers also give it considerable value as an ornamental plant.

 culinary

Like water chestnut, jicama is very refreshing when peeled and eaten raw. Tubers can be fried, braised, boiled, eaten in casseroles, used as a bamboo shoot, water chestnut or mooli substitute, added to custards, desserts and fruit salads or eaten as a snack. In California it is commonly sliced and added to salads, in Mexico it is marinated with lime then served topped with chile powder; sometimes sour orange is used as a lime substitute. Crunchiness is retained after cooking. The best-quality roots are about 4½ pounds in weight; older tubers become "woody" growing up to 7 ft. long and weighing 45 pounds, at this stage they become fibrous and inedible. Only the young pods are edible, boil them thoroughly before eating and use as green beans.

 varieties

Pachyrrhizus erosus is a scrambling perennial with attractive violet and purple flowers. Two major types are grown in Mexico, where it is a popular edible crop; Jicama de leche with dark skin and spindle-shaped roots, which is rather dry and Jicama de agua with light skin and a succulent, sweet, watery flavor to the tubers.

 cultivation

Propagation
From midspring, sow two seeds in a 4 in. pot filled with seed compost and place in a propagator or on a warm windowsill at 68°F. Thin after germination, leaving the strongest seedling and transplant regularly as the plants grow, supporting the stems with a stick. Plants grow rapidly: allow as much growing time as possible before they are planted outdoors (if that is what you intend to do); ideally the seeds should be sown around 6 to 8 weeks before the final frosts in spring. Although tubers can be stored at temperatures from 54–59°F for replanting, they are very sensitive to chilling. It is much easier to save or buy fresh seeds the following year.

Growing yam bean is day-length sensitive and the edible tubers are not formed until fall when there are fewer than 9 hours of daylight; unfortunately, this often coincides with the first frosts. Vines are best grown indoors in temperate climates, so they have enough energy to produce sizable tubers at the end of the growing season, before light and cold restrict growth.

If growing plants outdoors, warm the soil with cloches before planting the large ones, covering them with cloches for 2 to 3 weeks until they become acclimatized. Grow them like runner beans, along rows of stakes or up "wigwams," in a sunny position in well-prepared, deep, light, rich, moisture-retentive soil, incorporating plenty of well-rotted organic matter, if necessary. Pinch out growth tips if plants become too large, and remove the flower buds, too; this has the added advantage of encouraging tuber growth.

Maintenance
Spring Sow seeds early in the season.
Summer Keep plants well watered.
Fall Harvest after the first frosts.
Winter Order seed.

Protected Cropping
Grow in large tubs in the greenhouse or polyethylene tunnel border, then feed and water well during the growing season. A hot, humid environment encourages heavy cropping, so they are best grown under protection in temperate climates.

Harvesting and Storing
Cropping is most productive in temperate zones during hot summers. Harvest the tubers as late in the season as possible, once the top growth has been frosted. Harvest seed pods while immature.

Pests and Diseases
Bean seed weevil can be a problem; the seeds show evidence of tiny holes but usually germinate if sown. Alternatively, dry the seed, in silica gel, then freeze them for 48 hours.

 container growing

Plants can be grown in raised beds or very large containers, if preferred.

 warning

Mature seed pods contain rotenone: do not eat.

Pastinaca sativa. Apiaceae

PARSNIP

Biennial grown as annual for edible root. Hardy. Value: some carbohydrate, moderate vitamin E, smaller amounts of vitamins C and B.

This ancient vegetable is thought to have originated around the eastern Mediterranean. Exactly when it was introduced into cultivation is uncertain, as references to parsnips and carrots seem interchangeable in Greek and Roman literature: Pliny used the word *pastinaca* in the 1st century CE when referring to both. Tiberius Caesar was said to have imported parsnips from Germany, where they flourished along the Rhine — though it is possible that the Celts brought them back from their forays to the east long before that. In the Middle Ages, the roots were valued medicinally for treating problems as diverse as toothache, swollen testicles and stomach ache. In 16th-century Europe parsnips were used as animal fodder, and the country name of "madneps" or "madde neaps" reflects the fear that delirium and madness would be brought about by eating the roots.

Introduced to North America by early settlers, they were grown in Virginia by 1609 and were soon accepted by the Native North Americans, who readily took up parsnip growing. They were used as a sweetener until the development of beets in the 19th century; the juices were evaporated and the brown residue used as honey. Parsnip wine was considered by some to be equal in quality to Malmsey and parsnip beer was often drunk in Ireland. In Italy pigs bred for the best-quality Parma ham are fed on parsnips.

Avonresister

 varieties

Roots are "bulbous" (stocky, with rounded shoulders), "wedge" types (broad and long-rooted) or "bayonet" (similar, but long and narrow in shape).

"Alba" has small, thin, wedge- and bayonet-shaped roots and good canker resistance; top quality. "All American" has wedge-shaped roots and is sweet-tasting. "Arrow" should be sown in succession from midspring to midsummer for young roots and harvested from mid- to late summer for small roots. "Avonresister" is small with bulbous roots, is sweet-tasting, performs well on poorer soil and grows rapidly. It also has excellent resistance to canker and bruising. "Bugi Bijeli" is a Yugoslavian variety with a large, sweet root. "Cobham Improved Marrow" is wedge-shaped, medium in size and well-flavored, and resistant to canker. "Exhibition Long" is extra-long with an excellent flavor. "Gladiator" produces large, vigorous, well-shaped and fine-flavored roots with good canker resistance. "Javelin" is wedge- or bayonet-shaped, high-yielding and canker-resistant; "fanging" rarely occurs. "Student" has long slender roots and is very tasty. It originated around 1810 from a wild parsnip found in the grounds of the Royal Agricultural College, Cirencester, England. "Tender and True" is an old variety that is very tasty, tender and sweet. It has very little core. "White Gem" has wedge-shaped to bulbous smooth roots, with delicious flesh and good canker resistance. It is ideal for heavier soils.

cultivation

Propagation

Parsnip seed must always be sown fresh, as it rapidly loses the ability to germinate. Seeds are also renowned for erratic, slow germination in the cold, wet conditions which often prevail early in the year when they are traditionally sown.

To avoid poor germination, sow later, from mid- to late spring, depending on the weather and soil conditions, when the ground is workable and temperatures are over 45°F.

Warm the soil with cloches or floating row cover a few weeks before sowing. Rake in a granular general fertilizer at 2 oz./sq. yd. 1 to 2 weeks before sowing. Rake the seedbed to a fine texture before sowing. Sow *in situ* on a still day so the light, papery seeds are not blown away.

In dry conditions, water rows before sowing two to three seeds at the recommended final spacing in hills, thinning to leave the strongest seedling after germination. Sow radishes between the hills to act as a marker crop indicating where slower-germinating parsnip seeds are sown.

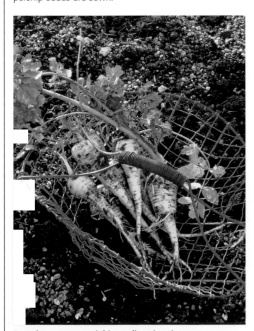

Parsnip — an essential ingredient in winter

Alternatively, parsnip seeds can be sown thinly in rows ⅕–⅓ in. deep. Sow shorter-rooted varieties in rows 6–8 in. apart, thinning them to 2–4 in., and larger types in rows 12 in. apart, thinning to 5–8 in.

In stony soil, make 6 × 36-in. hole with a crowbar, fill with finely sieved soil or compost, sow two to three seeds in the center of the hole and thin to leave the strongest seedling. Grow short-rooted varieties in shallow soils. **Zones 3 to 7.**

Growing

Parsnips thrive in an open or lightly shaded site on light, free-draining, stone-free soil which was manured the previous year.

Traditionally, parsnips are not grown on freshly manured soil as this causes "fanging," or forking of the roots; however, recent research has not supported this. Dig the plot and add plenty of well-rotted organic matter in fall or early winter the previous year. Deep digging is particularly important when growing long-rooted varieties.

The ideal pH is 6.5 to 7.0; lime where necessary, as roots grown in acid soil are prone to canker. Rotate with other roots

Keep crops weed-free, by hoeing or hand weeding carefully to avoid damaging the roots, or by mulching with well-rotted organic matter. Do not let the soil dry out, as erratic watering causes roots to split. Water at 3–4 gallons/sq. yd. every 2 weeks during dry weather when the roots are swelling.

Maintenance

Spring Rake the seedbed to a fine tilth, apply general fertilizer, sow seed in packs, "fluid sow" (see p. 645), or sow *in situ* when the soil is warm.
Summer Keep crops weed-free by mulching, hand weeding or careful hoeing.
Fall Harvest crops.
Winter Cover crops with straw or bracken before the onset of inclement weather. Dig the soil for the following year's crop.

Protected Cropping

Possible germination problems can be avoided by pregerminating and fluid-sowing seed, or by sowing in cell-packs under cover and transplanting before the tap root starts to develop.

Parsnip flowers attract beneficial insects

Harvesting and Storing

Most parsnips are a long-term crop and occupy the ground for around 8 months — a factor worth bearing in mind if your garden is small. Roots are extremely hardy and can remain in the ground until required.

Harvest from midfall onwards, covering plants with straw, bracken or hay for ease of lifting in frosty weather. Make sure you lift them carefully with a fork to avoid root damage.

Lift all your roots by winter and store them in boxes of moist sand, peat substitute or wood shavings in a cool shed.

Parsnips have a better flavor when they have been exposed for a few weeks to temperatures around freezing point. (This changes stored starch to sugar, increasing sweetness and improving the flavor.) Stored in a plastic bag in the refrigerator, they remain fresh for up to 2 months.

Wash, trim and peel roots, then cube and blanch in boiling water for 5 minutes before freezing them in plastic bags.

Pests and Diseases

Parsnip canker is a black, purple or orange-brown rot, often starting in the crown, which can be a problem during drought, when the crown is damaged or the soil is too rich. There is no chemical control. Sow crops later, improve drainage, keep the pH around neutral, rotate crops and sow canker-resistant varieties. Carrot fly can also be a problem.

 companion planting

Sow rapidly germinating plants such as lettuces between rows. Parsnips grow well alongside peas and lettuce, provided they are not in the shade.

Plant next to carrots and leave a few to flower the following year, as they attract beneficial insects.

 container growing

Shorter-rooted varieties can be grown in large containers of soilless potting mix. Longer types are grown in large barrels, making a deep hole in the potting mix, as described above for stony soil. Make sure that containers are well drained.

 medicinal

In Roman times, parsnip seeds and roots were regarded as an aphrodisiac.

Seeds only have a short life

 culinary

In 17th-century England, there are records of parsnip bread and "sweet and delicate parsnip cakes." They were often eaten with salt fish and were a staple during Lent.

Scrub or peel parsnips, and use boiled, baked, mashed or roasted with beef, pork or chicken. They combine particularly well with carrots.

Parsnips can be lightly cooked and eaten cold. Parboil and prepare like fries or slice into rings, dip in batter and eat as fritters. Grate into salads, add chopped and peeled to casseroles or soups. Or parboil, drain, then stew in butter and garnish with parsley. They are also good parboiled, then broiled with a sprinkling of Parmesan. Try steaming them whole, slicing them lengthwise and pan-glazing with butter, brown sugar and nutmeg, or garnishing them with chopped walnuts and a dash of sweet sherry.

Purée of Parsnips

Boil some parsnips and mix them with an equal quantity of mashed potatoes, plenty of salt and freshly ground black pepper, a little grated orange zest, a splash of thick cream and enough butter to make a smooth dish. Sprinkle with chopped Italian parsley and serve piping hot. (Puréed parsnips are also wonderful combined with carrots and seasoned with nutmeg.)

Curried Parsnip Soup

Serves 4 to 6

2 pounds parsnips
1 large onion, sliced
1 tablespoon butter
2 cloves garlic, crushed
1 good teaspoon curry powder
1 × 14 ounce can chopped tomatoes
4 cups vegetable stock
1 bay leaf
Sprig each of fresh thyme and parsley
4 to 6 teaspoons yogurt
Salt and freshly ground black pepper
Chopped fresh parsley, to garnish

Clean the parsnips and peel, if old. Chop them coarsely. Add the onion to a large soup pot with the butter and garlic and sauté over medium heat until lightly browned (this helps to give the flavor of Indian cuisine). Stir in the curry powder and continue to cook for 1 minute, stirring constantly.

Add the parsnips and stir, coating them well in the curry and onion mixture, and add the tomatoes, stock and herbs. Stir thoroughly. Season, bring to the boil and simmer, covered, for about 15 to 20 minutes, until the parsnips are tender.

Remove the herbs. Then liquidize the soup, adjust the seasoning and garnish with yogurt and parsley. This is delicious served with crusty bread.

HAMBURG PARSLEY

Petroselinum crispum var. *tuberosum.* Apiaceae

Also known as Parsley Root, Turnip-rooted Parsley. Swollen-rooted biennial, usually grown as annual for roots and leaves. Hardy. Value: root contains starch and sugar; leaves high in beta carotene, vitamin C and iron.

Hamburg parsley is an excellent dual-purpose vegetable. The tapering white root looks and tastes similar to parsnip and can be eaten cooked or raw. The finely cut, flat, dark green leaves resemble parsley; they are coarser in texture, but contribute a parsley flavor and can be used as garnish. As a bonus, it grows in partial shade, is very hardy and is an ideal winter vegetable.

Popular in Central Europe and in Germany, it is one of several vegetables and herbs known as *Suppengrun,* or "soup greens," which are added to the water when beef or poultry is boiled and later used for making sauce or soup. Introduced from Holland to England in the 18th century, this versatile vegetable enjoyed only a relatively brief period of popularity, but should certainly be more widely grown by America's gardeners.

Hamburg parsley roots

 cultivation

Hamburg parsley needs a long growing season to develop good-sized roots. Grow it in moisture-retentive soil in an open or semi-shaded position.

Propagation

As seeds are sown early in the year, it may be necessary to cover the bed with cloches or polyethylene before sowing to warm up the soil. Sow from early to midspring in rows ½ in. deep and 10–12 in. apart, thinning seedlings to a final spacing of 8 in.

They can also be sown in hills, planting three to four seeds in clusters 9 in. apart. Thin to leave the strongest seedling when they are large enough to handle.

Seeds can also be sown in cell-packs, but should be planted in their final position before the tap root begins to form.

To extend the harvesting season, make a second sowing in midsummer, which will provide crops early the following year. **Zones 4 to 9.**

Growing

Dig in plenty of well-rotted organic matter the fall before planting or plant in an area where the soil has been manured for the previous crop.

Rake the soil finely before sowing. Germination is often slow and it is important that the seedbed is kept free of weeds, particularly in the early stages.

Use a hoe with care as the plants become established to avoid damaging the roots. Mulching established plants is a sensible option as this stifles weed growth and conserves moisture. A 1 in. layer of well-rotted compost will perform the task perfectly. Root splitting can occur if plants are watered after the soil has dried out, so water thoroughly and regularly during dry periods to maintain steady growth.

Maintenance

Spring Sow seeds outdoors, warming the soil if necessary. Seeds can also be sown in cell-packs.
Summer Keep crops weed-free, water during drought and make a second sowing in midsummer for early crops the following year.
Fall Harvest as required.
Winter Cover crops with bracken or similar protection to make lifting easier in severe weather.

Harvesting and Storing

This is such a hardy vegetable that it can remain in the ground until required any time from early fall to midspring. When frosts are forecast, cover with straw, bracken or a similar material to make lifting easier. After removing the foliage, store in a box of sand or peat substitute in a cool shed or garage; some of the flavor is lost when roots are stored in this way, so they are better left in the ground, if possible.

Pests and Diseases

This tough vegetable is generally trouble-free, but it can suffer from parsnip canker. This appears as dark patches on the root. Control is impossible, but the following measures will help. Dig up and dispose of affected plants immediately, ensure that the soil is well drained, rotate crops and maintain soil at a pH around neutral.

 companion planting

When hill sowing, fill the spaces by planting "Tom Thumb" or a similar lettuce variety. Sowing radishes between hills is also useful, because their rapid germination indicates the position of the Hamburg parsley and prevents you accidentally removing any newly germinated seedlings when weeding.

The tops are also tasty

 container growing

Hamburg parsley can be grown in containers if they are deep enough not to dry out rapidly and provide sufficient space for the roots to form. Regular watering is vital and plants should also be kept out of scorching, bright sunshine.

 warning

Hamburg parsley should not be eaten in large amounts by expectant mothers or those with kidney problems.

 medicinal

The leaves are a good source of vitamins A and C and contain similar properties to traditional garnishing parsley. They reduce inflammation, are used for urological conditions such as cystitis and kidney stones, and help indigestion, arthritis and rheumatism. After childbirth the leaves encourage lactation; the roots and seeds promote uterine contractions. The leaves are also an excellent breath freshener — powerful enough to counter the effects of garlic!

 culinary

Hamburg parsley has a flavor reminiscent of celeriac, and is frequently used in Eastern European cooking.

Prepare for cooking by removing the leaves and fine roots, then gently scrubbing to remove the soil: don't peel or scrape. Try Hamburg parsley sliced, cubed and cooked like parsnips (sprinkle cut areas with lemon juice to prevent discoloration). It is delicious roasted, sautéed or fried like fries, as well as boiled, steamed or added to soups and stews. It can also be grated raw in winter salads.

Dried roots can be used as a flavoring. Dry them on a shallow baking sheet in an oven heated to 170°F; allow to cool before storing in an airtight jar, in a dark place. Wash the leaves and use as flavoring or garnish.

Croatian Hamburg Parsley Soup
Serves 8

1 pound Hamburg parsley
1 turnip, peeled
1 large onion, peeled
1 good-sized leek, cleaned
3 ½ tablespoons butter
2 ½ quarts vegetable stock
Salt and freshly ground black pepper
4 tablespoons sour cream
2 tablespoons each fresh chives and dill

Chop all the vegetables coarsely. Heat the butter in a heavy-bottomed pan and sauté the vegetables until softened. Stir to prevent burning. Pour over the stock, season with salt and pepper and simmer until the vegetables are tender.

Liquidize in a blender, then return to the pan. Stir in the sour cream and the herbs, allow to heat through again and adjust the seasoning. Do not allow to boil. Serve piping hot, with croutons.

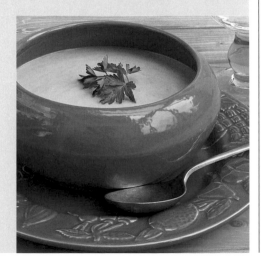

Phaseolus aureus. Papilionaceae

MUNG BEAN

Also known as green gram, golden gram. Annual grown for its seed sprouts and seeds. Tender. Value: sprouts: rich in vitamins, iron, iodine, potassium, calcium; seeds: rich in minerals, protein and vitamins.

This major Indian pulse crop was introduced to Indonesia and southern China many centuries ago and is grown throughout the tropics and subtropics, being sown towards the end of the wet season to ripen during the dry season. The leaves and stems are used to make hay and silage and the seeds are used for cattle feed. Mung beans came to prominence in the West with an increased interest in oriental cuisine: bean sprouts are an easy-to-grow major crop. Among other uses, their flour is a soap substitute and they serve as a replacement for soy beans in the manufacture of ketchup.

 varieties

Phaseolus aureus is a sparsely leaved annual to about 3 ft. with yellow flowers and small, slender pods containing up to 15 olive, brown or mottled seeds.

 cultivation

Propagation
Rake in a general fertilizer at 2 oz./sq. yd. about 10 days before sowing. Seeds can be broadcast or sown in rows on a well-prepared seedbed, thinning to 8–12 in. apart with 16–20 in. between the rows. **Zones 4 to 11.**

Growing
Mung beans flourish on rich, deep, well-drained soils and dislike clay. Add organic matter if necessary and lime to create a pH of 5.5 to 7.0. Water well throughout the growing season. Ideal growing conditions are between 86–97°F and with moderate rainfall.

Sprouting Seeds
Use untreated seeds for sprouting, as those treated with fungicide are poisonous. Remove any that are discolored, moldy or damaged. Soak them overnight in cold water and the following morning rinse in a colander. Place a layer of moist paper toweling or damp flannel over the base of a flat-bottomed tray or "seed sprouter," then spread a layer of mung beans about ½ in. deep over the surface.

Cover the container with plastic and put the bowl in a dark cupboard, or wrap it to exclude light.

Temperatures of 55–70°F should be maintained for rapid growth: an airing cupboard is ideal. Rinse the sprouts daily, morning and night.

Buy a "seed sprouter" or make one from a large yogurt pot or ice cream tub with holes punched in the bottom and use the lid as a drip tray. This makes for easier daily rinsing of the seedlings.

Shoots are so easy to grow

culinary

Bean sprouts can be eaten raw, in salads, with a suitable dressing, or lightly cooked for about 2 minutes only in slightly salted water. (Be warned: overcooked shoots lose their taste.)

To stir-fry, use only a little oil, stirring briskly for about 2 minutes. In Oriental cooking, bean sprouts combine well with other vegetables, eggs, red meat, chicken and fish and can be used to stuff savory pancakes, egg rolls and tortillas.

Stir-fried Mung Beans
Serves 2

1 bag mung beans
Peanut oil, for frying
2 cloves garlic, crushed
½ cup chicken stock
1 tablespoon light soy sauce
1 heaping teaspoon cornstarch
2 to 3 scallions, roughly chopped

Rinse the mung beans well. Heat the oil and the garlic in a wok, then add the mung beans. Fry for 1 minute, stirring constantly.

Cover with chicken stock and cook until tender and the liquid has evaporated. Then stir in the soy sauce and the cornstarch. Cook for 2 minutes more.

Garnish with the scallions and serve with rice.

Maintenance
Outdoors Broadcast or sow seed in rows; water when needed, as the soil dries out. Harvest before the pods split.

Sprouting Keep seeds moist. Harvest regularly.

Harvesting and Storing
Harvest shoots from 3 days onwards, when they are about 1–2 in. long. If the seed coats remain attached to the sprouts, soak them in water, then "top and tail," removing the seed and shoot tip. Store in the fridge. When growing for seed, gather before they split, to prevent the seeds being lost.

Pests and Diseases
Powdery mildew is a problem when plants are dry at the roots. Mulch and water regularly, remove diseased leaves immediately, spray with baking soda, improve air circulation by thinning crops and destroy plant debris at the end of the season.

medicinal

The seeds are said to have a cooling and astringent effect on fever and an infusion is used as a diuretic when treating beriberi. In Malaya it is prescribed for vertigo.

warning

Do not let sprouted seeds become waterlogged, as they rapidly become moldy.

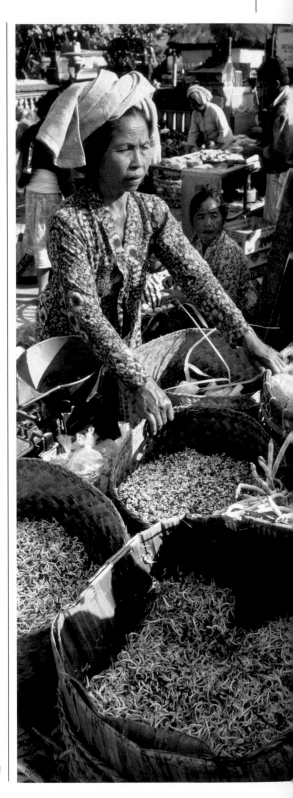

Somebody buy some, please!

RUNNER BEAN

Also known as Scarlet Runner. Perennial climber grown as annual in temperate climates for edible pods and seeds. Half hardy. Value: moderate levels of iron, vitamin C and beta carotene.

A native of Mexico, the runner bean has been known as a food crop for more than 2,200 years. In the late 16th century, Gerard's *Herball* mentions it as an ornamental introduced by the plant collector John Tradescant the Elder: "Ladies did not … disdain to put the flowers in their nosegays and garlands," and in the garden it was grown around gazebos and arbors. Vilmorin Andrieux commented in 1885: "In small gardens they are often trained over wire or woodwork, so as to form summer houses or coverings for walks." Philip Miller, keeper of Chelsea Physic Garden, is credited with being the first gardener to cook them.

It was the fashion in 17th-century England to experiment with soaking seeds. Mr Gifford, minister of Montacute in Somerset, noted in his diary: "May 10th 1679, I steep'd runner beans in sack five days, then I put them in sallet-oyle five days, then in brandy four days and about noon set them in an hot bed against a south wall casting all liquor wherein they had been infused negligently about the holes, within three hours space, eight of the nine came up, and were a foot high with all their leaves, and on the morrow a foot more in height … and in a week were podded and full ripe." You could try this for yourself — or perhaps you would prefer to stick to today's more conventional methods!

RUNNER BEAN

 ## varieties

Older cultivars were rather stringy unless eaten young; newer varieties are "stringless." Besides the traditional tall-growing climbers, there is also a choice of dwarf varieties that do not need supporting and are ideal for smaller gardens, early crops under cloches and in exposed sites.

Non-stringless Types
"Enorma" is ornamental, with red flowers. It has long pods and is very tasty. "Liberty" has good-quality pods to 45–20 in. long. "Painted Lady," a variety grown since the 19th century, has delicate red and white flowers and long pods.

Stringless Types
"Aintree" has red flowers that are followed by good-quality green pods. Tolerant of high temperatures. "Celebration" has pink flowers that are followed by plenty of straight, well-flavored, good-quality pods. "Desiree" has white flowers and seeds and is high-yielding and tasty. "Kelvedon Marvel" is tasty, matures early and crops heavily. "Lady Di" grows long, slim stringless pods with outstanding taste and

"White Lady"

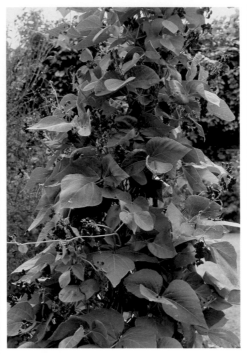

"Scarlet Emperor"

tenderness. "Red Rum" is very early, high-yielding, tasty and resistant to halo blight. "Scarlet Emperor" is a traditional "all rounder," tolerating a wide range of conditions. "Snowy" is white flowered and "sets" even in hot conditions where night temperatures are above 59°F; pods to 12 in. . "White Lady" is less likely to be attacked by birds. Its white flowers are followed by huge crops of straight fleshy pods (late). "Wisley Magic" is one of the heaviest yielding red-flowered varieties, producing masses of pods with a traditional flavor.

Dwarf Varieties
"Hammonds Dwarf Scarlet" is ideal for the small garden. The pods are easy to harvest but the tops may need to be pinched out. "Hestia" produces bicolored flowers and long, slim pods. Ideal for pots or containers.

 ## cultivation

Propagation
Runner beans are not frost-tolerant and need a minimum soil temperature of 50°F to germinate. Sow from late spring to early summer 2–3 in. deep, 6 in. apart in double rows 24 in. apart. To shelter pollinating insects they are better grown in blocks or several

short rows, rather than a single long one. Allow 3–6 ft. between rows for ease of harvesting, depending on the cultivar.

Climbing types can be encouraged to bush by pinching out the main stems when they are around 10 in.; the sideshoots can be pinched out at the second leaf joint for a bushy plant needing little or no staking. Seed sown outdoors crops in about 14 to 16 weeks, depending on climatic and cultural conditions. **Zones 4 to 10.**

Growing
Runner beans are not frost-hardy and are less successful in cooler areas unless you have a suitable microclimate. They flourish from 57–85°F, needing a warm, sheltered position to minimize wind damage and encourage pollinating insects.

Soil should be deep, fertile and moisture-retentive. Dig a trench at least 12 in. deep and 24 in. wide in late fall to early winter before planting, adding plenty of well-rotted organic matter to the backfill. Before sowing, rake in 2–3 oz./sq. yd granular general fertilizer.

Water well when flowering

"Painted Lady"

Keep crops weed-free during early stages of growth. Mulch after germination or after transplanting. Watering is essential for good bud set: the traditional method of spraying flowers has little effect. As the first buds are forming and again as the first flowers are fully open plants need 1–2 gallons/sq. yd. Crops should be rotated.

Climbers can be up to 10 ft. or more tall and a good sturdy support should be in place before sowing or transplanting. Traditionally, a "wigwam" of stakes, or a longer row of crossed stakes, were used; these may need supporting strings at the end of each row, like tent guy ropes. Do improvize: I once saw a wonderful structure like a V-shaped frame, designed so the beans would hang down and make picking easier. Use stakes, strong wooden stakes, steel tubes, or make frameworks of netting. There should be one stake or length of strong twine for each plant.

Maintenance

Spring Sow crops under cover or outdoors in late spring. Erect supports.
Summer Keep crops weed-free and well watered. Harvest regularly.
Fall Continue harvesting until the first frosts.
Winter Prepare the soil for the following year's crop.

Protected Cropping

For earlier crops and in cooler climates, sow in boxes or tall pots of seed or multipurpose compost under cover from midspring, harden off and plant out from late spring. Protect indoor and outdoor crops with cloches or floating row cover until they are established.

Harvesting and Storing

Harvest from midsummer to midfall. Picking is essential to ensure regular cropping, high yields and to avoid any "stringiness." Runner beans freeze well.

Pests and Diseases

Slugs, black bean aphid and red spider mite may prove troublesome.

Gray mold (*Botrytis*) and halo blight may cause problems in wet or humid weather.

Mice may eat seeds: dip in concentrated liquid fertilizer.

Root rots may kill plants in wet or poorly drained soils. Rotate crops to avoid this.

 companion planting

Runner beans are compatible with all plants except the *Allium* (onion) family.

Grow with corn to protect the latter from corn army worms. Nitrogen-fixing bacteria in the roots improve soil fertility. After harvesting, cut off tops, leave roots in the soil or add to compost piles. They thrive with brassicas; Brussels sprout transplants are sheltered and grow on once beans die back.

Late in the season, their shade can benefit celery and salad crops if enough water is available.

 container growing

Runner beans can be grown in containers at least 8 in. wide by 10 in. deep, depending on the vigor of the cultivar.

Sow seeds 2 in. deep and 4–5 in. apart indoors in late spring, moving the container outdoors into a sunny site. Water frequently in warm weather, less often at other times. Feed with liquid general fertilizer if plants need a boost.

Stake tall varieties, pinching out the growing points when plants reach the top of their supports. Otherwise use dwarf varieties.

 culinary

Wash, top and tail, pull off stringy edges, slice diagonally and boil for 5 to 7 minutes. Drain and serve with a pat of butter. Alternatively, cook whole and slice after cooking.

Runner Bean Chutney
Makes 3 pounds

Clare Walker and Gill Coleman give this recipe in *The Home Gardener's Cookbook*:

2 pounds runner beans
1 pound onions
1 level tablespoon salt
1 level tablespoon mustard seeds
½ cup golden raisins
1½ level teaspoons ground ginger
1 level teaspoon turmeric
6 dried red chiles, left whole
2½ cups spiced vinegar
1 pound turbinado sugar

Wipe, top, tail and string the beans and cut them into small slices. Place in a preserving pan with the peeled and finely minced onions. Add 1⅓ cups water, the salt and mustard seeds and simmer gently for 20 to 25 minutes until the beans are just tender.

Then add the golden raisins, ginger, turmeric, chiles and spiced vinegar, bring back to a boil and simmer for an additional 30 minutes, or until the mixture is fairly thick.

Stir in the sugar, allow to dissolve, then boil steadily for about 20 minutes until the chutney is thick. Pour into warm, dry jars, cover with thick plastic and seal with a lid, if available. Label and store in a cool, dry place for at least 3 months before using. The chiles can be removed before pouring into jars.

Phaseolus vulgaris. Papilionaceae
GREEN & DRY BEAN

Also known as Common, Bush, Pole, Snap, String, French Bean, Wax Bean, Haricot, Baked Bean, Flageolet, Kidney, Haricot Vert. Annual grown for edible pods and beans. Half hardy. Value: moderate potassium, folic acid, and beta carotene. Very rich in protein.

Evidence of the wild form, found in Mexico, Guatemala, and parts of the Andes, has been discovered in Peruvian settlements from 8000 BCE. Both bush and climbing varieties were introduced to Europe during the Spanish conquest in the early 16th century, though the dwarf varieties did not become popular for two more centuries. They were first referred to as "kidney beans" by the English in 1551, alluding to the shape of their seeds.

Gerard in his *Herball* calls them "sperage" beans and "long peason," while Parkinson wrote: "Kidney beans boiled in water and stewed with butter were esteemed more savory … than the common fava bean and were a dish more oftentimes at rich men's tables than at the poor." Another writer commented in 1681: "It is a plant lately brought into use among us and not yet sufficiently known."

In Europe, "haricot vert" was used in ships' stores in voyages of exploration during the early 1500s. When European colonists first explored the Americas, they found climbing beans planted with corn, providing starch and protein for indigenous tribes.

"The Prince"

 varieties

This group contains considerable variety. Plants are dwarf (ideal for smaller gardens or containers) or climbing, pods are flat, oval, or round in cross-section and are green, yellow (waxpods) or purple, or marbled. The seeds are colorful and often mottled. As well as being grown for the pods, seeds are eaten fresh as "flageolets," or dried as "white beans."

Pole Beans
"Borlotto Lingua di Fuoco" is an ornamental "fire tongue" form, with red-marked green pods. "Corona D'Oro" is high yielding with rounded, tender, golden-yellow pods. "Emerite" is one of the most productive of all pole beans. "Kwintus" produces tender, tasty pods. "Musica" can be sown early and is full of flavor. "Romano," an old variety, is tender, tasty and prolific, and excellent for freezing. "Trifonto Violetto" is an heirloom variety, and one of the prettiest. The long stringless beans are produces on plants with purple leaves and lavender flowers.

Drying Beans
"Cannellino" is a dwarf variety with white seeds. "Canadian Wonder," a Victorian variety, should be picked while young and tender, or dry for the red seeds. "Czar" produces long, rough pods; tasty when green or can be dried. "Saissons" has flat pods and tasty pale green seeds.

Dwarf or Bush Types
"Annabel" is high-yielding, round and tasty — perfect for the patio. The legendary Blue Lakes, known for their sweet, beany flavor, are now available as "Bush Blue Lake". "Chevrier Vert," a classic French flageolet from 1880, is tasty and tender. "Masai" has long thin pods, is robust, early, and high yielding, with good disease and cold tolerance. "Purple Queen" is delicious, producing heavy yields of glossy purple pods. "Royal Burgundy" germinates well in cold soil and has tasty, dark green

pods. Resistant to pea and bean weevil. Freezes well. "Royalty" crops heavily with dark purple pods that turn green when cooked and are delicately flavored. The dark green pods of "Sprite" freeze well. "Nickel" is a new breed of longstanding filet beans.

cultivation

Propagation

French beans dislike cold wet soils and are inclined to rot; for successful germination, do not sow until the soil is a minimum of 50°F.

For early sowings or in cold weather, warm the soil 3 to 4 weeks beforehand with cloches or black plastic.

Sow successively from midspring to early summer in staggered rows 1½ to 2 in. deep with 9 in. between the rows and plants for optimum yields. Climbing varieties should be in double rows 6 in. apart with 24 in. between rows. **Zones 4 to 11.**

Growing

French beans flourish in a sheltered, sunny site on a light, free-draining, fertile soil where organic matter was added for the previous crop. Alternatively, dig in plenty of well-rotted organic matter in late fall or winter before planting.

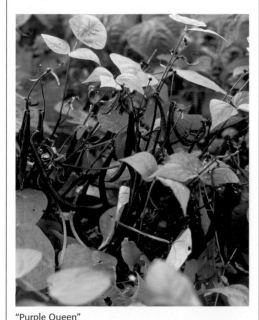

"Purple Queen"

The plants need a pH of 6.5 to 7.0; lime acid soils if necessary. Rake the soil to a medium tilth about 10 to 14 days before sowing, incorporating a balanced granular fertilizer at 1–2 oz. per square yard.

Keep crops weed-free or mulch when the soil is moist. Push twigs under mature bush varieties to keep pods off the soil, or support plants with pea sticks. Support climbing varieties in the same way as runner beans.

Keep well watered during drought; plants are particularly sensitive to water stress when flowers start to open and as pods swell. Apply 3–4 gallons per square yard per week.

Maintenance

Spring Sow early crops under cover or outdoors in late spring. Support climbers. Transplant when 2–3 in. tall.
Summer Keep crops weed-free, mulch, water in drought. Harvest regularly.
Fall Continue harvesting until the first frosts. Protect later crops with cloches or floating row cover.
Winter Prepare the soil for the following year's crop.

Protected Cropping

For earlier crops and in cooler climates, sow in boxes, packs, or pots of seed potting mix under cover from midspring. Warm the soil before transplanting. Harden off and plant out from late spring, depending on the weather and soil conditions. Protect crops sown indoors or *in situ* with cloches, polytunnels, or floating row cover until established.

For very early harvest, sow in pots in a heated greenhouse at 60°F from late winter. Sow four seeds near the edge of a 9–10 in. pot containing soilless potting mix with moderate fertilizer levels.

Seeds can also be pre-germinated on moist kitchen towel in an airing cupboard or similar. Keep moist with tepid water, ventilate in warm weather, and harvest in late spring.

Harvesting and Storing

Plants are self-pollinating, so expect a good harvest. Pick when pods are about 4–6 in. long, when they snap easily, before the seeds are visible. Pick regularly for maximum yields. Cut them with a pair of scissors or hold the stems as you pull the pods to avoid uprooting the plant.

Green beans are great when lightly boiled or steamed

For dried or white beans, leave pods until they mature, sever the plant at the base, and dry indoors. When pods begin to split, shell the beans and dry on paper for several days. Store in an airtight container.

French beans freeze well. Wash and trim young pods, blanch for 3 minutes, freeze in plastic bags or rigid containers. You should use within 12 months. They keep in a plastic bag in the refrigerator for up to a week and last about 4 days in a cool kitchen.

Pests and Diseases

Slugs, black bean aphid, and red spider mite can be troublesome. Gray mold (*Botrytis*) and halo blight may be problems in wet or humid weather. Mice may eat seeds. Root rots can kill plants in wet or poorly drained soils. Rotate crops. Bean leaf beetle is also a serious pest in the U.S.

companion planting

French beans do well with celery, corn, cucurbits, corn, and melons. Intercrop with brassicas.

container growing

French beans can be grown in containers that are at least 8 in. wide by 10 in. deep. Sow seeds 1½ to 2 in. deep indoors in midspring, moving the container outdoors into a sheltered, sunny site. Feed with liquid general fertilizer if necessary. Stake climbing varieties; pinch out growing points when plants reach the top of supports.

medicinal

One cup of beans per day is said to lower cholesterol by about 12 percent.

GREEN BEAN

culinary

Fresh green beans have such a delicate flavor that they hardly need more than boiling in water and serving as an accompaniment to meat and other dishes. Wash, top and tail pods, and cook whole in boiling salted water for 5 to 7 minutes, preferably within an hour of harvesting. Cut large flat-podded types into 1 in. slices. Alternatively, steam them, serve cold in salads, or try them stir-fried with other vegetables.

For white beans, place fresh beans in cold water, bring to a boil, remove from the heat, and allow to stand for an hour. Drain and serve as a hot vegetable, or in vinaigrette as a salad.

Mussel Soup with Green Beans
Serves 4

3 pounds mussels, cleaned and debearded
1¼ cups dry white wine
3 tablespoons olive oil
1 onion, finely minced
½ pound green beans, finely minced
Salt and freshly ground black pepper
3 plum tomatoes, peeled, seeded, and diced
Bunch fresh cilantro, leaves picked and chopped

Start by discarding any mussels that won't close when they are lightly tapped. Heat a large pan over high heat. Tip in the mussels and cover for 10 to 15 seconds, then pour over the wine and 1¼ cups of water. Cover and cook, shaking the pan every now and then, for 5 minutes or until the mussels have opened. Discard any that stay closed.

Tip the mussels into a colander set over a large bowl. Strain the cooking liquid and reserve. When cool enough to handle, remove the mussels from their shells and reserve, discarding the shells.

Heat 1 tablespoon of the oil in a pan and add the onion. Cook for a few minutes until softened, then pour in the reserved liquid and bring to a boil. Season to taste. Add the beans, mussels, and tomatoes and just warm through. Ladle into bowls, sprinkle with cilantro and drizzle over the remaining olive oil. Serve immediately.

Green Bean, Roquefort, and Walnut Salad
Serves 4

1¾ cups green beans, topped and tailed
2 cups Roquefort cheese
1 cup walnuts
1 small radicchio plus 2 "Little Gem" lettuces
3 tablespoons extra virgin olive oil
1 tablespoon balsamic vinegar
1 clove garlic, crushed
Salt and freshly ground black pepper

Green Bean, Roquefort, and Walnut Salad

Wash the beans and steam them over a pan of boiling water until just crunchy. Keep warm. Crumble the Roquefort and lightly crush the walnuts. Wash the lettuces thoroughly and shake dry. Make a dressing with the remaining ingredients.

Arrange the lettuces in a large bowl, top with the beans, walnuts, and cheese, and pour over the dressing. Toss and serve while the beans are still warm.

Phyllostachys spp. and others. Graminae/Poaceae

BAMBOO

Woody-stemmed, evergreen perennial. Hardy to tropical. Value: high in fiber, Vitamin C, E, and B6, and several other elements, including phosphorus, potassium, and zinc.

From creeping, grass-like species to giant fast-growing varieties climbing towards the heavens, bamboos are not only edible and ornamental but one of the most useful plants on earth. These fascinating, long-lived members of the grass family have influenced history and have many practical uses: from construction and scaffolding to the manufacture of fishing rods, paper, and medicine. Bamboo has also inspired works of art, and writings about bamboo in Chinese literature date back many centuries. Silkworm eggs were first smuggled out of the country in a bamboo stake and the Chinese have drilled to over 3,000 ft. for oil using bamboo stakes since at least 200 BCE. Bamboos rarely flower, but when they do, every specimen of that particular clone does so simultaneously, wherever it is in the world. Bamboo shoots play a prominent role in the diets of many countries — generations of pandas can't be wrong!

Harvest bamboo before this stage

 varieties

There are clump-forming and spreading species of bamboo, so choose garden specimens carefully — those with spreading roots are often vigorous and invasive.

Phyllostachys dulcis has masses of green stems that grow rapidly to around 26 ft. tall with a 13 ft. spread It is highly productive in hot summers — produces sweet shoots, is one of the best for eating, and thrives in sun or part shade. *P. edulis* can grow to a maximum of 65 ft. tall but is usually smaller. Clump forming and slow to establish, with green stakes. *Phyllostachys edulis Heterocycla* grows 65 ft. high with a spread of 16 ft.; not for the faint hearted or those with small gardens. Happy in sun or part shade, *P. aurea* grows to 10 ft., the young shoots are bright green, becoming pale creamy-yellow and matt yellow in sun. Very graceful, yet tough and vigorous in warm climates. *P. aureosulcata grows to* 10 ft tall. The green stakes with golden grooves often zigzag prominently at the base — very hardy and thrives in sun or part shade. *P. nigra*, the legendary black-caned bamboo, grows 16 ft tall and up to 39 ft. wide, though usually much smaller. Young canes are green and their transition to black is faster in sunshine; ideal in smaller gardens or containers. *P. nigra f. henonis* — the elegant canes of this clump-forming specimen reach 13ft. or more. It has dark green, glossy leaves and brown-yellow canes when mature and is excellent as a specimen plant. *P. nuda* grows to 5 ft. and is tough and vigorous with dark green stems. *P. rubromarginata* is compact and upright with slender, pale olive-yellow canes. Grows 5 ft. tall and is ideal for the smaller garden. *P. viridiglaucescens* grows to 13 ft. or more, in clumps up to 10 ft. wide. It is leafy and graceful with tall, glossy, green canes.

BAMBOO

Pleioblastus hindsii forms clumps to 7 ft. and sometimes dense thickets of olive-green canes up to 13 ft. tall. Good in sun and dense shade, for maritime conditions and as a windbreak in sun or shade. *Pseudosasa japonica* is adaptable, hardy and forms clumps to 10 ft. and occasionally dense thickets of olive-green canes to 16 ft. tall, which arch towards the tip. Good in shade, as a hedge or windbreak and easy to grow.

 cultivation

Propagation
Lift and divide clumps or rhizomes in spring, using a spade, and transplant in well-prepared ground.

Growing
Bamboos prefer rich, moist soils but are extremely tolerant, provided conditions are not waterlogged. Clear the ground of perennial weeds, add plenty of well-rotted organic matter to the soil and soak the root-ball in a bucket of water before planting slightly higher than the level of the plant in the pot, then water in well. Mulch well after planting, using well-rotted organic matter, then do so annually, each spring, after feeding with general fertilizer. Keep the soil moist, particularly during the first 2 to 3 years, until the plants are established. Bamboos in containers need regular watering during the growing season; do not let the roots dry out in winter, particularly during mild periods.

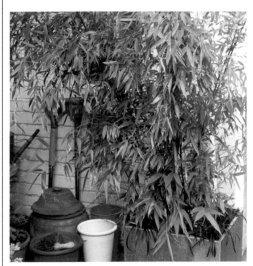

Bamboo can be grown in a container

Although regular harvesting thins the clump, remove about a third or more of the old and weak stems at the base in spring to encourage regrowth.

Maintenance
Spring Cut out stems that were damaged over winter. Harvest young shoots.
Summer Water if necessary during drought.
Fall Clear the ground ready for planting next spring.
Winter Order new varieties from plant catalogs.

Protected Cropping
Plants grown in containers can be protected under cover during winter and early spring, advancing shoot production for an earlier harvest.

 container growing

Grow in a multi-purpose potting mix; mix with added grit for stability and a good layer of drainage material in the base. In cold winters, wrap the pot with burlap or bubble wrap and put the pot in a sheltered position. In spring, feed with slow-release fertilizer and repot into a container one size larger, if necessary. Bamboos dislike being transplanted into pots which are considerably larger than the existing root ball.

Harvesting and Storing
Harvest shoots that are ½ in. or more in diameter — plants may take more than 5 years to produce canes of this size — removing a few from each clump so plant growth is not affected; up to one third of the new shoots can be removed without damaging the plants. New shoots grow rapidly, so check clumps daily and harvest from early to midspring, cutting shoots off at ground level with a sharp knife or clearing the soil and cutting at the point where they join the roots of spreading varieties. Shoots should be no more than 12 in. high; after this stage they become fibrous and inedible. Developing shoots that are blanched by covering with a box, bucket, or layer of mulch are tenderer when eaten.

Pests and Diseases
In temperate climates, bamboos are almost disease-free and are resistant to honey fungus. Rabbits, squirrels, and deer eat new shoots. Oriental bamboo spider mite can be a problem; spray to increase humidity or with an environmentally friendly insecticide.

 culinary

Most bamboos are edible but some are tastier than others. The sweetest are *Phyllostachys dulcis* and *Phyllostachys edulis*. Use the shoots immediately after harvest, in stir-fries and salads, or store them in a bowl of water; once they dry out, the taste deteriorates rapidly. Slice them lengthwise, removing the leafy outer sheath before cooking. Some varieties have a bitter flavor (called *egumi* in Japan) which can be removed by boiling in water for half an hour, either before or after the sheath has been removed. If there is still a hint of bitterness, cook the shoots again in fresh water. If you cannot find fresh bamboo shoots, you can buy them in jars or cans instead.

Fried Bamboo Shoot
Serves 3 to 4

1 tender bamboo shoot, about 12 in. long
2 teaspoons baking soda
1 teaspoon fenugreek seeds
4 dried red chilies
Salt
²/₃ vegetable oil

Rinse the bamboo shoot and chop it into small cubes. Add the baking soda and mix well.

Fry the fenugreek seeds and chilies in a dry pan until they release their flavor and add a little salt. Pour in the oil, add the cubed bamboo shoot, and continue cooking on a low heat. When the bamboo shoot dries up, add a couple of tablespoons of water and stir well. Serve piping hot.

PEA

Also known as Garden Pea, English Pea, Snap Pea, Sugar Pea, Snow Pea. Climbing or scrambling annual grown for seeds, pods, and shoot tips. Half hardy. Value: good source of protein, carbohydrates, fiber, iron, and vitamin C.

Like many legumes, peas are an ancient food crop. The earliest records are of smooth-skinned types, found in Mediterranean and European excavations dating from 7000 BCE. The Greeks and Romans cultivated and ate peas in abundance and it was the Romans who were said to have introduced them to Britain. In classical Greece they were known as *pison*, which was translated in English to "peason"; by the reign of Charles I they became "pease" and this was shortened to "pea" in the 18th century. During the reign of Elizabeth I types seen as "fit dainties for ladies, they come so far, and cost so dear" were imported from Holland.

In England "pease pudding," made from dried peas, butter and eggs, was traditionally eaten with pork and boiled bacon. It was obviously quite versatile, hence the nursery rhyme beginning, "Pease pudding hot, pease pudding cold, pease pudding in the pot nine days old." Peas were eaten dried or ground until the 16th century, when Italian gardeners developed tender varieties for cooking and eating when fresh. It took until the following century before this was accepted by fashionable England.

 varieties

Peas are usually listed according to the timing of the crop — early or late — but some descriptions refer to the pea itself, or to the pod.

Earlier varieties are lower-growing than later types, which are taller and consequently higher-yielding.

"Petit pois" are small and well flavored. "Semi-leafless" peas have more tendrils than leaves, becoming intertwined and self-supporting as they grow.

"Sugar peas" and "snow peas" — both varieties of *Pisum sativum* var. *macrocarpon* — are grown for their edible pods; snow pea pods are harvested before the pods fill and are used whole; sugar peas, also called snap peas, are harvested when the pods fill. Of these, the latter type are particularly succulent and sweet.

Early Peas

"Early Onward" is a heavy cropper with large blunt pods and wrinkled seeds. "Feltham First" is an excellent early round-seeded variety with large, well-filled pods. "Kelvedon Wonder" (early or main crop) produces pods packed with delicious peas. Dwarf.

Maincrop Peas

"Alderman," an old variety, produces heavy crops to 5 ft. with exquisite flavor. "Cavalier" produces huge crops and is highly resistant to mildew. Easy to harvest, with wrinkled seeds and fusarium resistance. "Darfon" is a high-yielding "petit pois" type, its pods packed with small peas. It resists downy mildew and fusarium. "Dorian" produces up to ten tasty peas per pod and harvests over a long period. "Hurst Green Shaft" is sweet-tasting and heavy-cropping, maturing over a long period. Wrinkle-seeded and downy mildew and fusarium-resistant.

"Early Onward"

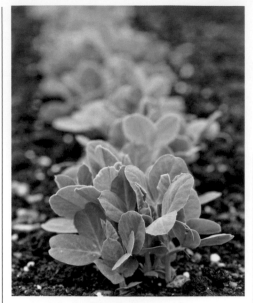
Leaves can be harvested for their shoot tips

Sugar Peas

"Oregon Sugar Pod" is sweet and tasty; harvest as the peas form. Fusarium-resistant. "Reuzensuiker" is a compact plant, needing little support. Its pods are wide and fleshy, and very sweet. "Sugar Snap" produces succulent, sweet edible pods or can be grown on for peas. Very sweet. Fusarium-resistant.

 cultivation

Propagation

Germination is erratic and poor on cold soils; do not sow outdoors when soil temperatures are below 50°F.

Sow earlies or second earlies successively every 14 to 28 days from midspring to midsummer. Avoid excessively hot times; these can affect germination.

According to the growing conditions, earlies mature after about 12 weeks, second earlies (or early maincrop) take 1 to 2 weeks longer, and maincrops take another 1 to 2 weeks longer again. As an alternative option, sow groups of earlies, second earlies, and maincrops in mid- to late spring; the length of time taken for each type to reach maturity will give you a harvest over several weeks.

In midsummer, with at least 12 weeks before the first frosts are expected, sow an early cultivar for harvesting in fall, and where winters are mild, sow earlies in mid- to late fall for overwintering. Cloche protection may be necessary later in the season.

Peas can be sown in single V-shaped rows 1–2 in. deep and 2 in. apart, double rows 9 in. apart or broad or flat rows 10 in. wide.

Peas can also be sown in strips 3 rows wide with the seeds 4 in. apart in and between the rows and with 18 in. between the strips, or in blocks 3–4 ft. wide with seeds 2–3 in. apart, or in potting mix in guttering that is then slid into place.

Yields are higher when plants are supported. Use pea stakes made from brushwood or netting. Place supports down one side of a single row, on either side or down the center of wide rows and around the outside of blocks of plants. **Zones 3 to 7.**

Growing

Peas are a cool-season crop, flourishing at 55–65°F, so crops will be higher in cooler summer temperatures. They do not tolerate drought, excessive temperatures, or waterlogged soil. Peas should be grown in an open, sheltered position on moisture-retentive, deep, free-draining soil with a pH of 5.5 to 7.0.

Incorporate plenty of organic matter in the fall or winter prior to sowing or plant where the ground was manured for the previous year's crop.

Keep crops weed-free by hoeing, hand weeding, or mulching (which also keeps the roots cool and moist). Hill up overwintering and early crops to provide extra support.

Where there are drought conditions, mostly in the West and Southwest, plants need watering from the outset. Elsewhere, established plants do not need watering until the flowers appear. For a good harvest, they will need 4 gallons per square yard each week until the harvest is complete.

Maintenance

Spring Sow early maincrops.
Summer Sow maincrops early in the season. Harvest, keep weed-free, and water. Sow earlies for a fall harvest.
Fall Sow early overwintering crops under cover. Prepare the ground for the following year.
Winter Sow early crops under cover.

Protected Cropping

Warm the soil before sowing treated seed in spring. Sow the seed of dwarf cultivars under cover in early spring. Remove the covers when the plants need supporting.

Early spring and late fall sowings can be made under cover, as flowers and pods cannot withstand frosty nights.

Harvesting and Storing

Harvest early types from late spring to early summer and maincrops from midsummer to early fall. Pick regularly to ensure a high yield when the pods are swollen. Harvest those grown for their pods when the peas are just forming. If peas are to be dried, leave them on the plant as long as possible, lifting just before the seeds are shed; hang in a cool airy place or spread the pods out on trays to dry until they split and the peas can be harvested. Store in airtight containers.

Freeze young peas of any variety. Shell and blanch for 1 minute. Allow to drain, cool, and freeze in plastic bags or containers. Use within 12 months.

A first-class pea support

Peas in a plastic bag in the refrigerator stay fresh for up to 3 days.

Pests and Diseases
Birds and mice can be a problem: net crops.

Pea moths are common, their larvae eating the peas. Protect with crop covers at flower bud stage. Fall, early, and midsummer sowings often avoid problems. Use bifenthrin or organic spray or cover with floating row cover.

Pea thrips attack developing pods, making pods distorted and silvery; peas do not develop. Spray with pyrethrum.

Mice may also be troublesome, eating seeds, particularly with over-wintered crops; trap them.

Powdery mildew, downy mildew, and fusarium wilt can be a problem: sow resistant varieties.

 companion planting

Peas grow well with other legumes, root crops, potatoes, cucurbits, and corn.

 container growing

Sow early dwarf varieties successionally through the season in large containers of soilless potting mix with moderate fertilizer levels. Provide support, keep weed-free and well watered.

 medicinal

Peas are said to reduce fertility, prevent appendicitis, lower blood cholesterol, and control blood sugar levels.

 culinary

Garden peas are eaten fresh or dried. When small and tender, they can be eaten raw in salads. Peas are traditionally boiled or steamed with a sprig of mint. Eat with butter, salt, and pepper or herbs. Serve in a cream sauce with pearl onions, with celery, orange, carrots, wine, or lemon sauce. Snow peas should be boiled for 3 minutes (or steamed), tossed in butter and served. Young pea shoot tips can be cooked and eaten.

Jean-Christophe Novelli's Cappuccino Soup
Serves 4

2 tablespoons butter
1 small onion, diced
¼ cup smoked pancetta, diced
1 pound fresh or frozen peas
3 cups light chicken stock
1 clove garlic
1 sprig fresh mint
A pinch of superfine sugar
4 tablespoons whole milk
Cep powder
Salt and freshly ground black pepper

Heat the butter in large pan, add the onion, and sweat gently until softened. Add the pancetta and quickly fry until crisp. Add the peas and stock, bring to a boil, and cook until the peas are soft to the touch. Pour into a blender, add the garlic, mint, sugar, and some seasoning and blitz until smooth.

Warm up the milk and froth up using cappuccino frother or a hand blender. Pour the soup into individual soup terrines or coffee cups. Top with frothed milk and finish with crispy pancetta and a dusting of cep powder to resemble a large cappuccino.

Pasta and Snow Pea Salad
Serves 4

1 pound pasta — penne or fusilli
4 tablespoons olive oil
²/₃ pound snow peas, topped and tailed
1 small onion, finely sliced
2 cloves garlic, crushed
8-oz. can tuna, drained and flaked
2 tablespoons heavy cream
2 tablespoons chopped fresh Italian parsley
Salt and freshly ground black pepper

Cook the pasta in boiling salted water for 10 minutes, or until *al dente*, and drain. Drizzle over 1 tablespoon of the oil and toss well. Allow to cool.

Meanwhile, cook the snow peas in a steamer for 2 to 3 minutes; they should remain crunchy. In a separate pan, heat the oil and sauté the onion for a couple of minutes, then add the garlic and continue cooking for 1 minute. Remove from the heat and allow to cool.

Put the pasta into a large serving bowl and mix in all the ingredients. Taste for seasoning and serve.

Portulaca oleracea subsp. *sativa.* Portulacaceae

PURSLANE

Also known as Summer Purslane. Annual grown for succulent shoot tips, stems, and leaves. Half hardy. Value: rich in beta carotene, folic acid, vitamin C; contains useful amounts of essential fatty acids.

Purslane has been grown for centuries in China, India, and Egypt, and is now widespread in the warm temperate and tropical regions of the world. It was once believed to protect against evil spirits and "blastings by lightning or planets and burning of gunpowder." Its name in Malawi translates as "buttocks of the wife of a chief," referring to the plant's succulent, rounded leaves and juicy stems! The cultivated form has an erect habit and larger leaves than the wild species.

 ## varieties

Portulaca oleracea subsp. *sativa* is a vigorous, upright annual growing to 18 in. tall with thick, succulent stems, spoon-shaped leaves, and bright yellow flowers. *P. o.* var. *aurea* is a yellow-leaved, less hardy form. It is more succulent, but has less flavor. Attractive in salads and as an ornamental.

 ## cultivation

Propagation
Sow in seed trays indoors in late spring and transplant seedlings into packs when large enough to handle. Harden off and plant when there is no danger of frost, 6 in. apart.

In frost-free climates or for later crops, sow directly, thinning to 6 in. apart. Sow in late spring for a summer crop and in late summer for fall cropping. **Zones 3 to 11.**

Growing
Easily cultivated, purslane thrives in a sunny, warm, sheltered site on light, well-drained soil. Add organic matter and sand to improve drainage if needed. Remove flowers as they appear.

Maintenance
Spring Sow protected crops, or *in situ* once the danger of frost is passed.
Summer Keep plants weed-free and water as necessary. Harvest regularly.
Fall Cut back mature plants to allow regrowth.
Winter In late winter sow early crops indoors.

Protected Cropping
To extend the season, sow in early to midspring and early to midfall under cover. Make earlier and late summer sowings under cover as a "cut and come again" crop.

Harvesting
Pick young shoot tips, stems, and leaves when about 1–2 in. long. "Cut and come again" crops are ready to harvest after about 5 weeks. Regular picking encourages young growth. As older plants deteriorate towards the end of the growing season, cut them back to within 2 in. of the ground, water them well and they should resprout. It self-seeds readily to be wary.

Pests and Diseases
Purslane is prone to slug damage, particularly when young. Damping off can be a problem if sown at low temperatures or in cold soil.

The *aurea* variety

 ## culinary

Wash thoroughly; growing close to the ground, leaves can be gritty. It can be lightly cooked, although the taste is not memorable. Older leaves can be pickled.

Purslane Salad
Serves 4

Use young buds and stems as well as the leaves.

4 ripe nectarines or peaches
Hazelnut oil
Handful purslane
15 hazelnuts, toasted
½ teaspoon coriander seeds, crushed

Slice the nectarines or peaches and arrange on a plate brushed with hazelnut oil. Add the purslane leaves. Trickle over a little more oil, sprinkle with the chopped nuts, and season with crushed coriander.

 ## container growing

Plant seedlings or sow seed in pots or containers when there is no danger of frost, using a soilless potting mix with a low fertilizer content. Continue to water regularly.

 ## medicinal

A traditional remedy for dry coughs, swollen gums, and, infused in water, for blood disorders. Research indicates that its high levels of fatty acids may help to prevent heart attacks and stimulate the body's immune system.

 ## warning

Expectant mothers and those with digestive disorders should not eat purslane in large quantities.

RADISH

Raphanus sativus. Brassicaceae

Annual or biennial grown for edible swollen roots, seed pods, and leaves. Hardy. Value: low in calories, moderate vitamin C, small amounts of iron, and protein.

Thought to be native to Asia, yet domesticated in the Mediterranean, this reliable little salad vegetable has been in cultivation for centuries. Depicted in the pyramid of Cheops, it was cultivated by the Egyptians in 2780 BCE and Herodotus noted that laborers working on the pyramids received "radishes, onions, and garlic" as their rations. By 500 BCE it was grown in China, reaching Japan 200 years later. Pliny records that "models of turnips, beets, and radishes were dedicated to Apollo in the temple at Delphi, turnips made of lead, beets of silver, and radishes of gold," while Horace wrote of "lettuces and radishes such as excite the languid stomach." John Evelyn, too, wrote: "Radishes are eaten alone with salt only, as conveying their pepper in them." The fiery flavor is due to the presence of mustard oil. Although radishes are usually red, there are also black-, purple-, yellow- and green-skinned types.

A bunch of organic radishes, including "White Icicle"

 varieties

The fast-growing salad types are ready to harvest in about 4 weeks. Larger, slow-growing types, often with long cylindrical roots, include large overwintering varieties and the oriental varieties known as "mooli" or "daikon."

Salad and overwintering radishes

"Cherry Belle" is round, with crisp, white, mild flesh. Tolerant of poorer soils, it is slow to go woody and keeps well. "China Rose" is a well-flavored winter variety with bright pink roots and white flesh. "French Breakfast 3" is long, mild, sweet, and tender. Harvest at maturity or it becomes hot and woody. "Hong Vit" is mild with pink stems. "Long Black Spanish," a winter variety, has wonderful dark skin and is extremely hot. "Mantang Long" has green and white skin, magenta flesh, and a sweet, nutty flavor. "München Bier" is grown for its tasty green pods, which are eaten raw or stir-fried. "Saisai" is an oriental leaf radish that came top in a taste test; tender, juicy, and succulent — use as young leaves in salads and stir-fries. "Scarlet Globe" is justifiably popular for its mild flavor and good quality; can be sown early under cover. "Short Top Forcing" is a bright red variety, excellent for winter sowing under cover.

Daikon or Mooli

"Daikon" and "mooli" are general terms for a group of long, white radishes (*Raphanus sativus* var. *longipinnatus*) that need cool temperatures and short day lengths to flourish.

"April Cross" is crisp, juicy, and mild. "Long White Icicle" is tender with a pungent, almost nutty taste. "Minowasa Summer," a Japanese variety, is long and mild. "Tsukushi" is a hardy, spring cross, white, with firm roots. Sow from late June for winter harvest.

 cultivation

Propagation

Radishes are one of the easiest and quickest vegetables to grow. Sow successively every 2 weeks from when the soil becomes workable, in early to midspring, to early fall. Sow thinly in rows ½ in. deep and 6 in. apart, thinning to 1 in. apart about 10 days after they appear. Alternatively, broadcast seed and thin to 1 in. apart. Radishes dislike being overcrowded.

Sow overwintering radishes in summer, ¼ inch deep in rows 9–12 in. apart; depending on the cultivar, thin to 6–9 in. Sow mooli/daikon from mid- to late summer.

Small radishes can be grown as "cut and come again" seedlings. Harvest when seedlings are 2–3 in. tall; if you allow them to grow to 8–9 in., the leaves can be cooked like spinach. **Zones 3 to 9.**

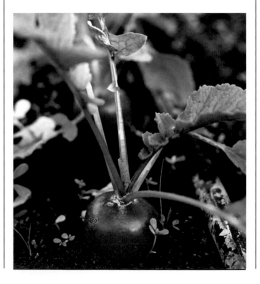

Growing

As radishes are a cool-weather crop, grow earlier and later crops in an open site, but plant summer crops in light shade, surrounded by taller plants. They flourish in a light, moisture-retentive, free-draining soil which was manured for the previous crop, with a pH of 6.5 to 7.5. Dig the ground thoroughly before preparing the seedbed and remove any stones, particularly when growing longer-rooted varieties.

Rake a slow-release granular fertilizer into the seedbed at 1 oz. per square yard before sowing the first crops and before planting winter varieties.

Rapid growth is essential for tasty, tender roots, so supply plenty of water and do not let the seedbed dry out. Overwatering encourages the production of leaves, rather than roots, and erratic watering causes roots to become woody or split. During drought, water weekly at 2 gallons per square yard. Hoe and hand-weed regularly.

Maintenance

Spring Sow crops outdoors when soil conditions allow.
Summer Sow successively; keep crops well watered and weed-free. Sow winter crops.
Fall Grow later crops under cover.
Winter Harvest overwintering crops. Sow early crops under cover.

Protected Cropping

Grow early and late crops of summer varieties under cloches to extend the cropping season. Ventilate and water thoroughly.

Grow summer crops under floating cloches to protect them.

 container growing

Radishes are easily grown in containers. These should be 6–12 in. wide by 8 in. deep. Use a soilless potting mix. Water well and liquid-feed with general fertilizer if necessary. They can also be sown in growing bags, thinning until they are 1–2 in. apart.

Harvesting and Storing

Pull immediately they mature, after 8 to 10 weeks, otherwise they will become woody or go to seed.

Thin the rows regularly for the best results

Later crops can be stored. Twist off leaves and store in boxes of dry sand or sawdust in a frost-free place. Overwintering types can be left in the ground and lifted as needed. Protect with straw or bracken. For ease of lifting, these can be allowed to grow over 14 in. long without being coarse.

Kept in a plastic bag in the refrigerator, radishes stay fresh for about a week.

Pests and Diseases

Flea beetle, cabbage fly, and slugs can be a problem.

 companion planting

Radishes grow well with chervil, peas, and lettuce and thrive with nasturtium and with mustard.

Because of their rapid growth, radishes make an excellent "indicator crop." Sown in the same row as slow-germinating crops like parsnips or parsley, they mark where the maincrop has been sown, make weeding easier, and can be harvested without disturbing the developing plants.

 medicinal

Radishes can be eaten to relieve indigestion and flatulence, as well as being taken as a tonic herb and an expectorant.

culinary

Radishes are usually eaten raw, whole, grated, or sliced into salads. Alternatively, wash and trim the root, remove the leaves and all but the bottom 1 in. of stalk to use as a "handle," and enjoy it with rough bread, creamy butter, salt, cheese, and a pint of good ale! (In Germany, you'll find them on the bar instead of peanuts.) They can also be sliced and used instead of onions in hamburgers.

Seedling leaves are eaten raw and older leaves are cooked like spinach.

Long white summer radishes and winter radishes can be eaten raw but are usually cooked and added to casseroles, stews, or curries.

Winter varieties are also pickled. Peel, then cube or slice in slightly salted water for about 10 minutes. Drain thoroughly and serve tossed in butter. Thin slices of winter varieties or larger summer types can be stir-fried.

For extra crispness, put them into a bowl of water with a few ice cubes for a couple of hours.

Slice radishes and tangerines, mandarins, or oranges into small pieces, sprinkle lightly with salt, chopped fennel leaves, and lemon juice. This interesting recipe is an acquired taste!

To make a "radish rose," remove the stalk and make a number of vertical cuts from the stalk almost to the root. Place in iced water for 30 minutes; the "petals" will open.

Immature green seed pods can be eaten raw, cooked or pickled. Pick when crisp and green. Scrape or peel and "top and tail" mooli or daikon before use. In India they are eaten cooked or raw. In Japan shredded mooli is a traditional accompaniment to *sashimi* (raw fish) and is eaten with *sushi*.

As with summer radishes, a thin slice makes an excellent and crunchy mustard substitute with a roast beef sandwich.

Radish and Scallop Soup
Serves 4

2 bunches radishes, topped and tailed
10 scallops, trimmed
2 scallions, chopped
2 tablespoons butter
2½ cups fish stock and milk combined
2 bay leaves
Pinch cayenne pepper
1 tablespoon chopped fresh parsley
4 tablespoons heavy cream

First wash the radishes thoroughly and cut into small dice. Then cut the scallops in half and set to one side.

In a soup pot, cook the onions in the butter until soft, then add the scallops. Cook them for 30 seconds on each side over a gentle heat then add the radishes.

Pour over the stock and milk mixture. Add the bay leaves, cayenne, and parsley and cook for 15 minutes over a gentle heat, just simmering.

Remove the soup from the heat. Remove the scallops from the soup, using a slotted spoon; cut them into slivers, and return them to the pan. Lastly, stir in the parsley and the heavy cream and serve immediately.

Rheum × hybridum. Polygonaceae
RHUBARB

Also known as Pieplant. Large perennial herb grown for pink or red edible stalks. Half hardy. Value: very low in calories, contains small amounts of vitamins.

The earliest records of rhubarb date from China in 2700 BCE and there are references to its cultivation in Europe in the early 1700s. It was originally grown for its medicinal use as a powerful purgative; the annual value of imports to England for this purpose was once estimated to be $300,000. It was first mentioned as a food plant in 1778 by the French, for making pies. Rhubarb was introduced to Maine around 1790; from there it spread to New England and Massachusetts. Forcing and blanching were discovered by chance at the Chelsea Physic Garden in 1817 after crowns were covered in debris when a ditch was cleared!

Plants tend to establish more rapidly if transplanted into 10 in. pots of multi-purpose potting mix for 3 months prior to planting out. Transplant, 2½ to 3 ft. apart, from late fall (the best time) to early spring, with the bud tip covered by 1 in. of soil. Plant cultivars which have large buds with the buds slightly above ground to prevent rotting. Plants remain productive for several seasons; their decline is marked by the production of masses of thin stalks.

Sow in rows about 1 in. deep and 12 in. apart, thinning to 6 in. Plant out the strongest in fall or the following spring. Eating quality will be variable. **Zones 3 to 7.**

Growing
Rhubarb flourishes in an open, sunny position in deep, fertile, well-drained soil with a pH of 5.0 to 6.0. It is ideal for cool temperate climates. It is very hungry, with deep roots, so ensure that the soil contains well-rotted manure or potting mix. On very heavy soils, plant on ridges or raised beds.

Mulch plants every winter with a good thick layer of well-rotted potting mix or manure. Do not allow them to flower unless you wish to save the seed, as this affects cropping the following year. Keep weed-free and watered, removing dead leaves instantly. In early spring, sprinkle a balanced general fertilizer around the crowns.

 varieties

A greater range of cultivars is to be found in specialized nurseries. "Early Champagne" ("Early Red") produces long, delicious scarlet stalks that are excellent for winemaking and early forcing. "Fulton's Strawberry Surprise" is vigorous and bright red and won joint first prize in an RHS (Royal Horticulture Society) taste test. "Merton Foremost" came second, "Grandad's Favorite" (vigorous, thick, sweet stems) was third and "Stein's Champagne" was fourth; bright red, vigorous stems — very tasty. "Glaskin's Perpetual" is vigorous, tasty, and crops over a long period. "The Sutton," introduced by Suttons Seeds in 1893, is tasty and good for forcing. "Timperley Early" is very early, vigorous, and bred for forcing. "Valentine" is hardy and vigorous with tender, rose-colored stalks. Perfect for pies and jams, it has

a wonderful flavor. "Victoria," a reliable old variety, is variable in size. Harvest from late spring.

 cultivation

Propagation
Rhubarb can be grown from seed, but the results are invariably poor. It is better to lift and divide mature crowns of known varieties or buy virus-free plants from a reputable nursery.

Plants can be divided every 2 or 3 years; if plants are any older, take divisions from the outer margins. Lift dormant crowns in winter after the leaves have died back and divide with a spade or knife. Each "set" should be about 4 in. across, with plenty of fibrous roots and at least one bud.

"Timperley Early"

RHUBARB

Maintenance

Spring Force early crops under a bucket or similar.
Summer Harvest stems.
Fall When stems die back, remove all plant debris.
Winter Mulch with well-rotted potting mix or manure.

Protected Cropping

For early crops lift a few crowns in late fall, leave them above ground and let them be frosted, then bring indoors into a cool place for forcing. Put in a large container packed with soil, or plant under greenhouse benches. Exclude light with an upturned box or bucket 15–18 in. high to allow for stem growth. They can also be forced in garbage bags. Keep potting mix moist. Dispose of exhausted forced crowns after harvest.

Alternatively, from late winter, cover *in situ* with a 6 in. layer of straw or leaves or with an upturned bin, bucket, or blanching pot covered with straw or strawy manure. Harvest in early to midspring. Do not harvest from a crown for at least 2 years after forcing.

Harvesting and Storing

Do not harvest until 12 to 18 months after planting, taking only a few stalks in the second season and more in later years. Cropping can last from early spring to midsummer. To harvest, hold the stems near the base and twist off. Avoid breaking the stems, as it can cause fungal problems. Do not over-pick; it can weaken the plant.

To freeze, chop the stems into sections and place on an open tray, then freeze for 1 hour before packing into plastic bags. This prevents the sections from sticking together. They can be stored for up to a year.

Pests and Diseases

Honey fungus may appear as white streaks in dead crown tissue; brown toadstools appear round the base. Dig out and burn diseased roots. Crown rot damages terminal buds and makes stems spindly. Dig out and burn badly infected plants. Do not replant in the area. Virus disease has no cure. Dig up and burn.

 ## companion planting

Rhubarb is reported to control red spider mite. A traditional remedy suggests putting rhubarb in planting holes to control clubroot. An infusion of leaves is effective as an aphicide and to check blackspot on roses.

Main course or dessert?

 ## culinary

Forced rhubarb is tender and needs less sugar. Cook stems slowly with sugar. Very little or no water is required; do not overcook them. Do not use aluminum pans.

Rhubarb can be stewed for fruit pies, canning or preserving, for fools, mousses, and rhubarb crumble, and is delicious served with duck. The flavor can be improved by adding orange juice, marmalade or cinnamon. It can also be puréed with apple. Claudia Roden's *Middle Eastern Food* demonstrates that it is unexpectedly wonderful stewed with beef or lamb in Persian *khoresh*.

Preserved Rhubarb

8 pounds rhubarb
8 pounds preserving sugar
Zest and juice of 2 lemons
½ cup blanched almonds

Cut the rhubarb into 1 in. lengths and cook gently in a preserving pan until the juices start to run. Add the sugar, lemon juice and zest, and the almonds. Stir until the sugar dissolves, then boil until a good color and thickened. Place into sterilized jars and seal.

Rhubarb Sorbet
Serves 4

1 pound rhubarb
¾ cup superfine sugar
Juice of ½ a lemon

Cut the rhubarb into 1 in. lengths and put into a heavy-bottomed pan. Add ¼ cup water. Warm gently until the juices run, then stir in the sugar and lemon juice, and simmer, covered, until tender. Freeze, whisking several times as it freezes, to break up the ice crystals. If you use an ice cream maker, churn until smooth. Remove from the freezer 15 minutes before serving and leave in the refrigerator.

 ## medicinal

Rhubarb is an astringent, stomachic, and potent laxative. Dioscorides recommended it for chest, stomach, and liver complaints, and ringworm. By the 16th century, in western Europe, it was taken as an infusion with parsley as a cure for venereal disease.

 ## warning

Do not eat the leaves, which are extremely poisonous!

Rorippa nasturtium-aquaticum. Brassicaceae
WATERCRESS

Also known as Summer Watercress. Usually aquatic perennial grown for pungent, edible leaves, and stems. Hardy. Value: excellent source of beta carotene, vitamins C and E, calcium, iron, and iodine.

This highly nutritious aquatic herb, a native of Europe, North Africa, and Asia, has been cultivated as a salad plant since Roman times and is grown throughout the world's temperate zones. It has become a weed in North America and New Zealand. Pliny records the Latin derivation of its original generic name as *Nasus tortus*, meaning "writhing nose" — referring to its spicy taste and pungent odor; *officinale* is often applied to plants with medicinal uses. Watercress was listed as an aphrodisiac in Dioscorides's *Materia Medica* of 77 CE.

It was mentioned in early Irish poetry around the 12th century — "Well of Traigh Dha Bhan, Lovely is your pure-topped cress," and, "Watercress, little green-topped one, on the brink of the blackbirds' well …" Early references to the shamrock are believed to be to watercress. Evidence to support this comes from Ireland's County Meath and Shamrock Well, the watercress of which was still remembered in the 1940s as "the finest in the district." Watercress was also known in Ireland as "St Patrick's Cabbage." The first records of commercial cultivation are from Germany, around 1750, France, between 1800 and 1811, and near Gravesend in England, around 1808.

cultivation

Found in and alongside fast-flowing rivers and streams, watercress has fleshy, glossy leaves on long stalks with 5 to 10 leaflets. Its long stems creep or float on the surface and root easily. Small whitish-green flowers appear in flat-topped clusters from midspring to early fall.

The best watercress is grown in pure, fast-flowing chalk or limestone streams with slightly alkaline water. This avoids the risk of contamination from pollution, which can cause stomach upsets.

Propagation
Propagated watercress is from store-bought material but the cutway "Aqua" can be grown from seed. Cuttings 4 in. long take about a week to root in a glass of water.

If you live by a fast-flowing stream, plant rooted cuttings 6 in. apart in the banks. Firm well to prevent them from being dislodged.

To grow watercress in the garden, dig a trench 24 in. wide and 24 in. deep, and put a 6 in. layer of well-rotted farmyard manure or potting mix into the base. (Do not use sheep manure, as it can carry dangerous liver fluke.) Mix in a little ground limestone if your soil is not alkaline, then cover with 3–4 in. of soil. Plant cuttings 6 in. apart in midspring. Alternatively, in spring, mark out an area, and dig in well-rotted organic matter and ground limestone, firm, and soak with water, then sprinkle seed thinly on the surface. Water daily.

Seeds can also be sown indoors from mid- to late spring, in a propagator or trays of peat-substitute seed potting mix on a window sill. Cover the seeds with $1/8$ in. of potting mix, keep it constantly moist at around 50–60°F.

Transplant three to four seedlings into a 3 in. pot when large enough to handle, then plant out 4–6 in. apart from midspring onwards. When plants deteriorate, replace them with fresh cuttings.

Growing
Plants grown in the garden need a bright, sheltered position away from direct sunshine; never allow them to dry out, or plants go to seed. As a cool-season crop, watercress grows most actively in spring and fall,

WATERCRESS

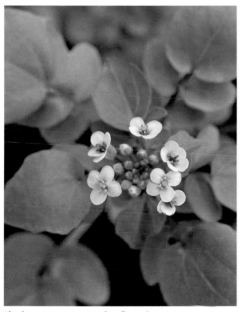

The leaves turn coarse after flowering

and during the winter in warmer climates. Occasional feeding with a dilute high-nitrogen liquid fertilizer or liquid fertilizer may be needed. Do not grow in stagnant or still water.

Maintenance
Spring Take cuttings or sow seed mid- to late spring.
Summer Do not let potting mix-grown plants dry out. Keep weed-free. Harvest as needed. Remove flower heads as they appear.
Fall Continue to harvest.
Winter Protect with cloches for continuous growth.

Protected Cropping
Cover plants with cloches, floating row cover, or plastic tunnels before the first frosts. Make a watercress bed in an unheated greenhouse over winter, or grow in pots.

Harvesting and Storing
Younger leaves near the stem tips have the best flavor. Harvest lightly during the first season and annually towards fall if plants are to be overwintered, cutting regularly for a constant supply of bushy shoots. Use leaves fresh or store in the salad compartment of a refrigerator for 2 to 3 days.

Pests and Diseases
Watercress is rarely troubled, but caterpillars of cabbage white butterfly may cause problems. Cover with netting.

 ## container growing

Grow in large pots or containers of moist peat-substitute potting mix, with a layer of gravel in the base, spacing 4–6 in. apart. Keep potting mix moist by standing the pot in a bowl of water which is replaced daily. Grow plants on a bright windowsill, but away from direct sunshine.

 ## medicinal

Watercress has been valued for its medicinal qualities since antiquity. It has been eaten to cure rheumatism, and used as a diuretic and as an expectorant for catarrh, colds, and bronchitis; it is a stimulant, a digestive, and a tonic to promote appetite, counteract anaemia, and to lower blood-sugar levels in diabetes.

 ## culinary

As with its relative, the radish, the hot, spicy taste of watercress comes from mustard oil. Remove discolored leaves and wash thoroughly, shaking off excess water. Eat in salads and stir-fries, or liquidize to make chilled soup. It makes a perfect garnish for sandwiches. Chop finely and add to butter, mashed potatoes, dumplings, or a white sauce. Also sauté in butter for 10 minutes and serve as a vegetable.

Among her many tastebud-tingling recipes, Jane Grigson suggests cutting orange segments into quarters and mixing with watercress, olive oil vinaigrette, and black pepper; add walnuts or black olives and eat as a salad with ham, duck, or veal.

Salmon with Watercress Sauce
Serves 6

6 salmon fillets, trimmed
4 tablespoons butter
4 tablespoons finely minced shallots
2 large bunches watercress, plus extra to garnish
2/3 cup heavy cream
Salt and freshly ground black pepper

Externally it can be used as a hair tonic. Rubbed on the skin it is said to remove rashes. Culpeper recommended the bruised leaves or juice for clearing spots and freckles and a poultice was said to heal glandular tumours and lymphatic swellings.

Traditionally it was taken as a spring tonic. In the past, in isolated parts of the British Isles where the diet was predominantly shellfish and salt meat, it was often grown to prevent scurvy, and was so mentioned by Philip Miller in his *Gardener's Dictionary* of 1731.

 ## warning

Gathering from streams is not recommended if sheep are grazing nearby, as there is a risk of liver fluke. Flukes can be destroyed by thorough cooking.

Steam the salmon fillets, covered, on a steamer rack over boiling water until cooked; this should take 10 minutes or so.

Meanwhile, prepare the sauce by melting the butter in a heavy skillet and sautéing the shallots until softened. Add the watercress and, constantly stirring, allow the watercress to wilt for about 2 minutes; it should retain its bright green color. Stir in the cream and seasoning and bring to a boil. Remove from the heat and blend in a liquidizer until smooth. Then reheat gently.

Arrange the salmon fillets in the center of individual plates and spoon sauce over each, garnishing with a little fresh watercress.

Scorzonera hispanica. Asteraceae

SCORZONERA

Also known as False Salsify, Spanish Salsify. Grown as perennial for shoots, flower buds, and flowers; annual for cylindrical tapering roots. Hardy. Value: contains indigestible carbohydrate inulin, which, when converted to fructose in storage, increases calorific content (27 calories per 100 g); small amounts of vitamins and minerals.

Scorzonera is very similar to salsify, though scorzonera is perennial, not biennial, its skin is darker, the roots narrower, and the flavor is not as strong. The name scorzonera may have come from the French *"scorzon"* or serpent, as the root was used in Spain to cure snake bites. Another interpretation suggests it comes from the Italian *"scorza,"* bark, and *"nera,"* black, describing the roots. Native to central and southern Europe through to Russia and Siberia, scorzonera was known by the Greeks and Romans, who took little interest in its cultivation; it arrived in England by 1560 and in North America by 1806. It is widely grown in Europe as an excellent winter vegetable. The leaves have been used as food for silkworms.

 varieties

"Duplex" produces long, tasty roots. "Flandria Scorzonera" has long roots, growing to 12 in., with strongly flavored flesh. "Habil" is long-rooted with a delicious flavor. "Lange Jan" ("Long John") has long, tapering, dark brown roots. "Long Black" is similar, but with black roots. "Russian Giant" lives up to its name, with long roots and a subtle, delicate flavor.

 cultivation

Propagation
Sow fresh seed *in situ* from mid- to late spring, in rows ½ to 1 in. deep with rows 6 in. apart. Alternatively, sow two or three seeds in hills 6 in. apart, thinning to leave the strongest seedling when large enough to handle. Or sow in late summer for use early the following fall. **Zones 5 to 10.**

Growing
It flourishes in a sunny position on a deep, light, well-drained soil which should have been manured for a previous crop. Do not grow on freshly manured or stony ground, as this causes "forking." A pH of 6.0 to 7.5 is ideal, so lime the soil if necessary.

The roots are very tasty when cooked

SCORZONERA

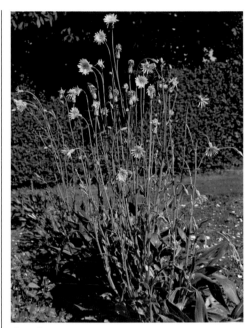

Flowering scorzonera

On heavy or stony soils, fill a narrow trench about 12 in. deep with finely sieved soil or free-draining potting mix, so that the roots grow straight. Dig soil deeply and rake in 2–3 oz. per square yard general balanced fertilizer 10 days before sowing.

Remove weeds around plants by hand, as roots bleed easily when damaged by a hoe. Mulching once the roots have established helps to smother weeds, conserves moisture and reduces the risk of bolting during dry weather. Water with 3 to 5 gallons per square yard per week.

Roots can be left in the ground to produce "chards" (edible shoots) the following spring. In fall cut off old leaves, leaving ½ to 1 in. above the soil. Hill up the roots to a depth of about 6 in. so the developing shoots are blanched during the winter. In late spring, scrape away the soil and harvest when the shoots are 5–6 in. long. They can also be blanched by covering to a similar depth with straw or leaves in early spring. Roots too small to harvest in the first year can be left to mature the following year.

Maintenance

Spring Sow thinly, from mid- to late spring. Thin when large enough to handle.
Summer Keep crops weed-free and water thoroughly as needed to keep soil moist.

Fall Leave roots in the ground and lift carefully with a fork as needed.
Winter Continue harvesting. Prepare the ground for the next crop.

Protected Cropping

Scorzonera is hardy, but protection with straw or cloches before the onset of severe weather makes lifting much easier.

Harvesting and Storing

Plants need at least 4 months to reach maturity and are ready to harvest from midfall to midspring. In a good year the roots may grow to 16 in., but are more usually about 8 in. long.

Roots can either be left in the ground until needed or lifted — with care, as they are easily damaged. Clean and store in boxes of sand or sawdust in a cool place. They last up to 1 week in a refrigerator. Mature plants flower in spring or summer of the second year. The edible buds can be harvested with about 3 in. of stem.

If, while lifting, you see that your crop has many forked roots, the remaining plants can be kept for their young shoots and buds.

Pests and Diseases

Scorzonera suffers few problems but may develop "white blister," which looks like glistening paint splashes. Affected plants become distorted. Spray with Bordeaux mixture or destroy.

 companion planting

Scorzonera repels carrot root fly and the flowers attract beneficial insects.

 container growing

In shallow or stony soils, plants can be grown in deep containers of soilless potting mix. Water regularly.

 medicinal

The name derived from the French reflects its reputation as an antidote to snake venom, "… and especially to cure the bitings of vipers (of which there may be very many in Spaine and other hot countries)," wrote Gerard in his *Herball* of 1636. This is not proven.

 culinary

Roots can be baked, puréed, dipped in batter, sautéed, and made into croquettes and fritters, deep-fried or served *au gratin* with cheese and breadcrumbs.

Boiling allows you to appreciate the flavor fully. They discolor when cut, so drop into water with a dash of lemon juice, then boil for 25 minutes in salted water with a tablespoon of flour added. Peel after boiling as you would a hard-boiled egg. Toss with melted butter and chopped parsley. Young "chards" can be served raw in salads. The flower stalks and buds are cooked and eaten like asparagus.

Sautéed Scorzonera

Allow 1 cup per person of cleaned scorzonera; it should not be peeled. Chop roughly and cook in a heavy skillet in a little extra virgin olive oil until *al dente*, turning to cook every side. Drain on paper towel and sprinkle with lemon juice mixed with 1 crushed garlic clove and 1 tablespoon finely minced Italian parsley.

Sechium edule. Cucurbitaceae
CHAYOTE

Also known as Vegetable Pear, Choko, Chow Chow, Christophine. Vigorous, scrambling, tuberous rooted perennial, grown for edible fruit and seed. Tender. Value: 90 percent water; low in calories; some vitamin C.

In good conditions, this climber spreads to 50 ft. and produces huge tubers. It originated in central America; "chayote" comes from the Aztec *chayotl*, while in the West Indies it is called "christophine" after Columbus, who reputedly introduced it to the islands. The pear-shaped fruits contain a single nutty-flavored seed, much prized by cooks.

varieties

"Ivory White" is a small, pale-skinned variety.

cultivation

Chayote needs rich, fertile, well-drained soil.

Propagation
Propagate cultivars from soft tip cuttings in spring at 65°F. Alternatively, plant the whole fruit laid on its side, at a slight angle, with the narrow end protruding from the soil.

Growing
Grow on mounds 12–16 in. high and 3 ft. apart; cover a shovel full of well-rotted manure with 6 in. of soil. Lightly mulch.

Alternatively, grow on beds 9 ft. square; dig in organic matter, plant seeds in the corners, and grow vines towards the center. Or, plant in 3 ft. wide ridges. Train the stems into trees, over trellising, fences, or 6 in. mesh netting. Water regularly in dry weather; optimum growth is during the wet season. A day length of just over 12 hours is required for flowering.

In the humid tropics, it grows better in moderate temperatures at altitude.

Germinating chayote fruit

Fruits are even better when suspended above ground

Harvesting and Storing

In tropical climates, plants last for several years, fruiting from 3 to 4 months after sowing, all year round. Harvest by cutting the stalk above the fruit with a knife. Fruit reaches its maximum size 25 to 30 days after fruit set. It will keep up to 3 months in a cool place.

Pests and Diseases

Root knot nematode causes wilting; powdery mildew can appear on leaves and stems; and red spider mite affects plants grown indoors.

 ## container growing

Propagate in spring from seed or cuttings. Repot into soilless potting mix with a high fertilizer content, adding well-rotted manure and grit to improve drainage. Water thoroughly, feed every 2 weeks with general liquid fertilizer, and, once established, with a high-potassium fertilizer. Train the growth on to a trellis.

 ## medicinal

Chayote is said to be good for stomach ulcers. It contains some trace elements.

Maintenance

Spring Sow seed or take cuttings.
Summer Feed and water.
Fall Harvest.
Winter Store fruit for next year's crop.

Protected Cropping

In cool temperate regions, grow indoors in bright light with moderate temperatures and humidity. In warmer areas, start off indoors and plant when the danger of frost has passed. Grow in the greenhouse bed or in containers.

 ## culinary

This versatile vegetable can be made into soups, boiled, candied, puréed (spiced with chili powder), or added to stews, curries, and chutneys. Its seeds can be cooked in butter, the young leaves cooked like spinach, and the tuber eaten when young. Its flesh stays firm after cooking. It makes a good substitute for avocado in a salad and is ideal for those on a diet.

For a stuffing, try a well-flavored bolognese sauce; add boiled chayote flesh and stuff back into halved chayote shells. Sprinkle with cheddar and bake in an oven preheated to 350°F for 30 minutes.

Chayote in Red Wine

Serves 6

Jane Grigson gives a recipe for this dessert.

¾ cup sugar
1 cup water
6 pear-sized chayotes, peeled and left whole
½ cup red wine
2 in. cinnamon stick
4 cloves
Lemon juice
Whipped cream and confectioners' sugar

Use a pan that will hold the chayote in a single layer. Put the sugar and water on to dissolve and simmer for 2 minutes. Carefully add the chayote, then the wine and spices.

Cover and simmer until tender. Remove the chayote to a bowl and arrange upright, like pears. Reduce the liquid until syrupy and add a little lemon juice to bring out the distinctive flavor. Strain the juice over the chayote and serve with whipped cream lightly sweetened with confectioners' sugar.

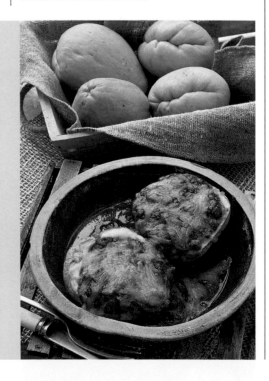

Solanum melongena. Solanaceae

EGGPLANT

Also known as Aubergine, Brinjal, Garden Egg, Guinea Squash, Pea Eggplant.
Short-lived perennial grown as annual for fruits. Tender.
Value: small amounts of most vitamins and minerals; very low in calories, with 3 percent carbohydrates and 1 percent protein.

This glossy-skinned fruit was known to sixteenth-century Spaniards as the "apple of love." In contrast, many botanists of the time called it *mala insana* or "mad apple," because of its alleged effects. The Chinese first cultivated eggplants in the fifth century BCE and they have been grown in India for centuries, yet they were unknown to the Greeks and Romans. Moorish invaders introduced them to Spain and the Spaniards later took them to the New World. "Eggplant" is a corruption of the Arabic name *al-badingan*.

 ## varieties

Fruits vary in shape from large, purple-skinned types to small, rounded white fruits 2 in. in diameter. Most modern F1 hybrids are bushy and grow about 2–3 ft. tall. Unlike older varieties, they are almost spineless.

"Black Beauty" produces high yields of good-quality dark purple fruits over a long period. "Calliope" is a dense, spineless plant. The white-skinned, purple striped fruits reach 4 in. at maturity. "Mohican" and "Baby Rosanna" grow golf-ball-sized fruit and are ideal for containers in the greenhouse or on the patio. "Diamond," from Ukraine, has dark purple fruit and flourishes in short summers and cool climates. The white and lavender-striped fruit of "Listada de

"Listada de Gandida"

Gandida" are very tasty. "Long Purple" produces good yields of dark purple fruits about 6 in. long. "Moneymaker" is a superb early variety with very tasty fruits. Tolerant of lower temperatures, it can be grown indoors as well as outside. "Ova" produces masses of small, white-skinned fruits. "Pintung Long" is one of the best — its ornamental, dark lavender fruits grow to 12 in. long and are tender and full of flavor. "Rossa Bianca," a classic gourmet variety, produces white, violet-tinted fruit with a mild, creamy taste. "Rosita" bears gorgeous glossy, lavender pink fruit that taste sweet. "Striped Toga" is unusual for its orange, green-striped fruit that are only 3 in. long at maturity. "Thai Green," with long, slender fruit, is renowned for its drought tolerance. "Thai Green Pea" is a tall plant covered with masses of tiny green fruit with a strong eggplant flavor. Ideal for stir-fries, curries, and soups. The fruit of "Thai Yellow Egg" are a bright golden yellow and egg-sized; perfect for Thai dishes. "Thai Long Green" grows highly ornamental slim, light lime-green fruit to 12 in. long: a gourmet variety; tender and absolutely delicious. "Violette di Firenze" needs warmth to ripen fully. Its unusual yet very attractive dark mauve fruits make this an ideal plant for growing in a "potager."

 ## cultivation

Eggplants need long, hot summers, and are the ideal crop for warm climates. In cooler regions, they will grow outside, but better harvests come from those protected indoors. Constant temperatures between 75–86°F with moderate to high humidity are needed for optimum flower and fruit production. Below 68°F growth is often stalled. **Zones 4 to 11.**

Propagation

Temperatures of 58–70°F are needed for good germination. Sow seed in early spring, in trays, pots, or packs of moist seed potting mix in a propagator or warm greenhouse or on a windowsill. Soaking seed in warm water for 24 hours before sowing helps germination. When three leaves appear, repot plants grown in seed trays into 2–3 in. pots, repotting as required until they are ready to plant outdoors or under cover. If you are growing eggplants outdoors, sow seeds 10 to 12 weeks before the last frosts are expected.

Growing

Eggplants flourish in a sunny, sheltered position on fertile, well-drained soil. Before planting, fork in a slow-release general fertilizer at 1–2 oz. per square yard, improve the soil with the addition of organic matter and, in cooler climates, warm the soil before planting and leave the cloches in place until the plants are established for 2 to 3 weeks, allowing them to "harden off" before removing the cloches.

Space plants 20–24 in. apart. "Pinch out" the growth tip when plants are 16 in. tall, or 9–12 in. for smaller varieties. Stake the main stem or support branches with string, if necessary, as fruit begins to mature. Mulch outdoor plants to conserve moisture and suppress weeds.

Feed plants with a liquid general fertilizer until they are established, then water with a high-potassium liquid

EGGPLANT

Beautiful in bloom and fruit

feed every 10 days, once the first fruits are formed. When the flowers begin to open, a light spray with tepid water helps pollination; for large, high-quality fruits, allow only four to five to form on each plant, after which any new side shoots should be removed.

Maintenance
Spring Sow seeds indoors.
Summer Once frosts are over, transplant outdoors. Retain four to six fruits per plant, harvesting as they mature.
Fall Protect outdoor crops from early frosts.
Winter Order seed for the following growing season.

Protected Cropping
When growing plants indoors, water them regularly with tepid water or dampen the paths on hot days. Keep the potting mix moist throughout the growing season, but take care to avoid waterlogging.

Harvesting and Storing
Harvest when the skin is shiny: overripe fruits have dull skin and are horribly bitter. Using a knife, cut the fruit stalks close to the stem. They will keep for 2 weeks in a cool, humid place or in a refrigerator.

Pests and Diseases
Eggplants are susceptible to the typical problems of crops grown indoors.

Check plants for aphids, whitefly, and red spider mite. Powdery mildew can stunt growth, and in severe cases leaves become yellow and die. Verticillium wilt turns lower leaves yellow; plants wilt, but recover overnight.

 companion planting

Eggplants flourish alongside the herbs thyme and tarragon, and peas.

 container growing

Eggplants can be grown in 8–12 in. pots or in growing bags. Keep temperatures around 58–65°F; water regularly, keep the potting mix moist and feed with a half-strength high-potassium fertilizer every other watering.

 culinary

The large "berries" contain a bitter quality in the flesh: slice large varieties, sprinkle with salt and leave for 30 minutes before rinsing. Small and newer varieties do not need this treatment. Rub cut surfaces with lemon juice to prevent discoloration.

Eggplants can be made into soups, puréed, stewed, stuffed, fried, and pickled. Slices can be dipped in batter to make fritters, or drizzled with olive oil and broiled or roasted. In the Middle East the skin is burned off over a naked flame, giving the flesh a smoky flavor.

In Provence, the vegetable stew *ratatouille* is made from eggplants, garlic, bell peppers, zucchini, onions, and coriander seeds, all cooked in olive oil. The Greek *moussaka* contains ground meat and eggplants. In the Caribbean, small white varieties are stewed in coconut milk and sweet spices. Oriental eggplants have a sweetness that does not suit European cooking; use them in stir-fries.

Sautéed Eggplants with Mozzarella
Serves 4

This dish goes well with plain meats.

4 small, long, thin eggplants
1 clove garlic, crushed
1 tablespoon chopped parsley
Salt and freshly ground black pepper

 medicinal

In Indian herbal medicine, white varieties are used to treat diabetes and as a carminative. The Sanskrit *vatin-ganah* means "antiwind vegetable." *Kama Sutra* prescribes it in a concoction for "enlarging the male organ for a period of 1 month." Neither claim is proven!

 warning

Always remove the fruit's bitter principle, as it irritates the mucous membranes.

¼ cup toasted breadcrumbs
3 tablespoons olive oil
1 cup buffalo mozzarella, cut into ¼-in. thick slices

Cut the eggplants in half lengthwise. Score the flesh deeply, but do not cut the skin. Arrange in a shallow pan, skin side down. Mix the garlic, parsley, salt and pepper, the breadcrumbs, and half the olive oil and press this into the scored eggplants. Drizzle over the rest of the oil and place in a preheated oven 350°F until tender, about 20 minutes. Raise the heat to 400°F and, as the oven warms, arrange the mozzarella on top of the eggplants. Return to the oven for 5 minutes. Serve this dish immediately the mozzarella melts.

POTATO

Solanum tuberosum. Solanaceae

Also known as Common Potato, Irish Potato. Perennial, grown as annual for edible starchy tubers. Half hardy. Value: rich in carbohydrates, magnesium, potassium; moderate amounts of vitamins B and C.

"Then a sentimental passion of a vegetable fashion must excite your languid spleen. An attachment à la Plato for a bashful young potato or a not too French French bean."
Sir William Gilbert (1836–1911)

The world's fourth most important food crop after wheat, corn, and rice, the potato is a nutritious starchy staple grown throughout temperate zones. Hundreds of varieties have been developed since 5000 BCE, when potatoes were first cultivated in Chile and Peru. The name derives from *batatas*, the Carib Indian name for the sweet potato, or from *papa* or *patata*, as it was called by South American Indians.

The Spaniards introduced potatoes to Europe in the 16th century and Sir John Hawkins is reputed to have brought them to England in 1563. Extensive cultivation did not start until Sir Francis Drake brought more back in 1586, after battling with the Spaniards in the Caribbean. Sir Walter Raleigh introduced them to Ireland and later presented some to Elizabeth I. Her cook is said to have discarded the tubers and cooked the leaves, which did not help its popularity!

In England and Germany, potatoes were considered a curiosity; in France they were believed to cause leprosy and fever. However, in 1773 the French scientist Antoine Parmentier wrote a thesis extolling the potato's virtues as a famine food after eating them while a prisoner of war in Prussia. He established soup kitchens to feed the malnourished; potato soup is now known as *Potage Parmentier*, and there is also *Omelette Parmentier*. He created "French fries," which were served at a dinner honoring Benjamin Franklin, who was unimpressed; it was Thomas Jefferson who introduced French fries to America at a White House dinner.

Parmentier presented a bouquet of potato flowers to Louis XVI, who is said to have worn one in his buttonhole. Marie Antoinette wore them in her hair, which made it highly fashionable. By the early 19th century, the potato had become a staple in France.

Ireland's climate and plentiful rain produced large crops. Potatoes were propagated from small tubers which were passed from one household to another, so the whole crop came from a few original plants. These were susceptible to potato blight, and devastating crop failure in the 1840s caused the death of more than 1.5 million people. Almost a million others emigrated to North America.

During the American Civil War, potatoes were sent to the prisons and front lines. By eating the potatoes in their skins, soldiers received adequate supplies of vitamin C. The common name "spud" came from a tool which was once used to weed the potato patch.

 varieties

Potatoes are classified as early, mid- or late season varieties. Early varieties grow rapidly, taking up less space for a shorter time than late season crops, so are better for small gardens. Yields are usually lower. They are also unaffected by some of the diseases afflicting maincrops. Midseason crops are planted about a month after earlies. Late season crops are for immediate consumption or winter storage.

Potatoes come in a huge range of shapes, sizes, colors and textures. The skin may be red, yellow, purple or white, and the flesh pale cream or yellow, mottled or blue. Their texture may be waxy or floury,

Do not eat the leaves!

"Maxine"

and their shapes are variously, knobbly, round, or oval. It is a wonderful time to grow potatoes. Hundreds of heritage varieties are available in catalogs; many from smaller, specialized producers and breeders are aiming to create more blight-resistant varieties. Grow some new varieties each year alongside your favorites for taste and performance. Use them or lose them!

"Arran Pilot" is an old favorite and a reliable cropper with tasty, firm, waxy flesh. "Belle de Fontenay" is a very old and rare French early variety that is excellent for salads. The yellow tubers are small and kidney-shaped with a waxy texture and fine flavor. "Cara" a late maincrop with pinkish-red tubers, is good for baking and very disease-resistant. "Charlotte" is a delicious second early salad variety with waxy flesh and a superb flavor hot and cold. "Desirée" is a popular maincrop with pink skin and pale yellow flesh that is good for fries and baking: crops well on most soils, but prefers medium to heavy; susceptible to mosaic and common scab "Golden Wonder," a late maincrop with floury, yellow flesh, is ideal for potato chips and good for baking but usually disintegrates when boiled. It grows well in moist, humid climates, is resistant to scab but susceptible to slug damage and drought. "Harlequin," a cross between "Charlotte" and "Pink Fir Apple," with pale yellow flesh, is an early maincrop salad potato with a delicious flavor — a taste test winner, both hot and cold. "Highland Burgundy Red" is an early maincrop with burgundy flesh and a mild taste. "Maris Bard" is a very early first early, with white skin and white waxy flesh. It is high-yielding and good under cover. Excellent quality and good virus resistance. "Maris Piper" is a prolific second early with waxy flesh when cooked. "Mayan Gold" is an early maincrop, "phureja"-type with different

"Maris Piper"

origins to traditional potatoes. Yellow-skinned with oval tubers, golden flesh, and a nutty flavor and creamy but dry texture, it is good for fries and pie toppings, but not for roasting. "King Edward," another famous high-yielding, good-quality maincrop, is good for baking but susceptible to blight, wart disease, and drought. "Lady Christl" is an excellent good-textured first early with good disease resistance. "Maxine" is a maincrop that produces high yields of large, round, red-skinned tubers. The white waxy flesh remains firm when cooked; excellent for French fries. "Mimi", a first early, produces tiny tubers that are superb in salads. Ideal for containers. First early "Pentland Javelin" produces high yields of oval, white-skinned tubers with white waxy flesh; resistant to common scab and golden eelworm. "Pink Fir Apple" is a wonderful old late maincrop. The unusual elongated tubers are pink-skinned with pale yellow flesh. Remaining firm when cold, they are good in salads and make good fries. "Ratte," a French classic early maincrop with a nutty flavor, is good for steaming. "Red Duke of York," a first early with delicious yellow flesh, is a good all-rounder with a long harvesting season. "Sarpo Axona" is similar to "Sarpo Mira" but with more regular-shaped tubers and creamier flesh. "Sarpo Mira" is heavy cropping with floury tubers that are good "all rounders" in the kitchen. It is also tolerant of a range of soils, not affected by slugs and 100 percent blight resistant. (Both late maincrops.) "Sharpes Express," one of the best first early potatoes, has a wonderful flavor and is good for fries and new potatoes. "Wilja" is a high-yielding second early with long white tubers and pale yellow waxy flesh. Good for salads and excellent for cooking. Resistant to blight, it also has some resistance to scab and blackleg.

cultivation

Propagation

Potatoes are normally grown from small tubers known as "seed potatoes." Buy "certified" virus-free stock from a reputable supplier to be certain of obtaining a good-quality crop.

First earlies are "sprouted" (or "chitted") about 6 weeks before planting to extend the growing season, which is particularly useful for early cultivars and in cooler climates. It is worth chitting second earlies and maincrops if they are to be planted late. Put a single layer of potatoes in a shallow tray or egg box with the "rose end" (where most of the "eyes" or dormant buds are) upwards, then put the tray in a light, cool, frost-free place to encourage growth. At 45°F it takes about 6 weeks for shoots around 1 in. long to form. At this stage, they are ready for planting. They can be planted when the shoots are longer, but need handling with care, as they are easily broken off. For a smaller crop but larger potatoes, leave three shoots per tuber on earlies; otherwise leave all of the shoots for a higher yield.

Plant earlies from midspring and maincrops from late spring, when there is no longer any danger of hard frosts and soil temperatures are 45°F.

Make trenches or individual holes 3–6 in. deep, depending on the size of the tuber. Plant them upright with the shoots at the top and cover with at least 1 in. of soil. Take care not to damage the shoots. Earlies can be planted a little deeper to give more protection from cooler weather. Ideally the rows should face north-south, so that both sides receive sunshine.

Plant earlies 12–15 in. apart with 15–20 in. between the rows and maincrops 15 in. apart with 30 in. between the rows. Alternatively, plant earlies 14 in. apart and second earlies and maincrops 12–15 in. apart in and between the rows. Spacing can be varied according to the size of the tubers and also according to their subsequent cropping potential.

While the traditional method of propagation is very common, seed is also available, which is easy to handle and produces healthy crops. Seeds are sown indoors before potting on, hardening off and transplanting. "Plantlets" produced by tissue culture are also available; these are healthy, virus-free and vigorous.

These, too, will need growing on before hardening off and then transplanting.

If cutting large potatoes in half, allow the cut surfaces to suberize for a couple of days before planting. I do not recommend the method I once saw being used — hollowing the tubers to leave a thin layer of flesh, then planting the skins only! **Zones 3 to 8.**

Growing

Potatoes flourish in an open, sunny, frost-free site on deep, rich, fertile, well-drained soil. They grow better in cool seasons, when temperatures are between 61–64°F, and are tolerant of most soils.

Lighter soils are better for growing earlies. Add organic matter to sandy soils. Alkaline soils or heavy liming encourages scab. Grow resistant varieties and lime acidic soils gradually to create a pH of 5 to 6, or cultivate in raised beds or containers. If necessary, dig in plenty of well-rotted organic matter in fall, then rake to a rough tilth 10 days before planting, adding a general granular fertilizer at 3–4 oz./sq. yd.

Potatoes are an excellent crop for new or neglected gardens; while the crop may not be large, the root system breaks up the soil and improves its structure.

"Mimi"

Keep crops weed-free until they are established, when the dense canopy of foliage suppresses weeds.

Potatoes are hilled up; this prevents exposure to light, which makes them green and inedible, and also disturbs germinating weeds. When the plants are about 8–9 in. tall, use a rake or spade to draw loose soil carefully around the stems to a depth of 4–5 in. Alternatively, begin hilling in stages when the plants are about 4 in. tall, adding soil every 2 to 3 weeks.

To avoid having to hill up, plant small tubers about 5 in. deep and 9–10 in. apart on level ground. Wide spacing means tubers are not forced to the surface, yet still produce a moderate crop.

Potatoes need at least 20 in. of rainfall over the growing season for a good crop. During dry weather water earlies every 12 to 14 days at 3–4 gallons/sq. yd. Except when there are drought conditions, do not water maincrops until the tubers are the size of marbles (check their development by scraping back the soil below a plant). At this point, a single, thorough soaking with at least 5 gallons/sq. yd. encourages the tubers to swell, increases the yield and makes them less prone to scab.

Fresh means full of flavor

Potatoes need a constant supply of water; erratic watering causes malformed, hollow or split potatoes. An organic liquid feed or nitrogenous top dressing helps plants to become established during the early stages of growth.

Early potatoes can be grown under black polyethylene, which also makes hilling unnecessary. Prepare the soil, lay a sheet of black polyethylene over the area, anchor the edges by covering with soil and plant your potatoes through crosses cut in the polyethylene. Alternatively, plant the potatoes, cover them with polyethylene and when the foliage appears, make a cut in the polyethylene and pull through.

Where early frosts and windy conditions do not occur and the ground is excessively weedy or wireworm is a problem, potatoes can be grown in a bed of compost and straw. Clear the ground and cover the soil with a good layer of well-rotted manure or compost. Space the potatoes as required and cover them with a 2–3 in. layer of straw or hay, adding more as the potatoes grow, to a maximum of 6 in. At this point, spread a 3–4 in. layer of lawn clippings over the area to exclude light from the developing tubers.

Rotate earlies every 3 and maincrops every 5 years.

Maintenance
Spring Chit potatoes before planting.
Summer Keep crops weed-free and water as necessary. Harvest and use, or store.
Fall Plant winter crops under cover. Prepare the soil for the following year.
Winter Harvest winter crops.

Protected Cropping
To advance early crops and protect them from frost, cover early potatoes with cloches or floating row covers, anchored by burying the edges under the soil. When the shoots appear, cut holes in the plastic and pull the foliage through. After 3 to 4 weeks cut the cover, leaving it in place to allow the potatoes to become acclimatized.

Protect the foliage and stems from heavy frosts by covering them at night with a layer of straw, bracken or newspaper, or a thin layer of soil. Light frosts do not generally cause problems.

For winter crops of new potatoes, in warm areas, plant earlies in midsummer and cover with cloches in fall. Alternatively, grow them in the borders of a frost-free greenhouse at 45–50°F. Provide warmth if necessary.

 companion planting

Growing horseradish in large sunken pots near to potatoes controls some diseases. Plant with corn, cabbage, beans and marigolds. Grow with eggplants, which are a greater attraction to Colorado beetle. Protect against scab by putting grass clippings and comfrey leaves in the planting hole or trench.

Harvesting and Storing
Earlies are ready to harvest from early to midsummer, second earlies from late summer to early fall and maincrops mature from early to midfall. Harvest earlies when they are about the size of a hen's egg: their readiness is often indicated by the flowers opening. Remove some soil from the side of a ridge and check them for size before lifting the root. Insert a flat-tined fork into the base of the ridge and lift the whole plant, bringing the new potatoes to the surface.

Harvest those grown under black plastic by folding back the sheeting: the crop of potatoes will be lying on the surface. Collect as required. Scrape away compost from those grown in containers to check their size before harvesting them.

Leave healthy maincrop potatoes in the soil for as long as possible, but beware of slugs! In early fall cut back the stem to about 2 in. above the soil, or wait until the foliage dies down naturally; leave the tubers in the ground for 2 weeks for the skins to harden before lifting.

Cut back the stems and work along the side of each ridge, lifting the potatoes with a fork. Harvest on a dry sunny day when the soil is moderately moist, leave in the sun for a few hours to dry, then brush off the soil. If the weather is poor, dry them under cloches or on trays indoors. Store healthy tubers in paper, gunny, or boxes in a dark, cool, frost-free place. They should keep until spring. Check tubers weekly, removing those that are damaged or diseased.

When harvesting, ensure that all potatoes, however small, are removed from the soil, to prevent future

POTATO

problems occurring with pests and diseases. New potatoes do not store, but can be frozen: blanch whole in boiling water for 3 minutes; cool, drain, pack into rigid containers and freeze. French fries can also be frozen.

Pests and Diseases

Common potato scab shows as raised, corky scabs on the surface of the tuber. It does not usually affect the whole potato and can be removed by peeling. It is common in hot, dry summers, on light, free-draining and alkaline soils. Water well in dry conditions, add plenty of organic matter to the soil before planting, avoid excessive liming, or rotating after the soil has been limed for brassicas. Do not put infected potatoes or peelings on the compost pile. Grow resistant cultivars.

Potato blight appears on the leaves as brown patches, often with paler margins. The infection can

"Maxine" leaves showing the first signs of blight

spread to the stems and through the tuber, making it inedible. The disease spreads rapidly in warm, humid conditions and maincrops are more susceptible. Grow resistant cultivars and avoid overhead watering; before the problem appears, apply a systemic fungicide every 2 weeks from midsummer. Alternatively, use copper sulfate sprays such as Bordeaux mixture. Hilling creates a protective barrier, slowing the infection of tubers. Lift early potatoes as soon as possible and in late summer, cut back the shoots of infected plants just above the ground and burn the infected material or put it in the garbage can. Leave tubers in the ground for 2 weeks before lifting.

With potato cyst eelworm ("golden nematode" or "pale eelworm") growth is checked and yields can be severely reduced; badly affected plants turn yellow and die. Lift and burn infected plants, rotate crops, and do not grow potatoes or tomatoes in the soil for at least 6 years. Try to grow resistant varieties.

Eelworms are about 1 in. long and golden brown in color. They tunnel into the tubers, making them inedible. They are fairly easy to control. Cultivate the soil thoroughly over winter to expose to the weather and birds, keep crops weed-free, and lift maincrops as early as possible.

Blackleg shows when the upper leaves roll and wilt and the stem becomes black and rotten at the base. The tubers may be rotten. It is more severe in wet seasons; do not plant on waterlogged land. Remove affected plants immediately; burn or put in the trash. Do not store damaged tubers.

Slugs tunnel into the tubers; damage is more severe the longer they remain in the ground. Use biological control.

 container growing

Potatoes can be grown in any container if it is at least 12 in. wide and deep and has drainage holes. It is possible to buy a potato barrel for this purpose — some models have sliding panels for ease of harvesting — but an old garbage can, flower pot or similar is just as good. Potatoes can also be grown in black garbage bags. Wider containers can, of course, hold more potatoes. Place a 4–5 in. layer of compost or good garden soil in a container, stand two to three chitted potatoes on the

surface and cover with a layer of compost about 4–6 in. deep. When the shoots are about 6 in. tall, cover with another 4–6 in. layer of compost, leaving the tips showing. Continue hilling until the shoots are 5–7 in. below the rim of the container.

Winter crops of first earlies can also be grown in containers. Plant in midsummer for harvesting at Christmas. Cover the stems or shoots in frosty weather or grow indoors.

Be sure to keep crops well fed and watered.

 other uses

Potatoes are made into flour and turned into bread. They can be boiled and the starch turned to glucose, which can be fermented to produce strong alcohol, like the poteen made in Ireland. In the past, they have also been a source of starch powder for whitening wigs. The juice of mature potatoes is particularly excellent for cleaning silks, cotton, wool and even furniture.

 medicinal

Potatoes are said to be good for rheumatism. One traditional cure for sciatica and lumbago is to carry a potato in your pocket.

The juice from a raw potato or the water in which potatoes have been boiled is said to relieve gout, rheumatism, lumbago, sprains and bruises.

Uncooked peeled and pounded potatoes are said to make a soothing plaster to scalds or burns when applied cold.

Potatoes contain little fat and provide more potassium *pro rata* than bananas, while the average potato contains as many calories as most apples or a glass of orange juice and can be eaten by those on a diet.

 warning

Green potatoes contain the toxic alkaloid solanine, which can cause vomiting and stomach upsets. Do not eat green potatoes. Be aware that the tomato-like fruits and leaves of the plant are also poisonous.

culinary

There are more than 500 ways of serving potatoes. They can be boiled, steamed, baked, roasted, mashed, sautéed, fried, and cooked *au gratin*. In the past, potatoes have been preserved and candied or mashed with butter, sherry, egg yolks, nutmeg, and a little sugar and baked until brown. Rub the skin from new potatoes under running water and boil for 12 minutes with a sprig of mint. Drain and toss in butter, then eat hot or cold in salads. Scrape old potatoes; peeling removes much of the vitamin C just below the surface.

Cut potatoes into ½ in. strips, wash in ice-cold water, drain and dry thoroughly. Fry until golden in a shallow frying basket in a pan one third full of oil at 250°F.

The difference between French fries and what British people call "chips" is their size and the method of cooking. French fries are very thinly sliced sticks and deep-fried in oil. "Chips" are sliced thickly and were originally cooked in animal fat. Nowadays, the only difference is the size. Steaming or microwaving generally retains the flesh color in unusual potatoes.

Mashed Potatoes with Olive Oil
Serves 4

For those on a diet, this at least has fewer calories than the traditional dish!

2 pounds potatoes, peeled
8 to 10 garlic cloves, unpeeled
8 tablespoons olive oil, preferably extra virgin
Salt and freshly ground black pepper

Put the potatoes and garlic cloves in a pan, cover with water and add salt. Bring to a boil and cook until tender, about 20 minutes, and then drain, reserving the potato cooking liquid. Boil this separately in the pan to reduce to roughly 1 cup. Meanwhile peel the garlic cloves.

Mash the potatoes and garlic. Return the pan to a gentle heat and beat in the olive oil and enough potato liquid to give the potatoes the right texture. Season with salt and pepper.

To make Irish champ, add ½ cup of cooked and roughly chopped cabbage or spring greens to the above.

Rösti
Serves 4

1 ½ pounds waxy potatoes
1 small onion, finely minced
¼ smoked bacon, diced
6 to 8 tablespoons olive oil
Salt and freshly ground black pepper

Clean the potatoes and boil them in lightly salted water until just tender. Drain, and when cool enough to handle, peel. Grate coarsely.

In a heavy pan, gently sauté the onion and bacon in half the fat. Fold this into the potatoes with the seasoning. Form the potatoes into one big "cake." In the same pan, heat the balance of the fat and gently slide the potatoes into the pan. Cook over high heat until the first side is browned. Place a plate over the pan and turn the potatoes on to the plate; then gently slide the "cake" back into the pan to allow the second side to cook. Serve piping hot. This classic Swiss dish can be eaten with Emmenthal melted on top (put the browned potatoes, covered with cheese slices, under the broiler for a few minutes).

Make smaller individual rösti if you prefer

Potato Salad with Goat Cheese Dressing

Potato Salad with Goat Cheese Dressing
Serves 4

The South Americans have excellent ways of cooking potatoes, including this rich salad which makes a good summer first course.

1 ½ pounds potatoes, fairly small
½ a red bell pepper, seeded and diced
1 small onion, peeled and finely minced
2 hard-boiled eggs, peeled and diced
Handful black olives, pitted
2 tablespoons chopped fresh Italian parsley

For the dressing:
⅔ cup well-flavored goat cheese
2 cloves garlic, peeled
2 tablespoons yogurt
2 tablespoons lemon juice
1 jalapeño pepper, seeded
¼ teaspoon turmeric
½ teaspoon ground cumin

Cook the potatoes in their skins in boiling water until tender; drain and peel.

Cut into generous dice and put into a serving dish. While the potatoes cook, mix the dressing ingredients in a blender, puréeing until smooth. Combine the potatoes with the red bell pepper and onion. Add the dressing and toss. Decorate the top with the diced eggs, olives and parsley.

Spinacia oleracea. Chenopodiaceae
SPINACH

Fast-growing annual, grown for highly nutritious leaves. Hardy. Value: high in iron, beta carotene and folic acid; rich in vitamins A and C.

Spinach is thought to be native to Southwest Asia. Unknown to the Greeks and Romans, it was first cultivated by the Persians, was grown in China by the 7th century CE and reached Europe around 1100, after its introduction to Spain by the Moors. The prickly-seeded form was known in 13th-century Germany and by the following century it was commonly grown by European monastery gardens. Smooth-seeded spinach was first described in 1522. Its first mention in England comes in William Turner's *New Herball*, in the 16th century: "An herbe lately found and not long in use." The name comes from Old French *espinache*, derived from its Arabic and Persian name.

Children were encouraged to eat spinach because of its effect on the comic book character Popeye the Sailor. The idea that it contains exceptional levels of iron originated from Dr E. von Wolf in 1870. His figures went unchecked until 1937, when it was discovered that the iron content was one-tenth that claimed by him as a result of a misplaced decimal point!

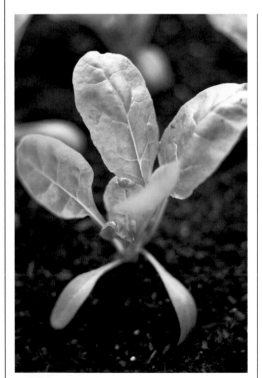

Harvest when young for "cut and come again" crops

 ## varieties

Traditionally there are two main groups. Prickly seeded varieties, which have lobed leaves, are regarded as hardier than the round, smooth-seeded types, which cope better with higher temperatures and are used for summer cropping. Modern cultivars are generally more adaptable. "Atlanta" has thick, deep green leaves for spring sowing. It does not overwinter well. "Bloomsdale" ("Bloomsdale Long Standing") is a Savoy-leaved (crinkled foliage) spinach with fleshy, tasty leaves. It is cold-tolerant, slow to bolt and crops over a long period. "Dominant" is a good all-rounder for spring or fall sowing: thick-leaved, prolific and resistant to bolting. "Giant Winter," a robust late fall and winter variety, withstands some frost and is highly disease-resistant. "Medania" is for summer cropping. It withstands hot, dry weather and is resistant to downy mildew. "Spartacus" is dark green, vigorous, yet slow to mature. Suitable for "cut and come again" crops. "Space" has smooth, dark green leaves and is resistant to downy mildew; ideal for any season. "Tetona,, has bright green, rounded leaves, is slow to bolt and ideal for early and late sowing or "baby" leaves; mildew resistant.

 ## cultivation

Spinach grows best in cool conditions, at temperatures around 60–65°F. It thrives in a bright position, but is better in light shade and moist ground if your garden is hot and sunny. **Zones 3 to 8.**

Propagation
Soak seed overnight to speed up germination. My friend Robert Fleming wraps seed in a wet paper towel and places it in a sealed container in the refrigerator for 5 days before planting. Germination usually takes 5 days. As a cool-season plant, it will not germinate above 86°F. Sow summer crops every 2 to 3 weeks from early to late spring for a summer harvest.

Sow in late summer, for cropping in winter until early summer. Sow *in situ* 1 in. apart and ½ to 1 in. deep in rows 12 in. apart. When large enough to handle, thin to 6–10 in. It also works as a "cut and come again" crop.

In colder areas, it is better to sow in seed trays or packs for transplanting.

Sow thinly in wide rows the width of a hoe or in rows 4 in. apart. Leave unthinned unless growth is slow, when they can be thinned to 2 in. apart. Plants can be thinned to 4–5 in. apart for larger leaves, though they are more inclined to bolt.

Growing

Spinach needs a rich, fertile, moisture-retentive soil, so, where necessary, dig in well-rotted organic matter before planting. On poor soils leaves are stunted, bitter and prone to bolt. The ideal pH is 6.5 to 7.5; lime acid soils.

Never allow the soil to dry out. Water regularly before the onset of dry weather and grow bolting-resistant cultivars. Water every 2 weeks with a high-nitrogen liquid fertilizer.

Maintenance

Spring Sow early crops successionally.
Summer Keep the soil moist and weed-free. Sow winter crops from late summer.
Fall Protect late crops under cloches; sow "cut and come again" crops indoors.
Winter Protect winter crops under cloches or floating row cover or sow in cold frames.

Protected Cropping

Hardy varieties for winter and early spring cropping are better protected in cold frames, cloches or under floating row cover.

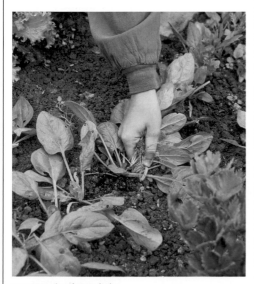

Harvest spinach regularly

Harvesting and Storing

Harvest from 5 weeks after sowing, cutting the outer leaves first. To harvest as a "cut and come again" crop, remove the heads 1 in. above the ground and allow them to resprout. Pick off the leaves carefully; the stems and roots are easily damaged. Alternatively, pull up whole plants and resow. Use the leaves fresh, or freeze. They can be washed and stored for up to 2 days in the refrigerator.

Pests and Diseases

Aphids and slugs can be troublesome, especially among seedlings. Downy mildew appears as yellow patches with fluffy mold on the underside of the leaf. Bolting caused by drying out or hot weather is most common cause of failure.

 ## container growing

Spinach is ideal for containers 8–18 in. wide and 12 in. deep. Water regularly in dry weather. Avoid scorching sunshine.

 ## companion planting

Good with beans, peas, corn and strawberries.

 ## medicinal

Spinach is said to be good for anemia, problems of the heart and kidney and in low vitality and general debility. Iron is in a soluble form, so any water left after cooking can be left to cool before drinking.

Research has shown that those who eat spinach daily are less likely to develop lung cancer. Of all the vegetable juices, spinach juice is said to be the most potent for the prevention of cancer cell formation.

 ## other uses

The water drained from spinach after cooking is said to make good matchpaper. It was used to make touchpaper for 18th- and 19th-century fireworks, as paper soaked in it smoldered well.

 ## culinary

Wash leaves thoroughly. Eat immediately after harvesting. Use young leaves raw in salads, lightly cooked or steamed. Place spinach in a pan without adding water, cover and stand on moderate heat so the leaves do not scorch.

After 5 minutes, stir and cook over high heat for 1 minute. Drain in a colander and cut with a knife or spatula.

Spinach can also be cooked with olive oil, cheese, cream, yogurt, ham, bacon and anchovies, besides being seasoned with nutmeg, pepper and sugar. All will bring out the flavor.

Scrambled Eggs with Raw and Cooked Spinach
Serves 6

2 pounds young spinach
2 tablespoons olive oil
Pinch grated nutmeg
2 tablespoons butter
12 eggs, lightly beaten with 1 tablespoon heavy cream
1 tablespoon chopped fresh chives
Salt and freshly ground black pepper

Wash the spinach and remove any tough stalks. Heat the oil in a heavy pan, then wilt most of the spinach, keeping back a couple of handfuls for decoration. Season with nutmeg, salt and pepper. Let sit and keep warm.

In the same pan, melt the butter and allow to just brown. Over a low flame, pour in the eggs and season. Stir constantly until just set (overcooked scrambled eggs are bad news!). Mound the eggs in the center of individual plates and sprinkle with chopped chives. Arrange the cooked spinach around the outside, then make an additional ring from the raw spinach leaves. Serve hot.

Stachys affinis. Labiatae

CHINESE ARTICHOKE

Also known as Japanese Artichoke, Crosne, Knotroot, Chorogi. Dwarf herbaceous perennial grown as annual for edible tubers. Hardy. Value: very high in potassium.

From the same family as mint, lavender and many other herbs, Chinese artichokes are not grown for their aromatic foliage but for the small, ridged tubers at the tips of creeping underground stems. A native of Japan and China, it has rough, oval leaves and white to pale pink flowers that appear in small spikes. It was introduced from Peking to France by a physician in the late 19th century. It has never been hugely popular, probably because a large area is needed for decent quantities, but it is worth trying, if only as a "novelty" crop.

 ## cultivation

Chinese artichokes flourish in an open, sunny site on light, fertile, yet moisture-retentive soil. **Zones 5 to 10.**

Propagation
For early crops, sprout the tubers in shallow trays or pots of potting compost in a moderately warm room, then plant out when soil is warm. Increase your stock by planting tubers individually in small pots of soilless compost with added organic matter, transplanting as required. Place in 8–9 in. pots for the rest of the growing season. Feed and water regularly.

Growing
In spring, plant the tubers vertically 1½ to 3 in. deep; on light soils up to 6 in. deep. Plant large tubers only,

Odd-looking, but edible

Lift the plants to harvest the tubers

12 in. apart each way or 8 in. apart in rows 16 in. apart. When they are 1–2 ft. high, hill up around the stems to about 3 in. Keep weed-free at first; as the plants mature, the leaf canopy naturally suppresses weed growth. Feed with a liquid general fertilizer every 2 weeks and remove flowering spikes to concentrate energy into fattening the tubers. Trim back the foliage. Rampant growth makes Chinese artichokes an ideal low-maintenance crop for a spare corner of the garden.

Maintenance
Spring Plant tubers when the soil has warmed.
Summer Keep crops weed-free, water and feed.
Fall Harvest after the first frosts, or about 5 months.
Winter Protect crops with hay, straw or burlap to enable harvesting to continue.

 ## culinary

The tubers have a delicate, nutty flavor. Only about 2 in. long, they are rather fiddly to cook. Boiling is simplest, but they can also be fried, stir-fried, roasted, added to soup or eaten raw in salads.

Creamed Chinese Artichokes
Serves 4

Jane Grigson, in her *Vegetable Book*, quotes this recipe from *La Cuisine de Madame Saint-Ange*.

1 pound Chinese artichokes
1 tablespoon butter
½ teaspoon lemon juice
1¼ heavy cream
Salt and freshly ground white pepper
Pinch nutmeg
Heavy cream, to serve

Boil the artichokes for about 5 minutes, drain, add the butter and lemon juice and cook gently for 5 to 7 minutes. Bring the cream to a boil, then add it to the artichokes, stirring in well. Season with nutmeg and salt and pepper. Cover and leave for 15 minutes over a moderate heat, until the cream has reduced by a quarter. Just before serving, stir in 3 spoonfuls of heavy cream and quickly remove from the heat.

Harvesting and Storing
Harvest as required from midfall to early spring, after the foliage has died back or when plants have been in the ground for 5 to 7 months. Lift them just before use, as they quickly shrivel. When forking through the ground during the final harvest, you should remove even the smallest tubers, or they will rapidly become weeds.

Pests and Diseases
Chinese artichokes are usually pest-free, but you should take precautions against lettuce root aphid, which can cause wilting.

Tetragonia tetragonoides (syn. *T. expansa*). Aizoaceae

NEW ZEALAND SPINACH

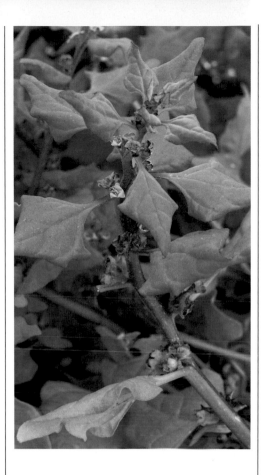

Also known as Botany Bay Greens. Creeping perennial, usually grown as annual for edible leaves. Half hardy. Value: high in iron, beta carotene and folic acid.

This plant was unknown in Europe until 1771, when it was introduced to the Royal Botanic Gardens at Kew by the great botanist Joseph Banks after his voyage on board the *Endeavour* with Captain Cook. By 1820 it was widely grown in the kitchen gardens of Britain and France, but it did not appear in New Zealand literature until the 1940s, and there is no evidence of its use by the Maoris. It is unrelated to the true spinach, but its leaves are used in a similar manner — hence the borrowed name — though their flavor is milder than that of true spinach. A low-growing perennial with soft, fleshy, roughly triangular, blunt-tipped leaves, about 2 in. long, it makes an attractive plant for edging and ground cover. It flourishes in hot dry conditions, without going to seed.

 ## cultivation

Propagation

The seed coat is extremely hard and germination is slow unless the seeds are soaked in water for 24 hours before sowing. Sow seeds individually, 1 in. deep in 3 in. pots indoors from mid- to late spring; repot as necessary. Plants are very cold-sensitive and so should be hardened off carefully before planting out once the danger of frost has passed.

Alternatively, sow seed *in situ* when there is no danger of frost, ½ to 1 in. deep in rows about 24 in. apart, thinning to a similar distance between plants. Seeds can also be sown, two or three per hill, 24 in. apart, thinning to leave the strongest. Pinch out tips of young plants to encourage bushy growth.

Plants usually self-seed and appear in the same area the following year. **Zones 4 to 8.**

Growing

New Zealand spinach flourishes in an open site on light, fertile soil with low levels of nitrogen and grows well in dry, poor conditions. It tolerates high temperatures, but is very susceptible to frost.

Keep seedlings weed-free with regular hoeing. Once plants have been properly established, their dense foliage will act as a ground cover and suppress weeds.

Water regularly during dry spells to encourage vigorous growth. It does not bolt in hot weather, but should be watered well to encourage growth. On poor soils, occasional feeding with a half-strength solution of general liquid fertilizer is beneficial, but take care not to overfeed.

Maintenance

Spring Sow seed under cover for transplanting once frosts are over.
Summer Keep crops weed-free, water and harvest as required.
Fall Protect plants to extend the growing season.
Winter Prepare the ground for planting in spring.

Protected Cropping

Protecting with cloches extends the harvesting season in cooler areas before frosts turn plants into a soggy mess.

Harvesting and Storing

The first young leaves and shoots are ready to harvest from about 6 weeks after sowing. Pick regularly to maintain a constant supply of young growth and to extend the harvesting season, which should last up to 4 months. Young leaves should be used immediately after cutting, can be stored for up to 2 days in a plastic bag in the fridge, or may be frozen. Wash, blanch for 2 minutes, allow to cool and drain before packing into plastic bags and placing in the freezer.

Pests and Diseases

New Zealand spinach is very robust but downy mildew may be a problem.

 ## container growing

Crops can be grown in large containers of soilless compost. Add grit to improve drainage. Water plants well throughout the growing season.

 ## companion planting

It is sometimes grown as a "green manure" to improve the soil structure.

 ## culinary

The young leaves and shoots are steamed, lightly boiled and eaten with a pat of butter, or eaten raw in salads. They are better eaten fresh, as the flavor deteriorates rapidly with age.

ASPARAGUS PEA

Also known as Winged Pea, Goa Bean. Sprawling annual winged bean, ornamental but grown for edible pods. Half hardy. Value: small amounts of protein, carbohydrate, fiber and iron.

A wildflower of open fields and wasteland in Mediterranean countries, this plant may have arrived in Great Britain with imported grain. It has since become naturalized. Gerard records its cultivation before 1569 for its dark crimson, pea-like flowers; only later were its edible merits discovered, but it has never gained widespread popularity. The 1807 edition of Miller's *Gardener's Dictionary* notes: "Formerly cultivated as an esculent plant, for the green pods ... it is now chiefly cultivated in flower gardens for ornament."

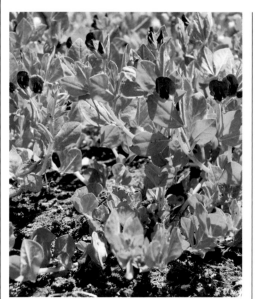
Asparagus pea in bloom

Maintenance
Spring Sow seed in mid- to late spring.
Summer Harvest regularly.
Fall Harvest until early fall.
Winter Prepare ground for the following year's crop.

Protected Cropping
In cooler areas, sow indoors for transplanting later.

Harvesting and Storing
Harvest from midsummer to early fall, when pods are 1 in. long. Pick regularly to prolong the harvest. Longer, older pods are stringy and inedible. Pods that do not bend easily are unsuitable for eating. Harvesting is easier in the evening, when the leaves close and the small green pods are more visible.

Pests and Diseases
Protect crops from birds using humming line or similar bird deterrents. They can also suffer from downy and powdery mildew.

 culinary

The subtle flavor is similar to asparagus. Wash the pods, top and tail if necessary, then steam for up to 5 minutes (check them after about 3 minutes, as they need only light cooking). Drain well before eating. Mix with butter and cream or serve on toast. Alternatively, cook them in butter until they are tender, drain and serve.

 cultivation

Propagation
Sow seed outdoors from mid- to late spring, once the soil warms and frosts are over. Rows should be 1 in. deep and 15 in. apart; thin to 8–12 in. apart once they are large enough to handle. In cooler areas, sow under cloches or in the greenhouse in trays or packs of moist seed compost. Harden off and transplant outdoors when plants are 2 in. tall, spacing them about 8–12 in. apart. **Zones 4 to 11.**

Growing
Asparagus peas flourish in an open, sheltered, sunny site on light, rich, free-draining soil. Keep weed-free and water as required. As they are lax in habit, growing up pea sticks or a similar support saves space and makes harvesting easier. Rotate them with other legumes.

Tragopogon porrifolius. Asteraceae
SALSIFY

Also known as Purple Salsify, Oyster Plant, Vegetable Oyster, Goat's Beard. Grown as biennial for shoots, flower buds and flowers; annual for cylindrical tapering edible roots. Hardy. Value: contains inulin, turning to fructose in storage; small amounts of vitamins and minerals.

It is difficult to know whether to grow this plant for its delicious roots, or to grow it as a fragile ornamental by letting it flower (the flowers are also edible). Its Latin and common names are apt; *tragos* means goat and *pogon*, beard, describes the tuft of silky hairs on the developing seedheads; *porrifolius* means "with leaves like a leek." "Salsify" comes from the old Latin name *solsequium*, from the way the flowers follow the course of the sun.

Salsify is a relatively recent crop. In the 13th century it was harvested from the wild in Germany and France. It was not cultivated until the early 16th century — in Italian gardens. The English plant collector John Tradescant the Younger recorded it in 1656. It was taken to North America in the late 19th century.

 ## varieties

The species *Tragopogon porrifolius* has a thin, creamy-white, tapering taproot up to 15 in. It has narrow leaves and long stems topped by beautiful dull purple flowers. These are followed by thistle-like seedheads. "Geante Noire de Russie" is an extremely long, black-skinned variety with white roots and a superb flavor. "Giant" is consistently long-rooted with a delicate taste of oysters. "Sandwich Island" is a selected type with strongly flavored roots and smooth skin.

Salsify roots aren't always easy to peel

 ## cultivation

Propagation
Always use fresh seed; its viability declines rapidly. Sow as early as possible, from early to midspring. Germination can be somewhat erratic, so it is better to sow two to three seeds in hills ½ to 1 in. deep and 4 in. apart with 12 in. between the rows. After germination, when the seedlings are large enough to handle, thin to leave the strongest seedling. Alternatively, sow the seeds in rows and thin to the above spacing. **Zones 5 to 11.**

Growing
Salsify thrives in an open situation on light, well-drained, stone-free soil which was manured for the previous crop (roots tend to fork when they are grown on freshly manured soil). On stony or heavy soils, dig a trench about 12 in. deep and 8 in. wide, filling it with finely sieved sandy soil or compost and sharp sand to give the roots room to grow.

Lighten heavier soils by thoroughly digging over the area the fall before planting, adding well-rotted organic matter and sharp sand. A pH of 6.0 to 7.5 is ideal; lime acid soils. Before sowing, rake the seedbed to a fine tilth and incorporate a slow-release general fertilizer at 2–3 oz./square yard.

Regular watering ensures good-quality roots and, importantly, stops bolting in dry conditions. It also prevents roots from splitting, which occurs after sudden rainfall or watering after drought. Salsify should be kept weed-free, particularly during the early stages of growth. Hand weed, as the roots are easily damaged. Alternatively, use an onion hoe or mulch moist soil with a layer of organic matter to stifle weed growth and conserve moisture. Roots can be left in the ground to produce edible shoots or "chards" the following spring. In fall, cut back the old leaves to within ½ to 1 in. of the soil and hill up to about 5–6 in. In midspring the following year, the shoots are ready to harvest when they appear. On heavier soils, "chards" can be blanched with a covering of bracken, straw or dry leaves at least 5 in. deep when new growth appears in spring. An upturned bucket or flower pots with the drainage holes covered work just as well.

Maintenance
Spring Rake over the seedbed, incorporating general fertilizer. Sow seeds in hills.
Summer Keep the crop weed-free, mulch and water during dry periods.
Fall Lift crops as required. Cut back the tops and cover those being grown for "chards."
Winter Dig over soil manured for the previous crop. Lift and store crops grown in colder areas.

Salsify in Batter

Harvesting and Storing

Harvest from midfall. Lift as required; protect roots with a layer of straw, bracken or a similar material before severe frosts or snow. They can be lifted in fall and stored in boxes of peat substitute, sand or sawdust, in a cool, frost-free garage, shed or cellar. Lift carefully with a garden fork; the roots "bleed" and snap easily.

If you begin lifting and find the crop misshapen, leave the roots buried in the ground and harvest the shoots and buds the following year. Next time, grow in sieved soil.

Harvest "chards" in early to midspring: scrape away the soil and cut the blanched shoots when they are 5–6 in. long. Or lift when 6 in. tall, without hilling, though they are not as tender.

Pests and Diseases

Salsify is usually trouble-free but may suffer from white blister, which looks like glistening paint splashes and can distort plants. Spray with Bordeaux mixture and destroy any plants that are badly affected. Aster yellows cause deformed new growth and the leaf veins or whole leaf become yellow. Control the aster leaf hopper, which spreads the disease.

 container growing

Salsify can be grown in containers, but it is impractical to produce them in large quantities. However, if you are desperate, fill a large wooden box, tea chest or plastic drum with sandy, free-draining soil or a soilless potting mix with added sharp sand. Ensure there are sufficient drainage holes. Keep crops weed-free and water regularly.

 companion planting

Salsify grows well with mustard and, planted near carrots, discourages carrot fly.

 medicinal

Salsify is said to have an antibilious effect and to calm fevers. In folk medicine, it is used to treat gall bladder problems and jaundice.

 culinary

Salsify has a delicate oyster-like flavor and can be cooked in a variety of ways (there is bound to be a recipe that suits you). Peel after boiling until tender, "skimming" under cold running water as you would a hard-boiled egg.

Cut roots discolor, so drop them into water with a dash of lemon juice, then boil for 25 minutes in salted water with lemon juice and a tablespoon of flour. Drain and skin, toss with melted butter and chopped parsley and indulge.

Try them with a light mornay sauce, deep-fried or served *au gratin* with cheese and breadcrumbs. Perhaps sautéing them in butter and eating with brown sugar is more to your liking?

Roots can also be baked, puréed, creamed for soup or grated raw in salads. They stay fresh in a fridge for about a week.

"Chards" can be served raw in salads or lightly cooked. Young flowering shoots can be eaten pickled, raw or cooked and eaten cold like asparagus, with oil and lemon juice. The subtle flavor makes them an excellent hors d'oeuvre.

Pick flower buds just before they open, with about 3 in. of stem attached, lightly simmer and eat when they are cool.

Salsify in Batter
Serves 4

1 ½ pounds salsify, topped, tailed and cleaned
Vegetable oil, for frying
Lemon wedges, to serve

For the Batter:
1 cup all-purpose flour
1 teaspoon baking powder
1 egg

1 tablespoon olive oil
¼ teaspoon harissa
½ teaspoon ground cumin
¼ teaspoon dried thyme
Salt and freshly ground black pepper

Cut salsify roots in half and boil in salted water for 30 minutes. Rinse under cold water. Peel and cut into 3 in. pieces.

Make the batter: whiz all the ingredients with ½ cup of water in a food processor for 30 seconds.

Heat the oil in a large skillet. Dip the salsify in the batter and fry in oil until crisp and golden, turning. Keep warm while cooking the remainder. Serve hot with lemon wedges.

Salsify in Ham with Cheese Sauce
Serves 4

8 salsify, peeled and trimmed
8 slices cooked ham
2 tablespoons butter
2 tablespoons flour
1 teaspoon Dijon mustard
1 ¼ cups milk
4 tablespoons grated Gruyère cheese
Pinch nutmeg
Salt and freshly ground black pepper

Boil the salsify for 5 minutes and drain. Cut into roughly 4 in. lengths. When cool enough to handle, wrap each in a slice of ham and arrange in a greased baking dish.

Melt the butter in a heavy pan and stir in the flour to make a roux. Cook for a minute or two and stir in the mustard. Slowly add the milk, then the Gruyère, and cook until the cheese is melted.

Season with nutmeg, salt and pepper and pour over the salsify. Bake in a preheated oven at 400°F for 20 minutes, until browned.

Valerianella locusta. Valerianaceae
LAMB'S LETTUCE

Also known as Corn Salad, Mâche, Lamb's Tongues. Low-growing, extremely hardy annual grown for edible leaves. Value: good source of beta carotene, vitamin C and folic acid. Very few calories.

In spite of its delicate appearance, lamb's lettuce is an extremely hardy plant, particularly valued as a nutritious winter salad crop. Its attractive bright green, rounded leaves have a slightly nutty taste. Depending on the authority, it was named lamb's lettuce because sheep are partial to it, or because it appears during the lambing season. Another name, corn salad, comes from its regular appearance as a cornfield weed.

Gerard wrote: "We know the Lamb's Lettuce as loblollie; and it serves in winter as a salad herb among others none of the worst." He also noted that "foreigners using it in England led to its cultivation in our gardens." It has been popular for centuries in France, where it is known as *salade de prêtre* (as it is often eaten in Lent), *doucette* ("little soft one," referring to the velvety leaves), and *bourcette*, describing their shape. In England it declined in popularity in the 1700s and a 19th-century commentator noted: "… it is indeed a weed, and can be of no real use where lettuces are to be had." Before the appearance of winter lettuce varieties, lamb's lettuce was the main winter salad; it was at one time classified in the same genus.

 ## varieties

There are two forms, the "large" or "broad-leaved" and the darker, more compact "green" type, which is popular in western Europe, but less productive.

"Cavallo" has deep green leaves and crops heavily. "Grote Noordhollandse" is very hardy. "Large Leaved" is tender and prolific. "Valeriana d'Orlanda" is an Italian variety with larger leaves than "Verte de Cambrai," which is a traditional French type with small leaves and good flavor. "Verte d'Etampes" has unusual, attractive savoyed leaves. "Vit" is very vigorous with a mild flavor.

 ## cultivation

Propagation
Lamb's lettuce can be grown as single plants or "cut and come again" seedlings. Sow seeds successively from mid- to late spring for summer crops in rows 4–6 in. apart and ½ in. deep, thinning when seedlings have three to four seed leaves to about 4 in. apart. Sow winter crops successively from mid- to late summer. Seeds can also be sown in wide rows, broadcast, or in seed trays or packs for transplanting. Leave a few plants to bolt, and transplant seedlings into rows. **Zones 4 to 9.**

Growing
Lamb's lettuce flourishes in a sheltered position in full sun or light shade and needs a deep, fertile soil for rapid and continuous growth. It tolerates most soils, provided they are not waterlogged. Create a firm seedbed and rake in a slow-release general fertilizer at 1–2 oz./sq. yd. before sowing in spring and summer. Overwintered crops growing on the same site should not need it.

Keep crops weed-free, particularly during the early stages, and water thoroughly to encourage soft growth.

Maintenance
Spring Sow successively.
Summer Continue sowing and harvesting; keep crops weed-free and water well.

Harvest before the plant starts flowering

LAMB'S LETTUCE

Productive even in winter

Fall Sow crops under cover. Continue harvesting.
Winter When growth is slower, do not overpick.

Protected Cropping
Although it is extremely hardy, growing lamb's lettuce under cloches, polyethylene tunnels or floating row cover, or in an unheated greenhouse, encourages better quality and higher productivity. Make the first sowings in early fall.

Harvesting and Storing
Harvest seedlings, pick leaves as required, or lift whole plants when they are mature — about 3 months after planting.

Do not weaken by removing too many leaves at one picking. This is particularly important with outdoor winter crops.

Leaves can be blanched for a few days before picking by covering with a box or pot to remove any bitterness.
Young flowers can be eaten in salads.

Pests and Diseases
Some varieties are susceptible to mildew. Protect seedlings from birds and slugs.

 ## companion planting

As plants take up very little space, lamb's lettuce is ideal sown between taller crops.

 ## container growing

Can be grown in 10 in. pots of soilless potting mix with a low fertilizer content. Sow seeds thinly ½ in. deep every 3 weeks from early spring to early summer and again from early to midfall, thinning to leave the strongest seedlings at a final spacing of 4 in. apart.

Keep the potting mix moist when plants are growing vigorously; reduce watering in cooler conditions.

 ## medicinal

With its high beta carotene, vitamin C and folic acid content, it is regarded by many as a winter and early spring tonic, and is useful when other nutritional vegetables are scarce.

 ## culinary

Thinnings can be used in salads. Wash the leaves thoroughly to remove soil. In 17th-century Europe, lamb's lettuce was often served with cold boiled beets or celery. The leaves are used as a substitute for lettuce and combine well with it, also complementing fried bacon or ham and beets. Leaves can also be cooked like spinach.

Lamb's Lettuce and Shrimp Salad
Serves 4

*A bag of lamb's lettuce, or a mixture of winter
    salad leaves*
16 to 20 large fresh shrimp, peeled
Toasted sesame seeds

For the vinaigrette:
Lemon juice
Balsamic vinegar
Extra virgin olive oil
Mustard
Salt and freshly ground black pepper
*Chopped fresh herbs, such as sage, parsley
    and chives*

Wash the salad leaves and arrange on individual plates. Season the shrimp with salt and pepper and coat generously with sesame seeds. In a heavy-bottomed skillet, gently cook them, turning after 3 minutes, when golden, to cook the other side. Arrange on the salad. Make the vinaigrette by mixing the ingredients to taste, sprinkle over and serve.

FAVA BEAN

Also known as Broad Bean, Horse Bean, Windsor. Annual grown for seeds, young leaf shoots and whole young pods. Value: low protein, good source of fiber, potassium, vitamins E and C.

They are thought to have originated around the Mediterranean, and the oldest remains of domesticated fava beans have been dated to 6800 to 6500 BCE. By the Iron Age, they had spread throughout Europe. The Greeks dedicated them to Apollo and thought that overindulgence dulled the senses; Dioscorides wrote that they are "flatulent, hard of digestion, causing troublesome dreams."

They may be the origin of the term "bean feast," being a major part of the annual meal given by employers for their staff. In the vernacular this has been changed to "beano." Great Britain has many folk sayings concerning the sowing date. Huntingdonshire country wisdom states: "On St Valentine's Day, beans should be in clay," and it was generally accepted that four seeds were sown — "One for rook, one for crow, one to rot, one to grow." Flowers were considered to be an aphrodisiac — "there ent no lustier scent than a beanfield in bloom" — while the poet John Clare wrote: "My love is as sweet as a bean field in blossom, beanfields misted wi' dew."

Hardy and prolific, they are the national dish of Egypt. An Arab saying goes, "Beans have satisfied even the pharaohs." How about you?

 ## varieties

Fava beans are classified as "dwarf," with small, early-maturing pods that are excellent under cloches or in containers, "longpods," which are also hardy, and "windsors," with broad pods that usually mature later and have a better flavor. There are green- and white-seeded forms among the longpods and windsors.

"Aquadulce" is a reliable hardy longpod for fall and spring sowing. "Aquadulce Claudia" is similar, with medium to long pods and white seeds, but less susceptible to blackfly; ideal for freezing. "Bunyard's Exhibition" is a reliable heavy cropper with a sweet subtle flavor and delicate texture. Good for freezing. "Imperial Green Longpod" produces pods around 15 in. long with up to 9 large green beans. "Masterpiece Green Longpod" is a good-quality, green-seeded bean that freezes well. "Jubilee Hyson" crops early with long pods of pale green beans; outstanding quality and flavor. "Red Epicure" has beautiful deep chestnut-crimson seeds. Some of the color is lost in cooking, but the flavor is superb. "Sweet Lorane" is a prolific, delicious small-seeded bean that is also cold-hardy. "The Sutton," a prolific dwarf variety, grows to around 12 in. high, is ideal for small gardens and under cloches — excellent flavor. "Witkiem Manita" is perfect for spring sowing, with sweet, succulent beans.

 ## cultivation

Propagation
As they germinate well in cool conditions, fava beans can be sown from mid- to late fall and overwintered outdoors for a midspring crop. Seedlings should be 1 in. high when colder weather arrives. "Aquadulce" cultivars are particularly suitable. When the soil is workable, sow every 3 weeks from late winter to late spring for successional cropping.

Pods filled with flavor

Plant seeds 2 in. deep in rows or make individual holes with 12 in. in and between the rows. Or grow them in staggered double rows, with 9 in. in and between the rows or in blocks 36 in. square with 8–20 in. between plants. Tall plants should be 12–15 in. apart. Sow extra seeds at the end of rows, for later use as transplants. **Zones 4 to 11.**

Growing

Fava beans flourish in an open, sunny site but overwintering crops need more shelter. Soils should be deeply dug, moisture-retentive and well-drained, having been manured for the previous year's crop.

Alternatively, add well-rotted organic matter in late fall before sowing. They need a pH of 6 to 7, so lime where necessary. Rotate with other legumes. Rake a granular general fertilizer into the seedbed 1 week before sowing. Mulch, hoe or hand weed regularly, especially at first.

Watering should be unnecessary except in drought, but for good-quality crops, plants need 4 gallons/sq. yd. per week from flower formation to harvest end.

Support taller plants with stakes. Planting several staggered rows allows plants to support one another. Dwarf types can be supported with brushwood.

Maintenance

Spring Sow early crops indoors, followed by later sowings until late spring.
Summer Harvest from late spring to late summer. Keep crops weed-free and water after flower formation.
Fall Sow outdoor crops for overwintering.
Winter Protect outdoor crops in severe weather.

Protected Cropping

Where plants cannot be overwintered outdoors, sow under cover in pots or boxes from midwinter. Harden off and plant out in midspring. Remove cloches from protected early crops when the beans reach the glass.

Harvesting and Storing

Pick when the beans begin to show, before the pods are too large (and tough). Pull with a sharp downward twist or cut with scissors. Pods harvested at 2–3 in. long can be treated as snap peas and eaten whole, but picking at this stage reduces yields. Fava beans freeze well, especially green-seeded varieties. Wash, blanch for 3 minutes, and freeze in plastic bags or rigid containers. Use within 12 months. Keep them in a plastic bag in the refrigerator for 1 week.

Pests and Diseases

Black bean aphid is the most common problem. Control by pinching off the top 3 in. of stem when the first beans start to form. This also encourages an earlier harvest.

Mice and Jays steal the seeds. Trap and tolerate.

 ## companion planting

Plant with summer savory to discourage black bean aphid and among gooseberries to discourage gooseberry sawfly. The flowers are very attractive to bees. Fava beans are a good "nurse" crop for developing maize and corn. Interplant with brassicas, which benefit from the nitrogen-fixing roots. Dig in plant debris as a "green manure" to increase soil fertility. Seedling beans protect early potato shoots from wind and frost.

 ## container growing

Grow dwarf cultivars in containers of low-fertilizer soilless potting mix at least 8 to–15 in. wide by 10 in. deep. Sow seeds 2 in. deep and 4–5 in. apart. Water regularly in warm weather, less at other times.

 ## culinary

Steam or lightly boil beans to eat with ham, pork and chicken. Eat with sautéed onions, mushrooms and bacon; dress with tomato sauce, warm sour cream or lemon butter and dill.

Fava beans with Summer Savory
Serves 4

A dish which reflects the pure tastes of summer

1 pound young fava beans, shelled weight
2 sprigs plus 2 tablespoons summer savory
2 tablespoons butter
Salt and freshly ground black pepper

Put the beans into a pan of boiling, salted water with the sprigs of summer savory and cook until just done, about 3 to 5 minutes. Drain and put the pan back on a gentle heat. Add the butter and toss well as it melts. Season with more summer savory and salt and pepper.

Bissara
Serves 4

An Algerian dish with subtle flavors, this is based on one from the late, great foodie, Arto der Haroturian.

1½ pounds young fava beans, shelled weight
1 small green chile, chopped
1 teaspoon paprika
1 teaspoon cumin seeds, crushed

2 cloves garlic, peeled
8 tablespoons extra virgin olive oil
Juice of ½ a lemon
Salt and freshly ground black pepper
A little olive oil, lemon juice and paprika, to garnish

Boil the beans in lightly salted water until just tender.

Drain and place in a food processor, together with the chile, paprika, cumin and garlic. Purée by slowly drizzling in the oil and lemon juice. Season and pour into a bowl.

Garnish with a little olive oil, lemon juice and paprika. Serve bissara with warm bread.

WASABI

Wasabia japonica. Cruciferae

Also known as Japanese Horseradish, Shan Kui. Hardy herbaceous perennial. Value: high in protein, potassium and moderate amounts of calcium and vitamin C.

This Japanese native, found in boggy ground by mountain streams, is highly prized for its horseradish-flavored roots, which are traditionally ground into a fine powder using a shark skin grater or *oroshi* before being turned into a paste. It has been cultivated in Japan since the 10th century CE; the highest prices are paid for natural water-grown *sawa* or semi-aquatic wasabi, the price and quality of field-grown or *oka* is correspondingly lower. At the time of writing, dried, field-grown wasabi rhizomes, cultivated on the Pacific coast of the U.S., are retailing at $40 per ounce. As demand outstrips supply beware of inferior products made of horseradish or Chinese mustard and food coloring — or grow your own.

A true vegetable delicacy

 varieties

Wasabia japonica grows up to 16 in. tall with glossy, almost heart-shaped leaves the size of small dinner plates, with coarsely-toothed margins and spikes of small white flowers in late spring.

 cultivation

Propagation

Repropagate plants every 2 years, as younger roots have a better flavor. Sow seeds in early spring in soilless potting mix; transplant into individual pots when the "true" leaves are large enough to handle.

Grow them in the greenhouse for the first year, standing in trays of water so the compost stays constantly moist. Plant out in late spring or early summer of the second year after acclimatizing plants to outdoor conditions.

Alternatively, divide healthy plants in early spring as they start into growth, grow them in an unheated greenhouse or cold-frame and plant out in late spring the following year. Small offsets can also be detached from well-established plants in spring.

Growing

The plants will grow in boggy ground of any pH, or in fresh, pollution-free, running water, in sunshine or part shade, particularly in warmer climates. Cultivation techniques are similar to watercress (see p. 178) and roots should be protected with bracken, straw or floating row cover over winter. The optimum water temperature is 50–55°F with air temperatures of 46–68°F, though plants still grow in less than perfect conditions.

Maintenance
Spring Sow seeds, divide or remove "offsets."
Summer Ensure plants remain moist. Harvest plants; retain divisions for replanting.
Fall Remove leaves as they die down.
Winter Cover plants to protect from frost.

Harvesting and Storing
Lift rhizomes as needed and use immediately, for the finest flavor.

Worth their weight in gold

 container growing

Grow in large pots of soilless potting mix kept constantly moist by standing in a bowl of water which is refreshed daily.

 medicinal

Wasabi is used to stimulate digestion, has antibacterial qualities, reduces mucus, and controls asthma and other congestive disorders. Isothiocyantates help detoxify the liver and gut; it is also a powerful antioxidant and has anticancer properties.

culinary

Use freshly dug rhizomes, as the flavor deteriorates rapidly once the root has been cut; it is similar but superior to horseradish and midgreen in color. Rhizomes harvested at 15 to 24 months old are considered to be the best. It is finely grated and turned into a paste and is the ideal complement to raw fish in *sashimi* or *sushi* dishes, added to soups or mixed with soy sauce to make dips. The leaves, flowers and leaf stems are also cooked and eaten. In Japan, the leaves and leaf stalks, flowers and rhizomes are soaked in salt water, mixed with sake lees and used to make a pickle called *wasabe-zuke*. Wasabi can also be bought in powdered form, in small cans. This recipe comes from *The Japanese Kitchen* by Kimiko Barber.

Wasabi and Avocado Dip
Serves 4

2 tablespoons wasabi powder
1 ripe avocado
2 tablespoons good mayonnaise
1 teaspoon light soy sauce
Salt (optional)

Mix the wasabi powder with 2 tablespoons water. Peel the avocado, remove the pit and roughly mash with a fork. Place the wasabi paste, mashed avocado mayonnaise and soy sauce into a food processor and whiz until smooth and creamy. Have a taste and season with salt if necessary.

Zea mays. Graminae

CORN

Also known as Maize, Corn on the Cob, Indian Corn, Baby Maize, Sweet corn. Annual grown for kernels of edible seeds. Half hardy. Value: high in carbohydrates and fiber, moderate protein and B vitamin content.

Wild plants of corn have never been found, but it is believed that the crop was first cultivated in Mexico around 7000 BCE. Primitive types, smaller than an ear of wheat, were found in caves at Tehuacan in southern Mexico dating from around 3500 BCE, yet they were bred by Mayan and Incan farmers almost to the size of modern varieties. Early American civilizations were based on corn, and life for the Aztecs revolved round the *milpa* or cornfield. Multicolored types with blue, scarlet, brown and almost black seeds predominated in South America. It became a staple crop in North America after 800 CE. The first types introduced to Europe in the 16th century from Central America were valued for both the cobs and the yellow meal. Corn flourished in Spain, France, Italy, the Balkans and Portugal.

Corn is a sweet form of maize, a starchy crop used for grain and fodder. The yellow-golden varieties are commonly cultivated for the kitchen, but those with multicolored seeds are extremely ornamental. Corn and maize are the third most important cereal in the world, after wheat and rice, and there are more than 500 different by-products. The seeds of corn also provide us with popcorn, with its exploding grains; starch extracted after milling has been used as laundry starch; the inner husks are used for making cigarette papers and the pith has been used for making explosives and packaging material. Best of all is delicious fresh corn eaten from the cob, dripping with butter; take the advice of Edward Bunyard: "The principle of the lathe is adopted in eating them."

varieties

"Normal" varieties were the first selections and have the best seed vigor. "Supersweets" have very high sugar levels, a longer storage life than "normal" varieties but poorer germination. "Sugar Enhanced" are not as sweet as "Supersweet" but are better for storing and "Extra Tender Sweets" are sweeter and more tender. If you aim to grow "supersweet" varieties they should be at least 250 feet from ordinary varieties to prevent cross pollination. Alternatively, grow sugar enhanced types — if cross pollination occurs, the cobs will be more like traditional varieties.

Supersweet Varieties

"Earlibird" has good vigor and is a top-quality variety for cob size and flavor. "Prelude" is vigorous and high yielding, with cobs up to 10 in. long. "Ovation" is a midseason variety with large tasty cobs up to 8 in. long. "Northern Xtra-Sweet" is good in cooler climates — one of the earliest to mature and with top-quality kernels. Do not let it overripen.

Extra Tender Sweet Varieties

"Swift," voted the best variety in independent trials, produces large cobs with exceptionally sweet, tender and succulent kernels. Does not need to be isolated from other varieties. "Lark" has moderate vigor, very sweet cobs and performs well in colder soils.

Sugar Enhanced Varieties

"Minipop" is a baby corn with sweet cobs. Plant in rows rather than blocks and harvest before they swell. Eat lightly steamed or with dips. "Tuxedo," a tall variety, performs well under drier conditions and is exceptionally drought resistant. "Sweet Nugget" grows to a moderate length, golden yellow cobs that taste very sweet. Ideal in cooler conditions.

Others

"Honey Bantam" grows exceptionally early, 7 in. long, with pretty yellow and white kernels that are very sweet indeed. "Kelvedon Glory" is an old variety with long, light golden cobs that are filled with flavor. "Red Strawberry" has tiny red kernels on compact cobs (only 2 in. long). Put them in the microwave and they explode into fluffy popcorn.

 ## cultivation

Propagation

Seeds do not germinate when soil temperatures are below 50°F. Better germination and earlier crops are achieved by sowing from midspring under cover in pots or packs. Plant two to three seeds 1 in. deep in pots of moist seed compost from mid- to late spring, at 55°F. After germination, thin to leave the strongest seedling. Corn is sensitive to root damage and disturbance, so thin with care, holding the strongest seedling while

removing weaker ones. Harden off and plant out once there is no longer any danger of frost.

Plants should be 14 in. apart in and between the rows or spaced 10–12 in. apart in rows 24 in. apart.

To avoid erratic germination, seeds can be pregerminated. Put a few sheets of tissue paper or similar material in the bottom of a seedtray, moisten with water, place seeds evenly over the surface and cover with another layer of moist tissue. Put the tray in a loosely knotted plastic bag in an airing cupboard or warm room. When the seeds swell and tiny rootlets have formed, sow a single seed 1 in. deep in a 4 in. pot of seed compost or sow singly outdoors. Sow a few in pots to replace those that do not germinate outdoors.

Alternatively, sow *in situ* from late spring to early summer. When the soil is workable, make a block about 4–5 ft., comprising four ridges of soil about 12 in. high with 14 in. between the top of each ridge. Hill sow two to three seeds in the furrow 14 in. apart each way and thin to leave the strongest seedling.

Extra protection is needed in the coldest climates such as Alaska and northern Minnesota: Cut a square of thin polyethylene slightly larger than the block. Spread over the furrows, dig a shallow trench around the edge and weigh the margins down with soil to hold in place. As seedlings emerge, cut crosses in the cover so they can grow through, or remove it and hill up around stem bases. Alternatively, sow on a level seedbed and protect crops with floating row cover or cloches, which should be removed as soon as the plants become too large.

"Supersweet" varieties need slightly warmer conditions for germination; soils should be at a minimum of 55°F. Because corn is wind-pollinated, plants are sown in blocks for effective germination.

The male tassels (flowers) at the top of the plant shed clouds of pollen on to the female tassels or "silks" below. These are clusters of pale green strands on the ends of the cobs which become sticky before pollination and each strand is attached to a single grain. Each must be pollinated, and sowing in a block ensures effective pollination. On a calm day tap the stems to help pollination. Mini varieties can be sown in rows. **Zones 4 to 10.**

"Minipop'

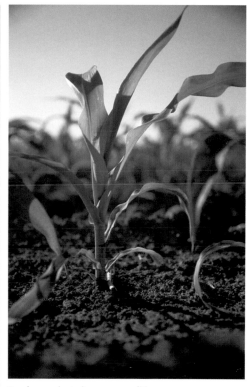

Seeds germinate in warm conditions

Growing

Corn needs a moisture-retentive, free-draining soil. Dig in plenty of organic matter several weeks before planting, or use ground manured for the previous year's crop. Ideally, the soil should be slightly acid, with a pH of 5.5–7.0. Plants need a long, warm growing season to succeed, so grow fast-maturing, early cultivars in cooler areas. The site should be open, sunny, warm and sheltered from cold winds and frosts.

Rake in a slow-release general fertilizer after transplanting or when preparing the seedbed. Keep compost moist throughout the growing season. Watering is particularly beneficial when they begin to flower, and when the grains begin to swell. Apply 4 gallons/sq. yd. per week. Stake plants when growing on exposed sites.

Corn is shallow-rooted, so take care when hoeing to avoid damaging the roots. It is much better to mulch with a layer of organic matter to suppress weeds and retain moisture. Mulch with black polyethylene on level ground. Do not remove sideshoots (tillers). Hill up to make plants more stable.

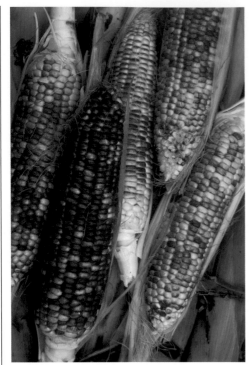

Corn can easily be part of an ornamental garden

Maintenance
Spring Sow seed under cover or outdoors.
Summer Sow seeds; keep crops weed-free and water. Harvest.
Fall Harvest.
Winter Prepare the ground for next year's crop.

Protected Cropping
When soil temperatures are below 50°F, sow from midspring under cover in pots or packs at 55°F. Harden off and plant out once there is no danger of frost.

Harvesting and Storing
Each plant usually produces one or two ears. Those sown *in situ* mature later than seed sown indoors. After pollination the silks begin to turn brown, an indication that the cob is maturing. Peel back the leaves and test for ripeness by pushing your thumbnail into a grain: if the liquid runs clear, it is unripe; if it is milky, it is ready to harvest; if it is thick, then it is over-mature and unsuitable for eating. To pick, hold the main stem in one hand and twist off the cob with the other. Corn is ideal for instant eating. Have a pot of water boiling before you harvest!

Freeze within at least 24 hours of picking, before the sugars in the seeds convert to starch. Supersweet varieties hold their sugar levels longer.

To freeze, blanch cobs for 4 to 6 minutes, cool and drain, before wrapping singly in foil or plastic wrap and placing in the freezer.

Cobs remain fresh for up to 3 days if they are stored in the refrigerator.

Pests and Diseases
Birds can pull up the seedlings and attack the developing cobs. Slugs attack seedlings. Smut appears as large galls on the cobs and stalks in hot dry weather. Cut off and burn the debris immediately after harvesting and do not grow corn on the site for at least 3 years. Frit fly larvae bore into the growing points of corn seedlings, which then develop twisted and ragged leaves. Growth is stunted and cobs are undersized. Use "dressed" seed and cultivate the ground thoroughly. Mice enjoy newly planted seeds, especially supersweet types. Trap, or buy a cat.

Enough to go around

Block planting results in good pollination

companion planting

Grow corn with or after legumes. Runner beans can be allowed to grow over corn plants. Intercrop corn with sunflowers, allowing cucurbits to trail through them.

The shade they provide is useful to cucumbers, melons, squashes, zucchini, marrows and potatoes. Brussels sprouts, kale, Savoy cabbages, rutabagas and broccoli can be interplanted. Grow lettuce and other salads, green beans and zucchini between the crops.

medicinal

Corn is said to reduce the risk of certain cancers, heart disease and dental cavities. Corn oil is reported to lower cholesterol levels more successfully than other polyunsaturated oils.

In parts of Mexico, corn is used to treat dysentery. It is also known in North American folk medicine as a diuretic and mild stimulant.

culinary

To serve whole, strip off outer leaves, leaving 2–3 in. of stalk on the ear. Pull off "silks." Boil in unsalted water, drain and eat hot with melted butter. Roasted corn is a favorite with most children — it tastes wonderfully succulent compared with the sogginess of canned corn.

Deep-fry spoonfuls of a mixture of mashed corn, salt, flour, milk and egg for 1 to 2 minutes or until golden brown to make corn fritters.

Seeds are ground, meal boiled or baked, the ear can be roasted or boiled or fermented, corn meal is cooked with water to create a thick mash, or dough.

Tortillas are made by baking in flat cakes until they are crisp. Polenta is made from ground corn.

Dry-milling produces grits, from which most of the bran and germ are separated. Cornflakes are rolled, flavored seeds. Multicolored corn adds color and flavor to sweet dishes and drinks.

Baby corns are particularly decorative and the perfect size for oriental stir-fries, where they combine well with snow peas.

Barbecued Corn on the Cob

This is the way to really taste the flavor of corn. Take 1 corn ear for each person. Boil them in salted water for 7 to 10 minutes and then drain.

Place each in the center of a piece of tinfoil. Use 1 tablespoon butter per corn ear and mix in 1 teaspoon fresh chopped herbs, kosher salt and freshly ground black pepper; spread over the corn ears. Season well and then seal the foil.

Lay the ears on a medium-hot barbecue or in a charcoal broiler (in which case, keep it covered) and roast for 20 minutes, turning the cobs once, halfway through cooking.

Corn Maque Choux
Serves 4

Cajun cooking has become popular in recent years and this dish reveals the true taste of corn.

1 tablespoon butter
1 large onion, roughly chopped
1 green bell pepper, seeded and diced
1 pound corn, cooked and stripped from the cob
2 tomatoes, peeled, seeded and diced
½ teaspoon Tabasco sauce
Salt and freshly ground black pepper

Heat the butter in a heavy pan and sauté the onion until softened. Add the pepper and continue cooking for 3 to 4 minutes. Toss in the corn and the remaining ingredients and, over low heat, simmer for 10 minutes. Adjust the seasoning and serve.

Corn Maque Choux

Succotash
Serves 4

Native North American cooked succotash, and many recipes for it still exist. "Silver Queen" is a particularly good variety to use for this dish.

3 to 4 tablespoons unsalted butter
⅔ pound fava beans, cooked
3 or 4 ears roasted corn
½ pound green beans, topped and tailed
1 medium red onion, finely minced
1 ¼ cups vegetable stock
½ red bell pepper, seeded and finely diced
1 beef tomato, peeled, seeded and chopped
Salt and freshly ground black pepper

Melt the butter in a heavy skillet and sweat the fava beans, corn, green beans and onion over medium heat for about 3 minutes.

Then add the stock and continue cooking for 5 minutes, before stirring in the remaining ingredients. Taste for seasoning, mix thoroughly and continue cooking for 5 minutes more. Serve hot.

HERBS
A-Z

Achillea ageratum
ENGLISH MACE

From the family Asteraceae.

Native to Switzerland, English mace is now cultivated in northern temperate countries. This culinary herb is little known and under used.

English mace belongs to the *Achillea* genus, named after Achilles, who is said to have discovered the medicinal properties of the genus. There is no direct historical record of English mace itself apart from the fact that it was discovered in Switzerland in 1798.

 varieties

Achillea ageratum
English Mace
Hardy perennial. Ht 12–18 in. when in flower. Spread 12 in. Clusters of small cream flowers that look very Victorian in summer. Leaves brightish green, narrow, and very deeply serrated. **Zone 6.**

 cultivation

Propagation
Cuttings
This is the best method for the propagation of a large number of plants. Take softwood cuttings in late summer; protect from wilting as they will be very soft. Use a bark-peat mix of potting mix. When well-rooted, harden off and plant out in the garden 12 in. apart.

Division
If you require only a few plants it is best to propagate by division. Either divide the plant in early spring — it is one of the first to appear — or in fall. Replant in the garden in a prepared site. As this is a hardy plant it will not need protection, but if you leave division until the frosts are imminent, winter the divided plants in a cold frame or cold greenhouse.

Pests and Diseases
Mace, in most cases, is free from pests and diseases.

Maintenance
Spring Divide established plants.
Summer Cut back flowers. Take softwood cuttings.
Fall Divide established plants if needed.
Winter Does not need protection.

Garden Cultivation
This fully hardy plant, which even flourishes on heavy soil, prefers a sunny, well-drained site. It starts the season off as a cluster of low-growing, deeply serrated leaves and then develops long, flowering stems in summer. Cut back after flowering for a fresh supply of leaves and to encourage a second flowering crop. When in flower this plant may need staking in a windy, exposed site.

Achillea ageratum **new spring growth**

Harvesting

Cut fresh leaves when you wish. For freezing — the best method of preserving — cut before flowering and freeze in small containers.

Pick the flowers during the summer. Collect in small bunches and hang upside down to dry. Both flowers and leaves dry particularly well.

 ## container growing

For a tall flowering plant this looks most attractive in a terracotta pot. Make sure it has a wide base to allow for its height later in the season. Use a soil-based compost mixed in equal parts with composted fine bark. Water regularly thoughout the growing season and give a liquid feed (according to manufacturer's instructions) in the summer months during flowering. Cut back after flowering to stop the plant from toppling over and encourage new growth. As this plant dies back in winter, allow the potting mix to become nearly dry, and winter the container in a cold greenhouse or cold frame.

 ## other uses

Flowers in dried flower arrangements.

 ## culinary

The chopped leaves can be used to stuff chicken, flavor soups and stews, and sprinkle on potato salads, rice, and pasta dishes. The leaf has a mild, warm, aromatic flavor and combines well with other herbs.

Chicken with English Mace in Foil
Serves 4

2 tablespoons yogurt
2 tablespoons Dijon mustard
4 chicken breasts
Salt and freshly ground black pepper
Bouquet garni herb oil (or olive oil)
6 tablespoons of chopped English mace leaves
Juice of 1 lemon

Preheat the oven to 375°F. Mix the yogurt and mustard together and coat the chicken pieces on all sides. Sprinkle with salt and pepper. Cut four pieces of foil and brush with herb or olive oil. Lay the chicken breasts in the foil and sprinkle each piece with a thick layer of English mace. Sprinkle with lemon juice. Wrap in the foil, folding the ends very tightly so no juices can escape. Lay the pockets on a rack in the oven, cook for 30 minutes. Serve with rice and a green salad.

YARROW

Achillea millefolium

Also known as Nosebleed, Millefoil, Thousand leaf, Woundwort, Carpenter's weed, Devil's nettle, Soldier's woundwort and Noble yarrow. From the family *Asteraceae*.

Yarrow is found all over the world in vacant lots, fields, pastures, and meadows. It is common throughout North America, Europe, and Asia.

This is a very ancient herb. It was used by the Greeks to control hemorrhages, for which it is still prescribed in homeopathy and herbal medicine today. The legend of Achilles refers to this property — it was said that during the battle of Troy, Achilles healed many of his warriors with yarrow leaves. Hence the name *Achillea*.

It has long been considered a sacred herb. Yarrow stems were used by the Druids to divine seasonal weather. The ancient Chinese text of prophecy, *I Ching, The Book of Changes*, states that 52 straight stalks of dried yarrow, of even length, were spilled instead of the modern way of using three coins.

It was also associated with magic. In Anglo-Saxon times it was said to have a potency against evil, and in France and in Ireland it is one of the Herbs of St John. On St John's Eve, the Irish hang it up in their houses to avert illness.

There is an old superstition, which apparently still lingers in remote parts of Britain and the United States, that if a young girl tickles her nostrils with sprays of yarrow and her nose starts to bleed, it proves her lover's fidelity:

"Yarrow away, Yarrow away, bear a white blow? If my lover loves me, my nose will bleed now."

Achillea millefolium

 varieties

Achillea millefolium
Yarrow
Hardy perennial. Ht 1–3 ft., spread 24 in. and more. Small white flowers with a hint of pink appear in flat clusters from summer to fall. Its specific name, *millefolium,* means "a thousand leaf," which is a good way to describe these darkish green, aromatic, feathery leaves. **Zone 2**

Achillea millefolium "Fire King"
Hardy perennial. Ht and spread 24 in. Flat heads of rich, red, small flowers in flat clusters all summer. Masses of feathery dark green leaves. This has an upright habit and is a vigorous grower. **Zone 2**

Achillea filipendulina "Gold Plate"
Hardy perennial. Ht 4 ft., spread 24 in. Large flat heads of small golden flowerheads in summer that dry well for winter decoration. Filigree green foliage. **Zone 3**

Achillea "Moonshine"
Hardy perennial. Ht 24 in., spread 20 in. Flat heads of bright yellow flowers throughout summer. Masses of small feathery gray/green leaves. **Zone 3**

Achillea filipendulina "Gold Plate"

cultivation

Propagation

Seed

For reliable results sow the very small seed under cool protection in fall. Use either a proprietary seeder or the cardboard trick (see p. 645) and sow into prepared seed or plug trays. Leave the trays in a cool greenhouse for the winter. Germination is erratic. Harden off and plant out in the garden in spring. Plant 8–12 in. apart, remembering that it will spread. As this is an invasive plant, I do not advise sowing direct into the garden.

Division

Yarrow is a prolific grower, producing loads of creeping rootstock in a growing season. To stop an invasion into areas where it is not wanted, divide by digging up a clump and replanting where required in the spring or early fall.

Pests and Diseases

Yarrow is usually free from both.

Maintenance

Spring Divide established clumps.
Summer Deadhead flowers, and cut back after flowering to prevent self-seeding.
Fall Sow seeds. Divide established plants.
Winter No need for protection, very hardy plant.

Garden Cultivation

Yarrow is one of nature's survivors. Its creeping rootstock and ability to self-seed ensure its survival in most soils.

It does well in seaside gardens, as it is drought-tolerant. Still, owners of manicured lawns will know it as a nightmare weed that resists all attempts to eradicate it.

Yarrow is the plant doctor of the garden, its roots' secretions activating the disease resistance of nearby plants. It also intensifies the medicinal actions of other herbs and deepens their fragrance and flavor.

Harvesting

Cut the leaves and flowers for drying as the plant comes into flower.

 ## culinary

The young leaves can be used in salads. Here is an interesting salad recipe:

Salad Made with Three Wild Herbs

Equal parts of yarrow, plantain, and watercress leaves
A little garlic
1/2 cucumber
Freshly chopped or dried chives and parsley

1 medium, boiled cold potato
Salad dressing consisting of lemon and cream, or lemon and oil, or lemon and cream and a little apple juice.

Select and clean herbs. Wash carefully and allow to drain. Cut the yarrow and plantain into fine strips. Cube the cucumber and potato into small pieces. Leave the watercress whole and arrange in a bowl. Add herbs and other vegetables, and salad dressing and mix well.

 ## container growing

Yarrow itself does not grow well in containers. However, the hybrids, and certainly the shorter varieties, can look stunning. Use a soilless potting compost mix and feed plants with liquid fertilizer during the flowering season, following the manufacturer's instructions. Cut back after flowering and keep watering to a minimum in winter. No variety is suitable for growing indoors.

 ## medicinal

Yarrow is one of the best-known herbal remedies for fevers. Used as a hot infusion it will induce sweats that cool fevers and expel toxins. In China, yarrow is used fresh as a poultice for healing wounds. It can also be made into a decoction for wounds, chapped skin and rashes, and as a mouthwash for inflamed gums.

 ## warning

Yarrow should always be taken in moderation and never for long periods because it may cause skin irritation. It should not be taken by pregnant women. Large doses produce headaches and vertigo.

 ## other uses

Flowerheads may be dried for winter decoration.

Traditionally the leaves of this unassuming herb were used to accelerate the decomposition of garden waste in a compost bin. The leaves were also used as a copper fertilizer.

Infusion of yarrow

MONKSHOOD

Also known as Friar's cap, Old woman's night-cap, Chariots drawn by doves, Blue rocket, Wolf's bane, and Mazbane. From the family Ranunculaceae.

Various species of monkshood grow in temperate regions. They can be found on shady banks, in deciduous woodlands, and in mountainous districts. They are all poisonous plants.

One theory for the generic name, *Aconitum*, is that the name comes from the Greek *akoniton*, meaning "dart." This is because the juice of the plant was used to poison arrow tips and was used as such by the Arabs and ancient Chinese. Its specific name *napellus* means "little turnip," a reference to the shape of the root. It was the name used by Theophrastus, the Greek botanist (370–285 CE), for a poisonous plant.

This plant has been known throughout history to kill both animals and humans. In the 16th century Gerard commented in his *Herball* on its "fair and good bluey flowers in shape like helmet which are so beautiful that man would think they were of some excellent virtue." Appearances should not be trusted. 150 years later, Miller in his garden dictionary wrote, "Monks Hood was in almost all old gardens and not to be put in the way of children less they should prejudice themselves therewith."

As recently as 1993 a British flower seller had to be hospitalized after handling monkshood outside pubs in Salisbury and Southampton.

 varieties

Aconitum napellus
Monkshood
Hardy perennial. Ht 5 ft., spread 12 in. Tall slender spires of hooded, light blue/indigo/blue flowers in late summer. Leaves midgreen, palm shaped, and deeply cut. There is a white flowered version, *A. napellus* "Albiflorus," which grows in the same way.
Zone 4

Aconitum napellus flowers

**Aconitum napellus subsp. napellus
Anglicum Group**
Monkshood
Hardy perennial. Ht 5 ft., spread 12 in. Tall slender spires of hooded, blue/lilac flowers are borne in early/midsummer. Leaves midgreen, wedge-shaped, and deeply cut. One of a few plants peculiar to the British Isles, liking shade or half-shade along brooks and streams. Among the most dangerous of all plants.

cultivation

Propagation
Seed
Sow the small seed under protection either in the fall (which is best) or spring. Use prepared seed or plug trays. Cover with perlite. Germination can be erratic, an all-or-nothing affair. The seeds do not need heat to germinate. In spring, when the seedlings are large enough to handle, plant out into a prepared, shady site 12 in. apart. Wash your hands after handling the seedlings; even better wear thin gloves. The plant takes 2 to 3 years to flower.

Division
Divide established plants throughout the fall, so long as the soil is workable. Replant in a prepared site in the garden — remember the gloves. You will notice when splitting the plant that the taproot puts out daughter roots with many rootlets. Remove and store in a warm dry place for planting out later.

Pests and Diseases
This plant rarely suffers from pests, and it is usually disease free.

Maintenance
Spring Plant out fall-grown seedlings.
Summer Cut back after flowering.
Fall Sow seeds, divide established plants.
Winter No need to protect. Fully hardy.

Garden Cultivation
In spite of the dire warnings this is a most attractive plant, which is hardy and thrives in most good soils.
  Position it so that it is not accessible. Plant at the back of borders, or under trees where no animals can eat it or young fingers fiddle with it. It is useful for planting in the shade of trees as long as the shade is not too dense.
  It is important always to teach people which plants are harmful, and which plants are edible. If you remove all poisonous plants from the garden, people will not learn which ones to respect.

Harvesting
Unless you are a qualified herbalist I do not recommend harvesting.

container growing

Because of its poisonous nature, I cannot whole-heartedly recommend that it be grown in containers. But it does look very attractive in a large container surrounded by heartsease *(Viola tricolor)*. Use a soilless compost mixed in equal parts with composted fine bark (see p. 643), water regularly throughout the summer months. Liquid feed in summer only.

warning

The symptoms of *Aconitum* poisoning are a burning sensation on the tongue, vomiting, abdominal pains, and diarrhea, leading to paralysis and death. Emergency antidotes, which are obtainable from hospitals, are atropine and strophanthin.

medicinal

This plant contains one of the most potent nerve poisons in the plant kingdom and is used in proprietary analgesic medicines to alleviate pain both internally and externally. These drugs can only be prescribed by qualified medical practitioners. Tinctures of monkshood are frequently used in homeopathy.

Under no circumstances should monkshood ever be prepared and used for self-medication.

Aconitum napellus in a meadow

Agastache
ANISE HYSSOP

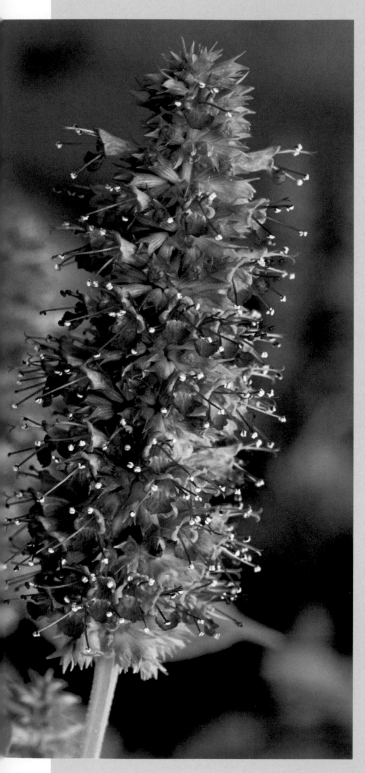

Also known as Giant Hyssop, Blue Giant Hyssop, Fennel Hyssop, Fragrant Giant Hyssop. From the family Lamiaceae.

Anise hyssop is a native of North America. *A. cana*, the Mosquito Plant originates from Mexico and *A. rugosa* is from Korea.

There are few references to the history of this lovely herb. According to Allen Paterson, Past Director of the Royal Botanical Garden in Ontario, it is a close cousin of the bergamots. It is common in North American herb gardens and is certainly worth including in any herb garden for its flowers and scent. The long spikes of purple or lilac flowers are big attractions for bees and butterflies.

 varieties

Agastache foeniculum
Anise Hyssop
Hardy perennial. Ht 36 in., spread 12 in. Long purple flower spikes in summer. Aniseed-scented midgreen oval leaves. **Zone 4**

Agastache cana
Mosquito Plant
Half-hardy perennial. Ht 36–48 in., spread 12 in. Pink tubular flowers in the summer with aromatic oval midgreen toothed leaves. **Zone 5**

Agastache rugosa
Korean Mint
Hardy perennial. Ht 3 ft., spread 12 in. Lovely mauve/purple flower spikes in summer. Distinctly minty scented midgreen oval pointed leaves. **Zone 5**

Agastache rugosa "Golden Jubilee"
Anise Hyssop Golden Jubilee
Hardy perennial. Ht 20 in., spread 12 in. Lovely mauve/purple flower spikes in summer. Anise-scented golden leaves. Prone to sun scorch, plant in partial shade. **Zone 5**

Agastache cana

ANISE HYSSOP

cultivation

Propagation

Seed

The small fine seeds need warmth to germinate: 65°F. Use the cardboard method (see p. 645) and artificial heating if sowing in early spring.

Use either prepared seed or plug trays or, if you have only a few seeds, directly into a pot of standard seed compost mixed in equal parts with composted fine bark. Cover with perlite. Germinates in 10 to 20 days.

One can also sow outside in the fall when the soil is warm, but the young plants will need protection throughout the winter months.

When the seedlings are large enough to handle, prick out and pot on using a potting compost mixed in equal parts with propagating bark. In midspring, when air and soil temperatures have risen, plant out at a distance of 18 in. apart.

Cuttings

Take cuttings of soft young shoots in spring, when all the species root well. Use a seed compost mixed in equal parts with composted fine bark. After a full period of weaning, cuttings should be strong enough to plant out in the early fall.

Semi-ripe wood cuttings may be taken in late summer, using the same compost mix. After they have rooted, repot, and winter in a cold frame or cold greenhouse.

Division

This is a good alternative way to maintain a short-lived perennial. In the second or third year divide the creeping roots in spring, either by the "forks back-to-back" method, or by digging up the whole plant and dividing it into several segments.

Pests and Diseases

This herb rarely suffers from pests or diseases, although seedlings can be prone to "damping off."

Maintenance

Spring Sow seeds.
Summer Take softwood or semi-ripe cuttings late in the season.
Fall Tidy up the plants by cutting back the old flower heads and woody growth. Sow seeds. Protect young plants from frost.
Winter Protect half-hardy species (and anise hyssop below 20°F) with either a floating row cover, bark or straw.

Garden Cultivation

All species like a lean, dry soil and full sun, and will adapt very well to most ordinary soils if planted in a sunny situation. All are short-lived and should be propagated each year to ensure continuity.

Anise hyssop, although hardier than the other species, still needs protection below 20°F. The Mexican half-hardy species need protection below 26°F.

Harvesting

Flowers
Cut for drying just as they begin to open.

Leaves
Cut leaves just before late spring flowering.

Seeds
Heads turn brown as the seed ripens. At the first sign of the seed falling, pick and hang upside down with a paper bag tied over the heads.

container growing

Not suitable for growing indoors. However, anise hyssop and Korean mint both make good patio plants provided the container is at least 10–12 in. in diameter. Use a potting compost mixed in equal parts with fine composted bark, and a liquid fertilizer feed only once a year after flowering. If you feed the plant beforehand, the flowers will be poor. Keep well watered in summer.

other uses

Anise hyssop, Korean mint, and Mexican giant hyssop all have scented leaves, which make them suitable for potpourris.

culinary

The two varieties most suitable are:

Anise Hyssop

Leaves can be used in salads and to make refreshing tea. Like borage, they can be added to summer fruit cups. Equally they can be chopped and used as a seasoning in pork dishes or in savory rice.

Flowers can be added to fruit salads and cups, giving a lovely splash of color.

Korean Mint

Leaves have a strong peppermint flavor and make a very refreshing tea, said to be good first thing in the morning after a night on the town. They are also good chopped up in salads, and the flowers look very attractive sprinkled over a pasta salad.

Korean mint tea

Alchemilla
LADY'S MANTLE

From the family Rosaceae.

Lady's mantle is a native of the mountains of America, Europe, and Asia. It is found not only in damp places but also in dry shady woods.

The Arab *alkemelych* (alchemy) is thought to be the source of the herb's Latin generic name, *Alchemilla*. The crystal dew lying in perfect pearl drops on the leaves has long inspired poets and alchemists, and was reputed to have healing and magical properties, even to preserve a woman's youth provided she collected the dew in May, alone, in full moonlight, naked, and with bare feet as a sign of purity and to ward off any lurking forces.

In the medieval period it was dedicated to the Virgin Mary, hence lady's mantle was considered a woman's protector, and nicknamed "a woman's best friend." It was used not only to regulate the menstrual cycle and to ease the effects of menopause, but also to reduce inflammation of the female organs. In the 18th century, women applied the leaves to their breasts to make them recover shape after they had been swelled with milk. It is still prescribed by herbalists today.

Alchemilla mollis

 varieties

Alchemilla alpina L.
Alpine Lady's Mantle
Known in the U.S. as Silvery lady's mantle.
Hardy perennial. Ht 6 in., spread 24 in. or more. Tiny, greenish-yellow flowers in summer. Leaves rounded, lobed, pale green, and covered in silky hairs. An attractive plant suitable for ground cover, rockeries, and dry banks. **Zone 3**

Alchemilla conjuncta
Lady's Mantle Conjuncta
Hardy perennial. Ht 12 in., spread 12 in. or more. Tiny, greenish-yellow flowers in summer. Leaves star-shaped, bright green on top with lovely silky silver hairs underneath. An attractive plant suitable for ground cover, rockeries, and dry banks. **Zone 3**

Alchemilla mollis AGM
Lady's Mantle (Garden variety)
Hardy perennial. Ht and spread 20 in. Tiny, greenish-yellow flowers in summer. Large, pale green, rounded leaves with crinkled edges. **Zone 3**

Alchemilla xanthochlora (vulgaris)
Lady's Mantle (Wildflower variety)
Also known as Lion's foot and Bear's foot, and Nine hooks. Hardy perennial. Ht 6–18 in., spread 20 in. Tiny, bright greenish-yellow flowers in summer. Round, pale green leaves with crinkled edges. **Zone 3**

Alchemilla mollis **flower**

cultivation

Propagation

Seed

Why is it that something that self-seeds readily around the garden can be so difficult to raise from seed? Sow its very fine seed in early spring or fall under protection into prepared seed or plug trays (use the cardboard method on p. 645), and cover with perlite. No bottom heat required. Germination can either be sparse or prolific, taking 2 to 3 weeks. If germinating in the fall, winter seedlings in the trays and plant out the following spring when the frosts are over, at 18 in. apart. Alternatively, sow in spring where you want the plant to flower. Thin the seedlings to 12 in. apart.

Division

All established plants can be divided in the spring or fall. Replant in the garden where desired.

Pests and Diseases

This plant rarely suffers from pests or diseases.

Maintenance

Spring Divide established plants. Sow seeds if necessary.

Summer To prevent self-seeding, cut off flowerheads as they begin to die back.

Fall Divide established plants if necessary.
Sow seed.

Winter No need for protection.

Garden Cultivation

This fully hardy plant grows in all but boggy soils, in sun or partial shade.

This is a most attractive garden plant in borders or as an edging plant, but it can become a bit of a nuisance, seeding everywhere. To prevent this, cut back after flowering and at the same time cut back old growth.

Harvesting

Cut young leaves after the dew has dried for use throughout the summer. Harvest for drying as plant comes into flower.

 ## container growing

All forms of lady's mantle adapt to container growing and look very pretty indeed. Use a soil-based compost, water throughout the summer, but feed with liquid fertilizer (following manufacturer's instructions) only occasionally. In the winter, when the plant dies back, put the container in a cold greenhouse or cold frame, and water only very occasionally. Lady's mantle can be grown in hanging baskets as a centerpiece.

Alchemilla mollis

Leaves laid out for drying

 ## medicinal

Used by herbalists for menstrual disorders. It has been said that if you drink an infusion of green parts of the plant for 10 days each month it will help relieve menopausal discomfort. It can also be used as a mouth rinse after tooth extraction. Traditionally, the alpine species has been considered more effective, although this is not proven.

 ## culinary

Tear young leaves, with their mild bitter taste, into small pieces and toss into salads. Many years ago Marks & Spencer had a yogurt made with lady's mantle leaves! I wish I had tried it.

 ## other uses

Excellent for flower arranging. Leaves can be boiled for green wool dye. They are also used in veterinary medicine for the treatment of diarrhea.

Allium

WELSH & TREE ONIONS

From the family Alliaceae.

These plants are distributed throughout the world. The onion has been in cultivation so long that its country of origin is uncertain, although most agree that it originated in Central Asia. It was probably introduced to Europe by the Romans. The name seems to have been derived from the Latin word *unio*, a large pearl. In the Middle Ages it was believed that a bunch of onions hung outside the door would absorb the infection of the plague, saving the inhabitants. Later came the scientific recognition that its sulfur content acts as a strong disinfectant. The juice of the onion was used to heal gunshot wounds.

Allium fistulosum

 varieties

There are many, many varieties of onion; the following information concerns the two that have herbal qualities.

Allium fistulosum
Welsh Onion
Also known as Japanese leek.
Evergreen hardy perennial. Ht 2–3 ft. Greenish-yellow flowers on second year's growth in early summer. Leaves are green hollow cylinders. This onion is a native of Siberia and extensively grown in China and Japan. The name Welsh comes from *walsch,* meaning foreign. **Zone 5**

Allium cepa Proliferum Group
Tree Onion
Also known as Egyptian onion, Lazy man's onions, Walking onion. Hardy perennial. Ht 3–5 ft. Small greenish-white flowers appear in early summer. It grows bulbs underground and then, at the end of flowering, bulbs in the air. Seeing is believing. It originates from Canada. It is very easy to propagate. **Zone 5**

 cultivation

Propagation
Seed
Welsh onion seed loses its viability within 2 years, so sow fresh in late winter or early spring under protection with a bottom heat of between 60°F and 70°F. Cover with perlite. When the seedlings are large enough, and after a period of hardening off, plant out into a prepared site in the garden at a distance of 10 in. apart. The tree onion is not grown from seed.

Division
Each year the Welsh onion multiply in clumps, so it is a good idea to divide them every 3 years in the spring.
Because the tree onion is such a big grower, it is a good idea to split the underground bulbs every 3 years in spring.

Bulbs
The air-growing bulbils of the tree onion have small root systems, each one capable of reproducing another plant. Plant where required in an enriched soil either in the fall, as the parent plant dies back, or in the spring.

Pests and Diseases
The onion fly is the curse of the onion family, especially in late spring and early summer. The way to try to prevent this is to take care not to damage the roots or leaves when thinning the seedlings and also not to leave the thinnings lying around, as the scent attracts the fly.
Another problem is downy mildew caused by cool, wet falls; the leaves become velvety and die back. Another disease is white rot, which can be introduced in contaminated soil. If you have either of the above diseases, burn the affected plants and do not plant in the same position again.

Allium cepa Proliferum Group

Other characteristic diseases are neck rot and bulb rot, both caused by a *Botrytis* fungus that usually occurs as a result of the bulbs being damaged either by digging or hoeing.

Onions are prone to many more diseases but, if you keep the soil fertile and do not make life easy for the onion fly, you will still have a good crop.

Maintenance

Spring Sow the seed, divide 3-year-old clumps of Welsh and tree onions. Plant bulbs of tree onions.
Summer Stake mature tree onions to stop them falling over and depositing the ripe bulbils on the soil.
Fall Mulch around tree onion plants with well-rotted manure. Use a small amount of manure around Welsh onions.
Winter Neither variety needs protection.

Garden Cultivation

Welsh Onions
These highly adaptable hardy onions will grow in any well-drained fertile soil. Seeds can be sown in spring after the frosts, direct into the ground. Thin to a distance of 10 in. apart. Keep well watered throughout the growing season. In the fall give the area a mulch of well-rotted manure.

Tree Onions
Dig in some well-rotted manure before planting. Plant the bulbs in their clusters in a sunny well-drained position at a distance of 12–18 in. apart.

In the first year nothing much will happen (unless you are one of the lucky ones). If the summer is very dry, water well.

In the following year, if you give the plant a good mulch of well-rotted manure in fall, it grows to 3–5 ft. and produces masses of small onions.

Harvesting

Welsh onions may be picked at any time from early summer onwards. The leaves do not dry well but can be frozen like those of their cousin, chives. Use scissors and snip them into a plastic bag. They form neat rings; freeze them.

The little tree onions can be picked off the stems and stored; lay them out on a rack in a cool place with good ventilation.

 culinary

Welsh onions make a great substitute for scallions, as they are hardier and earlier. Pull and use in salads or stir-fry dishes. Chop and use instead of chives.

Tree onions provide fresh onion flavor throughout the year. The bulbils can be pickled or chopped raw in salads (fairly strong), or cooked whole in stews and casseroles.

Pissaladière (A French Pizza)
Serves 4 to 6

4 tablespoons olive oil (not extra virgin)
20 tree onions, finely minced
1 clove garlic, crushed
1 dessertspoon fresh thyme, chopped
Salt
Freshly ground black pepper
¼ lb. once-risen bread dough
½ lb. ripe tomatoes, peeled and sliced
2 oz. canned anchovy fillets, drained and
  halved lengthwise
16 large black olives, halved and pitted

Heat the olive oil in a heavy skillet, add the onions, cover the pan tightly, and fry, gently stirring occasionally for 15 minutes. Add the garlic and the thyme and cook uncovered for 15 minutes, or until the onions are reduced to a clear purée. Season to taste and let cool.

Preheat the oven to 400°F. Roll the bread dough directly on the baking sheet into a circle 10 in. in diameter. Spread the puréed onions evenly over the dough, put the tomato slices on the onions, and top with a decorative pattern of anchovy fillets and olives.

Bake for 5 minutes. Reduce the oven temperature to 375°F and continue to bake for 30 minutes or until the bread base is well risen and lightly browned underneath.

Serve hot with a green herb salad.

 container growing

Welsh onions can be grown in a large pot using a soilless compost, but make sure the compost does not dry out. Feed regularly throughout the summer with a liquid fertilizer.

Tree onions grow too tall for containers.

 other uses

The onion is believed to help ward off colds in winter and also to induce sleep and cure indigestion. The fresh juice is antibiotic, diuretic, expectorant, and antispasmodic, so is useful in the treatment of coughs, colds, bronchitis, laryngitis, and gastroenteritis. It is also said to lower the blood pressure and to help restore sexual potency that has been impaired by illness or mental stress.

Allium schoenoprasum
CHIVES

From the family Alliaceae.

Chives are the only member of the onion group found wild in Europe, Australia and North America, where they thrive in temperate and warm to hot regions. Although they are one of the most ancient of all herbs, chives were not cultivated in European gardens until the 16th century.

Chives were a favorite in China as long ago as 3000 CE. They were enjoyed for their delicious mild onion flavor and used as an antidote to poison and to stop bleeding. Their culinary virtues were first reported to the West by the explorer and traveler, Marco Polo. During the Middle Ages they were sometimes known as rush-leeks, from the Greek *schoinos* meaning "rush" and *parson* meaning "leek."

Allium schoenoprasum f. *albiflorum*

 varieties

Allium schoenoprasum
Chives
Hardy perennial. Ht 12 in. Purple globular flowers spring and late summer. Leaves green and cylindrical. Apart from being a good culinary herb it makes an excellent edging plant. **Zone 3**

Allium schoenoprasum fine-leaved
Extra Fine-Leaved Chives
Hardy perennial. Ht 8 in. Purple globular flowers all summer. Very narrow cylindrical leaves, not as coarse as standard chives. Good for culinary usage. **Zone 3**

Allium schoenoprasum f. albiflorum
White Chives
Hardy perennial. Ht 8 in. White globular flowers all summer. Cylindrical green leaves. A cultivar of ordinary chives and very effective in a silver garden. Good flavor. **Zone 3**

Allium schoenoprasum "Forescate"
Pink Chives
Hardy perennial. Ht 8 in. Pink flowers all summer. Cylindrical green leaves. The pink flowers can look a bit insipid when planted too close to standard chives. Good in flower arrangements. **Zone 3**

Allium tuberosum
Garlic Chives, Chinese Chives
Hardy perennial. Ht 16 in. White flowers late summer. Leaf midgreen, flat and solid with a sweet garlic flavor when young. As they get older the leaf becomes tougher and the taste coarser. **Zone 3**

CHIVES

 ## cultivation

Propagation

Seed

Easy from seed, but they need a temperature of 65°F to germinate, so if sowing outside, wait until late spring for the soil to be warm enough. I recommend starting this plant in plug trays with bottom heat in early spring. Sow about 10 to 15 seeds per 1 in. cell. Transplant either into pots or the garden when the soil has warmed through.

Division

Every few years in the spring lift clumps (made up of small bulbs) and replant in 6 to 10-bulb clumps, 6 in. apart, adding fresh compost or manure.

Pests and Diseases

Aphids may be a problem on pot-grown herbs. Wash off gently under the tap or use a liquid insecticidal soap. Be diligent, for aphids can hide deep down low amongst the leaves.

Cool wet falls may produce downy mildew; the leaves will become velvety and die back from the tips. Dig up, split, and repot affected plants, at the same time cutting back all the growth to prevent the disease spreading.

Chives can also suffer from rust. As this is a fungus it is essential to cut back diseased growth immediately and burn it. DO NOT COMPOST. If it is very bad, remove the plant and burn it all. Do not plant any chives or garlic in that area.

Maintenance

Spring Clear soil around emerging established plants. Feed liquid fertilizer. Sow seeds. Divide established plants.
Summer Remove the flower stem before flowering to increase leaf production.
Fall Prepare soil for next year's crop. Dig up a small clump, pot, bring inside for forcing.
Winter Cut forced chives and feed regularly.

Garden Cultivation

Chives are fairly tolerant regarding soil and position, but produce the best growth planted 6 in. from other plants in a rich moist soil and in a fairly sunny position. If the soil is poor they will turn yellow and then brown at the tips. For an attractive edging, plant at a distance of 4 in. apart and allow to flower. Keep newly transplanted plants well watered in the spring, and in the summer make sure that they do not dry out, otherwise the leaves will quickly shrivel. Chives die right back into the ground in winter, but a winter cutting can be forced by digging up a clump in fall, potting it into a soilless potting compost mixed in equal parts with composted fine bark, and placing it somewhere warm with good light.

Harvesting

Chives may be cut to within 1 in. of the ground 4 times a year to maintain a supply of succulent fresh leaves. Chives do not dry well. Refrigerated leaves in a sealed plastic bag will retain crispness for up to 7 days. Freeze chopped leaves in ice cubes for convenience. Cut flowers when they are fully open before the color fades for use in salads and sauces.

 ## companion planting

Traditionally it is said that chives planted next to apple trees prevent scab, and when planted next to roses can prevent black spot. Hence the saying, "Chives next to roses creates posies."

 ## container growing

Chives grow well in pots or on a windowsill and flourish in a window box if partially shaded. Use a soil-based compost mixed in equal parts with composted fine bark. They need an enormous quantity of water and occasional liquid feed to stay green and succulent. Remember too that, being bulbs, chives need some top growth for strengthening and regeneration, so do not cut away all the leaves if you wish to use them next season. Allow to die back in winter if you want to use it the following spring. A good patio plant, easy to grow, but not particularly fragrant.

 ## medicinal

The leaves are mildly antiseptic and when sprinkled onto food they stimulate the appetite and help to promote digestion.

 ## other uses

Chives are said to prevent scab infection on animals.

 ## culinary

Add chives at the end of cooking or the flavor will disappear. They are delicious freshly picked and snipped as a garnish or flavor in omelets or scrambled eggs, salads and soups. They can be mashed into cream cheeses or sprinkled onto broiled meats. Add liberally to sour cream as a filling for baked potatoes.

Chive Butter

Use in scrambled eggs, omelets, and cooked vegetables and with broiled lamb or fish or on baked potatoes.

4 tablespoons chopped chives
½ cup butter, softened
1 tablespoon lemon juice
Salt and freshly ground black pepper

Cream the chives and butter together until well mixed. Beat in the lemon juice and season. Cover and cool the butter in the refrigerator until ready to use; it will keep for several days.

Ajuga reptans
AJUGA

Also known as Common or Creeping bugle, Bugle weed, Babies' shoes, Baby's rattle, Blind man's hand, Carpenter's herb, Dead men's bellows, Horse and hounds, Nelson's bugle, Thunder and lightning and Middle comfrey. From the family Lamiaceae.

The bugle found in Britain is a native of Europe. It is frequently found in mountainous areas and often grows in damp fields, mixed woodland and meadows. The bugle of North America is a species of *Lycopus* (gypsy weed).

Among the many folk tales associated with bugle is one that its flowers can cause a fire if brought into the house, a belief that has survived in at least one district of Germany.

varieties

Ajuga reptans
Bugle
Hardy evergreen perennial. Ht 1 ft., spread up to 3 ft. Very good spreading plant. Blue flowers from spring to summer. Oval leaves are dark green with purplish tinge. It is this plant that has medicinal properties.
Zone 3

Ajuga reptans "Atropurpurea"
Bronze Bugle
Hardy evergreen perennial. Ht 6 in., spread 3 ft. Blue flowers from spring to summer. Deep bronze/purple leaves. Very good for ground cover. **Zone 3**

Ajuga reptans "Multicolor"
Multicolored Bugle
Hardy evergreen perennial. Ht 5 in., spread 18 in. Small spikes of blue flowers from spring to summer. Dark green leaves marked with cream and pink. Good for ground cover. **Zone 3**

cultivation

Propagation
Seeds
Sow the small seed in fall, or spring as a second choice. Cover only lightly with soil. Germination can be erratic and slow.

Division
This method is easy and the only one suitable for cultivars as bugle produces runners, each one having its own root system. Plant out in fall or spring. Space 1 ft. apart, as a single plant spreads rapidly.

Pests and Diseases
Nothing much disturbs this plant!

Maintenance
Spring Clear winter debris around established plants. Dig up runners and replant in other areas. Sow seeds.
Summer Dig up runners to control established plants.
Fall Sow seed and dig up runners of established plants. Repot, using a soilless potting mix mixed in equal parts with composted fine bark, and winter in a cold frame. Alternatively, replant into a prepared site in the garden.
Winter No protection needed unless it is colder than −6°F.

Garden Cultivation
It will grow vigorously on any soil that retains moisture, in full sun, and it also tolerates quite dense shade. It will even thrive in a damp boggy area near the pond or in a hedgerow or shady woodland area. At close quarters bugle is very appealing and can be used as a decorative ground cover. Guard against leaf scorch on the variegated variety.

Harvesting
For medicinal usage the leaves and flowers are gathered in early summer.

container growing

Bugle makes a good outside container plant, especially the variegated and purple varieties. Use a soilless compost mixed in equal parts with composted fine bark. Also good in hanging baskets.

culinary

The young shoots of *Ajuga reptans* can be mixed in salads to give you a different taste. Not mine.

medicinal

An infusion of dried leaves in boiling water is thought to lower blood pressure and to stop internal bleeding. Nowadays it is widely used in homeopathy in various preparations against throat irritation, especially in the case of mouth ulcers.

other uses

In some countries it is gathered as cattle fodder.

Ajuga reptans "Artopurpurea"

Aloe vera

ALOE VERA

From the family Aloaceae.

There are between 250 and 350 species of aloe around the world. They are originally native to the arid areas of Southern Africa. In cultivation they need a frost-free environment. Aloe has been valued at least since the fourth century CE when Aristotle requested Alexander the Great to conquer Socotra in the Indian Ocean, where many species grow.

Flower spike of *Aloe vera (Aloe barbadensis)*

 ## varieties

Aloe vera (Aloe barbadensis)
Aloe vera
Half-hardy perennial. Grown outside: Ht 2 ft., spread 2 ft. or more. Grown as a house plant: Ht 1 ft. Minimum temperature 50°F. Succulent gray/ green pointed foliage, from which eventually grows a flowering stem with bell-shaped yellow or orange flowers. **Zone 10**

Aloe arborescens "Frutescens"
Half-hardy perennial. Grown outside: Ht and spread 6 ft. Minimum temperature 45°F. Each stem is crowned by rosettes of long, blue/green leaves with toothed edges and cream stripes. Produces spikes of red tubular flowers in late winter and spring. **Zone 8**

Aloe variegata
Partridge-breasted Aloe
Half-hardy perennial. A house plant only in temperate climates. Ht 1 ft., spread 4 in. Minimum temperature 45°F. Triangular, white-marked, dark green leaves. Spike of pinkish-red flowers in spring. **Zone 10**

 ## cultivation

Propagation
Seed
A temperature of 70°F must be maintained during germination. Sow the small seeds in spring onto the surface of a pot or tray, using a standard seed compost mixed in equal parts with sharp horticultural sand, and cover with perlite. Place in a propagator with bottom heat. Germination is erratic — 4 to 24 months.

Division
In summer gently remove offshoots at the base of a mature plant. Leave for a day to dry, then pot into 2 parts compost to 1 part sharp sand mix. Water in and leave in a warm place to establish. Give the parent plant a good liquid feed when returning to its pot.

Pests and Diseases
Overwatering causes it to rot off.

Maintenance
Spring Sow seeds. Give containerized plants a good dust! Spray the leaves with water. Give a good feed of liquid fertilizer.
Summer Remove the basal offshoots of a mature plant to maintain the parent plant. Repot mature plants.
Fall Bring in pots if there is any danger of frost.
Winter Rest all pot-grown plants in a cool room (minimum temperature 40°F); water sparingly.

Garden Cultivation
Aloes enjoy a warm, frost-free position — the full sun to partial shade — and a free-draining soil. Leave 3 ft. minimum between plants.

Aloe vera leaf

Harvesting
Cut leaves throughout the growing season. A plant of more than 2 years old has stronger properties.

 ## container growing

Compost must be gritty and well drained. Don't overwater. Maintain a frost-free, light environment.

 ## cosmetic

Aloe vera is used in cosmetic preparations, in hand creams, suntan lotions, and shampoos.

 ## medicinal

The gel obtained by breaking the leaves is a remarkable healer. Applied to wounds it forms a clear protective seal and encourages skin regeneration. It can be applied directly to cuts and burns, and is immediately soothing.

warning

It should be emphasized that, apart from external application, aloes are not for home medication. ALWAYS seek medical attention for serious burns.

Aloysia triphylla

LEMON VERBENA

From the family Verbenaceae.

Lemon verbena grew originally in Chile.

This Rolls Royce of lemon-scented plants was first imported into Europe in the 18th century by the Spanish for its perfume.

 varieties

Aloysia triphylla (*Lippia citriodora*)
Lemon Verbena
Half-hardy deciduous perennial. Ht 3–10 ft., spread up to 8 ft. Tiny white flowers tinged with lilac in early summer. Leaves pale green, lance shaped, and very strongly lemon scented. **Zone 8**

 cultivation

Propagation
Seeds
The seed sets only in warm climates and should be sown in spring into prepared seed or plug trays and covered with perlite; a bottom heat of 60°F helps. Prick out into 3½ in. pots using a standard seed compost mixed in equal parts with composted fine bark. Keep in pots for the first 2 years before planting specimens in the garden 3 ft. apart.

Cuttings
Take softwood cuttings from the new growth in late spring. The cutting material will wilt quickly so have everything prepared.
   Take semi-hardwood cuttings in late summer or early fall. Keep in pots for the first 2 years.

Pests and Diseases
If grown under protection you may have whitefly and red spider mite; either use the relevant predators or spray with a liquid insecticidal soap, but not both.

Maintenance
Spring Trim established plants. Take softwood cuttings. In warm climates sow seed.
Summer Trim lightly after flowering to remove the flowers. Take semi-hardwood cuttings.
Fall Protect from excessive wet and frosts.
Winter Keep plants frost free.

Garden Cultivation
Likes a warm humid climate. The soil should be light, free draining and warm. A sunny wall is ideal. It will need protection against frost and wind, and temperatures below 40°F. If left in the ground, cover the area around the roots with mulching material. In spring give the plant a gentle prune and spray with warm water to help revive it.

New growth can appear very late in spring so never discard a plant until late summer. Once the plant has started re-shooting, cut back all last year's growth to 1½ in. Cut off flowers once flowering has finished.

Harvesting
Pick the leaves any time before they start to wither and darken. Leaves dry quickly and easily, keeping their color and scent. Store in a damp-proof container.

 container growing

Choose a container at least 8 in. wide and use a soil-based compost mixed in equal parts with composted fine bark. Place the container in a warm, sunny, light, and airy spot. Water well throughout the growing season and feed with liquid fertilizer during flowering. Cut back last year's growth to 1½ in. in the spring only. In winter move the container into a cold greenhouse, and allow the compost to nearly dry out. The plant must be allowed to drop its leaves: this is not a sign that it is dead.

 medicinal

A tea last thing at night is refreshing and has mild sedative properties; it can also soothe bronchial and nasal congestion and ease indigestion. However, long-term use may cause stomach irritation.

 other uses

The leaves with their strong lemon scent are lovely in potpourris, linen sachets, herb pillows, sofa sacks. The distilled oil made from the leaves is an essential basic ingredient in many perfumes.

 culinary

Use fresh leaves to flavor oil and vinegar, drinks, fruit puddings, confectionery, apple gelatin, cakes, and stuffings. Infuse in finger bowls.
   Add a teaspoon of chopped, fresh leaves to homemade ice cream for a delicious dessert.

MARSH-MALLOW

Althaea officinalis

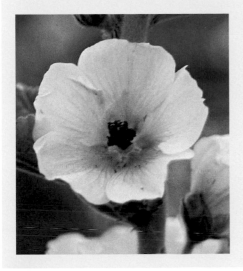

Also known as Mortification root, Sweet weed, Wymote, Marsh malice, Mesh-mellice, Wimote, and Althea. From the family Malvaceae.

Marsh-mallow is widely distributed from Western Europe to Siberia, from Australia to North America. It is common to find it in salt marshes and on banks near the sea. The generic name, *Althaea*, comes from the Latin *altheo*, meaning "I cure." It may be the *althea* that Hippocrates recommended so highly for healing wounds. The Romans considered it a delicious vegetable, used it in barley soup and in stuffing for suckling pigs. In the Renaissance era the herbalists used marsh-mallow to cure sore throats, stomach trouble and toothache. The soft, sweet marshmallow was originally flavored with the root of marsh-mallow.

 ## varieties

Althaea officinalis
Marsh-mallow
Hardy perennial. Ht 2–4 ft., spread 2 ft. Flowers pink or white in late summer/early fall. Leaves, gray-green in color, tear-shaped and covered all over with soft hair. **Zone 5**

 ## cultivation

Propagation
Seed
Sow in prepared seed or plug trays in the fall. Cover lightly with compost and winter indoors. Erratic germination takes place in spring. Plant out, 18 in. apart, when large enough to handle.

Division
Divide established plants in the spring or fall, replanting into a prepared site in the garden.

Pests and Diseases
This plant is usually free from pests and diseases.

Maintenance
Spring Divide established plants.
Summer Cut back after flowering for new growth.
Fall Sow seeds and winter the trays outside.
Winter No need for protection. Fully hardy.

Garden Cultivation
Marsh-mallow is highly attractive to butterflies. A good seaside plant, it likes a site in full sun with a moist or wet, moderately fertile soil. Cut back after flowering to encourage new leaves.

Harvesting
Pick leaves for fresh use as required; they do not preserve well. For use either fresh or dried, dig up the roots of 2-year-old plants in fall, after the flowers and leaves have died back.

 ## medicinal

Due to its high mucilage content (35 percent in the root and 10 percent in the leaf), marsh-mallow soothes or cures inflammation, ulceration of the stomach and small intestine, soreness of throat, and pain from cystitis. An infusion of leaves or flowers serves as a soothing gargle; an infusion of the root can be used for coughs, diarrhea and insomnia. The pulverized roots may be used as a healing and drawing poultice, which should be applied warm.

Decoction for Dry Hands
Soak 2 tablespoons of scraped and finely minced root in ½ cup of cold water for 24 hours. Strain well. Add 1 tablespoon of the decoction to 2 tablespoons of ground almonds, 1 teaspoon of milk and 1 teaspoon of cider vinegar. Beat it until well blended. Add a few drops of lavender oil. Put into a small screwtop pot.

 ## culinary

Boil the roots to soften, then peel and quickly fry in butter.

Use the flowers in salads. Leaves are also good in salads and may be added to oil and vinegar, or steamed and served as a vegetable.

Anethum graveolens
DILL

Also known as Dillweed and Dillseed. From the family Apiaceae.

A native of southern Europe and western Asia, dill grows wild in the grain fields of Mediterranean countries and also in North and South America. The generic name *Anethum* derives from the Greek *anethon*. "Dill" is said to come from the Anglo-Saxon *dylle* or the Norse *dilla*, meaning to soothe or lull. Dill was found amongst the names of herbs used by Egyptian doctors 5,000 years ago and the remains of the plant have been found in the ruins of Roman buildings in Britain.

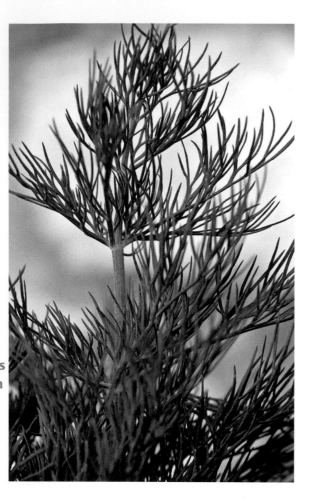

It is mentioned in the Gospel of St Matthew, where it is suggested that herbs were of sufficient value to be used as a tax payment — if only that were true today! "Woe unto you, Scribes and Pharisees, hypocrites! For ye pay tithe of mint and dill and cumin, and have omitted the weightier matters of the law."

During the Middle Ages dill was prized as protection against witchcraft. While magicians used it in their spells, lesser mortals infused it in wine to enhance passion. It was once an important medicinal herb for treating coughs and headaches, as an ingredient of ointments and for calming infants with whooping cough — dill water or gripe water is still called upon today. Early settlers took dill to North America, where it was known as the "Meeting House Seed," because the children were given the seed to chew during long sermons to prevent them feeling hungry.

varieties

Anethum graveolens
Dill
Annual. Ht 2–5 ft., spread 12 in. Tiny yellow/green flowers in flattened umbel clusters in summer. Fine aromatic feathery green leaves. **All zones**

cultivation

Propagation
Seed
Seed can be started in early spring under cover, using pots or module plug trays. Do not use seed trays, as dill does not like being transplanted, and if it gets upset it will bolt and miss out the leaf-producing stage.

The seeds are easy to handle, being a good size. Place four per plug or evenly spaced on the surface of a pot, and cover with perlite. Germination takes 2 to 4 weeks, depending on the warmth of the surrounding area. As soon as the seedlings are large enough to handle, the air and soil temperatures have started to rise, and there is no threat of frost, plant out 9 in. apart.

Garden Cultivation
Dill prefers a well-drained, poor soil in partial shade. Sow midspring into shallow rows on a prepared site, where they will be harvested. Protect seedlings from wind. When the plants are large enough to handle, thin out to a distance of about 8 in. apart to allow plenty of room for growth. Make several small sowings in succession so that you have a supply of fresh leaves throughout the summer. The seed is viable for 3 years.

The plants are rather fragile and it may be necessary to provide support. Twigs pushed into the ground around the plant and enclosed with string or raffia give better results than attempting to stake each plant.

In very hot summers, make sure that the plants are watered regularly or they will go to seed. There is no need to liquid feed, as this only promotes soft growth and in turn encourages pests and disease. The foliage is a food source for Black Swallow Tail Butterfly caterpillars.

Dill vinegar

Pests and Diseases

Watch out for aphids in crowded conditions. Treat with a liquid insecticidal soap if necessary. Be warned, slugs love dill plants.

Maintenance

Spring Sow the seeds successively for a leaf crop.
Summer Water well after cutting to promote new growth.
Fall (early) Harvest seeds.
Winter Dig up all remaining plants. Make sure all the seed heads have been removed before you compost the stalks, as the seed is viable for 3 years. If you leave the plants to self-seed they certainly will, and they will live up to their other name of Dillweed.

Harvesting

Pick leaves fresh for eating at any time after the plant has reached maturity. Since it is quick-growing, this can be within 8 weeks of the first sowing. Although leaves can be dried, great care is needed and it is better to concentrate on drying the seed for storage. Cut the stalks off the flower heads when the seed is beginning to ripen. Put the seed heads upside down in a paper bag and tie the top of the bag. Put in a warm place for a week. The seeds should then separate easily from the husk when rubbed in the palm of the hand. Store in an airtight container and the seeds will keep their flavor very well.

 ## container growing

Dill can be grown in containers, in a sheltered corner in partial shade. However, it will need staking. The art of growing it successfully is to keep cutting the plant for use in the kitchen. That way you will promote new growth and keep the plant reasonably compact. The drawback is that it will be fairly short-lived, so you will have to do successive sowings in different pots to maintain a supply. I do not recommend growing dill indoors — it will get leggy, soft and prone to disease.

 ## medicinal

Dill is an antispasmodic and calmative. Dill tea or water is a popular remedy for an upset stomach, hiccups, or insomnia, for nursing mothers to promote the flow of milk, and as an appetite stimulant. It is a constituent of gripe water and other children's medicines because of its ability to ease flatulence and colic.

 ## culinary

Dill is a culinary herb that improves the appetite and digestion. The difference between dill leaf and dill seed lies in the degree of pungency. There are occasions when the seed is better because of its sharper flavor. It is used as a flavoring for soup, lamb stews, and broiled or boiled fish. It can also add spiciness to rice dishes, and be combined with white wine vinegar to make dill vinegar.

Dill leaf can be used generously in many dishes, as it enhances rather than dominates the flavor of many foods.

Before it sets seed, add one flowering head to a jar of pickled gherkins, cucumbers, and cauliflowers for a flavor stronger than dill leaves but fresher than seeds. In America these are known as dill pickles.

Gravlax (Salmon marinaded with dill)

This is a traditional Scandinavian dish of great simplicity and great merit. Salmon treated in this way will keep for up to a week in the refrigerator.

1 ½ to 2 lbs. salmon, middle or tail piece
1 heaping tablespoon sea salt
1 rounded tablespoon caster sugar
1 teaspoon crushed black peppercorns
1 tablespoon brandy (optional)
1 heaping tablespoon fresh dill

Have the salmon cleaned, scaled, bisected lengthwise, and filleted. Mix remaining ingredients together and put some of the mixture into a flat dish (glass or enamel) large enough to take the salmon. Place one piece of salmon skin side down on the

 ## other uses

Where a salt-free diet must be followed, the seed, whole or ground, is a valuable replacement. Try chewing the seeds to clear up halitosis and sweeten the breath. Crush and infuse seeds to make a nail-strengthening bath.

bottom of the dish, spread more of the mixture over the cut side. Add the second piece of salmon, skin up, and pour over the remaining mixture. Cover with foil and place a plate or wooden board larger than the area of the salmon on top. Weigh this down with weights or heavy cans. Put in the refrigerator for 36 to 72 hours. Turn the fish completely every 12 hours or so and baste (inside surfaces too) with the juices.

To serve, scrape off all the mixture, pat the fish dry and slice thinly and at an angle. Serve with buttered rye bread and a mustard sauce called Gravlaxsas:

4 tablespoons mild, ready-made Dijon mustard
1 teaspoon mustard powder
1 tablespoon caster sugar
2 tablespoons white wine vinegar
6 tablespoons of vegetable oil
3 to 4 tablespoons of chopped dill

Mix the Dijon mustard with the mustard powder, caster sugar and vinegar, then slowly add the oil until you have a sauce the consistency of mayonnaise. Finally, stir in the dill. Alternatively, substitute a mustard and dill mayonnaise.

ANGELICA

Also known as European angelica, Garden angelica, and Root of the Holy Ghost. From the family Apiaceae.

Angelica in its many forms is a native of North America, Europe, and Asia. It is also widely cultivated as a garden plant. Wild angelica is found in moist fields and the countryside throughout Europe. American angelica is found in similar growing conditions in Canada and north-eastern and northern central states of America.

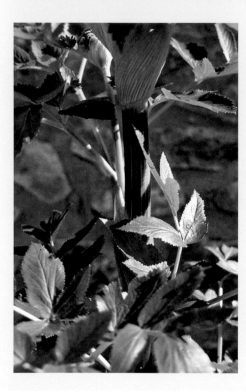

Angelica probably comes from the Greek *angelos*, meaning "messenger." There is a legend that an angel revealed to a monk in a dream that the herb was a cure for the plague, and traditionally angelica was considered the most effective safeguard against evil, witchcraft in particular. Certainly it is a plant no self-respecting witch would include in her brew.

Angelica is an important flavoring agent in liqueurs such as Benedictine, although its unique flavor cannot be detected from the others used. It is also cultivated commercially for medicinal and cosmetic purposes.

 varieties

Angelica archangelica
Angelica
Monocarpic (will live until it has successfully flowered and set seed). Ht 3–8 ft., spread 3 ft. in second year. Dramatic second-year flowerheads late spring through summer, greenish-white and very sweetly scented. Bright green leaves, the lower ones large and bi- or tri-pinnate; the higher, smaller and pinnate. Rootstock varies in color from pale yellowish-beige to reddish-brown. **Zone 4**

Angelica atropurpurea
American Angelica
Also known as Bellyache root, High angelica, Masterwort, Purple angelica, and Wild angelica. Biennial. Ht 4–5 ft. Flowers resemble those of *A. archangelica* — white to greenish-white, late spring through summer. Leaves large and alternately compound. Rootstock purple. The whole plant delivers a powerful odor when fresh. **Zone 5**

Angelica gigas
Korean Angelica
Monocarpic. Ht up to 4 ft., spread 3 ft. in second year.

Beautiful second or third year spherical deep red umbels with tiny white flowers in late summer. Palmate green foliage. **Zone 5**

Angelica polymorpha var. sinensis (Anglica sinensis)
Chinese Angelica
Also known as Dang Gui, Women's Ginseng. Monocarpic. Ht. up to 3 ft., spread 28 in. Umbels of small green and white flowers in summer. Palmate green foliage.

 cultivation

Propagation

Seed
The fresh seeds are only viable for 3 months from harvest. Sow in early fall, either where you want it to grow next year, or into plug trays that are placed outside to get the weather. There is no need to protect the seedlings from frost. Plant out in the following spring. If you cannot sow the seed fresh, mix them with horticultural sand and put them in to a plastic bag and then into the refrigerator. Once the seeds start to germinate in the bag, approximately 2 to 6 weeks, sow the seeds in groups of three into a prepared site in the garden 3 ft. apart. This plant

Angelica gigas

cannot be successfully transplanted once the taproot has developed, so choose your site with care.

Pests and Diseases
Remove blackfly easily with liquid insecticidal soap.

Maintenance
Spring Clear ground around existing plants. Plant out fall seedlings. Put old seed in refrigerator.
Summer Cut stems of second-year growth for crystallizing. Cut young leaves before flowering to use fresh in salads or to dry for medicinal or culinary uses. If in summer the leaves turn a yellowish-green, it is usually a sign that the plant needs more water.
Fall The ideal seed-sowing time.
Winter No need for protection.

Garden Cultivation
Angelica dislikes hot humid climates and appreciates a spot in the garden where it can be in shade for some part of every day. But it can be a difficult plant to accommodate in a small garden, as it needs a lot of space. Site at the back of a border, perhaps near a wall where the plant architecture can be shown off. Make sure that the soil is deep and moist. Add well-rotted compost to help retain moisture. Note that angelica dies down completely in winter but green shoots appear quickly in the spring. Angelica forms a big clump of foliage in the first summer and dramatic flowers the second or third, dying after the seed is set. A plant will propagate itself in the same situation if allowed to self-seed.

Harvesting
Harvest leaves — use fresh from spring onwards for culinary and medicinal; for drying, from early summer until flowering. Dry flowers in early summer for flower arrangements. Collect seeds when they begin to ripen. Harvest roots to dry for medicinal use in the second fall immediately after flowering.

 ## medicinal

It is used to treat indigestion, anemia, coughs, and colds; it has antibacterial and antifungal properties. It is said that a tea made from the young leaves is good for reducing tension and nervous headaches and that a decoction made from the roots is soothing for colds and other bronchial conditions. Reputedly crushed leaves freshen the air in a car and may help travel sickness.

 ## culinary

Candied Angelica

Angelica is now best known as a decorative confectionery for cakes. There is a bright emerald, apparently plastic, specimen sold commercially as angelica, which cannot compare with homemade, pale green candied angelica; this tastes and smells similar to the freshly bruised stem or crushed leaf of the plant.

Angelica stems
Granulated sugar
Caster sugar for dusting

Choose young tender springtime shoots. Cut into 3–4 in. lengths. Place in a pot with just enough water to cover. Simmer until tender, then strain and peel off the outside skin. Put back into the pan with enough water to cover and bring to a boil, strain immediately and allow to cool.

When cool, weigh the angelica stalks and add an equal weight of granulated sugar. Place the sugar and angelica in a covered dish and leave in a cool place for 2 days.

Put the angelica and the syrup which will have formed back into the pan. Bring slowly to a boil and simmer, stirring occasionally, until the angelica becomes clear and has good color.

Strain again, discarding all the liquid, then sprinkle as much caster sugar as will cling to the angelica. Allow the stems to dry in a cool oven (200°F). If not thoroughly dry they become moldy. Store in an airtight container between sheets of waxed paper.

Stewed Rhubarb

If when you cook rhubarb or gooseberries you add

young angelica leaves, you will need to add less sugar. Angelica does not sweeten the fruit but its muscatel flavor cuts through the acidity of the rhubarb.

2 lbs. rhubarb
1 cup angelica stems
Juice and rind of 1 orange
⅔ cup water
¼ cup sugar

Put all the ingredients in a pan, bring to the boil, then turn down the heat and simmer for 5 minutes.

 ## container growing

Angelica is definitely not an indoor plant, though if the container is large enough it can be grown as such. Do not over-fertilize and be prepared to stake when in flower. Be wary of the pot toppling over as the plant grows taller.

 ## warning

Large doses first stimulate and then paralyze the central nervous system. The tea is not recommended for those suffering from diabetes.

Anthriscus cerefolium
CHERVIL

From the family Apiaceae.

Native to the Middle East, South Russia, and the Caucasus, chervil can be cultivated in warm temperate climates. It is now occasionally found growing wild.

Almost certainly brought to Britain by the Romans, chervil is one of the Lenten herbs, thought to have blood-cleansing and restorative properties. It was eaten in quantity in those days, especially on Maundy Thursday.

Gerard, the Elizabethan physician who superintended Lord Burleigh's gardens, wrote in his *Herball* of 1597, "The leaves of sweet chervil are exceeding good, wholesome and pleasant among other salad herbs, giving the taste of Anise seed unto the rest."

 varieties

Anthriscus cerefolium
Chervil
Hardy annual (some consider it to be a biennial). Ht 12–24 in., spread 12 in. Flowers, tiny and white, grow in clusters from spring to summer. Leaves, light green and fern-like, in late summer may take on a purple tinge. When young it can easily be confused with cow parsley. However, cow parsley is a perennial and eventually grows much taller and stouter, its large leaves lacking the sweet distinctive aroma of chervil. **All zones**

Anthriscus cerefolium "Crispum"
Chervil curly leafed
Hardy annual. Grows like the ordinary chervil except that, in my opinion, the leaf has an inferior flavor. **All zones**

 cultivation

Propagation
Seed
The medium-size seed germinates rapidly as the air and soil temperatures rise in the spring provided the seed is fresh (it loses viability after about a year). Young plants are ready for cutting 6 to 8 weeks after sowing, thereafter continuously providing leaves as long as the flowering stems are removed.

Sow seed in prepared plug module trays if you prefer, and cover with perlite. Pot on to containers with a minimum 5 in. diameter. But, as a plant with a long taproot, chervil does not like being transplanted, so keep this to a minimum. It can in fact be sown direct into a 5 in. pot, growing it, like mustard and watercress, as a "cut and come again" crop.

Pests and Diseases
Chervil can suffer from aphids. Wash off gently with a liquid insecticidal soap. Do not blast off with a high-pressure hose, as this will damage the soft leaves.

Maintenance
Spring Sow seeds.
Summer A late sowing in this season will provide leaves through winter, as it is very hardy. Protect from midday sun.
Fall Cloche fall-sown plants for winter use.
Winter Although chervil is hardy, some cloche protection is needed to ensure leaves in winter, except in frost zones, where it is not possible to have foliage in winter.

Garden Cultivation
The soil required is light with a degree of moisture retention. Space plants 9–12 in. apart. Semi-shade is best, because the problem with chervil is that it will burst into flower too quickly should the weather become sunny and hot and be of no use as a culinary herb. For this reason some gardeners sow between rows of other garden herbs or vegetables or under deciduous plants to ensure some shade during the summer months.

Harvesting
Harvest leaves for use fresh when the plant is 6 to 8 weeks old or when 4 in. tall, and all the year round if you cover with a cloche in winter. Otherwise, freezing is the best method of preservation, as the dried leaves do not retain their flavor.

CHERVIL

Anthriscus cerefolium — a cut and come again plant

 culinary

It is one of the traditional *fines herbes*, indispensable to French cuisine and a fresh green asset in any meal, but many people elsewhere are only now discovering its special delicate parsley-like flavor with a hint of aniseed.

This is an herb especially for winter use because it is easy to obtain fresh leaves and, as every cook knows, French or otherwise, "Fresh is best." Use its leaf generously in salads, soups, sauces, vegetables, chicken, white fish, and egg dishes. Add freshly chopped towards the end of cooking to avoid flavor loss. In small quantities it enhances the flavor of other herbs. Great with vegetables.

Chervil with broad beans

 container growing

When grown inside in the kitchen chervil loses color, gets leggy, and goes floppy, so unless you are treating it as a "cut and come again" plant, plant outside in a large container that retains moisture and is positioned in semi-shade. Chervil looks good in a window box, but be sure that it gets shade at midday.

 medicinal

Leaves eaten raw are rich in Vitamin C, carotene, iron, and magnesium. They may be infused to make a tea to stimulate digestion and alleviate circulation disorders, liver complaints, and chronic catarrh, and fresh leaves may be applied to aching joints in a warm poultice.

 other uses

An infusion of the leaf can be used to cleanse skin, maintain suppleness, and discourage wrinkles.

Apium graveolens

CELERY LEAF

Also known as Wild celery, Smallage, Ajmud. From the family Apiaceae.

Wild celery has been used in both medicine and food for thousands of years. Seeds from this herb were found in the tomb of Tutankhamun (1327 CE). Today it can be found growing wild in marshy ground and by rivers in Europe and northern Africa. The whole plant strongly smells of celery — root, leaves, and seed — hence the latin *graveolens,* which means "strong-smelling." The salad celery, *Apium graveolens* var. *dulce* was originally bred in the 17th century from this wild form.

 varieties

Apium graveolens
Celery Leaf
Hardy Biennial. Ht 1–3½ ft., spread 6–12 in. Umbels of tiny green white flowers early in the second summer followed by ridged gray-brown seeds. The bright, aromatic, midgreen, cut leaves are very similar to its cousin French parsley, with which, when young, it is often confused. **Warmer zones.**

 cultivation

Propagation
Seed
Sow the fresh seed in early spring into pots or plug cell-packs using a standard seed compost. Cover with perlite, place under protection at 60°F. Germination takes 2 to 3 weeks. Alternatively sow seeds in late spring when the air temperature does not drop below 45°F at night into a well-prepared site that has been fed in the previous fall with well-rotted manure.

Pests and Diseases
Some years this herb has no problems at all then, in other years, it gets attacked by everything. If you see brown tunnel marks on the leaf, this is caused by the celery leaf miner. As soon as you see affected leaves remove them and burn them. If you have a bad infestation cut the plant back to 1¼ in. above the ground and make sure you remove all debris. Like parsley, it can be attacked by carrot fly in early summer. This fly attacks the roots and stem bases. To prevent this, cover the crop with a floating row cover, and only thin the seedlings in the early morning before the temperature rises. Cover immediately after thinning with a floating row cover to prevent the fly laying its eggs.

Maintenance
Spring Sow seeds under protection.
Summer Sow seeds into a prepared site. Remove flowers to maintain growth if seed not needed. Liquid feed plants.
Fall Harvest seeds. Feed the soil for next season's crops.
Winter Pick leaves. Only protect if temperatures fall below 23°F.

Garden Cultivation

Celery leaf is a hungry plant: it likes a good deep soil that does not dry out in summer. Always feed the chosen site well in the previous fall with well-rotted manure. If you wish to harvest celery leaf all year round have two different sites prepared. For summer supplies, a northern or eastern border is ideal because the plant needs moisture and prefers a little shade.

For winter supplies a more sheltered spot will be needed in a sunny position, for example against a sunny wall.

Harvesting

Pick the new young shoots throughout the growing season. Harvest the seeds in the late summer once they are fully ripe and start falling from the seed head. If you are saving the seed for sowing the following year be aware that celery is prone to disease and this can be harboured in the seed. So, for propagation, collect from healthy plants only. Dig up the roots of the second-year growth for use medicinally.

 ## companion planting

It is said that this herb helps repel the cabbage white fly from Brassicas.

 ## container growing

Celery leaf is ideal for containers. It can adapt to any deep container as it has a long taproot. Use a soilless compost. In summer place the container in partial shade to prevent the leaves from becoming tough. Feed and water regularly throughout the growing season.

 ## medicinal

The whole plant is used medicinally: roots, stem, leaf, and seeds. It is used to treat osteoarthritis, rheumatoid arthritis, and gout. Externally it is used to treat fungal infections. In the East it is used in Ayurvedic medicine to treat asthma, bronchitis, and hiccups.

 ## other uses

The essential oil made from the seed is used in perfumery and to make celery salt.

 ## warning

If the plant is infected with the fungus *Sclerotinia sclerotiorum*, contact with the sap can cause dermatitis in sensitive skin. Never take medicinally when pregnant.

Apium graveolens

 ## culinary

The young leaves are delicious in salads or when added to mashed potatoes. They are also great added to soups or sweated down with onions. In my opinion the mature, tough leaves are inedible. The seeds are also very useful: grind them in a mortar and pestle or add them whole to stews, casseroles, and soups. They are also lovely added to dough for flavorsome bread. In India it is an important minor spice.

Celery Seed Bread
Serves 4

3¾ cups wholewheat flour, plus extra for dusting
2 teaspoons of sunflower oil plus some extra for the grill pan
1 tablespoon of finely minced young celery leaves
1 pinch of salt
2 teaspoons celery seeds
Water to make the dough

Make a soft dough with the flour, sunflower oil, celery leaves, salt and celery seeds. Add water sparingly as one works the dough. Once the dough is easy to handle, divide into four equal-sized balls. Cover a board or surface with a dusting of flour, roll out each ball into a flat disk, adding a further dusting of flour if it sticks. By keeping the dough moving as you roll, you will prevent this happening.

Heat a grill pan to hot. Place the bread on the grill pan, reduce the heat and cook until the bread is covered in bubbles. Brush the upper surface with oil and turn over. Cook until bubbles appear on the surface. Cook the three remaining breads, serve warm with soups, pickles, or yogurts.

Armoracia rusticana
HORSERADISH

From the family Brassicaceae.

Native of Europe, naturalized in North America and Britain.

Originally the horseradish was cultivated as a medicinal herb. Now it is considered a flavoring herb. The common name means a coarse or strong radish, the prefix "horse" often being used in plants to donate a large, strong or coarse plant. In the 16th century it was known in England as Redcol or Recole. In this period the plant appears to have been more popular in Scandinavia and Germany, where they developed its potential as a fish sauce. In Britain horseradish has become strongly associated with roast beef.

Armoracia rusticana "Variegata"

varieties

Armoracia rusticana (Cochlearia armoracia)
Horseradish
Hardy perennial. Ht 2–3 ft., spread indefinite! Flowers white in spring (very rare). Leaves large green oblong. The large root, which is up to 24 in. long, 2 in. thick and tapering, goes deep into the soil. **Zone 3**

Armoracia rusticana "Variegata"
Hardy perennial. Ht 2–3 ft., spread also indefinite. Flowers white in spring (rare in cool climates). Leaves large with green/cream variegation and oblong shape. Large root which goes deep into the soil. Not as good flavor as *A. rusticana*. **Zone 3**

cultivation

Propagation
Root cuttings
In early spring cut pieces of root 6 in. long. Put them either directly into the ground, at a depth of 2 in., at intervals of 12 in. apart, or start them off in individual pots. These can then be planted out when the soil is manageable and frosts have passed.

Division
Divide established clumps in spring. Remember small pieces of root will always grow, so do it cleanly, making sure that you have collected all the little pieces of root. Replant in a well-prepared site.

Pests and Diseases
Cabbage white caterpillars may feed on the leaves during late summer. The leaves may also be affected by some fungus diseases, but this should not be a problem on vigorous plants and leaves should be simply removed and burnt.

Maintenance
Spring Plant cuttings in garden.
Summer Liquid feed with seaweed fertilizer.
Fall Dig up roots if required when mature enough.
Winter No need for protection, fully hardy.

Garden Cultivation
Think seriously if you want this plant in your garden. It is invasive. Once you have it, you have it. It is itself a most tolerant plant, liking all but the driest of soils. But for a good crop it prefers a light, well-dug, rich, moist soil. Prepare it the fall before planting with lots of well-rotted manure. It likes a sunny site but will tolerate dappled shade.

If large quantities are required, horseradish should be given a patch of its own where the roots can be lifted and the soil replenished after each harvest. To produce strong, straight roots I found this method in an old gardening book. Make holes 16 in. deep with a crow bar, and drop a piece of horseradish 2–3 in. long with a crown on the top into the hole. Fill the hole up with good rotted manure. This will produce strong straight roots in 2 to 3 years, some of which may be ready in the first year.

Harvesting
Pick leaves young to use fresh, or to dry.

If you have a mature patch of horseradish then the root can be dug up any time for use fresh. Otherwise dig up the roots in fall. Store roots in sand and make sure you leave them in a cool dark place over the winter.

Alternatively, wash, grate or slice, and dry. Another method is to immerse the whole washed roots in white wine vinegar.

companion planting

It is said that when grown near potatoes it improves their disease resistance. However, be careful that it does not take over.

Horseradish dye

other uses

Chop finely into dog food to dispel worms and improve body tone.

Traditionally, spray made from an infusion of the roots protects apple trees against brown rot.

The roots and the leaves produce a yellow dye for natural dyeing.

Slice and infuse in a pan of milk to make a lotion to improve skin clarity.

medicinal

Horseradish is a powerful circulatory stimulant with antibiotic properties. As a diuretic it is effective for lung and urinary infections. It can also help with coughs and sinus congestion. It can also be taken internally for gout and rheumatism, containing as it does potassium, calcium, magnesium and phosphorus. Grate into a poultice and apply externally to chilblains, stiff muscles, sciatica, and rheumatic joints, and to stimulate blood flow.

warning

Overuse may blister the skin. Do not use it if your thyroid function is low or if taking thyroxin. Avoid continuous dosage when pregnant or suffering from kidney problems.

culinary

The reason horseradish is used in sauces, vinegars, and as an accompaniment rather than cooked as a vegetable is that the volatile flavoring oil which is released in grating evaporates rapidly and becomes nothing when cooked. Raw it's a different story. The strongest flavor is from root pulled in the fall. The spring root is comparatively mild. Fresh root contains calcium, sodium, magnesium, and vitamin C, and has antibiotic qualities that are useful for preserving food.

It can be used raw and grated in coleslaw, dips, pickled beets, cream cheese, mayonnaise, and avocado fillings.

The young leaves can be added to salads for a bit of zip.

Make horseradish sauce to accompany roast beef and smoked oily fish.

Avocado with Horseradish Cream

Fresh horseradish root (approx. 6 in. long);
*   preserved horseradish in vinegar can be*
*   substituted. If it is, leave out the lemon juice*
1 tablespoon butter
3 tablespoons fresh breadcrumbs
1 apple
2 teaspoons yogurt
1 teaspoon lemon juice
Pinch of salt and sugar
1 teaspoon chopped fresh chervil
$1/2$ teaspoon each of fresh chopped tarragon
*   and dill*
3 to 4 tablespoons heavy cream
2 avocados (ripe) cut in half, pits removed

Peel and grate the horseradish. Melt the butter and add the breadcrumbs. Fry until brown, and add grated horseradish. Remove from heat and grate the apple into the mixture. Add yogurt, lemon juice, salt, sugar, and herbs. Put aside to cool. Chill in refrigerator. Just before serving gently fold the cream into the mixture and spoon into the avocado halves. Serve with green salad and brown toast.

Arnica chamissonis Less.
ARNICA

Also known as Mountain tobacco, Leopards bane, Mountain arnica, Wolfsbane, and Mountain daisy. From the family Asteraceae.

It is found wild in the mountainous areas of Canada, North America, and in Europe, where it is a protected species. Bees love it.

The name *Arnica* is said to be derived from the word *ptarmikos*, Greek for "sneezing." One sniff of arnica can make you sneeze.

The herb was known by Methusalus and was widely used in the 16th century in German folk medicine. Largely as a result of exaggerated 18th-century claims by Venetian physicians, it was, for a short time, a popular medicine.

 varieties

Arnica chamissonis
Arnica
Hardy perennial. Ht 1–2 ft., spread 6 in. Large, single, scented yellow flowers throughout summer. Oval, hairy, light green leaves. **Zone 4**

 cultivation

Propagation
Seed
Sow the small seed in spring or fall in either a pot, plug module, or seed tray, and cover with perlite. Place trays in a cold frame as heat will inhibit germination. The seed is slow to germinate, even occasionally as long as 2 years! Once the seedlings are large enough, pot them up and harden them off in a cold frame.

You can get a more reliable germination if you collect the seed yourself and sow no later than early fall. After potting up, winter the young plants under protection. They will die back in winter. Plant out in the following spring, when the soil has warmed up, 1 ft. from other plants.

Division
Arnica's root produces creeping rhizomes, which are easy to divide in spring. This is much more reliable than sowing seed.

Pests and Diseases
Caterpillars and slugs sometimes eat the leaves.

Maintenance
Spring Sow seeds. Divide creeping rhizomes.
Summer Deadhead if necessary. Harvest plant for medicinal use.
Fall Collect seeds and either sow immediately or store in an airtight container for sowing in the spring.
Winter Note the position in the garden because the plants die right back.

Garden Cultivation
Being a mountainous plant, it is happiest in a sandy acid soil, rich in humus, and in a sunny position. Arnica is a highly ornamental plant with a long flowering season. It is ideally suited for large rock gardens, or the front of a border bed.

Arnica chamissonis Less.

Harvesting
Pick flowers for medicinal use in summer, just before they come into full flower. For drying, pick in full flower, with stalks. Collect leaves for drying in summer before flowering. Dig up roots of second/third year growth after the plant has fully died back in late fall/early winter for drying.

 medicinal

Arnica is a famous herbal and homeopathic remedy. A tincture of flowers can be used in the treatment of sprains, wounds, and bruises, and also to give relief from rheumatic pain and chilblains, if the skin is not broken. Homeopaths say that it is effective against epilepsy and sea sickness, and possibly as a hair growth stimulant. It has also been shown to be effective against salmonella.

 warning

Do not take arnica internally except under supervision of a qualified herbalist or homeopath. External use may cause skin rash or irritation. Never apply to broken skin.

 other uses

Leaves and roots smoked as herbal tobacco, hence the name Mountain tobacco.

Artemisia abrotanum

SOUTHERNWOOD

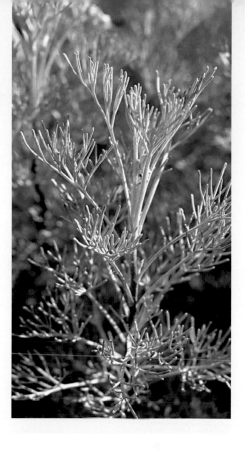

Also known as Lad's love and Old man. From the family Asteraceae.

This lovely aromatic plant is a native of southern Europe. It has been introduced to many countries and is now naturalized widely in temperate zones.

The derivation of the genus name is unclear. One suggestion is that it honors Artemisia, a famous botanist and medical researcher, sister of King Mausolus (353 CE). Another is that it was named after Artemis or Diana, the Goddess of the Hunt and Moon.

In the 17th century, Culpeper recommended that the ashes of southernwood be mingled with salad oil as a remedy for baldness.

 ## varieties

Artemisia abrotanum
Southernwood
Deciduous or semi-evergreen hardy perennial. Ht and spread 3 ft. Tiny insignificant clusters of dull yellow flowers in summer. The abundant olive-green feathery leaves are finely divided and carry a unique scent.

 ## cultivation

Propagation
Seed
Flowers in the central U.S. and further south with a warm climate.

Cuttings
Take softwood cuttings in spring from the lush new growth, or from semi-hardwood cuttings in summer. Use a standard seed compost mixed in equal parts with composted fine bark. Roots well. It can be wintered as a rooted cutting, when it sheds its leaves and is dormant. Keep the cuttings on the dry side, and in early spring slowly start watering. Plant out 2 ft. apart after the frosts have finished.

Pests and Diseases
It is free from the majority of pests and diseases.

Maintenance
Spring Cut back to maintain shape. Take cuttings.
Summer Take cuttings.
Fall Trim any flowers off as they develop.
Winter Protect the roots in hard winters with mulch.

Garden Cultivation
Southernwood prefers a light soil containing well-rotted organic material in a sunny position. However tempted you are by its bedraggled appearance in winter (hence its name, Old man) don't cut hard back as you may kill it. This growth protects its woody stems from cold winds. Cut the bush hard in spring to keep its shape, but only after the frosts have finished.

Harvesting
Pick leaves during the growing season for use fresh
Pick leaves for drying in midsummer.

 ## medicinal

It can be used for expelling worms and to treat coughs and bronchial catarrh. A compress helps to treat frost bite, cuts and grazes.

 ## culinary

The leaves can be used in salads. They have a strong flavor, so use sparingly. It also makes a good aromatic vinegar

 ## other uses

The French call it Garde Robe, and use it as a moth repellent. It is a good fly deterrent, too — hang bunches up in the kitchen, or rub it on the skin to deter mosquitoes.

 ## warning

No product containing southernwood should be taken during pregnancy.

WORMWOOD

Artemisia absinthium

Artemisia absinthium

Also known as Absinthe and Green ginger. From the family Asteraceae.

A native of Asia and Europe, including Britain, it was introduced into America as a cultivated plant and is now naturalized in many places. Found on waste ground, especially near the sea in warmer regions.

Legend has it that as the serpent slithered out of Eden, wormwood first sprang up in the impressions on the ground left by its tail. Another story tells that in the beginning it was called *Parthenis absinthium*, but Artemis, Greek goddess of chastity, benefited so much from it that she named it after herself — *Artemisia absinthium*. The Latin meaning of *absinthium* is "to desist from," which says it all.

Although it is one of the most bitter herbs known, it has for centuries been a major ingredient of aperitifs and herb wines. Both absinthe and vermouth get their names from this plant, the latter being an 18th-century French variation of the German *wermut*, itself the origin of the English name wormwood.

Wormwood was hung by the door where it kept away evil spirits and deterred night-time visitations by goblins. It was also made a constituent of ink to stop mice eating old letters.

It was used as a strewing herb to prevent fleas, hence:

> *"White wormwood hath seed, get a handful or twaine,*
> *to save against March, to make flea to refrain.*
> *Where chamber is sweeped and wormwood is strewn,*
> *no flea for his life, dare abide to be knowne."*

This extract comes from Thomas Tusser's *Five Hundred Pointes of Good Husbandrie*, written in 1573.

Finally, wormwood is believed to be the herb that Shakespeare had in mind when his Oberon lifted the spell from Titania with "the juice of Dian's bud," Artemis being known to the Romans as Dian or Diana.

 varieties

Artemisia absinthium
Wormwood
Partial-evergreen hardy perennial. Ht 3 ft., spread 4 ft. Tiny, yellow, insignificant flowerheads are borne in sprays in summer. The abundant leaves are divided, aromatic and gray/green in color. **Zone 5.**

Artemisia absinthium "Lambrook Silver"
Evergreen hardy perennial. Ht 32 in., spread 20 in. Tiny, gray, insignificant flowerheads are borne in long panicles in summer. The abundant leaves are finely divided, aromatic and silver/gray in color. May need protecting in exposed sites. **Zone 6.**

Artemisia pontica
Old Warrior
Evergreen hardy perennial. Ht 24 in., spread 12 in. Tiny, silver/gray insignificant flowerheads are borne on tall spikes in summer. The abundant, feathery, small leaves are finely divided, aromatic and silver/gray in color. This can, in the right conditions, be a vigorous grower, spreading well in excess of 12 in. **Zone 5.**

Artemisia "Powis Castle"
Evergreen hardy perennial. Ht 36 in., spread 4 ft. Tiny, grayish-yellow insignificant flowerheads are borne in sprays in summer. The abundant leaves are finely divided, aromatic and silver/gray in color. **Zone 6.**

cultivation

Propagation

Seed

Of the species mentioned above, only wormwood is successfully grown from seed. It is extremely small and best started off under protection. Sow in spring in a prepared seed or plug tray, using a standard seed compost mixed in equal parts with composted fine bark. Cover the seeds with perlite and propagate with heat, 60–70°F. Plant out when the seedlings are large enough to handle and have had a period of hardening off.

Cuttings

Take softwood cuttings from the lush new growth in early summer; semi-hardwood in late summer. Use a seed compost mixed in equal parts with perlite.

Division

As they are all vigorous growers, division is a good idea at least every 3 to 4 years to keep the plant healthy, to stop it becoming woody and to prevent encroaching. Dig up the plant in spring or fall, divide the roots and replant in a chosen spot.

Pests and Diseases

Wormwood can suffer from a summer attack of blackfly. If it gets too bad, use a liquid insecticidal soap, following manufacturer's instructions.

Maintenance

Spring Sow seeds. Divide established plants. Trim new growth for shape.
Summer Take softwood cuttings.
Fall Prune back semi-hardwood cuttings to within 6 in. of the ground. Divide established plants.
Winter Protect in temperatures below 23°F. Cover with a floating row cover, straw, bark, anything that can be removed in the following spring.

Garden Cultivation

Artemisias like a light well-drained soil and sunshine, but will adapt well to ordinary soils provided some shelter is given. Planting distance depends on spread.

Wormwood is an overpoweringly flavored plant and it does impair the flavor of dill and cilantro so do not plant nearby.

Harvesting

Pick flowering tops just as they begin to open. Dry. Pick leaves for drying in summer.

 ## container growing

Artemisia absinthium "Lambrook Silver" and *Artemisia pontica* (old warrior) look very good in terracotta containers. Use a soil-based compost mixed in equal parts with composted fine bark. Only feed in the summer; if you feed too early the leaves will lose their silvery foliage and revert to a more green look. In winter keep watering to the absolute minimum and protect from hard frosts.

 ## other uses

Wormwood can produce a yellow dye.

Antiseptic vinegar

This vinegar is known as the "Four Thieves" because it is said that thieves used to rub their bodies with it before robbing plague victims.

1 tablespoon wormwood
1 tablespoon lavender
1 tablespoon rosemary
1 tablespoon sage
4½ cups vinegar

Put the crushed herbs into an earthenware container. Pour in the vinegar. Cover the container and leave it in a warm sunny place for 2 weeks. Strain into bottles with tight-fitting, non-metal lids. This makes a very refreshing tonic in the bath, or try sprinkling it on countertops in the kitchen.

Moth-Repellent

Wormwood or southernwood can be used for keeping moths and other harmful insects away from clothes. The smell is sharp and refreshing and does not cling to your clothes like camphor moth-balls. Mix the following ingredients well and put into small sachets.

2 tablespoons dried wormwood or southernwood
2 tablespoons dried lavender
2 tablespoons dried mint

 ## medicinal

True to its name, wormwood expels worms, especially round- and threadworms.

 ## warning

Not to be taken internally without medical supervision. Habitual use causes convulsions, restlessness and vomiting. Overdose causes vertigo, cramps, intoxication and delirium. Pure wormwood oil is a strong poison, although with a proper dosage there is little danger.

Artemisia dracunculus
TARRAGON

Also known as Estragon. From the family Asteraceae.

A native of southern Europe, tarragon is now found in dry areas of North America, Southern Asia and Siberia.

***Dracunculus* means "little dragon." Its naming could have occurred (via the Doctrine of Signatures) as a result of the shape of its roots, or because of its fiery flavor. It was certainly believed to have considerable power to heal bites from snakes, serpents and other venomous creatures. In ancient times the mixed juices of tarragon and fennel made a favorite drink for the Kings of India.**

In the reign of Henry VIII, tarragon made its way into English gardens, and the rhyme, "There is certain people, and certain herbs, that good digestion disturbs," could well be associated with tarragon. I love, too, the story that Henry VIII divorced Catherine of Aragon for her reckless use of tarragon.

 cultivation

Propagation
Seed
Only the Russian and wild varieties produce viable seed. A lot of growers are propagating and selling it to the unsuspecting public as French tarragon. If you really want Russian tarragon, sow the small seed in spring, into prepared seed or plug module trays, using a standard seed compost mixed in equal parts with composted fine bark. No extra heat required. When the young plants are large enough to handle, transfer to the garden, 24 in. apart.

Cuttings
Both French and Russian tarragon can be propagated by cuttings.

Dig up the underground runners in spring when the frosts are finished; pull them apart, do not cut. You will notice growing nodules: these will reproduce in the coming season. Place a small amount of root (3–4 in.) each with a growing nodule, in a 3 in. pot, and cover with compost. Use a seed compost mixed in equal parts with perlite and place in a warm, well-ventilated spot. Keep watering to a minimum. When well-rooted, plant out in the garden after hardening off, 24 in. apart.

It is possible to take softwood cuttings of the growing

Artemisia dracunculus

 varieties

Artemisia dracunculus French
French Tarragon
Half-hardy perennial. Ht 3 ft., spread 18 in. Tiny, yellow, insignificant flowerheads are borne in sprays in summer but rarely produce ripe seed sets except in warm climates. The leaves are smooth dark green, long and narrow, and have a very strong flavor. **Zone 3.**

Artemisia dranunculus Russian
Russian Tarragon
Hardy perennial. Ht 4 ft., spread 18 in. Tiny, yellow insignificant flowerheads borne in sprays in summer. The leaves are slightly coarser and green in color, their shape long and narrow. This plant originates from Siberia, which explains why it is so hardy. **Zone 3.**

Artemisia dracunculus

tips in summer. Keep the leaves moist, but the compost on the dry side. It works best under a misting unit with a little bottom heat 60°F.

Division
Divide established plants of either variety in the spring.

Pests and Diseases

Recently there has been a spate of rust developing on French tarragon. When buying a plant, look for tell-tale signs — small rust spots on the underneath of a leaf. If you have a plant with rust, dig it up, cut off all foliage carefully, and discard the leaves. Wash the roots free from soil, and repot into fresh sterile soil. If this fails, place the dormant roots in hot water after washing off all the compost. The temperature of the water should be 111°F; over 114°F will damage the root. Leave the roots in the hot water for 10 minutes then replant in a new place in the garden.

Maintenance

Spring Sow Russian tarragon seeds if you must. Divide established plants. Take root cuttings.
Summer Remove flowers.
Fall Repot pieces of French tarragon root as insurance.
Winter Protect French tarragon. As the plant dies back into the ground in winter it is an ideal candidate for either a floating row cover, straw or a deep mulch.

Garden Cultivation

French tarragon has the superior flavor of the two and is the most tender. It grows best in a warm dry position, and will need protection in winter. It also dislikes humid conditions. The plant should be renewed every 3 years because the flavor deteriorates as the plant matures.

Russian tarragon is fully hardy and will grow in any conditions. There is a myth that it improves the longer it is grown in one place. This is untrue, it gets coarse. It is extremely tolerant of most soil types, but prefers a sunny position, 2 ft. away from other plants.

Harvesting

Pick sprigs of French tarragon early in the season to make vinegar. Pick leaves for fresh use throughout the growing season. For freezing it is best to pick the leaves in the midsummer months.

 ## container growing

French tarragon grows well in containers. Use a soilless compost mixed in equal parts with composted fine bark. As it produces root runners, choose a container to give it room to grow so that it will not become pot bound. At all times make sure the plant is watered, and in the daytime, not at night. It hates having wet roots. Keep feeding to a minimum: overfeeding produces fleshy leaves with a poor flavor, so be stingy. In winter, when the plant is dormant, do not water, keep the compost dry and the container in a cool, frost-free environment.

 ## medicinal

No modern medicinal use. Formerly used for toothache. Traditionally, a tea made from the leaves is said to overcome insomnia.

 ## culinary

Without doubt French tarragon is among the Rolls-Royces of the culinary herb collection. Its flavor promotes appetite and complements so many dishes — chicken, veal, fish, stuffed tomatoes, rice dishes and salad dressings, and of course is the main ingredient of sauce béarnaise.

Chicken Salad with Tarragon and Grapes
Serves 4 to 6

4½ cups cooked chicken
⅔ cup mayonnaise
⅓ cup heavy whipping cream
1 heaping teaspoon fresh chopped tarragon
  (½ teaspoon dried)
3 scallions, finely minced
1 small lettuce
½ cup green grapes (seedless)
A few sprigs watercress
Salt and freshly ground black pepper

Remove the skin from the chicken and all the chicken from the bones. Slice the meat into longish pieces and place in a bowl.

In another bowl mix the mayonnaise with the cream, the chopped tarragon, and the finely minced scallions. Pour this mixture over the chicken and mix carefully together. Arrange the lettuce on a dish and spoon on the chicken mixture. Arrange the grapes and the watercress around it. Serve with baked potatoes or rice salad.

ORACH

Atriplex hortensis

Atriplex hortensis var. *rubra*

From the family Chenopodiaceae.

The garden species of orach, *Atriplex hortensis*, originated in Eastern Europe and is now widely distributed in countries with temperate climates. In the past it was called mountain spinach and grown as a vegetable in its own right.

The red form, *Atriplex hortensis* var. *rubra*, is still eaten frequently in Continental Europe, particularly with game, and was used as a flavoring for breads.

The common orach, *Atriplex patula*, was considered a poor man's pot herb, which is a fact worth remembering when you are pulling out this invasive annual weed.

 varieties

Atriplex hortensis
Orach
Hardy annual. Ht 5 ft., spread 12 in. Tiny greenish (boring) flowers in summer. Green triangular leaves.

Atriplex hortensis var. rubra
Red Orach
Hardy annual. Ht 4 ft., spread 12 in. Tiny reddish (boring) flowers in summer. Red triangular leaves.

Atriplex patula
Common Orach
Hardy annual. Ht 3 ft., spread 12 in. Flowers similar to orach, the leaves more spear-shaped and smaller.

 cultivation

Propagation
Seed
For an early supply of leaves, sow under protection in early spring, into prepared plug module trays. Cover with perlite. When the seedlings are large enough and after hardening off, plant out into a prepared site 10 in. apart. Alternatively, in late spring, when the soil has started to warm and all threat of frost has passed, sow in rows 2 ft. apart, thinning to 10 in. apart when the seedlings are large enough. As this herb grows rapidly and the leaves can become

Atriplex hortensis

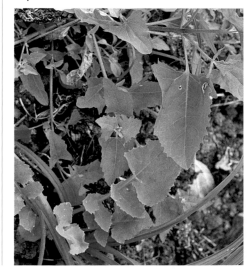

tough, it is advisable to sow a second crop in midsummer to ensure a good supply of young and tender leaves.

Pests and Diseases

Mostly pest and disease free, but it can suffer from leaf minor damage; bin or burn all affected leaves.

Maintenance

Spring Sow seeds.
Summer Cut flowers before they form.
Fall Cut seeds off before they are fully ripe to prevent too much self-seeding.
Winter Dig up old plants.

Garden Cultivation

This annual herb produces the largest and most succulent leaves when the soil is rich. So prepare the site with well-rotted manure. For red orach choose a site with partial shade as the leaves can scorch in very hot summers. Water well throughout the growing season. Red orach looks very attractive grown as an instant hedge or garden divider. Remove the flowering tips as soon as they appear. This will help to maintain the shape and, more importantly, prevent the plant from self-seeding. If you wish to save some seed for the following season, collect before it is fully ripe, otherwise you will have hundreds of orach babies all over your garden and next door.

Harvesting

Pick young leaves to use fresh as required. The herb does not dry or freeze particularly well.

 ## container growing

The red-leaved orach looks very attractive in containers; don't let it get too tall. Nip out the growing tip and the plant will bush out, and do not let it flower. Use a good potting compost. Keep the plant in semi-shade in high summer and water well at all times. If watering in high sun be careful not to splash the leaves as they can scorch, especially the red variety.

 ## medicinal

This herb is no longer used medicinally. In the past it was a home remedy for sore throats, gout and jaundice.

 ## culinary

The young leaves can be eaten raw in salads, and the red variety looks most attractive. The old leaves of both species ought to be cooked as they become slightly tough and bitter. It can be used as a substitute for spinach or as a vegetable, served in a white sauce. It is becoming more popular in Europe, where it is used in soups.

Red Orach Soup

1 pound potatoes
1 cup young red orach leaves
¼ cup butter
3½ cups chicken broth
1 clove garlic, crushed
Salt and freshly ground black pepper
4 tablespoons sour cream

Peel the potatoes and cut them into thick slices. Wash the orach and cut up coarsely. Cook the potatoes for 10 minutes in salted water, drain. Melt the butter in a pot with the crushed garlic and slowly sweeten; add the red orach leaves and gently simmer for 5 to 10 minutes until soft (if the leaves are truly young then 5 minutes will be sufficient).

Pour in the broth, add the parboiled potatoes and bring to a boil; simmer for an additional 10 minutes. When all is soft, cool slightly then purée in a blender or liquidize.

After blending, return the soup to a clean pan, add salt and pepper to taste and heat slowly (not to boiling). Stir in the sour cream, and serve.

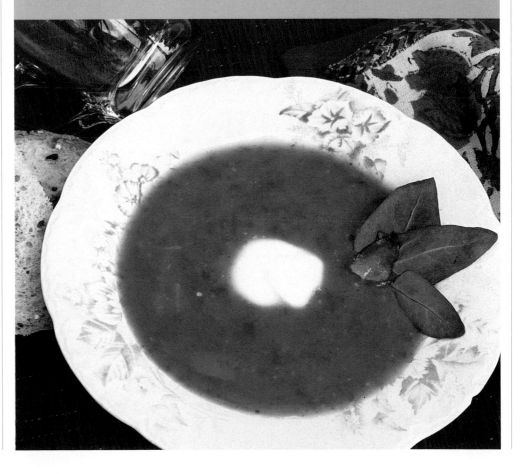

Ballota nigra
BLACK HOREHOUND

Also known as Stinking Horehound, Dunny Nettle, Stinking Roger, and Hairy Hound. From the family Lamiaceae.

Black horehound comes from a genus of about 25 species mostly native to the Mediterranean region. Some species have a disagreeable smell and only a few are worth growing in the garden. Black horehound is found on roadsides, hedge banks and in waste places throughout most of America, Australia, and Europe.

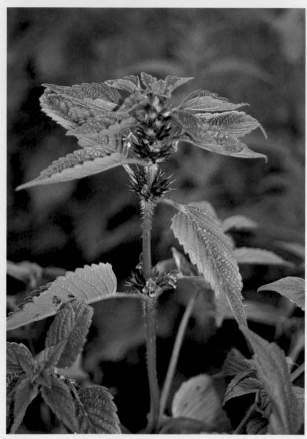

Ballota nigra, the black horehound, was originally called *ballote* by the ancient Greeks. It has been suggested that this comes from the Greek word *ballo*, which means "to reject," "cast," or "throw," because cows and other farm animals with their natural instincts reject it. The origin of the common name is more obscure, it could come from the Anglo-Saxon word *har*, which means "hoar" or "hairy."

 cultivation

Propagation
Seed
Sow the seeds direct into the prepared garden in late summer, thinning to 16 in. apart.

Division
Divide roots in midspring.

Pests and Diseases
Rarely suffers from any pests or diseases.

Maintenance
Spring Dig up established plants and divide; replant where required.
Summer When the plant has finished flowering, cut off the dead heads before the seeds ripen, if you wish to prevent it from seeding itself in the garden.
Fall Sow seed.
Winter No need to protect.

Garden Cultivation
Black horehound will grow in any soil conditions, though it prefers water-retentive soil. It tolerates full sun or part shade. In the garden, place it in a border. The bees love it and the flowers are attractive. Make sure it is far enough back so that you do not brush it by mistake because it does stink.

Harvesting
As this is a herbalist's herb, the leaves should be collected before flowering and dried with care.

 container growing

Not recommended, as it is such an unpleasant-smelling plant.

 medicinal

Black horehound was used apparently in the treatment of bites from mad dogs. A dressing was prepared from the leaves and laid on the infected part. This was said to have an antispasmodic effect. This is not an herb to be self-administered. Professionals use it as a sedative, antiemetic and to counteract vomiting in pregnancy.

 varieties

Ballota nigra
Black Horehound
Hardy perennial. Ht 16–40 in., spread 12 in. Purple-pink attractive flowers in summer. The leaves are green and medium-sized, rather like those of the stinging nettle. All parts of the plant are hairy and have a strong, disagreeable smell and taste. **Zone 4.**

Ballota pseudodictamnus
Half-hardy perennial. Ht 24 in., spread 12 in. White flowers with numerous purple spots in summer. Leaves white and woolly. This plant originated from Crete. The dried calyces look like tiny furry spinning tops; they were used as floating wicks in primitive oil lamps. **Zone 7.**

Bellis perennis

ENGLISH DAISY

Also known as Bruisewort, Eye of the Day, Common Daisy, English Daisy, and Barinwort. From the family Asteraceae.

This humble, attractive flower, beloved by generations of children, was traditionally used medicinally by eminent herbalists such as Gerard who, in the 17th century, called it bruisewort and used it as a cure for wounds and disorders of the liver. Currently its medicinal properties as a treatment for bruising are being researched.

 varieties

Bellis perennis
Daisy
Hardy perennial. Ht and spread 6–8 in. Numerous small flowers with yellow centers, white petals with a pink blush to the tips. Basal rosette of spoon-shaped, scalloped midgreen leaves. **Zone 3.**

Bellis perennis "Alba Plena"
Double-flowered Daisy
Hardy perennial. Ht and spread 6–8 in. Numerous small flowers with yellow centers, double white petals, which often have a pink blush. A basal rosette of spoon-shaped, scalloped midgreen leaves. **Zone 3.**

 cultivation

Propagation
Seed
Sow fresh seed in summer into prepared trays or plug cell-packs, using a standard seed compost. Cover with perlite, no extra heat is needed. Germination takes 10 to 20 days. Once the seedlings are large enough, repot using soilless potting mix. Alternatively plant out into a prepared site in early fall. They will flower in their second season.

The double varieties of the species are, in the majority of cases, sterile and can only be grown by division.

Division
Divide the creeping rhizomes in spring or fall. Once divided, either pot into soilless potting mix or replant into a prepared site in the garden.

Pest and Diseases
Rarely suffers in the garden from any pest or disease. Can be prone to powdery mildew in containers, this is usually caused by the compost drying out then being overwatered to compensate.

Maintenance
Spring Divide established plants.
Summer Sow fresh seed, deadhead flowers to maintain flowering.
Fall Divide established plants.
Winter No need for protection, fully hardy.

Garden Cultivation
This is a most tolerant plant; it will survive in most soils. When grown in an ideal situation it requires a loam that does not totally dry out in summer, in full sun to partial shade. When it is planted in the lawn it can be happily mown; this will encourage it to continue flowering.

Harvesting
Pick the leaves when young for using in salads. Pick the flowers in bud or just opening for use in salads and desserts. Dig up the roots for medicinal use in fall.

 container growing

Daisies look very attractive in a container. Use a soil-based compost so that it does not totally dry out on hot summer days.

 culinary

New young leaf shoots can be eaten raw or cooked. The flowering buds and flowers, just as they open, can be added to salads; they have a light, honey-bitter flavor which combines well with lettuce. They look most attractive in fruit salads.

 medicinal

An ointment made from the leaves can be applied to external wounds and bruising. A decoction made from the roots can ease the irritation of eczema. It is also used in homeopathic remedies to treat bruising.

 other uses

Traditionally, an insect-repellent spray was made from an infusion of the leaves.

Bellis perennis

Borago officinalis
BORAGE

Also known as Bugloss, Burrage, and Common Bugloss. From the family Boraginaceae.

Borage is indigenous to Mediterranean countries, but has now been naturalized in North America and Northern Europe. In fact one can find escapees growing happily on wasteland.

The origin of the name is obscure. The French *bourrache* is said to derive from an old word meaning "rough" or "hairy," which may describe the leaf, but the herb's beautiful, pure blue flowers are its feature and are supposed to have inspired the painting of the robes of the Madonna, and charmed Louis XIV into ordering the herb to be planted at Versailles.

The herb's Welsh name translates as "herb of gladness"; and in Arabic it is "the father of sweat," which we can accept as borage is a diaphoretic. The Celtic word *borrach* means "courage," however, and in this we have an association more credible by far. The Greeks and Romans regarded borage as both comforting and imparting courage, and this belief so persisted that Gerard was able to quote the tag, *Ego borage gaudia semper ago* in his *Herball*. It was for courage, too, that borage flowers were floated in stirrup cups given to the Crusaders. Clearly, the American Settlers also thought sufficiently highly of borage to take the seed with them on their long adventure. Records of it were found in a seed order of an American in 1631, where it was called burradge.

Borago officinalis "Alba"

 varieties

Borago officinalis
Borage
Hardy annual (very occasionally biennial). Ht 24 in. with hollow, bristly branches and spreading stems. The blue or purplish star-shaped flowers grow in loose racemes from early summer to midfall. The leaves are bristly, oval or oblong. At the base they form a rosette; others grow alternately on either side of the stem.

Borago officinalis 'Alba'
White Borage
Hardy annual. Ht 2 ft. White star-shaped flowers from late spring through summer. Bristly, oval, oblong leaves. Can be used in the same way as *B. officinalis*.

 cultivation

Propagation
Seed
Borage is best grown directly from seed, sown in spring and summer in its final position, as it does not like having its long taproot disturbed. But for an early crop it is as well to start the seeds under protection. In early spring sow singly in small pots. Transplant to final position as soon as possible after hardening off, when the seedling is large enough and all threat of frosts is over.

Pests and Diseases
Blackfly. If you are growing borage as a companion plant this will not worry you, but if it is becoming a nuisance then spray with liquid insecticidal soap.

A disease that can be unsightly at the end of the season, is a form of mildew. Dig the plant up and burn.

BORAGE

Maintenance

Spring Sow seeds. They germinate quickly and plants are fully grown in 5 to 6 weeks.

Summer Sow seeds. Look out for flower heads turning into seeds — collect or destroy if you do not want borage plants all over the garden. Deadhead flowers to prolong flowering season.

Fall As the plants begin to die back collect up the old plants. Do not compost the flower heads or next year you will have a garden full of unwanted borage.

Winter Borage lasts until the first major frost, and some years it is the last flowering herb in the garden.

Garden Cultivation

Borage prefers a well-drained, light, rather poor soil of chalk or sand, and a sunny position. Sow borage seeds 2 in. deep in midspring and again in late spring for a continuous supply of young leaves and flowers. Thin seedlings to 24 in. apart and from other herbs, as they produce lots of floppy growth.

I have used borage as an exhibit plant at flower shows. By continuously deadheading the flowers you can maintain a good supply of flowers for longer.

Harvesting

Pick flowers fresh or for freezing or drying when they are just fully opened. Cut the young leaves fresh throughout summer. They do not dry or freeze very successfully. Collect seed before the plant dies back fully. Store in a light-proof container in a cool place.

 ## companion planting

Borage is a good companion plant. The flower is very attractive to bees, helping with pollination, especially for runner beans and strawberries. Borage also attracts blackfly to itself, theoretically leaving the other plants alone. Equally, if planted near tomatoes it is said to control tomato worm.

 ## container growing

It is not suitable for container-growing indoors. However, when planted outside in large containers (like a half barrel), borage can be very effective combined with other tall plants like oxeye daisies, poppies, and cornflowers.

 ## culinary

Be brave, try a young leaf. It may be hairy, some would say prickly, but once in the mouth the hairs dissolve and the flavor is of cool cucumber. Great cut up in salads, or with cream cheese, or added to yogurt, or even in an egg mayonnaise sandwich. They give a refreshing flavor to cold drinks. Finally fresh leaves are particularly good to use in a salt-free diet as they are rich in mineral salts. Try them combined with spinach or added to ravioli stuffing.

The flowers are exciting tossed in a salad, floated on top of a glass of sweet liqueur, or crystallized for cake decoration. Also excellent as garnish for savory or sweet dishes, and on iced soups.

 ## medicinal

In the 1980s, borage was found to contain G.L.A., gamma linoleic acid, an even more valuable medicinal substance than evening primrose oil. But cultivation problems coincided with a dramatic slump in prices when waste blackcurrant pulp, provided a cheaper and richer source of GLA. So hopes for the future of borage as a commercial crop have diminished recently, but it deserves more medicinal research.

Borage tea is said to be good for reducing high temperatures when taken hot. This is because in inducing sweat, it lowers the fever. This makes it a good remedy for colds and flu, especially when these infect the lungs as it is also good for coughs. Leaves and flowers are rich in potassium and calcium and therefore good blood purifiers and a tonic.

Borage Tea

Small handful of fresh leaves
2 cups boiling water

Simmer for 5 minutes.

Natural Night-cap

3 teaspoons fresh borage leaves
1 cup boiling water
1 teaspoon honey
1 slice lemon

Roughly chop the borage leaves, put them into a warmed cup and pour over the boiling water. Cover with a saucer and leave the leaves to infuse for at least 5 minutes. Strain and add the lemon slice and honey. Drink hot just before retiring to bed.

 ## other uses

Dried flowers add color to potpourris. Children enjoy stringing them together as a necklace. Add to summer flower arrangements.

As a novelty burn the whole plant — nitrate of potash will emit sparks and little explosive sounds like fireworks.

Facial Steam for Dry, Sensitive Skin

Place two handfuls of borage leaves in a bowl. Pour over 5 cups of boiling water. Stir quickly with a wooden spoon. Using a towel as a tent, place your face about 12 in. over the water. Cover your head with towel. Keep your eyes closed and maintain for about 10 to 15 minutes. Rinse your face with tepid cool water. Use a yarrow infusion dabbed on with cotton wool to close pores.

 ## warning

Prolonged use of borage is not advisable. Fresh leaves may cause contact dermititis.

Brassica juncea
BROWN MUSTARD

Also known as Juncea, Brown Mustard, Indian mustard, Mustard Greens, and Chinese Mustard. From the family Brassicaceae.

This herb is mentioned more than once in the Bible; it has been used for thousands of years both medicinally and for culinary purposes.

Historically the Romans used the brown mustard as a pungent salad vegetable and the seeds of black mustard as a spice. The English name "mustard" is said to derive from the Latin, *mustem ardens*, which translates as "burning wine," a reference to the heat of mustard and the French practice of mixing unfermented grape juice with the ground seeds.

Brassica juncea "Rubra"

Brassica juncea "Red Frills"

 ## varieties

Brassica alba
White Mustard, Yellow Mustard
Hardy annual. Ht 12–24 in. Pale yellow flowers in summer followed by long seed pods with pale yellow seeds. Rough, bristly, oval, deeply lobed green leaves.

Brassica juncea
Brown Mustard
Hardy annual. Ht 16–40 in. Clusters of pale yellow flowers in summer followed by long seed pods with brown seed. Oval, lobed, olive-green leaves with pale green veins with crinkled edges.

Brassica juncea "Rubra"
Red mustard
Hardy annual. Ht 12 in. Yellow flowers in summer. Oval, red, purple-tinted leaves with indented edges, pungent mustard flavor. Good in salads and sandwiches.

Brassica juncea "Red Frills"
Mustard Red Frills
Hardy annual. Ht 6 in. Yellow flowers in summer. Attractive dark red, narrow, indented leaves with a mild mustard flavor, great for salads.

Brassica nigra
Black Mustard
Hardy annual. Ht 16–40 in. Pale yellow flowers in summer followed by long seed pods with dark brown seeds. Rough, bristly, oval, lobed green leaves.

 ## cultivation

Propagation
Seed
Sow seeds in the spring for seed and leaf production and the fall for leaf, into pots or plug cell-packs using a standard seed compost. Cover with perlite and place under protection at 60°F. Germination is in 5 to 10 days. Plant out after hardening off at a distance of 8 in. apart. Alternatively sow seeds in late spring or early fall into prepared open ground, when the air temperature does not go below 45°F at night. Germination takes 2 to 3 weeks. Once the seedlings are large enough, thin to 8 in. apart.

Pests and Diseases
All mustards can be attacked by flea beetle, which is a tiny, shiny, dark blue beetle that hops from plant to plant. A tell-tale sign that the plants are being attacked are small round holes on the leaves, which turn pale brown, making the leaves look unattractive. The adult beetles overwinter in leaf litter, emerging in the spring to attack lush seedlings. The other major attack comes in summer when there is a significant migration of adult beetles from oilseed rape fields into gardens; these can come in such numbers that they attack mature plants. The best organic method is to put a floating row cover over the plants so the beetles cannot attack the leaves.

Maintenance
Spring Sow seeds.
Summer Pick leaves and flowers.
Fall Harvest seeds, sow fall crop.
Winter Prepare ground for next season's crop.

Brassica juncea "Red Frills"

BROWN MUSTARD

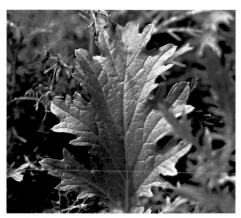

Brassica juncea

Garden Cultivation

All brassicas like to feed well, and mustard is no exception. However, do not become too enthusiastic and give them too much nitrogen, because this will make them soft and flabby and prone to attack from pests. Try and prepare your plant plots the fall before planting. Give the site a good feed of well-rotted manure and compost in the fall prior to sowing in the spring.

Harvesting

Pick young leaves as required and the flowers just as they open. The seed pods are harvested as they change color. Dry the pods in a light airy room until totally dried, remove from the pods and store in clean, dry jars which have a tight-fitting top.

 ## companion planting

Mustard is a good companion plant because it germinates quickly so can be sown next to slow germinators, for example parsley, to indicate the row. There is some evidence that mustard can be grown as a green manure. It is said to be effective in reducing soil-borne root diseases in pea crops.

 ## container growing

Mustard can successfully be grown in a container, using a standard potting compost. Place the container in partial shade. Water and feed regularly from spring until early fall.

 ## medicinal

Mustard has been and is still used to ease muscular pain, and treat respiratory tract infections. It is a warming stimulant with antibiotic effects. In China the leaves are eaten to ease bladder inflammation. In Korea, the seeds are used in the treatment of abscesses, colds, lumbago, rheumatism and stomach disorders. Current research has found that mustard seeds inhibit the growth of cancerous cells in some animal studies.

 ## culinary

The mustard leaves have a distinctive, warm peppery taste; the flowers also have a mild mustard flavor. Both are great in salads, stir-fry dishes, and they can transform a sandwich into a delight. Try a red mustard and ham sandwich.

Mustard seeds only get their pungency when they are crushed. When the seed is mixed with water and allowed to stand, the strength of flavor increases. If you mix the seed directly with vinegar or salt without previously soaking in water, you kill the flavor and if you boil the seed it will become bitter. The easiest and best way to use mustard seed is to make your own mustard. Use a combination of the black, brown and white seeds. This mustard is very versatile, complementing many dishes and enhancing the flavors of cheese, vegetables, poultry, red meat and fish. The seeds are also great added to salad dressings or sauces. When adding mustards to food, remember that the pungency of mustard is destroyed by heat, so add it to finished sauces or stews. Mustards are particularly good when combined with crème frâiche or cream cheese as dips for vegetables or pretzels.

Dill Mustard

1/3 cup black mustard seeds
2 tablespoons white mustard seeds
2 cups water
1/2 cup English mustard powder
2/3 cup cider vinegar
1/4 cup light brown sugar

 ## other uses

Mustard seeds have been suggested as a possible source of biodiesel in Australia.

 ## warning

Mustard seeds have been known to cause an allergic reaction. Prolonged contact with the skin can cause blistering.

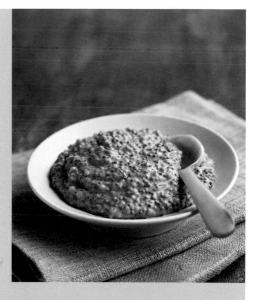

1 1/2 teaspoons salt
1 1/2 teaspoons turmeric
1/4 cup chopped dill, or other herb of your choice.

Place the mustard seed in a china or glass bowl, add in 2 cups water and soak for 24 hours prior to use. The next day add the mustard powder, vinegar, salt, and turmeric. When thoroughly mixed, place the bowl over a pot containing water, ensuring the water does not touch the bottom of the bowl. On a very low heat gently cook the mustard seed for 4 hours, stirring occasionally. Check from time to time that the water has not evaporated and never boil the mixture as the mustard will lose its flavor and become bitter. Once cooked allow to cool, then add the chopped dill. Cover the herb mustard and keep in the refrigerator.

AFRICAN BULBINE

Also known as Burn Jelly Plant, Snake Flower, Cat's Tail, Bulbinella, Ibhucu (Zulu), and Rooiwortel (Afrikaans). From the family Asphodelaceae.

This attractive drought-resistant herb is a native of South Africa and can be found growing wild in the desert grasslands of the Northern, Western and Eastern Capes. Indigenous plants play a pivotal role in Africa for traditional healing; this herb has been used by the Zulu for hundreds of years not only to cure rashes, to stop bleeding and as an antidote to poison, but also to treat their sick livestock.

 varieties

Bulbine frutescens
African Bulbine
Frost-tender, evergreen perennial. Ht 24 in., spread 3 ft. Attractive star-shaped yellow or orange single flowers, which grow in a linear cluster around the stem appearing sequentially throughout the summer. The flower has a characteristic hairy stamen. The leaves are succulent, cylindrical, narrow, and varying in length. They are glutinous when broken. **Zone 9.**

Bulbine latifolia (Bulbine natalensis)
Broad-leaved Bulbine
Frost-tender, evergreen perennial. Ht 24 in., spread 3 ft. Attractive star-shaped yellow flowers which grow on 24 in. flowering spikes throughout the summer. Dark green, aloe-like, pointed, succulent triangular leaves which form a basal crown. **Zone 9.**

 cultivation

Propagation
Seed
Sow fresh seed in spring, into prepared seed trays or module plugs, using a seed compost mixed in equal parts with perlite. Place in a well-shaded area at 68°F. Germination takes 10 to 20 days; however it is erratic as, like many herbs, it will happily self seed in a warm garden but, in a controlled situation, it sometimes will not perform. During germination, make sure that the compost does not dry out. Once the seedling is well-rooted repot using a seed compost mixed in equal parts with horticultural sand. Grow on until the plant has at least four well-developed leaves before either planting out in warm climates into a prepared site in the garden or potting up in cold climates to grow on as a container plant.

Cuttings
This is the easiest method of propagation in a cold climate. Cuttings can be taken from early spring for plants raised under protection or in late spring for plants grown outside. By looking at the plant you will note that it puts down roots where the clusters of leaves touch the soil. Using a sharp knife, take the cutting, removing some root at the same time. Put the cuttings into a small pot or large plug, using a seed compost mixed in equal parts with composted fine

AFRICAN BULBINE

Bulbine frutescens Yellow form

bark. Place the container in a warm position. It will root very quickly. Once the plant is established, either repot using a soilless potting mix mixed in equal parts with horticultural sand or, in warm climates, plant out into a prepared site in the garden.

Division
This plant grows rapidly in a container or garden and benefits from being divided. In spring or early summer, before dividing, remove all the flowering stems; this will make it easier to handle and also to see what one is doing. Divide established garden plants by using the two forks back-to-back method, replanting immediately into a prepared site. Container-raised plants will need to be removed from the pot, then, either using hands or two hand forks, tease the plant apart, repotting into a soilless potting compost mixed in equal parts with horticultural sand.

Pests and Diseases
This herb is rarely troubled by pests or diseases, with the exception of vine weevil if pot grown. There are two methods of getting rid of vine weevil organically. Either repot all the containers, checking each one for vine weevil grubs or, alternatively, watering the containers with a natural predator called *Steinernema krauseii* in late summer, early fall, when the night temperature does not fall

below 50°F and before the vine weevil grubs have grown large enough to cause serious damage. This predator is a nematode, a microscopic worm, which infects the weevil grubs with a fatal bacterial disease. Prior to using this nematode, make sure the compost in the containers is moist all the way down by watering well a few hours before you intend to add the biological control.

Maintenance
Spring In early spring remove flowering spikes, sow fresh seeds and divide established clumps.
Summer Remove flowering spikes that have finished flowering, take cuttings.
Fall Remove flowering spikes.
Winter Do not overwater, but do not allow the compost to become totally dry. Protect when temperatures drop below 32°F.

Garden Cultivation
This herb is a good drought loving plant; it can be planted out in cold climates in the early summer and then lifted before the frosts. Plant in a well-drained fertile soil that was fed with well-rotted manure in the previous spring. Position in full sun or semi-shaded and protected from cold winds.

Harvesting
The leaves can be picked for use throughout the year.

 container growing

This useful attractive herb, which can flower all year round, is ideal for growing in a warm conservatory as it requires a good light. Repot using a soilless potting compost mixed in equal parts with horticultural sand. Water regularly, and feed monthly, from spring until fall, with a liquid fertilizer following the manufacturer's instructions.

 medicinal

The leaves are filled with a clear gel similar in appearance and consistency to *Aloe vera*. This gel can be used directly on minor burns, wounds, cuts, abrasions, stings and rashes. It can also be used to treat eczema, cracked lips and herpes. An infusion or tincture made from the roots of *Bulbine latifolia* is taken to quell sickness and diarrhea, and it is also

used to treat urinary complaints and rheumatism. Currently the medicinal properties of this herb are under research, and the leaf gel is being used to aid the healing of postoperative scars.

 other uses

A red dye can be obtained from the roots of *Bulbine latifolia*.

 warning

Do not take internally when pregnant.

Bulbine frutescens Yellow form

BOXWOOD

Also known as Box and Bushtree. From the family Buxaceae.

Boxwood is a native plant of Europe, Western Asia, and North Africa. It has been cultivated widely throughout the world and is found in North America along the Atlantic coast, especially as an ornamental and hedging plant.

The common name, box, comes from the Latin *buxus*, which is in turn derived from the Greek *puxus*, meaning "a small box." At one time, boxwoods were widespread in Europe but the demand for the wood, which is twice as hard as oak, led to extensive felling. Its timber is close-grained and heavy, so heavy in fact that it is unable to float on water. The wood does not warp and is therefore ideal for boxes, engraving plates, carvings, and musical and navigational instruments.

It is not used medicinally now but the essential oil from boxwood was used for the treatment of epilepsy, syphilis, and piles, and also as an alternative to quinine in the treatment of malaria. A perfume was once made from its bark and a mixture of the leaves with sawdust has been used as an auburn hair dye.

When it rains, boxwood gives off a musky smell evocative of old gardens, delicious to most people, but not Queen Anne who so hated the smell that she had the box parterres in St James's Park (planted for her predecessors, William and Mary, in the last years of the 17th century) torn out.

 varieties

Buxus balearica
Balearic Boxwood – Half-hardy evergreen. Ht 6½ ft., spread 4½ ft. Suitable for hedging in mild areas. Has broadly oval, bright green leaves. Planting distance for a hedge 12–16 in. **Zone 8.**

Buxus microphylla
Small-leaved Boxwood – Hardy evergreen. Ht 3 ft., spread 4½ ft. Forms a dense mass of round/oblong, dark green, glossy leaves. Attractive cultivar "Green Pillow," which is good for formal shaping. Planting distance for a hedge 6–9 in. **Zone 5.**

Buxus sempervirens
Common Boxwood – Hardy evergreen. Ht and spread 15 ft. Leaves glossy green and oblong. Good for hedges, screening, and topiary. Planting distance for a hedge 15–18 in. **Zone 5.**

Buxus sempervirens "Elegantissima"
Variegated Boxwood – Hardy evergreen. Ht and spread 3 ft. Good variegated gold/green leaves. Susceptible to scorch in hard winter. Trim regularly to maintain variegation. Very attractive as a center hedging in a formal garden or as specimen plants in their own right. Planting distance for a hedge 12–16 in. **Zone 5.**

Buxus sempervirens "Latifolia Maculata"
Golden Boxwood – Hardy evergreen. Ht and spread 3 ft. The new growth is very golden, and as it matures it becomes midgreen. Planting distance for a hedge 12–16 in. **Zone 5.**

Buxus sempervirens "Suffruticosa"
Dwarf Boxwood – Hardy evergreen. Ht and spread 18 in. Evergreen dark shrub that forms tight, dense mass. Slow grower. This is the archetypal edging in a formal herb garden for patterns and parterres of the knots. It is trimmed to about 6 in. in height when used for hedging. Planting distance for hedge 6–9 in. **Zone 5.**

Buxus sempervirens 'Latifolia Maculata'

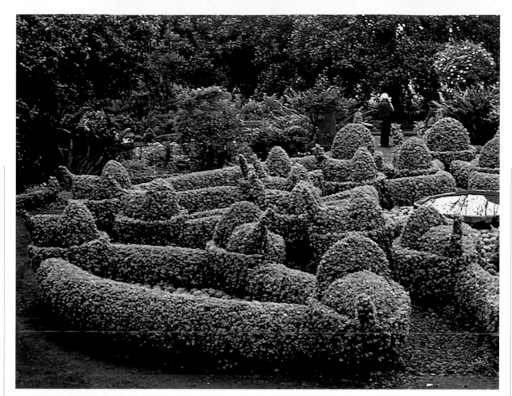

Buxus sempervirens 'Suffruticosa'

Buxus wallichiana

Himalayan Boxwood – Hardy evergreen. Ht and spread 6 ft. Slow growing. Produces long, narrow, glossy, bright green leaves. Planting distance for a hedge 12–16 in. **Zone 6.**

 cultivation

Propagation

Cuttings

Boxwood is cultivated from cuttings taken in spring from the new growth. Use a standard seed compost mixed in equal parts with composted fine bark. Keep the cuttings moist but NOT wet, and in a cool place, ideally in shade. They will take 3 to 4 months to root. If you have a propagator then they will take 6 to 8 weeks at 70°F. Use a spray to mist the plant regularly. When rooted, repot the young plants using a soilless potting mix or plant out, as per the distances mentioned under varieties. Alternatively, take semi-ripe cuttings in summer, using the same compost mix as above. Rooting time is approximately 2 months longer than for the softwood cuttings, but only 3 to 4 weeks longer with heat.

Pests and Diseases

Boxwood can be attacked by the green box sucker nymph, which is noticeable by a white deposit and curled leaves. Cut back the plant, then spray with insecticidal soap. Box blight, *Cylindrocladium buxicola* is a fungal disease that can cause serious defoliation. There is no reliable organic remedy. However, I know of one gardener who cut his boxwood plants back, then fed weekly with an organic fertilizer for one year and it recovered.

Maintenance

Spring Take stem cuttings. Trim fast growers such as *Buxus sempervirens* "Latifolia Maculata."
Summer Take semi-ripe cuttings. Trim hedges to promote new growth.
Fall Trim if needed but not hard.
Winter Does not need protection.

Garden Cultivation

Known for its longevity, it is not uncommon for it to live 600 years. Boxwood flourishes on limestone or chalk; it prefers an alkaline soil. But it is very tolerant of any soil provided it is not waterlogged. Boxwood is also fairly tolerant of position, surviving sun or semi-shade.

Boxwood hedges are a frame for a garden, outlining, protecting and enhancing what they enclose. Because one will be planting the boxwood plants closer together than when planting individual plants it is important first to feed the soil well by adding plenty of well-rotted manure or garden compost. Width of bed for a boundary hedge should be 24 in.; for small internal hedges 12 in. wide. Planting distances vary according to variety (see above).

If using common boxwood or golden boxwood, the more vigorous growers, trim in spring and prune at the end of summer or, in mild climates, in early fall. A late cut may produce soft growth that could be damaged by frost, which would then look ugly in winter. The slower varieties need a cut only in the summer. In general the right shape for a healthy, dense hedge is broad at the bottom, tapering slightly towards the top, rounded or ridged but not too flat, to prevent damage from heavy snow.

 container growing

Boxwood, especially the slow-growing varieties, lends itself to topiary and looks superb in containers. *Buxus sempervirens* "Elegantissima" looks very attractive in a terracotta pot. They are very easy to maintain. Use a soil-based compost. Feed with a liquid fertilizer in spring; water sparingly in winter.

 other uses

Boxwood is a favorite timber with cabinet makers, wood engravers and turners because it has a non-fibrous structure.

A mahogany box with boxwood detailing

 medicinal

It is advisable not to self-administer this plant; it should be used with caution. Boxwood is used extensively in homoeopathic medicines; a tincture prepared from fresh leaves is prescribed for fever, rheumatism, and urinary tract infections.

 warning

Animals have died from eating the leaves. All parts of the plant, especially the leaves and seeds, are poisonous. It is dangerous to take internally and should never be collected or self-administered. Symptoms of poisoning are vomiting, abdominal pain, and bloody diarrhea.

CALAMINT

Calamintha

From the family Lamiaceae.

Calamintha originated in Europe. It is now well established throughout temperate countries, but sadly it is still not a common plant. Calamint has been cultivated since the 17th century. Herbal records show that it used to be prescribed for women.

Calamintha nepeta

 varieties

Calamintha grandiflora
Calamint
Hardy perennial. Ht 15 in, spread 12 in. Square stems arise from creeping rootstock. Dense whorls of lilac pink flowers appear midsummer to early fall above mint-scented, toothed, oval green leaves. **Zone 5.**

Calamintha grandiflora "Variegata"
Hardy perennial. As *C. grandiflora* but with cream variegated leaves. **Zone 6.**

Calamintha nepeta
Lesser Calamint
Perennial. Ht 12–24 in., spread 12 in. Small purple/white flowers from summer to early fall. Stems and leaves pale gray and covered in fine downy hairs. Its wonderful aromatic scent attracts butterflies and bees. **Zone 5.**

Calamintha nepeta

Calamintha sylvatica subsp. ascendens
Mountain Balm, Mountain Mint
Hardy perennial. Ht 12 in., spread 8 in. Pale purple flowers in dense whorls from late summer to early fall. Leaves midgreen, oval, finely toothed and mint scented. A tisane can be made from the leaves. **Zone 5.**

 cultivation

Propagation
Seed
Sow calamint's fine seeds in spring or fall, either in their eventual flowering position or in trays, using a standard seed compost mixed in equal parts with composted fine bark and covered lightly with perlite. If fall sowing in trays leave them outside to overwinter, covered with a sheet of glass. As germination can be tricky, fall sowing is sometimes more successful because subjecting the seeds to all weathers — thereby giving the hot and cold treatment — can trigger the process (stratification, see p. 644). When the seedlings are large enough to handle, prick out and plant up into pots, using a potting compost mixed in equal parts with propagating bark. Alternatively plant them directly into the chosen site in late spring after hardening off.

Cuttings
Take cuttings of young shoots in spring. This is an especially good method for the variegated *grandiflora*. They take easily, but keep in the shade until fully rooted and do not allow to dry out. Plant out in their final position when fully hardened off.

Division
Once the plants are established they can be divided in the spring or fall, either by lifting the whole plant or by the double fork method. Replant immediately either into a prepared site or into pots using a potting compost mixed in equal parts with propagating bark. If this method is chosen in the fall, keep in a cold frame all winter.

Pests and Diseases
Rarely suffers from pests or diseases.

Maintenance
Spring Sow seeds. Take cuttings from new growth.
Summer Cut back after first flowering and keep the plant tidy. Give a feed of liquid fertilizer, which can promote a second flowering.
Fall Sow seeds. Cut back new growth after second flowering.
Winter Protect new growth in frosts below 25°F. Use a floating row cover, bracken, straw, or pine needles.

Garden Cultivation
These plants are indigenous to the limestone uplands and like a sunny position in well-drained soil that is low in nutrients. The leaves of *Calamintha grandiflora* "Variegata" scorch easily and need some shade.

Harvesting
Pick leaves either side of flowering for use fresh or dried.

 container growing

Unsuitable for growing indoors, but can look good in containers outside. Use a potting compost mixed in equal parts with propagating bark and a container with a diameter no less than 5 in. *Calamintha grandiflora* "Variegata" looks particularly striking in a terracotta pot.

 culinary

The young minty leaves of the lesser calamint can be added to salads and used to make a refreshing tea.

 medicinal

Infuse dried leaves as a tea for colic, and an invigorating tonic. Use fresh leaves in a poultice for bruises.

Calamintha nepeta

Calomeria amaranthoides

INCENSE PLANT

From the family Asteraceae.

This fascinating, highly aromatic herb is a native of Australia. Historically this plant came to England via the famous plant collector Sir Joseph Banks who gave some seed to Lady Hume, hence its former name _Humea elegans_, which was only changed in 1993 to _Calomeria amaranthoides_. Sadly it is now rarely grown in parks or large private gardens because of its tendency to cause skin irritation and because of its high pollen count, which can cause asthma attacks.

Pests and Diseases

As a container-grown plant, it suffers from aphids and red spider mite. Keep an eye out for these and use a horticultural liquid soap as soon as they appear.

Maintenance

Spring Prick out first year's plants. Repot second year's.
Summer Feed and water regularly. Collect seeds off second year's plants and sow immediately.
Fall Protect first year's plants.
Winter Protect plants from frost. Keep watering to a minimum.

Garden Cultivation

Do not plant outside until the night temperature no longer falls below 40°F. Plant in an area protected from the wind, even here, a stake is recommended. It prefers a light soil and a sunny position. All in all, it makes a better indoor plant, where the marvellous scent can be enjoyed.

Harvesting

Collect flowers for drying in summer.

 container growing

The incense plant is very ornamental and is the ultimate pot plant, growing to over 5 ft. It is, however, rarely seen because it needs a good deal of attention and protection. Use a good peat-free potting compost mixed in equal parts with composted fine bark. Regularly repot one size of pot at a time and regularly liquid feed throughout its short life until a pot size of 12 in. in diameter is reached. Place in full sun and water regularly throughout the growing season.

 other uses

Use in potpourris.

 varieties

Calomeria amaranthoides (_Humea elegans_)
Incense Plant
Tender biennial (sometimes annual). Ht up to 6 ft., spread 36 in. Tiny, delicate, coral flower bracts, very numerous on large branches. Large, oblong midgreen leaves. **Zone 8.**

 warning

Leaves can cause irritation and the same kind of burns as rue (see p. 387). The scent can cause breathing difficulties and when in flower, it has a high pollen count and can trigger asthma attacks.

 cultivation

Propagation
Seed
Being a biennial, this is grown from the small seed, which is viable for only a short time. Collect from the plants in the summer, when ripe, and sow immediately into prepared seed or plug module trays using a standard seed compost mixed in equal parts with composted fine bark. Leave the seeds uncovered. Overwinter in a cold frame and cover the seed tray with glass or plastic wrap. Germination is lengthy and very erratic. Pot on seedlings as soon as they appear, taking care not to injure the roots. Grow young plants in a cool, frost-free environment, and keep the roots almost dry through winter. In spring gradually encourage growth by watering and repotting.

CALENDULA

Calendula officinalis

Also known as Souci, Marybud, Bulls Eye, Holligold, and Pot Marigold. From the family Asteraceae.

Native of the Mediterranean and Iran. Distributed throughout the world as a garden plant.

This sunny little flower — the "merrybuds" of Shakespeare — was first used in Indian and Arabic cultures, before being "discovered" by the ancient Egyptians and Greeks. The Egyptians valued the marigold as a rejuvenating herb, and the Greeks garnished and flavored food with its golden petals. The botanical name comes from the Latin *calendae*, meaning "the first day of the month."

In India wreaths of calendula were used to crown the gods and goddesses. In medieval times they were considered an emblem of love and used as chief ingredient in a complicated spell that promised young maidens knowledge of whom they would marry. To dream of them was a sign of all good things; simply to look at them was thought to drive away evil humors.

In the American Civil War, calendula leaves were used by the doctors on the battlefield to treat open wounds.

Calendula officinalis

 varieties

Calendula officinalis
Marigold
Hardy annual. Ht and spread 24 in. Daisy-like, single or double flowers, yellow or orange: from spring to fall. Light green, aromatic, lance-shaped leaves. **All zones.**

Calendula officinalis Fiesta Gitana Group
Hardy annual. Ht and spread 12 in. Daisy-like, double flowers, yellow and/or deep orange: from spring to fall. Light green, lance-shaped leaves. **All zones.**

 cultivation

Propagation
Seeds
Sow in fall under protection directly into prepared pots or singly into plug module trays, in a standard seed compost mixed with equal parts composted fine bark, covering lightly with compost. Plant out in the spring after any frost, 12–18 in. apart. Alternatively in spring sow direct onto a prepared site in the garden.

Pests and Diseases
Slugs love the leaves of young calendulas. Keep night-time vigil with a torch and a bucket, or lay beer

CALENDULA

Calendula officinalis Fiesta Gitana Group

traps. In the latter part of the season, plants can become infested with blackfly. Treat in the early stages by brushing them off and cutting away the affected areas, or later on by spraying with a insecticidal soap. Very late in the season the leaves sometimes become covered with a powdery mildew, which should be removed and burnt.

Maintenance
Spring Sow seeds in the garden.
Summer Deadhead to promote more flowering.
Fall Sow seeds under protection for early spring flowering.
Winter Protect young plants.

Garden Cultivation
Calendula is a very tolerant plant, growing in any soil that is not waterlogged, but prefers, and looks best in, a sunny position. The flowers are sensitive to variations of temperature and dampness. Open flowers forecast a fine day. Encourage continuous flowering by deadheading. It self-seeds abundantly but seems never to become a nuisance.

Harvesting
Pick flowers just as they open during summer, both for fresh use and for drying. Dry at a low temperature. Pick leaves young for fresh use; they are not much good preserved.

Dried flowers make a colorful oil

container growing

Calendulas look very cheerful in containers and combine well with other plants. Well suited to window boxes, but not so in hanging baskets, where they will become stretched and leggy. Use a standard potting compost mixed in equal parts with composted fine bark. Pinch off the growing tips to stop the plant from becoming too tall and leggy. Deadhead flowers to encourage more blooms.

medicinal

Calendula flowers contain antiseptic, antifungal and antibacterial properties that promote healing. Make a compress or poultice of the flowers for burns, scalds, or stings. Also useful in the treatment of varicose veins, chilblains, and impetigo. A cold infusion may be used as an eyewash for conjunctivitis, and can be a help in the treatment of thrush. The sap from the stem has a reputation for removing warts, corns and calluses.

other uses

There are many skin and cosmetic preparations that contain calendula. Infuse the flowers and use as a skin lotion to reduce large pores, nourish and clear the skin, and clear up spots and pimples. The petals make a pale yellow dye (see p. 675).

culinary

Flower petals make a very good culinary dye. They have been used for butter and cheese, and as a poor man's saffron to color rice. They are also lovely in salads and omelets, and make an interesting cup of tea. Young leaves can be added to salads.

Sweet Calendula Buns
Makes 18

½ cup softened butter
½ cup superfine sugar, plus extra to sprinkle
2 eggs
½ cup self-rising flour
1 teaspoon baking powder
2 tablespoons fresh calendula petals

Put the butter, sugar, eggs, sifted flour, and baking powder into a bowl, and mix together until smooth and glossy. Fold in 1½ tablespoons of calendula petals. Turn the mixture into greased bun tins or individual paper cake cases. Sprinkle a few petals onto each bun with a little sugar. Bake in an oven 325°F for approximately 25 to 30 minutes.

Capparis spinosa
CAPER

Also known as Caper Bush, Kapparis, Tápara, Umabusane. From the family *Capparaceae*.

This trailing evergreen shrub is now naturalized in the Mediterranean but probably originated in the Middle East. It can be seen in the most unlikely places, from the ruins of ancient walls to the rubble alongside a newly built hotel. The Greek name *kapparis* is from the Persian *kabar*, hence "caper." The first recorded use of the caper bush was for medicinal purposes in 2000 BCE by the Sumerians. Since then it has been used not only medicinally, but also as a useful condiment in the kitchen.

 varieties

Capparis spinosa
Caper

Tender evergreen shrub. Ht up to 3 ft., spread up to 4½ ft. Masses of green buds (it is these that are pickled) are followed by very pretty solitary white, four-petalled flowers with long pink/purple stamens from early summer until fall. Leaves are oval, mid-green with a hint of brown, with two spines at the base of the leaf. The leaves grow on long stems which have been known to reach over 4½ ft. in length. **Zone 9.**

Capparis spinosa var. *inermis*
Spineless caper

Tender evergreen shrub. Ht and spread up to 4½ ft. Masses of edible green buds followed by solitary white four-petalled flowers with long pink/purple stamens from early summer until fall. Leaves are oval, midgreen with a hint of brown. **Zone 9.**

 cultivation

Propagation
Seed

Caper seeds are miniscule, and once germinated they take a long time to grow into transplantable seedlings. Fresh caper seeds germinate readily but only in low percentages. Once the seeds dry they become dormant and are notably more difficult to germinate, so patience is required. Start by immersing the dried seeds in hot water, 105°F, and leave to soak for 1 day. Carefully remove the seeds. Place them on some damp white kitchen towel, which makes them easier to see. Then put them into a sealed container and keep in the refrigerator for 2 to 3 months. After refrigeration, soak the seeds again in warm water overnight and then sow into prepared cell-packs, plug trays, filled with a seed compost mixed in equal parts with perlite. Sow the seeds on the surface of the compost and cover with perlite. Keep warm at a minimum of 50°F. Plants raised from seed will not flower until their fourth or fifth year.

Cuttings

The best and most reliable method is to raise plants

Capparis spinosa var. *inermis*

from cuttings. Take cuttings from the new spring growth. Put them into prepared cell-packs or plug trays filled with seed compost mixed in equal parts with composted fine bark for extra drainage. Put the tray on a heated propagator at 65°F, making sure the cuttings do not dry out. Once well-rooted repot using a soilless potting mix mixed in equal parts with propagating bark.

Pests and Diseases

This herb is rarely attacked by pests. Young cuttings and seedlings can keel over if the watering is too much or too little.

Maintenance

Spring Take cuttings.
Summer Harvest flowering buds.
Fall Sow fresh seed.
Winter Protect from excessive wet in winter.

Garden Cultivation

A simple rule of thumb is that the caper bush can be planted where the olive tree grows. It will thrive in lean, well-drained soil in a hot, sunny location with little or no water. It hates damp, cold, wet winters so if you live in northern Europe you will need to grow it in a container and place the container in a sheltered position for the winter. As an ornamental plant caper bushes can be an attractive loose groundcover, a specimen small shrub can be used as an espalier, which presents the flower buds well for picking. The caper bush is salt-tolerant and will flourish along shores. As flowers are borne on first-year branches, cut back plants back annually in the fall. It tolerates the cold down to 18°F, however the growing tips can be damaged even in slight frost. The damaged growing tips can be cut off in the spring.

Harvesting

The flower buds are picked early in the morning for pickling and salting. The roots are dug up in fall, the bark is then stripped from the roots and dried prior to use.

 ## container growing

If the plant is pruned well in the fall it will look wonderful growing in a container. For ease and self preservation, I advise growing the spineless variety, *Capparis spinosa* var. *inermis*. Repot using a soilless compost mixed in equal parts with horticultural grit.

 ## culinary

Throughout the Mediterranean you can buy fresh capers from the vegetable markets and stores from early summer for a few months. They are bright green tightly closed flower buds, the smallest having the best flavor. However, when eaten fresh they do not taste particularly good; the flavor comes only after they have been pickled. This is due to the development of an organic acid called capric acid, which is an important flavoring in the kitchen. When you buy capers fresh they will still have the stems attached, so remove them, place the capers on a plate or tray, cover with sea salt and each time you pass the plate, give it a shake. After 2 days place them in a colander and rinse well under running water. Pack the capers into jars, add a few fennel seeds to each jar and a few immature flowers. Fill the jar up with white wine vinegar and seal with a non-metallic top. Leave for a month before use.

 ## medicinal

The parts used medicinally are the bark from the roots and the flower buds. The bark is used to treat diarrhea and rheumatism. In South Africa the roots are reputedly used to treat insanity, snake bites, chest pains, jaundice and malaria. The buds are used to treat coughs.

 ## warning

Capparis spinosa has incredibly sharp spines: wear gloves when handling this plant.

The attractive stamens of *Capparis spinosa*

Carum carvi
CARAWAY

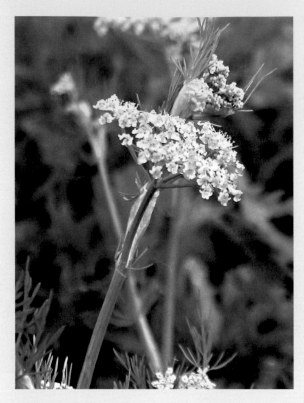

From the family Apiaceae.

Caraway is a native of Southern Europe, Asia, and India and thrives in all but the most humid warm regions. It is commercially and horticulturally cultivated on a wide scale, especially in Germany and Holland.

Both the common and species names stem directly from the ancient Arabic word for the seed, *karawya*, which was used in medicines and as a flavoring by the ancient Egyptians. In fact fossilized caraway seeds have been discovered at Mesolithic sites, so this herb has been used for at least 5,000 years. It has also been found in the remains of Stone Age meals, Egyptian tombs, and ancient caravan stops along the Silk Road.

Caraway probably did not come into use in Europe until the 13th century, but it made a lasting impact. In the 16th century when Shakespeare, in *Henry IV*, gave Falstaff a pippin apple and a dish of caraways, his audience could relate to the dish, for caraway had become a traditional finish to an Elizabethan feast. Its popularity was further enhanced 250 or so years later when Queen Victoria married Prince Albert, who made it clear that he shared his countrymen's particular predilection for the seed in an era celebrated in England by the caraway seed cake.

No herb as ancient goes without magical properties of course, and caraway was reputed to ward off witches and also to prevent lovers from straying, a propensity with a wide application — it kept a man's doves, pigeons, and poultry steadfast too!

 varieties

Carum carvi
Caraway
Hardy biennial. Ht in first year 8 in., second year 24 in.; spread 12 in. Flowers white/pinkish in tiny umbellate clusters in early summer. Leaves feathery, light green, similar to carrot. Pale, thick, tapering root comparable to parsnip but smaller. This plant is not particularly decorative. **Zone 4.**

 cultivation

Propagation
Seed
Easily grown; best sown outdoors in early fall when the seed is fresh. Preferred situation full sun or a little shade, in any reasonable, well-drained soil. For an acceptable flavor it must have full sun.

If growing caraway as a root crop, sow in rows and treat the plants like vegetables. Thin to 8 in. apart and keep weed free. These plants will be ready for a seed harvest the following summer; and the roots will be ready in their second fall. Caraway perpetuates itself by self-sowing and can, with a little control, maintain the cycle.

If you want to sow in spring, do it either direct in the garden into shallow rows after the soil has warmed, or into prepared plug module trays to minimize harmful disturbance to its taproot when potting up. Cover with perlite. Repot when seedlings are large enough to handle and transplant in the early fall.

Pests and Diseases
Caraway occasionally suffers from carrot root fly. The grubs of these pests tunnel into the roots. The only organic way to get rid of them is to pull up the plants and bin them. To prevent the fly laying the eggs in the first place cover the crop with a floating row cover.

Caraway seeds

Maintenance

Spring Weed well around fall-sown young plants. Sow seeds.
Summer Pick flowers and leaves.
Fall Cut seed heads. Dig up second-year plants. Sow seeds.
Winter Does not need much protection unless it gets very cold.

Garden Cultivation

Prepare the garden seedbed well. The soil should be fertile, free draining, and free of weeds, not least because it is all too easy to mistake a young caraway plant for a weed in its early growing stage. Thin plants when well established to a distance of 8 in.

Harvesting

Harvest the seeds in summer by cutting the seed heads just before the first seeds fall. Hang them with a paper bag tied over the seed head or over a tray in an airy place. It was once common practice to scald the freshly collected seed to rid it of insects and then dry it in the sun before storing. This is not necessary. Simply store in an airtight container. Gather fresh leaves when young for use in salads. They are not really worth drying. Dig up roots in the second fall as a food crop.

 container growing

Caraway really is not suitable for growing in pots.

 other uses

Pigeon fanciers claim that tame pigeons will never stray if there is baked caraway dough in their coot.

An infusion of caraway seeds

 medicinal

The fresh leaves, roots, and seeds have digestive properties. Chew seeds raw or infuse them to sharpen appetites before a meal, as well as to aid digestion, sweeten the breath, and relieve flatulence.

An infusion can be made from 3 teaspoons of crushed seeds with 1/2 cup of water.

 culinary

When you see caraway mentioned in a recipe it is usually the seed that is required. Caraway seed cake was one of the staples of the Victorian tea table. Nowadays caraway is more widely used in cooking, and in savories as well as sweet dishes. The strong and distinctive flavor is also considered a spice. It is frequently added to sauerkraut, and the German liqueur, Kummel, contains its oil along with cumin.

Sprinkle over rich meats, goose, Hungarian beef stew — as an aid to digestion. Add to cabbage water to reduce cooking smells. Add to apple pies, cookies, baked apples, and cheese.

Serve in a mixed dish of seeds at the end of an Indian meal to both sweeten the breath and aid the digestion.

Caraway root can be cooked as a vegetable, and its young leaves chopped into salads and soups.

Caraway and Cheese Potatoes
Serves 4

4 large potatoes
1/2 cup grated Gruyère cheese
2 teaspoons caraway seeds

Scrub but do not peel the potatoes. Cut them in half lengthwise. Wrap in a boat of greaseproof foil and sprinkle each half with some of the grated cheese and a little caraway. Preheat the oven to 350°F and cook for 35 to 45 minutes, or until the potatoes are soft.

Carlina acaulis

CARLINE

Also known as Carline thistle, Stemless thistle, Dwarf thistle. From the family Asteraceae.

This native herb of the Mediterranean is steeped in history. It is said that Charlemagne had a vision that the plant would ward off the plague, and in medieval times it was considered a good antidote to poisons. Today, in France, it is still known as *baromètre* because the flower closes at the approach of rain.

 ## varieties

Carlina acaulis
Carline
Short-lived hardy perennial. Ht 2–4 in., spread up to 6 in. Stemless, large solitary, creamy white flower, which is surrounded by creamy pointed flower bracts in late summer of the second season. Oblong, dark green pinnate prickly leaves. **Zone 5.**

Carlina vulgaris
Carline Thistle
Biennial. Ht 8–24 in., spread up to 6 in. Groups of two to five yellow to purplish-brown flowers each surrounded by cream, linear, stiff pointed bracts in the summer of the second season. Leathery dark green, narrow oblong, prickly leaves. Native to Britain and northwest Europe. Traditionally used as a purgative and in magical incantations. **All zones.**

 ## cultivation

Propagation
Seed
Sow fresh seed in fall into pots or plug cell-packs using a standard soilless seed compost. Cover lightly with compost, place in a cold frame. Germination takes 4 to 6 months. Plant out in spring once the seedlings are large enough to handle.

Division
Wearing gloves for protection from the prickles, divide plants in the second spring prior to flowering, using two small hand forks back-to-back. Replant in a prepared sunny site in the garden.

Pests and Diseases
Rarely suffers from pests and diseases.

Maintenance
Spring Divide first-year plants.
Summer Pick flowers for drying.
Fall Sow seeds.
Winter No need for protection, hardy to −40°F.

Garden Cultivation
This drought-tolerant, very hardy plant needs to be planted in full sun in a low-nutrient, free-draining soil. In the right conditions it will selfseed. It is now endangered in many Mediterranean countries; do not take from the wild.

Harvesting
Dig up the root of the second-year plant in early fall for making decoctions or drying. Pick the flower buds before they open for use in the kitchen. Pick the flowers when just opening for drying. Wear gloves to protect your hands.

Carlina vulgaris are popular in dried flower arrangements (right)

 ## container growing

This herb looks most attractive when flowering. Use a soilless potting compost mixed in equal parts with horticultural grit. Place the container in full sun.

 ## medicinal

A salve made from the root can be used to treat several skin complaints including acne. Today the roots are used in veterinary medicine to stimulate the appetite of cattle.

 ## other uses

The plant is popular in dried flower arrangements as the dried heads keep their appearance indefinitely.

 ## culinary

It may seem unbelievable when you look at this plant that the flower bud is quite edible. It is eaten in the same manner as the globe artichoke (*Cynara scolymus*). In Southern Italy there is a recipe for stuffing the small bud with cheese and eggs before it is fried. Before cooking, the prickles are brushed off with a stiff brush.

 ## warning

If the root is taken in large doses it is emetic and a purgative. Wear gloves when handling this plant.

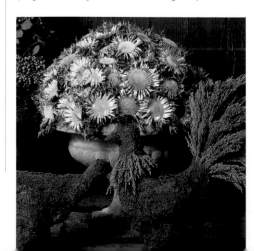

Catha edulis
KHAT

Also known as Bushman's tea, Qat, Chat and Miraa. From the family Celastraceae.

This herb is indigenous to East Africa. Historically the ancient Egyptians considered the khat plant a "divine food," which was capable of releasing humanity's divinity. The generic name *Catha* is derived from the Arabic name for this plant, *Khat*, and the specific name *edulis* is a Greek word meaning "edible."

 varieties

Catha edulis
Khat
Evergreen tropical and subtropical shrub or small tree. Ht up to 33 ft. Clusters of minute creamy-white to greenish flowers in spring. These are followed by three-lobed capsules, which split in late summer to release one to three narrowly winged seeds. Dark green shiny leaves with a dull underside. **Zone 10.**

 cultivation

Propagation
Seed
If you are able to obtain fresh seed, which is rarely available outside of Africa, sow in spring. Place the tray under protection at 68°F; germination takes 4 to 6 weeks. Once the seedling is established, repot using a potting compost mixed in equal parts with horticultural sand. Grow on in a container for 2 years before planting out into a prepared site in the garden or, in cold climates, potting on as a container plant.

Cuttings
In early summer take cuttings from the nonflowering shoots and insert into small pots or plug module trays using a seed compost mixed in equal parts with propagating bark. Once well-rooted, repot using a soil-based compost mixed in equal parts with horticultural sand. Grow on for 2 years before planting out into a prepared site. In cold climates grow on as a container plant.

Pests and Diseases
Rarely suffers from pests or diseases in warm climates. When grown as a container plant it can be prone to scale and red spider mite. To treat, either use the relevant predators or insecticidal soap following the manufacturers' instructions. Do not use both.

Maintenance
Spring In warm climates sow seed.
Summer Take cuttings from new growth.
Fall Cut back after flowering. Protect from excessive wet and cold weather.
Winter Protect from frost.

Garden Cultivation
In hot climates this herb can make an attractive garden plant, giving height in the border and all-year-round interest. Plant in full sun in a well-drained soil.

Harvesting
In early summer pick the new shoots as required for using fresh.

Bunches of khat shoots

 container growing

Khat can be grown successfully in a container using soilless compost mixed in equal parts with horticultural sand. Water and feed with a liquid fertilizer regularly throughout the growing season. Protect from frost and cold rains from fall onwards and reduce watering; do not allow the compost to totally dry out. In spring, reintroduce watering once the night temperature does not drop below 41°F. Place the container outside in a warm, sunny, sheltered position once the night temperature is above 50°F.

 medicinal

In Africa, this herb is used to treat chest complaints, asthma and coughs. It is taken in old age to stimulate and improve mental functions and communication skills. However, as with many beneficial medicinal herbs this can, and has been abused; see the warning.

 other uses

The bark is used as an insect repellent.

⚠ warning

This herb has been banned in many countries. In 1980, the World Health Organization classified khat as a drug of abuse that can produce mild to moderate psychic dependence. Overuse can cause aggression and develop personality problems. It should never be taken when pregnant or breastfeeding.

Cedronella canariensis

BALM OF GILEAD

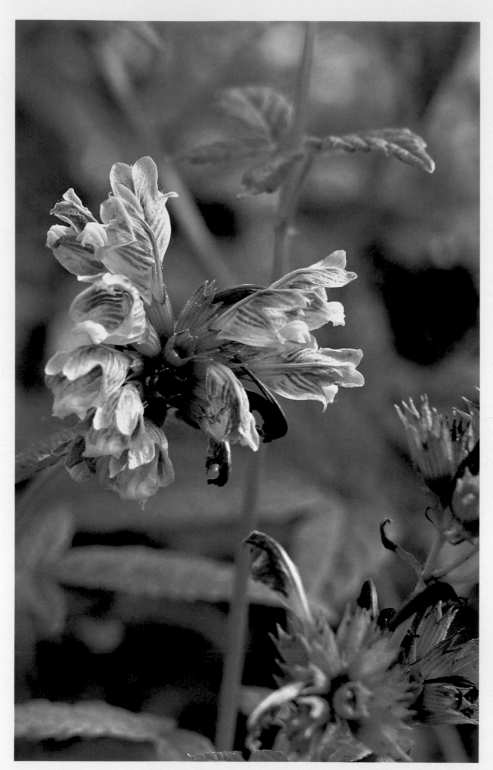

Also known as Canary balm. From the family *Lamiaceae*.

Although this herb originates from Madeira and the Canary Islands, as indicated by its species name, balm of Gilead is now established in many temperate regions of the world. Many plants have been called balm of Gilead, the common link being that they all have a musky, eucalyptus, camphor-like scent.

The Queen of Sheba gave Solomon a balm of Gilead, which was *Commiphora opobalsamum*, an aromatic desert shrub found in the Holy Land. Today this plant is rare and protected, its export prohibited.

The balm of Gilead mentioned in the Bible ("Is there no balm in Gilead; is there no physician there?") was initially held to be *Commiphora meccanensis*, which was an aromatic shrub. However some now say it was oleo-resin obtained from *Balsamodendron opobalsamum*, a plant now thought to be extinct. Whatever is the case, the medicinal balm of Gilead is *Populus balsamifera*. This is balsam poplar, a tree found growing in several temperate countries, which smells heavenly in early summer, while the herb now known as balm of Gilead is *Cedronella canariensis*. This is said to have a similar scent to the Biblical shrubs, perhaps the reason for its popular name.

Cedronella canariensis

 varieties

Cedronella canariensis syn. Cedronella triphylla
Balm of Gilead
Half-hardy perennial, partial evergreen. Ht 3 ft., spread 2 ft. Leaves with strong eucalyptus scent, three lobes and toothed edges, borne on square stems. Pink or pale mauve, two-lipped flowers throughout summer. Black seed heads. **Zone 10.**

 cultivation

Propagation
Seed
The fairly small seeds should be sown in spring directly on the surface of a prepared pot, plug, or seed tray. Use a standard seed compost mixed in equal parts with composted fine bark. Cover with a layer of perlite. It is a temperamental germinator, so bottom heat of 68°F can be an asset. If using heat, remember not to let the compost dry out, and only water with a fine spray when needed. The seedlings will appear anytime between 2 and 6 weeks. When two leaves have formed, prick out the seedlings and plant them in position 3 ft. apart.

Cuttings
More reliable than seed. They take readily either in early summer before flowering from new growth or in early fall from the semi-ripe wood. Use a standard seed compost mixed in equal parts with composted fine bark.

Pests and Diseases
Since it is aromatic, aphids and other pests usually leave it alone, but the seedlings are prone to damping off.

Maintenance
Spring Sow seeds under protection. In a warm garden a mature plant can selfseed; rub the leaves of any selfseedlings to see if it is balm of Gilead or a young nettle (but don't get stung!). At this stage their aroma is the only characteristic that tells them apart. Plants overwintered in containers should be repotted if root-bound and given a liquid feed.
Summer Cut back after flowering to keep it neat and tidy, and also to encourage new growth from which late cuttings can be taken.
Fall Take stem cuttings. Collect seed heads.
Winter Protect from frost.

Garden Cultivation
Balm of Gilead grows happily outside in sheltered positions. Plant in a well-drained soil in full sun, preferably against a warm, wind-protecting wall. The plant has an upright habit but spreads at the top, so plant approximately 3 ft. from other plants.

It is a tender plant that may need protection in cooler climates. If you get frosts lower than 29°F protect the plant for the winter, either by bringing it into a cool greenhouse or conservatory or by covering in an a floating row cover.

Harvesting
Pick leaves for drying before the flowers open, when they will be at their most aromatic. Either pick flowers when just coming into bloom and dry, or wait until flowering is over and collect the black flower heads (good for winter arrangements).

Seeds are ready for extraction when you can hear the flower heads rattle. Store in an airtight container to sow in the spring.

 container growing

Balm of Gilead makes an excellent container plant. A 9–10-in. pot will be required for a plant to reach maturity. Use a soil-based compost mixed in equal parts with composted fine bark. Liquid feed a mature plant monthly throughout summer.

When grown in a conservatory, the scent of the leaves perfumes the air, especially when the plant is watered or the sun shining on it. Flowers are long lasting and give a good show during the summer. Keep watering to the absolute minimum in the winter months.

 medicinal

Crush the leaves in your hand and inhale the aroma to clear your head.

Rub the leaves on skin to try and deter mosquitoes.

Said to be an aphrodisiac when applied ... no comment.

 other uses

Dried leaves combine well in a spicy or woody potpourri with cedarwood chippings, rosewood, pineneedles, small fir cones, cypress oil, and pine oil.

Add an infusion of the leaves to bath water for an invigorating bath.

Centella asiatica

GOTU KOLA

Also known as Pennywort, Spadeleaf, Brahmi, Tiger Herb, Tiger Grass. From the family Apiaceae.

This herb is indigenous to the subtropical and tropical areas of India, where it is known as Tiger Herb. This is because it is said that wounded tigers roll in the leaves, to help themselves heal. It can also be found in marshlands and alongside rivers in Pakistan, Sri Lanka, South Africa, Hawaii and Florida. It has been an important Ayurvedic medicinal herb for thousands of years, and its Ayurvedic name is Brahmi, or "knowledge." It was traditionally used to promote wound healing and slow the progress of leprosy, senile decay and loss of memory. It was also reputed to prolong life; for example, a Sinhalese proverb says "Two leaves a day keep old age away." In China, Gotu kola is one of the reported "miracle elixirs of life." This was attributed to a healer named Li Ching Yun who reputedly lived 256 years by taking a tea brewed from Gotu kola and other herbs. It did not become important in Western medicine until the 1800s.

 varieties

Centella asiatica
Gotu Kola
Tender perennial creeping plant. Ht 3 in., spread indefinite. The tiny magenta flowers in summer are surrounded by green bracts, which grow in small umbels near to the soil surface. Bright green kidney-shaped leaves with indented margins. **Zone 8.**

 cultivation

Propagation
Seed
In warm climates this herb will happily self-seed. However, in cool climates it rarely sets seed and, when you propagate from the seeds, the germination is very spasmodic. So, it is much easier to raise plants from cuttings.

Cuttings
As this plant tends to root where the stems touch the ground, and it is prolific when growing in damp conditions, it is easy to propagate any time during the growing season from spring until early fall. Separate the plantlet from the main plant by cutting the stem above the ground, and then gently tease the small roots from the ground. You can then, depending on the size of the root, either repot into small pots or trim the roots and ease them into a plug tray using a seed compost mixed in equal parts with vermiculite. Once rooted, which takes place very quickly in summer, repot using a soilless potting mix with vermiculite in equal parts, and winter in a frost-free environment.

Division
Divide established plants in summer, either replanting into a prepared site in the garden or repotting using a soilless potting mix with vermiculite in equal parts.

Pests and Diseases
When grown as a container plant it can be prone to red spider mite. If this is the case introduce *Phytoseiulus persimilis*, its natural predator, or treat regularly with insecticidal soap following the manufacturer's instructions. Do not use both.

Centella asiatica leaves

Centella asiatica **flowers**

Maintenance

Spring Take cuttings and repot container-raised plants.
Summer Take cuttings. Do not allow the plants to dry out at this time of year.
Fall Protect young plants and container-grown plants from frost.
Winter Cut off any damaged leaves to prevent the spread of disease.

Garden Cultivation

This plant will only grow successfully outside all year round in tropical or subtropical climates. For those in cooler and cold climates it will tolerate temperatures as low as 50°F; below this, it must be grown under protection. Its appearance changes, depending on growing conditions. In shallow water, the plant puts forth floating roots and the leaves rest on top of the water. In dry locations, it puts out numerous small roots and the leaves are small and thin.

Harvesting

Pick the leaves to use fresh from spring until late summer. Pick the leaves for drying in late spring.

 ## container growing

It will adapt happily to being grown in containers, and looks very interesting in a hanging basket where it will cascade. Plant in a soilless potting mix with vermiculite in equal parts. Place the container in partial shade, not full sun. Water and feed regularly from early spring until early fall with a liquid fertilizer following the manufacturer's instructions. This is especially important if you are picking the leaves regularly.

 ## medicinal

This is one of the most important medicinal herbs I grow. It is a rejuvenating, diuretic herb that clears toxins and reduces inflammation. It is being used in the treatment of rheumatism and rheumatoid arthritis. It is commonly used to treat depression, but be warned that it has been reported to also cause depression in well-adjusted individuals.

 ## other uses

As a beauty aid, Gotu kola stimulates the production of collagen and this helps improve the tone of veins near the surface of the skin. It is now being used in face creams which claim to be antiwrinkle and skin-firming.

 ## warning

Excessive use of this herb taken internally or externally can cause itching, headaches, and even unconsciousness. Avoid Gotu kola if you are pregnant or breastfeeding, using tranquillizers or sedatives, or have an overactive thyroid.

 ## culinary

When picking leaves for use in the kitchen, choose the new young tender leaves; the mature ones are dry and tough, especially if grown in dry conditions. Add the young leaves to salads, sandwiches, and stir-fry dishes where the dry, slightly spicy flavor combines well with fish and vegetables.

Eastern Herb Salad
Serves 4

1 cucumber, peeled, seeded and cut into
    ½ in. dice
Salt and freshly ground black pepper
2 cloves garlic, crushed
Juice of 1 lemon
3 tablespoons extra virgin olive oil
2 tablespoons young gotu kola leaves, roughly
    chopped
4 tablespoons purslane leaves, removed from the
    stalks and lightly chopped
2 tablespoons Italian parsley, roughly chopped
2 tablespoons cilantro leaves, roughly chopped
2 tablespoons mint, roughly chopped
1 red onion, finely minced
5 ripe tomatoes, peeled, seeded and
    roughly chopped
3 pita breads, toasted and broken into small
    pieces or five slices of white bread, toasted then
    cut into strips

Place the diced cucumber in a colander, sprinkle with salt and leave to drain for 20 minutes. In a large bowl, mix together the garlic, lemon juice, and the olive oil to make a dressing. Add the herbs, the diced vegetables, the pieces of bread and toss well to coat with the dressing. Season with salt and pepper, serve immediately. This salad does not keep.

Centaurea cyanus

CORNFLOWER

Also known as Blue Bottle, Bachelors Buttons. From the family Asteraceae.

Cornflowers are the national flower of Estonia. Historically it is said that Chiron, an ancient Greek Centaur, taught mankind the healing value of this herb. It was regarded as a good remedy against the poison of scorpions and also as a healing wash for wounds. This pretty traditional European flower is better known as a wild flower, which nearly became extinct in the UK due to the introduction of chemical weed controls in farming.

 ## varieties

Centaurea cyanus
Cornflower
Hardy annual. Ht 12–32 in., spread 6 in. Stunning single and double blue, daisy-like flowers in summer. Lance-shaped, gray-green leaves. The lower leaves are often toothed and covered in fine cotton. There are hybrids with pink, white, or purple flowers.

 ## cultivation

Propagation
Seed
In early spring sow seeds into prepared module plug trays using standard seed compost. Place the tray in a warm position; extra bottom heat is not required. Germination takes 14 to 21 days. Be careful not to overwater as the seedlings are prone to damping off. Repot or plant out when all threat of frost has passed. Alternatively, for the best results, sow in spring where you want the plant to grow and when the air temperature does not go below 50°F at night.

Pests and Diseases
Rarely suffers from pests or diseases.

Maintenance
Spring Sow seeds.
Summer Pick flowers for display and drying.
Fall Harvest seeds.
Winter Prepare garden for next season's sowing.

Garden Cultivation
Plant in a well-drained soil in a sunny position. If you wish to create a meadow effect, in the fall prior to sowing, prepare the ground well by clearing all the grass and weeds in a 12 in. square area for each plant. Sow 15 seeds per patch, thinning to preferably two plants. In fall, allow the plants to die back and self seed naturally.

Harvesting
For use in the kitchen or for drying pick the flowers in summer when they are just half open, before the center stems are visible. When drying, tie into small bunches of about 10 flowers per bunch and dry fast, otherwise the color will fade and the heads will start to crumble.

Centaurea cyanus

 ## companion planting

The blue flowers reputedly attract pollinating insects more than other colors, which is beneficial for increasing yield in the vegetable garden.

 ## container growing

They can be grown in large containers using a soilless potting compost. They look stunning on their own, or mixed with other tall wild flowers like oxeye daisies or poppies. When growing in a container it is worth tying some dark green sewing thread around the established plants to hold them in place and to minimize the damage from high winds or heavy rain.

 ## culinary

The petals of the flowers are edible; they look lovely sprinkled over green salads or over cold rice dishes.

 ## medicinal

The flower is the part used medicinally; it is considered a tonic and stimulant. The famous French eyewash Eau de Casselunettes was traditionally made from the distilled flowers because of their eye-brightening properties.

 ## other uses

The juice extracted from the petals makes a good blue ink which, when mixed with alum-water, can be used in watercolor paintings. It also makes a very good fabric dye. The dried flowers make up for their lack of scent by looking striking in arrangements or when added to potpourri.

Centranthus ruber
RED VALERIAN

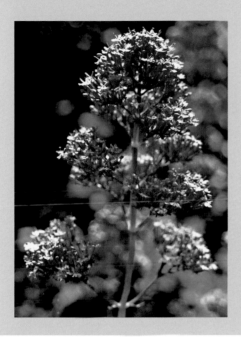

Also known as Jupiter's Beard, American Lilac, Bloody Butcher, Bouncing Bess, and Bouncing Betsy. From the family Valerianaceae.

A native of central and southern Europe, cultivated widely in temperate climates and has now become widely naturalized. This cheerful plant was a great ornament in Gerard's garden, but he described it in 1597 as "not common in England." However, by the early 18th century it had become well known.

butterflies. As an ornamental, it thrives in poor, well-drained, low-fertile soil, and especially on chalk or limestone. It likes a sunny position and self-seeds prolifically.

container growing

Make sure the container is large enough and use a soilless compost. No need to feed, otherwise you will inhibit its flowers. Position the container in a sunny spot and water regularly.

culinary

Very young leaves are eaten in France and Italy. They are incredibly bitter.

medicinal

A drug is obtained (by herbalists only) from the root, which looks like a huge radish and has a characteristic odor. It is believed to be helpful in cases of hysteria and nervous disorders because of its sedative and antispasmodic properties.

warning

Large doses or extended use may produce symptoms of poisoning. Do not take for more than a couple of days at a time, without seeking medicinal advice.

varieties

Centranthus ruber
Red Valerian
Perennial. Ht 2–3 ft., spread 18–24 in. in. Showy red fragrant flowers in summer. They can also appear in all shades of white and pink. Fleshy, pale green, pointed leaves. **Zone 5**.

cultivation

Propagation
Seed
Sow the small seeds in early fall in seed or plug module trays, using a standard seed compost mixed in equal parts with composted fine bark. Cover lightly with soil and leave outside over winter, covered with glass. As soon as you notice it germinating, remove the glass and place in a cold greenhouse. Prick the seedlings out when large enough to handle and repot using the same mix of compost. Leave the pots outside for the summer, maintain watering until the fall. No need to feed. Plant out 24 in. apart.

Pests and Diseases
This plant does not suffer from pests or diseases.

Maintenance
Spring Dig up self-sown seedlings and replant if you want them.
Summer Deadhead to prevent self-seeding.
Fall Sow seeds. Plant previous year's seedlings.
Winter A very hardy plant.

Garden Cultivation
Red valerian has naturalized on banks, crumbly walls, rocks, and along coastal regions. It is very attractive to

Centranthus ruber

CHAMOMILE

Chamaemelum nobile

From the family Asteraceae.

"I am sorry to say that Peter was not very well during the evening. His mother put him to bed and made some chamomile tea and she gave a dose of it to Peter, one tablespoon full to be taken at bedtime."—The Tale of Peter Rabbit by Beatrix Potter

Chamomile grows wild in Europe, North America, and many other countries. As a garden escapee, it can be found in pastures and other grassy places on sandy soils.

The generic name, *Chamaemelum*, is derived from the Greek *khamaimelon*, meaning "earth apple" or "apple on the ground."

 ## varieties

Chamaemelum nobile
Roman Chamomile
Also known as garden chamomile, ground apple, low chamomile, and whig plant. Hardy perennial evergreen. Ht 4 in., spread 18 in. White flowers with yellow centers all summer. Sweet-smelling, finely divided foliage. Ideal for ground cover. Can be used as a lawn, but because it flowers it will need constant cutting. **Zone 4.**

Chamaemelum nobile "Flore Pleno"
Double-flowered Chamomile
Hardy perennial evergreen. Ht 3 in., spread 12 in. Double white flowers all summer. Sweet-smelling, finely divided, thick foliage. Good for ground cover, in between paving stones, and lawns. More compact habit than Roman chamomile, and combines well with chamomile "Treneague." **Zone 4.**

Chamaemelum nobile "Treneague"
syn. Anthemis nobile "Treneague"
Chamomile Treneague
Also known as lawn chamomile. Hardy perennial evergreen. Ht 2½ in., spread 6 in. Nonflowering. Leaves are finely divided and very aromatic. Ideal for ground cover or mow-free lawn. Plant in well-drained soil, free from stones, 4–6 in. apart. **Zone 4.**

Anthemis tinctoria
Dyers Chamomile
Also known as yellow chamomile. Hardy perennial evergreen. Ht and spread 3 ft. Yellow daisy flowers in the summer. Leaves are midgreen and fern like. Principally a dye plant. **Zone 4.**

Matricaria recutita
German Chamomile
Also known as scented mayweed, wild chamomile. Hardy annual. Ht 24 in., spread 4 in. Scented white flowers with conical yellow centers from spring to early summer. Finely serrated aromatic foliage. The main use of this chamomile is medicinal. **All zones.**

 ## cultivation

Propagation
Seed
Dyers, Roman, and German chamomiles can be grown from seed. In spring, sow onto the surface of a prepared seed or plug tray. Use a standard seed compost mixed in equal parts with composted fine bark. Cover with perlite. Use bottom heat 65°F. Harden off and plant out or repot.

Cuttings
Double-flowered chamomile and chamomile 'Treneague' can only be propagated by cuttings and division. Take cuttings in the spring and fall from the offsets or clusters of young shoots. They are easy to grow as they have aerial roots.

Division
All perennial chamomiles planted as specimen plants will benefit from being lifted in the spring of their second or third year and divided.

Pests and Diseases
As all the chamomiles are highly aromatic they are not troubled by pests or diseases.

Chamaemelum nobile "Flore Pleno"

Maintenance

Spring Collect offshoots, sow seeds. Fill in holes that have appeared in the chamomile lawn. Divide established plants. Give a liquid fertilizer feed to all established plants.

Summer Water well. Do not allow to dry out. In the first season of a lawn, trim the plants to encourage bushing out and spreading. In late summer collect flowers from the dyers chamomile and cut the plant back to 2½ in. to promote new growth.

Fall Take cuttings. Divide if they have become too invasive. Cut back to promote new growth. Give the final feed of the season.

Winter Only protect in extreme weather.

Garden Cultivation

All the chamomiles prefer a well-drained soil and a sunny situation, although they will adapt to most growing conditions.

As a lawn plant, chamomile gets more credit than it deserves. Chamomile lawns are infinitely less easy to maintain in good condition than grass lawns. There is no selective herbicide that will preserve chamomile and kill the rest of the weeds. It is a hands-and-knees job with no short-cuts. Prepare the site well, make sure the soil is light, slightly acid, and free from weeds and stones. Plant young plants in plug form. I use a mix of double-flowered and "Treneague" chamomile at a distance of 4–6 in. apart. Keep all traffic off it for at least 12 weeks, and keep it to the minimum during the whole of the first year.

If all this seems daunting, compromise and plant a chamomile seat. Prepare the soil in the same way and do not sit on the seat for at least 12 weeks. Then sit down, smell the sweet aroma, and sip a cool glass of wine. Summer is here.

Harvesting

Leaves
Gather in spring and early summer for best results. Use fresh or dry.

Flowers
Pick when fully open, around midsummer. Use fresh or dry. Dyers chamomile flowers should be harvested in summer for their yellow dye.

 companion planting

Chamomile is said to be the plants' physician because when it is planted near ailing plants, it apparently helps them to revive. Roman Chamomile, when planted next to onions, is said to repel flying insects and improve the crop yield.

Traditional Chamomile Infusion
Bring 2 cups water to a boil. Add a handful of chamomile leaves and flowers. Cover and let it stand for half a day. This infusion was traditionally used as a spray to prevent damping off. It was also added to the compost heap as an activator to accelerate decomposition.

 container growing

I would not advise growing chamomiles indoors, as they get very leggy, soft, and prone to disease. But the flowers can look very cheerful in a sunny window box. Use chamomile "Flore Pleno," which has a lovely double flower head, or the nonflowering chamomile "Treneague" as an infill between bulbs, with a standard potting compost mixed in equal parts with composted fine bark.

 cosmetic

Chamomile is used as a final rinse for fair hair to make it brighter. Pour 3½ cups boiling water over one handful of chamomile flowers and steep for 30 minutes. Strain, cover and allow to cool. It should be poured over your hair several times.

 medicinal

German chamomile's highly scented dry flower heads contain up to 1 percent of an aromatic oil that possesses powerful antiseptic and antiinflammatory properties. Taken as a tea, it promotes gastric secretions and improves the appetite, while an infusion of the same strength can be used as an internal antiseptic. It may also be used as a douche or gargle for mouth ulcers and as an eye wash. An oil for skin rashes or allergies can be made by tightly packing flower heads into a preserving jar, covering

Chamomile Tea

with olive oil, and leaving in the sun for 3 weeks. If you suffer from overwrought nerves, add five or six drops of chamomile oil to the bath and this will help you relax at night.

Chamomile Tea

1 heaping teaspoon chamomile flowers (dried or fresh)
1 teaspoon honey
Slice of lemon (optional)

Put the chamomile flowers into a warm cup. Pour on boiling water. Cover and leave to infuse for 3 to 5 minutes. Strain and add the honey and lemon, if required. Can be drunk either hot or cold.

 other uses

Dyers chamomile can be used as a dye plant. Depending on the mordant, its color can vary from bright to olive/brown yellow (see p. 675). German and double-flowered chamomile are best for herb pillows and potpourri.

 warning

When taken internally, excessive dosage can produce vomiting and vertigo.

Chenopodium bonus-henricus

GOOD KING HENRY

Also known as All good, Good King Harry, Good neighbour, Wild spinach, Lincolnshire asparagus and Mercury. From the family Chenopodiaceae.

Good King Henry comes from a genus *(Chenopodium)* that is distributed all over the world and is found growing in all climates. This species *(C. bonus-henricus)* is native to Europe.

Good King Henry was popular from Neolithic times until the 19th century. Its curious name is not taken from the English king, Henry VIII, as might be expected, but from King Henry IV of Navarre, and to distinguish it from the poisonous Bad Henry (*Mercurialis perennis*).

Gerard in the 16th century observed that Good King Henry grew in untilled places and among rubbish near common ways, old walls, hedges and fields, and it still does — colonies of the herb can be found on many medieval sites.

 varieties

Chenopodiaceae, the goosefoot. family, includes 1,500 rather unattractive plants, some of them important edible plants, for example, spinach and beet.

Chenopodium bonus-henricus
Good King Henry
Perennial. Ht 24 in., spread 18 in. Tiny greenish-yellow flowers in early summer. Leaves green and arrow-shaped. Very occasionally a variegated form is found; but the yellow variegation will be difficult to maintain. **Zone 5.**

Chenopodium album
Fat Hen
Also known as lambs' quarters, white goosefoot., common pigweed, all good and muckweed. Annual. Ht 2–3 ft. Flowers small, greenish-white, summer to midfall. Green lance-shaped leaves. Its seeds have been identified at Neolithic villages in Switzerland and in the stomach of the Iron Age Tollund Man. Rich in fat and albumen, it appears to have been a food supplement for primitive man. **All zones.**

☠ Chenopodium ambrosioides
American Wormseed
Also known as Mexican tea, and in China as fragrant tiger bones. Annual. Ht 2–4 ft. Small greenish flowers from late summer to late fall. Green lance-shaped leaves. This is native to tropical Central America. Introduced through Mexico, it has become naturalized as far north as New England in the United States. It was introduced into Europe in the 18th century. Mexican Tea was once included in the United States pharmacopoeia but is now restricted to American folk medicine and mainly used for its essential oil, Chenopodium oil, against roundworm and hookworm. **All zones.**

Warning: *Chenopodium ambrosioides* is poisonous. Use under strict supervision. It causes deafness, vertigo, paralysis, incontinence, sweating, jaundice and death.

GOOD KING HENRY

 ## cultivation

Propagation

Seeds
Sow the fairly small seeds early in spring in prepared seed or plug trays for an early crop. Use a standard seed compost mixed in equal parts with composted fine bark and cover with perlite. No extra heat required. When the seedlings are large enough to handle and after hardening off, plant out in the garden 10 in. apart. Can be sown direct in late spring into prepared soil in the garden in late spring in ½ in. rows. Allow 18 in. between rows. Cover the seeds with ¼ in. soil. Germination in warm soil, 10–14 days. When large enough to handle, thin to 10 in. apart.

Division
Divide established plants in the spring. You will find even small pieces will grow.

Pests and Diseases
Does not usually suffer from these.

Maintenance
Spring Lift and divide established plants. If you wish to grow as an asparagus, blanch the shoots from early spring onwards. As they emerge, hill up with soil. Divide and repot container-grown plants.
Summer Give a liquid feed if a second crop of leaves is required.
Fall Cut back dying foliage and give the plant a mulch of compost.
Winter No need for protection.

Garden Cultivation
Good King Henry will tolerate any soil, but if planted in a soil rich in humus, dug deep and well drained in a sunny position, the quality and quantity of the crop will be much improved. Sow directly.

Keep well watered in dry months. In fall cover beds with a thin layer of manure. Beds should be renewed every 3 to 4 years.

Harvesting
Allow plants 1 year to develop before harvesting. From midspring the young shoots can provide an asparagus substitute crop. They should be cut when they are about 6 in. long. Harvest the flowering spikes as they begin to open. Later in the season gather the larger leaves as a spinach substitute as required. Freeze only when used as an ingredient in a cooked dish.

 ## container growing

Can be grown outside in a large container, in a soil-based potting compost mixed in equal parts with composted fine bark. Needs to be kept well watered throughout the summer and fed once a week to maintain a supply of leaves. Divide each spring and repot the divisions in fresh compost.

 ## medicinal

The seeds have a gentle laxative effect, making them

suitable relief for a slightly constipated condition. A poultice (or ointment) cleanses and heals skin sores.

 ## other uses

Good King Henry is a cough remedy for sheep. The whole plant is used to fatten poultry. Seed is used commercially in the manufacture of shagreen, an artificially granulated untanned leather, often dyed green. The whole plant of fat hen can be used as a red or golden dye (above).

 ## warning

Sufferers of kidney complaints or rheumatism should avoid medicinal preparations containing extracts from this plant.

 ## culinary

The leaves of Good King Henry and fat hen are rich in iron, calcium and vitamins B1 and C, and are particularly recommended for anemic subjects. Like all low-growing leaves, good King Henry must be washed with great care; the slightest suspicion of grit in the finished dish will ruin the meal. Use two or three changes of water.

Eat young leaves raw in salads. Alternatively, cook in casseroles, stuffings, soups and savory pies. The leaves are more nutritious than those of spinach or cabbage.

Steam flower spikes and toss in butter before serving, like broccoli.

To blanch the shoots, dip in hot water, rinse immediately in cold water. Alternatively, cut shoots 6 in. long. Steam or boil very quickly. Peel if necessary. Serve hot with melted butter, or cold with a vinaigrette.

The seed of fat hen can be ground into flour and used to make into a gruel.

Convallaria majalis

LILY OF THE VALLEY

Also known as Our Lady's Tears, Fairy's Bells, May Lily, Ladder to Heaven and May Bells. From the family Convallariaceae.

Lily of the Valley is a native of Europe, North America and Canada and has been introduced throughout the world in moist cool climates.

According to European folk tales, Lily of the Valley either originated from the Virgin Mary's tears, shed at the foot of the Cross, or from those shed by Mary Magdalen when she found Christ's tomb.

From the Middle Ages onwards the flowers formed the traditional part of a bride's bouquet and are associated with modesty and purity.

In the 16th century they were used medicinally and called Convall Lily. The Elizabethan physician Gerard has this amazing recipe: "Put the flowers of May lilies into a glass and set it in a hill of ants, firmly closed for 1 month. After which you will find a liquor that when applied appeaseth the paine and grief of gout."

 varieties

☠ **Convallaria majalis**
Lily of the Valley
Hardy Perennial. Ht 6 in., spread indefinite. White, bell shaped, scented flowers, late spring to early summer. Mid- to dark green oval-shaped leaves. **Zones 3 to 7.**

☠ **Convallaria majalis "Flore Pleno"**
Double Flowered Lily of the Valley
Hardy Perennial. Ht 9–12 in., spread indefinite. Creamy white, double, bell-shaped, scented flowers that are larger than the species, late spring to early summer. Mid- to dark green oval-shaped leaves.
Zones 3 to 7.

☠ **Convallaria majalis "Fortin's Giant"**
Fortin's Giant Lily of the Valley
Hardy Perennial. Ht 18 in., spread indefinite. White, larger than the species, bell-shaped, scented flowers, late spring to early summer. Mid- to dark green, wide oval-shaped leaves. A robust growing form of the Lily of the Valley. Widely thought to be a triploid form.
Zones 3 to 7.

☠ **Convallaria majalis var. rosea**
Pink Lily of the Valley
Hardy Perennial. Ht 6 in., spread indefinite. Pale pink, bell shaped, scented flowers, late spring to early summer. Mid- to dark green oval-shaped leaves.
Zones 3 to 7.

☠ **Convallaria majalis "Vic Pawlowski's Gold"**
Vic Pawlowski's Gold Lily of the Valley
Hardy Perennial. Ht 6 in., spread indefinite. White, bell shaped, scented flowers, late spring to early summer. Mid- to dark green oval-shaped leaves with attractive thin golden strips running the length of the leaves. This has a more consistent and better variegation than *Convallaria majalis* "Albostriata." **Zones 3 to 7.**

LILY OF THE VALLEY

 cultivation

Propagation

Seeds
Ripe seeds are seldom formed, and the scarlet berries are highly poisonous, so better to propagate by division.

Division
The plant produces crowns on creeping rhizomes. Divide in the fall after the plant has finished flowering and the leaves have died back.

Pests and Diseases
Lily of the Valley is free from most pests and diseases.

Maintenance
Spring In very early spring, bring pots into the house for forcing.
Summer Do nothing!
Fall When the plant has died back fully dig up the rhizomes for splitting. Repot crowns for forcing.
Winter No need for protection.

Garden Cultivation
Unlike its name, it should be grown not in an open valley but in partial shade. Ideal for growing under trees or in woodlands or in the shade of a fence provided there is not too much competition from other plants.

To get the best flowers, prepare the site well. The soil should be deeply cultivated with plenty of well-rotted manure, compost or leaf mold. Plant in fall, 6 in. apart, before the frosts make the soil too hard. Place the crowns upright in the prepared holes with the tips just below the soil.

Harvesting
Pick the flowers when in full bloom for drying so that they can be added to potpourri.

 container growing

This plant can be happily grown in pots as long as it is kept in the shade and watered regularly. Use a soilless potting mix mixed in equal parts with propagating bark. Feed with liquid fertilizer only during flowering. In winter let the plant die down, and keep it in a cool place outside.

Convallaria majalis

 medicinal

This plant, like the foxglove, is used in the treatment of heart disease. It contains cardiac glycosides which increase the strength of the heartbeat while slowing and regulating its rate, without putting extra demand on the coronary blood supply.

 culinary

None — all parts of the plant are poisonous.

 warning

Lily of the Valley should only be used as prescribed by a qualified practitioner and it is restricted. All parts of the plant are poisonous.

 other uses

The flowers of the Lily of the Valley are often used in bridal arrangements not only for their wonderful scent but also because in the language of flowers they signify a "return to happiness." I did not know this fact when I married over 30 years ago where I wore a wreath of Lily of the Valley flowers in my hair and carried them as my bouquet.

An essential oil is obtained from the flowers and used in the perfumery industry. The leaves can be used to make a natural dye. The young leaves in spring will give a green dye and the mature fall leaves will give a yellowish brown dye.

Lily of the Valley soap and cream

Coriandrum sativum
CILANTRO

Also known as Chinese parsley, Yuen sai, Pak chee, Fragrant green, Dhania (seed), Dhania pattar and Dhania sabz (leaves). From the family Apiaceae. In the U.S. the leafy greens of this plant are called cilantro, but the seeds of the same plant are called coriander.

A native of southern Europe and the Middle East, cilantro was a popular herb in England up until Tudor times. Early European settlers in America included seed among the beloved items they took to the New World, as did Spaniards into Mexico.

Cilantro has been cultivated for over 3,000 years. Seeds have been found in tombs from the 21st Egyptian Dynasty (1085–945 BCE). The herb is mentioned in the Old Testament — "when the children of Israel were returning to their homeland from slavery in Egypt, they ate manna in the wilderness and the manna was as coriander seeds" — and it is still one of the traditional bitter herbs to be eaten at the Passover when the Jewish people remember that great journey.

Cilantro was brought to Northern Europe by the Romans who, combining it with cumin and vinegar, rubbed it into meat as a preservative. The Chinese once believed it bestowed immortality and in the Middle Ages it was put in love potions as an aphrodisiac. Its name is said to be derived from *koris,* Greek for "bedbug," since the plant smells strongly of the insect.

 varieties

Coriandrum sativum
Tender annual. Ht 24 in. White flowers in the summer. The first and lower leaves are broad and scalloped, with a strong, strange scent. The upper leaves are finely cut and have a different and yet more pungent smell. The whole plant is edible. This variety is good for leaf production. **Warmer zones.**

Coriandrum sativum "Leisure"
Tender annual. Ht 24 in. Much as *C. sativum*; whitish flowers in summer; also suitable for leaf production. **Warmer zones.**

Coriandrum sativum "Sabor"
Tender annual. Ht 28 in. Flowers white with a slight pink tinge in summer. This variety is best for seed production. **Warmer zones.**

 cultivation

Propagation
Seed
Cilantro is grown from seed. Thinly sow its large seed directly into the soil in shallow rows. Lightly cover with fine soil or compost, and water. Look for results after a period of between 5 and 10 days. Seed sowing may be carried out as often as required between early spring (indoors), and late fall. When large enough to handle, thin out the seedlings to leave room for growth.

Sowing into seed trays is not recommended because cilantro plants do not transplant well once the tap root is established. If they get upset they bolt straight into flower, missing out the leaf production stage altogether.

If a harvest of fresh leaves is required, space the plants 2 in. apart; if of seed, 21 in. apart.

Pests and Diseases
Being a highly aromatic plant, cilantro is usually free from pests. In exceptional circumstances it is attacked by aphids. If so, do not be tempted to pressure hose the pests off, as this will destroy the leaves. Either wash off gently under the tap, and shake the plant carefully to remove excess water on the leaves, or use a liquid insecticidal soap.

Coriandrum sativum

Maintenance

Spring Sow seeds.
Summer Sow seeds, cut leaves.
Fall Cut seed heads. Sow fall crop in mild climates. Dig up old plants.
Winter Once the seed heads have been collected, the plant should be pulled up.

Garden Cultivation

Cilantro grows best in a light, well-drained soil, in semi-shade and a dry atmosphere. It is difficult to grow in damp or humid areas and needs a good dry summer if a reasonable crop is to be obtained. However, do not allow the soil to dry out because this will cause the plant to bolt. Plants also bolt readily in hot conditions. Make repeated sowings throughout the summer to ensure a constant supply of the leaves.

When the plant reaches maturity and the seed sets and begins to ripen, the plant tends to loll about on its weak stem and needs staking. On ripening, the seeds develop a delightful orangey scent, and are used widely as a spice and a condiment. For this reason alone, and because the flavor of home-grown seeds is markedly superior to those raised commercially, cilantro deserves a place in the garden. If you live in a mild, frost-free climate, sow in the fall for an over-winter crop; but make sure the plants are in full sunlight.

Harvesting

Pick young leaves any time. They should be 4 in. in height and bright green. Watch seed heads carefully, as they ripen suddenly and will fall without warning. Cut the flower stems as the seed smell starts to become pleasant. Cover bunches of about six heads in a paper bag. Tie the top of the bag and hang upside down in a dry, warm, airy place. Leave for 10 days. The seeds should come away from the husk quite easily and be stored in an airtight container. Coriander seeds keep their flavor well.

container growing

Cilantro can be grown in containers inside with diligence, but the plants produced will be weak and straggly. It is ideal for growing in large, deep pots outside, in partial shade on a patio or by a kitchen door. Fill the container with a standard potting compost mixed in equal parts with composted fine bark, water well, then sow the seeds thinly and cover lightly with compost. Once the leaves are large enough, start cropping. To maintain a supply prepare another large container and sow 20 days later. Water your containers regularly in the morning, not at night, as like many other herbs, cilantro does not like having wet feet. Do not allow the compost to dry out because this will cause the plant to bolt to seed.

medicinal

Cilantro is good for the digestive system, reducing flatulence, stimulating the appetite and aiding the secretion of gastric juices. It is also used to prevent gripe caused by other medication such as senna or rhubarb. Bruised seed can be applied externally as a poultice to relieve painful joints and rheumatism.

CILANTRO

culinary

The leaves and ripe seeds have two distinct flavors. The seeds are warmly aromatic, the leaves have an earthy pungency.

Cilantro seeds are used in garam masala (a mixture of spices) and in curries. Use ground seed in tomato chutney, ratatouille, frankfurters, curries, apple pies, cakes, cookies and marmalade. Add whole seeds to soups, sauces and vegetable dishes.

Add fresh lower leaves to curries, stews, salads, sauces and as a garnish. Delicious in salads, vegetables and poultry dishes. A bunch of cilantro leaves with a vinaigrette dressing goes particularly well with hard-boiled eggs.

Mushrooms and Cilantro
Serves 2

1 pound button mushrooms
2 tablespoons cooking oil
1 cup dry white wine
2 teaspoons coriander seeds
1 clove garlic
2 tablespoons tomato paste
Salt and freshly ground black pepper
Cilantro leaf for garnish

Wipe mushrooms and slice in half. Put the oil, wine, coriander seeds and garlic in a large pot. Bring to a boil and cover and simmer for 5 minutes. Add the mushrooms and tomato paste. Cook for 5 minutes, by which time the vegetables should be tender. Remove the mushrooms and put in a serving dish. Boil the liquid again for 5 minutes and reduce it by half. Pour over the mushrooms. When cool, sprinkle with some chopped cilantro leaf.

Crithmum maritimum

SEA FENNEL

Also known as Samphire, Crest marine, Krítamo. From the family Apiaceae.

This native of the Atlantic, Mediterranean and Black Sea is mentioned in Shakespeare's *King Lear*, where it is referred to as that "dreadful trade" of the samphire gatherer. Rock samphire was at one time cultivated in English gardens for its seed pods and sold in London, where it was called crest marine.

 container growing

Sea fennel will grow happily in containers. Use a soilless compost mixed in equal parts with grit. Place in a sheltered, sunny position.

 medicinal

This herb is very high in vitamin C; it also has digestive and purgative properties. It is under research for treating obesity and is in a number of herbal products.

 culinary

The leaves can be eaten fresh or cooked. Prior to cooking, remove any leaves that have begun to turn slimy and any hard parts of the stalk. The leaves have an aromatic salty flavor which combines well in salads or cooked in butter. They can also be used to make sauces and aromatic pickles.

 varieties

Crithmum maritimum
Sea Fennel
Hardy perennial. Ht 12 in., spread 8 in. Flat umbels of tiny white-green flowers in summer. Aromatic, succulent sea-green, triangular leaves with long rounded linear lance-shaped segments which grow in small groups along the branch. **Zones 7.**

 cultivation

Propagation
Seed
In fall sow fresh seeds into prepared small pots or module plug trays, using a seed compost mixed in equal parts with river sand, under protection at 50°F. Germination takes 2 to 3 weeks; if there is no germination within this period, place the container in a refrigerator for 4 weeks, then return to 50°F. Germination should occur within 4 to 6 weeks. Once the seedlings are large enough, repot using a soilless potting mix mixed in equal parts with horticultural grit. Winter seedlings in a frost-free environment. Plant out in the following spring.

Division
Divide established plants in spring. In the garden, dig up the whole plant, then divide. Once divided, replant in to a well-prepared site. Container-raised plants can be divided gently so as not to destroy the crown, and repotted into a soilless potting mix mixed in equal parts with horticultural grit.

Pests and Diseases
These plants, being aromatic, are not prone to pest damage. However, in cold wet winters, when grown in soil that does not drain well, they can be prone to rot.

Maintenance
Spring Divide established plants. Pick young leaves.
Summer Pick leaves until it starts to flower.
Fall Sow fresh seeds.
Winter Protect from hard frosts below 26°F.

Garden Cultivation
As this is a seaside plant that grows literally in the crevices between rocks, it is essential to prepare the site well, making sure it is well drained, adding extra grit if necessary. Plant in a sunny position and protect from cold winds. In winter cover the crown with straw, not mulch or compost, which would cause it to rot.

Harvesting
In early summer pick the leaves either to use fresh or to pickle.

 other uses

The seeds produce a fragrant oil which is widely used in modern perfumery and medicine. A number of leading manufactures of face creams purport to having included this herb for hydrating the skin.

Curcuma longa
TURMERIC

Also known as Indian saffron, Haldi, Haridra. From the family Zingiberaceae.

Of all the herbs I grow, this is one of the most traditional and versatile. The exact origin of turmeric is not known. It most probably came from western India where records show it has been used for at least 2,500 years. The yellow and yellow-orange colors obtained from the roots are sacred and auspicious. It is important in Hindu and Buddhist ceremonies, being associated with fertility and prosperity, and brings good luck if applied to a bride's face and body as part of the purification ritual before a wedding. The roots may be given as a present on special occasions, such as a visit to a pregnant woman. The use of turmeric is prohibited in a house of mourning.

 varieties

Curcuma longa
Turmeric
Tropical, subtropical, herbaceous perennial. Ht 3 ft., spread indefinite. The yellow/white flowers, with pink tinges to the tips of the petals, appear surrounded by pale green bracts in spring on a single stem. The flowers are sterile and do not produce viable seed. Aromatic long, up to 24 in., mid green, oval leaves. The root is a large rhizome. **Zone 9.**

 cultivation

Propagation
Cuttings
A word of warning before you start taking root cuttings: wear gloves and an apron because, once the root is cut, it produces a yellow sap which will stain your fingers and can permanently stain cloth.

Unless you live in the tropics, the best source for fresh turmeric root is from Asian and Caribbean stores. However, be aware that the quality can be variable. Often, after it has been air-freighted, the cold temperatures have killed the growth, alternatively it may have been treated with chemicals to inhibit sprouting. Choose a fresh, plump, juicy-looking root which has a tooth bud growing on one side. Choose a shallow container not much larger than the root; fill with a seed compost mixed in equal parts with horticultural grit. Place the root in the container with the tooth bud facing up, and cover the roots with compost making sure the tooth bud is peeping through the compost. Place the pot in a plastic bag, seal, and place in a warm place or in a propagator at 68°F. The shoots should emerge in 3 to 4 weeks but may take longer depending on the warmth. Once the shoots emerge, remove the plastic bag. Keep the container in a warm place, minimum temperature 64°F, but not in direct sunlight until fully established.

Only repot one size up, using a potting compost mixed in equal parts with horticultural grit when the plant looks as if it is bursting out of the container; it likes being pot bound.

Division
If you live in the tropics, or have a plant raised in a container, it can be divided in the spring. In the garden

Curcuma longa flower with its green bracts

use two forks back-to-back to divide the rhizome. Once divided replant into a prepared site in the garden. Pot-raised plants should be lifted from the container and excess compost removed so you can see the rhizome. Choose a section of rhizome with a growing bud; slice the root using a sharp knife. Pot the cutting into a small container which just fits the cutting using a seed compost mixed in equal parts with horticultural grit.

Pests and Diseases

Red spider mite can be an occasional problem on older plants when grown indoors; regular misting and keeping the leaves well-washed will reduce this. If it gets out of hand use a insecticidal soap spray following the manufacturer's instructions.

Maintenance

Spring Divide rhizomes.
Summer Pick leaves as required.
Fall Cut back on watering of container plants.
Winter Grow on at a minimum of 64°F.

Garden Cultivation

This herb can only be grown outside in the tropics. It requires a minimum temperature of 64°F at night. It is suitable for growing in a conservatory, heated greenhouse or a well-lit east- or west-facing window, not in direct midday sun, as this will cause leaf scorch.

Harvesting

Outside the tropics, this only produces a small amount of fresh rhizome, so is most usefully used medicinally or as a cosmetic. Harvest the rhizome in late summer/early fall. Only turmeric rhizome, when cured commercially, has the aroma and color necessary for cooking. The leaves can be used as a flavoring; pick as required throughout the growing season.

 ## container growing

Turmeric is ideal for growing in a container in cool and cold climates. However, you will not be able to harvest much useful root from your plant, although you will be able to use the leaves for flavoring. Pot using a soilless potting compost mixed in equal parts with horticultural grit. Be mean with the container size; do not over pot,

as this can cause the rhizome to rot in cool climates. In summer, place the plant in partial shade, water and liquid fertilize regularly. In dry weather plants will benefit from a daily light misting with rainwater. In the fall cut back on the watering, keeping the compost fairly dry. Keep the plant frost free at a minimum of 64°F.

 ## medicinal

Turmeric has been used medicinally for thousands of years; it is an important Ayurvedic herb used to treat inflammation, coughs and gastric disorders. It is also a very good first-aid remedy in the home; a paste can be used as a quick household antiseptic, for cuts, grazes and minor burns. It is also used as a decoction to calm the stomach and can be applied externally to remove hair and alleviate itching.

 ## other uses

Turmeric has been used as dye for centuries, it is used to color medicine, confectionery, paints, varnishes, silk and cotton.

 ## warning

If the roots are cut, the yellow sap will stain fingers or cloth indelibly.

 ## culinary

Turmeric is an essential ingredient in Indian cuisine. It is used in virtually every Indian meat, vegetable and lentil dish with the exception of greens, because when cooked with green vegetables it turns them gray and bitter. Turmeric has been known as poor-man's saffron as it offers a less expensive alternative yellow coloring. The flavor of the cured turmeric can vary, and this is dependent on how it is used. When added to oil before the main ingredient, the flavor is pungent, when added after the main ingredient it is more subtle.

The leaves have a warm, rich, sweet aroma and can be used fresh to wrap fish or candies before steaming.

Cymbopogon citratus
LEMON GRASS

Also known as Fever grass, Bhustrina and Takrai. From the family Poaceae.

This important culinary and medicinal herb, which can be found throughout the tropics, is indigenous to Southeast Asia where it is used extensively to produce an essential oil. It is also a snake repellent and a versatile garden plant. There are records showing that the Persians were using it as a tea in the first century CE. I have been lucky enough to see it growing and flowering naturally in the Caribbean where they primarily use it for reducing fevers.

 varieties

Cymbopogon citratus
Lemon Grass
Half-hardy perennial, evergreen in warm climates. Ht 4½ ft., spread 3 ft. Lax panicles of awnless spikelets appear throughout the summer. However, it rarely flowers in cold climates or in cultivation. Lemon-scented linear, gray/green leaves up to 3 ft. in length. Robust cream/beige stake-like stems. **Zone 9.**

Cymbopogon nardus
Citronella Grass
Half-hardy perennial, evergreen in warm climates. Ht 5 ft. and spread 3 ft. Lax panicles of awnless spikelets appear throughout the summer. However it rarely flowers in cold climates. Lemon-scented drooping, flat, blue/gray/green leaves up to 2 ft. in length. This species is cultivated for its medicinal and insect-repellent properties. It is also grown around buildings in Africa, as a snake repellent. The oil is used to perfume soaps. **Zone 9.**

Cymbopogon martini var. motia
Palmarosa, Rosha, Indian Geranium
Half-hardy perennial, evergreen in warm climates. Ht 4½ ft. and spread 3 ft. Lax panicles of awnless spikelets appear throughout the summer. However, it rarely flowers in cold climates. Rose-scented linear gray/green leaves up to 20 in. in length. The oil made from this species is used to perfume cosmetics and soap. It is also used in Ayurvedic medicine to treat fevers and infectious diseases. **Zone 9.**

 cultivation

Propagation
Seed
In spring, sow seeds into prepared seed or module plug trays and place under protection at 68°F. Germination takes 15 to 25 days. Once the seedlings are large enough, repot using a soilless potting mix and grow on until well established. Either plant in the garden in warm climates or, in cool climates, grow on as a container plant.

Cuttings
Take cuttings, in spring, from a plant that is more than a year old, which has an established crown. Gently remove the swollen lower stems from the crown. Remove any grass from the stem and cut the stem back to 4 in. Place in a prepared module plug tray or a very small pot using a seed compost; do not be tempted to over pot the cutting as this will cause it to rot. Place under protection or in a warm position away from cold draughts. Once rooted, pot into a small pot using a soilless potting mix.

Division
In the garden use two forks back-to-back and gently tease the plant apart, replanting immediately into a prepared site. Divide container plants either with your fingers, or two small forks, teasing the crown apart, repotting into a pot which fits snugly around the roots. This plant is happiest when pot bound. Use a soilless potting compost.

Pests and Diseases
Outside the tropics this herb can be prone to rot and mildew. To prevent this, in winter, keep container-grown plants nearly dry and in a well-ventilated, frost-free room.

Lemon grass stems

Maintenance

Spring Sow seeds. Divide or take root cuttings of established plants. Feed container-raised plants regularly.
Summer Do not allow the plants to dry out. Maintain feeding until late summer.
Fall In cool climates, to prevent disease, cut back the grass leaving the stems.
Winter Protect from frost. Keep watering to the minimum.

Garden Cultivation

Lemon grass can be grown outside where the night temperature does not fall below 48°F. Plant in any soil, including a heavy soil, as long as the summers are hot and wet and the winters are warm and dry. In low light levels the plant can become dormant. In spring, prune back all the old growth and thick stalks to 4 in.

Harvesting

The fresh leaves and lower stems can be cut throughout the summer to use fresh or to dry. The stems can be stored whole in the refrigerator in a plastic bag for up to 2 weeks. Alternatively the stems and the leaves can be frozen for use within 5 months.

 container growing

An excellent container plant. Use a soilless potting mix which should not be allowed to dry out in summer. In winter, bring the plant into a frost-free environment of 40°F minimum. When the light levels and night temperatures drop the plant will go "dormant," the grass gradually turns brown and the outside leaves shrivel. Reduce the watering to a minimum and cut back the grass to 4 in. above the stems. In early spring, as the day lengthens and the temperatures rise, you will notice new grass starting to grow. Cut off all dead growth. Repot if necessary and liquid feed weekly.

 medicinal

A tea made from fresh leaves is very refreshing as well as being a stomach and gut relaxant. It is also a good antidepressant and helps lift the spirits if one is in a bad mood. The essential oil is antiseptic, antibacterial, antifungal and deodorizing.

 other uses

Valued for its exotic citrus fragrance, it is commercially used in soaps, perfumes and as an ingredient in sachets. Also used as an insect repellent.

△ warning

Do not take the essential oil internally without supervision.

 culinary

The fresh leaves and stalks have been traditionally used in Thai, Vietnamese and Caribbean cooking. The lemon flavor complements curries, seafood, garlic and chilies.

Vegetable and Lemon Grass Soup
Serves 4

2 tablespoons light olive oil
1 large onion, finely minced
2 cloves garlic, finely sliced
4 carrots, scrubbed then finely sliced or, if in a hurry, grated.
2/3 cup button mushrooms, sliced
4 to 6 stems of lemon grass, cut into 1½ in. lengths and bruised
1 teaspoon ginger, finely grated
3½ cups chicken or vegetable broth
1 tablespoon very finely minced lemon grass leaves
Salt to taste

Heat the oil in a heavy-bottomed pot, add the onions, garlic and carrots, stir-fry for 3 minutes, stirring all the time. Add the mushrooms and stir-fry for an additional minute. Pour in the water, stir and add the lemon grass stems, ginger and salt to taste. Bring to a boil, then reduce the heat, cover and simmer for about 4 to 7 minutes until all the vegetables are cooked but still crunchy.

With a slotted spoon, remove the lemon grass stalks, add the very finely minced lemon grass leaves, stir and serve.

PINKS

Dianthus gratianopolitanus

Also known as Clove pink, Gillyflower, and Dianthus. From the family Caryophyllaceae.

Dianthus comes from the words *dios*, meaning divine, and *anthos*, meaning flower. Both the Romans and Greeks gave pinks a place of honor and made coronets and garlands from the flowers. In the 17th century it was recognized that the flowers could be crystallized, and the petals started being used in soups, sauces, cordials and wine.

 varieties

Dianthus deltoides
Maiden Pink
Evergreen hardy perennial. Ht 6 in., spread 12 in. Small cerise, pink or white flowers are borne singly early summer. Small, narrow, lance-shaped, dark green leaves. **Zone 5.**

Dianthus gratianopolitanus
Cheddar Pink
Evergreen hardy perennial. Ht 6 in., spread 12 in. Very fragrant pink/magenta flat flowers are borne singly early summer. Small, narrow, lance-shaped, gray/green leaves. This variety is protected in the UK. **Zone 5.**

Dianthus plumarius
Pinks
Evergreen hardy perennial. Ht 6 in., spread 12 in. Very fragrant flowers, white with dark crimson centers, are borne singularly all summer. Loose mats of narrow, lance-shaped, gray/green leaves. This species is related to the Cheddar pink and the origin of the garden pink. **Zone 5.**

 cultivation

Propagation
Seed
Sow the small seeds when fresh in the fall into prepared seed or plug module trays using a standard seed compost, and cover with perlite. Winter seedlings in a cold frame prior to planting out in the following spring 12 in. apart. Pinks raised from seed can be variable in height, color and habit.

Cuttings
Take stem cuttings in spring and heel cuttings in early fall. Place the cuttings into prepared plug module trays or a small pot using a seed compost mixed in equal parts with fine composted bark. Do not overwater the cuttings while they are rooting as this will cause them to rot.

Division
Established plants can be divided in early fall after flowering.

Layering
Established plants can be layered in late summer and then lifted in the following spring.

Pests and Diseases
During propagation young plants can be prone to rot; this is usually caused by fungus due to the compost being too wet. Infected plants must be removed as soon as this is spotted as it can spread to other plants very quickly. Aphids can be a problem; spray with insecticidal soap.

Maintenance
Spring Lift layers. Take stem cuttings.
Summer Deadhead flowers.
Fall Take heel cuttings. Divide established plants. Sow seed. Layer established plants.
Winter No need for protection.

Garden Cultivation
Pinks prefer to be planted in a well-drained soil, which does not become waterlogged in winter, and in full sun.

Harvesting
Pick the flowers just as they open for either using the petals fresh or for crystallizing.

 container growing

Pinks grow well in containers. Use a soilless compost mixed with 25 percent composted fine bark and 25 percent fine horticultural grit.

 culinary

Before eating the petals, they must be removed individually from the flower. You will notice that each petal has a white heel (see below); this must also be removed as it is very bitter. The prepared petals can be added to salads, sandwiches and fruit pies. They can be used to flavor jams, sugars and syrups. The crystallized petals can be used to decorate cakes and desserts.

 medicinal

An excellent nerve tonic can be made from the petals, either as a cordial or infused in white wine.

 other uses

Add dried petals to potpourris, scented sachets and cosmetic products.

Dianthus flowers, showing the bitter-tasting white heel

FOXGLOVE

Digitalis purpurea

Also know as Fairy fingers, Fairy gloves and Deadmen's bells. From the family Scrophulariaceae.

Foxgloves are a common wild flower in temperate climates throughout the world, seeding freely in woods and the countryside. The principal common name is probably derived from the Anglo-Saxon *foxglue* or *foxmusic* after the shape of a musical instrument. In 1542 Fuchs called it Digitalis after the finger-like shape of its flowers, but he considered it a violent medicine. It was not until the late 18th century, after William Withering used foxglove tea in Shropshire as an aid for dropsy, that its reputation as a medicinal herb grew.

Digitalis purpurea f. *albiflora*

Pests and Diseases
Foxgloves rarely suffer from pests or diseases.

Maintenance
Spring Thin seedlings from fall sowing.
Summer If self seeding is not required, remove flowering spikes after flowering.
Fall Sow fresh seeds. Dig up self-sown seedlings for potting on or replanting.
Winter No need for protection.

Garden Cultivation
This is one of the most poisonous plants in the flora, so choose its position with care. Foxgloves will grow in most conditions, even dry exposed sites, but do best in semi-shade and a moist but well-drained acid soil enriched with leaf mold. Water well in dry weather and remove the center spike after flowering to increase the size of the flowers on the side shoots.

Harvesting
Do not harvest unless you are a trained herbalist or pharmacist.

 ## container growing

Foxgloves are not ideally suited for growing in containers, mainly because of their flowering spike, which can be damaged in high winds. If you do wish to grow them in a container use a soilless compost and water regularly throughout the summer months.

 ## medicinal

Foxgloves are grown commercially for the production of a drug, the discovery of which is a classic example of a productive marriage between folklore and scientific curiosity. Foxgloves contain glycosides which are extracted from the second-year leaves to make the heart drug digitalis. For more than 200 years digitalis has provided the main drug for treating heart failure. It is also a powerful diuretic.

 ## warning

The whole plant is poisonous — seeds, leaves and roots. Even touching the plant can cause rashes, headaches and nausea. DO NOT USE without medical direction.

 ## varieties

Digitalis purpurea
Foxglove, wild, common
Short-lived perennial, grown as a biennial. Ht 3–5 ft., spread 2 ft. Flowers all shades of pink, purple and red in second summer. Rough, mid- to dark green leaves.
Zone 4.

Digitalis purpurea f. *albiflora*
White Foxglove
Short-lived perennial, grown as a biennial. Ht 3–5 ft., spread 24 in. Tubular white flowers all summer in the second season. Rough, mid- to dark green leaves.
Zone 4.

cultivation

Propagation
Seed
For the best germination, sow the very fine seeds in fall, using the cardboard method (see p. 645), either directly onto the prepared ground, or into pots or plug module trays, which have been filled with a standard seed compost. Sow on the surface and do not cover the seeds with compost. Place the container in a cold frame, cold greenhouse or under the eaves of the house. Winter the seedlings in the containers, only protecting if temperatures fall below 14°F. In the following spring either prick out or plant in the garden 18 in. apart. They will flower in the second season.

Echinacea
ECHINACEA

Also known as Coneflower, Purple coneflower and Black Sampson. From the family Asteraceae.

Echinacea is an herb that has been used by the Native American Indians for hundreds of years for everything from snake bites and wounds to respiratory infections. Its generic name *Echinacea* comes from the Greek *echinos*, "hedgehog," referring to the central golden cone, which becomes more pointed and prickly as the flower matures. It is only in the past decade that modern research has confirmed its medicinal properties; however there is still some argument over its validity. Despite this, it remains in much demand. This has had a major impact on the wild species, which has now become endangered due to over collection.

Echinacea pallida

Echinacea purpurea

 varieties

Echinacea angustifolia
Narrow-leafed Echinacea, Black Sampson
Hardy herbaceous perennial. Ht 2 ft., spread 12 in. Single flowers with long, thin purple or, rarely, white petals and a spiky central cone, borne throughout the summer until early fall. Midgreen linear leaves. In its natural habitat this echinacea has become an endangered species. The Native American Indians regarded this herb as a cure-all. **Zone 4.**

Echinacea pallida
Echinacea, Coneflower
Hardy herbaceous perennial. Ht 4 ft., spread 18 in. Single flowers with long mauve/pink, narrow, drooping petals and a spiky central cone, throughout the summer until early fall. The leaves are oval, narrow, dark green and veined. **Zone 4.**

Echinacea purpurea
Echinacea, Purple Coneflower
Hardy herbaceous perennial. Ht 4 ft., spread 18 in. Single honey-scented flowers with long mauve/pink, narrow, drooping petals and a spiky central cone, throughout the

summer until early fall. The leaves are oval, narrow, dark green and deeply veined. This species is cultivated for its medicinal properties. **Zone 3.**

 cultivation

Propagation

Seed

Sow seeds in early spring into prepared seed trays, plug cell-packs or a small container using a seed compost mixed in equal parts with perlite. Cover the seeds with perlite. Place in a warm position or in a propagator at 65°F. If no germination has occurred after 28 days, place the container outside for an additional 21 days, then place back under cover, out of direct sunlight. Germination should then occur within the next 20 days. Once the seedlings are large enough, pot into a soilless potting mix with composted fine bark in equal parts. Once rooted, harden off, plant out into a prepared site in the garden 12 in. apart.

Division

Divide established plants in the late fall when all the foliage has died back and the plant is dormant. Use the two forks back-to-back method. Replant immediately either into a prepared site in the garden, or alternatively, repot using a soilless potting compost mixed in equal parts with composted fine bark. Container-raised plants can also be divided at this time of year.

Pests and Diseases

Echinacea, in general, is not prone to pests and diseases. In spring, young plants can be attacked by slugs and snails, so it is worth doing a couple of night patrols with a flashlight to remove any that you may find in the crown of the plant. In a damp, warm late summer it can suffer from powdery mildew; if this happens cut off any affected parts, discard them and do not add to the compost.

Maintenance

Spring Sow seeds. Feed established plants lightly with well-rotted manure.
Summer Cut back stems as the blooms fade to encourage further flower production.
Fall Divide established plants.
Winter No need for protection from the cold, only from excessive wet.

Echinacea purpurea

Garden Cultivation

Echinacea grows wild on the fertile plains of North America, so, to keep it thriving in the garden, plant in a fertile loam soil which is free draining and in plenty of sun. It will adapt to most soils with the exception of excessive wet conditions and cold wet clay soils, which can cause the roots to rot. After flowering, cut back the plants, leaving 3 in. of growth above ground, collect the seeds and keep the flower heads for drying. Lightly mulch established plants with well rotted manure in the spring. Spring growth and young echinacea plants are a snail delicacy, so it is worth checking around the plants daily in spring.

Harvesting

Pick the flowers and leaves during flowering before the cone is fully formed and the petals have started to fall back. When the petals have died back pick the seeds heads, dry well. If you wish to use the plant medicinally, dig up the roots of 4-year-old plants of *Echinacea angustifolia*, or *purpurea*, or *pallida* in fall for drying and for making fresh tinctures.

 container growing

Echinacea adapts happily to being grown in containers. Use a soilless potting compost mixed in equal parts with composted fine bark. Divide pot-bound plants in the fall, or replant in a pot one size up. Place in full sun for the growing season. Feed regularly with a liquid fertilizer following the manufacturer's instructions. In winter, if you live in a damp, wet, cold climate, place the container under the eves of the house, or by a wall, to shelter it from the rain.

 medicinal

Echinacea has the ability to raise the body's resistance to infections by stimulating the immune system. It is reputedly very effective in preventing colds and flu or reducing their severity. A tincture made from the root is used to treat severe infections, and a decoction made from the root can be used as a gargle to treat sore throats and other throat infections. A decoction, or the juice extracted from the flowers, can be used externally to treat minor wounds, burns, boils and skin infections, including chilblains.

 other uses

The cone part of the flower head dries very well and looks most attractive in floral arrangements.

 warning

If you are allergic to plants in the Asteraceae family, for example chrysanthemums, marigolds or daisies, then you could be allergic to echinacea.

People who are suffering from progressive systemic autoimmune disorders should not take this herb without full consultation.

Dried roots and flowers

Echium vulgare
VIPER'S BUGLOSS

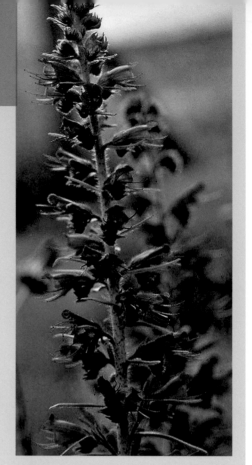

Also known as Bugles, Wild borage, Snake flower, Blue devil, Blueweed, Viper's grass and Snakeflower. From the family Boraginaceae.

This plant originates from the Mediterranean region and is now widespread throughout the northern hemisphere, being found on light porous stones on semi-dry grassland, moorlands, and waste ground. It is regarded as a weed in some parts of America. To many farmers this will seem an understatement; they consider it a plague.

The common name, viper's bugloss, developed from the medieval Doctrine of Signatures, which ordained that a plant's use should be inferred from its appearance. It was noticed that the brown stem looked rather like a snake skin and that the seed is shaped like a viper's head. So, in their wisdom, they prescribed it for viper bites, which for once proved right; it had some success in the treatment of the spotted viper's bite.

 ## varieties

Echium vulgare
Viper's Bugloss
Hardy biennial. Ht 2–4 ft. Bright blue/pink flowers in the second year. The leaves are midgreen and bristly.
All zones.

 ## cultivation

Propagation
Seed
Viper's bugloss is easily grown from seed. Start it off in a controlled way in spring by sowing the small seed into a prepared seed or plug module tray. Cover the seed with perlite. When the seedlings are large enough to handle, and after a period of hardening off, plant into a prepared site in the garden at about 18 in. apart.

Pests and Diseases
It rarely suffers.

Maintenance
Spring First year, sow seeds; second year, clear round plants.
Summer Second year, pick off flowers as they die so that they cannot set seed.
Fall First year, leave well alone. Second year, dig up plants and discard. Do not compost unless you want thousands of viper's bugloss plants all over your garden.
Winter No need to protect first-year plant.

Garden Cultivation
This colorful plant is beautifully marked. Sow the seed in spring directly into the garden. It will grow in any soil and is great for growing in dry soils and on sea cliffs. With its long taproot, the plant will survive any drought but cannot easily be transplanted except when very young. The disadvantage is that it self-seeds and is therefore invasive.

Harvesting
Gather flowers in summer for fresh use.

 ## container growing

Because it is a rampant self-seeder, it is quite a good idea to grow it in containers. For the first year it bears only green prickly leaves and is very boring. However, the show put on in the second year is full compensation. Use a soilless compost; no need to feed. Over-feeding will prohibit the flowering. Very tolerant of drought; nevertheless do water it regularly. Dies back in winter of first year — leave the container somewhere cool and water occasionally.

 ## culinary

The young leaves are similar to borage, but they have lots more spines. It is said you can eat them when young, but I haven't tried this. The flowers look very attractive in salads. They can also be crystallized.

 ## medicinal

The fresh flowering tips can be chopped up for making poultices for treating whitlows and boils. Infuse lower leaves to produce a sweating in fevers or to relieve headaches.

Echium vulgare

CARDAMOM

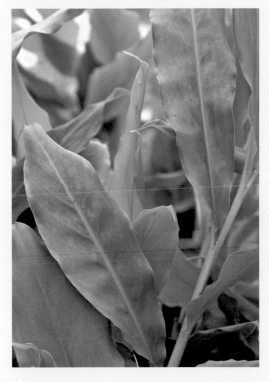

Also known as Ela, Ilaichi.
From the family Zingiberaceae.

Cardamom is indigenous to southern India where it grows abundantly under the forest canopy. Until the 19th century, the world's supply of cardamom came mainly from the wild, in an area known as the Cardamom Hills in Western Ghat, India. The fruits have been traded in India for at least 1,000 years. It was known as the Queen of Spices, with black pepper being the King. Cardamom is the third most expensive spice after saffron and vanilla. It is traded internationally in the form of whole fruits, and to a lesser extent as seeds. Early Arabs enjoyed cardamom seeds in their coffee, a practice which continues today, and which explains why cardamoms are mentioned so often in Sir Richard Burton's translation of *The Arabian Nights*. In India it is common practice to offer cardamoms at the end of a meal, as a digestive and for freshening the breath.

Division
Divide established plants in late spring, early summer. Replant into a prepared site in a tropical garden or tropical greenhouse. Alternatively, if dividing a potted plant, replant using a soilless potting compost mixed equally with composted fine bark. Plants in the tropics that have been divided take 3 years to flower; however, it rarely flowers outside the tropics, even when raised in a tropical house, due to the light levels.

Pests and Diseases
Red spider mite can be an occasional problem in older plants; regular misting with soft rain water and keeping the leaves well-washed will reduce this. If it gets out of hand use a insecticidal soap spray following the manufacturer's instructions.

If plants are too cold their leaves turn brown. If the leaves develop brown tips at any time (even if the plant is kept warm) it is a sign of overwatering. If the leaf develops creamy patches, this can be caused by too much sun and is a form of scorch.

Maintenance
Spring Divide established plants or pot plants.
Summer Spray leaves with rain water.
Fall Sow fresh seeds.
Winter Protect from cold weather.

 ## varieties

Elettaria cardamomum
Cardamom
Tropical, subtropical, evergreen perennial. Ht 9 ft., spread indefinite. In summer the flowers grow on a single stem. They are creamy white, with deep purple lines over the lower lip. They are followed by pale green to fawn fruits, each having three chambers, containing several small aromatic seeds which start white and ripen to black. Aromatic, up to 2 ft. long, midgreen, lance-shaped leaves. The root is a thick branching rhizome. **Zone 8.**

 ## cultivation

Propagation
Seed
Outside the tropics it is very difficult to get fresh seed, which remains viable for only 7 to 10 days once harvested; therefore it is far easier to propagate by division. If you can get fresh seed, sow in fall into prepared plug cell-packs, using a seed compost. Place in a warm place or propagator at 75°F. Germination takes 14 to 21 days. Plants raised from seed take 3 to 5 years to flower.

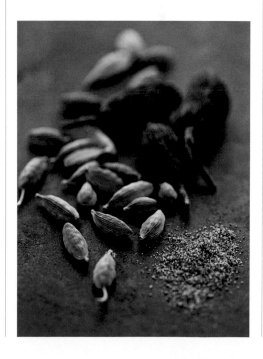

Cardamom fruits and the smaller seeds contained within them

CARDAMOM

Garden Cultivation

When grown outdoors in the tropics, it is grown in the shade of the trees, in a deep fertile soil. It needs a minimum annual rainfall of 60 in., and a short dry season. It takes 3 years before the plant will flower and set seed.

In the northern hemisphere it is best grown as a potted plant indoors or in a heated greenhouse, even in hot summers as it needs a minimum temperature of 64°F.

Harvesting

In tropical climates the fruit is harvested by hand from the third year onwards. In cool climates pick fresh leaves for use as required.

 ## container growing

Cardamom can only be grown indoors in climates outside the tropics and subtropics. It will not flower, although you can use the leaves for flavoring. Grow your plant in soilless potting compost mixed in equal parts with composted fine bark. Cardamoms can be fussy: they do not like drafts, sudden changes of temperature or direct sunlight. Grow them in a warm, steamy, shady place, like a warm bathroom and mist the plant daily with rainwater. Alternatively, stand the pot on a big saucer of pebbles which are kept moist, to encourage a humid atmosphere around the plant. In winter, keep the plant warm at a minimum of 68°F and cut back on the watering, but do not allow the plant to dry out. Regularly liquid feed during the growing season with a general-purpose foliage fertilizer following the manufacturer's instructions.

 ## medicinal

The medicinal properties of cardamom are found in the seeds, which have pain-relieving, antiinflammatory, and antispasmodic properties that are often used to treat urine retention and stomach disorders. In Ayurvedic medicine it is often used to improve the flavor and quality of medicine and as an expectorant.

Seeds extracted from the pod, chewed after a meal, freshen the breath and aid digestion.

 ## other uses

Cardamom oil made from the seeds is used in cosmetics, soaps, lotions and perfumes.

 ## culinary

In India and throughout South Asia the cardamom fruit is used not only in savory dishes, where it is an essential ingredient in garam masala, but also in candies where it is often combined with rose water and thickened milk. The bright lime green pods are the best culinary variety and the true cardamom. There are brown pods that are confusingly also called cardamom, but these come from a plant called *Amomum subulatum*, and they are used in savory dishes, especially rice dishes.

The leaves don't smell the same as the seeds; they have a sweet aromatic scent and can be used to wrap around fish, rice or vegetables to add flavor while cooking. The stalks are useful to tie together to make a neat pocket. They keep fish beautifully moist.

Garam Masala

There are many versions of Garam masala, some are spicy, some are hot; here is a fragrant version that is good with chicken and vegetables.

2 teaspoons cardamom seeds (removed from pods)
1 teaspoon cumin seeds
1 teaspoon whole black peppercorns
2 x 2 in. cinnamon sticks
½ teaspoon whole cloves
¼ teaspoon nutmeg, grated.

Heat a small skillet and add each spice individually with the exception of the nutmeg. As each one starts to smell fragrant, remove it from the pan onto a plate and allow to cool. Put all the cooled spices into a mortar and pestle or an electirc blender and grind to a fine powder. Add the finely grated nutmeg. Store in a glass jar with an airtight lid in a dark cupboard. Use within 4 weeks.

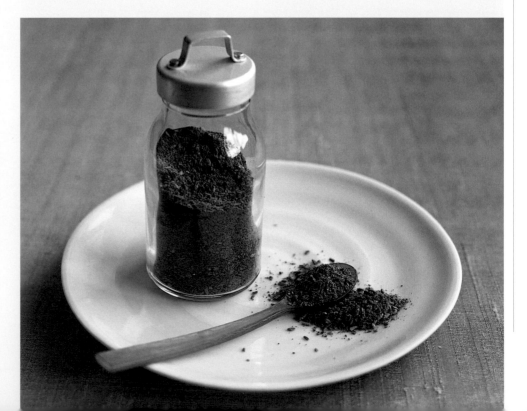

Equisetum arvense
HORSETAIL

Also known as Mare's tail, Shave grass, Bottle brush and Pewter wort. From the family Equisetaceae.

The Horsetail is a plant left over from prehistoric times. By the evidence of fossil remains, it has survived almost unchanged since the coal seams were laid. The Romans always used it to clean their pots and pans, not just to make them clean but also, thanks to the silica, to make them nonstick. The plant was used in the Middle Ages as an abrasive by cabinet makers and to clean pewter, brass and copper, and for scouring wooden containers and milk pans.

Equisetum arvense fertile shoots

varieties

Equisetum arvense
Horsetail
Hardy perennial. Ht 18 in. The plant does not flower. It grows on thin creeping rhizomes producing 8 in. long gray/brown fertile shoots with 4 to 6 sheaths in spring. The shoots die off and the spores are spread just like those of ferns. **Zone 6.**

cultivation

Propagation
I am not sure that this is necessary because it is so invasive, but if you do require a supply of horsetail it may be of merit.

Cuttings
Take root cuttings in summer and place into prepared seed or plug module trays using a standard seed compost mixed in equal parts with fine composted bark. Plant into a prepared site the following spring.

Pests and Diseases
This herb is pest and disease free.

Maintenance
Spring Remove any fertile shoots to prevent the plant spreading.
Summer Cut back plants as they begin to die back to prevent the spores spreading.
Fall Cut down to the ground.
Winter No need for protection; very hardy.

Garden Cultivation
If horsetail is to be introduced into the garden at all, and to be honest I do not recommend it, it is best to confine it to a strong container.

Harvesting
Pick the green/brown shoots that look like minute Christmas trees in summer for drying.

container growing

This is the only sane way to grow this herb. Choose a large tough container; garbage cans are ideal. Fill it with a soil-based potting compost. If you wish to sink it into the garden make sure that the rim is at least 6 in. above the surface so that the rhizomes cannot penetrate or creep over the top. Be sure to cut back in summer to prevent spread by the spores. No need to feed and it requires little watering. It can look attractive!

culinary

It has been eaten as a substitute for asparagus, but I do not recommend it unless you are stuck on a desert island and there is no other food available.

medicinal

This plant is a storehouse of minerals and vitamins, so herbalists recommend it in cases of amnesia and general debility. It also enriches the blood, hardens fingernails and revitalizes lifeless hair. Its astringent properties help to strengthen the walls of the veins, tightening up varicose veins and help guard against fatty deposits in the arteries.

other uses

The dried stems can be used to scour metal and polish pewter and fine woodwork. The whole plant yields a yellow ocher dye.

warning

If you wish to take horsetail medicinally do not self-administer; consult a herbalist.

Eriocephalus africanus
SOUTH AFRICAN WILD ROSEMARY

Also known as Wild rosemary, Snowbush, Kapokbos. From the family Asteraceae.

This amazing drought-loving plant, which is well known in the Cape of South Africa, has a special place in my herb farm because, while the majority of my herbs are becoming dormant in winter, it goes into full flower, which lifts everyone's spirits during the short gray days of the winter months. These flowers are followed by the most attractive seedheads, which are covered in white tufts, hence its Afrikaans name *Kapokbos*, which is derived from *Kapok*, meaning "snow." I had been growing this herb for a number of years before realizing its full potential as a medicinal herb; for example it has been used for many hundreds of years by the Khoi people of southwestern Africa as a diuretic.

 varieties

Eriocephalus africanus
South African Wild Rosemary
Half-hardy evergreen shrub. Ht and spread 3 ft. Clusters of small white flowers with magenta centers from early to late winter, which are followed by seeds covered in masses of tiny white hairs that make them look fluffy. Small, needle-like, silver-haired, oval, slightly succulent, aromatic leaves which grow in tufts along the branch. **Zone 9.**

 cultivation

Propagation
Seed
In spring, sow fresh seeds into prepared plug cell-packs, or small containers using a seed compost mixed in equal parts with perlite. Place in either a warm place or a propagator at 68°F, germination takes 10 to 15 days. Once large enough to handle, repot using a soilless potting mix mixed with 25 percent horticultural sand. In cool climates, winter young plants in a frost-free environment prior to planting out in the following spring.

Cuttings
In late spring, take softwood cuttings from the growing tips and insert into prepared plug cell-packs, using a seed compost mixed in equal parts with perlite. In cool climates grow under protection for the first year prior to planting out in the following spring.

Pests and Diseases
Very rarely suffers from pests or diseases. In cold climates excessive water in winter can cause the plant to rot.

Maintenance
Spring Prune after flowering in late spring to encourage new growth. Sow seeds. Take cuttings.
Summer Feed container-grown plants regularly.
Fall In cold climates protect from heavy fall rains.
Winter Protect from excessive wet in winter and when temperatures fall consistently below 37°F during the day.

Garden Cultivation
This amazingly drought-tolerant herb will adapt to most

SOUTH AFRICAN WILD ROSEMARY

Eriocephalus africanus seedhead

soils with the exception of heavy cold clay and marshy types of soil. The ideal situations are full sun and a well-drained soil. It makes an ideal coastal plant as it likes the sea spray and wind. In Mediterranean and other warm climates it can be grown as a hedge, or clipped into ball shapes. In situations where temperatures fall below 37°F at night it is advisable to grow this herb in a container.

Harvesting
Pick the leaves to use fresh or to dry after flowering from spring until early fall. The twiggy branches are also used in some medicinal decoctions; pick these as and when required. Harvest the seeds when they start to drop.

 ## companion planting

Because this herb flowers in winter it is a most beneficial late nectar plant and therefore attracts beneficial insects to the garden, which increases pollination of late-flowering plants.

 ## container growing

This wild rosemary makes a spectacular container plant as it cascades beautifully over the pot; another plus is that it does not mind a bit of neglect. Use a soilless compost mixed with river sand (75 percent loam, 25 percent sand). Repot every spring and give the plant a good "hair cut" after flowering. Water regularly throughout the summer and feed monthly with a general-purpose liquid fertilizer from spring until first flowering in early fall.

 ## medicinal

Wild rosemary has traditionally been used as a medicine for many ailments like coughs and

 ## culinary

The leaves can be used in a very similar way to rosemary *(Rosmarinus officinalis)*, especially with lamb dishes and vegetable stews as the flavor is fairly similar.

Special Lamb Stew
Serves 4 to 6

½ cup dried chickpeas, soaked overnight,
   or use tinned
4 tablespoons light olive oil
1 large onion, finely minced
11 pounds lean lamb, cubed
2 lemons, juice only
2 bay leaves
3 sprigs South African wild rosemary, roughly 4 in. long
3 leeks, cleaned and chopped
1 cup spinach
¾ cup French flat-leaf parsley
1 fresh lime, sliced
Salt and black pepper

Strain the soaked chickpeas, cook in fresh unsalted water for 15 to 20 minutes, drain, rinse under cold fresh water and let sit. Alternatively, open can, drain, rinse under cold fresh water and let sit.

Heat 2 tablespoons of olive oil in a large, heavy pan,

colds, flatulence and colic, and as a diuretic and a diaphoretic. It is said to have similar qualities to rosemary *(Rosmarinus officinalis)*. An infusion of the leaves can be used in the bath to help one relax, and also in a foot bath to stimulate the start of the menstrual period and to relieve swollen legs. An infusion of the leaves and twigs can be used to control dandruff and to stimulate hair growth.

 ## other uses

When dried it can be added to sachets and potpourris.

 ## warning

Do not take medicinally during pregnancy.

slowly saute the onion, add the lamb and brown on all sides, season with salt and pepper, pour over the lemon juice, add enough boiled hot water to just cover the meat. Add the bay leaves and South African wild rosemary. Cover and simmer for 30 minutes. Heat the remaining oil, saute the leeks, spinach and parsley until just cooked. Add this to the meat together with the chickpeas and sliced lime. Check that the liquid just covers the lamb, adding extra if required. Simmer all the ingredients for an additional hour, checking from time to time that nothing is sticking to the bottom of the pan. Just before serving, remove the remaining twigs of South African wild rosemary and find the limes, which can be used to decorate the serving plate. Serve with rice and either a green salad or green beans.

ASAFOETIDA

Ferula assa-foetida

Also known as Devil's dung, Food of the Gods and Hing. From the family Apiaceae.

This herb, indigenous to the Middle East, has for thousands of years been renowned for its gum resin which is extracted from its tuberous roots. Asafoetida gets its name from the Persian *aza*, "resin," and the Latin *foetidus*, "stinking," which is highlighted by one of its common names, Devil's dung. Ironically it is also called Food of the Gods, because minute quantities of the sulfur-smelling resin can enhance the flavor of many foods.

 ## varieties

Ferula assa-foetida
Asafoetida
Perennial. Ht 6 ft., spread 4½ ft. Flowers from the fourth year in early spring, with flat umbels of tiny yellow flowers, followed by small brown seeds. The flowering spikes can reach 12 ft. Large finely divided green/gray sulfuric, garlic-scented leaves. This plant often dies after flowering. **Zone 7.**

 ## cultivation

Propagation
Seed
Sow fresh seeds in late summer, into prepared plug cell-packs or small pots using a seed compost mixed in equal parts with vermiculite. Once the seedlings are large enough repot using a soilless potting mix mixed in equal parts with horticultural sand.

Pests and Diseases
Rarely suffers from pests or diseases. Container-raised plants can be attacked by aphids, however. Treat with a insecticidal soap spray following the manufacturer's instructions.

Maintenance
Spring Stake flowering spikes when grown on an exposed site.

Summer Sow seeds; harvest root from fourth year on.
Fall Mulch established plants with well-rotted manure.
Winter Protect from excessive wet.

Garden Cultivation
Plant in a warm, well-drained soil and a sunny position. Because of the height when in flower and because it dislikes being moved, position the plant with care. Do give it some protection from the prevailing wind, bearing in mind that it flowers in early spring.

Harvesting
Harvest the seed and resin in the summer from 4-year-old plants. Cut off the stems, and make successive slices through the roots. A milky smelly liquid will exude from the cuts. When dry it forms a resin which turns from creamy, grayish-white to reddish-brown as it is exposed to the air. One root, after successive slicing, can yield up to 2¼ lb. of resin.

 ## container growing

Only pot up one size of pot at a time; this plant does not like being over potted. Use a soilless potting mix mixed in equal parts with horticultural sand. Place the container in full sun and liquid feed regularly throughout the growing season following the manufacturer's instructions.

 ## medicinal

In Ayurvedic and Eastern herbal medicine asafoetida gum resin is used to treat bloating, wind, indigestion and constipation. It also helps lower blood pressure and thins the blood. Owing to its foul taste and smell it is usually taken in pill form.

 ## other uses

A mixture of garlic and asafoetida apparently makes the ultimate insect repellent. I think it would also make the ultimate human repellent. In Afghanistan it is said that asafoetida when rubbed over boots keeps snakes away.

 ## warning

Do not administer to very young children or babies.

 ## culinary

Asafoetida is used throughout southern India in the preparation of beans, peas and lentils, which are collectively known as *dal*. The best way to use asafoetida in the kitchen is to buy it already prepared in an airtight container. Add a minute pinch of resin to hot oil before adding the other ingredients; this calms the aroma and balances the other ingredients.

Filipendula
MEADOWSWEET

Also known as Bridewort, Meadow queen, Meadow-wort, and Queen of the meadow. From the family Rosaceae.

Meadowsweet can be found growing wild in profusion near streams and rivers, in damp meadows, fens and marshlands, or wet woodlands to 3,300 ft. altitude. It is a native of Europe and Asia that has been successfully introduced into, and is naturalized in, North America.

varieties

Filipendula ulmaria
Meadowsweet
Hardy perennial. Ht 2–4 ft., spread 2 ft. Clusters of creamy-white flowers in midsummer. Green leaf made up of up to 5 pairs of big leaflets separated by pairs of smaller leaflets. **Zone 4.**

Filipendula ulmaria "Aurea"
Golden Meadowsweet
Hardy perennial. Ht and spread 12 in. Clusters of creamy-white flowers in midsummer. Bright golden yellow, divided leaves in spring that turn a lime color in summer. Susceptible to sun scorch. **Zone 4.**

Filipendula ulmaria "Variegata"
Variegated Meadowsweet
Hardy perennial. Ht 18 in. and spread 12 in. Clusters of creamy-white flowers in midsummer. Divided leaf, dramatically variegated green and yellow in spring. Fades a bit as the season progresses. **Zone 4.**

Filipendula vulgaris
Dropwort
Hardy perennial. Ht 2–3 ft., spread 18 in. Summertime clusters of white flowers (larger than meadowsweet). Fern-like green leaves. **Zone 4.**

cultivation

Propagation
Seed
Sow in prepared seed or plug module trays in the fall. Use a standard seed compost mixed in equal parts with composted fine bark. Cover lightly with compost (not perlite) and winter outside under glass. Check from time to time that the compost has not become dry as this will inhibit germination. Stratification is helpful but not essential (see p. 644). Germination should take place in spring. When the seedlings are large enough to handle, plant out, 12 in. apart, into a prepared site.

Division
The golden and variegated forms are best propagated by division in the fall. Dig up established plant and tease the plantlets apart; they separate easily. Replant in a prepared site, 12 in. apart, or repot decorative varieties in a soilless potting compost.

Pests and Diseases
Meadowsweet can be prone to powdery mildew; cut back and remove infected leaves.

Maintenance
Spring Remove winter debris around new growth.
Summer Cut back after flowering.
Fall Divide established plants, sow seed for wintering outside.

Winter No need for protection.

Garden Cultivation
Meadowsweet adapts well to the garden, but does prefer sun/semi-shade and a moisture-retentive soil. If your soil is free-draining, mix in plenty of well-rotted manure and/or leaf mold, and plant in semi-shade.

Harvesting
Gather young leaves for fresh or dry use before flowers appear. Pick flowers just as they open, use fresh or dry.

container growing

Golden and variegated meadowsweet look attractive in containers, but use a soilless potting mix to make sure moisture is retained. Position in partial shade to inhibit drying out and sun scorch. The plant dies back in winter so leave it outside where the natural weathers can reach it. If you live in an extremely cold area, protect the container from damage by placing in a site protected from continuous frost, but not warm. Liquid feed only twice during flowering.

other uses

A black dye can be obtained from the roots by using a copper mordant (see also p. 675). Use dried leaves and flowers in potpourris.

medicinal

The whole plant is a traditional remedy for an acidic stomach. The fresh root is used in homeopathic preparations and is effective on its own in the treatment of diarrhea. The flowers, when made into a tea, are a comfort to flu victims.

culinary

A charming local vet gave me meadowsweet vinegar to try. Much to my amazement it was lovely, and combined well with oil to make a different salad dressing, great when used with a flower salad.

The flowers make a very good wine, and add flavor to meads and beers. Add the flowers to stewed fruit and jams to impart a subtle almond flavor.

Galega officinalis
GOAT'S RUE

Also known as French lilac, Italian fitch and Professor-weed. From the family Papilionaceae.

This ancient herb, indigenous to central and southern Europe and western Asia, has been used for hundreds of years to treat plagues and infections. Historically it was also recommend for snake bites. The name *Galega* comes from the Greek *gala*, meaning "milk" because of its reputation for increasing lactation. The common name goat's rue originates from the leaves, which smell unpleasant when crushed.

Maintenance
Spring Sow seeds, divide established plants.
Summer Cut back if growing too straggly; this will promote a second flowering.
Fall Collect seeds for drying.
Winter No need for protection.

Garden Cultivation
This full, hardy herb will grow in most soils. It prefers a deep soil that does not dry out in summer and allows the roots to become well established. This is important as they act as an anchor to stop it from being blown over in the summer when it is in full flower. If the plant becomes invasive or outgrows its position, cut it back hard; this will keep it under control and encourage flowering at a lower height, which can look most effective.

Harvesting
All the aerial parts of the plant are harvested in summer just before flowering, then dried for medicinal use.

 ## varieties

Galega officinalis
Goat's Rue
Herbaceous perennial. Ht 3–5 ft., spread up to 3 ft. Attractive clusters of white or mauve flowers in summer, followed by long seed pods. Green, compound, divided, lance-shaped leaflets. **Zone 3**

 ## cultivation

Propagation
Seed
Sow the easy-to-handle seeds in the spring into prepared seed or plug module trays using a seed compost, and cover with perlite. Germination takes 10 to 20 days without extra heat. Once the seedlings are strong enough, either pot using a soilless potting compost or alternatively in midspring, when the air and soil temperature has risen, plant out at a distance of 30 in. apart.

Division
This is a good method of propagation for this herb as it prevents the plant from becoming too large and it encourages it to put on new growth. In the second or third year, divide the root ball either by using two forks back-to-back or by digging up the whole plant and dividing. Once divided replant in a well-prepared site.

Pests and Diseases
Rarely suffers from pests. However, it is prone to powdery mildew, especially when planted against a wall or fence.

Leaves of *Galega officinalis*

 ## container growing

I do grow this herb in a container for exhibiting at the flower shows, using a soilless potting compost. However, for home display, I would not recommend it as it needs repotting at least three times in the growing season. Also, it grows very tall, requiring a large container, which makes it awkward to handle.

 ## medicinal

Used medicinally to reduce blood sugar levels and as a useful diuretic. It is also used to increase lactation in nursing mothers.

 ## other uses

The leaves and stem are used as an animal food supplement to increase milk yield.

 ## warning

Only to be used under professional supervision when treating diabetes.

Galium odoratum

SWEET WOODRUFF

Also known as New mowed hay, Rice flower, Ladies in the hay, Kiss me quick, Master of the wood, Woodward, and Woodrowell. From the family Rubiaceae.

This is a native of Europe and has been introduced and cultivated in North America and Australia. It grows deep in the woods and in hedgerows.

Records date back to the 14th century, when woodruff was used as a strewing herb, as bed-stuffing, and to perfume linen.

On May Day in Germany, it is added to Rhine wine to make a delicious drink called "Maibowle."

varieties

Galium odoratum syn. *Asperula odorata*
Sweet Woodruff
Hardy perennial. Ht 6 in., spread 12 in. or more. White, star-shaped flowers from spring to early summer. The green leaves are neat and grow in a complete circle around the stem. The whole plant is aromatic. **Zone 4.**

cultivation

Propagation

Seed
To ensure viability, only use fresh seed. Sow in early fall into prepared seed or plug module trays, and cover with compost. Water in well. Seeds require a period of stratification (see p. 644). Once the seedlings are large enough, either pot or plant out as soon as the young plants have been hardened off. Plant 4 in. apart.

Root Cuttings
The rootstock is very brittle and every little piece will grow. The best time to take cuttings is after flowering in the early summer. Lay small pieces of the root, 1–1½ in. long, evenly spaced, on the compost in a seed tray. Cover with a thin layer of compost, and water. Leave in a warm place, and the woodruff will begin to sprout again. When large enough to handle, split up and plant out.

Pests and Diseases
This plant rarely suffers from pests and diseases.

Maintenance
Spring Take root cuttings after flowering.
Summer Dig up before the flowers have set, to check spreading.
Fall The plant dies back completely in fall. Sow seeds.
Winter Fully hardy plant.

Garden Cultivation
Ideal for difficult places or underplanting in borders, it loves growing in the dry shade of trees right up to the trunk. Its rich green leaves make a dense and very decorative ground cover, its underground runners spreading rapidly in the right situation.

It prefers a rich alkaline soil with some moisture during the spring.

Harvesting
The true aroma (which is like new-mown hay) comes to the fore when it is dried. Dry flowers and leaves together in early summer.

container growing

Make sure the container is large enough, otherwise it will become root-bound very quickly. Use a soilless compost mixed in equal parts with composted fine bark. Only feed with liquid fertilizer when the plant is flowering. Position the container in semi-shade and do not overwater.

culinary

Add the flowers to salads. The main ingredients for a modern-day May Wine would be a bottle of Riesling, a glass of sherry, sugar, and strawberries, with a few sprigs of woodruff thrown in an hour before serving.

medicinal

A tea made from the leaves is said to relieve stomach pain, act as a diuretic, and be beneficial for those prone to gall stones.

Sweet woodruff tea

warning

Consumption of large quantities can produce symptoms of poisoning, including dizziness and vomiting.

GINKGO

Ginkgo biloba

Also known as Maidenhair tree and Bai guo. From the family Ginkgoaceae.

This beneficial herb is a living fossil, thought to be one of the oldest trees on the planet, dating back to when dinosaurs lived. Chinese monks are credited with keeping the tree in existence, as a sacred herb. The name *Ginkgo* is derived from the Japanese word *ginkyo*, meaning "silver apricot," referring to the fruit, and *biloba* translates as "two-lobed," which refers to the split in the middle of the fan-shaped leaf blades.

 ## varieties

Ginkgo biloba
Ginkgo
Hardy deciduous tree. Ht 130 ft., spread 65 ft. It is dioecious, meaning that it bears male catkins and female flowers on different trees in early summer. The female flowers are followed by small fruits. Fan-shaped green leaves are sometimes whole, but often have a single, central, vertical slit. **Zone 4**

 ## cultivation

Propagation
Seed
In fall, prepare the seeds by removing the pith; wear gloves, as the pith can cause dermatitis, then wash in a mild detergent. Sow immediately, singly into small pots using a soilless seed compost mixed in equal parts with horticultural grit. Cover with grit and place in a cold frame. Germination takes 4 months or longer. Grow on in a container for a minimum of 4 years before planting into the garden. You will only know the sex of your seed-raised plant when it flowers, which takes approximately 20 years.

Cuttings
Take cuttings from new growth in summer or semi-ripe growth in early fall. Place in a seed compost mixed in equal parts with horticultural grit. Keep frost-free until rooted. Grow as a container plant in exactly the same way as a seed-raised plant.

Pests and Diseases
Rarely suffers from pests or diseases.

Maintenance
Spring Repot or top dress container-raised plants.
Summer Take cuttings from new growth.
Fall Sow fresh seeds. Take cuttings.
Winter Hardy; no extra protection needed.

Garden Cultivation
Plant in full sun to partial shade in any fertile soil with the exception of heavy, cold, wet clay. To produce fruit a male and female tree need to be planted near each other.

Harvesting
In fall, pick the leaves for drying as they turn color from green to yellow. Also harvest the ripe small fruits from the female tree, and extract the kernel (nut) which is dried for medicinal use or used fresh in the kitchen.

 ## container growing

Once the young plant is more than 2 years old, use a soilless potting compost mixed in equal parts with river sand. Water and liquid feed regularly throughout the growing season.

 ## medicinal

Ginkgo is one of the bestselling Western herbal medicines and is taken to improve the memory. The dried leaves are used to improve circulation, ease tinnitus and in the treatment of asthma. Currently the leaves are being researched as a treatment for Alzheimer's disease.

 ## warning

If taken in excess, it can cause a toxic reaction. Wear gloves when preparing fresh nuts. Children can be allergic to cooked nuts. The fruits have an upleasant smell that people compare to vomit or rancid butter.

 ## culinary

There is current debate regarding the toxicity of the fresh nut, as to whether it can be eaten raw or whether it needs to be cooked. I would err on the side of caution as most recipes say cooked, where it is used in soups and stir-fries, and roasted. These nuts are available from Eastern supermarkets, where they are often called "White Nuts."

Glcyrrhiza glabra
LICORICE

Also known as Liquorice, Sweet licorice, and Sweetwood. From the family Papilionaceae.

This plant, which is a native of the Mediterranean region, is grown commercially throughout the temperate zones of the world and extensively cultivated in Russia, Iran, Spain, and India. It has been used medicinally for 3,000 years and was recorded on Assyrian tablets and Egyptian papyri. The Latin name *Glycyrrhiza* comes from *glykys*, meaning "sweet," and *rhiza*, meaning "root."

It was first introduced to England by Dominican friars in the 16th century and became an important crop. The whole of the huge cobbled courtyard of Pontefract Castle was covered by top soil simply to grow liquorice. It is sad that Pontefract cakes are made from imported liquorice today.

 ## varieties

Glycyrrhiza glabra
Licorice
Hardy perennial. Ht 4 ft., spread 3 ft. Pea-like, purple/blue and white flowers borne in short spikes on erect stems in late summer. Large greenish leaves divided into oval leaflets. **Zone 7**

 ## cultivation

Propagation
Seed
The seedlings often damp off. In cooler climates the seed tends not to be viable. Root division is a much easier method.

Division
Divide when the plant is dormant, making sure the root has one or more buds. Place into pots half filled with a soilless potting compost. Cover with compost. Water well and leave in a warm place until shoots appear. Harden off, then plant out in early spring or fall. If the latter, winter in a cold greenhouse or cold frame.

Maintenance
Spring Divide established plants.
Summer Do nothing.
Fall Divide established plants if necessary.
Winter In very cold winters protect first-year plants.

Garden Cultivation
Licorice needs a rich, deep, well-cultivated soil.

Plant pieces of the root, each with a bud, directly into a prepared site 6 in. deep and 3 ft. apart in early spring or in fall during the dormant season, if the ground is workable and not frosty. Licorice does best in long, hot summers, but will need extra watering if your soil is very free draining.

Harvesting
Harvest roots for drying in early winter from established 3- or 4-year-old plants.

 ## container growing

Never displays as well as in the garden. Use a soil-based compost. Feed throughout the growing season and water until it dies back.

 ## culinary

Licorice is used to flavor Guinness and other beers.

 ## medicinal

The juice from the roots provides commercial licorice. It is used either to mask the unpleasant flavor of other medicines or to provide its own soothing action on troublesome coughs. The dried root, stripped of its bitter bark, is recommended as a remedy for colds, sore throats, and bronchial congestion.

Licorice is a gentle laxative and lowers stomach acid levels, so relieving heartburn. It has a remarkable power to heal stomach ulcers because it spreads a protective gel over the stomach wall and in addition it eases spasms of the large intestine. It also increases the flow of bile and lowers blood cholesterol levels.

 ## warning

Large doses of licorice cause side effects, notably headaches, high blood pressure and water retention.

Licorice sticks

CURRY PLANT

Helichrysum italicum

From the family Asteraceae.

This plant is from southern Europe and has adapted well to damper, cooler climates. It is the sweet curry scent of its leaves that has caused its recent rise in popularity.

 varieties

Helichrysum italicum syn. *H. angustifolium*
Curry Plant
Hardy evergreen perennial. Ht 24 in., spread 3 ft. Clusters of tiny mustard-yellow flowers in summer. Narrow, aromatic, silver leaves. Highly scented. Planting distance for hedging 2 ft. **Zone 8**

Helichrysum italicum "Dartington"
Dartington Curry Plant
Hardy evergreen perennial. Ht 18 in., spread 24 in. Compact plant with clusters of small yellow flowers in summer. Gray/green, highly scented, narrow leaves (half the size of *H. italicum*). Its compact upright habit makes this a good plant for hedges and edging in the garden. Planting distance for hedging 1 ft. **Zone 8**

Helichrysum italicum "Korma"
Korma Curry Plant
Hardy evergreen perennial. Ht 24 in., spread 3 ft. Broad clusters of small bright yellow flowers, produced on upright white shoots. Narrow, aromatic, silver leaves. Planting distance for hedging 24 in. **Zone 8**

 cultivation

Propagation
Seed
I have not known any *H. italicum* to set good seed. For this reason I advise cuttings.

Cuttings
Take softwood cuttings in spring and semi-ripe ones in fall. Use a seed compost mixed in equal parts with composted fine bark.

Pests and Diseases
Pests give this highly aromatic plant a wide berth, and it is usually free from disease.

Maintenance
Spring Trim established plants after frosts to maintain shape and promote new growth. Take softwood cuttings.

The silver leaves of *Helichrysum italicum* "Korma"

Summer Trim back after flowering, but not too hard.
Fall Take semi-ripe wood cuttings.
Winter If the temperature falls below 14°F, protect from frost.

Garden Cultivation
The curry plant makes an attractive addition to the garden and it imparts a strong smell of curry even if untouched. It is one of the most silvery of shrubs and makes a striking visual feature all year round.

Plant in full sun in a well-drained soil. Do not cut the curry plant as hard back as lavender cotton, but it is worth giving it a good hair cut after flowering to stop the larger ones flopping and to keep the shape of the smaller ones.

If it is an exceptionally wet winter, and you do not have a free-draining soil, lift some plants, and keep in a cold greenhouse or cold frame.

Harvest
Pick leaves at any time for using fresh. Or before flowering for drying. Pick the flowers when fully open, in summer, for drying.

 container growing

All the curry plants grow happily in large containers (at least 8 in. in diameter). Use a soil-based compost mixed in equal parts with composted fine bark. Place in the sun to get the best effect, and do not overwater.

 culinary

There are not many recipes for the curry plant in cooking, and in truth the leaves smell stronger than they taste, but a small sprig stuffed into the cavity of a roasting chicken makes an interesting variation on tarragon. Add sprigs to vegetables, rice dishes, and pickles for a mild curry flavor. Remove before serving.

 other uses

The bright yellow button flowers can be used to add color to potpourris.

Hesperis matronalis

SWEET ROCKET

Also known as Damask violet and Dame's violet. From the family *Brassicaceae*.

This sweet-smelling herb is indigenous to Italy. It can now be found growing wild as a garden escapee. The old Greek name *Hesperis* was used by Theophrastus, the Greek botanist (370 to 285 CE). It is derived from *hesperos*, meaning "evening," which is when the flowers are at their most fragrant. This plant has been put on the invasive plant list in some areas of the U.S.

 ## varieties

Hesperis matronalis
Sweet Rocket
Hardy biennial; very occasionally perennial, sending out new shoots from the rootstock. Ht 2–3 ft., spread 10 in. The four-petalled flowers are all sweetly scented and come in many colors — pink, purple, mauve and white — in the summer of the second year. The leaves are green and lance shaped. **Zone 4**

There is a double-flowered form of this plant — *Hesperis matronalis* double-flowered. It can only be propagated by cuttings or division and needs a more sandy loam soil than sweet rocket.

 ## cultivation

Propagation
Seed
Sow the seed in the fall in prepared seed or plug trays, covering the seeds with perlite. Winter the young plants in a cold greenhouse for planting out in the spring at 18 in. apart. Propagated this way it may flower the first season as well as the second. Alternatively, sow seed in the garden in late spring.

Pests and Diseases
This herb is largely free from pests and diseases.

Maintenance
Spring Sow seed outdoors.
Summer In the second year deadhead flowers to prolong flowering.
Fall Sow seed under protection.
Winter No need to protect.

Garden Cultivation
It likes full sun or light shade and prefers a well-drained fertile soil. The seed can be sown direct into a prepared site in the garden in late spring, thinning to 12 in. apart, with a further thinning to 18 in. later on if need be.

Harvesting
Pick leaves when young for eating. Pick flowers as they open for using fresh or for drying.

 ## container growing

Sweet rocket is a tall plant. It looks attractive if three or four 1-year-old plants are potted together, positioned to make the most of the scent on a summer evening. Use a standard potting compost mixed in equal parts with composted fine bark and water well in summer months. No need to feed.

 ## culinary

Young leaves are eaten occasionally in salads. Use sparingly because they are very bitter. The flowers look attractive tossed in salads. They can also be used to decorate desserts.

 ## other uses

Add dried flowers to potpourris for pastel colors and sweet scent.

Hesperis matronalis

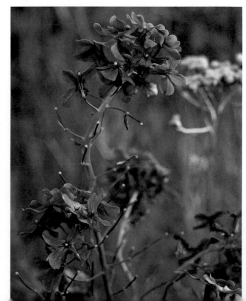

Helleborus niger
CHRISTMAS ROSE

Also known as Black Hellebore. From the family Ranunculaceae.

This ancient herb has had many stories attributed to its beauty and its medicinal properties. It is said to be one of Britain's oldest cultivated plants and it is thought to have been introduced by the Romans when they invaded these isles. There is an old legend, associated with the common name Christmas rose, that it sprouted in the snow from the tears of a young shepherdess who had no gift to give Jesus, the newborn King. An angel, upon hearing her weeping, appeared and brushed away the snow to reveal the most beautiful flower, the Christmas rose.

 varieties

☠ *Helleborus niger*
Christmas Rose
Evergreen perennial. Ht and spread 12 in. Large, outward-facing pink, purple or white flowers with golden stamens from very early in the New Year until April. Leathery, deep green, divided basal leaves. **Zone 4**

☠ *Helleborus foetidus*
Stinking Hellebore
Evergreen perennial. Ht and spread 18 in. Clusters of nodding cup-shaped pale green, red-margined flowers from very early in the New Year until April. Deeply divided, dark green leaves. This variety is used in homeopathy in the treatment of headaches, psychic disorders, enteritis and spasms. **Zone 5**

 cultivation

Propagation
Seed
Sow fresh seed in late summer into prepared seed trays, plug cell-packs, or small pots using a soilless seed compost mixed in equal parts with river sand. A word of warning about purchased seed: it must be fresh, old seed is nearly impossible to germinate. Cover with grit, and place the container outside for the winter as the seed needs frost to break its dormancy. Do not worry if the container becomes immersed in snow, as melting snow will aid germination. Germination will be erratic and may take a further season so do not throw away the sown seed after one winter.

Once it has germinated, grow on for one season in its container prior to planting in a well-prepared site in the garden. As this plant hates being transplanted choose your site with care. Alternatively, as anyone who has grown this plant successfully in the garden will know, hellebores will happily self seed. This is by far the easiest way to raise the plants from seed. When each seedling has at least one true leaf, carefully lift it and transplant into a prepared site that has moist, fertile soil in dappled shade. All seed-raised plants will take 3 to 5 years to flower.

Division
Hellebores hate their roots being disturbed, and are slow to re-establish after division. In early fall, choose a

CHRISTMAS ROSE

Helleborus niger

well-established plant and, with two forks back-to-back, tease very gently a clump away from the main plant. Carefully firm the soil in around the remaining clump and give the plant a feed with some well-rotted compost. As the original clump has had minimal disturbance it should flower in the early spring. Replant the divided section with the roots down, not spread out, into a well-prepared site that has had some new well-rotted compost dug in, and in partial dappled shade. It is unlikely to flower in the following spring but should do so the year after.

Pests and Diseases

Hellebores suffer from two diseases, black death and black spot. If you notice black streaking between the leaf veins, and seriously distorted stems and leaves, then this is most probably black death virus. Dig up the plants immediately to prevent it spreading and destroy, do not compost. Black spot fungus is identifiable by large, irregular, brown or black spots on the leaves and stems which cause the leaf to die. Remove these leaves and burn or discard — again, do not compost.

Hellebores can also suffer from root rot, a fungus that thrives on waterlogged soils. If you notice your plants are not thriving and you know you have very wet soil, then dig up the plants, and add some grit or bark to improve the drainage before replanting.

Maintenance

Spring Transplant self-sown seedlings into permanent positions.
Summer Sow fresh seed.
Fall Divide established plants.
Winter No need for protection, fully hardy.

Garden Cultivation

The Christmas rose should be planted in a deep, fertile, well-draining but moisture-retaining soil, in partial dappled shade. Under deciduous trees is ideal. In the fall, it is worth feeding the plants with well-rotted compost or leaf mold which will encourage it to flower profusely in the New Year.

Harvesting

The root is harvested in fall, then dried for medicinal use.

 companion planting

As this herb flowers so early, it is very beneficial for early insects as an early nectar plant; it attracts beneficial predators, which makes it a good companion near the vegetable patch.

Helleborus niger

 container growing

Because the Christmas rose has a very long taproot, choose containers that are deep. Use a soil-based potting compost mixed with 25 percent sand, and place the container in partial shade. Feed weekly throughout the growing season with a liquid feed following the manufacturer's instructions. Repot up one size of pot, or alternatively divide established plants in fall once the plant is dormant. Remember, if you have divided the plant then it is unlikely to flower in the following spring.

 medicinal

Helleborus niger is a very poisonous plant that is toxic when taken in all but the smallest doses. So this herb should not be self-administered and should only be taken under professional guidance. This herb contains properties similar to *Digitalis*, and was traditionally used as a heart stimulant and to treat dropsy, nervous disorders and hysteria. The best and safest way to take this herb is homeopathically, where it is used to treat headaches, psychic disorders, enteritis and spasms.

 warning

Highly poisonous and toxic plant, not to be self-administered.

HOPS

Humulus lupulus

Also known as Hopbind and Hop vine. From the family Cannabaceae.

Native of the Northern temperate zones, cultivated commercially, especially in North America, Northern Europe, and Chile.

Roman records from the first century AD describe hops as a popular garden plant and vegetable, the young shoots being sold in markets to be eaten rather like asparagus. Hop gardens did not become widespread in Europe until the ninth century. In Britain the hop was a wild plant and used as a vegetable before it became one of the ingredients of beer. It was not until the 16th century that the word hop and the practice of flavoring and preserving beer with the strobiles or female flowers of *Humulus lupulus* were introduced into Britain by Flemish immigrants, and replaced traditional bitter herbs such as alehoof and alecost.

During the reign of Henry VIII, parliament was petitioned against the use of the hop, as it was said that it was a wicked weed that would spoil the taste of the drink, ale, and endanger the people. Needless to say the petition was thrown out. The use of hops revolutionized brewing since it enabled beer to be kept for longer.

Hops have also been used as medicine for at least as long as for brewing. The flowers are famous for their sedative effect and were either drunk as a tea or stuffed in a hop pillow to sleep on.

Humulus lupulus female flowers

varieties

Humulus lupulus
Common Hop

Hardy perennial, a herbaceous climber. Ht up to 20 ft. There are separate female and male plants. The male has yellowish flowers in branched clusters. They are without sepals and have five tepals and five stamens. The female plant has tiny greenish-yellow, scented flowers, hidden by big scales (see left), which become papery when the fruiting heads are ripe. These are the flowers that are harvested for beer. The midgreen leaves have three to five lobes with sharply toothed edges. The hollow stems are covered with tiny hooked prickles which enable the plant to cling to shrubs, trees, or anything else. It always entwines clockwise. **Zone 3**

Humulus lupulus "Aureus"
Golden Hop

Hardy perennial, a herbaceous climber. Ht up to 20 ft. The main difference between this plant and the common hop is that the leaves and flowers are much more golden, which makes it very attractive in the garden and in dried flower arrangements. It has the same properties as the common hop. **Zone 3**

cultivation

Propagation
Seed

Beer is made from the unpollinated female flowers. If you grow from seed you will not know the gender for 2 to 3 years, which is the time it takes before good flowers are produced. Obtain seed from specialist seedsmen.

Sow in summer or fall. The seed is on the medium to large side so sow sparingly; if using plug module trays, one per cell. Push the seed in and cover it with the compost. Then cover the tray with a sheet of glass or plastic wrap, and leave somewhere cool to germinate — a cold frame, a cold greenhouse, or a garage. Germination can be very erratic. If the seed is not fresh you may need to give the hot/cold treatment to break dormancy.

Warning: As the seed will be from wild hops these should not be grown in areas of commercial hop growing, because they might contaminate the crop.

Humulus lupulus **male flowers**

Cuttings
Softwood cuttings should be taken in spring or early summer from the female plant. Choose young shoots and take the cuttings in the morning as they will lose water very fast and wilt.

Division
In spring dig up and divide the root stems and suckers of established plants. Replant 3 ft. apart against support.

Pests and Diseases

The most common disease is hop wilt. If this occurs, dig up and burn. Do not plant hops in that area again. Leaf miner can sometimes be a problem. Remove infected leaves immediately. Japanese beetles can be a serious defoliating pest. The golden variety sometimes suffers from sun scorch. If this occurs, prune to new growth, and change its position if possible the following season.

Maintenance

Spring Divide roots and separate rooted stems and suckers in spring. Repot container-grown plants. Check trellising. Take cuttings.
Summer Sow seed late in the season. Take cuttings.
Fall Cut back remaining growth into the ground. Give the plants a good feed of manure or compost. Bring containers into a cool place. Sow seed.
Winter No need for protection.

Garden Cultivation

For successful plants the site should be sunny and open, and the soil needs to be rich in humus and dug deeply. It is not generally necessary to tie the plants if good support is at hand. A word of warning: you must dominate the plant. Certainly it will need thinning and encouraging to entwine where you want it to go rather than where it chooses. But remember that it dies back completely in winter. Cut the plant into the ground each fall and then give it a good feed of manure or compost.

Harvesting

Pick young fresh side shoots in spring. Gather young fresh leaves as required.

Pick male flowers as required. Pick ripe female flowers in early fall. Dry and use within a few months, otherwise the flavor becomes unpleasant.

 container growing

Hops, especially the golden variety, can look very attractive in a large container with something to grow up. Use a soilless compost mixed in equal parts with composted fine bark, and feed regularly with a liquid fertilizer from late spring to midsummer. Keep well watered in the summer months and fairly dry in winter. It can be grown indoors in a position with good light such as a sunroom, but it seldom flowers. Provide some form of shade during sunny periods. During the winter months, make sure it has a rest by putting the pot in a cool place, keeping the compost on the dry side. Repot each year.

 other uses

The leaves can be used to make a brown dye. If you live close to a brewery it is worth asking each fall for the spent hops, which make either a great mulch or a layer in a compost heap.

 culinary

In early spring pick the young side shoots, steam them (or lightly boil), and eat like asparagus. The male flowers can be parboiled, cooled, and tossed into salads. The young leaves can be quickly blanched to remove any bitterness and added to soups or salads.

 warning

Contact dermatitis can be caused by contact with the flower. Also, hops are not recommended in the treatment of depressive illnesses because of their sedative effect.

 medicinal

Hop tea made from the female flower only is recommended for nervous diarrhea, insomnia, and restlessness. It also helps to stimulate appetite, dispel flatulence and relieve intestinal cramps. A cold tea taken an hour before meals is particularly good for digestion. It can be useful combined with fragrant valerian for coughs and nervous spasmodic conditions. Recent research into hops has shown that it contains a certain hormone, which accounts for the beneficial effect of helping mothers improve their milk flow.

To make a hop pillow, sprinkle hops with alcohol and fill a small bag or pillowcase with them (which all in all is bound to knock you out).

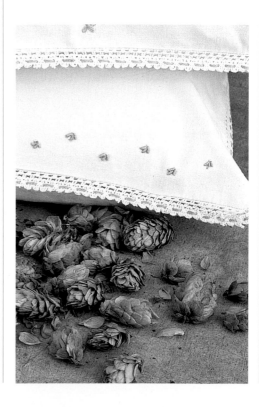

Hop pillow

Hyoscyamus niger

HENBANE

Also known as Devil's eye, Hen pen, Hen penny, Hog bean, Stinking Roger, Symphoniaca, Jusquiamus, Henbell, Belene, Hennyibone, Hennebane, Poisoned tobacco, and Stinking nightshade. From the family Solanaceae.

This native of Europe has become widely distributed worldwide and is found growing wild and on roadsides in well-drained sandy or alkaline soils.

Two famous deaths are attributed to henbane. Hamlet's father was murdered by a distillation of henbane being poured in his ear, and in 1910 Dr Crippen used hyoscine, which is extracted from the plant, to murder his wife. Every part of the plant is toxic.

Henbane has been considered to have aphrodisiac properties and is the main ingredient in some love potions and witches' brews. It was also placed by the hinges of outer doors to protect against sorcery.

 ## varieties

 ### Hyoscyamus niger
Henbane
Annual/biennial. Ht up to 32 in., spread 12 in. Flowers bloom in summer, are yellow/brown or cream, funnel-shaped, and usually marked with purple veins. Leaves are hairy with large teeth, and the upper leaves have no stalks. The whole plant smells foul. **All zones**

Hyoscyamus albus
White Henbane
Annual. Ht 12 in., spread 12 in. Its summer flowers are pale yellow marked with violet veins, funnel-shaped. Leaves are identical to *H. niger*. **All zones**

 ## cultivation

Propagation
Seed
Sow the fairly small seeds on the surface of pots or trays in spring, and cover with perlite. Germination takes 10 to 15 days. If you want henbane to behave like a biennial, sow in early fall, keeping the soil moist until germination (which can be erratic, but on average takes about 14 to 21 days). Winter the young plants in a cold frame or cold greenhouse. Plant out the following spring at a distance of 12 in. apart.

Pests and Diseases
This plant in the main is free from pests and diseases.

Maintenance
Spring Sow seed.
Summer Deadhead flowers to maintain plant (wear gloves).
Fall Sow seed for second-year flowers.
Winter Protect young plants.

Garden Cultivation
Choose the site for planting henbane with care, because it is poisonous. It will tolerate any growing situation but shows a preference for a well-drained sunny site. Sow seeds in late spring. When the seedlings are large enough to handle, thin to 12 in. apart. It can look striking in a mixed border.

Harvesting
Collect seed when the head turns brown and begins to open at the end.

 ## container growing

Inadvisable to grow such a poisonous plant this way.

 ## medicinal

This plant was used for a wide range of conditions that required sedation. The alkaloid hyoscine, which is derived from the green tops and leaves, was used as a hypnotic and brain sedative for the seasick, excitable, and insane. It was also used externally in analgesic preparations to relieve rheumatism and arthritis. The syrup has a sedative effect in cases of Parkinson's disease.

 ## warning

The whole plant is poisonous. Children have been poisoned by eating the seeds or seed pods. Use preparation and dosage only under strict medical direction.

ST JOHN'S WORT

Hypericum perforatum

Also known as Warrior's wound, Amber, Touch and Heal, Grace of God, and Herb of St John. From the family Clusiaceae.

This magical herb is found in temperate zones of the world in open situations on semi-dry soils. Whoever treads on St John's Wort after sunset will be swept up on the back of a magic horse that will charge round the heavens until sunrise before depositing its exhausted rider on the ground.

Besides its magical attributes, *Hypericum* has medicinal properties and was universally known as the Grace of God. In England it cured mania, in Russia it gave protection against hydrophobia, and the Brazilians knew it as an antidote to snake bite. St John's Wort ("wort," incidentally, is Anglo-Saxon for "medicinal herb") has been used to raise ghosts and exorcise spirits. When crushed, the leaves release a balsamic odor similar to incense, which was said to be strong enough to drive away evil spirits. The red pigment from the crushed flowers was taken to signify the blood of St John at his beheading, for the herb is in full flower on June 24, St John's Day.

 ## varieties

Hypericum perforatum
St John's Wort
Hardy perennial. Ht 1–3 ft., spread 1 ft. Scented yellow flowers with black dots in summer. The small leaves are stalkless and covered with tiny perforations (hence *perforatum*), which are in fact translucent glands. This is the magical species. **Zone 3**

 ## cultivation

Propagation
Seed
Sow very small seed in spring into prepared seed or plug module trays, and cover with perlite. Germination is usually in 10 to 20 days depending on the weather. When the seedlings are large enough to handle and after a period of hardening off, plant out 12 in. apart.

Division
Divide established plants in the fall.

Pests and Diseases
Largely free from pests and diseases.

Maintenance
Spring Sow seeds.
Summer Cut back after flowering to stop self-seeding.
Fall Divide established clumps.
Winter No need for protection, fully hardy.

Garden Cultivation
Tolerates most soils, in sun or light shade, but it can be invasive in light soils.

Harvesting
Harvest leaves and flowers as required.

 ## container growing

Can be grown in containers, but it is a bit tall so you do need a large clump for it to look effective. Use a soilless potting mix. Water in the summer months. Only feed with liquid fertilizer twice during the growing season, otherwise it produces more leaf than flower.

 ## other uses

The flowers release a yellow dye with alum, and a red dye with alcohol.

 ## warning

St John's Wort has sometimes poisoned livestock. Its use also makes the skin sensitive to light.

 ## medicinal

Oil extracted by macerating the flowers in vegetable oil and applied externally eases neuralgia and the pain of sciatica, varicose veins, ulcers, and sunburn. Only take internally under supervision.

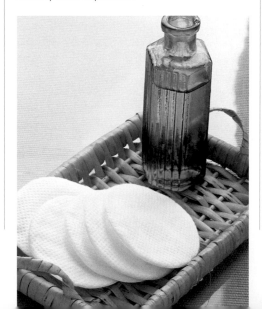

St. John's Wort oil

HYSSOP

Hyssopus officinalis

"Purge me with Hyssop and I shall be clean."
(Psalm 51, verse 7)

From the family Lamiaceae.

Hyssop is a native of the Mediterranean region, where it grows wild on old walls and dry banks. It is found as a garden escapee elsewhere in Europe and has been cultivated in gardens for about the last 600 years. It was one of the herbs taken to the New World by the colonists to use in tea, in herbal tobacco, and as an antiseptic.

Hyssopus officinalis subsp. *aristatus*

There has been much to-ing and fro-ing about whether common hyssop is the one mentioned in the Bible. Some say it was oregano or savory. However, present thinking is that hyssop is flavor of the month, especially since it has been discovered that the mold that produces penicillin grows on its leaf. This may have acted as an antibiotic protection when lepers were bathed in hyssop.

The Persians used distilled hyssop water as a body lotion to give a fine color to their skin.

Hippocrates recommended hyssop for chest complaints, and today herbalists still prescribe it.

 ## varieties

These are the common hyssops, readily available from nurseries and garden centers.

Hyssopus officinalis
Hyssop, Blue Hyssop
Hardy semi-evergreen perennial. Ht 32 in., spread 36 in. Blue flowers from summer to early fall. Small, narrow, lance-shaped leaves, aromatic, and darkish green. **Zone 3**

Hyssopus officinalis f. albus
White Hyssop
Hardy semi-evergreen perennial. Ht 32 in., spread 36 in. White flowers from summer to early fall. Small, narrow, lance-shaped leaves, aromatic, and darkish green in color. **Zone 3**

Hyssopus officinalis subsp. aristatus
Rock Hyssop
Hardy, semi-evergreen, perennial. Ht 12 in., spread 24 in. Dark blue flowers from summer to early fall. Small, narrow, lance-shaped leaves, aromatic, and darkish green. **Zone 3**

Hyssopus officinalis "Roseus"
Pink Hyssop
Hardy, semi-evergreen, perennial. Ht 32 in., spread 36 in. Pink flowers from summer to early fall. Small, narrow, lance-shaped leaves, aromatic, and darkish green. **Zone 3**

 ## cultivation

Propagation
Seeds
In early spring sow the small seeds in plug module or seed trays under protection, using a standard seed compost mixed in equal parts with composted fine bark. Cover with perlite. If very early in spring, a bottom heat of 60–70°F would be beneficial. When the seedlings are large enough, either pot or transplant into the garden after a period of hardening off. Plant at a distance of 12 in. apart. All varieties can be grown from seed with the exception of rock hyssop, which can only be grown from cuttings. However, if you want a guaranteed pink or white hyssop, cuttings are a more reliable method.

Cuttings
In late spring or early summer, take softwood cuttings from the new lush growth and nonflowering stems.

Pests and Diseases
This genial plant rarely suffers from pests or diseases.

Maintenance
Spring Sow seeds. Trim mature plants. Trim hedges.
Summer Deadhead flowers to maintain supply, trim after flowering to maintain shape. Trim hedges.
Fall Cut back only in mild areas.
Winter Protect in cold, wet winters and temperatures that fall below 23°F. Use a floating row cover, straw, bracken, etc.

Garden Cultivation
This attractive plant likes to be planted in conditions similar to rosemary and thyme, a well-drained soil in a sunny position. The seeds can be sown directly into

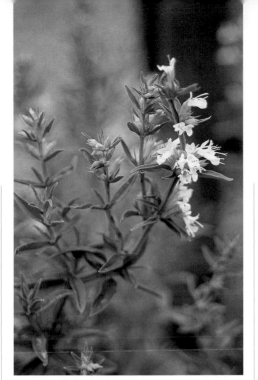

Hyssopus officinalis f. *albus*

the ground in very late spring or early summer, when the soil is warm. Thin to 12 in. apart if being grown as specimen plants. If for hedging, 7 in. As all parts of the plant are pleasantly aromatic and the flowers very attractive, plant it where it can be seen and brushed against. The flowers are also attractive to bees and butterflies. For these reasons hyssop makes a very good hedge or edging plant. Trim the top shoots to encourage bushy growth. In early spring, trim the plant into a tidy shape with scissors. To keep the plant

flowering in summer, remove the dead heads. Cut back to 8 in. in fall in mild areas, or trim back after flowering in cold areas. Keep formal hedges well clipped during the growing season.

Harvesting

Cut young leaves for drying in summer. The flowers should be picked during the summer too, when they are fully opened. The scent is generally improved with drying.

 ## companion planting

It is said that when grown near cabbages it lures away cabbage whiteflies. When planted near vines, it is reputed that the blue flowers of Hyssop attract the pollinating insects, so helping to increase the yield.

 ## container growing

Hyssop is a lovely plant in containers. It is happy in plenty of sunshine and prefers a south-facing wall. It also likes dry conditions and its tough leaves are not

affected by the fumes of city centers, making it ideal for window boxes. Equally, it is good on a patio as the scent is lovely on a hot summer's evening. Give it a liquid feed only during the flowering period. Cut back after flowering to maintain shape.

 ## medicinal

An infusion is used mainly for coughs, whooping cough, asthma and bronchitis, and upper respiratory catarrh. It is also used for inflammation of the urinary tract. Externally it can be used for bruises and burns. It was once a country remedy for rheumatism.

 ## warning

Hyssop should not be used in cases of nervous irritability. Strong doses, particularly those of distilled essential oil, can cause muscular spasms. This oil should not be used in aromatherapy for highly strung patients, as it can cause epileptic symptoms. Do not use continuously for extended periods, or during pregnancy.

 ## culinary

The flowers are delicious tossed in a green salad. In small amounts, leaves aid digestion of fatty foods, but as they are somewhat pungent, use them sparingly. The herb has a slightly bitter, minty taste and is therefore good flavoring in salads or as an addition to game, meats, soups, stews, and stuffings. A good idea is to add a teaspoon of chopped leaf to a Yorkshire pudding batter. Hyssop is still used in Gascony as one of the herbs in bouquet garni and for flavoring a concentrated purée of tomatoes preserved for the winter. It is used in continental sausages and also added to fruit pies, 1/4 teaspoon hyssop being sprinkled over the fruit before the top crust goes on.

When making a sugar syrup for fruit, add a sprig of hyssop as you boil the sugar and water; it adds a pleasant flavor, and the sprig can be removed before adding the fruit. When making cranberry pie, use the leaves as a lining for the dish.

Basque-Style Chicken
Serves 6

4 sweet bell peppers (2 red, 2 green)
Hyssop olive oil
3 1/2 lb. chicken
5 tablespoons dry white wine
6 onions
4 cloves garlic
4 medium tomatoes, peeled and roughly chopped
1 bouquet garni with a sprig of hyssop
Salt and freshly ground black pepper

De-seed and slice the peppers into thin strips. Gently fry them in a small amount of oil until soft. Remove from pan and put to one side. Joint the chicken and gently fry in the oil, turning all the time. Transfer to a Dutch oven, and season with salt and pepper, moisten with the wine, and leave over a gentle heat to finish cooking. Slice the onions and peel the garlic cloves, and soften without coloring in the olive oil in the skillet. Then add the tomatoes, bell peppers, and

bouquet garni, and season. When reduced almost to a cream, turn into the Dutch oven over the chicken and keep on a low heat until ready to serve, about an additional 20 to 30 minutes.

ELECAMPANE

Inula helenium

Also known as Allecampane, July campane, Elicompane, Dock, Sunflower, Wild sunflower, Yellow starwort, Elfdock, Elfwort, Horse elder, Horse heal, and Scabwort. From the family Asteraceae.

Elecampane originates from Asia whence, through cultivation, it spread across Western Europe to North America and now grows wild from Nova Scotia to Ontario, North Carolina, and Missouri.

Sources for the derivation of the principal common name, Elecampane, and the generic/species name, *Inula helenium*, are not altogether satisfactory, but I have found three possible explanations.

Helen of Troy was believed to be gathering the herb when she was abducted by Paris, hence *helenium*.

Down through the ages the herb was considered as good medicinally for horse or mule as for man; it was even sometimes called horselene. *Inula* could come from *hinnulus*, meaning "a young mule."

Finally, the Romans called the herb *Enula Campana* (Inula of the fields) from which Elecampane is a corruption.

According to the Roman writer Pliny, the Emperor Julius Augustus enjoyed elecampane so much he proclaimed, "Let no day past without eating some of the roots candied to help the digestion and cause mirth." The Romans also used it as a candied sweetmeat, colored with cochineal. This idea persisted for centuries, and in the Middle Ages, apothecaries sold the candied root in flat pink sugary cakes, which were sucked to alleviate asthma and indigestion and to sweeten the breath. Tudor herbalists also candied them for the treatment of coughs, nasal congestion, bronchitis, and chest ailments. Their use continued until the 1920s as a flavoring in candies.

I have discovered an Anglo-Saxon ritual using elecampane — part medicinal, part magical. Prayers were sung of the *Helenium* and its roots dug up by the medicinal man, who had been careful not to speak to any disreputable creature — man, elf, goblin, or fairy — he chanced to meet on the way to the ceremony. Afterward the elecampane root was laid under the altar for the night and eventually mixed with betony and lichen from a crucifix. The medicine was taken against elf sickness or elf disease.

There is an ancient custom in Scandinavia of putting a bunch of elecampane in the center of a nosegay of herbs to symbolize the sun and the head of Odin, the greatest of Norse gods.

ELECAMPANE

Inula helenium

 varieties

Inula helenium

Elecampane
Hardy perennial. Ht 5–8 ft., spread 3 ft. Bright yellow, ragged, daisy-like flowers in summer. The leaves are large, oval-toothed, slightly downy underneath, and of a midgreen color. Dies back
fully in winter. **Zone 4**

Inula hookeri

Hardy perennial. Ht 30 in., spread 18 in. Yellowish-green, ragged, daisy-like flowers slightly scented in summer. Lance-shaped hairy leaves, smaller than *I. magnifica*, and midgreen in color. Dies back fully in winter. **Zone 4**

Inula magnifica

Hardy perennial. Ht 6 ft., spread 3 ft. Large, ragged, daisy-like flowers. Lots of large, dark green lance-shaped rough leaves. May need staking in an exposed garden. This is often mistaken for *I. helenium*; the leaf color is the biggest difference, and on average *I. magnifica* grows much larger. Dies back fully in winter. **Zone 4**

 cultivation

Propagation

Seed
The seed is similar to dandelion; when the plant has germinated you can see the seeds flying all over the garden, which should be all the warning you need. In spring sow on the surface of a pot or plug module tray. Cover with perlite. Germination is 2 to 4 weeks, depending on the sowing season and seed viability. Prick out and plant 3–5 ft. apart when the seedlings are large enough to handle.

Root Division
If the plant grows too big for its position in the garden, divide in the fall when the plant has died back. As the roots are very strong, choose the point of division carefully. Alternatively, remove the offshoots that grow around the parent plant; each has its own root system, so they can be planted immediately in a prepared site elsewhere in the garden. This can be done in fall or spring.

Pests and Diseases

It rarely suffers from disease, although if the fall is excessively wet, as the leaves die back, they may suffer from a form of mildew. Simply cut back and destroy the leaves.

Maintenance

Spring Sow seed. Divide established plants.
Summer Remove flowerheads as soon as flowering finishes.
Fall Cut back growth to stop self-seeding and to prevent the plant becoming untidy. Remove offshoots for replanting. Divide large plants.
Winter The plant dies back so needs no protection.

Garden Cultivation

Plant in a moist, fertile soil, in full sun, sheltered from the wind (elecampane grows tall and would otherwise need staking). It can look very striking at the back of a border against a stone wall, or in front of a screen of deciduous trees. In a very dry summer it may need watering.

Harvesting

Dig up second- or third-year roots in the fall; they can be used as a vegetable, or dried for use in medicine.

The flowers are good in fall flower arrangements and dry well upside down if you cut them just before the seeds turn brown.

 container growing

Elecampane grows too big for most containers and is easily blown over.

 culinary

Elecampane has a sharp, bitter flavor. Use dried pieces or cook as a root vegetable.

 other uses

Your cat may be interested to know that scientific research indicates that elecampane has a sedative effect on mice.

 medicinal

The main use is for respiratory complaints, at one time specifically for tuberculosis. It is still employed in folk medicine as a favorite constituent of cough remedies, and has always been popular both as a medicine and as a condiment.

In America, elecampane oil is used for respiratory infections, intestinal catarrh, chronic diarrhea, chronic bronchitis, and whooping cough.

A decoction of the root has long been used externally for scabies, herpes, acne, and other skin diseases, hence its country name Scabwort. Recent research shows that the lactines found in the roots are powerful agents against bacteria and fungi.

Elecampane oil

IRIS

From the family Iridaceae.

All those mentioned are native to the northern hemisphere and are cultivated in varying conditions, from dry light soil (orris — *Iris* "Florentina") to damp boggy soils (blue flag iris — *Iris versicolor*).

The Greek word *iris*, meaning "rainbow" and the name of the Greek goddess of the rainbow, was appended to describe the plant's variable colors. The iris is one of the oldest cultivated plants — it is depicted on the wall of an Egyptian temple dating from 1500 CE.

In this very large family, three stand out for their beneficial herbal qualities. Orris has a violet-scented root, which has been powdered and used in perfumes since the times of the ancient Egyptians and Greeks. The Latin *Iris* "Florentina" depicts its association with Florence in the early Middle Ages. It is said to be the fleur de lys of French heraldry.

The blue flag iris is the common wetland plant, native to eastern North America and exported from there to Europe. Employed by the Native Americans and early settlers as a remedy for gastric complaints, it was included in the U.S. Pharmacopeia and is still believed in folk medicine to be a blood purifier of use in eruptive skin conditions. Sometimes the plant is known as liver lily because of its purifying effect.

The root of the yellow flag iris, a native of the British Isles, was powdered and used as an ingredient in Elizabethan snuff. It was taken to America and Australia by the earliest settlers.

Iris pseudacorus

 varieties

Iris "Florentina"
Orris
Also known as Florentine iris and orris root. Hardy perennial. Ht 2–3 ft. Spread indefinite. Large white flowers tinged with pale lavender and with a yellow beard appearing in early to midsummer. Green, sword-shaped leaves. The rootstock is stout and rhizomatous with a violet scent. Grows well throughout Europe and North America, except in the warm moist climates of Florida and the Gulf Coast. **Zone 4**

Iris germanica
Purple Iris
Also known as garden iris and flag iris. Hardy perennial. Ht 2–3 ft., spread indefinite. The fragrant flowers are blue/violet, occasionally white, and form early to midsummer. Leaves are grayish-green and sword-shaped. The root is thickish rhizome. There are many cultivated varieties. It is grown commercially for the rhizomes and, like *Iris* "Florentina," is used in perfumery and pharmaceutical preparations. **Zone 4**

Iris pseudacorus
Yellow Iris (Yellow Flag)
Perennial. Ht 16 in. to 5 ft., spread indefinite. Flowers are bright yellow with radiating brown veins and very slightly scented. They appear early to midsummer. The root is a thick rhizome from which many rootlets descend. **Zone 4**

Iris versicolor
Blue Flag Iris. Also known as flag lily, fleur de lys, flower du Luce, liver lily, poison flags, snake lily, water flag, and wild iris.
Hardy perennial. Ht 12–39 in., spread indefinite. Flowers claret-purple-blue in summer. Large, sword-shaped, green leaves. Root large and rhizomatous. **Zone 4**

Iris "Florentina"

 ## cultivation

Propagation

Seed

All the irises produce large seeds, which take some time to germinate and often benefit from a period of stratification. As the seeds are of a good size, sow directly into a 3 in. pot in fall, using a standard seed compost mixed in equal parts with composted fine bark. Water well, and cover the pots with cling film (to stop the mice eating the seed). Put outside to get the weather. Check that the compost remains damp. If there is any danger of it drying out, stand the container in water. This is especially important for blue and yellow flag irises.

Division

Divide the rhizome in late spring or early fall. This suits all the varieties. Replant immediately in a prepared site. Leave a decent distance between plants; spread is indefinite.

Pests and Diseases

The only major pest is the iris sawfly, which is attracted to waterside irises. The darkish-gray larvae feed along the leaf-margins, removing large chunks. Pupation takes place in the soil beneath or near the host plants, and the adult sawflies are on the wing during early to midsummer. Pick off the larvae. This is an annual pest and there is not much to be done to prevent it.

Maintenance

Spring Divide roots of mature plants.
Summer Collect the seeds as soon as ripe.
Fall Sow seeds and leave outside. Divide roots.
Winter Fully hardy; no need for protection.

Garden Cultivation

Orris and Purple Iris prefer a well-drained, rich soil and a sunny situation. When planting, make sure that part of the rhizomes is exposed.

Yellow and Blue Flag Irises are marsh-loving plants, ideal for those with a pond or ditch or piece of boggy ground. They grow happily in semi-shade but need full sun in order to produce the maximum bloom. In deep shade they will not flower at all but will spread quickly by stout underground rhizomes. A measure of control will be necessary.

Harvesting

The full violet fragrance of orris will not be apparent until the roots are 2 years old. Dig up these rhizomes in fall and dry immediately.

Gather yellow flag flowers and roots for use as a dye, in early summer and fall respectively. Dig up blue flag roots in fall and dry.

 ## container growing

These irises grow on strong rhizomes, so make sure that the container is strong enough, large enough, and shaped so that it will accommodate the plant happily and not blow over. For the bog lovers use peat in the compost mix — 75 percent peat mixed with 25 percent composted fine bark, but put lots of gravel and broken crocks in the bottom of the container to make up for loss of weight. For the dry gang, use a soilless compost. Do not let either compost dry out. They become pot bound very quickly, so split and repot every year.

 ## other uses

The violet-scented, powdered root of orris is used as a fresh scent to linen, a base for dry shampoos, a base for tooth powders, in face-packs, as a fixative in potpourris, and as a dry shampoo.

Flowers of yellow flag make a good yellow dye, while the rhizomes yield a gray or black dye when used with an iron mordant.

 ## medicinal

Orris and yellow flag are rarely used medicinally nowadays. However, herbalists still use the blue flag as a blood purifier acting on the liver and gall bladder to increase the flow of bile, and as an effective cleanser of toxins. It is also said to relieve flatulence and heartburn, belching and nausea, and headaches associated with digestive problems.

 ## culinary

Apparently, if you roast the seed of the yellow flag iris, they make an excellent coffee substitute. Apart from this little gem, I cannot find any culinary uses for irises.

 ## warning

Always wash your hands well after handling this plant as it can cause uncontrollable vomiting and violent diarrhea. Large doses of the fresh root can cause nausea, vomiting, and facial neuralgias.

Isatis tinctoria
WOAD

Also known as Dyers woad, Glastum. From the family Brassicaceae.

This ancient dye plant for cloth and wool has been used for thousands of years. It was the only source of blue dye available in Europe until the end of the 16th century, when indigo *(Indigofera tinctoria)* became available from India via the spice trade. There is a resurgence in interest in this herb not only because of recent films on Picts, Celts and Romans, but also due to current research into its medicinal properties.

 varieties

Isatis tinctoria
Woad
Hardy biennial. Ht in first year 18 in., second year when in flower 4 ft., spread 18 in. Clusters of numerous small, bright yellow, honey-scented flowers in the second summer, which are followed by pendulous black seeds. Lance-shaped, lightly toothed, blue/green leaves. The taproot in the second season can be 5 ft. long.

 cultivation

Propagation
Seed
Sow fresh seeds in fall into prepared plug cell-packs or small pots using a seed compost mixed in equal parts with perlite. Place the container in a cold greenhouse or cold frame. Germination takes 3 to 4 weeks. In the spring, plant out into a prepared site 12 in. apart. Alternatively, sow in late spring, when the night time temperature does not fall below 48°F, direct into a well-prepared site. Once the seedlings have emerged, thin to 12 in. apart.

Pests and Diseases
Woad seedlings can be attacked by the flea beetle. To prevent this, in spring, cover with a fine floating row cover for the first season only.

Maintenance
Spring Protect new seedlings from flea beetle. Mulch second-year plants.
Summer Harvest seeds and roots of second-year plants.
Fall Sow fresh seeds.
Winter No need for protection; fully hardy.

Garden Cultivation
Plant in a sunny position in a well-drained, well-fed soil. Be aware that this herb has a very long taproot and hates being transplanted once the plant starts to become established. In late summer, collect the seeds before they fall as it is renowned for self-seeding.

Harvesting
In late summer pick the leaves, either to dry for medicinal use, or to ferment and then dry for use as a dye. Dig up the roots of the second year's growth in late summer, then dry for medicinal use. Harvest the seeds in late summer as they turn dark brown and before they drop.

 container growing

Being biennial, this herb looks very boring for the first year and when it goes to flower in the second it becomes very tall, which does not make it an ideal container plant.

 medicinal

In Chinese medicine the root of this herb is known as *ban lang gen*, and it is used to treat meningitis and mumps. However be aware that woad is very astringent and poisonous and should only be taken internally under supervision. In 2006, the *New Scientist* reported that Italian biochemists have discovered that woad contains more than 60 times the amount of glucobrassicin, a type of glucosinolate, in the leaves than broccoli, which might help in the prevention of cancer.

 other uses

Traditional blue dye plant.

 warning

Astringent and poisonous when taken internally. It is classed as a noxious weed in Australia and the U.S.

Woad dye

Jasminum officinale
JASMINE

Also known as Common jasmine, Yasmine, Chambeli, Jessamine and Mogra. From the family Oleaceae.

The scent of the jasmine flower wafting over the night air is very evocative. The jasmine flower symbolizes femininity. Traditionally Italian girls include jasmine in their bridal head dresses. There is a lovely story that the Duke of Tuscany in the 17th century introduced this herb from China, and one of his gardeners gave his betrothed a piece as a token of his love and was promptly dismissed for this misdemeanor. However, his betrothed planted the cutting and their garden was soon festooned with jasmine, which was much sought after by the girls of the village for its aphrodisiac properties.

 ## varieties

Jasminum officinale
Jasmine
Hardy deciduous, occasionally semi-evergreen, climber. Ht up to 30 ft., spread up to 10 ft. Small fragrant white flowers all summer, followed by black poisonous berries. Pinnate midgreen leaves with three to nine leaflets.

Jasminum grandiflorum
Royal Jasmine, Spanish Jasmine, Jati
Tender evergreen climber. Ht up to 15 ft. Clusters of highly scented white flowers with a pink tinge all summer. Pinnate dark green leaves with seven or nine leaflets.

 ## cultivation

Propagation
Seed
In fall, extract the seeds from the berries, and sow into prepared pots or plug cell-packs using a standard soilless seed compost mixed in equal parts with coarse horticultural sand. Cover with sand, and then place outside for the winter. The seeds need frost to break their dormancy. Germination takes 4 to 6 months, but it can be erratic, so be patient and do not discard the container.

Cuttings
Take cuttings from semi-ripe growth in summer into prepared plug cell-packs or a small pot, using a seed compost mixed in equal parts with propagating bark. Place in a cold frame or cold greenhouse. Once rooted, repot into a soilless potting compost, winter in a cold frame, plant out in the following spring.

Pests and Diseases
Rarely suffers from pests or diseases.

Maintenance
Spring Prune established plants.
Summer Take cuttings from semi-ripe growth.
Fall Sow seeds.
Winter No need for protection, fully hardy.

Garden Cultivation
This sturdy climber, once established, will outgrow a trellis or need continual pruning if grown on a house, therefore is best grown over an arbour, porch, or a large old tree stump in a fertile soil and a sunny position. Prune in spring.

Harvesting
Pick flowers early in the morning, just as they open, for use as a flavoring, for infusions or for making oils.

 ## container growing

As this is a vigorous climber it is not ideally suited to container growing.

 ## medicinal

In Ayurvedic medicine a juice pressed from the leaves is used to remove corns. The leaves are also used as a gargle for mouth ulcers. An infusion made from the flowers is used to cool inflamed and bloodshot eyes. The essential oil made from the flowers is considered an antidepressant and relaxant.

 ## other uses

The essential oil is used in perfumes and in several food flavorings.

 ## warning

Do not take jasmine essential oil internally. The berries are poisonous.

Jasminum officinale berries

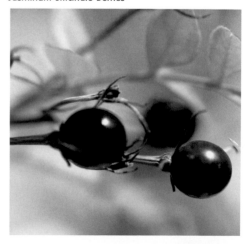

Juniperus communis

JUNIPER

Juniperus communis "Compressa"

From the family Cupressaceae.

Juniper is widely distributed throughout the world and grows either as a shrub or a small tree. It is a native of the Mediterranean region, but also grows in the Arctic, from Norway to the Soviet Union, in the North and West Himalayas and in North America. It is found on heaths, moorlands, open coniferous forests and mountain slopes.

This widely distributed plant was first used by the ancient Greek physicians and its use has continued right up to the modern day. It was believed to cure snake bites and protect against infectious diseases like the plague.

The English word "gin" is derived from an abbreviation of Holland's "geneva," as the spirit was first called. This in turn stems from the Dutch *jenever*, meaning juniper.

Juniperus communis "Hibernica"
Irish Juniper
Hardy evergreen perennial tree. Ht 10–20 ft., spread 1–2 ft. Leaves small and bluish/silvery-green, sharply pointed and aromatic. Columnar in shape and with a hint of silver in certain lights. Very slow growing.

Juniperus communis "Hornibrookii"
Juniper Hornibrookii
Hardy evergreen perennial tree. Ht 12–18 in., spread 6 ft. Leaves small and darkish green, sharply pointed and aromatic. A big carpeting plant.

Juniperus communis "Prostrata"
Prostrate Juniper
Hardy evergreen perennial tree. Ht 8–12 in., spread 3–6 ft. Leaves small and bluish-green, sharply pointed and aromatic. A smaller carpeting plant.

Juniperus communis berries

 ## varieties

Juniper is a conifer, a group of trees and shrubs distinguished botanically from others by its production of seeds exposed or uncovered on the scales of the fruit. True to form, it is evergreen and has needle-like leaves.

There are many species and varieties available, *Juniperus communis* being the main herbal variety. On the varieties detailed below, the flowers are all very similar: male flowers are very small catkins; female flowers are small, globose and berry-like, with usually three to eight fleshy scales. Over a period of 3 years, these turn blue and then finally black as they ripen.

Juniperus communis
Juniper
Hardy evergreen perennial. Ht 1–30 ft., spread 3–15 ft. The size of the plant is very dependent on where it is growing. Leaves small and bright green, sharply pointed and aromatic.

Juniperus communis "Compressa"
Juniper Compressa
Hardy evergreen perennial tree. Ht 6 ft., spread 1to 2 ft.. The leaves are small and bluish-green, sharply pointed and aromatic. Very slow growing with an erect habit, ideal for rock gardens or containers.

cultivation

Propagation

Seed

All the species can be propagated by seed. Sow seeds taken from ripe berries in a cold greenhouse, cold frame or cold conservatory in early fall. As junipers on the whole are extremely slow growing, it is best to grow the seedlings in a controlled environment for 1 or 2 years before planting out in a permanent position in the garden. Start in seed or plug module trays; then, when the seedlings are large enough, repot into small pots using a soil-based seed compost. This method is the easiest but to be sure of the plant's gender and leaf color, taking cuttings is more reliable.

Cuttings

It is quite easy to raise juniper from semi-hardwood cuttings taken from fresh current growth in either spring or fall.

Pests and Diseases

Various rusts attack juniper. If you see swellings on the branches with rusty, gelatinous extrusions, cut the branches out and burn them.

Honey fungus attacks many conifers. If this occurs, dig up the plant, making sure you have all the roots, burn it, and plant no further trees in that space.

Maintenance

Spring Plant out 2-year-old plants. Remove any leaders growing incorrectly in late spring/early summer.
Summer Take semi-hardwood cuttings. Harvest berries and store in a dry place.

Fall Sow seeds. Take cuttings.
Winter Winter young plants in cold frames, or provide added protection.

Garden Cultivation

Juniper likes an exposed, sunny site. It will tolerate an alkaline or neutral soil. Both male and female plants are necessary for berry production. The berries, which only grow on the female bush, can be found in various stages of ripeness on the same plant. Their flavor is stronger when grown in warm climates.

To maintain the shape of upright junipers, trim with hand pruners to ensure that there is no more than one leader, the strongest and straightest. Remember, when trimming, that most conifers will not make new growth when cut back into old wood, or into branches that have turned brown.

Harvesting

Harvest the berries when ripe in late summer. Dry them spread out on a tray, as you would leaves.

 ## container growing

Juniper is slow growing and can look most attractive in pots. Use a soilless compost, starting off with a suitable-sized pot, only potting up once a year if necessary. If the root ball looks happy, do not disturb it. Do not overwater. As the plant is hardy and evergreen, the container will need more protection than the plant during the winter months. Feed during the summer months only with a liquid fertilizer as per the manufacturer's guidelines.

 ## medicinal

Juniper is used in the treatment of cystitis, rheumatism and gout. Steamed inhalations of the berries are an excellent treatment for coughs, colds and catarrh.

 ## warning

Juniper berries should not be taken during pregnancy or by people with kidney problems. Internal use of the volatile oil must only ever be prescribed by professionals.

 ## culinary

Crushed berries are an excellent addition to marinades, sauerkraut and stuffing for guinea fowl and other game birds. Although no longer generally considered as a spice, it is still an important flavoring for certain meats, liqueurs, and especially gin.

Pork Chops Marinated with Juniper

Serves 4

Marinade
2 tablespoons olive oil
6 juniper berries, crushed
2 cloves garlic, crushed
Salt and freshly ground black pepper

Mix the oil, juniper berries, garlic and seasoning together in a bowl.

4 pork chops
4 tablespoons all-purpose flour
1 cup dry cider

Lay the pork chops in the bottom of a shallow dish and cover them with the marinade, turning the chops over once to make sure they are covered. Leave for a minimum of 3 hours, or if possible overnight. Remove the chops from the marinade, and reserve it. Heat a large skillet and add the reserved marinade. When hot, add the pork chops and cook over a moderate heat for about 20 minutes, turning the chops regularly. When all traces of pink have gone from the meat, remove from the heat, and put the chops on a plate. Return the pan to the heat and stir the flour into the remaining juices. Add the cider and bring to a boil. Return the chops to the sauce in the pan. Heat slowly, and serve with mashed potato and broccoli.

Laurus nobilis
BAY

Also known as Sweet Bay and Bay Laurel. From the family Lauraceae.

Bay is an evergreen tree native to southern Europe, and now found throughout the world.

That this ancient plant was much respected in Roman times is reflected in the root of its family name, Lauraceae, the Latin *laurus*, meaning "praise," and in its main species name, *Laurus nobilis*, the Latin *nobilis*, meaning "famous," "renowned." A bay wreath became a mark of excellence for poets and athletes, a symbol of wisdom and glory. The word laureate means "crowned with laurels" (synonym for bay), hence Poet Laureate, and the French *baccalauréat*.

The bay tree was sacred even earlier — to Apollo, Greek god of prophecy, poetry, and healing. His priestesses ate bay leaves before expounding his oracles at Delphi. As large doses of bay induce the effect of a narcotic, this may explain their trances. His temple had its roof made entirely of bay leaves, ostensibly to protect against disease, witchcraft, and lightning. Apollo's son Asclepius, the Greek god of Medicine, also had bay dedicated to him as it was considered a powerful antiseptic and guard against disease, in particular the plague.

In the 17th century, Culpeper wrote that "neither witch nor devil, thunder nor lightning, will hurt a man in the place where a bay-tree is." He also wrote that "the berries are very effectual against the poison of venomous creatures, and the stings of wasps and bees."

 varieties

Laurus azorica syn. Laurus canarinsis
Canary Island Bay
Perennial evergreen tree. Ht to 20 ft. Reddish-brown branches, a color that sometimes extends to the leaves. **Zone 9.**

Laurus nobilis
Bay
Also known as sweet bay, sweet laurel, laurel, Indian bay, Grecian laurel. Perennial evergreen tree. Ht up to 26 ft, spread 12 ft. Small, pale yellow, waxy flowers in spring. Green oval berries turning black in fall. The leaves may be added to broth, soups, and stews and are among the main ingredients of bouquet garni. *L. nobilis* is the only bay used for culinary purposes. **Zone 8.**

Laurus nobilis f. angustifolia
Willow Leaf Bay
Perennial evergreen tree. Ht up to 23 ft. Narrow-leafed variety, said to be hardier than *L. nobilis*. This is not strictly true. **Zone 8.**

Laurus nobilis "Aurea"
Golden Bay
Perennial evergreen tree. Ht up to 60 ft. Small, pale yellow, waxy flowers in spring. Green berries turning black in fall. Golden leaves can look sickly in damp, cooler countries. Needs good protection in winter especially from wind scorch and frosts. Trim in the fall/spring to maintain the golden leaves. **Zone 9.**

Umbellularia californica
Californian Laurel
Perenial evergreen tree. Ht up to 60 ft. Pale yellow flowers in late spring. Very pungent/aromatic leaves. Can cause headaches and nausea when the leaves are crushed. NOT culinary. **Zone 8.**

 cultivation

Propagation
Seed
Bay sets seed in its black berries, but rarely in cooler climates. Sow fresh seed in spring on the surface of either a seed or plug tray or directly into pots. Use a standard seed compost mixed in equal parts with composted fine bark. Keep warm: 68°F. Germination

is erratic, may take place within 10 to 20 days, in 6 months, or even longer. Make sure the compost is not too wet or it will rot the seeds.

Cuttings
Not a plant for the faint hearted. When I started propagating over 30 years ago I thought my bay cuttings were doing really well, but a year later not one had properly struck, and three-quarters of them had turned black and died. A heated propagator is a great help and high humidity is essential. Use either a misting unit or cover the cutting in plastic and maintain the compost or perlite at a steady moisture. Cuttings are taken in late summer/early fall 4 in. long.

Division
If offshoots are sent out by the parent plant, dig them up or they will destroy the shape of the tree. Occasionally roots come with them and these then can be potted up in a standard seed compost mixed in equal parts with composted fine bark. Place a plastic bag over the pot to maintain humidity. Leave somewhere warm and check from time to time to see if new shoots are starting. When they do, remove the bag. Do not plant out for at least a year.

Layering
In spring. A good way of propagating a difficult plant.

Pests and Diseases
Bay is susceptible to sooty mold, caused by the scale insect which sticks both to the undersides of leaves and to the stems, sucking the sap. Get rid of them by hand or use a liquid insecticidal soap. Bay sucker distorts the leaf so as soon as you see it, cut back the branch to clean growth.

Maintenance
Spring Sow seeds. Cut back standard and garden bay trees to maintain shape and to promote new growth. Cut back golden bay trees to maintain color. Check for pests and eradicate at first signs. Give container-grown plants a good liquid feed.
Summer Check that young plants are not drying out too much. In very hot weather, and especially in a city, spray-clean container-grown plants with water. Propagate by taking stem cuttings or layering in late summer.
Fall Take cuttings of mature plants. Protect container-grown and young garden plants. Cover garden plants in straw or bracken, if in a sufficiently sheltered position, or use a floating row cover.

Winter In severe winters the leaves will turn brown, but don't despair. Come the spring, it may shoot new growth from the base. To encourage this, cut the plant nearly down to the base.

Garden Cultivation
Bay is shallow rooted and therefore more prone to frost damage. Also, leaves are easily scorched in very cold weather or in strong, cold winds. Protection is thus essential, especially for bay trees under 2 years old. When planting out, position the plant in full sun, protected from the wind, and in a rich well-drained soil at least 3 ft. away from other plants to start with, allowing more space as the tree matures. Mulch in the spring to retain moisture throughout the summer.

Harvesting
Being evergreen, leaves can be taken all year round. It is fashionable now to preserve bay leaves in vinegars.

 ## culinary

Fresh leaves are stronger in flavor than dried ones. Use in soups, stews, and broths.

Add leaves to poached fish, like salmon.
Put on the coals of a grill.
Put fresh leaves in jars of rice to flavor the rice.
Boil in milk to flavor custards and rice pudding.

Bouquet Garni
I quote from my grandmother's cookbook, *Food for Pleasure*, published in 1950: "A bouquet garni is a bunch of herbs constantly required in cooking." The essential herbs in a bouquet garni are bay leaf, parsley, and thyme.

Laurus nobilis

Berries are cultivated for use in laurel oil and laurel butter. The latter is a vital ingredient of laurin ointment, which is used in veterinary medicine.

 ## container growing

Bay is a good container plant. Young plants benefit from being in a container indoors for the winter in cooler climates. Do not water too much, and let the compost dry out in the winter months. Large standard bays or pyramids look very effective in half barrels or containers of a similar size. They will need extra protection from frosts and wind, so if the temperature drops below 25°F bring the plants in.

To produce a standard bay tree, start with a young containerized plant with a straight growing stem. As it begins to grow, remove the lower side shoots below where you want the ball to begin. Allow the tree to grow to 8 in. higher than desired, then clip back the growing tip. Cut the remaining side shoots to about three leaves. When the side shoots have grown an additional four to five leaves, trim again to two to three leaves. Repeat until you have a leafy ball shape. Once established, prune with hand pruners in late spring and late summer to maintain it.

 ## other uses

Place in flour to deter weevils. Add an infusion to a bath to relieve aching limbs.

 ## medicinal

Infuse the leaves to aid digestion and increase appetite.

Lavandula
LAVENDER

From the family Lamiaceae.

Native of the Mediterranean region, Canary Isles, and India. Now cultivated in different regions of the world, growing in well-draining soil and warm, sunny climates.

Long before the world made deodorants and bath salts, the Romans used lavender in their bath water; the word is derived from the Latin *lava*, "to wash." It was the Romans who introduced this plant to Britain and from then on monks cultivated it in their monastic gardens. Little more was recorded until Tudor times when people noted its fragrance and a peculiar power to ease stiff joints and relieve tiredness. It was brought in quantities from herb farms to the London Herb Market at Bucklesbury. "Who will buy my lavender?" became perhaps the most famous of all London street cries.

It was used as a strewing herb for its insect-repellent properties and for masking household and street smells. It was also carried in nosegays to ward off the plague and pestilence. In France in the 17th century, huge fields of lavender were grown for the perfume trade. This has continued to the present day.

Lavandula stoechas subsp. *stoechas* f. *rosea* "Kew Red"

 ## varieties

This is another big family of plants that are eminently worth collecting. I include here a few of my favorites.

Lavandula angustifolia syn. *L. spica, L. officinalis*
Common/English Lavender
Hardy evergreen perennial. Ht 32 in., spread 3 ft. Mauve/purple flowers on a long spike in summer. Long, narrow, pale greenish-gray, aromatic leaves. One of the most popular and well known of the lavenders. **Zone 5.**

Lavandula angustifolia "Alba"
White Lavender
Hardy evergreen perennial. Ht 28 in., spread 32 in. White flowers on a long spike in summer. Long, narrow, pale greenish-gray, aromatic leaves. **Zone 5.**

Lavandula angustifolia "Bowles' Early"
Bowles Lavender
Hardy evergreen perennial. Ht and spread 24 in. Light blue flowers on a medium-size spike in summer. Medium-length, narrow gray-greenish, aromatic leaves. **Zone 5.**

Lavandula angustifolia "Folgate"
Folgate Lavender
Hardy evergreen perennial. Ht and spread 18 in. Purple flowers on a medium spike in summer. Leaves as above. **Zone 5.**

Lavandula angustifolia "Hidcote"
Hidcote Lavender
Hardy evergreen perennial. Ht and spread 18 in. Dark blue flowers on a medium spike in summer. Fairly short, narrow, aromatic, gray-greenish leaves. One of the most popular lavenders. Often used in hedging, planted at a distance of 12–16 in. **Zone 5.**

Lavandula x *intermedia* "Old English"

Lavandula angustifolia "Munstead"

Lavandula angustifolia "Loddon Pink"
Lavender Loddon Pink
Hardy evergreen perennial. Ht and spread 18 in. Pale pink flowers on a medium-length spike in summer. Fairly short, narrow, gray-greenish, aromatic leaves. Good compact habit. "Loddon Blue" is the same size, same height, with pale blue flowers. **Zone 5.**

Lavandula angustifolia "Munstead"
Lavender Munstead
Hardy evergreen perennial. Ht and spread 18 in. Purple/blue flowers on a fairly short spike in summer. Medium length, greenish-gray, narrow, aromatic leaves. This is now a common lavender and used often in hedging, planted at a distance of 12–16 in. **Zone 5.**

Lavandula angustifolia "Nana Alba"
Dwarf White Lavender
Hardy evergreen perennial. Ht and spread 12 in. White flowers in summer. Green-gray narrow short leaves. This is the shortest growing lavender and is ideal for hedges. **Zone 5.**

Lavandula angustifolia "Rosea"
Lavender Pink/Rosea
Hardy evergreen perennial. Ht and spread 18 in. Pink flowers in summer. Medium length greenish-gray, narrow, aromatic leaves. **Zone 5.**

Lavandula angustifolia "Twickel Purple"
Lavender Twickel Purple
Hardy evergreen perennial. Ht and spread 20 in. Pale purple flowers on fairly short spike. Medium length, greenish-gray, narrow, aromatic leaves. Compact. **Zone 5.**

Lavandula dentata
Fringed Lavender
Sometimes called French lavender. Half-hardy evergreen perennial. Ht and spread 24 in. Pale blue/mauve flowers from summer to early fall. Highly aromatic, serrated, pale green, narrow leaves. This plant is a native of southern Spain and the Mediterranean region and so needs protecting in cold damp winters. It is ideal to bring inside into a cool room in early fall as a flowering pot plant. **Zone 10.**

Lavandula x *intermedia* Dutch Group syn. *L. vera*
Lavender Vera
Hardy evergreen perennial. Ht and spread 18 in. Purple flowers in summer on fairly long spikes. Long greenish-gray, narrow, aromatic leaves. **Zone 5.**

Lavandula x *intermedia* "Old English"
Old English Lavender
Hardy evergreen perennial. Ht and spread 24 in. Light lavender-blue flowers on long spikes. Long, narrow, silver/gray/green aromatic leaves. **Zone 5.**

Lavandula x *intermedia* "Pale Pretender" syn. *L.* "Grappenhall"
Lavender Pale Pretender
Hardy evergreen perennial. Ht and spread 3 ft. Large pale mauve flowers on long spikes in summer. The flowers are much more open than those of other species. Long greenish-gray, narrow, aromatic leaves. **Zone 5.**

Lavandula x *intermedia* "Seal"
Lavender Seal
Hardy evergreen perennial. Ht 36 in., spread 24 in. Long flower stems, mid-purple. Long, narrow, silver/gray/green aromatic leaves. **Zone 5.**

Lavandula angustifolia "Twickel Purple"

Lavandula pendunculata subsp. *pedunculata*

Lavandula lanata
Woolly Lavender
Hardy evergreen perennial. Ht 20 in., spread 18 in. Deep purple flowers on short spikes. Short, soft, narrow, silver-gray aromatic foliage **Zone 6.**

Lavendula pedunculata subsp. *pedunculata* AGM
Lavender Pedunculata
Sometimes known as Papillon. Half-hardy evergreen perennial. Ht and spread 24 in. The attractive purple bracts have an extra mauve center tuft, which looks like two rabbit ears. The aromatic leaves are long, very narrow and gray. Protect in winter. **Zone 8.**

Lavandula stoechas
French Lavender
Sometimes called Spanish lavender. Hardy evergreen perennial. Ht 20 in., spread 24 in. Attractive purple bracts in summer. Short, narrow, gray/green, aromatic leaves. **Zones 7 to 9.**

Lavandula stoechas subsp. *stoechas* f. *leucantha*

White French Lavender
As *L. stoechas* except white bracts in summer. **Zones 7 to 9.**

Lavandula stoechas subsp. *stoechas* f. *rosea* "Kew Red"

Lavender Kew Red
Half-hardy evergreen perennial. Ht and spread 16 in. Cerise crimson flowers and pale pink "ears." Short, narrow, gray/green aromatic leaves. Prefers an acidic soil. **Zones 7 to 9.**

Lavandula viridis

Green Lavender, Lemon Lavender
Half-hardy evergreen perennial. Ht and spread 24 in. This unusual plant has green bracts with a cream center tuft. The leaves are green, narrow, and highly aromatic. Protect in winter. **Zone 9.**

Lavenders — Small

Grow to 18–20 in.:
L. angustifolia "Folgate," *L. angustifolia* "Hidcote," *L. angustifolia* "Loddon Pink," *L. angustifolia* "Munstead," *L. angustifolia* "Nana Alba," *L. angustifolia* "Twickel Purple"

Lavenders — Medium

Grow to 3ft.:
L. angustifolia "Bowles' Early," *L. x intermedia* "Old English"

Lavandula viridis

Lavenders — Large

28 in. and above:
L. angustifolia "Alba," *L. x intermedia* "Seal."

Half-hardy Lavenders

L. dentata (20 in.), *L. lanata* (20 in.), *L. stoechas* (20 in.), *L. stoechas* subsp. *stoechas* f. *leucantha* (20 in.), *L. pedunculata* subsp. *pedunculata* (24 in.), *L. viridis* (20 in.).

 ## cultivation

Propagation

Seed
Lavender can be grown from seed but it tends not to be true to species, with the exception of *L. stoechas*.

Seed should be sown fresh in the fall on the surface of a seed or plug tray and covered with perlite. It germinates fairly readily with a bottom heat of 40 to 50°F. Winter the seedlings in a cold greenhouse or cold conservatory with plenty of ventilation. In the spring, prick out and repot using a standard seed compost mixed in equal parts with composted fine bark. Let the young plant establish a good-size root ball before planting out in a prepared site in the early summer. For other species you will find cuttings much more reliable.

Cuttings
Take softwood cuttings from nonflowering stems in spring. Root in a standard seed compost mixed in equal parts with composted fine bark. Take semi-hardwood cuttings in summer or early fall from the strong new growth. Once the cuttings have rooted well, it is better to pot them up and winter the young lavenders in a cold greenhouse or conservatory rather than plant them out in the first winter. In the spring, plant them out in well-drained, fertile soil, at a distance of 18–24 in. apart or 12 in. apart for an average hedge.

Layering
This is easily done in the fall. Most hardy lavenders respond well to this form of propagation.

Pests and Diseases

The chief and most damaging pest of lavender is the rosemary beetle. The beetle and its larvae feed on the leaves from fall until spring. As soon as you see this

Lavandula angustifolia "Loddon Pink"

small shiny beetle, place some newspaper underneath the plant, then tap or shake the branches, which will knock the beetles and larvae on to the paper, making them easy to destroy.

The flowers in wet seasons may be attacked by gray mold (*Botrytis*). This can occur all too readily after a wet winter. Cut back the infected parts as far as possible, again remembering not to cut into the old wood if you want it to shoot again.

There is another fungus (*Phoma lavandulae*) that attacks the stems and branches, causing wilting and death of the affected branches. If this occurs dig up the plant immediately and destroy, keeping it well away from any other lavender bushes.

Maintenance

Spring Give a spring hair cut.
Summer Trim after flowering. Take cuttings.
Fall Sow seed. Cut back in early fall, never into the old wood. Protect all the half-hardy lavenders. Bring containers inside before frosts start.
Winter Check seedlings for disease. Keep watering to a minimum.

LAVENDER

Lavender herb jelly

Garden Cultivation

Lavender is one of the most popular plants in today's herb garden and is particularly useful in borders, edges, as internal hedges, and on top of dry walls. All the species require an open sunny position and a well-drained, fertile soil. But lavender will adapt to semi-shade as long as the soil conditions are met, otherwise it will die in winter. If you have very cold winter temperatures, it is worth growing lavenders in containers to move inside in winter.

Trim a lavender bush to shape every year in the spring, remembering not to cut into the old wood as this will not re shoot. After flowering, trim back to the leaves. In the early fall trim again, making sure this is well before the first fall frosts, otherwise the new growth will be too soft and be damaged. By trimming this way, you will keep the bush neat and encourage it to make new growth, so stopping it becoming woody.

If you have inherited a straggly mature plant then give it a good cut back in fall, followed by a second cut in the spring and then adopt the above routine. If the plant is aged, I would advise that you propagate some of the fall cuts, so preserving the plant if all else fails.

Harvesting

Gather the flowers just as they open, and dry on open trays or by hanging in small bunches. Pick the leaves any time for use fresh, or before flowering if drying.

 container growing

If you have low winter temperatures, lavender cannot be treated as a hardy evergreen. Treated as a container plant, however, it can be protected in winter and enjoyed just as well in the summer. Choose containers to set off the lavender; they all suit terracotta. Use a soil-based compost mixed in equal parts with composted fine bark. The ideal position is sun, but all lavenders will cope with partial shade, though the aroma can be impaired. Feed regularly through the flowering season with liquid fertilizer, following the manufacturer's instructions. Allow the compost to dry out in winter (not totally, but nearly), and slowly reintroduce watering in spring.

 medicinal

Throughout history, lavender has been used medicinally to soothe, sedate, and suppress. Nowadays it is the essential oil that is in great demand for its many beneficial effects. The oil was traditionally inhaled to prevent vertigo and fainting. It is an excellent remedy for burns and stings, and its strong antibacterial action helps to heal cuts. The oil also kills diphtheria and typhoid bacilli as well as streptococcus and pneumococcus.

Add 6 drops of oil to bath water to calm irritable children and help them sleep. Place 1 drop on the temple for a headache relief. Blend for use as a massage oil in aromatherapy for throat infections, skin sores, inflammation, rheumatic aches, anxiety, insomnia, and depression.

 other uses

Rub fresh flowers onto skin or pin a sprig on clothes to discourage flies. Use flowers in potpourri, herb pillows, and linen sachets, where they make a good moth repellent.

Left: Lavender sachets make good presents and can be used as moth repellents

 culinary

Lavender has not been used much in cooking, but as there are many more adventurous cooks around, I am sure it will be used increasingly in the future. Use the flowers to flavor an herb jelly, or a vinegar. Equally the flowers can be crystallized.

Lavender Cookies

¼ cup superfine sugar
½ cup butter
¾ cup self-rising flour
2 tablespoons fresh chopped lavender leaves
1 teaspoon lavender flowers removed from spike

Cream the sugar and butter together until light. Add the flour and lavender leaves to the butter mixture. Knead well until it forms a dough. Gently roll out on a lightly floured board. Sprinkle the rolled dough with the flowers and lightly press in with the rolling pin. Cut into small rounds with cutter. Place cookies on a greased cookie sheet. Bake in a hot oven 450°F for 10 to 12 minutes until golden and firm. Remove at once and cool on a wire tray.

Levisticum officinale
LOVAGE

Also known as Love parsley, Sea parsley, Lavose, Liveche, Smallage, and European lovage. From the family Apiaceae.

This native of the Mediterranean can now be found naturalized throughout the temperate regions of the world, including Australia, North America, and Scandinavia.

Lovage was used by the ancient Greeks, who chewed the seed to aid digestion and relieve flatulence. Knowledge of it was handed down to Benedictine monks by the Romans, who prescribed the seeds for the same complaints. In Europe a decoction of lovage was reputedly a good aphrodisiac that no witch worthy of the name could be without. The name is likely to have come from the Latin *ligusticum*, after Liguria in Italy, where the herb grew profusely.

Because lovage leaves have a deodorizing and antiseptic effect on the skin, they were laid in the shoes of travelers in the Middle Ages to revive their weary feet, like latter-day odor eaters.

 ## varieties

Levisticum officinale
Lovage
Hardy perennial. Ht up to 6 ft, spread 3 ft. or more. Tiny, pale, greenish-yellow flowers in summer clusters. Leaves darkish green, deeply divided, and large toothed. **Zone 3.**

A close relation, **Ligusticum scoticum**, shorter with white clusters of flowers, is sometimes called lovage. It can be used in the same culinary way, but lacks its strong flavor and the growth.

 ## cultivation

Propagation
Seed
Sow under protection in spring into prepared plug or seed trays and cover with perlite; a bottom heat of 60°F is helpful. When the seedlings are large enough to handle and after a period of hardening off, transplant into a prepared site in the garden about 2 ft. apart.

Division
The roots of an established plant can be divided in the spring or fall. Make sure that each division has some new buds showing.

Pests and Diseases
Leaf miners are sometimes a problem. Watch out for the first tunnels, pick off the affected leaves and destroy them, otherwise broad, dry patches will develop and the leaves will start to wither away. To control heavy infestations, cut the plant down to the ground, burning the affected shoots. Feed the plant and it will shoot with new growth. The young growth is just what one needs for cooking.

Maintenance
Spring Divide established plants. Sow seeds.
Summer Clip established plants to encourage the growth of new shoots.
Fall Dry seeds. Divide roots.
Winter No need for protection.

Garden Cultivation
Lovage prefers a rich, moist but well-drained soil. Prior to first planting, dig over the ground deeply and manure well. The site can be either in full sun or partial shade. Seeds are best sown in the garden in the fall. When the seedlings are large enough, thin to 2 ft. apart. It is important that lovage has a period of dormancy so that it can complete the growth cycle. Lovage is a tall plant, so position it carefully. It will reach its full size in 3 to 5 years. To keep the leaves young and producing new shoots, cut around the edges of the clumps.

Harvesting
After the plant has flowered the leaves tend to have more of a bitter taste, so harvest in early summer. I personally believe that lovage does not dry that well and it is best to freeze it (see p. 671 and use the parsley technique).

Harvest seed heads when the seeds start to turn brown. Pick them on a dry day, tie a paper bag over their heads, and hang upside down in a dry, airy place. Use, like celery seed, for winter soups. Dig the root for drying in the fall of the second or third season.

 ## container growing

Lovage is fine grown outside in a large container. To keep it looking good, keep it well-clipped. I do not advise letting it run to flower unless you can support it. Remember at flowering stage, even in a pot, it can be in excess of 5 ft. tall.

medicinal

Lovage is a remedy for digestive difficulties, gastric catarrh and flatulence. I know of one recipe from the West Country — a teaspoon of lovage seed steeped in a glass of brandy, strained and sweetened with sugar. It is taken to settle an upset stomach!

Infuse either seed, leaf or root and take to reduce water retention. Lovage assists in the removal of waste products, acts as a deodorizer, and aids rheumatism Its deodorizing and antiseptic properties enable certain skin problems to respond to a decoction added to bath water. This is made with 1¾ to 2¼ oz. of rootstock in 2 cups of water. Add to your bath.

warning

As lovage is very good at reducing water retention, people who are pregnant or who have kidney problems should not take this herb medicinally.

Lovage, brandy and sugar settles an upset stomach

Lovage soup

culinary

Lovage is an essential member of any culinary herb collection. The flavor is reminiscent of celery. It adds a meaty flavor to foods and is used in soups, stews, and broths. Also add fresh young leaves to salads, and rub on chicken, and around salad bowls. Crush seeds in bread and pastries, sprinkle on salads, rice and mashed potato. If using the rootstock as a vegetable in casseroles, remove the bitter-tasting skin.

Lovage Soup
Serves 4

2 tablespoons butter
2 medium onions, finely minced
2 cups potatoes, peeled and diced
4 tablespoons finely minced lovage leaves
3½ cups chicken or vegetable broth
1 cup milk or cream
Grated nutmeg
Salt and freshly ground black pepper

Melt the butter in a heavy pan and gently sauté the onions and diced potatoes for 5 minutes until soft. Add the chopped lovage leaves and cook for 1 minute. Pour in the broth, bring to a boil, season with salt and pepper, cover, and simmer gently until the potatoes are soft (about 15 minutes). Purée the soup through a strainer or liquidizer and return to a clean pan. Blend in the milk or cream, sprinkle on a pinch of nutmeg and heat through. Do not boil or it will curdle. Adjust seasoning. This soup is delicious hot or cold. Serve garnished with chopped lovage leaves.

Lovage and Carrot
Serves 2

3 carrots, grated
1 apple, grated
2 teaspoons chopped lovage leaves
2 tablespoons mayonnaise
½ cup plain yogurt
1 teaspoon salt (if needed)
Lettuce leaves
1 onion sliced into rings
Chives

Toss together the grated carrots, apple, lovage, mayonnaise, and yogurt. Arrange the lettuce leaves on a serving dish and fill with the lovage mixture. Decorate with a few raw onion rings, chives, and tiny lovage leaves.

Lovage as a Vegetable

Treat lovage as you would spinach. Use the young growth of the plant stalks and leaves. Strip the leaves from the stalks, wash, and cut the stalks up into segments. Bring a pan of water to a boil and add the lovage. Bring the water back to a boil, cover, and simmer for about 5 to 7 minutes until tender. Strain the water. Make a white sauce using butter, flour, milk, salt, pepper, and grated nutmeg. Add the lovage. Serve and wait for the comments!

Lonicera
HONEYSUCKLE

Also known as Woodbine, Beerbind, Bindweed, Evening Pride, Fairy Trumpets, Honeybind, Irish Vine, Trumpet Flowers, Sweet Suckle, and Woodbind. From the family Caprifoliaceae.

"Come into the garden, Maud,
I am here at the gate alone;
And the woodbine spices are
wafted abroad,
And the musk of the rose is blown."
Alfred Lord Tennyson (1809–1892)

Honeysuckle grows all over northern Europe, including Britain, and can also be found wild in North Africa, Western Asia, and North America.

Honeysuckle, *Lonicera*, receives its common name from the old habit of sucking the sweet honey-tasting nectar from the flowers. Generically it is said to have been named after the 16th-century German physician, Lonicer.

Honeysuckle was among the plants that averted the evil powers abroad on May Day and took care of milk, the butter, and the cows in the Scottish Highlands and elsewhere. Traditionally it was thought that if honeysuckle was brought into the house, a wedding would follow, and that if the flowers were placed in a girl's bedroom, she would have dreams of love.

Honeysuckle's rich fragrance has inspired many poets, including Shakespeare, who called it woodbine after its notorious habit of climbing up trees and hedges and totally binding them up.

"Where oxlips and the nodding violet grows
quite over-canopied with luscious woodbine . . ."
A Midsummer Night's Dream

The plant appeared in John Gerard's 16th-century *Herball*; he wrote that "the flowers steeped in oil and set in the sun are good to anoint the body that is benummed and grown very cold."

 varieties

There are many fragrant climbing varieties of this lovely plant. I have only mentioned those with a direct herbal input.

Lonicera x americana (Miller)
American Honeysuckle
Deciduous perennial. Ht up to 23 ft. Strongly fragrant yellow flowers starting in a pink bud turning yellow and finishing with orangish-pink throughout the summer. The berries are red, and the leaves are green and oval, the upper ones being united and saucer-like. **Zone 6.**

Lonicera caprifolium AGM
Deciduous perennial. Ht up to 20 ft. The buds of the fragrant flowers are initially pink on opening; they then change to a pale white/pink/yellow as they age and finally turn deeper yellow. Green oval leaves and red berries, which were once fed to chickens. The Latin species name, *caprifolium*, means goats' leaf, reflecting the belief that honeysuckle leaves were a favourite food of goats. This variety and *Lonicera periclymenum* can be found growing wild in hedgerows. **Zone 5.**

Lonicera etrusca
Etruscan Honeysuckle
Semi-evergreen perennial. Ht up to 12 ft. Fragrant, pale, creamy yellow flowers which turn deeper yellow to red in fall and are followed by red berries. Leaves oval, midgreen, with a bluish underside. This is the least hardy of those mentioned here, and should be grown on a sunny wall, and protected in winter where temperatures fall below 23°F. **Zone 7.**

Lonicera japonica
Japanese Honeysuckle
Semi-evergreen perennial. Ht up to 33 ft. Fragrant, creamy white flowers turning yellow as the season progresses, followed by black berries. The leaves are oval and midgreen in color. It is apt to build up an enormous tangle of shoots and best allowed to clamber over tree stumps or a low roof or walls. Attempts to train it tidily are futile. Still used in Chinese medicine. This species is invasive in the U.S. **Zone 5.**

Lonicera periclymenum
Deciduous perennial. This is the taller grower of the two common European honeysuckles, and reaches a

HONEYSUCKLE

Lonicera periclymenum

Deciduous perennial. This is the taller grower of the two common European honeysuckles, and reaches a height of 23 ft. It may live for 50 years. Fragrant yellow flowers appear midsummer to midfall, followed by red berries. Leaves are oval and dark green with a bluish underside. **Zone 5.**

cultivation

Propagation

Seed

Sow seed in fall thinly on the surface of a prepared seed or plug tray. Cover with glass and winter outside. Keep an eye on the compost moisture and only water if necessary. Germination may take a long time, it has been known to take two seasons, so be patient. A more reliable alternative method is by cuttings.

Cuttings

Take from nonflowering, semi-hardwood shoots in summer and root in a standard seed compost mixed in equal parts with composted fine bark. Alternatively, take hardwood cuttings in late fall, leaving them in a cold frame or cold greenhouse for the winter.

Layering

In late spring or fall honeysuckle is easy to layer. Do not disturb until the following season when it can be severed from its parent.

Pests and Diseases

Grown in too sunny or warm a place, it can become infested with aphids, blackfly, caterpillars, and red spider mites. Use a insecticidal soap, and spray the pests

Lonicera caprifolium

according to the manufacturer's instructions. To prevent powdery mildew, avoid dryness around the root.

Maintenance

Spring Prune established plants.
Summer Cut back flowering stems after flowering. Take semi hardwood cuttings.
Fall Layer established plants. Lightly prune if necessary.
Winter Protect certain species in cold winters.

Garden Cultivation

This extremely tolerant, traditional herb garden plant will flourish vigorously in the most unpromising sites. Honeysuckle leaves are among the first to appear, sometimes midwinter, the flowers appearing in very early summer and deepening in color after being pollinated by the insects that feed on their nectar. Good as cover for an unsightly wall or to provide a rich summer evening fragrance in an arbor.

Plant in fall or spring in any fertile, well drained soil, in sun or semi-shade. The best situation puts its feet in the shade and its head in the sunshine. A position against a shady wall is ideal, or on the shady side of a support such as a tree stump, pole, or pergola. Prune in early spring, if need be. Prune out flowering wood on climbers after flowering.

Harvesting

Pick and dry the flowers for potpourri just as they open. This is the best time for scent although they are at their palest in color. Pick the flowers for use in salads as required. Again the best flavor is before the nectar has been collected, which is when the flower is at its palest.

container growing

This is not a plant that springs to mind as a good pot plant, certainly not indoors. But with patience, it makes a lovely mop head standard if carefully staked and trained. The compost should be a soil-based one. Water and feed regularly throughout the summer and in winter keep in a cold frame or greenhouse and water only occasionally.

warning

The berries are poisonous. Large doses cause vomiting.

Honeysuckle tea

culinary

Add flowers to salads.

medicinal

An infusion of the heavy perfumed flowers can be taken as a substitute for tea. It is also useful for treating coughs, catarrh and asthma. As a lotion it is good for skin infections. Recent research has proved that this plant has an outstanding curative action in cases of colitis.

other uses

Flowers are strongly scented for potpourri, herb pillows and perfumery. An essential oil was once extracted from the plant to make a very sweet perfume but the yield was extremely low.

Honeysuckle flowers

Malva
MALLOW

Also known as High Mallow, Country Mallow, Billy Buttons, Pancake Plant, and Cheese Flower. From the family Malvaceae.

Native to Europe, Western Asia, and North America, it can be found growing in hedgebanks, field edges, and on road sides and wastelands in sunny situations.

The ancient Latin name given to this herb by Pliny was *malacho*, which was probably derived from *malachi*, the Greek word meaning

"to soften," after the mallow's softening and healing properties. Young mallow shoots were eaten as vegetables, and it was still to be found on vegetable lists in Roman times. Used in the Middle Ages for its calming effect as an antidote to aphrodisiacs and love-potions. The shape of its seed rather than its flowers suggested the folk name.

Sow seeds in the garden.
Summer Trim after flowering. Take cuttings.
Fall Sow seed under protection.
Winter Hardy enough.

Garden Cultivation
Mallows are very tolerant of site, but prefer a well-drained and fertile soil (if too damp they may well need staking in summer), and a sunny position (though semi-shade will do). Sow where it is to flower from late summer to spring. Press gently into the soil, 24 in. apart, and cover with a light compost. Cut back stems after flowering, not only to promote new growth, but also to keep under control and encourage a second flowering. Cut down the stems in fall.

Harvesting
Harvest young leaves for fresh use as required throughout the spring. For use in potpourris, gather for drying in the summer after first flowering.

 ## container growing

Malva moschata is the variety to grow in a large container. It can look very dramatic and smells lovely on a warm evening. Water well in the growing season, but feed only twice. Maintain as for garden cultivation.

 ## medicinal

Marshmallow (*Althaea officinalis*) is used in preference to the mallows (*Malva* sp.) in herbal medicine. However, a decoction can be used in a compress, or in bath preparations, for skin rashes, boils, and ulcers, and in gargles and mouth washes.

 ## varieties

Malva sylvestris
Common Mallow
Biennial. Ht 18–24 in., spread 24 in. Flower, dark pink or violet form, early summer to fall. Midgreen leaves, rounded at the base, ivy shaped at stem.
Zone 4.

Malva moschata
Musk Mallow
Perennial. Ht 12–32 in., spread 24 in. Rose/pink flowers, late summer to early fall. Midgreen leaves — kidney-shaped at base, deeply divided at stem — emit musky aroma in warm weather or when pressed.
Zone 4.

Malva pusilla
Dwarf Mallow
Also known as cheese plant, low mallow and blue mallow. Annual. Ht 6–12 in., a creeper. Purplish-pink, trumpet-shaped flowers from early summer to midfall. Leaves rounded, slightly lobed and greenish. North American native. **All zones.**

cultivation

Propagation
Seed
Sow in prepared seed or plug trays in the fall. Cover lightly with compost (not perlite). Winter outside, covered with glass. Germination is erratic but should take place in the spring. Plant out seedlings when large enough to handle, 24 in. apart.

Cuttings
Take cuttings from firm basal shoots in late spring or summer. When hardened off the following spring, plant out 24 in. apart into a prepared site.

Pests and Diseases
Mallows can catch hollyhock rust. There is also a fungus that produces leaf spots and a serious black canker on the stems. If this occurs dig up the plants and destroy them. This is a seed-borne fungus and may be carried into the soil, so change planting site each season.

Maintenance
Spring Take softwood cuttings from young shoots.

 ## culinary

Young tender tips of the common mallow may be used in salads or steamed as a vegetable. Young leaves of the musk mallow can be boiled as a vegetable. Young leaves of the dwarf mallow can be eaten raw in salads or cooked as a spinach.

Mandragora
MANDRAKE

Mandragora fallalis

Mandrake root

Also known as Devil's Apples, Satan's Apples. From the family Solanaceae.

Mandrake is indigenous to the Mediterranean. It is steeped in myth and magic. Historically it is recorded that in 200 BCE the Carthaginians created a bait for the Romans who were invading their city, made from wine spiked with mandrake juice. This rendered the Romans insensible and the city was saved. It has been used in witchcraft to make barren women fertile and it is also mentioned in the Bible, Genesis 30, where Rachel, the second wife of Jacob becomes fertile after her sister found mandrake growing in a field.

Maintenance
Spring Sow seeds and cuttings of *Mandragora autumnalis*.
Summer Check watering.
Fall Sow seeds and take cuttings of *Mandragora officinarum*.
Winter Protect from excessive wet.

Garden Cultivation
Plant in a well-drained, deep, fertile soil in partial shade. Because mandrake has a very long tap root, up to 4 ft., it dislikes being transplanted, so choose your site carefully. In summer, the plant will become dormant if the soil dries out.

Harvesting
Dig up the roots in fall or spring when the plant is dormant for medicinal use.

 varieties

☠ Mandragora officinarum
Mandrake, Satan's Apple
Hardy herbaceous, perennial. Ht 6–12 in., spread 12 in. Small bell-shaped, very pale blue flowers in spring, followed by aromatic round, yellow, toxic fruits in late summer. Large, up to 12 in. long, oblong, rough green leaves. **Zone 6.**

☠ Mandragora autumnalis
Hardy herbaceous, perennial. Ht 6–12 in. and spread 12 in. Small bell-shaped pale blue/violet flowers in fall, followed in the third year by aromatic round, yellow, toxic fruits in late summer. Large, oblong, hairy, dark green leaves. **Zone 6.**

 cultivation

Propagation
Seed
Sow the fresh seeds *M. officinarum* in fall and *M. autumnalis* in spring, into prepared plug cell-packs, using a soil-based seed compost mixed in equal parts with coarse horticultural sand. Cover with coarse sand and place in a cold frame. Germination can take anything from 4 months to 2 years. Once the seedling is large enough to handle, repot, and grow on for 2 years prior to planting in the garden.

Cuttings
In the early spring (fall for *M. autumnalis*) when you can see the new shoots appearing, clear around the plant to expose the crown and the top of the roots. Choose a side with new shoot appearing and, using a sharp knife, slice the root including a new shoot. Place the cutting into a small pot filled with a soilless potting compost mixed in equal parts with coarse horticultural sand. Place the container in a warm position until rooted. Grow on for 2 years prior to planting into a prepared site.

Pests and Diseases
Slugs can decimate a plant overnight. So check regularly at night and remove any that are found.

 container growing

Mandrake's long tap root makes it particularly unsuitable for growing in containers. It is possible, but the plant will be smaller and rarely set fruit. Use a soilless potting compost that has been mixed in equal parts with coarse horticultural sand.

 medicinal

Both the species mentioned have the same medicinal properties. Today, mandrake is rarely used in herbal medicine. However, tinctures made from the root are still widely used in homeopathy as a treatment for asthma and coughs.

 warning

The whole plant, including the root, is toxic. Only take under professional supervision. Not to be taken in any form during pregnancy.

Marrubium vulgare

WHITE HOREHOUND

Also known as Horehound and Maribeum. From the family Lamiaceae.

Common throughout America and Europe, the plant grows wild everywhere from coastal to mountainous areas.

The botanical name comes from the Hebrew *marrob*, which translates as "bitter juice." The common name is derived from the old English *har hune*, meaning "a downy plant."

varieties

Marrubium vulgare
White Horehound
Hardy perennial. Ht 18 in., spread 12 in. Small clusters of white flowers from the second year in midsummer. The leaves are green and wrinkled with an underside of a silver woolly texture. There is also a variegated version. **Zone 4.**

cultivation

Propagation
Seed
The fairly small seed should be sown in early spring in a seed or plug tray, using a standard seed compost mixed in equal parts with composted fine bark. Germination takes 2 to 3 weeks. Prick out into pots or transplant to the garden after a good period of hardening off.

Cuttings
Softwood cuttings taken from the new growth in summer usually root within 3 to 4 weeks. Use a standard seed compost mixed in equal parts with composted fine bark. Winter under protection in a cold frame or cold greenhouse.

Division
Established clumps benefit from division in the spring.

Pests and Diseases
If it is very wet and cold in winter, the plant can rot.

Maintenance
Spring Divide established clumps. Prune new growth to maintain shape. Sow seed.
Summer Trim after flowering to stop the plant flopping and prevent self-seeding. Take cuttings.
Fall Divide only if it has dangerously transgressed its limits.
Winter Protect only if season excessively wet.

Garden Cultivation
White horehound grows best in well-drained, dryish soil, biased to alkaline, sunny, and protected from high winds. Seed can be sown direct into a prepared garden in late spring, once the soil has started to warm up. Thin the seedlings to 12 in. distance apart.

Harvesting
The leaves and flowering tops are gathered in the spring, just as the plants come into flower, when the essential oil is at its richest. Use fresh or dried.

container growing

Horehound can be grown in a large container situated in a sunny position. Use a compost that drains well and do not overwater. Only feed after flowering, otherwise it produces lush growth that is too soft.

other uses

Traditionally an infusion of the leaf was used as a spray for cankerworm in trees. Also the infusion was mixed with milk and put in a dish as a fly killer.

medicinal

White horehound is still extensively used in cough medicine, and for calming a nervous heart; its property, marrubiin, in small amounts, normalizes an irregular heart beat. The plant has also been used to reduce fevers and treat malaria.

A Traditional Cold Cure
Finely chop nine small horehound leaves. Mix 1 tablespoon of honey and eat slowly to ease a sore throat or cough. Repeat several times if necessary.

Traditional Cough Candies

½ cup fresh white horehound leaves
½ teaspoon crushed aniseed
3 crushed cardamom seeds
1½ cups white sugar
1½ cups moist brown sugar

Put the horehound, aniseed and cardamom into 2 cups of water and simmer for 20 minutes. Strain through a filter. Over low heat, dissolve the sugars in the liquid; boil over medium heat until the syrup hardens when drops are put into cold water. Pour into an oiled tray. Score when partially cooled. Break up and store in wax paper.

LEMON BALM

Melissa officinalis

Also known as Balm, Melissa, Balm Mint, Bee Balm, Blue Balm, Cure All, Dropsy Plant, Garden Balm, and Sweet Balm. From the family Lamiaceae.

This plant is a native of the Mediterranean region and Central Europe. It is now naturalized in North America and as a garden escapee in Britain.

This ancient herb was dedicated to the goddess Diana, and used medicinally by the Greeks some 2,000 years ago. The generic name, *Melissa*, comes from the Greek word for bee and the Greek belief that if you put sprigs of balm in an empty hive it would attract a swarm; equally, if planted near bees in residence in a hive they would never go away. This belief was still prevalent in medieval times when sugar was highly priced and honey a luxury.

In the Middle Ages lemon balm was used to soothe tension, to dress wounds, as a cure for toothache, mad dog bites, skin eruptions, crooked necks, and sickness during pregnancy. It was even said to prevent baldness, and ladies made linen or silk amulets filled with lemon balm as a lucky love charm. It has been acclaimed the world over for promoting long life. Prince Llewellyn of Glamorgan drank melissa tea, so he claimed, every day of the 108 years of his life. Wild claims apart, as a tonic for melancholy it has been praised by herbal writers for centuries and is still used today in aromatherapy to counter depression.

Melissa officinalis "Aurea"

 varieties

Melissa officinalis
Lemon Balm
Hardy perennial. Ht 30 in., spread 18 in. or more. Clusters of small, pale yellow/white flowers in summer. The green leaves are oval, toothed, slightly wrinkled and highly aromatic when crushed. **Zone 5.**

Melissa officinalis "All Gold"
Golden Lemon Balm
Half-hardy perennial. Ht 24 in., spread 12 in. or more. Clusters of small, pale yellow/white flowers in summer. The leaves are all yellow, oval in shape, toothed, slightly wrinkled, and aromatic with a lemon scent when crushed. The leaves are prone to scorching in high summer. More tender than the other varieties. **Zone 6.**

Melissa officinalis "Aurea"
Variegated Lemon Balm
Hardy perennial. Ht 24 in., spread 12 in. or more. Clusters of small, pale yellow/white flowers in summer. The green/gold variegated leaves are oval, toothed, slightly wrinkled, and aromatic with a lemon scent when crushed. This variety is as hardy as common lemon balm. The one problem is that in high season it reverts to green. To maintain variegation keep cutting back; this in turn will promote new growth, which should be variegated.

 cultivation

Propagation
Seed
Common lemon balm can be grown from seed. The seed is small but manageable, and it is better to start

LEMON BALM

it off under protection. Sow in prepared seed or plug trays in early spring, using a standard seed compost mixed in equal parts with composted fine bark, and cover with perlite. Germination takes between 10 and 14 days. The seeds dislike being wet so, after the initial watering, try not to water again until germination starts. When seedlings are large enough to handle, prick out and plant in the garden, 18 in. apart.

Cuttings
The variegated and golden lemon balm can only be propagated by cuttings or division. Take softwood cuttings from the new growth in late spring/early summer. As the cutting material will be very soft, take extra care when collecting it.

Division
The rootstock is easy to divide (fall or spring). Replant directly into the garden in a prepared site.

Pests and Diseases
The only problem likely to affect lemon balm is a form of fungus similar to mint rust; cut the plant back to the ground and dispose of all the infected leaves, including any that may have accidentally fallen on the ground.

Maintenance
Spring Sow seeds. Divide established plants. Take cuttings.
Summer Take cuttings. Keep trimming established

plants. Cut back after flowering to reduce self-seeding.
Fall Divide established plants, or any that may have encroached on other plant areas.
Winter Protect plants if the temperature falls below 23°F. The plant dies back, leaving but a small presence on the surface of the soil. Protect with a bark or straw mulch or a floating row cover.

Garden Cultivation
Lemon balm will grow in almost any soil and in any position. It does prefer a fairly rich, moist soil in a sunny position with some midday shade. Keep all plants trimmed around the edges to restrict growth and encourage fresh shoots. In the right soil conditions this can be a very invasive plant. Unlike horseradish, the established roots are not difficult to uproot if things get out of hand.

Harvesting
Pick leaves throughout the summer for fresh use. For drying, pick just before the flowers begin to open when flavor is best; handle gently to avoid bruising. The aroma is rapidly lost, together with much of its therapeutic value, when dried or stored.

 ## container growing

If you live in an area that suffers from very cold winters, the gold form would benefit from being

grown in containers. This method suits those with a small garden who do not want a takeover bid from lemon balm. Use a soilless compost mixed in equal parts with composted fine bark. Only feed with liquid fertilizer in the summer, otherwise the growth will become too lush and soft, and aroma and color will diminish. Water normally throughout the growing season. Allow the container to become very dry (but not totally) in winter, and keep the pots in a cool, protected environment.

 ## medicinal

Lemon balm tea is said to relieve headaches and tension and to restore the memory. It is also good after meals to ease the digestion, flatulence and colic. Use fresh or frozen leaves in infusions because the volatile oil tends to disappear during the drying process. The isolated oil used in aromatherapy is recommended for nervousness, depression, insomnia and nervous headaches. It also helps eczema sufferers.

 ## other uses

This is a most useful plant to keep bees happy. The flower may look boring to you but it is sheer heaven to them. So plant lemon balm around beehives or orchards to attract pollinating bees.

 ## culinary

Lemon balm is one of those herbs that smells delicious but tastes like school-boiled cabbage water when cooked.

Add fresh leaves to vinegar. Add leaves to wine cups, teas and beers, or use chopped with fish and mushroom dishes. Mix freshly chopped with cream cheeses.

It has frequently been incorporated in proprietary cordials for liqueurs and its popularity in France led to its name "Tea de France." It is used as a flavoring for certain cheeses in parts of Switzerland.

Lemon balm with cream cheese

Mentha
MINT

From the family Lamiaceae.

The *Mentha* family is a native of Europe that has naturalized in many parts of the world, including North America, Australia, and Japan.

Mint has been cultivated for its medicinal properties since ancient times and has been found in Egyptian tombs dating back to 1,000 BCE. The Japanese have been growing it to obtain menthol for at least 2,000 years. In the Bible the Pharisees collected tithes in mint, dill, and cumin. Charlemagne, who was very keen on herbs, ordered people to grow it. The Romans brought it with them as they marched through Europe and into Britain, from where it found its way to America with the settlers.

Its name was first used in Greek mythology. There are two different stories, the first that the nymph Minthe was being chatted up by Hades, god of the Underworld. His queen Sephony became jealous and turned her into the plant, mint. The second that Minthe was a nymph beloved by Pluto, who transformed her into the scented herb after his jealous wife took umbrage.

Mentha x *piperita* f. *citrata*

 varieties

The mint family is large and well known. I have chosen a few to illustrate the diversity of the species.

Mentha aquatica
Water Mint
Hardy perennial. Ht 6–24 in., spread indefinite. Pretty purple/lilac flowers borne all summer. Leaves soft, slightly downy, midgreen in color. The scent can vary from a musty mint to a strong peppermint. This should be planted in water or very wet marshy soil. It can be found growing wild around ponds and streams. **Zone 5.**

Mentha arvensis var. piperascens
Japanese Peppermint
Hardy perennial. Ht 2–3 ft., spread 24 in. and more. Loose purplish whorls of flowers in summer. Leaves, downy, oblong, sharply toothed and green-gray; they provide an oil (90 percent menthol), said to be inferior to the oil produced by *M.* x *piperita*. This species is known as English mint in Japan. **Zone 5.**

Mentha x gracilis syn. Mentha x gentilis
Ginger Mint
Also known as Scotch mint. Hardy perennial. Ht 18 in., spread 24 in. The stem has whorls of small, two-lipped, mauve flowers in summer. The leaf is variegated, gold/green with serrated edges. The flavor is a delicate, warm mint that combines well in salads and tomato dishes. **Zone 5.**

Mentha longifolia Buddleia Mint Group

MINT

Mentha longifolia Buddleia Mint Group
Buddleia Mint
Hardy perennial. Ht 32 in., spread indefinite. Long purple/mauve flowers that look very like buddleia (hence its name). Long gray-green leaves with a musty minty scent. Very good plant for garden borders. **Zone 6.**

Mentha longifolia subsp. schimperi
Desert Mint, Eastern Mint
Hardy perennial. Ht 24–32 in., spread indefinite. Long pale mauve flowers in summer. Long narrow gray-green leaves with a highly pepperminted scent and flavor used to make tea. Plant in free-draining soil. **Zone 6.**

Mentha x piperita
Peppermint, White Peppermint
Also known as mentha d'Angleterre, mentha Anglais, pfefferminze and Englisheminze. Hardy perennial. Ht 12–24 in., spread indefinite. Pale purple flowers in summer. Pointed leaves, darkish green with a reddish tinge, serrated edges. Very peppermint scented. This is the main medicinal herb of the genus. There are two species worth looking out for — M x piperita black peppermint, with leaves much darker, nearly brown, and M x piperita "Black Mitcham" with dark brown, tinged with reddish-brown leaves. **Zone 6.**

Mentha x piperita f. citrata
Eau de Cologne Mint
Also known as orange mint and bergamot mint.

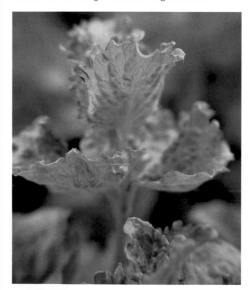

Mentha spicata var. *crispa*

Hardy perennial. Ht 24–32 in., spread indefinite. Purple/mauve flowers in summer. Purple-tinged, roundish, dark green leaves. A delicious scent that has been described as lemon, orange, bergamot, lavender, as well as eau de cologne. This plant is a vigorous grower. Use in fruit dishes with discretion. Best use is in the bath. **Zone 5.**

Mentha x piperita f. citrata "Chocolate"
Chocolate Peppermint
Hardy perennial. Ht 16–24 in., spread indefinite. Pale purple flowers in summer. Pointed dark green-brown leaves with serrated edges. Very peppermint scented with deep chocolate undertones. Great in desserts. **Zone 5.**

Mentha x piperita f. citrata "Lemon"
Lemon Mint
Hardy perennial. Ht 18–24 in. in., spread indefinite. Purple whorl of flowers in summer. Green serrated leaf, refreshing minty lemon scent. Good as a mint sauce, or with fruit dishes. **Zone 5.**

Mentha requienii
Corsican Mint
Also known as rock mint. Hardy semi-evergreen perennial. Ground cover, spread indefinite. Tiny purple flowers throughout the summer. Tiny bright green leaves, which, when crushed, smell strongly of peppermint. Suits a rock garden or paved path, grows naturally in cracks of rocks. Needs shade and moist soil. **Zone 8.**

Mentha spicata
Spearmint
Also known as garden mint and common mint. Hardy perennial. Ht 18–24 in. in., spread indefinite. Purple/mauve flowers in summer. Green pointed leaves with serrated edges. The most widely grown of all mints. Good for mint sauce, mint gelatin, mint julep. **Zone 5.**

Mentha spicata var. crispa
Curly Mint
Hardy perennial. Ht 18–24 in. in., spread indefinite. Light mauve flowers in spring. When I first saw this mint I thought it had a bad attack of aphids, but it has grown on me! The leaf is bright green and crinkled, its serrated edge slightly frilly. Flavor very similar to spearmint, so good in most culinary dishes. **Zone 5.**

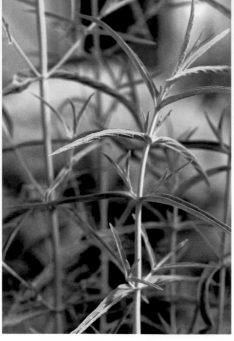

Mentha longifolia subsp. *schimperi*

Mentha spicata var. crispa "Moroccan"
Moroccan Mint
Hardy perennial. Ht 18–24 in. in., spread indefinite. White flowers in summer. Bright green leaves with a texture and excellent mint scent. This is the one I use for all the basic mint uses in the kitchen. A clean mint flavor and scent, lovely when served with yogurt and cucumber. **Zone 5.**

Mentha suaveolens
Apple Mint
Hardy perennial. Ht 24–40 in., spread indefinite. Mauve flowers in summer. Roundish hairy leaves. Tall vigorous grower. Gets its name from its scent, which is a combination of mint and apples. More subtle than some mints, so good in cooking. **Zone 5.**

Mentha suaveolens "Variegata"
Pineapple Mint
Hardy perennial. Ht 18–24 in. in., spread indefinite. Seldom produces flowers, all the energy going into producing very pretty cream and green, slightly hairy leaves that look good in the garden. Not a rampant mint. Grows well in hanging baskets. **Zone 6.**

Mentha suaveolens "Variegata"

Mentha x piperita f. *citrata* "Chocolate"

Mentha x *villosa* var. *alopecuroides*
Bowles' mint

Bowles' Mint
Hardy perennial. Ht 24–40 in., spread indefinite.
Mauve flowers, round, slightly hairy green leaves,
vigorous grower. Sometimes incorrectly called apple
mint. Has acquired reputation as the "connoisseur's
culinary mint." Not sure I agree, but mint tastes
do vary. **Zone 5.**

Pycnanthemum pilosum
Mountain Mint
Hardy perennial. Ht 36 in., spread 24 in. Knot-like
white/pink flowers, small and pretty in summer.
Leaves long, thin, pointed, and gray-green with a good
mint scent and flavor. Not a *Mentha*, so therefore not
a true mint, and does not spread. Looks very attractive
in a border, and is also appealing to butterflies. Any
soil will support it provided it is not too rich. **Zone 5.**

 ## cultivation

Propagation
Seed
The seed on the market is not worthwhile — leaf flavor is
inferior and quite often it does not run true to species.

Cuttings
Root cuttings of mint are very easy. Simply dig up a
piece of root. Cut it where you can see a little growing
node (each piece will produce a plant) and place the
cuttings either into a plug or seed tray. Push them
into the compost (a standard seed compost mixed in
equal parts with composted fine bark). Water in and
leave. This can be done any time during the growing
season. If taken in spring, in about 2 weeks you should
see new shoots emerging through the compost.

Division
Dig up plants every few years and divide, or they will
produce root runners all over the place. Each bit of
root will grow, so take care.

Corsican mint does not set root runners. Dig up a
section in spring and divide by easing the plant apart
and replanting.

Pests and Diseases
Mint rust appears as little rusty spots on the leaves.
Remove them immediately, otherwise the rust will
wash off into the soil and the spores spread to other
plants. One sure way to be rid is to burn the affected
patch. This effectively sterilizes the ground.

Another method, from an old gardening book, is to dig
up the roots in winter when the plants are dormant,
and clean off the soil under a tap. Heat some water to
a temperature of 105° to 111°F and pour into a bowl.
Place the roots in the water for 10 minutes. Remove
the runners and wash at once in cold water. Replant in
the garden well away from the original site.

Maintenance
Spring Dig up root if cuttings are required. Split
established plants if need be.
Summer Give plants a hair cut to promote new
growth. Control the spread of unruly plants.
Fall Dig up roots for forcing. Bring in containers.
Winter Sterilize the roots if rust is evident during the
growing season.

Garden Cultivation
Mint is one of those plants that will walk all over the plot
if not severely controlled. Also, mint readily hybridizes
itself, varying according to environmental factors.

If choosing a plant in a nursery or garden center rub
the leaf first to check the scent. Select a planting site
in sun or shade but away from other mints. Planted
side by side they seem to lose their individual scent
and flavor. To inhibit spread, sink a large bottomless
container (bucket or custom frame) in a well-drained
and fairly rich soil to a depth of at least 12 in.,
leaving a small ridge above soil level. Plant the
mint in the center.

Harvesting
Pick the leaves for fresh use throughout the growing
season. Pick leaves for drying or freezing before the
mint flowers.

 ## companion planting

Spearmint or peppermint planted near roses may
deter aphids. Buddleia mint will attract hoverflies,
which are predators of greenfly.

 ## container growing

Mint is good in containers. Make sure the container
is large enough, use a soil-based compost mixed in
equal parts with composted fine bark, and do not
let the compost dry out. Feed regularly throughout
the growing season with a liquid fertilizer. Place the
container in semi-shade.

Forcing
One good reason for growing mint in containers is to
prolong the season. This is called forcing. In early fall
dig up some root. Fill a container, or wooden box lined
with plastic, with compost. Lay the root down its length
and cover lightly with compost. Water in and place in
a light, warm greenhouse or warm conservatory (even
the kitchen windowsill will do). Keep an eye on it, and
fresh shoots should sprout within a couple of weeks.
This is great for fresh mint sauce out of season.

MINT

Fresh mint tea

 other uses

Pick a bunch of eau de cologne mint, tie it up with string, and hang it under the hot water tap when you are drawing a bath. You will scent not only your bath, but the whole house. It is very uplifting (unless you too have a young son, who for some reason thinks it is "gross").

 medicinal

Peppermint is aromatic, antiseptic, antispasmodic, antiinflammatory, antibacterial, antiparasitic, and is also a stimulant. It can be used in a number of ways for a variety of complaints including gastro-intestinal disorders where antispasmodic, anti-flatulent, and appetite-promoting stimulation is required. It is particularly useful for nervous headaches, and as a way to increase concentration. Externally, peppermint oil can be used in a massage to relieve muscular pain.

 warning

The oil may cause an allergic reaction. Avoid prolonged intake of inhalants from the oil, which must never be used by babies.

 culinary

For many years, French foodies have made fun of the British custom of eating mint sauce with lamb. Mint has not been used very much in traditional cooking. But slowly, even in France, this herb is gaining favor. Mint is good in vinegars and jellies. Peppermint makes a great tea. And there are many many uses for mint in cooking with fish, meat, yogurt, fruit, and so on. Here is a recipe for chocoholics like me:

Chocolate Mint Mousse
Serves 2

½ cup plain dark chocolate
2 eggs, separated
1 teaspoon instant coffee
1 teaspoon fresh chopped mint, either Moroccan, spearmint or curly
Whipped cream for decoration
4 whole mint leaves

Melt the chocolate either in a microwave, or in a double boiler. When smooth and liquid, remove from heat. Beat egg yolks and add to the chocolate while hot (this will cook the yolks slightly). Add coffee and chopped mint.

Leave the mixture to cool for about 15 minutes. Beat the egg whites (not too stiff) and fold them into the cooling chocolate mixture. Spoon into containers. When you are ready to serve put a blob of whipped cream in the middle and garnish with whole leaves.

Mentha pulegium
PENNYROYAL

Also known as European Pennyroyal and Pudding Grass. From the family Lamiaceae.

Pulegium is derived from the Latin *pulex*, meaning "flea" because both the fresh plant and the smoke from the burning leaves were used to exterminate the insect. Long ago, the wise women of the village used pennyroyal to induce abortion. It has since been medicinally used to facilitate menstruation. In the 17th century the herbalist John Gerard called it pudding grass. He claimed it would purify corrupt water on sea voyages.

Mentha pulegium "Upright"

 ## varieties

Mentha pulegium
Pennyroyal
Also known as Cunningham mint and creeping Pennyroyal. Semi-evergreen hardy perennial. Ht 6 in., spread indefinite. Clusters of mauve flowers in summer. Bright green, oval, highly peppermint scented leaves. **Zone 6.**

Mentha pulegium "Upright"
Pennyroyal Upright
Semi-evergreen hardy perennial. Ht 12 in., spread indefinite. Clusters of mauve flowers in summer. Bright green, oval, highly peppermint scented leaves. **Zone 6.**

The American pennyroyal or rock pennyroyal (*Hedeoma pulegioides*) has a similar aroma and usage as the European species.

 ## cultivation

Propagation
Seed
Sow the very fine seed in late spring, using the cardboard technique (see p. 645), into prepared plug module trays using a standard seed compost. Cover with perlite. Place under protection at 64°F; germination takes 10 to 20 days. Leave in the cell-packs to become well established before planting out in early summer 12 in. apart.

Cuttings
This plant roots where it touches the ground. In spring dig up a plant, divide it into small sections including some root, and put into prepared plug cell-packs or small pots using a standard seed compost mixed in equal parts with composted fine bark.

Division
Established or invasive plants can be divided in spring and early fall.

Pests and Diseases
Pennyroyal likes a well-drained soil; when grown in damp conditions it can suffer from mildew. Remove infected plants. If grown in a container cut back on the watering.

Maintenance
Spring Sow seed, divide established plants.
Summer Cut back after flowering.
Fall Divide established plants. Dig up a plant as insurance against a wet winter and winter in a cold frame or greenhouse.
Winter This mint hates wet winters, it will stand temperatures below 18°F only in a well-drained soil.

Garden Cultivation
Plant in a well-drained fertile soil in a sunny position. This may seem a contradiction, but it does like to be watered well in summer.

Harvesting
Pick leaves as required to use fresh. Pick either side of flowering for freezing. Not worth drying.

 ## container growing

Both species can be happily grown in containers. Use a soil-based compost mixed in equal parts with composted fine bark.

 ## culinary

This mint has a very strong peppermint flavor so use sparingly. A good substitute for peppermint in ice water.

 ## medicinal

A hot infusion from the leaves of this plant is an old-fashioned remedy for colds and head colds. The essential oil from this plant is highly toxic and should only be used by professionals, as if incorrectly self-administered it can cause irreversible kidney damage.

 ## other uses

The fresh leaves rubbed onto bare skin is an excellent insect and mosquito repellent. Equally, if you have been bitten by a horsefly or mosquito and rub the fresh leaves onto the bite it alleviates the itching.

 ## warning

Not to be medicinally used in pregnancy or if suffering from kidney disease. May cause contact dermatitis.

Monarda
BERGAMOT

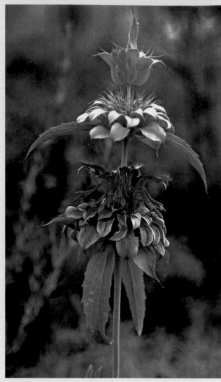

Monarda citriodora

Also known as Oswego Tea, Bee Balm, Blue Balm, High Balm, Low Balm, Mountain Balm, and Mountain Mint. From the family Lamiaceae.

This beautiful plant with its flamboyant flower is a native of North America and is now grown horticulturally in many countries throughout the world.

The species name *Monarda* honors the Spanish medicinal botanist Dr Nicholas Monardes of Seville who, in 1569, wrote an herbal on the flora of America. The common name, bergamot, is said to have come from the scent of the crushed leaf which resembles the small, bitter Italian Bergamot orange *(Citrus bergamia)*, from which oil is produced that is used in aromatherapy, perfumes and cosmetics.

The wild or purple bergamot *(Monarda fistulosa)* grows around the Oswego river district near Lake Ontario in the United States. The Indians in this region used it for colds and bronchial complaints as it contains the powerful antiseptic, thymol. They also made tea from it, hence Oswego tea, which was drunk in many American households, replacing Indian tea, following the Boston Tea Party of 1773.

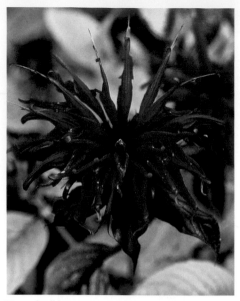

Monarda didyma

Monarda citriodora
Lemon bergamot; Wild Bee Balm
Hardy annual. Ht 24 in., spread 18 in. Beautiful mauve surrounded by pale mauve bracts. Intense lemon-scented leaves.

Monarda "Croftway Pink"
Bergamot Croftway Pink
Hardy perennial. Ht 3 ft., spread 18 in. Soft pink flowers in summer. Aromatic green leaves. **Zone 4.**

Monarda didyma
Bergamot (Bee Balm Red)
Hardy perennial. Ht 32 in., spread 18 in. Fantastic red flowers throughout summer. Aromatic, midgreen foliage. **Zone 4.**

Monarda "Schneewittchen"
Bergamot Snow Maiden
Hardy perennial. Ht 32 in., spread 18 in. Very attractive white flowers throughout summer. Aromatic, midgreen, pointed leaves. **Zone 6.**

 varieties

There are too many species and cultivars of bergamot to mention here, so I have included a short selection:

Monarda "Beauty of Cobham"
Bergamot Beauty of Cobham
Hardy perennial. Ht 30 in., spread 18 in. Attractive dense two-lipped pale pink flowers throughout summer. Toothed midgreen aromatic leaves. **Zone 4.**

Monarda "Blaustrumpf"
Bergamot Blue Stocking
Hardy perennial. Ht 32 in., spread 18 in. Attractive purple flowers throughout summer. Aromatic, green, pointed foliage. **Zone 4.**

Monarda "Cambridge Scarlet"
Bergamot Cambridge Scarlet
Hardy perennial. Ht 3 ft., spread 18 in. Striking rich red flowers all summer. Aromatic midgreen leaves. **Zone 4.**

Monarda "Cambridge Scarlet"

cultivation

Propagation

Seed
Only species will grow true from seed. Cultivars (i.e., named varieties) will not. Sow the very small seed indoors in the spring on the surface of either seed or plug trays or on individual pots, using a standard seed compost mixed in equal parts with composted fine bark. Cover with perlite. Germination is better with added warmth: 65°F. Thin or transplant the strongest seedlings when large enough to handle. Harden off. Plant in the garden at a distance of 18 in. apart.

Cuttings
Take first shoots in early summer, as soon as they are 3–4 in. long.

Division
Divide in early spring. Either grow on in pots, or replant in the garden, making sure the site is well prepared with well-rotted compost. Planting distance from other plants 18 in.

Pests and Diseases

Bergamot is prone to powdery mildew. At the first sign, remove leaves. If it gets out of hand, cut the plant back to ground level.

Young plants are a *bonne bouche* for slugs!

Maintenance

Spring Sow seeds of species. Divide roots. Dig up 3-year-old plants, divide and replant.
Summer Take cuttings of cultivars and species, when you need them.
Fall Cut back to the ground, and give a good feed with manure or compost.
Winter All perennial bergamots die right back in winter. In hard winters protect with a mulch.

Garden Cultivation

Bergamot is a highly decorative plant with long-lasting, distinctively fragrant flowers that are very attractive to bees, hence the country name bee balm. All grow well in moist, nutrient-rich soil, preferably in a semi-shady spot; deciduous woodland is ideal. However, they will tolerate full sun provided the soil retains moisture. Like many other perennials, bergamot should be dug up and divided every 3 years, and the dead center discarded.

Harvesting

Pick leaves as desired for use fresh in the kitchen. For drying, harvest before the flower opens. Cut flowers for drying as soon as they are fully opened. They will then dry beautifully and retain their color.

It is only worth collecting seed if you have species plants situated well apart in the garden. If near one another, cross-pollination will make the seed variable — very jolly provided you don't mind unpredictably mixed colors. Collect the flower heads when they turn brown.

 ## container growing

Bergamot is too tall for a window box, but it can look very attractive growing in a large pot, say 14–18 in. across, or tub as long as the soil can be kept moist and the plant be given some afternoon shade.

 ## other uses

Because the dried bergamot flowers keep their fragrance and color so well, they are an important ingredient in potpourris. The oil is sometimes used in perfumes, but should not be confused with the similarly smelling bergamot orange.

 ## medicinal

Excellent herb tea to relieve nausea, flatulence, menstrual pain, and vomiting.

Aromatherapists have found bergamot oil good for depression, as well as helping the body to fight infections.

 ## culinary

Pick the small flower petals separately and sprinkle a green salad with them at the last moment. Put fresh leaf into black tea for an Earl Grey flavor, and into wine cups and lemonade. The chopped leaves can be added sparingly to salads and stuffings, and can also be used to flavor jams and jellies.

Pork Fillets with Bergamot Sauce
Serves 2

2 large pork fillets
6 tablespoons butter
2 shallots, very finely minced
2½ tablespoons flour
4 tablespoons chicken or vegetable stock
4 tablespoons dry white wine
3½ tablespoons chopped bergamot leaves
Salt and freshly ground black pepper
1 tablespoon heavy cream

Preheat the oven to 400°F.

Wash the pork. Pat dry, season, and smear with half the butter. Roast in a shallow greased pan for 25 minutes. Allow to rest for 5 minutes before slicing. Arrange slices in a warmed serving dish.

While the fillets are in the oven, sweat the shallots in the remaining butter until soft. Stir in the flour and cook for about a minute, stirring all the time. Whisk in the broth. Simmer until it thickens, stirring occasionally. Then slowly add the wine and 3 tablespoons of the chopped bergamot. Simmer for several minutes then season to taste. Remove from heat, stir in the cream, pour over arranged pork slices, and garnish with remaining chopped bergamot. Serve with mashed potato, and fresh green vegetables such as broccoli.

Murraya koenigii
CURRY TREE

Also known as Indian bay, Nim leaves, Kahdi patta and Karapina. From the family Rutaceae.

The curry leaf trees are indigenous to India, and they have naturalized in forests and wasteland throughout the subcontinent, except in the higher parts of the Himalayas. Curry leaves are closely associated with South India where the word "curry" originates from the Tamil *kari* for spiced sauces. The use of curry leaves as a flavoring for vegetables is described in early Tamil literature dating back to the first century CE. These leaves are absolutely necessary for the authentic flavor of Southern Indian and Sri Lankan cuisine. Please do not confuse this herb with *Helichrysum italicum* (see p. 304), which is known in Europe as the curry plant.

 varieties

Murraya koenigii
Curry Leaf, Kahdi Patta
Tropical, subtropical, evergreen shrub or small tree. Ht 14–18 ft., spread up to 15 ft. Clusters of small creamy white, sweetly scented, star-shaped flowers from late summer, followed by small black edible fruit, the seed of which is poisonous if digested. Oval, soft, glossy, pinnate aromatic leaves, each leaf divided into 11 to 21 leaflets. The bark is dark brown, nearly black, and the wood is grayish-white, hard and close grained.
Zone 10.

 cultivation

Propagation
Seed
Sow fresh ripe seed in fall into prepared plug module trays using a seed compost mixed in equal parts with perlite. Cover the seeds with perlite, put in a warm place or propagator at 68°F. Germination is erratic, approximately 2 to 4 months.

Cuttings
Take semi-ripe stem cuttings in late spring or early summer. Place the cuttings into prepared plug-module trays using a standard seed compost mixed in equal parts with perlite. If you do not have a covered propagator, either cover the cuttings in white plastic or place in a white plastic bag and put in a warm place. Check the bag regularly and do not allow the compost to dry out; equally do not overwater. The cuttings should root in about 1 month. Once rooted, remove the bag or covering, grow on until fully rooted, then repot into a small pot, using a soil-based potting compost mixed in equal parts with horticultural grit.

Division
Plants grown outside in the garden often set suckers. In summer, using a spade, these can be removed gently, including some root. Planting into a pot that fits the size of root using a soil-based potting compost mixed in equal parts with horticultural grit. Replant in the garden after two seasons.

Pests and Diseases
Being an aromatic plant, it is often unaffected by pests. When grown as a pot plant it can be attacked by scale insects. Rub them off by hand, or use a insecticidal soap spray following the manufacturer's instructions.

Maintenance
Spring Take cuttings. Increase the watering of pot-raised plants.
Summer Feed container-raised plants weekly. Take cuttings. Remove suckers.
Fall Sow fresh seeds.
Winter In areas outside the tropics, cut back on watering, protect from frost.

Garden Cultivation
Only in the tropics or subtropics can this herb be grown in the garden. Plant in a fertile, light soil in partial shade. Young plants need to be watered daily for the first 3 years. In dry hot climates protect from the midday sun. This tropical plant will need protection when the night temperatures fall below 55°F.

Harvesting
Pick the fresh leaves for cooking and medicine as required. The leaves freeze well.

 container growing

In cool climates, this herb makes an ideal container

plant. It prefers to be pot bound, so do not over pot. Use a soilless potting compost mixed in equal parts with horticultural grit. Place the container in partial shade. Water daily and feed weekly throughout the growing season. As the plants grow, keep trimming them regularly to maintain a supply of young leaves for cooking. Water very sparingly during the winter months and do not feed. Reintroduce water and feed as soon as the light levels and temperatures increase in the spring and move the plants to a warm, light place (around 64–68°F).

medicinal

Curry leaves have been used in both Ayurvedic and Hindu medicine for many cures. A paste is made from the leaves to cure eruptions and bites. Fresh leaves eaten raw are reputedly a good cure for dysentery, or drunk as an infusion it is said to stop vomiting. The traditional use of the curry leaf to treat diabetes has attracted a great deal of interest. Recent medicinal research has found special compounds which could be used to make an effective new medicine for treatment of diabetes.

other uses

The twigs from the branches make a good toothbrush. This is a very popular method for cleaning the teeth as it is said that it helps to strengthen the gums and the teeth. The hard wood is used to make agricultural tools.

warning

Seed is poisonous if ingested.

Murraya koenigii

culinary

Curry leaves are usually used fresh but can be found dried or in powder form. In some recipes the leaves are oven-dried, toasted immediately before use, or quickly fried in butter or oil; this scented oil is then poured on top of many dishes to add richness and flavor. Equally, the leaves can be dropped into hot oil before adding the main ingredient. Since South Indian cuisine is dominantly vegetarian, curry leaves seldom appear in nonvegetarian food; the main applications are thin lentil or vegetable curries and stuffings for samosas. Because of their soft texture, they are not always removed before serving. Personally, I love the flavor of the leaves and have adapted many dishes to include them. This is a winter family favorite.

Curried Parsnip Soup
Serves 6

8 curry leaves plus 6 leaves for garnish
¼ cup butter
1 tablespoon light olive oil
2 medium onions, chopped
2 cloves garlic, chopped
1 teaspoon ground ginger
1 teaspoon turmeric
1½ pounds parsnips, peeled, chopped into small pieces.
4 cups vegetable broth

Heat a nonstick skillet and quickly fry four of the curry leaves, remove as soon as you can smell the wonderful aroma. Crush the leaves up. Return the skillet to the heat, add the butter and oil. Once the butter has melted add the onions and cook gently until they become translucent. Add the garlic and fry for 2 minutes, then add the ginger, dried curry leaves, fresh curry leaves, and turmeric, stir then add the parsnips. Toss them so they are covered in the wonderful spices and then transfer all this to a pot with the broth. Stir, bring to a very gentle simmer, cook for about 1 hour stirring from time to time. Remove from the heat, then liquidize or food process, return to the pot, gently warm, do not boil. Serve in soup bowls garnished with a curry leaf.

Myrrhis odorata
SWEET CICELY

Also known as Anise, Myrrh, Roman Plant, Sweet Bracken, Sweet Fern, and Switch. From the family Apiaceae.

Sweet Cicely was once cultivated as a pot shrub in Europe and is a native of this region and other temperate countries.

The Greeks called sweet cicely *seselis* or *seseli*. It is logical to suppose that "Cicely" was derived from them, "sweet" coming from its flavor.

In the 16th century John Gerard recommended the boiled roots as a pick-me-up for people who were "dull." According to Culpeper, the roots were thought to prevent infection by the plague. In South Wales, Sweet Cicely is quite often seen growing in graveyards, planted around the headstones to commemorate a loved one.

In the Lake District, sweet bracken (Cicely) was not only used in desserts but also for rubbing upon oak panels to make the wood shine and smell good.

Myrrhis odorata

 varieties

Myrrhis odorata
Sweet Cicely
Hardy perennial. Ht 2–3 ft., spread 24 in. or more. The small white flowers appear in umbels from spring to early summer. The seeds are long, first green, turning black on ripening. The leaves are fern-like, very divided, and smell of aniseed when crushed. **Zone 4.**

The following plant is called Sweet Cicely in North America. It is unrelated to the European one, but used in a similar way:

Osmorhiza longistylis
Also known as anise root, sweet anise and sweet chervil. Perennial. Ht 18–36 in. Inconspicuous white flowers appear in loose compound umbels in summer. The leaves are oval to oblong and grow in groups of three. The whole plant has an aniseed odor. Its roots used to be nibbled by children for their anise licorice flavor.

cultivation

Propagation

Seed
Sow the seed when ripe in early fall. Use prepared plug or seed trays and, as the seed is so large, sow only one per plug and cover with compost. Then cover the trays with glass and leave outside for the whole winter.

The seed requires several months of cold winter temperatures to germinate. Keep a check on the compost, making sure it does not dry out. When germination starts bring the trays into a cold greenhouse. A spring sowing can be successful provided the seed is first put in a plastic bag mixed with a small amount of damp sharp sand, refrigerated for 4 weeks, and then sown as normal in prepared seed or plug trays. When the seedlings are large enough to handle, which is not long after germination, and after the frosts are over, transplant to a prepared site in the garden, 24 in. apart.

Root Cuttings
The taproot may be lifted in spring or fall, cut into sections each with a bud, and replanted either in prepared plug trays or direct into a prepared site in the garden at a depth of 2 in.

Division
Divide the plant in fall when the top growth dies down.

Pests and Diseases
Sweet cicely is, in the majority of cases, free from pests and diseases

Maintenance
Spring Take root cuttings.
Summer Cut back after flowering, to produce new leaves and to stop self-seeding.
Fall Sow seeds. Divide established plants. Take root cuttings.
Winter No need for protection.

Garden Cultivation
It is one of the first garden herbs to emerge after winter and is almost the last to die down, and is therefore a most useful plant. If you have a light well-drained poor soil you may find that Sweet Cicely spreads all around the garden, and when you try to dig out established plants that the taproot is very long; even a tiny bit remaining will produce another plant. On the soil at my farm, which is heavy clay, it is a lovely, well-behaved plant, however, remaining just where it was planted in a totally controlled fashion. The situation it likes best is a well-draining soil, rich in humus, and light shade. If the seed is not wanted for propagation or winter flavoring, the whole plant should be cut down immediately after flowering. A new batch of leaves will soon develop. Sweet Cicely is not suitable for growing in humid areas because it needs a good dormant period before winter to produce its root and lush foliage.

Harvesting
Pick young leaves at any time for fresh use. Collect unripe seeds when green; ripe seeds when dark brown. Dig up roots for drying in fall when the plant has died back.

The foliage and seed do not dry or freeze, but the ripe seed stores well in a dry container.

 ## container growing

As this herb has a very long taproot it does not grow happily in a container. But it can be done. Choose a container that will give the root plenty of room to grow, and use a soilless compost mixed in equal parts with composted fine bark. Place it in a semi-shady place and keep it well watered throughout the growing season.

 ## medicinal

This herb is now rarely used medicinally. The boiled root is said to be a tonic for both the teenager and the elderly alike.

Sweet Cicely wine

 ## culinary

The root can be cooked as a vegetable and served with butter or a white sauce, or allow to cool and chop up for use in salads. Alternatively, it can be eaten raw, or peeled and grated, and served in a French salad dressing. It is difficult to describe the flavor — think of parsnip, add a hint of aniseed. The root makes a very good wine.

Toss unripe seeds, which have a sweet flavor and a nutty texture, into fruit salads. Chop them into ice cream. Use ripe seeds whole for flavoring cooked dishes such as apple pie, otherwise use them crushed.

The leaf flavor is sweet aniseed. Chop finely and stir in salads, dressings and omelets. Add to soups, stews and to boiling water when cooking cabbage

Add to cream for a sweeter, less fatty taste. It is a valuable sweetener, especially for diabetics, but also for the many people who are trying to reduce their sugar intake.

When cooking tart fruit, such as rhubarb, plums, gooseberries, red- or blackcurrants, add 4 to 6 teaspoons of chopped Sweet Cicely leaf. Or, as I do sometimes, mix a handful of large fresh leaves with some lemon balm and add to a boiling water in which the fruit is to be stewed. It gives a delightful flavor and helps to save almost half the sugar needed.

CATNIP

Also known as Catnep, Catmint, Catrup, Catswart, and Field Balm. From the family Lamiaceae.

The genus name may have derived from the Roman town Nepeti, where it was said to grow in profusion.

The Elizabethan herbalist, Gerard, recorded the source of its common name: "They do call it *herba cataria* and *herba catti* because cats are very much delighted herewith for the smell of it is so pleasant unto them, that they rub themselves upon it and wallow or tumble in it and also feed on the branches and leaves very greedily."

This herb has long been cultivated both for its medicinal and seasoning properties, and in the hippie era of the late 1960s and 1970s for its mildly hallucinogenic quality when smoked.

Nepeta x faassenii "Alba"

Nepeta cataria

 varieties

Nepeta cataria, Nepeta x faassenii, and **Nepeta racemosa** are all called catnip, which can be confusing. However, the first is the true herb with the medicinal and culinary properties and, just to be even more confusing, it is known also as dog mint!

Nepeta camphorata
Camphor Catnip
Hardy perennial. Ht and spread 23–30 in. Very different from ordinary catmint and very fragrant. Tiny white blooms all summer. Small, silvery gray, aromatic foliage. Prefers a poor, well-drained, dryish soil, not too rich in nutrients, and full sun. However, it will adapt to most soils except wet and heavy ones. **Zone 8.**

Nepeta cataria
Dog Mint, Nep-in-a-Hedge
Hardy perennial. Ht 3 ft., spread 24 in. White to pale pink flowers from early summer to early fall. Pungent aromatic leaves. This plant is the true herb. In the 17th century it was used in the treatment of barren women. **Zone 3.**

Nepeta x faassenii "Alba"
Hardy perennial. Ht and spread 18 in. Loose spikes of white flowers from early summer to early fall. Small grayish-green aromatic leaves form a bushy clump. **Zone 4.**

Nepeta racemosa "Walker's Low"
Hardy perennial. Ht and spread 32 in. Spikes of lavender blue/purple flowers from late spring to fall. Small, mildly fragrant, grayish leaves. Marvellous edging plant for tumbling out over raised beds or softening hard edges of stone flags. Combines especially well with old-fashioned roses. **Zone 4.**

 cultivation

Propagation
Seed
Sow its small seed in spring or late summer, either where the plant is going to flower or on to the surface of pots, plug or seed trays. Cover with perlite. Gentle bottom heat can be of assistance. Germination takes 10 to 20 days, depending on the time of year (faster in late summer). Seed is viable for 5 years. When large enough to handle, thin the seedlings to 12 in. The seed of *N. camphorata* should be sown in fall to late winter. It will usually flower the following season.

Cuttings
Take softwood cuttings from new growth in late spring through to midsummer. Do not choose flowering stems.

Division
A good method of propagation, particularly if a plant is becoming invasive. Divide established plants in spring. But beware of cats! The smell of a bruised root is irresistible. Cats have been known to destroy a specimen replanted after division. If there are cats around, protect the newly divided plant.

Nepeta racemosa "Walker's Low"

Pests and Diseases

These plants are aromatic and not prone to pests. However, in cold wet winters, they tend to rot off.

Maintenance

Spring Sow seeds. Take cuttings. Divide established plants.

Summer Sow seeds until late in the season. Cut back hard after flowering to encourage a second flush. Take cuttings.

Fall Cut back after flowering to maintain shape and produce new growth. If your winters tend to be wet and cold, repot and over-winter this herb in a cold frame.

Winter Sow seeds of *Nepeta camphorata*.

Garden Cultivation

The main problem with catnip is the love cats have for it. If you have ever seen a cat spaced-out after feeding (hence catnip) and rolling on it, then you will understand why cat lovers love catnip, and why cat haters who grow it get cross with cat neighbors. The reason why cats are enticed is the smell; it reminds

them of the hormonal scent of cats of the opposite sex. Bearing all this in mind, make your choice of planting site carefully. Nepetas make very attractive border or edging subjects. They like a well-drained soil, sun, or light shade. The one thing they dislike is a wet winter; they may well rot off. Planting distance depends on species, but on average plant 20 in. apart. When the main flowering is over, catnip should be cut back hard to encourage a second crop and to keep a neat and compact shape.

Harvesting

Whether you pick to use fresh or to dry, gather leaves and flowering tops when young.

 companion planting

Planting *Nepeta cataria* close to vegetables is said to deter flea beetle.

 container growing

N. x *faassenii* and all *N. racemosa* look stunning in large terracotta pots. The gray-green of the leaves and the blue-purple of the flowers complement the terracotta, and their sprawling habit in flower completes the picture. Use a soilless compost mixed in equal parts with composted fine bark. Note that both varieties tend to grow soft and leggy indoors.

Nepeta racemosa "Walker's Low"

 culinary

Use freshly picked young shoots in salads or rub on meat to release their mintish flavor. Catnip was drunk as a tea before China tea was introduced into the West. It makes an interesting cup!

 other uses

Dried leaves stuffed into toy mice will keep kittens and cats amused for hours. The scent of catnip is said to repel rats, so put bunches in hen and duck houses to discourage them. The flowers of *Nepeta* x *faassenii*, and *Nepeta racemosa* are suitable for formal displays.

 medicinal

Nepeta cataria is now very rarely used for medicinal purposes. In Europe it is sometimes used in a hot infusion to promote sweating. It is said to be excellent for colds and flu. It soothes the nervous system and helps one to sleep. It also helps to calm upset stomachs and counters colic, flatulence, and diarrhea. An infusion can be applied externally to soothe scalp irritations, and the leaves and flowering tops can be mashed for a poultice to be applied to external bruises.

Ocimum basilicum
BASIL

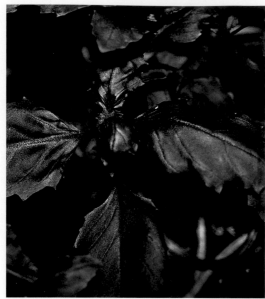

Ocimum basilicum var. *purpurascens*

Also known as Common Basil, St Joseph Wort, and Sweet Basil. From the family Lamiaceae.

Basil is native to India, the Middle East, and some Pacific Islands. It has been cultivated in the Mediterranean for thousands of years, but the herb only came to Western Europe in the 16th century with the spice traders, and to America and Australia with the early European settlers.

This plant is steeped in history and intriguing lore. Its common name is believed to be an abbreviation of *Basilikon phuton*, Greek for "kingly herb," and it was said to have grown around Christ's tomb after the resurrection. Some Greek Orthodox churches use it to prepare their holy water, and put pots of basil below their altars. However, there is some question as to its sanctity — both Greeks and Romans believed that people should curse as they sow basil to ensure germination. There was even some doubt about whether it was poisonous or not, and in Western Europe it has been thought both to belong to the Devil and to be a remedy against witches. In Elizabethan times sweet basil was used as a snuff for colds and to clear the brain and deal with headaches, and in the 17th century Culpeper wrote of basil's uncompromising if unpredictable appeal — "It either makes enemies or gains lovers but there is no in-between."

 varieties

Ocimum basilicum
Sweet Basil
Annual. Ht 18 in. A strong scent. Green, medium-sized leaves. White flowers. Without doubt the most popular basil. Use sweet basil in pasta sauces and salads, especially with tomato. Combines very well with garlic. Do not let it flower if using for cooking. **All zones.**

Ocimum basilicum "Cinnamon"
Cinnamon Basil
Annual. Ht 18 in. Leaves olive/brown/green with a hint of purple, highly cinnamon-scented when rubbed. Flowers pale pink. Comes from Mexico and is used in spicy dishes and salad dressings. **All zones.**

Ocimum basilicum "Green Ruffles"
Green Ruffles Basil
Annual. Ht 12 in. Light green leaves, crinkly and larger than sweet basil. Spicy, aniseed flavor, good in salad dishes and with stir-fry vegetables. But it is not, to my mind, an attractive variety. In fact the first time I grew it I thought its crinkly leaves had a bad attack of aphids. Grow in pots and protect from frost.

Ocimum basilicum "Horapha"
Thai Basil, Horapha Basil (Rau Que)
Annual. Ht 16 in. Leaf olive/purplish. Stems red. Flowers with pink bracts. Aniseed in scent and flavor. A special culinary basil from Thailand. Use the leaves as a vegetable in curries and spicy dishes.

Ocimum basilicum "Napolitano"
Lettuce-leaved Basil
Annual. Ht 18 in. Leaves very large, crinkled, and with a distinctive flavor, especially good for pasta sauce.

Ocimum tenuiflorum

Ocimum basilicum "Cinnamon"

Originates in Naples region of Italy and needs a hot summer in cooler countries to be of any merit.

Ocimum basilicum var. *purpurascens*

Purple Basil, Dark Opal Basil
Annual. Ht 12 in. Strongly scented purple leaves. Pink flowers. Very attractive plant with a perfumed scent and flavor that is especially good with rice dishes. The dark purple variety that was developed in 1962 at the University of Connecticut represents something of a breakthrough in herb cultivation, not least because,

Mixed basils growing around a tree on the Sinai Peninsula

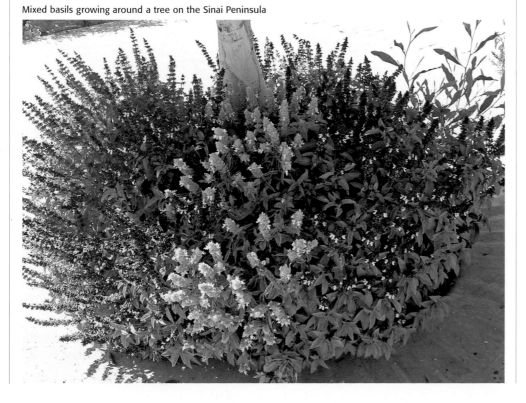

almost exclusively, herbs have escaped the attentions of the hybridizers. The variety was named an All-America Selection by seedsmen. **All zones.**

Ocimum basilicum var. *purpurascens* **"Purple Ruffles"**

Purple Ruffles Basil
Annual. Ht 12 in. Very similar to straight purple basil (above), though the flavor is not as strong and the leaf is larger with a feathery edge. Flowers are pink. It can be grown in pots in a sunny position outside, but frankly it is a pain to grow because it damps off so easily. **All zones.**

Ocimum x citriodorum

Lemon Basil (Kemangie)
Annual. Ht 12 in. Light, bright, yellowish-green leaves, more pointed than other varieties, with a slight serrated edge. Flowers pale, whitish. Lemon basil comes from Indonesia, is tender in cooler climates, and susceptible to damping off. Difficult to maintain but well worth the effort. Both flowers and leaves have a lemon scent and flavor that enhance many dishes. **All zones.**

Ocimum basilicum "Horapha"

Ocimum minimum

Bush Basil
Annual. Ht 12 in. Small green leaves, half the size of sweet basil. Flowers small, scented and whitish. Spread from Chile throughout South America, where, in some countries, it is believed to belong to the Goddess Erzulie and is carried as a powerful protector against robbery and by women to keep a lover's eye from roving. Excellent in pots on the windowsill. Delicious whole in green salads and with ricotta cheese. **All zones.**

Ocimum minimum "Greek"

Greek Basil (Fine-leaved Miniature)
Annual. Ht 9 in. This basil has the smallest leaves, tiny replicas of the bush basil leaves but, despite their size, they have a good flavor. As its name suggests, it originates from Greece. It is one of the easiest basils to look after — especially good in a pot. Use leaves unchopped in all salads and in tomato sauces. **All zones.**

Ocimum tenuiflorum syn. *Ocimum sanctum*

Sacred Basil, Kha Prao, Tulsi
Annual. Ht 12 in. A small basil with olive/purple leaves with serrated edges. Stems deep purple. Flowers mauve/pink. The whole plant has a marvellously rich scent. Originally from Thailand, where it is grown around Buddhist temples. Can be used in Thai cooking with stir-fry hot peppers, chicken, pork or beef. The Indian-related form, is considered kingly or holy by the Hindus, sacred to the gods Krishna and Vishnu. It was the herb upon which to swear oaths in courts of law. It was also used throughout the Indian subcontinent as a disinfectant against malaria. **All zones.**

cultivation

Propagation

Seed

All basils can be grown from seed. Sow direct into pots or plug trays in early spring and germinate with warmth. Avoid using seed trays because basil has a long taproot and dislikes being transplanted. Plugs also help minimize damping off, to which all basil plants are prone (see below).

Water well at midday in dry weather even when transplanted into pots or containers: basil hates going to bed wet. This minimizes the chances of damping off and will prevent root rot, a hazard when air temperature is still dropping at night.

Plant out seedlings when large enough to handle and the danger of frost has passed. The soil needs to be rich and well drained, and the situation warm and sheltered, preferably with sun at midday. However, prolific growth will only be obtained usually in the greenhouse or in large pots on a sunny patio. I suggest that you plant basil in between tomato plants for the following reasons:

1. Being a good companion plant, it is said to repel flying insects, so may help to keep the tomatoes pest-free.
2. You will remember to use fresh basil with tomatoes.
3. You will remember to water it.
4. The situation will be warm and whenever you pick tomatoes you will tend to pick basil, which will encourage bushy growth and prevent it flowering, which in turn will stop the stems becoming woody and the flavor of its leaves bitter.

Ocimum basilicum

Pests and Diseases

Aphids and whitefly may be a problem with pot- grown plants. Wash off with liquid insecticidal soap. Seedlings are highly susceptible to damping off, a fungal disease encouraged by overcrowding in overly wet conditions in seed trays or pots. It can be prevented by sowing the seed thinly and widely and guarding against an over-humid atmosphere.

Maintenance

Spring Sow seeds in early spring with warmth and watch out for damping off; plant out around the end of the season. Alternatively, sow directly into the ground after any frosts.

Summer Keep pinching out young plants to promote new leaf growth and to prevent flowering. Harvest the leaves.

Fall Collect seeds of plants allowed to flower. Before first frosts, bring pots into the house and place on the windowsill. Dig up old plants and dig over the area ready for new plantings.

Garden Cultivation

Garden cultivation is only a problem in areas susceptible to frost and where you can't provide for its great need for warmth and nourishment. In such areas plant out after the frosts have finished; choose a well-drained, rich soil in a warm, sunny corner, protected from the wind.

Harvesting

Pick leaves when they are young and always from the top to encourage new growth. If freezing to store, paint both sides of each leaf with olive oil to stop it sticking to the next leaf and to seal in its flavor. If drying, do it as fast as you can. Basil leaves are some of the more difficult to dry successfully and I do not recommend it. The most successful course, post-harvest, is to infuse the leaves in olive oil or vinegar. As well as being very useful in your own kitchen, both the oil and the vinegar make great Christmas presents (see also page 672). Gather flowering tops as they open during the summer and early fall. Add them fresh to salads, or dry to potpourris.

 ## container growing

Basil is happy on a kitchen windowsill and in pots on the patio, and purple basil makes a good centerpiece in a hanging basket. In Europe basil is placed in pots outside houses to repel flies. Use a standard potting

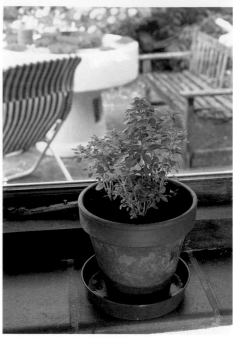

Ocimum minimum "Greek"

compost mixed in equal parts with composted fine bark. Water containers before midday but do not overwater. If that is not possible, water earlier in the day rather than later and again do not overwater.

 ## medicinal

Once prescribed as a sedative against gastric spasms and as an expectorant and laxative, basil is rarely used in herbal medicines today. However, leaves added to food are an aid to digestion and if you put a few drops of basil's essential oil on a sleeve and inhale, it can allay mental fatigue. For those that need a zing it can be used to make a very refreshing bath vinegar, which also acts as an antiseptic.

 ## other uses

Keep it in a pot in the kitchen to act as a fly repellent, or crush a leaf and rub it on your skin, where the juice repels mosquitoes.

Basil oil

culinary

Basil has a unique flavor, so newcomers should use with discretion otherwise it will dominate other flavors. It is one of the few herbs to increase its flavor when cooked. For best results add at the very end of cooking.

Hints and Ideas

1. Tear the leaves, rather than chop. Sprinkle over green salads or sliced tomatoes.

2. Basil combines very well with garlic. Tear into French salad dressing.

3. When cooking pasta or rice, heat some olive oil in a pot, remove it from the heat, add some torn purple basil leaves, toss the pasta or rice in the basil and oil, and serve. Use lemon basil to accompany a fish dish — it has a sharp lemon/spicy flavor when cooked.

4. Add to a cold rice or pasta salad.

5. Mix low-fat cream cheese with any of the basils and use in baked potatoes.

6. Basil does not combine well with strong meats such as goat or vension. However, aniseed basil is very good with stir-fried pork.

7. Sprinkle on fried or broiled tomatoes while they are still hot as a garnish.

8. Very good with French bread and can be used instead of herb butter in the traditional hot herb loaf. The tiny leaves of Greek basil are best for this because you can keep them whole.

9. Sprinkle on top of pizzas.

10. Basil makes an interesting stuffing for chicken. Use sweet basil combined with crushed garlic, breadcrumbs, lemon peel, beaten egg, and chopped nuts.

Pesto Sauce
One of the best-known recipes for basil, here is a simple version for 4 people.

1 tablespoon pine nuts
4 tablespoons chopped basil leaves
2 cloves garlic, chopped
6 tablespoons sunflower oil or olive oil (not virgin)
1 cup Parmesan cheese
salt

Blend the pine nuts, basil and chopped garlic until smooth. Add the oil slowly and continue to blend the mixture until you have a thick paste. Season with salt to taste. Stir the sauce into the cooked and drained pasta and sprinkle with Parmesan cheese.

Pesto sauce will keep in a sealed container in the refrigerator for at least a week. It can also be frozen but it is important, as with all herbal mixtures, to wrap the container with at least two thicknesses of plastic wrap to prevent the aroma escaping.

Oenothera
EVENING PRIMROSE

Also known as Common Evening Primrose, Evening Star, Fever Plant, Field Primrose, King's Cure-all, Night Willowherb, Scabish, Scurvish, Tree Primrose, Primrose, Moths Moonflower and Primrose Tree. From the family Onagraceae.

A native of North America, evening primrose was introduced to Europe in 1614 when botanists brought it from Virginia as a botanical curiosity. In North America it is regarded as a weed, but elsewhere as a pretty garden plant.

The generic name, *Oenothera*, comes from the Greek *oinos*, meaning "wine" and *thera*, "hunt." According to ancient herbals the plant was said to dispel the ill effects of wine, but both plant and seed have been used for other reasons — culinary and medicinal — by American Indians for hundreds of years. The Flambeau Ojibwe tribe were the first to realize its medicinal properties. They used to soak the whole plant in warm water to make a poultice to heal bruises and overcome skin problems. Traditionally, too, it was used to treat asthma, and its medicinal potential is under research. Oil of evening primrose is currently attracting considerable attention worldwide as a treatment for nervous disorders, in particular multiple sclerosis. There may well be a time in the very near future when the pharmaceutical industry will require fields of this beautiful plant to be grown on a commercial scale.

The common name comes from the transformation of its bedraggled daytime appearance into a fragrant, phosphorescent, pale yellow beauty with the opening of its flowers in the early evening. All this show is for one night only, however. Towards the end of summer the flowers tend to stay open all day long. (It is called evening star because the petals emit phosphorescent light at night.) Many strains of the plant came to Britain as stowaways in soil used as ballast in cargo ships.

Oenothera fruticosa subsp. *glauca*

varieties

Oenothera biennis
Evening Primrose
Hardy biennial. Ht 3–4 ft., spread 3 ft. Large evening-scented yellow flowers for most of the summer. Long green oval or lance-shaped leaves. This is the medicinal herb, and the true herb. **Zone 4.**

Oenothera fruticosa subsp. *glauca*
Perennial. Ht 20 in., spread 18 in. Small clusters of trumpet-shaped golden flowers, buds and flowers, often tinged with red. Lance-shaped midgreen leaves. The flowers are edible.

Oenothera macrocarpa
Hardy perennial. Ht 4 in., spread 16 in. or more. Large yellow bell-shaped flowers, sometimes spotted with red, open at sundown throughout the summer. The small to medium green leaves are of a narrow oblong shape. **Zone 4.**

cultivation

Propagation
Seeds
Sow in early spring on the surface of pots or plug trays, or in late spring direct into a prepared site in the garden. Seed is very fine so be careful not to sow it too thick. Use the cardboard method (see p. 645). When the weather has warmed up sufficiently, plant out at a distance of 12 in. apart. Often the act of transplanting *O. biennis* will encourage the plant to flower during the first year. This variety is a prolific self-seeder. So once it has been introduced into the garden, it will stay there.

EVENING PRIMROSE

Pests and Diseases
This plant rarely suffers from pests or diseases.

Maintenance
Spring Sow seed.
Summer Deadhead plants to cut down on self-seeding.
Fall Dig up old roots of second-year growth of the biennials.
Winter No need to protect.

Garden Cultivation
Choose a well-drained soil in a dry, sunny corner for the best results. It is an extremely tolerant plant, happy in most situations, and I have known the seedlings of *O. biennis* to appear in a stone wall, so be forewarned.

Harvesting
Use leaves fresh as required. Best before flowering. Pick the flowers when in bud or when just open. Use fresh. Picked flowers will always close and are no good for flower arrangements. Collect the seeds as the heads begin to open at the end. Store in jar for sowing in the spring. Dig up roots and use fresh as a vegetable or to dry.

 container growing

The lower-growing varieties are very good when grown in window boxes and tubs. Tall varieties need support from other plants or stakes. None are suitable for growing indoors.

 culinary

It is a pot herb — roots, stems, leaves, and even flower buds may be eaten. The roots can be boiled — they taste like sweet parsnips, or alternatively pickled and tossed in a salad.

 other uses

Leaf and stem can be infused to make an astringent facial steam. Add to hand cream as a softening agent.

Evening Primrose soap

 medicinal

Soon this plant will take its place in the hall of herbal fame. It can have startling effects on the treatment of premenstrual tension. In 1981 at St Thomas's Hospital, London, 65 women with PMS were treated. Of those, 61 percent experienced complete relief and 23 percent partial relief. One symptom, breast engorgement, was especially improved — 72 percent of women reported feeling better. In November 1982, an edition of the prestigious medical journal *The Lancet* published the results of a double-blind crossover study on 99 patients with ectopic eczema, which showed that when high doses of evening primrose oil were taken, about 43 percent of the patients experienced improvement of their eczema. Studies of the effect of the oil on hyperactive children also indicate that this form of treatment is beneficial.

True to the root of its generic name, the oil does appear to be effective in counteracting alcohol poisoning and preventing hangovers. It can help withdrawal from alcohol, easing depression. It helps dry eyes and brittle nails and, when combined with zinc, the oil may be used to treat acne.

But it is the claim that it benefits sufferers of multiple sclerosis that has brought controversy. It has been recommended for MS sufferers by Professor Field, who directed MS research for the UK Medical Research Council.

Claims go further. It is said to be effective in guarding against arterial disease; the effective ingredient, gamma-linolenic acid (GLA), is a powerful antiblood clotter.

It is also said to aid weight loss; a New York hospital discovered that people more than 10 percent above their ideal body weight lost weight when taking the oil. It is thought that this occurs because the GLA in evening primrose oil stimulates brown fat tissue.

In perhaps the most remarkable study of all, completed in Glasgow Royal Infirmary in 1987, it helped to relieve the symptoms of 60 percent of patients suffering from rheumatoid arthritis. Those taking fish oil, in addition to evening primrose oil, fared even better.

The scientific explanation for these extraordinary results is that GLA is a precursor of a hormone-like substance called PGEI, which has a wide range of beneficial effects on the body. Production of this substance in some people may be blocked. GLA has also been found in oil extracted from blackcurrant seed and borage seed, both of which are now a commercial source of this substance.

Oenothera biennis

Origanum
OREGANO & MARJORAM

Also known as Wild Marjoram, Mountain Mint, Winter Marjoram, Winter Sweet, Marjolaine and Origan. From the family Lamiaceae.

For the most part these are natives of the Mediterranean region. They have adapted to many countries, however, and a native form can now be found in many regions of the world, even if under different common names. For example, *Origanum vulgare* growing wild in Britain is called wild marjoram (the scent of the leaf is aromatic but not strong, the flowers are pale pink); while in Mediterranean countries wild *Origanum vulgare* is known as oregano (the leaf is green, slightly hairy and very aromatic, the flowers are similar to those found growing wild in Britain).

Oregano is derived from the Greek *oros*, meaning "mountain," and *ganos*, meaning "joy" and "beauty." It therefore translates literally as "joy of the mountain." In Greece it is woven into the crown worn by bridal couples.

According to Greek mythology, the King of Cyprus had a servant called Amarakos, who dropped a jar of perfume and fainted in terror. As his punishment the gods changed him into oregano, after which, if it was found growing on a burial tomb, all was believed well with the dead. Venus was the first to grow the herb in her garden.

Origanum vulgare "Compactum"

Aristotle reported that tortoises, after swallowing a snake, would immediately eat oregano to prevent death, which gave rise to the belief that it was an antidote to poison.

The Greeks and Romans used it not only as scent after taking a bath and as a massage oil, but also as a disinfectant and preservative. More than likely they were responsible for the spread of this plant across Europe, where it became known as marjoram. The New Englanders took it to North America, where there arose a further confusion of nomenclature. Until the 1940s, common marjoram was called wild marjoram in America, but is now known as oregano. In certain parts of Mexico and the southern states of America, oregano is, confusingly, the colloquial name for a totally unrelated plant that has a similar flavor.

Sweet marjoram, which originates from North Africa, was introduced into Europe in the 16th century and was incorporated in nosegays to ward off the plague and other pestilence.

varieties

Origanum amanum

Hardy perennial. Ht and spread 6–8 in. Open, funnel-shaped, pale pink or white flowers borne above small heart-shaped, aromatic, pale green leaves. Makes a good alpine house plant. Dislikes a damp atmosphere. **Zone 9.**

Origanum x applii

Winter Marjoram

Half-hardy perennial. Ht 9 in., spread 12 in. Small pink flowers. Very small aromatic leaves which, in the right conditions, are available all year round. Good to grow in a container. **Zone 10.**

Origanum dictamnus

Ditany of Crete

Hardy perennial. Ht 5–6 in., spread 16 in. Prostrate habit, purplish pink flowers that appear in hop-like clusters in summer. The leaves are white and woolly and grow on arching stems. Pretty little plant, quite unlike the other origanums in appearance. Tea made from the leaves is considered a panacea in Crete. **Zone 8.**

Origanum "Kent Beauty"

Hardy perennial. Ht 6–8 in., spread 12 in. Whorls of tubular pale pink flowers with darker bracts appear in summer on short spikes. Round, oval and aromatic leaves on trailing stems, which give the plant its prostrate habit and make it suitable for a wall or ledge. Decorative more than culinary. **Zone 8.**

Origanum "Kent Beauty"

Origanum laevigatum

Hardy perennial. Ht 9–12 in., spread 8 in. Summer profusion of tiny, tubular, cerise/pink/mauve flowers, surrounded by red/purple bracts. Aromatic, dark green leaves, which form a mat in winter. Decorative more than culinary. **Zone 8.**

Origanum majorana

Sweet Marjoram

Also known as Knotted Marjoram or Knot Marjoram. Half-hardy perennial. Grown as an annual in cool climates. Ht and spread 12 in. Tiny white flowers in a knot. Round pale green leaves, highly aromatic. This is the best variety for flavor. Use in culinary recipes that state marjoram. The leaf is also good for drying, retaining a lot of its scent and flavor. **Zone 10.**

Origanum onites

Pot Marjoram

Hardy perennial. Ht and spread 18 in. Pink/purple flowers in summer. Green aromatic leaves that form a mat in winter. Good grower with a nice flavor. Difficult to obtain the true seed; grows easily from cuttings, however. **Zone 8.**

Origanum "Rosenkuppel"

Hardy perennial. Ht 24 in. Clusters of small dark pink flowers in summer. Dark green, oval, slightly hairy leaves. Can be used in cooking, but has an inferior flavor to *Orgianum onites*.

Origanum rotundifolium

Hardy perennial. Ht 9–12 in., spread 12 in. Prostrate habit. The pale pink, pendant, funnel-shaped flowers appear in summer in whorls surrounded by yellow/green bracts. Leaves are small, round, midgreen and aromatic. Decorative more than culinary. **Zone 8.**

Origanum vulgare

Oregano

Also known as Wild Marjoram

Hardy perennial. Ht and spread 18 in. Clusters of tiny tubular mauve flowers in summer. Dark green, aromatic, slightly hairy leaves, which form a mat in winter. When grown in its native Mediterranean, it has a very pungent flavor, which bears little resemblance to that obtained in the cooler countries. When cultivated in the garden it becomes similar to pot marjoram. **Zone 4.**

Origanum vulgare "Aureum Crispum"

Origanum vulgare "Aureum"

Golden Marjoram

Hardy perennial. Ht and spread 18 in. Clusters of tiny tubular mauve/pink flowers in summer. Golden, aromatic, slightly hairy leaves, which form a mat in winter. The leaves have a warm aromatic flavor when used in cooking; combines well with vegetables. **Zone 5.**

Origanum vulgare "Aureum Crispum"

Golden Curly Marjoram

Hardy perennial. Ht and spread 18 in. Clusters of tiny tubular mauve/pink/white flowers in summer. Leaves, small, golden, crinkled, aromatic and slightly hairy, which form a mat in winter. The leaves have a slightly milder savory flavor (sweeter and spicy) that combines well with vegetable dishes. **Zone 5.**

Origanum vulgare "Compactum"

Compact Marjoram

Hardy perennial. Ht 6 in., spread 12 in. Lovely large pink flowers. Smallish green aromatic leaves, which form a mat in winter, have a deliciously warm flavor and combine well with lots of culinary dishes. **Zone 5.**

Origanum vulgare "Gold Tip"

Gold-Tipped Marjoram

Also known as Gold Splash

Hardy perennial. Ht and spread 12 in. Small pink flowers in summer. The aromatic leaves are green and yellow variegated. Choose the garden site carefully: shade prevents the variegation. The leaves have a mild savory flavor. **Zone 5.**

Origanum vulgare subsp. hirtum "Greek"

Greek Oregano

Hardy perennial. Ht and spread 18 in. Clusters of tiny tubular white flowers in summer. Gray/green hairy leaves, which are very aromatic and excellent to cook with. **Zone 5.**

Origanum vulgare "Nanum"

Dwarf Marjoram

Hardy perennial. Ht 4 in., spread 6 in. White/pink flowers in summer. Tiny green aromatic leaves. It is a lovely, compact, neat little bush, great in containers and at the front of an herb garden. Good in culinary dishes. **Zone 5.**

cultivation

Propagation

Seed

The following can be grown from seed: *O. vulgare, O. majorana, O. vulgare* subsp. *hirtum* "Greek." The seed is very fine, so sow in spring into prepared seed or plug trays. Use the cardboard trick (see p. 645). Leave uncovered and give a bottom heat of 60°F. Germination can be erratic or 100 percent successful. Watering is critical when the seedlings are young; keep the compost on the dry side. As the seed is so fine, thin before pricking out to allow the plants to grow. When large enough, either repot, using a standard seed compost mixed in equal parts with composted fine bark, or if the soil is warm enough and you have grown them in plugs, plant into the prepared garden.

Cuttings

Apart from the three species mentioned above, the remainder can only be propagated successfully by cuttings or division. Softwood cuttings can be taken from the new growing tips of all the named varieties in spring. Use a standard seed compost mixed in equal parts with composted fine bark.

Division

A number of varieties form a mat during the winter. These lend themselves to division. In spring, or after flowering, dig up a whole clump and pull sections gently away. Each will come away with its own root system. Replant as wanted.

Pests and Diseases

Apart from occasional frost damage, marjorams and oreganos, being aromatic, are mostly pest free.

Maintenance

Spring Sow seeds. Divide established plants. Take softwood cuttings.

Summer Trim after flowering to stop plants becoming straggly. Divide established plants in late summer.

Fall Before they die down for winter, cut back the year's growth to within 2½ in. of the soil.

Winter Protect pot-grown plants and tender varieties.

Garden Cultivation

O. majorana and *O.* x *applii* need a sunny garden site and a well-drained, dry, preferably chalk, soil. Otherwise plant them in containers. All the rest are

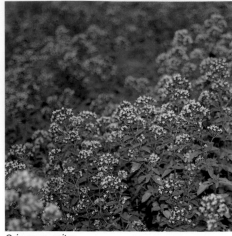

Origanum onites

hardy and adaptable, and will tolerate most soils as long as they are not waterlogged in winter. Plant gold varieties in some shade to prevent the leaves from scorching. For the majority, a good planting distance is 10 in., closer if being used as an edging plant.

Harvesting

Leaves

Pick leaves whenever available for use fresh. They can be dried or frozen, or be used to make oil or vinegar.

Flowers

The flowers can be dried just as they open for dried flower arrangements.

 container growing

The oreganos look great in containers. Use a soilless compost mixed in equal parts with composted fine bark. Make sure that they are not overwatered and that the gold and variegated forms get some shade at midday. Cut back after flowering and give them a liquid fertilizer feed.

 medicinal

This plant is one of the best antiseptics owing to its high thymol content. Marjoram tea helps ease bad colds, has a tranquillizing effect on nerves, and helps settle upset stomachs. It also helps to prevent sea sickness. For temporary relief of toothache, chew the leaf or rub a drop of essential oil on the gums. A few drops of essential oil on the pillow will help you sleep.

 other uses

Make an infusion and add to the bath water to aid relaxation.

 culinary

Marjoram and oregano aid the digestion, and act as an antiseptic and as a preservative. They are among the main ingredients of bouquet garni, and combine well with pizza, meat and tomato dishes, vegetables and milk-based desserts.

Red Mullet with Tomatoes and Oregano

Serves 4 to 6

4 to 6 red mullet, cleaned
3 tablespoons olive oil
1 medium onion, sliced
1 clove garlic, chopped
1½ cups tomatoes, peeled and chopped
1 green or red bell pepper, seeded and diced
1 teaspoon sugar
1 teaspoon chopped fresh oregano or
*   ½ teaspoon dried oregano*
Freshly ground salt and black pepper
Oil for baking or pan frying

Rinse the fish in cold water and drain on paper towels. Heat the olive oil in a pan and cook the onion and garlic slowly until golden brown; add the tomatoes, bell pepper, sugar and oregano, and a little salt and pepper. Bring to a boil, then simmer for 20 minutes until thickened.

Bake or fry the fish. Brush them with oil, place in an oiled ovenproof dish and cook at a moderately hot temperature, 375°F for 7 to 8 minutes. Serve with the sauce.

Papaver
POPPY

From the family Papaveraceae.

The poppy is widely spread across the temperate zones of the world. For thousands of years grain and poppies and civilizations have gone together. The Romans looked on the poppy as sacred to their corn goddess, Ceres, who taught men to sow and reap. The ancient Egyptians used poppy seed in their baking for its aromatic flavor.

The field poppy grew on Flanders Fields after the battles of World War I and became the symbol of Remembrance Day.

Papaver rhoeas

 ## varieties

Papaver commutatum AGM
Ladybird Poppy
Hardy annual. Ht 12–36 in., spread 18 in. Red flowers in summer, each with black blotch in center. Leaf oblong and deeply toothed. Native of Asia Minor. **All zones.**

Papaver rhoeas
Field Poppy
Also known as common poppy, corn poppy, blind eyes, blind man, red dolly, red huntsmen, poppet, old woman's petticoat, thunderbolt, and wartflower. Hardy annual. Ht 8–24 in., spread 18 in. Brilliant scarlet flower with black basal blotch from summer to early fall. The midgreen leaf has three lobes and is irregularly toothed. **All zones.**

Papaver somniferum
Opium Poppy
Hardy annual. Ht 12–36 in., spread 18 in. Large pale lilac, white, purple or variegated flowers in summer. The leaf is long with toothed margins and bluish in color. There is a double-flowered variety, *P. somniferum* var. *paeoniiflorum*. **All zones.**

Meconopsis cambrica
Welsh Poppy
Hardy perennial. Ht 1–24 in. Yellow flowers in summer. Green leaves are divided into many leaflets. It differs from *Papaver* in that seeds are released through slits in the seed heads, not through pepper-pot heads.

 ## cultivation

Propagation
Seed
Sow the very fine seed in fall onto the surface of prepared seed or plug trays, using a standard seed compost mixed in equal parts with composted fine bark. Cover with glass and leave outside for winter stratification. In spring, when seedlings are large enough, plant out into the garden in groups.

Pests and Diseases
Largely pest and disease free.

Maintenance
Spring Plant out in garden.
Summer Deadhead flowers to prolong flowering and prevent self-seeding.
Fall Sow seed. Dig up old plants.
Winter No need to protect.

Garden Cultivation
Poppies all prefer a sunny site and a well-drained fertile soil. Sow in the fall in a prepared site; press seed into the soil but do not cover. Thin to 8–12 in. apart. Remove the heads after flowering to prevent self-seeding.

Harvesting
The ripe seeds can be collected from both field and opium poppies, the seed of which is not narcotic. It must be ripe, otherwise it will go moldy in store.

 ## container growing

Use a standard potting compost mixed in equal parts with composted fine bark. Place in full sun out of the wind, and water well in the summer. Avoid feeding as this will produce lots of soft growth and few flowers.

 ## medicinal

The unripe seed capsules of the opium poppy are used for the extraction of morphine and the manufacture of codeine.

 ## other uses

The oil extracted from the seed of the opium poppy is used not only as a salad oil, and for cooking, but also for burning in lamps, and in the manufacture of varnish, paint and soap.

 ## warning

All parts of the opium poppy, except the ripe seeds, are dangerous and should be used only by trained medical staff.

 ## culinary

Sprinkle the ripe seeds on bread, cakes, and cookies for a pleasant nutty flavor. Add to curry powder for texture, flavor, and as a thickener.

SCENTED GERANIUMS

From the family Geraniaceae.

These form a group of marvellously aromatic herbs which should be used more. Originally native to South Africa, they are now widespread throughout many temperate countries, where they should be grown as tender perennials.

The generic name, *Pelargonium*, is said to be derived from *pelargos*, "a stork." With a bit of imagination one can understand how this came about: the seed pods bear a resemblance to a stork's bill.

 ## varieties

There are many different scented geraniums. I am mentioning a few typical of the species that I have a soft spot for. They are very collectable plants. **All can be grown outdoors only in Zone 10.**

Pelargonium "Attar of Roses"
Half-hardy evergreen perennial. Ht 12–24 in., spread 12 in. Small pink flowers in summer. three-lobed, midgreen leaves that smell of roses.

Pelargonium "Atomic Snowflake"
Half-hardy evergreen perennial. Ht 12–24 in., spread 12 in. Small pink flowers in summer. Intensely lemon-scented, roundish leaves with silver gray/green variegation.

Pelargonium capitatum
Half-hardy evergreen perennial. Ht 12–24 in., spread 12 in. Small mauve flowers in summer, irregular three-lobed green leaves, rose scented. This is now mainly used to produce geranium oil for the perfume industry.

Pelargonium "Chocolate Peppermint"
Half-hardy evergreen perennial. Ht 12–24 in., spread 3 ft. Small white/pink flowers in summer. Large, rounded, shallowly lobed leaves, velvety green with brown marking and a strong scent of chocolate peppermints! This is a fast grower so pinch out growing tips to keep shape.

Pelargonium "Clorinda"
Half-hardy evergreen perennial. Ht and spread 3 ft. Large pink attractive flowers in summer. Large rounded leaves, midgreen and eucalyptus-scented.

Pelargonium crispum
Half-hardy evergreen perennial. Ht and spread 12–24 in. Small pink flowers in summer. Small three-lobed leaves, green, crispy crinkled and lemon scented. Neat habit.

Pelargonium crispum "Peach Cream"
Half-hardy evergreen perennial. Ht and spread 12–24 in. Small pink flowers in summer. Small three-lobed leaves, green with cream and yellow variegation, crispy crinkled and peach-scented.

Pelargonium crispum "Variegatum"
Half-hardy evergreen perennial. Ht and spread 12–24 in. Small pink flowers in summer. Small three-lobed leaves, green with cream variegation, crispy crinkled, and lemon-scented.

Pelargonium denticulatum
Half-hardy evergreen perennial. Ht and spread 3 ft. Small pinky-mauve flowers in summer. Deeply cut palmate leaves, green with a lemon scent.

Pelargonium denticulatum "Filicifolium"
Half-hardy evergreen perennial. Ht and spread 3 ft. Small pink flowers in summer. Very finely indented green leaves with a fine brown line running through, slightly sticky and not particularly aromatic, if anything a scent of balsam. Prone to whitefly.

Pelargonium Fragrans Group
Half-hardy evergreen perennial. Ht and spread 12 in. Small white flowers in summer. Grayish green leaves, rounded with shallow lobes, and a strong scent of nutmeg/pine.

Pelargonium Fragrans Group "Fragrans Variegatum"
Half-hardy evergreen perennial. Ht and spread 12 in. Small white flowers in summer. Grayish green leaves with cream variegation, rounded with shallow lobes and a strong scent of nutmeg/pine.

Pelargonium graveolens
Rose Geranium
Half-hardy evergreen perennial. Ht 24–40 in. Spread up to 3 ft. Small pink flowers in summer. Fairly deeply cut green leaves with a rose/ peppermint scent. One of the more hardy of this species, with good growth.

Pelargonium "Lady Plymouth"
Half-hardy evergreen perennial. Ht and spread 12–24 in. Small pink flowers in summer. Fairly deeply cut grayish green leaves with cream variegation and a rose/peppermint scent.

Pelargonium "Atomic Snowflake"

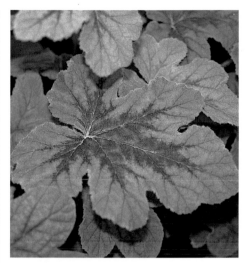

Pelargonium "Chocolate Peppermint"

Pelargonium "Lemon Fancy"

Half-hardy evergreen perennial. Ht 12–24 in., spread 12–18 in. Smallish pink flowers in summer. Small roundish green leaves with shallow lobes and an intense lemon scent.

Pelargonium "Lilian Pottinger"

Half-hardy evergreen perennial. Ht 12–24 in., spread 3 ft. Small whitish flowers in summer. Leaves brightish green, rounded, shallowly lobed with serrated edges. Soft to touch. Mild spicy apple scent.

Pelargonium "Mabel Gray"

Half-hardy evergreen perennial. Ht 18–24 in., spread 12–18 in. Mauve flowers with deeper veining in summer. If I have a favorite scented geranium, this is it: the leaves are diamond-shaped, roughly textured, midgreen and oily when rubbed and very strongly lemon-scented.

Pelargonium odoratissimum

Half-hardy evergreen perennial. Ht 12–24 in., spread 3 ft. Small white flowers in summer. Green, rounded, shallowly lobed leaves, fairly bright green in color and soft to touch, with an apple scent. Trailing habit, looks good in large containers.

Pelargonium "Prince of Orange"

Half-hardy evergreen perennial. Ht and spread 12–24 in. Pretty pink/white flowers in summer. Green, slightly crinkled, slightly lobed leaves, with a refreshing orange scent. Prone to rust.

Pelargonium quercifolium

Oak-Leafed Pelargonium

Half-hardy evergreen perennial. Ht and spread up to 3 ft. Pretty pink/purple flowers in summer. Leaves oak-shaped, dark green with brown variegation, and slightly sticky. A different, spicy scent.

Pelargonium "Rober's Lemon Rose"

Half-hardy evergreen perennial. Ht and spread up to 3 ft. Pink flowers in summer. Leaves grayish-green — oddly shaped, lobed and cut — with a rose scent. A fast grower, so pinch out the growing tips regularly to maintain shape.

Pelargonium "Royal Oak"

Half-hardy evergreen perennial. Ht 15 in., spread 12 in. Small pink/purple flowers in summer. Oak-shaped, dark green leaves with brown variegation, slightly sticky with spicy scent. Very similar to *P. quercifolium*, but with a more compact habit.

Pelargonium tomentosum

Half-hardy evergreen perennial. Ht 12–24 in., spread 3 ft. Small white flowers in summer. Large rounded leaves, shallow lobed, velvet gray-green in color with a strong peppermint scent. Fast grower, so pinch out growing tips regularly to maintain shape. Protect from full sun.

Mixed *Pelargonium*

 cultivation

Propagation

Seed

Although I have known these plants to be grown from seed, I do not recommend this method. Cuttings are much more reliable for the majority. However, if you want to have a go, sow in spring in a standard seed compost mixed in equal parts with composted fine bark at a temperature no lower than 59°F.

Cuttings

All scented geraniums can be propagated by softwood cuttings which generally take very easily in the summer. Take a cutting about 4–6 in. long and strip the leaves from the lower part with a sharp knife. At all costs do not tear the leaves off as this will cause a hole in the stem and the cutting will be susceptible to disease, such as blackleg. This is a major caveat for varieties such as *Pelargonium crispum* "Variegatum." Use a sharp knife and slice the leaf off, insert the cutting into a tray containing equal parts seed compost and composted bark. Water in and put the tray away from direct sunlight. Keep an eye on the compost, making sure it does not thoroughly dry out, but only water if absolutely necessary. The cuttings should root in 2 to 3 weeks. Pot up into separate pots containing a standard potting compost mixed in equal parts with composted fine bark. Place in a cool greenhouse or cool conservatory for the winter, keeping the compost dry and watering only very occasionally. In the spring repot into larger pots and water sparingly. When they start to produce flower buds give them a liquid feed. In early summer pinch out the top growing points to encourage bushy growth.

Pests and Diseases

Unfortunately pelargoniums suffer from a few diseases.

1. Cuttings can be destroyed by blackleg fungus. The cutting turns black and falls over. The main cause of this is too much water. So keep the cuttings as dry as possible after the initial watering.

2. Gray mold (*Botrytis*) is also caused by the plants being too wet and the air too moist. Remove damaged leaves carefully so as not to spread the disease, and burn. Allow the plants to dry out, and increase ventilation and spacing between plants.

3. Leaf gall appears as a mass of small proliferated shoots at the base of a cutting or plant. Destroy the plant, otherwise it could affect other plants.

4. Geraniums, like mint and comfrey, are prone to rust, especially on *P.* "Prince of Orange." Destroy the affected plants, or it will spread to others.

SCENTED GERANIUMS

5. Aphids. Be vigilant. If you catch them early enough, you will be able to control them by spraying with a liquid insecticidal soap. Follow manufacturer's instructions.

Maintenance

Spring Sow seed. Trim, slowly introduce watering, and start feeding. Repot if necessary.

Summer Feed regularly. Trim to maintain shape. Take cuttings.

Fall Trim back plants. Bring in for the winter to protect from frost.

Winter Allow the plants to rest. Keep watering to a minimum.

Garden Cultivation

Scented pelargoniums are so varied that they can look very effective grown in groups in the garden. Plant out as soon there is no danger of frost. Choose a warm site with well-drained soil. A good method is to sink the repotted, over-wintered geraniums into the soil. This makes sure the initial compost is correct, and makes it easier to dig up the pot and bring inside before the first frost.

Harvesting

Pick leaves during the growing season, for fresh use or for drying. Collect seeds before the seed pod ripens and ripen in paper bags. If allowed to ripen on the plant, the pods will burst, sprinkling the seeds everywhere.

 container growing

Scented pelargoniums make marvellous pot plants. They grow well, look good, and smell lovely. Repot as in "Propagation," using a standard potting compost mixed in equal parts with composted fine bark. Place so that you can rub the leaves as you walk past.

 other uses

In aromatherapy, geranium oil is relaxing but use it in small quantities. Dilute two drops in 2 teaspoons of soy oil for a good massage, or to relieve pre-menstrual tension, dermatitis, eczema, herpes or dry skin.

 warning

None of the crispums should be used in cooking as it is believed that they can upset the stomach.

 culinary

Before artificial food flavorings were produced, the Victorians used scented pelargonium leaves in the bottom of cake tins to flavor their sponge cakes. Why not follow suit? When you grease and line the bottom of a 8 in. sandwich tin, arrange approximately 20 leaves of either *P.* "Lemon Fancy," *P.* "Mabel Gray," or *P. graveolens*. Fill the pan with a sponge cake mix of your choice and cook as normal. Remove the leaves with the lining paper when the cake has cooled. Scented pelargonium leaves add distinctive flavor to many dishes although, like bay leaves, they are hardly ever eaten, being removed after the cooking process. The main varieties used are *P. graveolens*, *P. odoratissimum*, *P.* "Lemon Fancy," and *P.* "Attar of Roses."

Geranium Leaf Sorbet

12 scented Pelargonium graveolens *leaves*
6 tablespoons caster sugar
1¼ cups water
Juice of 1 large lemon
1 egg white, beaten
4 leaves for decoration

Wash the leaves and shake them dry. Put the sugar and water in a pot and boil until the sugar has dissolved, stirring occasionally. Remove the pan

from the heat. Put the 12 leaves in the pan with the sugar and water, cover and leave for 20 minutes. Taste. If you want a stronger flavor bring the liquid to a boil again, add some fresh leaves and leave for an additional 10 minutes. When you have the right flavor, strain the syrup into a rigid container, add the lemon juice and let cool. Place in the freezer until semi-frozen (approximately 45 minutes) — it must be firm, not mushy — and fold in the beaten egg white. Put back into freezer for an additional 45 minutes. Scoop into individual glass bowls, and decorate each with a geranium leaf.

Rose Geranium Punch

5 cups of apple juice
1 cup sugar
6 leaves of Pelargonium graveolens
6 drops of green vegetable coloring (optional)
4 limes

Boil the apple juice, sugar and geranium leaves for 5 minutes. Strain the liquid. Cool and add coloring if required. Thinly slice and crush limes, add to the liquid. Pour onto ice in glasses and garnish with leaves.

Rose Geranium Butter

Butter pounded with the leaves makes a delicious filling for cakes and cookies. It can also be spread on bread and topped with apple gelatin.

Perilla frutescens

SHISO

Also known as Beefsteak plant, Chinese basil, Wild Sesame, Rattlesnake weed, Egoma and Zi Su. From the family Lamiaceae.

The common name "beefsteak plant" is in reference to the large purple shiso leaves looking like a slice of raw beef. This name originated in the U.S., where it has become a naturalized wild plant in many southern and eastern states. Shiso has been used in Chinese medicine for thousands of years to treat morning sickness. Until recently, however, the culinary uses of this Far Eastern herb were relatively unknown in Western countries. Even in the early 1980s purple shiso was being used in the UK only as a spectacular spot bedding plant rather than in the kitchen. It has now become a chef's designer herb, often served in baby leaf form, which intensifies its unique flavors.

Perilla frutescens var. purpurascens

 varieties

Perilla frutescens var. *frutescens*
Zi su, Egoma
Hardy annual. Height up to 5 ft., spread 24 in. Mauve flowers in summer. Large aromatic, green with a hint of brown, leaves that have a deep purple underside. This is an important culinary and medicinal herb from Korea.

Perilla frutescens var. *crispa* AGM
Green Shiso, Aojiso and Perilla
Hardy annual. Height up to 4 ft., spread 24 in. Pink flowers during summer. Aromatic, anise-flavored, deeply cut, bright green leaf that has crinkled edges.

Perilla frutescens var. *purpurascens*
Purple Shiso, Beefsteak Plant
Hardy annual. Height up to 4 ft., spread 24 in. Pink flowers in summer. Deeply cut, aromatic, dark purple leaf with crinkled bronzed edges. There can be considerable variation in seed-raised plants; the flowers can be red and the leaves smoother.

 cultivation

Propagation
Seed
In spring, sow seeds into prepared seed trays, module plugs or small pots using a seed compost mixed in equal parts with perlite, and place under protection at 68°F. Germination takes 1 to 2 weeks. Do not overwater once germinated as seedlings are prone to damping off, especially when the nights are cold. Once large enough to handle, repot using a potting compost mixed in equal parts with composted fine bark. Grow on until seedlings are large enough to plant out into a prepared site 12 in. apart. Alternatively sow into prepared open ground in late spring, when the air temperature does not go below 45°F at night. Germination takes 14 to 20 days.

Pests and Diseases
Beware of caterpillars, especially in late summer. Hand pick off as soon as spotted.

Maintenance
Spring Sow seeds.
Summer Keep pinching out the growing tips to

SHISO

Perilla frutescens var. *frutescens*

maintain shape and to produce a bushy plant.
Fall Harvest leaves, then seeds.
Winter Clean the seed for next year's sowing.

Garden Cultivation

Plant in a fertile well-drained soil on a site that has been prepared with well-rotted compost or leaf mold in the previous fall. Plant in the late spring, in sun or partial shade. In arid climates, regular irrigation will be necessary.

Harvesting

Pick leaves to use fresh as required throughout the growing season. Pick flowering tops in late summer. Harvest the seeds in late fall.

 container growing

This herb looks lovely growing in containers, especially the purple-leaved varieties. Plant in a potting compost mixed in equal parts with composted fine bark. Place the container in a sunny position. Water regularly and liquid feed weekly through the summer, following the manufacturer's instructions.

 medicinal

Shiso has been used for centuries in Oriental medicine. It is a pungent, aromatic, warming herb. An infusion of the plant is useful in the treatment of asthma, colds, coughs and lung afflictions, constipation, food poisoning and allergic reactions, especially from seafood. An infusion made from the stems of this herb is a traditional Chinese remedy to alleviate morning sickness; however this should only be taken under the guidance of a Chinese doctor or fully trained herbalist.

 other uses

When walking or hiking in the country, rub the leaves directly on your skin and clothes and on to your dog to repel ticks. Before using, rub a bit on the back of your hand to see if you are allergic to it.

 warning

Do not take medicinally during pregnancy. Can cause contact dermatitis. Do not plant where horses or cattle can eat this plant as it can cause respiratory failure.

 culinary

This herb is one of the few aromatic plants to have established itself in Japanese cuisine, although it is a relatively newcomer to the European kitchen. It is sometimes confused with basil *(Ocimum)*, however the flavor is very different being, in my opinion, a mixture of cumin, mint and nutmeg with a hint of plums for the purple variety and anise for the green variety. Purple shiso is used as a dye for pickling fruit and vegetables, as a side dish with rice in the form of a dried powder, as an ingredient in cake mixes and as flavoring in beverages. The flower heads are used as a condiment with sushi. Green leaf shiso, the variety most commonly seen in Japanese markets, is used as a vegetable. The leaves are used as a wrapping for rice cake, in salads and tempura. The seeds from this variety are used as a condiment and with pickles. The essential oil extracted from the leaf and flowering parts contains a substance which is used in confectionery that is many times sweeter than sugar.

Shiso, Mooli and Kiwi Fruit Salad

1 mooli (This is a Japanese white radish which has a crunchy texture and a mild peppery flavor and can be found in large supermarkets, or in Asian or Caribbean stores.)

Lemon juice
3 tablespoons light olive oil
1 tablespoon white wine vinegar or rice vinegar
3 kiwi fruits, peeled and sliced
A good handful (approx 24 tips) of young purple shiso new growing tips, 6 tips put aside and the remainder finely minced
Salt and freshly ground black pepper

Peel and slice the mooli thinly, sprinkling the slices with lemon juice to prevent discoloration. Make the dressing with the oil and vinegar, season to taste. Arrange the sliced kiwi fruit and the mooli on a plate. Sprinkle with the chopped shiso, then drizzle the dressing over the salad, and decorate with the remaining purple shiso tips.

Persicaria odorata
VIETNAMESE CILANTRO

Also known as Rau Ram, Laksa Plant and Vietnamese Mint. From the family Polygonaceae.

Vietnamese cilantro is indigenous throughout the tropics and subtropics of South and Eastern Asia, where it is used in the kitchen and as an herbal remedy. It is a member of the knotweed family of plants that are notoriously invasive and more often than not considered as weeds. It should not be confused with a native wild flower found in Northwest Europe called *Persicaria bistorta*, common bistort, which has pink flowers and leaves that smell of vegetables when crushed, as opposed to the warm fragrant spicy scent of the tropical Vietnamese cilantro leaves.

 ## varieties

Persicaria odorata
Vietnamese Cilantro
Tropical evergreen perennial. Ht. 18 in., spread indefinite. Attractive small creamy white flowers in summer until late fall, rarely produced under cultivation and in cold climates. Highly aromatic leaves when crushed, narrow-pointed with a brown/maroon V-shaped marking near the base.

Persicaria bistorta
Common Bistort
Hardy perennial. Ht. 8 in. to 3 ft., spread indefinite. Dense clusters of small pink flowers in summer until early fall. Hairless, triangular, midgreen leaves.

Medicinally the root of this species is used to staunch blood flow and contract tissues. It is one of the most astringent of all medicinal plants.

 ## cultivation

Propagation

Cuttings
Cutting can be taken from spring until late summer. Take the cutting just below the stem joint, place in prepared module plug trays or a small pot filled with a standard seed compost. Put in a sheltered warm position, bottom heat is not required; it will root within 10 days in midspring. Alternatively, as this plant will root anywhere that the stem touches the ground, it is possible to take a stem cutting with some roots attached. Grow on in exactly the same way as taking a standard cutting. Once the cuttings are fully rooted in warm climates plant out into the garden into a prepared site; in cool and cold climates repot and grow on as a container plant.

Division
Garden and container-grown plants will need dividing to keep the plant healthy and productive and also to stop it either invading the garden or outgrowing the pot. With both situations you can be as vigorous as you like, either replanting divisions into a prepared site in the garden or repotting into a soilless potting compost.

Pests and Diseases
This highly aromatic plant rarely suffers from any pests or diseases.

Persicaria odorata flower

VIETNAMESE CILANTRO

Maintenance

Spring Reintroduce regular watering. Take cuttings.
Summer Cut back to produce new growth.
Fall Protect from frosts.
Winter In cool and cold climates cut back on watering.

Garden Cultivation

As this herb is a tropical plant it will need protection when temperatures fall below 45ºF at night. It can be grown outside in summer, planted in a rich fertile soil, in partial shade, but it will need lifting well before the first hint of frost. Be warned in warm climates: if you introduce this plant to your garden it will be more invasive than mint.

Harvesting

Pick the leaves to use fresh as required throughout the growing season.

 container growing

Vietnamese cilantro grows very happily in containers; use a soilless potting compost. Place the container in a warm greenhouse, conservatory or on a windowsill. Protect from the midday sun as this will scorch the leaves, which will then taste bitter. To maintain good-quality leaves, either divide the plant annually or replant in a container one size up. Water and liquid feed regularly from spring until fall. Outside the tropics, it is wise to reduce the watering and stop feeding in the winter months.

 medicinal

Throughout the Far East, Vietnamese cilantro is used to treat indigestion, flatulence and stomach aches. It is also reputedly eaten by Buddhist monks to suppress sexual urges.

 other uses

Currently in Australia there is interesting research into the essential oil of Vietnamese cilantro, called Kesom oil, for use in food flavoring.

 culinary

In some countries this herb goes under the name Vietnamese mint, which is a misnomer in all aspects as it is certainly not a member of the mint family (Lamiaceae), nor does it in any way have a mint flavor. The first time I ate the leaves of this herb I was totally taken by surprise. To begin with, the taste is mild with a hint of lime and spice, then as the flavor developed it became hot and peppery. This herb is never cooked, it is used as a fresh leaf condiment, always added at the end of cooking. In Asia, it is usually eaten raw as a salad or herb accompaniment. It combines well with meat, vegetables and fruit. It is important in Vietnamese cooking being used copiously with noodle soups (pho) where large heaps of the leaves are dipped into the soup using chopsticks. Personally, I like it sprinkled over stir-fried vegetables, which then gives the dish an extra zing.

Stir-fried Vegetables
Serves 4

½ oz. dried Chinese mushrooms, soaked in warm water for 20 minutes
4 tablespoons sesame seed oil
½ cup white cabbage, washed and finely sliced
½ cup carrots, peeled and sliced into thin strips
½ cup cucumber, cut into thin strips
½ cup bamboo shoots
4 tablespoons chicken or vegetable broth
2 tablespoons soy sauce
pinch of sugar
Salt and freshly ground black pepper to taste
10 Vietnamese cilantro leaves, finely minced

Drain the Chinese mushrooms and cut into small pieces. Heat the oil in a large skillet or wok, add the cabbage, stir-fry for 2 minutes. Add the mushrooms, carrots, cucumber and bamboo shoots, stir-fry for an additional 2 minutes. Add the broth, soy sauce, and sugar, salt and pepper to taste. Stir-fry for 2 minutes to heat through. Add the chopped Vietnamese cilantro leaves and serve with rice or noodles.

Petroselinum
PARSLEY

Also known as Common Parsley, Garden Parsley, and Rock Parsley. From the family Apiaceae.

Best-known of all garnishing herbs in the West. Native to central and southern Europe, in particular the Mediterranean region, now widely cultivated in several varieties throughout the world.

The Greeks had mixed feelings about this herb. It was associated with Archemorus, the Herald of Death, so they decorated their tombs with it. Hercules was said to have chosen parsley for his garlands, so they would weave it into crowns for victors at the Isthmian Games. But they did not eat it themselves, preferring to feed it to their horses. However, the Romans consumed parsley in quantity and made garlands for banquet guests to discourage intoxication and to counter strong odors.

It was believed that only a witch or a pregnant woman could grow it, and that a fine harvest was ensured only if the seeds were planted on Good Friday. It was also said that if parsley was transplanted, then misfortune would descend upon the household.

varieties

Petroselinum crispum
Parsley
Hardy biennial. Ht 12–16 in. Small creamy white flowers in flat umbels in summer. The leaf is brightish green and has curly toothed edges and a mild taste. It is mainly used as a garnish. **Zone 5.**

Petroselinum crispum Flat-leaf
Flat-leaf Parsley
Also known as Broad-Leafed Parsley. Hardy biennial. Ht 18–24 in. in. Small creamy white flowers in flat umbels in summer. Flat dark green leaves with a stronger flavor than *P. crispum*. This is the one I recommend for culinary use.

Petroselinum crispum var. tuberosum
Hamburg Parsley
Also known as Turnip-Rooted Parsley. Perennial, grown as an annual. Root length up to 6 in. Leaf, green and very similar to French parsley. This variety, probably first developed in Holland, was introduced into England in the early 18th century, but it was only popular for 100 years. The plant is still frequently found in vegetable markets in France and Germany, where it is sold as a root vegetable. **Zone 5.**

Warning: In the wild there is a plant called fool's parsley (Aethusa cynapium), which both looks and smells to the novice like French parsley. Do not be tempted to eat it as it is extremely poisonous.

cultivation

Propagation
Seed
In cool climates, to ensure a succession of plants, sow seedlings under cover only in plug trays or pots. Avoid seed trays because it hates being transferred. Cover with perlite. If you have a heated propagator, a temperature of 65°F will speed up germination. It takes 4 to 6 weeks without bottom heat and 2 to 3 weeks with. When the seedlings are large enough and the air and soil temperature have started to rise (about midspring), plant out 6 in. apart in a prepared garden bed. Alternatively, in late spring sow into a prepared site in the garden, in rows 12–18 in. apart and about 1 in. deep. Germination is very slow. Keep

Parsley seed tea

the soil moist at all times, otherwise the seed will not germinate. As soon as the seedlings are large enough, thin to 3 in. and then 6 in. apart.

Pests and Diseases

Slugs love young parsley plants. There is a fungus that may attack the leaves. It produces first brown then white spots. Where this occurs the whole stock should be destroyed. Get some fresh seed.

Maintenance

Spring Sow seed.
Summer Sow seed. Cut flower heads as they appear on second-year plants.
Fall Protect plants for winter crop.
Winter Protect plants for winter picking.

Garden Cultivation

Parsley is a hungry plant, it likes a good deep soil, not too light and not acid. Always feed the chosen site well in the previous fall with well-rotted manure. If you wish to harvest parsley all year round, prepare two different sites. For summer supplies, a western or eastern border is ideal because the plant needs moisture and prefers a little shade. For winter supplies, a more sheltered spot will be needed in a sunny place.

The seeds should be sown thinly, in rows. If at any time the leaves turn a bit yellow, cut back to encourage new growth and feed with a liquid fertilizer. At the first sign of flower heads appearing, remove them if you wish to continue harvesting the leaves. Remember to water well during hot weather. In the second year parsley runs to seed very quickly. Dig it up as soon as the following year's crop is ready for picking, and remove it from the garden.

Hamburg or turnip parsley differs only in the respect that it is a root not a leaf crop. When the seedlings are large enough, thin to 8 in. apart. Water well all summer. The root tends to grow more at this time of year, and unlike a lot of root crops the largest roots taste the best. Lift in late fall, early winter. They are frost resistant.

Harvesting

Pick leaves during first year for fresh use or for freezing (by far the best method of preserving parsley).
   Dig up roots of Hamburg parsley in the fall of the first year and store in peat or sand.

 container growing

Parsley is an ideal herb for containers, it even likes living inside on the kitchen windowsill, as long as it is watered, fed, and cut. Use a standard potting compost mixed in equal parts with composted fine bark. Curly parsley can look very ornamental as an edging to a large pot of nasturtiums. It can also be grown in hanging baskets, (keep well watered), window boxes (give it some shade in high summer), and containers. That brings me to the strawberry jar, the one with six holes around the side. Do not use it. As I have already said, parsley likes moisture, and these containers dry out too fast as the holes in the side are small and make it very difficult to water; also, parsley has too big a taproot to be happy.

 medicinal

All parsleys are a rich source of vitamins, including vitamin C. They are also high in iron and other minerals and contain the antiseptic chlorophyll. It is a strong diuretic suitable for treating urinary infections as well as fluid retention. It also increases mothers' milk and tones the uterine muscle.

Parsley is a well-known breath freshener, being the traditional antidote for the pungent smell of garlic. Chew raw, to promote a healthy skin. Use in poultices as an antiseptic dressing for sprains, wounds and insect bites.

 other uses

A tea made from crushed seeds kills head lice vermin. Pour it over the head after washing and rinsing, wrap your head in a towel for 30 minutes and then allow to dry naturally. Equally, the seeds or leaves steeped in water can be used as a hair rinse.

 warning

Avoid medicinal use during pregnancy. There is an oil produced from parsley, but it should be used only under medical supervision.

 culinary

Parsley is a widely used culinary herb, valued for its taste as well as its rich nutritional content. Cooking with parsley enhances the flavor of other foods and herbs. In bland food, the best flavor is obtained by adding it just before the end of cooking. As so many recipes include parsley, here are some basic herb mixtures.

Fines Herbes

You will see this mentioned in a number of recipes and it is a classic for omelets.

1 sprig parsley, chopped
1 sprig chervil, chopped
Some chives cut with scissors
1 to 2 leaves French tarragon, chopped

Combine all the herbs and add to egg dishes.

Fish Bouquet Garni

2 sprigs parsley
1 sprig French tarragon
1 sprig fennel (small)
2 leaves lemon balm

Tie the herbs together in a bundle and add to the cooking liquid.

Boil Hamburg parsley as a root vegetable or grate raw into salads. Use in soup mixes; the flavor resembles both celery and parsley.

Phlomis fruticosa

JERUSALEM SAGE

From the family Lamiaceae.

Originates from the Mediterranean region but is now cultivated widely as an ornamental garden plant.

The generic name, *Phlomis*, was used by Dioscorides, a Greek physician in the first century whose *Materia Medica* was the standard reference on the medical application of plants for over 1,500 years.

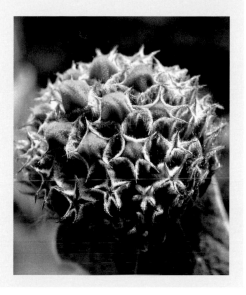

Winter Protect outside plants if the winter temperature is persistently below 23°F.

Garden Cultivation
Jerusalem sage is an attractive plant, making a fine mound of gray-furred leaves that cope with all but the most severe winter. A prolific summer flowerer, happy in a dry, well-drained, sunny spot. Cut back each year after flowering (late summer) and you will be able to control and maintain its soft gray dome all year round. Do not trim in the fall as any frost will damage and in some cases kill the plant.

Harvesting
Pick leaves for drying before plant flowers.

 ## container growing

Jerusalem sage is happy in a large container using a soilless compost mixed in equal parts with composted fine bark. Be mean on the feeding and watering as it is a drought-loving plant. Trim back especially after flowering to restrict its rampant growth. Protect during the winter in a cool greenhouse or conservatory. Keep watering to the absolute minimum.

 ## other uses

The slightly aromatic leaves are attractive in a potpourri.

 ## culinary

Although not listed amongst culinary herbs, the leaves are pleasantly aromatic. In Greece the leaves are collected from the hillside and, once dried and bundled together with other related species, are hung up for sale. The dried leaves can be used in stews and casseroles.

 ## varieties

Phlomis fruticosa AGM
Jerusalem Sage
Hardy evergreen perennial. Ht and spread 4 ft. Whorls of hooded yellow flowers in summer. Gray/green oblongish leaves, slightly wrinkled. **Zone 8.**

Phlomis italica
Narrow-Leaved Jerusalem Sage
Hardy evergreen perennial. Ht 36 in., spread 30 in. Whorls of lilac/pink flowers in midsummer, borne at the ends of shoots amid narrow, woolly, gray/green leaves. **Zone 8.**

Phlomis italica

 ## cultivation

Propagation
Seeds
Sow the medium-sized seed in the fall into either seed or plug trays and cover with a thin layer of compost. Winter in a cold greenhouse or cold frame. Does not need stratification nor heat, just cool temperature. Germination is erratic. When the seedlings are large enough to handle, prick out into pots using a potting compost mixed in equal parts with composted fine bark. Plant the young plants into the garden when there is no threat of frosts.

Cuttings
Take softwood cuttings in summer from nonflowering shoots; they root easily.

Division
If an established plant has taken over its neighbor's spot, dig up and divide it in the spring; replant into a prepared site.

Pests and Diseases
This plant is mostly free from pests and diseases.

Maintenance
Spring Divide established plants if need be.
Summer Cut back after flowering to maintain shape.
Fall Sow seeds.

Phytolacca americana
POKE

Phytolacca americana

Also known as Poke Root, Red Ink Plant, Virginia Poke weed, Pigeon Berry, Coccum, Indian Poke, American Poke and Cancer Root.
From the family Phytolaccaceae.

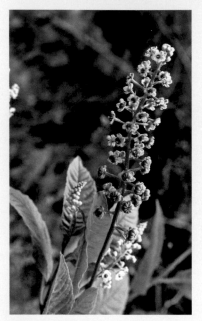

This herbaceous plant is a native to the warmer regions of America (especially Florida), Africa and Asia. It has been introduced elsewhere, particularly in the Mediterranean region.

Its generic name is derived from two Greek words: *phyton*, meaning "plant" and *lac*, meaning "lake," referring to the purple/blue dye that flows from some of the phytolaccas when crushed.

The herb was introduced to European settlers by the Native Americans, who knew it as pocan or coccum, and used it as an emetic for a number of problems. It acquired a reputation as a remedy for internal cancers and was called cancer root.

Summer Cut off the flowers if you do not want berries.
Fall Sow seeds. Divide established plants.
Winter Dies back into the ground; no protection needed.

Garden Cultivation
Plant poke in sun or shade in a moist, fertile soil, sheltered from the wind. This plant can look marvelos in a garden, especially in fall.

Harvesting
It can be used as a pot herb, the young shoots being picked in the spring. But because it is easy to confuse the identity of species, and toxicity varies among them, only do this if you really know what you are doing. So it is better to err on the side of caution and pick some nice fresh sorrel or red orach instead.

 ## container growing

It is a tall plant, and when in berry is sufficiently heavy to unbalance even a large pot. Keep the poisonous berries out of reach of children. If you choose to try it, use a soil-based compost mixed in equal parts with composted fine bark and water well during the summer months.

 ## medicinal

Herbalists prescribe it for the treatment of chronic rheumatism, arthritis, tonsillitis, swollen glands, mumps and mastitis. An extract from the roots can destroy snails. This discovery is being explored in Africa as a possible means to control the disease bilharzia, which is carried by water snails.

 ## warning

POISONOUS. When handling either seeds, roots or the mature plant, gloves should be worn. It is toxic and dangerous. It should be used only by professionally trained herbalists.

 ## varieties

☠ *Phytolacca americana* syn. *P. decandra*
Pokeweed
Hardy perennial. Ht and spread 4–10 ft. Shallow, cup-shaped flowers, sometimes pink, flushed white and green, borne in terminal racemes in summer. They are followed by round fleshy blackish-purple berries with poisonous seeds that hang down when ripe. Oval to lance-shaped midgreen leaves, tinged purple in fall. There is a variegated form with green and white leaves.

Phytolacca polyandra syn. *P. calvigera*
Hardy perennial. Ht and spread 4 ft. Clusters of shallow, cup-shaped, pink flowers in summer, followed by rounded blackish berries with poisonous seeds. Has brilliant crimson stems, oval to lance-shaped, midgreen leaves that turn yellow in summer through fall. This plant is a native of China. **Zone 5.**

 ## cultivation

Propagation
Seed
Wearing gloves, sow the seeds fresh in the fall or spring in prepared seed or plug trays. Cover with perlite. If sown in the fall, winter the young plants in a cold greenhouse or cold frame. In the spring, after a period of hardening off, plant them out in a prepared site in the garden, 3 ft. apart.

Division
Both species have large root systems that can be divided (wearing gloves) either in fall or spring.

Pests and Diseases
Largely free from pests and diseases.

Maintenance
Spring Sow seeds. Divide established plants.

Polemonium caeruleum
JACOB'S LADDER

Polemonium reptans

Also known as Blue Jacket, Charity, Jacob's Walking Stick, Ladder to Heaven, Greek Valerian. From the family Polemoniaceae.

This herb is steeped in history. It was known to the ancient Greeks as *Polemonium* and they administered a decoction made from the root mixed with wine in cases of dysentery, toothache, and against the bites of poisonous animals. As late as the 19th century it was known as Valeranae Graecae or Greek Valerian and was being used in some European pharmacies. It was predominantly used as an antisyphilitic agent and in the treatment of rabies. To confuse things, the American Shakers called it "Abscess" and used it for pleurisy and fevers.

 ## varieties

Polemonium caeruleum
Jacob's Ladder
Hardy perennial. Ht and spread 18–24 in. Clusters of attractive cup-shaped lavender-blue flowers in summer. The midgreen leaves are finely divided into small lance shapes. **Zone 2.**

Polemonium reptans
Also known as false Jacob's ladder or American Greek valerian. Hardy perennial. Ht 8–18 in. and spread 12 in. Clusters of attractive cup-shaped blue flowers in summer. The silver/green leaves are finely divided into small lance shapes. Native of Eastern North America. The root of this species is bitter in flavor and is employed as an astringent and as an antidote against snake bites. **Zone 2.**

 ## cultivation

Propagation
Seed
For flowering early the following spring, sow the fairly small seeds in fall into a prepared seed or plug module tray using a standard seed compost. Winter the seedlings in a cool/cold, but frost-free greenhouse. Prick out in spring, when the threat of frosts has passed, then plant directly into the garden after hardening off, at a distance of 12 in. apart.

Division
Divide established plants in the spring. Dig the whole plant up and ease it in half using two forks back-to-back. Replant in a prepared site in the garden.

Pests and Diseases
These plants rarely suffer from pests or diseases.

Maintenance
Spring Sow seeds if not previously done, divide established plants if needed.
Summer Deadhead flowers and, after flowering, cut back to prevent self-seeding.
Fall Sow seeds under protection.
Winter Established plants are hardy and should not need protection.

Garden Cultivation
Jacob's ladder prefers a rich, moisture-retentive soil, with added lime in a sunny position. However it is a most tolerant plant and will adapt to most soils with the exception of those that are very dry.

Harvesting
Cut the flowers just as they open for drying. Dry either in small bunches or individual sprays.

 ## container growing

This herb looks most attractive grown in a container. Use a soilless potting compost and place the container in semi-shade to help prevent the compost from drying out. Feed regularly only when the plant is flowering using a liquid fertilizer and following the manufacturer's instructions.

 ## medicinal

This herb is rarely used in modern herbal medicine.

 ## other uses

The dried flowers do not smell, but do look attractive in potpourris.
When the roots are combined with olive oil, it makes a black dye.

Polemonium caeruleum

Polygonatum
SOLOMON'S SEAL

Also known as David's Harp, Jacob's Ladder, Lady's Lockets, Lily of the Mountain, Drop Berry, Seal Root, or Sealwort. From the family Convallariaceae.

This plant's generic name *Polygonatum* is derived from *Poly,* meaning "many" and *gonu,* meaning "knee joint," which may refer to the many-jointed rhizome.

King Solomon, wiser than all men, gave his approval to the use of the roots (which are said to resemble cut sections of Hebrew characters) as a poultice for wounds, and to help heal broken limbs.

 varieties

☠ *Polygonatum* x *hybridum*
Solomon's Seal
Hardy perennial. Ht 12–30 in., spread 12 in. White waxy flowers tipped with green hang from arching stems in spring to summer and are followed by blue/black berries. Oval to lance-shaped, midgreen leaves.

☠ *Polygonatum odoratum* syn. *Polygonatum officinale*
Angular Solomon's Seal
Hardy perennial. Ht 24 in., spread 12 in. Produces pairs of fragrant tubular bell-shaped, green-tipped white flowers in spring, which are followed by blue/black berries. Oval to lance-shaped midgreen leaves.
Zone 4.

 cultivation

Propagation
Seed
In fall, sow fresh seeds into prepared seed or plug module trays using a standard seed compost mixed in equal parts with fine composted bark. Cover with compost then with glass and leave outside for the winter. Remove the glass as soon as germination starts in early spring. Once the seedlings are large enough to handle, plant out into a well-prepared site, and water regularly throughout the first season.

Division
This is a far more reliable method of propagation. Divide established plants in spring or fall. Replant into a prepared site in the garden.

Pests and Diseases
If you notice clean-cut holes in the leaves it is likely to be the sawfly caterpillar. This will not irreversibly damage the plant, but it can look devastated. Pick the larvae off or treat with soft insecticidal soap, although this is unlikely to completely eradicate the caterpillars.

Maintenance
Spring When the soil is damp, divide established plants.
Summer Make sure the soil does not dry out, and water if necessary.
Fall Sow fresh seeds, divide established plants.
Winter Protect with a layer of mulch if the winter has a prolonged frost below 14°F.

Garden Cultivation
Plant in a cool shady position in fertile well-drained soil. Dig the soil over before planting with some well-rotted leaf mold, and each winter top dress with extra leaf mold. This plant looks much better planted in large drifts than as single plants.

Harvesting
In the fall, after the foliage has died back, dig up and dry the roots for medicinal use from a well-established 3-year-old plant.

 container growing

Solomon's seal can be successfully grown in a container. Use a soilless potting compost and top dress in fall with well-rotted leaf mold. Position the container in semi-shade and water regularly throughout the summer months.

 medicinal

The powdered roots and rhizomes make a good poultice for bruises, inflammation and wounds and a good skin wash for rashes and blemishes.

 other uses

The plant has for centuries been employed as a cosmetic to clear freckles and as a skin tonic.

 warning

All parts of the plant are poisonous and should be taken internally only under the supervision of a qualified medicinal or herbal practitioner. Large doses can be harmful.

Primula veris
COWSLIP

Also known as St Peter's Keys, Palsywort, Coweslop, Fair Bells and Keys of Heaven. From the family Primulaceae.

This traditional herb is a native of Northern and Central Europe. In America the plant that is called cowslip is in fact the English marsh marigold *(Caltha palustris)* and is not to be confused with the above. A legend of northern Europe is that St Peter let his keys to Heaven drop when he learned that a duplicate set had been made. Where they fell the cowslip grew, hence the common name Keys of Heaven.

Dried cowslips

 varieties

Primula veris
Cowslip
Hardy perennial. Ht and spread 6–8 in. Tight clusters of fragrant tubular, yellow flowers produced on stout stems in spring. Oval midgreen leaves. Cowslips are often mistaken for oxlip (*P. elatior*), which is a hybrid of the cowslip and the primrose (*P. vulgaris*). Oxlips have large pale yellow flowers in a one-sided cluster. **Zone 5.**

 cultivation

Propagation
Seed
Sow fresh seed in fall on to the surface of prepared plug module trays or small pots, using a standard seed compost. Cover with perlite or a piece of glass. Place in a cold frame or cold greenhouse. Germination takes 4 to 6 weeks. If covered with glass, remove immediately when you see the seeds break. Winter the young plants in the cold frame or cold greenhouse before planting out in the following spring. If you sow old seed in winter you will need to stratify the seed

(the cold treatment; see p. 644) to enable the seed to germinate.

Division
All *Primula* divide easily and this is by far the easiest method of propagation. Divide established plants in early fall either using two hand forks back-to-back or by digging up a clump, dividing by hand and replanting into a prepared site 6 in. apart.

Ensure plants bought come from a cultivated source and are not dug from the wild.

Pests and Diseases
The scourge of all *Primula* plants, when grown in containers, is the vine weevil. To eradicate in pots water with nematodes, following the manufacturer's instructions, in spring and fall when the soil temperature does not fall below 40°F.

Maintenance
Spring Clear winter debris from around plants.
Summer Deadhead if you do not require seeds.
Fall Collect fresh seeds and sow. Divide established plants.
Winter No need for protection.

Garden Cultivation
Plant cowslips in semi-shade or sun, in a moist but well-drained soil. They look better grown in clumps and drifts rather than singularly.

Harvesting
I am sure I do not need to remind you, please do not dig up wild plants. This is prohibited in many countries. Pick leaves and flowers as required to use fresh. Dig up the roots of cultivated cowslips for drying in fall.

 container growing

Cowslips adapt happily to being grown in containers outside. Use a soilless potting mix. Protect the container from the midday sun.

 culinary

Use young leaves and flowers in salads, the leaves can also be added to meat stuffings. The flowers can be used to make wine.

 medicinal

A tea made from the flowers is a simple remedy for insomnia and nervous tension. Cowslip syrup was a country remedy for palsy, hence the common name palsywort. The roots have a high saponin content and are used to treat whooping cough and bronchitis.

 warning

Primula veris is renowned for causing contact dermatitis.

Primula vulgaris
PRIMROSE

Primrose tisane

Also known as Early Rose, Easter Rose, First Rose and May Flower. From the family Primulaceae.

This herald of spring is a native of Europe. The name Primrose originates from the Latin *prima*, meaning "first" and *rosa*, meaning "rose."

In the Middle Ages, concoctions were made from primroses which were used as a remedy for gout and rheumatism.

Due to the encouragement of sympathetic farming practices, one can now again see this once-endangered wild flower in the hedgerows. However it is still illegal to pick or dig this flower in the wild.

soil. They look better grown in clumps and drifts rather than singly. When growing primroses in a wild garden, delay cutting the grass until midsummer, which is after the plants have self-seeded.

Harvesting
In spring pick young leaves and flowers to use fresh. In summer collect seed for immediate sowing.

 ## varieties

Primula vulgaris
Primrose
Hardy perennial. Ht and spread 6 in. The fresh yellow, sweetly scented flowers with darker yellow centers are borne singly on hairy stems in early spring. Midgreen, wrinkled, oval leaves. **Zone 6.**

 ## cultivation

Propagation
Seed
Sow fresh seed, while it is still green and before it becomes dry and turns brown, in late summer on to the surface of prepared plug module trays or small pots, using a standard seed compost. Cover with perlite or a piece of glass. Place in a cold frame or cold greenhouse. Germination takes 4 to 6 weeks. If covered with glass, remove when you see the seeds break. Winter the young plants in the cold frame or cold greenhouse before planting out in the following spring. If you sow dry brown seeds in winter you will

need to stratify the seed (the cold treatment, see p. 644). Be patient, it can take 2 years to germinate.

Division
All *Primula* divide easily, and this is by far the easiest method of propagation. Divide established plants in early fall either using two hand forks back-to-back or by digging up a clump, dividing by hand and replanting into a prepared site 6 in. apart.

Pests and Diseases
The scourge of all *Primula* plants, when grown in containers, is the vine weevil. To eradicate in pots, water with nematodes, following the manufacturer's instructions, in spring and fall when the soil temperature does not fall below 40°F.

Maintenance
Spring Plant out fall-germinated plants.
Summer Sow fresh seed.
Fall Divide established plants.
Winter No need for protection.

Garden Cultivation
Plant primroses in semi-shade, under a deciduous tree or near hedgerows, in a moist but well-drained

 ## container growing

Primroses adapt happily to being grown in containers outside and are a great pick me up as they flower early in spring. Use a soilless potting mix. Position the container in semi-shade.

 ## culinary

The flowers are lovely in green salads, and they can be crystallized to decorate desserts and cakes. The young leaves make an interesting vegetable when steamed and tossed in butter.

 ## medicinal

Medicinally this herb is rarely used today. However, if nothing else is available, a tisane made from the leaves and flowers can be used as a mild sedative.

 ## warning

Primulas are renowned for causing contact dermatitis.

PROSTANTHERA

Prostanthera

Also known as Mint Bush. From the family Lamiaceae.

These highly attractive aromatic shrubs are natives of Australia.

I have fallen in love with these most generous of flowerers. When I was exhibiting one in flower at the Chelsea Flower Show, some member of the public fell in love with it in equal measure and tried to liberate it from my display!

I can find no historical references other than in the RHS *Dictionary of Gardening*, which states that the generic name, *Prostanthera*, comes from *prostithemi*, "to append," and *anthera*, meaning "anther," the pollen-bearing part of the stamen. This therefore alludes to the appendages usually borne by the anthers.

Prostanthera ovalifolia

Pests and Diseases
Over-watering young plants causes root rot — a killer.

Maintenance
Spring Take cuttings.
Summer Cut back after flowering only if necessary.
Fall Protect from frosts.
Winter Protect from hard frosts and excessive water.

Garden Cultivation
In cool climates with persistent frosts they are better grown in a container. However, if your climate is mild, plant out in the spring in a warm corner, in a lime-free, well-draining soil at a distance of 2–3 ft. apart. Rain combined with frost is the killer in winter. If you want to make a low hedge out of *Prostanthera cuneata* then plant specimens 18 in. apart.

Harvesting
Pick leaves in the summer after flowering for drying and inclusion in potpourris.

 container growing

This is a real crowd puller when in flower, and even when not, makes a most attractive aromatic plant. Use a soilless compost mixed with 25 percent composted fine bark and 25 percent peat. Keep young plants on the dry side, but water freely in the growing season.

 medicinal

I am sure that a plant such as *P. cuneata* that gives off as much scent, and has obviously so much oil in the leaf, will one day have some use.

Prostanthera lasianthos

 varieties

Prostanthera cuneata
Evergreen half-hardy perennial. Ht and spread 2–3 ft. Very attractive white flowers with purple spots that look rather like little orchids; late spring, early summer. Round, dark green, slightly leathery and shiny, mint-scented leaves. Can withstand a minimum temperature of 28°F. **Zone 10.**

Prostanthera lasianthos
Victorian Christmas bush.
Evergreen large shrub. Ht 3–18 ft. Profuse sprays of white pale lilac flowers. Long narrow toothed menthol-scented green leaves. **Zone 9.**

Prostanthera ovalifolia
Evergreen tender perennial. Reaches a height and spread of 4 ft. in its native country. Attractive purple flowers on short leafy racemes throughout spring and summer. Dark green aromatic leaves. Can only withstand a minimum temperature of 41°F. **Zone 10.**

Prostanthera rotundifolia "Rosea"
Evergreen half-hardy perennial. A small tree up to 10 ft. tall in its native country; in cooler climates it's a lot smaller. Pretty mauve/purple flowers in spring that last a long time. The dark green leaves (not as dark as *P. cuneata*) are round and mint-scented. Withstands a minimum temperature of 32°F. **Zone 10.**

 cultivation

Propagation
Cuttings
Take cuttings in spring or late summer. Use a standard seed compost mixed in equal parts with composted fine bark. When the cuttings are well-rooted, in 8 to 12 weeks, repot again using the same mix and keep in containers for the first year.

SELF HEAL

Prunella vulgaris

Also known as Carpenter's Herb, Sticklewort, Touch and Heal, All Heal, Woundwort, Hercules' Woundwort, Blue Curls, Brownwort and Hock Heal. From the family Lamiaceae.

This herb is found growing wild throughout all the temperate regions of the northern hemisphere, including Europe, Asia and North America. It is found on moist, loamy, well-drained soils, in grassland, pastures and open woodland, especially in sunny situations. Now introduced into China and Australia.

In strict 16th-century adherence to the Doctrine of Signatures, whereby it was believed that every plant bore an outward sign of its value to mankind, people noted that the upper lip of the flower was shaped like a hook, and as billhooks and sickles were a main cause of wounds in their agrarian society, they decided that the purpose of the herb was to heal wounds (hence Self Heal). They also saw the shape of the throat in the flower, which was why it was introduced to treat diseases of the throat such as quinsy and diphtheria, a propensity with a precedent in ancient Greece, where physicians used it to cure sore throats and tonsillitis.

 ## varieties

Prunella vulgaris
Self Heal
Hardy perennial. Ht 2–12 in., spread 6–12 in. Clusters of blue/purple flowers all summer. Oval leaves of a bright green. There is a much rarer white-flowered species, *Prunella laciniata*, which has very deeply cut leaves.

 ## cultivation

Propagation
Seed
Sow the small seeds into prepared seed or plug trays in either spring or fall and cover with perlite; no extra heat is required. If an fall sowing, winter the young plants in a cold frame. In spring, when the plants are large enough, plant out at a distance of 6–8 in. apart.

Division
This plant grows runners that have their own small root systems and is, therefore, easy to divide. Dig up in the spring or fall, and split and replant either in the garden or amongst grass.

Garden Cultivation
This plant, which is easy to establish, makes a colorful ground cover with attractive flowers. It is happy in full sun to semi-shade and will grow in most soils, including those that are rather acid, though it does best if the soil is fertile. It can be grown in a lawn, and while the mower keeps its spread and height in check, it will still flower and be much visited by bees and butterflies.

Pests and Diseases
In most cases it is free from pests and diseases.

Maintenance
Spring Sow seed. Divide established plants.
Summer Cut back after flowering to curtail self-seeding.
Fall Divide established plants. Sow seeds.
Winter No need for protection, fully hardy.

Harvesting
Harvest for medicinal use only. Dry both the leaves and flowers.

 ## container growing

Self heal can be grown in containers using a soilless compost. However, as it looks a bit insipid on its own, it is better combined with plants like heartsease, poppies and cowslips. Water well during the growing season, but only feed with liquid fertilizer twice otherwise it will produce too lush a growth.

 ## medicinal

Used in herbal medicines as a gargle for sore throats and inflammation of the mouth. A decoction is used to wash cuts and to soothe burns and bruises.

Prunella vulgaris

Pulmonaria
LUNGWORT

Also known as Pulmonaria, Jerusalem Cowslip, Adam and Eve, Lady Mary's Tears, Spotted Bugloss, and Spotted Comfrey. From the family Boraginaceae.

Lungwort is a native plant of Europe and northern parts of the U.S. The markings on the leaves were attributed to the Virgin Mary's milk or her tears; however the generic name, *Pulmonaria*, comes from *pulmo*, meaning "lung." The Doctrine of Signatures, which held that each plant must be associated either by appearance, smell or habit, with the disease which it was said to heal, thought that the leaves resembled a diseased lung so used it to treat various lung disorders with some success.

 ## varieties

Pulmonaria angustifolia
Semi-evergreen hardy perennial. Ht 21 in., spread 12–18 in. Pink flowers which turn to bright blue in spring. Lance-shaped midgreen leaves with no markings. **Zone 3.**

Pulmonaria longifolia
Hardy perennial. Ht 12 in., spread 18 in. Pink flowers which turn purplish-blue in spring. Lance-shaped, slightly hairy, dark green leaves with white spots. **Zone 4.**

Pulmonaria officinalis
Lungwort
Semi-evergreen hardy perennial. Ht 12 in., spread 24 in. Pink flowers which turn blue in spring. Oval leaves with blotchy white/cream markings on a midgreen slightly hairy surface. **Zone 6.**

Note The American native Virginia bluebells, *Mertensia virginica,* is known as smooth lungwort. It belongs to the same Boraginaceae family, but does not have the same medicinal properties.

 ## cultivation

Propagation
Seed
This plant rarely produces viable seed. However it has been known to self-seed erratically around the garden.

Division
This is by far the easiest way to propagate this herb. Divide established plants either after flowering in late spring or alternatively in early fall using the two forks back-to-back technique.

Pests and Diseases
In long, dry, hot summers this herb can be prone to powdery mildew. Cut back and burn infected growth, and then water the plant well.

Maintenance
Spring Dig up and replant seedlings.
Summer Water well, especially if the ground is drying out.
Fall Divide established plants.
Winter No need for protection; fully hardy.

Garden Cultivation
Lungwort prefers to be planted in semi-shade and in a moist but free-draining soil, which has been well fed with leaf mold or well-rotted compost the season prior to planting. The leaf mold is particularly important if you live in a drought area or if your soil is prone to becoming excessively dry in summer.

Harvesting
For medicinal use, pick the leaves after flowering for drying.

 ## container growing

Lungwort can be grown successfully in a container as long as it has enough room for the creeping rhizomes to spread. Use a soilless potting compost in a frost-hardy container. Winter the plants outside; if brought in they become prone to mildew.

 ## medicinal

Lungwort is a soothing expectorant. The silica contained in the leaves was traditionally used to restore the elasticity of the lungs. Externally the leaves have been used for healing all kinds of wounds.

 ## warning

Like many in the Boraginaceae family, lungwort has leaves that can cause contact dermatitis.

Lungwort potpourri

Rheum palmatum
CHINESE RHUBARB

 Also known as Da Huang. From the family Polygonaceae.

To many people rhubarb may seem a curiously English fruit; it is in fact a vegetable and an important medicinal herb, native to China and Tibet where it has been used for over 2,000 years to treat many digestive problems. It was first mentioned in the Shen Nong *Canon of Herbs* which was written in the Han dynasty (206 CE to AD 23).

 medicinal

The rhizomes are used to improve digestion, for liver and gall bladder complaints, and as a laxative. It can be made into a mouthwash for mouth ulcers but it tastes revolting! In homeopathy it is used to treat teething children.

 other uses

Traditionally an infusion of the leaves was used as an effective spray to control aphids and to check black spots on roses. As this infusion is poisonous when used in the kitchen garden, the gardeners would not harvest the treated vegetables for a minimum of 7 days.

 varieties

☠ *Rheum palmatum*
Chinese Rhubarb
Herbaceous perennial. Ht up to 6 ft in flower, spread 24–30 in. Panicles of deep red flowers in summer followed by three-winged fruit. Large, up to 36 in., palmate, lobed midgreen leaves. Nearly round green stems are NOT edible. **Zone 5.**

 cultivation

Propagation
Division
The easiest method of propagation is by root division. To start, buy a plant from a reputable nursery. Once you have an established plant, over 3 years old, it can then be divided as necessary. Do this when the plant is dormant, in late fall. Lift the crown, then with a sharp knife or spade, divide the crown into 4 in. sections including as much root as possible and a new bud with each section. Pot up immediately into a soil-based potting compost with the bud tip just below the surface of the compost. Leave the container in a cold frame or cold greenhouse until early spring, then plant out into a previously prepared site at a distance of 30 in. apart.

Pests and Diseases
Rhubarb can suffer from crown rot, which causes the rotting of the stalks and leaves. If you see infected plants, dig up and burn and do not replant in that position again.

Maintenance
Spring Plant out divided plants.
Summer Remove flower heads once they form seeds to prevent self-seeding.
Fall Divide established plants. Feed plants with well-rotted manure.
Winter No need for protection, fully hardy.

Garden Cultivation
Plant in a sunny position, in a deep fertile soil that has been fed with well-rotted manure in the previous fall. If you are growing this herb for use medicinally it will need to stay in position for at least 6 years, so choose your site with care.

Harvesting
In the fall lift 6-year-old rhizomes for medicinal use. Either dry or create tinctures.

 container growing

Rhubarb is not ideally suited for growing in containers because of its long root system.

 culinary

Chinese rhubarb is not a culinary herb.

 warning

The leaves are very toxic; on no account eat them. Do not take as a medicine during pregnancy or when breastfeeding.

Ground Chinese rhubarb root

Ricinus communis
CASTOR BEAN

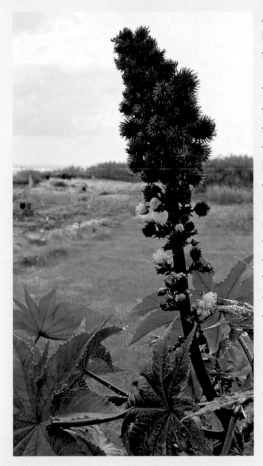

Also known as Palma-Christi, Eranda, and Rendi. From the family Euphorbiaceae.

The castor oil plant is one of the first medicinal plants known to man. Its seeds have been found in Egyptian tombs and it is mentioned in papyrus scrolls written in 1500 CE. The Greek historian Herodotus noted its use as a lamp oil, a purpose for which it is still employed in the temples of Southern India. The lampblack produced by the combination of castor oil with wicks dipped in herbal preparations, has provided the universal eye cosmetic of India known as kohl. In the 18th century this herb became popular in Europe as a laxative.

Pests and Diseases
This herb rarely suffers from disease and is not affected by pests; because the leaves have insecticidal properties, it actually repels insects.

Maintenance
Spring Sow seeds.
Summer Stake flowering heads in exposed sites.
Fall Harvest seeds.
Winter When grown as an annual, feed soil where the plant was grown.

Garden Cultivation
This frost-tender fast-growing evergreen shrub is often grown just for its attractive foliage in the garden. Plant in a sheltered position in full sun, in a rich fertile soil. It may need support in exposed areas.

Harvesting
The seed capsules can be gathered throughout the year when nearly ripe and then put out in the sun to dry and mature before the oil is extracted.

 ## companion planting

It is reputedly a good mole repellent.

 ## medicinal

The oil extracted from the seeds is well known for its strong laxative properties. It is also used as a massage oil in India where it is used on tender joints.

 ## other uses

The oil extracted from the seeds is used in numerous ways: in the manufacture of high-grade lubricants, as a fabric coating, as a leather preservative and in the manufacturing of inks, dyes and fibres.

 ## warning

Do not eat the seeds: they are extremely poisonous. Do not take castor oil during pregnancy. Wear gloves when handling this plant, because it can cause an allergic reaction.

 ## varieties

☠ *Ricinus communis*
Castor oil plant
Half-hardy evergreen shrub, grown as an annual in cool climates. Ht up to 12 ft. The separate male and female flowers are borne together in dense upright branching heads. The male flowers have yellow stamens and the green petal-less female flowers have beard-like red stigmas, which are followed by fruits each containing 3 seeds. The seeds are poisonous. The large palmate leaves when young are often red, turning green as they mature. **Warmer zones.**

 ## cultivation

Propagation
Seed
Sow the large, fresh seeds, in early spring individually into prepared pots or module plug trays using a standard seed compost mixed in equal parts with perlite. As the seeds are large, push them into the compost and cover with perlite. Place under protection at 70°F; germination takes 14 to 21 days. Once large enough to handle, repot using a standard soilless potting mix. Plant into a prepared site in the garden once the night time temperature does not drop below 50°F. When grown in cool climates it will die with the first frosts. Wearing gloves, clear the plant from the ground, dig the site over and feed with well-rotted manure.

Rosmarinus officinalis
ROSEMARY

Rosmarinus officinalis "Majorca Pink"

From the family Lamiaceae.

Rosemary is a shrub that originated in the Mediterranean area and is now widely cultivated throughout the temperate regions. The ancient Latin name means sea-dew. This may come from its habit of growing close to the sea and the dew-like appearance of its blossom at a distance. It is steeped in myth, magic and folk medicinal use. One of my favorite stories about rosemary comes from Spain. It relates that originally the blue flowers were white. When the Holy family fled into Egypt, the Virgin Mary had to hide from some soldiers, so she spread her cloak over a rosemary bush and knelt behind it. When the soldiers had gone by she stood up and removed her cloak and the blossoms turned blue in her honor. Also connected to the Christian faith is the story that rosemary will grow for 33 years, the length of Christ's life, and then die.

In Elizabethan days, the wedding couple wore or carried a sprig of rosemary as a sign of fidelity. Also bunches of rosemary were tied with colored ribbon tipped with gold and given to guests at weddings to symbolize love and faithfulness.

Rosemary was burnt in sick chambers to freshen and purify the air. Branches were strewn in courts of law as a protection from jail fever. During the plague people used to wear it in neck pouches to sniff as they traveled, and in Victorian times it was carried in the hollow handles of walking sticks for the same reasons.

 varieties

Rosmarinus officinalis
Rosemary
Evergreen hardy perennial. Ht and spread 3 ft. Pale blue flowers in early spring to early summer and then sometimes in early fall. Needle-shaped dark green leaves are highly aromatic. **Zone 8.**

Rosmarinus officinalis var. albiflorus
White Rosemary
Evergreen hardy perennial. Ht and spread 32 in. White flowers in early spring to early summer and then sometimes in early fall. Needle-shaped dark green leaves are highly aromatic. **Zone 8.**

Rosmarinus officinalis var. angustissimus "Benenden Blue"
Benenden Blue Rosemary
Evergreen hardy perennial. Ht and spread 32 in. Dark blue flowers in early spring to early summer and then sometimes again in early fall. Leaves are fine needles and fairly dense on the stem, good aroma. **Zone 8.**

Rosmarinus officinalis "Blue Lagoon"

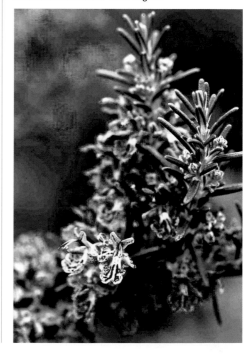

Rosmarinus officinalis "Aureus"
Golden Rosemary

Evergreen hardy perennial. Ht 32 in., spread 24 in. It hardly ever flowers, but if it does they are pale blue. The thin needle leaves are green splashed with gold. If you did not know better you would think the plant was suffering from a virus. It still looks very attractive. **Zone 8.**

Rosmarinus officinalis "Blue Lagoon"
Blue Lagoon Rosemary

Evergreen hardy perennial. Ht 16 in., spread 32 in. Striking small dark blue flowers in spring. Short dark green needle-shaped aromatic leaves. Arching semi-prostate habit. **Zone 8.**

Rosmarinus officinalis "Boule"
Boule Rosemary

Evergreen hardy perennial. Ht 12 in., spread 32 in. Small mid-blue flowers in spring. Short, dark green needle-shaped aromatic leaves with a white underside. Prostate hanging habit. Ideal for walls and containers. **Zone 8.**

Rosmarinus officinalis "Fota Blue"
Fota Blue Rosemary

Evergreen hardy perennial. Ht and spread 32 in. Very attractive dark blue flowers in early spring to early summer and then sometimes again in early fall. Very well-spaced, narrow, needle-like dark green leaves; the plant has a fairly prostrate habit. **Zone 8.**

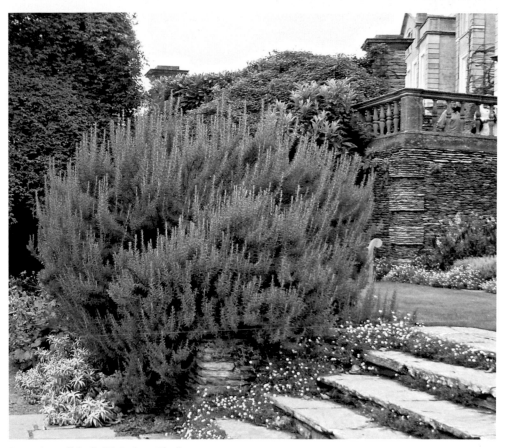

Rosmarinus officinalis "Sissinghurst Blue"

Rosmarinus officinalis "Majorca Pink"
Majorcan Pink Rosemary

Evergreen half-hardy perennial. Ht and spread 32 in. Pink flowers in early spring to early summer and then sometimes again in early fall. The needle-shaped dark green leaves are highly aromatic. This is a slightly prostrate form of rosemary. **Zone 8.**

Rosmarinus officinalis "Miss Jessopp's Upright"
Miss Jessopp's Upright Rosemary

Evergreen hardy perennial. Ht and spread 2m. Very pale blue flowers in early spring to early summer and then sometimes again in early fall. This rosemary has a very upright habit, making it ideal for hedges (see p. 382). The leaves are dark green needles spaced closely together, making the plant very bushy. **Zone 8.**

Rosmarinus officinalis "Primley Blue"
Primley Blue Rosemary

(Not Frimley, which it has been incorrectly called for a few years.)
Evergreen hardy perennial. Ht and spread 32 in. Blue flowers in early spring to early summer and then sometimes again in early fall. The needle-shaped dark green leaves are highly aromatic. This is a good hardy bushy variety. **Zone 8.**

Rosmarinus officinalis "Roseus"

Rosmarinus officinalis Prostratus Group
Prostrate Rosemary

Evergreen hardy perennial. Ht 12 in., spread 3 ft. Light blue flowers in early spring to early summer and then sometimes again in early fall. The needle-shaped dark green leaves are highly aromatic. This is a great plant for trailing on a wall or bank. **Zone 8.**

Rosmarinus officinalis "Roseus"
Pink Rosemary

Evergreen half-hardy perennial. Ht and spread 32 in. Pink flowers in early spring to early summer and then sometimes again in early fall. The needle-shaped dark green leaves are highly aromatic. **Zone 8.**

Rosmarinus officinalis "Severn Sea" AGM
Severn Seas Rosemary

Evergreen half-hardy perennial. Ht and spread 32 in. Mid-blue flowers in early spring to early summer and sometimes again in early fall. Highly aromatic needle-shaped dark green leaves. The whole plant has a slightly prostrate habit with arching branches. **Zone 8.**

Rosmarinus officinalis "Sissinghurst Blue" AGM
Sissinghurst Rosemary

Evergreen hardy perennial. Ht 5 ft., spread 3 ft. Light blue flowers in early spring to early summer and then sometimes again in early fall. The plant has an upright habit and grows very bushy. The needle-shaped dark green leaves are highly aromatic. **Zone 8.**

cultivation

Propagation

Seed

Rosmarinus officinalis can, with care, be grown from seed. It needs a bottom heat of 80–90°F to be successful. Sow in the spring in prepared seed or plug trays, using a standard seed compost mixed in equal parts with composted fine bark, and cover with perlite. Having got it to germinate, be careful not to overwater the seedlings as they are prone to damping off. Harden off the young plant slowly in summer and repot. Keep it in a pot for the first winter, and plant out the following spring into the required position at a distance of 2–3 ft. apart.

Cuttings

As cultivated varieties do not come true from seed, this is a more reliable method of propagation as it ensures that you achieve the variety you require.

Softwood: Take these in spring off the new growth. Cut lengths of about 6 in. Use a standard seed compost mixed in equal parts with composted fine bark.

Semi-hardwood: Take these in summer from the nonflowering shoots, using the same compost as for softwood cuttings.

Rosmarinus officinalis "Fota Blue"

Rosmarinus officinalis Prostratus Group

Layering

Layer established branches in summer.

Pests and Diseases

Rosemary beetle and its larvae feed on the leaves from fall until spring. Place some newspaper underneath the plant, then tap or shake the branches, which will knock the beetles and larvae on to the paper, making them easy to destroy.

Maintenance

Spring Trim after flowering. Sow seeds of *Rosamarinus officinalis*. Take softwood cuttings.
Summer Feed container plants. Take semi-hardwood cuttings. Layer plants.
Fall Protect young tender plants.
Winter Put a mulch, or straw or agricultural fleece around all plants.

Garden Cultivation

Rosemary requires a well-drained soil in a sheltered sunny position. It is frost hardy but in cold areas it prefers to grow against a warm, sunny wall. If the plant is young it is worth giving some added protection in winter. If trimming is necessary cut back only when the frosts are over; if possible leave it until after the spring flowering. Sometimes rosemary looks a bit scorched after frosts, in which case it is worth cutting the damaged plants to healthy wood in spring. Straggly old plants may also be cut back hard at the same time. Never cut back plants in the fall or if there is any chance of frost, as the plant will be damaged or even killed. On average, despite the story about rosemary growing for 33 years, it is best to replace bushes every 5 to 6 years.

Harvesting

As rosemary is evergreen, you can pick fresh leaves all year round as long as you are not greedy. If you need large quantities then harvest in summer and either dry the leaves or make an oil or vinegar.

Hedges

Rosemary certainly makes an effective hedge; it looks pretty in flower, smells marvelous and is evergreen. In fact it has everything going for it if you have the right soil conditions which, more importantly than ever, must be well drained and carry a bias towards lime. The best varieties for hedges are *R.o.* "Primley Blue" and *R.o.* "Miss Jessopp's Upright." Both are upright, hardy and bushy. *R.o.* "Primley Blue" has a darker blue flower and I think is slightly prettier. Planting distance 18 in. apart. Again, if you need eventually to trim the hedge, do it after the spring flowering.

companion planting

If planted near carrots it is reputed to repel carrot fly. It is also said to be generally beneficial to sage.

container growing

Rosemary does well in pots and this is the preferred way to grow it in cold districts. The prostrate and less hardy varieties look very attractive and benefit from the extra protection offered by a container. Use a soilless compost mixed in equal parts with composted fine bark, and make sure the compost is well drained. Do not overwater, and feed only after flowering.

Rosmarinus officinalis "Boule"

ROSEMARY

Rosemary infusion

other uses

Put rosemary twigs on the grill; they give off a delicious aroma. If you have a wood-burning stove, a few twigs thrown onto it makes the whole house smell lovely. Rosemary is used in many herbal shampoos and the plant has a long reputation as a hair tonic. Use an infusion in the final rinse of a hair wash, especially if you have dark hair, as it will make it shine. (Use chamomile for fair hair.)

medicinal

Like many other essential oils, rosemary oil has antibacterial and antifungal properties, and it helps poor circulation if rubbed into the affected joints. The oil may be used externally as an insect repellent. It also makes an excellent remedy for headaches if applied directly to the head. Rosemary tea makes a good mouthwash for halitosis and is also a good antiseptic gargle. Drunk in small amounts it reduces flatulence and stimulates the smooth muscle of the digestive tract and gall bladder and increases the flow of bile. Put a teaspoon of chopped leaves into a cup and pour on boiling water; cover and leave it to stand for 5 minutes. An antiseptic solution of rosemary can be added to the bath to promote heathy skin. Boil a handful in 2 quarts of water for 10 minutes.

warning

The oil should not be used internally. Also, extremely large doses of the leaf are toxic, possibly causing abortion, convulsions and, very rarely, death.

culinary

This is one of the most useful of culinary herbs, combining well with meat, especially lamb, casseroles, tomato sauces, baked fish, rice, salads, egg dishes, apples, summer wine cups, cordials, vinegars and oils.

Vegetarian Goulash
Serves 4

2 tablespoons rosemary olive oil
2 medium onions, sliced
2 teaspoons whole-wheat flour
1 tablespoon paprika
1 ¼ cups hot water mixed with 1 teaspoon
   tomato paste
14-oz. can Italian tomatoes
2 sprigs rosemary, 4 in. long
1 ¼ cups cauliflower sprigs
1 ¼ cups new carrots, washed and cut
   into chunks
1 ¼ cups new potatoes, washed and cut into
   halves
½ green bell pepper, seeded and chopped
½ cup sour cream or Greek yogurt
Salt and freshly milled black pepper

Heat the rosemary oil in a flameproof casserole or Dutch oven, fry the onions until soft, then stir in the flour and three-quarters of the paprika. Cook for 2 minutes. Stir in the water, tomatoes and sprigs of rosemary. Bring to a boil stirring all the time. Add all the vegetables and the seasonings. Cover and bake in the preheated oven (375°F) for 30 to 40 minutes. Remove from the oven, carefully take out the rosemary sprigs and stir in the sour cream or yogurt, plus the remaining paprika. Serve with fresh pasta and/or garlic bread.

SORREL

Rumex acetosa seed

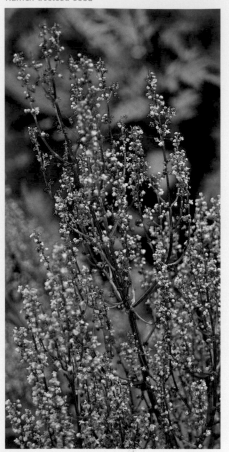

Also known as Bread and Cheese, Sour Leaves, Tom Thumbs, Thousand Fingers and Sour Sauce. From the family Polygonaceae. Sorrel is a native plant of Europe, Asia and North America. It has naturalized in many countries throughout the world on rich, damp, loamy, acid soils. The generic name, *Rumex*, comes from the Latin *rumo,* "I suck." Apparently, Roman soldiers sucked the leaves to relieve thirst, and their doctors used them as a diuretic.

The name sorrel comes from the old French word *surelle,* meaning "sour." The Tudors considered the herb to be one of the best English vegetables; Henry VIII held it in great esteem. In Lapland, sorrel juice has been used instead of rennet to curdle milk.

Rumex scutatus

spring. Sow into prepared seed or plug trays, using a standard seed compost mixed in equal parts with composted fine bark, and covering the seeds with perlite. Germination is fairly quick, 10 to 20 days without extra heat. When the seedlings are large enough and the soil has started to warm up, plant out 12 in. apart.

Division
Sorrel is easy to divide and it is a good idea to divide broad-leaf sorrel every other year to keep the leaves succulent. Fall is the best time to do this, replanting in a prepared site.

Pests and Diseases
Wood pigeons, slugs and occasionally leaf miners attack sorrel, but should cause no problems with established plants. Remove the affected leaves, and put out traps for the slugs.

Maintenance
Spring Sow seed, under protection, in early spring and outdoors from midspring.
Summer Cut off flowers to maintain leaf production and prevent self-seeding. In a hot summer, water regularly to keep the leaves succulent.
Fall Divide established plants.
Winter Fully hardy.

Garden Cultivation
This perennial herb likes a rich acid soil which retains moisture in full sun to partial shade. Sow the seeds in late spring into a prepared site. When germinated,

 varieties

Rumex acetosa
Sorrel
Also known as broad-leafed sorrel, common sorrel, garden sorrel, meadow sorrel, and confusingly (see below), French sorrel. Hardy perennial. Ht 2–4 ft., spread 12 in. The flowers are small, dull and inconspicuous; color greenish, turning reddish-brown as the fruit ripens. The midgreen leaves are lance-shaped with two basal lobes pointing backwards. **Zone 3.**

Rumex acetosella
Sheep's Sorrel
Hardy perennial. Ht 6–12 in., spread indefinite (can be very invasive). The flowers are small, dull and inconspicuous; color greenish, turning brown as the fruit ripens. The midgreen leaves are shaped like a

barbed spear. It grows wild on heaths and in grassy places, but is rarely found on chalky soil. **Zone 3.**

Rumex scutatus
Buckler-Leaf Sorrel
Also known as French sorrel. Hardy perennial. Ht 6–18 in., spread 24 in. The flowers are small, dull and inconspicuous; color greenish, turning brown as the fruit ripens. The midgreen leaves are shaped like squat shields. **Zone 3.**
Rumex scutatus "Silver Shield" is a variegated form of *Rumex scutatus.*

 cultivation

Propagation
Seed
For an early crop start off under protection in early

they seedling out to a distance of 3 in. and finally to a distance of 12 in. apart. Can be grown under cloches to provide leaf throughout the year. The plant tends to go to seed quickly so, to keep the leaves fresh and succulent, remove flowerheads as they appear. In really warm summers or generally warm climates, sorrel leaves tend to become bitter as the season progresses. A mulch will keep the soil cooler and, once the season cools down, the flavor will improve. Grow buckler-leaf sorrel with its smaller leaf, as it is less susceptible. If sorrel is causing a problem in your garden simply add a few applications of lime to eradicate it.

Harvesting
Pick young leaves throughout the growing season for fresh use and for freezing. Sorrel does not dry well.

 container growing

The buckler variety makes a good low-growing pot plant. Use a soilless compost mixed in equal parts with composted fine bark, and make sure the container has room for the plant to spread. It is a very useful culinary herb, so for those with a small garden or who live on a chalk soil this makes an ideal container plant. Remember to keep cutting off flowers to keep leaves tender. Water well in the growing season, and feed with liquid fertilizer, especially if you are picking a lot.

 medicinal

Sorrel is considered to have blood cleansing and blood improving qualities in a similar way to spinach, which improves the haemoglobin content of the blood. It also contains vitamin C. A leaf may be used in a poultice to treat certain skin complaints, including acne.

 other uses

Sorrel is a good dye plant; with an alum mordant it makes a yellow or green dye (see also pages 675). Use juice of the leaf to remove rust, mold and ink stains from linen, wicker and silver.

 warning

Care has to be taken that sorrel is not used in too great a quantity or too frequently. Its oxalic acid content may be damaging to health if taken in excess. Very large doses are poisonous, causing severe kidney damage. The herb should not be used medicinally by those predisposed to rheumatism, arthritis, gout, kidney stones or gastric hyperacidity. The leaf may cause dermatitis.

Rumex scutatus "Silver Shield"

Sorrel and lettuce soup

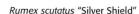 culinary

This is an excellent herb with which to experiment. Use sparingly in soups, omelets, fish sauces and with poultry and pork. It is useful for tenderizing meat. Wrap it around steaks or add pounded leaf to a marinade. Eat leaves raw in salads, especially the buckler-leaf sorrel, but reduce the vinegar or lemon in any accompanying dressing to compensate for the increased acidity. Cook like spinach, changing the cooking water once to reduce acidity.

A Green Sauce

Wash a handful each of sorrel and lettuce leaves and a handful of watercress. Cook in a little water with a whole peeled onion until tender. Remove onion and discard. Allow the (mushy) leaves to cool then add 1 tablespoon of olive oil, 1 tablespoon of wine vinegar, pepper and salt. Stir until creamy. Serve with fish or cold poultry.

Sorrel and Lettuce Soup
Serves 4

½ cup sorrel
½ cup lettuce
¼ cup Italian parsley
4 tablespoons butter
½ cup potatoes, peeled and sliced
1 cup chicken broth
4 tablespoons thin cream

Wash the sorrel, lettuce and Italian parsley, pat dry and roughly chop. Heat the butter in a heavy pan and add the sorrel, lettuce and parsley. Stew very gently for about 5 minutes, and then add the potato. Mix all together, pour over the heated broth and simmer covered for 25 minutes. Put in a liquidizer, or, if you are a purist, through a coarse food mill. Return to the pan and heat gently (do not boil). Swirl in some cream just before serving.

Ruta graveolens
RUE

Also known as Herb of Grace and Herbygrass. From the family Rutaceae.

Rue is a native of Southern Europe, especially the Mediterranean region, and is found growing in poor, free-draining soil. It has established itself in North America and Australia in similar conditions. It has also adapted to cooler climates and is now naturalized in Northern Europe. Rue was known as herb of grace, perhaps because it was regarded as a protector against the Devil, witchcraft and magic.

It was also used as an antidote against every kind of poison from toadstools to snake bites. The Romans brought it across northern Europe to Britain, where it did not gain favor until the Middle Ages, when it was one of the herbs carried in nosegays by the rich as protection from evil and the plague. Also, like rosemary, it was placed near the judge before prisoners were brought out, as protection from the pestilence-ridden jails and jail fever.

It was famous for preserving eyesight and was said to promote second sight, perhaps acting on the third eye. Both Leonardo da Vinci and Michelangelo are supposed to have said that their inner vision had been enhanced by this herb.

Ruta graveolens

 varieties

Ruta graveolens
Rue
Hardy evergreen perennial. Ht and spread 24 in. Yellow waxy flowers with four or five petals in summer. Small rounded lobed leaves of a greeny blue color. **Zone 5.**

Ruta graveolens "Jackman's Blue"
Rue Jackman's Blue
Hardy evergreen perennial. Ht and spread 24 in. Yellow waxy flowers with four or five petals in summer. Small rounded lobed leaves of a distinctive blue color. **Zone 5.**

Ruta graveolens "Variegata"
Variegated Rue
Hardy evergreen perennial. Ht and spread 24 in. Yellow waxy flowers with four or five petals in summer. Small rounded lobed leaves with a most distinctive cream/white variegation, which is particularly marked in spring, fading in the summer unless the plant is kept well clipped. I have known people mistake the variegation for flowers and try to smell them, which shows how attractive this plant is. Smelling it at close quarters is not, however, a good idea as this plant, like other rues, can cause the skin to blister. **Zone 6.**

Ruta graveolens "Jackman's Blue"

 cultivation

Propagation

Seed

In spring sow the fine seed using the cardboard trick (see p. 645) in prepared plug or seed trays. Use a standard seed compost mixed in equal parts with composted fine bark, and cover with perlite. You may find that a bottom heat of 68°F is helpful. Germination can be an all or nothing affair, depending on the source of the seed. Young seedlings are prone to damping off, so watch the watering, and just keep the compost damp, not wet. Unlike many variegated plants, the variegated rue will be variegated from seed. When the seedlings are large enough, plant out into a prepared site in the garden at a distance of 18 in.

Cuttings

Take cuttings of new shoots in spring or early summer. "Jackman's Blue" can only be propagated from cuttings. Use a standard seed compost mixed in equal parts with composted fine bark for the cuttings; again, do not overwater.

Pests and Diseases

Rue is prone to whitefly followed by black sooty mold. Treat the whitefly with a liquid insecticidal soap as soon as the pest appears, following manufacturer's

Ruta graveolens "Variegata"

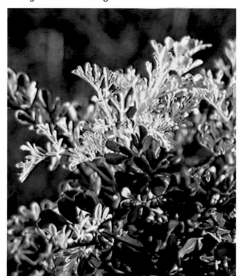

instructions. This should then also control the sooty mold.

Maintenance

Spring Cut back plants to regain shape. Sow seed. Take softwood cuttings.

Summer Cut back after flowering to maintain shape.

Fall The variegated rue is slightly more tender than the other two varieties, so protect when frosts go below 23°F.

Winter Rue is hardy and requires protection only in extreme conditions.

Garden Cultivation

All the rues prefer a sunny site with a well-drained poor soil. They are best positioned away from paths or at the back of beds where people won't brush against them accidentally, especially children, whose skin is more sensitive than adults. In the spring, and after flowering in the summer (not fall), cut back all the plants to maintain shape, and the variegated form to maintain variegations.

Harvesting

Pick leaves for use fresh. No need to preserve.

 container growing

Rue can be grown in containers; use a soilless compost mixed in equal parts with composted fine bark. Position the container carefully so that one does not accidentally brush the leaves. Although it is drought tolerant, in containers it prefers to be watered regularly in summer. Allow to dry in winter, watering only once a month. Feed plants in the spring with liquid fertilizer following the manufacturer's instructions.

 warning

Handling the plant can cause allergic reactions or phytophotodermatitis. If you have ever seen a rue burn, it really is quite serious, so do heed this warning. To minimize this risk do not take cuttings off the plants either when they are wet after rain or when in full sun, as this is when the plant is at its most dangerous. Wait until the plant has dried out or the sun has gone in; alternatively wear gloves.

Must only be used by medical personnel and not at all by pregnant women, as it is abortive. Large doses are toxic, sometimes precipitating mental confusion, and the oil is capable of causing death.

 culinary

I seriously cannot believe that people enjoy eating this herb; it tastes incredibly bitter. It can be added finely minced with discretion to egg, fish or cheese dishes.

 medicinal

This ancient medicinal herb is used in the treatment of strained eyes, and headaches caused by eye strain. It is also useful for nervous headaches and heart palpitations, for treating high blood pressure and helping to harden the bones and teeth. The antispasmodic action of its oil and the alkaloids explains its use in the treatment of nervous digestion and colic. The tea also expels worms.

Salvia
SAGE

From the family Lamiaceae.

"How can a man grow old who has sage in his garden?" **Ancient Proverb**

This large family of over 750 species is widely distributed throughout the world. It consists of annuals, biennials and perennials, herbs, sub-shrubs and shrubs of various habits. It is an important horticultural group. I have concentrated on the medicinal, culinary and a special aromatic species.

The name *Salvia* is derived from the Latin *salveo*, meaning "I save" or "I heal," because some species have been highly regarded medicinally. The Greeks used it to heal ulcers, consumption and snake bites. The Romans considered it a sacred herb to be gathered with ceremony. A special knife was used, not made of iron because sage reacts with iron salts. The sage gatherer had to wear clean clothes, have clean feet and make a sacrifice of food before the ceremony could begin. Sage was held to be good for the brain, the senses and memory. It also made a good gargle and mouthwash and was used as a toothpaste.

There are many stories about why the Chinese valued it so highly, and in the 17th century Dutch merchants found that the Chinese would trade three chests of China tea for one of sage leaves.

Salvia lavandulifolia

 varieties

I have only chosen a very few species to illustrate; they are the main ones used in cooking and medicine — with two exceptions, with which I begin.

Salvia argentea AGM
Silver Sage
Hardy biennial. Ht up to 18 in. in second season. Pale pinkish-white flowers in second season. Splendid large silvery gray leaves covered in long silvery white hairs. Protect from excessive rainwater.

Salvia elegans "Scarlet Pineapple" syn. S. rutilans
Pineapple Sage
Half-hardy perennial. Ht 36 in., spread 24 in. Striking red flowers, mid- to late summer. The leaves are green with a slight red tinge to the edges and have a glorious pineapple scent. This sage is subtropical and must be protected from frost. In temperate climates it is basically a house plant and if kept on a sunny windowsill can be used throughout the year. It can only be grown from cuttings. This is an odd sage to cook with; it does not taste as well as it smells. It is fairly good with apricots as a stuffing for pork, otherwise my culinary experiments with it have not met with great success. **Zone 8.**

Salvia lavandulifolia
Narrowed-Leaved Sage
Also known as Spanish Sage. Hardy evergreen perennial. Ht and spread 18 in. Attractive blue flowers in summer. The leaves are green and textured, small, thin, and oval in shape and highly aromatic. This is an excellent sage to cook with, very pungent. It also makes a good tea. Can only be grown from cuttings. **Zone 5.**

Salvia officinalis
Sage
Also known as common sage, garden sage, broad-leaved sage, and sawge. Hardy evergreen perennial. Ht and spread 24 in. Mauve/blue flowers in summer. The leaves are green and textured, thin and oval in shape and highly aromatic. This is the best-known sage for culinary use. Can be easily grown from seed. There is also a white-flowering sage, *Salvia officinalis* "Albiflora," which is quite rare. **Zone 5.**

Salvia officinalis broad-leaved

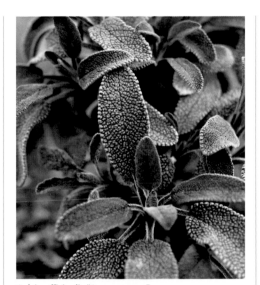

Salvia officinalis "Purpurascens"

Salvia officinalis broad-leaved
Broad-Leaved Sage

Hardy evergreen perennial. Ht and spread 24 in. Very rarely flowers in cool climates; if it does, flowers are blue/mauve in color. The leaves are green and textured, larger than the ordinary sage, with an oval shape and highly aromatic. Good for cooking. Can only be grown from cuttings. **Zone 6.**

Salvia officinalis "Purpurascens" AGM
Purple/Red Sage

Hardy evergreen perennial. Ht and spread 28 in. Mauve/blue flowers in summer. The leaves are purple and textured, a thin oval shape and aromatic. If you clip it in the spring, it develops new leaves and looks really good but flowers only a small amount. If you do not clip it and allow it to flower it goes woody. It you then cut it back it does not produce new growth until the spring, so can look a bit bare. So what to do? There is also a variegated form of this purple sage *Salvia officinalis* "Purpurascens Variegata." Both of these can only be grown from cuttings. **Zone 8.**

Salvia officinalis "Tricolor"
Tricolor Sage

Half-hardy evergreen perennial. Ht and spread 16 in. Attractive blue flowers in summer. The leaves are green with pink, white and purple variegation, with a texture. They are small, thin, and oval in shape and highly aromatic. It has a mild flavor, so can be used in cooking. Can only be grown from cuttings. **Zone 8.**

Salvia viridis var. comata
Painted Sage, Red-topped Sage

Hardy annual. Ht 18 in. Striking red, blue, purple-pink bracts and tiny bicolored flowers in summer. Green, oval rough-textured leaves.

Salvia officinalis "Tricolor"

 cultivation

Propagation
Seed

Common and painted sage can be grown successfully in the spring from seed sown into prepared seed or plug trays using a standard seed compost mixed in equal parts with composted fine bark and covered with perlite. The seeds are a good size. If starting off under protection in early spring, warmth is of benefit — temperatures of 60–70°F. Germination takes 2 to 3 weeks. Repot or plant out when the frosts are over at a distance of 18–24 in. in. apart.

Cuttings

This is a good method for all variegated species and the ones that do not set seed in cooler climates. Use

Salvia viridis var. comata

a standard seed compost mixed in equal parts with composted fine bark. Take softwood cuttings in late spring or early summer from the strong new growth. All forms take easily from cuttings; rooting is about 4 weeks in summer.

Layering

If you have a well-established sage, or if it is becoming woody, layer established branches in spring or fall.

Pests and Diseases

Sage grown in the garden does not suffer over much from pests and disease. Sage grown in containers, especially pineapple sage, is prone to red spider mite and leaf hopper. When you see these pests, treat with a liquid insecticidal soap as per the instructions.

Maintenance

Spring Sow seeds. Trim if needed, and then take softwood cuttings.
Summer Trim back after flowering.
Fall Protect all half-hardy sages, and first-year plants.
Winter Protect plants if they are needed for fresh leaves.

Salvia viridis var. comata

Salvia argentea

Garden Cultivation

Sage, although predominately a Mediterranean plant, is sufficiently hardy to withstand any ordinary winter without protection, as long as the soil is well drained and not acid, and the site is as warm and dry as possible. The flavor of the leaf can vary according to how rich, damp, etc, the soil is. If wishing to sow seed outside, wait until there is no threat of frost and sow direct into prepared ground, spacing the seeds 9 in. apart. After germination thin to 18 in. apart. For the first winter cover the young plants with a floating row cover or a mulch. To keep the plants bushy prune in the spring to encourage young shoots for strong flavor, and also after flowering in late summer. Mature plants can be pruned hard in the spring after some cuttings have been taken as insurance. Never prune in the fall as this can kill the plant. As sage is prone to becoming woody, replace the plant every 4 to 5 years.

Harvesting

Since sage is an evergreen plant, the leaves can be used fresh any time of the year. In Mediterranean-type climates, including the southern states of America, the leaves can be harvested during the winter months. In cold climates this is also possible if you cover a chosen bush with a floating row cover as this will keep the leaves in better condition. They dry well, but care should be taken to keep their green color. Because this herb is frequently seen in its dried condition people assume it is easy to dry. But beware, although other herbs may lose some of their aroma or qualities if badly dried or handled, sage seems to pick up a musty scent and a flavor really horrible to taste — better to grow it in your garden to use fresh.

 ## companion planting

Sage planted with cabbages is said to repel cabbage white butterflies. Planted next to vines it is reputed to be beneficial.

 ## container growing

All sages grow happily in containers. Pineapple sage is an obvious one as it is tender, but a better reason is that if it is at hand one will rub the leaves and smell that marvellous pineapple scent. Use a soilless compost mixed in equal parts with composted fine bark for all varieties, feed after flowering, and do not overwater.

 ## other uses

The dried leaves, especially those of pineapple sage, are good added to potpourris.

Sage tea

 ## medicinal

For centuries, sage has been esteemed for its healing powers. It is a first-rate remedy as a hot infusion for colds. Sage tea combined with a little cider vinegar makes a gargle which is excellent for sore throats, laryngitis and tonsillitis. It is also beneficial for infected gums and mouth ulcers. The essential oil is obtained by steamed distillation of the fresh or partially dried flower stems and leaves. It is used in herbal medicine but more widely in toilet waters, perfumes and soap, and to flavor wine, vermouth and liqueurs.

 ## warning

Extended or excessive use of sage can cause symptoms of poisoning. Although the herb seems safe and common, if you drink the tea for more than a week or two at a time, its strong antiseptic properties can cause potentially toxic effects.

Salvia officinalis "Purpurascens"

culinary

This powerful healing plant is also a strong culinary herb, although it has been misused and misjudged in the culinary world. Used with discretion it adds a lovely flavor, aids digestion of fatty food, and being an antiseptic it kills off any bugs in the meat as it cooks. It has long been used with sausages because of its preservative qualities. It also makes a delicious herb gelatin, or oil or vinegar. But I like using small amounts fresh. The original form of the following recipe comes from a vegetarian friend of mine. I fell in love with it and have subsequently adapted it to include some other herbs.

Hazelnut and Mushroom Roast
Serves 4

A little sage oil
2/3 cup long grain brown rice
1 ¼ cups boiling water
1 teaspoon salt
1 large onion, peeled and chopped
½ cup mushrooms, wiped and chopped
2 medium carrots, pared and roughly grated
1/2 teaspoon coriander seed
1 tablespoon soy sauce
½ cup wholemeal breadcrumbs
1 ¼ cup ground hazelnuts
1 teaspoon chopped sage leaves
1 teaspoon chopped lovage leaves
Sunflower seeds for decoration
A 2-lb. loaf tin, lined with waxed paper

Preheat the oven (350°F).

Heat 2 teaspoons of sage oil in a small pot, toss the rice in it to give it a coating of oil, add boiling water straight from the kettle and the teaspoon of salt. Stir, and let the rice cook slowly for roughly 40 minutes or until the liquid is absorbed.

While the rice is cooking, heat 1 tablespoon of sage oil in a medium sized frying-pan, add the onions, mushrooms, carrots, the coriander seed and soy sauce. Mix them together and let them cook for about 10 minutes.

Combine the cooked brown rice, breadcrumbs, hazelnuts, sage and lovage; mix with the vegetables and place the complete mixture in the prepared loaf pan. Sprinkle with the sunflower seeds and bake in the oven for 45 minutes. Let cool slightly in the pan. Slice and serve with a homemade tomato sauce and a green salad.

Sambucus

ELDERBERRY

Also known as Boun-tree, Boon-tree, Dogtree, Judas Tree, Scores, Score Tree, God's Stinking Tree, Black Elder, Blackberried, European Elder, Ellhorne and German Elder. From the family Caprifoliaceae.

Elder grows worldwide throughout temperate climates. Its common name is probably derived from the Anglo Saxon *Ellaern* or *Aeld*, which mean "fire" or "kindle," because the hollow stems were once used for getting fires going. The generic name, *Sambucus*, dates from ancient Greek times and may originally have referred to *sambuke*, a kind of harp made of elderwood. Pipes were made from its branches too, possibly the original Pan pipes. People thought that if you put it on the fire you would see the Devil. They believed it unlucky to make cradle rockers out of it, that the spirit of the tree might harm the child. Again, farmers were unwilling to use an elder switch to drive cattle and one folktale had it that elder would only grow where blood had been shed. Planting it outside the back door was a sure way of protecting against evil, black magic, and keeping witches out of the house, which would never be struck by lightning. It was thought that Christ's cross was made of elderwood.

Sambucus nigra

 varieties

☠ *Sambucus canadensis*
American Elder
Also known as black elder, common elder, Rob elder, sweet elder. Deciduous hardy perennial. Ht 5–12 ft. Numerous small white flowers in flat cymes throughout summer. Berries are dark purple in early fall; its leaves are long, sharply toothed and bright green. **Zone 3.**

Warning: All parts of the fresh *S. canadensis* can poison. Children have even been poisoned by chewing

or sucking the bark. Once cooked, however, flowers and berries are safe. Some Native American tribes use a tea made from the root-bark for headaches, mucous congestion, and to promote labor in childbirth.

☠ *Sambucus canadensis "Aurea"*
Deciduous hardy perennial. Ht and spread 12 ft. Creamy white flowers in summer, red fruits in early fall. Large golden yellow leaves. **Zone 3.**

☠ *Sambucus ebulus*
Dwarf Elder
Also known as blood Elder, danewort, wild elder, walewort. Deciduous hardy perennial. Ht 2–4 ft., spread 3 ft. White flowers with pink tips in summer.

spread 3 ft. White flowers with pink tips in summer. Black berries in early fall. Its green leaves are oblong, lance-shaped, and toothed around the edges. Dwarf elder grows in small clusters in Europe and in Eastern and Central States of America.

Warning: All parts of *S. ebulus* are slightly poisonous and children should be warned not to eat the bitter berries. It has a much stronger action than its close relative, common *S. nigra*. Large doses cause vertigo, vomiting and diarrhea, the latter, denoted colloquially as "the Danes," being the origin of Danewort. Nowadays *S. ebulus* is rarely used and should be taken internally only under strict medical supervision.

Sambucus nigra
Common Elder
Also known as European elder, black elder, bore tree. Deciduous hardy perennial. Ht 20–23 ft, spread 15 ft. Spreading branches bear flat heads of small, star-shaped, creamy-white flowers in late spring and early summer, followed in early fall by drooping purplish-black juicy berries. The leaves of *Sambucus nigra* are purgative and should not be taken internally; decoctions have an insecticidal effect. **Zone 5.**

Sambucus nigra "Aurea"
Golden Elder
Deciduous shrub. Ht and spread 20 ft. Flattened heads of fragrant, star-shaped, creamy-white flowers from early to midsummer. Black fruits in early fall. Golden yellow, oval, sharply toothed leaves usually in groups of five. **Zone 5.**

☠ *Sambucus racemosa*
Red Elder
Deciduous hardy perennial. Ht and spread 10–13 ft. Brown bark and pale brown pith. Flowers arranged in dense terminal panicles of yellowish cream. *Racemosa* refers to the flower clusters. The fruits are also distinct in being red in drooping clusters. It rarely fruits freely. Red berried elder is native to central and southern Europe. It has naturalized in Scotland, the northern U.S. and Canada. The fully ripe fruits are used medicinally. Bitter tasting, they may be used fresh or dried, and are high in vitamin C, essential oil, sugar and pectins. Fruits are a laxative and the leaves are a diuretic. This is the most edible and tasty of the elders. **Zone 3.**

Warning: The seeds inside the berries of *S. racemosa* are poisonous before being cooked.

Elderflower sorbet

cultivation

Propagation
Seed
Sow ripe berries 1 in. deep in a pot outdoors using a soil-based seed compost. Plant seedlings in semi-shade in the garden when large enough to handle.

Cuttings
Take semi-hardwood cuttings in summer from the new growth. Use a seed compost mixed in equal parts with composted fine bark, and winter these cuttings in a cold frame or cold greenhouse. When rooted, either pot on or plant out into a prepared site 12 in. apart.
Take hardwood cuttings of bare shoots in fall and replant in the garden 12 in. apart. The following fall lift and replant.

Pests and Diseases
Rarely suffers from pests or diseases apart from black-fly, which can be treated with insecticidal soap.

Maintenance
Spring Prune back golden and variegated elders.
Summer Take semi-ripe cuttings.
Fall Take hardwood cuttings. Prune back hard.
Winter Established plants do not need protection.

Garden Cultivation
Elder tolerates most soils and *S. nigra* is very good for chalky sites. They all prefer a sunny position. Elder grows very rapidly indeed and self-sows freely to produce new shoots 4 ft.. long in one season. It is short-lived. It is important to dominate elder otherwise it will dominate your garden. Cut back in late fall, unless it is gold or variegated, when it should be pruned in early spring before growth begins.

Harvesting
Handle flower heads carefully to prevent bruising, spread out to dry with heads down on a fine net without touching one another. Pick the fruits in fall, as they ripen, when they become shiny and violet.

container growing

Golden varieties of elder can look good in containers, as long as the containers are large enough and positioned to give the plants some shade, to stop the leaves scorching. Use a soilless compost. Keep well watered, feed with a liquid fertilizer.

other uses

Elderflower water whitens and softens the skin, removes freckles. The fruits make a lavender or violet dye when combined with alum. The flowers and berries of *Sambucus nigra* are used in industry for cosmetics. The wood from the adult plant is highly prized by craftsmen.

medicinal

Elderflowers reduce bronchial and upper respiratory catarrh and are used in the treatment of hay fever. Externally a cold infusion of the flowers may be used as an eye wash for conjunctivitis and as a compress for

culinary

Only American elder is used for culinary purposes, and its berries should not be eaten raw, nor fresh juice used. Be sure to cook very slightly first.

Elderflower Cordial
Pick flowers on a dry sunny day, as the yeast is mainly in the pollen.

4 quarts water
3 cups sugar
Juice and thinly peeled rind of 1 lemon
2 tablespoons cider or wine vinegar
12 elderflower heads

Bring the water to a boil and pour into a sterilized container. Add the sugar, stirring until dissolved. When cool add the lemon juice and the rind, vinegar and elderflowers. Cover with several layers of cheesecloth and leave for 24 hours. Filter through cheesecloth into strong, sterilized glass bottles. This drink is ready after 2 weeks. Serve chilled.

chilblains. A gargle made from elderflower infusion or elderflower vinegar alleviates tonsillitis and sore throats. Elderflowers have a mild laxative action and in Europe have a reputation for treating rheumatism and gout. The berries are a mild laxative and sweat-inducing. "Elderberry Rob" is traditionally made by simmering the berries and thickening with sugar as a winter cordial for coughs and colds.

Elderberry Conserve (for neuralgia and migraine)

2 cups elderberries
2½ cups sugar

Boil the elderberries with the least quantity of water to produce a pulp. Pass through a strainer and simmer the juice gently to remove most of the water. Add the sugar and stir constantly until the consistency of a conserve is produced. Pour into a suitable container. Take 2 tablespoons as required.

warning

Use parts of plants from this genus with care; many are poisonous. See warnings under relevant species.

Sambucus nigra

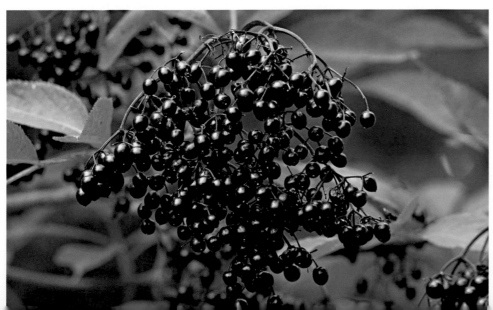

Sanguisorba minor

SALAD BURNET

Also known as Drumsticks, Old Man's Pepper and Poor Man's Pepper. From the family *Rosaceae*.

This herb is a native of Europe and Asia. It has been introduced and naturalized in many places elsewhere in the world, especially Britain and the United States. Popular for both its medicinal and culinary properties, it was taken to New England in the Pilgrim Fathers' plant collection and called pimpernel. It is found in dry, free-draining soil in grassland and on the edges of woodland. The name *Sanguisorba* comes from *sanguis*, meaning "blood," and *sorbere*, meaning "to soak up." It is an ancient herb, which has been grown in Britain since the 16th century. Traditionally it was used to staunch wounds. In Tudor times salad burnet was planted along borders of garden paths so the scent would rise up when trodden on.

Sanguisorba minor flower heads

 cultivation

Propagation

Seed
Sow the small flattish seed in spring or fall into prepared seed or plug trays and cover the seeds with perlite; no need for extra heat. If sown in the fall, winter the seedlings under protection and plant out in spring to a prepared site, 12 in. apart. If spring sown allow to harden off and plant out in the same way. When used as an edging plant it needs to be planted at 8 in. intervals.

Division
It divides very easily. Dig up an established plant in the early fall, cut back any excessive leaves, divide the plant and replant in a prepared site in the garden.

Pests and Diseases
This herb is, in the main, free from pests and diseases.

Maintenance
Spring Sow seeds.
Summer Keep cutting to stop it flowering, if being used for culinary purposes.
Fall Sow seeds if necessary. Divide well-established plants.
Winter No protection needed, fully hardy.

 varieties

Sanguisorba minor
Salad Burnet
Evergreen hardy perennial. Ht 8–24 in., spread 12 in. Produces small spikes of dark crimson flowers in summer. Its soft midgreen leaves are divided into oval leaflets. **Zone 4.**

Sanguisorba officinalis
Great Burnet
Also known as drumsticks, maidens hairs, red knobs, and redheads. Perennial. Ht up to 4 ft., spread 24 in. Produces small spikes of dark crimson flowers in summer. Its midgreen leaves are divided into oval leaflets. This wild plant is becoming increasingly rare due to modern farming practices. **Zone 4.**

Garden Cultivation

This is a most attractive, soft-leaf evergreen and is very useful in both kitchen and garden. That it is evergreen is a particular plus for the herb garden, where it looks most effective as an edging plant. It also looks good in a wild flower garden, where it grows as happily as in its original grassland habitat. With no special requirements, it prefers chalky soil, but it will tolerate any well-drained soil in sun or light shade. It is deep rooting and very drought resistant. The art with this plant is to keep cutting, which stops it flowering and encourages lots of new growth.

Harvesting

Pick young tender leaves when required. Not necessary to dry leaves (which in any case do not dry well), as fresh leaves can be harvested all year round.

 container growing

Salad burnet will grow in containers, and will provide an excellent source of soft evergreen leaves throughout winter for those with no garden. Use a soilless compost. Water regularly, but not too frequently; feed with liquid fertilizer in the spring only. Do not over-feed otherwise the leaf will soften and lose its cool cucumber flavor, becoming more like a spinach. For regular use the plant should not be allowed to flower. Cut back constantly to about 6 in. to ensure a continuing supply of tender new leaves.

 medicinal

Chewing the leaf assists digestion. An infusion of the whole plant is used for treating hemorrhoids and diarrhea.

Infusion of salad burnet

 culinary

The leaves of salad burnet have a nutty flavor and a slight taste of cucumber. The young leaves are refreshing in salads and can be used generously — they certainly enhance winter salads. Tender young leaves can also be added to soups, cold drinks, cream cheeses, or used (like parsley) as a garnish or to flavor casseroles — add at the beginning of cooking. The leaves also make an interesting herbal vinegar. Salad burnet combines with other herbs, especially rosemary and tarragon. Serve in a sauce with white fish.

 other uses

Because of its high tannin content, the root of great burnet can be used in the tanning of leather.

Salad Burnet Herb Butter

This butter is lovely with broiled fish, either cooked under the broiler or on the grill, and adds a cucumber flavor.

1 1/2 tablespoons chopped salad burnet
1 tablespoon chopped garden mint (spearmint)
6 tablespoons butter
Salt and freshly ground black pepper
Lemon juice

Mix the chopped herb leaves together. Melt the butter in a pot, add the herbs and simmer on a very low heat for 10 minutes. Season the sauce to taste with salt and pepper, and a squeeze (no more) of lemon. Pour over broiled fish (flounder or sole).

 warning

Great burnet should never be taken in large doses.

Santolina
LAVENDER COTTON

Also known as Santolina and French lavender. From the family Asteraceae.

Cotton lavender is a native of Southern France and the Northern Mediterranean area, where it grows wild on calcareous ground. It is widely cultivated, adapting to the full spectrum of European and Australian climates and to warm-to-hot regions of North America, surviving even an Eastern Canadian winter on well-drained soil.

The Greeks knew cotton lavender as *abrotonon* and the Romans as *habrotanum,* both names referring to the tree-like shape of the flying branches. It was used medicinally for many centuries by the Arabs. It was valued in medieval England as an insect and moth repellent and vermifuge.

The plant was probably brought into Britain in the 16th century by French Huguenot gardeners, who were skilled in creating the knot garden so popular among the Elizabethans. Cotton lavender was used largely in low clipped hedges, and as edging for the geometrical beds.

Santolina chamaecyparissus "Small-Ness"

 varieties

Despite its common name, this is not a member of the *Lavandula* family, but is a member of the daisy family.

Santolina chamaecyparissus
Lavender Cotton
Hardy evergreen shrub. Ht 2½ ft., spread 3 ft. Yellow button flowers from midsummer to early fall, silver coral-like aromatic foliage. **Zone 7.**

Santolina chamaecyparissus "Lemon Queen"
Lavender Cotton Lemon Queen
As "Edward Bowles," but feathery, deep-cut gray foliage. **Zone 7.**

Santolina chamaecyparissus "Small-Ness"
Hardy evergreen shrub. Ht and spread 18 in. Aromatic, deeply cut blue/green foliage. Very neat, tight habit.

Santolina pinnata subsp. *neapolitana*
Lavender Cotton Neopolitana
As "Edward Bowles."

Santolina pinnata subsp. *neapolitana* "Edward Bowles"
Lavender Cotton Edward Bowles
Hardy evergreen shrub. Ht 2½ ft., spread 3 ft. Cream button flowers in summer. Feathery, deep-cut, gray/green foliage. **Zone 7.**

Santolina rosmarinifolia subsp. *rosmarinifolia* "Primrose Gem"
Lavender Cotton Primrose Gem
Hardy evergreen shrub. Ht 24 in., spread 3 ft. Pale yellow button flowers in summer. Finely cut green leaves. **Zone 6.**

Santolina rosmarinifolia subsp. *rosmarinifiolia* "Primrose Gem"

Santolina rosmarinifolia* subsp. *rosmarinifolia
Cotton Lavender, Holy Flax, Virens
As "Primrose Gem." Bright yellow button flowers in summer. Finely cut, bright green leaves. **Zone 6.**

 ## cultivation

Propagation
Seed
Seed is not worth the effort as germination is poor.

Cuttings
Take 2–3 in. soft stem cuttings in spring before flowering, or take semi-ripe stem cuttings from midsummer to fall. Use a standard seed compost mixed in equal parts with composted fine bark. They root easily without the use of any rooting compound.

Pests and Diseases
Compost or soil that is too rich will attract aphids.

Maintenance
Spring Cut straggly old plants hard back. Take cuttings from new growth.
Summer I cannot stress enough that after flowering the

Santolina pinnata subsp. *neapolitana*

plants should be cut back or the bushes will open up and lose their attractive shape.
Fall Take semi-ripe cuttings, protect them from frost in a cold frame or greenhouse.
Winter Protect in only the severest of winters.

Garden Cultivation
This elegant aromatic evergreen is ideal for the herb garden as a hedging or specimen plant in its own right. Plant in full sun, preferably in sandy soil. If the soil is too rich the growth will become soft and start to lose color. This is particularly noticeable with the silver varieties.

Planting distance for an individual plant 18–24 in., for hedging 12–15 in. Hedges need regular clipping to shape in spring and summer. Do not cut back in the fall in frosty climates, as this can easily kill the plants. If temperatures drop below 5°F protect with a floating row cover or a layer of straw, spruce or bracken.

Harvesting
Pick leaves and dry any time before flowering. Pick small bunches of flower stems for drying, in late summer. They can be dried easily by hanging the bunches upside down in a dry, airy place.

 ## container growing

Cotton lavender cannot be grown indoors, however as a patio plant, a single plant clipped to shape in a large terracotta pot can look very striking. Use a soilless compost mixed in equal parts with composted fine bark. Place pot in full sun. Do not over-feed with liquid fertilizer or growth will be too soft.

 ## culinary

Cotton lavender (*S. chamaecyparissus*) makes an interesting addition to shortbread cookies instead of rosemary. Interesting being the operative word.

 ## medicinal

Although not used much nowadays, it can be applied to surface wounds, hastening the healing process by encouraging scar formation. Finely ground leaves ease the pain of insect stings and bites.

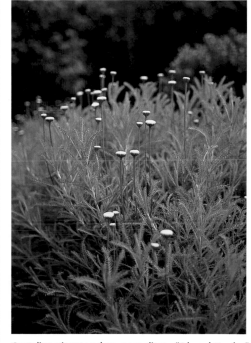

Santolina pinnata subsp. *neapolitana* "Edward Bowles"

 ## other uses

Lay in drawers, under carpets, and in closets to deter moths and other insects, or make an herbal moth bag

Herbal Moth Bag

A handful of wormwood
A handful of spearmint
A handful of cotton lavender
A handful of rosemary
1 tablespoon of crushed cilantro

Dry and crumble the ingredients, mix together and put in a cheesecloth or cotton bag.

Herbal moth bag, using
cotton lavender

Saponaria officinalis
SOAPWORT

Also known as Bouncing Bet, Bruisewort, Farewell Summer, Fuller's Herb, Joe Run By the Street, Hedge Pink, Dog's Clove, Old Maid's Pink and Soaproot. From the family Caryophyllaceae.

Soapwort, widespread on poor soils in Europe, Asia, and Northern America, was used by medieval Arab physicians for various skin complaints. Fullers used soapwort for soaping cloth before it went on the stamps at the mill, and sheep were washed with a mixture of the leaves, roots and water before being shorn.

 container growing

S. ocymoïdes is the best variety for container growing. Use a soilless compost. Water well during the growing season, but only feed twice. In winter keep in a cold greenhouse with minimum watering.

 medicinal

It has been used not only for treating skin conditions such as eczema, cold sores, boils, and acne, but also for gout and rheumatism. It is probably effective due to the antiinflammatory properties of its saponins.

 warning

This herb should only be prescribed by a qualified herbalist because of the high saponin content, which makes it mildly poisonous.

 other uses

The gentle power of the saponins in soapwort makes the following shampoo ideal for upholstery and delicate fibers.

Soapwort Shampoo

½ oz. dried soapwort root or two large handfuls of whole fresh stems
3 cups water

Crush the root with a rolling pin or roughly chop the fresh stems. If using dried soapwort, prepare by soaking first overnight. Put the soapwort into an enamel pan with water and bring to a boil, cover and simmer for 20 minutes, stirring occasionally. Allow to stand until cool and strain through a fine strainer.

Soapwort Shampoo

 varieties

Saponaria officinalis
Soapwort
Hardy perennial. Ht 1–3 ft., spread 2 ft. or more. Compact cluster of small pretty pink or white flowers in summer to early fall. The leaf is smooth, oval, pointed and midgreen in color. **Zone 3.**

Saponaria officinalis "Rubra Plena"
Double-Flowered Soapwort
Hardy perennial. Ht 3 ft., spread 12 in. Clusters of red, ragged, double flowers in summer. The leaves are midgreen and oval in shape. **Zone 3.**

Saponaria ocymoides AGM
Tumbling Ted
Hardy perennial. Ht 1–3 in., spread 16 in. or more. Profusion of tiny, flat, pale pink/crimson flowers in summer. Sprawling mats of hairy oval leaves. **Zone 4.**

 cultivation

Propagation
Seed
Only soapwort and tumbling Ted can be grown from seed. Sow in fall into prepared seed or plug trays and cover with compost. Place glass over container and leave out over winter. Usually germinates in spring, but can be erratic. When large enough, plant 24 in. apart.

Cuttings
Softwood cuttings of the nonflowering shoots can be taken from late spring to early summer.

Division
The creeping rootstock is easy to divide in the fall.

Garden Cultivation
Plant it in a sunny spot, in a well-drained poor soil; in rich soil it can become very invasive. Do not plant near ponds because the creeping rhizomes excrete a poison.

Pests and Diseases
Soapwort is largely free from pests and disease.

Maintenance
Spring Take cuttings.
Summer Cut back after flowering to encourage a second flowering and to prevent self-seeding.
Fall Divide established plants. Sow seed.
Winter Fully hardy.

Harvesting
Pick the leaves when required. Dig up the roots in the fall and dry for medicinal use.

Scutellaria
SKULLCAP

Also known as Helmet Flower, Mad Dog Weed, Blue Skullcap and Blue Pimpernel. From the family Lamiaceae.

The various varieties of skullcap are natives of different countries. They are found in America, Britain, India, and one grows in the rain forests of the Amazon.

The name *Scutellaria* is derived from *scutella*, meaning "a small shield," which is exactly how the seed looks.

The American Indians used *Scutellaria lateriflora* as a treatment for rabies. In Europe it was used for epilepsy.

Scutellaria lateriflora

 ## varieties

Scutellaria galericulata
Skullcap

Hardy perennial. Ht 6–20 in., spread 12 in. and more. Small purple/blue flowers with a longer spreading lower lip in summer. Leaves bright green and lance-shaped with shallow round teeth. This plant is a native of Europe. **Zone 5.**

Scutellaria minor
Lesser Skullcap

As *S. galericulata* except ht 8–12 in., spread 12 in. and more. Small purple/pink flowers. Leaves lance-shaped with four rounded teeth. Found on wet land. **Zone 5.**

Scutellaria lateriflora
Virginian Skullcap

As *S. galericulata* except ht. 12–24 in., spread 12 in. and more. Leaves oval and lance-shaped with shallow, round teeth. Native of America. **Zone 5.**

 ## cultivation

Propagation
Seed

Sow the small seeds in fall into prepared seed or plug trays and cover the seeds with compost. Leave the tray outside under glass. If germination is rapid, winter the young seedlings in a cold greenhouse. If there is no germination within 10 to 20 days, leave well alone. The seed may need a period of stratification. In the spring, when the plants are large enough, plant out into a prepared site in the garden 12 in. apart.

Scutellaria galericulata

Root Cuttings

Take cuttings from the rhizomatous root. In spring dig up an established clump carefully, for any little bits of root left behind will form another plant. Ensure each cutting has a growing node; place in a seed tray and cover with compost. Put into a cold greenhouse to root.

Division

Established plants can be divided in the spring.

Pests and Diseases

Skullcap is normally free from pests and disease.

Maintenance

Spring Divide established plants. Take root cuttings.
Summer Cut back to restrain.
Fall Sow seeds.
Winter: No need for protection, fully hardy.

Garden Cultivation

Tolerates most soils but prefers a well-drained, moisture-retentive soil in sun or semi-shade. Make sure this plant gets adequate water.

Harvesting

Dry flowers and leaves for medicinal use only.

 ## container growing

It can be grown in containers but ensure its large root system has room to spread. Use a soilless compost. Feed only rarely with liquid fertilizer or it will produce too lush a growth and inhibit flowering. Leave outside in winter in a sheltered spot, allowing the plant to die back.

 ## medicinal

S. lateriflora is the best medicinal species; the two European species are a little less strong. It is used in the treatment of anxiety, nervousness, depression, insomnia and headaches. The whole plant is effective as a soothing antispasmodic tonic and a remedy for hysteria. Its bitter taste also strengthens and stimulates the digestion.

 ## warning

Should only be dispensed by a trained herbalist.

SAVORY

From the family Lamiaceae.

Savory is a native of southern Europe and North Africa, especially around the Mediterranean. It grows in well-drained soils and has adapted worldwide to similar climatic conditions. Savory has been employed in food flavoring for over 2,000 years. Romans added it to sauces and vinegars, which they used liberally as flavoring. The Ancient Egyptians, on the other hand, used it in love potions. The Romans also included it in their wagon train to northern Europe, where it became an invaluable disinfectant strewing herb. It was used to relieve tired eyes, for ringing in the ears, indigestion, wasp and bee stings, and for other shocks to the system.

Satureja spicigera

varieties

Satureja coerulea AGM
Purple-Flowered Savory
Semi-evergreen hardy perennial. Ht 12 in., spread 8 in. Small purple flowers in summer. The leaves are darkish green, linear and very aromatic. **Zone 6.**

Satureja hortensis
Summer Savory
Half-hardy annual. Ht 8–12 in., spread 6 in. Small white/mauve flowers in summer. Aromatic leaves, oblong, pointed, and green. A favorite on the Continent and in America, where it is known as the bean herb. It has become widely used in bean dishes as it helps prevent flatulence. **All zones.**

Satureja montana
Winter Savory
Also known as mountain savory. Semi-evergreen hardy perennial. Ht 12 in., spread 8 in. Small white/pink flowers in summer. The leaves are dark green, linear and very aromatic. **Zone 5.**

Satureja spicigera
Creeping Savory
Perennial. Ht 3 in., spread 12 in. . Masses of small white flowers in summer. The leaves are lime greenish and linear. This is a most attractive plant and is often mistaken for thyme or even heather. **Zone 5.**

cultivation

Propagation
Seed
Only summer and winter savory can be grown from seed, which is tiny, so it is best to sow into prepared seed trays under protection in the early spring, using the cardboard method (see p. 645). The seeds should not be covered as they need light to germinate. Germination takes about 10 to 15 days — no need to use bottom heat. When the seedlings are large enough, and after a period of hardening off (making quite sure that the frosts have finished), they can be planted out into a prepared site in the garden, 6 in. apart.

Cuttings
Creeping, purple-flowered and winter savory can all be grown from softwood cuttings in spring, using a standard seed compost mixed in equal parts with composted fine bark. When these have rooted they should be planted out — 12 in. apart for creeping savory, 6 in. apart for the others.

Division
Creeping savory can be divided, as each section has its own root system similar to creeping thymes. Dig up an established plant in the spring after the frosts have finished and divide into as many segments as you require. Minimum size is only dependent on each having a root system and how long you are prepared to wait for new plants to become established. Replant in a prepared site.

Pests and Diseases
Being an aromatic plant, savory is, in the main, free from pests and diseases.

Maintenance
Spring Sow seed. Take softwood cuttings. Divide established plants.
Summer Keep picking and do not allow summer savory to flower, if you want to maintain its flavor.
Fall Protect from prolonged frosts.
Winter Protect.

Garden Cultivation
All the savories featured here like full sun and a poor, well-drained soil. Plant summer savory in the garden in a warm, sheltered spot and keep picking the leaves to

Satureja montana

stop it getting leggy. Do not feed with liquid fertilizer, otherwise the plant will keel over.

S. montana can make a good edging plant and is very pretty in the summer, although it can look a bit sparse in the winter months. Again, trim it from time to time to maintain shape and promote new growth. Creeping savory does not like cold wet winters, or for that matter clay soil, so on this nursery I grow it in a pot (see below). If, however, you wish to grow it in your garden, plant it in a sunny rockery or a well-drained, sheltered corner.

Harvesting

For fresh use, pick leaves as required. For drying, pick those of summer savory before it flowers. They dry easily.

 ## container growing

All savories can be grown in containers, and if your garden suffers from prolonged cold wet winters it may be the only way you can grow this delightful plant successfully. Use a soilless compost mixed in equal parts with composted fine bark. Pick the plants continuously to maintain shape, especially the

summer savory, which can get straggly. If you are picking the plants a lot they may benefit from a feed of liquid fertilizer, but keep this to a minimum as they get over eager when fed. Summer savory, being an annual, dies in winter; creeping savory dies back; the winter savory is a partial evergreen. So, the latter two will need protection in winter. Place them in a cool greenhouse or conservatory. If the container cannot be moved, wrap it up in paper or a frost cloth. Keep watering to the absolute minimum.

 ## culinary

The two savories that are used in cooking are winter and summer savory. The other varieties are edible but their flavor is inferior. Summer and winter savory combine well with vegetables, legumes and rich meats. These herbs both stimulate the appetite and aid digestion. The flavor is hot and peppery, and so the leaves should be added sparingly in salads.

Summer savory can replace both salt and pepper and is a great help to those on a salt-free diet. It is a pungent herb and until one is familiar with its strength it should be used carefully. Summer savory also makes a good vinegar and oil. The oil is used commercially as a flavoring, as is the leaf, which is an important constituent of salami.

The flavor of winter savory is both coarser and stronger; its advantage is that it provides fresh leaves into early winter.

 ## medicinal

Summer savory is the plant credited with medicinal virtues and is said to alleviate the pain of bee stings if rubbed on the affected spot. Infuse as a tea to stimulate appetite and to ease indigestion and flatulence. It is also considered a stimulant and was once in demand as an aphrodisiac. Winter savory is also used medicinally but is inferior.

Beans with Garlic and Savory
Serves 3 to 4

1 cup dried white beans
1 Spanish onion
1 carrot, scrubbed and roughly sliced
1 stick celery
3 tablespoons olive oil
1 tablespoon white wine vinegar
1 clove garlic, crushed
2 tablespoons chopped summer savory
2 tablespoons chopped French parsley

Soak the beans in cold water overnight or for at least 3 to 4 hours. Drain them and put them in a pot with plenty of water. Bring to a boil slowly. Add half the peeled onion, the carrot and celery, and cook until tender. As soon as the beans are soft, drain and discard the vegetables. Mix the oil, vinegar and crushed garlic. While the beans are still hot, stir in the remaining half onion (thinly sliced), the chopped herbs, and pour over the oil and vinegar dressing. Serve soon after cooling. Do not chill.

HOUSELEEK

Sempervivum

Also known as Bullocks eye, Hen and chickens, Jupiter's eye, Jupiter's beard, Live for ever, Thunder plant, Aaron's rod, Healing leaf, Mallow rock and Welcome-husband-though-never-so-late. From the family Crassulaceae.

Originally from the mountainous areas of central and southern Europe, now found growing in many different areas of the world, including North America.

The generic name *Sempervivum* comes from the Latin *semper vivo* meaning "to live for ever." The species name, *tectorum*, means "of the roofs," there being records dating back 2,000 years of houseleeks growing on the tiles of houses. The plant was said to have been given to man by Zeus or Jupiter to protect houses from lightning and fire. Because of this the Romans planted courtyards with urns of houseleek, and Charlemagne ordered a plant to be grown on every roof. This belief continued throughout history and in medieval times the houseleek was thought to protect thatched roofs from fire from the sky and witchcraft. In the Middle Ages the plant was often called Erewort and employed against deafness. When the settlers packed their bags for America they took houseleek with them.

Sempervivum tectorum with offsets

 varieties

This genus of hardy succulents had 25 species 40 years ago. Now, due to reclassification, it has over 500 different varieties. As far as I am aware only houseleek has medicinal properties.

Sempervivum tectorum AGM
Houseleek
Hardy evergreen perennial. Ht 4–6 in. (when in flower) otherwise it is 2 in., spread 8 in. Flowers are star-shaped and pink in summer. The leaves, gray/green in color, are oval, pointed and succulent. **Zone 4.**

Some other *Sempervivum* worth collecting:

Sempervivum arachnoideum AGM
Cobweb Houseleek
Hardy evergreen perennial. Ht 4–5 in., when in flower, otherwise it is 2 in., spread 4 in. Flowers are star-shaped and pink in summer. The leaves, which are gray/green in color, are oval, pointed and succulent. The tips of the leaves are covered in a web of white hairs. **Zone 5.**

Sempervivum "Commander Hay" AGM
Hardy evergreen perennial. Ht 4–6 in., when in flower, otherwise it is 2 in., spread 8 in. Flowers star-shaped, pink in summer. The leaves are deep maroon in color, oval, pointed and succulent. **Zone 4.**

Sempervivum "Commander Hay"

Sempervivum montanum

Hardy evergreen perennial. Ht 3–6 in., when in flower, otherwise 2 in., spread 4 in. Flowers star-shaped and deep red in summer. Leaves gray/green in color, oval, pointed and succulent. **Zone 5.**

cultivation

Propagation

Seed

Most species hybridize readily, so seed cannot be depended upon to reproduce the species true to type. When you buy seed it often says, "mixture of several species and varieties" on the package. It can be good fun to sow these as long as you do not mind what you get; it is even more fun trying to name them as they develop.

The seed is very small, so start off in a seed or plug tray in spring. Sow on the surface. Do not cover except with a sheet of glass. No need for bottom heat. Use a standard seed compost mixed in equal parts with composted fine bark.

Offsets

All the houseleeks produce offsets that cluster around the base of the parent plant. In spring gently remove them and you will notice each has its own root system. Either put straight into a pot, using a standard seed compost mixed in equal parts with composted fine bark, or plant where required. Plant 9 in. apart.

Pests and Diseases

Vine weevil, this scourge of the garden, is very destructive to a number of plants and one of these is houseleek. You will know they have been when you see rosettes lying on their sides with no roots. See p. 660 for methods of destroying the pests.

Maintenance

Spring Sow seeds. Pot up or replant offsets.
Summer Collect seeds from flowering plants if they are required.
Fall Remove offsets if the plant is becoming too invasive, and repot for following season's display.
Winter No need for protection.

Garden Cultivation

Basically the soil should be well-drained and thin, as houseleeks prefer very little to no soil. They will grow anywhere, on weathered rocks and screes and of course rock gardens. Another good place to plant them is between paving stones, or in between other creeping plants like thymes. They can take many years to flower, and when they do they die, but by then there will be many offsets to follow.

Harvesting

Pick leaves to use fresh as required. There is no good way of preserving them.

Mixed Sempervivum in flower

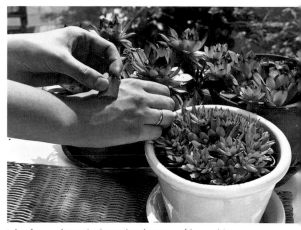

Juice from a houseleek soothes burns and insect bites

container growing

If the Romans could do it, so can we. Houseleeks do look good in containers and shallow stone troughs. The compost must be poor and very well drained. Use a soilless compost mixed with 50 percent horticultural grit and 25 percent composted fine bark. No need to feed, and do not overwater.

medicinal

The leaves are an astringent and when broken in half can be applied to burns, insect bites and other skin problems. Press the juice from the leaf onto the infected part. My son, when he goes on hikes or is building dens, always has some in his pockets for when he gets stung by nettles as houseleeks are more soothing than dock when applied.

To soften skin around corns, bind one leaf for a few hours, soak feet in water in attempt to remove corn. Repeat as necessary.

Infuse as a tea for septic throats, bronchitis and mouth ailments. It is also said that chewing a few leaves can ease toothache.

culinary

The leaves can be added to salad dishes. I think it would be polite to say that it is an acquired taste.

GOLDENROD

Solidago

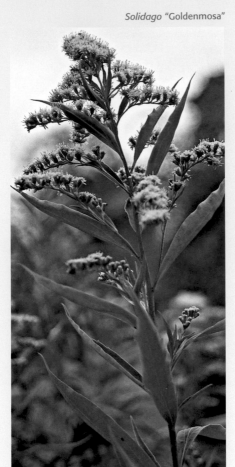

Solidago "Goldenmosa"

Also known as Woundwort, Aaron's rod, Cast the spear and Farewell summer. From the family Asteraceae.

This plant is widely distributed throughout Europe including the British Isles, and North America. It is common from the plains to the hills, but especially where the ground is rich in silica.

Its generic name, *Solidago*, is derived from the Latin word *solido*, which means "to join" or "make whole," a reference to the healing properties attributed to goldenrod.

The plant, originally called Heathen Wound Herb in Britain, was first imported from the Middle East, where it was used by the Saracens, and it was some time before it was cultivated here. In Tudor times it was available in London but at a price, its expense due to the fact that it was still available only as an import. Gerard wrote, "For in my remembrance, I have known the dry herb which comes from beyond the sea, sold in Bucklesbury in London for half a crown an ounce," and went on to say that when it was found growing wild in Hampstead wood, no one would pay half a crown for 100 cwt of it, a fact which the herbalist felt bore out the old English proverb, "Far fetch and dear, bought is best for ladies."

From Culpeper, around the same time, we know that goldenrod was used to fasten loose teeth and as a remedy for kidney stones (which it still is).

 varieties

Solidago odora
Sweet Goldenrod
Also known as aniseed-scented goldenrod, blue mountain tea, common goldenrod and woundweed. Perennial. Ht 2–4 ft., spread 2 ft. Golden-yellow flowers on a single stem from midsummer to fall. The green leaf is linear and lance-shaped. **Zone 6.**

Solidago nemoralis
Gray Goldenrod
Also known as dyer's weed, field goldenrod and yellow goldenrod. Perennial. Ht 2–3 in., spread 2 ft. Yellow flowers on large terminals on one side of the panicle. Leaves grayish-green or olive-green. **Zone 3.**

Solidago "Goldenmosa"

Solidago virgaurea
Goldenrod
Also known as European goldenrod. Perennial Ht 12–24 in., spread 24 in. Small yellow flowers from summer to fall. The green leaves are lance-shaped. **Zone 3.**

Solidago "Goldenmosa" AGM
Golden Mimosa
Perennial. Ht 3 ft., spread 2 ft. Sprays of mimosa-like yellow flowers from summer to fall. Lance-shaped green leaves. Attractive border plant. Has no herbal use. **Zone 4.**

GOLDENROD

 cultivation

Propagation

Seeds

Sow in plug or seed trays in spring. As seed is fine, sow on the surface of a standard seed compost mixed in equal parts with composted fine bark, and cover with perlite. Germination within 14 to 21 days without bottom heat. Prick out, harden off, and plant out into prepared site in the garden at a distance of 18 in. Remember, the plant will spread.

Division

Divide established plants in spring or fall. Dig up the plant, split into required size, half, third, etc., and replant in a prepared site in the garden.

Pests and Diseases

This plant rarely suffers from pests or diseases.

Maintenance

Spring Sow seeds.
Summer Enjoy the flowers. If you have rich soil, the plants may become very tall and need support in exposed sites.
Fall Divide mature plants.
Winter No need for protection.

Garden Cultivation

It is an attractive plant and has been taken into cultivation as a useful late-flowering ornamental. It is ideal for the herbaceous border, as it spreads rapidly to form clumps.

In late summer, sprays of bright yellow flowers crowd its branching stems amongst sharply pointed hoary leaves. When planting in the garden, it prefers open conditions and soils that are not too rich and are well drained. It tolerates sites in sun, semi-shade and shade, and, being a wild plant, it can be naturalized in poor grassland.

Sow seed thinly in spring or fall in the chosen flowering position, having prepared the site, and cover lightly with soil. When the seedlings are large enough, thin to 12 in. distance apart. (The plant will spread and you may have to do a second thinning.) If sown in the fall, the young plants may, in very cold temperatures, need added protection. Use a mulch that they can grow through the following spring, or which can be removed.

Solidago virgaurea

Harvesting

Collect the flowering tops and leaves in summer. Dry for medicinal use.

Goldenrod in potpourri

 container growing

Goldenrod can be grown in containers, but being a tall plant, it looks much more attractive in a garden border. Use a soilless compost mixed in equal parts with composted fine bark, and in the summer only give it liquid fertilizer and water regularly.

In winter, as the plant dies back, move the container into a cool and airy place that is completely protected from frost, but not warm. Keep the compost on the dry side.

 medicinal

Goldenrod is used in cases of urinary and kidney infections and stones, and catarrh. It also helps to ease backache caused by renal conditions because of its cleansing, eliminative action. It is used to treat arthritis. A cold compress is helpful on fresh wounds because of its antiinflammatory properties.

Sweet goldenrod is used as an astringent and as a calmative. The tea made from the dried leaves and flowers can be used to improve the taste of other medicinal preparations. Native Americans applied lotions made from goldenrod flowers to bee stings.

BETONY

Stachys officinalis

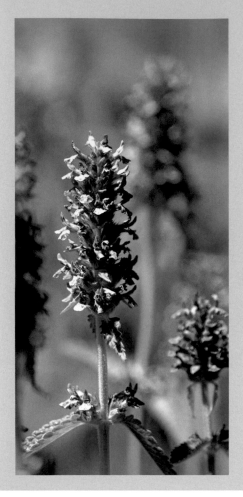

Also known as Lousewort, Purple betony, Wood betony, Bishop's wort and Devil's plaything. From the family Lamiaceae.

This attractive plant, native to Europe, is still found growing wild in Britain.

Betony certainly merits inclusion in the herb garden, but is thought by some to be one of the plant world's frauds. There are so many conflicting stories, all of which are well worth hearing. I leave it to you to decide what is fact or fiction.

The ancient Egyptians were the first to attribute magical properties to betony. In England, by the 10th century, the Anglo-Saxons had it as their most important magical plant, claiming it as effective against the Elf sickness. In the 11th century it was mentioned in the *Lacnunga* as a beneficial medicinal plant against the Devilish affliction of the body. Later, Gerard wrote in his *Herball*, "Betony is good for them that be subject to the falling sickness," and went on to describe its many virtues, one of them being as "a remedy against the biting of mad dogs and venomous serpents."

In the 18th century it was still used in the cure of diverse afflictions, including headaches and drawing out splinters, as well as used in herbal tobacco and snuff. Today, betony retains an important place in folk medicine, though its true value is seriously questioned. We owe the name to the Romans, who called the herb first *Bettonica* and then *Betonica*.

varieties

Stachys officinalis
Betony
Hardy perennial. Ht 24 in., spread 10 in. Dense spikes of pink or purple flowers from late spring through summer. Square hairy stems bear aromatic, slightly hairy, round, lobed leaves. **Zone 4.**

Stachys officinalis "Alba"
White Betony
Hardy perennial. Ht 24 in., spread 10 in. White flowers from late spring through summer. **Zone 4.**

cultivation

Propagation
Seed
Grows readily from seed, which it produces in abundance. Sow in late summer or spring in planting position and cover very lightly with soil. Alternatively, sow seeds in trays and prick out seedlings into small pots when large enough to handle.

Division
Divide roots of established plants in spring or fall, replant at a distance of 12 in. from other plants. Alternatively repot using a standard seed compost mixed in equal parts with composted fine bark.

Pests and Diseases
Apart from the occasional caterpillar, which can be picked off, this plant is pest and disease free.

Maintenance
Spring Sow seeds. Divide established plants.
Summer Plant out spring seedlings.
Fall Cut back flowering stems, save seeds, divide established plants.
Winter No protection needed.

Garden Cultivation
A very accommodating plant, it will tolerate most soils, but prefers some humus. Flourishes in sun or shade, and in fact it will put up with all but the deepest of shade. A wild plant, but it has for centuries been grown in cottage gardens.

other uses

The fresh plant provides a yellow dye. A hair rinse, good for highlighting graying hair, can be made from an infusion of the leaves.

 warning

Care must be taken if it is taken internally because in any form the root can cause vomiting and violent diarrhea.

Betony leaves

 medicinal

Today opinions differ as to its value. Some authorities consider it is only an astringent while others believe it is a sedative. It is however now chiefly employed in herbal smoking mixtures and herbal snuffs. As an infusional powder, it is used to treat diarrhea, cystitis, asthma and neuralgia. Betony tea is invigorating, particularly if prepared in a mixture with other herbs. In France it is recommended for liver and gall bladder complaints.

Dried leaves, flowers and root of betony

In the wild flower garden it is a very colorful participant and establishes well either in a mixed bed or in grassland. It is also an excellent plant for the woodland garden.

Harvesting

Collect leaves for drying before flowering in late spring and early summer. Use leaves fresh either side of flowering. Pick flowers for drying and for use in potpourris just as they start to open. Collect through flowering season to use fresh.

Collect and save seed in early fall. Store in a dry, dark container.

 container growing

Betony grows to great effect in half a beer barrel and combines well with other wild flowers such as poppies, oxeye daisy, chamomile. Use a soilless compost mixed in equal parts with composted fine bark. I do not advise it for growing indoors or in small containers.

STEVIA

Stevia rebaudiana

Also known as Sweet leaf, Yerba dulce, Honeyleaf and Caa'-ehe. From the family Asteraceae.

This fascinating and controversial subtropical and tropical herb is indigidous to South and Central America where it has been used for hundreds of years. In the 16th century the invading Spaniards noticed that the Guarani Indians of Paraguay were using this herb not only to sweeten their drinks, but also in herbal remedies and for making snacks. The Indians had many local names for stevia, one of which was Caa'-ehe; this and all the other local names have some form of reference to the sweetness of the leaf. In 1931. two French chemists, Bridel and Lavieille, extracted "stevioside" from the leaf, a compound which is 300 times sweeter than sucrose, which is now being used in many countries throughout the world.

 varieties

Stevia rebaudiana
Stevia
Subtropical evergreen perennial, grown as an annual in cold climates. Ht and spread 18 in. Clusters of small white flowers in late summer, early fall. Midgreen, oval leaves with serrated edges, which have an intense sugary taste, with a liquorice after taste, when eaten. **Zone 11.**

 cultivation

Propagation
Seed
Sow fresh seeds in spring into prepared module plug trays or small pots using a standard seed compost mixed in equal parts with perlite. Cover the seeds with perlite. Place under protection at 65°F; germination is erratic. As soon as the first few seeds emerge, remove from the heat, keep the container warm and the remaining seeds may germinate over the next few months. Once the seedlings are large enough, repot using a soilless potting compost mixed in equal parts with composted fine bark.

Cuttings
This is, by far, the most reliable method of propagation for this herb. Take semi-ripe cuttings from non-flowering shoots in early summer and place into prepared module plug trays using a seed compost mixed in equal parts with propagating bark. Place in a warm environment (bottom heat is not necessary), and it should root within 2 weeks. Once rooted, repot using the same methods as for seed-raised plants.

Pests and Diseases

This herb, when grown in the tropics, rarely suffers from pests and diseases. In cold climates, it is difficult to winter as it is prone to mildew and rot, especially if overwatered. If it is grown under protection in spring and summer, make sure that the leaves do not become scorched and watch out for aphids, especially on new growth. If the infestation becomes invasive, spray with an insecticidal soap following the manufacturer's instructions.

Maintenance

Spring Sow seeds.
Summer Take cuttings.
Fall Bring plants inside to protect from frost.
Winter Cut back on the watering of container plants in cool and cold climates.

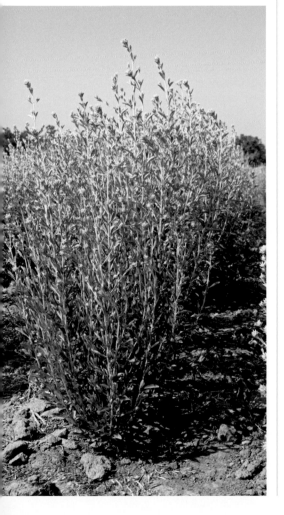

Garden Cultivation

Outside the tropics this herb can only be grown as an annual in the garden. Plant in full sun — it will not tolerate shade — in a light fertile soil that does not dry out in summer. If you know your soil is prone to drying, after planting add a good deep mulch, preferably leaf mold or well-rotted compost.

Harvesting

Pick the leaves to use fresh as required from spring until late summer. Pick the leaves for drying in early summer.

 ## container growing

Stevia is ideally suited for growing in a container. Plant in a soilless potting compost mixed in equal parts with composted fine bark. Place the container in a warm sunny position. Water and feed regularly throughout the growing season. In fall, in cold and cool climates, bring the container into a warm greenhouse, conservatory or well-lit windowsill. Cut back the plant to 4 in. and reduce the watering to minimal, but not totally dry. Re-introduce watering and repot one size up in the spring. Place the container outside once all frosts have passed.

 ## medicinal

For today's society this herb has phenomenal potential in the treatment of obesity, high blood pressure and for those, such as diabetics, who require a natural sweetener and for those on a low carbohydrate diet. Due to lack of clinical trials it is not yet recognized, however there is currently lots of different scientific research being carried out worldwide and I would not be surprised to find it being included in many herbal preparations in the near future.

 ## warning

This herb is banned for sale as a food or food ingredient in the UK and EU. In the U.S., it is sold as a dietary supplement and a sweetener.

 ## culinary

I have read many arguments regarding the safety of stevia in food production, and they have left me puzzled and frustrated. The Japanese, who have banned all artificial sweeteners, have been using stevia as a commercial sweetener for the past 30 years without a single case of documented stevia toxicity or adverse reaction, yet it has been banned by the U.S. and European agencies, although the U.S. have agreed that it can be used as a food supplement in the home.

The leaves can be used fresh or dried; they have a sweet, slightly licorice flavor. The flavor and intensity of the sugar content can vary due to growing position, sun strength, watering and age of plant. To test how strong the fresh leaves are, place a minute amount on the end of your tongue, this will immediately indicate strength. Alternatively, take one leaf, pour over 1 cup of boiled water, let it stand for 10 minutes, then taste the water with a teaspoon. If it's not sweet enough for your taste or recipe add another leaf, reheat the water to just below boiling, let it stand for an additional 10 minutes then taste again. Repeat this until you get the flavor you want. Always start with a few leaves because you can add but you cannot take away once you have created a sweet water. Once you have the flavor you require you can then use this sweet water in drinks, with fruit, water ices and other desserts.

Stevia rebaudiana under cultivation

Sutherlandia frutescens
CANCER BUSH

Also known as Kankerbos, Kankerbossie, Unwele, Phetola Mukakana and Lerumo-lamadi. From the family Papilionaceae.

The first time I saw this plant flower I knew that it was special, however I had no idea how special until I heard the BBC world news in November 2001 where it was proclaimed as a beneficial herb in the treatment of AIDS. This native of South Africa is regarded as the most profound and multi-purpose of their native medicinal plants. It has been used for centuries as a medicine; the Zulu sangomas, or traditional healers, know it as *unwele*, "the great medicine," which they used to ward off the effects of the devastating 1918 influenza pandemic which claimed 20 million lives worldwide. While the Afrikaaners call it the *kankerbossie* or cancer bush, because of its properties in treating people suffering with internal cancers and wasting.

varieties

Sutherlandia frutescens
Cancer Bush
Evergreen tender shrub. Ht up to 4 ft., spread 3 ft. Bright scarlet flowers, from early to midsummer, which grow in terminal clusters and are followed by inflated seed pods that are pale green, ripening to beige, tinged with red, in which there are small flat black seeds. Each gray, silver, slightly hairy leaf is divided into 13 to 21 leaflets. **Zone 9.**

cultivation

Propagation
Seed
The cancer bush self-seeds readily around the garden. However, as with many herbs that do this, it does need encouragement when grown under controlled conditions in a greenhouse or cold frame. Sow either in fall using fresh seed, or in the following spring with dried seeds. Prepare the seeds in exactly the same way that one would prepare the seeds of sweet peas, as they are from the same botanical family. Prior to sowing, scarify the seeds lightly by rubbing them gently on sandpaper and then soak them overnight in hand-hot water. Finally sow the prepared seed into cell-packs, or small pots, using a standard seed compost mixed in equal parts with perlite. Cover the seeds with just perlite as this helps prevent damping off. Place under protection at 60°F; germination takes 2 to 3 weeks. When sowing in the fall, winter the seedlings in a frost-free environment. Once the seedlings are large enough, repot using a soilless compost mixed in equal parts with horticultural sand. Harden off prior to planting in the garden or before growing on in a container. Plants raised from seed will take 3 years before they flower.

Cuttings
Take cuttings from nonflowering shoots from April until June. Put into prepared cell-packs or very small pots, using a standard seed compost mixed in equal parts with perlite. Place the cuttings in a warm position or on a propagator at 60°F; rooting takes 2 to 3 weeks. Once roots have established, repot using a soilless potting compost mixed in equal parts with horticultural sand.

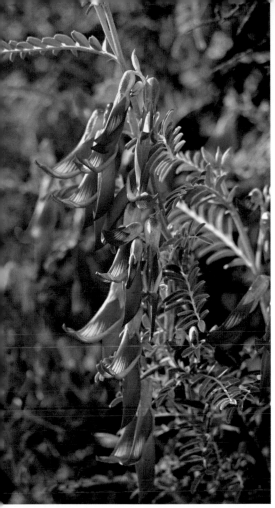

Sutherlandia frutescens

Pests and Diseases

The plant is quite pest resistant in the garden. When container grown, however, it can be prone to red spider mite *(Tetranychus urticae)*. The best way to control this is to use a biological predator *Phytoseiulus persimilis,* which feeds on the eggs and the active stages of red spider mite. This predator does not work well in cold weather, therefore use from late spring until early fall, well before the first frosts.

Container plants in the winter can suffer from powdery mildew, usually due to poor air circulation and the root ball being too dry. It also can suffer from downy mildew, which again is especially a problem in cold damp falls where the air circulation is stagnant and the plant's leaves have not been picked up. To prevent mildew, check the plants regularly, and lift the container off the floor onto bricks, to stop osmosis from the damp floor. Make sure that the root ball is just damp but not over-dry or sodden and, if the leaves do drop, make sure that they are removed and not left to rot on the surface of the pot.

Maintenance

Spring Sow seeds.
Summer Harvest leaves. Take cuttings.
Fall Harvest leaves and seeds. Bring in containers.
Winter Protect from frosts. Check air circulation.

Garden Cultivation

This stunning plant makes a very good focal point in the garden. In the northern hemisphere and areas where the night temperature falls constantly below 50°F, it can only be grown as an annual, or as a container plant that is sunk into the border for the growing season and lifted in the fall before the first frosts. With either method, plant in full sun in any good fertile, free-draining soil.

The cancer bush, once established, is fast growing; it is not particularly long-lived, approximately 5 years, so it is worth taking cuttings each summer as insurance.

Harvesting

The leaves are harvested in summer and then dried for medicinal use.

 companion planting

The cancer bush is a member of the legume (pea) family. Plants of this family fix atmospheric nitrogen via their roots in the soil, which then becomes a benefit for other plants.

 container growing

This herb grows happily in containers; use a soilless potting compost mixed in equal parts with horticultural sand. Water regularly and feed weekly with a liquid fertilizer throughout the growing season. In winter, in cool and cold climates, cut back on the watering and place in a frost-free environment that has good air circulation.

 medicinal

The cancer bush is a traditional Cape remedy that is taken as a bitter tonic and used for numerous conditions including chickenpox, piles, backache and rheumatism.

In 2001, the Medical Research Council of South Africa performed clinical trials to assess the immune-boosting properties of the cancer bush to support the anecdotal evidence that this plant can improve the quality of life of thousands of people both with HIV and full-blown AIDS. A multi-disciplinary team headed by Dr. Nigel Gericke, a botanist, medical doctor and indigenous plant specialist, found that *Sutherlandia* contained a powerful combination of molecules which have been identified and used in the treatment of patients with cancer, tuberculosis, diabetes, schizophrenia and clinical depression, and as an antiretroviral agent.

 warning

This herb should be taken under supervision only.

Seed pods

Symphytum
COMFREY

Also known as Knitbone, Boneset, Bruisewort, Knitback, Church bells, Abraham, Isaac-and-Jacob (from the variation in flower color) and Saracen's root. From the family Boraginaceae.

Native to Europe and Asia, it was introduced into America in the 17th century, where it has naturalized.

Traditionally known as Saracen's root, common comfrey is believed to have been brought to England by the Crusaders, who had discovered its value as a healing agent — mucilaginous secretions strong enough to act as a bone-setting plaster, and which gave it the nickname Knitbone.

The Crusaders passed it to monks for cultivation in their monastic herb gardens, dedicated to the care of the sick.

Elizabethan physicians and herbalists were never without it. A recipe from that time is for an ointment made from comfrey root boiled in sugar and licorice, and mixed with coltsfoot, mallow and poppy seed. People also made comfrey tea for colds and bronchitis.

Symphytum ibericum

But times have changed. Once the panacea for all ills, comfrey is now under suspicion medicinally as a carcinogen. In line with its common name "Bruisewort," research in America has shown that comfrey breaks down the red blood cells. At the same time, the Japanese are investigating how to harness its beneficial qualities; there is a research program into the high protein and vitamin B content of the herb.

Symphytum x uplandicum

Symphytum officinale
Comfrey (Wild or Common)
Hardy perennial. Ht and spread 3 ft. White/purple/pink flowers in summer. This is the best medicinal comfrey and can also be employed as a liquid feed, although the potassium content is only 3.09 percent compared to 7.09 percent in "Bocking 14." It makes a first-class composting plant, as it helps the rapid breakdown of other compost materials. **Zone 5.**

Symphytum x uplandicum
Russian Comfrey
Hardy perennial. Ht 3 ft., spread indefinite. Pink/purple flowers in summer. Green lance-shaped leaves. This is a hybrid that occurred naturally in Upland, Sweden. It is a cross between *S. officinale*, the herbalist's comfrey, and *S. asperum*, the blue-flowered, prickly comfrey from Russia. A very attractive form is *S. x uplandicum* "Variegatum," with cream and green leaves. **Zone 5.**

Symphytum x uplandicum "Bocking 4"
Hardy perennial. Ht 3 ft., spread indefinite. Flowers near to violet in color, in spring and early summer. Thick, solid stems. Large green lance-shaped leaves. Not a particularly attractive plant but it contains almost 35 percent total protein, the same percentage as in soybeans. Comfrey is an important animal feed in some parts of the world, especially in Africa. **Zone 5.**

Symphytum x uplandicum "Bocking 14"
Hardy perennial. Ht 3 ft., spread indefinite. Mauve flowers in spring and early summer. Thin stems. Green oval leaves, tapering to a point. This variety has the highest potash content, which makes it the best for producing liquid manure. **Zone 5.**

 ## varieties

Symphytum "Hidcote Blue"
Comfrey Hidcote Blue
Hardy perennial. Ht 20 in., spread 24 in. Pale blue flowers in spring and early summer. Green lance-shaped leaves. Very attractive in a large border. **Zone 5.**

Symphytum ibericum
Dwarf Comfrey
Hardy perennial. Ht 10 in., spread 40 in. Yellow/white flowers in spring. Green lance-shaped leaves. An excellent ground cover plant, having foliage through most winters. This comfrey contains little potassium and no allantoin, the crucial medicinal substance. **Zone 5.**

cultivation

Propagation

Seed
Not nearly as reliable as root cuttings or division. Sow in spring or fall in either seed or plug trays. Germination slow and erratic.

Root Cuttings
In spring, dig up a piece of root, cut into 1 in. sections, and put these small sections into a prepared plug or seed tray.

Division
Use either the double spade method or simply dig up a chunk in the spring and replant it elsewhere.

Pests and Diseases

Sometimes suffers from rust and powdery mildew in late fall. In both cases cut the plant down and burn the contaminated leaves.

Maintenance

Spring Sow seeds. Divide plants. Take root cuttings.
Summer Cut back leaves for composting, or to use as a mulch around other herbs in the growing season.
Fall Sow seeds.
Winter None needed.

Garden Cultivation

Fully hardy in the garden, all the comfreys prefer sun or semi-shade and a moist soil, but will tolerate most conditions. The large taproot can cause problems if you want to move the plant. When doing this make sure you dig up all the root because any left behind will reappear later.

Harvesting

Cut leaves with shears from early summer to fall to provide foliage for making liquid feed. Each plant is able to give four cuts a year if well fed. Cut leaves for drying before flowering. Dig up roots in fall for drying.

Liquid Manure

Use either *S. x uplandicum* or *S. x uplandicum* "Bocking 14" to make a quickly available source of potassium for the organic gardener. One method of extracting it is to put 14 pounds of freshly cut comfrey into a 20 gallon tapped, fiberglass water barrel. Do not use metal as rust will add toxic quantities of iron

Powdery mildew on comfrey leaf

oxide to the liquid manure. Fill up the barrel with rain or tap water and cover with a lid to exclude the light. In about 4 weeks a clear liquid can be drawn off from the tap at the bottom. Ideal feed for tomatoes, onions, gooseberries, beans and all potash-hungry crops. It can be used as a foliar feed.

The disadvantage of this method is that the liquid stinks, because comfrey foliage is about 3.4 percent protein, and when proteins break down they smell.

An alternative is to bore a hole into the side (just above the bottom) of a plastic garbage can. Stand the container on bricks, so that it is far enough off the ground to allow a dish to be placed under the hole. Pack it solid with cut comfrey, and place something (a heavy lump of concrete) on top to weigh down the leaves. Cover with a lid, and in about 3 weeks a black liquid will drip from the hole into a dish.

This concentrate can be stored in a screw-top bottle if you do not want to use it immediately. Dilute it 1 part to 40 parts water, and if you plan to use it as a foliar feed, strain it first.

container growing

Comfrey is not suitable for growing indoors, but it can be grown on a patio as long as the container is large enough. Situate in partial shade and give plenty of water in warm weather.

culinary

Fresh leaves and shoots were eaten as a vegetable or salad and there is no reason to suppose that it is dangerous to do so now, although it may be best to err on the side of caution until suspicions are resolved (see "Warning" below).

medicinal

Comfrey has received much attention in recent years, both as a valuable healing herb, a source of vitamin B12 and self-proliferate allantoin, and as a potential source of protein. Comfrey is also useful as a poultice for varicose ulcers and a compress for varicose veins, and it alleviates and heals minor burns.

warning

Comfrey is reported to cause serious liver damage if taken in large amounts over a long period of time.

other uses

Boil fresh leaves for golden fabric dye (see p. 675).

Comfrey is a good feed for racehorses and helps cure laminitis. For curing septic sores on animals, make a poultice between clean pieces of cotton and tie to the affected places.

Comfrey dye

WINTER TARRAGON

Also known as Mexican tarragon, Spanish tarragon and Sweet mace. From the family Asteraceae.

The first time I saw winter tarragon was over 15 years ago in Florida, where I found it on sale in a garden center. Until then I had never seen an edible *Tagetes* and was amazed by the power and the anise flavor of the leaves, which proved to be great in cooking.

Winter tarragon is indigenous to southern and central Mexico. Historically it is said that the Aztecs used it to flavor *chocólatl*, a coca-based drink and it is still popular today with the Tarahumara Indians of Chihuahua. It is revered by the modern Huichol Indians as a shamanic trance "tobacco," which is used in their religious rituals.

 ## varieties

Tagetes lucida
Winter Tarragon, Mexican Tarragon
Tender herbaceous perennial. Ht 32 in. in warm climates only, spread 18 in. Sweetly scented yellow flowers in late summer. Rarely flowers in cold temperatures. Narrow lance-shaped aromatic midgreen toothed leaves, which have strong aniseed scent and flavor. This herb, in cool climates, dies back in early spring, reappearing in early summer. **All zones.**

Tagetes patula
Wild Mexican marigold, French marigold
Half-hardy annual. Ht 4 ft., spread 18 in. Clusters of single yellow flowers, midsummer until first frosts.

Aromatic, deeply divided, lightly toothed midgreen leaves. This species is said to deter nematodes in the soil, and whitefly from tomatoes. The leaves have been used to flavor food; medicinally it is a diuretic and it improves the digestion. Externally it has been used to treat sore eyes and rheumatism. The flowers have been used to feed poultry and to color dairy produce and textiles. **All zones.**

 ## cultivation

Propagation
Seed
Sow the seeds in early spring into prepared seed or plug module trays using a standard seed compost mixed in equal parts with perlite. Place under protection at 68°F; germination takes 3 to 7 days. Once the seedlings are large enough, repot into a soil-based compost mixed in equal parts with horticultural sand. Alternatively sow in late spring, into prepared open ground, when the air temperature does not fall below 50°F at night; germination takes 2 to 4 weeks.

Cuttings
Take tip cuttings in early summer, place the cutting into prepared plug module trays using a standard seed compost mixed in equal parts with perlite. Place in a warm environment until rooted, about 2 to 3 weeks. Once fully rooted, repot into a soil-based compost mixed in equal parts with horticultural sand.

Pests and Diseases
Rarely suffers from pests. In cold, damp climates it will

WINTER TARRAGON

die back in late winter; make sure at this time of year that the leaves do not become too damp because this could rot the crown. If you notice mildew, cut off all the remaining growth, raise the container up onto some bricks and put in a well-aired, frost-free place.

Maintenance
Spring Sow seeds. Cut back any winter growth.
Summer Take cuttings.
Fall Lift garden plants and bring in containers once the night temperature falls below 50°F.
Winter Cut back the watering to minimal.

Garden Cultivation
Winter tarragon can only be grown successfully outside all year round in a tropical or subtropical climate. In cooler climates it must be grown as an annual or lifted in winter. Plant in a well-drained fertile soil in a sunny position.

Harvesting
The leaves can be picked as required throughout the growing season for using fresh. Alternatively pick in midsummer for drying.

 container growing

Winter tarragon is ideal for growing in a container in cool and cold climates. Pot up using a soilless compost mixed in equal parts with horticultural sand. Once the night temperature falls below 50°F, bring the container into a frost-free environment and cut back the watering to minimal but not totally dry. Repot each spring, after removing any winter growth. Only repot one size up at a time as this herb likes being pot bound.

 medicinal

The leaves of this herb are used as a relaxant and to treat diarrhea, indigestion, malaria and feverishness. It also has the reputation of being a very good hangover cure.

 other uses

Burnt leaves make a good insect repellent. The juice from crushed leaves when applied to ticks makes them easy to remove.

 warning

Not to be taken medicinally when pregnant or breast feeding. If taken in excess it can cause hallucinations.

Tagetes patula

 culinary

Winter tarragon makes a good substitute for French tarragon (*Artemisia dracunculus*), not only in winter, when French Tarragon has died back into the ground, but also where it is difficult to grow, i.e., in humid climates. The leaves of this tarragon are much stronger and more anise than the French variety so use with care until you get used to it.

Chicken and Winter Tarragon Pocket
Serves 2

2 skinless organic chicken breasts
2 cloves garlic, peeled and sliced
6 x 4 in. sprigs winter tarragon, leaves
  removed and chopped
1 oz. butter
²⁄₃ cup white wine
Extra-wide aluminum foil

Preheat the oven to 425°F. Cut two pieces of aluminum foil 14 in. x 20 in. Place them on top of each other. Then fold in half and seal the two long sides leaving the top open. Place the chicken breasts in the foil bag, with the garlic, chopped tarragon and butter. Check the sides of the bag are well sealed then pour in the white wine and seal the top. Place this on a baking sheet and put in the preheated oven for 25 minutes. Once cooked, place the foil bag onto a plate or serving dish before opening to catch all the juices. Serve with baked potatoes and a crisp green salad.

Tanacetum balsamita
ALECOST

Also known as Costmary, Bible Leaf, English Mace and Sweet Mary. From the family Asteraceae.

The first syllable in the common name, "alecost," is derived from the use to which its scented leaves and flowering tops were used in the Middle Ages, namely to clear, preserve and impart an astringent minty flavor to beer. The word "cost" derives from *kostos*, the Greek for spicy so therefore "alecost" literally means a spicy herb for ale. With the demise of its use in beer it has now become a rare plant in Europe, however, in North America it can be found as a garden escape growing wild in the Eastern and mid-West states.

 varieties

Tanacetum balsamita
Alecost
Perennial. Ht. 3 ft. and spread 18 in. Clusters of small white yellow-eyed daisy flowers from July to September. Oblong, silver/green mint-scented leaves. **Zones 6 to 9.**

Tanacetum balsamita subsp. *balsamitoides*
Camphor plant
Perennial. Ht. 3 ft. and spread 18 in. Clusters of small white yellow-eyed daisy flowers from July to September. Oblong, silver/green camphor-scented leaves. **Zones 6 to 9.**

 cultivation

Propagation
Seed
Although possible, as it is difficult to obtain viable seed I recommend raising this plant from division.

Division
Divide established plants in spring or early fall. Either plant out directly into the prepared garden or repot into individual pots using a potting compost mixed in equal parts with composted fine bark. If you have a very wet cold soil it is better to winter fall divided plants in pots, in a cold frame or cold greenhouse.

Pests and Diseases
Both species rarely suffer from pest or diseases.

Maintenance
Spring Divide established plants.
Summer Dead head flowers.
Fall Cut back the flowers. Divide established plants.
Winter Tidy up dead leaves as these will spread disease if left to rot. Protect pot grown plants from excessive wet.

Garden Cultivation
Both species will adapt to most conditions. However, they prefer a fertile, well-drained soil. Plant at a distance of 2 ft. from other plants and, if possible, in a sunny position because when planted in shade they will not flower.

Harvesting
Pick Alecost leaves for culinary use throughout the growing season. For drying pick the leaves in late spring, before flowering, which is when the leaves have the best sweet scent.

 container growing

This herb is not ideal for growing in containers, year round, as it grows tall and rapidly outgrows its pot, so requiring regular repotting throughout the growing season.

 culinary

Alecost leaves have a sharp bitter tang which can be overpowering so use sparingly. Add finely minced leaves to carrots, salads, game, poultry, stuffings and fruit cakes.

 medicinal

lly a tea made from the leaves of this herb was used to ease the pain of childbirth. It was also used as a tonic for colds, catarrh, stomach upsets and cramps.

Rub a fresh leaf of Alecost on a bee sting or horse fly bite to relieve the pain.

 other uses

The leaves and flowers can be used in home brewing to clear, flavor and preserve the beer. Dried leaves make a good addition to potpourri, they can also be added to linen bags where they not only smell good but also act as a good moth repellent.

Fresh or dried leaves of Alecost can be added to baths for a refreshing soak.

⚠ warning

Do not use camphor in any culinary dishes.

Tanacetum cinerariifolium

PYRETHRUM

Also known as Dalmatian Pellitory. From the family Asteraceae.

This plant is a native of Croatia and can be found growing wild in the hills above the Adriatic sea. It is now cultivated commercially in many parts of the world, including Japan, South Africa and parts of central Europe for its insecticidal properties. Originally the insecticide was known as Dalmatian insect powder because for many hundreds of years the eastern coast of the Adriatic was known as Dalmatia. The insecticide is now known as Pyrethrum and can be found in many proprietary products.

 ## varieties

Tanacetum cinerariifolium syn. *Chrysanthemum cinerariifolium*
Hardy perennial. Ht 12–15 in., spread 8 in. Daisy-like flower, white petals with a yellow center. Leaves green/gray, finely divided, with white down on the underside. **Zone 6.**

Tanacetum coccineum syn. *Chrysanthemum roseum*
Hardy perennial. Ht 12–24 in., spread 12 in. Large flowerhead which can be white or red, and sometimes tipped with yellow. Very variable under cultivation. Vivid green leaves. Native of Iran. It was known as Persian Insect Powder, but it is not as strong as *T. cinerariifolium* so fell out of favor. An attractive garden plant. **Zone 5.**

 ## cultivation

Propagation
Seeds
In spring sow into a prepared seed or plug tray and cover with perlite. Germination is easy and takes 14 to 21 days. In late spring, when the young plants are large enough and after a period of hardening off, plant out into a prepared site in the garden 6–12 in. apart.

Division
Established clumps can be dug up in the spring or fall and divided.

Pests and Diseases
Mostly free from pests and diseases.

Maintenance
Spring Sow seed. Divide established plants.
Summer Deadhead flowers to prolong season if not collecting seed.
Fall Divide established plants if necessary.
Winter Fully hardy.

Garden Cultivation
Pyrethrum likes a well-drained soil in a sunny spot; it is drought tolerant and fully hardy in most winters.

Harvesting
The flower heads are collected just as they open and dried gently. When they are quite dry, store away from light. The insecticide is made from the powdered dried flower.

 ## container growing

This herb is very well suited for growing in containers, especially terracotta. Use a soil-based compost mixed in equal parts with composted fine bark. Water well during the summer months, but be lean on the liquid fertilizer, otherwise the leaves will become green and it will stop flowering.

 ## medicinal

This herb is rarely used medicinally. Herbalists have found the roots to be a remedy for certain fevers. Recent research has shown that the flowerheads possess a weak antibiotic.

 ## other uses

This is a useful insecticide because it is nontoxic to mammals and does not accumulate in the environment or in the bodies of animals. It acts by paralyzing the nervous system of the insects, and can kill pests living on the skin of man and animals. Sprinkle the dry powder from the flowers to deter all common insects, pests, bed bugs, cockroaches, flies, mosquitoes, aphids and ants. Traditionally the dried flowers were mixed with methylated spirits and water and used as a garden spray. When buying it in a proprietary product, do read the instructions carefully as Pyrethrum is harmful to many beneficial pollinating insects.

 ## warning

When used as an insecticide, it can kill helpful insects and fish, as well as pests. Can cause contact dermititis.

Tanacetum parthenium
FEVERFEW

Also known as Featherfew in America and Febrifuge. From the family Asteraceae.

The common name suggests that this herb was used in the treatment of fevers and the old herbalists even call it febrifuge, however, strange as it may seem, the herb was hardly ever employed for this purpose. In the 17th century Culpeper advised it use for pains in the head and colds and nowadays it is used in the treatment of migraines.

Feverfew in sachets makes a good moth repellant

 varieties

Tanacetum parthenium syn. Chrysanthemum parthenium
Feverfew
Hardy herbaceous perennial. Height up to 4 ft., spread 18 in. Clusters of small white yellow-eyed daisy flowers from early summer until the first frosts. The leaf is midgreen, lobed and divided with lightly serrated edges. **Zone 4.**

Tanacetum parthenium "Aureum"
Golden Feverfew
Hardy herbaceous perennial. Height 8–18 in., spread 18 in. Clusters of small white yellow-eyed daisy flowers from early summer until the first frosts. The leaf is golden, lobed and divided with lightly serrated edges. Excellent edging plant. **Zone 5.**

 cultivation

Propagation
Seed
The fine, thin and fairly small seeds tend to stick together especially if they are damp. Mix the seed with a small amount of perlite or dry sand prior to sowing. Sow seeds in fall or spring, into prepared pots or cell-packs using a standard seed compost; do not cover. Place in a cold frame, germination 2 to 4 weeks. Fall sowings, winter in the cold frame. Plant out when large enough to handle 12 in. apart.

Cuttings
Take stem cutting in summer, making sure there are not flowers on the cutting material.

Division
Divide established plants in fall or spring, replanting into a prepared site.

Pests and Diseases
Aphids are the only real problem for feverfew.

Maintenance
Spring Sow seeds.
Summer As flowering finishes, cut back to restore shape and minimize self-seeding. Take stem cuttings.
Fall Divide established plants. Sow seeds.
Winter No need for protection, frost hardy.

Garden Cultivation
Plant in a well-drained fertile soil in a sunny position. Feverfew is drought tolerant and will adapt to most soils and conditions, however if planted in shade they are unlikely to flower. Golden feverfew can suffer from sun scorch; if this occurs cut back and the new growth will be unaffected.

Harvesting
Pick the leaves before flowering to use fresh or to dry. Pick the flower heads just as they open for drying.

 container growing

Both forms of Feverfew look attractive in containers. Use a soilless compost mixed in equal parts with composted fine bark.

 culinary

The young leaves can be added to salads; however they have a very bitter taste so use sparingly.

 medicinal

Feverfew is a renowned remedy for certain types of migraines. Because they are so bitter place two to three fresh leaves in between a slice of bread, this will make them more palatable. Do not take for a prolonged period and do not over-eat.

 other uses

A decoction made from the leaves is a good basic household disinfectant. The dried leaves make a good moth repellent when placed in a sachet.

 warning

One side effect associated with taking feverfew is ulceration of the mouth.

Tanacetum vulgare
TANSY

Also known as Bachelor's buttons, Bitter buttons, Golden buttons, Stinking Willy, Hind heel and Parsley fern. From the family Asteraceae.

Tansy is a native to Europe and Asia, and it has managed to become naturalized elsewhere, especially in North America.

The name derives from the Greek *athanasia*, meaning "immortality." In ancient times it was used in the preparation of the embalming sheets and rubbed on corpses to save them from earthworms or corpse worm.

 varieties

Tanacetum vulgare
Tansy
Hardy perennial. Ht 3 ft., spread 1–2 ft. and more. Yellow button flowers in late summer. The aromatic leaf is deeply indented, toothed and fairly dark green. **Zone 3.**

Tanacetum vulgare var. crispum
Curled Tansy
As *T. vulgare* except ht 2 ft., and the aromatic leaf is crinkly, curly and dark green. **Zone 3.**

Tanacetum vulgare "Isla Gold"
Tansy Isala Gold
As *T. vulgare* except ht 2 ft., and the leaf is golden in color. **Zone 3.**

Tanacetum vulgare "Silver Lace"
Tansy "Silver Lace"
As *T. vulgare* except ht 2 ft., and the leaf starts off white-flecked with green, progressing to full green. If, however, you keep cutting it, some of the variegation can be maintained. **Zone 3.**

 cultivation

Propagation
Seed
Sow the small seed in spring or fall in a prepared seed or plug tray using a standard seed compost, and cover with perlite. Germination takes 10 to 21 days. Plant out 18 in. apart when the seedlings are large enough to handle. If sown in the fall, protect over winter.

Division
Divide root runners in either spring or fall.

Pests and Diseases
Aphids are the only real problem for tansy.

Maintenance
Spring Sow seed. Divide established clumps.
Summer Cut back after flowering to maintain shape and color.
Fall Divide established clumps. Sow seeds.
Winter The plant is fully hardy and dies back into the ground for winter.

Garden Cultivation
Tansy needs to be positioned with care as the roots spread widely. The gold and variegated forms are much less invasive and very attractive in a semi-shaded border. They tolerate most conditions provided the soil is not completely wet.

Harvesting
Pick leaves as required. Gather flowers when open.

 container growing

Because of its antisocial habit, container growing is recommended. Use a soilless compost and a large container, water throughout the growing season, and only feed about twice during flowering. In winter keep on the dry side in a cool place.

 medicinal

Can be used by trained herbalists to expel roundworm and threadworm. Use tansy tea externally to treat scabies, and as a compress to bring relief to painful rheumatic joints.

 warning

Use tansy only under medical supervision. It is a strong emmenagogue, provoking the onset of a period, and should not be used during pregnancy. An overdose of tansy oil or tea can be fatal.

 other uses

Rub into the coat of your dog or cat to prevent fleas. Hang leaves indoors to deter flies. Put dried sprigs under carpets. Add to insect-repellent sachets. Sprinkle chopped leaves and flowers to deter ants and mice. It produces a yellow/green woollen dye.

Tanacetum vulgare "Isla Gold"

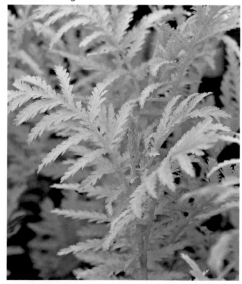

Taraxacum
DANDELION

Also known as Pee in the bed, Lions teeth, Fairy clock, Clock, Clock flower, Clocks and watches, Farmers clocks, Old mans clock, One clock, Wetweed, Blowball, Cankerwort, Lionstooth, Priests crown, Puffball, Swinesnout, White chicory, Wild chicory and Piss-a-beds. From the family Asteraceae.

Dandelion is one of nature's great medicines and it really proves that a weed is only a plant out of place! It is in fact one of the most useful of herbs. It has become naturalized throughout the temperate regions of the world and flourishes on nitrogen-rich soils in any situation to a height of 11,000 ft.

There is no satisfactory explanation why it is called dandelion, dents lioness, tooth of the lion in medieval Latin, and *dent de lion* in French. The lion's tooth may be the taproot, the jagged leaf or the flower parts.

The Arabs promoted its use in the 11th century. By the 16th it was well established as an official drug. The apothecaries knew it as *Herba taraxacon* or *Herba urinari*, and Culpeper called it piss-a-beds, all referring to its diuretic qualities.

 varieties

Taraxacum officinale **agg.**
Dandelion
Perennial. Ht 6–9 in. Large, brilliant yellow flowers 2 in. wide, spring to fall. The flower heads as they turn to seed form a fluffy ball (dandelion clock). Leaves oblong with a jagged edge. **Zone 3.**

Taraxacum kok-saghyz **Rodin**
Russian Dandelion
Perennial. Ht 12 in. Similar to the above. Extensively cultivated during World War II: latex was extracted from the roots as a source of rubber. **Zone 3.**

Taraxacum mongolicum
Chinese Dandelion
Perennial. Ht 10–12 in. Similar to the above. Used to treat infections, particularly mastitis. **Zone 3.**

 cultivation

Propagation
Seed
Grow as an annual to prevent bitterness developing in the plant. Sow seed in spring on the surface of pots or plug trays. Do not use seed trays as the long taproot makes it difficult to prick out. Cover with a fine layer of perlite. Germination will be in 3 to 6 weeks, depending on seed freshness and air temperature. Plant out when large enough to handle.

Root
In spring and fall, sections of the root can be cut and put in pots, seed trays or plug trays. Each piece will sprout again, just like comfrey.

Pests and Diseases
Dandelion is rarely attacked by either pest or disease.

Maintenance
Spring Sow seeds for use as an fall salad herb. Take root cuttings.
Summer Continually pick off the flower buds if you are growing dandelion as a salad crop.
Fall Put an up-turned flower pot over some of the plants to blanch them for fall salads. Sow seed for spring salad crop. Take root cuttings.
Winter No protection is needed. For salad crops,

however, if temperatures fall below 15°F, cover with floating row cover or 3 in. of straw or bracken to keep the leaves sweet.

Garden Cultivation

If the dandelion was a rare plant, it would be thought a highly desirable garden species, for the flowers are most attractive, sweet smelling and a brilliant yellow, and then form the delightful puff balls. Up to that point all is fine. But then the wind disperses the seed all over the garden. And it is very difficult to eradicate when established since every bit of root left behind produces another plant. So, it finds no favor at all with gardeners.

In general, details on how to grow dandelions are superfluous. Most people only want to know how to get rid of them. The easiest time to dig up the plants completely is in the early spring.

Harvesting

Pick leaves as required to use fresh, and flowers for wine as soon as they open fully. Dig up roots in fall for drying.

Dandelion wine

 ## container growing

Dandelions do look attractive growing in containers, especially in window boxes, if you can stand neighbors' remarks. But in all seriousness the containers will need to be deep to accommodate the long taproot.

 ## medicinal

It is one of the most useful medicinal plants, as all parts are effective and safe to use. It is regarded as one of the best herbal remedies for kidney and liver complaints. The root is a mildly laxative, bitter tonic, valuable in treating dyspepsia and constipation. The leaves are a powerful diuretic. However, unlike conventional diuretics, dandelion does not leach potassium from the body as its rich potassium content replaces what the body loses.

The latex contained in the leaves and stalks is very effective in removing corns and in treating warts and verrucas. Apply the juice from the plant daily to the affected part.

The flowers can be boiled with sugar for coughs, but honey has a greater medicinal value.

 ## other uses

As an herbal fertilizer, dandelion has a good supply of copper. Pick three plants completely: leaves, flowers and all. Place in a bucket, pour over 1 quart of boiling water, cover and allow to stand for 30 minutes. Strain through an old pair of tights or something similar. This fertilizer will not store.

A dye, yellow-brown in color, can be obtained from the root and dandelions are excellent food for domestic rabbits, guinea pigs and gerbils.

There is one thing for which they are useless, however — flower arrangements. As soon as you pick them and put them in water, their flowers close tight.

 ## culinary

Both the leaves and root have long been eaten as a highly nutritious salad. In the last century, cultivated forms with large leaves were developed as a fall and spring vegetable. The leaves were usually blanched in the same way as chicory. Dandelion salad in spring is also considered a blood cleanser, owing to its diuretic and digestive qualities. The leaves are very high in vitamins A, B, C and D, the A content being higher than that of carrots. The flowers make an excellent country wine and dandelion roots provide, when dried, chopped and roasted, the best-known substitute for coffee.

Dandelion and Bacon Salad
Serves 4

½ pound young dandelion leaves
4 tablespoons olive or walnut oil
1 tablespoon white wine vinegar
sugar
¼ pound bacon, diced
1 clove garlic, crushed
½ in. slice white bread, cubed
Salt and freshly ground black pepper
Oil for cooking

Wash and dry the leaves and tear into the salad bowl. Make a vinaigrette using olive oil and vinegar, and season to taste, adding a little sugar if desired. Fry the bacon, crushed garlic and bread in oil until golden brown. Pour the contents of the pan over the leaves and turn the leaves until thoroughly coated. Add the vinaigrette and toss again and serve at once.

Teucrium chamaedrys L.
WALL GERMANDER

Also known as Ground oak and Wild germander. From the family Lamiaceae.

This attractive plant, native of Europe, is now naturalized in Britain and other countries in the temperate zone. It is found on dry chalky soils.

The Latin *Teucrium* is said to have been named after Teucer, first king of Troy. It is the ancient Greek word for "ground oak," its leaves resembling those of the oak tree.

In medieval times, it was a popular strewing herb and a remedy for dropsy, jaundice and gout. It was also used in powder form for treating head colds, and as a snuff.

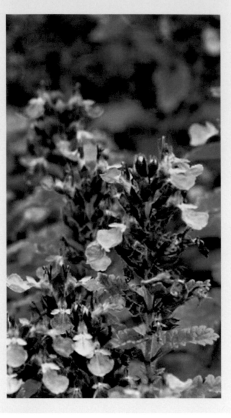

Pests and Diseases
Wall germander rarely suffers from pests or diseases.

Maintenance
Spring Sow seeds. Take softwood cuttings. Trim established plants and hedges. Divide established plants.
Summer Trim plants after flowering, take semi-hardwood cuttings.
Fall Trim hedges.
Winter Protect when temperatures drop below 23°F.

Garden Cultivation
Wall germander needs a well-drained soil (slightly alkaline) and a sunny position. It is hardier than lavender and cotton lavender, and makes an ideal hedging or edging plant. To make a good dense hedge, plant at a distance of 6 in. If you clip the hedge in spring and fall to maintain its shape, you will never need to cut it hard back.

It can also be planted in rockeries, and in stone walls where it looks most attractive. During the growing season it does not need extra water, even in hot summers, nor does it need extra protection in cold winters.

Harvesting
For drying for medicinal use, pick leaves before flowering, and flowering stems when the flowers are in bud.

 varieties

Teucrium chamaedrys L.
Wall Germander
Evergreen hardy perennial. Ht 18 in., spread 8 in. Pink flowers from midsummer to early fall. The leaves are midgreen and shaped like miniature oak leaves with crumpled edges. **Zones 5 and 6.**

Teucrium fruticans
Tree Germander
Evergreen hardy perennial. Ht 3–6 ft., spread 6–12 in. Blue flowers in summer. The leaves are aromatic, gray/green with a white underside. **Zone 8.**

Teucrium x lucidrys
Hedge Germander
Evergreen hardy perennial. Ht 18 in., spread 8 in. Pink flowers from midsummer to early fall. The leaves are dark green, small, shiny and oval. When rubbed, they smell pleasantly spicy. **Zone 5.**

 cultivation

Propagation
Seed
Sow the small seeds in spring. Use a prepared seed or plug tray and a standard seed compost mixed in equal parts with composted fine bark. Cover with perlite. Germination can be erratic — from 2 to 4 weeks. When the seedlings are large enough to handle, plant in a prepared site 8 in. apart.

Cuttings
This is a better method of propagating germander. Take softwood cuttings from the new growth in spring, or semi-hardwood in summer. Ensure compost does not dry out or become sodden.

Division
The teucriums produce creeping rootstock in the spring and are easy to divide. Dig up the plants, split them in half, and replant in a chosen site.

 container growing

Looks good in containers. Use a soilless compost mixed in equal parts with composted fine bark. Only feed in the flowering season. Keep on the dry side in winter.

 culinary

Used extensively in the flavoring of liqueurs.

 medicinal

Its herbal use today is minor. However, there is a revival of interest, and some use it as a remedy for digestive and liver troubles, anemia and bronchitis.

Teucrium scorodonia

WOOD SAGE

Also known as Gypsy sage, Mountain sage, Wild sage and Garlic sage. From the family Lamiaceae.

This plant is a native of Europe and has become naturalized in Britain and other countries in the temperate zone.

There is not much written about wood sage apart from the fact that, like alecost, it was used in making ale before hops were introduced. However, Gertrude Jekyll recognized its value, and with renewed interest in her gardens comes a revival of interest in wood sage.

 ## varieties

Teucrium scorodonia
Wood Sage
Hardy perennial. Ht 12–24 in., spread 10 in. Pale greenish-white flowers in summer. Soft green heart-shaped leaves, which have a mild smell of crushed garlic. **Zone 6.**

Teucrium scorodonia "Crispum"
Curly Wood Sage
Hardy perennial. Ht 14 in., spread 12 in. Pale greenish-white flowers in summer. The leaves are soft, oval and olive green with a reddish tinge to their crinkled edges. Whenever it is on show it causes much comment. **Zone 6.**

 ## cultivation

Propagation
Wood sage can be propagated by seed, cuttings or division. Curly wood sage can only be propagated by cuttings or division.

Seed
Sow the fairly small seed under protection in fall or spring in a prepared seed or plug tray. Use a standard seed compost mixed in equal parts with composted fine bark, and cover with perlite. Germination can be erratic, taking from 2 to 4 weeks. When the seedlings are large enough to handle, repot and winter under cover in a cold frame. In the spring, after a period of hardening off, plant out in a prepared site in the garden at a distance of 10 in.

Cuttings
Take softwood cuttings from the new growth in spring, or semi-hardwood cuttings in summer.

Division
Both wood sages produce creeping rootstock. In the spring they are easy to divide.

Pests and Diseases
In the majority of cases, it is free from pests and diseases.

Maintenance
Spring Sow seeds. Divide established plants. Take softwood cuttings.
Summer Take semi-hardwood cuttings.

Fall Sow seeds.
Winter No need for protection, the plants die back for the winter.

Garden Cultivation
It grows well in semi-shaded situations, but also thrives in full sun on sandy and gravelly soils. It will adapt quite happily to clay and heavy soils, but not produce such prolific growth.

Harvesting
Pick young leaves for fresh as required.

 ## container growing

I have grown curly wood sage most successfully in containers. The plain wood sage does not look quite so attractive. Use a soilless compost mixed in equal parts with composted fine bark, and plant in a large container — its creeping rootstock can too easily become pot-bound. Only feed twice in a growing season, otherwise the leaves become large, soft and floppy. When the plant dies back, put it somewhere cool and keep it almost dry.

 ## medicinal

Wood sage has been used to treat blood disorders, colds and fevers, and as a diuretic and wound herb.

 ## culinary

The leaves of ordinary wood sage have a mild garlic flavor. When young and tender, the leaves can be added to salads for variety. But go easy as they are slightly bitter.

THYME

Thymus

From the family Lamiaceae.

This is a genus comprising numerous species that are very diverse in appearance and come from many different parts of the world. They are found as far afield as Greenland and Western Asia, although the majority grow in the Mediterranean region.

This ancient herb was used by the Egyptians in oil form for embalming. The Greeks used it in their baths and as an incense in their temples. The Romans used it to purify their rooms, and most probably its use spread through Europe as their invasion train swept as far as Britain. In the Middle Ages drinking it was part of a ritual to enable one to see fairies, and it was one of many herbs used in nosegays to purify the odors of disease. Owing to its antiseptic properties, judges also used it along with rosemary to prevent jail fever.

Thymus vulgaris

Mixed thymes

 ## varieties

There are so many species of thyme that I am only going to mention a few of interest. New ones are being discovered each year. They are eminently collectable. Unfortunately their names can be unreliable, a nursery preferring its pet name or one traditional to it, rather than the correct one.

Thymus caespititius
Caespititius Thyme
Evergreen hardy perennial. Ht 4 in., spread 8 in. Pale pink flowers in summer. The leaves narrow, bright green and close together on the stem. Makes an attractive low-growing mound, good between paving stones. **Zone 7.**

Thymus camphoratus
Camphor Thyme
Evergreen half-hardy perennial. Ht 12 in., spread 8 in. Pink/mauve flowers in summer, large green leaves smelling of camphor. Makes a beautiful compact bush. **Zone 7.**

Thymus cilicicus **Boiss. & Bail.**
Sicily Thyme
Evergreen hardy perennial. Ht 2 in., spread 8 in. Pink flowers in summer. The leaves are bright green, narrow and pointed, growing close together on the stem with an odd celery scent. Makes an attractive low-growing mound, and is good between paving stones. **Zone 9.**

Thymus citriodorus
Lemon Thyme
Evergreen hardy perennial. Ht 12 in., spread 8 in. Pink flowers in summer. Fairly large green leaves with a strong lemon scent. Excellent culinary thyme, combines well with many chicken or fish dishes. **Zone 5.**

Thymus citriodorus "Golden King"

Golden King Thyme

Evergreen hardy perennial. Ht 12 in., spread 8 in. Pink flowers in the summer. Fairly large green leaves variegated with gold, strongly lemon scented. Excellent culinary thyme, combines well with many dishes, like chicken, fish and salad dressing. **Zone 6.**

Thymus citriodorus "Silver Queen"

Silver Queen Thyme

Evergreen hardy perennial. Ht 12 in., spread 8 in. Pink flowers in the summer. Fairly large leaves, gray with silver variegation, a strong lemon scent. Excellent culinary thyme, combines well with many dishes, like chicken and salad dressing. **Zone 6.**

Thymus Coccineus Group

Coccineus Thyme

Also known as creeping red thyme. Evergreen hardy perennial, prostrate form, a creeper. Red flowers in summer. Green small leaves. Decorative, aromatic and good ground cover. **Zone 4.**

Thymus comosus

Evergreen hardy perennial. Ht 4 in., spread 8 in. Attractive clusters of pink flowers in summer. Small midgreen round leaves. Excellent for growing in gravel. **Zone 5.**

Thymus doerfleri

Doerfleri Thyme

Evergreen half-hardy perennial. Ht 1 in., spread 8 in. Mauve/pink flowers in summer, gray, hairy, thin leaves, which are mat forming. Decorative thyme, good for rockeries, hates being wet in winter. Originates from the Balkan Peninsula. **Zone 8.**

Thymus herba-barona

Thymus "Jekka"

Thymus doerfleri "Bressingham"

Bressingham Thyme

Evergreen hardy perennial. Ht 1 in., spread 8 in. Mauve/pink flowers in summer. Thin, green, hairy leaves, which are mat forming. Decorative thyme, good for rockeries, hates being wet in winter. **Zone 8.**

Thymus "Doone Valley"

Doone Valley Thyme

Evergreen hardy perennial. Ht 3 in., spread 8 in. Purple flowers in summer. Round variegated green and gold leaves with a lemon scent. Very decorative, can be used in cooking if nothing else is available. **Zone 7.**

Thymus "Fragrantissimus"

Orange-Scented Thyme

Evergreen hardy perennial. Ht 12 in., spread 8 in. Small pale pink/white flowers in summer. The leaves are small, narrow, grayish green, and smell of spicy orange. Combines well with stir-fry dishes, poultry — especially duck — and even treacle pudding. **Zone 6.**

Thymus herba-barona

Caraway Thyme

Evergreen hardy perennial. Ht 1 in., spread 8 in. Rose-colored flowers in summer. Dark green small leaves with a unique caraway scent. Good in culinary dishes especially stir fry and meat. It combines well with beef. **Zone 4.**

Thymus "Jekka"

Jekka's Thyme

Evergreen hardy perennial. Ht 4 in., spread 12 in. Clusters of small pink and white flowers in early summer. Prolific midgreen aromatic leaves. Spreading habit. Good culinary flavor. **Zone 6.**

Thymus polytrichus subsp. britannicus

Wild Creeping Thyme

Also known as mother of thyme and creeping thyme.

Evergreen hardy perennial. Ht 1 in., spread 8 in. Pale mauve flowers in summer. Small dark green leaves which, although mildly scented, can be used in cooking. Wild thyme has been valued by herbalists for many centuries. **Zone 4.**

Thymus "Porlock"

Porlock Thyme

Evergreen hardy perennial. Ht 12 in., spread 8 in. Pink flowers in summer. Fairly large green leaves with a mild but definite thyme flavor and scent. Excellent culinary thyme. Medicinal properties are antibacterial and antifungal. **Zone 4.**

Thymus pseudolanuginosus

Woolly Thyme

Evergreen hardy perennial. Ht 1 in., spread 8 in. Pale pink/mauve flowers for most of the summer. Gray hairy mat-forming leaves. Good for rockeries and in stone paths or walls. Dislikes wet winters. **Zone 5.**

Thymus pulegioides

Broad-Leaved Thyme

Evergreen hardy perennial. Ht 3 in., spread 8 in. Pink/mauve flowers in summer. Large round dark green leaves with a strong thyme flavor. Good for culinary uses, excellent for ground cover and good in hanging baskets. **Zone 4.**

Thymus pulegioides "Aureus"

Golden Thyme

Evergreen hardy perennial. Ht 12 in., spread 8 in. Pale pink/lilac flowers. Green leaves that turn gold in summer, good flavor, combining well with vegetarian dishes. **Zone 6.**

Thymus pulegioides "Bertram Anderson"

Bertram Anderson Thyme

Evergreen hardy perennial. Ht 4 in., spread 8 in. Pink/mauve flowers in summer. More of a round mound than "Archer's Gold" and the leaves are slightly rounder with a more even golden look to the leaves. Decorative and culinary, it has a mild thyme flavor. **Zone 6.**

Thymus "Redstart"

Redstart Thyme

Evergreen hardy perennial. Ht 2 in., spread 8 in. Bright red flowers in summer. Small dark green round leaves. Decorative, aromatic and good ground cover. **Zone 4.**

Thymus serpyllum var. *albus*
Creeping White Thyme
Evergreen hardy perennial, prostrate form, a creeper. White flowers in summer. Bright green small leaves. Decorative aromatic and good ground cover. **Zone 4.**

Thymus serpyllum "Annie Hall"
Annie Hall Thyme
Evergreen hardy perennial, prostrate form, a creeper. Pale pink flowers in summer. Small green leaves. Decorative, aromatic and good ground cover. **Zone 4.**

Thymus serpyllum "Goldstream"
Goldstream Thyme
Evergreen hardy perennial, prostrate form, a creeper. Pink/mauve flowers in summer. Green/gold variegated small leaves. Decorative, aromatic and good ground cover. **Zone 4.**

Thymus serpyllum "Lemon Curd"
Lemon Curd Thyme
Evergreen hardy perennial, prostrate form, a creeper. White/pink flowers in summer. Bright green lemon-scented small leaves. Decorative, aromatic and good ground cover. Can be used in cooking if nothing else available.

Thymus serpyllum "Minimalist"
Minimalist Thyme
Evergreen hardy perennial, prostrate form, a creeper. Pink flowers in summer. Tiny leaves, very compact. Decorative, aromatic and good ground cover. Ideal for growing between pavings and alongside paths. **Zone 4.**

Thymus 'Redstart'

Thymus comosus

Thymus serpyllum "Pink Chintz"
Pink Chintz Thyme
Evergreen hardy perennial, prostrate form, a creeper. Pale pink flowers in summer. Gray/green small hairy leaves. Decorative, aromatic, good ground cover. Does not like being wet in winter. **Zone 4.**

Thymus serpyllum "Rainbow Falls"
Rainbow Falls Thyme
Evergreen hardy perennial, prostrate form, a creeper. Purple flowers in summer. Variegated green/gold small leaves. Decorative, aromatic and good ground cover. **Zone 4.**

Thymus serpyllum "Russetings"
Russetings Thyme
Evergreen hardy perennial, prostrate form, a creeper. Purple/mauve flowers in summer. Small green leaves. Decorative, aromatic and good ground cover. **Zone 4.**

Thymus serpyllum "Snowdrift"
Snowdrift Thyme
Evergreen hardy perennial, prostrate form, a creeper. Masses of white flowers in summer. Small green round leaves. Decorative, aromatic and good ground cover. **Zone 4.**

Thymus vulgaris
Common (Garden) Thyme
Evergreen hardy perennial. Ht 12 in., spread 8 in. Mauve flowers in summer. Thin green aromatic leaves. This is the thyme everyone knows. Use in stews, salads, sauces, etc. Medicinal properties are antibacterial and antifungal. **Zone 4.**

Thymus vulgaris "Silver Posie"
Silver Posie Thyme
Evergreen hardy perennial. Ht 12 in., spread 8 in. Pale pink/lilac flower. The leaves have a very pretty gray/ silver variegation with a tinge of pink on the underside. This is a good culinary thyme and looks very attractive in salads. **Zone 4.**

Thymus zygis
Zygis Thyme
Evergreen half-hardy perennial. Ht 12 in., spread 8 in. White attractive flowers. Small thin gray/green leaves which are aromatic. This is an attractive thyme which is good for rockeries. Originates from Spain and Portugal, therefore does not like cold wet winters. **Zone 7.**

Upright Thymes
Up to 12 in.:
T. caespititius, T. cilicicus Boiss. & Bail., *T.* "Jekka," *T. pulegioides* "Bertram Anderson"

12 in. and above:
T. camphoratus, T. citriodorus, T. "Fragrantissimus,'" *T.* 'Porlock,' *T. vulgaris*

Creeping Thymes
T. Coccineus Group, *T. Doerfleri, T.* "Doone Valley," *T. Herba-barona, T. pseudolanuginosus* and all *T. serpyllum*.

 cultivation

Propagation
To maintain the true plant, it is better to grow the majority of thymes from softwood cuttings. Only a very few, such as *T. vulgaris* and *T.* 'Fragrantissimus,' can be propagated successfully from seed.

Seed
Sow the very fine seed in early spring using the cardboard technique (see p. 645) on the surface of prepared trays (seed or plug), using a standard seed compost mixed in equal parts with composted fine bark. Give a bottom heat of 60–70°F. Do not cover. Keep watering to the absolute minimum, as these seedlings are prone to damping off disease. When the young plants are large enough and after a period of hardening off, plant out in the garden in late spring/ early summer, 9–15 in. apart.

Cuttings
Thymes are easily increased by softwood cuttings from new growth in early spring or summer. The length of

the cutting should be 2–3 in. Use a standard seed compost mixed in equal parts with composted fine bark. Winter the young plants under protection and plant out the following spring.

Division
Creeping thymes put out aerial roots as they spread, which makes them very easy to divide in late spring.

Layering
An ideal method for mature thymes that are getting a bit woody. Use either the strong branch method of layering in early fall or mound layer in early spring.

Pests and Diseases
Being such an aromatic plant, it does not normally suffer from pests but, if the soil or compost is too rich, thyme may be attacked by aphids. Treat with a liquid insecticidal soap. All varieties will rot off if they become too wet in a cold winter.

Maintenance
Spring Sow seeds. Divide established plants. Trim old plants. Layer old plants.
Summer Take cuttings of nonflowering shoots. Trim back after flowering.
Fall Protect tender thymes. Layer old plants.
Winter Protect containers and only water if absolutely necessary.

Garden Cultivation
Thymes need to be grown in poor soil, in a well-drained bed to give their best flavor. They are drought-loving plants and will need protection from cold winds, hard and wet winters. Sow seed when the soil has warmed and there is no threat of frost. Thin on average to 8 in. apart.

It is essential to trim all thymes after flowering; this not only promotes new growth, but also stops the plant from becoming woody and sprawling in the wrong direction.

In very cold areas grow it in the garden as an annual or in containers and then winter with protection.

Harvesting
As thyme is an evergreen it can be picked fresh all year round provided you are not too greedy. For preserving, pick before it is in flower. Either dry the leaves or put them in a vinegar or oil.

container growing

All varieties suit being grown in containers. They like a free-draining poor soil (low in nutrients); if grown in a rich soil they will become soft and the flavor will be impaired. Use a soilless compost mixed in equal parts with composted fine bark; water sparingly, keeping the container bordering on dry, and in winter definitely dry — only watering if absolutely necessary, when the leaves begin to lose too much color. Feed only occasionally in the summer months. Put the container in a sunny spot, which will help the aromatic oils come to the leaf surface and impart a better flavor. Trim back after flowering to maintain shape and promote new growth.

medicinal

Thyme has strong antiseptic properties. The tea makes a gargle or mouthwash, and is excellent for sore throats and infected gums. It is also good for hangovers. The essential oil is antibacterial and antifungal and used in the manufacture of toothpaste, mouthwash, gargles and other toilet articles. It can also be used to kill mosquito larvae. A few drops of the oil added to the bath water helps ease rheumatic pain, and it is often used in liniments and massage oils.

warning

Although a medical dose drawn from the whole plant is safe, any amount of the volatile oil is toxic and should not be used internally except by prescription. Avoid altogether if you are pregnant.

culinary

Thyme is an aid to digestion and helps break down fatty foods. It is one of the main ingredients of bouquet garni; it is good, too, in broths, marinades and stews; and a sprig or two with half an onion makes a great herb stuffing for chicken.

Poached Trout with Lemon Thyme
Serves 4

4 trout, cleaned and gutted
Salt
6 peppercorns (whole)
4 fresh bay leaves
1 small onion, cut into rings
1 lemon
1 sprig lemon thyme
1 tablespoon chopped lemon thyme leaves
½ cup white wine
2 tablespoons fresh snipped garlic chives
⅓ cup butter

Place the trout in a large skillet. Sprinkle with salt and add the peppercorns. Place one bay leaf by each trout. Put the onion rings on top of the trout, cut half the lemon into slices and arrange this over the trout, add the thyme sprig, and sprinkle some of the chopped thyme leaves over the whole lot. Pour in the wine and enough water just to cover the fish. Bring it to a boil on top of the stove and let it simmer uncovered for 6 minutes for fresh trout, 20 minutes for frozen.

Mix the remaining chopped lemon thyme and garlic chives with the butter in a small bowl. Divide this mixture into four equal portions. When the trout are cooked lift them out gently, place on plates with a slice of lemon and the herb butter on the top. Serve with new potatoes.

NASTURTIUM

Also known as Garden nasturtium, Indian cress and Large cress. From the family Tropaeolaceae.

Nasturtiums are native to South America, especially Peru and Bolivia, but are now cultivated worldwide.

The generic name, *Tropaeolum*, is derived from the Latin *tropaeum*, meaning "trophy" or "sign of victory." After a battle was finished, a tree-trunk was set up on the battlefield and hung with the captured helmets and shields. It was thought that the round leaves of the nasturtium looked like shields and the flowers like blood-stained helmets.

It was introduced into Spain from Peru in the 16th century and reached London shortly afterwards. When first introduced it was known as *Nasturcium indicum* or *Nasturcium peruvinum*, which is how it got its common name, Indian cress. The custom of eating its petals, and using them for tea and salads, comes from the Orient.

 varieties

Tropaeolum majus
Nasturtium
Half-hardy annual. Ht and spread 12 in. Red/orange flowers from summer to early fall. Round, midgreen leaves. **All zones.**

Tropaeolum majus Alaska Series
Nasturtium Alaska (Variegated)
Half-hardy annual. Ht and spread 12 in. Red, orange and yellow flowers from summer to early fall. Round, variegated (cream and green) leaves. **All zones.**

Tropaeolum majus "Peaches & Cream"
Nasturtium Peaches & Cream
Half-hardy annual. Ht 8 in., spread 12 in. Cream and orange flowers from summer to early fall. Round, midgreen leaves. **All zones.**

A few special species of interest:

Tropaeolum peregrinum
Canary Creeper
Tender perennial. Climber: Ht 6 ft. Small, bright yellow flowers with 2 upper petals that are much larger and fringed from summer until first frost. Gray/green leaves with 5 lobes. In cool areas, best grown as an annual. **Zone 9.**

Tropaeolum polyphyllum
Hardy perennial. Ht 2–3 in., spread 12 in. or more. Fairly small yellow flowers from summer to early fall. Leaves gray-green on trailing stems. A fast-spreading plant once established. Looks good on banks or hanging down walls. **Zone 8.**

Tropaeolum speciosum
Flame Creeper
Hardy perennial. Climber: Ht 9 ft. Scarlet flowers in summer followed by bright blue fruits surrounded by deep red calyxes in fall. Leaves green with six lobes. This very dramatic plant should be grown like honeysuckle with its roots in the shade and head in the sun. **Zone 8.**

Tropaeolum majus "Peaches & Cream"

NASTURTIUM

 ## cultivation

Propagation

Seed

The seeds are large and easy to handle. To have plants flowering early in the summer, sow in early spring under protection directly into prepared pots or cell trays using a standard seed compost, and cover lightly with compost. Plugs are ideal, especially if you want to introduce the young plants into a hanging basket; otherwise use small pots to allow more flexibility before planting out. When the seedlings are large enough and there is no threat of frosts, plant out into a prepared site in the garden, or into containers.

Cuttings

Take cuttings of the perennial varieties in the spring from the new soft growth.

Pests and Diseases

Aphids and caterpillars of cabbage white butterfly and its relatives may cause a problem. If the infestation is light, the aphids may be brushed off or washed away with soapy water.

Maintenance

Spring Sow seed early under protection, or after frosts in the garden.
Summer Deadhead flowers regularly to prolong the flowering season.
Fall Dig up dead plants.
Winter Plan next year.

Garden Cultivation

Nasturtiums prefer a well-drained, poor soil in full sun or partial shade. If the soil is too rich, leaf growth will

Trapaeolum majus

be made at the expense of the flowers. They are frost-tender and will suffer if the temperature falls below 40°F.

As soon as the soil has begun to warm and the frosts are over, nasturtiums can be sown directly into the garden. Sow individually 8 in. apart. For a border full of these plants, sow 6 in. apart. Claude Monet's garden at Giverny in France has a border of nasturtiums sprawling over a path that looks very effective.

Harvesting

Pick the flowers for fresh use only; they cannot be dried. Pick the seed pods just before they lose their green color (for pickling in vinegar). Pick the leaves for fresh use as required. They can be dried, but personally I don't think it is worth it.

 ## companion planting

This herb attracts blackfly away from vegetables such as cabbage and broad beans. It also attracts hover flies, whose larvae attack aphids. Further, it is said to repel whitefly, woolly aphids and ants. Altogether it is a good tonic to any garden.

 ## container growing

This herb is excellent for growing in pots, tubs, window boxes and hanging baskets. Use a standard potting compost mixed in equal parts with composted fine bark. Do not feed, because all you will produce are leaves not flowers, but do keep well watered, especially in hot weather.

 ## medicinal

This herb is rarely used medicinally, although the fresh leaves contain vitamin C and iron as well as an antiseptic substance, which is at its highest before the plant flowers.

 ## warning

Use the herb with caution. Do not eat more than ½ oz. at a time or 1 oz. per day.

 ## culinary

I had a group from the local primary school around the farm to talk about herbs. Just as they were leaving I mentioned that these pretty red flowers were now being sold in supermarkets for eating in salads. When a little boy looked at me in amazement, I suggested he try one. He ate the whole flower without saying a word. One of his friends said, "What does it taste like?" With a huge smile he asked if he could pick another flower for his friend, who ate it and screamed, "Pepper pepper.." The seeds, flowers and leaves are all now eaten for their spicy taste. They are used in salads also as an attractive garnish. The pickled flower buds provide a good substitute for capers.

Nasturtium Cream Cheese Dip

¼ pound cream cheese
2 teaspoons tender nasturtium leaves, chopped
3 nasturtium flowers

Blend the cream cheese with the chopped leaves. Put the mixture into a bowl and decorate with the flowers. Eat this mixture as soon as possible because it can become bitter if left standing.

Urtica
NETTLE

Also known as Common nettle, Stinging nettle, Devil's leaf and Devil's plaything. From the family Urticaceae.

This plant is found all over the world. It is widespread on waste-land especially on damp and nutrient-rich soil.

The generic name *Urtica* comes from the Latin *uro*, meaning "I burn." The Roman nettle *Urtica pilulifera* originally came to Britain with the invading Roman army. The soldiers used the plants to keep themselves warm. They flogged their legs and arms with nettles to keep their circulation going.

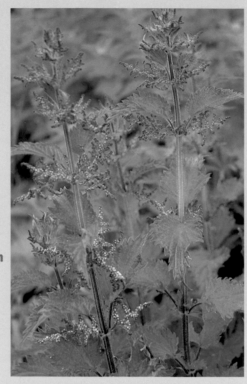

The use of nettles in the making of fabric goes back for thousands of years. Nettle cloth was found in a Danish grave of the later Bronze Age, wrapped around cremated bones. It was certainly made in Scotland as late as the 18th century. The Scottish poet, Thomas Campbell, wrote then of sleeping in nettle sheets in Scotland and dining off nettle tablecloths. Records show that it was still being used in the early 20th century in Tyrol.

In the Middle Ages it was believed that nettles marked the dwelling place of elves and were a protection against sorcery. They were also said to prevent milk from being affected by house trolls or witches.

Settlers in New England in the 17th century were surprised to find that this old friend and enemy had crossed the Atlantic with them. It was included in a list of plants that sprang up unaided. Before World War II, vast quantities of nettles were imported to Britain from Germany. During the war there was a drive to collect as much of the home-grown nettle as possible. The dark green dye obtained from the plant was used as camouflage, and chlorophyll was extracted for use in medicines.

 varieties

Urtica dioica
Stinging Nettle
Hardy perennial. Ht 5 ft., spread infinite on creeping rootstock. The male and female flowers are on separate plants. The female flowers hang down in clusters, the male flower clusters stick out. The color for both is a yellowish green. The leaves are green toothed and have bristles. This is the variety that can be eaten when young. **Zone 3.**

Urtica pilulifera
Roman Nettle
Hardy perennial. Ht 5 ft., spread infinite on creeping rootstock. This looks very similar to the common stinging nettle, but its sting is said to be more virulent. **Zone 3.**

Urtica urens
Small Nettle
Hardy annual. Ht and spread 12 in. The male and female flowers are in the same cluster and are a greenish white in color. The green leaves are deeply toothed and have bristles. **Zone 3.**

Urtica urentissima
Devil's Leaf
This is a native of Timor and the sting said to be so virulent that its effects can last for months and may even cause death. A plant of interest, but not for the garden. **Zone 3.**

Urtica dioica in flower

cultivation

Propagation

Seed
Nettles can be grown from seed sown in the spring. But I am sure any of your friends with a garden would be happy to give you a root.

Division
Divide established roots early in spring before they put on much leaf growth, and the sting is least strong.

Pests and Diseases

Rarely suffers from pests and disease, well not ones that one would wish to destroy!

Maintenance

Spring Sow seeds, divide established plants.
Summer Cut plants back if they are becoming invasive.
Fall Cut back the plants hard into the ground.
Winter No need for protection, fully hardy.

Garden Cultivation

Stinging nettles are the scourge of the gardener and the farmer, the pest of children in summer, but are very useful in the garden, attracting butterflies and moths, and making an excellent caterpillar food. They will grow happily in any soil. It is worth having a natural corner in the garden where these and a few other wild flowers can be planted.

Harvesting

Cut young leaves in early spring for use as a vegetable.

medicinal

The nettle has many therapeutic applications but is principally of benefit in all kinds of internal hemorrhages, as a diuretic in jaundice and hemorrhoids, and as a laxative. It is also used in dermatological problems including eczema.

Nettles make a valuable tonic after the long winter months when they provide one of the best sources of minerals. They are an excellent remedy for anemia. Their vitamin C content makes sure that the iron they contain is properly absorbed.

Nettle hair conditioner

other uses

Whole plants yield a greenish/yellow woollen dye. Traditionally the old gardeners used nettles to make a spray to get rid of aphids, especially blackfly. They soaked the nettles in rain water for a period of time, then used the steeped water to spray the infected plants, it was also said to be a good plant tonic.

Nettles have a long-standing reputation for preventing hair loss and making the hair soft and shiny. They also have a reputation for eliminating dandruff.

Nettle Rinse and Conditioner

Use this as a final rinse after washing your hair, or massage it into your scalp and comb through the hair every other day. Store it in a small bottle in the refrigerator.

1 big handful-size bunch of nettles
2 cups water

Wear rubber gloves to cut the nettles. Wash thoroughly and put the bunch into an enamel pot with enough cold water to cover. Bring to a boil, cover and simmer for 15 minutes. Strain the liquid into a pitcher and allow to cool.

warning

Do not eat old plants uncooked, they can produce kidney damage and symptoms of poisoning. The plants must be cooked thoroughly to be safe.

Handle all plants with care; they do sting.

culinary

Nettles are an invaluable food, rich in both vitamins and minerals.

In spring the fresh leaves may be cooked and eaten like spinach, made into a delicious soup, or drunk as a tea.

When cooked, I am pleased to say, nettles lose their sting.

Nettle Soup

Serves 4

½ pound young nettle leaves
¼ cup oil or butter
1 small onion, chopped
½ pound cooked potatoes, peeled and diced
1 teaspoon each (mix, fresh, chopped) sweet marjoram, sage, lemon thyme
2 teaspoons fresh chopped lovage
3 cups milk
2 tablespoons cream and French parsley, chopped (optional)

Pick only the fresh young nettle leaves, and wear gloves to remove from stalks and wash them. Heat the oil in a pot, add the chopped onion, and slowly sweat until clear. Then add the nettles and stew gently for about an additional 10 minutes. Add the chopped potatoes, all the herbs and the milk and simmer for an additional 10 minutes. Allow to cool then put all the ingredients into a liquidizer and blend. Return to a pot over gentle heat. Add a swirl of cream to each bowl and sprinkle some chopped French parsley over the top. Serve with French bread.

VALERIAN

Also known as All heal, Set all, Garden heliotrope, Cut finger and Phu. From the family Valerianaceae.

This herb is indigenous to Europe and West Asia and is now naturalized in North America. It can be found in grasslands, ditches, damp meadows and close to streams. The name may come from the Latin *valere*, "to be healthy," an allusion to its powerful medicinal qualities. The root is the medicinal part of this herb which, when dug up, literally stinks, hence another of its common names "phu." But to cats the scent of this herb is sheer elixir, even more than catmint *(Nepeta cateria)*, and it is said the Pied Piper of Hamelin carried the root to entice the cats to eat the rats of Hamelin. A tincture of valerian was employed in the World Wars I and II to treat shell-shock and nervous stress.

 varieties

Valeriana officinalis
Valerian
Hardy herbaceous perennial. Ht up to 4½ ft., spread 3 ft. Clusters of small, sweetly scented white flowers that are often tinged with pink in summer. Leaves are midgreen, deeply divided and toothed around the edges. Short conical rootstock which, when broken or cut, exudes a strong, rather unpleasant aroma. **Zone 5.**

Other varieties of special interest and well worth looking out for are:-

Valeriana jatamansii syn. *Valeriana wallichii*
Spikenard, Nard, Indian Valerian, Tagara
Hardy herbaceous perennial. Ht 4–10 in. and spread 18 in. Clusters of small white flowers in summer. Midgreen, toothed, heart-shaped leaves. In India the roots are used medicinally to treat hysteria, hypochondria and as a tranquilizer, and an essential oil is extracted from the sweet-smelling roots for use in perfumery. I was given this plant by Roy Lancaster, the well-known plantsman, who collected it in 1978 on one of his expeditions to the Himalayas. It has happily adapted to our climate. He grows his plant, from which he gave me a cutting, in the garden and I am growing it in a container using a soil-based compost mixed with 25 percent horticultural grit. This herb is often confused with, and medicinally substituted for, *Nardostachys grandiflora* (see below). **Zone 5.**

Nardostachys grandiflora
Nard, Spikenard, Musk Root
Hardy herbaceous perennial. Ht and spread 10–12 in. Clusters of small pink to pale purple flowers in summer. Narrow, basal, lance-shaped, midgreen leaves. The roots of this plant have a sweet musk scent. This herb is a member of the Valerianaceae family, and often confused with *Valeriana jatamansii*. It is indigenous to the alpine Himalayas and has been used for thousands of years as a nervine tonic. It is mentioned in the Song of Solomon and was the substance used to anoint the feet of Jesus at the Last Supper. **Zone 7.**

Valeriana jatamansii

 cultivation

Propagation

Seed

In spring, sow the fairly small seeds into prepared seed or module plug trays, using a standard seed compost. Press the seeds into the soil, cover with perlite. Do not cover with soil as this will delay germination. Place in a cold frame or cold greenhouse. Germination takes 3 to 4 weeks. Plant out when large enough to handle, 24 in. apart.

Division

Divided established plants in the fall, or early spring, using two forks back-to-back, replanting into a well-prepared site.

Pests and Diseases

Valerians rarely suffer from pests and diseases.

Maintenance

Spring Sow seeds. Divide established plants.
Summer Cut back after flowering to prevent self-seeding.
Fall Divide established plants if required.
Winter A very hardy plant, does not need protection.

Garden Cultivation

The roots of this herb like to be kept cool and damp in summer, so plant in any soil that does not dry out in high summer, in sun or partial shade. Choose the position in your garden with care and remember, if you have to move the plant, that the scent of the broken roots will attract all the neighborhood cats.

Harvesting

Dig up the roots of a second- or third-year plant. Wash and remove the pale fibrous root. Cut the root into manageable slices for drying.

 companion planting

It is said that valerian makes a good companion plant when planted near vegetables, the roots release phosphorus and stimulate earthworm activity.

 container growing

Valerian can be grown in a container, but make sure that it is large enough to accommodate the root system. Use a soilless potting compost. Position the container in partial shade so that the compost does not dry out. Water regularly throughout the growing season, especially in summer. Divide the plants each fall; this will prevent the roots rotting in the pots in wet winters.

 medicinal

This herb has been used for thousands of years as a sedative and relaxant. The dried roots are prepared into tablets, powder, capsules or tinctures which are then used as a safe, nonaddictive relaxant that reduces nervous tension and anxiety and promotes restful sleep.

This is an extremely useful herb for treating anxious or restless pets. I have had a number of cats and dogs and one dog in particular, Hampton, hated going in the car. After treating him with a few drops of valerian tincture, diluted in some water, prior to the journey he became much less frightened and slept peacefully throughout the journey, which made the family vacation even more enjoyable. I have also used it with the cats, especially if one had been injured in a fight, before cleaning their wounds or taking them to the vet for treatment. Cats are notoriously fussy about their food, but adore valerian, which they find very soothing. Make a decoction by crushing one teaspoon of dried root, which is then added to 1 quart of cold water. Leave for 24 hours. Strain the decoction into a clean, sterilized bottle. This will keep for 48 hours in a refrigerator. For a medium-sized, stressed or anxious cat, add 3 drops of the decoction to a small amount of water, which they will drink with relish.

 other uses

An infusion of the root sprayed onto the soil is said to attract earthworms. The root has been used as a bait in rat traps and to catch wild cats. Add the mineral-rich leaves to the compost heap.

 warning

Do not take for an extended period. Do not take during pregnancy.

Verbena officinalis

VERVAIN

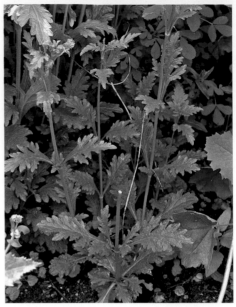

Verbena officinalis

Also known as Holy herb, Simpler's joy, Pigeon's grass, Burvine, Wizard's herb, Herba sacra, Holy plant, European vervain, Enchanter's plant and Herba the cross. From the family Verbenaceae.

This herb is a native of Mediterranean regions. It has now become established elsewhere within temperate zones and, for that matter, wherever the Romans marched.

It is an herb of myth, magic and medicine. The Egyptians believed that it originated from the tears of Isis. The Greek priests wore amulets made of it, as did the Romans, who also used it to purify their altars after sacrifice. The Druids used it for purification and for making magic potions.

Superstition tells that when you pick vervain, you should bless the plant. This originates from a legend that it grew on the hill at Calgary, and was used to staunch the flow of Christ's blood at the Crucifixion.

In the Middle Ages it was an ingredient in a holy salve, a powerful protector against demons and disease: "Vervain and Dill hinders witches from their will."

Garden Cultivation

Vervain can be sown direct into the garden in the spring in a well-drained soil and a sunny position. It is better to sow or plant in clumps because the flower is so small that otherwise it will not show to advantage. But beware its capacity to self-seed.

Harvesting

Pick leaves as required. Cut whole plant when in bloom. Dry leaves or whole plant if required.

 ## container growing

Vervain does nothing for containers, and containers do nothing for vervain.

 ## medicinal

Vervain has been used traditionally to strengthen the nervous system, dispel depression and counter nervous exhaustion. It is also said to be effective in treating migraines and headaches of the nervous and bilious kind. Chinese herbalists use a decoction to treat suppressed menstruation, and for liver problems and urinary tract infections.

 ## varieties

Verbena officinalis
Vervain
Hardy perennial. Ht 2–3 ft., spread 1 ft. or more. Small pale lilac flowers in summer. Leaves green, hairy and often deeply divided into lobes with curved teeth. This plant is not to be muddled with lemon verbena (*Aloysia triphylla*). **Zone 4.**

 ## cultivation

Propagation
Seed
Sow the small seeds in early spring in a prepared seed or plug tray using a standard seed compost. Cover with perlite. No need for extra heat. When the seedlings are large enough, and after hardening off, plant out in a prepared site, 12 in. apart.

Division
An established plant can be divided either in the spring or fall. It splits easily with lots of roots.

Pests and Diseases
If soil is too rich or high in nitrates, aphids can attack.

Maintenance
Spring Sow seeds. Divide established plants.
Summer Cut back after flowering to stop it self-seeding.
Fall Divide established plants.
Winter No need for protection; fully hardy.

 ## culinary

In certain parts of France, a tea is made from the leaves. Use with caution.

 ## warning

Avoid during pregnancy.

HEARTSEASE

Viola tricolor

Also known as Wild pansy, Field pansy, Love lies bleeding, Love in idleness, Herb trinity, Jack behind the garden gate, Kiss me behind the garden gate, Kiss me love, Kiss me love at the garden gate, Kiss me quick, Monkey's face, Three faces under a hood, Two faces in a hood and Trinity violet. From the family Violaceae.

Heartsease is a wild flower in Europe and North America, growing on wasteland and in fields and hedgerows.

In the Middle Ages, due to the influence of Christianity and because of its tricolor flowers — white, yellow and purple — heartsease was called Trinitaria or Trinitatis Herba, the herb of the Blessed Trinity.

In the traditional language of flowers, the purple form meant memories, the white loving thoughts, and the yellow, souvenirs.

Viola tricolor

 varieties

Viola arvensis
Field Pansy
Hardy perennial. Ht 2–4 in. The flowers are predominantly white or creamy, and appear in early summer. The green leaves are oval with shallow, blunt teeth. **Zone 4.**

Viola lutea
Mountain Pansy
Hardy perennial. Ht 3–8 in. Single-colored flowers in summer vary from yellow to blue and violet. The leaves are green and oval near the bottom of the stem, narrower further up. **Zone 4.**

Viola tricolor
Heartsease
Hardy perennial, often grown as an annual. Ht 6–12 in. Flowers from spring to fall. Green and deeply lobed leaves. **Zone 4.**

 cultivation

Propagation
Seed
Sow seeds under protection in the fall, either into prepared seed, plug trays or pots using a standard seed compost. Do not cover the seeds. No bottom heat required. Winter the seedlings in a cold frame or cold greenhouse. In the spring harden off and plant out at a distance of 6 in. apart.

Maintenance
Spring Sow seed.
Summer Deadhead flowers to maintain flowering.
Fall Sow seed for early spring flowers.
Winter No need to protect.

Garden Cultivation
Heartsease will grow in any soil, in partial shade or sun. Sow the seeds from spring to early fall where they are to flower. Press into the soil but do not cover.

Harvesting
Pick the flowers fully open from spring right through to late fall. Use fresh or for drying. The plant has the most fascinating seed capsules, each capsule splitting into three. The best time to collect seeds is midday when the maximum number of capsules will have opened.

 container growing

Heartsease look very jolly in any kind of container. Pick off the dead flowers as this appears to keep the plant flowering for longer.

 medicinal

An infusion of the flowers has long been prescribed for a broken heart. Less romantically, it is also a cure for bed-wetting. An ointment made from it is good for eczema and acne, and also for curing milk rust and cradle cap. Herbalists use it to treat gout, rheumatoid arthritis, and respiratory disorders. An infusion of heartsease leaves added to bath water has proved beneficial to suffers of rheumatic disease.

 warning

In large doses, it may cause vomiting.

 other uses

Cleansing the skin and shampooing thinning hair.

 culinary

Add flowers to salads and to decorate sweet dishes.

Viola
VIOLET

From the family Violaceae.

There are records of sweet violets growing during the 1st century CE in Persia, Syria, and Turkey. It is a native not only of these areas but also of North Africa and Europe. Violets have been introduced elsewhere and are now cultivated in several countries for their perfume.

This charming herb has been much loved for over 2,000 years and there are many stories associated with it. In a Greek legend, Zeus fell in love with a beautiful maiden called Io. He turned her into a cow to protect her from his jealous wife Juno. The earth grew violets for Io's food, and the flower was named after her.

The violet was also the flower of Aphrodite, the goddess of love, and of her son, Priapus, the god of gardens. The ultimate mark of the reverence in which the Greeks held sweet violet is that they made it the symbol of Athens.

For centuries perfumes have been made from the flowers of sweet violet mixed with the violet-scented roots of orris, and the last half of the 19th century saw intense interest in it — acres were cultivated to grow it as a market garden plant. Its main use was as a cut flower. No lady of quality would venture out without wearing a bunch of violets. It was also customary in gardens of large country houses to move the best clump of violets to a cold frame in late fall to provide flowers for the winter.

 ## varieties

Viola odorata
Sweet Violet
Also known as garden violet. Hardy perennial. Ht 3 in., spread 6 in. or more. Sweet-smelling white or purple flowers from late winter to early spring. Heart-shaped leaves form a rosette at the base, from which long-stalked flowers arise. *Viola odorata* is one of the few scented violets. It has been hybridized to produce Palma violets, with a single or double flower, in a range of rich colors. A recent revival in interest in this plant means it is being offered again by specialist nurseries. **Zone 5.**

Viola reichenbachiana
Wood Violet
Hardy perennial. Ht 2–8 in., spread 6 in. or more. Pale lilac/blue flowers in early spring. Leaves are green and heart-shaped. The difference between this plant and the common dog violet is the flowering time; there is also a slight difference in flower color but it is difficult to discern. **Zone 5.**

Viola riviniana
Common Dog Violet
Also known as blue mice, hedging violet, horse violet, and pig violet. Hardy perennial. Ht 2–8 in., spread 6 in. or more. Pale blue/lilac flowers in early summer. Leaves are green and heart-shaped. This violet does not grow runners. **Zone 5.**

 ## cultivation

Propagation
Seed
The small seed should be sown in early fall in prepared seed or plug trays. Use a soil-based seed compost; I have found violets prefer this. Water in and cover with a layer of compost, and finally cover with a

sheet of glass or plastic wrap. Put the trays either in a corner of the garden or in a cold frame (because the seeds germinate better if they have a period of stratification, though it will still be erratic). In the spring when the seedlings are large enough to handle, prick out into pots. If grown in cells allow a period of hardening off. Plant out as soon as temperatures have risen at a distance of 12 in.

Cuttings
These can be taken from the parent plant, with a small amount of root attached, in early spring and rooted in cell trays, using a standard seed compost mixed in equal parts with composted fine bark. Harden off and plant out into a prepared site in the garden in late spring when they are fully rooted. Water in well.

When using runners to propagate this plant, remove them in late spring and replant in a prepared site in the garden, 12 in. apart. Plant them firmly in the ground, making sure that the bottom of the crowns are well embedded in the soil; water in well. Runners can be grown on in pots in early fall. Remove a well-rooted runner and plant in a pot of a suitable size. Over-winter in a cool greenhouse, watering from time to time to prevent red spider mite. Bring into the house in the spring to enjoy the flowers. After flowering, plant out in the garden into a prepared site.

Division
Divide well-established plants as soon as flowering is over in early summer. It is a good idea to plant three crowns together for a better show and as an insurance policy against damage when splitting a crown. Replant in the garden in exactly the same way as for runners.

Pests and Diseases
The major pest for container-grown violets in warm weather is red spider mite. To keep this at bay, spray the leaves with water. If it is persistent, use a liquid insecticidal soap as per the manufacturer's instructions. In propagating violets, the disease you will most probably come across is black root rot, which is encouraged by insufficient drainage in the compost. Young plants can also be affected by damping off root rot, which is caused usually by too much water and insufficient drainage.

Maintenance
Spring Take cuttings from established plants. Remove runners, pot or replant in the garden.

Viola riviniana

Summer Divide well-established plants, and replant.
Fall Sow seed. Pot up root runners for wintering under cover.
Winter Feed the garden with well-rotted manure.

Garden Cultivation
Violets thrive best in a moderately heavy, rich soil in a semi-shaded spot. If you have a light and/or gravelly soil, it is a good idea to add some texture — a mulch of well-rotted manure — the previous fall. In spring dig the manure in.

Plant out in the garden as soon as the frosts have finished, allowing 12 in. between plants. When they become established, they quickly create a carpet of lovely sweet-smelling flowers. There is no need to protect any of the above-mentioned violets, they are fully hardy.

Harvesting
Pick the leaves in early spring for fresh use or for drying. Gather the flowers just when they are opening, for drying or crystallizing. Dig up the roots in fall to dry for medicinal use.

 container growing

Violets make good container plants. Use a soil-based compost mixed in equal parts with composted fine bark. Give them a liquid feed of fertilizer (following the manufacturer's instructions) after flowering. During the summer months, place the container in partial shade. In winter they do not like heat, and if it is too warm they will become weak and fail to flower. So, it is most important that they are in a cool place with temperatures no higher than 45°F. There must

VIOLET

also be good air circulation, and watering should be maintained on a regular basis.

 culinary

The flowers of sweet violet are well known in crystallized form for decorating cakes, desserts, ice-cream, and homemade candies. They are also lovely in salads, and make an interesting oil — use an almond oil as base. The flowers of common and dog violet can also be added to salads and used to decorate desserts. Their flavor is very mild in comparison to sweet violet, but they are just as attractive.

 medicinal

Only sweet violet has been used medicinally. Various parts are still used, most commonly, the rootstock. It is an excellent, soothing expectorant and is used to treat a range of respiratory disorders, such as bronchitis, coughs, whooping cough, and head colds. It also has a cooling nature and is used to treat hangovers. Made into a poultice, the leaves soothe sore, cracked nipples. Also they have a reputation for treating tumors, both benign and cancerous. Strong doses of the rhizome are emetic and purgative.

The flowers have a reputation for being slightly sedative, so can be helpful in cases of anxiety and insomnia.

 other uses

The flowers of sweet violets are used in potpourris, floral waters, and perfumes.

Sweet violet perfume

Vitex agnus-castus
CHASTE TREE

Also known as Monks pepper, Lygos, Hemptree, Agnus castus, Abraham's tree, and Chaste berry. From the family Verbenaceae.

This aromatic shrub, indigenous to the Mediterranean and Central Asia, has been used medicinally for thousands of years. The first known records of its medical use were made in the fourth century CE by Hippocrates; he used it to treat female disorders, particularly the diseases of the uterus. Historically the Christian monks used to chew the leaves and grind the dried berries over their food to reduce their libido. *Agnus castus* translates as "chaste lamb," which is the Christian symbol of purity. In Germany in the 20th century Dr Gerhard Madaus conducted scientific research into the plant's effects on the female hormonal system. He subsequently developed a medicine made from the dried berries called "Agnolyt," which is still available today.

varieties

Vitex agnus-castus
Chaste tree
Deciduous shrub. Ht and spread 10–15 ft. Upright panicles of fragrant, tubular violet blue flowers in late summer until midfall, which are followed by small round orange/red fruit. Dark green, aromatic leaves are divided into 5 or 7 lance-shaped leaflets. **Zone 6 and 7.**

cultivation

Propagation
Seed
The best time to sow the seeds is in the late fall when they are fresh. Sow into prepared plug module trays or small containers using a standard seed compost mixed in equal parts with perlite. Once the seedlings are large enough to handle, repot using a standard potting compost mixed in equal parts with composted fine bark. Place the container in a frost-free environment for the winter. Do not think it is dead when all you are left with is a twig for the first winter; new shoots will appear in the spring if you do not overwater. It will flower in the fourth or fifth summer.

Cuttings
The easiest and the most reliable method of propagation is by softwood cuttings taken in the late spring, early summer from nonflowering shoots. Prepare module plug trays or a small pot using a standard seed compost mixed in equal parts with perlite. Place the cuttings in a sheltered, warm environment; they do not need bottom heat. Once rooted, repot in exactly the same way as the seedlings and again winter in a frost-free environment. It will flower in the second or third summer.

Pests and Diseases
As the whole plant is aromatic, it is rarely attacked by pests. Over-watering of young container plants can cause rotting in winter, especially in cold and cool climates.

Maintenance
Spring Prune back last year's growth to 2 in.
Summer Take cuttings in early summer.
Fall Sow seeds.
Winter Protect from excessive wet.

CHASTE TREE

Garden Cultivation

This most attractive aromatic shrub is worthy of a place in the garden: it smells good, looks good, and does you good — what more can you ask of a plant? Plant in a fertile soil; it will tolerate, dry soils, moist soils but not cold, heavy clay soils. When living in cold areas, plant against a warm, sunny wall; the wall will help cut down the rainfall by 25 percent and give added protection and warmth in winter. Allternatively, plant in full sun in a sheltered position. It will not tolerate shade.

Harvesting

The leaves are picked in early summer for use fresh or for drying. Stems are cut in late summer or fall and are dried. Roots are lifted, from plants over 5 years old, in late summer and fall and dried. The fruits are harvested in fall for use fresh or for drying. However this plant rarely sets fruit in cool or cold climates.

 ## companion planting

Good late-nectar plant for butterflies, which is therefore beneficial for late pollination.

 ## container growing

From experience I know that this plant adapts happily to being grown in a container. Use a soil-based compost mixed in equal parts with composted fine bark. Feed the container throughout the growing season with a liquid feed following the manufacturer's instructions. In winter allow the plant to drop its leaves, then clear away any fallen debris to prevent disease. Place the container in a sheltered spot. In wet conditions raise the pot on bricks so it does not become waterlogged.

 ## medicinal

Vitex agnus-castus is one of the most important herbs for treating menstrual and menopausal problems and infertility. The key part of the plant used is the berries, which are taken in tablet or tincture form. It is used to regulate the hormones, for increasing female fertility, for regulating irregular periods, and during the menopause to balance the hormones. It is also used to relieve spasms of pain, especially PMS, and to treat migraines and acne associated with the menstrual cycle.

 ## other uses

The flowers are used in the making of perfume. A yellow dye is obtained from the leaves, the seed, and the roots.

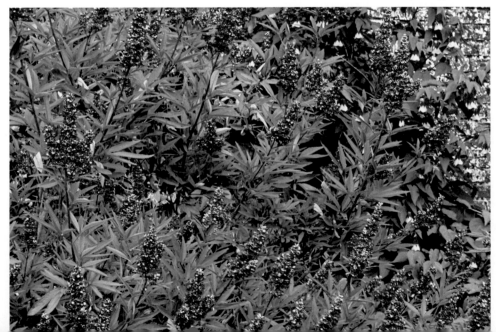 ## warning

Do not take excessive doses. Do not take *Vitex agnus-castus* during pregnancy. Do not take when taking any other product or drug that affects the female hormone system, such as HRT or the contraceptive pill.

Vitex agnus-castus

 ## culinary

The small aromatic fruit when dried is often used as a pepper subsitute; the flavor is milder and spicier. Today, it is rare to find chaste tree berries in recipes, although they can appear in a Moroccan spice mixture called *ras el hanout*, which translates as "top (or head) of the store," referring to the best combination of spices the seller can provide.

Ras el Hanout
No two recipes for this combination of spices are the same.

1 tablespoon dried chaste berries
2 cinnamon sticks, broken into several pieces
1 tablespoon cloves
1 tablespoon coriander seeds
1 tablespoon cumin seeds
1 tablespoon fenugreek
1 tablespoon fennel seeds
1 oz. dried Damask rose petals; these are
    available in Middle Eastern food stores

Place all the ingredients in a heavy-bottomed metal skillet and place over low heat. Do not let them burn, but cook until the seeds begin to pop in the pan. As soon as they start, shake or toss gently, cook for an additional minute, then allow to cool slightly. Remove all the ingredients from the skillet and grind the mixture in a coffee grinder, mini food processor, or mortar and pestle. Store in an airtight container, in a cupboard, and use this mixed spice within 2 weeks with meat, vegetable, and rice dishes.

GINGER
Zingiber officinale

Also known as Sweet ginger, Ginger, Shunthi, and Adrak. From the family Zingiberaceae.

Ginger is a very ancient herb. Confucius (551–479 CE) was known to have eaten fresh ginger with every meal as a digestive and carminative, and it has been used in India from the Vedic period (1500 CE) when it was called Maha-aushadhi, which means "the great medicine." Together with black pepper, ginger was one of the most commonly traded spices during the 13th and 14th centuries. Arabs carried the rhizomes on their voyages to East Africa and Zanzibar to plant at coastal settlements. During this time in England, ginger was sought after, and one pound in weight of ginger was equivalent to the cost of a sheep.

Zingiber officinale roots

 varieties

Zingiber officinale
Ginger
Tropical, subtropical, deciduous perennial. Ht 5 ft., spread indefinite. The yellow/green flowers, with a deep purple and cream lip in summer, grow on a single stem and are followed by red fleshy fruits, each having three chambers containing several small black seeds. Commercially cultivated plants are often sterile. Aromatic long, midgreen, lance-shaped leaves. The root is a thick branching rhizome. **Zone 9.**

 cultivation

Propagation
Seed
Rarely grown from seed as root cuttings are very simple and quick.

Cuttings
Unless you live in the tropics, the best source for fresh ginger is from a good grocer. However, be aware that the quality can be variable. For example, air-freighted rhizomes can be often killed by the cold temperatures or they may have been treated with chemicals to inhibit sprouting. Choose a fresh plump, juicy-looking root with a stout horn-like growing bud. Fill a pot with seed compost mixed in equal parts with vermiculite. Slice the root 2 in. below the bud, place in the container with the bud facing up, gently push the root into the compost, being careful not to break the bud. The compost should just cover the bud. Place the pot in a plastic bag and seal, put in a warm place or on a propagator at 68°F. In about 3 weeks, maybe longer depending on the warmth, shoots will emerge. As soon as they do, remove the plastic bag. Keep the container warm and out of direct sunlight until the plant is fully established. Then repot, one size up, using a soil-based potting compost mixed in equal parts with composted fine bark.

Division
Divide established plants in the spring. Use a spade to remove a clump, which includes some rhizomes, from the established plant in the garden, replanting into a prepared site in the garden. Alternatively, for container-raised plants, ease off some rhizomes either by hand or using two small forks, repotting into a container

that is just big enough. Use a soilless potting compost mixed in equal parts with composted fine bark.

Pests and Diseases

Red spider mite can be an occasional problem in older plants: regular misting and keeping the leaves well-washed will reduce this. If it gets out of hand, use a insecticidal soap following the manufacturer's instructions. If you live in the northern hemisphere you might find it difficult to over-winter plants due to the low light levels.

Maintenance

Spring Take cuttings from fresh roots. Divide established plants.
Summer Feed container-grown plants regularly.
Fall Harvest roots, cut back on watering container-raised plants.
Winter Protect from frost. Minimum temperature 68°F.

Garden Cultivation

When grown outdoors in the tropics it needs a minimum annual rainfall of 120 in., temperatures of 86°F or over, a short dry season and a deep, fertile soil. It usually takes 5 to 9 months to produce a crop.

Zingiber officinale

In colder regions it is best grown as a container plant either indoors, in a conservatory or a heated greenhouse. However, it rarely flowers outside of the tropics.

Harvesting

Outside the tropics one can only produce a small amount of fresh rhizome. The rhizome can be harvested in late fall. The leaves can be used as a flavoring; pick as required throughout the growing season. A fresh rhizome can be stored in the refrigerator for up to 2 weeks. Freshly grated ginger can be frozen.

 container growing

Container-raised plants do not produce much useful rhizome, although you can use the leaves in the kitchen for flavoring foods. Grow your plant in a soilless potting compost mixed in equal parts with composted fine bark. In summer keep the compost damp and warm, place the container in a slightly shaded position and feed during the growing season weekly with a general-purpose liquid fertilizer. In dry weather plants will benefit from being lightly misted with rainwater daily. In the fall cut back on the watering, keeping the plant fairly dry over the winter at a minimum of 68°F.

 medicinal

Ancient Indian and Chinese herbalists used this herb for many aliments. It has a wide range of demonstrated health-giving properties; it both stimulates the heart and settles the stomach. It will improve your digestion and circulation, reduce any inflammatory process in your body and improve the absorption of anything you eat. Ginger works best when treating post-operative nausea and morning sickness, although its effectiveness in treating sea-sickness and other forms of motion sickness is questioned by some scientists, and I personally can vouch that it did not help me.

Fresh rhizomes are said to help to reduce inflammation in conditions like osteo- and rheumatoid arthritis. In Ayurvedic medicine it is used as a cure for cholera, anorexia and "inflamed liver."

 culinary

When you buy fresh ginger, choose roots, which are often called "hands," that are plump, not shrivelled. Fresh ginger, peeled and ground or grated into a pulp, is used in many types of curries and spicy foods. In India it is used in curries, in China it is often used with seafood and mutton, in Japan it is pickled and is known as *gari* and *beni-shoga* and eaten with sushi. In European cooking, ginger is mainly used in sweet preparations, spiced breads, cookies and cakes. Many countries make liqueurs and drinks from the root; the Europeans make ginger beer and green ginger wine, and in China they make a liqueur called Canton, to name just a few.

Salmon, Watercress and Fresh Ginger
Serves 2
I love the combination of fish and ginger. Here is a very simple recipe that does not fail.

2 fillets of salmon, boned
1 tablespoon grated ginger
1 clove garlic, finely chopped
1 tablespoon chopped cilantro leaf
juice of ½ lemon
1 bunch watercress, washed and chopped
Olive oil and balsamic vinegar dressing
  (3 tablespoons olive oil, 1 tablespoon vinegar)
2 pieces of foil large enough to encapsulate the
  salmon fillets.

Preheat the oven to 400°F. Place the fillets of fresh salmon onto an individual piece of foil, sprinkle each fillet with the ginger, garlic and cilantro and finish with the lemon juice. Wrap loosely with the foil, bake in the oven for about 14 minutes or until the fresh fish is cooked. Serve on the watercress that has been drizzled with an oil and balsamic vinegar dressing.

FRUITS

In this section, fruit is defined as plant flesh that we are induced by the plant to eat, in order to distribute its seeds. Included is the closely allied group of nuts, which are in fact the seeds themselves. Presumably the plants are satisfied if a small percentage of the nut seeds are distributed to grow elsewhere.

The fruits covered in the three chapters Orchard Fruits, Soft, Bush, and Cane Fruits and Tender Fruits are determined by the manner in which we most usually grow them in temperate gardens. Those that require some protection or cover, such as the annual, perennial, and tender fruits, are mostly fruits that are not hardy enough outdoors for the UK and northern European gardener, but are achievable in much of the U.S., southern Europe, and Australia. Of course, we commonly grow many of these, such as melons, grapes, and even lemons, quite easily with the aid of a greenhouse, in cooler regions. I've also included many exotic tropical and subtropical fruits on sale in supermarkets and abroad which may be grown (or eaten!) out of curiosity and interest.

Most of these were once grown and fruited in Victorian stovehouses, and can often be fruited at home with a modest heated greenhouse or conservatory. Failing that, most of these make spectacular, educational, and decorative houseplants. (Please keep in mind, however, the potential final height and size of your humble date palm seedling before you start dreaming of ever ripening a crop!)

The chapter on Shrub and Flower Garden Fruits includes those forgotten and unsung heroes that are called upon only in times of shortage and famine, and by those country folk who appreciate the sharp, strong flavors these piquant fruits offer. The potential of these fruits has often been overlooked; many of them are worthy of deliberate cultivation, and with only a little breeding and selection they could become sweet and tender attractions for our delectation. The strawberry today is gigantic and succulent compared to those of two centuries ago; we can only imagine what new fruits we may conjure from nature's raw materials in the future.

ORCHARD FRUITS

When fruits are mentioned, these are probably the first that come to mind: apples, pears, plums, and cherries — the tree fruits, as they are known. They consist of two main groups: the pome fruits, which are the apple- and pear-like members, and the stone fruits, which are the plums, cherries, peaches, and apricots. The pomes have small seeds in a core around which the "stalk" from immediately behind swells, enclosing them with flesh. The stone fruits have a single seed in a hard shell around which the flesh forms. Both of these groups are related, as they are both members of the Rosaceae family. Mulberries and figs come from different families. Nonetheless, all are similar in hardiness, size and manner of cultivation to orchard trees.

Most of these fruits have been cultivated since ancient times. They were nearly all known to the Romans, who spread them throughout their empire. However, much knowledge of their cultivation was then lost during the Dark Ages. The monasteries, and a few noblemen, maintained fruit gardens and orchards, but the common people reverted to farming and cropping from the wild, with little interest in fruit cultivation. Indeed, fruits were often seen as poor fare compared to meat, and more suited for animal feed. If it was not for the ease with which many of these fruits could be fermented to make intoxicating beverages, they would probably have been even more neglected. After the Norman Conquest of England the new lords proved to be more interested in fruit than the Saxons they had defeated, bringing many of their own improved varieties with them from France. Orchards became more widely planted, and the wealthy vied with one another in collecting the greatest number and variety and in having the earliest and longest-lasting fruits.

In the 16th century, Henry VIII brought many new fruit varieties from the Netherlands and France, and the streets of London became full of homegrown and imported favorites. The impetus of completely different and new fruits from the New World aroused more enthusiasm for horticulture, reviving interest in the old fruits as well as the new discoveries. As old trusted varieties were exported to the colonies, new species and varieties were imported. These produced new varieties, which followed the old abroad at the same time as descendants of the first wave were already returning.

By the Victorian era the number of varieties in cultivation had escalated from a few hundreds to many tens of thousands, if you counted local varieties worldwide. The great cities were served by the immense orchards and market gardens that surrounded them.

Every gentleman aspired to a house with grounds that would include an orchard at the very least.

In the 20th century, after two World Wars, the labor to maintain great gardens and orchards was not available and the land was needed for more basic crops. Orchards were used for cereals and more exciting fruits became available from abroad. The British orchard all but disappeared from many counties. Houses with grounds and orchards were demolished to make way for office buildings at 10 to the acre.

However, the green movement, combined with people's increasing awareness of the utility of trees, the value of fruit, and the ecological advantages of permanent culture as opposed to annual crops, have all caused a reawakening of interest in orchard fruits. More are now being planted than for nearly a century.

CULINARY AND DESSERT APPLES

Malus domestica from the family Rosaceae

Tree up to 33 ft. Life span: medium to long. Deciduous, hardy, sometimes self-fertile. Fruits: up to 6 in., spherical, green to yellow or red. Vitamin value: vitamin C.

Malus domestica apples are complex selections and hybrids of *M. pumila* with *M. sylvestris* and *M. mitis*. Thus the shape of the fruit varies from the spheres of "Granny Smith" to the flattened buns of "Bramley," or the almost conical "Spartan," and "Golden Delicious." The color can be green, yellow, scarlet orange, or dark red to almost purple. The texture can vary from crisp to soft and they may be juicy or dry, acid or insipid, bitter, bland, or aromatic. All apples have a dent in the stalk end, the remains of the flower at the other, and a central tough core with several brown seeds. These are edible in small amounts, though there is a recorded death from eating a quantity, since they contain small amounts of cyanide.

The trees will often become picturesque landscape features, particularly when seen in an orchard. They frequently become twisted or distorted when left to themselves. They have soft downy or smooth leaves, never as glossy as pear leaves. The flowers are often pink- or red-tinged as well as snow white.

Apples are native to temperate Europe and Asia. They have been harvested from the wild since prehistory and were well known to the ancient Phoenicians. When Varro led his army as far as the Rhine in the first century BCE, every region had its apples. The Romans encouraged their cultivation, so although Cato had only noted a half dozen varieties in the second century BCE, Pliny knew of three dozen by the first century CE. The Dark Ages caused a decline in apple growing in Britain and only one pomerium (orchard), at Nottingham, is mentioned in the Domesday Book. However, interest increased after the Norman invasion. Costard and Pearmain varieties are first noted in the 12th and 13th centuries, and by the year 1640 there are nearly five dozen varieties recorded by Parkinson. By 1669, Worlidge has the number up to 92, mostly cider apples. *Downing's Fruits*, printed in 1866, has 643 varieties listed. Now we have more than 5,000 named apple varieties, representing about 2,000 actually distinguishable clones. Several hundred are easily obtainable from specialist nurserymen, though only a half dozen are grown on a commercial scale.

This sudden explosion in numbers was most probably due to the expansion of the colonies. The best varieties of apple trees from Europe mutated and crossed as they were propagated across North America, and then later Australia, and these then returned to be crossed again.

Apples are now grown extensively in every temperate region around the world. The first apples in North America, supposedly, were planted on the Governor's Island in Boston Harbor, but the Massachusetts Company had requested seeds in 1629, and in 1635 a Mr Wolcott of Connecticut wrote he had made 500 hogsheads of cider from his new apple orchard.

CULINARY AND DESSERT APPLES

 ## varieties

Medium to large "McIntosh," first introduced to the U.S. in 1870, has very tender red skin and crip white flesh with a delicious aroma and a sweet-tart tang. It's a favorite for eating fresh, and also valued for cider and baking. The self-fertile trees bear young and abundantly. The most widely grown apple in the U.S., favored by home gardeners and commercial orchards alike, is the large, tapered "Red Delicious." Solid and crisp, it has a mild, sweet flavor. "Winesap" and "Stayman Winesap" are old American apples with juicy, firm, yellowish flesh of wonderful winelike flavor that is as good in cooking as it is fresh. The youngster "Fuji" was introduced into the United States in 1962, but it's already a firm favorite, thanks to the outstanding honeyed sweetness of its crisp, white flesh. It doesn't need as many hours of winter chill as other varieties, and the fruit takes up to 200 days to mature, so it's popular with gardeners in milder-winter areas. The round, red, sometimes striped "Jonathan" is another old American variety, first

described in New York in 1862. Its sprightly, refreshing flavor holds up well in cooking and baking. The huge red fruits of "Rome" are excellent for all uses, but they're especially appreciated by cooks, who may only have to peel two or three apples for a pie. A late season "McIntosh" type, "Cortland" has been a favorite in America for almost a century. It's extremely cold hardy and will tolerate temperatures as low as −40°F. The pure white flesh has a delicious tanginess. "Liberty" and "Freedom" are part of a new generation of disease-resistant apples bred for carefree vigor. Both are resistant to nearly all major apple diseases and will flourish in the home garden without weed or chemical sprays. The oldest variety known and easily available is "Court Pendu Plat" (midwinter, dessert) which may go back to Roman times and is recorded from the 16th century. It is still grown because it flowers late, missing frosts. "Nonpareil" and "Golden Pippin" also come from the 16th century and keep until midspring. However, they are rarely available, though there are a dozen and a half part-descendants all called "Golden Pippin." "Golden Reinette" (midwinter, dessert) is still popular in

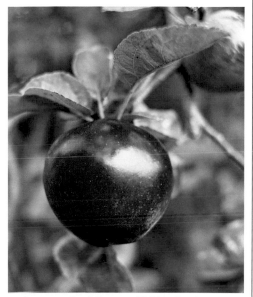

Apples exposed to full sun are highly colored, most aromatic and sweetest

Europe and dates from before 1650. The large green "Flower of Kent" (1660) has nearly disappeared. This was the apple that prompted Sir Isaac Newton in his discoveries of the laws of motion and gravity. "Ribston Pippin" (midwinter, dessert) has one of the highest vitamin C contents and superb flavor. It was bred in 1707 and does not like wet, heavy soils. From 1720 comes "Ashmead's Kernel," one of the best-tasting, late-keeping dessert apples, but it is a light cropper. "Orleans Reinette" (midwinter, dessert) has been known since 1776. It is juicy, very tasty with a rough skin and is not very good on wet, cold sites. "Bramley's Seedling" (midwinter, culinary) raised in 1809, has one of the highest vitamin C contents of cooking varieties. It grows large, so have it on a more dwarfing stock than others. "Egremont Russet" (late fall), bred in 1872, is one of the best russets, a group of apples with scentless, roughened skin and crisp, firm flesh, which is sweet and tasty but never over-juicy or acid. The ubiquitous "Golden Delicious," so much grown commercially in Europe, is a conical yellow. It actually tastes pretty good when grown at home, but must be waxed for keeping as otherwise it shrivels. It was found in West Virginia in 1916. "Discovery" was introduced in 1962. It is an early scarlet fruit with creamy white flesh that comes in late summer to early fall. The flowers are fairly frost tolerant and it is scab resistant. It is rapidly dominating the early apple market because it will keep better longer than most other early varieties.

These were fairly well thinned — but they would have been bigger and better if I'd been even more ruthless

cultivation

Apples are much-abused trees. They prefer a rich, moist, well-drained loam, but are planted almost anywhere and yet often still do fairly well. What they will not stand is being waterlogged, or growing on the site of an old apple tree or near to others that have been long established, and they do not thrive in dank frost pockets. Pollination is best served by planting more than three varieties, as many apples are mutually incompatible, having diploid or triploid varieties with irreconcilable differences in their chromosomes. Crab apples usually prove good pollinators for all apple trees.

A shady wall will grow apples but, surprisingly, pears might be a better choice

Choosing a variety

Start your apple orchard with the one you like best to eat, if it can be successfully grown in your area. Then you can branch out and explore the flavors of other varieties, including many old treasures that you'll never find on a supermarket counter. Most apples will grow well in Zones 4 through 8, but some can withstand winter cold as low as −50°F and others will set a good crop in other mild winter areas. Varieties also differ in the requirements for "winter chill," a period of cold that is vital for a good fruit set. Any trees stocked at your local nursery should thrive in your climate. Disease resistance is the new "watchword" in apple growing. Research stations are working on new releases that

"James Grieve"

combine good-tasting fruit with an ability to shrug off scab, cedar-apple rust, mildew, and other common apple problems. "Liberty," "Freedom," "Redfree," and "Williams Pride" are some of this new wave of flavorful, disease-resistant introductions.

 ## container growing

On very dwarfing stocks apples are easily grown in large pots. They need hard pruning in winter and in summer the lengthening shoots should be nipped out, thus tip-bearing varieties are not really suitable. Special varieties have been developed for containers, which supposedly require little pruning. In cold-winter areas, surround the container with a cylinder of chicken wire or wire fence, and fill it with leaves or straw for insulation.

Maintenance

Spring Weed, mulch, fertilize as needed.
Summer Thin fruits, summer prune, spray with seaweed solution, apply greasebands.
Fall Use poor fruits first, pick best for storage.
Winter Hard prune, add copious compost, remove mummified fruits.

Propagation

Apple seeds rarely make fruiting trees of value; however, many of our best varieties were chance seedlings. Apples are grafted or budded onto different rootstocks depending on site and size of tree required. Few grow

CULINARY AND DESSERT APPLES

them from cuttings on their own roots or as standards on seedling stocks as these make very large trees only suitable for planting in grazed meadows. Half-standards are more convenient for the home orchard and these get big enough on M25 stock at about 17 ft. high and 21 ft. apart. At the other extreme, the most dwarfing stock is M27, useful for pot culture, but these midgets need staking all their lives and the branches start so low you cannot mow or grow underneath them. M9 produces a 7 ft. tree, still needing staking but good for cordons. On such very dwarfing stocks the trees do badly in poor soil and during droughts. M26 is bigger, growing to 9 ft. and still needs a stake but is probably the best for small gardens. It needs 10 ft. on each side. MM106 is better on poor soils, and on good soils is still compact at about 14 ft., needing 15 ft. between trees.

Pruning and Training

Apple trees are often left to grow and produce for years with no pruning other than remedial work once the head has formed. They may be trained and hard pruned summer and winter, back to spur systems, on almost any shaped framework, though rarely as fans. For beauty and productivity, apples are best as espaliers; to achieve the maximum number of varieties, as cordons; for ease and quality, as open goblet-pruned small trees. Some varieties, especially many of the earliest fruiters, are tip bearers. These are best pruned only remedially as hard pruning will remove the fruiting wood. They can be grown on a replacement system as for peaches (see p. 470) but it is hard work. Removing crowded and congested, damaged and diseased apples improves the size and quality of those remaining and prevents biennial bearing. Thin after the June drop occurs and again twice after, disposing of the rejects to destroy any pests.

Pests and Diseases

Apples are the most commonly grown fruit tree in much of the temperate zone. They have thus built up a whole ecosystem of pests and diseases around themselves. Although they have many problems they still manage to produce enormous quantities of fruit for many years. The commonplace pests require the usual remedies (see p. 656–658), but apples suffer from some annoy-ing specialities. Holes in the fruits are usually caused by one of three pests. Codling moth, Oriental fruit moth, and apple maggot tunnel through the fruit, which often causes it to drop when young.

Once the first is damaged the rest will soon follow — don't delay; gather them NOW

You may see entry holes surrounded by sawdustlike frass. Codling moth is found across the country. Oriental fruit moth is widespread, affecting fruit everywhere except the Midwest, Texas, and some southern states. Apple maggots are a problem mainly in the Northeast and Great Lakes areas. They are controlled by red sticky traps, permitted sprays as the blossom sets, and hygiene. Cedar-apple rust, a disease that depends on eastern red cedar and other junipers as an alternative host, causes orange spots on apple leaves and fruits. Plant resistant varieties, or spray with sulfur or copper to control. Many varieties are scab-resistant. If it occurs, it affects first the leaves, then the fruits, and, like brown rot and canker, is spread by mummified apples and dead wood.

All of these problems, and mildews, are best controlled by hygiene, keeping the trees vigorous, well watered and mulched, and open pruned. Woolly aphids can be sprayed or dabbed with soft soap. Sticky non-setting tree bands control many pests all year round.

Harvesting and Storing

Early apples are best eaten right after harvest. They rarely keep for long. Most midseason apples are also

An early then a second thinning means these "Discovery" apples are nearly perfect

best eaten off the tree as they ripen, but many will keep for several weeks if picked just underripe and stored cool. Late keepers must hang on the trees till hard frosts are imminent, then if they are delicately picked and kept cool in the dark they may keep for 6 months or longer. They are best picked with a cupped hand and gently laid in a tray, traditionally padded with dry straw. (This may mold if dampened so better to use shredded newspaper.) Do not store early varieties with lates nor near pears, onions, garlic, or potatoes. The fruits must be free of bruises, rot and holes and the stalk must remain attached for them to store well. If apples are individually wrapped in paper they keep longer.

 companion planting

Apples are bad for potatoes, making them blight-prone. They are benefited by Alliums, especially chives, and penstemons and nasturtiums nearby are thought to prevent sawfly and woolly aphids. Stinging nettles nearby benefit the trees and, dried, they help stored fruits keep.

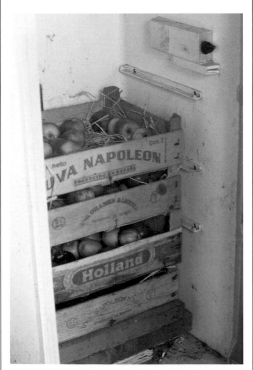

An old fridge makes a good mouse-proof insulated store

Apple surpluses can easily be dried as rings or pieces

CULINARY AND DESSERT APPLES

 culinary

Apples can be pureed and frozen, juiced and frozen, dried in thin rings, made into cider, or stewed and made into tarts, pies, and jellies, especially with other fruits, which their pectin helps set. The juice is delicious fresh and can be frozen for out-of-season use, and made into cider or vinegar. Cooking apples are different from dessert apples: much larger, more acid, and less sweet raw. Most break down quickly when heated, and few retain their texture, unlike most of the dessert types. "McIntosh," "Granny Smith," "Rome," and "Cortland" are excellent for cooking or eating due to their hint of tartness.

Flying Saucers
Per person

1 large cooking apple
Approx. 2 tablespoons mincemeat
Pat of butter
1 tablespoon sesame seeds
Cream or custard, to serve

Wash, dry and cut each apple in half horizontally. Remove the tough part of the core but leave the outside intact. Stuff the hollow with mincemeat, then pin the two halves back together with wooden toothpicks. Rub the outside with butter and roll in sesame seeds, then bake in a baking sheet in a preheated oven at 375°F for 30 minutes or until it "lifts off" nicely. Serve immediately with cream or custard.

 other uses

Apple wood is used for mallet heads, golf clubs, and in engraving. It is delicately scented when burned, and is useful for smoking foods and as fire logs.

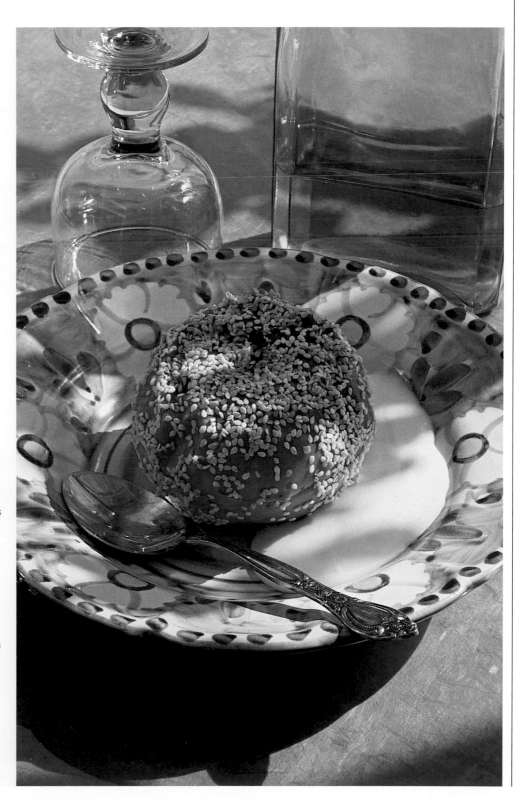

Malus pumila **from the family Rosaceae**

CRAB AND CIDER APPLES

Trees up to 33 ft. Life span: long. Deciduous, often self-fertile. Fruits: ½ to 3 in., spherical, yellow, green, or red. Value: make tonic alcoholic beverages.

Crab apples grow wild and have smaller, more brightly colored fruits than cultivated varieties. The fruits make delicious jellies. Cider apples are more like eating and cooking apples, with fruits in-between in size but similarly bitter and astringent. Selected crab apples are grown ornamentally and are useful pollinators for other apples, so they may be found on semi-dwarfing stocks as small trees. Cider apples were always grown on strong or seedling stock, gaining immense vigor, which they needed to tower above animals grazing underneath.

Crab apples have been used since prehistory and doubtless hard cider has been made for as long.

"Kingston Black"

 varieties

In the United States, many culinary and dessert apples, including "McIntosh" and "Winesap," are also used for cider. True cider apples, including the cold-hardy American varieties "Centennial," "Dolgo," "Wealthy," and "Chestnut," are interesting for the home gardener to experiment with, evoking a rich heritage of homemade apple cider and crab apple jelly, not to mention a bounty of spring blossoms. "Wealthy," developed in 1861 in Minnesota, at its best is a sweet strawberry-flavored variety, soft with creamy flesh, but can be less exciting depending on conditions. "Prairie Spy," introduced in 1914, is very sweet with little acidity. It is vigorous and hardy, with firm-fleshed, crisp, and juicy fruits. Many crabs are well-known ornamentals, such as "John Dowie," which has long golden-orange fruits, and "Golden Hornet," with bright yellow fruits. Most are mixed hybrids of *Malus pumila* with the European native *M. sylvestris,* which has sour, hard, green fruits and is sometimes thorny, and *M. mitis,* from the Mediterranean region, which has softer leaves and sweeter, more colored fruits. *M. baccata,* the Siberian crab, and *M. manchuria,* from China, are widely planted for their bright red fruits. Cider apples are more improved and closer to *M. domestica* hybrids.

 cultivation

Tougher than the finer apples, these may be grown almost anywhere not waterlogged or parched. Crab apples are extremely cold tolerant. Most varieties are hardy in Zones 3 through 8, and some will thrive as far north as Zone 2.

Growing under Glass
Neither the crab nor the cider apple is happy

"John Downie"

CRAB AND CIDER APPLES

permanently under glass. They need a winter chill, otherwise they crop badly.

Maintenance

Spring Weed, mulch, and fertilize as needed.
Summer Keep trees deeply mulched to conserve moisture in soil.
Fall Pick fruit.
Winter Prune, and spread the compost.

Propagation

Although some crab apples can be grown from seed they are not reliable. Named varieties are grafted on to rootstocks suitable for the size and site intended. Neither crab nor cider apple varieties are usually available on the most dwarfing rootstocks, but on more vigorous stock they make large trees.

Pruning and Training

Crab apples are usually worked as half-standards on semi dwarfing stock and are only pruned remedially in winter, unless they are nonresistant to apple scab, in which case they will defoliate every year. Cider apples are worked as standards on strong growing stocks and make big trees. Likewise, cider apples should only be pruned remedially after forming a head.

Pests and Diseases

Although these can suffer from the same problems as dessert and culinary apples, the crops are rarely badly affected. Crab apples are usually remarkably productive whatever care they get. For cider apples many problems such as scab are also mostly irrelevant.

Harvesting and Storing

Crab apples can be picked underripe for jellying, but you can wait as the birds do not go for them as fast as softer fruits. Cider apples are left as long as possible to get maximum sugar and to soften. If they are shaken down they bruise, so they are then best pressed immediately, not stored in heaps to soften further.

 companion planting

The plants that benefit dessert and culinary apples (see p. 450) also associate well with these varieties. Crab and cider apples are often grown in hedgerows and meadow orchards, content with grass underneath.

Malus baccata

A grape press for extracting juice from apples works better if they're pulped first

 container growing

Crab apples can be fruited in pots, even in the small pots in which garden centers sell them. Cider apples are shy and less likely to produce heavy crops.

other uses

Pressed apple pulp can be dried and stored till late winter for wild bird and livestock food.

 culinary

Crab apples make delicious tart jellies by themselves, or mixed with other fruits which have less pectin and so do not set so easily. Cider apples are used solely to make hard cider. They are cleaned, crushed, and pressed and the juice is fermented, often with the addition of wine yeast and sugar. After fermentation, hard cider may be flat, cloudy, sweet, or sparkling, green or yellow, depending on local taste. Ciders are made from several varieties of apple, to give a blend of acidity, sweetness, and tannin. (Palatable hard cider can be made from a mixture of dessert and cooking apples.) Some hard cider is made into vinegar, deliberately.

Crab Apple Jello

Makes approx 7½ lbs.

12 cups crab apples
Approx. 6 cups sugar

Chop the apples, then simmer them in water to cover until soft. Strain through a jelly bag and measure the juice. Add three-quarters of the volume in sugar. Return to the heat and bring to a boil, stirring to dissolve the sugar. Boil until setting point is reached, then skim and pour into warm, sterilized jars. Cover while still hot.

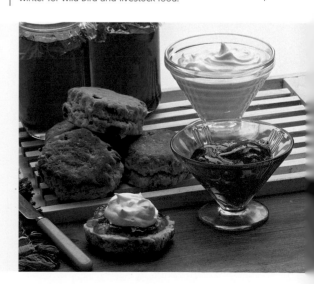

Pyrus communis from the family Rosaceae

CULINARY AND DESSERT PEARS

Tree up to 65 ft. Life span: very long. Deciduous, hardy, rarely self-fertile. Fruits: up to 3 x 7 in. Value: potassium and riboflavin.

Pears very closely resemble, and are related to, apples, but there are no known natural hybrids between them. Pears have a fruit that elongates at the stalk end, which stands proud, whereas an apple's stalk is inset in a dent in the top of the fruit. Some pears such as "Conference" and "Bartlett" will set fruit parthenocarpically (that is, they fruit freely without pollination). However, these fruits are usually not as good as fertilized ones, being misshapen and, of course, lacking seeds. Pear trees resemble apples but have shiny leaves, more upright growth and the fat stems usually have a glossier brown hue and more angled buds than apple. Pears on their own roots make very big trees, too big to prune, spray, or pick, and the fruit is damaged when it drops. Pears are thus usually worked on quince roots, which makes them smaller, more compact trees.

Pears are native to Europe and Asia. The first cultivated varieties were selected from the wild in prehistory. The ancient Phoenicians, Hebrews, and pre-Christian Romans grew several improved sorts; by the time of Cato there were at least a half dozen distinct fruits, Pliny records 41 and Palladius 56. A list of fruits for the

Grand Duke Cosimo III, in late medieval Italy, raises the number to 209, and another manuscript lists 232. In Britain in 1640 only five dozen were known. This had risen to more than 700 by 1842. In 1866 the American author T. W. Field catalogued 850 varieties. The rapid increase in numbers and quality, from poor culinary pears to fine desserts, was mainly the work of a few dedicated breeders in France and Belgium at the end of the eighteenth century, who selected and bred most modern varieties.

 varieties

As pears are used more for eating raw than in cooking, and dessert pears can be cooked, but not vice versa, it is not worthwhile growing purely culinary pears. "Comice" (late season) is by far the best dessert pear. No other approaches it for sweet, aromatic succulence, and the fruits can reach a magnificent weight. These are very choice and deserve to be espaliered on the best warm wall. "Bartlett/ Williams' Bon Chretien" (early/midseason) is widely grown for canning, but is an excellent table fruit — if a bit prone to scab. It is also parthenocarpic as is "Conference"

(early/midseason). The latter is a reliable cropper on its own and is scab-resistant. Beautiful, light green "Anjou" and its ruddy counterpart "Red Anjou," are mild, fine-textured pears with delicate, melting, white flesh. Their fine flavor gets even sweeter a few weeks after picking. Both need a pollinator, and "Bosc" is a good one. This golden-brown pear has russetted skin and aromatic, tender white flesh. For low-maintenance gardens, "Seckel" is the perfect choice. Its brownish skin and small size may look like nothing special, but this tiny morsel, often called "sugar pear," offers a few bites of spicy-sweet, fine-grained flesh with a moutwatering aroma. Along with its delicious taste come an iron constitution: the variety is widely

adaptable to almost any conditions, and it's naturally semi-dwarf, needing no pruning. It bears heavy crops and is less troubled by disease than other varieties. There are hundreds of other pear varieties, many of which are cooking, not dessert, and several species that have more ornamental than edible value: Birch-leaved Pear, *P. betufolia*, Chinese Sand or Duck Pear, *P. sinensis,* and Three-lobed-leaved Pear, *P. trilobata*, are popular.

cultivation

Dessert pears need a rich, well-drained, moist soil, preferably light and loamy. The blossoms and fruitlets need protection from frosts as they flower early in spring. Pollination is best ensured by planting a mixture of varieties. Do not plant deep as pears are prone to scion rooting, which allows them to make big, less fruitful trees. Most pears will thrive in Zones 5 through 8. Some are more cold-hardy, such as "Stacey," which bears small, sweet fruits after −50°F winters, and will do well as far north as Zone 2. A few varieties are more tender, and best in Zones 6 through 9. The unusual "Pineapple," which has a tropical flavor, is for mild-winter regions, including the Deep South. As with other fruits, read the catalog description to make sure the variety you are considering will do well in your area.

Growing under Glass

Pears appreciate a warm wall, but are not easy under glass as they do not like to get too hot and humid; they are thus difficult to grow in the tropics.

Ornamental and Wildlife Value

Why plant an ornamental flowering tree when you can plant a pear? They are just smothered with blossoms

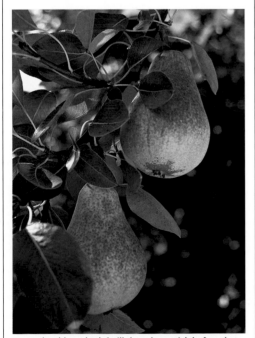

Pears should not be left till they drop; pick before that point to color and ripen indoors

"Kumoi"

and buzzing with bees in early spring. Overripe pears that hang on the trees or fall to the ground will attract butterflies as well as wasps and yellow jackets.

Maintenance

Spring Weed, mulch, and fertilize as needed; protect flowers against frosts.
Summer Thin fruit.
Fall Pick fruit.
Winter Prune hard or not at all; compost heavily.

Propagation

Pears do not come true from seed, reverting to their unproductive forms. They may root from cuttings and can occasionally be layered, but get too big on their own roots. Normally they are grafted on to quince rootstocks. For heavy, damp soils and for big trees, pear seedling stock was always used, but there is little demand for this nowadays. Pears have been grafted on to apple stocks and even on to hawthorn. As some varieties do not bond readily with quince stock they are "double-worked", or grafted on to a mutually compatible intergraft on the quince.

Pruning and Training

Grown as trees or bushes, pears can be left to themselves except for remedial pruning. They tend to throw double leaders, which need rationalizing. Alternatively, though you should not prune in summer, they respond better than most fruits to hard winter pruning thus they can be trained to an endless variety of forms. As they benefit from the shelter of a wall, they are commonly espaliered, and are more rewarding for less work than a peach in the same position. There are many specialized training forms for pears in addition to the cordon, espalier, and fan, and equally intricate and specialized pruning methods. Pears will take almost any shape you choose, and you will not go far wrong if you then shear almost all long growths off in winter. Take care not to let them root from or above the graft, which destroys the benefit of the rootstock!

other uses

The bark contains a yellow dye and arbutin, an antibiotic. The leaves have been used medicinally for renal and urinary infections. The wood is hard and uniform, so loved by carvers. It is beautifully scented.

 companion planting

Pears are hindered by grass, so this should not be allowed near them in their early years. However, the growing site may be seeded to grass later, especially if they are situated in rather too heavy and/or damp conditions.

Espaliered "Beurre Hardy" is happy on this sunny wall where it pollinates a "Doyenne du Comice" close by

Pests and Diseases

Pears suffer fewer problems than apples. However, ripening is poor in very cool or hot weather and results in hard or mealy fruits. Leaving the fruit too long on the tree causes formation of gritty stone cells in the fruits and leaving too long in storage causes them to rot. Pear midge causes the fruitlets to blacken and drop off; inspection reveals maggots within. These are remedied by the hygienic removal and disposal of affected fruits; running poultry underneath in orchards is as effective. Fireblight causes damage resembling scorching. It usually starts from the blossoms. Prune and burn damaged parts immediately, cutting back to clean wood. Scab is a problem in stagnant sites. It affects the fruits before the leaves, which is the opposite to apples. Sprays are usually unnecessary with the more resistant varieties. Good open pruning and healthy growth, not overfed with nitrogen, reduce attacks. Always remove all mummified fruits and dead wood immediately. Leaf blistering is usually caused by minute mites. These used to be controlled with lime and sulphur sprays before bud burst. Modern soft-soap sprays have also proved to be effective.

Harvesting and Storing

Early pears are best picked almost, but never fully, ripe. They should come off when lifted to the horizontal. Left on the tree they get gritty. Watch them carefully while they finish ripening. They will slowly ripen if kept cool, faster if warm. Late pears should be left until bird damage is too great, and picked with a stalk. Kept in a cool, dark place, late varieties last for months, ripening up rapidly if brought into the warm. Do not wrap them with paper as one does with apples, and take care not to store the two fruits near each other as they will cross-taint.

 container growing

Pears have often been fruited in tubs. They are amenable to hard pruning, and so respond better than most other fruits to this and to the cramped conditions of a pot.

Pear gluts are easily turned into sweet syrup!

CULINARY AND DESSERT PEARS

culinary

Pears are exquisite as dessert fruits and may be used in much the same way as apples, sliced and used in pies, baked, stewed or puréed. They are delicious pickled with onions and spices in vinegar.

Pear Islands
Serves 4

4 large pears
⅓ cup superfine sugar
Half bottle sweet Muscat wine
2 level tablespoons cornstarch
Splash of milk
Dark chocolate, to taste

Peel, halve, and core the pears. Dissolve two-thirds of the sugar in the wine over a gentle heat and poach the pears in this syrup. Place the pear halves on an oiled baking sheet, dredge with the rest of sugar and pop under a hot broiler for a minute or two until the tops caramelize. In the meantime, blend the cornstarch with a little milk and stir it into the syrup. Return to the heat and cook gently, stirring, until thick. Pour the sauce into a serving bowl, grate on some dark chocolate and set the pear halves into this. Serve piping hot or chilled.

Pyrus from the family Rosaceae

CIDER PEARS

"Blakeney Red"

Tree up to 65 ft. Life span: very long. Deciduous, rarely self-fertile. Fruits: up to 4 × 3 in., variable, pear-shaped, yellow, brown, or red. Value: make a healthy tonic beverage.

Cider pear fruits are smaller and hardier than their culinary and dessert cousins, while the trees are generally enormous. As these fruits were wanted in quantity for pressing, they were selected for large trees that would stand well above grass and the depredations of stock. The fruits are bitter and astringent, containing a lot of tannin, even though they may often look very appealing. They are pressed for the juice, which ferments to an alcoholic beverage.

Cider pears may have been brought to Britain by the Romans, but they were introduced in force by the Normans. Normandy was by then well established as a perry-growing region and the Normans found parts of the West and Midlands of England equally suitable. Many of the original pear orchards would probably still have been planted for perry without the Norman influence, as early pears tended to be unpalatable raw anyway. The colonists of North America certainly did not start off without perry pears. By 1648 a booklet entitled *A Perfect Description of Virginia* describes a Mr Kinsman regularly making 40 or 50 butts of perry from his orchard. Whereas hard cider has remained a popular drink, perry waned in the 19th century. It is now coming back into fashion as large hard cider makers have started selling it.

 varieties

There are some 200 to 300 perry pear varieties known, though these are called by twice as many names, each district having its own local variation. The "Thorn Pear" is recorded from 1676 and grows on a very upright tree. Other early varieties such as "Hastings" and "Brown Bess" could be eaten or made into perry. Later varieties such as "Holmer" are more single purpose and almost inedible. In the 19th century, breeders thought dual-purpose pears would be useful and produced "Blakeney Red" and "Cannock." The "Huffcap" group all make very big trees with fruits of a high specific gravity; "Rock" varieties make even stronger perry, but are still often called "Huffcaps."

 cultivation

Perry pears are less demanding than culinary or dessert pears and will do quite well in fairly poor soils. They do not like shallow or badly drained sites.

Growing under Glass
These are fairly hardy and will make big trees, so are generally not likely to thrive under glass.

Perry pears are not good eating

Perry pears are smaller, more acidic and often more brightly colored than dessert pears

Ornamental and Wildlife Value

Perry pears make a mass of flowers and are tall attractive trees that live for several hundred years, making them very suitable as estate and orchard trees, but too big for most gardens except on modern dwarfing stock. The flowers are good for insects and the fruits are eaten by birds in winter.

Maintenance

Spring Cut grass, fertilize as needed.
Summer No maintenance needed.
Fall Cut grass, collect fruits.
Winter Prune and spread compost.

Propagation

Perry pears were often grown from seed or grafted on to stocks grown from seeds in order to get large trees. Now they can be had on dwarfing stocks, such as quince, and are more manageable.

Pruning and Training

Once the initial shape is formed these are only pruned remedially, though care should always be taken to ensure that such large trees are sound.

Pests and Diseases

These suffer the same few problems as dessert and culinary pears which make little impression on the immense crops. Fireblight is a risk, but there is little one can do with such large trees.

Harvesting and Storing

Immense crops are produced; a ton or even 2 per tree is possible, after a wait of several decades. One tree in 1790 covered three-quarters of an acre and produced 6 tons per year. Perry pears do not keep and rot very quickly. Perry is usually pressed from one variety only, with sugar and yeast added. Dessert and culinary pears do not make a perry of any value, but can be made into a pear wine.

 ## companion planting

Young trees were usually cropped between cereals or hops and then grassed down as they matured, often grazed by geese.

 ## culinary

Perry pears are not normally very good for eating even when they are cooked, though "Blakeney Red" was once considered good for baking.

Pressless Perry Wine

18 cups whole pears, chopped
6 cups sugar

 ## container growing

Although they would resent it by being short-lived and light-cropping, it should be possible to grow these in large tubs.

 ## other uses

The wood is useful for carving and, as firewood, scents the room.

4 quarts water
Approx. 1 teaspoon wine yeast

Boil the water and add the pears. Stir in half the sugar, and bring back to a boil, then allow to cool to 70°F before adding the yeast. Seal with a fermentation lock and keep warm for 1 week, then strain and add the remaining sugar to the liquor. Reseal with the lock and ferment in a warm place until all action has stopped. Siphon off the lees (sediment) and store in a cool place for 3 months, then bottle and store for a year before drinking.

QUINCES

Tree up to 20 ft. Self-fertile, deciduous, hardy, long-lived. Fruits: 2 x 5 in., yellow and fragrant.

These are small, bushy trees, often twisted and contorted. There are two forms: a lower mounded one with lax branches, more suited to ornamental and wildlife use, and a stiffer, erect type, which bears larger fruits and is better for orchards. The leaves are downy underneath, resembling apple leaves more than pear. They turn a gorgeous yellow in fall. The decorative pink and white flowers resemble apple blossoms, but appear singly on short shoots, 6–8 in. long, that grow before the flower opens, so they are rarely bothered by late frost. In some varieties the unfurled flower bud looks like an ice-cream cone with strawberry stripes, or a traditional barber's pole. The quinces are hard fruits somewhat resembling pears in shape and color, often covered with a soft down when young, inedible when raw, but delicious and aromatic when cooked. Because they have long been used as rootstocks for pears and other fruits, they are sometimes found as suckers, surviving long after the scion has passed away.

Quinces are old fruits, still much grown in many parts of Europe though originally from Persia and Turkestan. Dedicated by the ancients to the Goddess of Love, they were promulgated by the Roman Empire as one of their favored crops and were well known to Pliny and Columella. In 812 CE Charlemagne encouraged the French to grow more and Chaucer refers to them by the French name as *coines*. Their pulp makes *Dulce de Membrillo* or *Marmelo*, still popular in Portugal and Spain, and the origin of the marmalade we now make from citrus fruit.

 varieties

"Smyrna" is one of the most attractive varieties in flower and fruit, with golden-yellow, pear-shaped fruit that is aromatic and tender. Introduced in 1897, it is still a favorite for desserts, preserves, and jellies. The very old "Orange" is a sturdy growing tree with bright yellow fruit that can weigh as much as a pound. "Champion" grows 12–15 ft. tall and is cold hardy and reliable.

 cultivation

Quinces are hardy in Zones 5 through 10. Their shallow

Cydonia quinces may be confused with *Chaenomeles*

roots grow well in almost any soil. Quinces thrive in moist soil and flourish as waterside specimens. They prefer a warm site, doing badly in cold or exposed places. Plant them at least 10 ft. apart. They will only need staking in their first years of life. They are self-fertile.

Ornamental and Wildlife Value

Quinces make excellent small specimen trees as the flowers, fruits, fall colors, and the knotted branches give year-round interest. The flowers feed beneficial insects while the fruits are relished by birds and other wildlife after the apples and pears have long gone.

Maintenance

Spring Spray with fertilizer; weed and mulch well.

QUINCES

 culinary

Quinces can be made into aromatic clear jello, jelly, or a pulpy cheese that goes well with both sweet and savory dishes. Pieces of quince (if you can hack them off) keep their shape when cooked, adding both texture and aroma to apple and pear dishes.

Quince Cheese
Makes about 4 lb.

1 small orange (unwaxed)
6 cups ripe quinces, chopped
A little water
Approx. 4 cups sugar
1 or 2 drops orange-flower or rose-petal water
(optional)

Finely chop the orange and simmer with the quinces, with just enough water to cover them, until they are a pulp. Strain the pulp and add its own volume in sugar. Bring to a boil and cook gently for about 1½ hours. Add the orange-flower or rose-petal water, if desired. Then put into oiled, warmed bowls, seal, and store for 3 months or more before using. Turn the cheese out of the bowl and slice for serving with cooked meats or savory dishes.

Summer Spray monthly with seaweed solution and weed.
Fall Remove rotten fruit and pick best for storing.
Winter Prune out dead and diseased wood; add plenty of compost.

Propagation
Quinces can be grown from seed. Better fruits will always result from buying a ready-formed tree of an already named variety.

Pruning and Training
Quinces can be trained but the twisted growth makes this difficult. They are best grown as bushes or standards, with pruning restricted to removing dead, diseased, and crossing wood. Trees will sucker from the roots, growing into a thicket of branches, but you can cut back the sucker to train the plant as a small tree.

Pests and Diseases
There are no widespread problems for quinces. Even the birds and wasps will ignore the fruits for most of the fall. Fireblight may cause the leaves and branch tips to suddenly wilt as if scorched. Cut off at least 12 in. below the signs of disease.

Harvesting and Storing
Pick the fruits in fall before they drop and keep them in a cool airy place. Do not store with apples or pears or vegetables as they may taint.

Cydonia quinces are very pear-like, but much firmer

 companion planting

Like pears and apples, quinces may be expected to benefit from underplantings of chives, garlic, and the pungent herbs.

 container growing

There is little to be gained by growing quinces under glass. They can be grown against a wall with some success and could be grown in pots and taken indoors by those living in harsh climates, but the fruit hardly merits such effort.

 other uses

The wood is hard and prunings make good kindling. The fruits are excellent room perfumers and can be used as bases for pomanders.

PLUMS

Tree 20 ft. Long-lived, deciduous, hardy, slender, thorny, not usually self-fertile. Fruits: ovoid, usually 1–2 in. in any color. Value: rich in magnesium, iron, and vitamin A.

Plums come in more variation than most other fruits. They differ in season, size, shape, color, and taste. We have mixed hybrids, descendants of plums originally selected from 15 or more different wild species. The European plum, *Prunus domestica*, is thought to be predominantly a hybrid between *P. cerasifera*, the cherry plum or "Myrobalan," and *P. spinosa*, "Sloe." It is a small to medium, slender, deciduous tree with small white blossoms.

The European plum came from Western Asia and the Caucasus. It naturalized in Greece first and then throughout most of the temperate zone. Plum stones were ordered in 1629 for planting in Massachusetts, and plums became widely cultivated in the temperate parts of North America. Some American plums returned to Europe; California, for example, became famous for exporting prunes — late, dark-skinned plums, which are dried on the tree.

"Czar"

 ## varieties

There are hundreds of good varieties, which ripen through the season. "Victoria" is fully self-fertile, pollinates many others and is always worth having. It has golden-yellow-fleshed, large, yellow, ovoid fruits, flushed with scarlet. "Oullin's Gage" is self-fertile. A plum with a richer, sweeter flavor, it flowers late, missing frosts. Self-fertile "Stanley" is a vigorous, spreading tree that gives bumper crops of tender freestone fruit year after year. Originally grown in Missouri, "Bluefree" is a good companion to "Stanley," which pollinates it well. It bears early and is extremely cold hardy. "Mount Royal," an exceptional pollinator for all European plums, is extraordinarily cold hardy, thriving in northern Wisconsin and Minnesota. Its sweet, meaty fruit is excellent for eating fresh or for canning and freezing. The very sweet fruits of the "French Improved" make it the leading prune plum in California. "Seneca" is a wonderful dessert plum, with very sweet, freestone flesh. It is resistant to brown rot. The reliable, early-ripening "Italian Prune" is self-fertile, but crops are even larger with a pollinator. "Empress" and "President" cross-pollinate well. Both are vigorous, upright trees and heavy bearers. Luther Burbank raised a sweet, yellow plum with incomparable flavor called "The Pearl." It is believed to be the result of a cross between a "Reine Claude" gage and "Prune d'Agen," an ancient plum brought back to Europe by Benedictine monks returning from the Crusades in Persia.

"Victoria"

 ## cultivation

European plums are hardy in Zones 4 through 9. They usually bloom later and ripen later than Japanese plums. Plums like a heavier, moister soil than many other fruits. Even on a shady wall some do well.

Growing under Glass and in Containers
Susceptible to spring frost, brown rot, and wasps, plums are worth growing under glass. They are best confined to large pots so they can spend some time outdoors, as they do not relish hot conditions.

Maintenance
Spring Protect blossoms from frost; weed, mulch.
Summer Put out pest traps.
Fall Remove mummified plums.
Winter Prune if needed.

Propagation
Graft on "Pixy" and other new dwarfing stocks, unless you have a big orchard. Plums can be grown from pits, but take years to fruit and do not come true.

Pruning and Training
Plums make good high standards because, eventually, heavy fruiting branches weep. Overladen branches will need propping. Plums are usually grown as a short standard or bush. Leave them alone once a head is formed, except to cut out dead and diseased wood. They can be usefully trained on walls if on dwarfing stock. Plums prefer herringbone, not fan shapes.

Pests and Diseases
Brown rot may cause spots on fruits that rapidly enlarge, sometimes followed by gray mold. Picking up dropped fruit helps control the disease. Sulfur sprays in summer may be necessary. Bacterial leafspot may disfigure leaves and cause small spots or cracks in fruit. Spray copper after buds open to prevent it. Apple maggots may tunnel intro fruit. To keep under control, hang red sticky ball traps in trees and collect any dropped fruit. Plum curculio may burrow into fruit, leaving small semi-circular scars on the skin and causing fruit to drop prematurely. A pyrethrin spray in early spring may help.

 ## culinary

Plums can be turned into jam, juice or cheese, or frozen if pitted first, and are Epicurean preserved in plum brandy syrup.

Prunes in Semolina
Serves 4

³/₄ cups dried prunes
½ cup plum brandy
½ cup water
3 cups milk
Twist of lemon rind
½ teaspoon salt
2 heaping tablespoons semolina
2 teaspoons honey
2 medium eggs, separated
Grated nutmeg, to taste

Soak the prunes in the brandy and water overnight. Strain off the juice and simmer it down to syrup. Put the fruits and syrup into the bottom of a pudding basin. Boil the milk, lemon rind, salt, and semolina for 10 minutes, stirring continuously.

Cool a little, remove the lemon rind and stir in the honey and egg yolks. Whip the egg whites and fork them in. Immediately pour the mixture over the back of a spoon onto the fruit and syrup. Grate nutmeg over the surface and bake in a preheated oven at 400°F for 20 minutes, or until the top is browning.

Delicious cold for breakfast or hot for dinner.

Harvesting and Storing
Plums picked underripe for cooking will keep for days, but often have poor flavor. Many varieties can be quite easily peeled, and this avoids some of the unfortunate side effects of too many plums.

 ## companion planting

Plant a ground cover of white clover beneath the tree to help control insect pests. Curculios are reportedly kept off by surrounding plum trees with garlic.

Double "Victoria"
Serves 6 to 8

2 cups Victoria plums, halved and pitted
⅙ cup honey
¼ cup flaked blanched almonds

for the sponge cake:
1 cups sifted self-rising flour
³/₄ cup vanilla-flavored superfine sugar
½ cup softened butter
2 eggs
pinch of salt

Place the plums in a buttered pudding dish and drizzle with the honey. Beat together the sponge ingredients in a mixer until creamy and light in color. Dollop the sponge mixture over the fruit, smooth, and garnish with almonds. Bake in a preheated oven at 375°F for 35 minutes or until golden brown and firm to the touch.

Prunus italica from the family Rosaceae

GREENGAGES

Tree/bush 13–16 ft.. Hardy, long-lived. Fruits: 1–1½ in., green to red.

Greengages are like plums, fruiting in midseason with sweet, greeny yellow or golden, lightly scented flesh. The fruits are smaller, firmer, more rounded and less bloomed than plums. They have a deep crease down one side and frequently russet spotting. The trees are sturdy, not often thorny, and bushier than most plums, though not quite as hardy.

Wild greengages are found in Asia Minor. Possibly introduced to Britain and Northern Europe by the Romans, they disappeared from cultivation during the Saxon period or Middle Ages and were not reintroduced until 1725. Originally known in France as the "Reine Claude," the first greengage was brought to Britain by, and named after, Sir Thomas Gage, who lived in Bury St Edmunds, Suffolk — less than 20 miles from where I now write. He was fortunate to live in East Anglia as the conditions suit greengages, which need a drier, warmer summer than plums. The original greengage almost always came true from seed, but there are some larger-fruited selections, and also some good crosses between gages and plums.

"Mirabelle"

 varieties

The old "Greengage" is original, but can be unreliable; an improved seedling is "Cambridge Gage." The "Transparent Gage" is another old variety from France and is honeyed in its sweetness. It has almost transparent, golden-yellow flesh and is heavily spotted with red. It fruits in late summer. The true "Mirabelle" is very similar, smaller fruited and of dwarf growth, but is rarely found except in southern France. (Sometimes the yellow "Myrobalan" plums may erroneously be called "Mirabelles" to make a sale!) "Denniston's Superb" comes from the U.S. and is close to the original in flavor, but is larger fruited, hardier, regular cropping and most valuable of all, self-fertile. "Jefferson" is similar, later, but not self-fertile.

"Reine Claude de Bavay" possibly has a plum as one parent. It fruits 2 weeks or so after the previous varieties, in early fall. It makes a most delicious jam, a touch more acid and tasty if the fruit is picked a week or so early. "Golden Transparent," another hybrid, is a large, round, transparent yellow. It ripens late and needs to be grown against a wall in most cool areas, but is self-fertile. "Oullin's Golden Gage" is self-fertile. A plum with a richer, sweeter flavor, it flowers late, missing frosts.

 cultivation

Greengages grow best in a warm, sunny climate. They will thrive in Zones 7 through 9. Some varieties have better cold tolerance, such as "Greengage," which will flourish to central Iowa. They need a lighter soil than plums but

GREENGAGES

Prunelle liqueur is a warming drink akin to brandy

still need it to be rich, moist and well aerated. They are easiest to tend as standards at least 20 ft. apart. In colder areas they need a wall. Some, such as "Denniston's Superb," "Early Transparent Gage," "Jefferson's Gage" or "Oullins Golden Gage," will fruit on a shady wall.

Growing under Glass and in Containers
Greengages, especially the choicer "Mirabelle" or "Transparent" varieties, are worth growing in pots as this is the only way to restrict their growth. They can then be taken under cover for the flowering and ripening periods. Greengages will need a rest in winter.

Ornamental and Wildlife Value
As for plums (see p. 463).

Harvesting and Storing
Picked fully ripe off the tree they are delectable, but do not last, especially if wet. They can be jammed, turned into cheeses, juiced or frozen if pitted first.

Pruning and Training
They are usually grown as low standards or bushes with remedial pruning in late spring once the shape has formed. Overladen branches need propping, but not as much as for plums. As they also tend to irregular bearing, thinning of heavy crops is sensible, but not as effective as for most fruits. Gages are best worked like plums in a herringbone pattern on a wall, and summer pruned.

Maintenance
Spring Protect blossom from frost; weed, mulch, spray with with fertilizer, then prune.
Summer Put out wasp traps.
Fall Remove mummified fruits.
Winter Protect buds from birds with floating row covers or nets.

Pests and Diseases
As greengages are so sweet they suffer particularly from bird damage, and the buds are attacked as well as the fruits! The damage caused also allows dieback to get a foothold, so trees need netting or floating row covers over the winter in bird-infested areas. Wasps also make a mess of the crop, so be prepared to be ruthless!

Propagation
Gages are usually grafted on to Myrobalan stocks, but newer dwarfing stocks mean that it is easier to fit them on to walls. Cuttings can be taken in late fall with some success and the oldest varieties come nearly true from stones.

 ## companion planting

Greengages benefit from being positioned on the sheltered, sunny side of the larger plums.

 ## other uses

Prunelle (left) is a liqueur from Alsace and Angers, made from "Mirabelles." Slivovitsa, an eau-de-vie, comes from the Balkans.

 ## culinary

They make the best plum jams. True Mirabelle jam is almost apricot flavored, but even better.

Greengage jam
Makes 4 pounds

4 cups greengages
4 cups sugar
A little water

Wash, halve and pit the gages. Crack a few stones, extract the kernels and add these to the fruit. Pour in enough water to cover the bottom of the pan and simmer until the fruit has softened. Add the sugar and bring rapidly to a boil, then carefully skim, jar and seal.

Prunus species **from the family Rosaceae**

DAMSONS
BULLACES AND JAPANESE PLUMS

"Zwetsche"

Tree/bush up to 16 ft. Long-lived, some self-fertile. Fruits: 1 in. or more. Some vitamin value.

Bullaces (*P. insititia*) have globular, bluey-black or greeny-yellow fruits, which ripen in late fall, at least a month later than most other plums. The fruits are small and generally too acid to eat raw, but make good preserves. The trees are sometimes thorny.

Damsons (*P. damascena*) are closely related to bullaces, with larger, blue-black fruit which more closely resemble plums. However, they are more oval, with less bloom, and have a sweet, spicy flavor once cooked. Damson trees are compact and are reasonably self-fertile.

The Cherry Plum or Myrobalan (*P. cerasifera*) is less

brittle and can be woven into hedges; it is often used as a windbreak. The white flowers open at the same time as the leaves, which are glossier than those of other plums. They are self-fertile. The fruits are yellow, red or purple, spherical and a little pointed at the bottom. They have a sweet, juicy, if somewhat insipid flesh and make good jam.

Japanese plums (*P. salicina* and *P. triflora*) are large, conical, orangey-red or golden fruits without much flavor. They blossom early and are vulnerable to cold, but they are also more productive and tolerant of a wider range of warm conditions than ordinary plums, so are extensively grown in Australia, South Africa and the U.S. They have shiny, dark twigs, white flowers on bold spurs and leaves that turn a glorious red in fall.

Bullaces are native to Europe and Asia Minor, but the current apparently wild stock has probably been inadvertently selected over the centuries. Damsons come from Damascus, or certainly that region, and were brought to Europe during the Crusades in the 12th century, supposedly by the Duke of Anjou, after a pilgrimage to Jerusalem. Cherry plums come from the Balkans, Caucasus and Western Asia and were introduced to Britain in the 16th century. Some of these went to the New World and were interbred with American native species to cope with the harsher climatic conditions. Japanese plums, originally natives of China, were introduced to Japan about 1500 and only to the U.S. in 1870. Being rather tender, they have never really expanded into Europe.

 varieties

American plum, also called Goose, Hog, or Yellow Plum, grows in spreading thickets of small, graceful trees with clouds of fragrant, white blossoms in early spring. The abundant red and yellow fruit is only an inch across, but it makes a pleasingly tart nibble and is excellent in jellies and preserves. "Red Diamond" is a very cold-hardy variety

with juicy, red-purple fruit. Beach plums are likewise small but deliciously sweet. The purple, red, and yellow fruit grows on a thorny shurb that is found on sandy beaches. The large, sweet fruit of Japanese plums have made them a favorite in American markets and for home gardeners. "Black Amber" has large, almost black fruit with sweet, firm, amber flesh. There are several ornamental forms of cherry plums that may fruit; some have pink flowers, many are purple-leaved.

 cultivation

These plums gorw well in average, well-drained soil. Beach plum, cherry plum, and American wild plum will also grow in lean soils, and beach plum flourishes in sandy soils. Japanese plum varieties do best in warm climates. They are hardy in Zones 6 through 9, with several varieties thriving in Zone 5 and some low-chill

"Farleigh"

selections doing well in Zone 10. The prolific "Santa Rosa" and "Satsuma" are hardy in Zones 5 through 9. American plums ae extremely tolerant of cold, but less so of heat. Wild plum grows well in Zones 3 through 6, and beach plum in Zones 4 through 6. American-Japanese crosses incorporate the cold tolerance of the American parent and the heat tolerance of the Japanese parent, and generally thrive in Zones 4 through 9.

Growing under Glass and in Containers

As most of these plum types are hardy and culinary, it seems unprofitable to fruit them under cover. If only small quantities are required then these plums could be tried in pots.

Ornamental and Wildlife Value

The trees are not imposing until they flower, then they froth and foam. Later their displays of fruiting profligacy are quite stupendous. Great masses of fruits continue to feed the wildlife through many months.

Maintenance

As for plums (see p. 463).

Propagation

Most types do well on Myrobalan stocks and many on their own roots. Japanese plums can bear in 3 years, others in five. Those on their own roots can be grown from suckers, and seedlings of most will come nearly true.

Pruning and Training

As for plums, these are best left alone except for remedial work.

Pests and Diseases

These varieties of plums are generally not as susceptible to brown rot as true plums.

Harvesting and Storing

American and Japanese plums are supposedly mellowed and taste better raw after frosts, but the birds will have eaten them by then.

 companion planting

Avoid anemones, which harbor plum rust.

 other uses

As hedges and windbreaks the bullaces and cherry plums are excellent. Damsons can be planted in sheltered sections.

Myrobalans

 culinary

Almost all of these fruits are now used culinarily only for jamming, jellying, fruit cheeses, winemaking and liqueurs.

Damson Cheese

Makes 5 pounds

6 cups damsons
About 4½ to 5 cups light brown sugar

Wash the fruit and then simmer till soft with just enough water to prevent burning. Strain and boil the pulp with three-quarters its own weight of sugar. Skim off any scum. Cook until the scum has finished rising and the jam is clear. Pot the pulp in warmed oiled bowls and seal.

APRICOTS

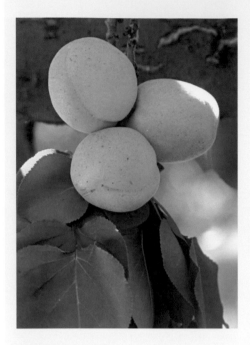

Tree up to 20 ft. Hardy, deciduous, self-fertile. Fruits: 1½ × 2 in., yellow/orange. Value: rich in vitamin A and potassium.

This small tree has white flowers (occasionally tinged with pink) very early in spring, well before the leaves emerge. These are spade-shaped and often glossy. The young shoots can also appear glossy, as if varnished in red or brown. The leaves are more similar to those of a plum than those of a cherry or peach, and apricot fruits closely resemble some plums, but the stone is more spherical and the flavor distinct. Some think that "Moorpark," one of the commonest varieties, is a plumcot (a plum-apricot hybrid).

The first apricots came from China or Siberia, not Armenia, where Alexander the Great found them. The fruits became loved by the Romans, but they never succeeded in transplanting any to northern Europe. Apricots reached Britain in the 13th century and were introduced again, more successfully, in the sixteenth. "Bredase" may be the oldest variety in cultivation; it closely resembles descriptions of Roman apricots.

varieties

Introduced in 1830, "Blenheim" is a perennial favorite with medium to large, very juicy fruit and sweet, aromatic flavor. It is superb for eating fresh or for canning and drying. "Perfection" bears very large fruit of good texture and flavor. Self-fertile "Stark Tilton" is a leading commercial variety also good for home gardens. "Early Golden" is prolific and does especially well in the South and Southwest. Disease-resistant and cold-hardy varieties from the Harrow Research Station in Canada include "Harglow," "Hargrand," "Harlayne," "Harogem," and "Harval." "Moorpark" is exquisite; the traditional variety, it ripens a little later.

cultivation

Like most stone fruits, apricots need a cold winter period to rest and warm summers to ripen the fruit. The plants themselves are tough, but the flowers are so early that they are always in danger from frost. The soil should not be heavy nor the site wet. Apricots are generally hardy in Zones 5 through 8, but some, such as "Sweet Pit" are extremely cold tolerant and grow well as far north as Zone 3.

Growing under Glass and in Containers
Grown under glass, apricots are more sure to crop if allowed a cold resting period, so do not plant in continuously heated greenhouses. A better plan is to confine them in large pots. Keep these outside unless very cold, bring them under glass for flowering and take them back outside again once the weather is warm.

Ornamental and Wildlife Value
Apricots are not noticeable trees, though the flowers are pretty enough. Ornamental varieties and Hunzas are attractive but unfruitful. Their earliness makes the flowers useful to bees and beneficial insects.

Pruning and Training
The least work is to grow apricots as trees, only removing dead and diseased wood as necessary. Cut out all the dieback until no discoloration is seen. The wood is brittle, so watch for overladen branches and prop or prune early. On walls, build a fan of old wood with fruiting spurs. Prune the frame and any dieback in late winter, then prune again in summer to restrict the growth.

Pests and Diseases
Apricots are vulnerable to many of the same diseases and pests as peaches. Canker and borers may plaugue the tree, but are not always fatal. Oozing sap and

Apricots grown in cool climates are still delicious

"New Large Early"

interesting formations of hardened resin on branches and possibly trunk are symptomatic of these problems. If you can cut or gouge out the damaged area, do so. Clip off infected branches at at least 12 in. below the point of infection. Aphids, scale and other insects may infest the tree, causing a decline in vigor and possibly a reduction in crop size. Since apricots are so prolific, insect attacks can usually be overlooked.

Propagation
Apricot trees are obtained budded on to suitable rootstocks. Successful trees have been raised from stones.

Maintenance
Spring Cover flowers on frosty nights; weed, mulch and spray with fertilizer as needed.
Summer Thin the fruits early, summer prune, bag fruits against wasps and birds.
Fall Keep weeded, tie in new shoots.
Winter Protect from very hard frosts, prune out dieback.

Harvesting and Storing
Apricots ripened on the tree are heavenly, but soon turn overripe. Picked young enough to transport, they never develop full flavor. Thus they are best eaten straight away, made into jams, or frozen.

 culinary

Apricots make scrumptious jam and can be preserved in brandy and syrup. Unlike the majority of *Prunus* fruits, most apricots have kernels that are sweet and edible and can be used to make ratafia cookies.

Apricot Sponge cake
Serves 6 to 8

2 cups apricots
Pat of butter
Coarse, light brown sugar

For the sponge cake:
¼ cup butter,
⅓ cup light brown sugar,
½ cup white self-rising flour
1 large egg
A splash of milk
1 teaspoon real vanilla extract

Halve and pit the apricots (score or remove the skin if you prefer) and place in a buttered pie pan, cut side up. Sprinkle with coarse sugar. Cream together the butter and sugar, stir in the egg, then fold in the flour, together with the milk, if the mixture is stiff, and the vanilla extract. Spoon the sponge cake mixture over the apricots and cook in a preheated oven at 375°F for about half an hour. When cold, turn out and serve with whipped cream.

  companion planting

Do not grow tomatoes, potatoes or oats near apricots, but they benefit from Alliums nearby, especially garlic and chives.

other uses

The wood is brittle, but of use as kindling.

Apricot halves freeze easily

PEACHES

Tree/bush up to 16 x 16 ft. Generally short-lived. Self-fertile, deciduous. Fruits: 2½ to 3½ in., yellow, orange, red. Value: rich in vitamin A, potassium and niacin.

Peach trees are small and resemble willows, with long, lightly serrated leaves. They bloom before the leaves appear. The smaller the flowers, the darker rose colored they are, with the largest being lightest pink. Flowering 2 weeks later than almonds, they are closely related, the almond having a tough, inedible, leathery skin over a smooth stone. The skin has a partition line along which it easily splits. Most peach stones are ribbed or perforated with small holes in the shell. In varieties known as clingstones the flesh clings to this shell; in others, the freestones, the fruit is free and easier to enjoy without having to tease it off the stone. The flesh may vary from white to yellow; there are even blood peaches with red staining. The texture varies with cultivar, soil and climate. The skin color can be from dull green through yellows and orange to dark red. The most distinctive feature of peaches is the soft downy fluff on the skin.

The peach was known in 300 CE to the Greek philosopher Theophrastus, who thought it came from Persia, and so it became named. Early Hebrew writings make no reference to it, nor is there a Sanskrit name, so it seems likely peaches did not reach Europe to any extent until shortly before the Christian period. Dioscorides mentions the peach during the first century, as does Pliny, who states that the Romans had imported it only recently from Persia.
Peaches are, in fact, of Chinese origin. They are mentioned in the books of Confucius from the first century CE, and can be traced back to the 10th century CE in artistic representations. The Chinese still have an immense number of varieties and these were initially spread by seed. The stones produce trees with ease, but, of course, do not come true. The variability

may have accounted for the slow spread to Europe. However, this was more likely to have been because peaches were initially tried in hot countries at too-low altitudes. Thus the trees did not get their winter dormancy and would have fruited badly, effectively discouraging further experiments. Pliny indeed mentions that peach trees were taken from Egypt to the island of Rhodes, but this transplantation did not succeed; they were then brought on to Italy.

It took till the middle of the 16th century for peaches to reach England and in 1629 a quantity of peach stones was ordered by the Governor of the Massachusetts Bay Colony of New England. The peach found its new home in North America highly suitable and spread abundantly. In fact, it spread so rapidly through the wild that it was thought to be a native fruit. Peaches spread so widely that they had conquered much of South America by Darwin's time. He spotted them on islands in the mouth of the Paraná, along with thickets of similarly fugitive orange trees.

PEACHES

varieties

Grown from a seed in Georgia in 1870, "Elberta" and its many selections (including "Early Elberta," "Fantastic Elberta," "Compact Elberta," "Fay Elberta," and others) is the post popular peach in America. The large, yellow fruit has a beautiful blush and juicy, yellow, freestone flesh. It is self-fruitful and makes a good pollinator. "Red Haven" is the leader among early peaches. Its offspring, "Compact Red Haven" is better in northern and central regions. "Hale Haven" the parent of "Red Haven," was developed in Michigan and is a peach of exceptional quality. "Golden Jubilee," "Redskin," and "Reliance," other favorites of home gardeners and commercial growers, produce a bounty of freestone fruit. Modern, disease-resistant varieties are like those developed at the Harrow Research Station in Canada: "Harbelle," "Harbrite," Harcrest," "Harken," and others. "Peregrine" is a good choice for a blush tree and has yellowish white flesh of excellent flavor. It is freestone and ripens midseason.

cultivation

Peaches ideally need a well-enriched, well-aerated, but moist piece of soil. They prefer open gravelly soils to heavy, and need to be planted at least 20 ft. apart. Dwarf types can be planted closer together. Peaches grow well in Zones 6 through 9, with some cold hardy varieties thriving in Zone 5. Like apricots, they bloom early and their buds and blossoms are susceptible to frost and cold damage. Late flowering varieties include "Jayhaven," "Red Haven," "Cresthaven," "Nectar," and "Emery." If they take (peaches do not always), they establish quickly and need no staking after the first year. They need copious quantities of compost annually and mulches are obligatory to ensure the constant moisture they demand. Where they are planted against walls, great care must be taken to ensure adequate water constantly throughout the season or the fruits will split. However, they are most intolerant of any waterlogging. Peaches also should not be planted near to almonds, as the two fruits may hybridize, resulting in bitter nuts.

It's worth thinning "Peento" or flat peaches to get bigger fruits

Growing under Glass and in Containers

If growing under glass, the greenhouse must be unheated in winter to give peaches a dormant rest period. More problems occur under cover — the red spider mite can be especially troublesome unless a high humidity is maintained. Peaches are good subjects for large pots as they can take heavy pruning if well fed and watered. Pots enable them to be kept under cover during the winter and through flowering and then brought out all summer, thus avoiding peach leaf curl and frost damage. The flowers must be protected from frosts and so must the young fruitlets. The flowers are more susceptible to frost damage after pollination and the fruitlets likewise for an additional 2 weeks.

Ornamental and Wildlife Value

The peach is a pleasure to have. The willowy leaves are held well into fall and the sight of a good crop of fruits is magnificent. The blossoms are wonderful too; peaches in bloom are a joy.

One — or better two — of these must go, or all will be small

Thinning to wide spacing gives bigger, more luscious fruits

Pruning and Training

Peaches fruit on young shoots, thus it is essential to have plenty of these growths. They are best obtained by a severe pruning operation late each winter. This makes the pruning more akin to that of blackcurrants than to that of most other tree fruits. Basically the top ends of the higher branches are removed to encourage prolific growth from the lower branches and stubs. This also serves to keep the peach bushes lower and more manageable.

On walls and under cover, peaches are usually fan-trained. Selected young shoots are allowed to spring from a main frame and then tied in to replace the previous growths, once those have fruited. More important than pruning is thinning. Peaches are prone to overcropping, breaking branches and exhausting themselves. Thin the fruits hard, removing those touching or anywhere near each other. Do this very early and then again later.

Maintenance

Spring Protect tree from leaf disease with Bordeaux sprays before buds open and blossom. Protect blossoms from frost. Hand-pollinate. Weed, mulch and spray with fertilizer as needed.

Summer Thin the fruits early, and often. Protect fruits from birds and wasps.

Fall Remove mummified fruits from the trees.

Winter Prune hard. Spray with Bordeaux mixture.

Propagation

Peaches can be raised from stones, but the results are haphazard and take years to fruit. Budded on to suitable stocks, peaches will normally fruit in their third year. Plum stocks are more resistant to wet, but for warmer, drier conditions seedling apricot or peach rootstocks are better.

Pests and Diseases

Peaches suffer most losses from birds and wasps. Small net or muslin bags will protect the crop. Earwigs can get inside the fruits and eat the kernel out, but are easily trapped in rolls of corrugated paper around each branch. Protect the bark from animals. Peaches are susceptible to myriad diseases. Brown rot affects the ripening fruit and causes it to mold; it's worst during wet, humid summers. Leaf curl, leaf spot, and powdery mildew may affect the leaves, thus weakening the leaves if the disease is widespread. Spraying with Bordeaux mixture prevents peach leaf curl if done several times as the buds are opening. Peach scab can affect the fruits, cauing clustered olive green spots near the stem end of the fruit about halfway to maturity. Weekly sulfur sprays will help control brown rot and scab. Other maladies, including cankers, crown gall, and viruses, may besiege your peach trees. Because of these problems, the useful life of peach trees is 10 to 12 years. Disease-resistant varieties include "Raritan Rose," "Elberta," and "Reliance."

Harvesting and Storing

A truly ripe peach is a bag of syrup waiting to burst. If picked under-ripe the flesh never develops the full gamut of flavor, or the juiciness. A good peach is a feast, drink and all. As with so many fruits, they are best eaten straight off the tree. They can be picked a few days early if handled with absolute care. Kept cool, they may last. The slightest bruising, however, and they decompose.

 companion planting

Peaches are benefited by Alliums, especially garlic and chives. Clover or alfalfa leguminous green manures give the richness they need. Nettles nearby are reputedly helpful at preventing the fruit from molding.

 other uses

Peach stones are used for making activated charcoal for filters. The wood is brittle, but the prunings make good kindling. In some countries, gluts of peaches are used for feeding the local livestock.

Pick just before they drop, peel and eat sun-warm

Home-grown peach preserves are exotic fare for the table

culinary

Peach jam, which is potentially more aromatic than plum, is easily over-cooked and the perfume lost. Make it set more easily and sooner by adding apple purée. Fruits that are ripening but starting to rot are best prepared then cooked in syrup. This, if not consumed immediately, can be frozen for winter use. Over-ripe fruits can be juiced, which is the nectar of the gods, and unripe peaches that never look like ripening make excellent chutney.

Peach Macaroon Cheesecake
Serves 4 to 6

1 cup macaroons
1 cup vanilla wafers
⅓ cup butter, melted
5 cups peaches
½ oz. gelatin
1 cup cottage cheese
½ cup yogurt
¼ cup honey or peach jam
Few drops vanilla extract
½ cup alpine strawberries

Crush the macaroons and wafers and mix with the butter. Press into a pie pan. Peel, slice and chill the peaches. Simmer the skins and stones in minimal hot water, strain and dissolve the gelatin in the warm liquid. Beat the cream cheese, yogurt, honey or jam and vanilla, then stir in the gelatin. Immediately pour over the biscuit base, chill and leave to set. Top with peach slices and alpine strawberries.

Prunus persica from the family Rosaceae

NECTARINES

Early Rivers

Tree up to 16 ft. Generally short-lived, self-fertile, deciduous. Fruits: up to 3 in., greenish yellow/orange and red. Value: rich in vitamin A, potassium and niacin, as well as riboflavin and vitamin C.

In almost every way nectarines and peaches are identical. However, there are several subtle and fascinating differences. Nectarines are more difficult to grow and are less hardy. The fruits are smaller, on average, than peaches. The flesh is firmer and less melting than a peach and more plum-like, less prone to falling apart while you eat it. Nectarines have a definite, almost peculiar, rich, vinous flavor quite distinct and in addition to that of a well-ripened peach. The color of some nectarines also makes them distinguishable from peaches, as many of the older varieties have a greenish or sometimes even a purplish hue over a quite yellowish or greenish ground. Most noticeably, nectarines do not have that downy fuzz on the skin so typical of peaches, but instead are smooth and shiny; indeed they closely resemble a very large, plump plum.

Darwin noted how peach trees occasionally spontaneously produced nectarines, and also the converse; he even noted the case of a nectarine tree that produced a fruit that was half peach, half nectarine and then reverted to peaches. Despite the peach's long history of cultivation, however, rather strangely, no mention is made of nectarines by pre-Christian authors. Pliny mentions an unknown fruit, a duracina, but the first, if indirect, reference is by Cieza de Leon, who lived in the early 16th century and described a Caymito of Peru as being "large as a nectarine." They were seen growing amongst peaches in Virginia in 1720 and A. J. Downing listed 19 varieties in the U.S. by 1857. Many dozens of nectarine varieties are now in cultivation, and travelers also report local varieties of nectarine in most of the world's peach-growing areas, so their spontaneous emergence is not really a rare phenomenon.

 varieties

"Red Gold" reaching about 15 ft. tall, is a vigorous grower, and an abundant bearer. The sweet flavor of "Sunglo," a 1962 California introduction, is a commercial favorite. "Goldmine" is a beauty, with smaller fruits blushed red over a white skin.

 cultivation

Nectarines need even better conditions than peaches do. Good water control is critical to prevent the fruit splitting, so thick mulches are obligatory. In any cool region they must be given a wall or extra shelter. Nectarines grow well in Zones 6 through 9, with some especially cold-hardy varieties, such as "Hardired," "Garden Delight," and "Mericrest," thriving in Zone 5. "Mericrest" is one of the hardiest nectarines, surviving cold as low as −20°F. It's a self-fruitful and a late bloomer, a consideration in areas where capricious spring frosts are a possibility.

Growing under Glass and in Containers
Nectarines are more suited than many plants to culture under glass, preferring warmer conditions than peaches. However, they need a cool period of rest each winter or they become unfruitful, so they are best grown in large pots moved outside after cropping and brought back into a cool greenhouse in mid-to-late winter. Being dry under cover prevents peach leaf curl, keeps the frost off the flowers and fruitlets and gets them an early start. But they

will only fruit successfully if religious attention is given to watering and ventilation. Hand pollination is desirable.

Pruning and Training

Exactly as for the peach (see p. 472).

Propagation

Nectarines sometimes come from peach stones and vice versa. More often they occur when a peach bud produces a sport. Most varieties are budded on suitable stocks as for peaches.

Pests and Diseases

Away from the Pacific coast, plum curculios can easily do much damage to their smooth skins. Spray against peach leaf curl.

Ornamental and Wildlife Value

Nectarines are attractive, with the long, glossy leaves being held late into the season. The pink flowers are beautiful and appreciated by early insects; the lack of fruits reduces their wildlife interest. Nectarines need spraying to prevent peach leaf curl in many areas, so cannot be left to themselves.

Maintenance

As for the peach (see p. 472).

Harvesting and Storing

Also as for the peach (see p. 472).

"Lord Napier"

 culinary

Nectarines can be used in similar ways to peaches, but as their skin is not fuzzy it is less of a barrier and makes them more toothsome to eat fresh. The firm flesh is also less melting and reduces one's need for a bib to catch half the juice as with a ripe peach. This makes the nectarine a civilized fruit for eating at the dinner table, and this is only enhanced by the succulent vinous flavor.

Nectarine Melba
(all quantities according to taste)

Nectarines
Honey
Vanilla pod
Vanilla ice cream
Frozen raspberries
Bitter chocolate and nutmeg

Halve, peel and pit, say, one ripe nectarine per person. Poach half of them, those that are the least decomposingly ripe, in a syrup made by gently warming the vanilla pod in the honey. Poach the nectarines very gently until they are tender but not breaking down, then drain and chill well. Create a bed of vanilla ice cream, interspersed with the chilled ripest halves. Lay the poached halves on this base. Crush the frozen raspberries in the drained honey syrup. Chill, then pour over the nectarines, followed by a generous grating of bitter chocolate and a hint of nutmeg.

 companion planting

Again as for the peach.

 other uses

As for peaches.

SWEET CHERRIES

Tree up to 33 ft. Long-lived, deciduous, not self-fertile. Fruits: 1 in., yellow, red, black, rich in riboflavin

Although described as sweet cherries, some varieties, and particularly wild ones, are not actually sweet. They are tall trees, often reaching over 30 ft., with white blossoms, occasionally pink, which are a massive display at about the same time as the peach. The leaves are plum-like with a lengthening and thinning at the tip. Dangling in pairs on long pedicels, the near-spherical fruits hang in groups along the fruiting branches. The flesh is cream or yellow, sweet or bitter, but once ripe is rarely acid.

The wild form native to Europe, known as the bird cherry or mazzard, is of little value as fruit except in Central Europe, where it is used for liqueurs. Mazzards, little improved from the wild version, still survive and have richly flavored black fruits only slightly larger than the wild. They make good seedling stocks for better varieties, though if left to themselves they can grow to 60 ft. or more high. Gean fruits were thought to have softer more melting flesh and varieties called Bigarreau had a crisp texture. Years of continuous selection and cross breeding have given us sweet cherries of mixed parentage. One group, the Duke or Royal cherries, have some sour cherry (Morello) blood, which serves to make them tasty and lightly acid as well as generally more hardy.

 varieties

There are countless varieties, but finding combinations compatible for pollination is difficult, so most useful cherries for private orchards are partly self-fertile. "Bing" is the quintessential sweet cherry, big dark, and delicious. The large, spreading tree isn't as prolific as "Angela" and other varieties, but it is the standard for flavor. "Black Tartarian" also has sweet, thick, tender flesh with rich flavor and its bumper crops are outstanding. "Van" is another "Bing" lookalike, but firmer and short-stemmed. Young trees bear early. Pollinate with "Bing," "Stella," or "Royal Ann," an old French variety, which tends to overbear, but this only reduces fruit size, not quality. "Stella" is fully self-fertile, a vigorous and upright tree with sweet, dark red fruits. "Rainer" is another premier yellow cherry with red blush.

 cultivation

Sweet cherries are very particular to soil and site. They need plentiful moisture at the roots but loathe waterlogging and need a very rich but well-aerated soil. Poor soil conditions can be helped by growing through grass. Sweet cherries flourish in warm, dry climates, but they will also grow in marginal areas. Many varieties will grow in Zones 5 through 7 or 8.

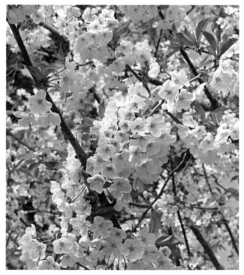

"Merton Glory"

SWEET CHERRIES

Sweet cherries rarely ripen unless protected from birds

Growing under Glass and in Containers

As the trees get so big and are particular to site and weather, pot cultivation is the most effective way to get cherries. In this way you avoid damage to the flowers from frost or rain and likewise protect the fruits. Do let the trees have a cool dormant period in winter.

Ornamental and Wildlife Value

Sweet cherries are quite staggering to behold in blossom, as if festooned with snow.

Propagation

Normally budded on to strong-growing rootstocks, which make for big trees, they are now offered on dwarfing stocks such as "Colt." This makes them smaller and easier to constrain. Stones grow, but the trees take years to fruit and get tall by then.

Pruning and Training

Prune as little as possible after the initial head formation. Most pruning should be done during the dormant season and then only to remove any dead and diseased growth.

Pests and Diseases

Cherries really suffer from bird damage, but escape the wasps by fruiting early in summer. Bacterial canker can kill the tree, and there are several virus diseases.

Maintenance

Spring Protect the flowers, weed, mulch and spray liquid fertilizer monthly. Prune if necessary.
Summer Protect the fruits from birds with netting or floating row covers.
Fall No maintenacne needed
Winter Remove dead wood.

 culinary

Sweet cherries often do not make as good culinary dishes as sour cherries because many lack acidity. Their jams and jellies are better combined with redcurrant or whitecurrant juice for this reason.

Pickled Cherries
Makes about 6 pounds

4 cups cherries
2 cups sugar
1 cup vinegar
6 cloves
¾ in. piece fresh ginger, peeled and chopped
Hint of ground cinnamon

Wash and stone (if desired) the cherries. Dissolve the sugar in the heated vinegar and add the spices. Simmer the cherries in the spiced vinegar for a few minutes, then pack them into warmed jars, and cover with the vinegar. Seal and store.

Eat with pâtés, cold meats and especially quiches.

Cherry Jam
10 cups cherries
3 lemons, squeezed
7 cups sugar

Harvesting and Storing

Sweet cherries are prone to cracking of the fruit. Moisture or the lack of it at the time the fruit is maturing can ruin a crop. Too little water causes shriveled fruit; too much causes the cherries to swell and split. A thick mulch and irrigation can help with insufficient rainfall, but if a deluge comes when your cherries are ripening, there's nothing much you can do. Cherries can be picked and kept for several days if absolutely dry. Leave them on the stems and do not pack them deep. They can be frozen, but are fiddly as they are better pitted first.

 companion planting

They are normally grown in grass sward, include clover and alfalfa, to give more fertility. Cherries supposedly suppress wheat and make potatoes prone to blight.

Wash the fruit thoroughly; remove stalks and stones. Put the fruit into a pan with the lemon juice and simmer gently for 30 to 35 minutes. Warm the sugar and add it to the cherries over a gentle heat and allow the sugar to dissolve. Then bring the jam to a rapid boil and continue boiling until setting point is reached; this will take about 15 minutes. Test for setting point, remove from the heat and leave for 5 minutes. Pot and cover. Store in a dry place.

 other uses

Sweet firewood.

"Stella"

Prunus cerasus from the family Rosaceae

SOUR CHERRIES

Also Morello cherries, pie cherries, tart cherries, and others. Tree up to 27 ft. Long-lived, deciduous, self-fertile. Fruits: ¾ in., crimson to black. Value: rich in vitamin A.

Sour or Morello cherries are similar to sweet cherries, except they are not sweet, so are useful only for culinary purposes. The trees are smaller than sweet varieties, with slightly lax, more twiggy branches and greener foliage that does not have such a red tinge when young. The fruits have shorter stalks, tend to have lighter colors and are more acid.

Sour cherries were selected from *Prunus cerasus* (also known as *P. acida*), which grew wild around the Caspian and Black Seas. In about 300 CE sour cherries were known to the Greek Theophrastus and proved so popular with the Romans, who developed at least half a dozen different varieties, that by the time of Pliny, in the first century AD, sour cherries had already long reached Britain. However, during the Dark Ages, the art of their cultivation was lost and the trees had to be re-introduced to England in the 16th century by Henry VIII, who had them brought from Flanders. They were soon adopted by the growers of Kent and by 1640 they had over two dozen varieties. The first cherries to reach the New World, the "Kentish Red," were planted by the Massachusetts colonists.

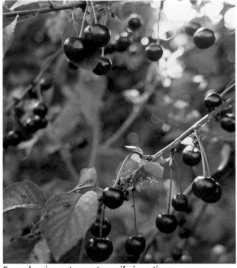

Sour cherries get sweeter — if given time

 varieties

Before World War II, more than 50 varieties of Morello and sour cherry were in cultivation, and almost every country had its own wide choice. Now only in the upper Midwest are they grown commercially. "Montmorency" is the typical sour cherry for pie — richly flavored with a good tang and firm flesh that doesn't get mushy during cooking. The 15 ft. tall tree is self-fertile and spreading in habit. "Early Richmond" is a heavy producer that ripens more than a week earlier than other sour cherries. The vigorous tree is self-fertile and the fruit is clear, bright red. "Noth Star" is a cross between the English "Morello" cherry and the Siberian cherry, which, as you might expect, gives it exceptional cold tolerance. It is cold hardy to −40°F. The naturally dwarf tree bows under the weight of the heavy crops of mahogany red fruit. "Meteor" is another cross with Russian blood, developed in Minnesota and usually hardy to −50°F. Its tart, bright red fruits are similar to "Montmorency."

 cultivation

Much the same conditions are needed as for pears, with an increased demand for nitrogen and even more water than needed by sweet cherries. Though the trees will do badly if they are waterlogged, they are more tolerant of poor drainage than sweet cherries. Sour cherries can take quite a bit more winter cold than sweet cherries, but they are much less tolerant of heat. Most varieties thrive in Zones 3 through 5, with some hardy in Zone 2.

Growing under Glass and in Containers
Although this would be possible, it would usually be more worthwhile to nurture sweet cherries, especially as sour cherries will even crop on a cold wall in cool areas.

Ornamental and Wildlife Value
Not as elegant or floriferous a tree as the sweet cherry, so of less ornamental value. Sour cherries are well-loved by birds and the early flowers are good for insects.

Maintenance
As for sweet cherries (p. 477).

Propagation
As for sweet cherries.

Pests and Diseases
Sour cherries are susceptible to cracking like sweet cherries. They may also be bothered by cherry leaf spot, powdery mildew, and brown rot.

Pruning and Training
Sour cherries fruit on younger wood than do sweet cherries and thus they can be pruned harder. However, it is usually more convenient to stick to removing dead, diseased and congested growths. Pruning should be done in winter while the trees are dormant. Usually grown as standards, they are ideal as low bushes for picking and bird protection, although they can also be trained as fans. They will even crop well on cold walls.

Harvesting and Storing
Cut the cherries off the tree rather than risk damage by pulling the stalks. Commercial harvest is done by shaking the trees. Morellos were one of the first fruits to be stored frozen and are one of the best. They can be frozen without sugaring and retain their flavor superbly.

 ## companion planting

As for sweet cherries.

 ## other uses

The prunings make good kindling.

 ## culinary

They are primarily a culinary fruit and make fabulous pies, tarts, jams and cakes.

Black Forest Gâteau
Serves 6 to 8

2 cups black cherries
⅓ cup honey
4 tablespoons kirsch
Little water

For the sponge cake:
½ cup butter
½ cup fine light brown sugar
1 cup white flour
2 large or 3 medium eggs
1 heaping teaspoon baking powder
1 heaping teaspoon cocoa powder

For the filling:
2 cups heavy cream
1 heaping teaspoon sugar
1 heaping teaspoon cocoa powder
1 teaspoon vanilla extract
4 squares dark chocolate, grated

Wash and pit the cherries. Dissolve the honey and kirsch in sufficient hot water just to cover the pitted fruits. Simmer till they soften, then strain (keeping the syrup) and chill. Mix the sponge cake ingredients and divide between three oiled or lined sandwich pans. Bake in a preheated oven at 325°F for about half an hour. Turn out and cool, then soak the sponge cakes in the syrup. Whip the cream, then stir in the sugar, cocoa powder and vanilla. Build up alternate layers of sponge cake, cream filling and fruit. Finish off with a covering of filling and grated chocolate.

MULBERRIES

Tree up to 30 ft. Long-lived, hardy, deciduous, usually self-fertile. Fruits: 1½ to 2¼ in., purple, also red through pink.

Mulberry trees are medium-sized trees with a round domed crown, formed by their habit of having no terminal bud on their overwintering twigs. They can become big, gnarled and picturesque in advanced old age. The leaves are heart-shaped, toothed and occasionally lobed, lightly downy underneath but rough on top. The black mulberry, *Morus nigra*, fruits are like loganberries, of a blackish dark red through purple when ripe and stain all they touch. The white mulberry, *Morus alba*, fruits are red or pinkish white, and slightly inferior to eat. There is a red mulberry (which can be almost black), native to North America, and several similar species in hotter climates.

Black mulberries are thought to be native to western Asia. Known at least since the time of the Greeks, they failed to become popular until the Roman Emperor Justinian encouraged them for the production of silk. The trees appeared all over the empire and *M. nigra* was not superseded by *M. alba*, the more productive variety for feeding silkworms, until the 16th century. Exceptionally long-lived, the black mulberry may attain some stature; giants found in many parts of the world were planted during the 17th and early 18th centuries in vain attempts to foster local silk industries. Some mulberries, such as *M. alba* var. *tatarica*, the Russian mulberry, seed freely and become weeds. The red mulberry was native to the Northern Missouri region and along the Kansas river system, where it was an esteemed fruit.

varieties

"Illinois Everbearing" is a favorite for its sweet but tangy blackberry-like taste. "Downing," "Wellington," "Black Persian," and "New American" all have long, sweet, black fruits. The honey sweet, lavender-white fruit of the *M. alba* variety "Lavender" are excellent for drying. the Red Mulberry (*M. Rubra*) has red/black fruits and lovely fall color with bright yellow leaves; it is said to have the preferable fruit. The White Mulberry (*M. alba*) has wider leaves and is grown for silkworm fodder, though the fruit is quite edible, often red or pinkish and sweet.

cultivation

Mulberries succeed in any well-drained soil. The tree is so adaptable to even the worst conditions of drought and poor soil that it is the second most common weed tree in New York City. Cold-hardiness of various mulberries varies, but most can be grown in Zones 5 through 8.

Growing under Glass and in Containers
This may be feasible, but I've not heard or read of it.

Ornamental and Wildlife Value
Mulberries become gnarled and attractively grotesque as they age. The traditional situation is in the middle of a lawn with a circular wooden seat around the trunk. The berries are much appreciated by birds and small children.

White mulberries

culinary

The fruits can be made into jams or jellies, though they are usually combined and bulked out with apples, and the wine is an old country favorite.

Mulberry No Fool
Per person

Clotted or thick fresh heavy cream
Some honey
A pot of tea
Cookies
A mulberry tree in fruit and a sunny day off

Take a bowl with a large portion of clotted or thick cream, honey and the tea and cookies. Sit peacefully under the mulberry tree, savoring the tea and cookies while waiting for enough fruits to fall to fill your bowl. Eat them with the cream and honey. In emergencies, canned or fresh fruit of any sort and a patio umbrella can be usefully substituted for the mulberries and tree!

Pests and Diseases
No significant pests or diseases bother the trees, other than the usual hazards of birds and small children.

Maintenance
Spring Cut grass and spray liquid fertilizer as needed.
Summer Pick the fruits as they ripen and drop.
Fall Cut grass and enjoy the seat occasionally,
Winter Thin and remove dead and diseased growths.

Propagation
Cuttings of newly ripened 10–12 in. growth with a heel taken in December are ideal. Layering is possible as are (supposedly) whole branch cuttings.

Pruning and Training
Mulberries can be pollarded hard to give the maximum foliage needed for feeding silkworms. If left to themselves, they make congested heads, so thin out twiggy, dead and diseased growths. Their narrow forks, big heads and brittle wood mean old trees should be carefully inspected and excess weight removed by a competent tree surgeon.

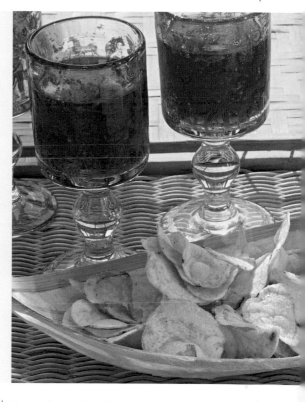

Harvesting and Storing
Mulberries are aromatic and mouth-watering when fresh and ripe, but decompose rapidly, so are really only of use as they drop, and will not store or travel, though they can be frozen. An easy way to harvest the fruit cleanly is to spread several sheets beneath a tree and shake the branches. The ripe fruit will fall like rain.

companion planting

Mulberries must be grown in a grass sward if there is to be any hope of getting clean fruit. They were one of the traditional trees to support grapevines in Classical times.

other uses

Of course you can try silkworm production and the foliage is palatable to other animals. The fruits will certainly make dye!

FIGS

"Brown Turkey"

Tree/bush up to 30 x 20 ft. Hardy, self-fertile. Fruits: pear-shaped, 2 x 4 in., brownish green.

Fig leaves are large and distinctive, but vary in exact shape with each variety. Although figs are deciduous, young plants tend to be almost evergreen and are then more tender. Figs can be grown as trees or bushes, but are most often grown as free-standing shrubs. Almost all fig cultivars set the fruit parthenocarpically, without actual fertilization. However, some old and mostly inferior varieties in hot climates have female fruiting plants and male caprifigs that are separately and specifically cultivated to produce female fig wasps. These wasps will crawl through the minute end hole into the fruits to pollinate them.

Figs are indigenous to Asia Minor and were one of the first fruits to be brought into cultivation. They thus became an intrinsic part of the diet of the Mediterranean basin long before Classical times, though the Greeks claimed they were given to them by the goddess Demeter. Cato knew of six different figs, and two centuries later, in about 60 AD, Pliny notes no fewer than 29 varieties! Figs were certainly brought to England by the Romans as remains have been found, though the plants were not officially introduced until the early 16th century. There are more than 600 fig species. Many of the varieties that we encounter today are ornamentals such as the India Rubber Plant (*Ficus elastica*), the Weeping Fig (*F. benjamina*) and the Fiddle Leaf Plant (*F. lyrata*).

varieties

"Brunswick" produces large fruits that are most tasty a couple of days after picking; "Brown Turkey" is reliably prolific; "White Marseilles" has pale fruits. Planted in San Diego, California, by Franciscan missionaries, "Black Mission" is the oldest and still the most popular fig for drying and shipping. The pear-shaped, fine-quality fruits have sweet, red flesh that is excellent fresh, dried, or canned. Self-fertile "Conadria" bears heavily in cooler climates.

cultivation

Varieties vary in hardiness, but even if the tops are lost many will regrow from the roots if these are protected from the frost. Thus figs may be planted a little deep to encourage stooling. Often grown against a wall, they can be cropped in the open in warm areas. "Brown Turkey" and "Celeste" are cold hardy to Zone 6, but most other figs do best in Zones 8 to 9 or 10. Some gardeners in cold-winter areas outside of normal hardiness zones dig up their figs and lay them on their sides to winter over, buried under a thick layer of insulating materials. Too much nitrogen will promote abundant undesirable soft growth.

Growing under Glass and in Containers
Figs fruit and ripen much more reliably under glass, and with heat and care three crops a year are possible.

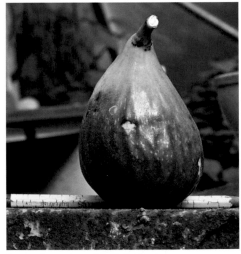
You rarely see them this big in the stores

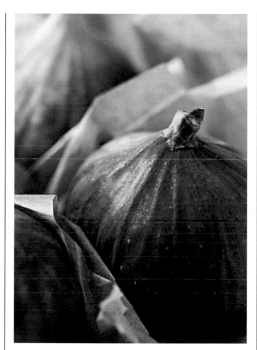

Okay, well, sometimes you do

 culinary

Figs are delicious fresh and they can be made into jams, jellies, cheeses and chutneys.

Savory and Sweet Figs
Serves 4 as a snack or canapé

12 dried figs
1 cup mild hard cheese, broken into chunks
Pinch of celery seeds
1 shallot, thinly sliced
1 square dark cooking chocolate
¼ cup marzipan
2 tablespoons each golden raisins and raisins
A little Cointreau or sweet liqueur
Honey

Stuff half the figs with small chunks of cheese, a sprinkling of celery seeds and a thin slice of shallot.

Grate the chocolate and marzipan. Mix in the dried fruit and liqueur, then stuff the remaining figs with this mixture. Smear all the figs with honey and put them in an oiled dish in a preheated oven at 350°F for 10 to 15 minutes. Serve the figs hot or cold.

Figs can be grown confined in large pots and can make excellent foliage plants for house or patio, though they will need careful watering and training.

Ornamental and Wildlife Value
The very attractive foliage adds a luxuriant touch to a garden. Of little use to wildlife in colder climes, figs are much more valuable in hotter countries.

Maintenance
Spring Remove frost protection, weed, spray liquid fertilizer as needed, and thin the fruits.
Summer Protect the fruits carefully from wasps and birds; make layers.
Fall Remove all fruits of all sizes before the first frosts arrive.
Winter Prune, take cuttings, protect from frost.

Propagation
Layers can be made during summer. Usually 8 in. well-ripened or old wood cuttings taken during the early winter will root, especially if given bottom heat. Seeds produce plants that are unlikely to fruit well.

Pruning and Training
The most fruitful wood is well-ripened, short-jointed and sturdy; long soft shoots are unproductive and better removed. Figs can be pruned any time during dormancy, but are best left until growth is about to start in spring. More importantly, remove any fruit or fruitlet in fall to prevent these starting into growth, failing and thereby spoiling the second crop that could otherwise succeed.

Pests and Diseases
Fig plants have few problems except birds and wasps. Weeding must be thorough near the trunks to prevent rodents nibbling the bark. Under cover, on walls or in pots they may suffer from red spider mites.

Harvesting and Storing
Most fig varieties bear two crops per year, in early summer and early fall. In some varieties, the first crop is heavy and the second light; in others, the pattern is reversed. In colder areas, any fruits formed in fall for the first crop will probably be killed by cold. In hotter regions figs can be dried and will keep well.

 companion planting

One of the few plants to get on well with rue.

 other uses

Figs are known by many for their syrup, administered as a laxative. Also valuable as a food, they contain nearly half their weight in sugar when dried.

A promising crop of "Rouge de Bordeaux" — needs thinning out with the odd one!

SOFT, BUSH AND CANE FRUITS

The reasons for the names of these fruits are fairly self-evident: *soft*, because they are not hard fruits such as apples; *bush* is self-descriptive and *cane* refers to the slender branches. (The term *vine* is applied differently depending on region; in some places it is used solely for grapes, in others to plants with long, flexible branches, even Cucurbits.)

Most of these fruits come from the Rosaceae family. They are shrubby perennials, not tree-like, and thus fairly compact, or can be kept so, quick to crop, and small-fruited. Most are found growing naturally on the woodland's edge and thrive given moist root runs with plentiful humus-rich compost and thick mulches of leafy material. Most will grow and even crop in light shade, though, of course, they usually produce sweeter, better-tasting fruit given more sun. Grapes will most obviously require much more sun than do the other plants of this group.

The majority of these fruits have been gathered from the wild native species since prehistory and their "cultivation" will have occurred inadvertently around sites of human habitation, from waste heaps and primitive latrine arrangements. (Both, of course, afford remarkably well-fertilized ground, and thus select for strains that could use such conditions.)

Being fast-growing plants and quick to crop, the proximity and opportunity would have created more, but still inadvertent, selection. Such a process would have produced much improved "cultivars," spread by migrating peoples, and these may well have influenced wild populations. Certainly now some wild fruits such as the blackberry are just such hybrids in most areas, and it may well be that some supposed native species are, in reality, escaped cultivars from our distant past.

Thus the cropping potential of some wild fruits may have been raised over the millennia by our own unintended selection. In any case, the wild forms of most of these fruits were so productive and available in such vast quantities that they were simply not brought into cultivation until the end of the Middle Ages, with the important exception of grapes, which have been tended since prehistory. Some, such as the strawberry, have undergone intense development and hybridization and so have improved dramatically, while others, such as aronia, have remained almost unaltered. Many closely related edible species are available, which could be crossed with cultivated forms, so improved fruits may be only be an experiment or two away. The tayberry is the result of one such crossing, and is better by far than all its similar predecessors.

Fragaria hybrids from the family Rosaceae
JUNE-BEARING STRAWBERRIES

Herbaceous. 1 ft. Life span: short. Self-fertile. Fruits: up to 2 x 2 in., red, conical. Value: some vitamin C and half as much iron as spinach.

This most delicious of fruits really needs no introduction! Modern strawberries are hybrids based on *F. chiloensis*, "Chilean Pine," and *F. virginiana*, "Scarlet Virginian." The first contributed larger fruit with a pineapple tang and was brought to Europe in 1712; the latter, first mentioned in Massachusetts in 1621, provides the superior flavor, and is still grown commercially as "Little Scarlet" for jam-making. These two were first combined in the 19th century, with intensive development since. Every region has its favorite varieties.

 ## varieties

There are far too many to list and new improved ones are continually becoming available. Popular U.S. varieties include "Robinson," "Surecrop," "Guardian," "Sparkle," "Allstar," "Earliglow," and "Lateglow."

 ## cultivation

Most strawberry varieties will thrive in Zones 4 through 8. "Arking" and some other varieties are suited for southern gardens in Zone 9, and "Cyclone" and other cold-tolerant varieties flourish as far north as Minnesota and the Dakotas. All preparation is well repaid. Strawberries need a very rich soil, full of humus, and benefit from slow-release phosphates, such as bone meal. Well-rotted manure or compost will give you better cropping. The more space you give them, the better they will do and the less work they will be; 2 ft. each way is the minimum.

Growing under Glass
They do not like the hot dry conditions under cover, and these also encourage red spider mites. However, the advantages of protection from birds, prevention of rain damage, and earlier crops mean that they are widely grown under glass and plastic.

Growing in Containers
Many containers, often tower shaped, are sold specifically for strawberries. The small amount of root run, hot in an above-ground position, and usually dry because of the low water-holding capacity, make these poor growing conditions for strawberries. However, strawberries can be grown successfully in pots and containers. They need regular feeding as well as copious automatic watering.

Maintenance
Spring Weed, root first runners, and spray liquid fertilizer.
Summer Weed, straw, protect from birds and mold; pick.
Fall Establish new plants, tidy up the best, eradicate old.
Winter Rake up old leaves, mulch, and compost.

Straw is essential to stop such low berries getting muddy

JUNE-BEARING STRAWBERRIES

Extra early crops indoors planted in the tubs of other fruits such as citrus and grapevines

Propagation

While some varieties can be grown from seed, runners are the best choice. These are best taken from quality plants that have been reserved for propagation and disbudded; half a dozen good ones, or many more poor, can be had thus. The first plantlet on an early runner is chosen, pinned or held to the ground — or preferably rooted into a pot of compost for an easier transplantation. Start new beds in late summer or early fall to allow them to establish; they can then crop well the next summer. Late fall or spring plantings should be disbudded the first summer to build up their strength for a massive crop the next.

Pruning and Training

Strawberries will become relatively unproductive after 3 or 4 years, so in practice a continual annual replacement of a quarter or a third of the plants is best. Replacing all every four years or so means years of gluts and years of shortages, as they are all the same age. Mulching is essential for clean crops. Do not mulch too early — only when the first green fruits are seen swelling. Remove surplus runners regularly.

Pests and Diseases

Major losses are from birds and mold. Individual bunches can be protected from both with jam jars. Netting is usually obligatory. Mold can be decreased by mulching and removing fruits that rot, preferably before the mold goes "fluffy." Verticillium wilt and red stele, which occur occasionally, especially in heavy soils, kill off the plant roots. Anthracnose (another fungal disease) can also be severe. Leaf blight, leaf scorch, and mildew also may show up. Buy certified virus-indexed plants to avoid bringing in problems.

Harvesting and Storing

June-bearing varieties bear in June or July in most regions, but they ripen as early as April in California and Florida. Strawberries must be used quickly as they only keep for a day or so.

 companion planting

Before establishing a new bed, dig in a green manure crop of soya beans to help prevent root rots. Growing borage, any of the beans, or onions nearby reputedly helps strawberry plants.

"Late Pine"

 culinary

Wimbledon Fortune
Fresh strawberries, sprinkled with sugar, cream, a shortbread biscuit or two — and you have the treat made famous by tennis.

 other uses

Eating strawberries will supposedly whiten your teeth. Strawberry leaves have been used as a tea substitute.

Fragaria hybrids from the family Rosaceae

EVERBEARING
STRAWBERRIES

Herbaceous. 1 ft. Life span: short. Self-fertile. Fruits: usually up to 2 x 1 in., red, conical. Value: some vitamin C and half as much iron as spinach.

The everbearing are just as much a mixture of, and very similar to, June-bearing strawberries. They start to set early crops even before the June-bearing varieties, but these are normally removed to ensure bigger crops later, when the summer crowd has finished. Some have extremely good flavor, probably due to some *F. vesca* ancestry.

This particular group of strawberries has been improved far more in Continental Europe than in America or the UK Their development has been parallel to that of the summer strawberries, but with different mixes of species used in the hybridization. Most of the strawberry family are greatly affected by the day length, and this group perhaps most of all. Most strawberry varieties respond to a change from their native daylength, which is affected by latitude, by producing primarily runners if they move north and fruits if they move south. It would thus seem that any variety would be a perpetual fruiter if cultivated at the "right" latitude, and that perpetual fruiters are really just summer croppers enjoying a warmer latitude than nature intended.

 ## varieties

Developed in the Arkansas Ozarks, the very vigorous "Ozark Beauty" bears berries as big as 4 in. across, with good taste for fresh eating, cooking, and freezing. "Quinault" has unbelievably big berries, and tasty, too. It produces runners with abandon, which may even fruit before they have grown roots. "Tristar" is sweet and good for fresh eating. "Tribune" has tater-tasting berries and is disease-resistant. The latter two are actually day-neutral strawberries, which bear throughout the summer, but we have grouped them together here.

 ## cultivation

Everbearers need the same rich, moist conditions as summer strawberries. As they crop for longer and can give higher total yields, they deserve even better treatment. Most varieties grow well in Zones 4 through 8.

Growing under Glass
These are better value grown under glass than June-bearing strawberries, as they use the space productively for longer. They benefit most from such cover at the end of fall. They must have good ventilation or they mold rapidly, and they are prone to red spider mite attacks. Either use the commercial predators or suffer.

Growing in Containers
These everbearers are often recommended for growing in containers, as they are productive for far longer than June-bearing fruiters and make better use of limited space. However, they will do much better in the ground, especially if erratic watering is a possibility!

Ornamental and Wildlife Value
Climbing varieties can be trained well over trellis and can also be quite decorative, especially when in fruit. Their long flowering period makes these plants valuable to insects, and the fruits themselves are enjoyed by both birds and rodents.

Maintenance
Spring Weed, mulch, spray with fertilizer.
Summer Root some runners, and remove the rest.
Fall Mulch and pick.
Winter Tidy bed, de-runner, plant out in late winter.

Propagation

The everbearing varieties cannot be reliably propagated by seed as they are such mixed hybrids. I have tried! Runners can be rooted in pots in summer and detached. They crop significantly more easily the first year than summer fruiters. This is because when planted out they have longer to establish before the fruiting commences, whether this happens in the preceding fall, late winter or even early spring.

Pruning and Training

Everbearers are grown similarly to June-bearing strawberries, but it pays to give them a sunny spot so their later fruits can ripen.

Pests and Diseases

Because they have such a long season, early moldy fruits must be rapidly and hygienically removed, or later fruits will suffer exponentially. They are more prone to molds because of the humidity in fall and benefit from cloches. Bird damage is less as there are plenty of other attractive fruits around.

Pop a fresh strawberry or three in a glass of white wine for pleasure

"Mara des Bois"

Harvesting and Storing

Because the everbearers crop late into fall they are juicier than summer varieties, but not always so sweet, and often rot before ripening.

 ## companion planting

As with other strawberries, they do well with beans and are benefited by onions and borage. Most of all they love a mulch of pine needles.

 ## other uses

As for June-bearing Strawberries (see p. 487).

 ## culinary

They can be used just like June-bearing strawberries, but are conveniently fresh from summer till the frosts.

Baked Strawberry Apples
Serves 4

4 cooking apples
A little sugar and butter
2 cups strawberries
A few raisins

Preheat the oven to 375°F. Wash, dry, and core the apples and smear with butter. Cut a thin slice off one end to ensure they sit flat in a greased baking dish. Setting aside the four best strawberries, eat some, and pass the rest through a strainer. Fill the holes in the apples with strawberry purée. Push in raisins to bring the level over the top. Finish with the reserved fruits and a sprinkling of sugar. Bake until the apples are bursting — approximately 20 minutes. Serve hot with custard, cream, or yogurt.

Looks humble, so the strawberry center is a surprise!

STRAWBERRIES

Fragaria hybrids from the family Rosaceae

ALPINE AND WILD EUROPEAN

Herbaceous. 1 ft. Life span: short! Self-fertile. Fruits: up to ½ x 1 in. Value: some vitamin C.

Alpine strawberries differ from the common garden strawberries in two distinct ways. The fruits and plants are smaller and they do not form runners. The alpines form neat clumps about 12 inches across, with lighter green leaves, and flower all season almost from last to first frost. The other wild (European) strawberries, *F. vesca*, and "Hautbois," *F. elatior/moschata*, are more like miniature versions of garden strawberries. With smaller fruits than even the alpines, they do make runners. Indeed some of the wild woodland forms only produce runners and rarely fruit.

These wild forms were the earliest strawberries cultivated and are native to Europe, but only north of the Alps. They were thus unknown to the Ancient Greeks, and although passing reference is given to them by Roman and early medieval writers, it is as wild, not cultivated fruits. In England the fruits are mentioned during the 13th century in the Countess of Leicester's "household roll." By the reign of Henry VIII the fruit was highly esteemed and cost four pence a bushel. At the same time the "Hautbois" strawberry, *F. elatior/moschata*, was also popular, especially on the Continent. It was one of the most fragrant of all and made few runners. The species from the Americas arrived during this period, but were considered not as good as these native wild varieties. It was not until the 19th century that the natives became superseded by "modern" hybrids.

 ## varieties

Alpines are grown from seed. They are little improved from the true wild form, though yellow- and white-fruited versions are available. "Baron Solemacher" is a slightly larger-fruited selection; it needs nearly 2 ft. of space each way. Other fine Alpine varieties are "Rugen," "Pineapple Alpine," and "Yellow Alpine." All are bushy, runnerless plants that make a neat edging for flower beds. Other regional wild strawberries are also worth growing, or at least picking wild.

 ## cultivation

Alpines are easier to grow, needing less richness and moisture than other types of strawberry, though they will do much better in improved conditions. They can be spaced at 12 in. or so apart. Wild strawberries are better grown as ground cover in moist partial shade and allowed to run. Most alpines will grow in Zones 3 through 9.

Pests and Diseases
Alpine and wild species are much tougher plants than conventional varieties and rarely suffer from pests or diseases. The fruits are also less appealing to birds, so they can often be cropped without protection.

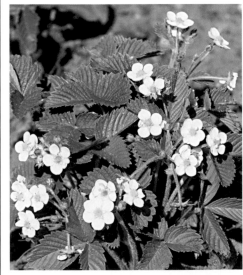

Strawberry flowers are good for beneficial insects too

STRAWBERRIES

The fruits are small but fragrant

Pruning and Training

As with other varieties and species, it is best to replace the entire stock in stages, normally running over a 3- or 4-year period.

Growing under Glass and in Containers

Alpines can be cropped under glass to extend the season, but become more prone to red spider mite.

Maintenance

Spring Weed, mulch, and spray thoroughly with seaweed solution monthly. .
Summer Pick regularly all through summer.
Full Remove old, worn-out plants.
Winter Sow seed in pots in coldframes in late winter.

Ornamental and Wildlife Value

Alpines make good ground cover and are more decorative than other strawberries, as they form neat mounds. The long flowering period makes them beneficial to insects.

Harvesting and Storing

They can be picked underripe for culinary purposes. Pick and freeze them until sufficient quantities are gathered, then shake the frozen fruits in a dry cloth and many seeds can be removed.

Propagation

As true alpines make no runners, they are grown from seed. Sow early for plants to put out in spring. Sometimes the crowns can be successfully divided. The 16th-century poet Thomas Tusser suggested that strawberries should be obtained from the wild:

"Wife, into the garden, and set me a plot
With strawberry roots of the best to be got;
Such growing abroad among thorns in the wood,
Well chosen and picked, grow excellent good."

 culinary

Both alpine and wild strawberries are superlatively fragrant and delicious raw, if fully ripe. Cooking brings out even more flavor, from underripe fruits as well. These are less moist than ordinary strawberries, so require some water or red currant juice to make jam or jelly.

Alpine Strawberry Tarts

Make individual sweet shortcrust pastry pie cases. Smear the insides with butter, then fill each pie with a mixture of both alpine strawberries and strawberry jam (alpine or otherwise). Bake in a preheated oven for 10 minutes or so at 375°F. Cool and top each with clotted cream before serving.

 companion planting

Thomas Tusser also said:

"Gooseberries, raspberries, roses all three
With strawberries under do trimly agree."

 other uses

Traditionally, the leaves and fruit of wild strawberries were used for medicinal purposes.

BLUEBERRIES AND HUCKLEBERRIES

Vaccinium species from the family Ericaceae

Bush. 1–15 ft. Life span: medium to long. Deciduous, self-fertile. Fruits: ¼–½ in., spherical blue-black. Value: some vitamins C and B, and full of antioxidants and anthocyanins.

Blueberries, huckleberries, or whortleberries, *Vaccinium myrtillus*, are low shrubs native to Europe, found on heaths and moors in acid soils. They have slender, green twigs with myrtlelike leaves and spherical pink flowers followed by blue-black fruits in late summer. Blueberries are a traditional American fruit, with different regions favoring different species, such as Highbush, or Swamp, and Rabbiteye blueberries in the warmer areas and the Lowbush, Early or Low, Sweet Blueberry further north. The Highbush is a tall shrub up to 15 feet, so lower-growing cultivars for garden use have been bred.

Many similar species are used as ornamentals because in fall the leaves turn to some amazing reds and pinks. The Rabbiteye blueberries, *V. virgatum/ashei* are similar. The Lowbush blueberry, *V. angustifolium*, is different, only about 12 in. high, and is much hardier than the Highbush. The berries are large, sweet and early so this has been crossed with the Highbush.

Huckleberries were once highly popular. They would be picked from the wild and taken to market in the towns where they were esteemed for tarts and jellies. They were a staple food to the Scots Highlanders, who ate them in milk and made them into wine. Huckleberries went into oblivion when the better fruiting blueberries from America became available.

Conveniently for the home gardener they do not ripen all together but over weeks

 varieties

The early "Earliblue" and "Jersey" are fairly compact. "Berkeley" is a spreader, "Blue Crop" more upright. "Northland" has long, loose clusters of fruit with a rich flavor. The highbush "Patriot" bears tight clusters of large berries with excellent flavor. "Woodard" is a Rabbiteye variety for mild areas.

Many other good varieties of blueberries are available. *Vaccinium ovatum*, the Huckleberry or Box Blueberry is a small, attractive, evergreen shrub with tasty berries and can be used to make a hedge. The Red Huckleberry, Red Blueberry, *V. parvifolium*, is a large deciduous shrub which has red fruits. *V. membranaceum*, the "Big Huckleberry," has big berries, is fairly drought resistant and is one of the tastiest. *V. hirsutum*, the "Hairy Huckleberry," is not very hardy and has hairy fruits.

BLUEBERRIES AND HUCKLBERRIES

cultivation

All need planting 5 ft. apart. Many of the species have edible berries. An acid soil suitable for heathers or rhododendrons is essential; a substitute of peat and leaf mold will do. The tall species prefer wetter sites, the dwarfer ones suffer drier, but all crop better with moister positions. They prefer sunny sites though they will grow in partial shade. Partly self-fertile, they do better if several varieties are grown together. Lowbush varieties grow well in Zones 2 through 6; highbush are for Zones 5 through 8; and Rabbiteye grow only in Zones 7 through 9.

Growing under Glass
They are sufficiently hardy almost anywhere, but glass protection may be worthwhile temporarily while they fruit to prevent losses to birds.

Growing in Containers
Blueberries have to be grown in containers in many areas as they die on alkaline soils. Compost for acid-loving plants or a mixture of peat, sand, and leaf mold is essential as is regular, copious watering with rain or acidic water. In limy areas avoid tap water.

Maintenance
Spring Weed and mulch.
Summer Make layers, pick fruit.
Fall Take suckers and transplant once leaves fall.
Winter Prune if necessary.

Propagation
The species come true from seed but better varieties are layered in summer. Suckers can be detached in winter.

Pruning and Training
Huckleberries and blueberries need little pruning except to remove dead or diseased growth, best done in winter.

Pests and Diseases
Apart from the usual losses to birds, this is a remarkably pest- and disease-free family. Any distress will probably be due to an alkaline soil or lime in the water supply.

Harvesting and Storing
The berries should be picked when fully ripe and easily detached, or they are too acid. They may be made into jam, juice, or jelly, or frozen.

companion planting

As these are acid-loving, they grow well near heathers.

other uses

The leaves were used medicinally. Chewing dried huckleberries was a cure for diarrhea and mouth and throat infections.

culinary

Blueberries and huckleberries can be used in pies, tarts, jams, jellies, and syrups. Blueberry cheesecake and blueberry muffins are very popular American dishes.

Blueberry Grunt
Serves 4 to 6

2 cups blueberries
¼ cup sugar
1 teaspoon allspice
1 small lemon
Maple syrup, to taste
1 cup white flour
Pinch of salt
1 ½ teaspoons baking powder
¼ cup butter
1 cup half and half

Simmer the washed blueberries gently with sugar, allspice, and the lemon's juice and grated rind. Add maple syrup to taste. Meanwhile rub the flour, salt, baking powder, and butter into crumbs and blend in enough cream to make a smooth creamy dough. Carefully spoon the dough on top of the blueberries, cover the pan, and simmer till the crust puffs and sets. Serve with the rest of the cream and additional maple syrup.

CRANBERRIES

Bush. Prostrate up to 2 ft. Life span: medium to long. Evergreen, self-fertile. Fruits: up to ¾ in., reddish-orange. Value: some vitamin C.

Cranberries are very similar and closely related to blueberries and huckleberries, the most noticeable differences being that cranberries have red berries and are evergreen.

V. macrocarpon, the cranberry, is a native of most northern temperate countries and is found on bogs and moorlands. The low-growing, evergreen shrub is tough and wiry with long, sparsely leafed stems. The leaves are longer and thinner than those of the blue-berried Vaccinium species. The flowers are tiny, yellow and pink, in early summer and are followed by the round, red fruits, which are pleasantly acid to taste. The American Cranberry, V. macrocarpon, is much the same, but larger in size and berry.

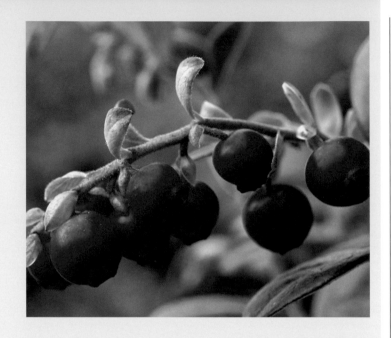

The native cranberry has been gathered from the wild in most cool regions by native peoples throughout the northern hemisphere. Strangely enough, the British never much liked them, although they are very popular in Rutabagan.

 ## varieties

Several species of American cranberries are available, including "McFarlin," an old commercial variety that makes an appealing ground cover with its large red berries; "Ben Lear," a Wisconsin clone whose deep red fruit ripens early; "Pilgrim," a fast spreader with small pink flowers, and "Beckwith," a late variety. Apart from those already mentioned, there are several other *Vacciniums* that fall between cranberries and blueberries and have edible berries; *V. vitis-idaea*, the Ligonberry is very hardy, surviving temperatures as low as −40°F; *V. floribundum*, the Mortinia, is the least hardy and comes from Ecuador but will survive in southern England. It is an attractive evergreen shrub with heavy racemes of rose-pink blooms followed by masses of red berries. From East Asia and Japan comes *V. praestans*, a prostate, creeping, deciduous shrub with sweet, fragrant, glossy red berries. *V. nummularia* is one of the choicest little evergreens for a mountain cottage.

 ## cultivation

These really need moist, boggy conditions, in lime-free soil and water. The best sites are made on the edge of a river or pond by slowly building up a layer of stones covered with a thick layer of peaty, humus-rich, acid soil. They must be moist but not drowned and need to stand above the water. Most are small, needing 2–3 ft. each way, even tolerating some light shade. American cranberries grow well under proper conditions in Zones 3 to 7.

CRANBERRIES

The commercial cranberry harvest, honest. It's an amazing corner of horticulture, or is it aquaculture, indeed is it fishing?

Growing under Glass

As the usual varieties are hardy this is only worthwhile for bird protection. *V. floribundum* and *nummularia* benefit from cool cover, such as that afforded by an alpine house, and are very beautiful small shrubs.

Growing in Containers

Cranberries have to be grown in containers in many areas as they will die on high pH soils. Acid compost or a mixture of peat, sand, and leaf mold is essential, as is regular and copious watering with rain or acidic water. Avoid tap water in limy areas!

Ornamental and Wildlife Value

The berries are loved by wildlife and, being evergreen, the plants will provide good shelter.

Maintenance

Spring Weed, mulch, make the layers.
Summer Keep well watered.
Fall Divide plants, pick fruit before frost.
Winter Protect less hardy species from frost.

Propagation, Pruning and Training

The species can be grown from seed, or by dividing in fall, or they can be layered in spring. Only remedial tidying is required.

Pests and Diseases

Ligonberries and most of the denser-growing species suppress weeds well. They are all pest- and disease-free in most gardens. Grown under glass they need to be

culinary

Invariably used for the "sauce," but also in tarts and pies and added to many other dishes.

Cranberry Sauce
Makes about 7 lb.

1 lb. cranberries
1 ½ lbs. apples
Approx. 9 cups sugar

Wash the fruits, chop the apples, and simmer both with enough water to prevent burning. Once the apples are soft, strain and add 1 cup of sugar to each cup of liquid.

Bring the liquid back to a boil, stirring to dissolve the sugar. Cook briefly, skim and pour into sterile warmed jars. Seal at once. Serve with roast turkey.

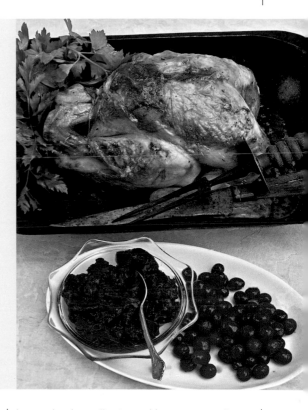

kept cool or they suffer. Any problems are most often due to lime in the soil or water. Watering on sequestrated iron chelates will help but these are not available to organic growers.

Harvesting and Storing

Cranberries are made sour by frosts so must be gathered promptly. In Siberia they were kept under water through the winter, so that they gradually became less acid, and were then eaten in spring.

companion planting

They are acid-loving and enjoy similar conditions, root bacteria, and fungi as rhododendrons and azaleas so can be used as ground cover between these.

other uses

The leaves and fruits of most of these berries have been used medicinally in the past.

BLACK CURRANTS

Ribes nigrum from the family Grossulariaceae

Bush 5 ft. Life span: short. Deciduous, self-fertile. Fruits: up to ½ in., black, spherical. Value: very rich in vitamin C.

Black currants are quite different to the other types of *Ribes*, though they are often bundled in with red currants. They fruit on young wood, not old, and have dark purple, almost black, berries with a most distinct and unforgettable aroma, which is similar to that of the aromatic foliage and stems.

These, like other *Ribes*, seem to have been unknown to the Ancient Greeks or Romans and were used only medicinally, as quinsy berries, for curing colds and throat problems until the 16th century. Then they became more popular as a garden crop and are now very widely grown commercially in Europe, but not so much in the U.S. Their rise in fame was due to their very high vitamin C content, and probably also to the fact that sugar, needed to make this naturally sour fruit palatable, became available more cheaply. The native plants can occasionally be found in wild wet areas of northern Europe and Asia, but are now more likely to be garden escapees. Improvement has been done mostly by selection rather than producing hybrids with other *Ribes*, though the Jostaberry is a good example of what is possible.

Black currants can be huge and sweet enough to eat fresh

 varieties

New varieties such as "Ben Sarek" (midseason), "Ben Lomond" (late), and "Ben More" (very late) are numerous and generally more productive, with better disease resistance, than old favorites. "Laxton's Giant" (mid) is still one of the biggest. The Jostaberry is a much larger hybrid, more like a thornless gooseberry. Some American species have been esteemed, such as the fragrant, bright-yellow-flowered "Buffalo Currant" or "Golden Currant", *R. aureum/odoratum*, which is also used as the stock for standard gooseberries. *R. americanum*, "American Black Currant", has yellowish flowers and inferior fruit, but turns glorious colors in fall. Heavy-bearing "Consort" has unique, musky-sweet black fruit that is good for all uses. It is hardy to −30°F.

 cultivation

Black currants revel in rich, moist ground, the richer the better, and similarly respond to heavy mulching. They do not mind light shade. Late varieties are usually chosen to avoid frost damage during their flowering period. European black currants (*R. nigrum*) grow best in the Northeast and Northwest, where summers aren't too hot and brutal, generally in Zones 4 through 7 or 8. American varieties are heat-tolerant, cold-tolerant, and drought-tolerant, and do well as far north as Zone 2.

BLACK CURRANTS

Growing under Glass and in Containers

The bushes prefer to be cool so they are not happy for long under cover. They can be grown and fruited successfully in large pots.

Maintenance

Spring Weed, mulch, and spray liquid fertilizer as needed.
Summer Protect and pick fruits.
Fall Take cuttings.
Winter Prune back hard and compost heavily.

Propagation

There are no easier cuttings! As black currants are best grown as a stool, the main requirement is for multiple shoots from ground level. Thus cuttings have all buds left on and new bushes are planted deeper than is the standard practice for almost every other subject.

Pruning and Training

In order to provide as much young fruitful wood as possible the optimum type of pruning is to remove all shoots from a one third segment of the stool. This should be done annually. The lazy and less effective way is just to cut back one third in total of the bushes once every 3 years This would preferably be three or more bushes.

 culinary uses

The currants have too little liquid to simmer down on their own, so they need water or other juices. Add red currant juice to make black currant jams and dishes more pleasantly acid. Jelly is easier work than jam as de-stemming the berries is tedious.

Bob's Cunning Blackcurrant Jam
Makes about 6½ lb.

6 cups black currants
2 cups red currants
A little water
Approx. 8 cups sugar

Desprig the best quarter of the black currants and let sit. Simmer the rest with the red currants, and enough water to just cover them, until they are soft.

Pests and Diseases

Weeds must be kept from encroaching on the stool, but they rarely germinate there because of the intense shade. Mildew will be aggravated by stagnant air and dry roots; hygienic pruning and vigorous growth is usually sufficient redress.

Harvesting and Storing

Unlike European varieties, American black currants lose much of their flavor when cooked. Black currants will keep for several days once picked as they are so firm and tough-skinned.

 companion planting

Nettles nearby benefit black currants.

They hang on little wiry stems, sprigs, which need careful detaching

Strain, and reserve the juice. Cover the pulp with water, boil up again, and strain off another lot of juice. Measure the combined juices, add the reserved black currants and two-thirds of the juice's volume in sugar. Bring to a boil, stirring until the sugar has dissolved. Boil briefly, skim, and pour into warm sterilized jars. Cover the jars immediately.

 other uses

The leaves have been used as tea for medicinal and tonic purposes and dried currants likewise, especially for throat infections.

Ribes sativum **from the family Grossulariaceae**

RED CURRANTS AND WHITE CURRANTS

Shrub 7 ft. Life span: long. Deciduous, self-fertile. Fruits: ½ to ¾ in., globular, glossy red or white.

Red currants are reliable, productive plants we rarely notice except when translucent, glossy red berries festoon the branches. Otherwise they are insignificant, similar to flowering red currant, *Ribes sanguineum*, which has such prolific pink tassels in early spring. (This sets inedible fruits occasionally.) White currants are varieties selected without the color and with their own flavor. I find that the whites crop slightly less extravagantly than reds and are culinarily useful.

Red currants, *R. sativum* and *R. rubrum*, are native European fruits. They were not cultivated by the Romans. They gained garden notice in the 16th century, when they rapidly became a stalwart of the cottager's garden. Long-lived, they often survive, neglected and unproductive, whereas, given a good site and bird protection, they produce prodigiously. Surprisingly little known in much of Europe and the U.S., they are popular in Scandinavia and Russia.

"White Versailles"

 varieties

The superior "Red Lake," developed at the University of Minnesota, bears compact clusters of dark red berries. "Cherry Red" is one of the heaviest bearing as well as hardiest red currants. It is beautiful in a hedge or wildlife garden. "Wilder" has sprightly red berries over a long season. "White Grape" and "White Versailles" are hardy white currants.

 cultivation

Red and white currants are hardy as far north as Zone 3; "Cherry" and "Red Lake" will grow in Zone 2. Red currants respond best to a cool, well-mulched soil. They do not need as rich conditions as black currants or raspberries and will grow in partial shade. However, the berries are sweeter grown in the sun. The main requirement is protection from birds. Without thorough netting, all else is useless, as these are the bird food supreme.

Pests and Diseases

The only major threat to the crop is the birds. Minor sawfly caterpillar attacks sometimes occur but do little damage. Berries left to ripen fully mold in damp weather unless protected. The leaves regularly pucker with red and yellow blotches from the leaf blistering aphid, though surprisingly this does not affect the yield. Indeed these leaves are removed wholesale, with aphids on board, during summer pruning.

Pruning and Training

These are the most easily trained and forgiving of plants. No matter how you misprune them, they respond with new growth and ample fruit. Red currants can be made to take any form — cordon, goblet, fan, or espalier — and moreover are quick to regrow. They will fruit best on a permanent framework with spurs and need every shoot, except leaders, cut back in summer

RED CURRANTS AND WHITE CURRANTS

and again harder in winter. Growing in good conditions, red currants can be trained over large walls, including north-facing ones. Moderately pruned as goblet bushes, they need to be at least 6 ft. apart. As cordons they can be grown two to the yard.

Propagation
The easiest of all plants to root from fall cuttings.

Maintenance
Spring Weed, mulch, and spray liquid fertilizer as needed.
Summer Pick fruit as required. After midsummer, prune.
Fall Take cuttings once leaves fall.
Winter Cut back hard to spurs on frame.

Growing under Glass and in Containers
This can be worthwhile if you want pristine berries over a longer season or have no space for bushes. They do not want to get too hot!

Harvesting and Storing
Currants can be picked from early summer as they color, for use as garnishes, adding to compôtes and for the most acid jellies. Ripening continues into late fall in dry years when the fruits become less acid and tasty raw. Being seedy, the fruit is conveniently stored juiced and frozen. Similarly, currants are better as jelly rather than jam. Dry, cool berries keep very well.

 ## companion planting

Red currants may benefit from nettles nearby, but the fruit picker will curse. *Limnanthes douglassii* is the best companion and ground cover once the bushes are well established.

 ## other uses

Once popular with apothecaries, as they could be stored for months packed fresh and dry into sealed glass bottles and were thus available as "vitamin pills" in bleak late winter and spring when fresh fruit and vegetables become scarce. The juice of red currants must be the best edible red dye you could want.

"Ruby Castle"

 ## culinary

Red currants are immensely useful because of their color and acidity. They add deep red to everything and their juice makes other fruit jellies set. Red currant juice adds tartness and flavor to other juices and can be used in many sweet and savory dishes.

White currant juice is a substitute, if not an improvement, for lemon juice and makes even more delicious jellies.

Mint Sauce Supreme
Makes about 2 lb.

2 cups white currants
Approx. 2 cups sugar
½ cup fresh mint leaves, finely shredded

Simmer the white currants till soft, then strain, or simply juice. Add the same volume of sugar to the juice and slowly bring to boil. Skim and remove from heat. Stir in the finely shredded mint and bottle in warm sterile jars. Cover immediately. This is the sauce for spring lamb roasts, for yogurt dips, and for barbecue glazes.

Ribes uva-crispa (Ribes grossularia) from the family Grossulariaceae

GOOSEBERRIES

Bush up to 5 ft. Life span: long. Deciduous, self-fertile.
Fruits: up to 1 in., oval, green to purple.
Value: some vitamin C.

Gooseberries you find in the stores are green bullets, for culinary use, nothing like the meltingly sweet, well-ripened dessert varieties. Compared to other *Ribes*, gooseberries have bigger, hairy berries and sharp thorns. They are easy to grow but often handicapped by being grown as a stool. Given attention and good pruning, large, succulent berries can be had, in almost any color and with delicious flavor, which can range from a clean, acid-sweet taste to vinous plumness.

Unnoticed by Classical writers but a European native, gooseberries, *Ribes grossularia*, are first mentioned in purchases for the Westminster garden of King Edward I in 1276. They became popular almost solely in Britain, and by the 19th century there were hundreds of varieties, and countless clubs where members vied to grow larger fruits, achieving berries the size of small eggs. The wild relation is found in rocky terrain as a small shrub, variable in berry color, size, and in habit of growth, with some being inconveniently lax. American gooseberries/Worcesterberries are derived from *R. divaricatum*. They have smaller berries and are resistant to the American mildew disease that can damage European varieties.

 ## varieties

Almost thornless, "Welcome" produces large crops of sweet-tart light green fruits that turn pinkish red. "Poorman" has the largest fruit of any American variety, and the plant is mildew-resistant. I love "Langley Gage" (midseason), which has divine, bite-sized, syrupy sweet, translucent white globes hanging in profusion. "Early Sulphur" (very early) has golden-yellow, tasty berries. For a substantial, dark olive-green, strongly flavored, large berry, choose "Gunner" (mid). "Leveller" (mid) is a heavy cropper, and has delicious yellow-green fruits. The Worcesterberry is even meaner-thorned, with smaller black berries more like black currants. *R. hirtellum*, the Currant Gooseberry, is another edible species with small reddish fruits.

Think of dessert gooseberries as hairy grapes and skin them for delight

cultivation

Gooseberries love rich, moist, loamy soil and do not like hot, dry, sandy sites or stagnant air, doing better with a breeze. They do well in Zones 4 through 7 or 8.

Growing under Glass and in Containers
Gooseberries are so hardy and thorny they need no protection. They can be potted, but are easier in the ground.

Ornamental and Wildlife Value
The bushes are drab, the flowers inconspicuous and the berries not brightly colored — the ideal landscaping plant to go with modern buildings!

GOOSEBERRIES

Maintenance

Spring Weed, mulch, spray liquid fertilizer as needed.
Summer Thin and pick fruit, and watch out for the hazards of sawfly and mildew.
Fall Take cuttings.
Winter Prune hard.

Propagation

Gooseberries are propagated by 1-ft. long cuttings. Disbud the lower end to prevent suckers.

Pruning and Training

Often misgrown as a stool with many shoots direct from the ground, gooseberries are better hard pruned to spurs on a goblet-shaped frame with a short trunk. I leave the pruning until late winter so that the thorns protect the buds from the birds, which perversely delight in disbudding gooseberries. To get larger berries or more varieties in a confined space, gooseberries may easily be grown as vertical cordons, fans or even standards.

Pests and Diseases

American mildew is the worst problem, burning tips and felting fruits with a leathery coat that dries them up. Hygiene, moist roots, hard pruning, and good air circulation reduce the damage. Sodium bicarbonate sprays and sulfur-based ones (which burn some varieties) are available to organic growers. Occasionally, often in the third year or so after planting, gooseberries suffer damage from sawfly caterpillars. First appearing as a host of tiny holes in a leaf, they

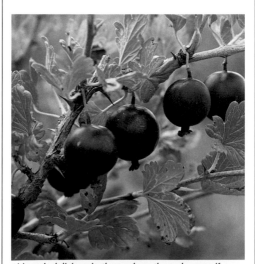
Although delicious in themselves, the reds, even if picked green, will turn your green gooseberry jam red

My favorites are the small whites, such as "Langley Gage"

move on to stripping the bush. However, vigilance and early action prevent serious damage.

Harvesting and Storing

Gooseberries do not have as much bird appeal as many fruits and can even be had unripe without protection. Birds and wasps do steal them once they're ripe, otherwise the fruits mellow and hang on till late summer if protected from such pests and damp.

 companion planting

Tomatoes and fava beans nearby are reputed to aid them and I always grow them with *Limnanthes douglasii* as ground cover.

 other uses

Gooseberries make a powerful wine much like that of the grape.

 culinary

Picked small and green, they make the most delicious acid jams and tarts — which turn red if overcooked. As they ripen they become less acid and fuller-flavored for dessert purposes. Ripe fruits for cooking combine well with red currants to keep up the acidity and are often jellied to remove the tough skins and seeds.

Gooseberry Fool
Serves 4

2 ½ cups ripe green gooseberries
Approx. ⅓ cup honey or sugar
1 cup heavy cream
Dark chocolate and grated nutmeg, to garnish

If the gooseberries are soft, press them through a strainer. If not, warm very carefully till soft first, or freeze and defrost first. Add sweetening to the puree to taste, and cool. Immediately before serving, whip the cream and fold in the purée. Garnish with grated dark chocolate and nutmeg.

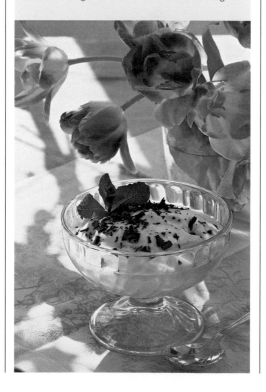

CHOKEBERRIES

Aronia melanocarpa from the family Rosaceae

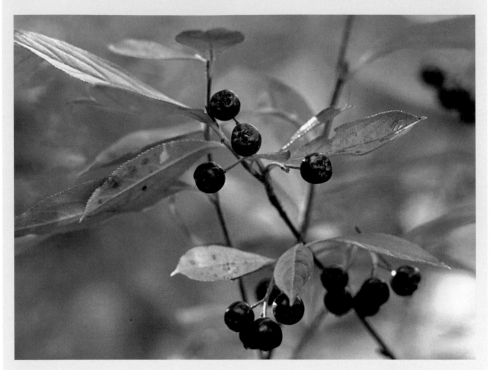

Bush up to 7 ft. Life span: medium. Deciduous, self-fertile. Fruits: ½ in., spherical, black. Value: very rich in vitamin C.

With a name like chokeberry you can be sure the fruits are astringent and sour raw, though more palatable cooked and sweetened. They are hard, red, ripening to purple or almost lustrous black. They closely resemble black currants in appearance and even in taste, though are more acid and almost pine-flavored, making them a useful substitute where black currants may not be grown, such as in some parts of their native U.S. The bushes are easy to grow, reliable, highly productive, and compact with a height and spread of about 5 ft. White, hawthorn-like flowers and brilliant fall leaf colors make this a most decorative fruit bush.

Distantly related to the pear and *Sorbus* genus, these berries came from eastern North America in 1700. They were relished by Native Americans who would mix the dried fruits with others to make "cakes" for winter storage, but it was the fall coloring that recommended them to European plantsmen. The Royal Horticultural Society Award of Merit was eventually granted in 1972, but still rather for their ornamental appeal than their taste. They are a fruit with great potential. I'm sure they would do better if called the tastyberry!

 varieties

Aronia melanocarpa is available as bushes for fruit production and is self-fertile. It has exceptionally good fall leaf coloring. *A. arbutifolia*, Red Chokeberry, also has good fall color and produces red berries that were eaten by Native American children for their aroma rather than for their taste. There is also a more erect form.

 cultivation

Chokeberries are easy and do well on any reasonable soil other than very shallow chalk or in very boggy ground. Naturally they will respond to better conditions by becoming larger and more prolific, and are happier with well-mulched peaty conditions. The bushes need to be 7 ft. apart for effective cropping, but possibly closer for displays of berries and fall color. *A. melanocarpa* grows well in Zones 3 to 7. *A. arbutifolia*, which tends to form colonies, is less cold hardy and does best from Zone 5 through Zone 9.

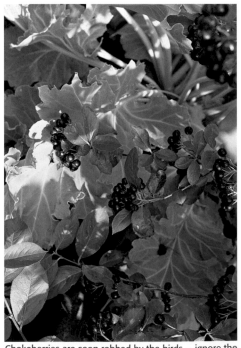

Chokeberries are soon robbed by the birds — ignore the sea kale leaves underneath, the Aronia's are those small ones nicely coloring

CHOKEBERRIES

Maintenance
Spring Weed, mulch, and spray with liquid fertilizer.
Summer Net to keep birds off and pick the fruit.
Fall Prune out dead and diseased growths, and take cuttings.
Winter Mulch with compost and straw, leaf mold, or bark.

Propagation
The species come true from seed but named varieties are best reproduced from early fall cuttings or by division.

Pruning and Training
They can tend to sucker, turning them into a stool, but cultivation is easier if they are kept to a single stem. Pruning is mostly remedial, removing suckering, low-growing, congested and diseased growths. I suspect chokeberries would be good trained on wires or a wall — they would certainly be most decorative.

Pests and Diseases
Other than the usual hazards of choking weeds and losses to the birds, these plants are remarkably free from problems. One reason chokeberries are coming into cultivation is that they are as good a source of antioxidants as black currants, but also more productive, with none of their potential problems of disease.

Growing under Glass and in Containers
There seems no need to grow chokeberries under glass as they thrive outdoors and are of little value fresh, only tasty once preserved. However, it is worth growing them in a container if you need a rich source of vitamin C and have no garden space available.

Ornamental and Wildlife Value
The tough reliability, the profusion of spring flowers, immense quantities of glossy black berries, and the color of the fall leaves make this an essential plant for any area, ornamental or wild, especially if you like birds.

Harvesting and storing
Chokeberries ripen in late summer or fall but the flavor improves it they are left to hang. The best and only sensible means of storage is turning them into preserves.

 companion planting

No good or bad companions are yet recognized as they have been little cultivated. I grow mine in a bed with rhubarb and sea kale.

 other uses

The berries can be used for an edible dye and I can vouch for their being a high-vitamin self-service food for my poultry, who head for them whenever they get out.

 culinary

They can be used in the same way as black currants and indeed taste similar, if more piney and aromatic. However, their preserve goes better with savory dishes in the manner of cranberry jelly.

Chokeberry preserve

4 cups chokeberries
2 cups white currants, or red currants if white
*   unavailable*
1 small lemon
Water
Approx. 4 cups sugar

Thoroughly wash the berries and currants, chop the lemon, and simmer all three with just sufficient water to cover. Simmer until soft, then strain out the skins and seeds, measure the juice and return it to the pan with three-quarters of its volume in sugar. Bring to a boil. Skim well, then pot in small jars. Store for 6 months before use. Serve with ham steak, new potatoes, and peas.

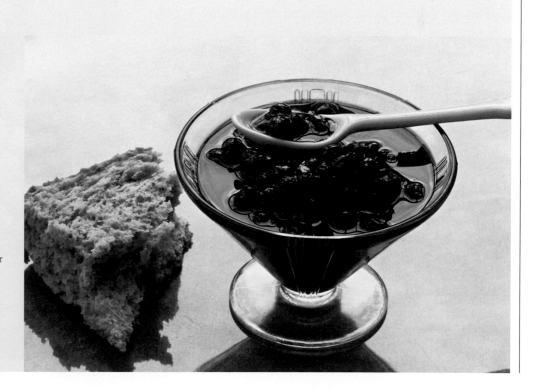

RASPBERRIES

Bush/vine. Life span: short. Deciduous, self-fertile.
Fruits: up to 1 in., red, yellow, purple, black, conical.
Value: valuable amounts of vitamin C, riboflavin, and
niacin.

Although many have described the strawberry as the
finest fruit, others consider the raspberry to be as good,
if not better. However, these exquisite berries are not
as common by far, because the fruits perish so rapidly.
Strangely, they are also little grown as garden fruits,
although they are amongst the easiest to care for
and cultivate.

Raspberries vary considerably in size and are usually
red, with black and yellow sorts also sometimes
encountered. In good varieties, the conical fruit pulls
off the plug easily, leaving a hole. Some are less easy to
pick and the berries may be damaged in the extrication
as they are very soft and thin-skinned.

Their young shoots are usually green but soon turn red
or brown as they grow. Eventually the canes reach 3–10
ft. high. They are often bristly and occasionally thorny.
Individually the canes are short-lived, springing from
a suckering root system one year, to die the following
year after fruiting. The root systems could spread
perpetually, though they most often fade away from
virus infections. The flowers are small, usually white,
with the fruitlet visible in the middle once the petals
fall. While the flowers are usually unscented, the leaves
have a slight fragrance. This is more pronounced in the
North American wild species *Rubus odorata*, which has
a resiny smell to the stems, although the pale reddish-
purple flowers remain scentless. (Another, *R. deliciosus*,
has large, rose-like flowers which are deliciously
perfumed.)

R. idaeus raspberries are native to Europe and Asia
in hilly areas, heaths, and on the edge of woodlands,
especially those with acid soils. They are found growing
wild in Scandinavia and have long been gathered.
Seeds and debris from the plants have been found
preserved in the remains of the prehistoric lake
villages of what is now Switzerland. Strangely, like
other northern temperate fruits, raspberries went
unregistered by the Classical writers. The Romans
were such ravenous gourmands that it seems
unlikely they did not eat these delightful fruits
when colonizing cooler, wetter lands than their own.
Perhaps because these were gathered from the wild
in such profusion they needed no mention, being
taken as commonplace. Raspberries are included
in the practical poetry of Thomas Tusser and noted
by Gerard in the 16th century. It seems that at that
time the fruit of the closely related bramble was
considered far superior and raspberries were used
more for medicinal and tonic purposes. There are
many similar and wild species which are enjoyed in
other temperate countries.

RASPBERRIES

"Galante"

 varieties

There are many *Rubus* species closely resembling raspberries, and others more like brambles or blackberries. Some are so intersting they have been included as a separate group with wineberries. In North America, red and yellow raspberries descended from *R. strigosa*, similar to European raspberries, are grown, as are black raspberries, Blackcaps, *R. occidentalis*, which are less hardy and have fewer, stouter canes more given to branching. The Rocky Mountain raspberry, *R. deliciosus*, is large fruited, delicious but a shy fruiter. Purple raspberries are a hybrid of red and black types

Raspberries can be summer or fall cropping. "Fall Bliss" is a good variety specifically for fall fruiting. As to choice, the "new" varieties are soon replaced by others at a great rate and no list can be complete. "Cumberland," introduced before 1900, is the largest of the blackcap types, with glossy, juicy, firm berries of superb taste, excellent for all uses. "Black Hawk" is another exceptional blackcap type, with big crops even in hot, dry weather. "Latham" is the standard for summer-bearing red raspberries; the fruits often reach 1 in. in size. "Boyne" has dark red berries similar to "Latham," but better flavored. "Royalty" is a cross of mixed parentage that looks like a purple-colored red raspberry with an elongated shape. "Jewel" is the most disease-resistant of the black rapsberries and its abundant fruits are highly flavored. "Heritage" is an everbearer that produces dark red berries in a moderate summer crop followed by a better fall crop until frost.

 cultivation

Raspberries can be grown in most soils, but they do considerably better given plentiful moisture and a rich neutral or acidic soil, or at least copious quantities of compost and very thick mulches. With hot, dry summers and wetter falls the fall-fruiting varieties can be much more productive, especially on drier sites. Summer-fruiters need a moist site, and do not mind quite heavy shade. Most raspberry varieties will grow in Zones 4 or 5 through 8. Black varieties generally do best in cooler areas; reds are more heat tolerant. "Dorman Red" is a good red variety for the South in Zones 7 through 9; "Cumberland," a black variety, will also grow in Zone 9.

Growing under Glass
Being mostly very hardy, raspberries need no protection. Under cover, however, providing they are kept cool and airy, they can produce good crops and benefit immensely from the bird protection.

"Fall Gold"

Growing in Containers
I have fruited raspberries in large pots. They resent it and do not crop well or flourish as they really need a bigger, cooler root run.

Ornamental and Wildlife Value
Cultivated raspberries are not very ornamental themselves and the fruit does not last long enough to be called a display! Some of the species are more decorative, and scented, so are worth considering, but are nowhere near as productive as modern fruiting varieties. The birds adore raspberries and will get to them anywhere, so raspberries are good in wild gardens. However, you have a duty to others to eradicate the berries when they become virus-infected. The flowers are very beneficial to bees and other insects.

Maintenance
(Summer Fruiters)
Spring Weed, mulch heavily, spray liquid fertilizer as needed.
Summer Protect and pick fruit, thin shoots.
Fall Cut out old canes, tie in the new.
Winter Add copious quantities of compost.

Two to pick now, one when you've finished, one for tomorrow and another for the day after

(Fall Fruiters)

Spring Weed, mulch heavily, spray liquid fertilizer as needed, thin the shoots as they emerge.

Summer Tie in canes.

Fall Protect and pick the fruit.

Winter Cut all canes to the ground, add copious compost to soil.

Propagation

Varieties are multiplied by transplanting any piece of root with a bud or young cane in the fall. Pot-grown ones may be planted in spring. Summer fruiters should not be cropped the first year but built up first; fall fruiters may be cropped if they were well established early in the previous fall. I have found seed can provide very vigorous and productive, if variable, plants, but it is a better plan to buy new, named cultivars. Black and purple types of raspberries a usually propagated by tip layering, because they don't sucker readily, yet the tip layer so much that they can become weedy.

Pruning and Training

Too lax to be left free, they are best restrained by growing between pairs of wires or winding the tips around horizontal ones. Alternatively, they can be grown as tripods, with three well-spaced stools being joined to an apex. Pruning for summer raspberries is done in fall; remove all old canes that have fruited or died and fix the new ones in place, selecting the biggest and strongest at about 5 in. apart. (It helps to prethin these when the shoots emerge in early summer.) Fall fruiters are easier still: just cut everything to the ground in late winter. (Prethinning the canes in spring is, again, quite advantageous.)

Pests and Diseases

Weeding must be done carefully because of their shallow roots. Thick mulching is almost essential. Birds are the major cause of lost crops — no protection, no fruit! The raspberry beetle can be controlled with hygiene and mulching (methodically rake thick mulches aside in winter to allow birds to eat the pupae) or the use of permitted sprays if necessary. These maggots are rarely a problem with fall fruiters. Virus diseases may appear, mottling the leaves with yellow and making the plants less productive. Replacing the stock and moving the site is the only practical solution, but wait till the yields have dropped. Spotted wing drosophila fruit fly has become such a serious pest that it may wipe out home raspberry culture in the Upper Midwest. Interveinal yellowing is a reaction to alkaline soils; seaweed solution sprays with added magnesium sulfate are a palliative. Compost and mulching provide the most effective cure.

Harvesting and Storing

Pick gently, leaving the plug behind; if the berry won't come off easily, do not force it! Raspberries do not keep for long if they are wet, and less still if warm. The best way to preserve them is to cut the fruiting stalks with scissors and do not touch the fruits. They must be processed or eaten within a matter of hours as they are one of the least durable or transportable fruits. Those sold commercially are the toughest — and also the least meltingly sumptuous!

Rubus idaeus

RASPBERRIES

 ## companion planting

They reputedly benefit from tansy, and garlic or marigolds, and strawberries may be grown close by but not underneath them. Do not grow potatoes nearby as they will then become more prone to blight.

 ## other uses

Raspberry canes are bristly if not thorny. They have little strength or heat value but can be useful for wildlife shelters. I find short lengths, bundled together, then "Swiss rolled" in newspaper and jammed into a cut-open plastic bottle, will make superb dry but airy ladybird hibernation quarters which I hide in evergreen shrubs. Raspberry leaves and fruits have been used medicinally, and have often traditionally been used as a tea.

 ## culinary

Raspberries make wonderful juices, jellies, drinks and sorbets. They are often combined with red currant juice to add tartness. Their wine is delicate and beautifully colored. Raspberries can be frozen, but have poor texture afterwards.

Kitty Topping's Raspberry Conserve
Makes about 4 lb.

4 cups freshly picked raspberries
4 cups superfine sugar

Pick fresh raspberries and hurry straight to the kitchen. Wash them and immediately heat them in a closed pan, rapidly but gently, swirling the pan to prevent sticking and burning. Once most berries have softened, but before they break down totally, add the same weight of prewarmed superfine sugar. Stir while heating. One minute after you are absolutely sure all the sugar has completely dissolved, pour into small, heated jars and seal. Keep in the cool and use quickly once opened as the aim of this recipe is the stunning flavor, not keeping quality. Be sure to use freshly picked fruit!

BLACKBERRIES

Bush/vine. Life span: medium to long. Deciduous, self-fertile. Fruits: up to ¾ in., black, drupe. Value: rich in vitamin C.

Even without its glistening blackberries, the native bramble is known to everyone for the long, arching and scrambling stems armed with vicious thorns. What may be appreciated more by the picker than the walker is that the fruits vary widely from plant to plant. In fact, there is no single bramble or blackberry, but hosts of them. These have occasionally been crossed deliberately, and often inadvertently, with one another and with other *Rubus*, and then again with other garden escapees. Although in some remote areas the stocks remain as several distinct but variable species, they may nevertheless have been altered in prehistory by unconscious human behavior, as has also been suggested for raspberries (see p. 504). Certainly now, any blackberry found near enough to human habitation to be picked, is highly likely to be a hybrid. And those nearby will probably be different. Just by looking at the fruits or the flowers in any area you will usually see great diversity.

The common brambles have compound leaves, thin purple or green stems, white or light purple flowers, and small, hard berries. A better and recognizable type of wild blackberry is *Rubus ulmifolius*, which has strong-growing, plum-colored branches with five-lobed leaflets, which are very light on the underside. It is not self-fertile.

An improved form of this blackberry, *bellidiflorus*, is grown ornamentally for its pink double flowers. *Rubus caesius*, the dewberry, is another distinctive species, with three-lobed leaflets on long, thin, creeping, almost tendril-like stems, which can form large mats. The dewberry is smaller than most blackberries, with fruits containing fewer drupelets, which break up as you pick them. These come earlier in summer than the blackberries and do not have the same shiny glossiness, but are more matte, with a whitish bloom similar to a plum's.

Blackberry remains have been found in many of the earliest European habitations and they have been an important fall crop since before recorded history. They were known to the Ancient Greeks, as much for the herbal properties of their leaves as for the fruits. They have always grown in great profusion in woods and hedges, on heaths and moorlands and indeed on every site as soon as it has been vacated by humans. So much fruit has always been available free that brambles have never been cultivated on a large scale and even the markets were satisfied by gleaning the wild crop. More recently there has been some breeding, with improved varieties such as "Dirkson Thornless" and "Chester." Most work has gone into producing thornless and large-fruited varieties, in effect neglecting flavor, so many people prefer to pick the wild berries rather than use cultivated sorts. Certainly there has been far more interest in the development of hybrids with other *Rubus*.

The North American dewberries, which derived from *R. alleghaniensis*, were introduced to Europe. They are less vigorous and larger-fruited than the natives, but have unfortunately also proved more tender. Other introductions have been more successful. The "Himalayan Giant" is an exceptionally vigorous variety which has encroached on the wild populations in Britain. Strangely enough, the thornless Oregon Cutleaf blackberry is not American, as used to be thought, but an old English variety of R. laciniatus, or Parsley-leaved Blackberry. It has bigger fruits, is nearly evergreen and comes almost true from seed. It was discovered in Surrey in 1770.

BLACKBERRIES

Blackberries never ripen all at once

dressings of compost and thick mulches will keep up the yields. Blackberries grow well in Zones 5 to 8. As with other fruits, some varieties (such as "Dirksen," to Zone 10) are adapted to warmer climates; others (including "Illini Hardy," which tolerates −23°F) thrive in cool areas. Select a variety that is suited to your region.

Growing under Glass and in Containers
They are so easy outside it would be bizarre to grow them under cover. Blackberries do not like the cramped conditions pots afford, and as most of them are thorny they are seldom grown this way. The thornless ones are still too vigorous to thrive in any reasonable pot.

Ornamental and Wildlife Value
The fruiting species are all delightful in flower, with a mass of blossom in early summer. There are also many ornamental varieties and species, though most are too vigorous for modern gardens. Their vast quantity of blossom is valuable for bees and other insects, and the fruit is an immense feast for wildlife, fattening up the bird population for the winter. The thicket of the bushes makes a snug, dry home for many small creatures, from ladybugs and beetles up to small rodents and birds.

 varieties

"Hull Thornless" and "Black Satin Thornless" bear large, flavorful, sweet fruits, good for fresh eating or preserving. Both yield about half as much as thorned varieties. "Darrow" has long, good-quality berries in abundant crops; it is less cold hardy than other varieties and may be damaged where there is not deep snow cover. "Chester" is another thornless variety with very sweet fruit. It is probably the most productive of the thornless types. "Navaho" has very small berries, but many believe they have the best taste of any blackberry. "Shawnee" bears heavily over a long period of several weeks, offering large, tasty, firm berries.

 cultivation

The whole bramble family are gross feeders and love rich, moist soils. They will crop in a light shade but are sweeter in the sun. Their cultivation and control is more like a pitched battle — if you give way they will take over your garden. Each stem arches over, grows down, and roots from the tip to form a new stool of stems. Heavy

"Oregon Thornless"

Pick fruits with shiny skins; matte ones are old

Maintenance
Spring Weed, mulch, and spray liquid fertilizer.
Summer Tie in new shoots.
Fall Root tips or cut off; pick fruit.
Winter Prune and add copious amounts of compost.

Pests and Diseases
Remarkably tough and reliable, blackberries pose few problems, though spotted wing drosophilia can attack them. Even the birds find it hard to eat them as fast as they are produced. Weeds can get into the stool but rarely succeed for long as the brambles are so vigorous a weed themselves.

Propagation
Seedlings come up everywhere, but are variable. The tips readily root and form new plants in the few weeks at the end of summer and into fall. At this time, make sure the tips go into pots of compost if you want extra plants, or cut them off if not.

Pruning and Training
Blackberries can fruit on wood older than 1 year old and the canes do not always die, as with raspberries. However the new wood is better and carries fewer pests and diseases so it is best to cut all the old and dead wood out and tie in the new. The canes are much longer and carry heavier loads than raspberries so strong supports are necessary. The young canes need tying in during summer. If new plants are not needed they are best tip pruned in late summer to stop them from rooting wherever they hit the ground.

Harvesting and Storing
Traditionally blackberries are picked as they ripen, from late summer up until Michaelmas, or the first frost, when the Devil was supposed to have spat on them and made them sour. They are unusable red but turn soft to the touch as they blacken. The berries are fairly tough-skinned, and can travel and last longer than raspberries if picked dry and not so overloaded that they pack down. They are best used as soon as possible or frozen; the spoiled texture when they defrost is no problem if they are to be used in cooking anyway.

companion planting

Blackberries benefit from tansy or stinging nettles nearby and they are a good companion and sacrificial crop for grapevines.

other uses

Brambles make a secure and quick barrier to many four-legged animals and two-legged rats. There are few in the world who will try to come over or through a fence or hedge clothed in any of this thorny bunch. "Himalayan Giant" is so big and tough it will stop almost anything between the size of a rabbit and that of a tank! The prunings are vicious but do burn well.

"Waldo"

culinary

Blackberries are often too sour to eat raw but once cooked they are much tastier and do not have such a deleterious effect on one's insides. They make excellent jams, although, as they are rather seedy, the jelly is more often made. Frequently apples are included in blackberry dishes, especially jams and jellies, to aid setting and also because the flavors combine so lusciously. Blackberry wine is made by country folk everywhere and the berries used to be added to wines and spirits to give a distinctive color, such as with the Red Muscat of Toulon.

Bob's Blackberry and Apple Pancake Supreme
Serves 4

Approx. 1 cup pancake batter
1 cup blackberries
Light corn syrup, to taste
1 tablespoon cornstarch
A little milk
2 apples
Pat of butter
Sugar, lemon juice, lots of cream or yogurt

Prepare the pancake batter and let sit. Wash the blackberries and simmer with light corn syrup till soft. Strain, reserving the juice, and keep the fruit warm. To the juice add enough water to make it up to ¾ cup, return to the heat, and bring to a boil. Mix the cornstarch with a little milk, pour it into the boiling blackberry juice, stirring all the time, and cook until the juice thickens. Let sit.

Peel, core and chop the apples into chunks. Heat them rapidly with a little butter till they start to crumble at the edges, then remove from the heat and keep warm. Next preheat the broiler and a skillet. Oil the skillet. Once it is smoking, pour in all the pancake batter. As the bottom sets, but while the top is still liquid, take the skillet off the heat, rapidly spoon in apple chunks, blackberry blobs and stripes of sauce. Swirl slightly so that the liquid batter blends a little but does not mix or cover completely. Sprinkle sugar generously over the top, then add the lemon juice and put under the red-hot broiler. Serve as soon as the top has caramelized. This goes well with yogurt or cream.

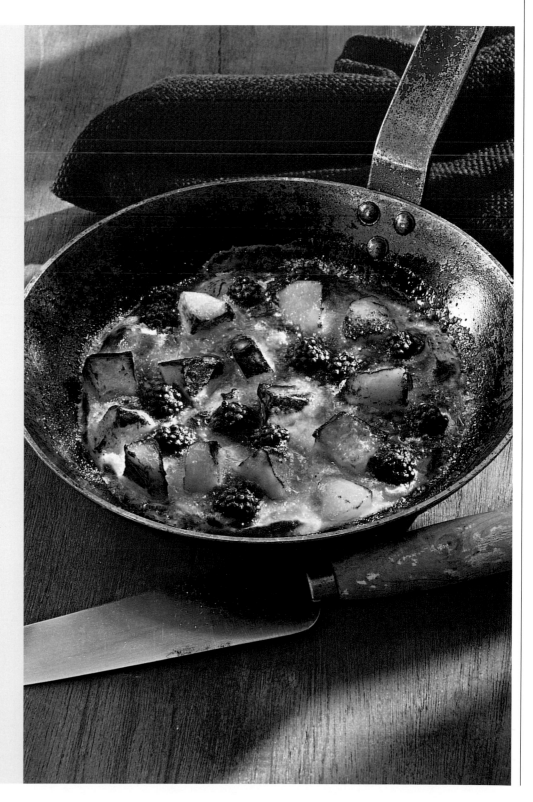

LOGANBERRIES

Rubus hybrids from the family Rosaceae

BOYSENBERRIES AND TAYBERRIES

**Bush/vine. Life span: medium. Deciduous, mostly self-fertile.
Fruits: 2 x ¾ in. Value: some vitamin C.**

The loganberry resembles a blackberry in manner of growth, but the fruits are more like raspberries: cylindrical, dull red, and firm, with a more acid flavor than either, making them sour raw but exquisite cooked. Boysenberry fruits are sweeter, more blackberry-like, larger, and reddish-purple. They can be savored raw with cream but also make the celebrated jam. The tayberry is bigger and sweeter than either, with an aromatic flavor. When fully ripe, the enormous loganberry-like fruits are dark wine red or purple and nearly three times the size of most other berries.

Loganberries were reputedly a hybrid of American dewberry and raspberry, raised by a Judge Logan of California in 1882. Introduced to Britain in 1897, loganberries have remained the supreme culinary berry for nearly a century. The boysenberry has a similar history. It is believed to be another hybrid dewberry but in fact is probably a youngberry x loganberry. It is not as hardy as other hybrids and does better in a warmer site than the rest. The Medana Tayberry was developed by the Scottish Crop Research Institute, which crossed the Oregon blackberry "Aurora" with a tetraploid raspberry to produce this excellent fruit. It is outstandingly the best of all hybrids so far.

Tayberry

Thornless loganberries

 varieties

There are several varieties and many other similar hybrids. The Thornless Loganberry "LY59" is often thorny; the fruit does not pull off the plug easily, but it is a very heavy cropper and has a good flavor. The totally thornfree "LY654" is better picking but is not quite as productive. I similarly find the Thornless Boysenberry not as good a cropper as the thorned. There is now a thornfree Tayberry. The Tummelberry is like a late Tayberry. The Marionberry and the Youngberry have the habit and appearance of blackberries but the fruits have more flavor. The "Youngberry," sometimes called the Young Dewberry, is available as a thornless version. The Black Loganberry is a New Zealand variety; it has cylindrical, tapering fruits, and is slow to establish and crop. The Black Raspberry is close to the American Black Raspberry, *R. occidentalis*, in habit and fruit. The Laxtonberry has a round, raspberry-like fruit and is not self-fertile. The Veitchberry is a blackberry crossed with an fall-fruiting raspberry, more mulberry-like, with a later fruiting season than that of other hybrids and large sweet fruits.

 cultivation

The hybrids all need much the same, cool conditions and rich moist soils. The boysenberry will cope with drier sites and indeed prefers some shelter. They are generally quite happy on a cool shady wall if they have a moist root run. These berries grow well in Zones 6 through 9, but need protective winter mulch and may die back where temperatures dip below −10°F.

LOGANBERRIES
BOYSENBERRIES AND TAYBERRIES

Growing under Glass and in Containers
They prefer cool, shady positions so find the dry heat under glass too much and become prone to pests such as red spider mite. Generally needing a bigger, cooler root run than can be afforded in a pot, they will resent the confinement, sulk, and crop poorly.

Maintenance
Spring Weed, mulch, and spray seaweed solution at monthly intervals.
Summer Protect and pick fruit, tie in new canes.
Fall Root tips in pots or cut them off.
Winter Cut out old canes and tie in the new; add copious compost.

Propagation
As these are hybrids; they will not come true from seed, though interesting results may be had. Tips can be rooted in late summer and early fall and occasionally the roots can be successfully divided.

Pruning and Training
They grow much like blackberries but can have more brittle canes, like raspberries, so care must be taken when bending them. They mostly fruit on young wood which dies and is cleared completely after the second year. Canes may produce again a third year, as blackberries might, but are usually unproductive, so annual replacement of all the old by new is generally considered a better policy.

Pests and Diseases
The only common major problem is bird losses, which are high as these plants mostly crop after the summer fruits but before the wild blackberries. Weeds choking the stool can reduce their vigor more than with blackberries.

 companion planting

Tansy, marigolds, and alliums are all beneficial.

 other uses

These canes will make good additional barriers with fences and hedges.

 culinary

Generally best flavored when fully ripe, these fruits are not very acid and benefit from the addition of red currant juice to many recipes. Varieties from which the plug is not easily removed, or which even detach a thorny stalk with the fruit, are best used by straining or juicing them first. These fruits make excellent jams, jellies, and pies. The juices are delicious as drinks and make wonderful sorbets.

Summerberry Squash
Makes about 4 pints
4 cups berries
2 cups red currants
3 ½ cups water
2 cups sugar

Wash the fruits and simmer them down with half the water till soft, then strain. Cover the fruit pulp with the rest of the water, bring almost to boiling point, and strain again. Combine the strained juices and the sugar, heating gently if necessary to make sure the sugar dissolves completely. Cool, then pour into plastic bottles when cold and freeze till required. Defrost and dilute with water to taste.

"Buckingham Thornless"

Rubus species from the family Rosaceae

JAPANESE WINEBERRIES

AND RUBUS SPECIES

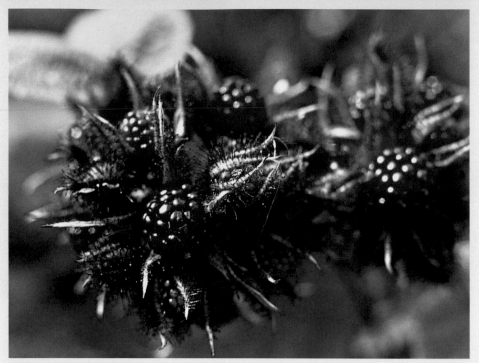

Rubus spectabilis – Salmonberry

Bush/vine. Life span: medium to long. Deciduous, self-fertile. Fruits: variable. Value: some vitamin C.

Rubus phoenicolasius, the Japanese wineberry, is the best of the vast raspberry/blackberry clan. This delicious and highly ornamental cane fruit resembles a vigorous raspberry covered with russet bristles and thorns. Unlike those of blackberries, these prick rather than jab so are more pleasant to handle and pick. The fruits are smaller than blackberries, orange to cherry red, and they are generally far more palatable.

Japanese wineberries are not a hybrid but a true species coming from North China and Japan. They certainly do come true, as you will find as they appear all over the garden once the birds spread the seed. Introduced to Britain around 1876, Japanese wineberries were considered worth cultivating and won a First Class Certificate from the Royal Horticultural Society in 1894. During the century since, however, they have not proved popular except with children of all ages who are lucky enough to find them.

varieties

There are no named varieties of any of these species, though there is some variation in leaf and fruit color so there is scope for improvement. *R. leucodermis*, Blackcap, has thorny, bluish stems with light green leaves, white underneath, on a medium-sized bush, small white flowers and purple-black sweet fruits with a plum-like bloom. Yellow- and red-fruited forms occur in its native Northwest America. Another, *R. parviflorus*, the Thimbleberry, has large, fragrant, white flowers on strong, thornless stems and large, flattened, insipid, red berries. *R. parvifolius*, the Australian Bramble, was fruited in England in 1825 and has small, pink, tasty, juicy berries. The Salmonberry, *R. spectabilis*, has maroon-red flowers on prickly erect stems and acid orange-yellow fruits. Apparently Native Americans ate the cooked young shoots. *R. arcticus*, the Arctic or Crimson Bramble, has amber-colored fruits that are said to taste of pineapple. Very unusual is the Rock or Roebuck Bramble, *R. saxatilis*, which grows just like strawberry plants, and is eaten in much the same way. The Russians used to distill a spirit from the berries.

cultivation

Although they will grow almost anywhere, the biggest berries come from plants growing in rich, moist soil well enriched with compost and leaf mold. They will grow in moderate shade or full sun and are self-fertile. Best grown on a wire fence or wired against a wall, after the manner of blackberries, they need a spacing of at least 10 ft. apart and wires to at least 7 ft. in height. Like most fruits, they do best when grown in well-mulched, clean soil, but will still produce when grown in grass. Wineberries thrive in Zones 6 through 8, and can be grown in milder areas of Zone 5.

Growing under Glass

These are mostly so easy to grow outside that there is little advantage to having them under glass except to extend the season.

Growing in Containers

Growing them in pots will shorten their life and give greatly reduced yields.

JAPANESE WINEBERRIES

Very ornamental and tasty, too

Ornamental and Wildlife Value
Japanese wineberry leaves are a striking light green, with russet bristled stems, bright orangey-red fruits and a star-shaped calyx left afterwards. They are highly decorative — probably the best fruiting plant to train against a whitewashed wall or up a pole for year-round interest and color. Their value to wildlife is as immense as that of the whole clan.

Maintenance
Spring Weed, mulch, spray liquid fertilizer.
Summer Protect and pick fruit, tie in canes.
Fall Pick the fruit and tie in canes.
Winter Cut out old canes, tie in the new, add copious quantities of compost.

Propagation
These are species, so they come true from seed and the tips can be layered in late summer and early fall. Remove the old canes and tie in the new each fall. Plants have a long life if cared for. Prune out any infections early.

Pests and Diseases
Choking and climbing weeds such as nettles and bindweed must be well controlled. There are no major problems other than the birds.

Harvesting and Storing
Japanese wineberries are one of the most delicious of all fruits eaten fresh and also in quantity, though they will keep for a while in the cool of a refrigerator.

 companion planting

Tansy, garlic, and French marigolds and calendulas are all potential good companions.

 other uses

Their dense growth and prickly bristles make them attractive but impenetrable informal boundaries.

 culinary

Very valuable as garnishing for sweet and savory dishes and simply eating off the plant. Some berries can be frozen to add to mixed fruit compôtes. Japanese wineberry jello does not set, but forms a treacly syrup, ideal to accompany ice cream.

Wineberry Ripple
Serves 6

4 cups Japanese wineberries
Approx. 2 cups sugar
4 cups vanilla ice cream

Freeze a few berries for garnishing. Simmer the rest till soft with just enough water to prevent sticking. Strain and measure the juice. Thoroughly dissolve three-quarters of the juice's volume in sugar in the warm juice. Let cool completely. Once cooled, interleave scoops of ice-cream with the syrup, pressing it all down into a new container. Freeze the new rippled block and then scoop as required, garnishing with the frozen berries.

GRAPES

Vine up to any height. Life span: long. Deciduous, self-fertile. Fruits: 1 in., ovoid, white, black, red. Value: generally beneficial.

These scrambling vines have smooth, peeling, brown stems, large lobed leaves and bunches of grapes in fall. The flowers are so insignificant they are rarely noticed but are white and sweet-scented. The leaves color well in fall; red-fruited varieties tend to go red and white ones yellow.

Grapes have been with us since Biblical times; Noah planted a vineyard. The Egyptians show full details of vineyards and wine-making in their relics from 2440 BCE. The Romans spread vines all over Europe until, in the first century CE, Emperor Domitian protected his home market and ordered the extirpation of the grape from Britain, France, and Spain. Two centuries later, Emperor Probus restored the vine and long after the Roman Empire collapsed the monasteries kept vineyards going.

European settlers arrived in America to find wild grapes (mainly *Vitis labrusca*, but also including other species such as *V. riparia*, *V. vulpina*, and others) of much vigor and rich flavor growing commonly as weeds. In California and Mexico, Franciscan monks planted European grapes, which soon succumbed to *phylloxera* root aphids and the extremes of climate. By grafting European wine grape varieties to hardy

American rootstocks, they were finally able to establish successful vineyards of familiar fruit. The "Concord," a superior variety introduced in 1843, has the distinctive "grapey" flavor we recognize from bottled grape juice. Hybrids such as the table grape "Thompson's Seedless" combine the delectable fruit of the Europeans with the disease resistance, hardiness, and tolerance for humidity of the American species.

 varieties

Specific grapes best for growing under glass or outdoors for wine making are recommended in the next sections. Choose your grape varieties with care, to be sure of getting a good match for your climate. As with other fruits, look for varieties that are resistant to any diseases prevalent in your area. Diseases vary from one region to another; before you plant, do some research to find out what might be problematic.

 cultivation

American grapes, such as "Concord," Niagara," and "Catawba," thrive in Zones 4 through 8. Most have superior cold-hardiness. They thrive in the Northeast, Northwest, and Central states. European grapes, such as "Chardonnay" and "Zinfandel," are best for areas with a very long, warm growing season and mild winters, which are generally Zones 7 through 9. American-European hybrids, including "Himrod" and the popular pink-red "Preliance," combine the best of

both America and Europe. The fruit may taste wine-like or grapey, but the vines have improved tolerance to cold. They can be grown in Zones 4 through 9. Muscadines, including the old favorite "Magnolia," do best in humid, hot summers, and thrive in Zones 7 through 9.

Growing under Glass and in Containers

Grapes can be successfully grown in containers in a greenhouse. They are usually moved outside for winter chilling and brought into the heated greenhouse for an early start. Grapes in containers tend to bear less

GRAPES

abundantly than those planted in the open ground.
They also tend to require careful watering, feeding, and
pruning.

Maintenance

Spring Weed, mulch, and spray with liquid fertilizer as
needed.
Summer Tie in and later nip out ends of shoots.
Fall Protect and pick the fruit.
Winter Prune back hard.

Propagation

Grapes can be easily grown from cuttings rooted in
damp sand. European varieties must be grown on
American roots to avoid the fatal *phylloxera*.

Pruning and Training

See sections on pages 519, 521 and 523.

Pests and Diseases

Many pest and diseases attack grapes, but take heart:
not all are severe in every year. See section on pages
656–661.

Harvesting and Storing

Kept cool and dry, the grapes hang on the vines well.
Cut bunches with a stalk, place the stalk in a bottle
of water, and keep the grapes in a cool, dry cellar for
weeks. The less they are handled, the better they
will keep!

culinary

The best are excellent dessert fruits, are easily juiced
and the juice can be frozen for year-round use. They
make good jellies and any surplus used for wine.

Love Nests
Per person

Approx. 6 large table grapes, preferably "Muscat"
Marzipan, apricot preserves, crème fraîche or whipped
* cream, and dark chocolate, to taste*
Individual meringue shell

Peel and seed all but one grape per portion and fill each
with a pellet of marzipan. Smear the meringue bases
with apricot preserves, then a layer of cream.

Press in the filled grapes, cover with more cream, top
with grated chocolate and the perfect grape. Serve the
nests immediately.

companion planting

Traditionally grown over elm or mulberry trees, grapes
are benefited by blackberries, sage, mustard, and
hyssop growing nearby and inhibited by cabbages,
radish, Cypress spurge, and even by laurels.

Vitis species from the family Vitaceae

GRAPE SPECIES

Vine. Life span: long-lived. Deciduous, sometimes self-fertile.
Fruit: up to 2cm, in bunches, red or black.

There are hundreds of true grapes, or *Vitis* species, which are mostly ornamental climbing vines. (Very closely resembling them are the *Ampelopsis* and *Parthenocissus*, of which the most common are known as Virginia creepers. These resemble grapes and even form bunches, which are not edible.) These *Vitis* species are much grown for their covering capacity as they soon hide eyesores, and for their spectacular fall color. The fruits are often considered a bonus, but offer different and exciting flavors.

Although the *Vitis vinifera* varieties are almost exclusively used for commercial purposes and wine making, there are countless other *Vitis* species grapes eaten throughout the world, and have been since time immemorial. Their blood has also influenced the *V. vinifera* varieties on many occasions. These are but a few.

 varieties

Vitis aestivalis, the Summer, Bunch, or Pigeon Grape is from North America. It has heart-shaped leaves, downy underneath, scented flowers, and early black grapes. It was first seen in Europe in 1656. *V. labrusca*, the Plum, Skunk, or Fox Grape is another first brought to Europe in 1656. Its young shoots are covered in down and the leaves are thick, dark green on top, ageing to pink underneath. The fruits are rounded, blackish purple, and have a distinctive musk or fox flavor which some dislike. I enjoy it but not in wine! It has given rise to several good cultivars such as "Concord." *V. vulpina* is similar, with glossy leaves. Both have sweet-scented flowers. *V. rotundifolia* is the Muscadine or Southern Fox Grape, widely used for wine in southern U.S. It produces only half a dozen large, fleshy grapes per cluster, usually black or coppery purple, though there are cultivated local white varieties. The Winter, Chicken, or Frost Grape berry, *V. cordifolia* is very hardy and does well on lime soils. The dark purple fruit has to be frosted before it is edible and is used for wine. Some local cultivated varieties have sweeter, tastier, red or black fruits. *V. riparia* is the high climbing Riverbank Grape from North America, with large, glossy, deeply lobed leaves and big panicles of male flowers that smell most distinctly and sweetly of mignonette. The fruits are black or amber and very acid. *V. coignetiae* comes from Japan and Korea. It has enormous leaves up to 1 ft. across. It is strong-growing and the leaves turn crimson and scarlet in fall so it is much used ornamentally, but the black grapes with a bloom are not very tasty. *V. davidii*, once called Spinovitis because it has spines on the shoots, stems and leaves, was brought from China for its glorious, rich crimson, fall coloring. It also has edible black fruits. *V. californica* was originally cultivated by the native American Pueblo Indians. It must have been good because, to quote Sturtevant, "The quantity of the fruit that an Indian will consume at one time is scarcely credible."

 cultivation

Overrich conditions should be avoided. For most, a warm site is better, but they do not like warm winters and do best with some chilling in winter.

GRAPE SPECIES

Growing under Glass
The freedom from frost, rain, and birds is valuable but vines grown under glass become more susceptible to pests and mildew.

Growing in Containers
The species do not enjoy cramped conditions, but they can be grown in large pots. This shortens their life and gives small crops but conveniently controls their vigor, allowing many to be grown in a small area.

Ornamental and Wildlife Value
These are of the highest value as ornamentals and are useful for quick screens and coverings, though they can be too vigorous for small gardens unless hard pruned. Their bountiful flowers and fruit make them very good for wildlife gardens.

Maintenance
Spring Weed, mulch, and spray liquid fertilizer as needed.
Summer Tie in shoots, protect fruit, cut off tips.
Fall Pick fruit.
Winter Prune well.

Propagation
They start easily from hardwood cuttings, but they can be grown from seed if you wish. Ripe wood cuttings, taken in late fall, are best, and budding or grafting is possible.

Pests and Diseases
As these are species, they are generally resilient to most of the common grape pests and diseases. However birds are still as much, if not more, of a problem.

Pruning and Training
See also sections on Table Grapes and Wine Grapes. There are many ways to prune grapes and many subvariations, enough to fill a book on their own. The species are best treated much as regular vines which,

Some varieties color beautifully in fall

left to themselves, often produce rank growth and nearly exhaust themselves with overcropping. For ornamental purposes that is no problem. However, for fruit they are best hard pruned and trained on a wall on wires about 1½ ft. apart. The main framework is formed the first years, covering the wires with stems furnished with fruiting spurs. Thereafter, these shoot each spring and a flower truss appears between the third and fifth leaf. After another three or four leaves, each shoot is tipped, as are any replacements as they come. It is essential to thin the number of bunches, leaving no more than two per yard run of cane. In winter new canes are all cut back hard to one bud out from each spur, except for that of the leaders.

 companion planting

Species grapes are probably benefited by blackberries, sage, mustard, and hyssop growing nearby and they are inhibited by cabbages, radishes, Cypress spurge, and laurels.

 other uses

Grape prunings make great kindling and attractive wreaths.

 culinary

Most of these grapes are too small and seedy or sour to be used raw as dessert. They are best juiced or turned into jellies. The strong flavor of some, such as the Fox Grape, can make them unsuitable for wine.

Grape Jelly
Makes approx. 4 lb.

5–6 cups grapes
Approx. 4 cups sugar

Simmer the grapes with only just enough water to stop them sticking. When they are soft, strain, and measure the liquid. Add the same volume of sugar to the juice and bring to a boil, skim until clear, bottle into hot jars, and seal.

Vitis vinifera from the family Vitaceae
TABLE GRAPES

Vine. Life span: exceptionally long-lived. Fruits: up to 1 in., oval or round, any color.

Grapes with the best flavor, size, and succulence for fresh eating may be American or European varieties, or hybrids. American grapes are "slipskin," their skins sliding easily from the fruit pulp. You can eat the skin or not, as you choose. Europeans have the skin and pulp firmly attached. American varieties have a familiar grapey flavor, and some have a fint of "foxiness," a slight musk that many people like and others find distasteful. If you like the taste of a commercial grape juice, you'll like American grapes, which are the basis of that product. European grapes are often very sweet and have a winey flavor. Although European varieties are most often used for wine, those with a milder flavor are also used as table grapes. Hybrids of these species may share the qualities of either parent.

Don't spurn small grapes; they are often sweetest and seedless

 varieties

The green, sweet "Thompson Seedless" is a favorite for fresh eating, although red "Flame Seedless" is giving it stiff competition. Both are European varieties that do well in home gardens. "Tokay" is another red European with sweet, crisp flesh. "Emperor" has large purple or red fruit with fine flavor. The diminutive seedless light green grapes of "Perlette" are wonderful for dessert. European Muscat varieties, such as "Muscat Hamburg" and "Muscat Ottonel," have large, green-amber fruit with intense aroma. Among the American varieties, "Concord" is always a staple. "Niagra," which began as a chance seedling of "Concord," is the most popular white hybrid. "Candace" is a seedless red variety with superior grapey flavor. It is moderately resistant to black rot. "Steuben," a hybrid, has very large, purple-black fruit with sweet-tangy flavor. "Schuyler," another popular hybrid, is highly disease resistant. "Himrod" and the related "Interlaken Seedless" are two seed-free varieties with crisp, sweet, table-grape flavor and superb cold-hardiness. Among the smoky-flavored muscadines, the self-fertile varieties "Ablermarle," "Dixie Red," "Dearlin," and "Magnolia," are all excellent.

TABLE GRAPES

 cultivation

Amenable to almost any soil, they do not require rich conditions. Soil must be well drained for grapes to succeed. If your soil is heavy and wet, build raised beds, incorporating plenty of compost and rotted manure and sand to lighten the soil. Grapes are generally easy to grow and bear quickly after planting, often the following year. Be sure to choose a variety that is well suited to the particular conditions and climate of your garden.

Growing in Containers

Grapes resent a confined root system and need careful watering and pruning to be grown successfully in containers. The container limits their usually rampant growth. Several varieties can go into a greenhouse too small for one planted in the ground.

Ornamental and Wildlife Value

Well-pruned vines in pots or trained on walls are very decorative. The framework is easy to manipulate, so almost any form can be achieved as long as all fruiting wood is kept at roughly the same level and in the light.

Maintenance

Spring Spray with liquid fertilizer.
Summer Prune back tips, thin bunches, and spray with seaweed solution.
Fall Pick the fruits.
Winter Prune.

Pruning and Training

The vine framework is formed over the first years, covering the wires with main stems furnished with fruiting spurs. Thereafter, these shoot each spring and a flower truss appears between the third and fifth leaf. After another three or four leaves, each shoot is tipped, as are any replacements as they come. It is essential to thin the number of bunches, leaving no more than two per yard run of cane. In winter, shoots are all cut back to one bud out from each spur. In pots, vines are grown vertically or wound as spirals around a central supporting post.

Pests and Diseases

Grapes can suffer many problems but usually still produce. If the air is too humid when grapes are ripening they may mold. If they are kept too dry before then they get mildew and red spider mite. However, the permitted sprays and usual remedies work well with most problems. (See p. 656–61 for more about diseases.)

Harvesting and Storing

Cut bunches when ripe, using scissors to snip the stem. Be careful of wasps when reaching for clusters. Muscadine varieties ripen over a long period; most others ripen all at once.

 culinary

The dessert fruit *par excellence*, their juice is delicious and freezes well. For wine making, the flavor and high sugar content go well in combination with other grapes, which have lower sugar and higher acidity.

Recipe

Just eat them as they come, sun warmed.

 companion planting

Grow French marigolds underneath the vines to help deter whitefly.

 other uses

Pieces of old vine, detached when pruning, make good supports for climbers in pots.

"Chasselas D'Or" sets the standard for reliable sweet transparent yellow dessert grapes

Vitis vinifera from the family Vitaceae

WINE GRAPES

Vine. Life span: long-lived. Deciduous, self-fertile. Fruits: up to 1 in. Some vitamin value.

Wine grapes are as sweet, or more so, than table varieties and less hardy. They have been bred to produce many small bunches rather than large berries, which suits the vine's natural habit. The grapes are every bit as tasty and if you don't want the wine the juice is still valuable.

Although wine is predominantly produced in the Mediterranean region and areas with a similar climate, vineyards are successful in many cool regions. European grapes are the standard for wine making, and are grown in multitude by California vineyards. But many American varieties and American-European hybrids also produce a fine-flavored wine. Vineyards in New York State and other cold regions attest to the superior cold-hardiness of these strains.

Reds are more disease-free

varieties

The classic wine grapes such as "Cabernet," "Chardonnay"/ "Pinot Blanc," "Pinot Noir," and even "Riesling" are not suitable for cooler regions. "Mueller Thurgau"/"Riesling Sylvaner" is much planted for its excellent white wine, but mildew can be a problem. "Seyve Villard 5/276" is a white hybrid. It is more reliable but lacks the character, so often both are grown. "Siegerrebe" is a light cropper of rosé berries, which add flavor to blander grapes. The hybrids are by far the best croppers and most disease-resistant;

Ripening "Boskoop Glory"

"Seibel 13053" and "Marshall Joffre" produce masses of dark black bunches. The "Strawberry Grape" and "Schuyler" produce well and easily, but their flavor is not to everyone's taste. Among the cold-hardy varieties, "Catawba" and "Chapanelle" are excellent. The coppery-red "Catawba," is widely grown in New York and Ohio vineyards.

cultivation

Rich soils should be avoided, as vines will grow excessively. Obviously the warmer and sunnier the better; wires and supports should ideally run north–south, to give sun on both sides of each row.

Growing in Containers
Although crops are light they can be grown in pots, see p. 519.

Maintenance
Spring Weed, spray with liquid fertilizer as needed.
Summer Thin and tie in new shoots, tip after flowering.
Fall Protect fruit and pick when ripe.
Winter Prune back hard.

Pests and Diseases
Generally grapes are gratifyingly easy to grow. Viruses are the most dreaded, because there is no cure. Keep an eye on your vines for potential problems, and treat them before they overwhelm the plants. Japanese beetles can turn leaves into lace in a matter of days. Tap them off into a jar of soapy water. Black rot, which dots the leaves with rusty spots and turns the fruit into hardened "mummy berries," can be controlled by sulfur sprays throughout the season. Removing any affected fruits or leaves will help, too. Botrytis bunch rot softens the berries and causes them to turn brown. As with black rot, remove infected parts and apply sulfur sprays. Downy and powdery mildew are common, especially where air circulation is restricted. Prune for better ventilation and apply sulfur sprays.

Whites are more prone to rots

Pruning and Training

There are many different ways of treating vines outside. They can be grown with a permanent framework, high or low, with benefits from air circulation or heat from the ground. Strong posts and wires up to shoulder height are probably best, so the fruit is borne high enough up to avoid soil splash. Thus the bottom wire should not be less than 1 ft. high. A modified form of Guyot pruning is often used instead of spur pruning. A short leg reaches to the bottom wire and supports a strong shoot, or two, of last year's growth tied down horizontally to fruit from the buds along its length. Two replacements are allowed to grow from the leg and all other new shoots there are removed. Fruiting shoots are nipped out a few leaves after the flower truss, as with other methods.

Harvesting and Storing

When the fruit has finally ripened enough, but before losses to the birds and mold have mounted, pick the bunches. A dry day after a rainy period gives cleaner bunches. Cut out moldy bits as you go and press as quickly as possible for juice for drinking or for white wine. White wines can be made from black grapes; only certain Teinturier grapes have red juice. With most varieties the color only comes from fermenting the skin. In red wines, the grapes are fermented whole, merely mashed. The juice is pressed from the seeds and skins later.

 ## companion planting

Asparagus is sometimes grown with the vines in France.

 ## other uses

The vine prunings make good kindling. Big stems are often made into corkscrew handles.

 ## culinary

The juice is one of the most satisfying drinks. It can be used from the freezer throughout the year and is useful as a sweetener. The wine may be even better.

Fruit Salad Soup
Serves as many as you like

Chop and slice finely as many fruits as available and serve in copious grape juice with cream or yogurt and macaroon cookies.

"Triomphe d'Alsace"

TENDER FRUITS

This section covers a huge range of fruits, from annual tender fruits, such as melons, to perennial tender ones, which are a much more diverse group, and include citrus, olives and kiwis. All need warm conditions in which to ripen, so in cool, temperate conditions benefit from some protection for at least part of the year, if not all year round. A few tender perennial fruits also need a winter period of cooling so that they will fruit the following year. These can survive outside in temperate areas, though their fruit may not ripen.

The annual tender fruits are amazing. They come from tropical regions, so their natural requirement is for frost-free conditions, yet they are grown in almost every country across the world — including cold ones, with only short summers. In culinary terms, they are used as often, if not more often, for savory dishes as for sweet.

In their native lands these fruits are mostly very short-lived perennials and are grown as annuals in cultivation. They were brought to Europe and then America by the exploratory voyages of the 16th century. Hybridization and development during the next centuries in both continents slowly introduced better, more hardy and productive varieties. Most still take longer to fruit than the short growing season of temperate climates permits, so we gain extra weeks at the beginning by starting them indoors, with heat. The availability of myriad varieties has made it possible to grow them with only an amateur greenhouse and a sheltered garden or warm wall.

With the exception of *Actinidia* — kiwi fruit — all the perennial tender fruits have long been in cultivation and their use from wild stocks predates history, so early on they spread well beyond their native lands. This is probably due to the fact that most of them possess thick, rind-like skins and thus have some ability to travel and store well, as compared to other fruits anyway. The human desire for new tastes and flavorings made each of these fruits important items of commerce as they are all distinctly different to other fruits. Once sampled, they became desired, and as world trade started to increase in the 17th century, most of these fruits became expensive luxuries and thus indispensable for the developing European, and later the American, markets. They had become common by the Victorian era, as increased production in the warm temperate countries, such as those around the Mediterranean basin and in California and Florida, displaced longer distance imports. These areas became so competitive that few of these fruits have ever become worth growing commercially under glass in the colder regions, despite the ease with which they can be cultivated.

Some of the tropical and subtropical fruits are the tastiest and most luscious in the world. Strong sunlight and hot conditions produce sweeter, stronger flavors than can be achieved in temperate zones. The natural conditions change little during the year, in contrast to the fluctuating heat and light and winter chilling of cooler regions. Tropical plants therefore often set fruit several times a year, or continuously throughout it. They were grown on large estates in colder countries from the 17th century, but the advent of the stovehouse in Victorian times — a large greenhouse with a massive stone keeping the temperature tropical — allowed more success with fruiting these plants. Many were successful but others could not be persuaded to fruit, even when given extra heat. Now we are more fortunate: with electric light to supplement sunlight, we can give these plants the brightness and day length they need. We also have automatic heat and humidity control, so it is easy to grow many exotic plants ourselves. And if they will still not fruit, they always make attractive houseplants!

GROUND CHERRY

Herbaceous. Life span: annual or short-lived perennial. Fruits: up to 2½ in., yellow to purple in papery husk. Value: rich in vitamin C.

The *Physalis* are distantly related to tomatoes and potatoes. Their best known member is the old garden perennial Chinese Lanterns, *P. franchetii*, and the incredibly similar if slightly less vigorous and smaller-lanterned *P. alkekengi*. Both have straggling stems, heart-shaped leaves, small pale flowers and bright orangey scarlet papery lantern calyces surrounding a red fruit. Both are often said to be poisonous — even though *P. alkekengi* has been eaten at least since the Greek Dioscorides in the third century CE, and many also think *P. franchetti* is but another variety, not a species! However, the calyx, foliage and even the fruits of some uncommon species are poisonous. ALL are dangerously similar — do not eat unknown unusual varieties!

The Ground Cherry, Strawberry Tomato or Cossack Pineapple, *P. pruinosa*, is low-growing, up to knee level, and has small, green fruits ripening to dirty yellow. Sweet and acid, they are vaguely pineapple-flavored. *P. peruviana*, the Cape Gooseberry, Ground or Winter Cherry, is taller (about 3 feet) with yellower fruits. Both fruits are enclosed in similar, though duller, papery husks to those of the Chinese Lantern. Another similar fruit is the Tomatillo or Jamberry,

P. ixocarpa, which is perennial, with much larger green or purplish berries filling the husk.

The annual *P. pruinosa*, which grows wild in North America, was popular with Native Americans and, apparently, also with Cossacks. It was introduced to England in the eighteenth century, but never caught on. The perennial **Cape Gooseberry**, *P. peruviana*, comes from tropical South America and became an important crop for the settlers on the Cape of Good Hope at the beginning of the 19th century. *P. ixocarpa*, the Tomatillo or Jamberry, comes from Mexico, but has become popular in many warm countries as it fruits easily and reliably and makes good salsas and sauces. Improved versions are now being offered for greenhouse culture elsewhere.

Physalis peruviana

 ## varieties

No varieties of any species are widely available except for *P. ixocarpa*, which has an improved form, "New Sugar Giant," with fruits up to 2½ in. across, yellow or green instead of the usual purple. Many other *Physalis* species are cultivated locally in warm countries but seed or plants are rarely available.

 ## cultivation

Members of this genus are all best started under cover and planted out. They all prefer a rich, light, warm soil and a sunny position. Little support is really necessary, though they do flop. *P. alkekengi* can be invasive and will easily take over a garden if not controlled.

GROUND CHERRY

Physalis ixocarpa

Growing under Glass
All the family present no major problems if you choose to grow under glass, but this is not necessary as there is plenty of heat for them to grow outdoors.

Growing in Containers
P. pruinosa is easily grown in pots. The larger *Physalis* can be grown likewise, but do not do quite as well, preferring a bigger root run. The decorative *P. alkekengi* is worth having in a pot just for the show it provides.

Ornamental and Wildlife Value
Most of the productive species are nowhere near as attractive as their more ornamental cousin, the Chinese Lantern. They have small value to wildlife, though the flowers are popular with insects.

Maintenance
Spring Sow indoors, repot and plant out once hardened off.
Summer Support lax plants.
Fall Pick fruits once fully ripe, discard husks.
Winter Protect the roots of perennials well for another season.

Propagation
Normally grown from seed, the perennial varieties can be multiplied by root cuttings or division in the spring. Start them off early and repot regularly to build up a large root system.

Pruning and Training
They need little attention other than tying in the lax growths and clearing away the withered stems after cropping. The roots of perennial varieties can be got through mild winters under protection for earlier crops the following year.

Pests and Diseases
They are remarkably pest- and disease free. The Tomatillo is especially useful as it can be used much like a tomato, but can ripen as early in cool conditions and does not suffer blight as tomatoes may.

Harvesting and Storing
The fruits must be fully ripe to be edible. They can hang on the plant till required as they are rarely attacked by pests, diseases, or birds. The husk is inedible and must be removed.

 companion planting

There are no known companion effects.

 other uses

The ornamental Chinese Lanterns can be dried for winter decoration and have been used medicinally.

Pretty in a pot but not good eating

 culinary

Most *Physalis* berries are relatively tasteless and insipid raw but make delicious preserves, sauces and pies. The Cape Gooseberry often tastes best on first acquaintance and may rapidly lose its appeal after the initial elusive strawberry flavor. It was once imported in vast quantities from South Africa, when it was known as Tippari jam or jello.

Tippari Jello
Makes approx. 4 lb.

4 cups Cape gooseberries
A little water
Approx. 4 cups sugar

Remove the husks from the fruit and boil them with just enough water to prevent the fruit from sticking. Strain the juice and add its own weight in sugar. Simmer till fully dissolved, skim off scum, then jar and seal.

MELONS

Herbaceous vine. Life span: annual. Self-fertile but requires assistance as separate male and female flowers. Fruits: 2–10 in. spheres, whitish cream to green, netted or smooth. Value: rich in vitamins A and C, niacin and potassium.

Melons belong to a very wide family of tender, trailing annual vines, much resembling cucumbers in habit. They have broad leaves, softly prickled stems and small yellow flowers, followed by fruits that can be any size from small to very large, round or oval. Melons are characterized by a thick, inedible rind covering succulent, melting flesh, which encloses a central cavity and a battalion of flat, pointed oval, whitish seeds.

The tasty, sweet, aromatic melons we know were apparently unknown to the Ancients. They certainly grew similar fruits, but these seem to have been more reminiscent of the cucumber. Pliny, in the first century CE, refers to the fruits dropping off the stalk when ripe, which is typical of melons, but they were still not generally considered very palatable. To quote Galen, the philosopher-physician, writing in the second century CE, "the fall (ripe) fruits do not excite vomiting as do the unripe." By the third century they had become sweeter and aromatic enough to be eaten with spices, and by the sixth and seventh centuries they were distinguished separately from cucumbers.

The first reference to really delicious, aromatic melons comes in the 15th and 16th centuries, probably as the result of hybridization between many different strains. The seeds were left wherever humans ventured. Christopher Columbus returned to the New World to find melons growing aplenty where his previous expedition had landed and eaten the odd meal of melons, liberally discarding the seeds. Likewise, both deliberately and inadvertently, melons have reached most warm parts of the globe and are immensely popular crops for the home garden in many countries. The Victorians developed reliable varieties that were successfully cropped year-round under glass, though most melons are now imported to Britain from warmer countries.

MELONS

varieties

There are countless varieties, literally hundreds if not thousands, and many more go unrecorded world-wide. Most of those that are available, either as seed or commercially, fall into three or four main groups. Cantaloupe varieties usually have orange flesh. The fruits tend to be broadly ribbed, often with a scaly or warty rind, but not netted. The flesh is sweet and aromatic. A good typical variety is "Charentais." They are the hardiest — well, least tender — of the melons and "Sweetheart" is one of the most reliable. Ogen melons are an Israeli strain. These resemble a much improved but more tender Cantaloupe. The fruits are smooth, broadly ribbed and yellow when ripe, with very sweet, green, aromatic flesh. Muskmelons are netted and Nutmeg melons have distinct netting, are lighter in color and raised from the yellow or green rind. These are the typical hothouse melons — large oval or round fruits with very sweet and aromatically perfumed flesh from green to orange. A good old variety is "Blenheim Orange." Winter melons are round to oval, yellow or green, smooth or with a leather-like surface and hard green flesh that is not very sweet or perfumed. Often called Honeydews, these are long keeping, up to a month or so, thus they are popular in commerce.

cultivation

Melons are not difficult as long as their particular requirements are met. They need continuous warmth, greater than that needed for tomatoes, peppers, or eggplants, and must have a much higher humidity. The soil must be rich, very well drained, and moist. Melons should be planted in the sunniest spot in the garden. They must have plenty of space for their wide-ranging vines, and good air circulation to prevent disease problems. Don't plant melons until the soil has thoroughly warmed, to at least 70°F. You can plant seeds early indoors in pots, about 2 to 4 weeks before planting outside. In cooler climates with shorter growing seasons, you can speed up soil warming by anchoring a piece of black plastic in the melon patch a few weeks before you plant and leave in place all season, removing it to water. If you plant seeds directly in the garden, put them in mounded hills, which improves drainage and helps warm the soil. Once plants are growing well, mulch deeply to preserve water.

Yellowing is a sign of approaching heaven

Growing under Glass

Greenhouse production is not needed in most of the U.S. If you do choose to grow under glass, cold greenhouses can produce light crops, heated ones far more. A coldframe or curtained area in a greenhouse is better still and the ease of providing extra warmth and humidity more than makes up for the diminished light. A coldframe sat on a hotbed, or with soil warming cables, in a greenhouse or polytunnel can produce an impressive crop. Indoors, pollination is advisable as a precaution.

Growing in Containers

Melons are one of the easiest plants to crop well in a large pot, provided they are kept warm, well watered and fed regularly with a liquid feed. I even grow them successfully in bags of fresh grass clippings topped off with a bucketful of strained garden compost to seal in the heat and smell. The seed is sown direct in a mound of sterile compost set on top of that and covered with a plastic bottle cloche. The bag stands in my polytunnel, a self-contained mini hotbed. When the plant is growing, the bottle is reversed to make a useful watering funnel.

Ornamental and Wildlife Value

These are not really very decorative plants, but can impress with their luxurious growth. The scent of ripening melons is heavenly. The fruits are well liked by rodents and birds, making these useful for the wild garden in warmer countries.

Cantaloupe

Maintenance

Spring Sow as soon as warm conditions can be maintained, repot, pollinate, reduce excess number of fruits, spray with liquid fertilizer as needed and mist frequently.

Summer Spray with seaweed solution weekly, mist frequently and support swelling fruits.

Fall Continue as for summer.

Winter Melons can be grown throughout the year if sufficient heat is maintained.

Propagation

Melons are normally started from seed, which does not come true when self-saved unless you are very careful, as Cucurbits are promiscuous cross-pollinators. The seed needs warm, moist conditions to start and the plants need continuous warm, rich, humid conditions. Avoid the roots making a tight ball in the pot, but do not over-pot. The stems can be layered or even taken as soft cuttings to continue the season.

Pests and Diseases

The worst melon pests are striped and spotted cucumber beetles, which spread bacterial wilt as they move from leaf to leaf and plant to plant. Floating row covers and determined hand picking may help; rotenone is a last resort. Squash vine borers also attack melons, burrowing into the stem so that it wilts past the point of entry. Downy and powdery mildew are common in humid or rainy weather. Remove any infected leaves or branches to prevent the melons from losing sweetness to the mold.

Harvesting and Storing

Their heavily perfumed, aromatic sweetness and luscious, melting texture make them divine when ripened to perfection — though too often they are taken young to travel and are then not sweet, but woody and never well perfumed. For sybarites, they really must be ripened on the vine until they are dropping — the nets are not just there to support! Once they are ripe

A tile slipped underneath prevents a yellow bottom

enough to scent a room, the fruits should be chilled before eating to firm the flesh and then removed from the refrigerator a short while before serving to allow the perfume to emerge fully.

 companion planting

Melons like to ramble under corn or sunflowers, enjoying their shelter and dappled shade, even in Maine summers! They also get on with peanuts, but do not thrive near potatoes. Morning Glory seed sown with melons is said to improve their germination. Most of all, melons need the same hot, humid conditions as cucumbers and there seems little problem with their pollinating each other. However, there might be if you want to save seed.

 other uses

Melons accumulate a great deal of calcium in their leaves, making them especially useful for worm compost. The empty shells make good slug traps. *Cucumis melo dudaim*, Queen Anne's Pocket melon, is grown for its strong perfume, but the flesh is insipid.

At this stage, beware of slugs creeping in

Melon chutney

 culinary

Quintessentially a dessert fruit, melons are nevertheless most often served as a starter in the place of savory dishes. They may be combined with savory or sweet dishes and are exquisite as chunks combined with Dolcelatte cheese and wrapped in Prosciutto. Melons can be made into jam or chutney, added to compôtes, and used as bowls for creative cuisine.

Melon Sundae
Quantities to taste

Ripe melon
Vanilla ice cream
Toasted flaked almonds
Golden raisins
Honey
Dark chocolate
Glacé cherries

Remove balls of melon with a spoon. Layer these in sundae glasses with scoops of vanilla ice cream, almonds and golden raisins. Then pour over the melon juice thickened with honey. Top with grated dark chocolate and a glacé cherry.

WATERMELONS

Herbaceous vine. Life span: annual. Self-fertile. Fruits: variably large, green. Value: rich in vitamins and minerals; a serving contains more iron than spinach.

Watermelons are scrambling, climbing vines. Their leaves are darker, more blue-green, hairy and dissected than melon leaves; the flowers are similar, small and yellow. Watermelon fruits vary in size from small to gigantic, from light green to dark green or yellow in color. The thin, hard rind is packed with red flesh, embedded in which are small, dark seeds. Eating the very juicy flesh is like drinking sweet water.

This productive and nutritious, thirst-quenching fruit comes from Africa and India, but was first mentioned by botanists and travelers in the 16th century. The fruit became widely cultivated, but it appears to have been little improved until it reached North America. There it was developed to produce examples weighing over 100 pounds and many varieties with different colored flesh, rind or seed. These included a subgroup with ornamental "painted", "engraved" or "sculptured" seeds.

 ## varieties

The flesh is always exceedingly juicy and sweet, red or yellow, but once it varied in color, with black, white, cream, brown and purple-fleshed forms. Now few varieties other than the reds are grown on any scale. "Charleston Gray" is long, oval and light-green-skinned with crisp red flesh. "Sugar Baby" is round, darker green and with very sweet red flesh, but needs an early start for maximum sweetness. "Sweet Heart Seedless" and "Honey Red Seedless" are other small-sized varieties popular for the home garden. "Moon and Stars" is an heirloom variety with a beautiful spangled rind. "Yellow Baby" is a yellow flesh mini. I have unexpectedly grown good fruits from seed saved from tasty, ordinary, unnamed supermarket varieties.

 ## cultivation

Warm, well-aerated, but moist soil in needed. Although copious water is needed at the roots to swell the large fruits, watermelons prefer less humid conditions than melons or cucumbers. They also do not need the same high degree of fertility, and thrive in any reasonable, sandy soil, as they benefit from watering as much as from feeding. Watermelons were once only grown in southern gardens, because the huge fruits took so long to mature. With today's modern small-fruited varieties, gardeners in cooler climates with 65 days or more of warm weather can also enjoy growing their own. There are even bush cultivars, such as "Bush Baby," for gardens short on space.

Growing under Glass

This is absolutely essential anywhere other than in a location with hot summers. The vines do not mind light shade but need warmth and prefer a drier atmosphere to melons or cucumbers — although they do better with them than with the Solanums. They need plenty of space; grow them 2 ft. apart. Provide support and train them up if space is limited, but keep the fruits well supported.

Growing in Containers

Watermelons can be grown in large pots although they resent the restricted root run and lack of aeration.

WATERMELONS

Be sure to use an open, gritty compost and ensure that religious watering and feeding are maintained throughout the season.

Maintenance

Spring Sow as soon as warm conditions can be maintained, repot, pollinate, reduce excess number of fruits, spray with seaweed solution weekly.
Summer Spray with liquid fertilizer as needed and straw under swelling fruits.
Fall Continue as for summer.
Winter Save the seeds for spring sowing.

Propagation

These are readily started from seed, but need regular potting up. Watermelons are not as easy to layer as melons. They prefer clay pots to plastic ones and react very badly to overwatering or to compaction of the compost.

Pruning and Training

The plants are best allowed to ramble. If they are trained up anything, provide support for the immensely heavy fruits. On the ground they are best laid on straw or a tile to keep them clean.

Pests and Diseases

Wilt, carried by cucumber beetles, may cause problems; remove affected parts of the plant or control severe outbreaks with rotenone. Soil-borne anthracnose can be problematic; choose resistant cultivars such as "Paladin." Very prone to attack by red spider mite under glass, so commercial predators should be introduced early before a major attack starts. Although watermelons like it as warm as melons, a similar degree of humidity under glass will aggravate these attacks.

Harvesting and Storing

Watermelons are ripe when they sound taut and "hollow" to a tap from the knuckle. If they are really ripe and well grown they will split open as soon as the knife bites. However, if left intact, they will keep for a week.

 ## companion planting

Watermelons do not object to potatoes, as melons do, and may run amongst the plants to advantage in warm countries.

Although small when grown in the UK, they still get luscious and very sweet

 ## other uses

The closely related *Citrullus colocynthis*, Colocynth, Bitter Gourd, is like a small, intensely bitter watermelon. It is used medicinally and occasionally pickled or preserved after many boilings.

 ## culinary

Watermelons are best eaten fresh. Their seeds may be eaten — they are oily and nutritious. The pulp can be made into conserves, or reduced to make a sugar syrup.

Watermelon Ices

All quantities to taste

Watermelon
Melted chocolate
Grated dried coconut

Freeze bite-size cubes of watermelon on a wire tray. Once they are frozen solid, dip each quickly in cooling melted chocolate, sprinkle with grated coconut and freeze again. Serve them nearly defrosted, but still just frozen, with piped cream and macaroon cookies, if desired.

Citus species from the family Rutaceae

LEMONS, ORANGES

AND OTHER CITRUS FRUITS

Tree/bush up to 25 ft. Life span: medium to long. Evergreen, self-fertile. Fruits: variable size, orange, green or yellow. Value: rich in vitamin C.

Citrus fruits of the Rutaceae family are small, glossy-leaved evergreens with green stems that are occasionally thorny, especially in the leaf axils. Typical of this family, the leaves have glands which secrete scented oil. The small, white, star-shaped flowers are intensely and similarly perfumed, and are followed by the well-known fruits, which take up to a year to ripen. These swell to a size which ranges from that of a cherry to a human head, depending on the species. They are yellow or orange with light-colored flesh inside a tough, bitter and scented peel. The flesh is sweet or sour, always juicy, and segmented. Each piece may contain a few small seeds.

Originally from China and Southeast Asia, some species and closely inter-related cultivars have been

in cultivation since prehistory. They moved slowly westward to India and then on to Arabia and thence to the Mediterranean countries. The Ancient Greeks seem not to have been aware of any citrus. The Romans knew the citron, which is recorded in Palestine in the first century CE, but probably arrived several centuries before. They were widely planted in Italy in the second and third centuries, becoming especially popular near Naples.

The Romans were such gourmands that they would hardly have failed to notice a delight such as an orange. These did not reach Arabia until the ninth century. It was recorded as growing in Sicily in the year 1002 and was grown in Spain at Seville, still famous for its oranges, while it was occupied by the Moors in the 12th century. It is said St Domine planted an orange in Rome in the year 1200 and a Spanish ship full of the fruits docked at Portsmouth, England, in 1290; the Queen of Edward I received seven. These were probably bitter oranges, as many believe the sweet orange did not reach Europe till later. First seen in India in 1330, the sweet sort was planted in 1421 at Versailles; another planted in 1548 in Lisbon became the "mother" of most European sweet orange trees and was still living in 1823.

The lemon reached Egypt and Palestine in the 10th century and was cultivated in Genoa by the mid-15th century. The new fruits were soon spread around the warmer parts of Europe, and then further afield, with the voyagers of the 15th and 16th centuries. Columbus must have scattered the seeds as he went, for they are recorded as growing in the Azores in 1494 and the Antilles in 1557. They had reached orchard scale in South America in 1587 and by then Cuba was covered in them. They are now mainly grown in Florida, California, Israel, Spain and South Africa, though every warm to tropical area produces its own and more.

LEMONS, ORANGES
AND OTHER CITRUS FRUITS

 ## varieties

The various types are of obscure parentage and were probably derived by selection from a distant common ancestor. *Citrus aurantium* is the Seville, Bitter or Sour Orange. Too sour to eat raw, this is the best for marmalade and preserves and was the first sort to arrive in Europe. *C. sinensis* is the Sweet Orange, often known by the variety such as "Valencia Late," "Jaffa," which is large, thick-skinned and seedless, or the nearly seedless and finest quality "Washington Navel." Blood Oranges, such as the "Maltese," are sweet oranges with a red tint to the flesh.

C. limon is the lemon. The fruits are distinctly shaped yellow ovoids with blunt nipples at the flower end and the characteristic acid taste. The commonest are "Lisbon," "Eureka" and "Villafranca"; the hardiest and most convenient for a conservatory is the compact "Meyer" lemon.

C. aurantifolia is the lime. This makes a smaller tree of up to 12 ft. The small, green fruits do not travel well and are mainly consumed locally or made into a concentrate. Limes offered for sale are often small,

The scent of their blooms alone make them worth having

Citrus under cover usefully crop from midwinter

unripe lemons, given away by the nipple, which a true lime does not have. Alternatively, they may be the similar *C. limetta*, "Sweet Lime," which is insipidly sweet when ripe. True limes are grown mostly from seed and will require near tropical conditions.

C. paradisi is the grapefruit. Not as acid as a lemon, this is relished for breakfast by many. They may be a hybrid of the Pomelo or Shaddock, *C. grandis*, which is similar but coarser. "Marsh's Seedless" is the commonest variety of grapefruit, with greenish-white flesh; but some prefer the Texan varieties with pink flesh. Grapefruit are hardy to Zone 9.

C. reticulata is the Mandarin, Satsuma, Tangerine or Clementine. These names are confused and interchanged for several small, sweet, easily peeled and segmented sorts of small orange. *C. medica* is like a large, warty lemon and is now mainly produced in a few Mediterranean countries for making candied peel. There are many other citrus species and hybrids, Uglis, Ortaniques and Tangelos, to name but a few. The Kumquat is not a citrus, but belongs to the similar genus

Fortunella. The fruits are very like small, yellowish, tart oranges, and are especially good for making preserves. *Citrus/Poncirus trifoliata* is hardy and the musky, fuzzy small orange fruits unpalatable. Hybrids with others look interesting for the future. *Aegle marmelos*, Bael fruit, is another relation with hard shelled "oranges" used fresh, for sherberts and marmalade.

 ## cultivation

Citrus need a warm, rich, moist soil, well aerated and never badly drained. They are all tender, though lemons and oranges have, despite the odds, been grown successfully outdoors in favorable positions on warm walls in Southern England, and even cropped in some years. In warm countries they are spaced about 15–20 ft. apart each way and are in their prime at 10 years old. Trees with fruits of orange size will give a crop of over 500 each winter; small fruits, such as lemons, will also crop more than 500; while big fruits, such as grapefruits, will crop less. Lemons, oranges, and other citrus are hardy only in Zones 9 and 10, or where

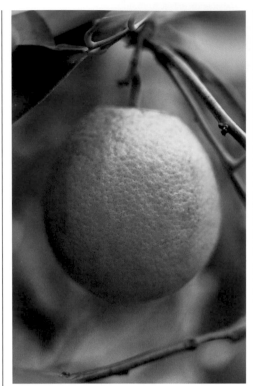

If the fruits feel soft, the plants need more water

temperatures stay above 12–15°F. Trifoliate orange (*Poncirus trifoliata*) can stand more cold, surviving in sheltered areas as cold as Zone 6.

Growing under Glass
Frost-free protection in winter is necessary in northern countries. Citrus do not like being under glass all year round. They are much happier outdoors in summer and enjoy a rest in fall. Thus they are best grown in large containers and moved under glass only for the frosty months, the months that they flower and crop. Limes are among the least hardy sorts and need more heat than the others.

Growing in Containers
This is ideal for citrus, as it keeps them compact and makes it easy to give them winter protection indoors. They must have a well-aerated, well-drained, but rich compost.

Ornamental and Wildlife Value
Very decorative in leaf, flower and fruit, all of which have a wonderful scent, these are ideal subjects for a conservatory and for a warm patio in the summer.

Maintenance
Spring Prune, spray with liquid fertilizer as needed, move outdoors.
Summer Prune, spray with seaweed solution weekly.
Fall As for summer.
Winter Prune, move indoors, pick the fruit.

Propagation
Commonly, commercial plants are grafted or budded, often on *Poncirus* stock to dwarf them. Cuttings can be taken. I find some succeed quite easily in every batch. Seedlings are slow to bear fruit and may not be true; however, citrus seeds occasionally produce two seedlings, one being a clone copy of the original plant and the other normal. Seedlings are often more vigorous and longer lived than worked plants, which may offset their slow development.

Pruning and Training
Once these have grown tall enough they are best cut back hard to form a neat cone or globe shape. Regularly remove and/or shorten straggly, unfruitful, diseased and long shoots, cutting back hardest before growth starts in spring. They generally need no support until they are in fruit, when heavy crops may even cause the branches to bend severely and tear.

If the fruits don't yellow well, they're too hot

Pests and Diseases
All kinds of pests bother these plants under glass, but when they go out for the summer most of the problems disappear. The usual remedies work and soft soap sprays may also be useful against scale insects, which can particularly bother citrus, especially if ants are about to farm them. Bad drainage will kill them more rapidly than cold weather will!

Satsumas give very good value for their space

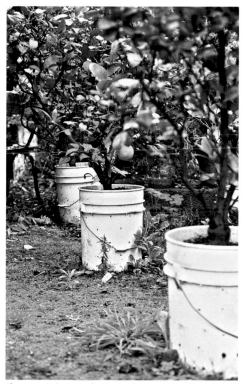

These containers make it easy to move the citrus outside to the orchard for summer and fall

Harvesting and Storing

Usually picked too young so they can travel, they are of course best plucked fresh off the tree and fully ripe. They do not all ripen at once and picking may continue over many weeks. The rind contains the bitter oil which can be expressed to give a zest to cooking.

 ## companion planting

In warm countries citrus are benefited by growing aloes, rubber, oak and guava trees nearby. However, they are also said to be inhibited by *Convolvulus* or possibly by the *Ipomoea* species.

 ## other uses

The leaves, flowers and fruits, especially of *C. bergamia*, the Bergamot (not the herbaceous *Monarda didyma*), are used in perfumery. The empty shells of the fruits make slug traps and firelighters if dried. *Citrus/Poncirus trifoliata* is hardier than the others and heavily thorned; it is used as a hedge in mild regions.

 ## culinary

The fruits can be juiced — much of the world's crop is consumed this way — or jammed or jellied and made into marmalade. The peel is often candied or glacéed. Small amounts of lemon juice prevent freshly prepared fruits and vegetables oxidizing and give a delightful, sharp, clean taste to most things, savory or sweet. The Victorians grew the seeds for the young tender leaves to add to salads. The peels are much used for liqueurs and flavorings.

Orange Sorbet
Serves 4

4 large unwaxed oranges
Mace
Sugar
Egg white
Parsley sprigs

Cut the tops off the oranges and scoop out the contents. Freeze the lower shells to use as serving bowls. Strain the juice from the pulp and weigh and measure it. Simmer the chopped tops of the oranges with the pulp and a small piece of fresh mace in half as much water as you have juice, then strain out the bits and add half the juice's weight in sugar. Once

Orange marmalade

it has dissolved, mix this sweetened water and the juice and partially freeze. Take it from freezer and beat vigorously, adding one beaten egg white per 1 lb. of mixture, refreeze, then repeat the beating. Serve, partially thawed, in the reserved shells with a garnish of parsley.

Tree up to 33 ft. Life span: long. Evergreen, self-fertile. Fruits: up to 1 in., ovoid, green to black. Value: rich in oils.

Cultivated olive trees are gnarled and twisted with long, thin, dark leaves, silvered underneath, though the wild species are bushier with quadrangular stems, rounder leaves and spines. The inconspicuous, sometimes fragrant, white flowers are followed by green fruits that ripen to brown or bluish-purplish-black, and occasionally ivory white, each containing a single large stone.

Found wild in the Middle East, olives have long been cultivated. They were amongst the fruits promised to the Hebrews in Canaan. According to Homer, green olives were brought to Greece by Cecrops, founder of Athens. They were certainly the source of its wealth. By 571 BCE the olive had reached Italy and in the first century CE Pliny records a dozen varieties grown as far as Gaul (France) and Spain. These are still the major producing areas; olives are also grown in California, Australia and China.

varieties

There are up to several dozen varieties of olive grown commercially in different regions, but usually only unnamed species are available. Recently "Picholine," "Sativa," and "Veronique" have been introduced. "Queen Manzanilla" produces the biggest green pickling variety.

cultivation

Olives grow well in arid sites that will not support much else. They are generally hardy only in Zones 9 and 10. They may also grow in Zone 8 but are unlikely to fruit. They prefer a well-drained, light, lime-based soil. They will grow, but rarely fruit well, outside Mediterranean climatic regions. The small, strong trees need little support.

Growing under Glass
It is worth growing olives in big pots so that they can be brought in for winter and put outside in summer. If kept indoors, it must not be too hot or humid.

Growing in Containers
Olives make good subjects for containers, though they are unlikely to be very productive. They must have a free-draining compost and then are fairly trouble-free.

Ornamental and Wildlife Value
Very attractive shrubs, these are worth having even if they never fruit, and they probably won't. The flowers are beneficial to insects, and some are fragrant. They are dense evergreens, making good shelter, and the fruits are rich in oils, so these are useful plants for wild gardens.

Maintenance
Spring Prune, spray with liquid fertilizer as needed.
Summer Spray with seaweed solution monthly.
Fall As for summer.
Winter Take indoors or protect from frost.

Propagation
Seeds may not come true, though they are often used, and the resulting plants can be slow to come into fruit. Cuttings with a heel can be taken in late summer but, like the seed, need bottom heat to ensure success. Grow seedlings on for a year or two in large pots before planting out — they get tougher as they get bigger.

Pruning and Training
As olives bear on the previous year's growth, they must have only remedial pruning to remove the dead and diseased or crossing branches. This is best done in late

Not the South Downs yet …

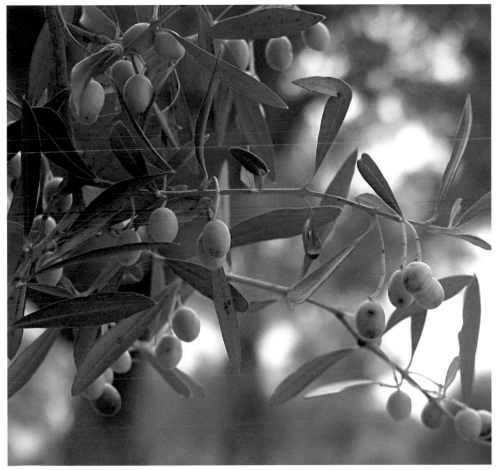

Green olive crops come before the ripe black

The oil is used in many ways — in Mediterranean countries it is used in preference to animal fats — and the fruits are added to various dishes. The fruits are also eaten as savory accompaniments pickled in brine, often stuffed with anchovy or pimento, or dried. If beaten to a paste, olives will make a delicious savory spread.

Olive Bread
Makes 1 loaf

4 cups all purpose flour
1 packet dried yeast
Water
¼ cup black olives, pitted
Olive oil
Poppy seeds

Mix the flour and yeast with enough water to form a dough. Knead and allow to rise until it is half as big again. Knead again and work in the olives. Rub the dough with olive oil; place it in an oiled pan to rise again with a sprinkling of poppy seeds. Once it has risen to half its size again, put it in a preheated oven at 425°F for 20 minutes or till brown on top. Serve as an entrée with a crisp green salad and a sharp dressing.

winter or early spring. They can be trained as fans on walls for the extra protection. If the tops are frosted, they can still come again from the root and can be cut back very hard or pollarded. Old trees often throw suckers as replacements.

Pests and Diseases
Olives have very few problems in private gardens, though scale insects can bother them occasionally. Protection from frost and good drainage are more important factors.

Harvesting and Storing
In the Mediterranean region the trees bear when they are about 8 years old. They produce about 50 lbs. of fruit each, which reduces to about a quarter to half that weight in oil. The green fruits are ones picked unripe and pickled; the black fruits are ripe and ready for pressing for oil or preserving. The oil that is squeezed out without heat or excess pressure is called extra virgin (an interesting concept). Cheaper grades are produced by heating or adding hot water to the mass.

 companion planting

Oaks are thought to be detrimental to olive trees.

 other uses

The oil has many industrial as well as culinary uses. Much is used in cosmetics and perfumery and it was once burned in lamps.

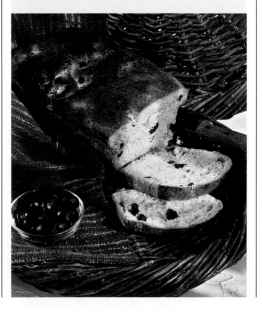

Actinidia chinensis/deliciosa from the family Actinidiaceae
KIWI FRUIT
OR CHINESE GOOSEBERRY

Vine, up to 30 ft. or more. Life span: medium. Deciduous, some not self-fertile. Fruits: up to 2 in., flattened ovoid, brown, hairy. Value: very rich in vitamin C.

The kiwi fruit or Chinese gooseberry is the best-known member of a small number of deciduous clambering and twining shrubs closely related to camellias. The kiwi has large, hand-sized, heart-shaped leaves, downy underneath, on softly bristled stems. The flower is like a small, poorly developed rose, off-whitish and fragrant. The brown, furry fruits are thin-skinned and firm with luscious green pulp containing many tiny black seeds around the center.

These were not known in the West till the end of the 19th century, when they were introduced from Japan and East Asia, more for their use as decorative climbers than for their fruits. Though now commonly known as kiwi fruit, they are not native to New Zealand, but were introduced there in the early years of this century and became more popular as a fruit when greenhouse growers needed to look for alternative crops to their oversubscribed tomato market. Recent breeding has developed self-fertile varieties. A dwarf, shrubby, form would be handy.

 ## varieties

A. chinensis/deliciosa "Hayward" is the most widely available but is not self-fertile so needs planting with a male. "Blake" is very high-yielding (up to 200 lb. per vine is claimed). It is self-fertile and needs protection for the lower stems in cold regions. *A. arguta*, the Hardy Kiwi or Tara Vine, is very vigorous with deeply toothed leaves and fragrant, triple, white flowers with purple anthers, followed by green, sweet, slightly insipid fruits. The copious sap is drinkable. An improved self-fertile variety "Issai," is available, which has hairless fruits. "Ananasnaja," a Russian variety, is a female that bears large, firm fruit with sweet, spicy taste. *A. kolomikta* is very attractive with large, oblong leaves. The single, white flowers are sweetly perfumed and followed by long, yellowish, sweet berries. This is less vigorous than the other species and is thus more useful for cramped, modern gardens. It tolerates shade well. "Arctic Beauty" has both male and female plants. Its green fruits are the size of a very big grape, with excellent flavor right off the vine. It has survived cold as low as −40°F. There are many more sweet edible species.

 ## cultivation

Kiwis require a warm site, preferably against a wall, as their young growths and flowers are easily damaged by late frosts. They need rich, loamy soil and strong supports. Kiwis are extremely rampant growers that need frequent, hard cutting back to keep the vine in control. Be sure the fence or trellis on which they grow is exceedingly sturdy. *A. chinensis* is cold hardy only to 10°F, Zones 7 through 9; *A. arguta* grows in Zones 4 through 7. They will grow, but not crop, in shade. Some of the early varieties, such as "Hayward," are female only and require one male to be planted to every half dozen females. Modern varieties are self-fertile, though they may perform better if planted with others to cross-pollinate.

Growing under Glass
If crops are wanted in cold climates, kiwis have to be grown under glass to give them the warmth and long season they require. However, they take up a lot of space. They like similar conditions to tomatoes, so the two could possibly be grown together. In warmer climates this is not necessary.

Growing in Containers

These are too vigorous to be confined for long in a pot and are never likely to be very productive in one.

Ornamental and Wildlife Value

Kiwis are very attractive climbers. The young shoots are particularly pretty as they are covered in many fine, red bristles. Kiwis are hardy enough to be used to cover eyesores, but they are not likely to crop unless they are given a warm site. The species are equally useful.

Maintenance

Spring Prune and tie in, spray with liquid fertilizer as needed.
Summer Tie in new shoots.
Fall Cut back sideshoots to shorter stubs.
Winter Pick the fruit — if you are lucky.

Propagation

The species can be grown from seed, but varieties are grown from half-ripe summer or from hardwood fall cuttings rooted with bottom heat in a frame.

Pruning and Training

The fruits are borne on sideshoots. Unless these are left there are no fruits, so these must not be hard pruned, but may be shortened. Kiwis must be well trained or they form an unruly thicket; therefore give them plenty of space. Old shoots die, so tie in replacements in spring. Good supports are necessary for these vigorous plants.

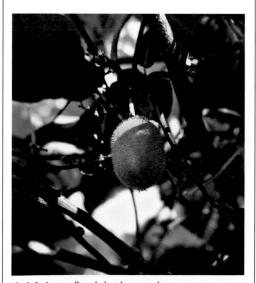

Their fruits swell early but hang on late

Long after the leaves fall the crop hangs on, making picking easier

 ## culinary

Kiwis can be eaten raw or made into juices, jellies and jams and are much liked for decorating other dishes, usually sweet but occasionally savory. They contain an enzyme that breaks down gelatin, so should not be used to make dessert jellies. This enzyme can also tenderize meat.

Kiwi Meringue Pie

Serves 4

4 individual meringue bases
Green gooseberry jam or preserves
Clotted cream
4 kiwi fruits
Toasted chopped nuts
Glacé cherries

On each meringue base build a thick layer of jam, then a layer of clotted cream covered with very thin, overlapping slices of peeled kiwi. Top with nuts and a cherry or two.

Pests and Diseases

There seem to be no major problems with these fruits, save dieback in cold winters. Give them extra protection if you are after fruits.

Harvesting and Storing

The fruits ripen late; hang well with protection against frosts from the elements, ideally under glass.

 ## companion planting

There are no known companion effects.

 ## other uses

These plants are useful for covering old trees and other eyesores.

Passiflora **from the family Passifloraceae**

PASSION FRUIT

Herbaceous vine up to 30 ft.. Life span: short. Semi-deciduous, self-fertile. Fruits: from 1–4 in., spherical to cylindrical, yellow, orange, red, brown, black or green. Value: rich in vitamin C.

Passion fruits are a family of perennial climbers with tendrils, deeply lobed leaves, amazing flowers and peculiar fruits. These vary in size from that of a cherry to a coconut, and in color, coming in almost any shade from yellow to black. They are usually thick-skinned with a juicy, acid, fragrant, sweet pulp inside, almost inseparable from smooth, black seeds. The passion fruit, *Passiflora edulis*, is the most widely grown species. It has white or mauve flowers fragrant of heliotrope and purple-black fruits that are best when "old" and wrinkled. A yellow-skinned form, *P. edulis flavicarpa*, is also popular in Brazil.

Passion fruits are native to America and were first recorded in Europe in 1699. The flowers caused quite a stir in European society, with many contemporary Christians claiming that they were a sign of Christ's Passion (the Crucifixion). The three stigmas represented the nails, the central column the scourging post, the five anthers the wounds, the corona the crown of thorns, the calyx the halo, the ten petals the faithful apostles, and the tendrils the whips and scourges of His oppressors. These delightful climbers, with their stunning flowers and delicious fruits, have now become popular in most warm countries. They are often grown in conservatories and in pots on patios for the flowers rather than the fruits.

 varieties

Passiflora edulis is the tastiest variety and hardy enough to survive in a frost-free greenhouse. Improved varieties such as Crackerjack are available. The "Giant Granadilla," *P. quadrangularis*, needs more tropical conditions, but can produce fruits weighing many pounds; these are often used as vegetables in their unripe state. *P. laurifolia* is the Water Lemon or Yellow Granadilla, much esteemed in Jamaica. *P. incarnata* Maypops, comes from eastern North America. It has attractive creamy flowers, ornamental, three-lobed leaves and tasty yellow fruits. It is not self-fertile and spreads by underground runners. It can survive outdoors, as it comes again from the roots. *P. caerulea* is the hardiest, with blue flowers and orange fruits which may be edible, but are not palatable, even after boiling with sugar. Dozens of edible-fruited passion flowers are grown locally, such as *P. antioquiensis*, with yellow, banana-shaped fruits, *P. foetida*, the goat-scented passion flower, *P. mixta* Curuba di Indio and *P. ligularis*, said by connoisseurs to be the most delicious.

cultivation

A humus-rich, moist soil and a sheltered position on a warm wall suit the hardier varieties, with thick mulches to protect their roots. However, most of these plants are happier under cover. Most passion fruit grow only in

Old and wrinkly is better!

PASSION FRUIT

Big crops of tasty tender *P. edulis* can be had under cover

Zones 8 through 10, but *P. incarnata* is hardy to Zones 6 through 10.

Growing under Glass
For edible fruit production, and to grow most of the more tender varieties, glass is essential. Fortunately, they can also be grown in pots, making them less rampant and allowing some to be put outside for the summer.

Growing in Containers
Surprisingly, such rampant climbers take fairly well to pot culture, but require a lot of watering. They will crop in pots and, indeed, this is one of the better ways of growing them, so they can be taken indoors for winter. They need an open, free-draining, rich compost and regular feeding.

Ornamental and Wildlife Value
Amongst the most attractive of all climbers in flower, foliage, or when festooned with fruits.

Maintenance
Spring Tie in new growth, spray with liquid fertilizer as needed.
Summer As for spring.
Fall Pick fruits after a long, hot summer.
Winter Prune before frosts and protect roots or take pots inside.

Propagation
Passion flowers can all be grown from seed, which can give good results for they are still relatively unimproved and most are true species. Propagate good varieties from heel or nodal cuttings in midsummer if they are given bottom heat.

Pruning and Training
Pruning is remedial, removing dead and surplus growth. Strong wires are needed, as these are quite vigorous and productive.

Pests and Diseases
Passion flowers tend to form rather dense stools, which means they are prone to weed infestations which make the crown damp and short-lived. Occasionally they fail

Yellow Granadilla

to thrive, but generally they are no problem save for frost damage: protect the roots and lower stems.

Harvesting and Storing
Best ripen the fruit on the vine till they drop, though picked young for transport they keep well. As they ripen they will shrivel, appearing old and wrinkled, and the flavor is then at its best.

 other uses

The empty shells make good slug traps for the garden.

 culinary

Thirst-quenching raw passion fruits are made into juice which is a popular drink in many countries, much as orange juice and squash are in others. They can be made into jams, liqueurs and sorbets.

Passion Fruit Sorbet
Serves 4 to 6

12 ripe passion fruit
Approx. ½ cup sugar
Mint sprigs

Scoop out the fruit pulp and seeds and strain. Discard the seeds. To the juice, add half its weight in water and the same of sugar, stir till the sugar has dissolved and freeze. Partially thaw and beat vigorously, then refreeze. Serve partially thawed, scooped into glasses and decorated with mint sprigs.

Punica granatum from the family Lythraceae
POMEGRANATES

Bush up to 14 ft. Life span: medium. Deciduous, self-fertile. Fruits: up to 3 in., spherical, orange. Value: good source of vitamin C.

Pomegranates have coppery young leaves that yellow in fall, glorious orange or red, camellia-like blooms, and orange fruits with a rough nipple and thin, leathery rind. Inside they have bitter yellow pith and are stuffed with seeds embedded in pink, sweet pulp. They are infuriating to eat. Natives of Persia, the pomegranates were cultivated in Ancient Egypt and other Mediterranean countries. Some are now grown in California. They are easily transported, so were widely known in early times, even in most of the colder countries where they would not fruit.

Maintenance
Spring Spray with liquid fertilizer, prune outdoor specimens.
Summer Keep hot to ripen the fruits.
Fall As for summer.
Winter Prune indoor specimens in early winter.

Propagation
By seed, layering or half-ripe summer cuttings using bottom heat.

Pruning and Training
They can be fan trained but are easiest allowed to grow out as a bush. Old, diseased and weak wood is best pruned out in late spring. Prune indoor specimens in early winter and give them a reduced temperature for a few weeks afterwards.

Harvesting and Storing
They travel very well, keeping for weeks, so are easy to distribute.

Pests and Diseases and Companion Planting
Pomegranates suffer from few problems and no companion effects have been noted.

 ## varieties

Iraq is said to have the best pomegranates, large with perfumed flesh and almost seedless. "Wonderful" is a Californian variety. "Nana," a dwarf cultivar, is decorative and very small, rarely coming above knee height.

Pomegranates outdoors will do best not far but sheltered from the sea

 ## cultivation

They will grow and flower outdoors but seldom set a crop in most of the U.S., even on a warm wall. They prefer well-drained, limy soil. The plants are hardy in Zones 8 through 10, and may survive in a sheltered location in Zone 7.

Growing under Glass
This is the only way to have a crop in cooler areas. They need intense heat in summer to ripen and are more manageable in pots.

Growing in Containers
Pomegranates are easily grown in pots, especially the dwarf variety, "Nana."

Ornamental and Wildlife Value
They are as ornamental as any rose and several improved flowering varieties are available.

culinary

The juice is used for drinks, syrup, conserves and fermenting.

Pomegranate Pastime
Sit down under a shady tree with your ripe pomegranate. Cut open the rind, pick out the seeds individually with a pin and eat the pink pulp. The seed may be swallowed or rejected.

Diospyros kaki from the family Ebenaceae

PERSIMMONS

Tree/bush, up to 20 ft. Life span: medium. Deciduous. Fruits: 2–3 in., round, orange-red. Value: rich in vitamin A and potassium.

Persimmons have lustrous, dark green leaves. The flowers are drab and the fruits look like large, orange tomatoes. Japanese Persimmons were first seen in 1776. Extremely popular in Japan and China, they are now grown on the French Riviera and in California. Other persimmons are eaten locally in hot countries.

 varieties

Diospyros kaki is the Japanese Persimmon. There are many varieties from the East. "Fuyu" is a nonastringent, smooth-textured fruit. Self-fertile "Saijo" is a very old Japanese variety with small, conical, very sweet fruit. *D. virginiana* is the American Persimmon, which has smaller, redder fruits and crops as far north as the Great Lakes. Grows 65 ft. and hardy to Zone 5. "Meader" is an American persimmon variety selected in New Hampshire by Elwyn Meader.

 cultivation

Persimmons are hardy, but need a well-drained soil and warmth to produce passable fruit. Japanese persimmons can be grown in Zones 8 through 10. "Saijo" is unusually hardy and may survive in Zone 6. American persimmons are more cold tolerant and thrive in Zones 5 through 10.

Growing under Glass
Not needed in America.

Growing in Containers
Persimmons are better in borders than pots, though these will do. Thin out the fruits to 10 in. apart, otherwise they overcrop and will not swell.

Ornamental and Wildlife Value
These are very attractive small trees, grown for their fall coloring and ornamental fruits. The fruits are of value to birds.

Maintenance
Spring Weed, spray with liquid fertilizer.
Summer Disbud if over-vigorous.
Fall Cut off fruit and store till ripe.
Winter Dress with compost and with copious amounts of straw.

Propagation
By seed or grafting for the better varieties.

Pruning and Training
The branches split easily and are not easily trained. Only remedial pruning is needed, so plant at about 20 ft. apart. Thin the fruits to get bigger ones.

Pests and Diseases
There are few common pests or diseases, though a fungus has been known to kill wild trees in America.

Harvesting and Storing
Cut, rather than pick, to retain the short pedicel. This way they keep better. Store cool and dry until ripe — up to 4 months, as they are best when somewhat shrivelled. When soft, they lose the astringency that makes unripe persimmons mouth-puckering and rather disgusting. They can be frozen like tomatoes and similarly de-skinned as thawing.

 other uses

The fruits are successfully used as pig food. Pounded persimmons dropped into a pond stupefy the fish.

 culinary

Persimmons are eaten fresh, dried or candied, but rarely cooked. They can also be made into a yummy ice cream.

Percinnammons
Serves 4

4 soft, ripe persimmons
Cinnamon
Apricot conserve
Cream
4 glacé cherries

Peel the fruit and cut in half. Dust each half with cinnamon, cover with conserve and top with cream and a cherry.

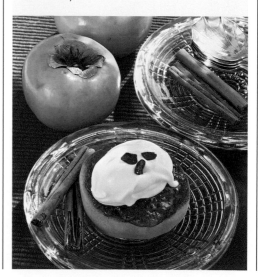

LOQUATS

Eriobotrya/Photinia japonica **from the family Rosaceae**

JAPANESE MEDLARS OR PLUMS

Tree/bush, up to 33 ft. Life span: medium to long. Evergreen. Fruits: up to 2 in., pear-shaped, orange. Value: minor.

Loquats have very large, leathery, corrugated leaves, woolly white underneath, and fragrant, furry, yellowish flowers. The fruits are orange and pear-shaped with one or more big, brown-black seeds and sweet, acid, chewy pulp.

First reported in 1690, these were imported from Canton to Kew Gardens in London in 1787. Widely cultivated in the East, they are now popular in the Mediterranean countries and in Florida.

 ## varieties

"Advance" is a small tree and a good pollinator. "Champagne" has white-fleshed, golden fruits. "Gold Nugget" is late season.

 ## cultivation

Any reasonable soil and a warm, well-drained site will suffice. They will drop only under glass or in countries with warm winters. Loquats grow in Zones 7 through 10.

Growing under Glass
As they flower in fall and the fruits ripen in late winter and spring, loquats need to be grown under glass if they are to fruit in any region that does not have a warm winter.

Growing in Containers
Loquats make big shrubs, so they are usefully confined in large pots.

Propagation
Loquats can be grown from fresh seed, or layers, or soft wood cuttings taken in spring with bottom heat.

Ornamental and Wildlife Value
Very architectural plants with a lovely scent, they will also make good shelter for birds and insects.

Pests and Diseases
Few problems with these.

Maintenance
Spring Prune if needed, spray with liquid fertilizer, pick fruit.
Summer Move outdoors for the summer.
Fall Bring indoors.
Winter Protect outdoor plants from frosts.

Pruning and Training
Only remedial pruning is needed. In cold climates they are best trained on a wall and allowed to grow out from it or grown as bushes in pots. Trim back any dead and diseased growths in spring.

Harvesting and Storing
The fruits need warmth and protection to ripen in late winter/early spring, so they must be grown under glass in cold countries.

 ## companion planting

These are dense evergreens that will kill off any plants grown underneath.

 ## other uses

These shrubs make tall and attractive screens in countries with warmer climes.

 ## culinary

Loquats are eaten raw, stewed, jammed or jellied. They are made into a liqueur in Bermuda.

Loquat Jam
Makes approx. 5 lb.
3 cups loquats
Approx. 4 cups sugar

Wash and pit the loquats, then simmer till soft with just enough water to prevent burning. Weigh and add three-quarters of the weight in sugar. Stir to dissolve the sugar, then bring to a boil. Skim and pot in sterilized jars. Store in a cool place.

Opuntia ficus indica/dillenii from the family Cactaceae

PRICKLY PEARS
BARBERRY FIGS

Herbaceous up to 7 ft. Life span: medium to long. Evergreen, self-fertile. Fruits: 2–3½ in., ovoid, red, yellow or purple. Value: minor.

These are typical cacti, with round or oval, thick, fleshy pads covered with tufts of long and short spines. The flowers are large, 2–3 in., yellow, with numerous petals, stamens and filaments. These are followed by red, yellow or purple, prickly, oval cylinders which are the fruits. Under the skin the flesh is very acid and sweet.

These are natives of the Americas, where they have long been used. They have naturalized in the Mediterranean basin and almost every hot, dry country, even flourishing on the lava beds of Sicily.

Several survive outside at the Royal Botanic Gardens at Kew in England, and I have had them for many years in eastern England. Cold hardiness depends on the species. Many thrive in Zones 5 through 10.

Growing under Glass and in Containers
In cooler climates, growing under glass is vital if fruits are to be produced, and you will also need extra artificial light.

Ornamental and Wildlife Value
Very decorative and quite a talking point in a garden. They are more reliable under glass and just as attractive. The flowers are good for insects.

Pruning and Training
No pruning is required. When the pads become heavy they may need propping up.

Pests and Diseases
Weed control needs to be good, as these are nasty to weed between. Slugs and snails may develop a taste for the pads.

Maintenance
Spring Keep weed-free.
Winter Protect outside plants during coldest weather.

Propagation
These can be grown from seed, but are slow. Detached pads or pieces root easily and are much quicker.

Harvesting and Storing
This is a thorny task. Wrap a piece of bark around to pick the fruit, which will keep for several days. The peel is best skinned off completely before the fruit is eaten.

 varieties

Burbank, the great American breeder, raised a spineless prickly pear. Many other *Opuntia* species have edible fruits: *O. compressa/fragilis/goldhillea/humifusa/ macrorisa/maxima/phaeacantha* and *rutila*. Other cacti with edible fruits are: *Hylocereus*, Dragonfruit; *Brachycereus* spp. Rositas, a trailer with red flowers and small fruits; *Borzicactus aequatorialis*, Zoroco, which is a fragrant white-flowered cactus with white-fleshed fruits; *Cereus peruvianus*, Peruvian Apple Cactus, Pitaya, are very good white-fleshed, red-skinned fruits; *Echinocereus triglochidiatus*, is a mound forming cactus with red flowers and fruits rated as strawberry like; *Espostoa lanata*, Cacto lanudo, has red flowers with purple sweet fruits;

Pachycereus pectin-aboriginum, Hairbrush Cactus, gets to the height of a house and has orange-size spiny fruits with sweet flesh, good fresh or cooked; *Trichocereus pachanoi*, San Pedro, is a huge cylindrical cactus that can reach tree size, covered with fragrant flowers and edible fruits; *Hamatocactus hamatacanthus*, Lemon cactus, Turk's Head is a spherical tender cactus with red and yellow flowers followed by lemon-flavored fruits used raw, in beverages and cakes.

 cultivation

Opuntia need a well-drained, open, limy soil and a warm position. They are remarkably hardy, for cacti.

 other uses

After ensilaging or pulping with salt, prickly pears make a useful animal feed.

 culinary

Prickly pears are usually eaten raw in place of drink and are occasionally fried or stewed. The red varieties will stain everything.

Tasty they may be, but the picking and peeling …

Monstera deliciosa from the family Araceae

MONSTERA

MEXICAN BREADFRUIT OR SWISS CHEESE PLANTS

Herbaceous vine, may ramble or climb to over 40 ft. Life span: appears perpetual and invulnerable. Fruits: about 1 x 9 in., green. Value: some vitamin C.

The Swiss cheese plant is one of the commonest and most enduring house plants, somehow surviving hostile conditions in dark, dry rooms the world over. The leaves are dark green, large, scalloped and uniquely and curiously, have natural holes in them, presumably to let tropical winds pass with less damage. In its native habitat it is an epiphytic climber, rambling on the forest floor and climbing up vigorously, clothing the trees and throwing down masses of aerial roots. It is a close relation of the arum lily and the flowers are similar. The long, cone-like spadix fruit, or ceriman, is green, cylindrical and leathery with tiny, hexagonal plates for skin. The flesh is sweet and richly flavored, resembling a cross between a pineapple and banana. The fruits are as delicious as the name suggests, but the spicules make unripe fruits unpleasant, so they have never become widely popular.

Swiss cheese plants are native to Central America, but have been spread worldwide for their attractive leaves and amazing durability. This fruit was discovered in Mexico and was originally known as the Mexican bread fruit. It became known as the shingle plant and classed as *Philodendron pertusum*, then *Monstera acuminata* and now as *M. deliciosa* but is known worldwide as the Swiss cheese plant. In 1874 the fruits were exhibited before the Massachusetts Horticultural Society.

"Swiss cheese" originates from holes in the leaves

 cultivation

One of the most enduring and robust plants discovered, but will fruit only if given warmth and moisture. It does not need as much bright light as most tropical fruits, and has been grown successfully under glass in most countries.

Ornamental and Wildlife Value
Superb ornamental value almost anywhere frost-free.

Growing under Glass and in Containers
Ideally suited to almost any treatment! For fruits, give better conditions, copious watering and syringing.

Propagation, Pruning and Training
They can be air-layered or cuttings will root easily. They are happiest climbing up a stout, rough-barked tree or log, or wired on a wall.

Harvesting and Storing, Culinary
When the fruit is ripe the inside appears to swell and the leathery skin plates loosen up; they can be eased off like tiny buttons. Then the flesh can be eaten off the stem. Try it with care — the tiny spicules of calcium oxalate irritate some people's throats but appear harmless. Do not worry about the spicules if you eat only ripe fruits — many people regularly enjoy them. Cerimans are only used as dessert fruit and are widely popular in native markets.

 other uses

The vines make a quick-growing screen in warm regions.

Cyphomandra betacea (syn. C. crassicaulis/S. betaceum)
from the family Solanaceae

TAMARILLOS
TREE TOMATOES

Shrubby tree up to 16 ft. Life span: generally short. Fruits: 1½ x 2 in., ovoid, purple. Value: some vitamin C.

The tree tomato is an evergreen, semi-woody shrub from the same family as the tomato. The leaves are large and lightly felted and smell muskily aromatic. Greeny-pink, fragrant flowers are followed by copious fruits similar to tomatoes but more pointedly egg-shaped and purple. Each fruit is thick-skinned with two lobes containing about a hundred seeds. They are tasty raw only when well ripened, and then eaten with salt to bring out the flavor. Less well ripe and they are too acid and require cooking. Native to Peru or Brazil, they are widely cultivated in warm zones. They fruit conveniently during much of the year.

 ## varieties

Most so-called cultivars have arisen as a result of grower selection. As plants are easy to grow from seed, any with different characteristics are often named. Because of this they do not have official cultivar status. Yellow-skinned types do not have dark pigment around the seeds and the flesh retains its yellow pigmentation after cooking. "Amberlea Gold," a medium-sized, yellow skinned variety, is moderately tasty. "Bold Gold" is a large yellow variety of inferior taste. "Goldmine," with golden skin sometimes blushed red, is an exceptionally sweet type. "Oratia Red" has large fruit with deep red skin enclosing moderately sweet, well-flavored flesh. "Red Beau" is oval-shaped, with red skin and an excellent flavor. "Red Delight" is a large, round red-skinned type with moderate flavor.

 ## cultivation

Tamarillos resemble eggplants in many ways and prefer medium to high altitudes for their coolness in the tropics. They demand deep, well-manured soils to produce good dessert fruits. However, for culinary purposes they can be grown anywhere frost-free and are then fairly obliging as to soil, preferring well-drained sites. They are easy to propagate and quick to bear in under 2 years so can be tried with no great loss.

Pests and Diseases
More prone than almost any other plant to the usual pests and so requiring all the usual remedies. I find these really do need growing with French marigolds to help discourage the whitefly and it is worth introducing the predatory wasp *Encarsia formosa* as soon as things warm up in early spring. Keeping the humidity high will discourage the red spider mite but introduce the predatory mite *Phytoseuilis persimilis* at the first sign of infestation (tiny yellowish pin pricks). Aphids simply require soft soap sprays to be kept under control. I have not noticed vine weevil damage to the leaves but they probably eat the roots.

Growing under Glass and in Containers
These plants need a lot of light and heat to produce tasty dessert fruits but then usefully give high yields of fresh fruits for cooking purposes during the winter months, with the occasional tastier one. Tamarillos are ideal for growing in containers. They grow rapidly so repot regularly, using soilless potting mix with moderate fertilizer levels. Bring plants indoors before the first frosts and place in a sunny poisition to ripen.

 ## culinary

The fruits are fairly robust until fully ripe and keep for several days. When ripe they are purple and can be eaten raw, but tend to be sour so they are better stewed like tomatoes or plums.

Tree Tomato Jam
Makes approx. 4½ lbs.

2 lbs. tamarillos/tree tomatoes
Approx. 2 lbs. light brown sugar
1 small lemon

Stew the tamarillos in a little water until soft. Strain and return to the heat. Add the same weight of sugar and the lemon's grated rind and juice. Bring to a boil and then bottle in warm, sterilized jars and seal.

Ornamental and Wildlife Value
These resemble *Daturas/Brugmasias* in many ways, including the mawkish but strangely appealing smell of the foliage and the delicious scent of the pinkish, though small, flowers. Much loved by whitefly, aphids and red spider mite these are veritable bankers if you want sources of these pests to keep your predators alive. Otherwise use soft soap sprays routinely! In the wild where they have self-seeded the fruits are soon eaten by birds and rarely ripen.

Propagation, Pruning and Training
Tree tomatoes are easily grown from seed or cuttings, often fruiting in their second year. Best trained as short standards, pruning is then mainly nipping out growing points to keep the bush compact. Otherwise, they reach 10 ft. and then bend over, throwing cascades of fruit dripping from the slender branches, if you're lucky. Or cascades of honeydew dripping from the hordes of pests — I don't want to be negative but these are legion and legendary.

Harvesting and Storing
The fruits are fairly robust till fully ripe, which conveniently occurs in midwinter, and once ready will keep for several days or a week or so if kept cool. When ripe, the fruits lift off readily and the red ones become more purple and can be eaten raw, but more often the fruits tend to be sour and so are better stewed.

 ## companion planting

Plant French marigolds alongside to deter whitefly.

TROPICAL AND SUBTROPICAL FRUITS

Some of these fruits are the tastiest and most luscious in the world. Strong sunlight and hot conditions produce sweeter, stronger flavors (indeed, often excessively so) than in temperate zones. The natural conditions change little during the year, usually being hot, bright, and dry, followed by hot, bright, and wet, or by more of the same, rather than the fluctuating heat and light and winter chilling of cooler regions. Tropical plants therefore often set fruit several times a year, or continuously throughout it. Thus tropical fruits are a more reliable source of food than those of cooler areas and less reliance has to be put on storage till the next harvest.

The original species of many tropical fruits have disappeared, to be replaced, even in the wild, by our partially selected stock. This happened far back in prehistory; there is no wild date or banana that corresponds to the cultivated varieties. Many of these long-cultivated plants have been turned into clones, superior varieties propagated vegetatively, often without seed, or not coming true from seed. This handicaps the gardener as only inferior forms can be had from seed; to get better sorts, living plant material has to be obtained. With international restrictions this can be difficult.

However, some tropical fruits are still species, little changed from the original, and useful to the gardener, for if the fruits can be obtained, it may be possible to grow the plant. We can find some fruits in ethnic stores and even occasionally in more adventurous supermarkets. Modern refrigeration and air travel now permit us to enjoy a tremendous range of fresh exotic fruits. The availability and range is constantly extended, but, of course, our predecessors discovered and enjoyed these fruits before us, and they also wanted them back home after travelling abroad.

The first tropical fruits probably reached northern Europe in Roman times, but were then forgotten until rediscovered by late medieval travelers. To be enjoyed fully, many needed to be ripened longer on the plant than early long-distance transport allowed. The colonization of the Canary Islands during the Renaissance enabled exotic fruits to be cultivated within reach of the European market, and this was given further impetus by the newly discovered New World fruits.

These new, expensive, luxury fruits were so desirable that owners of large estates in colder countries encouraged their gardeners to try them even though they needed more than a frost-free greenhouse or simple winter protection to grow, let alone fruit. Surprisingly, just as they had succeeded with orangeries, they met with more success; for example, pineapple plants were grown in Britain as early as 1690. However, it required the Industrial Revolution to provide the iron, glass and heat for serious home production.

The stove house was just that — a large glass greenhouse with a massive stove keeping the temperature tropical; different sections were arid and dry or steamy moist. With steam- or water-heated pipes, the stove could be moved to a separate boiler room. The Victorian age saw British-grown pineapples, bananas and mangosteens gracing many a table. Nothing seemed impossible to these horticultural pioneers.

Along with private extravagance, public botanic gardens were built, and specimens were obtained of many plants. Of course when kept in pots, some grew far too big to be considered. Many were successful, but others could not be persuaded to fruit even in extra heat. Now we are more fortunate: with electric light to supplement sunlight we can give these plants the brightness and day length they need. We also have automatic heat and humidity control, so it is easy to grow many exotic fruits ourselves. And if they still will not fruit, they always make attractive house plants.

PINEAPPLES

Ananas comosus from the family Bromeliaceae

Herbaceous, 3 x 3 ft. Life span: short-lived, perennial. Fruits: average 4 x 8 in., dull orange or yellow. Value: rich in vitamins C and A.

Pineapples need little description; they are the most distinctive of fruits — there is nothing else like them. They are Bromeliads, like many houseplants. They resemble common garden yuccas, being nearly cylindrical with a tuft of narrow, pointed leaves emerging from the top. The skin of the fruit is green to yellow, with many slightly raised protuberances. Wild species have serrated, thorny-edged leaves and set seed. Modern cultivars are seedless, with smoother leaves and smaller fruits; those of traditional varieties weighed up to 20 lb.

Cultivated and selected from the wild by the people of Central America for thousands of years, the fruits were sensational in 1493 to the crew of Columbus. The first fruit, surviving the voyage back, was regarded as nearly as great a discovery as the New World itself. Pineapple motifs appeared, sometimes distorted, throughout European art — often as knobs on pew ends. By 1550 pineapple was being preserved in sugar to be sent back to the Old World as an exotic, and profitable, luxury. By the end of the 16th century pineapples had been spread to China and the Philippines and were naturalizing in Java, and soon after were colonizing the west coast of Africa. An enterprising M. Le Cour of Holland succeeded in growing them under glass in 1686 and was supplying plants to English gardeners in 1690. Within a few years

there was a craze for pineapples, with noblemen's gardeners growing them under glass on deep hotbeds of horse dung and leather wastes as far north as Scotland. The Victorians raised the cultivation of pineapples to a high level with the regulated heat from steam boilers.

 varieties

There have been hundreds of varieties, but most have disappeared as a few commercial cultivars monopolized trade. Pineapples are now grown most intensively in Hawaii, but also in Australia, Malaysia, and South Africa. "Smooth Cayenne," or "Kew Pine," was widely grown for many years, but connoisseurs preferred "Queen" and "Ripley." Long gone is the favorite British hothouse variety "Enville."

 cultivation

A tropical plant, the pineapple is happiest in Hawaii. It needs very high soil and fairly high air temperatures; high humidity during the growing season except when ripening; as much light as possible; and a very

The juice acts as high fiber!

rich, open, fibrous compost in quantity. In plantations pineapples have about a square yard of ground each, so generous pots are required! Never let them chill below 70°F or "cook" above 90°F.

Ornamental Value
They are easy to root and grow as houseplants, but require lots of heat and care to fruit well.

Maintenance
Spring Pot up cuttings and mature plants.
Summer Root cuttings or crowns.
Fall Tidy and dry off plants for winter.
Winter Keep warm!

Propagation
Suckers from healthy plants are best, fruiting in a year and a half or so. Pups, the shoots produced at the bottom of the fruit, seeds, and even stem cuttings can be used, but take longer to grow and fruit. The crown from a fruit is easily rooted; cut it off whole with a thin shoulder, pry off the shoulder, and pull off the lower withered leaves individually. Root over heat in a gritty compost. Keep the foliage moist in a plastic bag, but be careful of mold.

Pruning and Training
Young plants rooted in summer need repotting in spring, growing on for a year and repotting the following spring to fruit that summer or fall. Repot annually, and remove superfluous shoots and fruited stumps if you have any. If happy, pineapples may grow and produce for 5 to 10 years.

PINEAPPLES

Pests and Diseases
The main pests are white scale and mealybugs, controlled by sprays of soft soap or by the use of commercial predators.

 companion planting

A secret of success is apparently to grow pineapples with a light top dressing of banana skins.

 other uses

Pineapple leaves have a strong fiber used for thread and fishing lines and pinya cloth to make the national dress shirt of Filipino men.

Pineapples have many culinary uses, but do not use fresh pineapple in jello as it prevents setting. It can also be used as a meat tenderizer. See below for a recipe suggestion.

 culinary

Picked underripe and kept cool, they can be stored for several weeks. They make tasty jam, delicious juice, and are best known canned. Although a fruit, they add sweetness and texture to many savory dishes, from Chinese to curries, and can even be fried with ham.

Pineapple-baked Ham
Serves 4

1 canned ham
1 large pineapple
Garlic (optional)

Carefully empty the meat from the can in one piece. Using a very sharp knife, carefully extract the pineapple from its skin, first slicing off the top shoulder. Leave the skin intact. (Slice and chill the pineapple flesh for dessert, cutting out the tough central core.) Insert the ham in the hole created, pin the shoulder back on to seal, and bake for at least an hour in a preheated oven at 400°F. (Garlic lovers may rub the ham over before insertion.)

To serve, turn the pineapple on its side to cut circles of ham with a pineapple rind. Serve with pureed corn and baked sweet potatoes.

Musa species from the family Musaceae
BANANAS

Tree/herbaceous plant, 10–30 ft. and nearly as wide. Life span: perpetual as vegetative clones but sterile. Fruits: up to 12 in., green to yellow or red. Value: nutritious and rich in starch.

Banana plants form herbaceous stools of shoots like small trees. Each enormous shoot unfurls sheaths of gigantic, oblong leaves up to 15 ft. long. A mature shoot disgorges one flower stalk, which hangs down under its mighty bunch of many "combs" or "hands" of bananas. The hands point upward, sheltered by succulent, purple bracts the size of plates, along the length of the stalk, and a mass of male flowers adorns the end. One bunch can hold about a dozen combs, each with over a dozen fingers. Bananas are the most productive food crop, giving about 40 times the yield of potatoes. The fruits are green, ripening yellow or red, sweet, notoriously shaped and unforgettably scented.

The Ancient Egyptians had the culinary Abyssinian banana (*Musa ensete*), but early travelers from Europe soon discovered sweeter, more edible bananas in most tropical and semitropical regions. The hardier, the smaller Chinese banana, was brought from the East Indies for cultivation in the Canary Islands by 1516 — and, it has been suggested, was introduced to the Americas from there, but evidence of indigenous bananas discounts this. Most cultivated bananas are probably descendants of *M. sapientum*, *M. acuminata*, and *M. balbisiana*, wild bananas thought to come from eastern Asia and Indo-Malaysia. *Musa maculata* and *M. rosacea* descendants

are popular in parts of Asia and worldwide there exist many other species. In prehistoric cultivation, seed-bearing species were replaced by selected hybrids with big, seedless fruits propagated vegetatively. These superior sorts multiplied and by the 19th century there were countless local varieties of bananas in most hot countries. Many of these have now been lost and replaced by a few high-yielding commercial cultivars.

 ## varieties

Common cultivars are "Robusta," "Lacatan," and "Gros Michel," the latter pair being old varieties that survived the Panama disease that destroyed many. However, they are tall and need hot, moist conditions such as those of Jamaica, where "Gros Michel" was introduced in 1836. The "Chinese Banana" (*M. cavendishii*), also known as "Dwarf" or "Canary Island Banana," is hardier, smaller, and particularly tasty with shorter, delicate fruits, making it widely grown for domestic use, and well suited for greenhouse culture. A new, medium-sized and more productive hybrid, "William," is taking over commercially. Plantains are separate varieties, possibly descendants of *M. paradisiaca*, larger and slightly horn-shaped. Plantains are most often used for cooking, not dessert purposes; thus cooking bananas are sometimes referred to as plantains.

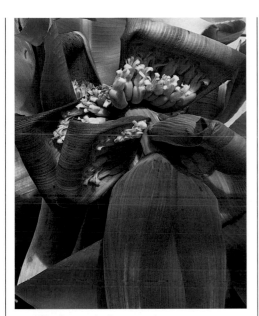

No pollination required or wanted

 cultivation

In warm enough climates bananas need a rich, quite heavy, deep, well-drained soil with copious moisture. Freedom from strong winds is also essential. The smallest varieties are usually planted about 10 ft. apart, the larger proportionately more.

Growing under Glass and in Containers
In cooler climates the "Canary"/"Chinese"/"Cavendish" is best, as it is very compact and fruits at less than 10 ft. Keep the temperature above 65°F in winter and under 85°F in summer. Potted plants can go out for summer.

Maintenance
Spring Repot or top dress, thin, and root suckers.
Summer Top dress, thin suckers.
Fall Cut fruits, remove old shoot, thin suckers.
Winter Keep warm.

Propagation
Some ornamental and inferior varieties grow from seed. The best edible plants are bits of rhizome with a bud or sterile hybrids, propagated by suckers. Viable buds will resemble enormous, sprouting bulbs. They root easily in a gritty compost over heat in a moist atmosphere.

 culinary

Bananas are best matured off the tree and kept in a warm room. Most are at their best when yellow. They can be dried, made into flour, or fermented to produce a sweet liqueur.

In hot countries, bananas are a staple food, being used as a vegetable and a source of flour, as well as a fruit.

Banana Custard Pie
Serves 4

6 oz. graham crackers
⅓ cup butter, melted
1 tablespoon strawberry jam
1¼ cups milk
1 tablespoon honey
1 tablespoon cornstarch
Dash of vanilla extract
3 or 4 bananas, sliced and chilled
Grated nutmeg

Crush the graham crackers and mix with most of the butter. Press into a pie dish and freeze. Spread the frozen surface with the remaining butter, paint with the jam and refreeze. Heat the milk and honey, mix

the cornstarch with a drop of water and the vanilla, then pour the hot milk on to the flour mixture. Return to the heat, stirring continuously, until thickened, then allow to cool. Put chilled banana slices into the cooled custard, mix together and pour into the biscuit case. Top with grated nutmeg and chill until required.

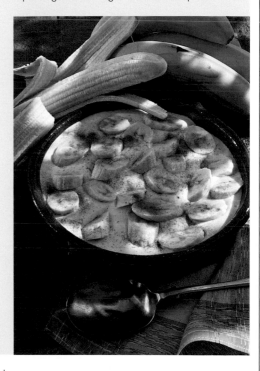

Pruning and Training
Bananas fruit continuously if growing happily. A stem will flower and fruit in about a year and a half. Only one main shoot and a replacement are allowed; all others should be removed, and once the main shoot has fruited it is cut out. The clump or stool may live as long as a human being, but is replaced commercially every dozen years or so.

Pests and Diseases
No major problems for private gardeners.

 other uses

Often used in beauty preparations and shampoos. The foliage will provide good animal fodder.

My plastic tunnel is not quite tall enough

Phoenix dactylifera from the family Arecaceae

DATE PALMS

Tree 80 x 20 ft. Life span: as long as a human being. Fruits: just under 1 x 2 in., blue, brown, or yellow. Value: rich in vitamins A, B1, and B2, and some B3.

Date palms are tall trees with ferny leaves, the russet dead leaf bases protecting the trunk. Separate male and female plants are required for fruiting, which is prolific. Each tree annually bears several bunches of three or four dozen strings, each string carrying two or three dozen dates, the total weight being up to 150 lb.

Dates have been cultivated in the Middle East for at least 4,000 years and all wild forms have disappeared. They have always

been one of the staple foods of the Arab peoples, much of whose lives were centered around the oases where the palms were found.

 culinary

Soft dates are partly dried, pitted, and pressed into cakes, then exported all over the world. Semi-soft dates are those we see at Christmas. Dry dates are hard, ground to a flour, and commonly found only in Arab markets. Dates can be used in cakes, cookies, and confectionery and with curries and savory dishes. They are also made into wine.

Stuffed Date Chocolates

28 dates
8 oz. real marzipan
5 squares of dark chocolate, melted
Powdered sugar

Pit the dates and stuff with marzipan. Dip in melted chocolate and cool on a tray dusted with powdered sugar.

 varieties

Numerous local varieties exist. "Deglet Noor" is from north Africa and is the world's most popular variety. "Saidi" is the common date; "Fardh" is favorite in Arabia, "Weddee" a feed date for donkeys and camels, "Farayah" a choice, long blue.

 cultivation

One of the few crops to revel in hot, even scorching, dry places, date palms still need irrigation to fruit well but can use brackish water. Date palms can be grown only in Zones 9 and 10.

Growing under Glass and in Containers
They are well suited to indoor life, though they may find it too humid with other fruits, and they get too big and need too much heat to produce good fruit. Date palms are easy to distribute as the small rootballs transplant with ease.

Ornamental and Wildlife Value

Choice ornamentals, they are popular in hotter climates both with people and wildlife. Birds love the fruits.

Propagation
For choice fruit, offshoots or suckers have to be potted up; however, for ornamental use, seedlings are easily germinated but grow slowly. Large trees are easily transplanted with small rootballs. One male will be needed to every fifty females.

 other uses

The palms have their sap extracted for sugar or fermenting. They may also be used as lumber.

Persea americana from the family Lauraceae
AVOCADOS
ALLIGATOR PEAR, VEGETABLE MARROW

Tree up to 30 x 20 ft. Life span: short, self-fertile. Fruits: 6 x 3 in., green. Value: rich in fats, proteins, vitamins A, B, and C, and thiamine.

This subtropical tree from Central America was originally introduced to Europe by the conquistadores and has since been planted in many parts of the world. Its anglicized name is a corruption of the Aztec word ahuacatl, which was used to describe both its fruit and the testicle. There are three main races: Guatemalan fruits are large with a warty skin, Mexican ones are small, and large, smooth-skinned types come from the West Indies. All have been hybridized, producing hundreds of cultivars suitable for Mediterranean to tropical climates.

varieties

"Ettinger" (Mexican x Guatemalan) produces oblong fruit with bright green, shiny skin. "Fuerte" (Mexican x Gutaemalan) is the most common cultivar, producing large fruit with green, textured skin. "Hass" (Guatemalan) is self-fertile, the skin dark purple when it is mature.

cultivation

Avocados flourish in shelter and sunshine. The ideal soil is a slightly acid, moisture-retentive, free-draining loam. Temperatures should be between 68–82°F with humidity greater than 60 percent all year round. Some can withstand down to 48°F. Allow 20 ft. between the trees and the rows. In exposed areas, plant windbreaks to prevent damage. During the growing season, apply 3 lb. to 4½ lb of general fertilizer in two or three doses. Mulch around the base to suppress weeds. Water during times of drought until trees are established.

Shape young trees to ensure a balanced crown. Remove diseased, damaged or crossing branches after fruiting. They withstand hard pruning. Plant several cultivars with overlapping or simultaneous flowering periods to produce fruit.

Growing under Glass
Grow in a greenhouse, maintaining moderate temperatures and humidity according to the cultivar. Flowers and fruit are rarely produced in cool temperate zones due to low light intensity and reduced daylight hours.

Growing in Containers
Repot young plants as the compost becomes congested. Every 2–3 years repot into a pot one size larger, using a loam-based potting mix with moderate fertilizer levels. Top-dress in the intervening years by removing the top 2–3 in. in the spring. Apply a general fertilizer every 2–3 weeks when plants are actively growing. Water as the compost surface dries out. Reduce watering in winter and do not feed. In spring, prune side branches to encourage bushy growth. During winter, they need a light, cool position with temperatures no lower than 60°F.

Maintenance
Spring Repot containerized plants.
Summer Feed, harvest, and water as necessary.
Fall Bring plants indoors in cool temperate zones.
Winter Reduce watering and stop feeding avocados.

Propagation, Pruning and Training
Avocados are propagated from seed. Choose healthy seeds, cut ½ in. from the pointed end, and dip in fungicide. Sow in a 6 in. pot of moist potting mix, with

culinary

Coat cut surfaces with lemon or lime juice to prevent discoloration. Avocado is delicious simply with olive oil and vinaigrette. The flavor also blends well with shrimp, crabmeat, and other seafood, or grapefruit and pineapple. Try it with bacon in a sandwich, or made into a fine salad.

Avocado Dip/Guacamole
Serves 6

3 avocados
1 large hard-boiled egg
1 plum tomato, skinned and seeded
1 small sweet red bell pepper
3 scallions
1 or more garlic cloves (optional)
1 tablespoon lemon or lime juice
Dribble of olive oil
Salt and pepper in moderation
A little ground coriander
As much chili powder as you like

Scoop out the flesh of the chilled avocados and blend with all the other ingredients. Chill and serve with crudités.

the cut end just above the surface. Germinate in a greenhouse or propagator and put in a bright position away from direct sunshine at 70–80°F. When the fourth leaf appears, remove from the propagator and leave for 2 weeks to acclimatize. Allow the stone to rot away from the roots. When they outgrow 12–16 in. pots, plant out into their final positions.

Harvesting and storing
Seed-raised trees fruit after 5 to 7 years; grafted plants 3 to 5 years. Remove fruit carefully using hand pruners.

Pests and Diseases
Use resistant rootstocks against avocado root rot. Those grown indoors may be attacked by whitefly: use sticky traps, the predator *Encarsia formosa*, or soft soap. Control red spider mite by maintaining humidity, and remove mealybugs by dabbing them with a paintbrush dipped in denatured alcohol.

Mangifera indica **from the family Anacardiaceae**

MANGO

Tree, variable size. Life span: as long as a human being. Fruits: variable in size, flat ovoids, green/yellow or red. Value: rich in vitamins A, B, and C.

Medium to large trees, with luxuriant masses of narrow leaves, these carry fruits that weigh anything from a few ounces to a couple of pounds. They have an inedible, tough skin, and an enormous, flat stone to which the fibrous flesh adheres.

Mangoes are native to India and exist there in countless variety. Doubtless early Europeans came across them, but they were first recorded by a Friar Jordanus in about 1300. Mangoes have now spread to most hot regions, including Florida.

 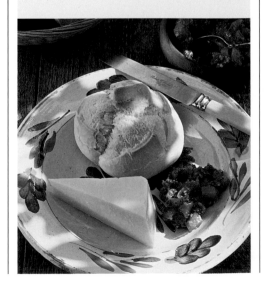

harvesting and storing, culinary

Mangoes soften and turn yellow, red, or purple as they ripen. Picked unripe, they travel well and are fine for culinary use. They are very messy to eat raw! They are widely used for chutneys, jams, pies, pickles and preserves.

Mango Chutney
Makes about 2 lb.

2 lb. green mangoes
¾ cup salt
2 cups vinegar
12 garlic cloves, peeled and chopped
½ cup golden raisins
¼ cup chopped dates
¼ cup blanched almonds
3-in. piece fresh ginger, chopped
2 teaspoons hot chili powder
2¼ cups brown sugar

Peel, pit, and chop the mangoes, sprinkle them with salt and keep cool overnight. Rinse and drain thoroughly. Mix all the ingredients except the sugar and simmer for several hours till soft. Add the sugar, bring to a boil, and bottle in a clean sterilized jar. Store for 6 months before use.

 ## varieties

India's favorite varieties are "Alphonso" and "Mulgoa." The West Indies prefer "Bombay" ("Peters") and "Julie." American varieties include anthracnose-resistant "Keitt"; the Hawaiian standard, "Haden"; small, purple-skinned "Manzanillo"; and the fall-ripening "Brooks Late."

 ## cultivation

Mangoes want a hot, dryish climate and deep, well-drained, rich soils. Excessive rain spoils pollination They want exceptionally deep and wide planting holes dug about 30 ft. apart. Mangoes will thrive only in Zone 10.

Growing under Glass and in Containers
As they are large when fruitful, the greenhouse would have to be big. They may be grown in pots for ornamental use but fruiting success seems unlikely.

Propagation
Mangoes raised from seed are often polyembryonic, giving several seedlings. Some are near-clones of the original, and some produce poor fruits with stringy texture and a turpentine taint! The best varieties are grafted or layered and will bear in about 4 years.

Young fruits are often pulled — but not this young

Pruning and Training
Remedial pruning of thin and poor growth is necessary once a head has formed, plus root pruning if the tree persists with strong, unfruitful growth.

 ## other uses

The seeds have been boiled and eaten in famines. The wood is poor, but used for packaging crates and firewood.

PAPAYAS

Carica from the family Caricaceae

Herbaceous, up to 20 ft. Life span: very short. Fruits: up to 12 x 6 in. Value: rich in papain, calcium, and in vitamins A and C.

Papayas (also known as pawpaws) are small herbaceous "trees" that resemble palms as they are unbranched with ornate, acanthus-like foliage clustered on top and up to 50 green "melons" underneath. There are male, female, and hermaphrodite plants. The fruits uncannily resemble melons, turning yellow-orange as they ripen. The flesh is usually pink with a central hole full of small round seeds and can weigh up to 5 lb.

Although it is indigenous to Central America, the papaya has rapidly spread to every warm country. Seeds were sent to Nepal as early as 1626 from the East Indies.

 ## varieties

"Solo" is a commercial dwarf, but most papayas are local varieties selected from seed and varying considerably. Grow them from fruit you like. *Carica candamarcensis*, or the Mountain Papaya, is hardier with coarser leaves and smaller fruit, which have blunt ridges and an applelike aroma. They are too acid to eat raw, but good cooked or as jam.

 ## cultivation

Papayas prefer deep, humus-rich soil, and to be planted about 10 ft. apart. They need support while young. You should eliminate most males and replace the whole lot every 5 years. Papayas are only successful in Zone 10.

Growing under Glass and in Containers
They are practical for tall, heated greenhouses, and highly ornamental, so also well worth growing as pot plants, but they do not fruit well easily.

Ornamental and Wildlife Value
Their foliage is very attractive and they're so easy to grow.

Propagation
Variable from seed; usually grown by sowing several to a hole and eliminating the poorest seedlings. (Only one male is needed to 50 females, but in fact they can be differentiated only when flowering.) Fruiting occurs within a year.

 ## other uses

Papain, the active ingredient, is used medicinally, and for chewing gum.

 ## culinary

Papayas are in season all year, and unripe ones keep for many days. Eaten as dessert or cooked as a side dish, papaya is delicious, especially the first time. However, most important, the fruit and leaves contain papain, which tenderizes meats cooked with them.

Papaya Breakfast Juice
Serves 2

1 ripe papaya
juice of 1 small lime
honey or sugar to taste

Scoop out the flesh and sift out the seeds of the papaya. Add lime juice and sweetener and liquidize. Serve immediately in frosted glasses with sugared rims as breakfast starters.

Psidium and *Acca* from the family Myrtaceae
GUAVAS
AND FEIJOAS

Tree 10–30 ft. Life span: short. Fruits: 2–3 in., yellow or red. Value: very rich in vitamin A and C, pectin, iron, potassium, and calcium.

Guavas are small trees or spreading shrubs with leathery leaves. The bark peels off the smooth, ruddy branches in flakes. The fruits are round, ripening from green to yellow or red, full of acid yellow or red pulp and many hard, round seeds.

Native to tropical America, guavas soon became popular the world over and were grown in orangeries.

 harvesting and storing, culinary

Guavas are best fresh off the tree, or picked early, as they soften. They are good for dessert, and cooked as pies, jam, and, of course, the jelly.

Guava Jelly
Makes approx. 4 lb.

2 lb. guavas
1 large lemon
Approx. 4 cups sugar

Simmer the washed, chopped guavas for 2 hours with a little water. Strain, measure, and bring back to the boil. Add the same volume of sugar and the juice of the lemon, reboil, pour into warmed sterilized jars, and seal.

 varieties

There are many species of guavas. *P. guajava* is the most common with yellow fruits. Many varieties of it are pyriferum — bearing somewhat pear-like fruits, which are a little acid and better for cooking. Some varieties are pomiferum, bearing apple-shaped fruits which are thought better. For dessert, gourmets choose *P. cattleianum*, the Strawberry Guava. This has a reddish-purple, plum-size, sweeter fruit on a hardier, shaggy-barked tree. *P. araca, P. montanum, P. pigmeum* and *P. polycarpon* are all reputed more delicious still. *Acca sellowiana* a.k.a. Feijoa is so similar as to be a variety of guava. It is smaller, with crimson and white flowers and fragrant fruit. It is hardy to Zone 8 and not self-fertile, and grown in California. Feijoas are rich sources of vitamin C.

 cultivation

Any good soil and a sunny site is all they require. In a warm climate they are normally planted at about 15 ft. apart. Tropical guavas thrive in Zone 10; strawberry guava in Zones 9 and 10. Feijoas are more

tolerant of cold and will grow in Zones 8 through 10, and possibly in Zone 7.

Growing under Glass and in Containers
Feijoa is most reliable, the "Strawberry Guava" next, but all guavas are easily grown under glass and/or confined in pots. They can be put outdoors during the warmer months of the year.

Propagation, Pruning and Training
Propagate by seeds for the species but also by suckers, layers, or grafts for better varieties. Some plants occasionally produce seedless fruits: note these and propagate from them. Nip out top shoots to promote bushiness; otherwise prune only remedially.

 other uses

The heavy wood is used for agricultural implements. The leaves and bark are a native cure for dysentery.

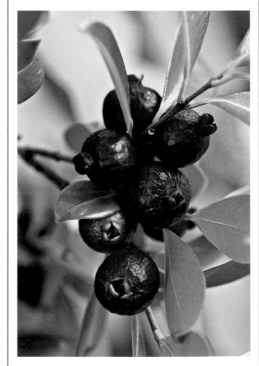

Strawberry guava — it really does taste of strawberry!

Artocarpus from the family Moraceae

BREADFRUIT
AND JACKFRUIT

Trees up to 90 ft. Life span: medium. Fruits: up to 8 in. diameter, leathery balls. Value: mostly starch.

Both breadfruit and jackfruit are attractive, tall trees with large, deeply incised leaves. From the branch ends hang green, round to ovoid fruits, which have a thin, warty rind and are white and starchy within. Some have about 200 fleshy edible seeds or more, some have none.

Breadfruit are native to the Pacific and East Indies; jackfruit come from the Asian mainland and Indian subcontinent. They were first noted in the voyages of the 16th century and soon taken to other hot regions, but never proved really popular. Breadfruit plants being taken to the West Indies played a part in the famous 1787 mutiny on *The Bounty*. When the water supply ran low, the valuable cargo was given water in preference to the crew.

 varieties

Artocarpus communis (*incisa* or *altilis*) is the Breadfruit proper, bearing a remarkable resemblance, once cooked, to bread. From the West Indies comes the Bread-nut Tree, which, when cooked, is claimed to rival a new loaf in both taste and texture. *A. integrifolia* (*heterophylla*) is the Jackfruit or Jakfruit. The fruit is much bigger, weighing up to 65 lb. These fruits strangely spring from older branches and direct from the trunk. When ripe they have a strong odor of very ripe melon.

A. odoratissima, the "Johore Jack" is smaller and esteemed for its sweetness and flavor.

 cultivation

Any reasonable soil and site in a hot and moist climate. They grow in Zone 10.

Growing under Glass and in Containers
The size of the fruiting tree makes it impractical to grow these in pots or under glass except for ornamental value.

Propagation, Pruning, and Training
They can be propagated by seed, but the best varieties come only by root suckers or by layering. Little pruning is required except remedial.

Harvesting and Storing
Breadfruit are eaten fresh after cooking, but used to be stored in pits where the pulp was fermented to make a nauseous soft "cheese," which would keep for several years.

 companion planting

The jackfruit tree is used to support pepper (*Piper nigrum*) and as a shade tree for coffee plantations.

 other uses

Jackfruit wood is like mahogany, valuable and useful. A yellow dye for clothing is extracted from the wood in India and the East. Breadfruit wood is light and used for box manufacture, and in Hawaii for surfboards.

 culinary

Breadfruit are usually eaten roasted, boiled or fried as a vegetable. The edible seeds are often preferred, when they occur. Jackfruit are eaten in the same way and have a stronger flavor. Breadfruit can be dried and ground to a flour offensive to some and may also be eaten raw, in soups or even ice cream.

Baked Breadfruit
Serves 2

Bake a breadfruit in a preheated oven at 190°C/375°F, until you can push a knife through it easily. Extract the pulp, seeds and all, and serve with curry or a savory sauce.

DURIANS
CIVET FRUIT

Durio zibethinus from family Malvaceae/Bombacaceae

Tree 100 ft. Life span: fairly long. Fruits: about 10 x 8 in., ovoid, green to yellow. Value: a little protein, a little fat; one-quarter to one third is fat and starch.

This is an infamous fruit, banned from airlines and loathed by most people on first acquaintance. It has an aroma similar to that of an overripe Gorgonzola cheese in a warm room. The flavor was long ago described as "French custard passed through a sewer pipe". The texture is like that of blancmange or custard, and the sweet flavor delicious and addictive. Once bravely tasted, the durian is unforgettable and "the sensation is worth a voyage to the East."

The trees are very large and upright with leaves not dissimilar to those of a peach. The fruits are round to ovoid, very large, weighing up to 10 lb., green initially, yellowing as they ripen, with a long stalk. They are covered in short, sharp spikes and resemble some brutal medieval weapon. The pulp is white with up to a dozen big seeds.

Durians come originally from Malaysia and spread to Southeast Asia in prehistoric times. Widely grown all over the region, they have never managed to become more than a curiosity elsewhere.

 ## harvesting and storing, culinary

Durians must be eaten fresh and they quickly spoil due to a chemical change (and the aroma gets worse!). They are best eaten raw but may be made into ice cream or jam, or juiced and drunk with coconut milk. The large, fleshy seeds are boiled or roasted and eaten as nuts.

Durian Delight
Serves 6

1 cup each unsweetened durian purée
½ cup honey,
1¼ cups yogurt
1 cup heavy cream
Dash of vanilla extract

Mix the ingredients and beat till smooth. Partially freeze, beat again and repeat this two or three times before freezing firm. Keep well sealed until immediately before eating!

 ## varieties

Local varieties exist with variation in size, shape, and flavor, but no widespread commercial clones are currently available.

 ## cultivation

The large trees need a deep, heavy soil to secure them, but they are not too difficult to please. They will grow in Zone 10.

Propagation, Pruning, and Training
Seeds, if fresh, germinate in about a week and come nearly true. Only remedial pruning work is necessary.

Growing under Glass and in Containers
Their size and their need for tropical heat and moisture make them difficult. They may make good pot specimens if fresh seed can be obtained.

Ornamental and Wildlife Value
Attractive trees in their native climate.

 ## other uses

Durians help get railway compartments to oneself. They are also reputed to be an aphrodisiac.

They can be located by the nose alone

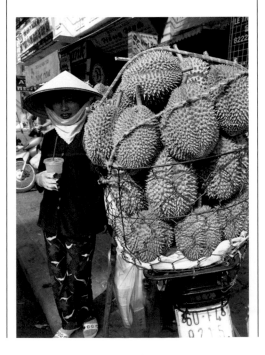

CHERIMOYAS
CUSTARD APPLES AND SOURSOPS

Annona from the family Annonaceae

Tree up to 20 ft. Life span: short. Fruits: variable in size, green and scaly. Value: all varieties rich in vitamins.

A family of small trees, known as custard apples or soursops, from the flavor and texture of the better fruits. Many have aromatic leaves and/or fragrant flowers. Despite the varying appearance of each species, the common names are often swapped or confused in different countries. The flesh is usually white, sweet, and acid, with up to 30 black seeds embedded in it and covered with a thin rind, which breaks off like scales when ripe.

Natives of the Americas, they are most popular there but have spread to other tropical and warm zones. They are grown in Madeira and the Canaries for the European trade.

other uses

Corossol tea was traditionally made from the leaves of *A. muricata.*

harvesting and storing, culinary

Picked underripe they keep for up to a week or so. They are usually eaten raw or used to flavor drinks and ices.

Soursop Sorbet
Serves 6

2 cups sugar
1 large ripe soursop
3-in. piece crystallized ginger

Dissolve the sugar in 2 cups of boiling water and chill. Squeeze the juice from the soursop pulp and strain. To each cupful add half a cup of sugar syrup. Partly freeze, beat, and refreeze. Repeat twice. After the final beating, mix in the chopped ginger.

varieties

Annona squamosa is the true Custard Apple or Sweet Sop, and is most common in the West Indies.
A. cherimolia is the Cherimoya. This is deciduous, more hardy, growing at high elevations in hotter areas
A. muricata, or Soursop, is evergreen with leaves that smell of black currants and large (up to 8 lb.) green fruits with soft spines in ridges and a sourer taste.
A. reticulata is the Bullock's Heart, so-called because of its ruddy color. It it has firm, sweet, yellow pulp rich in vitamin A. Numerous other species are grown all over the Americas.

cultivation

They will thrive in poor soils but give better crops with better treatment and prefer dryish, hilly conditions. They will grow in Zone 10.

Growing under Glass and in Containers
The cherimoya is worth growing even if it never fruits and custard apples are probably worth trying. Sour sops may not crop, but all are good value as pot specimens.

Propagation, Pruning and Training
They grow from seed, but best varieties are budded. Only remedial pruning and nipping out is required.

Averrhoa carambola from the family Oxalidaceae
STAR FRUIT

Tree up to 35 ft. Life span: medium. Fruits: up to 2 x 6 in. Cylindrical, star-shaped in cross section, yellow. Value: vitamins A and C.

Averrhoas are small trees with delicate, pinnate (walnutlike) foliage. A profusion of sprays of little white or pinkish flowers is followed by huge quantities of yellow, cylindrical, star-shaped fruits with five prominent angles, which weigh down the branches.

Natives of Indonesia and the Moluccas, averrhoas are still mostly grown in Southeast Asia and the Indian subcontinent. However, because of their decorative value, and being quite robust, they are now exported and appear almost everywhere.

harvesting and storing, culinary

They travel fairly well if picked just underripe and then keep for a week or two. Carambolas are more often used for making jelly and preserves than as dessert fruits. Their star shape makes excellent decorative garnishes in compotes and fruit salads. "Billings" are used for pickles and preserves and Billings jam is made after soaking overnight and straining to remove the acid bitterness. The flowers of both species were once made into conserves.

Camaranga or Carambola Jam
Makes about 4 lb.

2 lb. carambolas
4 cups white sugar

Cut the fruit up into finger-thick pieces and discard the sharp edges. Do not discard the seeds, as they improve the flavor. Add water to cover and boil until softening — about 15 minutes should be sufficient. Add the sugar and bring to a boil again for another 15 minutes, then bottle, and seal.

varieties

Carambolas are variable in taste. Some are much better than others, though they are all juicy. I have eaten them from European supermarkets, when they tasted like yellow soap, and also fresh, when they were amber and a joy. *Averrhoa bilimbi* or Billings are similar, resembling gherkin cucumbers, but are used more as vegetables and in curries, and for the popular billings jam.

cultivation

Adaptable to most warm, moist climates, and any reasonable, well-drained soil, they fruit prolifically with little attention. They will grow in Zone 10.

Ornamental and Wildlife Value
Burdened with yellow fruit, they are impressive.

Growing under Glass and in Containers
Carambolas are pretty plants, so make good specimens. If they fruit they will put on a terrific show.

Propagation
Usually they are grown from seed, but better varieties are grafted. Only remedial pruning is needed.

other uses

Carambola juice removes stains from linen and can be used for polishing brass. "Billings" also polishes brass.

SAPODILLAS

Achras sapota/Manilkara zapota from the family Sapotaceae

OR SAPOTAS, NASEBERRIES, BULLY TREES, CHIKKUS

Tree 14–52 ft. Life span: medium. Fruits: about 2½ in., rounded, brown.

Sapodilla makes a medium to big tree with glossy leaves. The fruit is a large, round berry with a rough, brown skin over luscious pulp similar to a pear's, containing a core with up to a dozen seeds much like an apple's — black, shiny, and inedible. The tree's milky sap can be tapped in the same way as rubber. Once collected, it is coagulated with heat and the sticky mass produced is strained out and dried to form chicle gum.

Still mostly grown in its native region of Central America, sapodilla is found wild in the forests of Venezuela. Sapodillas were more extensively planted when chicle gum started to be used for a booming new commodity — chewing gum. Now it is an important crop for Mexico and Central American countries. The naseberry is Jamaica's national fruit.

One of the great unknowns

 ## companion planting

Sapodilla trees are normally grown for the first 5 years with underplanted legume crops.

 ## other uses

Sapodilla wood is hard and durable, so it is used for handles and tools.

 ## culinary

Perfectly ripened, they are considered superb dessert fruit. The fruits keep up to a month or more in a cold refrigerator.

Chewing Gum

*4 oz. each of chicle gum, glucose, caramel
    paste, powdered sugar
1 cup sugar
Spearmint or mint flavoring, to taste*

Melt the gum carefully in a double boiler. Meanwhile boil ½ cup water, the sugar and glucose to exactly 255°F. Remove from the heat, add the caramel, and boil again. Off the heat, mix the syrup into the melted gum, beating steadily and briskly. Add the flavoring and pour on to a cold surface thickly coated with powdered sugar. Roll flat. When cold, cut into strips, wrap and label.

 ## varieties

Local varieties are cultivated for fruit, but there is little commercial demand, as it must be eaten absolutely ripe. However, there is a big demand for chicle gum; varieties selected for sap production can give up to 6½ lb. of gum per year.

 ## cultivation

Sapodilla prefers very hot, moist climates with rich soil. They will grow in Zone 10.

Propagation, Pruning and Training
Propagate by seed or preferably by grafting for better varieties. Only remedial pruning work seems necessary.

Growing under Glass and in Containers
The trees are variable in size and unlikely to crop well under glass, but they are attractive so should make good specimen pot plants.

Ornamental and Wildlife Value
Sapodilla has very attractive foliage and the fruits are enjoyed by wildlife.

Harvesting and Storing
Best finally ripened off the tree, when the fruit softens and mellows in a few days to a treacly, gummy consistency. Left on the tree, the fruits become veined with milk, which makes them too acid until bletted like medlars (see p. 577).

Nephelium lappaceum and *N. chinensis/litchi* from the family Sapindaceae

RAMBUTANS AND LITCHIS

Tree up to 60 ft. Life span: medium to long. Usually not self-fertile; male and female flowers often on separate trees. Fruits: 1–2 in., round, reddish or yellow.

Rambutan or ramtum trees are large and spreading, with pinnate leaves, and festooned with hairy, chestnut-like conkers. These fruits are apricot-sized, covered with red or orange-yellow soft spines like tentacles. Underneath the skin the flesh is wrapped around the single, inedible, brown seed. The flesh is sweet, acid, almost like pineapple with a hint of apricot — shame there is so little, as it is one of the best fruits I've ever tried.

Very similar yet more perfumed are litchees, lychees or litchis. These have a prickly, crackly shell and grow on a smaller tree. Originally from the Malay archipelago, rambutans are greatly appreciated in Southeast Asia where they are often grown in gardens, but, surprisingly, have never proved popular anywhere else. Litchis have long been a Chinese speciality, so they followed their people to many other suitable areas, such as Florida.

culinary uses

Litchis are often preserved in syrup or dried to perfumed "prunes". All the fruits are superb desserts. Litchis are often used to close a Chinese meal.

Litchi Sundae
Serves 4 to 6

4 cups litchis
2 cups vanilla ice cream
¼ cup blanched toasted almonds
Nutmeg
¼ cup coarse brown sugar
4 to 6 glacé cherries

Peel and pit the litchis, then chill them. Layer the fruit in tall glasses with ice cream and almonds and top with a flourish of nutmeg, sugar, and a cherry.

varieties

Many different varieties of rambutan and litchi are grown in their regions. The Pulassan, *Nephelium mutabile/chryseum*, is another species; native to Java It is similar but covered with warts instead of tentacles. *N. longana/Dimocarpus longan*, the Longan, is popular in Southern China; it is smaller, browny yellow and nearly smooth skinned with similar chewy flesh.

cultivation

They need tropical conditions. Litchis prefer lower humidity, rambutans more. They will grow in Zone 10.

Growing under Glass and in Containers

Sadly they are too large. They may possibly do as pot specimens for foliage, but are unlikely to fruit.

Ornamental and Wildlife Value
The fruit is exceptionally attractive to birds and also bats.

Propagation, Pests and Diseases
They come nearly true from seed, but the best varieties are budded. Bird and bat damage is a severe problem.

Harvesting and Storing
Both will ripen if picked early off the tree, so they are often found in temperate country shops. .

MANGOSTEEN

Garcinia mangostana **from the family Clusiaceae (Guttifereae)**

Tree 45 ft. Life span: long. Fruits: 2½ in., round, brownish. Value: small amounts of protein, mineral matter, and fat; approx. one-seventh sugar and starch.

The trees are small to medium-sized, cone-shaped, and have large, leathery leaves somewhat like a lemon's. The fruits are round, purplish-brown, about apple size, with a rosette of dead petals around the stalk and an odd flower-shaped button on the other end. If you cut the rind around the fruit's circumference, the top can be lifted off to reveal about half a dozen kernels of melting white pulp, tasting between grape and strawberry, tart and sweet, almost syrupy, and chewy. There is a seed contained in many kernels, which is not eaten.

Mangosteens are natives of Malaya and were described by Captain Cook in 1770 in detail, and with delight. They were introduced to Ceylon (now Sri Lanka) in 1800 and were successfully fruited in English greenhouses in 1855. Widely held to be the world's most delicious fruit, they may be found in gardens in every tropical area, but are nowhere grown on a commercial scale.

Not all segments have seeds

 ## varieties

There are many local varieties and also close relations, most of which are found in the East Indies. *Garcinia cambogia* has a smaller, yellow-pulped, yellow fruit. *G. cowa* is the Cowa-Mangosteen. Bigger, ribbed and apricot-colored, it is generally too acid for dessert but makes good preserves. Another, *G. indica*, the Cocum, Conca or Kokum, has a sour, purple pulp used to make a vinegar, and the seeds are pressed for cocum oil. *G. dulcis* is a yellow-fruited variety found in the Moluccas. *G. morella* is common in Southeast Asia and the plant also provides an orange-red resin, gamboge.

 ## cultivation

Mangosteens need deep, rich, well-drained soil, a sheltered site, shade when young, a hot, moist climate. They will grow in Zone 10.

Growing under Glass and in Containers

If it can be done in England in the mid-19th century, it can be done now.

Propagation

They are slow and unreliable from seed. They are then slow-growing, reaching only to the knee after 2 or 3 years. The best varieties are layered.

 ## companion planting

Mangosteens prefer tropically bright but not direct light, so they are planted in the shade of taller trees.

 ## harvesting and storing, culinary

Use a ladder to climb up and pick mangosteens as they bruise if they fall. They can be picked unripe and kept for a few days or may be made into conserves.

Mangosteen Ecstasy

If you are fortunate enough to have a mangosteen, just eat it!

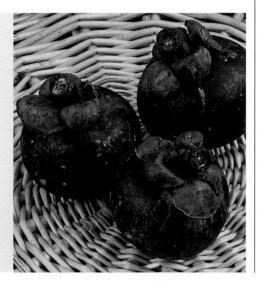

TRAVELERS' TALES TROPICAL FRUITS

There are many more fruits the inveterate traveler may come across in tropical and semi-tropical countries. Some of these are of more practical or commercial interest, such as the spices, while others are of such purely local interest they are rarely if ever recorded. Many may be unknown, as they are unpalatable by "modern" standards, or they may be delicious but hard to cultivate. As we move into a homogenized world of mass consumption, the numbers of varieties of even the most popular fruits is declining. Quaint, difficult and unusual fruits have already disappeared from all but local native markets and botanic and private gardens. If you travel far off the beaten track, you may come across the following, and others — but, when choosing to taste them, do not rely on my identification.

Aberia gardneri,
"Ceylon Gooseberry," Bixinea
Native to what is now Sri Lanka, this is a small, shrubby tree with large, purple-brown, round berries mostly used for making jams and preserves. Closely related is *A. caffra*, the Kai, Kau or Kei Apple of South Africa, which is yellow and so acid it is used as a pickle, omitting the vinegar.

Baccaurea dulcis/Pierardia motleyana,
Rambeh or Rambei, Euphorbiaceae
Found in Malaysia, especially Sumatra, and China, this has long, hanging bunches of large, yellow berries that are reputedly sweet-tasting, juicy and luscious.

Bactris/Guillielma utilis,
Peach Nut or Pewa, Palmaceae
A native of Central America, similar to a date palm, this has fruits like large dates. Usually cooked in salted water before eating, they taste of chestnuts. The best varieties are seedless. Other relations are the Prickly Palm, *B. major*, and the Tobago Palm, *B. minor*.

Blighia sapida,
Akee, Sapindaceae
A medium-sized tree from West Africa, grown in the West Indies, especially Jamaica, where the fruit, fried in butter, is considered excellent fare. The fruits are bright red, heart-shaped pods (see image above), which burst to reveal three glossy, black seeds the size of peas sitting in a yellowish cup, which is the tasty bit. The seeds are inedible, the pink flesh highly poisonous and even the edible bit is poisonous if under- or over-ripe. One wonders how this ever became popular!

Borassis flabellifer,
Borassus or Palmyra palm, Palmaceae
A tall palm like a date palm but with a shorter, fan-shaped leaves. It is widely distributed in the drier regions of Africa and Asia. The fruits contain much sap. This is also tapped from the trunk for boiling down into sugar or for fermenting.

Carissa grandiflora,
Natal Plum, Apocynaceae
This and *Carissa carandas* are large, thorny shrubs used as hedges in Natal. They have purple, damson-like fruits tasting of gooseberry which are widely used for pies and preserves. *C. carandas*, which is also used for pickling, prefers drier areas.

Chrysophylum cainito,
Star Apple, Sapotaceae
Noted by Cieza de León in Peru in 1532–50, this is a large, evergreen tree with purple-brown "apples", which, when cut through, have a star shape in the middle with about half a dozen shiny, brown seeds in a sweet/acid pulp.

Coccoloba uvifera,
Seagrape, Polygonaceae
A colonizer of tropical shores, this is a very salt-tolerant, small, evergreen shrub or tree found from Florida to Venezuela. The "grapes" are up to half an inch across, mild and sweet. They are eaten raw or jellied. The wood is hard and takes a polish well. It is often used as hedging or for good windbreaks.

Eugenia caryophyllus

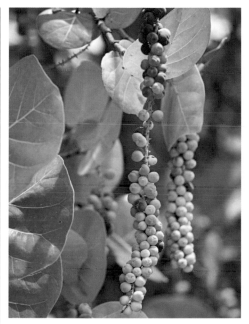

Coccoloba uvifera

Eugenia caryophyllus,
Cloves, Myrtaceae
Cloves are the dried flower-buds of this Indonesian tree. Other *Eugenia* species such as the Malay Apple, *E. Malaccensis*, the Rose Apple, *E. Jambos,* and the Surinam Cherry, *E. uniflora*, have edible fruits varying from yellow to red and purple. They are eaten raw and made into jams and liquers in tropical and subtropical countries.

Mimusops elengi,
Sapotaceae
This large East Asian tree has fragrant flowers. The 1 in. yellow berries are eaten when ripe and an oil is expressed from the seed. Other Mimusops are also grown for their similar fruits. *M. elata* of Brazil is the Cow Tree. Its apple-sized fruits contain a milk-like latex that resembles milk, when fresh, and is drunk with coffee, but soon congeals to a glue.

Pimenta dioica, Allspice,
Pimento, Myrtaceae
This small, evergreen West Indian tree has pea-size berries that are dried and valued unripe for their mixed spice flavor.

Piper nigrum,
Pepper, Piperaceae
Black and white pepper are the unripe and ripe (and de-corticated) seeds of this Indian climbing wine.

Spondias,
Spanish Hog or Brazilian Plum, Anacardiaceae
Distantly related to cashews and pistachios, the *Spondias* have edible fruits, most of them only when made into preserves, but some are eaten raw. They are purple to yellow, resembling a plum with a central "stone". The stone of the Spanish Plum, *Spondias purpurea*, is eaten by some people.

Tamarindus indica,
Tamarind Tree, Caesalpiniaceae
This large, handsome tree has brown pods containing very acid pulp used for beverages and in chutneys, curries, and medicine.

Vanilla planifolia,
Vanilla, Orchidaceae
Vanilla is the fruit of an orchid that is native to Central America but is mostly grown in Madagascar. The bean-like pods are cured and dried for flavoring.

Syzygium paniculatum

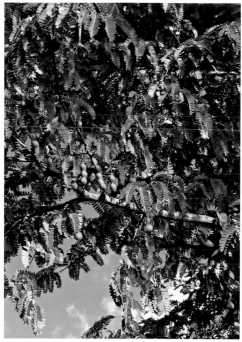

Tamarindus indica

Zizyphus jujuba,
Jujube, Chinese Date, Rhamnaceae
An East Indian native, this reached China and was improved to dessert quality. In China it is popular dried or preserved in syrup. Jujubes resemble large, yellowish or reddish cherries with thick, tough skin, a hard kernel and a pithy, acid pulp, rich in vitamin C. The thorny, shrubby trees survive in cooler climates and have been in Mediterranean countries since biblical times. *Z. vulgaris*, a native of the Middle East, is similar but less agreeable. *Z. lotus* is like a sweet olive and is thought to be the lotus Odysseus had trouble with.

Adansonia digitata
Baobab, Monkey Breadfruit, Bombacaceae
This large African tree has a swollen trunk often hollowed by age. The leaves are eaten as a vegetable and the fruits, up to 12 in. long, are fat, cylindrical, dark, and hairy. They have a floury white pulp that reputedly tastes like gingerbread, with small black seeds that have been ground and eaten in times of famine.

Antidesma bunius
Bignay
Coming from the Far East and Northern Australia, this tropical evergreen tree — originally from India — produces grape-like bunches of multicolored berries which are eaten raw, made into jams, or eaten with fish.

Billardiera longiflora
Appleberry, Pittosporaceae
An acid-loving, nearly hardy climber from Australasia, which has oblong dark blue berries with a pleasing taste. Many similar species are eaten by the native Australians.

Bixa orellana
Annatto, Lipstick tree, Bixaceae
This is a small evergreen tropical shrub-cum-tree that has heart-shaped leaves with peachy flowers followed by heart-shaped pods with seeds embedded in a colored flesh used as a lipstick, for dyeing hair and clothes, and commercially as the coloring Annatto.

Bouea macrophyla
Gandaria
This is just like a small mango gone very wrong. However, many in the Far East become addicted to its odd, though very juicy, taste.

Butyrospermum parkii
Shea Butter Tree, Sapotaceae
A native of central Africa, this small stout African tree has white fragrant flowers followed by plum-like fruits with a thick pericap that bleeds when green. Once fully ripe, this has some pulp, which is sweet and perfumed, but the fruits are gathered more for their seeds which have a high fat content and are used to make shea butter. The wood is resistant to termites.

Canarium commune
Chinese olive, Java almond
This is a closely related, rather attractive tree from Southeast Asia, which is grown for the tasty kernel.

Canarium edule/Dacryoides edulis
Safu, Burseraceae
The fruit is a large violet drupe that is too bitter to be eaten raw, but is fatty and nutritious once cooked. It is popular in West Africa.

Casimiroa edulis
Casimiroa, *White Sapote or Zapotl*
From South America (but not a Sapota or Sapodilla), this plant looks pretty much like an apple crossed with a mango, buttery custardy, tasting a bit like pear flesh, with white seeds and a bitter papery skin that must be avoided. Chill before eating and they will not keep long, going rock hard to too soft in days. Claimed to have medicinal values as well as vitamins A and C.

Cecropia peltata
Trumpet Tree, Monkey's Paw, Urticaceae
This stinging nettle relation is the tropical equivalent of elderberry as a weed; from South America, it takes over old human habitations. The small apple-sized fruits are watery and fig flavored.

Cicca acida
Malay Gooseberry, Euphorbiaceae
A small tree resembling a Carambola but with bunches of small greeny yellow berries, each with a hard seed and sour acid flesh eaten fresh but more often made into pickles.

Bixa orellana

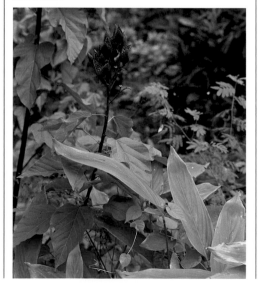

Cynometra cauliflora
Nam-Nam, Fabaceae
Popular in Malaysia, this tree relation of the beans has odd, wrinkled, kidney-shaped, small apple-sized pods concealing juicy yellow, sour, flesh wrapped around a big seed.

Dillenia indica
Chulta, Elephant Apple, Dilleniaceae
This is a tree with huge leathery leaves and strange fruits a bit like globe artichokes with acidic pulpy bits and is rather stringy. It is used for sherbets, curries, jello, making vinegar and, apparently, as treats for elephants.

Emblica officinalis
Indian Gooseberry, Euphorbiaceae
The fruits are small marbles of yellow or green. They are too acid to be eaten raw, but are amazingly rich in vitamin C, containing three hundred times as much as orange juice. They are often jammed and pickled and used to treat scurvy.

Euterpe oleracea
Acai Palm, Palmaceae
From the Amazonian basin, this plant has acid berries that are claimed to be incredibly health giving and so these are now appearing in smoothies and other tonic beverages.

Gnetum gnemon
Gnemon, Gnetaceae
A primitive plant from Java, this has what are technically cones, though not resembling a pine's; from these swell green "fruits" that are really seeds. When these turn orangey-red the skin or rind is edible and most often used in cakes and confectionery.

Grewia asiatica
Phalsa, Pharsa, Tiliaceae
This is a shrubby reddish tree from India and the East Indies, which has many small red berries that are too acid and dry to eat many of. However, they make the most delicious sorbets and syrups, and are very popular in northern India.

Harpephyllum caffrum
Kaffir Plum
A dark red fruit, used for jello, on a house-high tree with glossy leathery leaves. Its name is derived from the Arabic word kafir, for "disbeliever," though today it is used as a racial slur.

Heteromeles arbutifolia
Christmas Berry, Tollon, Rosaceae
This is an easy-to-grow, attractive pot plant closely resembling a holly with white scented flowers and red, holly-like berries. It is a unique plant, found only in California, where it makes a shrubby tree 30 ft. in height.

Irvingia gabonensis
Duika, Wild mango, Irvingiaceae
This is a large central African tree which has an inferior mango pulp, but the seed is oily and is used for cooking and soap-making. It is also used in Gabon chocolate or *pain de dika*.

Lansium domesticum
Langsat, Dokong, Longkong or Duku
Meliaceae
These are a tribe of small yellowish berries with parchment-like skins hanging like slim bunches of grapes from large Far Eastern trees. The Duku is the preferred choice, though has a bitter seed to be avoided; the kongs are not big ape relatives but bigger sweeter Dukus.

Lardizabala biternata
Zabal Fruit, Aquiboquil, Lardizabalaceae
These are sold in Chilean markets: a climber with dark evergreen leaves, clusters of purple black flowers are followed by finger-length purple sausages full of sweet pulp. Nearly hardy, this is a superb conservatory or cold greenhouse plant or even for the warmest garden.

Malpighia glabra/ punicfolia/ emarginata Acerola
Barbados Cherry, Malpighiaceae
Big evergreen tropical shrubs with pink or red flowers followed by thin-skinned juicy red berries with a very high vitamin C content that are mouth-puckeringly acid, so are used in drinks and tonics with much sweetening.

Mammea americana
Mammey Apple, Guttifereae
This is a large evergreen tropical tree with an orange- to grapefruit-sized russeted yellowish fruit; this contains one to four big seeds in firm juicy flesh which is best eaten stewed, though some eat them raw if very ripe.

Morinda citrifolia
Dog Dumpling, Rubiaceae
This is a handsome glossy foliaged, small tropical tree which almost continuously flowers, attracting hummingbirds whilst dropping strange, off-whitish, macabrely pineapple-like fruits which make ripe Camembert seem like fresh air. Yet these are believed to be very healthy medicine, especially if fermented first. The leaves are also used as poultices for pain, fever and headaches and the roots widely used for dye.

Owenia acidula
Australian Native Nectarine, Meliaceae
This is a small, tender, ornamental tree with pinnate foliage, white flowers and bluish black fruits with very acid red pulp, which is good for drinks, juices and jellies. The large stony seed is used for jewelry.

Parinarium curatefolium
Mupunda, Chrysobalanaceae
There are a number of other closely related fruits found in Africa. This is considered the best, with reddish-brown or greyish plum-sized drupes on a shrubby bush.

Parmentiera aculeata
Cucumber Tree, Bignoniaceae
A Central American small tree, this bears flowers directly from the trunk which turn into very cucumber-like fruits used raw, roasted and cooked.

Pereskia aculeata
Rose Cactus, Barbados Gooseberry, Cactaceae
These very floriferous plants closely resemble small trees with woody stems and deciduous leaves and are the least succulent of the cacti family. The highly perfumed flowers vary from orange to white through yellow and the fruits resemble orange or yellow cherries. They are popular for preserving in the West Indies.

Randia formosa
Raspberry Bush or Blackberry-jam Fruit, Rubiaceae
This South American tender shrub can be grown in a frost-free conservatory to fruit in a large pot. The white flowers are followed by woody shelled fruits with a jam- like sweet, sticky center. GOOD!

Salacca zalacca
Snakefruit, Salak, Palmaceae
Another palm tree fruit; coming in bunches of a couple of dozen, the "nuts" are an inch or so across and covered in what looks just like snakeskin with flesh tasting like a mixture of banana and pineapple all wrapped about a brown seed.

Sicana odifera
Musk Cucumber, Casabanana, Curuba or Coroa
Cucurbitaceae
This South American climbing vine resembles a lushly grown and prettier cucumber plant, but its tendrils really serve to glue themselves at the tips as well as twine. A perennial in Brazil and Ecuador, it can be grown very easily in more northern climates as an annual or conservatory subject. A very vigorous plant, it has yellow flowers and yellowish-red fruits with a sweetish flavor, but which are strongly fragrant — too strong for many. The fruits can be eaten young as vegetables and ripe as fruits, most commonly in jams.

Theobroma cacao
Cocoa, Sterculiaceae
The nibs are not eaten raw but fermented, dried and ground to make our chocolate. The trees are small natives of the Americas but now mainly grown in West Africa. The melon-like pods are green, ripening to red or yellow, and spring directly out of the trunk and main branches of the tree, following delightful fuschia-like pink flowers. Their pulp is sweet and edible also. Closely related is Pheng Phok, Chinese Chestnut, *Sterculia monosperma*, of which the nuts are much esteemed by the Chinese, who eat them boiled or roasted.

Yucca baccata
Eve's Date, Liliaceae
This is closely related to our Adam's Needle, the spiky garden perennial which flowers but rarely sets fruit. *Y. baccata* is too tender, or rather too loathing of damp, so needs to be grown under cover. The flowers need hand pollinating, then purple peach-sized, stubby cylindrical fruits form which have an aromatic bitter-sweet taste. The native Americans were fond of them fresh or dried and also ate the flowerbuds roasted or boiled.

SHRUB AND FLOWER GARDEN FRUITS

WILD GARDEN FRUITING TREES AND SHRUBS

Many of our familiar garden and countryside plants also bear fruit. Some of these are edible and can add variety and nutritional range to the diet. But first, I must insist that you never eat anything you are not sure of. Have it identified as safe by an expert on the spot. Also you must realize that although the fruits of some plants, such as yew, may not themselves be harmful, the foliage and seeds are deadly if ingested in quantity. Various parts may also be an irritant to some people.

However, such paranoid exclamations aside, there are many familiar plants that have edible, if not actually delicious, fruits. Although they might not seem at first glance very attractive or be popular with many of us today, some of these were once greatly esteemed by native peoples, and others were part of the country fare of our not-so-distant predecessors. With a little care and attention, these plants can provide us with fresh and unusual dishes, far exceeding in vitamins and flavor those made from the tired and flabby fruits usually offered for sale.

The plants at the beginning of this chapter are all excellent garden subjects, worthy of anyone's attention, which incidentally bear edible fruit. Some of the other plants with edible fruits are not attractive enough, or grow too big, for most gardens, but are of interest or value to insects or birds, and are more often planted in larger, public or wildlife gardens.

The ideal picturesque garden, often called the cottage garden, is typified these days by extravagant species at flower shows with odd mixtures of flowers, half of them out of season, grown elsewhere in pots and jammed full, with a camouflage of bark. The true cottager's garden was indeed a mixture of plants, but all with a purpose — to provide medicines, herbs, flavorings, fruits and, last of all, flowers.

Fruiting trees and shrubs can be easily cultivated with other plants underneath, and were the backbone of a true cottage garden. A mixture of plants that were found to grow happily together for both production and ornament was sensible, as it produced a mixed ecology, so there were rarely pest or disease problems. In addition, the plants grown in flower, shrub and wild gardens are often innately more reliable than those especially cultivated for fruits, as they are closer to the wild forms, with natural pest and disease resistance.

The biggest handicap for some of these plants has probably been their very attractiveness. If they had been a little less pretty, they might have been developed further for their fruits and have remained part of our diet.

Few of them are palatable raw, at least not to most people's taste, and all are better made into jams, jellies and preserves, but they have appealing and interesting flavors and are of inestimable value to the adventurous gourmet or those wishing to expand their dietary range. And for those interested in breeding, they offer plenty of opportunity for rapid improvement toward bigger, tastier and better fruits.

JUNEBERRIES
SHADBLOW, SASKATOON BERRY, AMELANCHIER

Amelanchier canadensis from the family Rosaceae

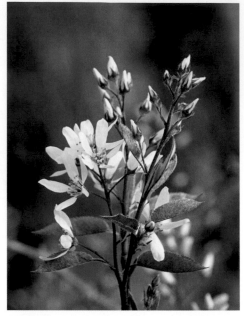

Tree/bush up to 20–30 ft. Life span: medium. Self-fertile. Fruits: ½ in., round, purple-black. Value: rich in vitamin C.

The Amelanchiers are small, deciduous trees or shrubs tending to suckering growth, most noticeable when absolutely covered with white blossoms. The fruits are purplish, spherical and about pea-size, but can be larger. *A. canadensis* is the best species and a native of North America. Though there are relatives in Asia and Europe, these are not as palatable. *A. vulgaris* grows wild in European mountain districts and was long cultivated in England, as much for the flowers as the fruits.

Frequently grown as a flowering shrub on lime-free sites

harvesting and storing, culinary

They can be eaten raw, but are better as jams or pies, or dried like raisins.

Snowy Mespilus Sponge Cakes
Makes about 10

2 oz. each butter, powdered sugar and white self-rising flour
1 large or 2 medium eggs
Dash of vanilla extract
Splash of milk
4 oz. dried amelanchier berries

Cream the butter and sugar, beat in the eggs and vanilla, fold in the sifted flour, then add enough milk to make a smooth mixture. Stir in the berries; pour into greased paper cups. Stand the cups on a metal tray and bake in a preheated oven at 375°F for 20 minutes or till firm.

varieties

Amelanchier canadensis was a favorite fruit of Native Americans. It was adopted by French settlers and became Poires in Canada. It has small, purple berries which are sweet. A. alnifolia, or Western Service Berry, is larger and found wild in the states of Oregon and Washington.

cultivation

Amelanchiers do best in moist but well-drained, lime-free soil. They are slow-growing, and some species tend to sucker. Most species grow in Zones 3 through 8.

Ornamental and Wildlife Value
Neat, compact, floriferous with good fall leaf colors, they are excellent shrub border plants.

Propagation, Pruning and Training
Sow seeds fresh for the species, but graft choice varieties in April onto Sorbus aucuparia stock. They may need to have suckers removed, otherwise prune only remedially.

Growing under Glass and in Containers
They are so hardy that it's not worth the space under cover. They could be delightful small specimens in pots.

Pests and Diseases
No particular problems affect these tough plants.

MYRTLE

Tree up to 15 ft. Life span: medium. Fruits: ½ in. usually black-blue.

Myrtle is one of 60 small evergreen shrubs which are densely and aromatically leafed, with white flowers.

***Myrtus communis* has long been grown in southern Europe and western Asia. It was highly revered and much enjoyed by the Ancient Greeks, whose mythology held myrtle sacred to Aphrodite, the goddess of love. As all other myrtles are native to South America or New Zealand, common myrtle may indicate a prehistoric link between the continents.**

 ## culinary

Myrtle berries are eaten raw or in pies and jams or dried. The jam has an aromatic flavor which goes well with savory dishes. The fresh flowers can be added to a salad. Mediterranean, especially Tuscan, cooking uses the dried fruits and flower buds as a spice. In Chile, Temo, *M. molinae*, seed was used to make a coffee.

Myrtle Jam
Makes approx. 4 lbs.

2 lb. myrtle berries
2 lb. sugar

Wash the berries and prick them with a darning needle. Simmer them until soft with just enough water to prevent burning. Add the sugar and bring to a boil then bottle in warm, sterilized jars and seal.

 ## varieties

Myrtus communis is grown for fruit and has ornamental forms such as *microphylla* and *tarentina* which are small, rarely reaching more than 25 in. high. Their foliage is aromatic when crushed, making them good for small patios or sunny windows, but they rarely fruit well. *M. ugni* is the "Chilean Guava Myrtle," which has delicious, mahogany red, pleasantly fragrant berries which are used to flavor water. These apparently fruit well in English greenhouses. *Luma apiculata*, "Arrayan," nearly hardy, from Chile, this small evergreen has beautiful leathery leaves, white flowers and then juicy aromatic sweet purple berries, good raw or as jam.

 ## cultivation

Myrtles need full sun and a well-drained soil. They are not averse to lime and are also good by the seaside. *M. communis*, *chequen* and *nummalaria* are the hardiest.

Myrtles come in several species and varieties, though rarely selected for cropping

Ornamental and Wildlife Value
Very attractive evergreens for mild regions. The flowers and berries are attractive to wildlife.

Pests and Diseases
As myrtles are very tough there are no real problems.

Propagation and Training
The species can be grown from seed, or half-ripe cuttings can be taken in late summer with some success. In early summer, clipping is usually preferred to pruning.

Growing under Glass and in Containers
These are very good subjects to have under glass and/or in containers, especially *M. ugni* or *M. communis tarentina*.

 ## other uses

Used in medicine. The dried leaves and wood are fragrant. The flowers are made into perfume and toilet water.

Berberis vulgaris from the family Berberidaceae

BARBERRIES
MAHONIAS, OREGON GRAPES

Bush up to 14 x 14 ft. Life span: short. Fruits: under ½ in., white, yellow, scarlet, purple or black.

The Berberis family contains hundreds of small- to medium-sized, spiny shrubs that have masses of berries in many colors. The leaves of most deciduous varieties turn bright shades in fall and the wood is usually yellow.

Various species are found all over the world. Our common barberry is now seldom relished, but was once widely popular. Indeed, the settlers in Massachusetts grew so many that in 1754 the province had to forbid further planting. Many states have now banned barberry planting because it can be invasive.

Growing under Glass and in Containers

They are hardy enough not to need protection, but do make good plants in containers.

Pests and Diseases
Barberries are an alternate host for wheat rust, so care should be taken not to plant near wheat.

 ## other uses

They make good hedges and game cover. A dye was made from the Yellow Barberry wood and roots.

 ## varieties

Berberis vulgaris is the Common Barberry, which once existed in many local forms and colors. One found in Rouen was seedless. Other species are enjoyed all over the world: *B. darwinii* is popular; *B. buxifolia*, the Magellan Barberry, is large and the best raw or cooked. *Mahonia* is now a separate genus, but is very similar, lacking the spines and having pinnate leaves. The flowers are yellow, usually scented, and the blue-black berries of *M. aquifolium* were made into preserves as Oregon grapes.

cultivation

They will grow anywhere not bone-dry or waterlogged, even tolerating salt spray. Most will grow in Zones 6 through 9, with some species and varieties hardy to Zone 3.

Ornamental and Wildlife Value
Some ornamental varieties are very attractive, though not as productive of berries, which are well liked by birds. Most varieties are excellent when used for wildlife gardens.

Propagation, Pruning and Training
The species grows from seed, layered or grafted. They can usually be cut to the ground and will recover.

Beautiful in flower and berry, and nice tart jello

 ## culinary

The berries can be pickled in vinegar, preserved in sugar or syrup, candied or made into jam. The leaves were once used as a seasoning.

Colonel Flowerdew's Bengal Chutney
Makes approx 3 lb.

6 cups grated apple
½ cup dried barberries
1 ¼ cups soft brown sugar
½ cup mustard seed
¼ cup light corn syrup
¼ cups each: chopped onions, chopped garlic,
  chopped fresh ginger and salt
½ oz. cayenne pepper
2 ½ cups vinegar

Mix all the ingredients and simmer till soft, say, 2 to 3 hours. Bottle in small sterilized jars for 6 months.

MEDLARS

Mespilus germanica **from the family Rosaceae**

Tree up to 30 ft. Life span: medium. Self-fertile. Fruits: 1–2 in., green to russet.

Medlars resemble pear trees but are smaller, have bigger leathery leaves, single, large, white flowers and fruits like giant, distorted rose hips. The brownish-green fruits have a rough "leafy" end, which shows the seed chambers. Medlars seldom ripen fully on the tree in cool regions and were eaten "bletted" — stored till at the point of decomposition. The taste is like that of rotten pear and they are now disdained. Originally from Persia, medlars became naturalized over much of Europe. Theophrastus mentions them in Greece in 300 CE and Pliny refers to the Romans having three sorts. Once very popular, they are now planted infrequently.

varieties

There are only a few left. Generally the bigger the tree, the larger the fruit tends to be. "Dutch" and "Monstrous" are the largest, "Royal" and "Nottingham" the tastiest and smaller. The seedless "Stoneless" has disappeared.

cultivation

Medlars are obliging and will grow in most places, generally preferring a sunny spot in a lawn or grass. They are hardy in Zones 6 through 10.

Growing under Glass and in Containers
The tree is hardy, so it is a waste to grow it under cover, but the twisted framework and general attractiveness make it a good specimen plant for pot growing.

Ornamental and Wildlife Value
Pretty flowers, large leaves and gorgeous fall golds make this a delightful specimen tree, with a twisted and contorted dark framework for winter interest.

Propagation, Pruning and Training
Medlars can be grown from seed, but are usually grafted on pear, quince or hawthorn stock. They are best pruned only remedially, as they fruit on the ends of the branches.

Pests and Diseases
Medlars rarely suffer from any problem.

A beautiful small tree in foliage, flower and fruit

 ## harvesting and storing, culinary

The fruits should be left on the tree till winter and then stored in a cool, dry place till they soften (blet). The pulp was once popular raw, mixed with liqueur and cream, but is better jammed or jellied.

Medlar Fudge
Makes about 4 lb.

2 lb. medlars
1 large or 2 small lemons
3 cloves
2 cups apple cider
Approx. 2½ cups light brown sugar
Honey or maple syrup to taste, cream and
  macaroons to serve

Wash and chop the fruit, add the cloves and cider and simmer until the fruit is soft. Strain and weigh the pulp. Add three quarters of its weight in sugar and bring back to a boil, then bottle and seal. When required, whip the fruit cheese with honey or maple syrup till soft, spoon into bowls and top with whipped cream and broken macaroons.

Chaenomeles japonica from the family Rosaceae

JAPANESE QUINCE
FLOWERING QUINCE

Shrub up to 10 x 10 ft. Life span: short. Self-fertile. Fruits: 1–2 in., round, green/red/yellow.

A tangled mass of dark, occasionally thorny branches covered with red, white, orange or pink blossom in early spring. This is followed later in the year by hard, roundish fruits, green flushing red or yellow.

This shrub arrived in Europe from Japan as late as 1800. It was rapidly accepted and is now widely planted in many varieties and hybrids, for its flowers, not the fruits. There is opportunity for developing a better culinary or even a dessert form.

harvesting and storing, culinary

Inedible — well, impenetrable anyway — until cooked, when they have an aromatic scent similar to, but different from, *Cydonia* quinces. They can be used for pies, baked or stewed or made into cheese or jello.

Japonica Jello
Makes approx. 8 lb.

4 lb. Japanese quinces
Approx. 8 cups sugar

Chop the fruit and simmer in 12 cups water until tender, then strain and weigh the pulp. Add 1 cup of sugar per 1 cup of pulp and return to the heat. Bring to boil, bottle and seal. Store for 3 months before use.

varieties

The botanical *C. japonica* has orange flowers, and true Japanese quince is *C. speciosa.* "Texas Scarlet" is a dense, spreading shrub with 3 in. fruit. "Thornless Cameo" has double flowers in a beautiful shade of peach. The fruits of "Toyo Nishiki" are as big as apples. *C. cathayensis* is larger, with green fruits up to 6 in. long.

cultivation

Hardier than *Cydonia* quinces, these are easy almost anywhere, even on shady walls. They thrive in Zones 4 through 9 or 10.

Growing under Glass and in Containers
Tough and unruly plants, they are better outdoors. I've found them dependable in pots to force for early flowers.

Ornamental and Wildlife Value
The displays of early flowers and long-lived fruit are exceptional, making these valuable shrubs. The flowers come in late winter, benefiting early insects, but the hard fruits often rot before the birds take them.

Propagation, Pruning and Training
Unlikely to come true from seed. Better varieties are easily layered or can be grafted. Winter cuttings may take; softwood cuttings are better but trickier. The shrubs have a congested form and are best left alone or tip-pruned in summer to control their size. I weave young growths like basket work to produce a tight surface that can be clipped.

Pests and Diseases
Other than weeds and congestion, they have no common problems.

Arbutus unedo **from the family Ericaceae**

STRAWBERRY TREE
CANE FRUIT, ARBUTE

Tree up to 20 ft. Life span: long. Fruits: about 1 in., spherical, red.

Arbutus unedo **is a small, evergreen tree often with gnarled, shedding bark, rich brown underneath. It has white, heather-like flowers in late fall as the previous year's crop of spherical fruits ripens. These are stubbily spiky, resembling litchis. The pulp is really no good raw, especially in cool regions, but may be better in warmer climes.** *Arbutus unedo* **is native to the Mediterranean. The Ancient Greek Theophrastus knew it was edible, but three hundred years later, the Roman Pliny did not regard it as worth eating. Ever since, it has been planted for its beauty, yet not really for the fruit, which have remained undeveloped. I gather the descriptive name** *unedo* **means "I eat one only."**

A. rubra (above); "Killarney" (top right)

 ## varieties

The ordinary Killarney Strawberry Tree is commonest and in few varieties; *Rubra* has pink flowers and abundant fruits. Other species are *A. canariensis*, whose berries are made into sweetmeats, and *A. menziesii*. Madrona, from California, has cherry-like fruits that are said once to have been eaten.

 ## cultivation

A. unedo prefers a mild climate or a warm site. It grows well in Zones 7 and 8. Although acid-loving, it does not mind some lime, but does better in a leaf-mold-rich woodland or acid soil. The other species are not as compliant.

Ornamental and Wildlife Value
One of the most highly prized, small, ornamental evergreens. Of slight value to wildlife, though the flowers are handy for insects late in fall.

Pests and Diseases
Few problems occur.

Growing under Glass and in Containers
So ornamental it is worth having under cover, but only if confined in a pot. Be careful to use rainwater.

 ## harvesting and storing, culinary

Harvested a year after the flowers, the fruits are made into sweets, confections, liqueurs and sherbets, but rarely eaten raw.

Killarney Strawberry Surprise
Serves 6

1½ cups graham cracker crumbs
½ cup (1 stick) butter
¼ cup strawberry jam
1 cup strawberries
2 tablespoons gelatin
1 large cup hot water
Killarney strawberries (arbutus fruits) to garnish

Propagation, Pruning and Training
Seed of the species comes true, layers are possible and winter cuttings may take. The strawberry tree needs little pruning and usually recovers if cut back hard.

 ## other uses

The hard, tough wood is turned into carved souvenirs of Killarney, especially small cudgels.

Break up the graham crackers and mix them with most of the butter. Press into a pie pan and chill. Once set, rub the biscuit crust with the rest of the butter, line with half the jam, then fill with strawberries. Dissolve the gelatin and the rest of the jam in a cup of hot water, then cool. Pour the jello over the fruit, swirl and chill. Garnish with Killarney strawberries and serve with cream.

Viburnum trilobum from the family Caprifoliaceae

HIGHBUSH CRANBERRIES

Shrub 14 ft. Life span: relatively short. Fruits: 1 in., round, scarlet.

A large, spreading shrub with maple-like leaves that give good fall color, and scarlet, glossy,

translucent berries in midsummer, very similar to the European Guelder Rose.

Viburnum is an immense genus of many species, some of which have berries that were once considered highly edible. The "Guelder Rose" (Snowball Tree, Whitten, Water Elder, V. opulus) is now forbidden fruit and as children we are warned how dangerous it is. Though the foliage is poisonous, the fruit was cooked and eaten by the poor for millennia. A native European fruit, it thrives in wet soils and damp hedgerows. Similar conditions suit most species.

varieties

V. trilobum, "Highbush Cranberry," which is very similar to V. opulus, is one of several edible wild North American species; V. lentago (Sweet Viburnum, "Nannyberry" or "Sheepberry") has sweet black berries; V. nudum ("Naked Viburnum" or "Withe Rod") is similar, with a deep blue berry; V. prunifolium ("Black Haw") is sometimes good enough even to eat raw.

V. lentago

cultivation

Very easy to please. Most species do best in moist, humus-rich soil. Highbush cranberry is hardy to Zone 3.

Growing under Glass and in Containers
Tough individuals, these are mostly hardy and need no glass, though other viburnums may be grown in pots so that their scented flowers may be enjoyed.

Ornamental and Wildlife Value
Most viburnums are grown for their pretty or scented flowers. The berrying sorts are often as decorative and both fruit and flowers are very useful for attracting insects and birds.

Propagation, Pruning and Training
Species come true from seed but are slow. Most varieties can be layered and some will strike from hardwood cuttings taken in winter.

Pests and Diseases
No common problem, just weeds and bird losses.

harvesting and storing, culinary

The berries are not eaten raw, save occasionally after frost, but can be made into sharp-tasting jams and jellies.

American Highbush Chutney
Makes approx. 2½ lb.

1 ½ lb. highbush cranberries
1 ¼ cups distilled vinegar
4 oz. each currants, golden raisins, raisins, sugar
½ oz. salt
2 teaspoons each cinnamon, allspice
Pinch of nutmeg

Wash the fruits and then remove each of the stalks. Simmer, with enough water to prevent burning, until soft. Add in the vinegar and the other ingredients, simmer until the chutney thickens. Store in sterilized jars for 3 months.

Fuchsia from the family Onagraceae

FUCHSIA

Semi-herbaceous shrub to 7 x 7 ft. Life span: short. Fruits: ½ in., round/oval purple-black.

This gloriously flowered plant needs little description, and most of us must have noticed the roundish oval, purple fruits it occasionally sets. As I have always searched for new fruits from far places, I was amused when I first saw fuchsia jello and learned that I had overlooked these berries, which are so close at hand, often edible and as delicious as many from distant shores.

The first fuchsia was recorded in 1703. Over the following century a few species arrived in Britain from South America with little remark, but in 1793 James Lee astutely launched his *F. coccinea*, the first with impressive flowers, and took the world by storm. Other species were introduced from New Zealand and now there is an amazing range of colors and forms of hybrids of many species. James Lee claimed he found this new Fuchsia in a sailor's window but it was actually supplied to him by Kew (labelled Coccinea) who got it from a Captain Firth in 1788. However, Pere Plumier wrote of *Fuchsia triphylla flore coccinea* in Plantarum Americanum Genera no P. 14, tab. 14, in 1703. What was so "astute" about launching *F. coccinea* was the way he did it — putting two on display, saying he would only sell one of the pair, for a guinea, which he did, and then replacing it with one of the three hundred he had propagated as soon as the client had left.

 harvesting and storing, culinary

Some are tasty raw, but all are best jellied or in pies.

Fuchsia Jello
Makes approx. 4 lb.

2 lb. fuchsia berries
Approx. 4 cups sugar
Juice of 1 lemon

Simmer the berries with sufficient water to cover. Once they have softened, strain and weigh. Add the same weight of sugar and the lemon juice. Bring back to boil, then transfer to sterilized jars.

 varieties

Fuchsia species *corymbiflora* and *denticulata* were eaten in Peru and *F. racemosa* in Santo Domingo. Fuchsia clubs and societies often have jello competitions. There appears to be no known poisonous variety — and I have tried many. As they are all bred for flowers, the berries are neglected and should be easily improved — there is enough variety to start with! *F. magellanica* is the hardiest, but rarely fruits.

 cultivation

Most fuchsias are hardy only in Zones 9 and 10, but *F. magellanica* may survive in Zone 7 if deeply mulched in winter. Even many less hardy species can be grown in cold regions if the roots are well protected, as fuchsias usually spring again from underground to flower and fruit. Make backup plants to be safe and keep these indoors. Fuchsias are amenable to almost any soil but prefer a sunny site.

Propagation, Pruning and Training
Seed produces mixed results; cuttings easy to train. Nip out tips in summer; cut back in winter.

Ornamental and Wildlife Value
Fuchsias are appealing. They can support large numbers of unwanted wildlife.

Growing under Glass and in Containers
An ideal plant for a cool or heated greenhouse or conservatory. Can be grown for years in large pots.

Pests and Diseases
They suffer from common pests.

Rosa from the family Rosaceae
ROSE HIPS

Clambering shrub up to 30 ft. Life span: short to medium. Usually self-fertile. Fruits: up to 1 in., ovoid, red, yellow or purplish black. Value: very rich in vitamin C.

There can be none of us who does not know roses and few who have never nibbled at the acid/sweet flesh of a rose hip. These are so rich in vitamin C that they were collected on a massive scale during World War II for rose-hip syrup for expectant mothers and babies. Rose stems are commonly thorny with a few exceptions such as the divine "Zéphirine Drouhin." The deciduous leaves vary from glossy to matte, the flower color is any you want save black or blue, though wild roses are almost all white or pink. The Eglantine rose leaves smell of apples after rain.

Rose hips and flowers are eaten in countries all over the world. The "Brier" or "Dog Rose," *Rosa canina*, and Eglantine or Sweetbrier, *R. rubiginosa*, are natives of Europe and temperate Asia. Their fruits have been eaten by country folk since time immemorial, but are now regarded with some disdain. However, eglantine sauce was made at Balmoral Castle from sweetbrier hips and lemon juice and was considered good enough for Queen Victoria. Roses are bred for flowers, not for their hips, so most varieties have small hips. However, a little selective breeding could produce hips as large as small apples within a few generations.

A little breeding and these could be as large and sweet as apples

 varieties

The Brier and Eglantine rose hips are the most common varieties used for hips, though *R. rugosa*, the Rugosa Rose, offers larger hips so is more rewarding. *R moyesii* has large flask-shaped hips and *R. omiensis* has pear-shaped, yellow and crimson fruits that ripen early. *R. spinosissima/pimpinellifolia*, the Scotch or Burnet Rose, is another European native, often found in maritime districts. It has a sweet, purplish-black fruit.

 cultivation

Most roses prefer heavy soil. Roses vary in cold hardiness, depending on species, but they are typically not assigned to particular hardiness zones because so many other factors affect their survival.

Propagation
Some species can be grown from seed. Cuttings taken in early fall are reliable for many varieties and most species.

Ornamental and Wildlife Value

Roses are *the* garden plant. At least one or more can fit into almost any garden anywhere to good effect.

Growing under Glass and in Containers

Only tender roses such as *R. banksiae* are happy under glass. Hardier varieties tend to become soft and drawn and suffer from pests. They must be kept moist at the roots, well-ventilated and shaded against scorch.

Maintenance

Spring Weed, mulch heavily and spray with liquid fertilizer as needed.
Summer Deadhead regularly, watch for aphids.
Fall Take cuttings.
Winter Cut back or tie in.

 ## culinary

Hips can be made into jellies, preserves and the famous syrup. The flower petals may be used as garnishes, preserved in sugar or syrup, used for rosewater flavoring, honeys, vinegars and conserves, pounded to dust for lozenges and they make good additions to salads. The leaves of *R. canina* have been used for tea (in desperation, one suspects).

Rose Hip Pie
Serves 6

for the dough:
2 cups self-rising flour
⅔ cup butter
1 large egg yolk
¼ cup brown sugar
Pinch of salt
Splash of water

for the filling:
2 cups rose hips
⅔ cup brown sugar
¼ cup honey
⅓ chopped stem ginger preserved in syrup
1 teaspoon cinnamon
Sprinkling of sugar and grating of nutmeg

Rub together the ingredients for the dough, making it a little on the dry side, and use it to line a pie dish. Wash, top, tail and halve the rose hips, extract every bit of seed and hairy fiber, rinse and drain. Mix with the sugar, honey, cinnamon and ginger and spoon on top of the dough. Decorate with dough offcuts and sprinkle with sugar and nutmeg before baking at 350°F for half an hour or until the dough is light brown on top.

Pruning and Training

This requires a chapter on its own just to list the methods! Basically, for most roses, plant them well apart, prune as little as possible and wind in growths rather than prune. Reduce tall hybrid bushes by a third to a half in height with hedge trimmers annually in late winter.

Pests and Diseases

Roses suffer from a host of common diseases, but provided they are growing reasonably well the only real threat to flower and hip production is aphids. Control these with jets of water and soft soap.

Harvesting and Storing

The berries need to ripen fully on the bush before being eaten raw, but are best taken before they soften for culinary use. All seed hairs must be removed!

Don't forget the petals for salads and garnish

 ## companion planting

Underplantings of Alliums, especially garlic or chives, help deter blackspot and pests. Parsley, lupines, mignonette and lavender are beneficial; catnip and *Limnanthes douglassii* are good ground cover underneath roses.

 ## other uses

Strong-growing roses such as *R. rubiginosa*, *R. spinosissima* or "Queen Elizabeth" make excellent stock- and people-proof hedges. The flower petals are dried for potpourri and used in confectionery, medicinally and in perfumery.

Cornus mas from the family Cornaceae

CORNELIAN CHERRY

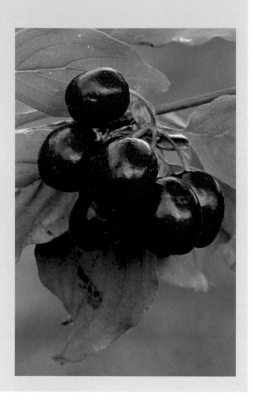

Tree/bush up to 25 ft. Life span: medium to long. Deciduous, self-fertile. Fruits: ½ in., ovoid, red.

Cornelian cherry fruits resemble small, red cherries but are generally too sour to eat raw, except for the occasional better one. The trees or large bushes are tall, deciduous, densely branched and suckering, common in hedgerows and old grasslands. The stems are greyish and the leaves are oval, coming to a point with noticeable veins. The flowers are primrose yellow and appear in small clusters early in spring before the leaves.

The Cornelian cherry is one of a genus of about a hundred, mostly small, shrubby plants up to 10 feet high, but ranging from creeping sub-shrubs to small trees. One of the two species native to Europe and western Asia, *Cornus mas* was once widely cultivated and rated very highly, though now it is rarely eaten even by country folk. There are species from North America and the Himalayas and it seems a shame they have not been cross-bred for better fruits. The Cornelian cherry really is a fruit that has stalled in development and probably would not take much further work to improve immensely.

 ## varieties

"Redstone" and "Russian Giant" produce better crops than the common species. The variety *C. mas macrocarpa* has somewhat larger fruits and is still available. There used to exist many other improved forms, now apparently lost. In France and Germany there are records of several varieties of Sorbets, as they were called — one that had a yellow fruit, some with wax-colored fruits, white fruits and even one with a fleshy, rounded fruit. Other *Cornus* such as *C. stolonifera*, the Red Osier, and *C. amomum*, "Kinnikinnik," are found in North America and are edible. The former was eaten more in desperation than for pleasure; the latter, found in Louisiana, is said to be very good. The berries of *C. suecica* used to be gathered by Native Americans, who froze them in wooden boxes for winter rations. *Cornus kousa chinensis* comes from China via Japan and is a smaller tree than *C. mas*. The flowers are grayish-purple backed by immense pale bracts; the fruits are more strawberry-like and juicy with better flavor. This species needs a moist, acid soil.

Cornus capitata

C. macrophylla and the tenderer *C. capitata* come from Asia and the Himalayas and are eaten raw and made into preserves in India. *C. canadensis (Chamaepericlymenum canadense)*, Bunchberry or Dwarf Cornel, is a different type altogether. A lime hater more resembling a soft dwarf raspberry in manner of growth, it has white flowers on low, soft shoots with vivid red fruits. These are pleasant enough, if tasteless, and can be added to summer desserts.

 ## cultivation

C. mas is easy to grow almost anywhere but prefers calcareous soil. Some species need acid conditions. Generally they are among the most reliable of shrubs, requiring little attention. They are cold hardy to Zone 5.

Maintenance
Spring Cut back ornamental stemmed varieties, weed, mulch and spray with liquid fertilizer.
Summer Make layers.
Fall Preserve fruit for winter.
Winter Take cuttings or suckers and prune.

CORNELIAN CHERRY

Cornus canadensis

harvesting and storing, culinary

In Germany the fruits were sold in markets to be eaten by children (who presumably liked them). They were widely made into pies, confectionery and sweetmeats, even used as substitutes for olives. In Norway the flowers were used to flavor spirits and in Turkey the fruits were used as flavoring for sherbets. It is noticeable that fruits vary on different bushes and some are more palatable raw than others.

Sorbet Sorbet
Serves 4

4 cups cornelian cherries
1 small lemon
Approx. 2½ cups sugar
2 or 3 small egg whites

Wash the fruits, slit the cherries, chop the lemon and simmer them till soft, just covered with water, in a deep pan. Strain and measure the juice, then dissolve just less than 1 cup of sugar per cup of juice. Bring back to a boil, cool and partially freeze. Remove from the freezer and beat, adding 1 beaten egg white for every 2 cups of sorbet. Repeat the freezing and beating one more time before freezing until required.

Growing under Glass and in Containers
They are hardy, so are hardly worth growing under glass unless you wish to force them for their early flowers. They will grow well in pots.

Ornamental and Wildlife Value
Many species are liked particularly for their fall color and some species and varieties are grown for their brightly colored stems. The flowers are early, benefiting insects, and birds and rodents love the berries. These factors render them one of the best backbone shrubs of a wild garden.

Propagation
The species come true from seed with some variation, but are slow. Suckers taken in fall are best; hardwood winter cuttings may take, but layering is more sure.

Pruning and Training
Generally only remedial pruning is needed — though, as these plants sucker, some root pruning may become necessary. Ornamental colored-stem varieties are best sheared to ground level in late winter.

Pests and Diseases
No common problems bother these tough plants.

other uses

Cornus sanguinea, the Cornel Dogwood, Dogberry or Pegwood, is a common European relation, not really edible, though the fruits were once used for oil and in brewing. *C. alba* varieties tolerate wet or dry situations and can be used to reinforce banks. Dogwoods grow stiff and straight, so were used for arrows.

HAWTHORN AND AZAROLE

Crataegus azarolus from the family Rosaceae

Tree/bush up to 25 ft. Life span: long. Deciduous, self-fertile. Fruits: up to 1 in., roundish, usually orange. Value: rich in vitamins C and B complex.

The azarole is a more palatable relation of the well-known hawthorn and is cultivated in many of the Mediterranean countries for its cherry-sized fruits. These are usually yellow to orange, but can occasionally be red or white. They are larger than a hawthorn haw and have an apple-flavored, pasty flesh with two or three tough seeds. Small, spreading trees or large shrubs, these are typical of the hawthorn genus, with clusters of large, white flowers that do not have the usual family scent.

The hawthorn family are remarkably hardy, tough plants for wet, dry, windswept or even coastal regions. They are survivors and various species can be found in almost every part of the world, many of which bear similar small, edible, apple-like fruits. Native to North Africa, Asia Minor and Persia, the azarole, *C. azarolus*, may be the *mespile anthedon* about which Theophrastus wrote. More popular in the Latin countries, it was brought to Britain in 1640. In 1976 it got an award of merit from the Royal Horticultural Society, but it has never really caught on, most probably because other more floriferous varieties and species were readily available.

Crataegus tomentosa

 varieties

The Azarole is the more productive of the species and is grown commercially for flavoring liqueurs. It is probably the best choice for a tree for preserves. The Armenian *C. tanacetifolia*, the Tansy-leaved Thorn or Syrian Hawberry, is another good choice. The berries are almost relishable raw as dessert and have an aromatic apple flavor, which is surprising, as they also closely resemble small yellow apples. They are pale green to yellow, with slight ribs like a melon, and a tassel of "leaves" at the end. The Common Hawthorn or Quickthorn Haw, *C. monogyna*, has one seed and is edible but not at all palatable, so is seldom eaten, save by curious children. Reputedly it was eaten raw when fully ripe by Scots Highlanders. The fruits are dark red and hang in immense festoons in fall. The flowers have a sweet perfume when new, but go fishy as they age — on some trees more than others. Equally common, *C. oxycantha/*
laevigata is very similar, usually with dark red flowers. There are several edible North American species. *C. tomentosa*, Black Thorn or Pear Thorn, has hard, orange-red, pear-shaped fruits; *C. flava* has yellow fruits; *C. douglasii* is a better species with small but sweet, black berries with yellow flesh. One identified as *C. coccinea* (now *mollis*, sub *mollis, pedicellata* or *intricata*) was very popular with Native Americans, who dried the large scarlet or purple fruits for winter use. Sometimes these fruits were mixed together with chokecherries and service berries before they were dried and pressed into cakes for storage. *C. mollis* also has amazingly big thorns.

 cultivation

The hawthorns are all extremely easy to please and require little skill or attention. They tend to lean when in the open. Hawthorns, including red azarole, are generally hardy to Zone 5, and some can take even

HAWTHORN AND AZAROLE

Common Hawthorn

The flowers of the Common Hawthorn once made a heady liqueur or wine. The young leaves and buds, known to schoolchildren as bread and cheese, had a nutty taste and made a welcome addition to salads. We are now told that both are slightly poisonous. However, the berries of Azarole, Common Thorn, and especially the Armenian or Syrian, will make excellent preserves, wines and jellies.

Hedge Jello
Makes approx. 6 lb.

6 cups haws
3 cups crab or cooking apples
1 cup elderberries
Approx. 6 cups sugar

Wash the fruits, chop the apples and simmer the

fruits together, just covered with water, for about 2 hours, till softened. Strain and weigh the juice. Add the same weight of sugar to the juice and bring back to a boil. Skim off the scum, jar and seal.

---

more extreme cold. The black hawthorn (*C. douglasii*) is found in the wild from Alaska to California and east into Minnesota.

Growing under Glass and in Containers
Because they are so hardy they do not need protection, but several of the ornamental varieties can be grown in pots for forcing to produce early flowers.

Ornamental and Wildlife Value
The shows of blossom and masses of bright fruits make these an excellent choice for larger shrub borders and informal gardens.

Propagation
This is more difficult than for many fruits. The haws need stratifying for winter and a year before sowing the next spring, and may also produce mixed offspring unless they are from a true species grown far from any others. Cuttings are difficult, so choice varieties are best obtained budded in May or grafted in April onto common stock.

Maintenance
Spring Weed, mulch and spray with liquid fertilizer as needed.
Summer No maintenance.
Fall Collect fruits before the birds do.
Winter Prune if necessary.

Pruning and Training
Very little is needed. Do not over-thin the branches, as hawthorns will naturally have a congested head.

Pests and Diseases
Hawthorns rarely suffer badly from problems, though they are occasionally defoliated by caterpillar attacks. These attacks may be easily avoided by diligent observation and prompt action.

other uses

Hawthorns make the best and most traditional hedge with a trimmed surface like fine tweed. The wood is heavy and hard and will burn with a good heat.

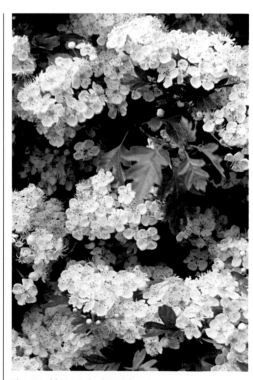

The May blossom is cheerful, too

MOUNTAIN ASH

ROWAN, WHITEBEAM

Tree, up to 50 ft. Life span: short. Deciduous, self-fertile. Fruits: up to ½ in., spherical, scarlet, in clusters. Value: very rich in vitamin C and pectin.

Mountain ashes or rowans are most attractive, small trees with distinctive, pinnate leaves, dark green above, lighter underneath. They have big heads of foamy, cream flowers like elderflowers, but smell unpleasant. In fall the branches bend under massive clusters of bright red to scarlet berries, which would hang through the winter if the birds did not finish them so quickly. The Latin name *aucuparia* means "bird catching" and refers to the fruit's early use as bait.

The *Sorbus* family is large and includes dwarf shrubs and large trees. They are spread all over the world and the majority are quite hardy. They color richly in fall and are widely grown for their attractive shows of fruits, also in yellow and white. Many new ornamental species were introduced from China during the 19th century, but little advance has been made in fruit quality since *S. aucuparia edulis* (*moravica* or *dulcis*) was first introduced in about 1800.

Rowan

 varieties

Sorbus aucuparia, the Rowan or Mountain Ash, has scarlet berries that birds love and which are generally too sour and bitter for our tastes. There are many other ornamental species and varieties, for example *S. aucuparia xanthocarpa*, which has yellow fruits. However, the common rowan is still the frequent favorite choice from the genus and much planted in metropolitan areas. The best variety by far for the gourmand is *edulis* which has larger, sweeter fruits carried in heavy bunches. *S. aria*, the Whitebeam, has similar red berries to a rowan and they were once eaten and used for wine. *Sorbus domestica*, the Service Tree, is a native of Asia Minor and was also once widely liked, but is now less common. It has smaller clusters of larger fruits of a brownish green, resembling small pears. They need to be bletted like medlars (see p. 577) before they are edible. There were pear-shaped and apple-shaped versions; the flavor and texture were improved after a frost and they were commonly sold in London markets. In Brittany they were used to make a rather poor cider. The Wild Service or Chequer Tree, *S. torminalis*, has smaller, still harder fruits, that would pucker even the hungriest peasant's mouth, but were once eaten by children. Note the seeds contain cyanides and should not be swallowed.

 cultivation

Mountain ashes are tolerant of quite acid soils and do not like chalky or limy ones, protesting by being short-lived. They generally prefer drier to wetter sites but, strangely, are commonly seen growing naturally by mountain streams and in wet, hilly country. Most mountain ash species are cold hardy to Zone 5, with *S. acuparia* being hardy to Zone 3.

Growing under Glass and in Containers

They are hardy and rather too large for growing inside. They can be grown, and fruited, in pots if only a small crop is desired.

Ornamental and Wildlife Value

Almost all the species and varieties are very attractive to us in flower and fruit, turning glorious shades of crimson in fall, but most unfortunately do lack a sweet scent. Rowans are valuable to the birds and insects and are pollinated by flies and midges.

Maintenance

Spring Weed, mulch and spray with liquid fertilizer.
Fall Pick fruit before the birds get them.
Winter Prune as necessary.

Service tree

Whitebeam

Propagation

Seed from the species may come true if the tree is isolated, but it must be stratified over winter first. Cuttings are rarely successful, so selected forms are budded in midsummer or grafted in early spring onto seedling rootstocks. The fruits of rowans are thought to get larger if the trees are grafted on to Service stock.

Pruning and Training

Pruning should be only remedial once a good head has formed, but watch for overladen branches and prop in time. The strongly erect growth of young trees can be bent down and into fruitfulness: pull them down gently with weights tied near the ends.

Pests and Diseases

Apart from bird losses, and being rather short-lived on alkaline soils, the members of this genus need little care and rarely suffer problems. They are thus well liked for amenity planting.

 ## other uses

Rowan bark was used in dyeing and tanning. The wood is strong and was used for handles. Service wood is tough and resists wear well. The berries of the Wild Service tree, *S. torminalis*, were also used medicinally.

 ## culinary

Rowan berries make a delicious jello, almost like marmalade, which goes well with venison, game and fatty or cold meats. They can be used in compôtes, preserves and syrups, and are sometimes added to apple dishes to liven them up. They have been used for fermenting and distilling liquor, and in emergencies the dried berries have been ground into meal to make a substitute for bread. Service fruits were used traditionally in quite similar ways.

Mountain Ash Jello

Makes approx. 4 lb.

2 lb. firm ripe rowan berries
1 small lemon
Approx. 4 cups sugar

Wash and de-stem the berries, add the chopped lemon and 2 cups of water and simmer till soft (for about an hour). Strain and add 1 cup of sugar to each cup of liquid. Bring back to a boil, skim and jar.

SLOES, BIRD CHERRIES, BEACH PLUMS

Tree/bush up to 30 ft. Life span: medium. Deciduous, self-fertile. Fruits: up to 1 in., ovoid, single stone, red to black. Value: rich in vitamin C.

Closely related to orchard plums and cherries, the wild *Prunus* species remain very much tough, hardy alternatives for difficult spots or wild gardens. Sloes are the fruits of the blackthorn, *P. spinosa*, which is a medium-sized shrub, many-branched, very thorny, with blackish bark. The fruits are black ovoids with a bloom that resembles plums, and hard, juicy, green flesh that is usually far too astringent to eat raw. However, like many children, I forever searched for a sweeter one.

Sloes are native to Europe, North Africa and Asia. The stones have been found on the sites of prehistoric dwellings, so they have long been an item of diet. They may be one of the ancestors of the damson and some of their "blood" has probably got into many true plums. The Bird Cherry is a native of Europe and Asia, especially grown in the north of England. The 16th-century herbalist Gerard claimed it was in "almost every hedge". Many ornamental *Prunus* species were later introduced in the 18th and 19th centuries; *P. maritima* was introduced by R. J. Farrer in 1800.

 ## varieties

Prunus padus, the Bird Cherry or Hag Berry, is a small tree with white, fragrant flowers in late spring; the double-flowered form, *P. padus plena*, is more heavily almond-scented. The leaves and bark smell of bitter almonds and contain highly poisonous prussic acid. The Sand Cherry (*P. besseyi*) is an American species native to the Great Plains and the Great Lakes region. It has shiny, silvery green, leathery leaves and bears small, sweet, purplish-black fruits in abundance. Hansen's Bush Cherry is an improved form of this wild fruit, good for wildlife gardens and with attractive red fall color. Another North American species is *P. virginiana*, the Choke Cherry. This is a tall shrub with glossy green leaves and variable red to purplish-black berries. *P simonii*, the Apricot Plum, from China, has large, attractive, red and yellow, scented fruits.

Bird Cherries

SLOES, BIRD CHERRIES, BEACH PLUMS

cultivation

Sloes and Bird Cherries are very hardy — *P. padus* is cold hardy to Zone 4; *P. besseyi* to Zone 2 — and good for making windbreaks. They like an exposed site and thrive on quite poor soil. Do mulch these heavily; water well while establishing on very sandy soils as these hold little water.

Growing under Glass and in Containers
Most of these are hardy and not tasty enough to merit space under cover. *P. americana* may be more fruitful if pot-grown, wintered outside and brought in for the spring through to fall.

Ornamental and Wildlife Value
All *Prunus* are good at flowering time, but few are worth space in most small, modern gardens. They are more use to the wild garden, as the flowers are early, benefiting insects, while the fruits are excellent winter fare for birds and rodents.

Pruning and Training
Minimal pruning is required and is best done in summer to avoid silver leaf disease. As hedges, blackthorn should be planted at 45°, staggered in two or three close rows, each laid in opposite directions. Most species can be trained as small trees, but leave beach plum bushes alone.

American Red Plum

Choke Cherries

Maintenance
Spring Weed, mulch, spray with liquid fertilizer.
Summer Prune if any pruning is needed.
Fall Protect fruits from the birds.
Winter Pick fruits.

Propagation
The species usually come true from seed. Choicer varieties have been developed for ornamental use and must be budded in summer or grafted in spring. Cuttings do not take.

Pests and Diseases
These wildest members of the *Prunus* family suffer least from pests or diseases.

other uses

Sloes are good hedging plants. Their leaves were formerly used to adulterate tea. Bird Cherries do well in a hedge. Their wood is hard and used for carving and especially liked for rifle butts. Sloe bark was once used for medicinal purposes.

culinary

Sloe berries are much used for liqueurs, especially gin-based ones, and to add color to port-type wines. All over Europe they are fermented for wine or distilled to a spirit. In France the unripe sloes are pickled like olives. They can be made into juice, syrup or jello. Bird Cherries have been used in much the same way but are inferior. The American species are used similarly. The Apricot Plum seems strangely under-rated.

Sloe Gin

Sloes
Brown sugar or honey
Peeled almonds
Gin, brandy or vodka

Wash and dry the sloes and prick each several times. Pack the sloes loosely into bottles. To each bottle add ¾ cup brown sugar or honey and a couple of almonds, then fill with gin (or brandy or vodka). Leave for several months before drinking.

Pinus edulis (syn. *P. pinea*) from the order Pinaceae

PINE NUTS
PIGNONS, PINONS, PINOCCHI

Tree up to 80 ft. Life span: long. Evergreen, self-fertile. Fruits: up to ½ in. long, ivory-white seeds inside a cone. Value: high in minerals and oils.

Pine kernels are more nuts than fruits as we eat the seed and not the surrounding part (in this case, the cone), but they are softer than true nuts. Most pine kernels come from the stone or umbrella pine. It is an attractive, mushroom-shaped tree with glossy, brown cones which expand in the sun, and drop the seeds. Each is in a tough skin which needs to be removed before they are eaten.

The pinyon pine is most widely used in America. The stone pine is indigenous to the Mediterranean region. Loved by the Ancient Greeks, it was dedicated to the sea god Poseidon.

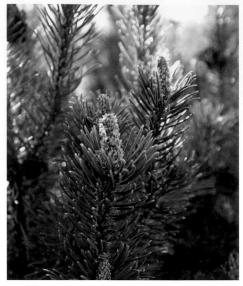

P. edulis

Pests and Diseases
Pines need companion bacteria and fungi, use soil from around another pine is used to inoculate new sites.

Pruning and Training
Pines are best left well alone.

Propagation
They can be grown from seed or grafted (with skill).

 ## varieties

Pinus pinea grows happily in northern regions, but without enough sun the cones do not ripen. *P. cembra*, the Swiss Stone Pine is native to Central Europe and Asia and the seeds are a staple food in Siberia.

Gerard's Pine

P. gerardiana, Gerard's Pine, comes from the Himalayas. *P. cembroides* is a native of North America and has pea-sized kernels that taste delicious roasted. *P. edulis*, from Mexico, is the best variety, but unlikely to fruit in Britain. Likewise the Araucaria Pine or Monkey Puzzle Tree, *A. aurucana*, which has edible kernels and grows but rarely fruits in cool climates. The Parana Pine, *A. angustifolia*, from South America, is not hardy and equally is too big for glass-house culture.

 ## cultivation

Pinyon pines are hardy to Zone 5. Stone pines need shelter to fruit in cold regions. They prefer to grow in sandy soil and acid conditions, and are hardy to Zone 8.

Growing under Glass and in Containers
Most pines grow too large unless confined and are unlikely to crop. *P. canariensis*, however, is a particularly pleasing indoor pot plant.

Ornamental and Wildlife Value
Very attractive if the space is available. Pine nuts will provide excellent food for many species of bird.

 ## other uses

Pines are a source of turpentine and resin.

 ## culinary

Pine nuts are roasted and salted in the same way as peanuts, and also used in marzipan, confectionery, salads and soups.

Piñon Truffle Salad
Quantities to taste

Pine nuts
Butter
Truffles
Walnut oil
Vinegar
Lettuce

Gently fry the kernels in butter till light brown. Remove from the heat; add finely sliced truffles, oil and vinegar. Cool the mixture and toss it in clean, dry lettuce leaves.

VERY WILD FRUITS

There are many other edible, if not palatable, fruits in gardens and parks, just waiting for breeders to improve them. The following are a few of the many that are occasionally eaten by some, but are not widely used. Please remember not to eat anything unless you are 100 percent sure of it and you have had it identified on the spot by an expert!

Asimina/Annona triloba
Pawpaw Annonacease
Pawpaw is a bottle-shaped fruit. Closely related to the papaya, it is much hardier; it is found as far north as Michigan and New York. A large, attractive, long-leafed, suckering bush, it is pest-resistant with fragrant, purple flowers. It prefers moist, not wet soils. Cultivars include "Sunflower," "Sweet Alice," "Zimmerman," "Taylor," and "Mary Foos Johnson." Male and female plants are needed; pollination is by flies. The fruits vary from 2–6 in. long, are green, ripening yellow to bronze, with yellow pulp, big brown seeds, and a resinous flavor, best cooked. They are slow-growing, slow-bearing, and long-lived. Zones 5 to 8.

Carpobrotus edulis
Hottentot Fig Aizoaceae
This resembles the mesembryanthemums, with which it was once classed. Native to South Africa, it is a low-growing succulent, found wild in maritime southwest England and southern Europe. Large, magenta or occasionally yellow flowers are followed by small, fig-like fruits, which can be eaten raw or cooked, pickled or preserved. The fleshy, triangular leaves can be eaten as saladings as can those of the similar *Mesembryanthemum crystallinum*.

Ceratonia siliqua
Carob Tree Leguminosae
The Locust Bean or St. John's Bread is an edible, purple-brown, beanlike pod that tastes so much like chocolate it can be ground up and used as a substitute. The seeds are not eaten, but are so exact in size and weight they were used for weighing gold and were the original "carat." This tree is native to the Mediterranean region, and preserved pods have been found at Pompeii. Nowadays the pods are used as animal feed. Zones 9 and 10.

Elaeagnus umbellata
Fall Olive Elaeagnaceae
A strong-growing, spreading, deciduous shrub from Asia with fragrant, yellow flowers and small, orange or red berries used like red currants or dried to "raisins". Many species in this genus bear edible fruits, and most of these have fragrant flowers. *E. commutata*, the "Silver Berry," has pasty, silver berries and silver leaves. *E. angustifolia*, "Oleaster" or "Wild Olive," has sweet berries, and is still popular in southeastern Europe. Zones 5 to 9.

Akebia quinata
Chocolate Vine
A hardy climber from China with attractive, five-lobed leaflets, and scented, chocolate-purple flowers in two sizes. These are followed by weird little purple sausage fruits, surprisngly edible — sweetish but pasty and insipid. This needs a warm spot to ripen the fruits, which have a yellowish pulp full of black seeds. *A. trifoliata/lobata* is similar. Zones 5 to 9.

Hovenia dulcis
Japanese Raisin Tree Rhamnaceae
I remember having this as a child. Resembling brown, candied angelica, the "fruit" is the dried, swollen flower stalk from behind the pea-sized seed of a small, attractive, Asian tree with glossy foliage. Zones 7 to 9.

Humulus lupulus,
"Hop" Cannabidaceae
I have to include this strange fruit or I will never be forgiven by my beer-swilling compatriots! A rampant climber closely related to *Cannabis*, this is a hardy native of southern Europe with maplelike leaves. Twining stems produce drooping, green-yellow, aromatic flower clusters that enlarge as they set. These are boiled to add their bitter, aromatic flavor to good ale and make it beer. The youngest shoots can be eaten in the manner of asparagus in early spring. Zones 4 to 8.

Rhus glabra
Smooth Sumac, Vinegar Tree Anacardiaceae
This small, easily grown, hardy shrub was introduced to the UK from North America in 1622. It is often grown for its spectacular foliage, which turns scarlet in fall. However, it can produce masses of fruits if both males and females are grown, and these were once eaten by Native Americans and children. They have a sour taste and were used as a substitute for vinegar and in teas. Dried and crushed, they were sprinkled over meat and fatty dishes as a seasoning. Some other members of the *Rhus* family have apparently had their fruits or foliage eaten, but as they are closely related to poison ivy, R. *toxicodendron*, great caution is advised! Zones 4 to 8.

Taxus baccata
"Yew" Taxaceae
The foliage is deadly without cure, the seed may be poisonous — but for centuries children have eaten the red, fleshy aril. However, it is advisable not to try this one. Zones 6 to 9.

Yucca filamentosaa
"Adam's needle" Agavaceae
A well-known, spiky, garden perennial, this flowers occassionally in Britain and rarely sets fruit. This can be as large as a peach in the plant's homeland, southwestern North America. Native Americans were fond of the fruit fresh or dried and ate the flower buds roasted or boiled. Zones 5 to 9.

Hippophae rhamnoides
"Sea Buckthorn" Elaeagnaceae
Often grown as an ornamental for its silver leaves, this tall, thorny shrub produces acid, orangey-yellow fruits if both sexes are planted. The fruits are too sour for most tastes, but have been eaten in famines and by children and are apparently widely collected in Russia, as they are very rich in vitamin C. They are used as a sauce with fish and meat in France, and in Central Europe they are made into a jello that is eaten with fish or cheese. Zones 4 to 9.

Gaultheria procumbens,
"Checkerberry," "Teaberry," Ericaceae
A low-growing, evergreen native of North America with white flowers and red berries, needing moist, acid soil and partial shade. The berries are odd raw, but can be cooked for jellies and pies and were once popular in Boston. Ironically, the leaves were once used as "tea". *G. humifosa* was also used, as was *G. shallon,* another taller, shrubbier version with great clusters of purple berries which were eaten dried by Native Americans. Zones 4 to 7.

Smilacina racemosa
"Treacle Berry" Convallariaceae
This delectable, herbaceous garden plant has scented, foamy, white flowers followed by apparently edible, sweet, red berries. One of the best of unknown fruits! Zones 3 to 7.

Tilia species
"Lindens" Tiliaceae
These enormous, well-known trees have sweet sap which was formerly boiled down to sugar. The fruits were once ground into a "chocolate", but this never caught on, as it kept badly. Can be grown to Zone 4, depending on species.

NUTS

Nuts are different from fruits. We eat the seeds of nuts and usually not the coverings, though we often find uses for these as well. With fruits, plants are giving us, the animals and birds who consume them, a sweet pulp so that we will, inadvertently, help distribute their seeds. This trade-off is easy for the plant, as the seeds are the expensive items to manufacture and the sugary pulp takes little resource.

However, when we eat nuts, we eat big seeds that are very expensive for the plant to make, as they are rich in oils, minerals, proteins and vitamins. They have a high dietary value to us, but of course this does not serve the plant well. The trade-off is that the plant "hopes" that if it produces a lot of nuts, some will escape the slaughter and be trampled underfoot or carried elsewhere and hidden but never recovered and thus start a fresh territory.

Squirrels are well known for assisting this process by burying nuts, but many other small mammals, particularly rodents, are also involved. Birds similarly hide nuts; there are plausible stories of birds that have filled attics with nuts, popping them in singly throughout the fall through a small space such as a knot hole.

Because of their high oil content and nutritional value, nuts have long been gathered from the wild. The rise of industry created greatly increased demand for nuts as a source of oils for lighting and lubrication and for turning into margarines, soaps and cosmetics. The pulps that remained were rich animal feeds and helped to fuel the expansion of farming in the 19th century. Nuts were no longer wild crops, but had become cultivated crops on a vast scale.

Although nut trees generally require little work, they mostly grow too big for the garden and are best grown agriculturally. (Of course they then suffer from a build-up of pests and diseases — problems associated with all crops if they are grown as monocultures.)

They are slow to come into production, though on the plus side they are mostly long-lived and make good timber. Many nut trees produce very hard or oily wood that lasts well. Walnut is one of the most prized of all timbers, so precious that it is used mostly as veneer.

Nuts suffer different pests from those that attack fruits. Bigger birds and rodents are more of a threat and, as nuts are larger, they are harder to protect or grow under cover (indeed, except as bonsai, many are almost impossible to keep small). Also, they are unfortunately more tender and susceptible to frost damage than many fruits. This, plus the need for a hot summer and fall to ripen the nuts, means that most nut trees are best grown in countries warmer than Britain.

One interesting connection between many of the nut trees covered in this chapter is how many of them have catkins and are wind-pollinated, even though these nut trees belong to entirely different families. This also means that they do not generally have scented flowers and give little nectar to insects, but they are, of course, a rich source of pollen.

From a commercial point of view, it is curious how almost all retail nut sales take place at Christmas, a period that serves to outsell the rest of the year put together.

ALMONDS

Prunus dulcis/amygdalus from the family Rosaceae

Tree up to 20 ft. Life span: short. Deciduous. Fruits: 2 in., pointed oval, in brown skin. Value: rich in protein, calcium, iron, vitamins B2 and B3 and phosphorus.

Almond trees resemble and are closely related to peaches, with larger, light pink blossoms appearing before long, thin leaves. Flowering 2 weeks earlier than peaches, they are often affected by frost. The wild varieties sometimes have spiny branches. The almond fruit has tough, inedible, leathery, greenish-brown, felted skin with a partition line along which it easily splits. The skin peels off a smooth, hard stone, full of small holes that do not penetrate the shell, containing the single, flat, pointed oval seed. Originally from the Middle East, almonds were known to the Ancient Hebrews and Phoenicians. Long naturalized in southern Europe and western Asia, they are now widely grown in California, South Africa and south Australia. Almond trees were introduced to England in 1548.

Almond orchards must be well away from peach trees

 varieties

Prunus dulcis dulcis is the Sweet Almond, *P. dulcis amara,* the Bitter Almond. The former is the much-loved nut; the latter is used for producing oil and flavorings and is too bitter for eating. It contains highly poisonous amounts of prussic acid. The variety "Texas" is especially tasty roasted and salted with the skin on. Self-fruited "Hall's Hardy" is a beautiful tree with a cloud of pale pink flowers and heavy crops of nuts. "Nonpareil" is the leading commercial variety. Ornamental varieties rarely bear fruit. "Robijn" is a new introduction, pink flowered, soft shelled and self-fertile.

 cultivation

Almonds want well-enriched, well-aerated, light soil, and to be at least 10 ft. apart. They need no staking after the first year. They want copious quantities of compost and mulches. Usually grown as trees. They should not be planted near peaches, as they may hybridize, resulting in bitter nuts. Hand-pollination is recommended. They are not completely self-fertile, so several trees should be planted together. Almonds can be grown in Zones 7 through 9. Like the related peach trees, almonds have a tendency to bloom early, which can be problematic in areas with unpredictable late spring weather. "Hall's Hardy" is reliable in Zone 6.

Growing under Glass
Almonds are rarely grown under glass because the necessary extra efforts of replenishment — pruning and tying in — are not usually well rewarded. The greenhouse must be unheated in winter to give them a dormant rest period. More problems occur under cover, and red spider mite can be troublesome unless high humidity is maintained.

Growing in Containers
Almonds can be grown in large pots, and take heavy pruning if well fed and watered. Pots enable them to be kept under cover during winter and through flowering and then brought out all through the summer, thus avoiding peach leaf curl and frost damage. The flowers must be protected from frosts and so too must the young fruitlets.

Ornamental and Wildlife Value
The almond is a real beauty — the fruiting tree as much as the many ornamental varieties.

Propagation
Almonds can be raised from stones, but take years to fruit and may produce a mixture of sweet and bitter

In the almond the outer flesh is leathery and peels away

Bitter Almond

fruits. Grafting on peach rootstocks are better.

Maintenance
Spring Protect blossoms from frost, hand-pollinate, weed, mulch and spray with liquid fertilizer as needed.
Summer Thin fruits early.
Fall Remove ripe and mummified fruits from the trees.
Winter Prune hard, spray with Bordeaux mixture.

Pruning and Training
Almonds fruit on young shoots, like peaches, but need to carry more fruits, so the trees are not pruned as hard. Commercially, every third year or so a few main branches are cut back hard and the top end of the remaining higher branches is removed to encourage prolific growth from the lower branches and stubs. This is best done in late winter, though it may let silver leaf disease in. It also keeps the bushes lower and more manageable. On walls and under cover, almonds may be fan trained, as for peaches (see p. 472). Thinning the fruits is not essential, but prevents biennial bearing.

Pests and Diseases
Earwigs can get inside the fruits and eat the kernel, but are readily trapped in rolls of corrugated paper around each branch. Protect the bark from animals such as rabbits and deer. Although we think of them as nuts, not fruits, almonds are closely related to peaches and are susceptible to some of the same diseases, including brown rot, borers, and peach leaf curl. Shot hole fungus and navel orange worm can also cause problems.

Harvesting and Storing
Once the nuts start to drop, knock them down, peel and dry. Commercially they are hulled, but the nuts will keep better intact. They can be stored in dry salt or sand for long periods.

other uses
The wood is hard and makes good veneers; the oil is used in cosmetics.

companion planting
Almonds are benefited by Alliums, especially garlic and chives. Clover or alfalfa and stinging nettles are also reputedly helpful.

culinary
The nuts are left with the brown skin on, or are blanched to provide a cleaner-tasting product. They may be eaten raw, cooked or turned into a milk.

Sirop d'Orgeat Milkshake
Quantities to taste

Sirop d'Orgeat
Ice-cold whole organic milk
Grated nutmeg

To one part Sirop d'Orgeat add approximately seven parts milk, mix well and top with the grated nutmeg.

Carya species from the family Juglandaceae
PECAN AND HICKORY NUTS

Tree up to 100 ft. Life span: medium to long. Deciduous, partly self-fertile. Fruits: up to 2 in., green-skinned, hard-shelled nuts.

Pecans are very large, fast-growing trees with pinnate leaves, male catkins and insignificant flowers followed by pointed, rounded, cylindrical fruits. These have a leathery skin that peels off to reveal a reddish, smooth shell enclosing the walnut-like kernel. Hickories are similar, though not as large in tree or fruit, with non-aromatic leaves and peeling bark, while the pecan has grey, resinous leaves. Hickories also prefer more humid conditions than pecans.

These are natives of North America and have been long enjoyed by Native Americans. They are grown in Australia, but rarely crop well elsewhere, though they are widely grown for their timber. The first trees were introduced to Britain in 1629.

Pecans

 varieties

Carya illinoinensis is the pecan, a fruit much like a walnut in most ways save that the reddish shell is smooth, not embossed. The trees grow up to 70 ft. high. Hickories are similar to pecans, with more flattened nuts, and the trees grow half as big again, which is pretty big. The Shellbark Hickory, *C. laciniosa/ alba*, and *C. ovata*, the Shagbark Hickory, are the more popular and productive sorts. American breeders have developed many good varieties of hickories. The shagbarks "Wurth," "Yoder," and "Wilcox" are good producers of flavorful, easily cracked nuts. "Missouri Mammoth" and "Keystone" are excellent shell barks, with nutmeats that crack clean of the shell. The pecan "Desirable" has large nuts with thin shells that crack cleanly; pollinate it with "Stuart." "Mohawk" bears very large pecans with very thin shells that crack into halves for fancy baking needs. "Cape Fear," "Cheyenne," and "Choctaw" are other good cracking and tasty pecans. "Hican" is a pecan and hickory hybrid with hickory flavor but a thinner shell; "Burton" is a worthy variety.

 cultivation

Plant pecans in deep, rich, moist soil; hickories tolerate a range of soils but do best in rich, well-drained sites. Pecans thrive in Zones 6 through 9, hickories in Zones 4 through 8.

Growing under Glass and in Containers
There is little practical possibility of getting these huge trees under cover. They resent being confined in pots and are unlikely to crop.

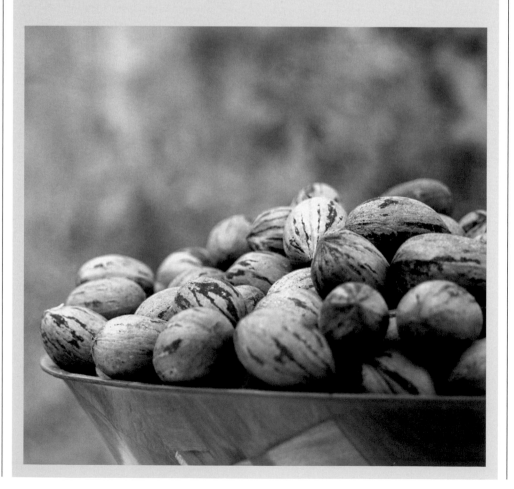

PECAN AND HICKORY NUTS

Bitternut Hickory

Harvesting and Storing

Ripe fruits are knocked down from the tree, husked (if the husk has not dropped off already) and dried. They do not store as well as walnuts, though they may keep up to a year if they are stored in a cool, dry place. Commercially they are hulled before storage and will keep up to 2 years at 5°F.

Pests and Diseases, Companion Planting

Disease is usually not a factor in drier areas, but in the humid Southeast, scab can be troublesome. Choose disease-resistant cultivars such as "Candy" and "Caddo." Black and yellow aphids may also inflict damage. A healthy tree will usually shrug off such attacks. Birds and squirrels will compete for the nuts.

 other uses

Hickories are planted for their tough, elastic timber and are renowned as fuel for smoking foods. Hickory bark was used for a yellow dye.

Ornamental and Wildlife Value

Given a suitable setting, these are large, attractive trees with decorative foliage that turns a rich yellow in fall.

Maintenance

No maintenance needed.

Propagation

Normally grown from seed, they are best pot-grown and then planted out as soon as possible in their final site, as they do not like to be transplanted. They are slow to establish and then fast-growing. Improved varieties are grafted or budded on seedling stock.

Pruning and Training

No pruning and training are required. Large specimens need staking for the first few years, as they are slow to take.

Square Nut

 culinary

Pecan nuts taste much like mild, sweet walnuts and to my taste are preferable. They are used raw or cooked in savory and sweet items, especially cakes and ice cream. Pecan pie is a legendary dessert. Hickory nuts are used similarly and can be squeezed to produce nut milk or oil.

Pecan Pie
Serves 4 to 6

6 oz. shortcrust pastry
¼ cup shelled pecans
3 oz. brown sugar
2 large eggs
1 cup light corn syrup
1 oz. maple syrup
½ teaspoon vanilla essence
¼ teaspoon salt

Roll out the dough and line a wide, shallow pie dish. Bake blind, weighed down with dried peas or similar, at 375°F for 20 minutes or until cooked. Cool and fill the case with pecans, arranged aesthetically. Beat together the other ingredients till the sugar is dissolved and pour over carefully without disturbing the nuts, which may float. Bake at 450°F for 10 minutes, then reduce the temperature to 350°F and cook for another 30 minutes. Cool and chill well before serving in slices with dollops of whipped cream.

WALNUTS

Tree 135 ft. Life span: long. Deciduous, partially self-fertile. Fruits: up to 2 in., green sphere enclosing nut. Value: rich in oil; the husks contain much vitamin C.

Walnuts are slow-growing, making massive trees up to 135 ft. eventually, with aromatic, pinnate foliage, silvery bark, insignificant female flowers and male catkins. All parts have a distinct sweet, aromatic smell. The fruits have a green husk around the nut, enclosing a kernel wrinkled like a brain.

***Juglans regia*, the common or Persian walnut, is native to western Asia. Introduced to the Mediterranean basin before the first century BCE, it became an important food in many regions and was also grown for timber. Walnuts reached Britain in the 16th century, if not in Roman times. The black walnut, *J. nigra*, comes from north-east America and was introduced to Britain in 1686. It is even bigger than the common walnut and widely grown for timber. The nuts are large, very hard to crack and a valuable dietary source of phosphorus.**

varieties

Named varieties of common English walnuts include "Franquette," once popular as a commercial variety on the West Coast, and slow to leaf out in spring so less susceptible to frost damage. "Chandler" bears large nuts with light-colored meats on a smaller tree. "Ambassador" is a Carpathian variety with plump, well-flavored kernels and heavy crops. "Thomas Black" is an excellent black walnut with large, thin-shelled nuts. There are several named varieties available from the U.S. They can grow half as high again as common trees, up to 150 ft. "Broadview" comes into cropping earlier than most after just 3 to 4 years. "Majestic" is a heavy cropper of big nuts on a very vigorous tree. "Rubis" produces attractive, different red-skinned kernels. Another American species, the White Walnut or Butternut, *J. cinerea*, introduced in 1633, is grown for timber and ornamental use.

cultivation

Walnuts prefer a heavy, moist soil. Black walnuts thrive in Zones 4 through 8, Persians in 5 through 9, and Capathian in 5 through 9. As pollination is difficult, it is best to plant several together. The old saying, "The wife, the dog and the walnut tree, the more you beat them the better they'll be", is advice that puzzles many. It is not to encourage fruitfulness, but rather to give the walnut a damaged bark, which then produces a more valuable distorted grain in the timber. (As to dog or wife, I suggest attention and treats probably develop better relationships with either.)

Growing under Glass and in Containers
Huge trees, these can hardly be housed. I have a 15-year-old bonsai walnut, but I doubt that it will ever fruit!

Ornamental and Wildlife Value
Very attractive and sweetly aromatic trees, they grow too big for most small gardens. They are very valuable to wildlife, especially rodents, squirrels, and birds.

Butternut

WALNUTS

Japanese

Maintenance
No maintenance needed.

Propagation
The species can be grown from seed, but are slow. Improved varieties are grafted or budded, and still take a decade to start to fruit, finally maturing around the century. They are best started in pots and moved to their final site while still small, as they resent being transplanted.

Pests and Diseases
There are few problems. Late frosts damage them, otherwise they are slow reliable croppers, each averaging 150 lb. annually.

Pruning and Training
Walnuts must be pruned only in fall, as they bleed in spring. Minimal pruning is required, but branches become massive, so remove badly positioned ones early. They need no stake after the first years.

Harvesting and Storing
The nuts are knocked down and the sticky staining husk is removed before drying. Walnuts can then be stored for up to a year. For pickling, pick the nuts green when a skewer can still be pushed through.

 companion planting

Varro, in the first century BCE, noted how sterile the land near walnut trees was. Walnut leaves and roots give off exudates that inhibit many plants and prevent their seeds from germinating. The American species are more damaging than the European and they are particularly bad for apples, *Solanaceae*, *Rubus* and many ornamentals.

 other uses

The foliage and husks have long been used as brown dyes and the oil as a hair darkener and for paints. The wood has always been valued for veneers and gun stocks, the more gnarled the better. Walnut trees were often planted near stables and privies, as their smell was thought to keep away flies. The walnut sap has traditionally been boiled to produce sugar.

Black Walnut

 culinary

Walnuts may be eaten either raw or cooked, often in confectionery or cakes, and associate particularly well with coffee or chocolate. They yield an edible, light oil. The young fruits may be pickled before the stone forms.

Walnut Aperitif or post-prandial liqueur

Young green walnuts
Brandy
Red wine
Sugar, as required

Wash and prick enough nuts to fill a wide-necked bottle. Fill with brandy, seal and store in a cool, dark place. After a year, decant the brandy into another bottle, refill the original bottle with red wine and reseal. After another year, decant the wine into the brandy, refill the walnut bottle with wine and reseal. After another year decant again, fill the walnut bottle with white sugar and reseal. After a year (making four in total,) discard the nuts and add the sugar syrup to the wine and brandy. Serve in sherry glasses before meals.

HAZELNUTS AND FILBERTS

Corylus species from the family Corylaceae

Tree/bush up to 20 ft. Life span: medium to long. Deciduous, partially self-fertile. Fruits: up to 1 in., pointed round, or oblong oval, brown nuts. Value: rich in oils.

These are shrubby trees, typical of woods and thickets, with dark stems, leaves rounded to a point and magnificent, yellow catkin male flowers in early spring. The gorgeous, carmine-red, female flowers are tiny, sea-urchin-like tentacles that protrude on warm days. The nuts are a pointed round or oblong oval. Hazelnuts have a husk around the bottom, while filberts (full-beards) are completely enveloped by the husk. The shell is thin and the kernel sweet. Wild hazels are *Corylus avellana*, but, being wind-pollinated, these have often been influenced by *C. colurna*, Turkish filberts, and *C. maxima* or filberts.

Hazelnuts of wild species were known in ancient times and filberts were introduced by the Romans from Greece. Pliny claims they came there from Damascus. The Romans may have brought filberts to Britain, but they were not noticed officially till introduced in 1759. Cob nuts were introduced earlier, in 1582, and the American hazelnut, *C. americana*, a similar, smaller nut with a thicker shell and heart-shaped leaves, arrived in 1798. Any appellation no longer signifies true breeding, as these all became interbred during the 19th century, giving us most of our current varieties.

Hazel catkins

 varieties

I adore Red-skinned Filberts; they are certainly small and fiddly, with tight, russet husks, but they are so delicious. Filberts are grown commercially in the Pacific Northwest. "Barcelona," popular in commercial orchards and home gardens, bears very large nuts that self-husk and are easy to crack out. Pollinate with "Duchilly," which bears large, long nuts. "Ennis" is a recent introduction for European filbert from Oregon State University. It has excellent flavor and produces more nuts and fewer "blanks" (empty nutshells) than older varieties. For the best flavor, however, you can't beat the wild hazelnut.

 cultivation

Hazelnuts thrive in stony, hilly ground or well-drained, loamy soil and will tolerate heavy, damp soils. Hazels need no support and are best planted severally to ensure pollination. They are an immensely easy crop for the lazy gardener, requiring even less effort than most.

Growing under Glass and in Containers
There seems no reason to grow them under cover and I suspect they would not like it anyway. They survive in pots quite well, looking attractive but seldom cropping.

Ornamental and Wildlife Value
These are not generally noticed, save when their catkins make a welcome display. The Twisted Hazel is attractively distorted and deformed and still crops well. The hazels will support many life forms, both large and small, and are also excellent plants for wild or native gardens.

HAZELNUTS AND FILBERTS

Maintenance
No maintenance needed.

Propagation
These can be grown from seed but do not come true. Layering or grafting is possible, but root suckers are best, detached in fall and potted up or planted *in situ* or a nursery bed for a year before their final move.

Pruning and Training
Traditionally hazels were grown on a low, flat, cartwheel frame. They are probably best trained to spurs on goblets, but are often left to be bushes or thickets. It is worth keeping them on a single trunk, uncongested, and removing the suckers, to prevent losing any of the nuts.

Pests and Diseases
Weedy growth underneath makes it hard to find nuts, so hazels are best planted in grass or mulched. In gardens they suffer few problems on a scale sufficient to damage crops, other than the attentions of birds, rodents, children and especially squirrels.

Kentish Cob

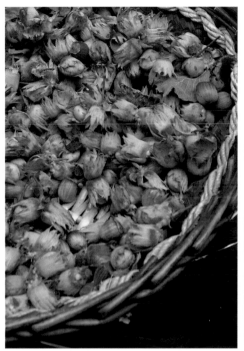
Kentish Cob

Harvesting and Storing
The nuts can be eaten a little unripe, but have to be fully ripe to keep. Ideally they should be allowed to fall off, but many are stolen by wildlife. They need to be dehusked and dried to keep well, though I never dehusk my Red-skinned Filberts. They will keep best, and for years, if packed in salt.

companion planting

They seem to associate naturally with bluebells and primroses, and truffles can be grown on their roots.

other uses

Hazels make good hedges and windbreaks. The foliage is eaten by many animals, including cows. The stems are tough and flexible, so are good for baskets and hurdles, and forked branches make divining rods. The wood is used for smoking fuel and I smoke my cheese with the shells.

culinary

Hazelnuts of all varieties are used in savory dishes, but more often in sweet dishes and confections. They are used for liqueurs and can be squeezed to express a light, edible oil.

Hazelnut Macaroons
Makes about 12

½ cup hazelnuts
½ light brown sugar
1 egg white
Drop of vanilla extract
Whipped cream, to serve

Grind three-quarters of the nuts in a food processor, then add the other ingredients and cream them together. Pour rounds of the mix on to rice paper on a baking sheet, place the remaining nuts on top and bake for 15 minutes at 350°F. Serve sandwiched with thick or clotted cream.

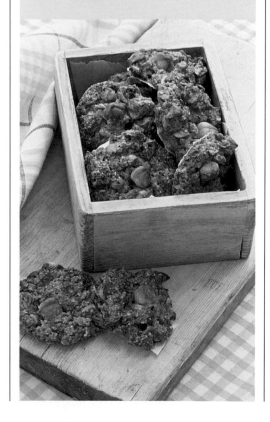

Castanea sativa **from the family Fagaceae**

SWEET OR SPANISH CHESTNUTS

Tree up to 120 ft. Life span: long. Deciduous, rarely self-fertile. Fruits: 2 in., prickly burrs containing two or three nuts. Value: rich in oils.

Sweet chestnuts make massive and beautiful trees. They have very large, serrated-edged leaves. The male flowers are long, yellow catkins, different from walnut or hazel catkins, as they are divided like pearls on a string. The fruits are brownish-russet, softly spiny burrs usually containing three brown nuts with thin, tough, leathery shells, flattened on one side and pointed.

Sweet chestnuts are native to the Mediterranean region. They were highly valued by the Romans for food and timber and became widely distributed. They fruit well only after hot summers in Britain, but are still capable of reaching a large size, so they have been planted for timber and were often coppiced. The major exporter of these nuts has always been Spain, though most southern European countries have their own production, as chestnuts have become a staple food. Madeiran nuts are said to be the biggest and were traditionally served to sustain the peasants for months each year.

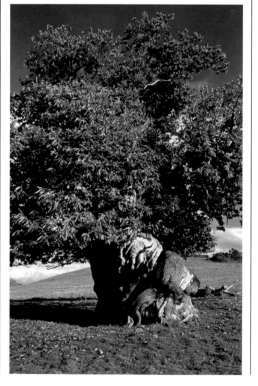

Castanea sativa – not for the smaller garden

 varieties

C. dentata was the American Sweet Chestnut, with smaller, richly flavored, sweeter nuts, but has been almost wiped out by a fungus, chestnut blight. Now American growers are breeding hybrids from the resistant *C. mollissima*, the Chinese Chestnut. Chinese-American crosses are taller than the Chinese species — they may reach 90 ft. — and include "Dunstan," which bears in 3 or 4 years after planting. "Revival" is a third-generation Chinese-American hybrid with very large, sweet nuts from which the brown membrane is easily removed. "Layeroka" is a Chinese-American hybrid and early ripening. *C. pumila*, the American Chinquapin, is rare in cultivation, and unlikely to fruit in Britain, but the nut is said to be very sweet. Other *Castanea* species are widely grown and the delicious nuts eaten with appreciation all around the world.

 cultivation

Sweet chestnuts are far too big for most gardens, rapidly reaching 100 ft. or even more. They thrive in light, well-drained loam or light, dry, sandy soil. Chinese and European chestnuts and their hybrids are hardy in Zones 5 through 8. They need no staking after the first year or so. If nuts are required rather than timber, plant on the sunny side of woodlands or windbreaks, ideally of yes or holm oak.

Maintenance
No maintenance needed.

Ornamental and Wildlife Value
Sweet chestnuts make statuesque trees and the large leaves color well in fall. The nuts are often rather too useful to wildlife.

Growing under Glass and in Containers
Far too big to grow under glass, they resent being confined in a pot and they are unlikely to ever fruit in one, but there's a challenge.

Pests and Diseases

In America, chestnut blight wiped out the best species; so far this is no problem elsewhere. Rodents, birds (especially rooks and pheasants) and squirrels soon take the nuts.

Propagation

They can be grown from seed and are fast-growing but still slow to fruit. The best varieties are budded or grafted, but hard to find in the U.S.

Pruning and Training

Minimal pruning is required and is best tackled in winter. Chestnuts get very large, so care must be taken to remove unsound branches.

Harvesting and Storing

The nuts are beaten down, the husks then removed and dried. They will keep for a year in cool, dry conditions; longer if totally dried first.

 companion planting

Chestnuts are considered healthier when they are grown near oak trees.

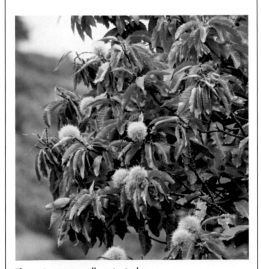

The nuts come well protected

 culinary

Chestnuts are not eaten raw, but are delicious roasted. They are made into marrons glacés (crystallized chestnuts), ground into flour and then made into oatmeal, puddings, breads, cakes, muffins and pies and they are also much used for savory dishes such as pâtés and in stuffing for meats. Sweet chestnuts are even made into liqueurs.

Chestnut Amber
Serves 4

1 cup chestnuts
1 ¼ cup milk
1 lemon
1 vanilla bean
⅓ cup breadcrumbs
2 tablespoons butter
¼ superfine sugar
2 eggs, separated
1 quantity piecrust, made from ¾ cup flour, ⅓ stick butter and water to mix

Roast the chestnuts for 20 minutes, cool and remove the skins. Simmer gently, with sufficient water to cover, until tender, then drain and strain to a purée. Simmer the milk with the lemon peel and vanilla bean for 15 minutes, then strain on to the breadcrumbs. Blend the butter and half the sugar, mix in the egg yolks and lemon juice and stir in the puréed chestnuts, breadcrumbs and milk. Line a deep dish with dough and fill with the mixture. Bake at 400°F for 25 minutes, or until firm and brown. Whip the egg whites to a stiff froth, add a teaspoon of sugar, whip again and spoon on top of the pie. Sprinkle with more sugar and then return to the oven until the meringue turns a delicious amber.

 other uses

Sweet chestnut has long been used for cleft paling. The wood is durable, but has "shakes" or splits in it. Often used for rough or external timber, such as coffins and hop poles, it makes a poor firewood but superior charcoal. The nuts were traditionally esteemed for the self-service fattening of swine.

Castanea dentata

PISTACHIOS

Pistacia vera from the family Anacardiaceae

Tree, up to 30 ft. Life span: medium. Deciduous, not self-fertile. Fruits: 1 in., pointed oval nuts. Value: rich in oil.

Pistachios are small, tender trees with gray bark and gray-green, slightly downy, pinnate leaves. The male and female flowers are borne on separate trees in the wild, but some cultivated varieties may be unisexual. It is hard to tell, as the flowers are inconspicuous though carried in panicles, which later become masses of small, pointed red fruits. These have a thin, green husk covering the thin, smooth, twin-shelled nut, housing a small, oval, green kernel that has a most appealing taste, especially after roasting and salting. Pistachios are usually the most expensive variety of nuts to buy.

Pistachios are natives of the Middle East and Central Asia and, with some close relations, have been cultivated since ancient times. They were grown in Italy in the late Roman period but were not introduced to Britain until the 16th and 17th centuries and then never proved hardy enough. The seed was distributed by the U.S. Patent Office in 1854 and the trees proved successful in many southern states, where the nuts are now produced in quantity, rivalling the output of the Mediterranean and Turkey.

 varieties

"Kerman" is a female plant that bears heavy clusters of excellent nuts, up to 50 lb. per tree. It can be single- or multi-trunked and is beautiful ornamental. Pollinate with "Peters," a male, nonfruiting variety. *P. terebinthus*, the Cyprus Turpentine Tree or Terebinth, is similarly not hardy. The whole plant is resinous, with nuts which start coral red, ripening to brown, and have edible, oily kernels, also green and pointed but smaller. It was used as a pollinator for pistachios as these shed pollen too early to fertilize themselves. Thus most seedling pistachios became hybrids of these two species. This has prevented much improvement of the pistachio nut. *P. lentiscus* is the evergreen "Mastic Tree." The nuts yield edible oil, but this tree is grown mainly for the resin that is obtained from bark incisions, used in turn for chewing gum and medicines.

 cultivation

Pistachios are not particular as to soil. In warmer countries they are useful for growing on poor, dry, hilly soil where other nuts will not thrive. Their greater value commercially also encourages this. Pistachios need a period of moderate cold to produce well. They are cold hardy to about 15°F and reliable in Zone 9 and possibly Zone 8. One male staminate tree is needed for six female pistillate trees, but as the pollen is shed early it needs to be saved in a paper bag until the pistils are receptive.

Mastic Tree

Pistacia vera

Growing under Glass and in Containers

Pistachios have been grown under glass and they make very attractive shrubs in large pots. However, good provision must be made for their pollination.

Ornamental and Wildlife Value

In warm countries or on a warm wall these are not unattractive, small trees. The unproductive Chinese Pistachio, *P. chinensis*, is a small, very pretty and hardy shrub. Pistachio nuts are readily taken by maurauding birds and mammals.

Maintenance

Spring Put out pots or uncover trees; weed, mulch, spray with seaweed solution.
Summer Water plants in pots regularly but minimally.
Fall Gather nuts if the summer has been hot.
Winter Bring in pots or protect trees.

Propagation

Although better varieties could be grown, pistachios seem to lack development. Continual cross-hybridization with terebinths has prevented improvement, but means that nuts come as true as their parents, which is not claiming a lot. Better varieties can be layered, budded or grafted.

Pruning and Training

Only remedial pruning is required and this is best done in midsummer. They can be trained against walls and are best fan-trained initially, then allowed to grow out to form a bush.

Pests and Diseases

No common pests or diseases are a problem for pistachios in garden cultivation, though under glass and on a warm wall they may suffer red spider mite attacks.

Harvesting and Storing

As these hang severally on panicles, they can be cut off to be dried and husked. They are best stored in their shells, which open automatically if they are roasted.

 other uses

P. terebinthus was long ago cultivated for producing first terebinth, the resin which oozes from the tree, and later turpentine. The wood is dark red and hard and used in cabinet making.

Pistacia terebinthus

 culinary

Pistachios can be eaten raw, but are most commonly roasted and salted, the shelling being left to the purchaser. They are much used as a coloring and flavoring for a wide range of foods, some savory and many sweet, including nougat and ice cream.

Pistachio Ice Cream

Serves 6

2 large egg yolks
¾ cup honey
1 teaspoon vanilla extract
2 cups cream
½ cup shelled pistachios
Natural green food coloring
Candied lemon slices and glacé cherries to taste

Whip the egg yolks, honey, vanilla and half the cream. Scald the remaining cream in a bain-marie, add the egg mixture and stir until the mixture thickens. Remove from the heat, cool, chill, then partially freeze. Remove from the freezer, beat vigorously and return. Repeat, but after the second beating mix in the nuts and coloring, then freeze again. Partially defrost before serving the ice cream scooped into glasses, garnished with lemon slices and cherries.

Anacardium occidentale from the family Anacardiaceae
CASHEWS

Tree up to 40 ft. Life span: medium. Semi-evergreen. Fruit: up to 3 in. long, weird. Value: kernels are nearly half fat and one-fifth protein.

Cashews are medium-sized, spreading trees with rounded leaves, related to pistachios. The cashew comes attached underneath the bottom of the much larger and peculiar fruits, cashew apples, which are juicy and astringent. The nut is grey or brown, ear-shaped and contains a white kernel within the acrid, poisonous shell.

Indigenous to South America, cashews were planted in the East Indies by the 16th century and **are now grown in many tropical regions, especially India and eastern Africa.**

 culinary

Cashew nuts are popular raw, i.e.,, already partially roasted, or roasted and salted. They are used in many sweet and savory dishes and can be liquified to make a thick sauce. Cashews are fermented to make wine in Goa. The cashew apple is the more valued part and is eaten fresh, preserved in syrup, candied and fermented to wine.

Cashew Pies
Makes 12

1 cup marzipan
A little powdered sugar
½ cup cashew nuts
¼ cup honey
1 teaspoon vanilla extract
A little milk
Glacé cherries

Roll the marzipan as dough and form individual pie cases in a tray dusted with powdered sugar. Liquify the other ingredients, adding just enough milk to ensure success. Pour into the marzipan cases, set a cherry in each and chill them to set.

 varieties

Other cashews are eaten: *A. humile*, the Monkey-nut, and *A. nanum* are from Brazil and have similar nuts. *A. rhinocarpus* is the Wild Cashew of Colombia and British Guyana.

 cultivation

Cashews grow in Zone 10 and will thrive in any reasonable soil.

Growing under Glass and in Containers
Plants dwarfed by large pots could probably be grown in a hot greenhouse or conservatory, if the seed could be found.

Ornamental and Wildlife Value
Cashews make interesting subjects for a collection or botanical garden.

Propagation
They are normally grown from seed, but this is difficult to obtain.

Pruning and Training
Only remedial pruning is necessary.

Pests and Diseases
No problems are known. The trees exude a gum obnoxious to insects, which was used in book-binding.

Harvesting and Storing
Once the nuts are picked from underneath the fruits, they have to be roasted and shelled, which, despite mechanization, is labour-intensive. This is because all the shell must be removed, as it contains an irritant in the inner membrane around the kernel, though this is rendered harmless by heat.

 other uses

The shells of the nuts contain an oil used industrially. The "apples" are then fermented to make a liquor. The sap makes an indelible ink.

Macadamia integrifolia (Macadamia ternifolia) from the family Proteaceae

MACADAMIAS
OR QUEENSLAND NUTS

Tree up to 60 ft. Life span: medium. Semi-evergreen. Fruits: up to 1 in., gray-husked nuts. Value: over 70 percent fat.

Macadamia trees are densely covered with narrow, glossy, holly-like, dark green leaves. The tassels of whitish flowers are followed by strings of small, hard, roundish, pointed nuts in grayish-green husks.

The kernel is finely flavored and of exquisite texture.

These nuts, despite the Greek-sounding name, are natives of north-eastern Australia. Not widely appreciated, they are mostly consumed in the United States from plantations in Hawaii. They were introduced to Ceylon, now Sri Lanka, in 1868.

 culinary

Most macadamia nuts are eaten roasted and salted, but they are also used in certain baked goods and confectionery.

Macadamia Slice
Serves 8 to 10

½ cup macadamia nuts
Powdered sugar
1 cup marzipan
2 teaspoons apricot jam
¼ cup chopped candied peel

Rinse and dry the macadamia nuts, if they are salted. Dust a rolling board with powdered sugar and roll out the marzipan thickly. Coat thinly with jam and cut into two equally shaped pieces and an approximate third. On one piece spread a layer of nuts and peel, then place one third of marzipan on top, sticky-side down. Smear the top with jam and add another layer of nuts and peel. Then put the last third on top (also sticky-side down). Carefully press and roll this sandwich flatter and wider until the nuts almost push through. Trim, cut into small portions and sprinkle the mixture with powdered sugar before presenting.

 varieties

"Mauka" and "Wiamanola" are two fine varieties with buttery rich flavor.

 cultivation

Macadamia nuts prefer tropical or subtropical, moist conditions. They are hardy in Zones 9 and 10. They are not particular as to soil and do best on the volcanic slopes of Hawaii. They thrive at medium elevations.

Growing under Glass and in Containers
If the seed could be obtained they might be grown under glass, in pots to constrain growth, though it is doubtful they would crop.

Ornamental and Wildlife Value
They are attractive, glossy, dark trees, but too tender for growing successfully outside subtropical zones.

Propagation
They are propagated by seed, but as the nuts are usually sold roasted and salted this may be difficult to find.

Pruning and Training
Only remedial pruning is necessary and they will form bushy trees.

Harvesting and Storing
The shells are very hard to crack, so the bulk crops are collected mechanically and taken to factories to be de-husked, shelled, roasted and salted before packaging and storing, when they will keep for up to a year or so.

Cocos nucifera from the family Arecaceae
COCONUTS

These attractive palms, so typical of dreamy, deserted islands, are spread by their floating, oval-husked nuts. The thick, fibrous husk is contained in a rind and itself encloses a thick-shelled, oval nut with a hollow kernel that is full of milk when under-ripe.

Palm, up to 90 ft. Life span: medium to long. Evergreen, not usually self-fertile. Fruits: 12 in. plus, green-brown, oval husk containing the nut. Value: 65 percent oil.

Venerated in the islands of the Pacific as a sacred emblem of fertility, coconuts are distributed and known around the world.

Each tree holds a huge weight of small head-crushing bombs

 ## varieties

The King Coconut of Ceylon is esteemed for its sweet juice. The Dwarf Coconut, *Nyiur-gading*, of Malaysia has small fruits, but crops when young and at only a few feet high. The Maldive Coconut is small and almost round; the Needle Coconut of the Nicobar Islands is triangular and pointed.

cultivation

Coconuts thrive by the sea in moist, tropical heat and rich, loamy soils and are planted about 33 ft. apart. They are suitable only in Zone 10, but they are interesting to grow from seed as houseplants.

Growing under Glass and in Containers
These are very attractive, easy plants to start with, rapidly outgrowing most places. The "Dwarf Coconut" may fruit, given good conditions, in only 4 years — thus, while still small enough to stay indoors!

Ornamental and Wildlife Value
Very attractive trees, these can be used for indoor display until they grow too large.

Propagation
Ripe nuts that are laid on their side and barely covered with compost will germinate readily in heat.

Harvesting and Storing
The nuts are used as they drop.

 ## companion planting

Coconuts are often grown in alternate rows with rubber trees, and with cacao while young. Climbing bell peppers, *Piper nigrum*, are grown up the coconut trunks.

 ## culinary

The milk is drunk fresh or fermented. The nut is eaten raw or cooked, often in the form of desiccated or shredded coconut.

Coconut Cookies
Makes approx. 10

1 egg white
1⅓ powdered sugar
¾ cup dried coconut
Rice paper
Glacé cherries
Crystallized angelica

Beat the egg white until stiff, then beat in the sugar and coconut. Spoon blobs of the mixture on to rice paper on a baking sheet. Garnish each with a cherry and angelica and bake at 350°F for 15 minutes or until they are browning.

Bertholletia excelsa from the family Myrtaceae

BRAZILS
OR QUEENSLAND NUTS

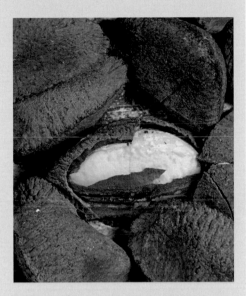

Tree up to 100 ft. Life span: long. Semi-evergreen. Fruits: up to 6 in.; brown, spherical shell containing many nuts. Value: 65 percent fat and 14 percent protein.

These are tall handsome trees found on the banks of the Amazon and Orinoco Rivers. They have large, laurel-like leaves and panicles of white flowers, which drop brown, spherical bombs with thick, hard cases. These need to be smashed to reveal inside a dozen or more nuts shaped like orange segments, each with its own hard shell enclosing the oval, brown-skinned, sweet, white kernel. Natives of Brazil, these are still mainly produced there and also in Venezuela and Guyana. They are grown ornamentally in other countries such as Ceylon, but rarely on a commercial scale.

Propagation
The nuts can be started off in heat, but actually take months to germinate.

 other uses

The oil expressed from the kernels is used industrially; bark once caulked ships.

 culinary

Most often Brazil nuts are eaten raw at Christmas time, but are also widely used in cooking, baking and confectionery.

Treacly Brazil Pie
Serves 6

8 oz. shortcrust dough
1/3 cup Brazil nuts
1/3 cup breadcrumbs
1/3 cup light corn syrup
Juice and grated rind of 1 lemon
Cream, to serve

Roll out three-quarters of the dough and line a pie pan with it. Use dried peas to weigh it down, and bake blind at 375°F for 10 minutes. Remove the peas and put a layer of nuts around the bottom of the case. Mix the other ingredients together and pour on top. Decorate with strips of dough and then bake for 20 minutes at 375°F. Serve the pie with dollops of whipped cream.

 varieties

Many consider the Sapucaya Nut superior; it is similar, though it comes from a different tree, *Lecythis zabucajo*.

You really don't want to climb a Brazil nut tree so you wait till they drop

 cultivation

Brazil trees thrive in deep, rich, alluvial soil in tropical conditions. They will grow in Zone 10.

Ornamental and Wildlife Value
Very attractive trees, but too large and requiring too much heat and warmth for widespread use.

Growing under Glass and in Containers
These can be grown from seed and kept dwarfed in containers, making interesting specimens, but are unlikely ever to fruit.

Harvesting and Storing
The individual nuts are obtained by cracking the spherical containers, which are sealed with wooden plugs. Inside their shells the nuts will keep for up to 2 years.

Pruning and Training
These need no special attention, but are slow. They are often not cultivated, but are gathered from the wild, as they take 15 years to start fruiting.

Arachis hypogaea from the family Leguminosae

GROUNDNUTS OR PEANUTS

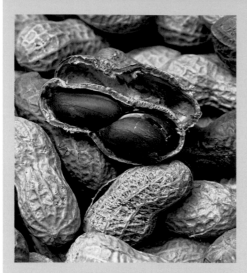

Herbaceous, 2 ft. Life span: annual. Self-fertile. Fruits: ½ in. small oval seeds. Value: rich in oil, protein and vitamins B and E.

Peanuts are always known and used as nuts, although they are in fact the seeds of a tropical, pea-like, annual plant. After pollination of the yellow "pea" flower, the stalk lengthens and pushes the seed pod into the ground, where it matures. The light brown husks shell easily to reveal a few red-skinned, whitish-yellow seeds.

Natives of tropical America, peanuts were brought to Europe in the 16th century and remained curiosities until the nineteenth. Useful for oil, animal feed and "nuts", they are now grown worldwide.

 ## culinary

Peanuts are commonly roasted and salted, and are much used in baking and confections, savory sauces and for their butter and edible oil. They should be kept dry until required.

Roasted Peanuts
Makes 2 lb.

4 cups peanuts, shelled weight
4 cloves garlic
6 to 8 canned anchovy fillets
3 tablespoons oregano

Boil the peanuts for 2 minutes and slip off their skins, then dry the nuts. Blend the garlic, anchovies and oregano. Coat the peanuts with this mixture and roast at 350°F for 10 minutes or so. Stir and cool.

 ## companion planting

Peanuts have been grown with rubber and coconuts.

 ## other uses

Peanut oil is used industrially.

 ## varieties

"Spanish Bunch" or "Virginia" varieties average fewer kernels than the better "Valencia" varieties, which have up to four. Mauritius peanuts are believed to be of superior quality.

 ## cultivation

Peanuts prefer loose, dryish, sandy soil. They need a long season of warmth to mature, and thus do best in southern gardens. Northern gardeners an choose earlier varieties and start the seeds indoors a month before the last spring frost date, to get a head start on the season. They are normally grown on ridges to make digging the crop easier.

Ornamental and Wildlife Value
Too pea-like to be attractive, they have curiosity value. The seeds are only too valuable to wildlife!

Pruning and Training
These require no care. The old varieties were more difficult.

Pests and Diseases
On a garden scale these are problem-free, save for rodent thefts.

Harvesting and Storing
The pods are dug in fall, thoroughly dried and shelled before storing. Commercially the bulk is pressed for oil and feedcake.

Propagation
Sow in pots in heat for growing on in large pots to fruition, or planting out in favorable areas. In warm areas they are grown outdoors, sown 3 in. deep, about 2 ft. apart each way.

Growing under Glass and in Containers
Peanuts are good subjects for greenhouses, or in large pots, which can be kept under cover at the start and end of the season and put out on the patio in summer.

Grow them in the ground, not pots

OTHER NUTS

Araucaria araucana,
Monkey Puzzle or Chile Pine, Auracariaceae
These well-known trees, with spiny, overlapping, dark green leaves festooning the long, tail-like branches. Where they have been planted severally, as at a school in Sussex, they reportedly set seed and the nuts were shed most years. In Chile the seeds are eaten raw, roasted or boiled. Closely related trees are also grown in Brazil and in Australia.

Brosimium alicastrum,
Maya Breadnut is a tall Caribbean tree with round yellow fruits containing a large edible seed. Not to be confused with the Breadnut which is the seedy form of the normally seedless Breadfruit, *Artocarpus* (see p. 561.)

Canarium ovata,
Pili Nut, Burseraceae
This is the legendary and rare Pili nut frustratingly rated as the best tasting of all nuts by those fortunate enough to have found it.

Castanospermum australe,
Moreton Bay Chestnut, Leguminosae
These poisonous Australian nuts are relished by native Australians, who leach them in water before drying and roasting the nuts to render them edible.

Coffea arabica,
Coffee, Rubiaceae
Small, evergreen trees, which once grew wild in Arabia and are now cultivated in most hot countries. Coffee "beans" are seeds from the cherry-like berries, roasted to oily charcoal, then leached with hot water.

Terminalia catappa,
Geranium tree, West Indian Almond
Has red geranium-like flowers followed by small flattened walnut-like fruits containing a very hard-to-get-at edible kernel much resembling almond.

Cordia sebestena,
Geiger tree
This is another Caribbean tree with hairy leaves, orange-red tubular flowers and sweet sticky fruits that can be eaten raw or cooked with sugar or even made into cough medicine.

Fagus sylvatica,
Beech, Fagaceae
A well-known tree that can reach 100 ft. and chokes out everything underneath with heavy, dry shade. Although parts of the tree are poisonous and have been used medicinally, an edible oil can be extracted from the seeds and they have been eaten raw and roasted to make "coffee". In sheer desperation, beech sawdust has been boiled, baked and mixed with flour to make "bread". A worthy subject for parks on acid or alkaline soil, but far too large for most gardens! The American Beech, *F. grandiflora*, is similar.

Myristica fragrans,
Nutmeg, Myristiceae
These nuts are only ever used as a spice. They are natives of the Moluccas Islands in Indonesia and are commercially grown in few other places save Grenada in the West Indies. The trees reach 55–65 ft. and have fruits resembling apricots or peaches which split, like almonds, revealing a nut surrounded by a reddish yellow aril. This is the spice, mace. Inside the thin shell is the brown nutmeg kernel which rattles when ripe. If still alive, they will germinate in heat after 3 months or so.

Quercus species,
Acorns, Fagaceae
Although acorns are not edible raw these have been ground, leached and cooked in times of hardship, some varieties were apparently relished, and with huge numbers of species these have great potential for breeding a new tasty nut or oil source. Acorns fatten swine but can kill horses! *Q. macrocarpa*, Bur Oak, has the biggest acorns, they also have a low tannin content and are easily made edible. The Cork Oak, *Q. suber* also bears more edible acorns.

Simmondsia chinensis,
Goat Nut, Jojoba
Grown mainly for the oil which is odorless and does not go rancid, the small nut like fruit can be eaten if desperate.

Xanthocerus sorbifolium,
Bob's Nuts, Sapidaceae
From China comes this pretty slow growing, very hardy tree much resembling a mountain ash with sprays of almost orchid-like flowers followed by green, smooth, small apple-sized capsules with thick hard walls that split and peel back to drop about a dozen or so black shelled nuts. These much resemble macadamias when roasted. Very good!! Apparently the flowers and foliage were also cooked and eaten.

PRACTICAL GARDENING

PLANNING YOUR VEGETABLE GARDEN

Several factors determine the planning and layout of a vegetable garden and the varieties that can be grown:

- the locality and climatic conditions
- the size and shape of the plot
- the number of people to be supplied with vegetables
- the duration of cropping
- the skill of the gardener, and the time available for maintaining the plot
- whether the vegetables are intended for use when fresh, stored or both

It is a good idea to list the vegetables you like, then decide how and where they can be grown to achieve the best results. In large gardens a vast range and volume of tasty vegetables can be produced using crop rotation and protected cropping to extend the growing season. Smaller sites allow fewer opportunities for self-sufficiency, but it is still possible to grow a good selection of high-value crops like asparagus and try unusual varieties. Even the tiniest gardens, balconies or patios are suitable, particularly with the use of containers, while areas surrounded by buildings sometimes create favorable microclimates for tender vegetables and early crops. Protected cropping provides further opportunities to defy the cold weather.

Before preparing a planting plan it is important to be aware of the advantages and disadvantages of the site, considering everything from aspect and shelter to soil quality and drainage. Choose a design that suits your site and taste: traditionally, plots were planned in beds and rows, but you may prefer the potager (or "edible landscape") developed by the French, or the raised bed system, which is ideal for intensive small- or large-scale cropping. It is essential to provide the best possible growing conditions for optimum production and the old saying, "the answer lies in the soil", is particularly relevant to vegetable growing.

Accurate timing is also a prerequisite. A cropping timetable should make full use of the ground for the full growing season. It is advisable to plan backwards from the intended harvesting date to work out when crops should be sown. The aim is to provide home-grown vegetables throughout the year, even if you have to rely on frozen or stored produce.

Top: Kitchen garden
Bottom: Is there a more glorious site for a garden than the foot of the Alps?

Site and Soil

Most vegetables are short-term crops, which are harvested before they reach maturity. To achieve the necessary rapid growth, the ideal site is warm and light with good air circulation. This is particularly important for the fertilization of wind-pollinated crops such as sweetcorn, and to discourage pests and diseases, which flourish in still conditions. However, it is worth noting that strong winds can reduce plant growth by up to 30 percent.

On a *gently sloping site* facing the sun, the soil warms faster in spring than in other aspects, making such an area perfect for early crops.

It is more difficult to work the soil on *steeper slopes*, especially if machinery is being used: crops should be planted across, rather than down the slope to reduce the risk of soil erosion during heavy rain. On *very steep slopes* the ground should be terraced.

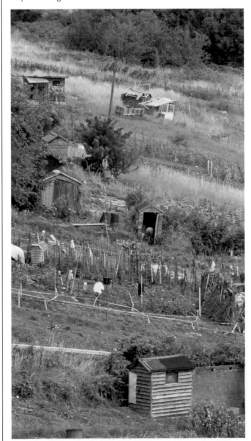

A sloping site is ideal for early crops

There's plenty of cropping potential here

The sight of a neat, well-tended vegetable garden burgeoning with healthy crops is immensely satisfying. Conditioned to believe that vegetables are functional and flowers beautiful, many fail to appreciate the beauty and bounty of a vegetable plot with its contrasting colors, forms and textures, neatly framed by well-kept paths.

The traditional design for a vegetable garden is based on a system of rows. This gives ease of access and maintenance, enables crops to be rotated regularly and for maximum production while preventing the build-up of pests and diseases. Large kitchen gardens were formerly attached to a "great house," with the gardeners' task to cultivate a wide range of crops and supply the household with vegetables throughout the year.

By way of contrast, most gardeners now have smaller gardens, and the basis for what they grow and how they grow is more a matter of choice than necessity.

This provides them with the opportunity to grow vegetables for their ornamental and culinary values so you can savor the flavor. For the same reasons, it may also be preferable to grow small quantities of a wider range of cultivars.

Color
Vegetables are not only eaten for their flavor and nutritional value but add welcome color to a meal. Consider the range of colors and tonal variation in a salad; it is generally greater than the range of flavors.

There are tones of green in lettuce, endive and cucumber, yellow in peppers, purple in beets and leaf lettuce and red in tomatoes and peppers. For centuries, only the French potager capitalized on this display of colors, but vegetables are at last more commonly used as design elements within ornamental planting schemes. The sight of vegetables dotted individually or grouped in the flower border has in recent years become a familiar sight. To the open mind and eye,

all vegetables are ornamental, even if their attraction is more obvious in some than in others. The contrasting red and green foliage of ruby chard is sumptuous, as is Bull's Blood beets, while purple- or yellow-podded Green beans and the mauve leaves of cabbage Red Drumhead create their own exotic magic. Red-skinned onions like Red Baron and the red-leaved lettuce Lollo Rosso are equally stunning. Squashes impress with their bold shapes and color (think of Turk's Turban) while tomatoes like the golden Yellow Perfection and striped Tigerella delight the eye. Flowers, fruits and companion plants add other color accents.

Form
While you may not consider the shape of certain vegetables to be interesting (rutabagas or potatoes, for instance), a good many have appealing foliage or a distinctive habit. The bold architectural leaves and sculptured form of globe artichokes are prized by garden designers, a "wigwam" of bicolored runner beans or trailing cucurbits makes a dramatic focal

Look closely and see a bud's true beauty

point, while the compact growth of parsley and chives is a neat edging for borders. Members of the onion family, leeks, and chives have spiky, linear leaves, which contrast well with the rounded shapes of lettuce and the feathery, arching growth of carrot tops. Celery and Brussels sprouts naturally have a distinguished upright habit. Perhaps the most unusual of all, e.g., a purple Brussels sprout, Rubine, which is planted as a single specimen in a container, looks like an angular, alien sculpture.

Texture

Texture is rarely considered a design feature, yet the different colors and forms of vegetable foliage are underlined by their texture. Consider the solidity of a compact cabbage head, wreathed in glaucous,

puckered leaves, or the soft billowing effect created by the dissected leaves of fennel or asparagus foliage. Exploiting such contrasts provides a foliage display as interesting as a bedding scheme or herbaceous border. Even after harvest the impact remains; the tall dried stems of sweetcorn look wonderful when frosted on a winter's day and the rustling sound as the wind blows through their dead leaves brings life to a desolate garden.

Vegetables as Bedding Plants

Many vegetables are grown as annuals and, as each crop matures and is harvested, the appearance of the vegetable garden changes. Often, the only constant elements are the framework of paths and hedges and a few long-lived perennial crops.

Such intensively grown crops are easier to maintain when grown in a formal pattern as this provides the ideal opportunity to arrange crops in brightly colored, bold patterns or emphasize their subtle qualities. Brightly colored chard, lettuce or kale or the fern-like foliage of carrots can be used to provide a foliage display rivalling any bedding plant.

Vegetables which have gone to seed look particularly spectacular; lettuces are upright and leafy, beets display their red-veined leaves and bold flower spikes while onions and leeks produce symmetrical globes of flowers which are invaluable for attracting pollinating insects. Some gardeners allow a few plants to go to seed to enjoy such effects, but would you be daring enough to create a planting scheme with the specific purpose of featuring vegetables in their later stages?

One approach to creating a bedding scheme is to group together plants with a similar life span, for a long-term display. Alternatively, with skilful planning, it is possible to plant crops taking different times to reach maturity, filling any gaps with suitable vegetables after harvest, to retain the impact of the design. The time scale can vary considerably, with radishes taking a mere five weeks, and sprouting broccoli and winter cabbages remaining in the ground for several months. The rapid changeover of these crops means that colors and flavors are constantly changing within the scheme; there is a fine example at the Eden Project in the UK (the largest indoor rainforest, under two large biomes).

Perennial vegetables such as asparagus, globe artichoke and rhubarb can be grown in separate beds or used as

permanent feature plants within the design. In smaller or irregularly shaped gardens, crop rotation allows a wide range of annual design patterns and planting arrangements. Growing vegetables purely for their ornamental value is an option which gardeners of such gardens should consider.

The Potager

Their love of food and appreciation of aesthetics motivated French gardeners to create the potager, or ornamental vegetable garden, with a more obvious visual appeal than the English kitchen garden. Simple, formal, geometric shapes such as four square-shaped raised beds dissected by straight paths form a permanent structure, enlivened with a succession of vibrantly colored leafy crops chosen for their culinary and visual qualities. The main paths are wide enough for a wheelbarrow, but narrower ones, and stepping stones, allow access for maintenance and picking. Vegetables are placed according to their height and habit, larger vegetables forming center pieces and smaller ones making up the rows. Climbing vegetables growing over ornamental tripods, arches or even canes provide height, and the whole area can be screened by trellis and can include vegetables in containers as additional features.

To maintain the symmetry, harvest plants with an eye to pattern: work evenly from both ends and from the center, or cut every other plant to keep the coverage balanced as far as possible. Make full use of successional cropping to ensure that the soil is always utilized and the pattern maintained.

Random Systems

Scattering vegetables individually or in groups among ornamental borders is becoming more popular. They should be planted according to their ultimate height with lower plants near the front of the border, using brightly colored vegetables strong enough to stand up to their brightly colored neighbors. Grow purple-pod climbing Green beans through shrubs instead of clematis, runner bean "Painted Lady" instead of sweet peas and purple-leaved cabbage alongside nasturtiums. Mini vegetables can be grown in window boxes or hanging baskets; try tomato "Tumbler" or grow climbers as trailing plants.

The only requirement for successful growth of vegetables among ornamental plants is adequate soil or compost fertility, which can easily be maintained with well-prepared soil and careful feeding.

PLANNING YOUR HERB GARDEN

Herbs are so versatile that they should appeal to anyone, be they a cook, a lover of salads, or someone just wanting to enjoy the rich scents of plants and watch the butterflies collecting nectar from the flowers. And there are herbs for every space; they will grow in a window box or in a pot on a sunny window ledge; and some can be grown indoors as houseplants as well as outside in gardens, small or large. The best way to grow herbs is the organic way. Quite apart from the fact that if you use natural products, the soil remains clean and free from chemical pollutants, in organic herb gardens there is no chance of contaminating a plant before you eat it. Organic methods also encourage bees and other insects to the garden, which in turn helps maintain the healthy natural balance of predator and pest.

Conditions

As herbs are basically wild plants tamed to fit a garden, it makes sense to grow them in conditions comparable with their original environment. This can be a bit difficult, for they come from all over the world. As a general rule, the majority of culinary herbs come from the Mediterranean and prefer a dry sunny place. But herbs really are adaptable and they do quite well outside their native habitat, provided you are aware of what they prefer.

Choosing the Site

Before planning your site, it is worth surveying your garden in detail. Start by making a simple plan and mark on it north and south. Show the main areas of shade — a high fence, a neighboring house and any high trees, noting whether they are deciduous or evergreen. Finally, note any variations in soil type — wet, dry, heavy etc. Soil is one of the most important factors and will determine the types of herb you can grow. For different soil types, see p. 633.

Use

Next, decide what you want from your herb garden. Do you want a retreat away from the house? Or a herb garden where the scents drift indoors? Or do you want a culinary herb garden close at hand to the kitchen door?

Assessing the position of your herbs before planting

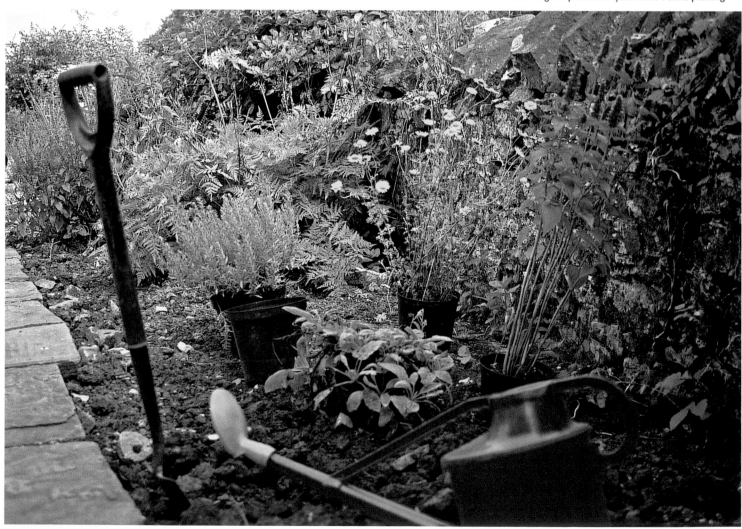

Style

Then think about what shape or style you want the garden to take. Formal herb gardens are based on patterns and geometric shapes. Informal gardens are a free-for-all, with species and colors, all mixed together. Informal gardens may look unplanned, but the best have been well planned. This is worth doing even if it is just to check the final height and spread of the plant. It can be misleading buying plants from a garden center — they are all neat, uniform and fairly small, and it is well worth investigating and trying to visualize their mature size.

The plants have to be accessible, either for using fresh or to harvest, so paths are a good idea. They also introduce patterns to the design and can help to define its shape. For convenience, herbs should be no more than 30 in. from a path, and ideally the beds no more than 3–4 ft. wide. If they are more than 4 ft. wide, insert stepping stones to improve access.

laying paths

There are a number of choices of materials you can use for paths.

Grass

A grass path is quite easy to achieve and looks very attractive. Another plus point is the minimal cost. Make it at least as wide as your lawn mower, otherwise you will be cutting it on your hands and knees with shears. It is a good idea to edge the path either with wood, metal or, more attractively, with bricks, laid on their side end to end. Disadvantages to this kind of path are that it needs mowing and will not take heavy traffic.

Gravel

Gravel paths really do lend themselves to being planted with herbs. Be sure to prepare them well otherwise a water trap will form, and the plants would be better off being aquatic.

First remove the topsoil carefully. Then dig out to a depth of 12 in., putting the soil to one side. It is advisable to put a wooden edge between the soil of the garden or lawn and the new path. This will stop the soil falling into the path, and keep the edge neat. Fill the newly formed ditch with 6 in. hard core. Mix the topsoil with peat, bark and grit in the ratio 3:1:1:1, and put this mix on top of the hard core to a depth of 3 in. Finish with 3 in. gravel or pea shingle. There are many colors of gravel available, most large garden centers stock a good range, or if you have a quarry nearby it is worth chatting them up.

Roll the path before planting. Herbs that will grow happily in gravel are creeping or upright thymes, winter savory, and pennyroyal. The disadvantage of gravel is that you will find that weeds will recur, so be diligent.

Bricks

Paths made out of bricks have become very fashionable. There is now a subtle range of colors available, and varied and original patterns can be created. For standard-size bricks, dig out to a depth of 4 in. As with the gravel path, include a wooden edge. Spread 2 in. of sharp sand over the base; level and dampen. Lay the brick on top of the sand in the desired pattern, leaving a 1/8–1/4 in. gap between the bricks. Settle them in, using a mallet or a rented plate vibrator.

If you wish to plant the path with herbs, it is as well at this juncture to leave out one or two bricks, filling the gaps later with compost and planting them when the path has settled. When the whole path has been laid, spread the joints with a mix 4:1 of fine dry sand and cement, and brush it in. The mixture will gradually absorb the moisture from the atmosphere, so setting the brick.

Paving stones

These can take up a lot of space and are expensive to lay over a large area. Garden centers now stock a large range in various colors and shapes. Also try building centers, you may get a better deal, especially if you require large quantities. Paving stones are ideal for the classic chequer-board designs and the more formal designs.

If you want the paving stones to lie flush with the ground, dig out the soil to the depth of the slab plus 2 in. Put 2 in. of sharp sand on to the prepared area, level off and lay the slabs on top, tapping them down, and making sure they are level. If the chosen area is already level and you want the slabs to be proud, then lay them directly in position with only a small layer of sand underneath.

alternative planting

Raised beds

If your soil is difficult, or if you wish to create a feature in the garden, raised beds are a good solution. Also, plants in raised beds are easier to keep under control and will not wander so much around the rest of the garden. Finally, they are more accessible for harvesting and stand at a good height for those in wheelchairs.

The ideal height for a raised bed is between 12 in. and 30 in. If you raise it over 3 ft. high you will need some form of foundation for the retaining walls, to prevent them keeling over with the weight of the soil. Retaining walls can be made out of old railway sleepers (which are not as cheap as they used to be and you must be sure to avoid creosote), logs cut in half, old bricks, or even red bricks — leave the odd one out and plant a creeping thyme in its place.

For filling a 1 ft. raised bed, the following ratios are ideal. First put a layer of hard core (rubble) on top of the existing soil to a depth of 3 in., followed by an 3 in.

Raised bed: ideal for confining plants that tend to roam

layer of gravel, and finally 6 in. of topsoil mix — made up of 1 part peat, 1 part bark, 1 part grit or sharp sand, with 3 parts topsoil.

Lawns

Many herbs are excellent ground cover and can make a fragrant lawn but, as already mentioned under chamomile (see p. 271), beware of planting too large an area to begin with. It can be an error costly in both time and money. Small areas filled with creeping herbs give great delight to the unsuspecting visitor who when walking over the lawn, discovers a pleasant aroma exuding from their feet!

It may sound repetitious, but it is worth saying that preparing your site well is the key to a good garden. Given a typical soil, prepare the site for the lawn by digging the whole area out to a depth of 12 in. and then prepare in exactly the same way as for the raised bed: 3 in. hard core, 3 in. gravel, 6 in. topsoil mix — this time, 1 part peat, 2 parts sharp sand, 3 parts top soil. Apart from chamomile, other plants that can be used for a herb lawn are Corsican mint, *Mentha requinni,* planted 4 in. apart, or creeping thymes (see p. 424–26 for varieties) and plant them about 9 in. apart.

HERB GARDENS

The gardens I have designed can be followed religiously, or adapted to meet your personal tastes, needs and of course space. It is with this last requirement in mind that I have specifically not put the exact size into the design and concentrated on the shape, layout and the relationship between plants. I hope these plans give you freedom of thought and some inspiration.

first herb garden

When planning your first herb garden, choose plants you will use and enjoy. I have designed this garden in exactly the same way as the one at my herb farm. Much as I would love to have a rambling herb garden, I need something practical and easy to manage, because the nursery plants need all my attention.

It is also important that the herbs are easy to get at, so that I can use them every day. By dividing the garden up into four sections and putting paving stones around the outside and through the middle, it is easy to maintain and provides good accessibility.

For this garden, I have chosen a cross-section of herbs with a bias toward culinary use, because the more you use and handle the plants, the more you will understand their habits. There is much contradictory advice on which herb to plant with which but many of these are old wives tales.

There are only a few warnings I will give: Do not plant dill or coriander near wormwood as it will impair their flavor. Also, different mints near each other cross-pollinate and over the years will lose their individual identity. Finally, if you plan to collect the seed from lavenders, keep the species well apart. Aside from that, if you like it, plant it.

1   Parsley *Petroselinum crispum*
2   Pineapple Mint *Mentha suaveolens* "Variegata"
3   Fennel *Foeniculum vulgare*
4   Lavander Munstead *Lavandula angustifolia* "Munstead"
5   Greek Oregano *Origanum vulgare* subsp. *hirtum* "Greek"
6   Alpine Strawberry *Fragaria vesca*
7   Purple Sage *Salvia officinalis* "Purpurascens"
8   Chives *Allium schoenoprasum*
9   Heartsease *Viola tricolor*
10 Golden Curly Marjoram *Origanum vulgare* "Aureum Crispum"
11 Salad Burnet *Sanguisorba minor*
12 Lemon Thyme *Thymus citriodorus*
13 Garden Thyme *Thymus vulgaris*
14 Roman Chamomile *Chamaemelum nobile*
15 Rock Hyssop *Hyssopus offinialis* subsp. *aristatus*
16 Buckler-Leaf Sorrel *Rumex scutatus*
17 Bergamot *Monarda didyma*
18 Dartington Curry Plant *Helichrysum italicum* "Dartington"
19 Rosemary *Rosmarinus officinalis*
20 Borage *Borago officinalis*
21 Variegated Lemon Balm *Melissa officinalis* "Aurea"
22 Apple Mint *Mentha suaveolens*
23 Winter Savory *Satureja montana*
24 Chervil *Anthriscus cerefolium*

herb bath garden

This may seem a bit eccentric to the conventially minded but when my back is aching after working in the nursery, and I feel that unmentionable age, and totally exhausted, there is nothing nicer than lying in a herb bath and reading a good book.

The herbs I use most are thyme, to relieve an aching back, lavender, to give me energy, and eau-de-cologne to knock me out. Simply tie up a bunch of your favorite herbs with string, attach them to the hot water tap and let the water run. The scent of the plants will invade both water and room. Alternatively, put some dried herbs in a muslin bag and drop it into the bath.

Remember when planting this garden to make sure that the plants are accessible. Hops will need to climb up a fence or over a log. Again, quite apart from the fact that the herbs from this garden are for use in the bath they make a very aromatic garden in their own right. Position a seat next to the lavender and rosemary so that when you get that spare 5 minutes, you can sit in quiet repose and revel in the scent.

1. Lavender Seal *Lavandula* x *intermedia* "Seal"
2. Lemon Verbena *Aloysia triphylla*
3. Benenden Blue Rosemary *Rosmarinus officinalis* var. *angustissimus* "Benenden Blue"
4. Gold Sage *Salvia officinalis* "Icterina"
5. Valerian *Valeriana officinalis*
6. Bronze Fennel *Foeniculum vulgare* "Purpureum"
7. Tansy *Tanacetum vulgare*
8. Golden Lemon Thyme *Thymus citriodorus* "Golden Lemon"
9. Double-Flowered Chamomile *Chamaemelum nobile* "Flore Pleno"
10. Houseleek *Sempervivum tectorum*
11. Black Peppermint *Mentha* x *piperita*
12. Orange-scented Thyme *Thymus* "Fragrantissimus"
13. Meadowsweet *Filipendula ulmeria*
14. Fennel *Foeniculum vulgare*
15. Pennyroyal *Mentha pulegium*
16. Creeping Hops *Humulus lupulus*
17. French Lavender *Lavandula stoechas*
18. Bay *Laurus nobilis*
19. Roman Chamomile *Chamaemelum nobile*
20. Lemon Balm *Melissa officinalis*
21. Porlock Thyme *Thymus* "Porlock"
22. Prostrate Rosemary *Rosmarinus officinalis* Prostratus Group
23. Golden Marjoram *Origanum vulgare* "Aureum"
24. Eau de Cologne Mint *Mentha* x *piperita* f. *citrata*
25. Comfrey *Symphytum officinale*
26. Lady's Mantle *Alchemilla mollis*
27. Yarrow *Achillea millefolium*
28. Lavender Grappenhall *Lavandula* x *intermedia* "Pale Pretender"
29. Silver Posie Thyme *Thymus vulgaris* "Silver Posie'

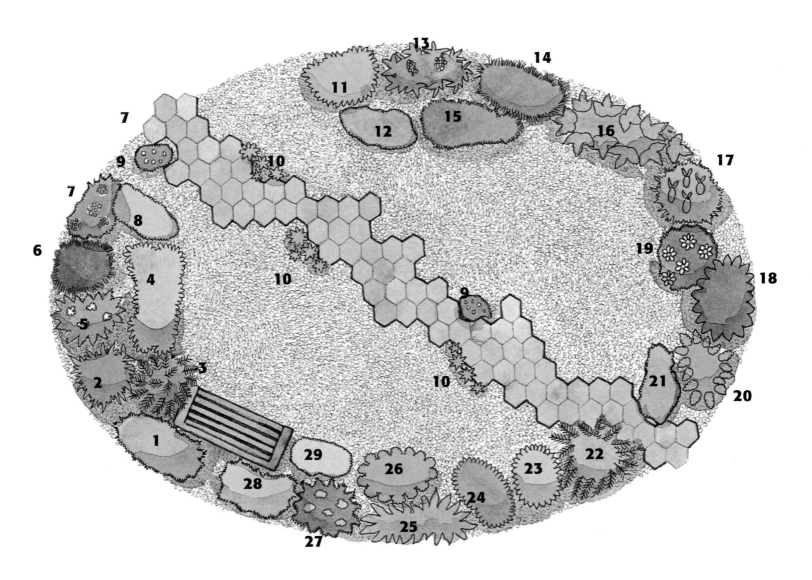

white herb garden

This garden gave me great pleasure to create. For me, it is a herb garden with a different perspective.

It has a row of steps going from the road to the front door of the house. Either side of the steps is a dwarf white lavender hedge. In spring before the lavender, and just before the Lily of the Valley, are in flower, the sweet woodruff gives a carpet of small white flowers. This is the start of the white garden, which then flowers throughout the year through to fall. It is a most attractive garden with a mixture of scents, foliage and flowers.

This planting combination can easily be adapted to suit a border. Even though it is not a conventional herb garden, all the herbs can be used in their traditional way. The garlic chives with baked potatoes, the horehound for coughs, the chamomile to make a soothing tea, and the lavender to make lavender bags or to use in the bath.

The great thing about a garden like this is that it requires very little work to maintain. The hedge is the only part that needs attention – trim in the spring and after flowering in order to maintain its shape.

1 Dwarf White Lavender *Lavandula angustifolia* "Nana Alba"
2 Sweet Woodruff *Galium odoratum*
3 Bergamot Snow Maiden *Monarda* "Schneewittchen"
4 Jacob's Ladder (white) *Polemonium caeruleum* subsp. *caeruleum* f. *album*
5 Yarrow *Achillea millefolium*
6 Foxgloves (white) *Digitalis purpurea* f. *albiflora* (POISONOUS)
7 Roman Chamomile *Chamaemelum nobile*
8 Lily of the Valley *Convallaria majalis* (POISONOUS)
9 White Thyme *Thymus serpyllum* var. *albus*
10 White Hyssop *Hyssopus officinalis* f. *albus*
11 Snowdrift Thyme *Thymus serpyllum* "Snowdrift"
12 Garlic Chives *Allium tuberosum*
13 Pyrethrum *Tanacetum cinerariifolium*
14 Sweet Cicely *Myrrhis odorata*
15 Valerian *Valeriana officinalis*
16 White Horehound *Marrubium vulgare*
17 Prostanthera *Prostanthera cuneata*

cook's herb garden

The best site for a culinary herb garden is a sunny area accessible from the kitchen. The importance of this is never clearer than when it is raining. There is no way that you will go out and cut fresh herbs if they are a long way away and difficult to reach. Another important factor is that the sunnier the growing position, the better the flavor of the herbs. This is because the sun brings the oils to the surface of the leaf of herbs such as sage, coriander, rosemary, basil, oregano and thyme.

The cook's herb garden could be made in the ground or in containers. If it is to be in the ground, make sure that the site is very well drained. Position a paving stone near each herbs so that it can be easily reached for cutting, weeding and feeding, and also to help contain the would-be rampant ones, such as the mints, which might otherwise take over.

Alternatively, the whole design could be adapted to be grown in containers. I have chosen only a few of the many varieties of culinary herb. If your favorite is missing, either add it to the design or substitute it for one of my choices.

1   Ginger Mint *Mentha* x *gracilis*
2   Chervil *Anthriscus cerefolium*
3   Coriander *Coriandrum sativum*
4   French Parsley *Petroselinum crispum* French
5   Chives *Allium schoenoprasum*
6   Corsican Rosemary *Rosmarinus officinalis* var. *angustissimus* "Corsican Blue"
7   Garden Thyme *Thymus vulgaris*
8   Angelica *Angelica archangelica*
9   Fennel *Foeniculum vulgare*
10 Winter Savory *Satureja montana*
11 Greek Basil *Ocimum minimum* "Greek"
12 Buckler-Leaf Sorrel *Rumex scutatus*
13 Bay *Laurus nobilis*
14 Sweet Cicely *Myrrhis odorata*
15 Garlic *Allium sativum*
16 Greek Oregano *Origanum vulgare* subsp. *hirtum* "Greek"
17 French Tarragon *Artemisia dracunculus*
18 Lovage *Levisticum officinale*
19 Garlic Chives *Allium tuberosum*
20 Lemon Balm *Melissa officinalis*
21 Moroccan Mint *Mentha spicata* var. *crispa* "Moroccan"
22 Dill *Anethum graveolens*
23 Parsley *Petroselinum crispum*
24 Lemon Thyme *Thymus citriodorus*
25 Sweet Marjoram *Origanum majorana*

salad herb garden

Herbs in salads make the difference between boring and interesting; they add flavor, texture, and color (especially the flowers).

Included in the design is a selection of salad herbs and salad herb flowers. There are two tall herbs in the middle, chicory and red orach (blue and red), which are planted opposite each other. Also, I have positioned the only other tall plant – borage – on

the outside ring, opposite the chicory so that the blue flowers together will make a vivid splash. To make access easy, there is an inner ring of stepping stones.

The herbs chosen are my choice and can easily be changed if you want to include a particular favorite. Remember to look at the heights; for instance, do not plant angelica in the outside circle because it will hide anything in the inner circle. Equally, in the inner circle make sure you do not plant a low growing plant next to a tall spreading herb because you will never find it.

This whole design can be incorporated in a small garden or on the edge of a vegetable garden to give color throughout the growing season. As the majority of these herbs are annuals or die back into the ground, the fall is an ideal time to give the garden a good feed by adding well rotted manure. This will encourage lots of leaves from the perennial herbs in the following season, and give a good kick start to the annuals when they are planted out in the following spring.

1 Chives *Allium schoenoprasum*	7 Buckler-Leaf Sorrel *Rumex scutatus*	13 Spearmint *Mentha spicata*
2 Caraway *Carum carvi*	8 Hyssop *Hyssopus officinalis*	14 Chicory *Cichorium intybus*
3 Borage *Borago officinalis*	9 Pot Marigold *Calendula officinalis*	15 Lemon Thyme *Thymus citriodorus*
4 Salad Burnet *Sanguisorba minor*	10 French Tarragon *Artemisia dracunculus*	16 Garlic Chives *Allium tuberosum*
5 Italian Parsley *Petroselinum crispum* French	11 Salad Rocket *Eruca vesicaria* subsp. *sativa*	17 Red Orach *Atriplex hortensis* var. *rubra*
6 Nasturtium *Tropaeolum majus*	12 Cowslips *Primula veris*	

medicinal herb garden

I would like this garden, not just for its medicinal use, but for the tranquillity it would bring. The choice of herbs is not only for internal use but for the whole being. I can imagine sitting on the seat watching the dragonflies playing over the pond.

Some of the herbs included are certainly not for self-administration, for instance blue flag iris, but this is a beautiful plant and would look most attractive with the meadowsweet and the valerian. Chamomile, peppermint, dill and lemon balm are easy to self-administer with care as they all make beneficial teas. One should not take large doses just because

they are natural, as some are very powerful. I strongly advise anyone interested in planting this garden to get a good herbal medicine book, see a fully trained herbalist, and always consult your doctor about a particular remedy.

1   Blue Flag Iris *Iris versicolor*
2   Meadowsweet *Filipendula ulmaria*
3   Valerian *Valeriana officinalis*
4   Horseradish *Armoracia rusticana*
5   Sage *Salvia officinalis*
6   Lady's Mantle *Alchemilla mollis*
7   Rosemary *Rosmarinus officinalis*
8   Dill *Anethum graveolens*
9   Chamomile *Chamaemelum nobile*
10 White Horehound *Marrubium vulgare*
11 Comfrey *Symphytum officinale*
12 Feverfew *Tanacetum parthenium*
13 Heartsease *Viola tricolor*
14 Lemon Balm *Melissa officinalis*
15 Garlic *Allium sativum*
16 Black Peppermint *Mentha* x *piperita*
17 Fennel *Foeniculum vulgare*
18 Pot Marigold *Calendula officinalis*
19 Lavender Seal *Lavandula* x *intermedia* "Seal"
20 Garden Thyme *Thymus vulgaris*
21 Houseleek *Sempervivum tectorum*

PLANNING THE FRUIT GARDEN

Planning your fruit garden means deciding your priorities — what do you want most? A little thought beforehand can save you a lot of wasted effort and ensure you actually get what you are after. With vegetables and bedding plants we have the luxury of burying our mistakes annually; with our trees and bushes we need to be more certain.

Although most of us get our garden fortuitously with our house, we usually have quite a wide choice of what we actually do with it, though the tendency is rarely to make radical changes. However, if we spend as much time and effort planning and remaking the garden as we do on decorating and furnishing the rest of our home it will turn out a mighty fine place!

Obviously the soil, climate, large trees, buildings and the rest of the hard landscape have to be worked around. But with skill and cunning, and modern materials, we can have almost any fruit we desire. Which fruits we actually choose to grow must depend on our budget as much as our climate. Obviously growing fruit in the open garden is easiest and cheapest, but a heated greenhouse allows for growing many more.

I think the first criterion for choosing fruit must be taste. After all, if you are growing for yourself, there is no point having poorly flavored varieties or ones that are widely available commercially. Go for those with flavor and sweetness, even if they are poor croppers. If you find you especially like a particular kind, you can always grow more.

Vine arches add a productive aesthetic

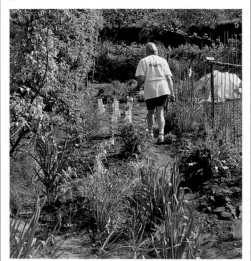

The Greater Plaited in his native surroundings

Freshness is invaluable and one's own fruits are the most truly fresh. It makes sense to choose fruits and varieties that are best eaten straight off the plant and thus rarely found in shops. Likewise dessert are preferable to cooking varieties as we eat them with all their vitamins and flavor while culinary fruits lose some in the cooking.

Of course, growing your fruit yourself guarantees freedom from unwanted chemical residues, and applying plentiful compost will ensure a good internal nutritional balance in the fruit. However, when choosing fruits, bear in mind that their dietary value can vary as much with variety as with type or growing conditions. For example, "Golden Delicious" apples contain a third or less vitamin C than "Ribston Pippin," while "Laxton's Superb" has only one sixth!

Economy must always be considered. Fruit growing requires higher investment initially than vegetables but running costs are lower. Similarly, soft fruit plants are cheaper than tree fruits individually, but require netting from birds in many areas. For maximum production, tree fruits produce as much weight from fewer plants per acre and usually require less maintenance, but are slower to crop, and live longer. Likewise vine fruits and cordons require more posts, ties and wires than trees or bushes. Any form of greenhouse or cover is costly, requiring upkeep, and of course heating uses much expensive energy.

The seasonal implications, and the time taken to maintain different fruits need to be considered, although in general fruit requires much less labor per yield than vegetable production. Initially the preparation and planting are heavy demands on time and energy but afterwards the workload is light, for the amateur if not for the professional. Fruit trees and bushes generally need mulching, thinning, picking and pruning, which are all light tasks and can be done upright in pleasant conditions. Growing the fruit is only half the battle, though. After picking we need to process and store the fruit and this takes more time than the growing! Don't plan to grow fruits that mature just when you go away on your annual vacation!

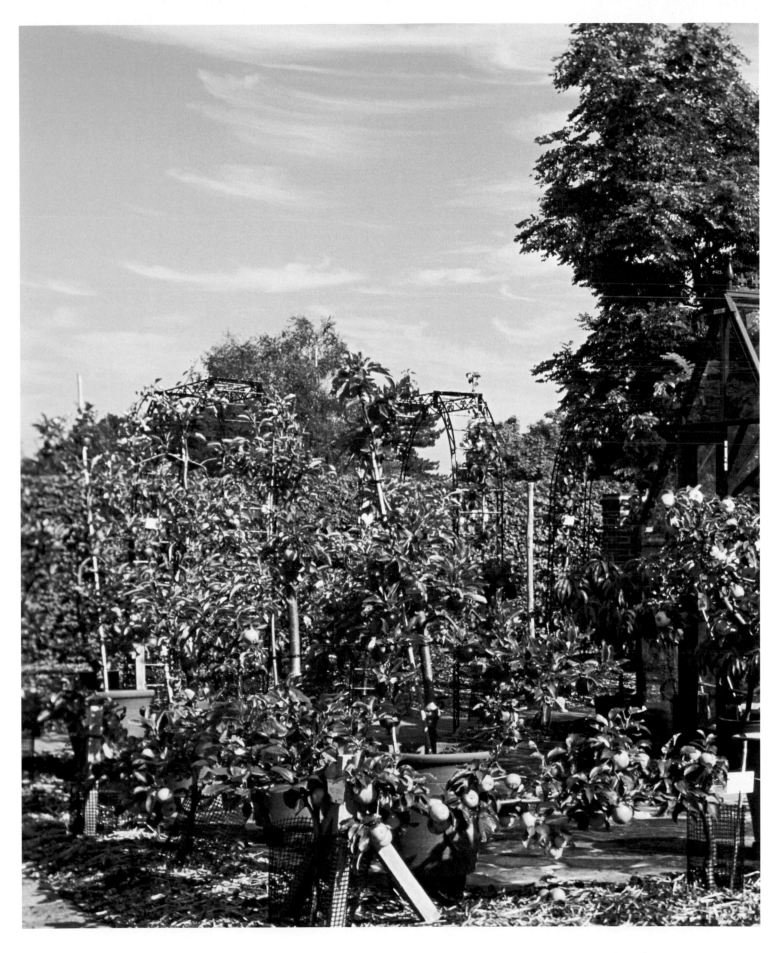

ORCHARDS

Orchards are devoted to the production of tree fruits, most frequently, privately and commercially, for apples, pears and plums. Other fruits are less common, only being widely grown in suitable areas — for example, cherries are little grown in wetter maritime regions but are common in drier zones such as Kent, in southeast England.

Orchards were always seeded down for convenience and soil preservation, though recent practice has been for bare cultivation, but this has been shown to be irresponsible. Initially weed-free conditions must be maintained in the orchard, but in general the preservation of bare soil is counterproductive. Most home orchard fruits will be best with a heavy mulch, ground cover or companion plants, or a grass sward.

For comfort and least cost, private orchards are still customarily planted with standard or semi-dwarf trees

A better way of staking

on strong rootstocks. Though more intensive plantings with more dwarfing stock are more productive, they also require much more pruning and training and are difficult to mow underneath!

Grass clippings are an excellent mulch if put on in thin layers, and are a good fertilizer if returned to the sward. However, orchards, and indeed most other swards, should not be composed solely of grasses, as these compete strongly for resources in the topmost layers and do not contribute much to the mineral levels. Include clovers, alfalfa and chicory seeds in your sowing mixture. Special blends are now available ready mixed. Traditionally orchards were combined with grazing livestock. Though no longer done on a commercial scale, the practice is still useful for amateurs. Running chickens underneath adds interest and fertility, and almost guarantees freedom from most pest problems. Cynics might add, "especially if you do not overfeed them!" Ducks control slugs and snails better than hens and do not scratch and damage so much, and

the drakes do not crow so they are preferable from that point of view. Geese are superb lawnmowers, converting grass into fertilizer and eggs as well as being the most noisy watchdogs. Be warned, though, as geese may severely damage young plants with thin bark if they are hungry.

Other forms of livestock are more dangerous to the home orchard. I suggest that no four-legged herbivorous animals are allowed anywhere near valued plants, unless each is individually and securely fenced and protected.

Orchards are also an enticement to two-legged rats and it has long been established best practice to surround them with a thick, impenetrable hedge of thorny plants such as quickthorn or blackthorn. This, and a narrow verge of long grass and native plants, simultaneously provides a good background ecology to help control all the other pests of the orchard. A fence or wall does not contribute in the same way, and is usually more expensive and surmountable.

ORNAMENTAL FRUIT GARDENS

A "Doyenne du Comice" pear espalier is also decorative

Trained fruit trees and bushes which can be bought ready-made in a host of interesting and architectural forms, such as espaliers and fans, create interest out of season as the framework of the plants becomes revealed. Attention to the appearance of the supports is essential as they are also disclosed for much of the time. Neatness and uniformity are thus of the greatest moment. Pergolas can look as beautiful clothed in grapevines as they do with any climber and even a fruit cage can be fashioned ornamentally from the right materials.

It is important in a fruit garden to allow for plentiful light and air — more than perhaps might be granted with a shrub garden. Wide paths aid such design and can be of grass sward where wear is light. Gravel is next choice for practicality and economy, and concrete or stone flags where the area is small or budget large.

More color and interest, with benefit to the main planting, is obtained by having suitable companion plants to provide shelter, ground cover, flowers for nectar and pollen for the beneficial insects, and sacrificial plants that give up their fruits that others may not be eaten. However, vegetables are not easily mixed in. They do not grow well surrounded by vigorous competitors such as fruiting plants, but most of the culinary herbs can be grown to advantage and use.

Wildlife Fruit Gardens

Although these may be as stylized and neat as any purely decorative garden, an accurate description of many so-called wild gardens is "unkempt". Indeed, the term is often used to justify total neglect.

However, if the aim is truly to provide more and better habitats for endangered native flora and fauna, then neglect is not enough. A wild garden needs to be managed so that we maximize the number and forms of life supported. The more fruiting and berrying plants we include, the more wildlife we attract, and we need to ensure other basic necessities for wild creatures.

The fruit helps immensely but shelter for nesting and hibernation, water and peace are also required. Dense brambles, shrubs and evergreens are mandatory, but do ensure the gardener can still gain access. Paths should be maintained to permit various tasks, but of course excess traffic will soon drive away most creatures.

Many garden soils are too rich for the more appealing wild flowers. To establish these it is frequently necessary to start them in pots and plant them out into sites prepared by removing the turf. Thus they should be kept away from the fruiting plants which require richer conditions.

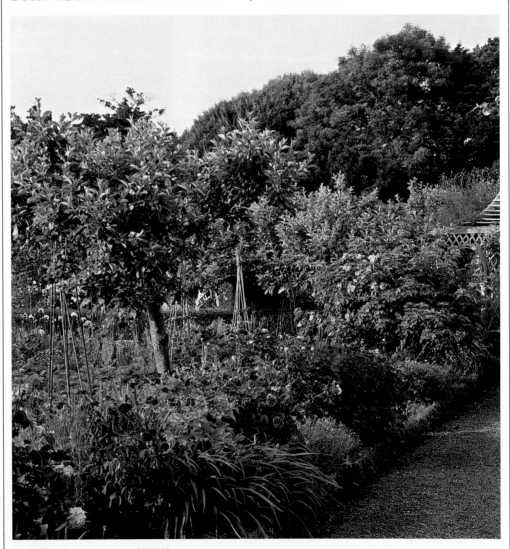

Fruits do well with flowers underneath

SITE, SOIL PREPARATION AND PLANTING

Most old gardening books started off with instructions to make a garden on a well-drained, south-facing slope of rich loamy soil. If only we had such a choice! We must often take what comes. And as we get small gardens with modern houses we rarely have much choice of positioning within them.

site

Shelter is the most important aid we can give our plants — good hedges, fences, windbreaks, warm walls, cloches, plastic sheets and even old curtains on frosty nights. But be careful not to overdo it and make the area stagnant. Drainage is occasionally necessary to prevent waterlogging, as few plants survive for long with drowning roots. But for most gardens, water is more often a problem in its absence. Growing on raised beds is ideal for draining away the water in areas with wet summers.

soil

For most crops, a neutral to slightly acid soil with moderate fertility and organic matter content is ideal. There are basically four types of soil.

Chalk or Limestone Soil

This soil tends to be light and very well drained. But its inability to hold moisture can cause problems in a hot summer. It is alkaline in character and it is sometimes difficult to lower its pH level, so some plants become stunted and leaves go yellowish in color, because the minerals, especially iron, become locked away. If you find the plants are not thriving, try a raised bed where you can introduce the soil they require.

Clay Soil

This soil is made up of tiny particles that stick together when wet, making the soil heavy. When dry, they set rock hard. Because it retains water and restricts air flow around roots, it is often known as "a cold soil." It may have a natural reserve of plant food, but even so it is better to work compost, gypsum (often sold as clay breaker) and horticultural grit into the top layer as this will help get the plants established and improve drainage. If you continue to do this every year, it will gradually become easier to cultivate, and extremely productive. Your efforts will be well rewarded.

Loam Soil

This soil is a mixture of clay, silt, and sand. It contains a good quantity of humus and is rich in nutrients. There are various types of loam: heavy, which contains more clay than loam and becomes wet in winter and spring; light loam, which has more sand than clay; and medium loam, which is an equal balance of clay and sand.

Sandy Soil

This is a very well-drained soil, so much so that plant nutrients are quickly washed away. A plus point is that it warms up quickly in the spring so is ideal for early crops. For hungry plants you will need to build the soil up with compost to help retain moisture and stop the leaching of nutrients. Plants such as the Mediterranean herbs and carrots will thrive on this soil.

Soil Acidity and Alkalinity

The natural acidity of the soil must be taken into account. Find out whether your soil is acid or alkaline using a reliable soil-testing kit, available from any good garden center. Soil acidity and alkalinity is measured on a pH scale ranging from 0 to 14; 0 is the most acid and 14 the most alkaline.

Acid soils (0 to 6.9 pH), on a sliding scale from acidic to nearly neutral, include sphagnum moss peat, sandy soil, coarse loam soil, sedge peat and heavy clay. Alkaline soils (7.1 to 14 pH) tend to contain chalk or lime and may be thin or shallow.

A reading that approaches either end of the pH scale indicates that the soil will tend to lock up the nutrients necessary for good growth. If it is very acid, you will need to add lime in the late fall to raise the pH. Fork the top 4 in. of the soil and dress with lime. Clay soils need a good dressing, but be careful not to over-lime sandy soils. It should not be necessary to do this more than once every 3 years unless your soil is very acid. Never add lime at the same time as manure, garden compost or fertilizer, as a chemical reaction can occur that will ruin the effects of both. As a general rule, either add lime 1 month before, or 3 months after manuring, and 1 month after adding fertilizers. If the soil is alkaline, dress it every fall with well-rotted manure to a depth of 2 in. to 4 in., and dig over in the spring.

Soil pH also influences the number and type of beneficial soil-borne organisms and the incidence of pests and diseases; worms dislike a low pH, but leather-

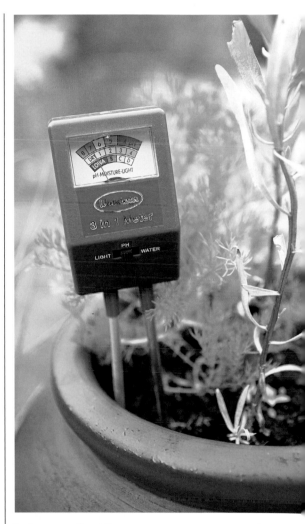

Testing your soil's acidity

jackets and wireworms are usually more common in acid conditions, as is the fungal disease clubroot.

Some plants and plant families have quite specific pH requirements; others are more tolerant. On the whole, we have unwittingly selected plants that grow happily in the average, mildly acid to slightly alkaline soils most of us have. Herbs and vegetables generally do best in a soil between 6.5 and 7.5 pH (fairly neutral). A few fruits such as blueberries need acid conditions. They resent lime in the soil and need to be cultivated in pots of ericaceous compost and watered with rain, not ground water. Brassicas benefit from a slightly alkaline soil to reduce the risk of clubroot.

preparation

The more you plan and the more carefully you prepare the site, the better the results and the more pitfalls avoided. Always work out schemes on paper. Draw a map of existing features and plan how you will fit in the new. For vegetables, plan your rotation (see p. 637). For fruits and perennial herbs, imagine walking round after 5 years when all the plants have grown up.

A good soil structure can be easily damaged by cultivating when it is excessively wet or dry and by using heavy machinery — even walking on wet soil causes compaction and smearing. To reduce the impact, lay a plank on the soil to disperse the weight. Once the soil is under cultivation, aim to stick to the path rather than tread on the soil.

Eliminating Weeds

If you don't weed thoroughly before you start, it will become much harder once the plants go in. Most weeds do not emerge until the spring, and continue well into the season. If you wish to get rid of them successfully, it is best to cover the plot with black plastic the previous fall. Dig a shallow trench around the area and bury the sides of the plastic in it to keep it secure. Starved of light, the weeds will eventually give up. This will take until the following spring, so if you do not like the sight of the black plastic, position a few paving stones (taking care not to make any holes because the weeds will find them and come through), cover the plastic with bark, and place terracotta pots planted up on top of the stones.

Alternatively, fork through the plot and remove weeds by hand. If you do not have the patience to use a plastic mulch, you can dig over the area, pulling out weeds by the roots. This works most easily when the soil is just moist, which is most often in fall. With less patience still, some may resort to a herbicide to kill all the weeds initially. There are no organic herbicides. We disapprove, but do understand the dilemma. If you consider you really need to, then purchase whatever a reputable supplier recommends and follow the instructions religiously! Even so, results will not be instant and may need repeat applications. There is no short cut to eradicating weeds.

Soil Cultivation

The soil structure essential for successful growth is created by incorporating different materials into the soil:

well-rotted compost improves moisture and nutrient retention, creates an open structure and aerates the soil; sharp sand helps drainage; and "green manures" improve the structure.

Digging is the most important method of cultivation prior to planting. In the vegetable garden it is an annual event. On heavier soils in cooler climates fall digging is beneficial as the winter frosts that follow help to break down these wet, sticky soils into a workable tilth. Sandy soils can be lightly forked over and it is advisable to cover them with compost or green manure to reduce the loss of nutrients during the winter rains and snows, or to leave the digging until spring. No matter what type of soil you have, it is beneficial to lay a good layer of well-rotted manure or garden compost over the surface in winter and dig it in the following spring. You can also use the "no-dig" method for vegetables: dig over the soil, remove weeds, then add organic matter on the surface annually and let nature build the structure.

Single digging consists of cultivating the soil to about 12 in., a good spade's depth and the average rooting zone of many plants. Double digging is used on poorly drained and previously uncultivated land. It encourages deep rooting and promotes rapid drainage. "Double" refers to the depth of cultivation, some 18–24 in. deep or approximately two spades' depths. When double digging it is important to ensure that the topsoil and subsoil are not mixed.

There should be no need to add extra fertilizers to the soil if it has been well-prepared. Too much fertilizer causes lank, soft, disease-prone growth.

If necessary, in the vegetable garden you can gradually improve the soil by planting a ground-breaking crop such as potatoes or Jerusalem artichokes. Potatoes are so good for this because they need a number of cultivations to "hill" and cover the tubers, so preventing weeds from becoming established. Potatoes also produce large, leafy tops, blocking the light that is so essential for the germination of many weeds.

planting

If this is a new garden, and you are planting fruit trees and bushes, herbs or perennial vegetables, it is worth laying the plants out on top of the prepared ground first, walking round and getting an overall view. Make any changes to the design now, rather than later. For details on buying plants, see p. 647.

Any stakes or supports must be in place beforehand, and for trees and bushes they must be strong enough to do the job and must last for a reasonable number of years. It is false economy to be mean on these, as it will be hard to correct when the plants are grown.

Remember that once the planting is done, the future is determined. So don't skimp on digging or preparation. Dig a wide planting hole: bigger is better! Don't mix in compost, manure or fertilizer: apply later once plants have established. Don't bury plants too deeply. Almost all wish to be planted at the same depth as they have grown or slightly shallower. For grafted fruit trees, don't bury the rootstock. Keep roots in their respective and different layers. Don't force them doubled up into a cramped hole, and never pack them all down in a flat layer unless they grew like that. Gently pack soil around roots, filling and firming as you go. It is better to over-firm! Then attach support if needed.

aftercare

For fruit trees and bushes, herbs and perennial vegetables, use a mulch to retain moisture and suppress weeds. Try a thick layer of organic matter or a plastic sheet or carpet mulch. In the fruit garden, whatever the final intention, do not allow a weed or grass within a circle as wide as the tree or bush is high for 3 years.

Good watering in dry spells is absolutely crucial! For long-term plants, water regularly for 3 years.

Add plenty of well-rotted organic matter to the soil

Rotation is a system whereby groups of vegetables are grown on a different section of the plot each year, so maintaining the balance of soil nutrients for successive crops. Growing crops in this way avoids the build-up of pests and diseases, assists in weed control and prevents the soil from deteriorating.

For crop rotation to be effective, a large area of ground is required, particularly when controlling soil-borne pests and diseases. White rot (which attacks the onion family), clubroot (which damages members of the cabbage family) and potato cyst eelworm remain dormant in the soil for many years and can survive on any weeds that are relatives. This makes good husbandry just as vital as crop rotation.

Planning
Before planting, first list the vegetables you want to grow and group them together according to their botanical relationship. Allocate each group to a plot, then compile a monthly cropping timetable for each space.

Rotational groups

Legumes	Onion family	Carrot and tomato families	Brassicas
Fava bean	Bulb onion	Carrot	Cabbage
Green bean	Garlic	Celery	Cauliflower
Pea	Leek	Pepper	Radish
Runner bean	Salad onion	Parsnip	Rutabaga
	Shallot	Potato	Turnip
		Tomato	

Next, allocate each rotation group to a plot of land ("plot A" etc), and draw up a month-by-month timetable for each space.

Plot A

Year 1	Year 2	Year 3	Year 4
Legumes	Onion family	Carrot and tomato families	Brassicas
Fava bean	Bulb onion	Carrot	Cabbage
Green bean	Garlic	Celery	Cauliflower
Pea	Leek	Parsnip	Radish
Runner bean	Salad onion	Pepper	Rutabaga
	Shallot	Potato	Turnip
		Tomato	

Plot B

Year 1	Year 2	Year 3	Year 4
Onion family	Carrot and tomato families	Brassicas	Legumes
Bulb onion	Carrot	Cabbage	Fava bean
Garlic	Celery	Cauliflower	Green bean
Leek	Parsnip	Radish	Pea
Salad onion	Pepper	Rutabaga	Runner bean
Shallot	Potato	Turnip	
	Tomato		

Plot C

Year 1	Year 2	Year 3	Year 4
Carrot and tomato families	Brassicas	Legumes	Onion family
Carrot	Cabbage	Fava bean	Bulb onion
Celery	Cauliflower	Green bean	Garlic
Parsnip	Radish	Pea	Leek
Pepper	Rutabaga	Runner bean	Salad onion
Potato	Turnip		Shallot
Tomato			

Plot D

Year 1	Year 2	Year 3	Year 4
Brassicas	Legumes	Onion family	Carrot and tomato families
Cabbage	Fava bean	Bulb onion	Carrot
Cauliflower	Green bean	Garlic	Celery
Radish	Pea	Leek	Parsnip
Rutabaga	Runner bean	Salad onion	Pepper
Turnip		Shallot	Potato
			Tomato

This timetable fully utilizes the land and provides continuity of cropping. As space becomes available, plant the crops due to follow immediately. Crops may come from different groups, which means that rotation from one plot to another is a gradual process, rather than a wholesale changeover on a set date. Wind-pollinated sweetcorn should be sown in blocks in any remaining space on the plot, bearing in mind it casts shade. Ensure it is not planted in the same place in successive years. Zucchini, squashes, cucumbers and melons can be treated similarly.

GROWING SYSTEMS

Bed system, with paths separating them

Random Planting

Vegetables can be grown as "edible bedding plants" scattered among flowering plants and borders in the ornamental garden. Swiss chard, cabbage "Ruby Ball," beets "Bull's Blood," fennel and Brussels sprout "Rubine" are particularly pleasing. (See also pages 618 to 619, "The Ornamental Vegetable Garden.")

The Potager

This is the French tradition of planting vegetables in formal beds; a practical and visually pleasing display.

Long-term Crops

Perennial vegetables such as asparagus are difficult to incorporate into a crop rotation programme. For this reason, they are often grown on a separate, more permanent site for several years before being replaced.

What shall I harvest today?

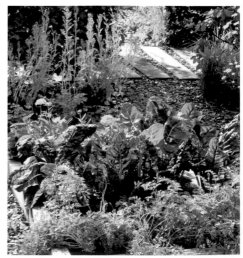

Rows

Traditionally, vegetables are grown in long straight rows, with plants close together within the rows, and paths to allow access. This has some drawbacks. Competition between plants for space in a row means that much of the plants' extension growth is into the pathways, causing leafy vegetables like cabbages, cauliflowers and lettuces to produce oval "hearts" rather than round ones.

Beds

These are effectively multi-row systems, with equidistant spacing of plants in and between the rows. Plants may be set in staggered rows, creating a diagonal pattern. Major paths between beds should always be wide enough to accommodate a wheelbarrow; access paths can be narrower. Pathways between the beds are slightly wider than those on the row system, but closer plant spacing means that more plants are grown per square yard and their growth and shape are more uniform. Close spacing ensures that weed growth is suppressed in its later stages and the soil structure remains intact, because there is less soil compaction when pathways are further apart.

Raised beds should be about 30 in. wide so that it is easy to reach into the center without overbalancing. After initial double digging, and the addition of organic matter, they will not be trodden on, allowing a good soil structure to form. Layers of well-rotted compost added annually will be further incorporated by worm activity. Where natural populations are low, they can be bought from specialist suppliers. You can't have enough!

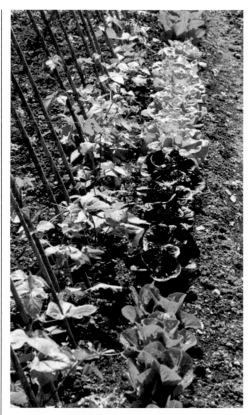

Any space can be utilized

Sowing for Continuity

The greatest challenge is to have vegetables ready for harvest throughout the year. Some, such as asparagus, have only a short harvesting period, while vegetables like cabbage, cauliflower and lettuce are available at almost any time, provided that there is successional sowing. Careful selection of cultivars also helps to achieve continuity; growing both rapidly maturing and slow-growing types extends the cropping period. The season for many root vegetables such as parsnips can be lengthened by growing a portion of the crop for eating fresh, and the remainder for storage. These can slowly be eaten over the winter period.

Successional Sowings

It is usually quick-maturing crops that are prone to gluts and gaps, often bolting and becoming inedible. To avoid this, sow sufficient seed for your needs a little and often, so that if something goes wrong, the problem is only a small one. A good guide is to sow a batch of each seed when the first "true" leaves of the previous sowing begin to emerge.

Intercropping

Spaces between slow-growing crops can be used as a seedbed for vegetables such as brassicas that will later need to be transplanted into permanent positions at wider spacings. This is only successful where the competition for moisture, nutrients, light and space is not too great. This can be partially solved by growing them between rows of deep-rooted crops, so that the roots are in different levels of the soil. To achieve this, it may also be necessary to space crops a little further apart than the usual spacings. Radishes sown on the same day as parsnips will have germinated, grown and been harvested before the parsnips have fully developed, achieving the maximum possible yield, covering the soil with vegetation and suppressing weed growth. This intercropping requires some flexibility in the cropping plan.

Catch Crops

These are rapidly-maturing vegetables and include radishes, lettuce and salad onions, all of which can be grown before the main crop is planted. Catch cropping is useful when growing tender crops such as tomatoes, sweetcorn and zucchini, which cannot be planted until the risk of late frost is well and truly over.

Extending the Season

The season for vegetables can be extended by growing them under cover at the beginning or end of their natural season; sowing early under cover hastens maturity while protection later in the season extends the cropping period. (For more detail, see p. 642–43, "Container Culture" and 653, "Protected Cropping.")

Pot-raised Plants

Raising plants in pots or cell-packs is useful for those that are frost tender and allows plants to mature while the ground is cleared of earlier crops. This saves time and space and gives more control over the growth and development of young plants. Brassicas, lettuces, leeks and onions can be grown in this way.

"The Hungry Gap"

Few vegetables mature from late winter to early spring – a period often referred to as "the hungry gap". In mild winter areas, careful planning allows this gap to be bridged; spring cauliflower, winter cabbage, celeriac, kale, leeks, and oriental vegetables can all be grown for harvesting during this period.

Raised beds are highly productive

POLLINATION AND COMPANION PLANTING

Almost all our fruits require their flowers to be pollinated. Many are self-fertile and can set by pollinating themselves, but crop better if cross-pollinated. Some of these — for example figs — have varieties that will produce fruit parthenocarpically, without pollination; thus they are often seedless. A few fruits, such as "Conference" pears, are partly parthenocarpic: if not pollinated by another variety, their fruits are different and oddly shaped.

Some fruits do not have male and female flowers on the same plant and so we have to grow a non-fruiting male to pollinate every half dozen or so females. Wild kiwis are good examples. For convenience, we have bred varieties that carry both sexes.

Some fruits and many nuts are wind-pollinated, others by bees and other insects. Under cover, neither of these natural pollinators exists and we have to assist. A rabbit's tail, a cotton ball or piece of wool lightly touched on each flower — moving pollen from flower to flower — should suffice. Lure more insects to help by growing attractant companion plants and this can add a bit of color and life as well.

Outdoors early in the year there are few insects about and for the earliest flowerers pollination is risky. Again, hand pollination is effective, but tedious. It is better to ensure insect pollination by increasing the numbers. Planting companion plants as attractants helps; taking up bee-keeping makes an enormous improvement.

To pollinate each other, not only do varieties have to be compatible, but they also have to flower at the same time. All reputable catalogues have a choice of suitable cross-pollenizers indicated. When in doubt, choose the wild species, which is often the best pollenizer for most of its varieties. Alternatively, simply plant more varieties. This is especially true for a few fruits which are not good pollinators themselves. For example, the apples "Cox's Orange Pippin" and "Bramley's Seedling" never crop together, but if you add a "James Grieve," all three fruit.

Companion planting is of immense benefit to most fruiting plants as it brings in and supports pollinating and predatory insects, and maintains them throughout the rest of the year. We must aim at having a continuity of flowers throughout the year as it is these that provide nectar and honey for the bees, hoverflies and other beneficial insects.

Of particular usefulness is *Limnanthes douglasii*, the poached egg plant, which is a low-growing, self-seeding,

There are three water butts hidden here

weed-suppressing, hardy annual. I find it especially beneficial under soft fruit and gooseberries. *Phacelia tanacetifolia*, *Convolvulus tricolor*, calendulas and clovers are all very good for beneficial insects.

Other plants can be good companions to our fruiting plants by repelling pests. French marigolds are one of the strongest and their smell will keep whitefly out of a greenhouse. Planted about the fruit garden, they disorient pests sniffing for their quarry. The aromatic herbs such as rosemary, thyme, sage, southernwood and lavender are all excellent companions as they not only camouflage the air with their perfume but they are long-flowering, also benefiting the various pollinators and predators.

Alliums are valuable companions. Their smell deters many pests, yet their flowers attract beneficial insects. They help protect the plants they grow with from fungi and are even claimed to improve the scent of roses. Garlic and chives are the easiest to grow and use in quantity at the base of the most fruit trees and bushes.

Many companion plants help access nutrients and make them available for our fruiting plants. Clovers, lupines and the other leguminous plants are especially

Hand pollinating should be called brush pollinating, really

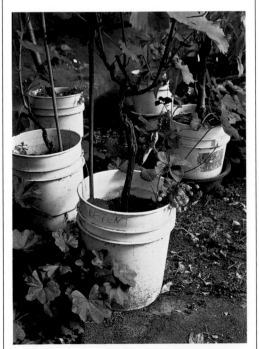

Strawberries hitch a ride with the grapes and peaches

good as they fix nitrogen from the air and the surplus will feed our crops. Alfalfa is exceptionally deep-rooted and brings up minerals from depths other plants cannot reach. It should be included in the seed mixture for orchard and wild garden swards. Similarly a few thistles and docks can be tolerated in those areas for the same purpose, but cut off flowers before they set seed. Clovers and chicory should be included whenever grass is seeded as the sward that is produced will be both richer and lusher.

In grass at the base of trees, dense shrubs and hedges, bulbous, spring-flowering plants can be fitted in with no difficulty. These areas can remain uncut till the bulbs' foliage dies down and their flowers will be a rich source of pollen and nectar for the earliest pollinators and

predators. Some ivy in the hedges will provide late flowers to feed the insects in fall before they hibernate.

Ground-cover plants provide habitats for ground beetles and many other useful creatures, but may also harbor slugs, snails and over-wintering pests. On the whole it is better to have such habitats kept as far as possible from soft fruit and seed beds — after all, the beetles, frogs and hedgehogs can walk further than slugs and snails!

Some plants are specifically helpful to others and a few hinder. These are noted with the entry for that particular fruit. For example, the Romans noticed that oaks were bad for olives, and cabbages were not good companions for vines, but rue benefited from the presence of figs.

CONTAINER CULTURE

Growing in containers is an ideal technique for fruits and vegetables that might otherwise be difficult, enabling you to control the size of the plant and conditions in which it is kept. Almost all herbs can be grown in containers. The individual plant entries give details of the best size of container for each crop and where to place it to receive the ideal growing conditions. This section provides more general information and advice on container growing.

Advantages of Containers

With attention to feeding and watering, almost any plant can be coaxed to grow in a container. Where room is limited, containers offer an alternative to ground space. They can also offer different condtions to those found in the ground. Tomatoes and cucumbers have long been grown under glass in containers to prevent any contact with disease-infected soil. If you have a chalky soil, lime-hating plants can be grown in containers of ericaceous compost and watered with rain water.

Portable containers allow you to respond to weather conditions, moving plants outdoors once spring frosts end, and putting them under shelter again at the onset of colder weather.

For large fruit plants, a container cramps the root system, preventing them growing too large or too quickly. Allied with pruning, this allows us to dwarf plants we would find too large to handle. Often this restriction is resented by the plant and, perversely, may result in earlier fruiting. The fruits may not be prolific, but a selection of containers can give several different varieties in a space otherwise occupied by one, allowing greater variety and a longer season.

Vegetables most suited to container culture are either rapidly maturing crops such as mini beets, carrots, lettuces, radishes and salad onions, or dwarf varieties of bush or climbing vegetables, including eggplants, beans, cucumbers, peas, peppers and tomatoes, as these need little support. Deep-rooted vegetables like sprouts, maincrop carrots and parsnips can be grown in containers at least 18 in. deep.

Choosing a Container

Choose the container to suit the plant. If it is a tall plant, make sure the container has a base wide enough to prevent it toppling over, even outside in a high wind. For vegetables, the chance of successful cropping is improved with large containers; they allow for a greater rooting depth, dry out slowly and provide adequate anchorage for crops that need staking.

Plastic containers (with drainage holes) are more moisture-retentive than those of wood or terracotta, but the latter are preferred by some plants, such as citrus.

If using unconventional containers — old watering cans, sinks, a half beer barrel — make sure they have drainage holes, and mesh fabric or broken pots in the bottom of the container to stop the holes clogging up.

Herbs can suit hanging baskets, but the position is crucial. They dislike high wind and full sun all day. Also, they are mostly fast growers and if too cramped or over- or under-watered they will drop their leaves.

Composts

Choosing the right compost is essential for healthy plants. Avoid using garden soil in containers. Instead use commercially available soilless potting mixes.

John Innes
This is loam-based and includes chemicals. On the plus side, it stays richer in nutrients longer, making feeding less critical; it holds water well and is a stable compost for a large, long-term plant. If it does dry out, it takes up water easily. The major watch point is that it is easy to overwater.

Peppers do well in containers and need little support

You must choose the correct one for the job. Loam-based composts are generally ideal for vegetables and fruits in containers, and organic matter can be added if required. This is not a suitable compost for hanging baskets, because it is heavy when wet.

Own Soil-based Mix
If you wish to make a soil-based compost of your own this recipe is fairly reliable.
4 parts good weed-free garden topsoil
3 parts well-rotted garden compost
3 parts moist peat
1 part horticultural sharp sand

Multipurpose Potting Compost
This is usually peat-based with added nutrients. The bags are light and the compost is clean and easy to use. On the negative side, you will need to feed regularly as nutrients are soon depleted; also the compost is light, so watch out that large plants do not fall over. The most frequent problem is that it takes up water poorly if ever it dries out.

Own Mix Bark, Peat, Grit
This is ideal for many herbs as well as some fruits and vegetables. The open mix helps prevent overwatering; the bark retains water, which protects against under-watering and keeps the compost open to help absorb water if ever it dries out completely. It is suitable for containers and hanging baskets alike. Another plus is that you know what nutrients are in it, so will be able to feed in a balanced way.

Alternative Composts
Peat-free composts are increasingly available as we become aware of the need to conserve our diminishing peat fields. They are generally made of coir, a by-product of coconuts, or composted bark. Coir is very free-draining and so some composts include a jelly that retains water, releasing it gradually. Coir compost is light, so there may be a stability problem with tall or large plants. A final minus point — the nutrients are soon depleted so you will need to feed from the start.

Composted bark has similar drawbacks if used straight, with no peat or soil: watering and nutrient loss. If the bark has not been composted for long enough, it can leach the nutrients and starve the plants. However, mixed with peat or soil, bark is a great asset.

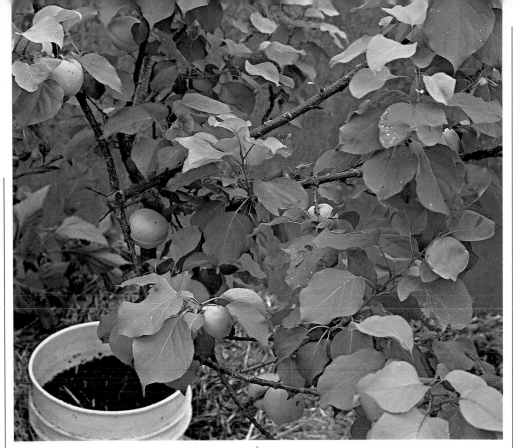
Apricots can be cropped in big buckets

Maintenance

Most plants need moist soil but drown if waterlogged and wilt if dry. Water stress due to drought, even for short periods, can greatly reduce the potential productivity of plants. If you cannot maintain consistent watering, install an automatic system of irrigation. It is best to water containers in the early morning or the evening, especially in summer, as this reduces the amount lost through evaporation.

Repotting into a larger container helps provide new nutrients, but this may become difficult with larger plants. The alternatives are top-dressing with an enriched mix of compost and organic fertilizer, or feeding little and often with a diluted liquid feed, or comfrey and nettle extract.

Liquid seaweed contains small amounts of nitrogen, phosphorous, potassium, and it is also rich in trace elements. It not only makes a good soil feed but, as the elements are easily taken in by the plant, it can also be sprayed on as a foliar feed.

Maintenance Calendar

Spring Pot on perennial plants if necessary (look for roots protruding from the bottom of the container). Use a pot the next size up. Carefully remove the plant from its old pot. Give it a good tidy up, removing any weeds and dead leaves. Place gravel or other drainage material in the bottom of the container and keep the compost sweet by adding a tablespoon full of granulated charcoal. As soon as the plant starts producing new growth or flowers, start feeding regularly with liquid feed. Prune fruits as needed. Plant pots of ornamental vegetables.

Summer Keep a careful eye on the watering; make sure the pots do not dry out fully. Move some plants out of the midday sun. Deadhead any flowers on herbs. Feed with liquid feed, on average once a week. Remove any pest-damaged leaves. Prune fruits as needed. Harvest vegetables.

Fall Cut back the perennial herbs. Weed containers and at the same time remove some of the top compost and re-dress. Bring any tender plants inside before the frosts. Start reducing the watering. Prune fruits as needed.

Winter Protect all container-grown plants from frosts. If possible move into a cold greenhouse, conservatory or garage. If the weather is very severe, cover the containers in a layer of burlap. Keep watering to a minimum. Prune fruits as needed.

PROPAGATION AND BUYING PLANTS

One of the great joys of gardening is propagating your own plants. Success is dependent on adequate preparation and the care and attention you give in the critical first few weeks. This section provides general instructions for the main propagation methods. Individual guidelines are given under each plant entry. Where space and time are short, or for larger perennial plants such as fruit trees and bushes, it may be easier to buy your plants.

seed

Most vegetables, annual herbs and annual fruits are usually grown from seed. There is a huge range of seed available from seed catalogues, or you can save your own. Seed is not always advisable for perennials, particularly fruits; a fruit seedling will not fruit until mature, which may be quick for some but takes many decades for most trees. Until the fruit is produced there is usually no way of telling what it will be like — and it may not be very good. Most of the best varieties will not come true from seed.

Seed can be sown outside, either directly where it is to mature or into a seedbed for transplanting. Alternatively, starting off the seeds in a greenhouse or on a windowsill gives you more control over the warmth and moisture they need, and enables you to begin propagating earlier in the season.

Types of Seed
Seeds are usually bought as packets of individual "naked" seeds; but vegetable seeds in particular may be available in other forms.

Pelleted seeds are individual seeds coated in a ball of clay, which moistens and disintegrates in the soil. They are easy to handle and sow at precise spacings, reducing the need for thinning. Sow at a depth of about twice their diameter and keep the soil moist but not waterlogged until germination.

Seed tapes and sheets are individual seeds encased at the correct spacing in tapes or sheets of tissue paper or gel. These substances are soluble when placed in moist soil. Tapes and sheets are quick to use and are precisely spaced so there is no need for thinning.

Primed seeds are in the first stages of germination and are used for those that are hard to germinate or need

Seedlings almost ready to be planted out

high germination temperatures, such as cucumbers. They arrive by mail in plastic packets to prevent moisture loss and are pricked out into pots or trays on arrival.

Preparation of Seed
Most seeds need air, light, particular temperatures and moisture to germinate. Some have a long dormancy, and some have hard outer coats and need a little help to get going. Here are two techniques. See individual plant entries for when to use these techniques.

Scarification
If left to nature, seeds that have a hard outer coat would take a long time to germinate. To speed up the process, rub the seed between two sheets of fine sandpaper. This weakens the coat of the seed so that moisture needed for germination can penetrate.

Stratification (vernalization)
Some seeds need a period of cold (from 1 to 6 months) to germinate. Mix the seed with damp sand and place in a plastic bag in the refrigerator or freezer.

After the appropriate length of time, sow on the surface of the compost and cover with perlite.

Sowing Outside
In an average season the seed should be sown in mid to late spring after the soil has been prepared and warmed. It is simplest to sow direct where the plants are to mature, and this is best for plants that resent root disturbance, such as many root vegetables. Alternatively you can use a seedbed if you need the space seedlings are to occupy for something else, and to save space as small plants are not at their final spacing until they mature.

Before starting, check your soil type (see p. 633), making sure that the soil has sufficient food to maintain a seedbed. Dig the bed over, mark out a straight line with a piece of string secured tightly over each row, draw a shallow row, ¼ to ½ in. deep (this will vary according to seed size), using the side of a fork or hoe, and sow the seeds thinly. For larger seeds, sow individually. If your soil is sticky clay, give the seeds a better start by adding a fine layer of horticultural sand along the row. Do not overcrowd the bed, otherwise the seedlings will grow leggy and weak and be prone to disease. For more precise details of seed spacing see individual plant entries

Protected Sowing

Sowing under cover is expensive and often labor-intensive, yet it allows seeds to be sown whatever the weather. It is most often used in cooler climates for tender crops that cannot be planted out until there is no longer any danger of frost.

Start with a thoroughly cleaned container. Old compost also provides ideal conditions for damping off fungi and fungus gnats, so remove any spent compost from the greenhouse or potting shed. Always use fresh compost.

Compost

It is best to use a sterile seed compost. Ordinary garden soil contains many weed seeds that could easily be confused with the germinating seed. The best compost for most seed sowing is 50 percent propagating bark: 50 percent peat-based seed compost. However, for plants that prefer a freer-draining compost, or for those that need stratification outside, a 25 percent peat-based seed compost: 50 percent propagating bark: 25 percent horticultural grit mix is ideal. And if you are sowing seeds that have a long germination period, use a soil-based seed compost or buy ready-mixed.

Sowing in Seed Trays

Fill a clean seed tray with compost to ½ in. below the rim and firm with a flat piece of wood. Do not press too hard as this will over-compress the compost and restrict drainage, encouraging damping off disease and attack by sciarid fly.

The gap below the rim is essential, as it prevents the surface-sown seeds and compost being washed over the edge when watering.

Water the prepared tray using a fine rose on the watering can so as not to disturb the seed. Do not overwater. The compost should be damp, not soaking. After an initial watering, water as little as possible, but never let the surface dry out. Once the seed is sown, lack of moisture can prevent germination and kill the seedlings, but too much excludes oxygen and encourages damping-off fungi and root rot.

Sowing Methods

There are three main methods, the choice dependent on the size of the seed. They are, in order of seed size, fine to large:

1 Scatter on the surface of the compost, and cover with a fine layer of perlite or vermiculite.
2 Press into the surface of the compost, either with your hand or a flat piece of wood the size of the tray, and cover with perlite or vermiculite.
3 Press down to one seed's depth, cover with potting mix.

The Cardboard Trick

When seeds are too small to handle, you can control distribution by using a thin piece of card cut to 4 in. x 2 in., and folded down the middle. Place a small amount of seed into the folded card and gently tap it over the prepared seed tray. This technique is especially useful when sowing into plug trays (see below).

Sowing in Plug (Module) Trays (Multi-cell Trays)

These plug trays are a great invention. The seed can germinate in its own space, get established into a strong seedling, and make a good root ball. When transplanting, the young plant remains undisturbed and will continue growing. This is very good for plants like cilantro, which hate being transplanted and tend to bolt if you move them. Another advantage is that the problem of overcrowding is cut to a minimum, and damping-off disease and fungus gnats are easier to control. Also, because seedlings in plugs are easier to maintain, planting out or transplanting is not so critical. Plug trays come in various sizes; for example, you can get trays with very small holes of ½ in. x ½ in. up to trays with holes of 1¼ in. x 1¼ in. To enable a reasonable time lapse between germination and transplanting, the larger are recommended.

Teasing two plantlets apart

Prepare the potting mix and fill the tray right to the top, scraping off surplus potting mix with a piece of wood level with the top of the holes. It is better not to firm the compost down. Watering in (see above) settles the mix enough to allow space for the seed and the top-dressing.

The principles of sowing in plug trays are the same as for trays. Having sown your seed, label the trays clearly with the name of the plant, and the date.

Sowing in Pots

Multi-sowing in pots speeds the growth of root and bulb vegetables. Sow up to six seeds (two for beets) into a 3–4 in. pot, leave the seedlings to develop and then transplant the potful of plants, allowing extra space within the rows. Thinning is not needed. This technique works well for beets, cauliflower, turnips, kohlrabi, leeks and onions.

Fluid Sowing

This is useful when weather and soil conditions make germination erratic. Seeds germinated under ideal conditions are sown, protected by a carrier gel. To germinate the seeds, place some moistened kitchen towel in the base of a plastic container. Scatter the

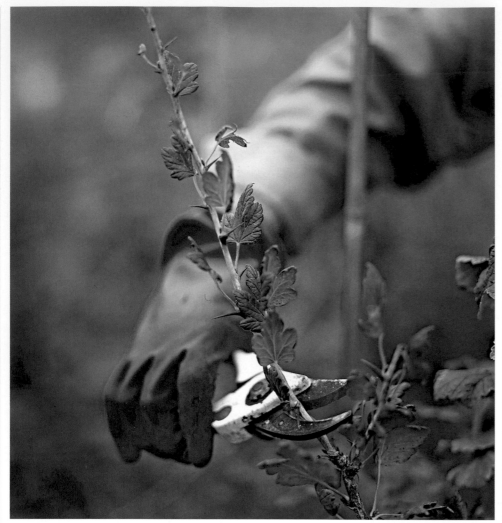

Taking a hardwood cutting

seeds evenly on the surface, cover with a lid or cling film and keep at 70°F. When the rootlets are about ¼ in. long they are ready to sow. Wash them into a fine mesh strainer. Mix carrier gel from half-strength fungicide-free wallpaper paste, scatter the seeds in the paste, and mix. Pour into a clear bag, cut off a corner and force the mixture through the hole. Cover the seeds with soil or vermiculite.

Seed Germination

Seeds need warmth and moisture to germinate. In a cold greenhouse, a heated propagator may be needed in early spring for seeds that germinate at warm to hot temperatures. In the house you can use a shelf near a radiator (never on the radiator), or a closet. Darkness does not hinder the germination of most seeds, but if you put your containers in a closet check them daily. As soon as there is any sign of life, place the trays in a warm light place, not in direct sunlight.

Hardening Off

When large enough to handle, prick out seed tray seedlings and repot individually. Allow them to root fully. Test plug tray seedlings by giving one or two

a gentle tug. They should come away from the cells cleanly, with the root ball. If they do not, leave for another few days.

When the seedlings are ready, harden them off slowly by leaving the young plants outside during the day. Once weaned into a natural climate, usually after 10 to 14 days, plant them directly to where they will mature.

Seed Storage and Viability

Once seed is harvested from the plant, it begins to deteriorate; even ideal storage conditions can only slow down the rate of deterioration. Viability (the ability to germinate) usually declines with age. Always use fresh seed, or store in cool, dark, dry conditions (definitely not the corner of the greenhouse) in airtight containers.

cuttings

Taking cuttings is the best way to propagate many fruiting plants and nonflowering herbs. This may be the only way to reproduce a particular variety or cultivar that will not come true from seed. For successful softwood

cuttings it is worth buying a heated propagator, which can be placed in a greenhouse or on a shady windowsill. For successful semi-ripe, hardwood and root cuttings, a shaded coldframe can be used. For specific details, see under the individual entry.

Softwood Cuttings

Softwood cuttings are usually taken between spring and midsummer, using the new, lush, green growth. To produce successful rooting material from herbs, prune the plant vigorously in winter to encourage new growth, and take cuttings as soon as there is sufficient growth.

Prepare a pot, seed tray, or plug tray with cutting compost — 50 percent bark, 50 percent peat. Firm the compost to within 1 in. of the rim. Collect the cuttings in small batches in the morning. Choose sturdy shoots with plenty of leaves. Best results come from nonflowering shoots with the base leaves removed. Cut the shoot with a knife, not scissors. Place the cutting at once in the shade in a polythene bag or a bucket of water; softwood cuttings are extremely susceptible to water loss.

To prepare the cutting material, cut the base of the stem just below a leaf joint, to leave a cutting of roughly 4 in. long. If the cutting material has to be under 4 in., take the cutting with a heel. Remove the lower leaves and trim the tail which is left from the heel. Trim the stem cleanly before a node, the point at which a leaf stalk joins the stem. Remove the leaves from the bottom third of the cutting with a knife, leaving at least two or three leaves on top.

Make a hole in the compost and insert the cutting up to its leaves. Do not overcrowd the container or include more than one species, because quite often they take different times to root. Label and date the cuttings clearly, and only water the compost from above if necessary. Keep out of direct sunlight in hot weather. If it is very sunny, heavy shade is best for the first week.

Place in a heated or unheated propagator, or cover the pot or container with a plastic bag supported on a thin wire hoop (to prevent the plastic touching the leaves), or with an upturned plastic bottle with the bottom cut off. If you are using a plastic bag, turn it inside out every few days to stop excess moisture from condensation dripping onto the cuttings. Spray the cuttings with water every morning for the first week. Average rooting time is 2 to 4 weeks. The cutting medium is low in nutrients, so give a regular foliar feed when the cutting starts to root. Harden off the cuttings gradually when they are rooted. Bring them out in stages to normal sunny, airy conditions. Pot them on using a prepared potting compost once they are weaned. Label and water well after transplanting. About 4 to 5 weeks after transplanting, when the plant is growing away, pinch out the top center of the young cutting. This will encourage the plant to bush out, making it stronger as well as fuller. Allow to grow on until a good-size root ball can be seen in the pot, then plant out.

Semi-hardwood or Greenwood Cuttings

These are usually taken from shrubby herbs such as rosemary and myrtle toward the end of the growing season (from midsummer to midfall). Use broadly the same method as for softwood cuttings, but the compost should be freer-draining. Make the mix equal parts peat, grit and bark. Once the cuttings have been inserted in the compost, place the pot, seed tray or plug tray in a cold greenhouse, cold frame or cool conservatory, not in a propagator, unless it has a misting unit. Average rooting time for semi-hardwood cuttings is 4 to 6 weeks. If the fall is exceptionally hot and the compost or cuttings seem to be drying out, spray once a week. Begin the hardening off process in the spring after the frosts. Give a foliar feed as soon as there is sufficient new growth.

Hardwood Cuttings

Taken in late fall or early winter after the plants are dormant, in exactly the same way as softwood cuttings, but with a freer-draining compost of equal parts peat, grit and bark. Keep watering to the absolute minimum. Winter in a cold frame, greenhouse or conservatory. Average rooting time can take as long as 12 months. For hardwood cuttings of hardy fruits, push cuttings into a slit trench lined with sharp sand in moist ground, firm well and keep them weed-free and protected from drying winds — a cloche is usually advantageous.

Root Cuttings

This method of cutting suits plants with creeping roots, such as bergamot, comfrey, horseradish, lemon balm, mint, soapwort and sweet woodruff. Dig up some healthy roots in spring or fall. Fill a container with cutting compost — 50 percent bark, 50 percent peat, firmed to within 1 in. of the rim. These cuttings lend themselves to being grown in plug trays. Water well. Cut 1½ to 3 in. lengths of root that carry a growing bud. For comfrey and horseradish, simply slice the root into sections, 1½ to 3 in. long, using a sharp knife to give a clean cut through the root. Make holes in the compost with a dibble. If using pots or seed trays these should be 1–2½ in. apart. Plant the cutting vertically. Cover with a small amount of compost, and a layer of perlite level with the top of the container. Label and date. Average rooting time is 2 to 3 weeks. Do not water until roots or top growth appears. Then apply liquid feed. Slowly harden off the cuttings when rooted. Pot on cuttings in seed trays and pots in a potting compost once they are hardened off. Label and water well after transplanting. About 2 to 3 weeks after transplanting, when you can see that the plant is growing away, pinch out the top center of the young cutting. This will encourage the plant to bush out, making it stronger as well as fuller. Allow to grow on until a good-size root ball can be seen in the pot. Plant out in the garden when the last frosts are over.

layering

Layering is a process that encourages sections of plant to root while still attached to the parent. Bay, rosemary, sage, and other evergreens suit this method. Blackberries root their tips anywhere they can in fall, and many plants will root where they touch the ground to form natural layers, which easily detach with roots in fall or spring.

To layer a plant, cultivate the soil around it during winter and early spring by adding peat and grit to it. In spring trim the leaves and side shoots of a young, low vigorous stem for 4–24 in. below its growing tip. Bring the stem down to ground level and mark its position on the soil. Dig a trench at that point. Roughen the stem at the point where it will touch the ground, and peg it down into the trench, then bend the stem at right angles behind the growing tip, so that it protrudes vertically. Return the soil to the trench to bury the stem. Firm in well and water. Keep the soil moist, especially in dry periods. Sever the layering stem from its parent plant in fall if well-rooted, and 3 to 4 weeks later nip out the growing tip from the rooted layer to make plant bush out. Check that the roots are established before lifting the layered stem. If necessary, leave for a further year. Replant either in open ground or in a pot. Label and leave to establish.

grafting

Some fruit plants are only propagated by grafting or budding small pieces onto more easily grown rootstocks. Often this is done with special rootstocks simply to influence growth or to get the maximum number of plants from limited material. Budding and grafting techniques, although essentially simple, are profoundly difficult to master without much practice and are beyond the scope of this book.

buying plants

Buying fruit, vegetable and herb plants has the advantage of ease and speed over growing them yourself, but is relatively costly and incurs a high risk of importing weeds, pests and diseases along with the plants, especially with pot-grown specimens.

To fill an average garden with plants does not require an immense investment but it is still quite enough to warrant care and budgeting. For fruit, specialist mail-order nurseries usually provide a greater choice, and are often cheaper than most local suppliers. Get several catalogues and compare them before ordering, and do so early.

For fruit trees and shrubs bare-rooted plants are easier to inspect than pot-grown ones for signs of health or disease. The root systems on well-grown, bare-rooted trees are usually more extensive than those of pot-grown plants. Furthermore, for larger growing trees, there is the danger of pot-grown specimens being root bound. However, for most smaller subjects, containerized plants from reputable suppliers are convenient and give good results.

Vegetables may be available pre-grown as seedlings, at the stage when they require transplanting; as plugs with three or four true leaves, which may need growing on; or as plants that are quite large (sold in strips or multi-packs, like bedding plants) and should be transplanted directly on arrival.

Misting unit

MAINTAINING THE GARDEN

To ensure that plants are productive and the crops are of high quality, vegetables, herbs and fruit need careful nurturing and diligent husbandry. Vegetables require more constant attention than either herbs or fruit. However, all plants benefit from regular checking so that any problems can be spotted early. (For watering, see p. 651; for pests and diseases, see p. 656–61.)

planting out

Plants that have been germinated or grown as cuttings in a greenhouse will need to be planted out after hardening off. The timing depends on the prevailing weather and soil conditions. All plants suffer a check in their growth rate after transplanting, caused by inevitable root disturbance and by the change in environment to somewhere cooler. Younger plants tend to recover rapidly while older ones take longer. To reduce stress, ensure there is plenty of water available, transplant on an overcast day into moist soil and provide shelter from strong sunshine until plants are established.

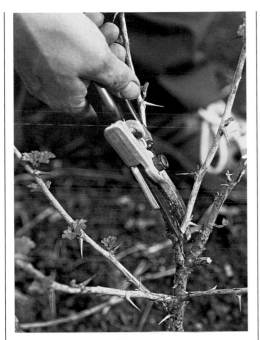

If you must prune, be ruthless

plant supports

These should be positioned before they are required by the plants. Plants growing tall without a support can be damaged or suffer a check in growth. Select a support according to the plant being grown. Peas climb with tendrils, preferring to twine round thin supports such as chicken wire or spindly twigs, while runner beans hug poles or canes. Vegetables without climbing mechanisms need to be tied to stakes with garden twine in a loose figure eight loop, positioning the stake on the windward side of the plant. Fruit trees trained against a flat surface need strong wires to which the branches can be tied.

pruning fruit trees

We prune for several reasons: to remove diseased, damaged and ill-placed growths, and to channel growth into fruit production. We may also prune to reduce the size of a plant as it becomes too large for the space available.

Excessive pruning, especially at the wrong time, is counter-productive. In general, pruning even moderate amounts from a tree or bush in fall and winter stimulates regrowth, proportionately as much as the amount removed. This is useful when the plant is young and we wish to form the framework by stimulating the growth of young, vigorous replacement shoots.

However such fall and winter pruning is not so suitable for more mature fruiting plants whose structure is already formed and from which we wish to obtain fruit. Most respond much better to summer pruning, which is cutting out three-quarters of every young shoot, bar the leaders. This redirects growth and causes fruit bud production on the spurs or short side shoots formed. These may be further shortened and tidied in the winter but then, as only a little is removed, vigorous re-growth is avoided.

Although it may seem complicated, pruning is easy once you've done it a few times. Use clean pruning shears, which have been sterilized with alcohol, or a sharp saw, and cover large wounds with a proprietary sealant to prevent water getting in.

Training the Basic Shape

The majority of our perennial woody fruiting plants can be trained and pruned to make a permanent framework which carries spurs, preferably all over. Growing just one such stem, branch or cordon on a weak rootstock allows us to squeeze many varieties into the same space as one full-sized tree. Such single-stemmed cordons do not produce very much fruit, especially as they are hard to support if they reach more than head height. Sloping these cordons at 45° serves to make them longer without going too high.

Growing two, three, or more branches is a better compromise. These can be arranged as espaliers (in tiers), fans (radiating from the center), or gridirons of almost any design. However, for the vast majority of trees and bushes, the shapes most commonly used are the modified central leader and open vase.

This bowl shape maximizes the surface area of fruiting growth exposed to the sun and air. To achieve it the main leader is removed from the middle and the branches trained as a bowl with a hollow center open to the sky. The number of main stems is customarily about five or six which divide from the trunk and redivide to form the walls of the goblet. The stem or trunk may be short, as is common with gooseberries, or taller, which is often more convenient. Where the branches of a tree divide from the trunk on a short trunk they are termed bushes, at waist to shoulder height they are called semi-dwarfs, and standards where they start higher still. Bushes, especially those on the more dwarfing stocks, tend to be too low to mow underneath but can always be mulched instead. Semi-dwarfs grow large, depending on stock, and are tall enough to mow underneath. Full standards make very big specimens and are only usually planted in parks and meadows.

Young unformed plants, whips, can be bought more cheaply than those with a good shape or form already trained. It is very satisfying to grow your own espalier or gridiron from a whip, but the result will depend on your skill and foresight.

Renewal Pruning

Some fruits need pruning on the renewal principle. Whole branches or shoots are removed at a year or two old, after they have fruited. Summer raspberries are typical, the old shoots being removed at ground level as the young are tied in. Grapevines can be constrained to two young branches emerging from the trunk, replaced each year. Peaches on walls also have young shoots tied in and old fruited ones removed. Blackcurrants have a third of growths from the ground removed annually.

Timing

A few plants are pruned only at certain times of year. Hollow-stemmed, tender and evergreen plants are pruned in spring once the hardest weather is over and *Prunus* (members of the cherry family or stone fruits) are pruned in summer, as otherwise they are liable to disease.

Working on steps requires two people, or beware …

FERTILITY AND WATER MANAGEMENT

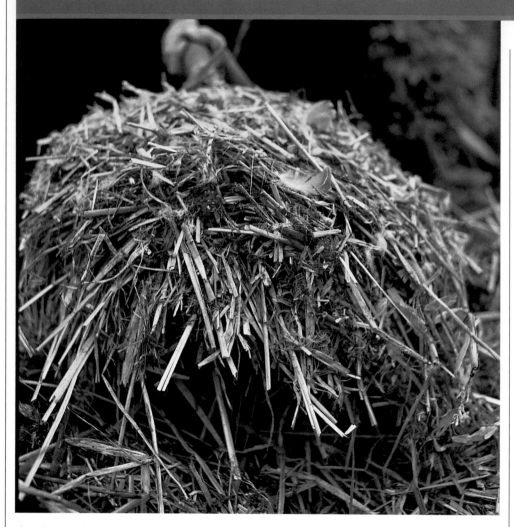

Good stuff for the compost heap

Plants have varying nutrient requirements according to the species. All need sufficiently fertile soil and water to grow and yield well. Fruits are ordinarily not as demanding as many vegetable crops; this is because they are mostly perennial. Growing in open ground, they make extensive root systems, which find the water and nutrients required. Annual and short-lived crops generally need much more attention to soil fertility and water provision because they have limited root systems. Plants in containers similarly require much care, and because of the confinement also readily suffer from any excess.

soil fertility

Soil fertility is the source of essential nutrients needed for healthy growth. There is no precise definition of a fertile soil, but ideally it has the following characteristics: a good crumbly structure; plenty of humus and nutrients; good drainage, moisture-retentive; a pH that is slightly acid to neutral. Nutrients are absorbed in solution by the roots and transported through the plant's system. The major elements include nitrogen, phosphorus, potassium, calcium, magnesium and sulphur. Minor, or trace, elements include iron, manganese, boron, zinc, copper, nickel, chlorine, and molybdenum. These are needed in minute quantities yet are still essential.

Nutrients are present in the soil as a result of the weathering processes on the mineral particles and the chemical breakdown or decay of organic matter and humus by bacteria and other micro-organisms. These release nutrients in a form available to plants. To function effectively they must have an open, well-drained soil with adequate supplies of air and water. Extra nutrients in the form of compost and fertilizer may be needed to provide sufficient nutrients to sustain healthy growth.

Fertility is best provided organically from materials that slowly convert to a usable form in the soil. Well-rotted farmyard manures, good compost, seaweed meal, hoof and horn meal, blood, fish and bone meal, bone meal, and fish emulsions are all eminently suitable.

If mineral shortages are suspected, then ground rock dusts provide cheap, slow-release supplies; potash, phosphate, magnesium (dolomitic) limestone, calcified seaweed and lime are all widely available, cheap and pleasant to apply. Wood ashes are extremely valuable to most fruiting plants. Seaweed extracts sprayed on the foliage can give rapid relief of mineral deficiencies.

Bulkier materials such as well-rotted manure and compost also provide much humus, which is essential for the natural fertility of the soil, its water-holding capacity and its buffering action (preventing the soil being too acid or alkaline). The humus content is conserved by minimal cultivation and refraining from soluble fertilizers.

More humus can be provided by growing green manures. These occupy the soil when other plants are dormant or if parts of the plot are empty throughout winter. Nutrients and water that would have leached away are combined with winter sunlight to grow dense covers of hardy plants. These also protect the soil surface from erosion and rain compaction. When the weather warms up, green manures are incorporated *in situ* by digging in or composting under a plastic sheet, or are removed and added to the compost heap.

Organic mulches such as well-rotted manures, composted shredded bark, leafmold, mushroom compost, straw or peat are all advantageous to most plants. They rot down at the soil surface aiding fertility and humus levels and suppress weeds if they are thick enough, but most importantly they conserve soil moisture.

Careful rotation in the vegetable plot can aid fertility. Plant "hungry" crops such as celery, leeks and members of the cabbage family, which require plenty of nitrogen, after peas, beans and other legumes, which fix nitrogen from the atmosphere using nitrogen-fixing bacteria in swollen nodules on their roots and release nitrogen into the soil.

watering

Vegetables and fruits crop to their full potential only when water is plentiful. Yields are reduced when plants suffer from drought stress. The soil is a plant's reservoir and different soils are able to retain different levels of water. Clays retain water very efficiently but dry out in summer, loams have a good balance between drainage and water retention, and sandy soils are very free-draining.

Water is lost from both soil and the leaves of plants and this loss is most rapid on hot, sunny days with drying winds. It is vital to reduce the loss of water from soil by:
• regularly incorporating well-rotted organic matter into the soil, to increase its moisture-holding capacity.
• deep cultivation to open up the soil and encourage deeper rooting. This allows plants to draw water from a greater soil depth.
• covering the soil surface with mulches such as well-rotted manure or black plastic to prevent moisture loss from the surface and upper soil layers.
• improving drainage on waterlogged soil; a high water table restricts root development, making plants prone to stress during drought. By improving the drainage system and lowering the water table, the roots are encouraged to penetrate to a greater depth, thereby leaving them more drought-tolerant.
• removing weeds, which compete with other plants for water. They should be removed at seedling stage.
• reducing plant density, particularly on dry, exposed sites, to allow each plant to draw water from a greater volume of soil.
• providing shelter, especially on exposed sites. Reducing wind speed reduces moisture loss from the soil and plants.
• being careful with accurate timing and frequency of application. Most plants have critical periods when adequate water supplies are very important for successful development and cropping.

Critical Watering Periods
Water before it is too late; if a plant is wilting it is already suffering badly!

Seeds and Seedlings
Water is essential for seed germination and rapid seedling development. Seedbeds should be moist, not waterlogged. Water seedlings using a fine rose on a watering can to provide a shower of tiny droplets and prevent plant damage.

Having easy access to water makes it less of a chore

Transplants
Plants often suffer from transplanting shock due to root damage after being moved, and the effects are more pronounced if the soil is dry. Water plants gently after moving them to settle moist soil around the roots. Liquid seaweed is a useful boost. Water woody plants until they have been established for up to 3 years, particularly evergreens, which cannot drop their leaves when under stress and so survive by going dormant.

Fruiting Crops
Fruits and vegetables, such as peas, beans and tomatoes, with edible fruits have two critical periods for water availability once they have established: when flowering (to aid pollination and fruit set) and when the fruit begins to swell.

Leaf and Root Crops
These need a constant water supply throughout their cropping life.

Methods of Watering
It is vital to maintain rapid growth in the growing season, particularly in annual plants, otherwise plant tissues can harden and growth can be affected. Growth check in cauliflowers can cause young plants prematurely to form a small, poorly developed curd, while other annuals will "bolt."

Always water thoroughly, soaking the soil to a reasonable depth. It is bad practice merely to wet the soil surface. This draws the roots up to form a surface mat while much is wasted by evaporation. A good soaking descends and draws the roots after it, thus they become deeper and more able to find other soil moisture on their own. Water in the evening if possible.

If you bury a length of hosepipe with the roots of a tree you can inject the water right where it is needed during the critical first few years. Likewise a pot or funnel pushed in nearby is a useful aid.

When time is limited and cash more abundant it is wise to invest in automatic watering equipment. Drip feeds and soaker hoses allow a constant and even supply of water close to the roots without the gardener's constant attention, and soon repay the investment. Overhead sprinklers are extremely inefficient as only about 20 percent of the water ever reaches the plant.

Mulching
Once the rains have drenched the soil a mulch prevents it evaporating away again. Any mulch helps, but the looser and thicker the better. Less than 2 in. is ineffective, and initial applications always pack down, so be prepared to add more after a few months. When organic material for mulching is in short supply, inorganic ones may be used. Sharp sand and gravel make excellent moisture-retaining mulches and are cheap and sterile.

Grass clippings are an excellent mulch, if applied in thin layers — though if applied too thickly in wet conditions they may make a nasty smelly mess. Clippings provide a rich source of nitrogen and encourage soil life. They soon disappear and need topping up. Continuous applications slowly make the soil less alkaline and more acid, which is often advantageous.

Weeds being kept down (neatly) with old carpet

GROWING IN GREENHOUSES

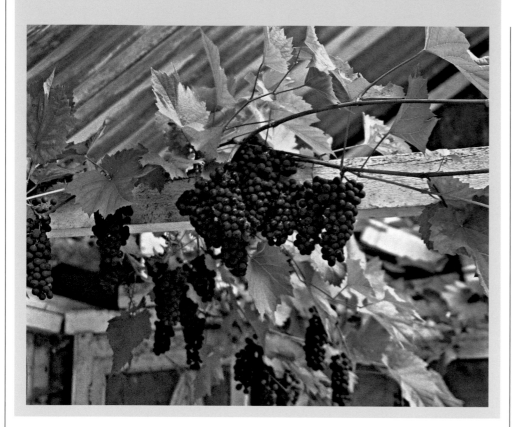

There is no substitute for walk-in cover, which is more valuable if heated and frost-free, and even more so if kept warm or even hot. If maintained as warm as a living room all year round, many exotic fruits and vegetables from oranges to eggplants become possible. It is not only summer crops that benefit. Lettuce, spinach and other hardy winter salads produce more tender, better-quality crops in an unheated greenhouse than outside.

Exotics such as passion fruits are best grown under cover as they would not crop otherwise. The extra heat ripens the fruit and also the wood, which often cannot ripen outdoors. Some plants take many months to crop each year and without cover they would never ripen before frosts come. Extra warmth and shelter allows us to have tender or delicate plants that would not survive in the open, but it also means we can have the same crop earlier than outdoors — for example strawberries or tomatoes.

Often it is best to grow plants in containers that are to go under cover as this allows for more variety in the same area, though each plant will necessarily yield less than if it was in the ground. Containers not only control the vigor of the plants but also make them portable so they can be moved under cover and outside as convenient. This suits many fruits such as the citrus, which really prefer to be outside all summer but need frost protection in winter.

This is why some plants are difficult. They need hot summers and warm falls and also cold winters to go dormant. Without dormancy they do not ripen wood or fruit well and often just fade away. It is quite easy to chill a greenhouse in a cold area for the couple of months required, but not of course if other tender plants are kept there, too.

The other requirement may be for extra light. Many plants need more light than can be had in winter through dirty glass. The physical barrier reduces light intensity by half. Fortunately, artificial lights are cheap to fit and run — compared to heating anyway. Some plants are very demanding; not only do they want more light and heat but they want enough hours of complete darkness every night as well. This requires the fitting of blinds to exclude daylight and light from any nearby streetlights, too! Similarly some plants find bright light too intense and need shading.

Fortunately most exotics are remarkably easy to grow. The biggest problems are usually the cost of heating and the eventual size of the plants.

Hygiene in the Greenhouse

Greenhouses should be cleaned annually in winter: wash thoroughly with disinfectant to kill overwintering eggs and fungal spores. If you have space, before introducing a new plant to the greenhouse, keep it in quarantine for a few weeks to prevent new problems being introduced.

Tomatoes are reliable under cover

PROTECTED CROPPING

Many crops need protecting at some point in their life. In some cases they need protecting from the elements, to provide conditions more conducive to growth; they may also need protecting from predators such as birds and rodents.

Protection from the Elements
A few simple structures can extend the growing season in spring and fall, accelerate growth and increase productivity.

Coldframes are ideal for raising seedlings or hardening off plants before transplanting outdoors. The lack of height limits the crops that can be grown in them. Cloches of glass or plastic are easily moved to provide shelter to those individual plants or small groups that need it most. Low polythene tunnels are like small cloches, are cheap, portable and versatile, but are of limited use because of their flimsiness and lack of height. Crop covers or floating row covers are flexible covers that can be laid immediately over the crop or suspended on hoops as "floating mulches." As the plants grow they are forced upwards. Fleece is lightweight, soft-textured spun polypropylene, which lasts for a year if it is kept clean, or sometimes longer if cared for. It is ideal for frost protection and for forcing early crops. Many crops, especially vegetables, can be grown under this, from sowing to harvesting, and it is an effective barrier against pests and diseases. More

light and air can penetrate through this than through plastic film. Plastic film is usually perforated with minute slits or holes for ventilation, but the crop may overheat on sunny spring days. The film is laid directly over the plants; as they grow, the flexible material is pushed upwards, splitting open the minute slits and increasing ventilation. It is often used in the early stages of growth. Plastic netting has a very fine mesh, filtering the wind and providing protection, but has little effect on raising temperature. It lasts for several seasons.

As many of these materials are manufactured in long, narrow rolls, the most effective way to use them is to grow crops in long, narrow strips. Insect-pollinated crops like zucchini, squashes, cucumbers, and tomatoes should have the covering removed or opened as the crop develops.

Protection from Predators
Fruit cages are covered with netting. They are necessary to protect soft fruit in areas with many birds. The most troublesome birds, such as blackbirds and pigeons, can be excluded with coarse 1 in. mesh, while smaller, insectivorous birds such as wrens and bluetits can still gain access. If all the net is wire, squirrels and rodents can also be stopped. If a finer mesh, down to about ½ in. is used then bees can still enter but large moths and butterflies are excluded.

Fruit cages have other uses. The netting itself makes a more sheltered environment enjoyed by the plants. Light frosts are kept off, and chill winds are reduced. In very hot regions, denser netting gives welcome shade and cooler conditions.

A fruit cage can even be reversed in principle to enclose all of a small garden and to confine ornamental seed- and insect-eating, but hopefully not inadvertently fruit-eating, birds. On a more prosaic level, it is practical to grow plants on a tall post and then run chickens underneath for their excellent pest control. If you have chickens, they can be running in the cage during most of the year when the plants are not in fruit.

Fruit cages can be hand-crafted from second-hand materials or easy custom-made ones are available. In areas of high wind, obviously, the most substantial materials have to be used. Permanent sides of wire mesh and a light net laid on wires for the roof are most practicable. Make sure you can remove the roof net easily if snows are forecast as a thick layer on top will break most cages.

Most fruit cage plants are natives of the woodland's edge and do not mind light shade, but few of them relish stagnant air so do not overcrowd them.

Cabbage plants protected with garden netting

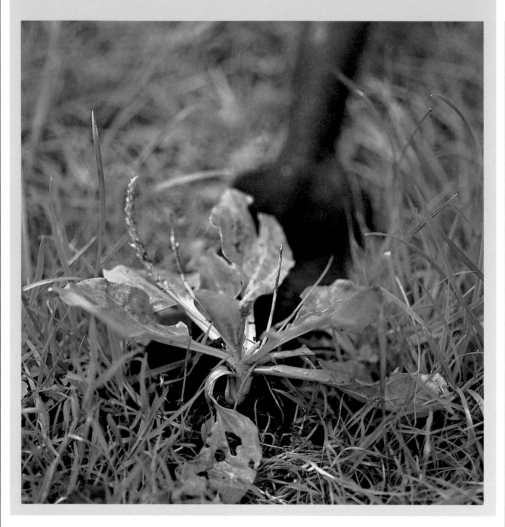

Any plant that grows in a place where it is not wanted is described as a weed. These compete with crops for moisture, nutrients and light, acting as hosts to pests and diseases, which can then spread to crops.

types of weeds

Knowledge of a weed's life cycle enables the gardener to control weeds effectively.
• Ephemeral weeds germinate, flower and seed rapidly, producing several generations each season and copious quantities of seed.
• Annual weeds germinate, flower and seed in one season.
• Biennial weeds have a life-cycle spanning two growing seasons.

• Perennial weeds survive for several years. They often spread through the soil as they grow, producing scores of new shoots and setting seed. New plants sprout from tiny fragments of root, rhizome or bulbils in the soil.

methods of control

There are four main methods of weed control: manual, mechanical, mulching and chemical. Wherever possible, keep the garden weed-free and if germination occurs, remove weeds immediately, before they flower and produce seed. The old saying, "One year's seed is seven years' weed" is, unfortunately, scientifically proven.

Complete elimination of weeds from an area before planting is invariably worthwhile and is much easier than trying later to weed among the plants (see p. 634).

Manual Weeding
Digging, forking, hoeing and hand weeding, are often the only practical ways to eradicate weeds in confined spaces.

Digging cultivates the soil to a depth of at least 12 in. Soil is turned over, burying surface vegetation and annual weeds. Perennial weeds should be removed separately and not buried among the surface vegetation.

Forking cultivates the soil around perennial weeds before they are lifted by hand. If this is undertaken carefully, roots can be removed without breaking into sections and forming new plants.

Hoeing kills germinating weed seeds, reduces moisture loss and minimizes soil disturbance. Hoeing is best undertaken in dry weather and the blade should penetrate no deeper than ½ in.

Hand-weed in dry weather when the soil is moist so that weeds are easily loosened from the soil; try to remove the whole plant. Remove weeds from the site to prevent them from rerooting.

Mechanical Weed Control
Machines with revolving rotary tines, blades or cultivator attachments are useful for preparing seedbeds and can also be used to control annual weeds between rows of vegetables. They should be employed carefully to avoid root damage. When clearing the ground of perennial weeds, the blades simply slice through the roots and rhizomes. While this increases their number initially, several sessions over a period of time should gradually exhaust and eventually kill the plants. This is only viable when there is plenty of time.

Biological Weed Control
Mulching is the practice of covering the soil around plants with a layer of organic or inorganic material to suppress weeds, reduce water loss (see also p. 651) and warm the soil. Choose your material carefully; straw harbors pests such as vine weevil and flea beetle and contains weed seeds, but is effective as an insulating layer over winter. It also draws nitrogen from the soil in the early stages of decay. Using rotted material like well-rotted farm manure or spent hops avoids this problem

Organic mulches are also limited where crops need to be hilled — a process that disturbs the soil. Inorganic materials like plastic sheeting, though effective, are unattractive but can at least be hidden beneath a thin layer of organic mulch.

Inorganic mulches suppress weeds and prevent seeds from germinating. They also conserve soil moisture by slowing evaporation; plastic films are the most effective for this purpose. They keep trailing crops clean. White plastic mulches hasten growth and ripening by reflecting light on to leaves and fruit; black plastic mulches warm the soil in spring. Sheet mulches are most effective when applied before the crop is planted, and the young plants are then planted through small holes in the sheet.

Organic mulches improve soil fertility and conserve its structure by protecting the surface from heavy rain and being trodden on, encouraging earthworm activity and adding organic matter and nutrients to the soil. They insulate the soil, keeping it cooler in summer and warmer in winter. Weeds that push their way through are easily removed. For effective weed control organic mulches should be about 4 in. deep, to block out the light.

In general, organic mulches improve soil fertility as they decay, while inorganic mulches are more effective against weeds as they form an impenetrable barrier.

Chemical Weed Control

Choose and use herbicides with extreme care and ensure they are suitable for the weeds to be controlled. **Follow the manufacturer's instructions carefully.**

• Residual herbicides form a layer over the soil, killing germinating weeds and seedlings.
• Contact herbicides only kill those parts of the plant that they touch. They are effective against annual weeds and weed seedlings, but are not recommended against established plants.
• Systemic or translocated herbicides are absorbed by the foliage, travelling through the sap system to kill the whole plant, including the roots. Glyphosate is often the active ingredient. Individual weeds can be "spot treated" using such herbicides in gel or liquid form.

Several chemical weed-control methods have been developed for use with vegetables and other edible plants but no single chemical is suitable for all crops. This gives the grower three options: stock a range of chemicals and change the type regularly; use chemicals only as a last resort; or grow organically. For edible plants the latter is almost invariably the best.

Using and Storing Weedkillers Safely

Always wear adequate protective clothing, such as face mask, goggles, rubber gloves and old waterproof clothes when mixing weedkillers. Dilute weedkillers according to the manufacturer's instructions, and never mix different chemicals together. Never dilute chemicals in a confined space, as they may give off toxic fumes.

As for mixing, always wear the specified protective clothing when applying weedkillers. Follow the manufacturer's instructions carefully and use only as recommended on the product label. Do not apply weedkillers in windy conditions; nearby plants may suffer serious damage. Do not apply weedkillers in very hot, still conditions when there is a high risk of spray travelling on warm air currents. If you are using a watering can to apply chemicals, ensure that it is obviously labelled and at no times use it for any other purpose.

Store chemicals in the original containers with the labels well secured so that the contents can be identified. Mark the container with the date of purchase, so that you know how long it has been stored. Never store dilute weedkillers for future use. Always store concentrates in cool, frost-free, dark conditions out of the reach of children and animals, in a locked cupboard in a workshop or shed.

Thoroughly wash protective clothing, sprayers, mixing vessels and utensils after use. Never use the same sprayer, mixing vessels and utensils for other types of chemical such as fungicides. The results could be disastrous!

grass management

Under woody perennial plants such as fruit trees and bushes, the most convenient ground cover is usually grass sward. Grass competes vigorously, especially if kept closely mowed as a lawn. However grass sward is simple to maintain, ornamental, hygienic and prevents worse weeds. The clippings themselves are a free source of mulching material and can contribute much fertility to our plants.

Grass sward is most productive of useful clippings when the grass is cut often and not too closely. Long grass grows more quickly, is more drought-resistant and suppresses turf weeds better than closely cropped. Cut your grass regularly and frequently with slightly greater height of cut and the longer, more vigorous grass soon chokes out most weeds. When seeding, it is sensible to include clovers in the grass seed mix as they have the advantage of fixing nitrogen from the air to aid the grasses. A clover grass mixture also stays greener for longer in hot dry summers and, if left to flower, the clovers attract bees and other beneficial insects.

If a soil test indicates a need for it, you should lime your turf every fourth year, providing you are not growing ericaceous plants or fine golf-green grasses. Most swards slowly become acid in the topmost layer; this encourages mosses and acid-loving weeds. If such weeds, say daisies, are increasing you need to add more lime, up to a couple of handfuls per square yard per year. You probably also need to raise the height of your cut. If weeds that like wet acid soils such as buttercups appear, then lime is desperately needed and probably better drainage as well.

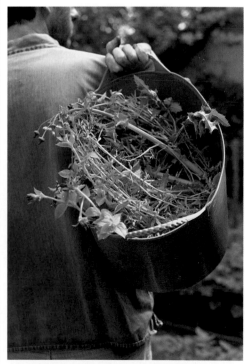

If they're in the wrong place, take them away!

PESTS AND DISEASES

can do to make the sun come out, the wind stop or the rain fall.

The second cause of loss is probably the gardener. We all leave action too late, skimp preparation and routine tasks, put plants in less than their optimum positions, and then over-crowd them as well. What we must remember is that our plants "want" to leaf, flower and crop. They are programmed as tightly as any computer, If we give them the right inputs they must produce the right output.

preventing problems

Organic gardeners avoid the use of artificial chemicals, relying on good management and natural predators to control pests and diseases, while working to create an environment in which they are unlikely to occur. If we give our plants the right conditions then they are also healthy and vigorous enough to shrug off most pests and disease. Healthy plants grow in a well-suited site and soil, with shelter and water when they are small, and are not overfed. Excess fertilizer makes plants soft and prone to problems. Keep them lean and fit with the correct compost and mulches.

Working with Natural Defenses
The most effective way to control pests is to persuade others to do it for you. The natural ecology always controls them in the long run. We can help it quickly reach a balance of more ladybugs, thrushes and frogs with fewer aphids, snails and slugs. Our allies require shelter, nest sites, food out of season, water and companion plants. If we provide these they increase in number and thus the pests decrease.

Timing can be of service. For example late raspberries usually escape the depredations of their fruit maggot. Having many fruits that ripen at the same time also reduces damage. When successive plants ripen they are picked clean by small numbers of pests which are overwhelmed by a glut, as may be the gardener!

Check plants daily if possible. Instant eradication is often the best remedy: either remove the affected part of the plant or wipe off the pest or disease as with aphids.

General Hygiene
Plant debris is a logical host for pests and diseases, particularly over winter, allowing them to survive in

The control of pests and diseases is done to preserve the yield or appearance of our crops, but we must ensure that the costs incurred do not outweigh the gains. It is ironic that commercial apples are sprayed to prevent scabby patches on their skin, which is now peeled and discarded to avoid the very residues left by many such sprays. Herbs in general suffer from few pests and diseases and in fact many can be used to protect other crops.

For the home gardener the main causes of loss of crops most years is the weather. There is very little we preparation for reemergence and reinfection the following year. Do everything possible to keep plants healthy by cleaning your greenhouse and equipment regularly. Dispose of organic matter immediately; compost healthy material and get rid of infected plants at once by burning or placing in the garbage can. When buying plants, ensure they come from a reputable source and, if possible, keep them in quarantine for a short while before introducing them to the greenhouse.

Winter is the perfect time to disinfect plant supports, particularly bamboo canes, which are hollow and often split with age, creating cracks and crevices which form suitable sites for fungi and insect eggs to overwinter. These can be sprayed or dipped in disinfectant.

Cultural Practices

Always use pasteurized compost for seed sowing and potting. Seedlings are particularly vulnerable, especially when sown under cover. Sow seeds thinly, do not irrigate with stagnant or cold water, ventilate the greenhouse, but avoid chilling plants or seedlings and do not allow compost to become waterlogged. Promote rapid germination and continuous growth to reduce the risk of infection at the time when seedlings and young plants are at their most vulnerable. Inspect plants regularly, particularly if a variety is prone to certain problems. Grow pest- and disease-resistant cultivars where possible. Rotate vegetable crops and always keep the garden weed-free. Handle plants with care, particularly when harvesting, as this is a common cause of infection. Regularly check stored crops as rot spreads rapidly in a confined space.

Yellow sticky trap

Copper rings

control methods

Barriers and Traps

The simplest method of protection is to use a barrier to prevent pests or disease reaching the plant. For example, netting stops birds and floating row cover stops many insects.

On fruit trees, traps of corrugated cardboard, carpet or old gunny sacks can be made by rolling strips around trunk or stem. These attract pests by replicating creviced bark. They hide within and can be dislodged in winter. Nonsetting sticky bands applied to aluminium foil wrapped tightly around trunk, branch or stem stop pests climbing up and down. Do remember to paint the support as well.

Sticky traps can be bought to lure flying pests to them with pheromone sex attractant "perfumes." Others use the smell of the fruit or leaf to entice the pest to a sticky end, or simply use colors like yellow. Jars of water with lids of foil containing pencil-sized holes trap wasps when baited with fruit juice or jam.

Organic Sprays

Soap spray suffocates most small insect pests and is remarkably safe for us and the environment. People used to employ ordinary household soap flakes but improved soft soaps are now sold for pesticidal use. Sprays based on plant oils or plant and fish oils are also available, alongside blends of surfactants and nutrients.

Biological Controls

Many predators are now available commercially. Apart from *Bacillus thuringiensis*, the bacterial control for caterpillars, few are effective outside the closed environment of a greenhouse. Most pesticides kill predators with the exception of insecticidal soaps and

Soft soap spray

pirimicarb (against aphids) and so should be avoided. Particularly useful are *Phytoseiulus persimilis*, the predatory mite that controls two-spotted or red spider mite and *Encarsia formosa*, a parasitic wasp, controlling greenhouse whitefly. All biological control methods are relatively expensive when compared with chemical alternatives, and nearly all depend on warm temperatures to work efficiently.

Chemical controls

Chemicals offer a quick and simple solution to many pest and disease problems but, before using them, it is worth considering the following. Many chemicals are toxic and can be harmful to humans, pets and wildlife. They should be applied with extreme care. Chemicals may remain in soil and plant tissue for long periods, affecting predators. Many pests and diseases, particularly whitefly and red spider mite, can develop a resistance to chemicals that are used persistently for long periods, so rendering controls less effective. Applying a range of chemicals can overcome this. Government legislation may make some chemicals unavailable in the future.

Always follow instructions with regard to safety, mixing and application. Apply chemicals in still, overcast conditions, usually in the early morning or evening. Protect surrounding plants from the chemical solution. Thoroughly clean equipment after use. Dispose of unwanted chemicals according to the manufacturer's recommendations. DO NOT POUR THEM DOWN THE DRAIN.

soil-borne pests

Cutworms

These grey-green caterpillars, approximately 2 in. long, appear from late spring until early fall. They burrow into root crops including beetroot, carrot, parsnip and potato, and any plant with a soft taproot, eating through plant stems at soil level.

Plants grown under cover seem less prone to damage, and heavy watering in early summer often kills young caterpillars. To control them, encourage birds by hanging feeders and bird boxes; cultivate the soil in winter to expose them to predators; encourage ground and rove beetles and use the biological control *Steinernema carpocapsae*.

Cabbage Root Fly

These white larvae, approximately ½ in. long, are found from late spring to midfall. They feed on the roots of brassicas just below soil level, stunting growth and causing plants to wilt, seedlings to die and tunnels to appear in root crops. As a preventive measure, grow under floating row cover. To control them, place a 5 in. collar of cardboard, plastic, carpet underlay or similar around the plant bases. Grow under floating row cover or mesh. Use biological control nematodes and practice crop rotation (see pp. 636–7).

Carrot Root Fly

These creamy-white maggots, approximately ½ in. long, appear from early summer until midfall. They are a common problem with carrots, but can also affect celeriac, parsnip, celery, parsley and other umbelliferous plants. Larvae burrow into the roots, causing stunted growth and reddish-purple coloration of the foliage.

Sow carrots late, after late spring, and harvest before late summer. Use resistant varieties and biological control. Place a barrier 25 in. high around crops or cover with floating row cover. Where plants are badly affected, pull them up and destroy them. Large herbs should overcome attacks so just pick off dead leaves and boost with a liquid fertilizer feed. Water after thinning, or thin when rain is forecast.

Leatherjackets

These grey-brown, wrinkled grubs, can be up to 1½ in. long. They eat through roots and through the stems of young plants just below soil level. Most crops are vulnerable, including Brussels sprouts, cabbage, cauliflower and lettuce. To discourage them, ensure the soil is well drained, dig over the ground in the early fall, especially if it has been fallow in the summer. The problem is often worse on new sites and usually diminishes with time. Use biological control nematode *Steinernema carpocapsae*, water ground, cover with polythene, then collect or leave for predators.

nematodes (eelworms)

Potato Cyst Nematode

These white to golden-brown, pinhead-sized cysts are found on roots in midsummer. Each can contain up to 600 eggs which can remain dormant in the soil for up to six years. Potatoes and tomatoes are affected, with weak and stunted growth, small fruits and tubers, yellow foliage, with the lower leaves dying first followed by premature death of the plants.

Rotate crops and grow resistant varieties like "Pentland Javelin," "Pentland Lustre," "Maris Piper" or "Kingston." Do not grow potatoes or tomatoes on infected soil for at least 6 years.

Stem and Bulb Nematode

These are microscopic pests that live inside the plant and move around on a film of moisture; most active from spring to late summer. The symptoms are weak, stunted growth, swollen bases on young plants, and later stems that thicken and rot. They affect a wide range of young plants from spring until late summer, particularly leek, onion, shallot and chives.

Rotate crops, practice good hygiene and management, and destroy infected crops.

Do not grow potatoes or tomatoes on infected soil for at least 6 years, and any other vulnerable crops on the site for at least 4 years.

A friend indeed

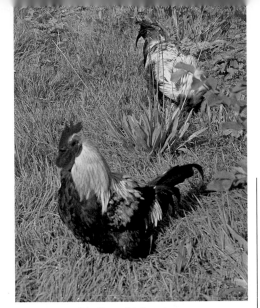

Hens soon get rid of weevil infestation

slugs

Slimy, with tubular-shaped bodies, usually up to 4 in. (the banana slug can grow to 10 in.), from creamy-white through grey to jet-black and orange, slugs are voracious feeders, making circular holes in plant tissue; damaged seedlings are usually killed. They tend to feed at night. Most soft plant tissue is vulnerable. Slugs are more of a problem on wet sites and clay soils; keep the soil well drained and weed-free. Remove all crop debris. Grow less susceptible cultivars. Remove slugs by hand at night and destroy them. Create a barrier of grit, sand, eggshell or soot around plants or cut a 4 in. section from a plastic bottle and place it as a "collar" around plants. Make traps from plastic cartons, half-buried in the ground and filled with beer or stout, or lay old roof tiles, newspaper or old lettuce leaves or other tempting vegetation on the ground and hand pick regularly from underneath. Attract natural predators like toads to the garden or use biological controls.

Chemical controls include applying aluminium sulfate in the spring as the slug eggs hatch and alternatives such as wool pellets or bran.

wireworms

These are thin, yellow larvae, pointed at each end, about 1 in. long. They make holes in the roots and tubers, and can cause foliage to collapse; seedlings are usually killed. A wide range of plants are attacked, particularly root crops and potatoes. Symptoms appear from spring until midsummer. More of a problem on newly cultivated soil, wireworms usually disappear after 5 years; avoid planting root crops until the sixth year. Lift root crops as soon as they mature. Cultivate the ground thoroughly well before planting.

soil-borne diseases

Clubroot

This is a soil-borne fungus that can remain in the soil for up to 20 years. It causes leaves to yellow and discolor, wilting rapidly in hot weather; the roots display swollen wart-like swellings, and become distorted. All members of the Brassicaceae family are vulnerable, including brassicas and weedy relatives. Clubroot is worse on acid soils, so lime to raise the pH and improve the drainage. Practice strict crop rotation, good management and hygiene, and grow your own plants instead of buying in, or at least purchase from a reputable source. Raise plants in pots. Rutabaga "Marian" has good resistance to clubroot, as do Kale "Tall Green Curled," Brussels Sprout "Chronos" and "Crispus," Calabrese "Trixie" and Cabbages "Kilaton" and "Kilaxy." Lift and dispose of affected plants immediately, and do not compost.

Common Scab

This fungus causes superficial damage to the under-ground parts of affected plants. Rough brown lesions appear on the surface of roots and tubers. It is more severe on alkaline soils and in dry summers. Common scab affects mainly potatoes, but can be found on radishes, beetroot, rutabaga and turnips. Avoid liming, do not grow potatoes on soil recently used for brassicas, apply organic matter and irrigate thoroughly in dry weather. Grow resistant potato cultivars like "Arran Pilot" and "King Edward." Avoid "Majestic" and "Maris Piper," which are very susceptible. Rotate crops.

Root Rot

This fungus is difficult to eradicate. It attacks beans and peas, causing shrivelled, yellowing leaves, stems and pods; roots rot and stems rot at the base. Plants collapse. Practice a minimum 3-year crop rotation; remove and burn infected plants; or grow in pots or raised bed, avoiding overcrowding and improving the soil with compost for better drainage and fertility.

Stem Rot

This fungus is difficult to eradicate. It attacks eggplant and tomato, causing yellow-brown cankerous lesions with black dots in and around the lesions, occurring at soil level. Remove and burn infected plants and crop debris, disinfect anything that comes into contact with diseased material, including hands and equipment. Improve growing conditions like drainage and feeding, avoid waterlogged soil, and always use fresh compost in pots.

Onion White Rot

This fungus is almost impossible to eradicate. Common on onions and leeks, it also attacks chives and garlic, causing discolored, yellowing leaves, which die slowly. Roots rot and plants fall over, becoming covered with a white felt-like mold. Do not grow susceptible crops for 8 years after an infection. Remove and burn infected plants immediately; do not compost any plant debris. Try biofumigation with chopped Caliente mustard 199 or water the soil with garlic solution.

air-borne pests

Aphids

These are dense colonies of winged and wingless insects, from pale-green through pink to greeny-black. They attack soft tissue on a wide range of plants, including brassicas, beans and peas, lettuces, potatoes and root crops. Shoot tips and young leaves become distorted; they leave a sticky coating on lower leaves, often accompanied by a black sooty mold. Pinch the growth tips from fava beans, destroy alternative hosts, and take care not to overfeed with high nitrogen fertilizers. Treat small infestations by squashing or, on sturdy plants, washing off with a jet of water; spray with soft soap, rotenone, pyrethrum-based insecticide; encourage natural predators like lacewings, ladybugs and their larvae and small birds like blue tits. On larger woody perennials these are more of an inconvenience than a real problem.

Cabbage Caterpillars

These are small, hairy, yellow and black caterpillars up to 2 in. long. Voracious feeders, the caterpillars eat

Greenfly

holes in the leaves and in severe cases leave plants totally defoliated. They attack all brassicas, including horseradish, and are a problem from late spring to fall. Inspect plants regularly, squash eggs or caterpillars as they are found, pick off caterpillars and grow crops under floating row cover or fine netting. Alternatively, spray regularly with pyrethrum when eggs are first seen, or use the biological nematode *Steinernema carpocapsae*.

Cabbage Whitefly

These small, white-winged insects are usually found on the leaf underside. Clouds of insects fly up whenever the leaves are brushed. The young leaves pucker and there is a sticky coating, often accompanied by a black mold. Whitefly attack all leafy brassicas, usually the outer leaves, so infestations can be tolerated. They can survive severe winter weather and are seen all year round. Remove and burn badly infected plants immediately after cropping, or add to local-authority recycling bin. Spray with sprays based on plant oils, fatty acids or pyrethrum.

Pea Thrips

These small, white to black-brown or yellow-bodied insects, usually on the leaf underside, are commonly known as "thunder flies." They cause distorted pods with a silvery sheen; peas fail to swell in the pod. The insects are often found on peas and also on fava beans. Remove and burn badly infected leaves or plants. Spray

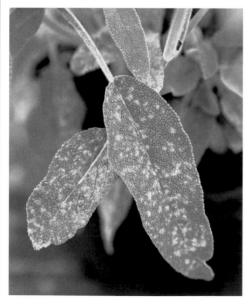

Powdery mildew

with sprays based on plants oils or pyrethrum, or use blue-colored traps or fleece.

Vine Weevils

The adult weevil is dark grey, beetle-like ½ to 1 in. long, with a very long snout. It takes rounded bits out of leaves, but most harm is done by the grubs, which are up to the same size with a grey-pink body and brown head. They destroy the roots of many plants. Adults can be trapped in rolls of corrugated cardboard, in bundles of sticks or under saucers, where they hide in the daytime. The grubs can be destroyed by watering on the commercially available predatory nematode.

Leaf Miners

These grubs are sometimes a problem on lovage, wild celery, certain sorrels and various mints. They eat through the leaf, creating winding tunnels in the leaves that are clearly visible. Pick off the affected leaves as you see them. If left, the tunnels will extend into broad dry patches and whole leaves will wither away.

air-borne diseases

Blight

This fungus infects leaves, stems and tubers and is worse in wet seasons. Severe epidemics led to the Irish potato famine. In midsummer brown patches appear on the upper and lower leaf surfaces, ringed with white mold in humid conditions; leaves become yellow and fall prematurely. In humid climates the fungus spreads rapidly over the foliage and stems which quickly collapse. Tubers show dark, sunken patches. The fungus attacks potatoes, tomatoes and closely related weeds. Remove and burn badly infected plant tops in late summer, avoid overhead watering and use resistant cultivars like "Cara," "Romano" and "Wilja" potatoes, plus "Sarpo" varieties. Do not store infected tubers. Early potatoes are more likely to escape infection. Hill, use a 4-year rotation, and remove all infected material from the soil and destroy.

Botrytis

This fungus infects flowers, leaves and stems and usually enters through wounds. Discolored patches appear on stems, which may rot at ground level; flowers and leaves become covered with woolly, grey fungal growth. It causes shadows on unripe tomato fruit called "ghost spot." Soft-leaved plants are particularly vulnerable including fava beans, brassicas, lettuces, potatoes and

Scale insect

tomatoes. Maintain good air circulation, handle plants with care to avoid injury and remove and burn badly infected plants. Use a greenhouse fan in winter, avoid high humidity or damp conditions, and don't water or spray leaves.

Downy Mildew

This is a fungus that infects leaves and stems, overwintering in the soil or plant debris. It causes discolored, yellowing leaves, which have grey/white moldy patches on the lower surface; plants often die slowly in the fall. Attacks brassicas including weed species, lettuce, spinach, peas and onions. Avoid overcrowding, remove and burn badly infected plants and maintain good air circulation. Rotate crops, choose resistant varieties like Lettuce "Chartwell" and Cabbage "Harmony," and maintain good garden hygiene.

Powdery Mildew

This common fungal disease can occur when the conditions are hot and dry, and the plants are overcrowded. Prevent it by watering well during dry spells, following the recommended planting distances, and clearing away any fallen leaves in the fall. Adding a mulch in the fall or early spring also helps. If your plant does suffer, destroy all the affected leaves.

Rust

If only small numbers are affected by pale spots or pustules, remove the leaves by hand. Avoid excess nitrogen, remove all diseased material and dispose of it away from the garden. Use resistant cultivars.

pests and diseases under cover

Red Spider Mite

The spider mites like hot dry conditions and can become prolific in a greenhouse. Look out for speckling on the upper surfaces of the leaves. Another telltale sign is cobwebs. At first sight, raise the humidity and use either a spray of horticultural soap, or the natural predator *Phytoseiulus persimilis*, but not both.

Scale Insects and Mealy Bugs

These are often noticeable as immobile, waxy, brown/yellow, flat, oval lumps gathered on the backs of leaves or on stems. These leaves also become covered with sticky black sooty mold. Rub off the scales gently before the infestation builds up, or use a horticultural liquid soap or biological controls.

Whitefly

Act as soon as you see the small white flies, either by introducing the natural predator *Encarsia formosa*, or by spraying with horticultural soap or plant invigorator.

Red spider mite

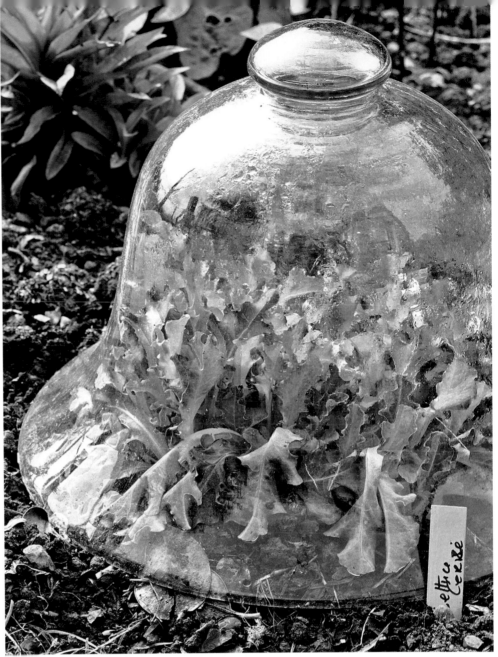

A bell jar can be used to protect crops

other pests

Birds

Birds damage many fruits and some vegetables. Netting or row cover is the answer. If the whole plant cannot be enclosed or moved under cover then protect each fruit or bunch with waxed paper or netting bags. Things that flash, such as pieces of foil and humming tape, all work as bird scarers but only for a short time. Scarecrows rarely work at all!

Ants

These farm aphids, which produce sticky secretions on which sooty mold forms. Use biological control *Steinernema feltiae*, or baits and sprays on hard surfaces.

Wasps

Wasps are valuable allies early in the year when they control caterpillars and other pests. Later they turn to fruit and need trapping with jars (see p. 657). Locate nests and call in pest controller. Protect fruit in muslin bags. Use wasp traps.

Rabbits

Only fencing the area will keep rabbits out. In case they get in, have a plank ramped against the fence so they are not trapped inside and eat even more. If the perimeter cannot be secured, surround or wrap each plant in wire netting.

DISEASE-RESISTANT VEGETABLES

This list shows vegetables (and varieties) that are either resistant or tolerant to disease. In most years, resistant plants are unaffected, but they will suffer in "epidemic" years when conditions are ideal and the disease thrives. Tolerant varieties continue to grow and crop despite being infected with little effect on their performance. Whether a variety is resistant or tolerant, the effect is the same: they will crop. This list covers a wide range of vegetables, but they won't necessarily overlap with the varieties mentioned in the A–Z of vegetables. The internet can be a good source of more information on disease resistance.

variety	resistant or tolerant to
Asparagus	
Jersey Knight	rust, crown and root rot
Eggplant	
Bonica	cucumber mosaic virus
	tomato mosaic virus
Dusky	tomato mosaic virus
Elondo	tomato mosaic virus
Bean (Dwarf/French/Bush)	
Aiguillon	common bean mosaic virus
Allegria	anthracnose
	common bean mosaic virus
Blauhilde	common bean mosaic virus
Cantare	anthracnose
	common bean mosaic virus
Copper Teepee	anthracnose
Daisy	common bean mosaic virus
Delinel	anthracnose
	common bean mosaic virus
Eva	cucumber mosaic virus
	bean yellow mosaic virus
Forum	anthracnose
	common bean mosaic virus
	halo blight
Green Arrow	anthracnose
	common bean mosaic virus
Helda	common bean mosaic virus
Hildora	common bean mosaic virus
Jersey	anthracnose
	common bean mosaic virus
Laguna	anthracnose
	common bean mosaic virus
Maxi	common bean mosaic virus
Modus	anthracnose
	common bean mosaic virus
	halo blight
Necktar Gold	common bean mosaic virus

variety	resistant or tolerant to
Necktar Queen	common bean mosaic virus
Nerina	common bean mosaic virus
Nomad	anthracnose
	common bean mosaic virus
Opera	anthracnose
	common bean mosaic virus
	halo blight
Purple Teepee	common bean mosaic virus
Safari	high disease resistance
Scuba	anthracnose
	common bean mosaic virus
Scylla	anthracnose
	common bean mosaic virus
Sonate	anthracnose
	common bean mosaic virus
Sonesta	anthracnose
	common bean mosaic virus
Speedy	common bean mosaic virus
Venice	anthracnose
	common bean mosaic virus
Bean (Runner)	
Armstrong	good disease tolerance
Galaxy	good disease tolerance
Red Rum	halo blight
Beetroot	
Kestrel	good disease resistance
	including eelworm
Solo	downy mildew
	powdery mildew
	leafspot
Broccoli (Sprouting)	
Express Corona	downy mildew
Ironman	crown rot
	downy mildew
	fusarium wilt
Shogun	downy mildew
Brussels Sprouts	
Bosworth	ringspot
Brigitte	good disease resistance
Brilliant	good disease resistance
Cascade	powdery mildew
Cavalier	light leaf spot
Cor Valiant OGC	ringspot
Cromwell	powdery mildew
Nautic	powdery mildew
Nautic	ring spot

variety	resistant or tolerant to
Odette	powdery mildew
Rampart	powdery mildew
	ringspot
Revenge	good disease resistance
Saxon	powdery mildew
	turnip mosaic virus
Sheriff	powdery mildew
Trafalgar	powdery mildew
Wellington	powdery mildew
Cabbage	
Brigadier	fusarium wilt
Kilaton	clubroot
Sherwood	leaf spot
Stonehead	powdery mildew
Cabbage (Chinese)	
China Express	downy mildew
China Pride	downy mildew
	soft rot
	virus
Harmony	clubroot
	downy mildew
	soft rot
Kiansi	virus
Calabrese	
Belstar	downy mildew
Emperor	black rot
	downy mildew
Gitano	downy mildew
Marathon	black rot
Matsui	downy mildew
Samson	downy mildew
Shogun	black rot
	downy mildew
Trixie	clubroot
Typhoon	downy mildew
Zen	downy mildew (moderate)
Carrot	
Artemis	cavity spot
Fly Away	carrot fly
Nantes Express	cavity spot
Nelson	cracking
	greentop
Resistafly	carrot fly
Senior	leaf spot
	powdery mildew

variety	resistant or tolerant to
Sytan	carrot fly

Cauliflower
variety	resistant or tolerant to
Candid Charm	clubroot
Clapton	clubroot

Celeriac
variety	resistant or tolerant to
Prinz	leaf spot
	hollowness

Celery
variety	resistant or tolerant to
Granada	celery leaf spot
Tango	stalk rot

Corn Salad
variety	resistant or tolerant to
Jade	powdery mildew
Vit	downy mildew
	powdery mildew

Zucchini
variety	resistant or tolerant to
Afrodite	good all round disease resistance
Astia	powdery mildew
Defender	cucumber mosaic virus
Firenza	powdery mildew
Optima	cucumber mosaic virus
	powdery mildew
Pasqualine	cucumber mosaic virus
	powdery mildew
Supremo	cucumber mosaic virus
Sylvana	good all round disease resistance
Tarmino	cucumber mosaic virus
Zucchino	cucumber mosaic virus

Cucumber
variety	resistant or tolerant to
Aidas	leaf spot
	scab gummosis
Bali	angular leaf spot
	scab
Bella	leaf spot
	scab gummosis
Birgit	gummosis
	leaf spot
	scab gummosis
Boyce	leaf spot
	scab gummosis
Burpee Hybrid	cucumber mosaic virus
	downy mildew
Burpless Tasty Green	downy mildew
	powdery mildew
Bush Champion	cucumber mosaic virus
Carmen	gummosis
	leaf spot
	powdery mildew
Crispy Saladin	cucumber mosaic virus
Cumlaude	powdery mildew
El Toro	gummosis
	leaf spot
Femdan	leaf spot

variety	resistant or tolerant to
Femdan	scab gummosis
Femspot	gummosis
	leaf spot
Flamingo	powdery mildew
Futura	powdery mildew
La Diva	downy mildew
	powdery mildew
Landora	scab gummosis
Marketmore	cucumber mosaic virus
	downy mildew
	powdery mildew
Mistral	powdery mildew
Muncher	cucumber mosaic virus
Passandra	downy mildew tolerant
	gummosis resistant
	powdery mildew
Pepinex	gummosis
	leaf spot
Petita	cucumber mosaic virus
	gummosis
	leaf spot
Silor	cucumber mosaic virus
	gummosis
	powdery mildew
Slice King	angular leaf spot
	downy mildew
	gummosis
	powdery mildew
Styx	powdery mildew
Superator	gummosis
	leaf spot
Swing	powdery mildew
Tiffany	powdery mildew
Tiger Cross	cucumber mosaic virus
Tokyo Slicer	cucumber mosaic virus
Tyria	gummosis
	leaf spot
	powdery mildew

Endive
variety	resistant or tolerant to
Eminence	basal rot

Gherkin
variety	resistant or tolerant to
Diamant	downy mildew
	powdery mildew
Sena	cucumber mosaic virus
	downy mildew
	powdery mildew

Kale
variety	resistant or tolerant to
Tall Green Curled	clubroot

Leek
variety	resistant or tolerant to
Apollo	rust
Fall Giant	
– Poribleu	rust
Fall Giant 2	
– Porvite	rust
Fall Mammoth	
– Tornado	rust (moderate)

variety	resistant or tolerant to
– Verina	rust
Fall Mammoth 2	
– Walton Mammoth	rust
Bandit	rust
Blue Green Fall	
– Ardea	rust
– Neptune	rust
– Pandora	virus
Einstein	white tip
Flexitan	rust
	white tip
Kajak	leaf spot
	virus
Oarsman	rust
Porbella	rust
Poribleu	rust
Poristo	rust
Swiss Giant – Zermatt	rust (moderate)

Lettuce
variety	resistant or tolerant to
Action	downy mildew
Amorina	downy mildew
Avoncrisp	downy mildew
Avondefiance	botrytis
	downy mildew
Beatrice	downy mildew
	root aphid
Belize	bolting
	downy mildew
	leaf aphid
	tipburn
Brandon	downy mildew
Bridgemere	downy mildew
Bubbles	downy mildew
Bughatti	downy mildew
Cassandra	downy mildew
	lettuce mosaic virus
Chartwell	downy mildew
Chatsworth	downy mildew
Claremont	downy mildew
Clarion	downy mildew
	virus
Columbus	downy mildew
Corsair	downy mildew
	lettuce mosaic virus
Cosmic	downy mildew
Counter	bremia
	tip burn
Crestand	downy mildew
	virus
Crispino	lettuce mosaic virus
Debby	downy mildew
	lettuce mosaic virus
Diana	downy mildew
Dynasty	downy mildew
	lettuce mosaic virus
Estelle	downy mildew
	leaf aphid
Fatima	bremia
	mosaic virus

variety	resistant or tolerant to
Fristina	downy mildew
	tipburn
Iceberg	big vein
Jewel	downy mildew
Lakeland	downy mildew (moderate)
	root aphid
Lilian	downy mildew
Little Gem	root aphid
Lizzy	downy mildew
	lettuce mosaic virus
Marcord	downy mildew
Milan	downy mildew
	mosaic virus
	root aphid
	tipburn
Multy	downy mildew
Musette	downy mildew
	lettuce mosaic virus
Nika	good disease resistance
Novita	downy mildew
Nymans	downy mildew
Pandero	downy mildew
Pinares	tipburn
Pinokkio	high disease resistance
Rachel	downy mildew
Revolution	bremia
Romance	lettuce mosaic virus
Romany	tipburn
Roxy	tipburn
Rushmore	downy mildew
Ruth	downy mildew
Sabrina	downy mildew
Saladin	downy mildew
	tipburn
Saladin Supreme	tipburn
Sierra	good disease resistance
Sigmahead	botrytis
Sonette	downy mildew
Sunny	downy mildew
	lettuce mosaic virus
Sylvesta	downy mildew
	leaf aphid
Targa	downy mildew
TinTin	downy mildew
	leaf aphid
	root aphid
Valdor	botrytis
Vienna	downy mildew
	leaf aphid

Marrow

variety	resistant or tolerant to
Badger Cross	cucumber mosaic virus
Tarmino	cucumber mosaic virus
Tiger Cross	cucumber mosaic virus
Zebra Cross	cucumber mosaic virus

Onion

variety	resistant or tolerant to
Feast	downy mildew
Golden Bear	botrytis
	downy mildew

variety	resistant or tolerant to
	white rot tolerant
Marco	good disease tolerance
Norstar	downy mildew

Parsnip

variety	resistant or tolerant to
Arrow	canker
Avonresister	canker
Cobham Improved	canker
Countess	canker
Excalibur	canker
Gladiator	canker
Javelin	canker
Lancer	canker
New White Skin	canker
Palace	canker
Panache	canker
Polar	canker
Tender & True	canker
White Gem	canker

Pea

variety	resistant or tolerant to
Ambassador	fusarium wilt
	pea enation virus
	powdery mildew
Avola	fusarium wilt
Cascadia	fusarium wilt
Cavalier	powdery mildew
Delikata	fusarium wilt
	powdery mildew
Green Shaft	downy mildew
	fusarium wilt
Jaguar	powdery mildew
Jessy	fusarium wilt
	powdery mildew
Kelvedon Wonder	fusarium wilt
	powdery mildew wilt
Kodiak	downy mildew
	fusarium wilt
Markana	fusarium wilt
Norli	fusarium wilt
Onward	fusarium wilt
Oregon Sugar Pod	fusarium wilt
	pea enation virus
	powdery mildew
Rondo	fusarium wilt
Spring	fusarium wilt
Starlight	downy mildew
Sugar Snap	fusarium wilt
Sugarbon	fusarium wilt
Twinkle	fusarium wilt
Zuccola	fusarium wilt

Pepper

variety	resistant or tolerant to
Anaheim	tobacco mosaic virus
Antaro	tobacco mosaic virus
Bell Boy	tobacco mosaic virus
Canape	tobacco mosaic virus
Gypsy	tobacco mosaic virus
Luteus	tobacco mosaic virus

variety	resistant or tolerant to
Midnight Beauty	tobacco mosaic virus
Ringo	tobacco mosaic virus
Unicorn	tobacco mosaic virus

Potato

variety	resistant or tolerant to
Accent	eelworm
	scab
Anya	blight (moderate)
	scab
Arran Pilot	blight (moderate)
	scab
Arran Victory	blight
Cara	blight
Catriona	scab
Charlotte	blight
	scab (moderate)
Colleen	blight
Cosmos	blight
Desirée	blight
	scab (moderate)
Duke of York	scab
Estima	blight (moderate)
	scab
Eve	blight
Foremost	blight (moderate)
	scab
Homeguard	scab
King Edward	scab
Lady Balfour	blight
Lady Christl	eelworm
	scab
Majestic	blight (moderate)
	scab
Marfona	blight
	scab (moderate)
Maris Bard	blight
	scab (moderate)
Maris Peer	blight
	scab (moderate)
Maris Piper	blight (moderate)
	eelworm
Markies	blight
Nadine	blight (moderate)
	eelworm
	scab
Orla	blight
Pentland Javelin	eelworm
	scab
Pink Fir Apple	scab
Pomeroy	blight
Premiere	blight
Ratte	scab
Remarka	blight
Rocket	eelworm
	scab (moderate)
Sarpo Axona	blight
Sarpo Mira	blight (100 percent resistant)
Saxon	blight (moderate)
	eelworm
	scab

variety	resistant or tolerant to
Sharpes Express	blight (moderate)
	scab
Swift	blight (moderate)
	scab
Valor	blight
Verity	blight
Wilja	blight (moderate)
	scab
Winston	fusarium wilt
	nematode
	scab

Spinach

variety	resistant or tolerant to
Bergola	downy mildew
Fiorano	downy mildew
	powdery mildew
Galaxy	downy mildew
	powdery mildew
Mazarka	downy mildew
Palco	downy mildew
Senic	downy mildew
	powdery mildew
Space	downy mildew
Tetona	downy mildew
Tornado	downy mildew
Trinidad	downy mildew
Triton	downy mildew

Squash (Butternut)

variety	resistant or tolerant to
Metro	powdery mildew

Rutabaga

variety	resistant or tolerant to
Marian	clubroot
	powdery mildew
Magres	powdery mildew
Virtue	clubroot
	powdery mildew
Willemsburger	clubroot

Sweetcorn

variety	resistant or tolerant to
Landmark	high disease tolerance
Tuxedo	high disease tolerance

Tomato

variety	resistant or tolerant to
Alexanovas	fusarium wilt
	tomato mosaic virus
Alicante	greenback
	powdery mildew
Amarel	blossom end rot
	tomato mosaic virus
Aviro	tomato mosaic virus
Cherry Wonder	fusarium wilt
	greenback
	leaf mold
	tomato mosaic virus
Craigella	greenback
Cristal	good disease resistance
Cumulus	fusarium wilt
	tomato mosaic virus
Cyclon	leaf mold

variety	resistant or tolerant to
	tomato mosaic virus
	verticillium wilt
Delicate	good all round resistance
Dombito	tomato mosaic virus
Dona	fusarium wilt
	tomato mosaic virus
	verticillium wilt
Estrella	fusarium wilt
	greenback
	leaf mold
	tomato mosaic virus
	verticillium wilt
Eurocross	greenback
	leaf mold
Falcorosso	fusarium wilt
	leaf mold
	tobacco mosaic virus
	verticillium wilt
Favorita	good all round disease
	resistance
Ferline	blight
	fusarium wilt
	verticillium
Golden Boy	alternaria stem canker
Golden Sweet	fusarium wilt
	rootknot nematode
Grenadier	fusarium wilt
	leaf mold
Herald	leaf mold
Husky Gold	fusarium wilt
	verticillium wilt
Ida	fusarium wilt
	leaf mold
	tomato mosaic virus
	verticillium wilt
Incas	blossom end rot
	fusarium wilt (high)
	verticillium wilt
Legend	blight
Libra	fusarium crown and root rot
Matador	greenback
Matina	greenback
Moravi	fusarium wilt
	leaf mold
	tobacco mosaic virus
	verticillium wilt
Nimbus	fusarium wilt
	tomato mosaic virus
	verticillium wilt
Olivade	good disease resistance
Piccolo	leaf mold
	tomato mosaic virus
Piranto	fusarium crown and root rot
Pixie	fusarium wilt
	tomato mosaic virus
	verticillium wilt
Primato	fusarium wilt
	leaf mold
	tomato mosaic virus
	verticillium wilt

variety	resistant or tolerant to
Royal des Guineaux	good all round disease
	resistance
Sakura	fusarium wilt
	tomato mosaic virus
Seville Cross	leaf mold
Shirley	cladosporium
	fusarium wilt
	greenback
	tomato mosaic virus
Sonatine	fusarium wilt
	leaf mold
	tomato mosaic virus
Sungold	fusarium wilt
	tomato mosaic virus
Typhoon	fusarium wilt
	leaf mold
	tomato mosaic virus
	verticillium

Turnip

variety	resistant or tolerant to
Oasis	turnip mosaic virus

Companion planting in action

GROWING SPROUTING SEEDS AND MICRO-GREENS

Onion sprouts

Sprouting seeds and micro-greens are eaten in salads, sandwiches or as a garnish for other dishes. Containing high levels of minerals, protein, fiber and enzymes, they are not only delicious but also nutrient-rich. The difference between the two is that sprouted seeds are harvested when the seed leaves are present and micro-greens when the first true leaves appear.

Suitable plants include: alfalfa, adzuki beans, amaranthus, beetroot, basil, fava beans, broccoli, buckwheat, cabbage, carrot, chard, coriander, celery, clover, fennel, kale, leek, lovage, *Mesembryanthemum chrystallinum*, mizuna greens, mustard salad, onion, oxalis, peas, radish, rape salad, red mustard, rocket, salad cress, salad mixes, shiso, soya bean, wheatgrass.

sprouting seeds

Seed sowing
They can be sown in a "seed sprouter," a clear glass jar with a muslin "lid" or a similar receptacle. Sterilize the equipment before use and after every 3 or 4 crops of seedlings by soaking for 10 minutes in a solution of 1 tablespoon of bleach or similar to a pint of water, before scrubbing and rinsing thoroughly.

To encourage germination, soak seeds for the time recommended on the seed packet at a 3:1 ratio of water to seed to start the germination process. Stir the seeds with a tablespoon or fork to ensure they are all moistened then place them in the sprouting container. Rinse the seeds thoroughly 2 to 3 times a day, using water under a high pressure and drain thoroughly to avoid disease problems. Keep the seedlings in a bright position, away from scorching sunlight and maintain the temperature between 55–70°F.

Harvesting and Storing
Harvest when the seedling leaves appear.

Ensure that sprouts are properly dry before storing in the refrigerator. Around 12 hours after their final watering, drain the seedlings thoroughly, using a salad spinner if possible and store them in a sealed plastic bag to prevent dessication. They will store for several days in the salad drawer of the fridge. When eating large quantities of sprouts, it is advisable to cook them first.

micro-greens

At the time of writing, micro-greens are very trendy and valued by top chefs for the subtle flavor of their stems. They are easy to grow and are the ideal way to make the most of half-used packets of seeds. Seedlings of a wide range of herbs and vegetables can be used as micro-greens, particularly those whose leaves are traditionally eaten at maturity. Do not use seedlings from plants with poisonous leaves like tomato, potato and rhubarb.

Seed sowing
Sow successively from spring to fall for a constant supply. Sow in seed trays in a 2 in. layer of compost. For larger volumes, make a wooden frame in a heated propagator in spring and fill it with compost to make a large seed-bed. Sow seeds close together over the surface of the compost, but not so densely that they are too congested and prone to disease. Cover with a layer of compost or vermiculite or perlite to reduce moisture loss and keep the stems clean and place the seed tray in a warm, bright place.

When growing seedlings on a windowsill, turn the trays every two or three days to maintain balanced growth and stop them from growing toward the light. Keep the compost moist but not waterlogged.

Harvesting and Storing
Harvest with a pair of scissors when the first true leaves appear, retaining as much of the stem as possible. Use new compost for each crop adding used material to your compost heap. Large seeds like peas can be germinated on several layers of moist kitchen towel.

Water 24 hours before storing as they deteriorate rapidly if refrigerated when wet. Micro-greens with soft stems are more vulnerable to damage through being wet when stored.

Small-scale sprouting is still productive

One of the pleasures of a productive garden is picking your produce and cooking or eating it fresh. However, there are myriad means of storing many crops, thus extending the season, and avoiding unmanageable gluts. See also details under individual crops.

when to harvest

Vegetables

While the majority of vegetables are not harvested until they reach maturity, others, like some lettuces, are harvested while semi-mature and others still, such as arugula, are harvested while juvenile. Some vegetables, again like lettuce, cannot be stored for long and so must be harvested and eaten fresh. Many other leafy vegetables, such as Brussels sprouts and sprouting broccoli, are hardy, surviving outdoors in the ground in freezing conditions. The flavor of Brussels sprouts even improves immeasurably after they have been frosted. Some root vegetables with a high moisture content are easily damaged in winter, even when protected by the soil. This is usually caused by rapid thawing after a period of cold weather. Carrots, parsnip and rutabaga are exceptions; they are very hardy and can be left in free-draining soils until required, depending on the region. In wet soils these crops would suffer winter loss by slug damage and rotting.

Herbs

Herbs can be harvested from very early on in their growing season. This encourages the plant to produce vigorous new growth and allows the plant to be controlled in shape and size. Most herbs reach their peak of flavor just before they flower. Snip off suitable stems early in the day before the sun is fully up, or even better on a cloudy day (provided it is not too humid). Cut whole stems rather than single leaves or flowers. Always use a sharp knife, sharp scissors or pruning shears, and cut lengths of 2–3 in. from the tip of the branch, this being the new, soft growth. Do not cut into any of the older, woody growth. Cut from all over the plant, leaving it looking shapely. Pick herbs that are clean and free from pests and disease. If herbs are covered in garden soil, sponge them quickly and lightly with cold water, not hot as this will draw out the oils prematurely. Pat dry as quickly as possible. Keep each species separately so that they do not contaminate each other.

Most annual herbs can be harvested at least twice during a growing season. Cut them to within 4–6 in.

of the ground, and feed with liquid fertilizer after each cutting. Give annuals their final cut of the season before the first frosts.

In the first year of planting, perennials will give one good crop; thereafter it will be possible to harvest two or three times during the growing season. Do not cut into the woody growth unless deliberately trying to prevent growth; again, cut well before frosts. There are of course exceptions: sage is still very good after frosts, and both thyme and golden marjoram (with some protection) can be picked gently even in midwinter.

Pick flowers for drying when they are barely open. Seed should be collected as soon as you notice a change in color of the seed pod; if, when you tap the pod, a few scatter on the ground, it is the time to gather them. Seeds ripen very fast, so watch them carefully.

Roots of herbs are at their peak of flavor when they have just completed a growing season. Dig them throughout fall as growth ceases. Lift whole roots with a garden fork, taking care not to puncture or bruise the outer skin. Wash them free of soil. Cut away any remains of top-growth and any fibrous off-shoots. For drying, cut large, thick roots in half lengthways and then into smaller pieces for ease.

Fruit

Without doubt most fruits are best, and certainly are enjoyed most, when they are plucked fully ripe off the tree or vine. Only a few, such as melons, are improved by chilling first. The majority are tastiest fresh and warmed by the sun. Some, such as pears, have to be carefully nurtured till they are fully ripe and need to be picked early and brought to perfection, watched daily, in a warm, not too dry, dim room. Medlars are similarly picked early and are then ripened, or bletted, to the point of rotting.

The best date for picking will vary with the cultivar, the soil, the site and the season, and can only be determined by experience as these factors all vary considerably. Of course, it will generally remain much the same in relation to other fruits nearby, which are also subject to the same conditions, i.e., in a late year, most fruits are late, which is pretty self-evident anyway.

On any tree, the sunny side ripens first. Fruit will also ripen earlier where extra warmth is supplied, so that growing sites next to a wall, window, chimney or vent, or close to the soil are good places for finding early fruits.

Likewise, when all the rest have gone, you may find some hidden in the shade.

If you want to store fruits for home use, they need to be picked at just the right stage. Most fruits store best when picked just under-ripe. They may keep much longer if picked even younger, but this is at the cost of flavor and sweetness.

storage conditions

Vegetables

In colder areas, vegetables overwintering in the ground need further protection. This can be provided by spreading a layer of loose straw or bracken over them to a depth of 8 in. and covering with a plastic sheet. While this is labor-saving, crops stored in this way are susceptible to attack by pests and diseases through the winter.

The traditional method for storing root vegetables is in a clamp or "pie." Low mounds of vegetables are laid on a bed of loose straw up to 8 in. thick. The top and sides of the mound are covered with a similar layer of straw, and then with a 6 in. layer of soil or sand. Clamps can be made outdoors on a well-drained site or under cover in a shed or outhouse; for extra protection outdoors, they can be formed against a wall or hedge. If crops are to be stored for a long period, find a site that receives as little sunlight as possible during the winter. Although storage conditions are very similar to those in the ground, harvesting from a clamp is much easier. However, losses from rodent damage and rotting can be high.

The length of time that vegetables may be stored depends on the type and cultivar as well as the storage conditions. When traditional methods are used, the main cause of deterioration is moisture loss from plant tissue; for instance, beetroot and carrot desiccate very rapidly. Fungal infection of damaged tissue is a common problem; onions and potatoes bruise very easily. Vegetables for storage should be handled carefully; only store those that are disease-free, check them regularly and remove any showing signs of decay immediately.

Fruits

Although we occasionally store some fruits, such as pears, for a period to improve their condition, predominantly we store fruit to extend the season so that we can enjoy them for as long as possible.

To be stored, all fruit must be perfect. Any blemish or bruise is where molds start. Choose varieties that are suitable for storing — many early croppers are notoriously bad keepers!

Common, long-keeping fruits such as apples and quinces can be stored at home for months, or even up to a year. The major problems, apart from the molds, are shrivelling due to water loss and the depredations of rodents and other big pests. A conventional root cellar is too large for most of us and the house or garage is too warm, too cold or too dry. Dead deep freezers and refrigerators make excellent, storage units. They are dark, keep the contents at the same constant temperature and will keep out night frosts easily. Most useful of all, they are rodent-proof.

Some ventilation is needed and can be obtained by cutting holes in the rubber door or lid seal. If condensation occurs it usually indicates insufficient

Dried herbs will keep for several months and see you tastily through the winter

ventilation, but too much draft will dry out the fruits. In mild climates, the unit can stand outdoors, as it needs no power. In a shed it is out of sight and better protected against the cold, but may then get too warm.

When putting fruits in storage it is usually best to leave them to chill at night in trays and to load them into the storage unit in the morning when they have dried off but before they have warmed up again. Similarly it is helpful to chill and dry off the fruits initially by leaving the storage unit open on chill, dry nights and closing it during the day for a week or two after filling.

Most fruits are best removed from storage some time before use, so any staleness can leave them. Care should be taken not to store early and late varieties together or any that may cross-taint. Obviously it is not a good idea to site your storage unit in the same place as strong-smelling things such as onions, paint or bleach! Likewise, although straw is a convenient litter, if it gets damp it taints the fruit. Shredded newspaper is safer, though it also has a slight whiff. Dried stinging nettles are reckoned good but dangerous to handle. Always inspect stored fruits regularly. They can spoil very quickly. Remember, if only one in 10 spoils every month, you have to start with two trays just to have one tray left after 6 months. So do not store any fruit long just for the sake of it, but store well what you will use.

Careful storage will cope with seasonal gluts

drying

Vegetables

Peas and beans can be harvested when almost mature and dried slowly in a cool place. Either lift the whole plant and hang it up or pick off the pods and dry them on a tray or newspaper. Beans can be collected and stored in airtight jars until required. They will need soaking for 24 hours before use. Storage areas should be frost-free. Chillies, green peppers, garlic and onions can be hung indoors where there is good air circulation. Peppers, tomatoes and mushrooms can be cut into sections and sun-dried outdoors where conditions allow, otherwise in the gentle heat of a closet or above a radiator.

Herbs

The object of drying herbs is to eliminate the water content of the plant quickly and, at the same time, to retain the essential oils. Herbs need to be dried in a warm, dark, dry and well-ventilated place. The faster they dry, the better the aromatic oils are retained. Darkness helps to prevent loss of color and unique flavors. The area must be dry, with a good air flow, to hasten the drying process and to discourage mold.

Suitable places for drying herbs include: a closet; attic space immediately under the roof (provided it does not get too hot); in the oven at a low temperature and with the door ajar (place the herbs on a brown piece of paper with holes punched in it and check regularly that the herbs are not over-heating; a plate-warming compartment; a spare room with curtains shut and door open. The temperature should be kept at 70–90°F.

Herb leaves should always be dried separately from each other, especially the more strongly scented ones. Spread them in a single layer on trays or slatted wooden racks covered with muslin or netting. Place the trays or frames in the drying areas so that they have good air circulation. Turn the herbs over by hand several times during the first 2 days.

Roots require a higher temperature — from 120–140°F. They dry more quickly and easily in an oven and require regular turning until they are fragile and break easily. Seed should be dried without any artificial heat and in an airy place. Almost-ripe seed heads can be hung in paper bags (plastic causes them to sweat) so the majority of seeds will fall into the bag as they mature. They need to be dried thoroughly before storing and the process can take up to 2 weeks.

An alternative method for flowers, roots or seed heads is to tie them in small bundles of 8 to 10 stems. Do not pack the stems too tightly together. Then hang them on coat-hangers in an airy, dark room until they are dry. The length of drying time varies from herb to herb, and week to week. The determining factor is the state of the plant material. If herbs are stored before drying is complete, moisture will be reabsorbed from the atmosphere and the herb will soon deteriorate. Leaves should be both brittle and crisp. They should break easily into small pieces but should not reduce to a powder when touched. The roots should be brittle and dry right through. Any softness or sponginess means they are not sufficiently dry and, if stored, will rot.

It is possible to dry herbs by microwave, but easy to over-dry and cook the leaves to the point of complete disintegration. Small-leafed herbs such as rosemary and thyme take about 1 minute, while the larger, moist leaves of mint dry in about 3 minutes. Add an eggcupful of water to the microwave during the process. Herbs lose their flavor and color if not stored properly. Pack the leaves or roots, not too tightly, into a dark glass jar with an air-tight screw top. Label with name and date. Keep in a dark cupboard; nothing destroys the quality of the herb quicker at this stage than exposure to light.

After the initial storing, keep a check on the jars for several days. If moisture starts to form on the inside of the container, the herbs have not been dried correctly. Return them to the drying area and allow further drying time.

Most domestic herb needs are comparatively small so there is little point in storing large amounts for a long time. The shelf life of dried herbs is only about 1 year so it is sufficient to keep enough just for the winter. If you have large, dark jars, thyme and rosemary can be left on the stalk. This makes it easier to use them in casseroles and stews and to remove before serving.

Fruit

Many fruits can be dried if they are sliced thinly and exposed to warm, dry air. Sealed in dark containers and kept cool and dry, they keep for long periods to be eaten, dried or reconstituted, when required. However, in the UK, and much of maritime Europe and North America, the air is too humid and so drying is not quick enough, not helped by the low temperatures in these regions. Solar-powered dryers — simply wire trays under glass — with good ventilation, allow fruit to be dried to a larger extent, but in the highest humidity regions the fruit may still go moldy before it dries.

Slicing the fruit thinly and hanging the pieces, separated by at least half their own diameter, on long strings over a cooking range provides the dry warmth and ventilation needed to desiccate most within a day or two, or even just overnight for the easier ones such as apple.

Oven-drying with artificial heat is risky as it can cook the fruit. It is possible, however, if the temperature is kept down and the door kept partly open. It may be convenient to finish off partly dried samples in the cooling oven after you have finished baking. The dying heat desiccates fruit well with little risk of caramelizing.

freezing

Vegetables

Only the best-quality vegetables should be frozen, and they should always be thoroughly cleaned and carefully packed. Vegetables should be fast-frozen. Most freezers have a fast-freeze switch, and keep the freezer door closed during freezing. Do not open the freezer door regularly or leave it open longer than necessary. Many vegetables need to be blanched before freezing, and others need to be shredded, puréed or diced, or frozen when young. See under individual vegetables for details.

Herbs

Freezing is great for culinary herbs as color, flavor and the nutritional value of the fresh young leaves are retained, and it is quick and easy. It is far better to freeze herbs such as fennel, dill, parsley, tarragon and chives than to dry them.

Pick the herbs and, if necessary, rinse with cold water, and shake dry before freezing, being careful not to bruise the leaves. Put small amounts of herbs into labelled, plastic bags, either singly, or as a mixture for bouquet garnis. Either have a set place in the freezer for them or put the bags into a container, so that they do not get damaged with the day-to-day use of the freezer.

There is no need to thaw herbs before use; simply add them to the cooking as required. For chopped parsley and other fine-leaved herbs, freeze the bunches whole in bags and, when you remove them from the freezer, crush the parsley in its bag with your hand.

Another way to freeze herbs conveniently is to put finely chopped leaves into an ice-cube tray and top them up with water. The average cube holds 1 tablespoon chopped herbs and 1 teaspoon water. The flowers of borage and leaves of variegated mints look very attractive frozen individually in ice-cubes for drinks or fruit salads.

Fruits

Most fruits freeze easily with little preparation. Obviously only the best are worth freezing as few fruits are improved by the process! Most fruits turn soggy when defrosted, but they are still packed full of sweetness, flavor and vitamins so are well worth having for culinary use, especially in tarts, pies, sauces and compôtes. A mixture of frozen fruits is marvelous if they are dechilled but not totally defrosted, so they retain their frozen texture like pieces of sorbet, served with cream.

For most fruits, merely putting them in sealed freezer bags or boxes is sufficient. However they then tend to freeze in a block. If you freeze them loose on open wire drying trays or greased baking trays, they can be packed afterwards and will stay separate. Fruits that are cut or damaged need to be drained first or, if you have a sweet tooth, they can be dredged in sugar, which absorbs the juice, before freezing them.

Stone fruits are best pitted before freezing as the stone can give an almond taint otherwise. The tough skins of fruits such as plums are most easily removed after freezing and before use. Carefully squeeze the frozen fruit under very hot water, when the skin will slip off.

Fruits lose value slowly in the freezer. The longer they are frozen the less use they are nutritionally.

Parsley can be frozen stored in a bag, or in ice cubes

juicing

Not all fruits can be juiced, but the majority can be squeezed to express the juice, or heated or frozen to break down the texture then strained. Sugar may be added to taste as it improves the color, flavor and keeping qualities. When the juice remains unheated, honey may be substituted, though it has a strong flavor of its own. Sweet juices such as apple can be mixed with tart ones like plum.

Fruit juices may be drunk as they are, added to cocktails, drunk as squashes diluted with water, and used in cooking. Grapes are the easiest to press and the most rewarding; they are best crushed first to break the skins. Most of the currants and berries can be squeezed in the same way. Apples and pears must be crushed first and then squeezed; they will go through the same juicing equipment as grapes, but more slowly than the more juicy fruits.

Pulpy, firm fruits such as black currants and plums are best simmered with water till they soften then the juice can be strained off. If you repeat the process and add sugar to the combined juices you also have the basis for jellies. Raspberries, strawberries and fruits with similar delicate flavors are best frozen then defrosted and strained, to obtain a pure juice unchanged by heating.

Suitable equipment for processing large amounts of fruit is widely available if the quantities are too large for kitchen tools.

Commercially juices are passed through microfine filters or flash pasteurized. At home they will ferment rapidly in the warm, last longer if kept cool in the refrigerator, and keep for months or years deep frozen.

HERB OILS, VINEGARS AND PRESERVES

Many herbs have antiseptic and antibacterial qualities, and were used in preserving long before there were cookbooks. Herbs aid digestion, stimulate appetite and enhance the flavor of food. I hope the following recipes will tempt you, because a variety of herb oils and vinegars can lead to the creation of unusual and interesting dishes. Herbs can make salad dressings, tomato-based sauces for pasta dishes, marinades for fish and meat, and can act as softening agents for vegetables, introducing myriad new tastes and flavors. They also make marvelous presents.

herb oils

These can be used in salad dressings, in marinades, sauces, stir-fry dishes and sautéing. Find some interesting bottles with good shapes. To start with, you need a clean glass jar, large enough to hold 2 cups, with a screw top.

Basil Oil
This is one of the best ways of storing and capturing the unique flavor of basil.

4 tablespoons basil leaves
2 cups olive or sunflower oil

Pick over the basil, remove the leaves from the stalks, and crush them in a mortar. For Greek basil, with its small leaves, simply crush in the mortar. Pound very slightly. Add a little oil and pound gently again. This bruises the leaves, releasing their own oil into the oil. Mix the leaves with the rest of the oil and pour into a small bowl. Put a little water into a small saucepan and place the bowl on the rim of the pan so that the bottom of the bowl does not touch the water. Bring the water to the boil, then turn down to simmer for 15 minutes. Stir the oil occasionally and check that the water does not boil dry. Remove the bowl from the heat, cover and allow to cool before straining into a sterilized bottle. Label and date. This oil will keep in a refrigerator for 1 month.

Adapt this recipe for dill, fennel (green), sweet marjoram, rosemary and garden or lemon thyme. Garlic also makes a very good oil. Use 4 cloves of garlic, peeled and crushed, and combined with the oil.

Bouquet Garni Oil

I use this oil for numerous dishes.

1 tablespoon sage
1 tablespoon lemon thyme
1 tablespoon Greek oregano
1 tablespoon French parsley
1 bay leaf
2 cups olive or sunflower oil

Break all the leaves and mix them together in a mortar, pounding lightly. Add a small amount of the oil to mix well, allowing the flavors to infuse, then proceed as for basil oil above.

Sweet Oils

Good with fruit dishes, marinades and puddings. Use almond oil, which combines well with scented flowers such as pinks, lavender, lemon verbena, rose petals and scented geraniums. Make as for savory oils above, mixing 4 tablespoons of torn petals or leaves with 2 cups almond oil.

Spice Oils

Ideal for salad dressings, they can be used for sautéing and stir-frying too. The most suitable herb spices are: coriander seeds, dill seeds and fennel seeds. Combine 2 tablespoons of seeds with 2 cups olive or sunflower oil, having first pounded the seeds gently to crush them in a mortar and mixed them with a little of the oil. Add a few of the whole seeds to the oil before bottling and labelling. Treat as for savory oils and store.

herbal vinegars

Made in much the same way as oils, they can be used in gravies and sauces, marinades and salad dressings.

10 tablespoons chopped herb, such as basil, chervil, dill, fennel, garlic, lemon balm, marjoram, mint, rosemary, savory, tarragon or thyme
2 cups white wine or cider vinegar

Pound the leaves gently in a mortar. Heat half the vinegar until warm but not boiling, and pour it over the herbs in the mortar. Pound further to release the flavors of the herb. Leave to cool. Mix this mixture with the remaining vinegar and pour into a wide-necked bottle. Seal tightly. Remember to use an acid-proof lid (lining the existing lid with greaseproof paper is a way around this). Put on a sunny windowsill and shake each day for 2 weeks. Test for flavor; if a stronger taste is required, strain the vinegar and repeat with fresh herbs. Store as is or strain through double muslin and rebottle. Add a fresh sprig of the chosen herb to the bottle for ease of identification.

To Save Time

1 bottle white wine vinegar (1 pt.)
4 large sprigs herb
4 garlic cloves, peeled

Pour off a little vinegar from the bottle and push in 2 sprigs of herb and the garlic cloves. Top up with the reserved vinegar if necessary. Reseal the bottle and leave on a sunny windowsill for 2 weeks. Change the herb sprigs for fresh ones and the vinegar is now ready to use.

Seed Vinegar

Make as for herb vinegar, but use 2 tablespoons of seeds to 20 oz. white wine or cider vinegar. Dill, fennel and coriander seeds make well-flavored vinegars.

Floral Vinegar

Made in the same way, these are used for fruit salads and cosmetic recipes. Combine elder, nasturtiums, sweet violets, pinks, lavender, primrose, rose petals, rosemary or thyme flowers in the following proportions:

10 tablespoons torn flower heads or petals
2 cups white wine vinegar

Pickled Horseradish

As a child I lived in a small village in the West of England where an old man called Mr Bell sat outside his cottage crying in the early fall. It took me a long time to understand why — he was scraping the horseradish root into a bowl to make pickles. He did this outside because the fumes given off by the horseradish were so strong they made one's eyes water.

Wash and scrape the skin off a good-size horseradish root. Mince in a food processor or grate it (if you can stand it!). Pack into small jars and cover with salted vinegar made from 1 teaspoon salt to 10 oz. cider or white wine vinegar. Seal and leave for 4 weeks before using.

Pickled Nasturtium Seeds

Poor man's capers!
Pick nasturtium seeds while they are still green. Steep in brine made from 3.5 oz. salt to 1 quart water for 24 hours. Strain the seeds and put 2 tablespoons of them into a small jar. Into a saucepan add 1 clove of peeled garlic, 1 teaspoon black peppercorns, 1 teaspoon dill seeds, 1 tablespoon English mace leaves and enough white wine vinegar to fill the jar. Slowly bring to simmering point. Then strain the vinegar and pour over the seeds. Seal the jars with acid-proof lids and leave for about 4 weeks. After opening, store in the refrigerator and use the contents quickly.

savory herb jelly

Use the following herbs: sweet marjoram, mints (all kinds), rosemary, sage, summer savory, tarragon and common thyme.

Makes 2 x 12-oz. jars

6 cups tart cooking apples or crab apples, roughly chopped, cores and all
3¾ cups water
2¼ cups sugar
2 tablespoons white wine vinegar
2 tablespoons lemon juice
1 bunch herbs, approx. 4 tablespoons chopped herbs

Put the apples into a large pan with the bunch of herbs and cover with cold water in a preserving pan. Bring to the boil and simmer until the apples are soft, roughly 30 minutes. Pour into a jelly bag and drain overnight.

Measure the strained juice and add 2¼ cups sugar to every 2½ cups fluid. Stir over gentle heat until the sugar has dissolved. Bring to the boil, stirring, and boil until setting point is reached. This takes roughly 20 to 30 minutes. Skim the surface scum and stir in the vinegar and lemon juice and the chopped herbs. Pour into jars, seal and label before storing.

sweet jellies

Follow the above recipe, omitting the vinegar and lemon juice, and instead adding ⅔ cup water. The following make interestingly flavored sweet jellies: bergamot, lavender flower, lemon verbena, scented geranium, sweet violet and lemon balm.

preserves

Coriander Chutney

Makes 2 x 1-lb. jars

6 cups cooking apples, peeled, cored and sliced
2 cups onions, peeled and roughly chopped
2 cloves garlic, peeled and crushed
1 red and 1 green pepper, deseeded and sliced
3¾ cups red wine vinegar
2¼ cups soft brown sugar
½ tablespoon whole coriander seeds
6 peppercorns tied securely in a piece of muslin
6 all-spice berries
¼ cup root ginger, peeled and sliced
2 tablespoons coriander leaves, chopped
2 tablespoons mint, chopped

Combine the apples with the onions, garlic and peppers in a large, heavy saucepan. Add the vinegar and bring to the boil, simmering for about 30 minutes until all the ingredients are soft. Add the brown sugar and the muslin bag of seeds and berries. Then add the ginger. Heat gently, stirring all the time, until the sugar has dissolved, then simmer until thick; this can take up to 60 minutes. Stir in the chopped coriander and mint and spoon into hot, sterilized jars. Seal and label when cool.

NATURAL DYES

Herbs have been used to dye cloth since the earliest records. In fact, until the 19th century and the birth of the chemical industry, all dyes were "natural." Then the chemical process, offering a larger range of colors and a more guaranteed result, took over. Now, once again, there is a real demand for more natural products and colors, which has resulted in a revival of interest in plants as a dye source.

The most common dyeing herbs are listed in the dye chart. You will notice that yellows, browns and greys are predominant. Plenty of plant material will be required so be careful not to over-pick in your own garden (and please do not pick other people's plants without permission! I plead from personal experience). To begin with, keep it simple. Pick the flowers just as they are coming out, the leaves when they are young and fresh and a good green; dig up roots in the fall and cut them up well before use.

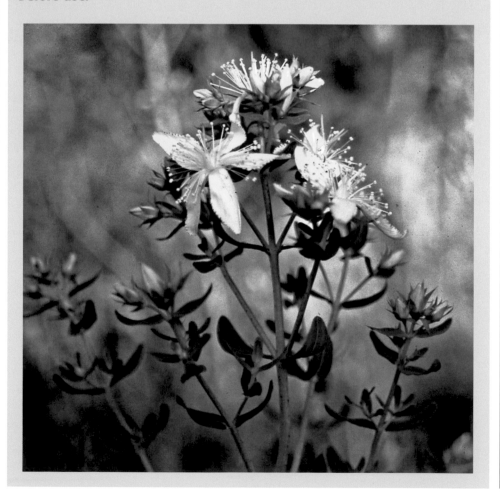

fabric

Any natural material can be dyed; some are trickier than others. It just takes time and practice. In the following sections I will explain the techniques connected with dying wool, the most reliable and easiest of natural materials. Silk, linen and cotton can also be dyed, but are more difficult.

preparation

First time, this is a messy and fairly lengthy process, so use a utility room, or clear the counters in the kitchen and protect all areas. Best of all keep it away from the home altogether. Some of the mordants used for fixing dye are poisonous, so keep them well away from children, pets and food. The actual dyeing process is not difficult, but you will need space, and a few special pieces of equipment:

1 large stainless-steel vessel, such as a canning bath
 (to be used as the dye-bath)
1 stainless-steel or enamel bucket and bowl
1 pair of tongs (wooden or stainless-steel; to be used
 for lifting)
1 measuring jug
1 pair rubber gloves essential for all but Jumblies –
 "Their heads are green and their hands are blue,
 And they went to sea in a sieve."
Mortar and pestle
Thermometer
Water; this must be soft, either rainwater or filtered
Scales

Dyeing comprises four separate tasks:

• Preparation of the material (known as scouring)

• Preparation of the mordant

• Preparation of the dye

• Dyeing process

preparation of the material (scouring)

Prepare the wool by washing it in a hot solution of soap flakes or a proprietary scouring agent in order to remove any grease. Always handle the wool gently. Rinse it several times, squeezing (gently) between each rinse. On the final rinse add 1¾ oz. of vinegar.

The flowers of St John's Wort produce a beige dye

preparation of the mordant

Mordants help "fix" the dye to the fabric. They are available from drug stores or dye suppliers. The list below includes some of the more common. Some natural dyers say that one should not use mordants, but without them the dye will run very easily.

Alum: Use 1–20 oz. dry wool

This is the most useful of mordants, its full title being potassium aluminium sulfate. Sometimes potassium hydrogen tartrate, cream of tartar, is added (beware! this is not the baking substance) in order to facilitate the process and brighten the color.

Iron: Use 2–20 oz. dry wool

This is ferrous sulfate. It dulls and deepens the colors. It is added in the final process after first using the mordant Alum. Remove the wool before adding the iron, then replace the wool and simmer until you get the depth of color required.

Copper: Use 3–20 oz. dry wool

This is copper sulfate. If you mix with 10 oz. of vinegar when preparing the mordant it will give a blue/green tint to colors.
WARNING: Wear gloves; copper is poisonous.

Chrome: Use 3–20 oz. dry wool

This is bichromate of potash and light sensitive, so keep it in the dark. It gives the color depth, makes the colors fast, and gives the wool a soft, silky feel. WARNING: Wear gloves; chrome is poisonous.

• Dissolve the mordant in a little hot water.

• Stir into 5 gallons of hot water 120°F.

• When thoroughly dissolved immerse the wet, washed wool in the mixture. Make sure it is wholly immersed.

• Slowly bring to the boil and simmer at 180–200°F for an hour.

• Remove from the heat. Take the wool out of the water and rinse.

preparation of the dye

No two batches of herbal dye will be the same. There are so many variable factors — plant variety, water, mordant, immersion time.

The amount of plant material required for dyeing is very variable. A good starting ratio is 1 lb. of mordanted wool in skeins to 1 lb. plant material.

* Chop or crush the plant material.

* Place loosely in a muslin or nylon bag and tie securely.

* Leave to soak in 5 gallons of soft, tepid water overnight.

* Slowly bring the water and herb material to the boil.

* Reduce heat and simmer at 180–200°F for as long as it takes to get the water to the desired color. This can take from 1 to 3 hours.

* Remove the pan from the heat, remove the herb material, and allow the liquid to cool to hand temperature.

dyeing process

* Gently add the wool.

* Bring the water slowly to the boil, stirring occasionally with the wooden tongs.

* Allow to simmer for a further hour.

* Remove pan from the heat and leave the wool in the dye-bath until cold, or until the color is right.

* Remove the wool with the tongs and rinse in tepid water until no color runs out.

* Give a final rinse in cold water.

* Dry the skeins of wool over a rod or cord, away from direct heat. Tie a light weight to the bottom to stop the wool kinking during the drying process.

dye chart

Common Name	Botanical Name	Part Used	Mordant	Color
Comfrey	Symphytum officinale	Leaves and stalks	Alum	Yellows
Chamomile, Dyers	Anthemis tinctoria	Flowers	Alum	Yellows
Chamomile, Dyers	Anthemis tinctoria	Flowers	Copper	Olives
Elder	Sambucus nigra	Leaves	Alum	Greens
Elder	Sambucus nigra	Berries	Alum	Violets/Purple
Goldenrod	Solidago canadensis	Whole plant	Chrome	Golden Yellows
Horsetail	Equisetum arvense	Stems and leaves	Alum	Yellows
Juniper	Juniperus communis	Crushed berries	Alum	Yellows
Marigold	Calendula officinalis	Petals	Alum	Pale Yellow
Meadowsweet	Filipendula ulmaria	Roots	Alum	Black
Nettle	Urtica dioica	Whole plant	Copper	Greyish-green
St John's Wort	Hypericum perforatum	Flowers	Alum	Beiges
Sorrel	Rumex acetosa	Whole plant	Alum	Dirty yellow
Sorrel	Rumex acetosa	Roots	Alum	Beige/pink
Tansy	Tanacetum vulgare	Flowers	Alum	Yellows
Woad	Isatus tinctoria	Leaves	Sodium dithionite, ammonia	Blues

YEARLY CALENDAR

This calendar gived general guidelines for a garden in a fairly temperate zone. But as any gardener knows, you cannot be precise. Each year is different — wetter, windier, hotter, drier, colder than the last. So use this calendar as a general guide, and check with the specific entry for each plant for more detailed information.

midwinter

Look back over the previous year, at successes and mishaps, and plan for the following season. Think about any structural changes as well as ordering seeds and plants. Keep an eye out for any weather damage in the garden, checking especially after heavy frost, snow, and gales.

Vegetables
Prepare cropping plants. Lime fall-dug plots if needed. Place early seed potatoes in shallow boxes with "eyes" up, and store in a light, frost-free place. Toward the end of the month, plant out shallots if soil is moist enough.

Under cover, sow radishes and carrots in growbags or in the borders of a cold greenhouse; sow lettuce for growing under cloches, and leeks.

Herbs
This is one of the quietest times. Keep an eye on the degrees of frost and protect tender herbs with an extra layer of floating row cover or mulch if necessary.

With a little bit of protection in the garden, bay, hyssop, rosemary, sage, winter savory, thyme, lemon thyme, chervil, and parsley can be picked.

Start parsley seed with heat. Outside, if not sown in the fall, sow sweet cicely, sweet woodruff, and cowslip, to enable a period of stratification. Force chives, mint and tarragon in boxes in the greenhouse.

Keep watering of containers to a minimum. Clean old pots ready for the spring "pot up".

Fruit
Make a health and hygiene check and examine each plant in your care for pests, diseases, and dieback. Check stores, remove and use any fruits starting to deteriorate before they go over and infect others.

late winter

As the days lengthen, and if the weather is not too unpleasant, this is a good time to have the final tidy up before the busy season starts. If you want to get an early start in the garden and you have prepared a site the previous fall, cover the soil now with black polythene. It will warm up the soil and force any weeds.

Vegetables
Sow fava beans, early peas, and spinach. Sow early-maturing cabbage and cauliflowers in pots from the middle of the month on. "Chit" maincrop potatoes. Sow cabbages, carrots, lettuces, and radishes under row covers.

Herbs
With a little bit of protection in the garden, bay, hyssop, rosemary, sage, winter savory, thyme, lemon thyme, chervil, and parsley can be harvested. Chives start to come up if they are under protection, and mint can be available if forced. Start borage, dill, and parsley seeds with heat, and sow chervil in a cold greenhouse.

Herbaceous perennial herbs, including chives, lemon balm, pot marjoram, mints, oregano, broad-leafed sorrel, and tarragon, can be divided now, as long as they are not too frozen and are given added protection after replanting.

As the containers have been brought in for the winter, new life may be starting. Dust off, and slowly start watering.

Outside, check that any dead or decaying herbaceous growth is not damaging plants. Check for wind and snow damage.

Fruit
Check stored fruits, remove and use any fruits starting to deteriorate before they go over and infect others. Spread compost or well-rotted manure under and around everything possible and add a good layer of mulch, preferably immediately after a period of heavy rain.

Lime most grass swards one year in four, more often on acid soil, but not amongst ericaceous plants or lime-haters! Once ground becomes workable, plant out hardy trees and shrubs that missed the fall planting. Sow the very earliest crops for growing under cover. Ensure good weed control, hoeing every 2 weeks or adding extra mulches on top.

Do major pruning work to trees and bushes missed earlier or damaged in winter (but not stone fruits or evergreens). Prune fall-fruiting raspberries to the ground.

Spray everything growing with diluted fertilizer solution at least once a month, and anything with deficiency symptoms more often. Spray peaches and almonds with Bordeaux mixture to protect against peach-leaf curl.

Examine each plant for pests, diseases, and dieback. Apply sticky bands and inspect sacking bands on apple trees, and others if they suffered from many pests.

Check straps and stakes after gales. On still, cold nights protect the blossoms and young fruitlets from frost damage with net curtains, plastic sheeting or newspaper.

early spring

Gradually uncover tender plants outside and look for hopeful signs of life. Give them a gentle tidy.

Vegetables
Plant onion sets in prepared ground. Sow beetroot, cabbage, carrots, parsnip, lettuce, and maincrop peas.

Plant lettuce under cloches or in plastic tunnels, sow salad onions in growbags in an unheated greenhouse for early crops. Sow early cabbages, cauliflowers and tomatoes under glass for transplanting later.

Herbs
Herbs available for picking include angelica, lemon balm, bay, chives, fennel, hyssop, mint, parsley, peppermint, pennyroyal, rue, sage, savory, sorrel, and thyme.

Toward the end of the month, start borage, fennel, coriander, sweet marjoram, rue, and basil seeds with heat. In a cold greenhouse sow chervil, chives, dill, lemon balm, lovage, parsley, sage, summer savory, and sorrel. Outside in the garden sow chervil, chives, parsley (cover with cloches), chamomile, tansy, caraway, borage, and fennel.

Check seeds that have been left outside from the

Planting seeds

The vegetable patch starts to flourish in spring

previous fall for stratification. If they are starting to germinate, move them into a cold greenhouse.

Take root cuttings from mint, tarragon, bergamot, chamomile, hyssop, tansy, sweet woodruff, and sweet cicely. Divide mint, tarragon, wormwood, lovage, rue, sorrel, lemon balm, salad burnet, camphor plant, thyme, winter savory, marjoram, alecost, horehound, and pennyroyal. This is a good time to start mound layering on old sages or thymes.

Tidy up all the pots, trim old growth to maintain shape. Start liquid feeding with fertilizer. Repot if necessary. Pot up new plants into containers for display later in the season.

In the garden, clear up all the winter debris, fork the soil over and give a light dressing of bonemeal. If your soil is alkaline, and you gave it a good dressing of manure in the fall, now is the time to dig it well in.

Remove black polythene, weed, and place a cloche over important sowing sites a week before sowing to raise the soil temperature and keep it dry.

When major frosts are over, you can cut lavender back and into shape. This is certainly advisable for plants 2 years old and older. Give them a good mulch. Equally, sage bushes of 2 years and older would benefit from a trim, but not hard back. Cut back elder and rosemary, neither of which minds a hard cutting back. Transplant the following if they need it: alecost, chives, mint, balm, pot marjoram, sorrel, horehound, and rue.

Fruit
Continue to spread a good layer of compost or well-rotted manure under and around everything possible. If you have acidic soil, spread wood ashes under and around plants, giving priority to gooseberries and culinary apples. Only use on acidic soils, as they raise the pH and will cause problems on alkaline soils. Plant out evergreen and the more tender hardy plants.

Protect them from frost and wind the first season. Sow plants grown under cover or for later planting out.

Maintain good weed control by hoeing every 2 weeks or adding extra mulch on top. Cut the grass at least every 2 weeks, preferably weekly, returning the clippings or raking them into rings around trees and bushes.

Spray everything growing with diluted fertilizer solution at least once a month, and anything with deficiency symptoms more often. Spray peaches and almonds with Bordeaux mixture against peach-leaf curl. Make a health and hygiene check on each plant in your care for pests, diseases, and dieback.

Prune back tender plants and evergreens. Protect the new growth against frost afterwards. Pollinate early-flowering plants and those under cover by hand. On still, cold nights protect the blossoms and young fruitlets from frost damage with net curtains, plastic sheet, or newspaper.

midspring

This is the main period for sowing outdoors, as soon as soil conditions permit. It is also now possible to prune back to strong new shoots the branches of any shrubs that have suffered in winter.

Vegetables
Dig plots occupied by winter greens and prepare for leeks; plant maincrop potatoes, cabbages, and cauliflowers (sown under cover in early spring, depending on location). Make further sowings of beet, radishes, spinach, carrots, cauliflower, maincrop peas, fava beans, and parsnips. Sow iceberg lettuce, scallions, and sea kale. Sow winter cauliflower, Savoy cabbage, kale, and broccoli into seedbeds. Transplant cabbages and cauliflowers sown in nursery beds in late winter. Pinch out the

growing tips of flowering fava beans.

Tomatoes sown and pricked out in early spring should be transferred to a coldframe and hardened off. Sow marrows, squashes and sweetcorn at the end of the month. Prepare greenhouse borders or growbags for tomatoes, and plant toward the end of the month.

Herbs
Herbs available for picking include: angelica, balm, bay, borage, caraway, chervil, chives, fennel, hyssop, lovage, pot marjoram, mints, parsley, pennyroyal, peppermint, rosemary, sage, winter savory, sorrel, thyme, tarragon, and lemon thyme.

Start basil seeds with heat. In the cold greenhouse sow borage, chervil, cilantro, dill, fennel, lemon balm, lovage, pot marjoram, sweet marjoram, sage, summer savory, winter savory, sorrel, buckler leaf sorrel, horehound, rue, bergamot, caraway, and garden thyme. Outside in the garden sow parsley, chives, hyssop, caraway, and calendula. Prick out the previous month's sown seeds, pot on, or harden off before planting out.

Take softwood cuttings of rue, mint, sage, southernwood, winter savory, thymes, horehound, lavender, rosemary, cotton lavender, and curry. Take root cuttings of sweet cicely, fennel, and mint. Divide pennyroyal, chives, lady's mantle, salad burnet, and tarragon.

You should be able to put all containers outside now; keep an eye on the watering and feeding. In the garden, if all the frosts have finished, the following will need cutting and pruning into shape: bay, winter savory, hyssop, cotton lavender, lavenders, rue especially variegated rue, southernwood, and thymes.

Fruit
Ensure good weed control, hoeing weekly or adding extra mulch on top. Cut the grass at least weekly, returning the clippings or raking them into rings around trees and bushes. Sow plants grown under cover or for later planting out. Plant out more tender hardy plants under cover or with protection.

Spread a good layer of mulch under and around everything possible, and spread wood ashes under and around fruit trees, giving priority to gooseberries and culinary apples. Spray everything growing with diluted fertilizer solution at least once a month, and anything with deficiency symptoms more often.

Water all new plants established within the previous 12 months whenever there has been little rain. Disbud or de-fruit new plants to give them time to establish. Pollinate plants under cover by hand. Tie in new growths of vines and climbing plants. Make a health and hygiene check weekly and examine each plant in your care for pests, diseases, and dieback. On still, cold nights protect the blossoms and young fruitlets from frost damage with net curtains, plastic sheet, or newspaper. Make layers of difficult subjects.

late spring

Vegetables
Sow string and runner beans, Chinese lettuce, carrots, zucchini, outdoor cucumbers, lettuce, turnips, spinach, and parsley. Plant out celeriac, celery, corn, and summer cabbage. Harvest asparagus, fava beans, cauliflowers, peas, radish, and spinach. Earth up potatoes. Under cover, transplant eggplants, outdoor cucumbers, tomatoes, peppers, and corn.

Herbs
Everything should be growing quickly now. The annuals will need thinning; tender and half-hardy plants should be hardened off under a cold frame or by a warm wall. A watch must be kept for a sudden late frost; basil is especially susceptible. Move container specimens into bigger pots or top-dress with new compost.

Nearly all varieties of herbs are available for picking. Outside, keep sowing cilantro, dill, chervil, parsley, sweet marjoram, basil, and any other annuals you require to maintain crops. Prick out and repot or plant out any of the previous month's seedlings.

Take softwood cuttings of marjorams, all mints, oregano, rosemarys, winter savory, French tarragon, and all thymes. Containers should now be looking good. Keep trimming to maintain shape; water and feed regularly. In the garden, trim southernwood into shape.

Cut second-year growth of angelica for candying. Cut thyme before flowering to dry.

Fruit
Maintain good weed control. Sow plants grown under cover or outdoors. Plant out tender plants under cover or with protection. Pollinate plants under cover by hand. Cut the grass at least every 2 weeks, preferably weekly, returning the clippings or raking them into rings around trees and bushes.

Water all new plants established within the last twelve months especially if there has been little rain. Disbud or de-fruit new plants. Spray everything growing with diluted fertilizer solution at least once a month, and anything with deficiency symptoms more often.

Examine each plant twice weekly for pests, diseases,

and dieback. Tie in new growths of vine and climbing plants. On still, cold nights protect the blossoms and young fruitlets from frost damage with net curtains, plastic sheet, or newspaper. Make layers of difficult subjects. Protect almost every ripening fruit from the birds.

early summer

Vegetables
Sow string and runner beans, Chinese lettuce, carrots, zucchini, outdoor cucumbers, lettuce, turnips, spinach, and parsley. Transplant celery, summer cabbage, and

Preparing the soil for seed sowing

tomatoes. Harvest asparagus, fava beans, cauliflowers, calabrese, peas, radish, spinach, and turnips. Under cover, transplant eggplants and corn; pollinate tomato plants.

Herbs
This is a great time in the herb garden. All planting is now completed. Plants are beginning to join up so that little further weeding will be needed. Many plants are now reaching perfection.

All herbs are available fresh. Outside in the garden sow basil, borage, chives, cilantro, dill, fennel, sweet marjoram, summer savory, winter savory, and any others you wish to replace, or keep going.

With all the soft new growth available this is a very busy month for cuttings. Make sure you use material from nonflowering shoots. Take softwood cuttings of all perennial marjorams, all mints, all rosemary, all sage, variegated lemon balm, tarragon (French), and all thymes. Also divide thymes and layer rosemary.

Plant up annual herbs such as basil and sweet marjoram into containers to keep near the kitchen. If you must plant basil in the garden, do it now. Nip out the growing tips of this year's young plants to encourage them to bush out.

Trim cotton lavender hedges if flowers are not required and to maintain their shape; clip box hedges and topiary shapes as needed. A new herb garden should be weeded thoroughly to give the new plants the best chance.

Cut second-year growth of angelica for candying. Cut sage for drying.

Fruit
Maintain good weed control. Plant out the tender plants or move them out for summer. Cut the grass at least every 2 weeks, preferably weekly, returning the clippings or raking them into rings around trees and bushes. Raise the height of cut of your mower. Spray everything growing with diluted fertilizer solution at least once a month, and anything with deficiency symptoms more often.

Water all new plants established within the previous twelve months especially whenever there has been little rain. Examine each plant twice weekly for pests, diseases, and dieback.

Start summer pruning. This applies to all red and white currants, gooseberries, and all trained apples and pears. From one third of each plant, remove approximately half to three-quarters of each new shoot, except for leaders. Prune grapevines back to three or five leaves after a flower truss. Tie in new growths of vine and climbing plants.

Fall's bounty

Also begin fruit thinning. To do this, remove every diseased, decayed, damaged, misshapen, distorted, and congested fruitlet. This applies to all apples, pears, peaches, apricots, quality plums, dessert grapes, gooseberries, figs, and especially to trained forms. Compost or burn rejected fruitlets immediately. Of course usable ones, such as the larger gooseberries, may be consumed.

Take softwood cuttings if you have a propagator. Make layers of difficult subjects. Protect almost every ripening fruit from birds.

midsummer

Vegetables

Sow final crops of beet, carrots, lettuce, turnips, spinach, and parsley. Sow scallions, spring cabbage, and sea kale for overwintering. Sow keeping onions in a seedbed for transplanting the following spring. In colder zones, plant leeks sown in coldframes in winter. Remove basal suckers from early trench celery, water well and earth up.

Under cover, harvest cucumbers and tomatoes regularly to encourage further fruiting, and pinch out the growing point when each stem contains about five or six trusses of fruit.

Herbs

The season is on the wane, the early annuals and biennials are beginning to go over. It is already time to think of next year and to start collecting seeds. Take cuttings of tender shrubs as spare shoots are available.

All herbs can be harvested fresh. Outside in the garden sow chervil, angelica (if seed is set), borage, cilantro, dill, lovage, and parsley. Take softwood cuttings of wormwood, scented geraniums, lavenders, and the thymes. Layer rosemary. Keep an eye on watering of containers as the temperatures begin to rise.

Cut all lavenders back after flowering to maintain their shape. If this is the first summer of the herb garden and the plants are not fully established it is important to make sure they do not dry out, so water regularly. Once established, many are tolerant of drought.

Harvest and dry lemon balm, horehound, summer savory, hyssop, tarragon, thyme, and lavender. Use lavender and rosemary for dyeing and potpourris. Harvest seed of caraway and angelica.

Fruit

Maintain good weed control. Cut the grass at least every 2 weeks, preferably weekly, returning the clippings or raking them into rings around trees and bushes. Raise the height of cut of your mower. Spray everything growing with diluted fertilizer solution at least once a month, and anything with deficiency symptoms more often. Water all new plants established within the previous 12 months especially if there has been little rain. Examine each plant for pests, diseases, and dieback. Tie in new growths of vines and climbing plants.

Continue summer pruning. For red and white currants, gooseberries, and all trained apples and pears, from the second third of each plant remove approximately half to three-quarters of each new shoot, except for leaders. Prune grapevines back to three or five leaves after a flower truss. Black currants may have a third to half of the old wood removed after fruiting. Stone fruits are traditionally pruned now to avoid silver-leaf disease.

Continue to thin fruits as in June. Take softwood cuttings if you have a propagator, and root tips of the black and hybrid berries. Protect almost every ripening fruit from the birds.

late summer

Vegetables

Sow turnips for spring "greens" and Japanese onions for overwintering in mild zones. Sow spring cabbage in nursery rows. To prevent wind-rock in fall and winter, draw soil around the stems of winter greens, particularly Brussels sprouts, kale, and broccoli. Earth up trench celery. Harvest maincrop onions, ensuring that the bulbs' outer skins are well-ripened before storing. Under cover, harvest cucumbers and tomatoes regularly and self-pollinate tomatoes.

Herbs

Traditionally a time for holidays, it is also time to harvest and preserve many herbs for winter use. Collect and dry material for potpourris, and collect seeds for sowing next year.

All herbs are available fresh. In the garden or greenhouse sow angelica, cilantro, dill, lovage, parsley, winter savory. Take softwood cuttings of bay, wormwood, rosemary, the thymes and lavenders, scented geraniums, balm of Gilead, pineapple sage, and myrtles.

If you are going away, make sure you ask a friend to water your containers for you. Give box, cotton lavender, and curry their second clipping and trim any established plants that are looking unruly. Maintain watering of the new herb garden and keep an eye on mints, parsley, and comfrey, which need water to flourish. There is no real need to feed your herbs if the ground has been well prepared, but if the plants are recovering from a pest attack they will benefit from a foliar feed of liquid fertilizer.

Harvest thyme, sage, clary sage, marjoram, and lavender for drying. Pick the mints and pennyroyal to freeze. Gather basil to make a basil oil. Collect the seed of angelica, anise, caraway, coriander, cumin, chervil, dill, and fennel.

Fruit

Maintain good weed control. Plant new strawberry plants, if you can get them. Cut the grass at least every 2 weeks, preferably weekly, returning the clippings or raking them into rings around trees and bushes. Lower the height of cut of your mower. Spray everything that is growing with diluted fertilizer solution at least once a month, and anything that has deficiency symptoms more often. Water all new plants established within the previous twelve months especially whenever there has been little rain. Sow green manures and winter ground cover on bare soil that is not mulched; grass down orchards. Check for pests, diseases, and dieback, and apply sticky bands and sacking bands to apple trees, and to others if they suffer from many pests.

Finish summer pruning. For red and white currants, gooseberries, and all trained apples and pears, for the last, unpruned third of each plant, remove approximately half to three-quarters of each new shoot, except for leaders. Prune grapevines back to three or five leaves after the fruit truss. Thin fruits as in June. Protect almost every ripening fruit from the birds. Root the tips of the black- and hybrid berries.

early fall

Vegetables

Order seed catalogues for the following year. In mild zones, plant out spring cabbages into permanent positions. Sow spinach for harvesting in spring. Lift maincrop carrots, beets, and potatoes, and store in a cool, dark place: later sowings may be left in the ground. Earth up celery before severe frosts. Lift tomato plants with fruits still attached and store; ripen on straw under cloches or in the greenhouse. Wrap green fruits in paper and store in the dark.

Plant thinnings from late-sown salads in frames or under cloches to provide crops during winter. Lettuces reaching maturity should be covered with cloches or frames; sow further crops in a coldframe. Fall is a good time to lay drains through waterlogged sites.

Herbs

Basil should be taken up and leaves preserved. Line out semi-ripe cuttings of box, cotton lavenders, etc., in coldframes, under cloches, or in polythene tunnels for hedge renewal in the spring.

Herbs that can be picked fresh include: lemon balm, basil, bay, borage, caraway, chervil, chives, clary sage, fennel, hyssop, calendulas, marjoram, the mints, parsley, pennyroyal, peppermint, rosemarys, sages, winter savory, sorrels, and the thymes. Sow outside in the garden or greenhouse angelica, chives, cilantro, parsley, and winter savory. Take softwood and semi-ripe cuttings of rosemary, thyme, tarragon, lavender, rue, cotton lavender, curry plant, and box. Divide bergamot.

At the beginning of the month give the shrubby herbs their final clipping (bay, lavender, etc). Do not leave it too late or the frost could damage the new growth. Put basil into a greenhouse or kitchen. Top-dress bergamots if they have died back. If lemon

verbena is to be kept outside make sure it is getting adequate protection. Toward the end of this month take in all containers, and protect tender plants like bay trees, myrtles, and scented geraniums. Harvest dandelion (roots), parsley, marigold, clary sage, and peppermint for drying or freezing. Collect seed of angelica, anise, caraway, chervil, and fennel.

Fruit

Maintain good weed control. Plant out pot-grown specimens and those that can be dug with a decent rootball or moved with little disturbance. Cut the grass at least every 2 weeks, preferably weekly, returning the clippings and fallen leaves or raking them into rings around trees and bushes. Sow green manures and winter ground cover on bare soil that is not mulched; grass down orchards. Spray everything that is growing with diluted fertilizer solution at least once a month, and anything that has deficiency symptoms more often.

Make a health and hygiene check. Apply sticky bands and sacking bands to apple trees, and to others if they suffer from many pests. On still, cold nights protect ripening fruits from frost damage with net curtains, plastic sheet, or newspaper. Protect first the tops then the stems and roots of more tender plants before frosts come. Bring indoors tender plants in pots or protect them. Take cuttings of plants as they start to drop their leaves. Prune early fruiting raspberries and hybrids, and black currants and other plants as they start to drop their leaves. Protect almost every ripening fruit from the birds. Root the tips of the black- and hybrid berries.

midfall

Vegetables

Lift potatoes, beet, and carrots for storing. Tie onions on to ropes when the skins have thoroughly ripened. Transplant lettuces sown in summer to a well-drained, protected site to overwinter in mild zones. Plant root cuttings of sea kale in pots of sand and leave them in a sheltered place until the spring. Cut down asparagus foliage as it turns yellow. Tidy the vegetable plot, removing all plant debris. Add organic matter to plots, and lime if necessary.

Sow lettuce in greenhouse borders or growbags for cutting in the spring. Continue harvesting green tomatoes, storing in a dark, frost-free place to ripen. Clear growbags used for cucumbers, peppers, and tomatoes in the summer and replant with winter lettuce.

Herbs

The best time in all but the coldest areas to plant hardy perennial herbs.

Basil, bay, borage, chervil, fennel, hyssop, marigold, marjoram, parsley, rosemary, sage, winter savory, sorrel, and the thymes can all be picked fresh. Sow parsley seed with heat. In the garden sow catmint, chervil, wormwood, chamomile, fennel, and angelica.

Take softwood and semi-ripe cuttings of bay, elder, hyssop, cotton lavender, southernwood, lavenders, the thymes, curry, and box. Take root cuttings of tansy, pennyroyal, the mints, and tarragon. Divide alecost, the marjorams, chives, lemon balm, lady's mantle, hyssop, bergamot, camphor plant, lovage, sorrel, sage, oregano, and pennyroyal.

Start reducing the watering of containers. Clear the garden and weed it well. Cut down the old growth and collect any remaining seed heads. Cut back the mints, trim winter savory and hyssop. Give them all a leaf mold dressing. Dig up and remove the annuals such as dill, coriander, borage, summer savory, and sweet marjoram, and the second-year biennials — parsley, chervil, arugula etc. Protect with cloches or floating row covers any herbs to be used fresh in winter, like parsley, chervil, lemon thyme, salad burnet. Dig up some French tarragon, repot in trays for forcing and protection.

Check the pH of alkaline soil every third year. Dress with well-rotted manure to a depth of 2–4 in. and leave the digging until the following spring. Dig over heavy soils; add manure to allow the frost to penetrate.

Fruit

Ensure good weed control. Plant out bare-rooted hardy trees and bushes if soil is in good condition and they are dormant. Cut the grass at least once every 2 weeks, preferably weekly, collecting the clippings with the fallen leaves or raking them into rings around trees and bushes. Spray everything that is growing with diluted fertilizer solution at least once a month, and anything that has deficiency symptoms more often.

Check plants for pests, diseases, and dieback. Top up the sticky bands and inspect the sacking bands on apple trees, and on others if they suffered from many pests. Check straps and stakes before the gales. On still, cold nights protect ripening fruits from frost damage with net curtains, plastic sheet, or newspaper.

Take cuttings of hardy plants as they start to drop their leaves. Prune early-fruiting raspberries and hybrids, and black currants and other plants as they start to drop their leaves. Protect first the tops then the stems and roots of more tender plants before frosts come. Check stores, remove and use any fruits starting to deteriorate before they go over and infect others. Protect almost every ripening fruit from the birds.

late fall

Vegetables

In mild zones, sow fava beans and round-seeded peas in the open: protect with cloches if necessary. Remove dying leaves from winter greens, allowing air to circulate between plants. Check stored vegetables regularly and remove any showing signs of decay. Use those that are slightly damaged immediately. Sow green manure. Lift and store crowns of chicory as well as sea kale.

Herbs

The days are getting shorter and frosts are starting. Planting of hardy herbaceous herbs can continue as long as soil remains unfrozen and in a workable condition.

Basil, bay, hyssop, marjoram, mint, parsley, rosemary, rue, sage, and thyme are available to pick fresh. Sow the following so that they can get a good period of stratification: arnica (old seed), sweet woodruff, yellow iris, poppy, soapwort, sweet cicely, hops (old seed), sweet violet. Sow in trays, cover with glass, and leave outside in a cold frame or corner of the garden where they cannot get damaged.

Cut back on all watering of container-grown plants. Give them all a prune, so that they go into rest mode for the winter. This is the time for the final tidy up in the garden. Cut back the remaining plants, lemon balm, alecost, horehound, and give them a dressing of leaf mold. Give the elders a prune. Dig up a clump of mint and chives, put them in pots or trays and bring them into the greenhouse for forcing for winter use.

Fruit

Keep on top of weeds. Plant out bare-rooted hardy trees and bushes if the soil is in good condition and they are dormant. Cut the grass at least every 2 weeks, collecting the clippings with the fallen leaves or raking them into rings around trees and bushes. Check plants for pests, diseases, and dieback. Top up the sticky bands and inspect the sacking bands on apple trees, and on others if they suffered from many pests.

Check straps and stakes before the gales. Spread a good layer of compost or well-rotted manure under and around everything possible, preferably after a period of heavy rain. On still, cold nights protect ripening fruits from frost damage with net curtains, plastic sheet, or newspaper. Protect first the tops then the stems and roots of more tender plants before frosts come.

Take cuttings of hardy plants as they start to drop their leaves. Prune late-fruiting raspberries, hybrid berries, currants and vines, trees, and bushes as the leaves fall. Check stores, remove and use any fruits starting to deteriorate before they go over and infect others. Protect almost every ripening fruit from the birds.

early winter

Vegetables

Plan next year's rotation of vegetables, ordering seeds as soon as possible. Prepare a seed-sowing schedule. Dig and store rutabaga and late-sown carrots. If heavy falls of snow or prolonged frosts are forecast, lift small quantities of vegetables such as celery, leeks, and parsnips and store under cover in a cool, easily accessible place. Finish digging before the soil becomes waterlogged. On clay soils, spread sand, old potting compost, or well-rotted leaf mold on the surface and dig in as soon as conditions are favorable, allowing the frost to break down the soil. Sow green manures on sandy soils or cover with compost to reduce leaching.

Herbs

Bay, hyssop, marjoram, oregano, mint (forced), parsley, chervil, rosemary, rue, sage, and thyme are all available for picking fresh. In the garden, remove all the dead growth that falls into other plants, add more protective layers if needed. Wrap and terracotta or stone ornaments in burlap if you live in extremely cold conditions. Bring bay trees in if the temperature drops too low. Keep an eye on the plants you are forcing in the greenhouse.

Fruit

Ensure good weed control, make sure no weeds are getting away, hoe at two week intervals or add extra mulch on top. Plant out bare rooted hardy trees and bushes if soil is good and they are dormant. Examine each plant in your care for pests and diseases.

Examine plants for pests, diseases, and dieback. Top up the sticky bands and inspect the sacking bands on apple trees, and on others if they suffered from many pests. Check straps and stakes before the gales. Spread a good layer of compost or well-rotted manure under and around everything possible, preferably after, but not immediately before, any heavy rain.

Peaches crop well in drier, warmer areas

GLOSSARY

Analgesic A substance that relieves pain.

Annual A plant that completes its life-cycle from germination to flowering and death in one growing season.

Antidote A substance that counteracts or neutralizes a poison.

Apothecary An old term for a person who prepared and sold drugs and administered to the sick.

Aromatherapy The use of essential oils in the treatment of medical problems and for cosmetic purposes.

Astringent A substance that contracts the tissues of the body, slowing down discharges of blood and mucus.

Atropine An alkaloid obtained from members of the Solanaceae family.

Base dressing An application of organic matter or fertilizer, applied to the soil prior to planting or sowing.

Bed system A method of planting vegetables in close blocks or multiple rows.

Beta carotene The orange-yellow plant pigment and precursor of vitamin A which protects against certain cancers and heart disease.

Biennial A plant that produces roots and leaves in the first growing season, then flowers, seeds and dies by the end of the second.

Blanch To exclude light from leaves and stems and prevent development of green coloration. In the culinary sense, to immerse in boiling water for the removal of skin or color, often as a preparation for freezing.

Bolt To flower and produce seed prematurely.

Brassica Member of the cabbage family (Brassicaceae), including broccoli, Brussels sprouts, cauliflower etc.

Broadcast To scatter granular substances such as seeds, fertilizer or pesticide evenly over an area of ground.

Bulb A modified plant stem, with swollen leaves acting as a storage organ.

Bulbil A small bulb, usually rising above the ground in the axil of a leaf or bract. Can also form underground.

Capping A crust forming on the surface of soil damaged by compaction, heavy rain or watering.

Carminative A substance that allays pain and relieves flatulence and colic.

Catch-crop A rapidly maturing crop sown among slow-growing vegetables to make maximum use of the ground.

Chitting Pre-germination of seeds before sowing. The same term is used for sprouting potatoes.

Clamp A structure made of earth for storing root vegetables outdoors.

Climber A plant which naturally grows upwards covering supports or other plants.

Cloche A small portable structure, often made of plastic or glass, used to protect early crops grown outdoors.

Cold frame A low-lying square or rectangular unheated structure, with a glass or plastic lid.

Columnar Column-shaped.

Compost Decomposed organic material used as soil conditioner, mulch, potting or seed-sowing medium.

Crop rotation A system in which crops are grown in different plots on a 3- or 4-year cycle, limiting the build-up of pests and diseases and making the best use of soil nutrients.

Cultivar A contraction of "cultivated variety," a group of cultivated plants which retain distinctive desirable characteristics when propagated.

Cultivate The practice of growing plants in soil or compost. Can also be used to describe methods of soil preparation.

Cut and come again crops Seedlings, mature or semi-mature varieties, where several harvests can be taken from one crop.

Damp down To wet the floors and benches in a greenhouse in order to increase humidity and lower high temperatures.

Deciduous Describes a plant that loses its leaves annually at the end of the growing season.

Decoction An extract of a herb (when the material is hard and woody, i.e., root, wood, bark, nuts) obtained by boiling a set weight of plant matter in a set volume of water for a set time.

Diuretic A substance that increases the frequency of urination.

Dormancy Temporary cessation of growth during unfavorable growing conditions.

Double digging A cultivation technique which penetrates to two spades depth, also known as trench digging or bastard trenching.

Hilling To draw the soil around the base for support or to cover a plant for the purpose of blanching.

Emetic A substance that induces vomiting.

Essential oil A volatile oil obtained from a plant by distillation, having a similar aroma to the plant itself.

Evergreen A plant that retains its leaves throughout the year.

F1 hybrid First-generation plants obtained by crossing two selected pure-breeding parents to produce uniform vigorous offspring.

Fanging A term used to describe the forking of a root vegetable.

Fertilizer A chemical or group of chemicals applied to the soil or plants to provide nutrition.

Fleece Lightweight, woven polypropylene cover used for crop protection.

Floating mulch (floating cloche) Sheets of flexible lightweight material placed over plants to provide protection.

Floating row cover A light, woven fleece used to cover crops and protect them from frost, wind, hail, birds, rabbits and other pests that eat or chew the leaves. It allows a light transmission of around 85 percent and can be permeated by rain.

Fluid sow A method for sowing germinated seeds into the soil using a carrier gel.

Folic acid Part of the vitamin B complex, found in leafy vegetables. Deficiency of folic acid causes anemia.

Friable Used to describe soil with a crumbly, workable texture, capable of forming good tilth.

Fungicide Chemical used for the control and eradication of fungi.

Genus A taxonomic classification used to describe plants with several similar characteristics.

Germination The chemical and physical changes which take place as a seed starts to grow.

Globose Spherical, globe-like.

Green manure A rapidly maturing, leafy crop grown for incorporation into the soil to improve its structure and nutrient levels.

Grow-bag A fabric container used instead of a plastic pot or a bag of compost used as a growing medium.

Half hardy A term that describes plants that tolerate low temperatures but not frost.

Hard Pan A layer of compacted soil that is impermeable to water and oxygen, and impedes root development and drainage.

Harden off To acclimatize plants gradually, enabling them to withstand cooler conditions.

Hardy A term that describes plants that can withstand frost without protection.

Haulm The foliage of plants such as potatoes.

Heart up The stage at which leafy vegetables, like cabbage and lettuce, swell to form a dense cluster of central leaves.

Heavy soil A soil with a high proportion of clay particles, prone to waterlogging in winter and drying in summer.

Herbicide A chemical used to control and eradicate weeds.

Herbaceous Relating to plants that are not woody and that die down at the end of each growing season.

Herbicide A substance that kills plants.

Humus The organic decayed remains of plant material in soils.

Hybrid A variety of plant resulting from the crossing of either two pure lines within a species or, less often, two distinct species or genera.

Infusion An infusion is made by pouring a given quantity of boiling water over a given weight of soft herbal material (leaves or petals) and left to steep for 10–15 minutes before straining.

Inorganic Term used to describe fertilizers made from refined naturally occurring chemicals, or artificial fertilizers.

Insecticide Chemical used to eradicate insects.

Intercropping The practice of planting fast-growing vegetable crops between slower-growing varieties (see *Catch-crop*).

Inulin An easily digestible form of carbohydrate.

John Innes compost Loam based growing medium made to standardized formulas.

Knot garden A decorative formal garden made popular in the 16th century and normally consisting of very low hedges in geometric patterns.

Leaching The downward washing and loss of soluble nutrients from topsoil.

Leaf mold Partially decomposed leaves.

Legume A single-podded fruit containing several seeds which splits on maturity, e.g., beans and peas.

Lime Calcium compounds used to raise the pH of the soil (i.e., make it less acidic).

Loam The term used for a soil of medium texture.

Maincrop The largest crop produced throughout the main growing season. Also used to describe the cultivars used.

Module A generic term for the containers used for propagating and growing young plants.

Mordant A substance used in dyeing that, when applied to the fabric to be dyed, reacts chemically with the dye, fixing the color.

Mulch A substance spread around a plant to protect it from weeds, water loss, heat, or cold, and in some cases to provide nutrient material. Materials ranging from sawdust and pine needles to black plastic can be used as mulches; bark and wood chips are most commonly employed and leaves and old straw can also be used. Mulches should only be applied to moist soil.

Nematocide Chemical used for the control and eradication of nematodes (eelworms).

Neutral Soil or compost with a pH value of 7, which is neither acid nor alkaline (see pH).

Nutrients Minerals which are essential for plant growth.

Organic Term used to describe substances which are derived from natural materials. Also used to denote gardening without the use of synthetic chemicals and composts, mulches and associated material.

Perennial Non-woody plants that die back and become dormant during winter, regrowing the following spring. Perennials usually survive for 3 or more years, sometimes much longer.

Perlite Expanded volcanic rock. It is inert, sterile and has a neutral pH value (i.e., it is neither acidic nor alkaline).

pH A measure of acidity or alkalinity. The scale ranges from 0 to 14, and is an indicator of the soluble calcium within a soil or growing medium. A pH below 7 is acid and above, alkaline.

Pinch out To remove the growing tip of a plant to induce branching.

Potager An ornamental vegetable garden.

Propagation The increase of plant numbers by seed or vegetative means.

Radicle A seedling root.

Rhizome A swollen underground stem that stores food and from which roots and shoots are produced.

Root The part of the plant which is responsible for absorbing water and nutrients and for anchoring the plant into the growing medium.

Root crops Vegetables grown for their edible roots, e.g., carrot and parsnip.

Runner A trailing shoot that roots where it touches the ground.

Salve A soothing ointment.

Saponin A substance that foams in water and has a detergent action.

Seed A ripened plant ovule containing a dormant embryo, which is capable of forming a new plant.

Seed leaves or cotyledons The first leaf or leaves formed by a seed after germination.

Seedling A young plant grown from seed.

Sets Small onions, shallots or potatoes used for planting.

Shoot A branch, stem or twig of a plant.

Shrub A perennial plant with woody stems growing from or near the base.

Sideshoot A branch, stem or twig growing from a main stem of a plant.

Single digging A cultivation technique which penetrates to one spade's depth.

Species A plant or plants within the same genus. These can be grown from seed and in the main run true to type.

Spore The reproductive body of a nonflowering plant.

Stale seedbed method A cultivation technique whereby the seedbed is created and subsequent weed growth is removed before crops are sown or planted.

Stamen The pollen-producing part of the plant.

Stigma The part of a pistil (the female organs of a flower) that accepts the pollen.

Subsoil Layers of less fertile soil immediately below the topsoil.

Sucker A stem originating below soil level, usually from the plant's roots or underground stem.

Systemic or translocated A term used to describe a substance which is absorbed by a plant at one point and then circulated through its sap system.

Tap root The primary anchoring root of a plant, usually growing straight down into the soil. In vegetables this is often used for food storage.

Tender Plant material which is intolerant of cool conditions.

Thinning The removal of seedlings or shoots to improve the quality of those which remain.

Thymol A bactericide and fungicide found in several volatile oils.

Tilth The surface layer of soil produced by cultivation and soil improvement.

Tincture A solution that has been extracted from plant material after macerating in alcohol or alcohol/water solutions.

Tisane A drink made by the addition of boiling water to fresh or dried unfermented plant material.

Top-dressing The application of fertilizers or bulky organic matter to the soil surface, while the plants are *in situ*.

Topsoil The upper, usually most fertile layer of soil.

Transpiration The loss by evaporation of moisture from plant leaves and stems.

Topiary The art of cutting shrubs and small trees into ornamental shapes.

Transplant To move a plant from one growing position to another, usually into a larger pot. Or to transfer seedlings from a seedbed or tray to a further pot, tray, or seedbed (also known as prick out or pot on).

Tuber A swollen underground stem used to store moisture and nutrients.

Umbel An inflorescence with stalked flowers arising from a single point.

Variety A term used in the vernacular to describe different kinds of plants. Also used in botanical classification to describe a naturally occurring variant of a plant.

Vegetative A term used to describe parts of a plant which are capable of growth; non-reproductive or nonflowering.

Vermifuge A substance that expels or destroys worms.

Vulnerary A preparation useful in healing wounds.

Weathering Using the effect of climatic conditions to break down large lumps of soil into small particles.

SEED SOURCES

When importing plants and seeds, both American and Canadian consumers must obtain an import permit and a phytosanitary certificate from the exporting country. In the U.S., visit www.aphis.usda.gov and in Canada, visit www.inspection.gc.ca. In both cases, there are restrictions under CITES (Convention on International Trade in Endagered Species of Wild Fauna and Flora) of importing endagered plants.

seed suppliers

Artistic Gardens/
Le Jardin du Gourmet
P.O. Box 75
St. Johnsbury Center, VT 05863-0075
www.artisticgardens.com

B & T World Seeds
Paguignan 34210
Aigues-Vives, France
www.b-and-t-world-seeds.com

Baker Creek Heirloom Seed Co.
2278 Baker Creek Road
Mansfield, MO 65704
www.rareseeds.com

Bountiful Gardens
1712-D South Main St.
(in the Evergreen Shopping Center)
Willits, CA 95490
www.bountifulgardens.org

Chiltern Seeds
Crowmarsh Battle Barns,
114 Preston Crowmarsh,
Wallingford, OX10 6SL, England
www.chilternseeds.co.uk

Heirloom Market at Comstock Ferre
263 Main Street
Wethersfield, CT 06109
www.heirloommkt.com

The Cook's Garden/Burpee®
W. Atlee Burpee & Co.
300 Park Avenue
Warminster, PA 18974
www.cooksgarden.com

Dixondale Farms
PO Box 129,
Department WP15
Carrizo Springs, TX 78834-6129
www.dixondalefarms.com

Ed Hume Seeds
P.O. Box 73160
Puyallup, WA 98373
www.humeseeds.com

Evergreen Seeds
P.O. Box 17538
Anaheim, CA 92817
www.evergreenseeds.com

Filaree Garlic Farm
83 Epley Rd,
Omak, WA 98841
www.filareefarm.com

Heirloom Tomatoes
5423 Princess Drive
Rosedale, MD 21237
www.heirloomtomatoes.net

Heritage Harvest Seed
P.O. Box 279
Carman, MB R0G 0J0
www.heritageharvestseed.com

Hole's
101 Riel Drive
St. Albert, AB T8N 3X4
www.holesonline.com

John Scheepers Kitchen Garden Seeds™
23 Tulip Drive, P.O. Box 638
Bantam, CT 06750
www.kitchengardenseeds.com

Johnny's Selected Seeds
955 Benton Avenue
Winslow, ME 04901
www.johnnyseeds.com

Kitazawa Seed Company
201 4th Street
Oakland, CA 94607
www.kitazawaseed.com

Mapple Farm
129 Beech Hill Road
Weldon, NB E4H 4N5
www.mapplefarm.com

Nourse Farms, Inc.
41 River Road
Whately, MA 01373
www.noursefarms.com

OSC Seeds
P.O. Box 7
Waterloo, ON, N2J 3Z6
www.oscseeds.com

Park Seed Co.
3507 Cokesbury Road
Hodges, SC 29653
www.parkseed.com

Peaceful Valley Farm & Garden Supply
P.O. Box 2209
Grass Valley, CA 95945
www.groworganic.com

Pinetree Garden Seeds
P.O. Box 300
New Gloucester, ME 04260
www.superseeds.com

Plants of the Southwest
3095 Agua Fria Road
Santa Fe, NM 87507
-and-
6680 4th Street NW,
Albuquerque NM 87107
www.plantsofthesouthwest.com

Richters Herbs
357 Highway 47
Goodwood ON, L0C 1A0
www.richters.com

Potato Garden
12101 2135 Road
Austin, CO 81410
www.potatogarden.com

Salt Spring Seeds
Box 444, Ganges P.O.
Salt Spring Island, BC V8K 2W1
www.saltspringseeds.com

Seeds of Change
P.O. Box 4908
Rancho Dominguez, CA 90220
www.seedsofchange.com

Seeds of Diversity Canada
40 King St S, Unit 304,
Waterloo, ON N2J 1N8
www.seeds.ca

Southern Exposure Seed Exchange
P.O. Box 460
Mineral, VA 23117
www.southernexposure.com

Tomato Growers Supply Company
P.O. Box 60015
Fort Myers, FL 33906
www.tomatogrowers.com

Vegetable Seed Warehouse
P.O. Box 572
Graniteville, SC 29829
www.vegetableseedwarehouse.com

Vermont Bean Seed Company
334 W. Stroud Street
Randolph, WI 53956
www.vermontbean.com

Vesey's Seeds Ltd.
P.O. Box 9000
Charlottetown, PE C1A 8K6
www.veseys.com

Wood Prairie Farm
49 Kinney Road
Bridgewater, ME 04735
www.woodprairie.com

suppliers of biological controls

Biological controls are also available from garden centers and other outlets.

Agralan
The Old Brickyard
Ashton Keynes
Swindon
Wilts SN6 8600015
United Kingdom
www.agralan.co.uk

ARBICO Organics
P.O. Box 8910
Tucson, AZ 85738-0910
www.arbico-organics.com

The Beneficial Insect Co.
P.O. Box 119
Glendale Springs, NC 28629
www.thebeneficial insectco.com

Buglogical
P.O. Box 32046
Tucson, AZ 85751-2046
www.buglogical.com

Gardener's Supply Company
128 Intervale Road
Burlington, VT 05401
www.gardeners.com

Green Home
850 24th Avenue
San Fransisco, CA 94121
www.greenhome.com

The Green Spot Ltd.
93 Priest Road
Nottingham, NH 03290-6204
www.greenmethods.com

Natural Insect Control
3737 Netherby Road
Stevensville, ON L0S 1S0
www.natural-insect-control.com

Planet Natural
1612 Gold venue
Bozeman, MT 59715
www.plaetnatural.com

soil testing

For information on local soil testing labs, contact municipal services of the Horticulture and Crop Science department of your local University Extension.

See also, www.certifiedorganic.bc.ca/rcbtoa/services/soil-testing-services.html for facilities in Canada and the United States.

SELECTED BIBLIOGRAPHY & OTHER RESOURCES

The Allotment Book
Andi Clevely
(Collins 2008)

The Allotment Book: Seasonal Planner and Cookbook
Andi Clevely
(Collins 2008)

Biodynamic Gardening
John Soper
(Souvenir press 1983)

Complete Book of Companion Gardening (new edn)
Bob Flowerdew
(Kyle Cathie 2004)

Collins Guide to the Pests, Diseases and Disorders of Garden Plants
Stefan Buczacki & K. M. Harris
(Harper Collins 1994)

The Complete Know and Grow Vegetables
J.K.A. Bleasdale & P.J. Salter
(Oxford Paperbacks 1991)

Control Pests
Richard Jones
(Impact Publishing 2007)

Create Compost
Pauline Pears
(Impact Publishing 2007)

Creative Vegetable Gardening
Joy Larcom
(Mitchell Beazley 2008)

Crops in Pots: 50 Great Container Projects Using Vegetables, Fruit and Herbs
Bob Purnell
(Hamlyn 2007)

Domestication of Plants in the Old World
Daniel Zohary & Maria Hopf
(Oxford Science Publications 1994)

Dye Plants and Dyeing
John & Margaret Cannon
(Herbert Press 1994)

Encyclopedia of Gardening (RHS) (Revised Edition)
Christopher Brickell
(Dorling Kindersley 2007)

The English Gardener
William Cobbett
(Cobbett 1833)

Gardening and Planting by the Moon 2008
Nick Kollerstrom
(Quantum/Foulsham; published yearly)

Growing Fruit and Vegetables on a Bed System the Organic Way (new edn)
Pauline Pears
(Search Press Ltd 2004)

The Half-hour Allotment (RHS)
Lia Leendertz
(Frances Lincoln 2006)

HDRA: Encyclopedia of Organic Gardening (Henry Doubleday Research Association)
Pauline Pears
(Dorling Kindersley 2005)

Jane Grigson's Vegetable Book
Jane Grigson
(Penguin 1988)

The Gardeners and Florists Dictionary or a Complete System of Horticulture: Volumes 1 & 2
Phillip Miller
(Charles Rivington 1724)

Gourmet Gardener (New Edition)
Bob Flowerdew
(Kyle Cathie 2007)

Grow Your Own Veg (RHS)
Carol Klein & Royal Horticultural Society
(Mitchell Beazley 2007)

The History and Social Influence of the Potato
Redcliffe Salaman
(Cambridge University Press 1984)

The Kitchen Garden: a Historical Guide to Traditional Crops
David Stuart (Hale 1984)

Maison Rustique, or the Countrie Farme
Charles Estienne & Richard Surflet
(1600)

Organic Gardening: The Natural No-dig Way
Charles Dowding
(Green Books 2007)

The Organic Salad Garden (New Edition)
Joy Larkcom & Roger Phillips
(Frances Lincoln 2003)

Oriental Vegetables
Joy Larkcom
(Frances Lincoln 2007)

The Ornamental Kitchen Garden
Geoff Hamilton
(BBC Books 1990)

Queer Gear; How to Buy and Cook Exotic Fruits and Vegetables
Michael Allsop & Carolyn Heal
(Century Hutchinson 1986)

RHS Pests and Diseases
Pippa Greenwood & Andrew Halstead
(Dorling Kindersley 2007)

Tropical Planting and Gardening
H.F. MacMillan
(Malayan Nature Society 1991)

The Vegetable Garden Displayed
Joy Larkcom
(RHS 1992)

Vegetables
Roger Phillips & Martyn Rix
(Pan Macmillan 1993)

Vegetables of South East Asia
G.A.C. Herklots
(Allen & Unwin 1973)

The Yellow Book: NGS Gardens Open for Charity (Revised Edition)
Stephen Anderton, Tim Wonnacott & Zac Goldsmith
(The National Gardens Scheme 2008)

North American gardeners are given guidance through a system of zones, of which zone 0 is the Arctic and zone 11 the southernmost part of the continent. A plant may be hardy to zones 7 to 9, which means you can leave it outdoors all winter if you live in Texas, but not if you live in Manitoba. Both countries recently revised their zone systems — the U.S. in 1990, Canada in 2000 — to incorporate changes in climate and advances in data collection. The key to using the zone system is simple: know the minimum winter temperature of your area and check the hardiness rating of plants before purchasing them. For more details, American gardeners should go to www.usna.usda.gov/Hardzone/index.html and Canadians can visit http://sis.agr.gc.ca/cansis/nsdb/climate/hardiness/index.html.

Hardiness Zones and Average Minimum Winter Temperatue Range

Zone	Temperature (°F)	Examples of Cities in This Zone	Temperature (°C)
1	below −50°F	Fairbanks, Alaska; Resolute, Nunavut	below −46°C
2	−50°F to −40°F	Pinecreek, Minnesota; Lloydminster, Alberta	−46°C to −40°C
3	−40°F to −30°F	Tomahawk, Wisconsin; Sidney, Montana; Dauphin, Manitoba	−40°C to 34°C
4	−30°F to −20°F	Minneapolis/St. Paul, Minnesota; Sherbrooke, Quebec	−34°C to −29°C
5	−20°F to −10°F	Mansfield, Pennsylvania; Sackville, New Brunswick	−29°C to −23°C
6	−10°F to 0°F	St. Louis, Missouri; Lebanon, Pennsylvania; Windsor, Ontario	−23°C to −18°C
7	0°F to 10°F	Little Rock, Arkansas; Griffin, Georgia, Victoria, BC	−18°C to −12°C
8	10°F to 20°F	Dallas, Texas; Gainesville, Florida; Chilliwack, BC	−12°C to −7°C
9	20°F to 30°F	Houston, Texas; Fort Pierce, Florida; Brownsville, Texas	−7°C to −1°C
10	30°F to 40°F	Miami, Florida; Victorville, California; Coral Gables, Florida	−1°C to 4°C
11	above 40°F	Honolulu, Hawaii; Mazatlan, Mexico	above 4°C

Aaron's rod, 402, 404
Abelmoschus esculentus, 120
Aberia gardneri, 568
Abraham, Isaac and Jacob, 412, 438
Absinthe, 242
Acca
  guavas, 560
Achillea ageratum, 212, 213
Achillea millefolium, 214, 623, 624
Achras sapota, 565
Aconitum napellus, 216, 217
Actinidia chinensis/deliciosa, 540, 541
Adam and Eve, 377
Adam's needle, 571
African bulbine, 254, 255
Agaricus arvensis, 14
Agaricus bisporus, 12, 13
Agaricus campestris, 14
Agastache foeniculum, 218, 219
Ajuga, 226
Ajuga reptans, 226
Alchemilla, 220, 221
Alecost
  container growing, 416
  culinary use, 416
  cultivation, 416
  medicinal use, 416
  pests and diseases, 416
  varieties, 416
Alfalfa, 148, 149
All good, 276
All heal, 376, 432
Allecampane, 314
Allium cepa, 18–23
Allium cepa Proliferum Group, 222
Allium fistulosum, 222
Allium porrum, 24–25
Allium sativum, 26–27
Allium schoenoprasum, 224–225
Allspice, 569
Almonds
  companion planting, 597
  culinary uses, 597
  cultivation, 596–597
  growing under glass or in containers, 597
  pests and diseases, 597
  sirop d'Orgeat milkshake, 597
  varieties, 596
Aloe vera, 227
Aloysia triphylla, 228
Alpinia galanga, 136–137
Althaea officinalis, 229
Althea, 229
Amber, 311
Amelanchier canadensis, 574
American cress, 42
American lilac, 273

American poke, 370
Anacardium occidentale, 608
Ananas comosus, 552, 553
Anchovies
  cress, anchovy and barley salad, 42
Anethum graveolens, 230, 231
Angelica
  candied, 233
  container growing, 233
  culinary use, 233
  cultivation, 232, 233
  medicinal use, 233
  pests and diseases, 233
  varieties, 232
Angelica archangelica, 232
Anise hyssop
  container growing, 219
  culinary use, 219
  cultivation, 219
  pests and diseases, 219
  varieties, 218
Anise, 346
Annona, 563
Anthriscus cerefolium, 234–235
Antiseptic vinegar, 243
Aphids, 659
Apium graveolens var. *dulce*, 30–33
Apium graveolens var. *rapaceum*, 34, 35
Apples
  baked strawberry apples, 489
  Bob's blackberry and apple pancake supreme, 511
  cider, 452–453
  crab, 452–453
  culinary, 446–451
  dessert, 446–451
Apricots
  apricot and horseradish sauce 39
  apricot sponge, 469
  companion planting, 469
  culinary uses, 469
  cultivation, 468–469
  growing under glass and in containers, 468
  pests and diseases, 468–469
  varieties, 468
Arachis hypogaea, 612
Araucaria araucana, 613
Arbute, 579
Arbutus unedo, 579
Armoracia rusticana, 38, 221
Arnica, 240
Aronia melanocarpa, 502, 503
Artemisia abrotanum, 241
Artemisia absinthium, 242, 243
Artemisia dracunculus, 244, 245
Artocarpus, 561
Arvi leaves, 88
Ascorbic acid, plant containing

bitter melon, 150
Asiatic yam, 110
Asimina, 559
Asparagus
  companion planting, 41
  culinary use, 41
  cultivation, 40, 41
  medicinal use, 41
  pests and diseases, 41
  steamed asparagus, 41
  varieties, 40
Asparagus lettuce, 132
Asparagus officinalis, 40, 41
Asparagus pea, 196
Asperula odorata, 301
Atriplex hortensis, 246, 247
Aubergine, 184
Autumn olive, 593
Averrhoa carambola, 564
Avocado
  avocado dip 557
  avocado with horseradish cream, 239
  culinary uses, 557
  cultivation, 557
  growing under glass and in containers, 557
  pests and diseases, 557
  varieties, 557
Azarole
  culinary uses, 587
  cultivation, 587, 586
  varieties, 586

Babies' shoes, 226
Baby maize, 206
Baby's rattle, 226
Baccaurea dulcis, 568
Bachelor's buttons, 419
Bacon
  custard marrow with bacon and cheese, 100
  dandelion and bacon salad, 421
  oca and bacon, 152
Bactris, 556
Baked bean, 164
Balkali havuci, 109
Ballota nigra, 248
Balm, 335
Balm mint, 335
Balm of Gilead
  container growing, 269
  cultivation, 269
  medicinal use, 269
  pests and diseases, 269
  varieties, 269
Balsam pear, 150
Bananas
  banana custard pie, 555
  culinary uses, 555

cultivation, 555
  growing under glass and in containers, 555
  pests and diseases, 555
  varieties, 554
Barbecued corn on the cob, 209
Barbarea verna, 42
Barberries, 576
Barberry figs, 547
Barley
  cress, anchovy and barley salad, 42
Basil
  basil oil, 672
  container growing, 352
  culinary use, 353
  cultivation, 352
  medicinal use, 352
  pesto sauce, 353
  pests and diseases, 352
  varieties, 350, 351
Batavian endive, 82
Bay
  container growing, 323
  culinary use, 323
  cultivation, 322, 323
  medicinal use, 323
  pests and diseases, 323
  varieties, 322
Beach plums, 590, 591
Bee balm, 335, 342
Beech, 613
Beerbind, 330
Beet
  companion planting, 47
  culinary use, 47
  cultivation, 46
  medicinal use, 47
  pests and diseases, 47
  spicy beet salad, 47
  varieties, 45
Beetroot, 45
Belene, 310
Belgian endive, 84
Bell pepper
  companion planting, 77
  culinary use, 78
  cultivation, 77
  fennel sautéed with peas and red bell peppers, 115
  medicinal use, 77
  Mrs Krause's pepper hash, 78
  pests and diseases, 77
  Puy lentils with roasted red bell peppers and goat's cheese, 139
  varieties, 76
  warm red and yellow bell pepper salad, 83
Bellis perennis 249
Berberis vulgaris, 576

Bergamot
  container growing, 343
  culinary use, 343
  cultivation, 343
  medicinal use, 343
  pests and diseases, 343
  pork fillets with bergamot
    sauce, 343
  varieties, 342
Bertholletia excelsa, 611
Beta carotene, plants containing
  asparagus, 40
  bell pepper and chilli, 76
  broccoli, 64
  Brussels sprout, 60
  cabbage, 57
  carrots, 106
  cucumber, 93
  endive, 82
  Fennel, 114
  green bean, 164
  Hamburg parsley, 157
  kale, 52
  lamb's lettuce, 199
  land cress, 42
  leeks, 24
  lettuce, 126
  New Zealand spinach, 195
  pumpkin and squash, 96
  purslane, 172
  runner bean, 161
  spinach, 192
  sweet potato, 124
  Swiss chard, 43
  tomato, 140
  watercress 178
Beta vulgaris subsp. *cicla*, 43, 44
Beta vulgaris subsp. *vulgaris*, 45–46
Betony
  container growing, 407
  cultivation, 406, 407
  medicinal use, 407
  pests and diseases, 406
  varieties, 406
Bhindi, 120, 121
Bible leaf, 416
Bilberries, 492
Billy buttons, 332
Bindweed, 330
Bird cherries, 590, 591
Biscuits
  coconut biscuits, 610
  lavender biscuits, 327
Bissara, 203
Bitter buttons, 419
Bitter melon
  culinary use, 151
  cultivation, 150, 151
  medicinal use, 151
  pelecing peria, 151

pests and diseases, 151
Black elder, 392
Black horehound
  container growing, 248
  cultivation, 248
  medicinal use, 248
  varieties, 248
Black truffle, 15
Blackberried, 392
Blackberries
  Bob's blackberry and apple
    pancake supreme, 511
  companion planting, 510
  culinary uses, 511
  cultivation, 509, 510
  growing under glass and in
    containers, 509
  pests and diseases, 510
  varieties, 509
Black currants
  Bob's cunning black currant jam,
    501
  companion planting, 501
  culinary uses, 501
  cultivation, 500–501
  growing under glass and in
    containers, 501
  pests and diseases, 501
  varieties, 500
Blewit, 15
Blight, 660
Blind man's hand, 226
Bloody butcher, 273
Blowball, 420
Blue balm, 335, 342
Blue curls, 376
Blue giant hyssop, 218
Blue jacket, 371
Blue pimpernel, 399
Blue rocket, 216
Blue skullcap, 399
Blue-stalk, 15
Blueberries
  blueberry grunt, 493
  companion planting, 493
  culinary uses, 493
  cultivation, 493
  growing under glass and in
    containers, 493
  pests and diseases, 493
  varieties, 492
Blueweed, 292
Boletus edulis, 14
Boneset, 412
Boon-tree, 392
Borage
  companion planting, 251
  container growing, 251
  cosmetic use, 251
  culinary use, 251

cultivation, 250
medicinal use, 521
pests and diseases, 250
varieties, 250
Borage tea, 521
Borago officinalis, 250, 251
Borassus flabelliter, 556
Borassus, 556
Borecole, 52
Botrytis, 660
Bottle brush, 259
Bottle gourd, 134
Boun-tree, 392
Bouncing Bess, 273
Bouncing Bet, 398
Bouncing Betsy, 273
Bouquet garni oil, 673
Box, 256
Boxwood
  container growing, 257
  cultivation, 257
  medicinal use, 257
  pests and diseases, 257
  varieties, 256
Boysenberries
  companion planting, 513
  culinary uses, 513
  cultivation, 512–513
  growing under glass and in
    containers, 513
  pests and diseases, 513
  varieties, 512
Brain fungus, 15
Braised chicory, 86
Braised lettuce, 131
Brambles
  companion planting, 510
  culinary uses, 511
  cultivation, 509, 510
  growing under glass and in
    containers, 509
  pests and diseases, 510
  varieties, 509
Brassica juncea 252
Brassica napus Napobrassica Group,
  50, 51
Brassica oleracea Acephela Group, 52,
  53
Brassica oleracea Botrytis Group, 54–56
Brassica oleracea Capitata Group, 57–59
Brassica oleracea Gemmifera Group,
  60–62
Brassica oleracea Gongylodes Group,
  63, 64
Brassica oleracea Italica Group, 65–67
Brassica rapa Pekinensis Group, 73–75
Brassica rapa Rapifera Group, 68, 69
Brazil nuts, 611
Brazilian plum, 569
Bread

olive bread, 487
Bread and cheese, 384
Breadfruit, 561
Bridewort, 299
Brinjal, 184
Broad bean, 201
Broccoli
  companion planting, 66
  culinary use, 67
  cultivation, 66
  penne with broccoli,
    mascarpone and dolcelatte, 67
  varieties, 65–66
Brown mustard 252–253
Brownwort, 376
Bruisewort, 398
Brussels sprout
  companion planting, 62
  culinary use, 62
  cultivation, 61–62
  pests and diseases, 62
  stir-fried sprouts, 62
  varieties, 60
Bugle, 226
Bugle weed, 226
Bugloss, 250
Bulbine frutescens 254–255
Bulgar wheat
  pumpkin kibbeh, 100
Bullace, 466, 467
Bullocks eye, 402
Bulls eye, 260
Bully trees, 565
Burrage, 250
Burvine, 434
Bushtree, 256
Butter
  chive butter, 225
  rose geranium butter, 362
Buxus sempervirens, 256, 257
Buying plants, 647

Cabbage
  colcannon, 59
  companion planting, 59
  culinary use, 59
  cultivation, 58
  czerwona kapusta, 59
  medicinal use, 58
  pests and diseases, 59
  varieties, 57
Cabbage caterpillars, 659
Cabbage root fly, 658
Cabbage whitefly, 660
Cacao, 571
Cakes
  apricot sponge, 469
  Black Forest gâteau, 479
  carrot and raisin cake, 109
  snowy mespilus sponge cakes,

574
Calabash
  culinary use, 135
  cultivation, 134–135
  medicinal use, 135
  pests and diseases, 135
  varieties, 134
Calabrese, 65
Calamint, 258
Calamintha, 258
Calcium, plants containing
  almonds, 542
  amaranth, 28
  burdock, 36
  horseradish, 38
  kale, 52
  land cress, 42
  mung bean, 159
Calendula
  container growing, 261
  culinary use, 261
  cultivation, 260, 261
  medicinal use, 261
  pests and diseases, 260, 261
  varieties, 260
  sweet calendula buns, 261
Calendula officinalis, 260
Calomeria amaranthoides, 259
Canary balm, 268
Cancer bush, 410–411
Cancer root, 370
Cane fruit, 579
Cankerwort, 420
Cantharellus cibarius, 14
Caper, 262–263
Capparis spinosa, 262–263
Capsicum, 76
Capsicum annuum, 76–78
Caraway
  caraway and cheese potatoes, 265
  container growing, 265
  culinary use, 265
  cultivation, 264, 265
  medicinal use, 265
  pests and diseases, 265
  varieties, 264
Carbohydrate, plants containing
  asparagus pea, 196
  corn, 206
  Jerusalem artichoke, 118
  lentil, 138
  mushrooms and edible fungi, 12
  pea, 169
  potato, 186
  sweet potato, 124
  yam, 110
Cardon, 101
Cardoon
  culinary use, 102
  cultivation, 101–102
  lamb tagine with cardoons, 102
  pests and diseases, 102
  varieties, 101
Carica, 559

Carissa grandiflora, 568
Carlina acaulis, 266
Carline, 266
Carob tree, 568
Carpenter's herb, 226, 376
Carpenter's weed, 214
Carpobrotus edulis, 593
Carrot root fly, 658
Carrots
  balkali havuci, 109
  carrot and raisin cake, 109
  companion planting, 108
  culinary use, 109
  cultivation, 107–108
  lovage and carrot, 329
  medicinal use, 108
  pests and diseases, 108
  varieties, 107
Carum carvi, 264–265
Carya species, 598–599
Cashews, 608
Cassava
  cassava chips, 147
  culinary use, 147
  cultivation, 146–147
  pests and diseases, 147
  varieties, 146
Cast the spear, 404
Castanea sativa, 604–605
Castanospermum australe, 613
Catha edulis, 267
Cat's tail, 254
Catnip
  companion planting, 349
  container growing, 349
  culinary use, 349
  cultivation, 348–349
  medicinal use, 349
  pests and diseases, 349
  varieties, 348
Catnep, 348
Catrup, 348
Catswart, 348
Caucasian wing-nut, 600
Cauliflower
  cauliflower soufflé, 56
  cauliflower with chillies and black mustard seeds, 56
  companion planting, 55
  culinary use, 56
  cultivation, 55
  medicinal use, 55
  pests and diseases, 55
  varieties, 54
Cauliflower mushroom, 15
Cedronella canariensis, 268–269
Celeriac
  companion planting, 35
  culinary use, 35
  cultivation, 34
  medicinal use, 35
  monkfish with celeriac, 35
  pests and diseases, 35
  varieties, 34
Celery

celery and zucchini with blue cheese dip, 33
  companion planting, 32
  culinary use, 33
  cultivation, 31, 32
  medicinal use, 32
  pests and diseases, 32
  varieties, 30
Celery cabbage, 73
Celery root, 34, 35
Celtuce, 132–133
Centaurea cyanus, 272
Centella asiatica, 270–271
Centranthus ruber, 273
Cep, 14
Ceratonia siliqua, 568
Ceylon gooseberry, 568
Chaenomeles japonica, 578
Chamaemelum nobile, 274–275
Chamomile
  companion planting, 275
  container growing, 275
  cosmetic use, 275
  cultivation, 274–275
  medicinal use, 275
  pests and diseases, 274
  varieties, 274
Chamomile tea, 275
Chanterelle, 14
Chariots drawn by doves, 216
Charity, 371
Chayote, 182
Checkerberry, 593
Cheese
  caraway and cheese potatoes, 365
  celery and zucchini with blue cheese dip, 33
  chicory with ham and cheese sauce, 86
  cucumber and cream cheese mousse, 95
  custard marrow with bacon and cheese, 100
  green bean, Roquefort and walnut salad, 166
  leek and ricotta pie, 25
  nasturtium cream cheese dip, 429
  penne with broccoli, mascarpone and dolcelatte, 67
  potato salad with goat's cheese dressing, 191
  Puy lentils with roasted red bell peppers and goat's cheese, 139
  salsify in ham with cheese sauce, 198
  sautéed eggplants with Mozzarella, 185
Cheese flower, 332
Cheesecake
  peach macaroon cheesecake, 473
Chenopodium bonus-henricus, 276
Cherimoyas, 563

Cherries
  cherry jam, 477
  ground, 526–527
  morello, 478–479
  pickled cherries, 477
  sweet, 476–477
Cherry plum, 466
Chervil
  container growing, 235
  culinary use, 235
  cultivation, 234
  fines herbes, 235
  medicinal use, 235
  pests and diseases, 234
  varieties, 234
Chewing gum, 565
Chicken
  Basque-style chicken, 313
  chicken salad with tarragon and grapes, 245
  chicken with English mace in foil, 213
Chicken of the woods, 15
Chickpea
  culinary use, 81
  cultivation, 80–81
  medicinal use, 81
  pests and diseases, 81
  puréed chickpeas, 81
  varieties, 80
Chicory
  braised chicory, 86
  chicory with ham and cheese sauce, 86
  companion planting, 85
  culinary use, 86
  cultivation, 84–85
  medicinal use, 85
  pests and diseases, 85
  varieties, 84
Chikkus, 565
Chile pine, 613
Chilli
  cauliflower with chillies and black mustard seeds, 56
  companion planting, 77
  culinary use, 78
  cultivation, 77
  medicinal use, 77
  Mrs Krause's pepper hash, 78
  pests and diseases, 77
  varieties, 78
Chinese artichoke, 194
Chinese cabbage
  companion planting, 75
  culinary use, 75
  cultivation, 74
  pests and diseases, 75
  sweet and sour Chinese cabbage, 75
  varieties, 74
Chinese date, 569
Chinese gooseberry, 540
Chinese keys, 137
Chinese leaves, 73

Chinese lettuce, 152
Chinese mushroom, 14
Chinese parsley, 280
Chives
  chive butter, 225
  companion planting, 225
  container growing, 225
  culinary use, 225
  cultivation, 225
  fines herbes, 368
  medicinal use, 225
  pests and diseases, 225
  varieties, 224
Chocolate
  Black Forest gâteau, 479
  chocolate mint mousse, 340
  stuffed date chocolates, 556
Chokeberries
  chokeberry preserve, 503
  companion planting, 503
  culinary uses, 503
  cultivation, 503
  growing under glass and in
    containers, 503
  pests and diseases, 503
  varieties, 502
Choko, 182
Chow Chow, 182
Christmas rose, 306–307
Christophine, 182
Chrysanthemum cinerariifolium, 417
Chrysanthemum parthenium, 418
Chrysophylum cainito, 568
Chufa, 612
Church bells, 412
Chutney
  American highbush chutney, 580
  Colonel Flowerdew's Bengal
    chutney, 576
  cilantro chutney, 673
  mango chutney, 558
  runner bean chutney, 163
Cicer arietinum, 80–81
Cichorium endivia, 82–83
Cichorium intybus, 84–85
Cider apples, 452–453
Cider pears
  companion planting, 459
  culinary uses, 459
  cultivation, 458, 459
  growing under glass and in
    containers, 458
  pests and diseases, 459
  pressless perry wine, 459
  varieties, 458
Cilantro
  container growing, 281
  cilantro chutney, 673
  culinary use, 282
  cultivation, 280–281
  medicinal use, 281
  mushrooms and cilantro, 282
  pests and diseases, 280
  varieties, 280
Citrullus lanatus/vulgaris, 532–533

Citrus fruit
  companion planting, 537
  culinary uses, 537
  cultivation, 535–536
  growing under glass and in
    containers, 536
  pests and diseases, 536
  varieties, 535
Civet fruit, 562
Clock, 420
Clock flower, 420
Clocks and watches, 420
Clove pink, 277
Cloves, 560
Clubroot, 659
Cobs
  companion planting, 603
  culinary uses, 603
  cultivation, 602–603
  growing under glass or in
    containers, 602
  pests and diseases, 603
  varieties, 602
Coccoloba uvifera, 568
Coccum, 370
Cochlearia armoracia, 238
Cocoa, 571
Coconuts, 610
Cocos nucifera, 610
Coffea arabica, 613
Coffee, 613
Colcannon, 59
Cold cure, 334
Colewort, 52
Collards, 52
Colocasia esculenta var.
  antiquorum, 87
Colocasia esculenta var.
  esculenta, 88–89
Comfrey
  container growing, 413
  culinary use, 413
  cultivation, 413
  liquid manure, use for, 413
  medicinal use, 413
  pests and diseases, 413
  varieties, 412
Common basil, 350
Common bean, 164
Common bugle, 226
Common bugloss, 250
Common evening primrose, 354
Common nettle, 430
Common parsley, 367
Common potato, 186
Common scab, 659
Containers
  advantages of, 642
  choosing, 642
  composts for, 642
  maintenance, 643
Convallaria majalis, 278–279
Coriandrum sativum, 280–281
Corn
  barbecued corn on the cob, 209

companion planting, 208
corn maque choux, 209
culinary use, 209
cultivation, 207, 208
medicinal use, 208
pests and diseases, 208
succotash, 209
varieties, 206, 207
Cornflower, 272
Corn on the cob, 206
Corn salad, 199
Cornelian cherry
  culinary uses, 585
  cultivation, 584
  varieties, 584
Cornus mas, 584
Corylus species, 602
Costmary, 416
Cough sweets, 334
Courgette, 96
Cowberries
  companion planting, 495
  culinary uses, 495
  cultivation, 494
  growing under glass and in
    containers, 495
  pests and diseases, 495
  varieties, 494
Coweslop, 373
Cowslip
  container growing, 373
  culinary use, 373
  cultivation, 373
  medicinal use, 373
  pests and diseases, 373
  varieties, 373
Crab apples
  companion planting, 453
  crab apple jelly, 453
  culinary uses, 453
  cultivation, 452 453
  growing under glass and in
    containers, 452
  hedge jelly, 587
  pests and diseases, 453
  varieties, 452
Crambe maritima, 90–91
Cranberries
  companion planting, 495
  cranberry jelly, 495
  culinary uses, 495
  cultivation, 494–495
  growing under glass and in
    containers, 495
  highbush, 580
  pests and diseases, 495
  varieties, 494
Crataegus azarolus, 586–587
Creeping bugle, 226
Cress, anchovy and barley salad,
  42
Crithmum maritimum, 92
Croatian Hamburg parsley soup,
  158
Crop rotation, 636

Crosne, 194
Cucumber
  companion planting, 85
  cucumber and cream cheese
    mousse, 95
  culinary use, 95
  cultivation, 94–95
  medicinal use, 95
  pests and diseases, 95
  varieties, 93
Cucumis melo, 528–531
Cucumis sativus, 93–95
Cucurbita maxima, 96–100
Cucurbita moschata, 96–100
Cucurbita pepo, 96–100
Culinary apples
  companion planting, 451
  container planting, 448
  culinary uses, 451
  cultivation, 448
  flying saucers, 451
  pests and diseases, 450
  varieties, 447–448
Culinary pears
  companion planting, 456
  container planting, 456
  culinary uses, 457
  cultivation, 455–456
  pear islands, 457
  pests and diseases, 456
  varieties, 454
Cure all, 335
Curried parsnip soup, 156
Curry plant, 304
Curry tree, 344–345
Custard apples, 563
Custard banana, 559
Cut finger, 432
Cutworms, 658
Cydonia oblonga, 460–461
Cydonia vulgaris, 460–461
Cynara cardunculus, 101–102
Cynara scolymus, 103–105
Cyperus esculentus, 612
Cyphomandra betacea, 549
Cyphomandra crassicaulis, 549
Czerwona kapusta, 59

Daisy, 249
Damask violet, 305
Dame's violet, 305
Damsons
  companion planting, 467
  culinary uses, 467
  cultivation, 467
  damson cheese, 467
  growing under glass and in
    containers, 467
  pests and diseases, 467
  varieties, 466
Dandelion
  culinary use, 421
  cultivation, 420–421
  dandelion and bacon salad, 421
  medicinal use, 421

pests and diseases, 420
varieties, 420
Dasheen
  culinary use, 89
  cultivation, 88–89
  palusima, 89
  pests and diseases, 89
  varieties, 88
Date palms, 556
Daucus carota complex *sativus*, 106–109
David's harp, 372
Dead men's bellows, 226
Deadmen's bells, 289
Dessert apples
  companion planting, 451
  culinary uses, 451
  cultivation, 448
  growing under glass, 448
  pests and diseases, 450
  varieties, 447–448
Dessert pears
  companion planting, 456
  culinary uses, 457
  cultivation, 455–456
  growing under glass, 455
  pear islands, 457
  pests and diseases, 456
  varieties, 454
Devil's eye, 310
Devil's leaf, 430
Devil's nettle, 214
Devil's plaything, 406, 430
Dhall, 80
Dhania, 280
Dhania pattar, 280
Dhania sabz, 280
Dianthus, 288
Digitalis 'American' foxglove, 289
Digitalis purpurea, 289
Dill
  container growing, 231
  culinary use, 231
  cultivation, 230–231
  gravlax, 231
  medicinal use, 231
  pests and diseases, 230
  varieties, 230
Dillseed, 230
Dillweed, 230
Dioscorea alata, 110–111
Diospyros kaki, 545
Dock, 314
Dog's clove, 398
Dogtree, 392
Doodhi, 134
Downy mildew, 660
Drop berry, 372
Dropsy plant, 335
Drumsticks, 394
Drying produce, 670–671
Dunny nettle, 248
Durians, 562
Durio zibethinus, 562

Dyes, 674–675

Early rose, 374
Easter rose, 374
Echinacea, 291–291
Echinacea, 291–291
Echium vulgare, 292
Eddoe, 87
Eggplant
  companion planting, 185
  culinary use, 185
  cultivation, 184, 185
  medicinal use, 185
  pests and diseases, 185
  sautéed eggplants with Mozzarella, 185
  varieties, 184
Eggs
  scrambled eggs with raw and cooked spinach, 193
  zucchini omelette, 100
Egyptian pea, 80
Elaeagnus umbellata, 593
Elderberry
  container growing, 393
  culinary use, 393
  cultivation, 393
  elderberry conserve, 393
  elderflower cordial, 393
  medicinal use, 393
  pests and diseases, 393
  varieties, 392
Elderberry conserve, 393
Elderflower cordial, 393
Elecampane
  container growing, 315
  culinary use, 315
  cultivation, 315
  medicinal use, 315
  pests and diseases, 315
  varieties, 315
Elephant's ear, 88
Elfdock, 314
Elfwort, 314
Ellhorne, 392
Enchanter's plant, 343
Endive
  companion planting, 83
  culinary use, 83
  cultivation, 82–83
  pests and diseases, 83
  varieties, 82
  warm red and yellow bell pepper salad, 83
English mace
  chicken with English mace in foil, 213
  container growing, 213
  culinary use, 213
  cultivation, 212
  pests and diseases, 212
  varieties, 212
English pea, 169
Enokitake, 13
Equisetum arvense, 295

Eriobotrya, 546
Eriocephalus africanus, 296–297
Escarole, 82
Essential fatty acids, plant containing
  purslane, 172
Estragon, 244
Eugenia caryophyllus, 569
European angelica, 232
European elder, 392
European lovage, 328
European pennyroyal, 341
European vervain, 434
Evening pride, 330
Evening primrose
  container growing, 355
  culinary use, 355
  cultivation, 354–35
  medicinal use, 355
  pests and diseases, 355
  varieties, 354
Evening star, 354

Fagus sylvatica, 613
Fair bells, 373
Fairy clock, 420
Fairy fingers, 289
Fairy gloves, 289
Fairy ring champignon, 15
Fairy trumpets, 330
Fairy's bells, 278
False salsify, 180
Farewell summer, 398, 404
Farmers clock, 420
Fat, plants containing
  avocado, 557
  brazils, 611
  cashews, 608
  macadamias, 609
Fava bean
  balkali havuci, 109
  bissara, 203
  fava beans with summer savory, 203
  companion planting, 203
  culinary use, 203
  cultivation, 201–202
  pests and diseases, 203
  varieties, 201
Featherfew, 418
Febrifuge, 418
Feijoas, 560
Fennel
  companion planting, 115
  culinary use, 115
  cultivation, 114–115
  fennel sautéed with peas and red bell peppers, 115
  fish bouquet garni, 368
  medicinal use, 115
  pests and diseases, 115
  varieties, 114
Fennel hyssop, 218
Fever plant, 354–355

Feverfew
  container growing, 418
  culinary use, 418
  cultivation, 418
  medicinal use, 418
  pests and diseases, 418
  varieties, 418
Fibre, plants containing
  asparagus pea, 196
  chickpea, 80
  corn, 206
  fava bean, 201
  lentil, 138
  okra, 120
  pea, 169
  soy bean, 116
Ficus carica, 482–483
Field balm, 348
Field mushroom, 14
Field pansy, 435
Field primrose, 354
Figs
  companion planting, 483
  culinary uses, 483
  cultivation, 482
  growing under glass and in containers, 483
  pests and diseases, 483
  savoury and sweet figs, 483
  varieties, 482
Filberts
  companion planting, 603
  culinary uses, 603
  cultivation, 602–603
  growing under glass or in containers, 602
  pests and diseases, 603
  varieties, 602
Filipendula, 299
Fines herbes, 368
Finocchio, 114
First rose, 374
Fish bouquet garni, 368
Flageolet, 164
Flammulina velutipes, 13
Floral vinegar, 673
Florence fennel, 114
Foeniculum vulgare var. *azoricum*, 106, 107
Folic acid, plants containing
  asparagus, 40
  beet, 45
  broccoli, 65
  Brussels sprout, 60
  Chinese cabbage, 73
  green bean, 164
  lamb's lettuce, 199
  mushrooms and edible fungi, 12
  New Zealand spinach, 195
  pumpkin and squash, 96
  purslane, 172
Foxglove
  container growing, 289
  cultivation, 289
  medicinal use, 289

pests and diseases, 289
varieties, 289
Fragaria hybrids, 486–491
Fragrant giant hyssop, 218
Fragrant green, 280
Freezing produce, 671
French artichoke, 103
French lavender, 396
Friar's cap, 216
Fruit
  definition, 443
  freezing, 671
  fruit salad soup, 523
  harvesting, 668
  jellying and jamming, 673
  juicing, 671
  orchard, 444–483
  shrub and flower garden, 572–593
  soft, bush and cane, 484–523
  storing, 669
  summerberry squash, 513
  tender, 524–549
  tropical, 549–571
  very wild, 593
Fruit garden
  aftercare, 635
  orchards, 630
  ornamental, 631
  planning, 628
  planting, 635
  preparation, 634–635
  pruning, 649
  site, 633
  soil, 633
  weeding, 654–655
Fuchsia, 581
Fuller's herb, 398
Fungi, edible
  culinary use, 17
  cultivation, 16
  medicinal use, 16
  pests and diseases, 16
  varieties, 13–15

Galangal languas, 136
Galangal soup, 137
Galega officinalis, 300
Galium odoratum, 301
Garbanzo, 80
Garcinia mangostana, 567
Garden angelica, 232
Garden balm, 335
Garden egg, 184
Garden heliotrope, 432
Garden nasturtium, 428
Garden parsley, 367
Garden pea, 169
Garlic
  beans with garlic and savory, 401
  companion planting, 27
  culinary use, 27
  cultivation, 26, 27
  medicinal use, 27
  pestou, 27

pests and diseases, 27
varieties, 26
Garlic sage, 423
Gaultheria procumbens, 593
Geraniums, scented
  container growing, 362
  culinary use, 362
  cultivation, 361
  geranium leaf sorbet, 362
  rose geranium butter, 362
  pests and diseases, 361
  rose geranium punch, 362
  varieties, 360–361
German elder, 392
Giant hyssop, 218
Giant puffball, 15
Gillyflower, 288
Ginger
  culinary use, 441
  cultivation, 440 441
  medicinal use, 441
  pests and diseases, 441
  varieties, 440
Ginkgo, 302
Ginkgo biloba, 302
Girasole, 118
Glasshouses, growing in, 652
Globe artichoke
  culinary use, 105
  cultivation, 103–104
  medicinal use, 104
  pests and diseases, 104
  risotto with artichokes, 105
  tart of artichoke bottoms, 105
  varieties, 103
Glossary, 682–683
Glycine max, 116
Glycine soja, 116
Glycyrrhiza glabra, 303
Goat's beard, 197
Goat's rue, 300
God's stinking tree, 392
Golden buttons, 419
Golden gram, 159
Goldenrod
  container growing, 405
  cultivation, 405
  medicinal use, 405
  pests and diseases, 405
  varieties, 404
Good King Harry, 276
Good King Henry
  container growing, 277
  culinary use, 277
  cultivation, 277
  pests and diseases, 277
  varieties, 276
Good neighbour, 276
Gooseberries
  companion planting, 499
  culinary uses, 499
  cultivation, 498–499
  gooseberry fool, 499
  growing under glass and in containers, 499

pests and diseases, 499
varieties, 498
Gotu kola, 270
Grace of God, 311
Grafting, 647
Gram, 80
Grape pears, 574
Grapes
  companion planting, 517, 519, 521, 523
  culinary uses, 517, 519, 521, 523
  cultivation, 517, 518, 519, 521, 522, 523
  grape jelly, 519
  growing under glass and in containers, 517, 519, 521, 522
  love nests, 517
  outside, grown, 522, 523
  pests and diseases, 517, 519, 521, 522
  succotash, 209
  varieties, 516, 518, 520, 522
  wine, for, 522, 523
Grass management, 655
Gravlax, 231
Greater galangal
  culinary use, 137
  cultivation, 136
  galangal soup, 137
  medicinal use, 137
  pests and diseases, 137
  uses of, 137
Greater yam, 110
Greek valerian, 371
Green artichoke, 103
Green bean
  companion planting, 165
  culinary use, 166
  cultivation, 165
  green bean, Roquefort and walnut salad, 166
  medicinal use, 165
  pests and diseases, 165
  succotash, 209
  varieties, 164
Green ginger, 242
Green gram, 159
Green sauce, 385
Greengages
  companion planting, 465
  culinary uses, 465
  cultivation, 465
  greengage jam, 465
  growing under glass and in containers, 465
  pests and diseases, 465
  varieties, 464
Ground cherry
  culinary uses, 526
  cultivation, 526
  growing under glass and in containers, 527
  pests and diseases, 527
  tippari jam, 527
  varieties, 526

Ground oak, 422
Ground-almond, 612
Groundnuts, 612
Grumolo, 82
Guavas, 560
Guillielma utilis, 556
Guinea squash, 184
Gumbo, 120, 121
Gypsy sage, 423

Hairy hound, 248
Ham
  chicory with ham and cheese sauce, 86
  pineapple-baked ham, 553
  salsify in ham with cheese sauce, 198
Hamburg parsley
  companion planting, 158
  Croatian Hamburg parsley soup, 158
  culinary use, 158
  cultivation, 157
  medicinal use, 158
  pests and diseases, 158
Haricot bean, 165
  beans with garlic and savory, 401
Haricot vert, 164
Harvesting, 668
Hawthorn
  culinary uses, 587
  cultivation, 587
  hedge jelly, 587
  varieties, 586
Hazelnuts
  companion planting, 603
  culinary uses, 603
  cultivation, 602, 603
  growing under glass or in containers, 502
  hazelnut and mushroom roast, 391
  hazelnut macaroons, 603
  pests and diseases, 603
  varieties, 602
Healing leaf, 402
Heartsease, 435
Hedge pink, 398
Helianthus tuberosus, 118, 119
Helichrysum italicum, 304
Helleborus niger, 306
Helmet flower, 399
Hen and chickens, 402
Hen pen, 310
Hen penny, 310
Henbane, 310
Henbell, 310
Hennyibone hennebane, 310
Herb dyes, 674, 675
Herb garden
  bath, 623
  conditions, 620
  cook's, 625
  designs, 622–627

first, 622
lawns, 621
medicinal, 627
paths, 621
planning, 620, 621
raised beds, 621
salad, 626
site, 620
style, 621
use of, 620
white, 624
Herb of Grace, 386
Herb of St John, 311
Herb oils, 672, 673
Herba the cross, 434
Herbal moth bag, 397
Herbal vinegars, 673
Herbygrass, 386
Hercules' woundwort, 376
Hesperis matronalis, 305
Hibiscus esculentus, 120, 121
Hickory nuts
  companion planting, 599
  culinary uses, 599
  cultivation, 598, 599
  growing under glass or in
    containers, 599
  pests and diseases, 599
  varieties, 598
High balm, 342
Highbush cranberries, 580
Hind heel, 419
Hippophae rhamnoides, 593
Hirneola auricula judae, 14
Hock heal, 376
Hog bean, 310
Holligold, 260
Holy herb, 434
Holy plant, 434
Honeybind, 330
Honeysuckle
  container growing, 331
  culinary use, 331
  cultivation, 331
  medicinal use, 331
  pests and diseases, 331
  varieties, 330
Hop vine, 308
Hopbind, 308
Hops
  container growing, 309
  culinary use, 309
  cultivation, 309
  medicinal use, 309
  pests and diseases, 309
  varieties, 308
Horehound, 334
Horse and hounds, 226
Horse bean, 201
Horse elder, 314
Horse heal, 314
Horse mushroom, 14
Horseradish
  avocado with horseradish cream, 239
  companion planting, 238

culinary use, 239
cultivation, 238
medicinal use, 239
pests and diseases, 238
pickled, 673
varieties, 238
Horsetail
  container growing, 295
  culinary use, 295
  cultivation, 295
  medicinal use, 295
  pests and diseases, 295
  varieties, 295
Hottentot fig, 593
Houseleek
  container growing, 403
  culinary use, 403
  cultivation, 403
  medicinal use, 403
  pests and diseases, 403
  varieties, 402
Hovenia dulcis, 569
Huckleberries
  companion planting, 493
  culinary uses, 493
  cultivation, 493
  growing under glass and in
    containers, 493
  pests and diseases, 493
  varieties, 492
Humea elegans, 259
Humulus lupulus, 308, 309
Hyoscyamus niger, 310
Hypericum perforatum, 311
Hypholoma capnoides, 14
Hyssop
  Basque-style chicken, 313
  companion planting, 313
  container growing, 313
  culinary use, 313
  cultivation, 312, 313
  medicinal use, 313
  pests and diseases, 313
  varieties, 312
Hyssopus officinalis, 312, 313

Ice cream
  pistachio ice cream, 607
Incense plant, 259
Indian corn, 206
Indian cress, 428
Indian poke, 370
Inula helenium, 314, 315
Iodine, plants containing
  globe artichoke, 103
  mung bean, 159
  samphire, 92
Ipomoea batatas, 124, 125
Iribia, 152
Iris
  container growing, 317
  culinary use, 317
  cultivation, 317
  medicinal use, 317

pests and diseases, 317
varieties, 316
Irish potato, 186
Irish vine, 330
Iron, plants containing
  alfafa, 148
  almonds, 596
  asparagus pea, 196
  bitter melon, 150
  broccoli, 65
  chickpea, 80
  endive, 82
  globe artichoke, 103
  Hamburg parsley, 157
  kale, 52
  land cress, 42
  lentil, 138
  mung bean, 159
  mushrooms and edible fungi, 12
  New Zealand spinach, 195
  okra, 120
  pea, 169
  plums, 462
  radish, 173
  runner bean, 161
  samphire, 92
  soy bean, 116
  spinach, 192
  strawberries, 488, 486
  Swiss chard, 43
  watermelon, 532

Jack behind the garden gate, 435
Jackfruit, 561
Jacob's ladder
  container growing, 371
  culinary use, 371
  cultivation, 371
  pests and diseases, 371
  Solomon's seal, 372
  varieties, 371
Jacob's walking stick, 371
Jams, jellies and conserves. *See also*
  Chutney
  Bob's cunning black currant jam,
    501
  camaranga or carambola jam, 564
  cherry jam, 477
  chokeberry preserve, 503
  crab apple jelly, 453
  cranberry jelly, 495
  damson cheese, 467
  elderberry conserve, 393
  fuchsia jelly, 581
  grape jelly, 519
  greengage jam, 465
  guava jelly, 560
  hedge jelly, 587
  Japonica jelly, 578
  Kitty Topping's raspberry
    conserve, 507
  loquat jam, 546
  mountain ash jelly, 589
  quince cheese, 461
  savoury herb jelly, 673

sweet jellies, 673
tippari jam, 527
Japanese artichoke, 194
Japanese medlars, 546
Japanese plums, 466, 467
Japanese quinces, 578
Japanese raisin tree, 569
Japanese wineberries
  companion planting, 515
  culinary uses, 515
  cultivation, 514, 515
  growing under glass and in
    containers, 514
  pests and diseases, 515
  varieties, 514
  wineberry ripple, 515
Japonica jelly, 578
Jerusalem artichoke
  artichoke soup, 119
  culinary use, 119
  cultivation, 118, 119
  medicinal use, 119
  pests and diseases, 119
  varieties, 118
Jerusalem cowslip, 377
Jerusalem sage, 369
Jew's ear, 14
Joe run by the Street, 398
Judas tree, 392
Juglans species, 600, 601
Jujube, 569
July campane, 314
Juneberries, 574
Juniper
  container growing, 321
  culinary use, 321
  cultivation, 321
  medicinal use, 321
  pests and diseases, 321
  pork chops marinated with
    juniper, 321
  varieties, 320
Juniperus communis, 320, 321
Jupiter's beard, 402
Jupiter's eye, 402
Jusquiamus, 310

Kaempferia galanga, 137
Kale
  companion planting, 53
  culinary use, 53
  cultivation, 52, 53
  pests and diseases, 53
  stir-fried kale, 53
  varieties, 52
Karela, 150
Keys of heaven, 373
Khat, 267
Kidney bean, 164
King stropharia, 13
King's cure-all, 354
Kiss me behind the garden gate,
  435
Kiss me love at the garden gate,
  435

Kiss me love, 435
Kiss me quick, 301, 435
Kiwi fruit
  companion planting, 541
  culinary uses, 541
  cultivation, 540, 541
  growing under glass and in
    containers, 541
  kiwi meringue pie, 541
  pests and diseases, 541
  shiso, mooli and kiwi fruit salad, 364
  varieties, 540
Knitback, 412
Knitbone, 412
Kohlrabi
  companion planting, 64
  culinary use, 64
  cultivation, 63, 64
  kohlrabi sautéed in butter, 64
  pests and diseases, 64
  varieties, 63
Korean mint, 219
Kumara, 124

Lactuca sativa, 126–131
Lactuca sativa var. augustana, 132–133
Lad's love, 241
Ladder to heaven, 278, 371
Ladies in the hay, 301
Lady Mary's tears, 377
Lady's fingers, 120, 121
Lady's lockets, 372
Lady's mantle
  container growing, 221
  culinary use, 221
  cultivation, 221
  medicinal use, 221
  pests and diseases, 221
  varieties, 220
Laetiporus sulphureus, 15
Lagenaria siceraria, 134, 135
Lamb
  honey-glazed lamb, 27
  lamb tagine with cardoons, 102
Lamb's lettuce
  companion planting, 192
  culinary use, 192
  cultivation, 199, 192
  lamb's lettuce and prawn salad,
    191
  medicinal use, 192
  pests and diseases, 192
  varieties, 192
Lamb's tongues, 191
Land cress, 42
Languas galanga, 136, 137
Langermannia gigantea, 15
Large cress, 428
Laurus nobilis, 322, 323
Lavandula, 224–327
Lavender
  container growing, 327
  culinary use, 327
  cultivation, 326
  lavender biscuits, 327

medicinal use, 327
pests and diseases, 326
varieties, 324–326
Lavender cotton
  container growing, 397
  culinary use, 397
  cultivation, 397
  medicinal use, 397
  pests and diseases, 397
  varieties, 396
Lavose, 328
Layering, 647
Leaf beet, 43
Leaf miners, 660
Leatherjackets, 658
Leeks
  companion planting, 24
  culinary use, 25
  cultivation, 24, 25
  leek and ricotta pie, 25
  pests and diseases, 25
  varieties, 24
Lemon balm
  container growing, 336
  culinary use, 336
  cultivation, 335, 336
  medicinal use, 336
  pests and diseases, 336
  varieties, 335
Lemon verbena, 228
Lemons
  companion planting, 537
  culinary uses, 537
  cultivation, 535, 536
  growing under glass and in
    containers, 536
  pests and diseases, 536
  varieties, 535
Lens culinaris, 138, 139
Lentil
  companion planting, 139
  culinary use, 139
  cultivation, 138, 139
  pests and diseases, 139
  Puy lentils with roasted red
    bell peppers and goat's cheese,
    139
  varieties, 138
Lentinula edodes, 13
Leopard's bane, 240
Lepista nuda, 15
Lettuce
  braised lettuce, 131
  companion planting, 129
  culinary use, 130
  cultivation, 127–129
  green sauce, 385
  medicinal use, 129
  pests and diseases, 129
  sorrel and lettuce soup, 385
  varieties, 126, 127
Levisticum officinale, 328, 329
Licorice, 303
Lily of the mountain, 372
Lily of the valley

container growing, 278
cultivation, 279
medicinal use, 279
pests and diseases, 279
varieties, 278
Limes, 535
Lincolnshire asparagus, 276
Lindens, 593
Linoleic acid, plants containing
  mushrooms and edible fungi, 12
Lion's mane, 13
Lions teeth, 420
Lionstooth, 420
Lippia citriodora, 228
Litchis, 566
Live for ever, 402
Liveche, 328
Loganberries
  companion planting, 513
  culinary uses, 513
  cultivation, 512, 513
  growing under glass and in
    containers, 513
  pests and diseases, 513
  varieties, 512
Lonicera, 330, 331
Loquats, 546
Louisiana yam, 124
Lousewort, 406
Lovage
  container growing, 328
  culinary use, 329
  cultivation, 328, 329
  lovage and carrot, 329
  lovage soup, 329
  medicinal use, 329
  pests and diseases, 328
  varieties, 328
  vegetable, as, 329
Love apple, 140
Love in idleness, 435
Love lies bleeding, 435
Love parsley, 328
Low balm, 342
Lungwort
  container growing, 377
  cultivation, 377
  medicinal use, 377
  pests and diseases, 377
  varieties, 377
Lycopersicon esculentum,
  140–145

Macadamia ternifolia, 609
Macadamias, 609
Mache, 199
Mad dog weed, 399
Magnesium, plants containing
  eddoe, 87
  plums, 462
  potato, 186
Mahonias, 576
Maize, 206
Mallow, 332
Mallow rock, 402

Malus domestica, 446–451
Malus pumila, 452, 453
Malva sylvestris, 332
Mangifera indica, 558
Mandragora spp., 333
Mandrake, 333
Mango, 558
Mangold, 45
Mangosteen, 567
Manilkara zapota, 565
Manihot esculenta, 146, 147
Manihot utilissima, 146, 147
Marasmius oreades, 15
Mare's tail, 295
Maribeum, 334
Marigold, 260
Marjolaine, 356
Marjoram
  container growing, 358
  culinary use, 358
  cultivation, 358
  history of, 356
  medicinal use, 358
  pests and diseases, 358
  varieties, 357
Marrow
  companion planting, 44
  culinary use, 100
  cultivation, 98–99
  custard marrow with bacon and
    cheese, 100
  medicinal use, 99
  pests and diseases, 99
  varieties, 97, 98
Marrubium vulgare, 334
Marsh malice, 229
Marsh-mallow, 229
Marybud, 260
Master of the wood, 301
Masur, 138
May bells, 278
May lily, 278
Mazbane, 216
Meadow queen, 299
Meadow-wort, 299
Meadowsweet
  container growing, 299
  culinary use, 299
  cultivation, 299
  medicinal use, 299
  pests and diseases, 299
  varieties, 299
Medicago sativa, 148
Medlar fudge, 577
Medlars, 577
Melissa, 335
Melissa officinalis, 335, 336
Melon
  companion planting, 530
  culinary uses, 531
  cultivation, 529, 530
  growing under glass and in
    containers, 529
  melon sundae, 531
  pests and diseases, 530

varieties, 529
Mentha, 337–340
Mentha pulegium, 341
Mercury, 276
Meringues
  kiwi meringue pie, 541
  love nests, 571
Mesh-mellice, 229
Mespilus germanica, 577
Middle comfrey, 226
Millefoil, 214
Mimusops elengi, 569
Mint
  chocolate mint mousse, 340
  companion planting, 339
  container growing, 339
  culinary use, 340
  cultivation, 339
  medicinal use, 340
  mint sauce supreme, 497
  pests and diseases, 339
  varieties, 337–339
Mint bush, 375
Momordica charantia, 150, 151
Momordica, 150
Monarda, 342, 343
Monkey head, 13
Monkey puzzle, 592
Monkey's face, 435
Monkfish with celeriac, 35
Monkshood
  container growing, 217
  cultivation, 217
  medicinal use, 217
  pests and diseases, 217
  varieties, 216
Monstera deliciosa, 548
Morchella esculenta, 15
Morel, 15
Moreton Bay chestnut, 613
Mortification root, 229
Morus alba, 480, 481
Morus nigra, 480, 481
Moths moonflower, 354
Mountain arnica, 240
Mountain balm, 342
Mountain daisy, 240
Mountain mint, 356, 339
Mountain sage, 423
Mountain tobacco, 240
Mrs Krause's pepper hash, 78
Muffins
  onion and walnut muffins, 21
Mulberries
  companion planting, 481
  culinary uses, 481
  cultivation, 481
  growing under glass and in
    containers, 481
  mulberry no fool, 481
  pests and diseases, 481
  varieties, 481
Mulching, 651
Mung bean
  culinary use, 160

cultivation, 159, 160
medicinal use, 160
pests and diseases, 160
stir-fried mung beans, 160
varieties, 159
Murraya Koenigii, 344, 345
Musa species, 554, 555
Mushrooms
  culinary use, 17
  cultivation, 16
  grilled shiitake mushrooms, 17
  hazelnut and mushroom roast,
    391
  medicinal use, 16
  mushroom soup, 17
  mushrooms and cilantro, 282
  mushrooms mélange, 17
  nature of, 12
  pests and diseases, 16
  species, 13–15
Mustard seeds
  cauliflower with chillies and
    black mustard seeds, 56
Mustard greens, 48
Myristica fragrans, 613
Myrrh, 346
Myrrhis odorata, 346, 347
Myrtle
  container growing, 575
  culinary use, 575
  cultivation, 575
  medicinal use, 575
  pests and diseases, 575
  varieties, 575
Myrtus communis, 575

Nameko, 13, 16
Naseberries, 565
Nasturtium
  companion planting, 429
  container growing, 429
  culinary use, 429
  cultivation, 429
  medicinal use, 429
  nasturtium cream cheese dip,
    429
  pests and diseases, 429
  varieties, 428
Nectarines
  companion planting, 475
  culinary uses, 475
  cultivation, 474, 475
  growing under glass and in
    containers, 474
  nectarine melba, 475
  pests and diseases, 475
  varieties, 474
Neeps, 51
Nelson's bugle, 226
Nematodes, 685
Nematoloma capnoides, 14
Nepeta, 348, 349
Nephelium chinensis/litchi, 566
Nephelium lappaceum, 566
Nettle

cosmetic use, 431
culinary use, 431
cultivation, 431
medicinal use, 431
nettle rinse and conditioner,
  431
nettle soup, 431
pests and diseases, 431
varieties, 430
New mowed hay, 301
New Zealand spinach
  companion planting, 195
  culinary use, 195
  cultivation, 195
  pests and diseases, 195
New Zealand yam, 152
Niacin, plants containing
  melons, 528
  mushrooms and edible fungi, 12
  nectarines, 474
  peaches, 470
  raspberries, 504
Night willowherb, 354
Noble yarrow, 214
Northern pawpaw, 559
Nosebleed, 214
Nutmeg, 513
Nuts, 594–613

Oca, 152
Ocimum basilicum, 350–353
Oenothera, 354, 355
Oil, plants containing
  cobs, 602
  coconuts, 610
  filberts, 602
  groundnuts, 612
  hazelnuts, 602
  hickory nuts, 598
  olives, 538
  peanuts, 612
  pecan nuts, 598
  pistachios, 606
  Spanish chestnuts, 604
  sweet chestnuts, 604
  walnuts, 600
Okra
  companion planting, 121
  culinary use, 121
  cultivation, 120, 121
  medicinal use, 121
  pests and diseases, 121
  varieties, 120
Old man, 241
Old man's clock, 420
Old man's pepper, 394
Old woman's night-cap, 216
Olea europaea, 538, 539
Olives
  companion planting, 539
  culinary uses, 539
  cultivation, 538, 539
  growing under glass and in
    containers, 538
  olive bread, 539

pests and diseases, 539
varieties, 538
One clock, 420
Onion
  companion planting, 20
  culinary use, 21
  cultivation, 19, 20
  medicinal use, 20
  onion and walnut muffins, 21
  onion tart, 21
  varieties, 18, 19
  See also, Tree onion, Welsh onion
Opuntia ficus indica/dillenii, 547
Orach
  container growing, 247
  culinary use, 247
  cultivation, 246
  medicinal use, 247
  pests and diseases, 247
  red orach soup, 247
  varieties, 246
Oranges
  companion planting, 537
  culinary uses, 537
  cultivation, 535, 536
  growing under glass and in
    containers, 536
  orange sorbet, 537
  pests and diseases, 536
  varieties, 535
Orchards, 630
Oregano
  container growing, 358
  culinary use, 358
  cultivation, 358
  history of, 356
  medicinal use, 358
  pests and diseases, 358
  red mullet with tomatoes and
    oregano, 358
  varieties, 359
Oregon grapes, 576
Origan, 356
Origanum, 356–358
Oswego Tea, 342
Our Lady's tears, 278
Oxalis tuberosa, 152
Oyster mushroom, 13
Oyster plant, 197

Paddy straw, 14
Padi-straw, 14
Pak chee, 280
Palmyra palm, 556
Palsywort, 373
Palusima, 89
Pancake plant, 332
Papain, plant containing
  papayas, 559
Papaver, 359
Papaya, 559
Parsley
  container growing, 368
  culinary use, 368

cultivation, 367, 368
fines herbes, 368
fish bouquet garni, 368
medicinal use, 368
pests and diseases, 368
varieties, 367
Parsley fern, 419
Parsley root, 157
Parsnip
companion planting, 156
culinary use, 156
cultivation, 155, 156
curried parsnip soup, 156
medicinal use, 156
pests and diseases, 156
purée of parsnips, 156
varieties, 154
Passiflora, 542, 543
Passion fruit
culinary uses, 543
cultivation, 542, 543
growing under glass and in
containers, 543
pests and diseases, 543
varieties, 542
Pasta
pasta and mangetout salad, 171
penne with broccoli, mascarpone
and dolcelatte, 67
Pastinaca sativa, 154–156
Paths, 621
Papayas, 559
Pe Tsai, 73
Pea
companion planting, 171
culinary use, 171
cultivation, 170, 171
fennel sautéed with peas and
red bell peppers, 115
medicinal use, 171
pasta and mangetout salad, 171
pests and diseases, 171
varieties, 169
Pea aubergine, 184
Pea thrips, 660
Peaches
companion planting, 472
culinary uses, 473
cultivation, 471, 472
growing under glass and in
containers, 471
peach macaroon cheesecake,
473
pests and diseases, 472
varieties, 471
Peanuts, 612
Pears
culinary, 454–457
dessert, 454–457
grape, 574
perry, 458, 459
sweet, 574
Pecan nuts
culinary uses, 599
cultivation, 598, 599

growing under glass or in
containers, 598
pecan pie, 599
pests and diseases, 599
varieties, 598
Pectin, plants containing
rowan, 588
service berries, 588
whitebeam, 588
Pee in the bed, 420
Peking cabbage, 73
Pelargonium, 360–362
Pelecing peria, 151
Penny bun, 14
Pennyroyal
container growing, 341
culinary use, 341
cultivation, 341
medicinal use, 341
pests and diseases, 341
varieties, 341
Peppers, 76
Percinnammons, 545
Perigord truffle, 15
Perilla frutescens, 363
Persea americana, 557
Persicaria odorata, 365
Persimmons, 545
Pesto sauce, 353
Pestou, 27
Pests and diseases
air-borne diseases, 660
air-borne pests, 695, 660
aphids, 659
blight, 660
botrytis, 660
cabbage caterpillars, 659
cabbage root fly, 658
cabbage whitefly, 660
carrot root fly, 658
clubroot, 659
common scab, 659
control of, 657–658
cutworms, 658
downy mildew, 660
leaf miners, 660
leatherjackets, 658
nematodes, 658
pea thrips, 660
potato cyst eelworm, 658
powdery mildew, 660
preventing problems from, 656–657
red spider mite, 661
root rot, 659
rust, 660
slugs, 659
soil-borne diseases, 659
soil-borne pests, 658
stem and bulb eelworm, 658
stem rot, 659
under cover, 661
vine weevils, 660
white rot, 659
wireworms, 659
Petroselinum, 367, 368

Petroselinum crispum var.
tuberosum, 157, 159
Pewter wort, 295
Phaseolus aureus, 159
Phaseolus coccineus, 161–163
Phaseolus vulgaris, 164–166
Phlomis fruticosa, 369
Phoenix dactylifera, 556
Pholiota nameko, 13
Phosphorus, plants containing
almonds, 596
chickpea, 80
Photinia japonica, 546
Physalis species, 526, 527
Phytolacca americana, 370
Pieplant, 176
Pierardia motleyana, 568
Pigeon berry, 370
Pigeon's grass, 434
Pignons, 592
Pimenta dioica, 569
Pimento, 76, 569
Pine kernels, 592
Pineapples
companion planting, 553
culinary uses, 553
cultivation, 552, 553
growing under glass and in
containers, 552
pests and diseases, 553
pineapple-baked ham, 553
varieties, 552
Pinks
container growing, 288
culinary use, 288
cultivation, 288
medicinal use, 288
pests and diseases, 288
varieties, 288
Pinocchi, 592
Pinon truffle salad, 592
Pinons, 592
Pinus pinea, 592
Piper nigrum, 610
Piss-a-beds, 420
Pissaladière, 223
Pistachios
culinary uses, 607
cultivation, 606
growing under glass or in
containers, 607
pests and diseases, 607
pistachio ice cream, 607
varieties, 606
Pistacia vera, 606, 607
Pisum sativum, 169–171
Plantain
salad made with three wild
herbs, 215
Planting out, 548
Pleurotus, 13
Plums
companion planting, 463
culinary uses, 463
cultivation, 462, 463

growing under glass and in
containers, 462
pests and diseases, 463
prunes in semolina, 463
varieties, 462
Poisoned tobacco, 310
Poke, 370
Poke root, 370
Polemonium caeruleum, 371
Polygonatum, 372
Polyporus sulphureus, 15
Pomegranates, 544
Poor man's pepper, 394
Poppy, 359
Pork
pork chops marinated with
juniper, 321
pork fillets with bergamot
sauce, 343
Portulaca oleracea subsp. *sativa*, 172
Pot marigold, 260
Potassium, plants containing
apricots, 468
asparagus, 40
beet, 45
Brussels sprout, 60
cardoon, 101
celeriac, 34
celery, 30
celtuce, 132
chickpea, 80
chicory, 84
Chinese artichoke, 194
cucumber, 93
eddoe, 87
endive, 82
fava bean, 201
Fennel, 114
green bean, 164
leeks, 24
melons, 528
mung bean, 159
mushrooms and edible fungi, 12
nectarines, 474
okra, 120
peaches, 470
pears, 454
potato, 186
soy bean, 116
sweet potato, 124
Swiss chard, 43
Potato
caraway and cheese potatoes,
265
colcannon, 59
companion planting, 189
culinary use, 191
cultivation, 188, 189
history of, 186
mashed potato with olive oil,
191
medicinal use, 190
pests and diseases, 190
potato salad with goat's cheese
dressing, 191

rösti, 191
tzimmes, 125
varieties, 186–188
Potato cyst eelworm, 658
Potiron, 96
Powdery mildew, 660
Prawns
lamb's lettuce and prawn salad, 200
Prickly pears, 547
Priests crown, 420
Primrose
container growing, 374
culinary use, 374
cultivation, 374
medicinal use, 374
pests and diseases, 374
varieties, 374
Primrose tree, 354
Primula veris, 373
Primula vulgaris, 374
Propagation
cuttings, 646
grafting, 645
hardening off, 646
layering, 645
seed, 644
sowing, 644–645
Prostanthera, 375
Protected cropping, 653
Protein, plants containing
alfalfa, 148
almonds, 596
asparagus pea, 196
brazils, 611
calabash, 134
cashews, 608
cassava, 146
chickpea, 80
corn, 205
groundnuts, 612
lentil, 138
oca, 152
pea, 169
peanuts, 612
radish, 173
soy bean, 116
Prunella vulgaris, 376
Prunes in semolina, 463
Pruning, 649
Prunus armeniaca, 468, 469
Prunus avium, 476, 477
Prunus cerasus, 478, 479
Prunus domestica, 462, 463
Prunus dulcis/amygdalus, 596, 597
Prunus italica, 464, 465
Prunus persica
nectarines, 474, 475
peaches, 470–473
Psidium, 560
Pterocarya fraxinifolia, 600
Pudding grass, 641
Puffball, 420
Pulmonaria officinalis, 377
Pumpkin
companion planting, 99

culinary use, 100
cultivation, 98–99
meaning, 96
medicinal use, 99
pests and diseases, 99
pumpkin kibbeh, 100
varieties, 97, 98
Punica granatum, 544
Purple betony, 406
Purslane, 172
Puy lentils with roasted red
bell peppers and goat's cheese, 139
Pyrethrum, 417
Pyrus communis, 454–457

Queensland nuts, 609
Quince
companion planting, 461
culinary uses, 461
cultivation, 460, 461
growing under glass and in
containers, 461
quince cheese, 461
varieties, 460
Japanese quinces, 578

Radicchio, 84
Radish
culinary use, 175
cultivation, 174
medicinal use, 174
pests and diseases, 174
radish and scallop soup, 175
varieties, 173
Raisins
carrot and raisin cake, 109
Rambeh/rambei, 568
Rambutans, 566
Raphanus sativus, 173–175
Raspberries
companion planting, 507
culinary uses, 507
cultivation, 505–507
growing under glass and in
containers, 505–506
Kitty Topping's raspberry
conserve, 507
pests and diseases, 506
varieties, 505
Red ink plant, 370
Red mullet with tomatoes and
oregano, 358
Red spider mite, 661
Red valerian, 273
Redcurrants
companion planting, 497
culinary uses, 497
cultivation, 496
growing under glass and in
containers, 497
pests and diseases, 496
varieties, 496
Rheum x hybridum, 176, 177
Rhubarb
companion planting, 177

culinary use, 177
cultivation, 176, 177
medicinal use, 177
pests and diseases, 177
preserved rhubarb, 177
rhubarb sorbet, 177
stewed, 233
varieties, 176
Rhus glabra, 502
Ribes grossularia, 498, 499
Ribes nigrum, 500, 501
Ribes sativum, 496, 497
Riboflavin, plants containing
nectarines, 474
pears, 454
raspberries, 504
sweet cherries, 476
Rice
risotto with artichokes, 105
Rice flower, 601
Roast peanuts, 612
Rock parsley, 367
Rock samphire, 92
Roman plant, 346
Root of the Holy Ghost, 232
Root rot, 659
Rorippa nasturtium-aquaticum,
178, 179
Rosa, 582, 583
Rose hips
companion planting, 583
culinary uses, 583
cultivation, 582, 583
pests and diseases, 583
rose hip tart, 583
varieties, 582
Rosemary
container growing, 382
culinary use, 383
cultivation, 382
hedges, 382
medicinal use, 383
pests and diseases, 382
varieties, 380, 381
vegetarian goulash, 383
Rosmarinus, 380–383
Rösti, 191
Rowan
culinary uses, 589
cultivation, 588
mountain ash jelly, 589
varieties, 588
Rubus fruticosus, 508–811
Rubus idaeus, 504–507
Rue
container growing, 387
culinary use, 387
cultivation, 387
medicinal use, 387
pests and diseases, 387
varieties, 386
Rumex, 384, 385
Runner bean
companion planting, 163
culinary use, 163

cultivation, 162
pests and diseases, 163
runner bean chutney, 163
varieties, 162
Rust, 660
Ruta graveolens, 386, 387
Rutabaga
companion planting, 51
culinary use, 51
cultivation, 50, 51
medicinal use, 51
neeps, 51
pests and diseases, 51
varieties, 50

Sage
companion planting, 390
container growing, 390
culinary use, 391
cultivation, 389
hazelnut and mushroom roast,
391
medicinal use, 390
pests and diseases, 389
varieties, 388, 389
Salad
chicken salad with tarragon and
grapes, 245
cress, anchovy and barley
salad, 42
dandelion and bacon salad, 421
green bean, Roquefort and
walnut salad, 166
lamb's lettuce and prawn salad,
200
pasta and mangetout salad, 171
pinon truffle salad, 592
potato salad with goat's cheese
dressing, 191
purslane salad, 172
salad made with three wild
herbs, 215
spicy beet salad, 47
warm red and yellow bell pepper
salad, 83
yellow yam salad, 111
Salad burnet
container growing, 395
culinary use, 395
cultivation, 394, 395
medicinal use, 395
pests and diseases, 394
varieties, 394
Salmon
gravlax, 231
salmon with watercress sauce,
179
Salsify
companion planting, 198
culinary use, 198
cultivation, 197, 198
medicinal use, 198
pests and diseases, 198
salsify in batter, 198
salsify in ham with cheese

sauce, 198
varieties, 197
Salvia, 388–391
Sambucus, 392, 393
Samphire, 92
Sanguisorba minor, 394, 395
Santolina, 396, 397
Sapodillas, 565
Saponaria officinalis, 398
Sapota, 565
Saracen's root, 412
Satureja, 400, 401
Savory
  beans with garlic and savory, 401
  fava beans with summer savory, 203
  container growing, 401
  culinary use, 401
  cultivation, 400, 401
  medicinal use, 401
  pests and diseases, 400
  varieties, 400
Savoury herb jelly, 673
Scabish, 354
Scabwort, 314
Scallops
  radish and scallop soup, 175
Scarlet runner, 161
Scarlet sumac, 502
Score tree, 392
Scores, 392
Scorzonera
  companion planting, 181
  culinary use, 181
  cultivation, 180, 181
  medicinal use, 181
  pests and diseases, 191
  sautéed scorzonera 181
  varieties, 180
Scorzonera hispanica, 180, 181
Scurvish, 354
Scutellaria, 399
Sea buckthorn, 593
Sea parsley, 328
Sea samphire, 92
Seagrape, 568
Seakale
  culinary use, 91
  cultivation, 90, 91
  pests and diseases, 91
  seakale gratinée, 91
  varieties, 90
Seakale beet, 43
Seal root, 372
Sealwort, 372
Sechium edule, 182
Seed vinegar, 673
Seeds, 644, 645
Self heal, 376
Sempervivum tectorum, 402
Service berries
  culinary uses, 589
  cultivation, 588
  varieties, 588
Set all, 432

Shads, 574
Shallots
  companion planting, 23
  culinary use, 23
  cultivation, 22, 23
  varieties, 22
Shampoo
  soapwort, 398
Shave grass, 295
Shiitake, 13
  grilled shitake mushrooms, 17
Shiso, 363
Siamese ginger, 136
Silver beet, 43
Silver chard, 43
Simpler's joy, 434
Sirop d'Orgeat milkshake, 597
Skullcap, 399
Sloes
  culinary uses, 591
  cultivation, 591
  sloe gin, 591
  varieties, 590
Slugs, 659
Smallage, 236
Smilacina racemosa, 593
Snake flower, 254
Snakeflower, 292
Snowy mespilus, 574
Soaproot, 398
Soapwort, 398
Sodium, plant containing
  Swiss chard, 43
Soil fertility, 650
Solanum melongena, 184, 185
Solanum tuberosum, 186–191
Soldier's woundwort, 214
Solidago virgaurea, 404, 405
Solomon's seal
  container growing, 372
  cultivation, 372
  medicinal use, 372
  pests and diseases, 372
  varieties, 372
Sorbet
  geranium leaf sorbet, 362
  orange sorbet, 537
  rhubarb sorbet, 177
  sorbet sorbet, 585
  sour sop sorbet, 563
Sorbet (cornelian cherry), 584, 585
Sorbus aucuparia, 588, 589
Sorrel
  container growing, 385
  culinary use, 385
  cultivation, 384, 385
  green sauce, 385
  medicinal use, 385
  pests and diseases, 384
  sorrel and lettuce soup, 385
  varieties, 384
Souci, 260
Soufflé
  cauliflower soufflé, 56

Soup
  artichoke soup, 119
  Croatian Hamburg parsley soup, 158
  curried parsnip soup, 345
  eddoe soup, 87
  galangal soup, 137
  lovage soup, 329
  mushroom soup, 17
  nettle soup, 431
  radish and scallop soup, 175
  red orach soup, 247
  sorrel and lettuce soup, 385
Sour cherries
  Black Forest gâteau, 479
  culinary uses, 479
  cultivation, 478, 479
  growing under glass and in containers, 479
  pests and diseases, 479
  varieties, 478
Sour leaves, 384
Sour sauce, 384
Sour sops, 563
South African wild rosemary
  companion planting, 297
  culinary use, 297
  cultivation, 296, 297
  medicinal use, 297
  pests and diseases, 196
  varieties, 296
Southernwood, 241
Soy bean
  culinary use, 117
  cultivation, 116, 117
  medicinal use, 117
  pests and diseases, 117
  soy bean and walnut croquettes, 117
  varieties, 116
Spanish chestnuts
  chestnut amber, 605
  companion planting, 605
  culinary uses, 605
  cultivation, 604, 605
  growing under glass or in containers, 605
  pests and diseases, 605
  varieties, 604
Spanish plum, 569
Spanish salsify, 180
Sparassis crispa, 15
Spice oils, 673
Spinach
  companion planting, 193
  culinary use, 193
  cultivation, 192, 193
  medicinal use, 193
  perpetual, 43
  pests and diseases, 193
  scrambled eggs with raw and cooked spinach, 193
  spinach beet fritters, 44
  varieties, 192
Spinacia oleracea, 192, 193

Split pea, 138
Spondias, 569
Spotted bugloss, 377
Spotted comfrey, 377
Sprouting broccoli, 65
Sprouts, 60
Squash
  acorn squash with balsamic vinegar, 100
  companion planting, 99
  culinary use, 100
  cultivation, 98–99
  meaning, 96
  medicinal use, 99
  pests and diseases, 99
  varieties, 97–98
St John's wort, 311
St Peter's keys, 373
Star fruit, 564
Stachys affinis, 194
Stachys officinalis, 406, 407
Star apple, 568
Starch, plants containing
  cassava, 146
  dasheen, 88
  eddoe, 87
Stem and bulb eelworm, 658
Stem lettuce, 132
Stem rot, 659
Stevia
  container growing, 409
  culinary use, 409
  cultivation, 408, 409
  medicinal use, 406
  pests and diseases, 409
  varieties, 408
Stevia rebaudiana, 408, 409
Sticklewort, 376
Stinging nettle, 430
Stinking horehound, 248
Stinking nightshade, 310
Stinking Roger, 248, 310
Stinking Willy, 119
Stir-fried mung beans, 160
Storage of produce, 669–671
Strawberries
  alpine strawberry tarts, 491
  alpine, 490, 491
  baked strawberry apples, 489
  June-bearing, 486, 487
  Killarney strawberry surprise, 579
  perpetual, 488, 489
  remontant, 488, 489
  wild European, 490, 491
  Wimbledon fortune, 487
Strawberry tree, 579
Stropharia rugosoannulata, 13
Stuffed date chocolates, 556
Stuffed tomatoes, 145
Succory, 84
Succotash, 209
Sugar loaf chicory, 84
Summer purslane, 172
Summer watercress, 178

Sunchoke, 118
Sunflower, 314
Sutherlandia frutescens, 412, 413
Swede, 50
Swedish turnip, 50
Sweet and sour Chinese cabbage, 75
Sweet balm, 224
Sweet basil, 350
Sweet bracken, 346
Sweet cherries
  cherry jam, 477
  companion planting, 477
  culinary uses, 477
  cultivation, 476, 477
  growing under glass and in
    containers, 477
  pests and diseases, 477
  pickled cherries, 477
  varieties, 476
Sweet chestnuts
  chestnut amber, 605
  companion planting, 605
  culinary uses, 605
  cultivation, 604, 605
  growing under glass or in
    containers, 605
  pests and diseases, 605
  varieties, 604
Sweet cicely
  container growing, 347
  culinary use, 347
  cultivation, 347
  medicinal use, 347
  pests and diseases, 347
  varieties, 346
Sweet fennel, 114
Sweet fern, 346
Sweet licorice, 303
Sweet calendula buns, 261
Sweet Mary, 416
Sweet oils, 673
Sweet pepper, 76
Sweet potato
  culinary use, 125
  cultivation, 124, 125
  medicinal use, 125
  pests and diseases, 125
  tzimmes, 125
  varieties, 124
Sweet rocket, 305
Sweet suckle, 330
Sweet weed, 229
Sweet woodruff, 301
Sweetcorn, 206
Sweetwood, 303
Swiss chard
  companion planting, 44
  culinary use, 44
  cultivation, 43, 44
  medicinal use, 44
  pests and diseases, 44
  spinach beet fritters, 44
  varieties, 43
Swiss cheese plant, 548
Switch, 346

Symphoniaca, 310
Symphytum officinale, 412, 413

Tamarillo
  culinary uses, 549
  cultivation, 549
  growing under glass and in
    containers, 549
  pests and diseases, 549
  tamarillo chutney, 549
  tree tomato jam, 549
  varieties, 549
Tamarind tree, 569
Tamarindus indica, 569
Tanacetum balsamita, 416
Tanacetum cinerariifolium, 417
Tanacetum parthenium, 418
Tanacetum vulgare, 419
Tansy, 419
Taraxacum officinale, 420, 421
Taro, 88
Tarragon
  chicken salad with tarragon and
    grapes, 245
  container growing, 245
  culinary use, 245
  cultivation, 244, 245
  fish bouquet garni, 368
  medicinal use, 245
  pests and diseases, 245
  varieties, 244
Tarts and pies
  alpine strawberry tarts, 491
  banana custard pie, 555
  cashew tarts, 608
  kiwi meringue pie, 541
  leek and ricotta pie, 25
  onion tart, 21
  pecan pie, 599
  rose hip tart, 583
  tart of artichoke bottoms, 105
Tayberries
  companion planting, 513
  culinary uses, 513
  cultivation, 512, 513
  growing under glass and in
    containers, 513
  pests and diseases, 513
  varieties, 512
Teaberry, 593
Tetragonia expansa, 195
Tetragonia tetragonoides, 195
Tetragonolobus purpureus, 196
Teucrium chamaedrys, 422
Teucrium scorodonia, 423
Theobroma cacao, 571
Thousand fingers, 384
Thousand leaf, 214
Three faces under a hood, 435
Thunder and lightning, 226
Thunder plant, 402
Thyme
  container growing, 427
  culinary use, 427
  cultivation, 426, 427

medicinal use, 427
  pests and diseases, 427
  poached trout with lemon thyme,
    427
  varieties, 424–426
Thymus, 424–427
Tiger nut, 559
Tilia, 593
Tom Thumbs, 384
Tomato
  companion planting, 144
  culinary use, 145
  cultivation, 142–144
  medicinal use, 144
  pests and diseases, 144
  red mullet with tomatoes and
    oregano, 358
  stuffed tomatoes, 145
  varieties, 141
Touch and heal, 311, 376
Tragopogon porrifolius, 197, 198
Treacle berry, 593
Treacly Brazil pie, 611
Tree onions
  container growing, 223
  culinary use, 223
  cultivation, 222, 223
  pests and diseases, 222
  varieties, 222
Tree primrose, 354
Trinity violet, 435
Tropaeolum majus, 428, 429
Trout
  poached trout with lemon thyme,
    427
Truffles, 191
  pinon truffle salad, 592
Trumpet flowers, 330
Trumpet gourd, 134
Tuber melanosporum, 15
Turnip
  companion planting, 69
  culinary use, 69
  cultivation, 68, 69
  medicinal use, 69
  pests and diseases, 69
  turnip tops, 69
  varieties, 68
Turnip rooted parsley, 157
Two faces in a hood, 435
Tzimmes, 125

Urtica, 430, 431

Vaccinium species
  blueberries, 492, 493
  cowberries, 494, 495
  cranberries, 494, 495
  huckleberries, 492, 493
Valerian, 432, 433
Valeriana officinalis, 432, 433
Valerianella locusta, 199, 200
Vanilla, 569
Vegetable garden

bedding plants, 619
  catch crops, 639
  colour, 618
  companion planting, 640, 641
  containers, use of, 642, 643
  crop rotation, 636
  form, 618
  growing systems, 638, 639
  intercropping, 639
  ornamental, 618, 619
  planning, 616, 617
  pollination, 640, 641
  potager, 619
  protected cropping, 653
  random systems, 619
  site, 633
  soil, 633
  texture, 619
Vegetable oyster, 197
Vegetarian goulash, 383
Velvet foot, 13
Velvet shank, 13
Verbena officinalis, 434
Vervain, 434
Viburnum trilobum, 580
Vicia faba, 201, 202
Vietnamese cilantro
  container growing, 366
  culinary use, 366
  cultivation, 365, 366
  medicinal use, 366
  pests and diseases, 365
  varieties, 365
Vine weevils, 660
Vinegar tree, 502
Viola, 436, 437
Viola tricolor, 435
Violet
  container growing, 437
  culinary use, 437
  cultivation, 436, 437
  medicinal use, 437
  pests and diseases, 437
  varieties, 436
Viper's bugloss, 292
Viper's grass, 292
Virgin Mary's milkdrops, 377
Virgin Mary's tears, 377
Virginia poke weed, 370
Viscid mushroom, 13
Vitamin A, plants containing
  apricots, 468
  dasheen, 88
  date palms, 556
  endive, 82
  mango, 558
  melons, 528
  morello cherries, 478
  nectarines, 474
  peaches, 470
  pineapples, 552
  plums, 462
  spinach, 192
Vitamin B, plants containing
  almonds, 596

azarole, 586
blueberries, 492
calabash, 134
cassava, 146
chickpea, 80
corn, 206
dasheen, 88
date palms, 556
endive, 82
groundnuts, 612
hawthorn, 586
hickory nuts, 598
huckleberries, 492
Jerusalem artichoke, 118
lentil, 138
mango, 558
mushrooms and edible fungi, 12
parsnip, 154
peanuts, 612
pecan nuts, 598
soy bean, 116
swede, 50
sweet potato, 124
tomato, 140
yam, 110
Vitamin C, plants containing
  apples, 446
  azarole, 586
  beach plums, 590
  bell pepper and chilli, 76
  bird cherries, 590
  bitter melon, 150
  blackberries, 509
  black currants, 500
  blueberries, 492
  boysenberries, 512
  brambles, 509
  broccoli, 64
  Brussels sprout, 60
  cabbage, 57
  calabash, 134
  cassava, 146
  cauliflower, 54
  celeriac, 34
  chervil, 234
  Chinese cabbage, 74
  chokeberries, 502
  cowberries, 494
  cranberries, 494
  dewberries, 508
  eddoe, 87
  fava bean, 201
  gooseberries, 498
  ground cherries, 526
  guavas, 560
  Hamburg parsley, 157
  hawthorn, 586
  huckleberries, 492
  Japanese wineberries, 514
  juneberries, 574
  kale, 52
  kiwi fruit, 540
  kohlrabi, 63
  lamb's lettuce, 192
  land cress, 42

leeks, 24
loganberries, 512
mango, 558
melons, 528
nectarines, 474
okra, 120
parsley, 367
parsnip, 154
passion fruit, 542
pea, 169
pineapples, 552
potato, 186
pumpkin and squash, 96
purslane, 172
radish, 173
raspberries, 504
rose hips, 582
rowan, 588
runner bean, 161
samphire, 92
seakale, 90
service berries, 588
sloes, 590
sorrel, 384
soy bean, 116
spinach, 192
strawberries, 488, 490
swede, 50
sweet potato, 124
Swiss cheese plant, 548
tamarillo, 549
tayberries, 512
tomato, 141
walnuts, 600
whitebeam, 588
Vitamin E, plants containing
  asparagus, 40
  avocado, 557
  Brussels sprout, 60
  cabbage, 57
  carrots, 106
  fava bean, 201
  groundnuts, 612
  kale, 52
  parsnip, 154
  peanuts, 612
  soy bean, 116
  tamarillo, 549
Vitis vinifera, 516, 517, 520, 521
Volvariella volvaceae, 14

Wall germander, 422
Walnuts
  companion planting, 601
  culinary uses, 601
  cultivation, 600, 601
  green bean, Roquefort and
    walnut salad, 166
  growing under glass or in
    containers, 300
  onion and walnut muffins, 21
  pests and diseases, 601
  soy bean and walnut
    croquettes, 117
  varieties, 600

walnut aperitif, 601
Water yam, 110
Watercress
  culinary use, 179
  cultivation, 178, 179
  medicinal use, 179
  pests and diseases, 179
  salad made with three wild
    herbs, 199
  salmon with watercress sauce,
    179
Watering, 651
Watermelon
  companion planting, 433
  culinary uses, 533
  cultivation, 532, 533
  growing under glass and in
    containers, 532
  pests and diseases, 533
  varieties, 532
  watermelon ices, 533
Wax bean, 164
Weeds
  control of, 654, 656
  types of, 654
Welcome-husband-though-never-so-
  late, 402
Welsh onions
  container growing, 223
  culinary use, 223
  cultivation, 222, 223
  pests and diseases, 222, 223
  varieties, 222
West Indian kale, 88
Wetweed, 420
White endive, 420
White flowered gourd, 134
White horehound, 334
White rot, 659
White yam, 110
Whitebeam
  culinary uses, 589
  cultivation, 588
  varieties, 588
Whitecurrants
  culinary uses, 497
  cultivation, 496, 497
  growing under glass and in
    containers, 497
  mint sauce supreme, 497
  pests and diseases, 497
  varieties, 496
Wild borage, 292
Wild endive, 420
Wild germander, 422
Wild marjoram, 356
Wild pansy, 435
Wild sage, 423
Wild spinach, 276
Wild sunflower, 314
Wimbledon fortune, 487
Wimote, 229
Windsor, 201
Winged yam, 110
Winter marjoram, 356

Winter mushroom, 13
Winter sweet, 356
Wireworms, 659
Wizard's herb, 434
Wolf's bane, 216
Wolfsbane, 240
Wood betony, 406
Wood blewit, 15
Wood sage, 423
Wood-ear, 14
Woodbind, 330
Woodbine, 330
Woodrowell, 301
Woodward, 301
Wormwood
  antiseptic vinegar, 243
  moth repellent recipe, 243
  container growing, 243
  cultivation, 243
  medicinal use, 243
  pests and diseases, 243
  species, 242
Woundwort, 214, 376, 404
Wymote, 229

Yam
  companion planting, 111
  culinary use, 111
  cultivation, 110, 111
  medicinal use, 111
  pests and diseases, 111
  varieties, 110
  yellow yam salad, 111
Yarrow
  container growing, 215
  culinary use, 215
  cultivation, 215
  medicinal use, 215
  pests and diseases, 215
  salad made with three wild
    herbs, 215
  species, 214
Yearly calendar, 676–681
Yellow starwort, 314
Yellow yam, 124
Yucca baccata, 571
Yuen sai, 280

Zea mays, 206–209
Zinc, plant containing
  lentil, 138
Zingiber officinale, 440, 441
Zizyphus jujuba, 569
Zucchini
  celery and zucchini with blue
    cheese dip, 33
  companion planting, 99
  culinary use, 100
  cultivation, 98–99
  medicinal use, 99
  pests and diseases, 99
  varieties, 97–98
  zucchini omelette, 100

ACKNOWLEDGMENTS

The authors and publisher wish to thanks the following for permission to quote recipes:

Onion and Walnut Muffins – Hudson Valley Cookbook by Wally Malouf; La Gasconnade – Goose Fat & Garlic by Jeanne Strang; Mrs Krause's Pepper Hash – Pennsylvania Dutch Country Cooking by William Woys Weaver; Risotto with Artichokes – The River Cafe Cookbook by Rose Gray and Ruth Rogers; Pelecing Peria – Indonesian Food and Cookery by Sri Owen; Chayote in Red Wine and Creamed Chinese Artichokes – The Vegetable Book by Jane Grigson; Tzimmes – Russian Cooking by Olga Phklebin.

Photography key:

AL = Alamy; BAL = Bridgeman Art Library; BF = Bob Flowerdew: FY = Fran Yorke; GAP = GAP Photos; GH = Geoff Hayes; GPL = Garden Picture Library; GWI = Garden World Images; JM = Jekka McVicar; LL = Lisa Linder; MG = Michelle Garratt; PC = Pete Cassidy; PG = Photolibrary Group; sf = Stockfood; SPL = Science Photo Library; WH = Will Heap

l = left; r = right; b = bottom; c = centre; t = top

1 David Chapman; 2 Tim Gainey/AL; 4/5 Anneke Doorenbosch/AL; 7 Private Collection © Chris Beetles, London, UK/BAL; 8 Loxton, Margaret/RONA Gallery, London, UK/BAL; 9 Robins, Thomas/© Cheltenham Art Gallery & Museums, Gloucestershire, UK/BAL

Vegetables
10 Mark Bolton/PG; 13 (t) botanica/PG, (b) AGStockUSA, Inc./AL; 14 (t l) Tim Spence/Lightshaft Ltd/PG, (t r) botanica/PG, (b) Michele Lamontagne/PL; 15 (l) PSL Images/AL, (r) botanica/PG; 16 (l) David Sanger Photography/AL, (r) blickwinkel/AL; 17 MG; 18 (l) Natural Visions/AL, (r) Jacqui Hurst/PL; 19 (l) David Marsden/Anthony Blake Photo Library, (r) Steffen Hauser/botanikfoto/AL; 20 (t) blickwinkel/AL, (b) Jacqui Hurst/PL; 21 (l) MG, (r) MG; 22 (l) Iain Bagwell/ALnthony Blake Photo Library, (r) Foodcollection.com/AL; 23 G&M Garden Images/AL; 24 (l) Howard Rice/PL, (r) Maxine Adcock/PL; 25 MG; 26 (l) Tim Hill/AL, (r) JTB Photo Communications, Inc./AL; 28 (l) J S Sira/PL, (r) Robert Harding Picture Library Ltd/AL; 29 (l) botanica/PG, (r) Martin Brigdale; 30 (l) Photofrenetic/AL, (r) Duncan Smith/SPL; 31 MG; 32 (l) Busse Yankushev/PL, (r) Inga Spence/AL; 33 corbis/PG; 34 Jacqui Hurst/PL; 35 MG; 36 Foodpix/PG; 37(t) MG, (b) Jo Whitworth/PG; 38 (l) Bloom Works Inc./AL, (r) Bob Gibbons/AL; 39 (l) Arco Images GmbH/AL, (r) Martin Brigdale; 40 (l) Arco Images GmbH/AL, (r) Michael Grant/AL; 41 Jean-Christophe Novelli; 42 Derek St Romaine; 43 (l) botanica/PG, (r) blickwinkel/AL; 44 MG; 45 (l) Rob Whitrow/PL , (r) Howard Rice/PL; 46 Michael Howes/PL; 47 MG; 48 Martin Brigdale; 49 (l) John Glover/PL, (r) Martin Brigdale; 50 Andy Williams/SPL; 51 (l) Nigel Cattlin/AL, (r) MG; 52 (l) Stephen Shepherd/PL, (r) vario images GmbH & Co.KG/AL; 53 (l) Geoff Kidd/SPL, (r) Martin Brigdale; 54 (l) Kieran Scott/ALnthony Blake Photo Library, (r) JUPITERIMAGES/ Polka Dot/AL; 55 (l) D. Hurst/AL, (r) Malcolm Case-Green/AL; 56 MG; 57 (l) O.D. van de Veer/AL, (r) John Glover/AL; 58 (t) Martin Hughes-Jones/AL, (b) John Daniels/ALrdea.com; 59 (l) MG, (r) MG; 60 John Martin/AL; 61 (l) foodpix/PG, (r) Nic Murray/AL; 62 (l) Adrian Davies/AL, (r) MG; 63 (l) STOCKFOLIO/AL, (r) Bon Appetit/AL; 64 (l) Holmes Garden Photos/AL, (r) MG; 65 (l) Nigel Cattlin/AL, (r) Howard Rice/PL; 66 (l) Marc Hill/AL, (r) Organics image library/AL; 67 MG; 68 (l) Garden World Images Ltd/AL, (r) Marie-Louise Avery/AL; 69 (l) Photo Agency EYE/AL, (r) Sue Atkinson/AL R C Studios/PG; 70 (t) Sue Wilson/AL, (r) Martin Brigdale; 71 (l) David Cavagnaro/PL, (r) Martin Brigdale; 72 MIXA Co., Ltd./AL; 73 (t) John Glover/AL, (b) Westend61 Ohg/PG; 74 Nigel Cattlin/AL; 75 MG; 76 (t) Martin Brigdale, (b) Jeff Morgan food and drink/AL; 77 Simon Fraser/SPL; 78 (l) Shannon99/AL, (r) Martin Brigdale; 79 (l) Shannon99/AL, (r) Martin Brigdale; 80 Nigel Cattlin/AL; 81 (t) blickwinkel/AL, (b) MG; 82 (t) Bon Appetit/AL, (b) Friedrich Strauss/PL; 83 (t) Images Etc Ltd/AL, (b) Maximilian Stock Ltd/Sf; 84 (t) Bon Appetit/AL, (b) Arco Images GmbH/AL; 85 botanica/PG; 86 (t) MG, (b) MG; 87 (l) blickwinkel/AL, (r) Richard Wainscoat/AL; 88 (l) Collections/PG, (r) MG; 89 (l) Kaktusfactory, Ninprapha Lippert/sf, (r) Lemonnier, Nicolas/sf; 90 (l) Philip Smith/AL, (r) Collection/PG; 91 (t) Brian Harris/AL, (b) MG; 92 Nigel Cattlin/AL; 93 Francois De Heel/PG; 94 (l) Christopher Burrows/AL, (r) Chris Burrows/PG; 95 (l) Collection/PG, (r) MG; 96 Piotr Adamczyk shapencolour/AL; 97 (l) Collection/PG, (c) Paul Hart/PL, (r) Carole Drake/PL; 98 (b) Shangara Singh/AL, (t) Foodcollection.com/AL; 99 Mark Winwood/PL; 100 (l) Winkelmann, Bernhard/sf, (r) MG; 101 (l) Collection/PG, (r) Le Scanff Mayer/PG; 102 (l) Collection/PG, (r) MG; 103 (l) Anneke Doorenbosch/AL, (r) Pernilla Bergdahl/PL; 104 (l) Collections/PG, (r) Paul Collis/AL; 105 (t) Lutterbeck, Barbara/sf, (b) FoodPhotogr. Eising/sf; 106 moodboard/AL; 107 (l) Maxine Adcock/PL, (c) Maxine Adcock/PL, (r) David Forster/AL; 108 (l) Mark Bolton/PL, (r) Hoff, Dana/sf; 109 (l) MG, (r) MG; 110 John Heseltine/Fresh Food Images; 111 (l) Michael Warren/PH, (r) MG; 112 Martin Brigdale; 113 (l) Kit Young/PL, (r) MG; 114 FoodStock/AL; 115 (l) Francois De Heel/PL, (r) MG; 116 (l) Bill Barksdale/

ALGSTOCKUSA/SPL, (r) D. Hurst/AL; 117 MG; 118 Neil Holmes/PL; 119 (l) Piotr & Irena Kolasa/AL, (r) MG; 120 (l) David Cavagnaro/PL, (r) Michael Warren/PH; 121 MG; 122 (l) David Cavagnaro/PL, (r) Nigel Cattlin/AL; 123 (l) Vietnam Images/AL, (r) Martin Brigdale, 124 (l) David Cavagnaro/PL, (r) Michele Molinari/AL; 125 MG; 126 (l) Jo Whitworth/PL, (r) Howard Rice/PL; 127 (l) Geoff Kidd/SPL, (r) John Swithinbank/PL; 128 (t) Sunniva Harte/PL, (b) botanica/PL; 129 Pernilla Bergdahl/PL; 130 Juliet Piddington/PL; 131 Martin Brigdale; 132 (t) Nigel Cattlin/AL, (b) Dufour Brigette Dit Noun/PG, 133 MG, 134 botanica/PG; 135 (l) Mark Bolton Photography/AL, (r) Bon Appetit/AL; 136 Tim Hill/AL; 137 MG; 138 (r) Itani/AL, (l) Foodpix/PG; 139 (t) MG, (b) AGStockUSA, Inc./AL; 140 John Glover/PL; 141 (l) Stephen Henderson (Burt Latino Com)/PL, (c) Sunniva Harte/PL, (r) David Cavagnaro/PL, 142 (l) botanica/PG, (r) Alec Scarsbrook/PL; 143 (t) botanica/Koenigsberg Diana/PG, (b) Michael Howes/PL; 144 (l) Mark Winwood/PL, (r) Michael Howes/PL; 145 MG; 146 botanica/PG; 147 (t) David R. Frazier PL, Inc./AL, (b) MG; 148 (l) Brian L Carter/PL, (r) Mark Gibson/AL; 149 (l) MG, (r) Joy Skipper/Fresh Food Images/PG; 150 (l) botanica/PG, (r) Anto V Chacko valiyakulam/AL; 151 (l) Henry Westheim Photography/AL, (r) MG; 152 (l) Steffen Hauser/botanikfoto/AL, (r) MG; 153 (l) Martin Brigdale, (r) Martin Brigdale; 154 (l) Bon Appetit/AL, (r) Maxine Adcock/PL; 155 (l) Jacqui Hurst/PL, (r) Steffen Hauser/botanikfoto/AL; 156 (l) David /AL, (r) MG; 157 (l) Foodcollection.com/AL, (r) imagebroker/AL; 158 (t) CuboImages srl/AL, (b) MG; 159 (t) Foodcollection.com/AL, (b) Tim Gainey/AL, 160 (l) NDisc/AL, (r) Neil McAllister/AL; 161 Howard Rice/PL; 162 (l) Niall McDiarmid/AL, (c) Anne Green-Armytage/PL, (r) Tommy Candler/PL; 163 (l) Anne Green-Armytage/PL, (r) MG; 164 (l) Anne Green-Armytage/PL, (r) Howard Rice/PL; 165 (l) Michael Howes/PL, (r) Mark Winwood/PL; 166 MG; 167 (l) botanica/PG, (r) Mark Bolton/PL; 168 (l) Juliette H Wade/PL, (r) Martin Brigdale; 169 (l) botanica/PG, (r) botanica/PG; 170 (l) Mark Turner/PL, (r) botanica/PG; 171 MG; 172 (t) MG, (b) Howard Rice/PL; 173 (l) MG, (r) Maxine Adcock; 174 (l) botanica/PG, (r) Juliet Greene/PL; 175 MG; 176 (l) Juliette Wade/PL, (r) Howard Rice/PL; 177 (t) Ray Roberts/AL, (b) MG; 178 David Cavagnaro/PL; 179 (l) Nic Murray/AL, (r) MG; 180 (l) Mayer/Le Scanff/PG, (r) Maximilian Stock Ltd/sf; 181 (l) Nigel Cattlin/AL, (r) Minowa Studio Co./sf; 182 (l) blickwinkel/AL, (r) imagebroker/AL; 183 (l) blickwinkel/AL, (r) MG; 184 (t) Westend 61/AL, (b) Juliette H Wade (Espalier Media

Ltd)/PG; 185 (l) Chris Burrows/PL, (r) MG; 186 Maxine Adcock/PL; 187 (l) botanica/PG, (r) Maxine Adcock/PL; 188 (l) Jacqui Hurst/PL, (r) Jo Whitworth/PL; 189 Maxine Adcock/PL; 190 Maxine Adcock/PL; 191 (t) MG, (b) MG; 192 (l) botanica/PG, (r) Inga Spence/AL; 193 (l) Dufour Brigette Dit Noun/PG, (r) MG; 194 (l) Andrea Jones/AL, (c) Dave Bevan/AL, (r) MG; 195 Arco Images GmbH/AL, 196 (l) Arco Images GmbH/AL, (c) Bon Appetit/AL, (r) FoodPhotography/sf; 197 (l) Nigel Cattlin/AL, (r) blickwinkel/AL; 198 MG; 199 (l) Sunniva Harte/PG, (r) Martin Hughes-Jones/AL; 200 (t) Arco Images GmbH/AL, (b) Foodcollection/sf; 201 (l) Mayer/Le Scanff/PG, (r) Maxine Adcock/PL; 202 PhotoCuisine RM/AL; 203 MG; 204 (l) Rich Iwasaki/AL, (r) Jonah Calinawan/AL; 205 (l) imagebroker/AL, (r) Martin Brigdale; 206 Mark Winwood/PL; 207 (l) Mark Winwood/PL, (r) LWA- JDC/PG; 208 (l) David Cavagnaro/PL, (c) botanica/PG, (r) Carole Drake/PL; 209 MG

Herbs
All photos by Jekka McVicar except:

212 (l) Sally Maltby; 213 (r) MG; 215 MG; 216 (r) Mediacolor's/Alamy, (l) Bickwinkel/AL; 217 Ron Niebrugge/Alamy; 218 (l) John Glover/Alamy, (r) Organica/Alamy; 219 MG; 220 (t) Mediacolor's/Alamy, (b) Torie Chugg; 221 (l) GH; (r) MG; 223 MG; 224 (l) Torie Chugg; 225 MG; 226 (b) Clive Nichols/Garden Picture Library; 227 (l) GH; 228 (l) GH, (b) MG; 229 (l) GH, (r) MG; 233 MG; 235 MG; 237 (l) WH; 239 (both) MG; 241 (b) MG; 243 (b) MG; 245 MG; 246 (b) Sally Maltby; 247 (b) MG; 248 GH; 251 MG; 253 (r) WH; 257 (r) MG; 259 (r) MG; 260 (l) Torie Chugg; (r) GH; 261 (b & r) MG; 262 Pat Behnke/AL; 263 (t) WH, (b) CuboImages srl/AL; 264 (b) MG; 265 MG; 266 Sara Taylor (b); 267 (t) David Hoffman Photo Library/AL; 269 (t) Sally Maltby, (b) MG; 271 (t) WH; 272 (r) GH; 273 (b) GH; 275 MG; 279 (c) John Glover/Alamy, (b) WH; 281 Organics image library/Alamy; 282 MG; 283 (b) WH; 284 Steve Baxter; 285 (t) Photo Dinodia/Garden Picture Library, (b) WH; 287 (t) D. Hurst/Alamy,(b) WH; 288 (b) MG; 289 Sally Maltby; 291 (t) Richard Bloom/GPL, (b) WH; 293 (r) Steve Baxter; 294 WH; 295 (l) Sally Maltby; 297 (b) WH; 298 (b) WH; 300 (b) Organica/Alamy; 301 (b) MG; 302 (t) Rob Walls/AL, (b) WH; 303 (b) MG; 304 (l) GH; 307 (b) Friedrich Strauss/

Garden Picture Library; 308 Mediacolor's/Alamy; 309 (b) MG; 310 GH; 311 (b) MG; 313 (t) GH, (b) MG; 314 GH; 315 (t) GH, (b) MG; 317 (r) MG; 318 (b) WH; 319 (t) Bickwinkel/AL; 320 (r) Woodystock/AL; 321 MG; 322 Torie Chugg; 323 (t) GH, (b) MG; 325 (r) Mark Bolton/GPL; 326 (r) GH; 327 MG; 329 MG; 330 GH; 331 (bl) GH, (t & br) MG; 332 (b) MG; 333 (r) WH; 334 (b) MG; 335 (r) GH; 336 MG; 339 Torie Chugg; 340 MG; 342 (br) GH; 343 MG; 345 (t) WH, (b) Fenix rising/AL; 347 MG; 349 (tr) MG; 350 (t) GH; 352 (t & br) MG; 353 MG; 354 (l) GH; 355 (t) WH; 358 (b) MG; 359 (b) MG; 362 MG; 363 Torie Chugg; 364 (r) WH; 366 WH; 367 GH; 368 (l) MG, (r) WH; 369 (bl) GH, (br) MG; 370 (r) Sally Maltby; 372 GH; 373 (t) TH Foto/Alamy; 374 (r) MG; 376 (b) Sally Maltby; 377 (b) MG; 378 (b) WH; 383 MG; 384 GH; 385 (t) MG, (b) GH; 386 (b) GH; 387 (t) GH; 390 (b) GH, (tr) MG; 391 MG; 392 John La Gette/Alamy; 393 (t) MG, (b) Dave Watts/AL; 394 (l) GH, (r) Organics image library/Alamy; 395 MG; 396 (b) GH; 397 (tr & bl) GH, (br) MG; 398 (t) GH, (b) MG; 401 (b) MG; 402 (t) GH; 403 (t) MG, (b) Sally Maltby; 404 (r) GH; 405 (b) WH; 406 Konrad Zelazowski/AL; 407 (tl) WH, (tr) Organica/Alamy, (br) MG; 409 (l) Fenix rising/AL, (r) WH; 411 (t) Chris & Tilde Stuart/FLPA, (b) Howard Rice/Garden Picture Library; 413 (t) GH, (b) MG; 414 Bickwinkel/AL; 415 (t) WH; 417 Sally Maltby; 418 (l) Sally Maltby, (r) MG; 421 MG; 423 (br) MG; 424 (t) GH; 425 (t) Torie Chugg; 427 MG; 429 (r) MG; 430 (t) GH; 431 MG; 432 GH; 433 (b) MG, 434 (r) Sally Maltby; 435 (b) MG; 437 (t) Neil Hardwick/AL, (b) MG; 439 (t) Eising/StockFood; 439 (b) Holmes Garden Photo/AL; 440 Paul Thompson Images/AL; 441 (t) Scherer, Tim/StockFood, (b) Humberto Olarte Cupas/AL

Fruit
442 PC; 444 PC; 446 BF; 447 (t) PC, (b) BF; 448 (l) GH, (r) PC; 449 PC; 450 (t) and (bl) BF, (br) PC; 451 MG; 452 (t) Mark Bolton/GAP, (b) Christina Bollen/GAP; 453 (t) Sally Maltby, (c) Jonathan Buckley/GAP, (b) MG; 454 PC; 455 (l) BF, (r) FY; 456 (l) FY, (r) PC; 457 WH; 458 (t) Dave Bevan/GAP, (b) Juliette Wade/GAP; 459 (t) Juliette Wade/GPL, (b) MG; 460 (t) Emma Lee, (b) Andrea Jones/AL; 461 (t) MG, (b) David Askham/AL; 462 (t) PC, (b) Christina Bollen/GAP; 463 (l) John Glover/GAP, (r) MG; 464 (l) imagebroker/AL, (r) PC; 465 MG; 466 Arco Images